AF668145

Computers Today

A Ravichandran

KHANNA BOOK PUBLISHING CO. (P) LTD.

Computer Today — A Ravichandran

Copyright © 2009 by **Khanna Book Publishing Co. (P) Ltd.**

Published by
Khanna Book Publishing Co. (P) Ltd.

Regd. Office:
1694-95 Nai Sarak
Delhi - 110 006 (India)
Tel. 011-23283211, 23256658
Telefax: 011-23256658
Website: www.khannaedu.com
E-mail: contact@khannaedu.com

ISBN 978-93-80016-29-0

FirstEdition 2009

Trade mark acknowledged. All trade marks mentioned in this book are acknowledged as trade marks of the respective owners and are used for editorial purposes only. No intention of trade mark infringement is intended upon any trade marked names appearing in the text.

All rights reserved. No part of this publication may be reproduced, stored in a retrieval system, or transmitted, in any form or by any means, electronic, mechanical, photocopying, recording and/or otherwise, without the prior written permission of the publishers.

Disclaimer. Every effort has been made to supply complete and accurate information. However, the publishers and the author assume no responsibility for its use, for any infringement of the intellectual property rights of third parties, errors or omissions. Nor is any liability assumed for damages resulting out of use of the information contained herein.

Printed in India by Seth Printers, Noida (U.P.)

Contents at a Glance

Unit 1 — Information Technology

Unit 2 — Hardware and Communications

Unit 3 — Software and Data Management

Unit 4 — Information Systems Development

Unit 5 — Information System

Unit 6 — Information Systems Resources Management

NOTES

CONTENTS

Unit 1 — Information Technology

Unit 2 — Hardware and Communications

Unit 3 — Software and Data Management

Unit 4 — Information Systems Development

Unit 5 — Information System

NOTES

CHAPTER 1

An Introduction to Computers

Learning Objectives

After going through this chapter, you should learn the following:

- Primary Key
- What is a Computer?
- Characteristics of Computers
- Main Parts of the Computer
- Computer Software
- Liveware
- What computers cannot do
- How does Computer Store Data
- Processing of Data
- Types of Computers
- The Need for Computer Literacy
- Computer Limitations
- Uses and Impact of Computers
- Data Processing
- Data Processing Systems

WHAT IS A COMPUTER?

There is a story that five blind men came across an elephant. Each one of them touched the different parts of its body. The one who touched the trunk said that the elephant was like a snake; the one who held the tail, said that it was like a rope. The ones holding other parts of its body said different things. Like elephant, a computer is made of different parts which when looked at from any user angle will give a different definition. We should just remember that a computer:

1. Cannot think
2. It has vast capabilities of calculations like addition, substraction, etc. and
3. It is totally under the control of the user.

So, we can say that a computer is a machine, totally at the command of the user, which can perform operations at a much higher speed than a human being.

So may times you have seen or heard that a telephone bill or an electricity bill has been wrongly prepared and the amount charged is enormous. It is not because of computer's mistake but it is so since the meter reading given to the computer was wrong, possibly the reading was wrongly taken by the meter reader who had gone to the house to read and record the meter reading.

Therefore, we understand that there is nothing magical about a computer. It is actually a friendly machine which is totally at your command. Do you remember the story Aladdin and the Magic Lamp? Just like the Genie of the magic lamp, a computer will obey your command. If you make a mistake in giving commands to the computer, it will carry out these commands giving wrong results.

CHARACTERISTICS OF COMPUTERS

A computer can be judged by various factor, among them are:

Speed

Computers provide the processing speed essential to our fast-paced society. The quick service we have come to expect - for bank withdrawals, telephone calls, and travel reservations, to name a few - is made possible by computers. Businesses depend on the speedy processing computers to handle high volume activities such as balancing ledgers and designing products.

The smallest unit of time in the human experience is, realistically, the second. Computer operations - for example, the execution of an instruction, such as multiplying pay-rate with numbers of hours worked - are measured in milliseconds, microsecond, nanoseconds and picoseconds (one thousandth, one millionth, one billionth, and one trillionth of a second respectively).

Although all computers are fast, but there is a wide diversity of computer speeds. The execution of an instruction on a very slow computer may be measured in less than a millisecond. Most computer can execute an instruction measured in microseconds range, but still to be broken in the picosecond barrier.

A computer speed is generally expressed in megahertz (MHz), millions of machine cycles per second. Thus a PC (Personal Computer) listed at 100 MHz has a processor capable of handling 100 million machine cycles per second. Another measure of computer speed is MIPS (one million instructions per second). MIPS is often a more accurate measure than clock speed, because some computers can use each tick of the clock more efficiently than others.

A third measure of speed is the megaflops (MFLOPS), which stands for one million floating point operations per second. It measures the ability of the computer to perform complex mathematical operations.

Accuracy

Errors do occur in computer based information systems, but precious few can be directly attributed to the computer system itself. The vast majority can be traced to a program logic error, a procedural error, or erroneous data. These are human errors. High accuracy implies small error, but accuracy is contrasted with precision e.g. three places of decimals properly computed are less precise but more accurate than four places of decimals containing an error. The accuracy of the results obtained from computer mainly depends on the method of programming and the way the results are interprted.

Reliability

Computers are extremely reliable. Where reliability is the measurement of the performance of a computer, measured against some predetermined standard for operation without the failure of it.

Reliability Of Computer = Serviceable Time/Serviceable Time + Down Time

where serviceable time is the total time during which a computer is in a state where it can operate normally, including time when the computer is idle, but not the time when it is unattended. Down time is the time when a computer is inoperable due to a machine fault.

Computer systems are particularly adept at repetitive tasks. They donot take sick leave and tea breaks, and they seldom complain anything below 99.9% serviceable time, the time when the computer system is in operation, is usually unacceptable. For some companies, any down time is unacceptable. These companies provide backup computers that take over automatically if the main computer fails.

Provides a Capability that would otherwise be Impossible

Computers operate on very high speed on data so that they can produce results in seconds, which is not possible otherwise. For example, computer can be used to provide management with up-to-the minute figures on all aspects of its business. This information can go long way in taking decisions by management.

Similary, computers enable companies to provide customers with instanteneous services, such as airline flight availability and charge account status. The result is that these companies can offer far more customer services than would be impossible without the computer.

Storage Capability

Since, various computer media can store millions of characters of data in a condensed form, there is a tremendous savings in the storage area required to maintain the vital records necessary in a business environment.

Intangable Benefits

There are many companies that utilize computers for intangible benefits such as flexibility, ability to accomodate growth, and the psychological factor that may give them a competitive edge in attracting consumers to buy their products or services.

Reduced Cost

With the ever-increasing advances being made in the state of the art, the cost of computer equipment has dropped drastically over the years. Hardware costs have been decreasing at an estimated anual rate of 30%. Thus, companies that at one time could not justify the cost of acquiring their own computer system may now find it not only feasible to acquire a system, but cost-effective as well.

MAIN PARTS OF THE COMPUTER

The main parts of the computer are :

Keyboard

Monitor

Central Processing Unit

All these parts are shown in the figure here. These parts are the other parts of the computer are mentioned here in brief. You will read about them details later.

Keyboard

The main input device for the computer. It allows you to type the information for the computer.

Monitor

The main output device which displays most of the actions being performed by the computer and also shows the results in the form of output.

Mouse

A pointing device which is used to click the options on the computer.

Central Processing Unit

It is where all the processing takes place.

Speakers

They are used to sound output coming from the computer.

CD drive

It is used to read and write CD ROMs and other types of CDs.

Floppy drive

It is used to read and write to the floppy disks.

Hard disk

A fixed drive of the computer, which stores all the information of the computer.

Central Processing Unit

Most of the things we learned so far has been pertaining to the items attached to the Central Processing Unit of the computer. Now we will go through the various components which are inside the CPU. Most of them are the various type of cards which are there and then there is microprocessor which controls the whole working of the system.

Microprocessor

As mentioned above it is the brain of the whole computer. This is where the whole processing takes place. All arithmetical, logical and other basic processing steps are done here. The thousands of instructions that the microprocessor executes one at a time to carry out the actions of each program is done here. In short a processor which is short for both microprocessor and central processor unit (CPU) is a piece of electronic circuitry that uses digital logic to perform the instructions of your software.

Semiconductors

A microprocessor is constructed of layer upon layer of electronic circuits that are liberally carved out of silicon.

Silicon is a very commonly element in the world. In fact, after oxygen, there is more silicon available than any other element and you can find it easily on the beach in rocks and sand. However, the silicon used for manufacturing integrated circuits is found in white quartz. Silicon is the primary building material used in manufacturing the electronic integrated circuits (chips) that are used to conduct the processor and ultimately the computer. It is used in electronic circuits because it is an excellent semiconductor. A semiconductor is a material that is neither a conductor nor an insulator but can be chemically altered to be either one.

Conductors and Insulators

A material that is a conductor allows electrical current to pass through it. Without getting too technical, materials like copper, aluminum or gold are good conductors of electricity because they have free electrons through which the current can pass. While, a material that does not allow an electrical current to pass through it is called an insulator. Insulators like rubber, wood or glass do not have many free electrons through which the current can pass.

Integrated Circuit

An integrated circuit (IC) is a combination of electronic components, such as transistors, capacitors and resistors. An IC is designed to fulfill some logical function and can be built to be a timer, counter, a bank of computer memory, or even a microprocessor.

The basic building block of an IC is a logic gate. A logic gate performs the Boolean algebra AND operation by testing two input signals (each stored in a transistor). If both the positive (representing true or 1) it sets the signal of a result value to positive. Otherwise, the value is set to negative (representing false of 0).

Main Parts of Microprocessor

The processor, which is also called the central processing unit (CPU), is made up of several parts. These parts work together to carry out the instructions and actions that translate to a word processing system or a game on your PC.

The primary parts of CPU, as shown in the figure here are as follows:

Control Unit (CU)

At the risk of being obvious, the control unit controls the functions of the CPU. It is kind of like the manager who coordinates the activities between the different parts of a factory. It tells the other parts of CPU how to operate, what data to use and where to put the results.

Protection Test (PTU)

This part of the CPU works with the control unit to monitor where or not functions are carried out correctly. It is like the quality control department of the CPU. If it detects something is not done properly, it generates an error signal.

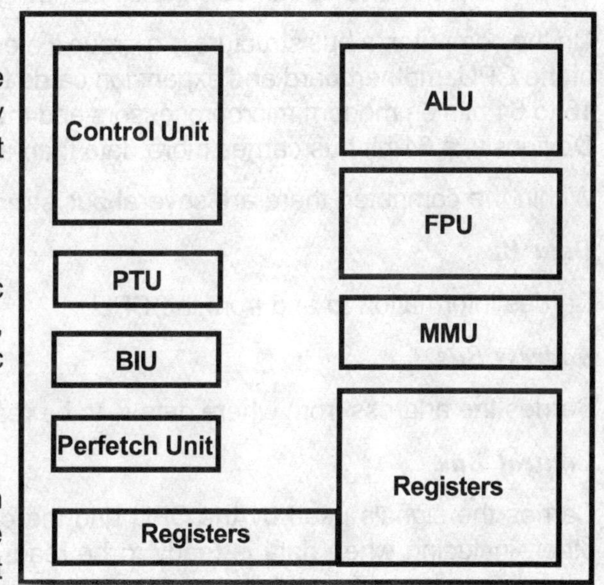

Arithmetic and Logic Unit (ALU)

The ALU performs of the calculation and comparative logic functions for the CPU, including all add, subtract, divide multiply, equal to, greater than, less than and other arithmetic and logic operations.

Floating Point Unit (FPU)

The FPU goes by several other names, including the math coprocessor, the numerical processing unit (NPU) and the numerical data processor (NDP). It handles all floating point operations for the ALU and CU. Floating point operations involve arithmetic on numbers with decimal places and high math operations involve arithmetic on numbers with decimal places and high math operations like trigonometry and logarithms.

Memory Management Unit (MMU)

The MMU handles the addressing and cataloging of where data is stored in system memory. Whenever the CPU needs something from memory, it requests it from the MMU. The MMU manages memory segmentation and paging allocations and translates all logical addressing into physical addressing.

Bus Interface Unit (BIU)

The BIU supervises the transfer of data over the bus system between the other components of the computer and the CPU. It also serves as the interface point for the CPU and its external bus, as well as handling all data transfers out of the control unit.

The Prefetch Unit

The unit preloads the instruction registers of the CPU with instructions from memory whenever the BIOS is idle. This allows the CPU to look ahead at future instructions. The prefetch unit does not analyze instructions, so on occasion it may bring in an unnecessary instruction because it assumes that the instructions will be carried out one after the other without branching or jumps.

Decode Unit

Many instructions are actually combinations of simpler instructions. The decode unit does just about what its name suggests. It decodes incoming instructions to their simplest form. While the prefetch unit retrieving more instructions, this unit decodes them to get them ready for the control unit.

Registers

Built into the CPU are a number of holding areas and buffers that are used to temporarily hold the data, addresses and instructions being passed around between the CPU's components. These are the registers.

CPU's Bus System

The bus, as it relates to the pathways on the computer an in the processor, carries the various signals, addresses and data that are transferred around the computer between its components. Although quite dissimilar, it can be related to the routes of our local transit company in many ways.

On the computer, a bus structure is a group if electronic transmission lines that connect the various components of the CPU, motherboard and expansion cards to each other. Bus structures have different sizes, ranging from 16 to 64 bits on modern microprocessors and their size determines the amount of data that can be transmitted. Obviously, a 64-bit bus carries more data than a 16-bit bus.

Within the computer, there are several bus structures, the most important of these are as follows:

Data Bus

Carries information to and from the CPU.

Address Bus

Carries the address from where data is to be read to where data is to be written.

Control Bus

Carries the signals used by the CPU and the other components of the computer to communicate with each other, including when data is ready to be read, when another device wishes to use the bus and the type of operation to be performed (read, write, interrupt).

Input/Output Devices

As we know, computer processes data which is fed into it and gives results in the form you like. You can feed in this data for processing using a number of input mediums available and take the resultant output on various other medias available. In this chapter we will read about all these input and output devices through which we can input the data and take the processed output.

Since output is dependent on the data which is inputted, it must be ensured that the data is correct else the result will be wrong too. If by mistake you type the bank account 9634 instead of 9631 then the amount would be credited to a different person. So one must ensure that the data is accurate. As you will read later in the chapter, there are devices which allow you to feed the directly to the computer whereas there are others which allow you to feed the data off line, record it in some media and then feed this media into the computer.

Input Concepts

On the basis of input, computer gives an output. Clerical kind of mistakes occasionally occur during the inputting of data, e.g., if Student Identification Number 6346 is wrongly inputted as 6364 can lead to the wrong result. Input phase is an excellent place to detect and correct errors. A right input protects computer files, i.e., inputted data which is stored in file on disks can be used later in some task. Accurate input is therefore vital to protect these files from "contamination". Data preparation is often labour intensive. This makes data preparation comparatively costly and therefore an important site for cost control. There are 3 important characteristics for a good data input

1. Timeliness
2. Accuracy and
3. Potential Usefulness

Data Preparation

There are two ways of entering the data into the computer. One is directly and second is indirectly. By direct, we mean typing directly into the computer and in the case of indirectly, we mean that the data has been prepared somewhere else and is now copied into the computer.

Transcriptive Data Entry

The data are prepared on documents at the source of the data. The data must then be transcribed to another medium that can be read and interpreted by a computer.

Source Data Entry

The data are prepared at the source in a machine readable form that can be used by a computer without a separate intermediate data transcription step. This type of data prepration reduces the number of errors during input process.

Output Concepts

The success of business today can depend to a large extent on how meaningful and timely the information a computer can produce, i.e., the output. So the two most important requirements of computer output are that it is meaningful and convenient to use.

Hard Copy

It is the output of the computer, which can be saved and read over and over. For example, the printer output.

Soft Copy

It is the output of the computer, which cannot be saved but just can be seen. For example, the output on the screen.

Storage Devices

Memory is not the only place where you store the data or program, since it is volatile. So you need to have storage devices which can store your data and programs permanently. For this we use so called storage units. These can be used for storing the data and then, maybe, transferring it to another computer or storage media.

COMPUTER SOFTWARE

Software is a program which cannot be seen but tell the computer what results to produce and a program is a set of instructions given to the computer to perform a certain task. There are two main types of software, namely:

(i) Application Software and **(ii) System Software**

System Software

The software used to operate and maintain a computer system and also used by a programmer to develop application software is known as **System Software**. It is written in a language which handles the computer hardware directly, whereas the application software works through the system software.

The Operating Systems like DOS, Windows fall into this category. Their job is not only to run the system but also to maintain it. Every comptuter system must have system software to make it work, without system software a computer cannot work.

Operating System (OS)

An operating system (OS) is a set of computer programs that manage the hardware and software resources of a computer. It processes raw data which is given to the computer as input. It then allocates and manages the tasks of the internal system resources of the computer. It is the operating system which performs basic tasks such as controlling and allocating memory, prioritizing system requests, controlling input and output devices, facilitating networking and managing file systems. Most operating systems come with an application that provides an interface to the operating system managed resources. These applications have had command line interpreters as a basic user interface, but more recently have been implemented as a Graphical User Interface (GUI) for ease of operation.

Operating Environments and shells

These are software programs that run top of the operating system and acts as homogenous user-interface between the applications and the operating system. They provide more facilities for input/output then the operating system. For example, Microsoft Windows on DOS, X-Windows for Unix, etc.

Device Drivers

These are special programs to extend the capabilities of operating system in order to support more Input/ Output devices like Mouse, Tape drives, etc.

Disk Directory and File Management Utilities

These are utility programs generated to manage data. These programs provide a good user-interface to ease the process of maintaining the files, directories and other system related settings.

Application Software

The computer does different type of jobs and for these different jobs, different applications are used. Each application needs to have its own set of programs and these programs combine together to form an Application Software. For example railway-ticketing, telephone-bill printing, salary and wages calculation, etc.

Application Software are of two types: **Ready Made Software** (Pre written application packages) and **Customized Software** (User written application packages).

User written application packages

User writing application packages are those that are designed and coded by the users of the package for their own use. For example, Payroll program, and Inventory control program for specific organization, etc.

Pre written application packages

Pre-written application packages are those packages that have been written by another person or group and made available to computer users. The following have been the most popular of these packages.

Word Processor

Word processor allows you to play with words. You can create documents, edit them, decorate them, add tables, graphs, pictures to them, etc., using a word processing program. Popular word processing programs are: Microsoft Word, Wordstar, WordPerfect, etc.

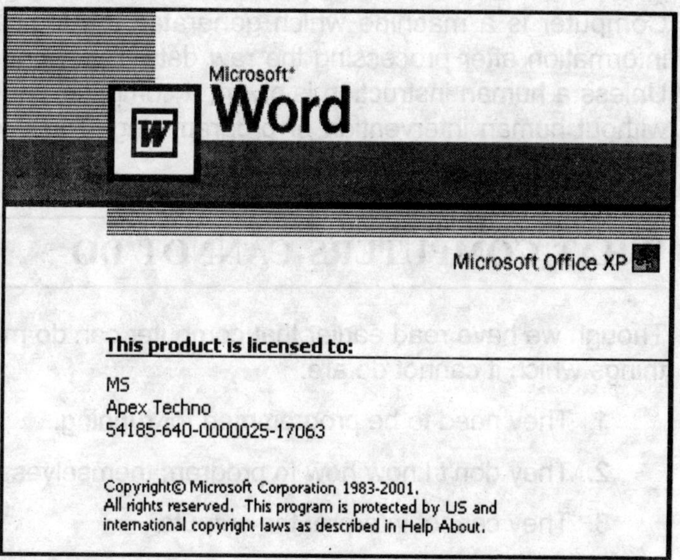

Data Manager

It stores, organizes, manipulates, retrieves, displays and prints data. Data Managers are important to Corporations and Central/State Governments as they keep track of the vast amounts of data that these organizations have to gather and store. Common among them are:

Database Management System (DBMS): A database is an integrated collection of well defined data and information, centrally controlled in all its aspects, created and stored in a typical structure for an organisation. In an organisation, the database could be, one or more, depending upon the needs and the operations of the organisation. The data structure and its storage should be such that it facilitates shareability, availability, evolvability and integrity of the data. The database separates a design of the information system from the data design and its management.

Relational Database Management System (RDBMS): A relational database management system (RDBMS), such as Access, stores data in related tables. For instance, a table containing employee data (names and addresses) may be related to a table containing payroll data (pay date, pay amount, and cheque number). Queries allow the user to ask complex questions (such as "What is the sum of all paychecks issued to Amitabh Bachchan in 2007") from these related tables, with the answers displayed as on-screen forms and printed reports.

Electronic Spreadsheet

A spreadsheet is a matrix of rows and columns. These columns and rows are used for entering text and numbers, which can then be used for calculations. An ideal software for accounting purposes and is very widely used for creating balance sheet, etc.

Graphics Packages

These are used for working with pictures and graphics instead of numbers and text. Computer-accessible data can readily be converted to graphic form on the screen as well as on paper using dot-matrix printers, ink-jet printers or plotters.

Communication Packages

It allows you to send and receive data over communication lines. The data/text can be transferred between two points, or it may involve communication through out a network of computers and work stations. Text extended at one office can be sent electronically to other sites. Users at these sites can retrieve and examine the text at their convenience. For example, PC-TALK, NICMAIL, Xpad, Radix, XTALK, etc.

Adobe

Licensed to:Amitabh Bachchan
ABCL Corp.
1039112129987586 7388

Adobe® PageMaker® 7.0

Ver. 7.0

LIVEWARE

Computer is a machine which generates the logical information after processing the raw data. But, above all it is the human which controls the whole process. Unless a human instruction is given, a computer cannot do anything. It cannot accept input, generate output without human intervention or programming. Thus, we say that the most important part of the computer is Liveware, i.e., the human being.

WHAT COMPUTERS CANNOT DO

Though we have read earlier that computer can do most of the things, but, it cannot do everything. Few of the things which it cannot do are:

1. They need to be programmed for running.
2. They don't know how to program themselves.
3. They cannot interpret the outputs.
4. They cannot take any decisions.
5. They cannot decided what input to take.

HOW DOES COMPUTER STORE DATA

Computer systems can store tremendous amounts of data, which can be located retrieved efficiently. A typical mainframe computer system will have many billions of characters stored and available for instant recall. High end PCs have access to about a billion characters of data. Most of this data is stored in Hard Disks which is fixed in the computer or the data can be fed in with the help of various storage devices like floppy disks, CD-ROMs, etc.

The storage capacity of disks depends on the number of tracks per inch of the surface and the bits per inch of track. Larger disks have more tracks and hence they have greater storage capacity. The total number of bytes that can be stored on a disk pack can be calculated as:

Number of cyclinders x ***Tracks per cyclinder*** x ***Sectors per track*** x ***Bytes per sector***

The total number of bytes that can be stored on a disk can be calculated as:

Number of sector x ***Sectors per cyclinder*** x ***Number of cyclinders*** x ***Number of heads***

For example, a hard disk drive having 14 heads, 723 cylinders and 51 sectors and each sector can store 0.5 KB has a storage capacity of 258 MB.

14 x 723 x 51 x 0.5 = 258,111.00 KB = 258 MB approx.

PROCESSING OF DATA

There are two type of processing. They are described next.

Batch Processing

It is a method in which data are gathered and batched through either an on line or off line data gathering process and processed periodically without user intervention.

Transaction Processing

It is an on-line method in which data are processed immediately, and files are updated as a transaction takes place. This allows the user to communicate with the computer during processing, through interactive programs which supply the results of processing so that they can be used when needed to control an operation or modify a process. This procedure is called real time processing. It is used in airlines offices to book and prepare a ticket.

TYPES OF COMPUTERS

Analog Computer: Analog computers are in which numerical magnitudes are represented by physical quantities, such as electric current, voltage or resistance, mechanical movements etc. Analog computers accepts data and then process it to produce analog data. Analog computer are machines designed to perform arithmetical functions upon numbers where the numbers are represented by physical quantity. For example, in mechanical analog computers the number are often represented by physical dimensions of the members forming the various functional units for instance by the angular rotation of the shaft or gear wheels.

In electrical analog machines voltages are used to represent the input variables.Essentially an analog computer must be able to accept inputs which vary with respect to time, and directly apply these inputs to various devices within the computer which perform the computing operations of addition, subtraction, multiplication, division and integration. The output from the system may be in the form of a graph produced by a plotting pen or a trace on a cathode-ray tube. The computing units of analog computers are able to respond immediately to the changes which they detect in the input variable and the connection of these various units in a particular fashion can cause an analog computer to perform very complex arithmetical functions at high speed while the actual process under study is in operation.

The ability to operate in real time mode means that analog computers has many application in the scientific and industrial fields in simulating various physical systems or automatically controlling industrial processes. They are widely used for research into design problems. Analog computers are used in manufacturing units where temperatures, pressure or flow of liquids are to be monitored continuously. It also used at service station where gasoline pump contains an analog processor that connect fuel flow measurements into quantity and price values.

Digital Computers: A digital computer operates on data in the form of digits, rather than the physical quantities used in analog computers. That is, its input must be discrete rather than continuous and may consist of combinations of numbers, characters and special symbols, written in appropriate programming language. Computers generate digital signals representing bit patterns, whereas standard telephone lines were designed to handle analog signals in the form of voices and other sound patterns to use telephone for data communication digital signals need to be converted to an analog format. Originally digital computers were mechanical devices employing cogs, gears and levers, they now depend upon electronic technique enabling them to deal automatically with a wide range of problems at a very high speeds. Some of the earlier digital computing devices were developed from punched card machines and the program was set up by means of connections on a plugboard, machines of this category are generally referred to as calculators, rather than computers.

Modern digital computers are usually based on the binary notation, numbers and letters being coded into group of digits consisting only of 1 or 0. Each of these digits is represented in an electronic circuit or magnetic store by a component in an on or off state. For example, passing current or not passing current, magnetized or not magnetized. Data in this form is processed in the CPU of the computer by gates (switches) which obey the instructions of the program.

The individual operations performed by a digital computer are very simple arithmetic or logical processes involving the manipulation of the bits in words or characters of information. The great power of any digital computer rets in the ability to store large volumes of data and to perform these various functions at extremely high speed. Arithmetic and logical circuits for processing data in binary form are constructed from simple basic units designed to perform the operations of Boolean algebra AND, OR, NOT etc. These simple units are used as building blocks in constructing the complex logic and control circuits required.

General purpose digital computers: It is also known as all purpose digital computer. Theoretically it can be used for any type of application. e.g., computers that are used for payroll, graphs, analysis etc.

Special purpose digital computers: A digital computer designed to solve problems of a restricted type. That is, special-purpose digital computer is designed to be especially efficient in a certain class of applications. For example, computers installed in washing machines.

THE NEED FOR COMPUTER LITERACY

There was a time when students wanted to learn computers, just to get jobs in US. Slowly it changed and computers became the IN thing. Everybody wanted to learn computers. Since, computers were used everywhere, a computer literate was finding it easier to get the job. While on other hand, girls, who were not planning to take up jobs, wanted to add an extra qualifications in their matrimonial status. But, all this has changed now. The jobs are plenty in India only. Computer knowledge has become the basic information need. Most of the graduate and post-graduate syllabus have computer related course.

What is it enough? No. The computer knowledge has to be given at basic level, i.e., Schools. I do not say that computers are not taught at schools. But, whatever is taught is not enough. It is still treated as an elective subject. Moreover, there is dearth of good computer teachers around. All schools want a good teacher first, i.e., they should have a B.Ed degree, even if they do not have MCA. Good teachers cannot teach good computers. Teachers who are good at computers, take up computer related jobs, like, software development, which is more attractive.

To make the computer education reach the masses, somebody has to devise a method to make the computer education, more user friendly. In fact, everyone from publisher to school to teacher to student, everyone should have a say in the development of this method. Only then it will succeed.

COMPUTER LIMITATIONS

Despite being the most powerful machine available to us these days, the computer still has its own limitations. Some it does perform abnormally, due to some reasons or others which may be baffling to the users. To ensure that the computers work normally, we have to see that the following are taken care of:

Programs must be Reliable

The most common problems faced by computers come from the use of faulty software. These are the software which are usually called the Pirated software. One person buys the original software and makes copies of them for others to use. It is possible that while copying something or the other is missed and you would not know about it immediately. Most of the popular computer software are subjected to the vigorous tests before releasing in public. It can be possible that a particular eventuality is not taken care of and that occurs for some unknown reason. This can give problem.

Application Logic must be Understood

Computer works on logic, if your logic is wrong, it will give bad results. It is like chess, where making a move you have to mentally sit on the opposite side and think of all the possible moves, before making your own move. Similarly, a program has to look into all the possible situations.

USES AND IMPACT OF COMPUTERS

There are lots of uses of computers. In fact, in our everyday life it is used in almost every step. Some of the places where it is used is listed below.

Business and Industry: For most of the companies, all the work relating to accounts is now done on computers, for accuracy and speediness. You can even have your correspondence on it. Computers are finding their place in automizing the production process too.

Health care: Lots of research in medicine is done using computers. Doctors now a days can see the complete inside of the human beings using the computers, which results in no fault operations.

Education: Computers can help in teaching too. In fact this books on computers was created using computers. Most of the schools now use computers for accounting, students record management, papers preparation and even results compilation.

Humanities: In recent years, computer usage has increased in people having interests in history, literature, music, graphics, arts and other branches of humanities.They use it to:

- ease manuscript preparation
- translate texts from one natural language to another
- conduct studies that would otherwise be impractical
- apply artistic talents to a new medium, and
- discover significant stylistic patterns in text.

Science and Technology: All the movements of the satellites are controlled using computers. Using computers and satellites you can predict the weather for the next few days. In fact, the biggest computer in India is with the Meteorological Department of India, at New Delhi.

Recreation and Entertainment: There are various programs available in computers which allow you to create animations. By learning about them you can become an expert animator. You may even make a movie of your own. Computers are used in cinema halls too, for tickets printing and seat allocation.

Government: America has used the computers in defence for the fullest with pin pointing the position of enemy targets. Most of the missiles these days are computer controlled. Government uses it planning and other information too.

Various uses of the computers are also shown on the next page.

Airlines booking	Banks	Business
Now you can book your ticket for a flight leaving New York while sitting in Melbourne. All the airlines are interconnected through computers. The same goes for Railways but it is restricted to individual countries only.	Computers in Banks have made it possible that you can get your account information while sitting at home only. For this your bank must be an e-bank, which most of them are. ATMs are another computer applications of banks.	For most of the companies, all the work relating to accounts is now done on computers, for accuracy and speediness. You can even have your correspondence on it.
Animation	**Cinema**	**Defence**
There are various programs available in computers which allow you to create animations. By learning them you can become an expert animator. You may even make a movie of your own.	Now-a-days most of the film editing is done by computers. You can add and delete film clips at a snap using computers. In fact, some movies are totally made using computers. Films like Toy Story are made using computers.	America has used the computers in defence for the fullest with pin-pointing the position of enemy targets. Most of the missiles these days are computer controlled.
DTP	**Education**	**Home**
It has revolutionized how composing for printing used to done. Now every book for printing is composed on computer since it is very easy to edit and read on screen.	Computers can help in teaching too. In fact, this book on computers was created using computers. Most of the schools now use computers for accounting, students record management, papers preparation and even results compilation.	At home it has become an additional entertainment media. You can use it for playing games, watching movies, listening to songs, writing letters, creating your own database of friends, etc., the options are unlimited.
Library	**Medicine**	**Space Technology**
Maintaining the records in library manually used to be a very cumbersome method. Computers have dramatically changed the way the cataloging is done in libraries.	Lots of research in medicine is done using computers. Doctors now-a-days can see the complete inside of the human beings using the computers.	All the movements of the satellites are controlled using computers.

DATA PROCESSING

There are several steps involved in processing of data. Data as such is the term given to all the facts that record an event, an activity or a situation. As isolated facts and figures may not be meningful in themselves, they can be processed in various specific ways in order to give them a useful maining.

Data processing involves the steps like sorting, relating, interpretting, and computing items of data in order to provoke meaningful and useful information. It will be evident that to arrive at certain figures, the data must be processed according to predefined procedures and rules arranged in a specific order. It would, for instance, be pointless to add the number of lengths of timber to number of hours worked, the answer would be meaningless. The term Data Processing System relates to an assembly of those steps in logical order.

The stepes by which information data (current and past paper work) is expressed as data processed and returned to individuals as updated and useful information, is known as Data Processing. The following steps are generally followed:

1. Prepration of source documents
2. Input of Data
3. Manipulation of Data
4. Output of information
5. Storage

Prepration of source documents

The first step is to obtain the relevant facts and figures and to set these out on source documents, for example, in a population survey, the name, address, age, sex, occupation, etc., must be first written down on to a survey sheet or some other document. These documents may be so designed that information is recorded in the required order.

Input Data

Once the data has been extracted from the source document, it must than be transferred into some form suitable for data entry into the computer so that processing can take place. The method will depend upon the input media and the devices.

Manipulation of Data

Information, inputs for processing may have to be classified or sorted. It is this form of operation, or data manipulation, rather than pure computation, with which data processing is mainly concerned. For example, in the population survey we may want to classify people by occupation or by age. We may wish to sort lists on alphabetical order or in any other order. We may require employees to be grouped by departments for a pay roll program. All these forms of data manipulation will produce results, which can be organised in the form of summaries.

Information Output

The objective of results or summaries is to provide meaningful information to Managers, Accountants, etc., and careful consideration, therefore, should be given to the presentation of results so that they can be understandable easily and quickly.

Data Storage

In most cases, the results of processing are retained for future use or reference. In many cases, it may be necessary after updating, to compare the latest figures with the previous figures, perhaps, over different periods of time. This means that data processing installations require a great deal of secondary storage space to store all the programs and the different sets of data.

DATA PROCESSING SYSTEMS

Current technology has produced many forms of data processing, and a company can select a form uniquely suited to its needs. Management must decide which hardware and data processing approach to adopt, a decision that will dictate the day-to-day operation of the data processing department and how users receive their computer prepared information.

Batch Processing

It is a widely used technique. It involves the regular processing of large amounts of data. In batch processing, data is collected for a predeterrnined period of time, after which it is processed. The processing of a payroll is a good example of batch processing. Payroll data is accumulated over 1-, 2-, or 4-week period and processed at regular intervals. Pay cheques are distributed to all employees on a predetermined schedule.

Online Processing

Batch processing requires that data be accumulated before it is processed by the computer, creating a delay between a transaction and its processing. Current technology can shorten this delay and process data almost immediately by using special hardware. These online devices allow direct communication with the computer and an uninterrupted flow of input data. The term offline describes the condition where direct communication with the computer is not possible. Online processing is used when delay in handling data is undesireable. Online processing is used by airlines and car rental agencies to accept and confirm customer reservations in seconds.

Time Sharing

One form of online processing allows the concurrent use of a computer by a group of individuals. This form of online processing is called time-sharing. Many users share a computer's resources at the same time. Schools often adopt time-sharing systems to support their computer curriculumns. Time sharing allows many students concurrent access to th same computer. The student can create an online link to the computer using a device called a terminal with a keyboard for inputting data and a TV screen for output data. The online link to the computer may use a leased line or a regular telephone line. The student receives a set of instructions on how to use the terminal and create the online link.

Remote Job Entry

The tim-shared processing of student program represents one type of telecommunications operation. Other types may use different input or output devices. For example, a busineeperson may want to imput data on computer cards and output information in a printed report, operations that require a computer device is called a remote job entry station.

A remote job entry (RJE) station is a device permitting transfer of data from a remote location to a distant computer system via telecommunications. An RJE may use computer cards or a keyboard for online processing. As processing occurs, information may be transmitted back to the RJE as a printed report. Printed reports are generally called hard copy because they are permanent, tangible processing records. Output that appears on a terminal's screen is called soft copy because it is impermanent and remains useful only while it is visible. RJE stations often have a terminal to expand the device's ability to handle input and output operations.

SUMMARY

1. A computer: cannot think, it has vast capabilities of calculations like addition, substraction, etc. and It is totally under the control of the user.
2. Though the first fully operational electronic computer was introduced to the world in 1946, but the historian assumes the starting of a computer age from 1951, when first commercial computer UNIVAC was introduced.
3. Computer is vastly used for Airlines booking, Banking business, Professional Business, Cartoons creations, Cinema editing, Defence applications, Desk Top Publishing, Education books and teaching, Home videos and games, Library management of books, Medicine records, Space Technology and Weather reporting.
4. The main parts of the computer are: Monitor, Central Processing Unit and Keyboard.
5. The block diagram shows all the parts of the computer.
6. Over the years personal computers have gone through various changes and have been named as XT, AT, etc.

7. There are various types of memories which are used by computers.
8. What is a Digital Computer?
9. What are the drawbacks of Analog Computers?
10. Write down some basic features of Super Computers.
11. What are the drawbacks of Super Computers?
12. What are the uses of Super Computers?
13. What are the uses of Main Frame Computers?
14. What are the uses of Mini Computers?
15. What are the Characteristics of Computers.
16. Classify the computers according to their size.
17. What computer cannot do?
18. Distinguish between RAM, ROM, PROM and EPROM. For a given computer, which type of memory would have the greater capacity to store data and programs: Cache or RAM? RAM or registers? registers or Cache?
19. What are the two types of computer memories, and how do they differ?
20. What purpose does the RAM serve when it is simply a volatile storage medium?
21. What do you mean by volatile memory? What can be done to overcome the problems of this kind of memory?
22. Operating system in most of the PCs is Windows.
23. There are various software available for creating multimedia.
24. Hardware is something which can be seen and touched whereas Software cannot be seen or touched.
25. A set of programs is called Software.
26. There are two types of system software and they are: Operating System; and Language Translators.
27. There are 3 types of translators: Assembler, Interpreter and Compiler.
28. Word processors are used for manipulating text.
29. Spreadsheets are used for calculations.
30. DTP packages are used for text and graphics.
31. Anti virus software are used for virus detection and removal.
32. For communicating with the computer, we use computer language called programming language.
33. The machine language is the only one that computer can understand directly.
34. A program written by a programmer in an assembly language is called a Source Program.
35. LOGO programming allows you to draw pictures on the screen.
36. COBOL is basically used for business applications.
37. PASCAL is a general purpose language.
38. JAVA programming is used on Internet.

MULTIPLE CHOICE QUESTIONS

1. Full form of RAM is:
   (a) Random Access Memory (b) Read And Memory (c) Read Access Memory
2. Central Processing Unit has:
   (a) Control Unit (b) Arithmetic Logic Unit **(c) Both**
3. Two main memories of computer are RAM and:
   (a) RAC **(b) R**OM (c) RAM
4. Capacity of RAM is measure in:
   (a) bytes (b) litres (c) grams
5. Which of the following is not a memory?
   (a) Flash (b) Bubble **(c) Tr**iple.
6. Which software is usually used for making overhead presentations?
   (a) Microsoft Frontpage (b) Microsoft Powerpoint (c) Microsoft Word

7. What is usually used for displaying information at public places?
   (a) Monitors (b) Overhead projections (c) Touch screen kiosks
8. Which is the most popular media for multimedia packaging?
   (a) Floppy disk (b) CD-ROM (c) Hard disk
9. Which is the most popular hardware for the multimedia creations?
   (a) PCs (b) Mini Computers (c) Mainframe Computers
10. What is MP3?
   (a) A mouse (b) A printer (c) A sound format
11. Can you create a multimedia project alone?
   (a) Yes (b) No
12. A computer language which is used for drawing pictures on the screen is:
   (a) LOGO (b) COBOL (c) BASIC
13. Computer program which controls the operations of computer is called:
   (a) Assembler (b) Operating System (c) Interpreter
14. A computer program used for Business applications is:
   (a) LOGO (b) COBOL (c) BASIC
15. A software package for creating printing artworks is called:
   (a) Word Processing (b) DTP (c) Spreadsheet
16. Computer understands the ________ language.
   (a) Machine (b) Assembly (c) High level language
17. Computer language used on Internet is
   (a) PASCAL (b) JAVA (c) BASIC

REVIEW QUESTIONS

1. What is the difference between Hardware and Software?
2. What are the different type of system software?
3. Describe the various language translators.
4. Which are the various popular software packages?
5. What are assembly and machine languages?
6. Describe briefly the following languages:

LOGO	FORTRAN	COBOL
BASIC	PROLOG	PASCAL
C	C++	JAVA

7. Describe the various functions of CPU.
8. What does CPU consist of ?
9. What is Internal memory?
10. What are Registers? What function do they play?
11. What happens inside ALU?

ANSWERS

Multiple Choice Questions

1. a	2. c	3. b	4. a
6. c	7. c	8. b	9. a
10. c	11. b	12. a	13 b
14. b	15. b	16. a	17. b

CHAPTER 2

Development of Computers

Learning Objectives

After going through this chapter, you should appreciate the following:

- Year wise development of computers
- Computer Generations
- First Generation Computers
- Second Generation Computers
- Third Generation Computers
- Fourth Generation Computers
- Fifth Generation Computers
- Personal Computers
- History of Personal Computers.
- Classification of Computers by Size
- Super Computers
- Mainframe Computers
- Minicomputers
- Laptops
- Supercomputers

INTRODUCTION

In the early days people started exchanging goods and in this process they felt the need of counting. This was done with the help of stones. Each stone represented a single unit. Stones could be counted before giving or taking the things.

Next, they started drawing lines on wall or on sand before selling or purchasing the goods. It was a simple but a lengthy process for large numbers they felt the need of a system to keep track of the numbers in a simple and easier way.

They used different ways to do so started evolving tools.

Abacus

In 3000 B.C. Abacus is the simplest form of a digital computer. It is interesting to note that it is still used in its larger version and its users can calculate at amazing speed. Abacus was invented by the Chinese.

Later it was modified by Egyptians and Indians. It is simply a rectangular wooden frame with horizontal rods which carry rounded moveable beads, which are used for counting. It has 10 rods with 5 beads in each.

Each rod has 2 sections, upper and lower. In lower section there are 4 beads representing a single unit. Upper section has 1 bead representing number 5. Counting is done by shifting of beads from one side to another.

If the beads in the upper part are placed just beside the cross bars, they denote the digit five. When the beads are placed far from the cross bar, i.e. beside the bar of the frame, they denote zero.

Similarly, the beads in the lower part denote the number 1, when they are placed beside the cross bar and zero when placed near the frame bar. The topmost line represents the unit digit, second line ten's, third line hundred's digit and so on.

Simple addition and subtraction can be carried out rapidly and efficiently by positioning the beads appropriately. It is interesting to note that the method of subtraction used in Abacus was based on the principle of complement of a number, a very important concept used in modern digital computer.

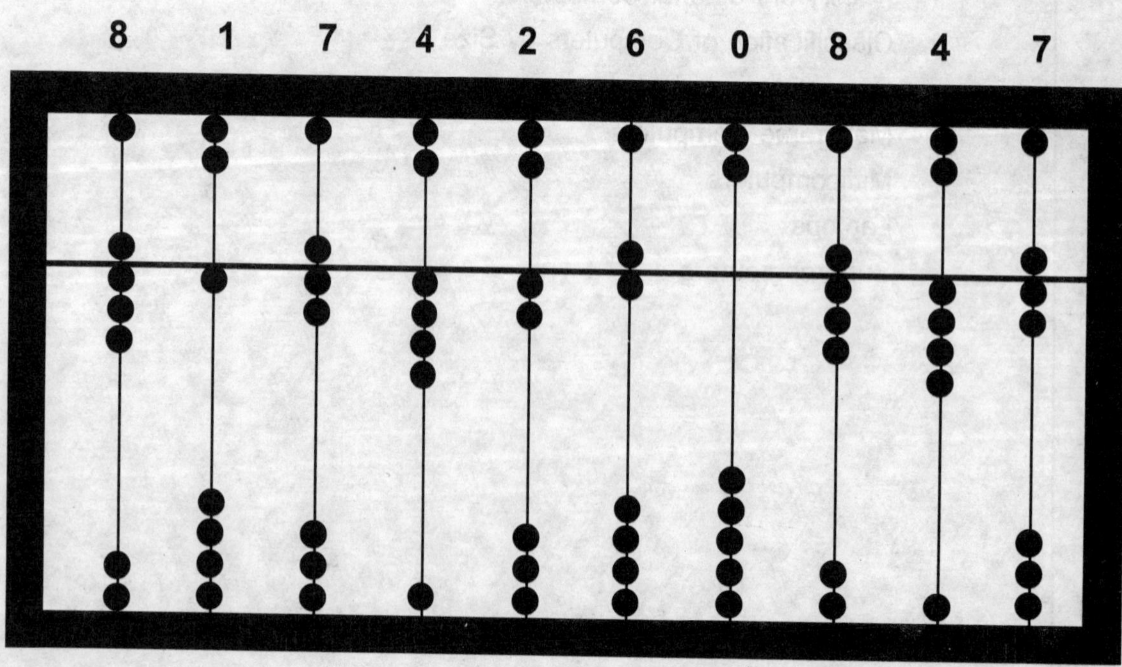

OTHER YEAR-WISE DEVELOPMENTS OF COMPUTERS

1600

Hindu Arabic math became popular in Europe.

1614

John Napier introduced logarithms.

1617

John Napier invented a machine which consisted of a set of numbered rods for doing multiplications. Each rod contained digits from 1 to 9.

Napier Bones

In the early 17th century John Napier, a Scottish mathematician, developed another calculating device known as Napier's Bones. John Napier is famous for development of logarithms. He used a set of eleven rods called Bones. The numbers were carved on them. In fact, Napier's Bones was very helpful in the work which involved multiplications. It was an analog device.

1642

A famous French mathematician Blaise Pascal developed the first mechanical calculating machine which was known as **Pascaline**. This machine had a number of teeth and wheels connected together by chains. Numbers were fed into the machine by dialing them on the wheels. It could add and do multiplications.

Pascal's Calculator

For inventing the first mechanical calculating machine in 1642, the credit goes to the great French Mathematician Blaise Pascal. His father was a tax collector and his job was very tiring and he had to keep late hours at night.

Blaise was highly motivated to ease his father's workload which involved endless computations. He started working and could develop a calculator in the year 1642, which was patented in the year 1645. His machine was the first calculator in the right sense and was able to add, subtract efficiently.

Pascal's calculator used gears, cog wheels and dials. Each wheel had 10 segments like that of millimeters on house energy meters. When one rotation is completed by one wheel the next wheel moves by one segment. The present day speedometers (called ode meters) can be compared to Pascal's machine. In Pascal's machine addition was straightforward and subtraction was done by the method of complement of numbers, a method used in modern computers. The adjacent figure shows a Pascal's machine.

The machine became very popular and was produced on mass scale. In fact, it paved the way for further development of calculators. Pascal was paid most benefiting tribute by Professor Nikalus Wirth at Zurich, in the year 1960, when he developed a programming language and named it PASCAL.

1671

Ad Gofried Leibrietzi – Modified or improved the Pascal's machine.

Leibnitz's Machine

The famous German Mathematician, Gottfried von Leibnitz, developed a calculating machine, which could multiply and divide numbers successfully. In fact, this machine was a modified model of Pascal's calculator. A new idea was used in Leibnitz's machine, i.e. the use of slide performing this shift mechanism. Moving a digit to the right or left is called a shift. When we multiply and divide two numbers manually, we work in steps moving from one column to next and so on. This was exactly what Leibnitz's machine could do.

Although Pascal's and Leibnitz's machines exhibited a sound principle, the under developed machine technology of 17th Century proved a hindrance in obtaining the required accuracy.

Though, the machines developed by Pascal and Leibnitz, could not gain popularity these machines were the forerunners of key-driven calculators developed in the 9th Century.

1801

Jacquard's Loom

The first example of robot controlled machine was Jacquard's loom in 1801. It was invented by Joseph-Marie Jacquard. This machine was capable of weaving complicated patterns which depended on the position of holes in punched cards that were supplied to the machine.

1792 – 1871

Charles Babbage, an English Mathematician, designed a machine, named **Difference Engine**. In 1833- 34, Babbage invented another machine with an automatic computing mechanism. He named it **Analytical Engine**. This machine could store the data in **Memory**, which became the base of Modern Computers. This is why he is known as the Father of Computers.

Charles Babbage – Difference Engine

The year 1823 could be considered a golden year in the history of Computer Science. It was in the year 1823, when an Englishman, Charles Babbage, a professor of mathematics of Cambridge University, developed and demonstrated a working model of a mechanical computer called Difference Engine. His Difference Engine could evaluate algebraic expressions correctly and was also able to produce mathematical and statistical tables correct up to 20 digits. During this period, mathematical and statistical tables were prepared by a group of clerks. Babbage's Difference Engine was based on the principle that for certain expressions, the difference between certain values of the expression at a certain stage becomes constant. For this work, Babbage is considered to be the father of modern digital computers. But even the utmost care an precautions could not eliminate human errors. Babbage had to spend several hours checking these tables. Soon he became dissatisfied and exasperated with this type of monotonous job. The result was that the started thinking to build a machine which could compute tables guaranteed to be error-free. In this process, Babbage designed Analytical Machine in 1833 which was an automatic computing machine designed to do additions at the rate of 60 per minute and had memory also. Unlike the modern computers, his Analytical Engine was to have five units – Store, Mill (ALU), Control, Input and Output.

Unfortunately, Babbage's Analytical Engine could not be completed due to under-developed technology of his time. In fact, Babbage could have designed a better machine during his life time itself by the contemporary technology could not assist and match his genius. His machine Analytical Engine was never built although he spent a lot of government funds and his own money. He died in the year 1871 without completing his project. No doubt, Babbage failed in his mission but he laid the foundation for the development of modern digital computers. It is said that Babbage was a genius at least hundred years ahead of his time. The drawing and notes left by Babbage for his Ar lytical Engine show the glimpse of modern electronic computers because his store can be compared with memory unit. Mil is compared with ALU and the rest are same.

1840

Augusta Ada suggested binary data storage rather than the decimal. She was a "First Programmer".

Lady Ada Lovelace

Babbage's life history would be incomplete without a mentions of an amateur mathematician who was his disciple, namely Ada Lovelace, the daughter of famous English poet, Lord Byron. She developed a special number system called Binary Number System for Babbage's machines. She sued to correspond regularly with Babbage giving him advice and sometimes scolding for his mistake. If Babbage is considered the father of modern computer science, then Lady Ada Lovelace must be thought of as first programmer in the world. While referring to the use of punch card in both Jacquard's loom and the Analytical Engine, she wrote The Analytical Engine weaves algebraic pattern as Jacquard's look weaves flowers and leaves.

1850

George Boole, an English Mathematician realized that complex mathematical problems could be solved by reducing them. The binary's system of 1's for positive answers and 0's for negative answered could be implemented. That is why the story of Boolean logic became fundamental to the design of computer circuity.

Boolean Algebra

A very important development took place in 1854, when an English Mathematician, George Boole, developed two-state algebra, called Boolean Algebra. It was able to solve logic problems where each variable has either of the two values, namely True/False. It implies that Boolean Algebra is binary is nature and hence could be applied to development of computers. It was Claude Shanon, an electrical engineer, who came up with is application to switching circuits that led to the simplification mathematics and logic. The circuits of present-day computers depend upon the application of this algebra.

1880

Herman Hollerith, a mathematician, invented a Tabulating Machine by using punch cards for the census (calculation of population) in USA. The cards used to have holes for different answers. When these cards passed through this machine, the machine could detect holes on cards, recognize numbers and it could make required calculations.

Hollerith Machines

The next significant step towards modern computing came from Dr. Herman Hollerith (1860-1929) of USA. He was working in USA Census as a statistician. Tabulation of Census manually is a gigantic task for big countries like India and USA. It was felt that the existing methods of tabulating information were inadequate and Census Bureau was at loss to understand how to complete this work. Moreover, with the next census due in 1890, with a higher population to deal with, some new methods were needed. Dr. Herman Hollerith, taking cue from Jacquard's punched cards system to control weaving looms suggested that information may be represented by combination of holes on punch cards. The ideas was accepted by the government and Hollerith was given a green signal to go ahead with the project. This machine could sense the punched holes, recognized the number and make the required calculations. The tabulations of these machines used electrical contacts which brushed these cards and made the contact through the holes in the cards as these cards passed through the machine. This is precisely what is done in present day computers. This resulted in completion of work relating to 1880 census by 1887, taking a time of 7 years. The information gained in 1890 census relating to 60 million people could be processed just in three years, a great success of Hollerith machines.

Punched cards machines were very popular in the first four decades of this century and even now is a common medium for feeding information into a computer.

1896

Hollerith established his own company named as Tabulating Machine Company. Later on, this company was incorporated into international Business Machine Corporation (IBM) which is the largest computer manufacturer in the world even today. One of the features of Hollerith's inventions was the use of electromechanical means of reading cards. Metallic plungers would feel for holes in the card and if they found a hole, they would go right through and dip into a bowl of mercury, thus completing an electrical circuit. This would cause a needle to point to the value read or cause a machine to add the figures. Hollerith realized that electricity was a much more convenient tool for transmitting results than mechanical means. For this work, he is considered as the father of modern data processing.

During the first three decades of 20th Century, many developments in the field of computers and electronics took place. In the field of data storage media the contribution of Valdemair Poulson cannot be forgotten. He developed various recording devices such as magnetic tapes and magnetic drums. The invention of Thermionic Valve (vacuum tube) by Lee de Forest in 1906 opened the gates for development of electronic computers.

Alan Turing, an English mathematician, made a very deep impact on computer science in 1937. He established theoretically that a complex problem having a logical solution can be split into a set of simple steps and can be solved easily. He helped England during the second world war to develop machines that could break secret codes. These code breaks were very useful to the British military forces when they intercepted messages from the German armies. Alan Turing is also famous for another idea of his. He published a paper in which he described that a computer was capable of solving any problem that required a finite number of mechanical steps. This came at the time when most of the scientists and engineers thought that for each different class of problems, a different machine had to be built.

1930-1939

The first electronic computer was built by Dr. John Vincent Atanasoff, a Professor of Physics and Mathematics at Iowa State College and Mr. Clifford Berry, his graduate assistant. This was known as "Atanasoff-Berry Computer" or ABC.

Eletro-Mechanical Computers

Until the 1930's the development of automatic computing was mostly in improving the technology of calculators. The machines made till then were adequate for the businessman to handle large amount of data that needed to be treated in the same way, what is now called data processing. In fact, all the calculating machines invented hitherto were basically mechanical machines. The first fully automatic calculating machine was designed by Dr. Howard Aiken and Grace Hopper of Harvard University in 1944.

It was developed with the collaboration of IBM (International Business Machine) Corporation. Its design was based on the techniques already developed for punched card machinery. It was known as Mark-I or Automatic Sequence Controller Calculator (ASCC). It used more than 3000 electrically controlled switches (relays). Although it was not a fully electronic device, it was quite fast and could add two to 20-digit numbers in a span of about 5 seconds. The output was obtained on punch cards through an electric typewriter.

Although this machine proved to be extremely reliable, it was very complex in design and huge in size. It had a shape like monster about 15 m long and 3 m high. It was basically an electro-mechanical device since both mechanical and electronic components were used in its design. Although its operations were not controlled electronically, Aiken's machine is often classified as computer because its instructions, which were entered by means of punched paper tape, could be altered. This machine was produced on mass scale and remained in use till 1959. After this, all the computers developed were electronic in which relays were replaced by valves, transistors, etc.

The growth of computer after the end of World War-II was very amazing but this development took in five distinct phases known as computer generations. In fact, the scientists and engineers were more conscious about the second World War. They started working to make computers that would help in artillery calculations and code breaking. For this purpose, the money was easily available to them. Several wartime computers made their appearance.

Some of them were the German ENIGMA and the British COLOSSUS which were used by the military for code breaking. However, the ENIAC from the USA was the first large electronic computer to become functional.

1939

Cloud Shanon brought the idea of Boolean Algebra to be adopted in computer field. He was able to establish that the Electronic Switching Circuits could be employed to perform logical and arithmetic operations. He was the first person to use Boolean Algebra in the designing of electrical circuits of computers. It was not long before on electro-mechanical computer based on relays was developed.

1944

IBM had made a computer and named it Harvard Mark – I. It worked electro mechanically without any manual efforts. It could perform three addition operations and one subtraction operation per second. As multiplication, it could perform one operation per second. It was a first computer and was also called Automatic Sequence Controlled Computer (ASCC).

1946

ENIAC (**E**lectronic **N**umeric **I**ntegrator **A**nd **C**alculator) computer was developed by Mr. Mauchly and Eckert. This was based on Mark 1, which was developed by Howard Aitken and Grace Hopper in 1930.

ENIAC

The first large scale, all valve computer, was called Electronic Numerical Integrator and Computer (ENIAC). It was made in 1946 by J.P. Eckert and J.W. Marchly at the University of Pennsylvania of USA. It was developed as a result of military need. It was voluminous in size and needed a space of 20ftx40ft. The power needed by the computer was enough to light up a small township. It was a very fast machine as compared to its ancestors which could perform 5000 additions or 350 multiplications in one second. It contained 18000 vacuum tubes, 70000 resistors, 10000 capacitors and 60000 switches. The ENIAC suffered from two shortcomings: first, it could store only a small amount of information and secondly, its programs were wired on boards which made the task of modifying a program quite difficult. However, whatever the shortcomings of ENIAC, it represented an impressive feat of electronic engineering and was used till 1955 to solve ballistic problems, i.e. problems dealing with the weapons.

1949

Mr. Maurice V.Wilkes of Cambridge built **E**lectronic **D**elayed **S**torage **A**utomatic **C**omputer (**EDSAC**), the first stored program computer.

EDSAC was modified by Mr. Mauchly, Eckert and Von Neumann and invented **E**lectronic **D**iscreter **V**riable **A**utomatic **C**ompuer (**EDVAC**), this was a second stored program computer.

EDSAC (1947-49)

The operation of ENIAC was seriously handicapped by the wiring board. This problem was later overcome by the new concept of Stored Program developed by Dr. John von Neumann in 1946. He delivered a series of lectures on Electronic Digital Computers and presented a report. The basic idea behind his report was the use of binary numbers to represent data and instructions; a sequence of instructions as well as data can be stored in the memory of the computer for the purpose of automatically directing the flow of operations. The EDSAC (Electronic Delayed Storage Automatic Computer) was the first computer which used Neumann's idea of stored program. It was developed by a group of scientists headed by Prof. Wilkers at the Cambridge University.

1950

Grace Hooper developed **UNIVAC I** compiler.

Turing built the **A**utomatic **C**omputing **E**ngine (**ACE**) which can be considered the first programmable digital computer.

EDVAC

This was another computer which used this idea of von Neumann. It was built in 1950 at Moore School in USA. The program and data were fed to the EDVAC though a punched paper tape. The Electronic Discrete Variable Automatic Computer (EDVAC) was designed on stored program concept.

The stored program concept considerably influenced the development of modern digital computers and because of this feature we often refer to modern digital computer stored program digital computers.

1951

Mauchly and Eckert built the first computer **UNIVAC I**, which was designed and sold commercially.

UNIVAC

The Universal Automatic Computer (UNIVAC) was the first digital computer which was not one of a kind. Many UNIVAC machines were produced, the first of which was installed in the Census Bureau in 1951 and was used continuously for 10 years. It was developed by Universal Accounting Company set up by Eckert and Mauchly. It was different from its predecessors in the sense that it was a self checking computer and used magnetic tape as input media. UNIVAC I is remembered even today for having predicted correctly the election of President Dwight Eisenhower of USA in year 1952. Another achievement of this computer was established in the year 1954, when GEC (General Electric Corporation) used it for business application for the first time and this Corporation undertook the mass scale production of the computer.

LEO (Lyons Electronic Office)

M.V. Wilkes developed this first commercial computer in 1951.

1957

International **B**usiness **M**achines (**IBM**) engineers developed **FORTRAN** (**For**mula **Tran**slation Language)

1959

Hooper developed the **COBOL** (**C**ommon **B**usiness **O**riented **L**anguage) programming language.

1960

IBM System/360 series of Mainframe Computers were introduced were based on Integrated Circuits (ICs) technology.

1965

Beginner's All-purpose Symbolic Instruction Code (BASIC) language was developed by Dr. John Kemeny. A mathematics Professor and his colleague, Dr. Thomas Kurtz.

1970

Memory Chip was introduced by Intel which could store a kilobit of information.

1975

H. Edward Roberts, an electrical engineer designed the first **Micro Computer**.

1977

The first **Apple Micro Computer** was invented by Mr. Stephen Wozniak, the Technical Expert and Steven Jobs.

1980

Persibal Computers were introduced.

From this point onward computers developed can be classified into various generations.

Beginning of Computer Age

Though the first fully operational electronic computer was introduced to the world in 1946, but the historian assumes the starting of computer age from 1951, when first commercial computer, UNIVAC was introduced. The remarkable thing about the computer age is that so much has happened in so much short time.

We have leapfrogged through four generations of technology in about 40 years - a span of time whose events are within the memories of many people today.

The first three computer generations are pinned to three technological developments.

- the vacuum tube
- the transistor and
- the integrated circuit

Each has drastically changed the nature and size of computers. We define the timing of each generation according to the beginning of commercial delivery of the hardware technology. Defining subsequent generations has become more complicated because the entire industry has become more complicated.

COMPUTER GENERATIONS

Computer generations can be derived on the basis of the various methods used in the making of the computer.

	Generations	*Based on*	*Period*
(i)	First Generation	Electronic Valves	1950
(ii)	Second Generation	Transistors	1960

(iii)	Third Generation	Integrated Circuits	1965
(iv)	Fourth Generation	Microprocessors	1975
(v)	Fifth Generation	Large Scale Integrated Systems	1980

First Generation Computers

J.P. Eckert and J.W. Muchly developed the first electronic computer known as UNIVAC I in 1951. General features of these computers were:

(i) Vacuum tubes were used in these computers.

(ii) Punched cards were used to feed the information and for the output punched cards and papers were used.

(iii) For External storage Magnetic tapes were used.

(iv) Assembly language and machine language were developed.

(v) The other computers which come into this category are NIVAC, EDVAC, UNIVAC UNIVAC I, IBM 650 etc.

The First generation computers were the voluminous computers. This generation began with the development of ENIAC, EDSAC, UNIVAC I etc. These machines were made possible by the invention of Vacuum Tube which was a fragile glass device that could control and amplify electronic signals. These computers were comparatively faster and used the idea of stored programs.

The first generation of computers, characterized by the use of vacuum tubes is generally thought to have begun on June 14, 1951 with the introduction of the first commercially viable electronic digital computer. The Universal Automatic Computer (UNIVAC 1), developed by Mauchly and Eckert for the Remington Rand Corporation, was installed in the U.S. Bureau of the Census in 1951. Later that year, CBS news gave the UNIVAC 1 national exposure when it correctly predicted Dwight Eisenhower's victory in the presidential election with only 5 percent of the votes counted.

In the first generation, vacuum tubes - electronic tubes about the size of light bulbs - were used as the internal computer components. However, because thousands of such tubes were required, they generated a great deal of heat, causing many problems in temperature regulation and climate control.

In addition although all the tubes had to be working simultaneously, they were subject to frequent burnout - and the people operating the computer did not know whether the problem was in the programming or in the machine.

Another drawback was that the language used in programming was machine language, which uses numbers. Using numbers alone made programming the computer difficult and time consuming.

After the success of UNIVAC, IBM made a commitment to develop and market computers. IBM's first entry into the commercial computer market was the IBM 701 in 1953. It was IBM 650, introduced in 1954, which brought fame to IBM. The IBM 650 was designed as a logical upgrade of existing punched card machines.

To supplement primary storage, first generation computers stored data on punched cards. IN 1957 magnetic tape was introduced as a faster more compact method of storing data.

The main drawbacks of the computers of first generation were:

(i) Large size

(ii) Slow Speed

(iii) Generated more heat

(iv) Unreliable

(v) Air conditioning required

(vi) Used in limited areas

(vii) Constant maintenance required

Second Generation Computers

Second Generation Computers were introduced between 1959 to 1965.

(i) The computers were based on transistor (transfer resistor) technology which replaced the vacuum tubes.

(ii) Punched cards and magnetic tape was used to input the data.

(iii) Output were taken on the punched cards and papers.

(vi) For external storage Magnetic core storage i.e. magnetic tape was used.

(v) FORTRAN, COBOL, BASIC, high level languages were developed.

(vi) Examples of second generation computers are: UNIVAC 1108, IBM 700, 1401, CDC-1604, 3600.

The transistor was invented as a smaller and more reliable successor to the vacuum tube. Although the transistor was invented in 1948, its applications to computers come only in 1950. The transistor was more reliable, less expensive, smaller than the smallest vacuum tube consumed very little power and produced much less heat.

Transistor, a small device that transferred electric signals across a resistor, was developed in this generation. It revolutionized electronics in general and computers in particular. Transistors were much smaller than vacuum tubes and they had numerous other advantages, they needed no warm up time, consumed less energy and were faster and more reliable. Another important development of this generation was the move from machine language to assembly language - also called symbolic languages. Assembly language used mnemonics (abbreviations) for instructions rather than numbers. For example, ADD for addition, MULT for multiplication and so on. This made programming less cumbersome.

Development of high level languages were also observed in this generation. FORTRAN (1954), COBOL (1959) and ALGOL (1960) were the few important high level languages used for programming. These languages are still widely used (in updated form). They are more English like.

Another major development of this generation was the invention of the first removable disk pack (1962) which supplemented magnetic tape systems and helped users to have fast access to desired data.

So we can say that the invention of the transistor signaled the start of the second generation of computers. These transistorized computers were more powerful, more reliable, less expensive, and cooler to operate than their vacuum tubed predecessors.

Honeywell established itself as a major player in the second generation of computers. Burrough, UNIVAC, NCR, CDC and Honeywell - IBM's biggest competitors during the 1960s - became known as the BUNCH. Example of second generation computers are Honeywell 400, PDP-8 (1963), IBM 7090, IBM 70941.

PDP-8 made by D.E.C. in 1963, is generally considered the first successful minicomputer. At a mere $18000, the transistor based PDP-8 was an instant hit. It confirmed the tremendous demand for small computers for business and scientific applications.

All these new development made the second generation of computers less costly to operate, and thus began a surge of growth in computer systems. Throughout this period computers were being used principally by businesses, university and government organizations. They had not filtered down to the general public. The real part of the revolution was about to begin.

Third Generation Computers

Third generation of computers included significant advances in machine hardware.

(i) The transistors were replaced with Integrated Circuits (ICs) or chip.

(ii) These included special Operating Systems which provided capabilities for automatic proceeding from one job to the next with human intervention and for multiprogramming.

(iii) With the help of Operating System made it possible for a machine to perform several jobs concurrently.

(iv) Instead of Punched cards, Monitors and keyboards were used to input and for output the data.

(v) Magnetic tape was replaced by Magnetic disks for external storage data.

(vi) Report Program Generator (RPG) and PASCAL, high level languages were developed.

(vii) Example: IBM –360, 370, ICL–1900.

One of the most abundant elements in the earth's crust (27% by weight) is Silicon, a non-metallic substances found in common beach sand as well as in particularly all rocks and clay. In India it is found abundantly at Kerala beach. It is principally used as a semiconducting material for making Silicon chip, the integrated circuit.

This element is important in the study of computers because the circuitry of the computer is etched on a chip of Silicon. It was in 1965, at Santa Clara Country (Silicon Valley) in U.S.A., when the production of Silicon Chip (IC) was started.

An integrated circuit (IC) is a complete electronic circuit on a small chip of Silicon. The chip may be less than 1/8 inch square and contains thousands or millions of electronic components. In 1965 integrated circuits began to replace transistors in computer. The resulting machines were called third generation computers.

ICs are made of silicon because it is a semiconductor i.e., it is an electrical conductor whose resistance decreases with rising temperature and the presence of impurities, in contrast to normal conductors for which the reverse is true. The chips were hailed as a generational breakthrough because they had desirable characteristics : reliability, compactness and low cost.

The beginning of the third generation was proclaimed by the IBM 360 in 1964. The numeral 360 represents 360 degrees i.e. the system and its peripheral units were all arranged in a circular form. The system 360 family of computers, designed for both business and scientific use, came in several models and sizes. System 360 was conceived as a family of computers with upward compatibility, when a company out grew one model it could move up to the next model without worrying about converting its data.

System 360 and other lines built around ICs made all previous computers obsolete but the advantages were so great that most users wrote the costs of conversion off as the price of progress. Perhaps the most far reaching contribution of the 360 series was the decision to unbundle the software i.e. to sell the software separately from the hardware. This approach led to the creation of today's software industry.

Software became more sophisticated and efficient in this generation, because several programs could run in the same time frame and with a resource sharing capabilities. Software systems were developed to support interactive processing, which used a terminal to put the user in direct contact with the computer. This kind of access caused the customer service industry to flourish, especially in areas such as reservations.

Fourth Generation Computers

These computers were based upon the development of Large Scale Integration (LSI) and very Large Scale Integration (VLSI).

(i) Modification of Input and output devices.

(ii) Introduction of microcomputers with the help of efficiency of circuits.

(iii) Magnetic disks became more popular for external storage.

(iv) Special Software were used to manage large data base.

(v) Another computers in this generation are: INTEL 4004 Apple Series I and II, Spectrum 7.

Through the 1970s computers gained dramatically in speed, reliability and storage capacity, but entry into fourth generation was evolutionary rather than revolutionary. Although most computer vendors would classify their computers as fourth generation, most people pinpoint 1971 as the generation's beginning. That was the year when large scale integration (LSI) of circuitry was introduced.

The fourth generation was, in fact, an extension of third generation technology. The base technology, though is still the integrated circuit. This is not to say that two decades have passed without significant innovations.

In fact, the computer industry has experienced a mind boggling succession of advances in the further miniaturization of circuitry, data communications, and the design of computer hardware and software computers today are 100 times smaller than those of the first generation and a single chip is far more powerful than ENIAC.

The enthusiastic reception of the Altair 8800 in 1975 and Apple II from Apple Computer, convinced IBM that there was market for microcomputers. IBM responded with its 1981 announcement of the IBM Personal Computer or PC.

Today, the IBM PC and its clones have become a powerful standard for the microcomputer industry.

Fifth Generation Computers

Fifth Generation Computers focused on connectivity.

(i) In the mid of 1990s Japanese described the powerful intelligent computers.

(ii) Later they cover the several research fields related to computer intelligence, artificial intelligence, expert systems and natural language.

(iii) The true focus in this generation has been connectivity.

(iv) This method of connecting of computers is called Networking.

(v) Networking used in developing of Internet

This all lead to most important computer of the century, called the Personal Computer. History of computers cannot be complete without the mention of these computers and how they have developed over the years.

The term fifth generation was coined by the Japanese to describe the powerful, intelligent computers they wanted to build by the mid 1990s. Later the term evolved to encompass several research fields related to computer intelligence, artificial intelligence, expert systems, and natural language.

But the true focus of this ongoing fifth generation is connectivity, the massive industry effort to permit users to connect their computers to other computers. The concept of the information superhighway has captured the imaginations of both computer professionals and everyday computer users.

History is still being made in the computer industry and it is being made incredibly rapidly. Whatever may be the speed of miniaturization of ICs, the basic components of a computer system (i.e. input, processing, output and storage) will be present in the computer, whatever the date or generation may be.

Personal Computers

Personal Computers were introduced by International Business Machine (IBM) in 1981. IBM has brought out different versions/models with variations of floppy disks, hard disks, chips etc. making them faster and faster.

The various versions of IBM PC computers are:

Model	***RAM Chip***	***Type of Chip***	***Floppy Drive 5¼"***	***Floppy Drive 3½"***	***Hard Disk***
PC	640 K	8088	2	Nil	Nil
PC-XT	640 K	8088	1	Nil	20 MB
PC-AT/286	1028 K	80286	1	1	40 MB
PC-AT/386	4 MB	80386	1	1	120 MB
PC-AT/486	8 MB	80486	1	1	260 MB
PC-Pentium	16 MB	Pentium	Nil	1	720 MB
PC-PIII	32 MB	Pentium–III	Nil	1	4.3 GB
PC-PIV	64 MB	Pentium-IV	Nil	1	20 GB
PC-V	256 MB	Penitum - V	Nil	1	80 GB

To understand the various terms used in the table, it is important to know the following terms:

1 byte	=	1 character (0 to 9 or a to z or a special character like $)
1 Kilobyte (KB)	=	1,000 Bytes approx.
1 Megabyte (MB)	=	1,000 Kilobytes approx.
1 Gigabyte (GB)	=	1,000 Megabytes approx.

HISTORY OF PERSONAL COMPUTERS

In the mid 1970s, a visionary band of programmers, engineers and hobbyists came together to launch a revolution that would change the way we perceive computers forever. That is, they wanted to build such a computer which was to be closer to user. It was named Personal Computer. Compared to other technologies, the personal computer has evolved over a short period of time. The development have been dramatic and they have not stopped. In the span of just two decades, the PC has grown from a hobbyists novelty to a tool of immense flexibility and capability that reaches into millions of homes and businesses.

The relatively low cost and almost unlimited applications for the PC have made it the darling of the business community. When you use a PC, the capabilities of a complete computer system are at your finger tips. Some are more powerful than computers that once handled the computing requirements of a large organization.

Personal computer as by name, and as by history too are personal, full of stories of success and failure and of individuals with whom we can readily identify. Various PCs introduced to the world since 1975 are :

The ALTAIR 8800

The Altair 8800 computer, introduced in 1975, was developed by Ed Roberts, owner of the MITS company in Albuquerque, U.S.A. The Altair was built around one of the earliest computer "chips" - 8080 microprocessor, a product of Intel. The Altair was a machine, loaded with switches and dials and no keyboard or screen.

Other personalities who were associated with Altair or similar type of machine in the year 1975 were Gary Kildall, Paul Allen and Bill Gates.

Gary Kildall, a consultant and computer science teacher wrote an operating system for a computer powered by the Intel 8080. He called his operating system Control Program for Micros (CP/M).

Bill Gates, a student of Harvard, in 1975 called Ed Robert, the inventor of Altair, and told him that he and Allen had developed a BASIC language that can be adapted for the Altari computer. Later in the third quarter of 1975 Allen, demonstrated the BASIC, he and Gates had developed, to Ed Roberts. Miraculously, it worked on the first try. In 1975, Bill Gates and Paul Allen formed Microsoft Corporation, which wrote system programs for Altair and Apple microcomputer and expanded BASIC for other computers.

Apple Computer

In 1977, this computer was developed by two young men in their twenties, named Steve Wozniak and Steve Jobbs. This computer became very popular for home and small business use. The company which they formed, Apple Computers, manufactured more small computers than any other computer manufacturer of the time. Over the years the company has grown tremendously and has Macintosh brand of computers available throughout the world. Their computers are, according to some users, better than those manufactured by IBM.

Steve Wozniak, with his friend Steve Jobs, built a complete computer on a circuit board in 1976. Unlike the Altair, Woznaik's and Job's computer did not had a case, lights, switches or any other amenities and was built around a MOS Technology 6502 microprocessor, a clone of a Motorola 6800. This computer was introduced to general public in 1977. Wozniak and Jobs called this computer as Apple.

The first Apple computer Apple I, was not a commercial success, Wozniak and Jobs produce the next generation of their computer - Apple II. The Apple II came in a case with a built in keyboard. For a monitor users hooked upto an ordinary TV set. The Apple II came with 4K of memory and could generate colour graphics, so it was the Apple II that anchored the early years of the company. In act, it was the combination of the Apple II and the spreadsheet software called VisiCalc, that caught the attention of the business community.

The IBM Personal Computer

Till 1980, in the history of the PC, there were no bets on any standard operating system and what to talk of any standard computer. In 1980 IBM observed that the personal computer market was too big to ignore. So it began development of its own personal computer. Also, IBM decided that the marke cannot wait for it to develop its own machine from the scratch. So it decided that to get to market as soon as possible, it must assembly a machine from widely available components. Because of the continuing availability of 8 bit devices, IBM decided on the 8-bit 8088, rather than more capable 8086 processor.

In August 1981, IBM unveiled the IBM PC. The standard configuration of the original PC included a system unit with Intel 8088 CPU, 16KB of memory, a keyboard and a port to connect an audiocassette player for storing programs and data. For a monitor, user had to connect the computer to a TV set. The expanded version included 64 KB of memory, one 160K floppy disk drive and still no monitor.

In 1983, IBM unveils the IBM PC XT. Essentially a PC with a hard disk drive and more memory, the XT is able to store an unprecedented volume of programs and data on its built in 10 MB harddisk drive. The excitement and media publicity over the PC XT and Lotus 1-2-3 fosters the feeling among business managers from large corporations to small businesses that, if they do not purchase a PC and Lotus 1-2-3, they will be missing the bandwagon and will provide their competitors with an edge.

In 1984, IBM unveils the IBM PC AT. The PC AT uses the Intel 80286 processor and is much faster than the earlier XT. The standard PC AT is equipped with 512 KB of 250 nsec RAM memory, a 30 MB hard disk and EGA colour graphics. IBM made its computer from nonproprietary part, this has opened the door for other manufacturers to do the same. Thus, other PC manufacturers emulated the IBM standard, producing IBM clones, copy cat computers that can run software designed for IBM computers. Almost all the major PC manufacturers today - Compaq, Dell, Gateway, AST and so many more - are IBM clones. In fact, clone computers now dominate the PC market having IBM with a market share that is small when compared to its original success.

or the analog unit is integrated as a part of the central processor of a digital computer which ultimately helps in getting input/output directly. The digital unit is able to exert control over the analog computer by means of instructions stored in the digital memory. These instructions can control the operation mode of the hardware units in the analog section, while the analog machine can interrupt the digital computer to initiate input/output operations. This type of system combines the properties of the true analog system with the accuracy, reliability, memory capacity and programming flexibility of the digital system.

Hybrid Machines are generally used in scientific applications or in controlling industrial processes, in both situations the user is able to exploit the machine's ability to process both discrete and continuous data using accurate digital subroutines where necessary and the analog machines for fast integration functions.

CLASSIFICATION OF COMPUTERS BY SIZE

Computers come in sizes from tiny to monstrous, in both appearance and power. The size of a computer that a person or an organization needs depends on the computing environments. Clearly, the National Weather service provided by Meteorological Department of India keeping watch on the weather fronts of many continents has requirements different from those of a two wheeler dealer's service department that is trying to keep track of its parts inventory. And the requirements of both of them are different from the needs of a salesperson using a small laptop computer to record client orders on a sales trip.

In general the classification of computers can be characterized by cost, size, storage capacity, number of users and processing speed. In many cases, there is a considerable amount of overlapping of these characteristics. So broadly, computers can be classified as

Super Computers SUPER COMPUTERS

Mainframe Computers MAINFRAME COMPUTERS

Mini MINICOMPUTERS

WORKSTATIONS

MICROCOMPUTERS OR PERSONAL COMPUTERS

Supercomputers, the biggest of all, have greater computing capacities than mainframe computers.

Mainframe computers have grater computing capacities than minicomputers and Minicomputers have greater computing capacities than microcomputers. Rapid advances in computer technology have blurred what used to be distinguishing characteristics (physical size, cost, memory capacity and so on).

Super Computers

The speed of a computer is limited by two things,

1. the switching time
2. the time taken by an electric pulse to go from one part of the computer to another.

The Switching time may be thought of as the time a transistor takes to go from a conducting state to nonconducting state or vice versa. Since the switching time is now only of one thousand millionth of a second, the time an electric pulse takes to travel from one part of the computer to another is becoming a more serious limitation. Nothing can travel faster than the speed of light and light can only travel one foot in a thousand millionth of a second. Thus it is not feasible to increase the speed of sequential computer (e.g. PCs, mainframe etc.) made with a single processor beyond a limit. The only alternative for achieving higher speed of computing is to use many processors to work in parallel. Also it is very important that everything is made as small as possible and the memory does not require too much space.

One of the problems with packing a very large numbers of silicon chips into a small space is that they use power and this means a lot of heat is generated in this space. An elaborate cooling system is a very important part of a supercomputer.

Motivation Force Behind Invention Of Supercomputer

Eventhough higher speed obtainable with supercomputer is the main motivating force for building supercomputers, there are other features also as :

Better Quality of Solution

When arithmetic operations are distributed to many computers, each one does a smaller number of arithmetic operations. Thus rounding errors are lower when supercomputers are used.

Better Algorithms

The availability of many processors which can work simultaneously leads to different algorithms which are not relevant for purely sequential computers (viz., computers with 80286, 80386, 80486 or pentium processor). It is possible to explore different facets of a solution simultaneously using several processors and solutions simultaneously. Using several processors and these give better insight to solutions of several physical problems.

Better storage distribution

Certain type of supercomputers provide much larger storage which is distributed. Access to the storage is faster in each processor (having internal memory). This feature is of special interest in many applications such as information retrieval computer aided design.

Greater reliability

In principle a supercomputer will work even if a processor fails. We can build a supercomputer's hardware and software for better fault tolerance.

Scientists using computers have realised that a 100 to 1000 fold increase in computing speed makes it possible to refine physical models such as those of complex molecules and crystals, verify thoeries and solve new problems in science.

A supercomputer is among those with the highest speed, largest functional size biggest physical dimensions or greatest monetary cost in any given period of time. Supercomputer has got the highest processing speed available at a given time for solving scientific and engineering problems. Supercomputers are specially designed to maximize the number of floating point instructions per second (FLOPS) which is usually more than 1 gigaflops per second.

A supercomputer contains a number of CPUs which operate in parallel to make it faster. Its processing speed lies in the range of 400 - 10,000 [Millions of Floating point Operation Per second (MFLOPS)]. Its word length is 64 - 96 bits. Supercomputers are typical designed with state-of-the-art computer architecture, including unique cooling systems to dissipate internal heat built up and the ability to execute program instructions concurrently instead of sequentially.

Drawbacks

Supercomputers are designed using multiprocessing to achieve much faster processing speed than mainframe, but they use this processing power to work on just one complex problem at a time instead of sharing processing time with many users, for example in meteorological department the fast processing speed of a supercomputer is used for a single purpose - forecasting the weather.

One of the problems of building computers of so much power is the tremendous amount of heat created by the machine. Every one of the major manufacturers of supercomputer, tackles this problem by cooling its machine with liquid coolants. Cray also designs some of their computers in a special curved shape that helps the machines to dissipate the heat generated by certain components.

Uses

Model Global Weather : Both long and short term weather forecasts require solution of large sets of non-linear partial differential equations. For short range forecasts these equations are to be solved in a very short time, based on measured values communicated to the forecasting centre, so that forecast are meaningful. Hundred of MFLOPS speed and large memory size have been found essential to solve such real time weather forecast.

Scientists build models of a computer processes and simulate the process in a supercomputer. One such process is nuclear fission. As a fissionable material approaches a critical mass, scientist want to know exactly what will happen during every millisecond of a nuclear chain reaction. A supercomputer is used to model the actions and reactions of literally millions of atoms as they interact.

There is a need of supercomputer to solve multi-variate mathematical problems of real physical processes, occurring in disciplines such a aerodynamics, seismology, metrology and plasma physics. Oil companies use supercomputers for petroleum exploration by analyzing rock formation and samples. Military strategists use supercomputers to simulate defence scenarios. Cinematic specialists use them to produce sophisticated movie animations. Supercomputer has limited use and because of its price tag, limited market. Only a few dozen of these machines are operational in India, mostly at research centres of some government agencies.

The largest commercial users of supercomputers are in the entertainment/advertising industry.

Examples of Supercomputers

CRAY - 3 (Control Data Corporation)

Cyber 205 (ETA Systems Incorporation)

PRAM (INDIA)

Supercomputers are able to reach the large volume and speed performances for beyond the theoretical limits of mainframes by using parallel processing, pipeline processing and vector processing. The speed at which computer operate, as measured by the number of basic operations performed per second, has undergone rapid and continual improvement. This has been mainly due to improvement in the technology of computing circuits and memory devices.

It can be concluded that the computer speed has increased linearly by factor of about 100 per decade since 1930. It is widely believed that the rate of increase in computer speed due to technology improvements in diminishing, which suggests that significant increases in speed can come only from improved algorithms or heuristics. For example, we can see that the rate of increase of the speed of the basic electronic circuits used in supercomputer has been relatively slow. For instance the arithmetic processor of CRAY - 1 supercomputer built in 1978 took 12nsec to add two floating point numbers whereas that of CRAY - YMP built in 1988 took 6nsec. But from this we cannot conclude that there is no future for supercomputer.

Now supercomputers are moving towards the mainstream, for activities as varied as stock analysis, automobile design, special effects for movies and even sophisticated artwork. CRAY RESEARCH and ETA SYSTEMS, INC., firms located in the Minneapolis are two primary builders of supercomputer in the United States. Nippon Electric Co., Hitachi are Japanese Supercomputer builders. India is also present in the field of building supercomputer. India's first supercomputer built was named as PARAM.

Mainframe Computers

Next step down from supercomputers, in terms of speed and storage capacity are mainframes. Mainframes are large, relatively expensive machines that offer extensive problem-solving capabilities. It can have memory capacities measured in gigabytes and more. The largest mainframes can process well over 100 MIPS. Their operating systems usually handle multiple applications within a timesharing environment. This provides many users with the ability to perform different processing tasks Data storage is primarily on hard disks, with tapes used as backup.

Mainframe is a large computer, in particular one to which other computers can be connected so that they can share facilities the mainframe provides. e.g; a System/370 computing system to which personal computers are attached so that they can upload and download programs and data.

The term mainframe usually refers to hardware only : main storage, execution circuitry and peripheral units.

Mainframe word-length may be 48, 60 or 64 bits. It has got a system memory (ie; RAM) of 64 to 256 MB, hard disk of capacity 1 -10 GB or more and processing speed of 30 - 100 Millions of Instructions per seconds. A substantial amount of peripherals can be attached to mainframe computer.

Mainframe computers are designed to handle tremendous amount of input, output and storage. Mainframe computers often act as host computers i.e., computers that serve as central receiving and switching computers in regional or national computer networks.

Mainframe act as a database server, that is, the database is controlled by mainframe computer that can handle the input and output needs of all terminals connected to it.

Uses

Mainframe computers are used in research organizations, large industrial banks, airline and railway reservations where large data base is required. Insurance companies use mainframe to process millions of policies.

Mainframe can serve as the heart of a teleprocessing system with remote connections all over the world.

Advantages

Ability to handle large computer applications viz., railways and airline reservation systems.

- A wide variety of memory sizes or terminal support option.
- Ability to execute computer programs written in wide variety of computer languages.

Disadvantages

- High cost
- Special power and air-conditioning requirements

Examples of Mainframe

IBM 4300, IBM 308 X, IBM 3090

HP 9000 - 8705/400

VAX 8842

Minicomputers

The next step down from mainframe computers, in terms of speed and storage capacity are minicomputers. It is an intermediate - size computer that can perform the same kind of applications as a mainframe but has less storage capacity, processing power and speed than a mainframe.

It is functionally intermediate between a microcomputer and a mainframe. Minicomputers are floor-standing or desktop devices, frequently connected to a mainframe to perform subsidiary operations. They are priced for purchase by smaller businesses and are sufficiently compact to be located in a typical office environment.

When Digital Equipment Corporation (DEC) began shipping its PDP series computer in the early 1960s the press dubbed these machines, minicomputers, because of their small size compared to other computers of the day.

Some minicomputers are uni-processor systems whereas some are multiprocessor system. The processing speed lies in the range 10 -30 MIPS. Memory capacity lies in the range of 8 - 256 MB and can easily range into gigabytes of temporary storage. Minicomputers have operating systems with multitasking and network capabilities enabling them to serve more than one user. It serves as a centralized storehouse for cluster of workstations or as a network server.

For example, a team of architects working on different subsystem within the same building could be directly linked to the office minicomputer that maintains everyone's files and documentation. A mini computer can support more than 100 terminals. Generally, the processing speeds and related capabilities of minicomputers exceed those of microcomputers and more peripheral devices can be attached to them. Minicomputer also tend to have more sophisticated operating systems than microcomputers and can usually be programmed in a wider variety of programming languages.

Uses

These are extensively used for payroll preparation, accounting and scientific computation.

- ☐ High-performance workstations with graphics I/O capability use minicomputers.
- ☐ Minicomputer are typically multi-user systems so are used in interactive applications in industries, research organizations, colleges and universities.
- ☐ Minicomputer are also used for real-time controls and engineering design work.

Supermini

The term supermini has been coined to describe minis at the top of the size-price scale. It is a large minicomputer. Physically it is a 32-bit minicomputer which support more simultaneous users (one hundred or more) and more peripheral devices and large memories than previous minicomputer.

Advantages of Minicomputers

- ☐ Its affordability ie., cost effectiveness small businesses that were unable to purchase an expensive central computer in past have found that they can now afford to purchase minicomputers.
- ☐ It is commonly used as dedicated computers ie., used exclusively for one processing function. For example, for program development or payroll preparation.

The major minicomputer manufacturers include DEC, Data General, IBM and HewlettPackard.

Workstations

Between minicomputers and microcomputer in terms of processing power is a class of computers known as workstations. A workstation looks like a personal computer and is typically used by only one person, much as is a personal computer. Although workstations are still more powerful than the average personal computer, the difference is the capabilities of these types of machines.

Difference between a Workstation and Microcomputer

Internally, workstations are constructed differently than microcomputers. They are generally based on another philosophy of CPU design called Reduced Instruction Set Computing (RISC), which results in faster processing of instructions.

- ☐ Microcomputer can run any of the four major operating systems:

  DOS UNIX OS/2 and Microsoft Windows NT, etc.

But workstations generally run the UNIX operating systems or a variation of it. The biggest manufacturer of workstation in Sun Microsystem, others are IBM, HP, DEC of Silicon Graphics.

Many people use the term workstation to refer to any computer or terminal that is connected to another computer. But this meaning is outdated and these days a workstation is a powerful RISC-based computer that runs the UNIX operating systems and is generally used by scientists and engineers.

Microcomputers And Personal Computers

The microcomputer is a scaled-down version of the mainframe. Microcomputer is a digital computer whose processing unit consists of one or more microprocessors, one or more input/output units and sufficient memory to execute instructions. The essential components of a microcomputer are often contained within a single enclosure. Microcomputers are usually desk-top or portable devices with a display, a keyboard and tape disk and diskette storage, they are designed primarily for stand-alone operation but can be used as workstations in terminal emulation mode. Every microcomputer is capable of performing jobs once handled by only the largest computers. A typical microcomputer memory unit stores upto 64 MB of data. Processing speeds of microcomputer are measured in megahertz instead of MIPS. A microcomputer running at 90 MHz is faster than one running at 33 MHz and works at approximately 90 MIPS.

The terms microcomputer and personal computer are interchangeable however, PC-which stands for personal computer-has a more specific meaning. In 1981, IBM called its first microcomputer the IBM PC. Within a few years, many companies were copying the IBM design creating "clones" or "compatibles" that aimed at functioning just like the original. For this reason, the term PC has come to mean the family of computers that includes IBMs and compatibles.

Personal computer is a type of microcomputer primarily intended for stand-alone use by an individual. It is a desk-top, floor - standing or portable microcomputer that usually consists of a system unit a display monitor, a keyboard, one or more diskette drives, internal hard disk storage, and an optional printer. PCs are designed primarily to give independent computing power to a single user and are inexpensively priced for purchase by individuals or small businesses. A few of the major personal computer manufacturers are APPLE, IBM, Compaq, Dell, AST and Hewlett-Packard.

Supermicros : The upper-end machines used by workers such as engineers, financial traders and graphics designers are small enough to fit on a desk top but approach the power of a mainframe.

Laptops

In recent years design changes have reduced the size of some microcomputers, making computer technology portable and affordable.

Laptop computers are roughly the size of a large notebook. Their power source - a battery- is completely self-contained yet can be recharged from an electrical outlet. Laptops, sometimes called notebook computers, can contains more than 500 MB of hard disk memory, 16+MB of RAM, floppy disk drives, keyboard, mouse and a colour monitor. Power adapters can be used to plug into any electrical outlet throughout the world. It can be connected with an additional battery or serial port, a network or fax equipment. Laptops are not as inexpensive as their size might suggests, many carry a price tag equivalent to full-size personal computer for business.

Personal Digital Assistants

Personal digital assistants (PDA's) are the smallest of portable computers. It is even smaller than the laptop computers and uses a pen or electronic stylus, rather than a keyboard for input. PDAs, also sometimes called palmtops, are much less powerful than notebook or desktop models. They are usually used for special applications such are creating spreadsheets, displaying important telephone numbers and addresses. Monitor is rather small and the only apparent form of output. It can recognize hand - printed text, storing it, such as a business letter, note or other document.

Basic mathematics problems such as addition and multiplication are calculated when the problems is written on the screen. It can also be connected to fax pager, printer or a disk drive to output or store data. The processing hardware is based on RISC technology. Because of their limited power PDAs usually have no disk drives rather they use small cards about the size of credit card to store programs and data. Its potential users are workers who cannot easily use a laptop computer because they are on their feet all day : Sales representatives, real estate agents, insurance agents, meter readers, and nurses.

The last generation of PDAs, called personal intelligent communicators PICs can use infrared light to communicate with nearby computers and may have cellular telephone and fax capabilities built in.

Micros Versus Minis, Mainframes And Supercomputers

Minicomputers, mainframes and supercomputers are computer systems. Micros also are computer systems. Each offers many input and output alternatives, i.e., ways to enter data to the system and to present information generated by the system. In addition each is supported by a wide variety of packaged software. There are, of course, obvious differences in size and capabilities of the two sets of computers.

Everything associated with minicomputers, mainframes and supercomputers is larger in scope than that associated with microcomputers :-

- ☐ execution of programs is faster;
- ☐ disk storage has more capacity;
- ☐ printer speeds are faster.

Computers in these three categories can service many terminals and, of course, they cost more.

Besides size and capability, the single most distinguishing characteristics of minicomputers, mainframe computers and supercomputers is manner in which easy type is used. The three larger computers, with their expanded processing capabilities, provide a computing resource that can be shared by many people. For example, finance, personal and accounting departments within a company share the resources of a mainframe, possibly all at the same time.

In contrast, most microcomputers are used by one user at a time.

Another important difference between micros and the other categories of computers is that you, in all probability will spend much of your working life within arm's reach of micro. You will be the person who turns on the systems, selects the software to be run, enters the data and requests the information.

SUMMARY

1. In 3000 B.C. Abacus is the simplest form of a digital computer. It is interesting to note that it is still used in its larger version and its users can calculate at amazing speed. Abacus was invented by the Chinese.
2. In the early 17th century John Napier, a Scottish mathematician, developed another calculating device known as Napier's Bones.
3. For inventing the first mechanical calculating machine in 1642, the credit goes to the great French Mathematician Blaise Pascal.
4. The famous German Mathematician, Gottfried von Leibnitz, developed a calculating machine, which could multiply and divide numbers successfully.
5. Charles Babbage developed a working model of a mechanical computer called Difference Engine.
6. Lady Ada Lovelace must be thought of as first programmer in the world.
7. **ENIAC** (**E**lectronic **N**umeric **I**ntegrator **A**nd **C**alculator) computer was developed by Mr. Mauchly and Eckert.
8. **EDSAC** was modified by Mr. Mauchly, Eckert and Von Neumann and invented **E**lectronic **D**iscreter **V**riable **A**utomatic **C**ompuer (**EDVAC**), this was a second stored program computer.
9. Beginner's All-purpose Symbolic Instruction Code (BASIC) language was developed by Dr. John Kemeny.
10. The first three computer generations are pinned to three technological developments. the vacuum tube, the transistor and the integrated circuit.
11. The First generation computers were the voluminous computers.
12. The Second generation computers were based on vacuum tubes.
13. The Third generation computers were based on Integrated Circuits (ICs).

14. The Fourth generation computers were based upon the development of Large Scale Integration (LSI) and very Large Scale Integration (VLSI).
15. Personal Computers were introduced by International Business Machine (IBM) in 1981.
16. A computer is made of different parts.
17. Computer is a machine, totally at the command of the user.
18. The first three computer generations were based on: vacuum tube, transistor and integrated circuit.
19. The computer is physically divided into 3 main parts: Monitor, Central Processing Unit and Keyboard.
20. CPU consists of 4 main units: Primay Storage, Arithmetic Logic Unit, Control Unit and Output Unit.
21. The main functions of the Primary storage are: Holding the data in its memory till it is required to be processed; Holding the result of the processed data and Holding program instructions which are required for processing.
22. Arithmetic Logic Unit is used to process Arithmetic and Logic problems.
23. Fourth generation computers were based on Micro chips and Fifth generation computers on Large Scale Integration Systems.
24. The latest Personal Computer is based on the Pentium V chip.
25. Various class of computer are: Mainframe Computers, Super Mini Computers, Mini Computers and Micro Computers or Personal Computers.
26. A PC's memory is made up of electronic components in which the PC temporarily stores data and instructions.

MULTIPLE CHOICE QUESTIONS

1. Herman Hollerith invented a tabulating Machine which used:
   (a) Punch cards (b) Memory (c) Teeth and wheels
2. Tabulating machine was invented in
   (a) 1940 (b) 1880 (c) 1671
3. First generation computers was developed by
   (a) J.P.Eckert (b) J.W.Muchly (c) Both
4. Second generation computers were based on
   (a) Transistors (b) Integrated (Circuits) (c) Electronic Valves
5. Pascal's machine was modified by
   (a) John Napier (b) Charles Babbage (c) Ad-Gofried Leibrietzi
6. John Napier's machine contained digits from
   (a) 1 – 9 (b) 0 – 9 (c) 1 – 10
7. ENIAC computer was developed in
   (a) 1930 (b) 1946 (c) 1940
8. Fifth generation computers were based on
   (a) Microprocessors (b) Integrated Circuits (c) Large Scale Integrated Systems
9. ENIAC computers was based on
   (a) Mark – 1 (b) Memory (c) Z2 machines
10. Personal Computers were introduced by
   (a) IBM (b) Apple Computers (c) Grace Hooper
11. What is called the 'Brain' of the computer?
   (a) The Control Unit (b) The Arithmetic Logic Unit (c) The Central Processing Unit
   (d) The Power Supply
12. RAM is considered volatile because
   (a) it may change at any time.
   (b) the contents of memory are lost when the computer is switched off.
   (c) the contents of memory are the same each time the computer is switched on.
   (d) the memory may be easily removed from the CPU.

13. What does RAM stand for?
 (a) Random Access Mail (b) Random Access Memory (c) Rational Access Memory
 (d) Random Authorization Mechanism
14. What is Computer Peripheral?
 (a) The power supply (b) The processor
 (c) A hardware connected to a computer
 (d) A silicon chip
15. What are the main components of the central processor?
 (a) The processor and the monitor (b) The arithmetic logic unit and the control unit
 (c) The processor and the control unit (d) The keyboard and the mouse

REVIEW QUESTIONS

1. Who developed Abacus?
2. How does Abacus works?
3. What is the use of Rods and Beads in Abacus?
4. Write a short note on the followings.
 (i) Napier Bones (ii) Pascal's Calculator (iii) Leirnitz's Machine
 (iv) Jacquard's Loom (v) Difference Engine (vi) Lady Ada Lovelace
 (vii) Boolean Algebra (viii) Hollerith Machines (ix) Electro-Mechanical Computers
 (x) EDSAC (xi) EDVAC (xii) UNIVAC
 (xiii) LEO (xiv) Analog Computer (xv) Hybrid Computers
 (xvi) The ALTAIR 8800
5. What is a Digital Computer?
6. What are the drawbacks of Analog Computers?
7. Write down some basic features of Super Computers.
8. What are the drawbacks of Super Computers?
9. What are the uses of Super Computers?
10. What are the uses of Main Frame Computers?
11. What are the uses of Mini Computers?
12. What are Workstations?
13. What are the Characteri

ANSWERS

Multiple Choice Questions

1. a	2. b	3. c	4. a
5. c	6. a	7,. b	8. b
9. a	10. c	11. c	12. b
13. b	14. c	15. a	

CHAPTER 3

Fundamentals of Computers

Learning Objectives

After going through this chapter, you should appreciate the following:

- Input to the Computer
  - Keyboard
  - Joystick or Paddle
  - Optical Recognition
  - Bar Codes
  - Light Pens
  - Touch Screen
  - Digitizer
  - Voice Recognizers
  - Graphics Tablet
  - Mouse
  - Source Data Automation
  - Scanners
  - MICR
  - Trackball
  - Touch Pad
  - Voice Input
  - Concept Keyboard
  - Microphone
- Storage Devices
  - Magnetic Tape
  - Hard Disk
  - Floppy Disk
- Central Processing Unit
  - The Control Unit
  - Memory
  - The Arithmetic Logic Unit
  - ROM
- Computer Output
  - Printers
  - Daisywheel Printers
  - Non-impact Printers
  - Laser Printers
  - Electrostatic Printers
  - Plotters
  - Drum Plotter
  - Audio-Response Voice Output
  - The Monitor
  - Terminals
  - Dot Matrix Printer
  - Line Printers
  - Inkjet Printers
  - Thermal Printers
  - Graphics Output Devices
  - Flatbed Plotters
  - Computer Output Microfilm System
  - Speech Synthesizers
  - Video Controller
  - Punched Cards and Card Readers
- CD ROM Technology
  - Read Only Disk CD-ROM
  - Erasable Disks
  - Recordable Disk
- Pentium V Architecture
  - Advancement in Motherboard Technology
  - Chipsets for the Pentium and Beyond
  - Itanium Processor
  - Xeon Processors Family

INPUT TO THE COMPUTER

On the basis of input, computer gives an output. Clerical kind of mistakes occasionally occur during the inputting of data, e.g., if Student Identification Number 6346 is wrongly inputted as 6364 can lead to the wrong result. Input phase is an excellent place to detect and correct errors. A right input protects computer files, i.e., inputted data which is stored in file on disks can be used later in some task. Accurate input is therefore vital to protect these files from "contamination".

Data preparation is often labour intensive. This makes data preparation comparatively costly and therefore an important site for cost control.

There are 3 important characteristics for a good data input

1. Timeliness
2. Accuracy and
3. Potential Usefulness

Timeliness

Timely data is data that is collected and processed fast enough for action to be taken. For example, in on-line system in electricity department data of voltage and current is input continuously. Whenever the data of voltage or current is below or above the danger mark, i.e., data is also processed simultaneously, alarm gets on and whole system is shut down.

Accuracy

Data must be accurate to save the informational needs of the alarm to get on. For example, alarm should not run on any other which are not equivalent to the specified value.

Potential Usefulness

Data as such is raw and is of no use unless it is logical, i.e., related to the requirement. When this data is processed it becomes an information which helps in making decision. So the preparation of computerized input is the first step in the creation of useful information.

Source Document

In most business information systems, source documents are prepared manually. Examples of source documents include employee application forms, deposit slips, invoices and sales tickets.

Advantages

1. As it can be prepared manually so it needs no computer background or training.
2. Source documents can serve as backup for computer files. This is because of usage of source document to create a computer file, so the source document could also be used to re-create the file in the event it is accidentally damaged or destroyed.
3. Source document helps in providing evidence to authenticity.
4. Source documents establish an audit trail. An audit trail is the data in the form of logical path linking a sequence of events, used for tracing the transactions that have affected the contents of a record.

Disadvantages

1. Source documents are rarely machine readable. So, for processing the source document data, the data must be transferred to binary form.

Inputting the Data

Within the central processing of any computer, information can be processed at very high speeds, but before the central processor can be set to work, the data and programs must be entered into the memory. This is done by means of input devices which provide a vehicle for communication, between the computer and the people who are concerned with its operation.

In real life data is created in many places and in many ways. Before data can be processed and stored, they must be translated into a form the computer can interpret. For this we need input devices. But there are some input data which can go directly to the computer for processing. Input in this category includes bar codes, speech that enters the computer through a microphone, and data entered by means of a device that converts motions to on- screen actions. Some input data, however goes, through a good deal of intermediate handling, such as when it is copied from a source document and translated to a medium that a machine can be read, such as a magnetic disk. In either case the task is to gather data to be processed by the computer - sometimes called raw data (unprocessed data) - and convert it into some form the computer can understand.

Input devices are used to put data and instructions into a computer. There are two main types of input device - **Direct** and **Manual**.

Direct Input devices can input large amounts of data quickly and accurately without any need for human intervention. **Bar code readers** and **optical mark** readers are both examples of direct input devices.

Manual input devices are used by people to enter data by hand. The most commonly used manual input devices are the **mouse** and **keyboard**.

Let us now talk about the various input devices in details.

KEYBOARD

The most common input medium in computer is Keyboard. Without it many consider the computer as incomplete. Let us see how the data is accepted by computer when fed in by the keyboard.

How Computer Accepts Input from the Keyboard

When we press a key on a keyboard key say the letter S, then a tiny computer chip inside either the computer or the keyboard called the keyboard controller, takes a note that a key has been pressed and places a code into part of its memory buffer, indicating which key was pressed. This code is called the key's Scan Code (identifying number). Now without specifying what has happened the keyboard controller signals (i.e. sends interrupt) the computer processing components that something has happened at the keyboard. The keyboard controller sends an interrupt request to the CPU (using the interrupt number 9 assigned to the keyboard interrupt) when it receives a complete keystroke.

Interrupts cause the CPU to put aside what it is doing and jump to an interrupt handling program. In this case the interrupt handles an integral part of the ROM-BIO software. When the computer's processing components receive an interrupt request, the program that is controlling the computer at that moment evaluates the request to determine the appropriate response. In the case of a key press, the program reads the memory location in the keyboard buffer that contains the scan code of the key that was pressed and places the keyboard letter in the computer's main memory.

The keyboard buffer can actually store a number of keystrokes at once. This is necessary because some time elapses between the pressing of a key and the computer's reading of that key from the keyboard buffer. Also programmers must put instructions into their programs to read keystrokes and program might be doing something else when the key is pressed. With the keystrokes stored in a buffer the program can react to them when convenient. Because reading the keyboard to get the scan code of a key action is a function of software, we can reassign scan codes to represent different letters or symbols.

Keyboard Keys

There are more keys on computer keyboard than on typewriter. Most commonly used keyboards has **101 keys** and more. With XT, 84 key keyboard was used but it has now become obsolete. The 101 key keyboard has the important keys:

Alphabetic Keys

These are alphabet keys from [A] to [Z]. As in typewriter, you can use [SHIFT] to make them capital, i.e., ABCDE, etc. So if you press a b c d e …. etc. With [SHIFT] key already pressed, you will get A B C D E …. etc. Similar results can be obtained by putting CAPS LOCK key ON.

a = [A]

[SHIFT] + [A] = A

For typing [A], you press [SHIFT] key and then while keeping [SHIFT] key pressed, press the "a". Otherwise for typing a, you don't need to press the [SHIFT] key, just press the a key.

Numeric Keys

The numeric keys (with the characters 0 to 9) are located on the computer's keyboard at two places. You can see them in the top row above the alpha keys (as in typewriter). A second set of these keys is provided on the right-hand side of the keyboard. The numeric keys in the top row can be used straightaway to type in numeric characters. By simultaneously holding down the Shift key (as in the typewriter), you can also type in special upper characters like ! % $ *, etc. However, to type numeric characters by using the keys on the right side, you will need to press the Num Lock key ON.

Function Keys

These keys are marked [F1] to [F10] in the 84 key format and to [F12] in the 101 format. These keys are used for specific purposes as defined in the computer (a computer program is a set of instructions given to a computer to perform a specific task) which you may be using. For example, in BASIC programming (BASIC is a computer language used for writing programs) [F3] will load the program, [F1] will list the program after loading and [F2] will run the program.

Arrow Keys

On 101 keys keyboard these are placed at two places. The first is called the cursor pad which works independently. The other is the numeric-cum-cursor pad. It is similar to the one on the 84 key keyboard. When the Num Lock key is not in the ON position, pressing the key of the numeric keypad moves the cursor in the direction shown on each key. Otherwise, this portion is used to enter numbers.

Special Keys including Spacebar

There are several other keys which serve some definite purposes. Some of these keys are available on the typewriter too. The special keys are:

Shift Key — It is used for typing capital letters and special characters. In combination with both Control and Alternate keys, it is sometimes used to execute a particular command too.

Control Key — On its own, this key does not have any purpose. However, combined with different keys, it performs some useful operations. For example, in WordStar software, Control if pressed alongwith B, will make the character Bold.

Backspace — It allows the cursor to go back by one character. Some types of computer programs allow the backspace to delete the last character. A cursor is usually a blinking line (_), on the screen, which shows where he character you type on your keyboard will appear.

Spacebar — As in the typewriter, the Spacebar is used to leave space between words.

Enter Key — It informs the computer that the line of the matter, you are typing, has come to an end. After that you begin typing from a new line. It is also used, while programming, to tell the computer to execute certain commands which you give. Thus, while writing a computer program, you can also use this key to indicate the end of a given command.

Del Key — If, by mistake, you have typed in something which you did not want to, you can erase the wrong character by pressing the DEL (short for Delete) key.

Various other types of keyboards which are available but very much in use are:

DVORAK Keyboard

The DVORAK Keyboard, named after its inventor August Dvorak, was invented in 1932. Through ergonomic studies of typists, he noticed that the QWERTY layout forces that majority of the work to be done by the weakest finger - the fourth and fifth fingers of the left hand. The stronger, quicker right hand and middle fingers are used only for the least frequently typed characters. The Dvorak keyboard layout, places the most frequently used characters in the center, i.e., on the home row (the vowels plus, d, h, t, n and s).

The next most frequently used characters are placed up one row because it is easier to reach up than down. Because this layout distributes the typing work load among the fingers according to their strengths, awkward strokes are reduced by 90%. Operators who are involved with word processing have found 75% improvement in their production after switching over to Dvorak keyboard.

PC users who want to try the Dvorak layout do not need to replace their QWERTY keyboard. The switch can be made electronically.

AZERTY Keyboard

The AZERTY layout of keyboards are used in some European typewriters. The term describes the sequences of the first six letters in the first row of alphabetic keys.

MOUSE

Don't be afraid, it is not a real one. It is so called since it resembling a "Rat". In fact, it is a pointing device. These days it is almost essential for personal computers. Click at any place on the monitor with mouse to point out the location where you want to input the information. All Windows-based programs use mouse, making working with computers easier as you are not required to type commands.

It is a pointing device that lets you move a cursor or pointer on the screen just by moving the mouse around on a flat surface. A mouse also allows you to create graphic elements on the screen, such as lines, curves and freehand shapes and makes using menus and message boxes easier.

Types of Mouse

There are three basic types of Mouse

1. Mechanical Mouse
2. Optomechanical Mouse
3. Optical Mouse

Mechanical Mouse

A mechanical mouse has a rubber or metal ball on its underside that can roll in all directions. Mechanical sensors within the mouse detect the direction of the rolling ball and make a movement of the screen pointer accordingly.

Optomechanical Mouse

Optomechanical mouse is also similar to a mechanical mouse except that it uses optical sensors to detect the movement of the ball on the Mouse Pad.

Optical Mouse

Optical mouse uses a laser beam to detect the movement of mouse on specially designed Mouse Pad. We must move the mouse along a special mat with a grid so that optical mechanism has a frame of reference. This type of mouse has no mechanical moving parts. Optical mouse respond more quickly and precisely than any other mouse. These are very expensive.

A mouse can be used for many applications ranging from games to designing products with graphics. It provides an alternative for people who are uncomfortable with a keyboard or it can be used in combination with a keyboard to enhance input operations.

The mouse is also used to draw sketches, diagram, etc., on the CRT screen. It is also moved on graphic tablet for drawing work and the same is also used to edit text. For editing text on the screen the cursor is quickly moved to the desired point of the screen by moving the mouse.

How to use the mouse

There are three simple techniques - clicking, double-clicking and dragging

Clicking

To click on something with the mouse means to move the pointer or cursor to the item on the screen and to press the release the mouse button once.

Double-Clicking

Press and release the mouse button twice in rapid succession.

Dragging

After positioning the mouse pointer over the item, then depress the button and hold it down as you move the mouse.

How Mouse Works

A mouse has a ball inside of it that extends just below the housing of the mouse itself. When you slide the mouse around on a flat surface such as a desktop or mouse pad the ball rolls. Movement of the mouse result in a corresponding movement of the pointer on the screen

On two sides of the ball at 90 angle each other are two small rollers or wheels that spin to match the speed of the ball. Sensors detect how much each roller spins and send this information to the computer in the form of changes to the current pointer position.

Like the keyboard, a mouse does not actually send a message directly to the program that the computer is running. Rather it sends an interrupt request to the CPU. The program that is running checks regularly to see whether a mouse event has occurred or not.

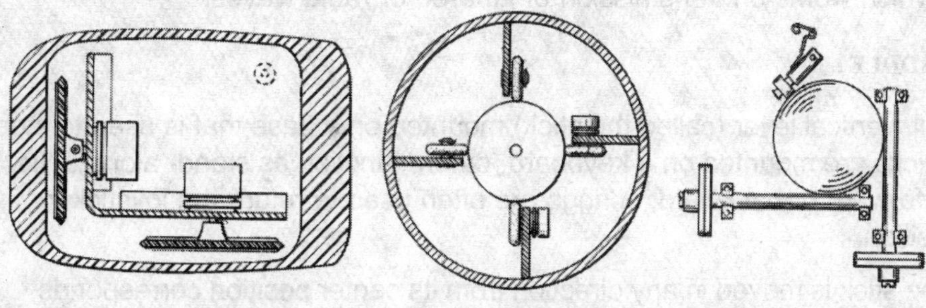

Mouse Diagram

Buttons on the Mouse

A mouse can have one, two or three buttons with a two or three- button mouse the primary or main button is the one on the left because most people are right-handed. We can reconfigure mouse device to make another button primary.

Mouse Connection to the computer

Every mouse is connected to the computer's bus, which is the backbone through which all the components of the computer communicate.

Some mouse devices are connected to the computer's bus through a special electronic card and other tie into the bus through a serial port.

A Serial Port is a socket to which you can connect external devices, viz., modem or mouse.

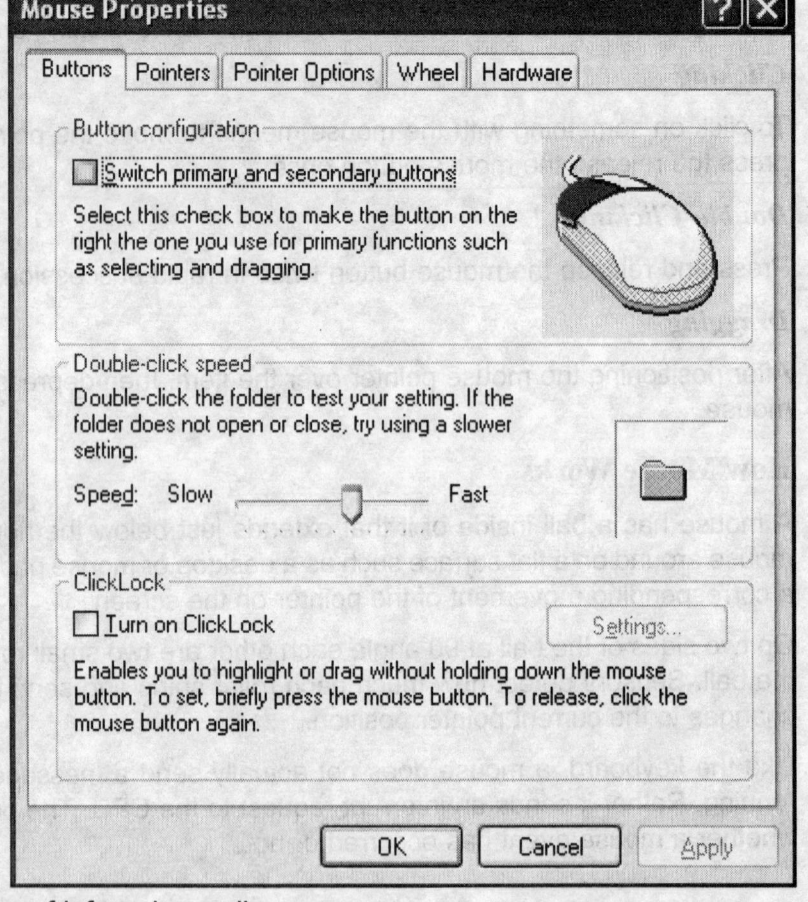

Advantages

1. It is simple device and very easy to use.
2. It is not that very expensive.
3. It moves the cursor faster than the arrow keys of keyboard do.

Drawbacks of a Mouse

1. The movement of the cursor is not very sensitive to movement of mouse.
2. If the contact between wheels and mouse pad is lost, the cursor does not move.
3. It is not useful in word-processing or in computer programming applications.
4. It requires space on tabletop or other hard surface to roll.
5. It requires serial port for connection with computer system.

A recent development in the wireless mouse or remote mouse, which works on transmission of infrared or radio waves.

JOYSTICKS (OR PADDLE)

It consists of a small, vertical lever (called the stick) mounted on a base that is used to steer the screen cursor around. Some joysticks are mounted on a keyboard, others function as stand- alone units. The joystick can be moved left or right, forward or backward, springs are often used to return the joystick to its home center position.

The distance that the stick is moved in any direction from its center position corresponds to screen cursor movement in that direction. Potentiometers mounted at the base of the joystick measure the amount of movement and springs return the stick to the center position when it is released. One or more buttons can be programmed to act as input switches to signal certain actions once a screen position has been selected.

It is difficult to use a joystick to control the absolute position of a screen cursor directly, because a slight movement of the shaft is amplified 5 to 10 times in the movement of the cursor. This makes the screen cursor's movement quite jerky and does not allow quick and accurate fine positioning. Thus, the joystick is often used to control the velocity of the cursor movement rather than the absolute cursor position.

Some joysticks have a third degree of freedom, the stick can be twisted clockwise and counter clockwise. Isometric Joystick is rigid strain gauges on the shaft and it measures slight deflections caused by force applied to the shaft.

Joyswitch

Joyswitch a variant of the joystick, is found in some home and arcade computer games. The stick can be moved in any of 8-directories up, down, left, right and four diagonals direction.

Source-Data Automation

Until recently, data entry has been synonymous with keystrokes. The keystroke will continue to be the basic mode of data entry for the foreseeable future, but recent innovations have eliminated the need for key-driven data entry (which were source of human errors) in many applications. In real sense, efficient data input means - reduction in the number of intermediate steps required between the origination of data and its processing. This is best accomplished by source-data automation - the use of special equipment to collect data at the source, as a by-product of the activity that generates the data, and send it directly to the computer.

For example, you have probably noticed the pre-printed bar codes on various products (viz., books), which can be used to send data about the product directly to the computer. You only need to pass the product over the laser scanner which would tell the computer about the price of product. Source-data automation eliminates keying, thereby reducing costs and opportunities for human-oriented mistakes. Since data about a transaction is collected when and where the transaction takes place, source data automation also improves the speed of the input operation.

Data entry is an area in which enormous potential exists for increase in productivity. The technology of data entry devices is constantly changing. New and improved methods of transcribing raw data are being invented and put on the market each month. For convenience we will divide this discussion into primary areas related to source-data automation.

Optical Recognition

There are two types of optical recognition devices.

1. Optical Character Recognition (OCR) and
2. Optical Mark Reading (OMR)

Optical Character Recognition (OCR)

A special kind of devices called scanners use the principle of OCR to input the printed matter on the paper or any other object. This matter can be in the coded form (bar codes) or simple text/ graphics (pictures). Bar Code Readers and Scanners come into this category of devices. OCR is a technique which permits the direct reading of printed character. Optical character recognition readers or scanners typically examine each character as if it were made up of a collection of minute spots. Once the whole character has been scanned, the pattern detected is matched against a set of patterns stored in the computer. Whichever pattern it matches, or nearly matches is considered to be the character read. Patterns which can not be identified are rejected.

The standard fonts used for OCR are :

OCR-A

OCR-A (American Standard) is a USA Standard character set for OCR.

OCR-A font size 1. It describes the International Standards Organization Recommendation.

OCR-B

OCR-B is a European Standard character set for OCR

A wide range of fonts, using ordinary inks can now be accepted by OCR scanner including many typewriter fonts. OCR software translates a scanned page of text into code that you can use in a word processor. So far, however, OCR works reliably on only printed text; deciphering handwriting is a far more challenging task. It is possible that a computer could be programmed to accept some signatures, but it is unlikely that it could ever be programmed to accept every type of signature.

Advantages of OCR

1. It eliminates some of the duplication of human efforts required to get data into the computer. This reduction in effort can improve data accuracy and can increase the timeliness of the information processed.

Disadvantages of OCR

1. When document to be read is poorly typed or have strikes or erasures over it makes difficult for OCR to recognize the characters.
2. It is expensive.

Optical Mark Recognition

It is an automatic optical sensing of marks recorded on a data medium. In this method special preprinted forms are designed with boxes which can be marked with a dark pencil or ink. These documents are applicable in areas where responses are one out of a small number of alternatives and the volume of data to be processed is large. Thus they are used for

1. Objective type answer papers in examinations (e.g; in UPSC) in which large number of candidates appear.
2. Market surveys, population survey s etc., where responses can be restricted to one or more out of a few possibilities.
3. Order forms containing a small choice of items.

These preprinted documents filled by user are passed under a light source and presence of mark is detected by measuring very accurately the infra-red light levels. A mark reader may be able to detect coloured marks. It can also be designed to be insensitive to certain colours. Now these particular colours could be safely used in the pre-printing of the documents without the risk of their being read as marks intended for recognition.

Mark reading is performed in two different ways:

1. One method relies on the conductivity of graphite to determine the presence of pencil mark. This reading process is sometimes referred to as mark sensing.

PAY ______ OR BEARER

RUPEES ______

Rs.

A/c. NO.		TR NO.		INTLS	

Bank of Punjab Ltd.
10166-67, Gurdwara Road,
Karol Bagh,
New Delhi - 110 005

DHS - KRB

222287″ 110237003: 10

2. In another method while evaluating the document OMR directs a thin beam of light on the surface of the paper. Lesser amount of light is transmitted through the dot as compared to the nearby surface, due to which the filled box is recognized. OMR can evaluate only those documents which are printed with marked positions in the specified areas. The UPSC situated at New Delhi is equipped with such computers.

Advantages of OMR

1. Information is entered at its source and no further transcription is required.
2. It minimizes the unreliability of data.

Disadvantages of OMR

1. They are read very slowly.
2. Documents use a forced-answer format that leaves no opportunity for additional information.
3. The data filled can be changed erased or double-coded (more than one box filled).
4. It requires accurate alignment of printing on forms and need good quality of expensive paper

SCANNERS

Whereas a keyboard, mouse or trackball requires manual input of data, scanners allow input of printed data. A scanner reads text, photographs and graphics from paper which are then converted into bit patterns for processing, storage or output.

Scanner is a device that examines a spatial pattern one part after another and generate analog or digital signals corresponding to the pattern. Scanners are often used in mark sensing, pattern recognition or character recognition. Practically scanner uses light for examining the spatial patterns.

In a scanner, as the image is scanned, it is converted into light and dark picture elements, or pixels, similar to newspaper photo. Colour scanners can assign a specific colour to a pixel. The pixel are then stored as bit patterns. This technique makes the images usable by word processing, desktop publishing, and graphic packages.

There are two types of scanners, Hand-held scanner and Flat-bed scanner

Hand-Held Scanner

These devices read data on price tags, shipping labels, inventory part number, book ISBNs, and the like. Hand-held scanner, sometimes called wand scanners, use either contact or laser technology.

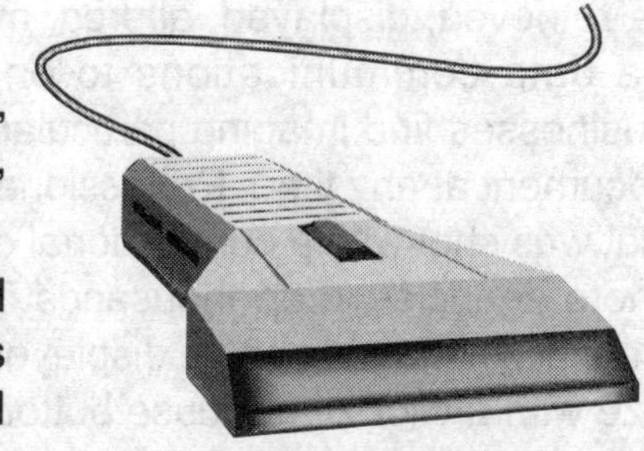

It has a set of light emitting diodes. It is placed over the material to be scanned and slowly dragged from the top to the bottom. The light emitted by the diodes are not reflected by black lines and are reflected by whole areas. The material is converted and stored in a bitmap.

Typical applications are to store images and reproduce them in publications.

Flat-bed Scanner

It consists of a box with glass plate on top, which is used for placing the document to be scanned. The light beam is situated below the glass plate and is moved from left to right horizontally. After scanning one line the beam moves up little and scans the next line.

The scanner can also store colour images.

BAR CODES

Bar Codes represent alphanumeric data by varying the width and combination of adjacent vertical lines. These zebra strips can be sensed and read by a bar code reader, a photoelectric device that reads the code by means of reflected light. When a bar code is scanned, the light source is reflected off the spaces between the marked bars. This returned light is then converted into bit patterns. A decoder in the scanning system translates the bit patterns into meaningful letters and numbers.

The bar code reader in a bookstore or grocery store is a part of a point-of-sale terminal. When you buy, say, a book at a bookstore, the checker moves it past the bar code reader. The bar code merely identifies the product to the store's computer; the code does not contain the price, which may vary. The price is stored in a file that can be accessed by the computer. This is because of the reason that it is easier to change the price once in the computer than to have to restamp the price on each book. The computer automatically tells the point-of-sale terminal what the price is; a printer prints the item description and price on a paper tape for the customer.

Bar coding has been described as in inexpensive and remarkably reliable way to get data into a computer. The advantage of bar codes over characters is that the position or orientation of the code being read is not a critical to the scanner.

Digital Camera

In recent years, source-data automation has expanded to allow the direct entry of graphic information, as well as text-based information via scanners. In a process called imaging, a scanner converts a drawing, a picture, or any document into computer- recognizable form by shinning a light on the image and sensing the intensity of the reflection at each point of the image. That is, the hard-copy image is translated into an electronic format that can be interpreted by and stored on computers. The electronic version of the image can then be stored, probably on disk, and reproduced on the screen when needed.

The image to be stored can be handwritten notes, a photograph, a drawing, an insurance form - anything that can be digitized. Once an image has been digitized and entered to the computer system, it can be retrieved, displayed, altered, merged with text, stored, and sent via data communications to one or several remote locations. Businesses find imaging particularly useful for documents, since they can view an exact replica of the original document at any time. Professional photo agencies are the another area where imaging is useful. Here the film that was shot with a conventional camera is processed onto optical disk instead of prints or slides. Professional photo agencies keep thousands of images on file, ready to be leased for a fee. Typically a couple of dozen small-size images can be displayed on the screen at one time; a particular image can be enlarged to full screen size with a click of a mouse button.

A digital camera can store many more pictures than an ordinary camera. Pictures taken using a digital camera are stored inside its memory and can be transferred to a computer by connecting the camera to it. A digital camera takes pictures by converting the light passing through the lens at the front into a digital image.

It does not by using a grid of tiny light sensors which concert the light that is falling on them into binary patterns of 0s and 1s. Different binary patterns are used to represent the different colours and shades of light that make up a picture. Pictures taken using a digital camera can be easily saved and transferred from one computer to another where they can be edited using special graphics software. Some digital camera can also capture short clips of moving images but for longer video clips a digital video camera is needed. However both of these types of camera are still quite expensive.

MICR (Magnetic-Ink Character Recognition)

This process is used by a special machine which reads coded numbers you see on your bank cheques. These days most cheques issued and used bear MICR numbers to speed up clearing of cheques.

It is a technology related to the recording of information on document by means of magnetized ink characters and automatic recognition of such characters by means of machines. In this technology the magnetic ink contains particle of magnetizable material (viz., iron oxide), which can be energized to facilitate automatic reading of printed characters. Magnetic ink document reader helps in translating the information read into a coded format usually for direct insertion into an input area of a computer's core storage in an order according to the digits recorded in a specified field, i.e., account number, etc.

When document having magnetic ink character are passed through a strong magnetic field the ink coded characters become magnetized and are recognized by the magnetic ink document reader.

Early in 1966, two standard MICR fonts (typographical styles) were accepted by International Standards Organization.

E13B Font

It is used in USA and UK. It consists of the numerals 0-9 and four special characters. This is used principally for bank cheques. The code number of the banks, the customer's account number and the cheque sequence number are all pre-printed in magnetic ink. When a cheque is submitted to a bank the amount of transaction is inscribed on it before the cheque is presented for computer processing.

The magnetized ink induces a current in a reading circuit. The current induced will be proportional to the area of ink being scanned. The patterns of the varying currents can then be compared with and identified as bit patterns of the selected character.

CMC7 Font

It originated in France and is used in Europe. It includes the digits 0-9, the letters of the alphabet, and five special characters. The symbols are made up of 7 magnetizable lines with six spaces of varying width between them.

A wide space generates a binary 1, a narrow space a 0.

Advantages of MICR

1. Since the magnetic ink characters are machine-readable, so they can be used directly for computer input.
2. Thickness, width or size of magnetic ink character has no side effects on processing or storing capability of the equipment.
3. The standard MICR code is readably by humans. Thus both individuals and MICR reading devices are able to interpret the number and symbols in the code, thereby making it easier to detect and correct across.
4. Cheques with magnetic ink character can be read even when these are over-stamped, folded or roughly handled.
5. It reduces or eliminates the amount of encoding necessary to prepare a document for computer processing.

Disadvantage of MICR

1. The magnetic strength, i.e., magnetic flux, of MICR characters tends to diminish over time, thus making MICR documents unreliable as input media when repeated processing is required.

Light Pens

A light pen is a small pen-shaped wand, which contains light sensors. The light pen is used to choose objects or commands on the screen either by pressing it against the surface of the screen or by pressing a small switch on its side. This sends a signal to the computer, which then works out the light pen's exact location on the screen. The advantage of a light pen is that pen is that unlike a touch screen it doesn't need a special screen on screen coating.

Light pens were developed early in the history of interactive computer graphics. It detects light pulses, rather than emitting light as its name implies. Light pens are sensitive to the short burst of light emitted from the phosphor coating at the instant the electron beam strikes a particular point. Other light source, such as the background light in the room, are usually not detected by a light pen.

The pen consists of a photocell placed in a small tube. As the user moves the tip of the pen over the screen surface, it is able to detect the light coming from a limited field of view. The light from the screen causes the photocell to respond when the pen is pointed directly at a lighted area. By reading the saved values, the graphic package can determine the coordinates of the pixel seen by the light pen.

Used like an ordinary writing pen, this electronic pen is used to enter data by writing on the screen. The data you write is displayed on the monitor.

Drawbacks

1. When a light pen is pointed at the screen part of the screen image is obscured by the hand and pen.
2. When used over several hours, a light pen can be tiring for inexperienced users, because it must be picked up, pointed and set down for each use.
3. Light pens require special implementation for some applications because they can't detect position within black area.
4. To be able to select positions in any screen area with a light pen we must have some non zero intensity assigned to each screen pixel.
5. The light pen is an aging technology with limited use. Unless properly adjusted, light pens sometimes detect false targets, such as fluorescent lights (i.e. background high timing in a room) or other nearby graphics primitives (e.g.; adjacent characters) and fails to detect intended targets.

Trackball

Trackball is a pointing device that works like an upside-down mouse. You rest your thumb on the exposed ball and your fingers on the buttons. To move the cursor around the screen, you roll the ball with your thumb. Because you do not move the whole device, a trackball requires less space than a mouse.

It is particularly used in notebook computers.

Touch Screens

Similar in use to the light pen is the touch-screen, which enables users to input instructions by merely touching on-screen prompts. The edges of the monitor of a touch-screen emit horizontal and vertical beams of light that criss-cross the screen. When a finger touches the screen, the interrupted light beams can pinpoint the location selected on the screen. Such screens are especially helpful when people are unfamiliar with computers. Information systems in shopping malls, airports, and amusement parks are now being developed using touch-sensitive screens as the only input hardware.

A touch screen can detect exactly where on its surface it has been touched. There are several ways in which this can be done. One common type of touch screen uses beams of invisible infra-red light which shine from top-to-bottom and side-to-side just in front of the screen. The beams of light form a grid that divides up the screen. When the screen is touched some of the beams are blocked and the exact position where the screen has been touched can be worked out by the computer. Touch screens are used in a lot of fast food chains and restaurants because they are easy to keep clean and re-program if changes need to be made to the menu.

Touch Pad

A small, touch-sensitive pad is used as a pointing device on some portable computers. By moving a finger or other object along the pad, we can move the pointer on the display screen. The touch pad is related to the touch screen, but activated by different means. The touch pad uses pressure sensitive materials to record data at the point where the pad is touched. Many appliances around the home, such as microwave ovens, use touch pads for programming time or temperature.

Digitizer

A digitizer, or graphics tablet, is similar to a light pen; however, instead of drawing on the screen, a separate tablet is used on which a special stylus is moved. Input tablets or digitizer tablet are typically found in CAD terminals or engineering workstations etc. These tablets are work surfaces that contain hundreds of copper wires in the form of a grid, which are connected to the computer. Each copper wire receives electric pulses.

A stylus or pen, which is sensitive to these pulses and signals to the computer to form drawings. By selecting commands on the digitizer, objects can be drawn or erased and coordinates can be marked on the screen. Light pens and digitizers are often used in the mechanical and architectural fields for drawing. The drawings are not made on the tablets directly but normally a sketch of drawing is traced on a per kept on tablet by this pen, to transmit to the computer.

Digitizers are also called Digitizing Tablets, Graphics Tablets, Touch Tablets or simply Tablets.

Advantages

1. The sketches displayed on the screen are neater and more precise than that on paper.
2. Digitizers provide a capability of interactive graphics.
3. The drawings can easily be changed and their effects can quickly be analyzed, thus saving user time.

Disadvantages

1. They are costly
2. They are suitable for applications which require high resolution graphics only.

Voice Input

Speaking to a computer, known as voice input or speech recognition, is another form of source input. Voice recognizers accept the spoken word through a microphone and convert it into binary code (0s and 1s) that can be understood by the computer. Most voice recognizer systems are speaker dependent - that is, they must be separately trained for each individual users. Therefore, a data base of words must be created for each person using the system. To create this database, each person using the system must repeat - as many as 20 times - each word to be interpreted by the system. This training is necessary because we seldom say a word the same way each time.

VOICE RECOGNIZERS

Voice recognizers are used in some graphic workstations as input devices to accept voice commands. The voice-system input can be used to initiate graphics operations or to enter data. These systems operate by matching an input against a predefined dictionary of words and phrases.

Voice recognizer apply a pattern-recognition approach to the wave forms created when we speak a word The wave form is typically separated into a number of different frequency bands and the variation over time of the magnitude of the wave form in each band forms the basis for the pattern matching. However, mistakes can occur in the pattern matching, so it is especially important that an application using a voice recognizer provide convenient correction capabilities.

The following 4 steps illustrate how voice recognition works

1. When you speak into a microphone, each sound is broken down into various frequencies.
2. The sounds in each frequency are digitized so they, can be manipulated by the computer.
3. The digitized version of the word is matched against similarly formed templates in the computer's electronic dictionary. The digitized templates in a form that can be stored and interpreted by computers in binary forms (0s and 1s).
4. When a match is found, the word is displayed on a computer screen or the appropriate command is performed. If no match is found, the speaker is asked to repeat the word.

Voice recognizers differ in :

1. whether or not they must be trained to recognize the waveforms of a particular speaker and
2. whether they can recognize connected speech opposed to single words or phases.
3. speaker-independent recognizer have very limited vocabularies, e.g., 50 to 100 words.

A dictionary is set up for a particular operator by having the operator speak the command words to be used into the system. Each word is spoken several times and the system analyzes the word and establishes a frequency pattern for that word in the dictionary along with the corresponding function to be performed. Later, when a voice command is given, the system searches the dictionary for a frequency pattern match.

The user of a recognizer must pause of a fraction of a second after each work to cue the system that a word end has occurred; the pause is typically 100 to 200 m sec, and can be longer if the set of possible words is large. Voice input is typically spoken into a microphone mounted on a head set. The microphone is designed to minimize input of other background sounds. If a different operator is to use the system the dictionary must be re-established with that operator's voice patterns.

Drawbacks

1. Their limited vocabulary (around 1000) makes them of little use for application such as word processing.
2. Compared to other input devices (e.g; floppy disk readers) the reliability of voice recognizer is low and tends to decrease for people with cold or poor pronunciation.
3. Voice recognizer must be calibrated to the user's voice level, tone and modulation of voice. This makes it difficult for more than one individual to use the same machine.

CONCEPT KEYBOARD

A concept keyboard is a flat board with a grid of programmable keys on its surface. A single key on its surface. A single key or a group of keys can set up to carry out a particular task. Paper overlays are placed on top of the keyboard with pictures drawn on them to represent what will happen it the keys in certain position are pressed.

Concept keyboards are often used with young children in primary schools who can't use an ordinary keyboard very well.

GRAPHICS TABLET

A graphics tablets consists of a flat surface and a pen, or stylus, which can be used to produce freehand drawings or trace around shapes. When the special pen touches the surface of the graphics tablet data about its position is sent to the computer. This data is used to produced on the screen an exact copy of what is being drawn on the surface of the graphic tablet.

MICROPHONE

A microphone is used to input sound into a computer system, Microphone are often used for voice recognition systems which convert sounds made by a user into commands that the computer can carry out. Systems like this are useful for people who can't use ordinary input devices such as the mouse and keyboard. As computers become more powerful in the future, voice recognition will be a much more common input method for all computer users.

VOICE INPUT DEVICES

It is the latest input device about which the computer users are very happy. It not types the data which you speak but also is capable of obeying the commands which you give to the computer. Through the process of voice synthesis the spoken words are converted into digital input for the computer and stored as such.

STORAGE DEVICES

In this section we discuss the devices which act as both input and output devices and those which can be used for storing data.

Secondary Storage

Although the central processing unit has internal memory but this memory cannot store both an application program and data indefinitely for processing; Also internal memory is semiconductor memory - which is costly and volatile in nature - where the data are lost when the electricity is interrupted or computer is switched off. Another limitation of primary storage is that the storage requirements for programs and data on which it operate exceeds the capacity of primary storage in all computer system.

For example, the RAM capacity of a large mainframe computer would not come close to meeting the data and program storage needs of even a small company. So it is necessary to extend the storage capabilities of a computer by using devices external to main-memory.

An external storage is also called secondary storage (or auxiliary storage) because it ,provides a second, longer-term storage for programs and data needed frequently but not currently active. It usually consists of disk units electronically connected to the system. An input/output operations is required to access or retrieve information stored in secondary storage. Secondary storage is necessary because primary storage can be used only temporarily. Data is placed in primary storage only when it is needed for immediate processing; where as data which is not being currently processed reside in the secondary memory. Also data in secondary storage remains there until overwritten with new data or deleted and is accessed when needed.

Secondary storages are used to store system programs (viz; operating system, assembler, interpreter, compiler and so on), data files, software packages and so on. The arithmetic and logical operations can not be performed directly on the data stored in secondary storage this is because the reason that central processing unit can not read informations directly from the secondary storage. The programs and data (residing in secondary storage) if needed by the central processing unit for processing are first transferred from the secondary to the RAM (primary memory). Then the CPU reads it from the RAM and processes it.

The characteristics of secondary storage are:

Nonvolatile Storage

Secondary storages are nonvolatile storages i.e., the data and programs remain intact when the computer is turned off. So secondary storages do not need continuous supply of electricity as do the primary storages require.

Capacity

Secondary storage devices have larger capacity as compare to primary storage. For example, Secondary storage like hard disk are available in few gigabits (GB) as compare to primary storage, which are still available in their maximum capacity in few megabytes (MB).

Cost Effectiveness

Secondary storages are less expensive in terms of per bit of information stored as compared to primary storage this is because of the reason of adoption of magnetic and optical technology for storing data into secondary storage; whereas primary storage uses semiconductor (CMOS) technology for storing data in RAM.

Reusability

The data which is not processed currently is stored in secondary storage for future use. So secondary storage devices stores a program for future use; gets a backup of programs during execution and helps in storing of information in files. Also data in secondary storage remains there until overwritten with data or deleted. After deletion of data, that space, in secondary storage can be used to store fresh data or programs.

Reliability

Data in secondary storage is basically safe since secondary storage is physically reliable. Also it is more difficult for unscrupulous people to temper with data on disk than data stored on paper in a file cabinet.

Storage Media

Over the years manufacturers have developed a variety of devices and media for the permanent storage of data and the programs. Paper tape, punched cards, the data cell, and a variety of others have become obsolete. Two main technologies are used to store data today:

1. Magnetic Storage, and
2. Optical Storage

Although devices that store data typically employ one or the other, some combine both technologies. The primary types of magnetic storage are:

1. Floppy disks (diskettes)
2. Hard disks
3. Magnetic tapes

The primary types of optical storage are:

1. CD-ROM
2. WORM
3. Magneto-optical media

The most common storage devices use magnetic technology. When data and program files are constantly changing, magnetic storage media are most often used. Magnetic-disk-or-tape drive record data by magnetizing small areas on the storage media. These magnetized areas store the binary codes representing data or programs instructions. When the file is no longer needed, the storage hardware overwrites the binary code and records new information in its place.

The three most common storage devices floppy disk drives, hard disk drives and tape drives - all use similar techniques for reading and writing data, because all use the same medium. The surface of diskettes, hard disk and magnetic tapes are all coated with a magnetically sensitive material (usually iron oxide) which reacts to a magnetic field. As the rea/write head passes over the disk's or tape surface, the direction of current in its electromagnetic aligns iron particles on the disk or tape in one of two polarities.

How Magnetic Media Works

The three most common storage devices - floppy disk drives, and tape drives - all use similar techniques for reading and writing data, because all use the same medium (on which data are stored). The surface of floppy disks, hard disks and magnetic tape are all coated with magnetically sensitive material (usually iron oxide) which reacts to a magnetic or rust field. The actual magnetic coating is quite thin; in fact, the thinner it is, the better it works. Just as a transistor can represent binary data as ON or OFF, the strength of a magnetic field can be used to represent data. But a magnet has one important property over transistor:

It retains its polarity without a continual source of electricity.

The surface of disks and magnetic tapes are coated with millions of tiny iron particles. Each of these particles can act as a magnet, taking on a magnetic field when subjected to an electromagnet so that they can write data to the medium, with the use of read/write heads of a disk drive. The read/write heads contain electromagnets that charge the medium as it passes over surface of disk. The read/write heads record strings of 1s and 0s by alternating the direction of the current in the electromagnets.

To read data from a magnetic surface, the process is reversed. The read/write head passes over the disk or tape while no current is flowing through the electromagnet. Since the storage medium has a magnetic charge but the head does not, so the storage medium charges the magnet in the head, which causes a small current to flow through the coil in one direction or the other, depending on the polarity of the particles. The disk drive senses the direction or the other, depending on the polarity of the particles. The disk drive senses the direction of the flow as the storage medium passes by the head.

Memory Hierarchy

Electronic memories (internal memory) are fast, but are expensive, so design tradeoffs have to be made. In fast electronic memory, the speeds are limited by the time it takes for a signal to propagate through the connected combinational logic circuits and to change the state of the storage elements. In slower memory units (external memory), which requires some form of physical movement, speeds are further limited by the mechanical characteristics of the devices.

Great changes in memory capacity, speed, and cost have been made over the years, and there will be more in the future. Memory speeds have historically had an inverse nonlinear relationship to cost. There are vast differences in speed and price among the various memory devices. We try to organize our system memories in ways that optimize processing speed and minimize cost. To do this we equip systems with different types of memories, each serving a different purpose. Registers are used to store information (temporarily) within the central processing unit. Their speed is needed to keep the processor running as fast as possible.

Instructions and data that are part of an executing program need to be accessed quickly (within nanoseconds). This ensures that CPU will not have to spend time waiting for information from memory.

Magnetic bubble memories are currently used mostly in secondary storage applications. It is faster than hard disks and magnetic tapes but are slower then internal memory.

Hard disks are used to store programs which you are developing or letters you are writing. In such storage you can usually wait a while (milliseconds or seconds) to view the stored program and change them.

Magnetic tapes are used for backup copies of programs, where internal memory can occupy upto 3 layers depending on how the system is designed.

External memory is often split into two classes based on access speed. Programs and data that are more frequently used by the system are typically stored online i.e; data is on disk devices. Whereas backup copies of important programs or data that will not be needed soon are stored offline i.e; on magnetic tapes or diskettes.

Organising and Accessing Stored Data

As a user of computer system, you just offer data as you are instructed to do; but in real sense data can not be dumped helter- skelter into a computer. System analyst has to decide how data from users will be received, organized and stored, and also in which manner data will be processed by the computer.

Organizing Data

To be processed by the computer, raw data is organized into a hierarchy. The six levels of the hierarchy of data organization are bit, character, field, record, file, and database. Each information system has a hierarchy of data organization, and each succeeding level in the hierarchy is the result of combining the elements of the preceding level. Bits - the first level - are handled automatically. The other five levels are important design considerations for any information processing activity.

Bits and Characters:

A character is represented by a group of bits that are configured according to an encoding scheme, viz; ASCII (7-bits) or EBCDIC (8-bits). On the one side the bit is the basic unit of primary and secondary storage, and on the other side character is the basic unit for human perception. In terms of data storage, a character is usually the same as a byte. A character is a letter, digit, or special character.

Fields

A field contains a set of related characters. It is the lowest level logical unit in the data hierarchy. For example, a single character viz; S has little meaning out of context. But when characters are combined to form a name (e.g; SUKHVIR or SATYAPAL), they form a logical unit.

A field is best described by example: first name, middle name, last name, address.

These are all fields. An address is not one, but four fields: Street name, city, state and pincode. Whereas the field is the general reference, the specific content of a field is called the data item.

Records

A record is a collection of related fields. Thus on the publisher mailing list, author's name, address, city, pincode, and phone number constitute a record.

Files

A file is a collection of related records. The term file is also used to refer a named area on a secondary storage device that contains a program, textual material or even an image. All the author records for the publisher compose a file. Figure 12.3 shows how the publisher data might look.

Database

A database is a collection of interrelated files stored together with minimum redundancy. For example, if records are kept in a traditional file environment and an author moves, his or her address must be changed in all files that maintain address data. In a database author address data are stored only once and are made available to all department. Therefore, only one update is needed.

Data Manipulation and Retrieval:

Data management encompasses the storage, retrieval, and manipulation of data. Many existing information systems are designed using traditional approaches to develop new information systems. In traditional, or flat file, processing files a re stored, merged, and processed by a key field (a unique identifies for a record). For example, in an author file the key might be "author's number"

In addition to organizing the expected data, a plan must be made to access the data on files.

File Plan

Now that you have a general idea of how data is organized, we need to consider what way would be appropriate to place data on a storage medium - tape or disk.

Consider these application examples to see how an access decision might be made.

1. When a student, makes a request for issuing a book on his/her card, a librarian checks the validity of the student from his account and takes appropriate decision. The librarian needs immediate access to the student record in the student file.
2. Reports of airline flight attendant next month schedules are computer-produced monthly and delivered to the attendants' home- base mailboxes. The schedules are put together from information based on flight records, whose entire file can be accessed monthly at a convenience of the airline and the computer-use plan.

As you can see, the question of access seems to come down to whether a particular record is needed right a way, as it is in example. As we will see, this immediate need for a particular record means access must be direct. It follows that the organization must also be direct, or at least indexed, and that the storage medium must be magnetic disk.

File Organization:

Based on the differences in the speed and method of access there are three major methods of storing files of data in secondary storage:

1. Sequential File Organization, in which records are organized in a particular order.
2. Direct File Organization, in which records are not organized in any special order.
3. Indexed Organization, in which records are organized sequentially, but indexes built into the file allow a record to be accessed either directly or sequentially.

Sequential File Organization:

Sequential file processing means records are in order according to a primary key field. If a particular record in a sequential file is wanted then all t he prior records in the file must be read before reaching the desired records. Tape storage is limited to sequential file organization. Operationally, the magnetic tape is same as the one in home and automobile tape decks.

Sequential files, used for sequential processing, contain records ordered according to a key field. If the key field in an employee record is employee name, the records are ordered and processed alphabetically by last name. A sequential file is processed from start to finish. The entire file must be processed, even if only one record is to be updated.

An example of direct access: Assume there are 13 address (0 through 12) available in the file. Dividing the keynumber 327, which is SUKHVIR employee number, by the prime number 13 yields remainder 2. Thus, 2, is the address for key 327. However, for the key 678, dividing by 13 yields remainder 2, a synonym, since this address has already been used by the key 327, which also has a remainder of 2. Hence the address becomes the next location i.e; 3.

Note, incidentally, that keys (and therefore records) need not appear in any particular order.

Direct File Organization

Direct access, allows the computer to go directly to the desired record by using a primary key; the computer does not have to read all preceding records in the file as it does if the records are arranged sequentially. Direct access requires disk storage, in fact, a disk device is called a direct-access storage device (DSAD) because the computer can go directly to the desired record on the disk. An added advantage of direct access organization is the ability to read, change, and return a record to its same place on the disk, this is called updating in place.

Indexed File Organization

It is useful in applications where a file needs to be in sequential order but, in addition, access to individual records is needed. In indexed file organization records are stored in the file in sequential order, but the file also contains an index. The index is like a directory, with the keys to all records listed in order (ascending or descending). To access a record directly, the record key (primary key) must be located in the index; the address associated with the key is then used to locate the record on the disk. To access the entire file of records sequentially, begin with the first record and proceed through the rest of records.

Magnetic Tape

Like your tape recorder's cassette, it has magnetic coated plastic material. It is very useful to store large volumes of data. While larger tape spools with magnetic tape units are used with mainframe computers, the small cassette tapes, similar to music cassettes are used with Personal Computers.

Physical Characteristics of a Magnetic tape

The tape is made of plastic material with iron oxide (ferrite) coating on one side of the tape, which is magnetically sensitive, and it is this surface that is used for the recording of data. The magnetized spots or bits are extremely small and not visible to the human eye.

One main advantage of tape is that large volumes of data can be condensed into a relatively small area. Typically magnetic tape is 1/2 inch wide and comes in reels which are 2400 to 3600 feet long and have a diameter of about 10 1/2 inch.

Representation of Data on a Magnetic Tape

Tracks run across the length of the tape with a tape having typically 7 to 9 tracks across its width. For IBM and IBM-compatible mainframe that use the 9-bit EBCDIC code, a tape would have 9 longitudinal tracks on channels or recording surfaces each capable of storing magnetized bits.

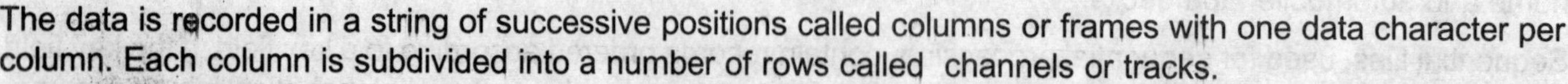

The data is recorded in a string of successive positions called columns or frames with one data character per column. Each column is subdivided into a number of rows called channels or tracks.

The magnetic state of each track within each frame is said to be binary in that the presence of a particular magnetic state or bit is:

1. taken to represents a 1
2. absence of bit represents a 0

At any point along the length of the tape, the combination of bits on the tracks represent a character For example, A to Z, a to z, 0 to 9

special characters like ;,;$@ etc.

Each track with a column contains 1 bit and the bit combinations in each column represent data characters according to the particular coding system such as ASCII (7 bit) EBCDIC (8 bit).

Three coding systems frequently used are the 7 track code, 9 track code and binary code.

1. In case of the 7 track code, 6 tracks are used for data bits and one track contains the parity bit used for increasing hardware operating accuracy.
2. In the case of 9 track code, 8 tracks are used for data bits and 9th is the parity bit.
3. In the binary coding system data is recorded in terms of the binary system rather in terms of alphabetic characters and decimal numeric values.

For example, if a particular machine utilizes 24-bit binary words and 7-track tape is being used, 4 columns of the tape can be used to encode each binary word.

Tape Density

The actual number of characters that can be represented in an inch of tape is called the tape density.

or

The number of columns or frames per inch of magnetic tape is a measure of the density of the tape.

Density is expressed in terms of bytes per inch (bpi). Here the term byte refers to the set of bits that can be entered in a single column of the tape.

Typical tape densities are in the range of 800 to 1600 dpi, although higher as well as lower densities are possible. Since there are enough tracks across the width of the tape to represent characters, so this density also gives the number of character per inch of tape.

If characters are packed onto a tape at a density of 800 dpi then a 2400 ft tape would hold

= 800x2400x12

= 23,04,00,00 character

A density of 1600 bpi would double this figure.

Magnetic Tape Units

The magnetic tape drive is a specialized input/output device used for reading and writing magnetic tapes. The file reel contains the tape to be read or be written on, and machine reel contains the tape that has already been processed.

The tape advances past the read/write head the rated speed of reading or writing is a function of two factors:

1. the recording density of the tape and
2. the linear speed of the tape drive

For example, if the recording density is 1600 bps and the speed is 200 inches per second rated read/write speed = 1600x200 = 320000 bps

Tape Records, Blocks and Interblock Gaps

Data is recorded on magnetic tape in the form of blocks. Where each block consists of a grouping of data written (or read) in one continuous operation. For example, a grouping of data written on magnetic tape in one continuous operation and which may include one or more records is called a block. Between physical disk or tape records, the computer automatically reserves some blank space called on interblock gap (IBG). It permits proper timing for accessing records and activating read/write heads.

Blocks are separated by a gap, which is a blank space about 1/2 inch in length. Gaps are required in order to differentiate different blocks of data. The greater the number of inter-record gaps, the smaller the storage capacity of the tape.

For example,

let each record = 800 bytes

density = 1600 bytes/inch

In case where two consecutive records have 1/2 inch gap, i.e., inter-record gap = 1/2 inch

then in one inch length of tape contains 800 bytes and 1/2 inch is a gap between two re cords. Therefore, only half of the length of tape is used for storing data. To circumvent this problem, records are often grouped in blocks. If records are blocked i.e; grouped together, one write command can transfer a number of consecutive records to the tape without requiring inter-record gaps between them. Gaps appropriately called interblock gaps are placed between successive blocks. In using magnetic tape the record size is not restricted and can be as long as it is suitable for the application involved.

Records can be of two-types:

1. Fixed length record - records are of same size.
2. Variable length record - records length differ.

For example, variable-length record is a record containing the transactions for the month for an individual flow of cheques. The record for a customer who wrote 40 cheques during the month is substantially shorter than the record of another customer who wrote 200 cheques.

Just as record-size can be variable so can be the number of records per block. So we can have fixed-length or variable-length records and fixed-length or variable-length blocks. Even though the block size is variable, but its size can not be unlimited. The programmer has to define the maximum limit on block size in each tape operation.

To distinguish variable length records written in a block, we have a control field at the beginning of each record, which contains the length of the record. The utilization of a tape's storage capacity increases as the number of records in a block is made larger

Blocking factor = number of records in a block.

For example, let number of records = 10

record capacity = 800 bytes

density = 1600 bpi

inter-record gap = 1/2 inch.

Buffer

In order to read a block from at ape or disk one specifies the length of block and also the address A in memory where the block is to be transferred. The block of data is packed in to the words A, A+1, A+2....

Similarly in order to write a block of data onto tape one specifies the starting address in memory and the number of consecutive words to be written. These input and output areas in memory will be referred to as buffers.

However, each time a read or write operation is executed for a particular storage device, a block of logical records is transferred. The apparent difference in a program's read and write statements and read and write commands issued for a particular device is resolved by using a buffer between external storage and the data area of a program.

A buffer is a section of main memory which is equal in size to the maximum size of a block of logical records used by a program. The data-management routines of the operating system use buffers for the "blocking" and "deblocking" of records.

There is two type of buffering

1. Single buffering
2. Multiple buffering

Single buffering

Consider the use of the Master sequence file as an input file. When the first Read statement is executed, a block of records is moved from external storage to a buffer. The first record in the block is then transferred to the program's data area.

For each subsequent execution of a READ statement the next successive record in the buffer is transferred to the data area. Only after every record in the buffer has been moved to the data area, in response to READ statements, does the next READ statement cause another block to be transferred to the buffer from external storage.

The new records in the buffer are moved to the data area as described previously and this entire process is repeated for each block that is read. In a similar fashion WRITE statements cause the transfer of program data to the buffer becomes full (corresponding to a block of logical records) then the block is written on the external storage device immediately after the preceding blocks of records.

Multiple buffering

Multiple buffering makes use of a queue of buffers which are normally controlled by the operating system. The need for more than one buffer arises because of the delay (which is in the order of milliseconds) necessary to read in or write out the next block of records. This delay in the execution of Read or Write statement, when a blocking factor i.e., number of records in a block is N and a single buffer is used.

However, if the program is executing in an environment where the desired response time is small and where processor and I/O activity need to be overlapped, then it is wise to eliminate this delay by using multiple buffers.

Parity and Error Control

In order to interpret correctly the data that are stored on a tape, the encoding scheme (EBCDIC, ASCII etc) that was used when data were written must be known. Additionally the technique used to record error-control bits has to be known in order for that information to be used.

One common technique for error control on magnetic tapes is parity. Odd parity : there must be an odd number of 1-bits represented for each character. If the bits making up a character's binary representation already have an odd number of 1-bits, then the parity bit (in 9th track) is a 0-bit.

If there is an even number of 1-bits, the parity bit for that character is 1-bit making the total number of 1-bits for that character's representation odd. Parity bits are written when data on the tape are written, then they are checked when the tape is read to verify that an error has not occurred.

Blocking

Data are read from or written to a tape in groups of characters called blocks or physical records. A block is the smallest amount of data that can be transferred between secondary memory and primary memory in one access. A block may contain one or more records. In order to read or write data properly the tape medium must be moving at a constant speed when it passes by the head mechanism.

Because requests to read or write blocks do not arrive at a tape drive at a constant rate, there must be a gap (interblock gap) between each pair of blocks, forming a space to be passed over as the tape slows from read/write speed and as the tape accelerates to read/write speed. Because the tape is not moving at a constant speed while the read/write head is positioned at a gap, a gap can not contain user data.

The block size can significantly affect the amount of data that can be stored on a tape.

Case I

Time required to access full tape with 1 record per block

(a) to find the length of the block:

We have found the total number of blocks = 46753 blocks

% of length consumed where data are stored = 100 - 97.4 = 2.6%

length of blocks in inches = 2.6/100 * 28800 = 749 inches

length of one blocks = total length of blocks/number of blocks

749/46753 = 0.016 inch 749

time required to access full tape with 1 record per block and a delay in each gap is

= 46753 * 0.016/200 + 46753 * 0.004 = 190.75 sec.

Case II

Time required to access the same collection of records with 20 records per block is

number of blocks = 46753/20 = 2338 blocks

length of each block = 34.8 * 28000/100*31304 = 0.32 inch

2338 blocks * 0.32 inch/block/200 inch/sec. + 2338 blocks * 0.004 sec./gap * 1 gap/block = 10.55 sec.

A program that accesses a file of data stored on a tape can execute no faster than that file can be accessed.

The blocking factor (number of records per block) used when a file is written must be known when that file is later read.

Why not just have one block include all of the records of the file?

This approach certainly would minimize the number of blocks, and also minimize the number of gaps and the time required to access the file. The problem with this approach is that regardless of the block size, there must be space allocated in main memory to hold the contents of a block prior to writing the block onto the tape (for the output file) or prior to reading the block into a program (for an input file).

The size of a buffer or a file is the same as that file's block size. When a program requests a record from tape file with a blocking factor (number of records/block) of one record per block, the tape is accessed, one block is moved into the buffer and the record is available.

When there is more than one record per block, a program still requests a read of one record at a time but the entire block must be brought into the buffer at once. Selection of the appropriate blocking factor for a tape file thus involves:

1. trade-offs between the time required to access the tape.
2. the cost of main memory buffer space, and

3. the number of accesses to secondary storage.

Blocking is a technique that increases the speed of input/output operations and makes more effective use of storage space on disk and tape. A group of logical records is included within one block to maximize the efficient use of a disk or tape area, i.e., reading in a block of 20 disk records is more efficient than reading in each disk record separately. Even though a disk or tape file may be blocked, the program processes records in the standard way, i.e., one logical record at a time

By indicating Block Contains N Records for an input disk or tape the computer is able to read the full block correctly. Similarly by indicating the number of records in a block for an output disk or tape the computer is able to create the correct block of records. Thus Block contains clause of a disk or tape file is the only entry required to read or write a block of records.

Suppose we have an input file with the following file description (FD) entries:

1. FD Transaction-File
2. Labels records are standard
3. Record contains 20 characters
4. Block contains 15 records

With a record size of 20 and block 15, 300 character (20x15) are read into the input area reserved for this file. For the initial read the first 20 characters in main-memory are processed and for the next read the next 20 characters in main-memory are processed. For the next read the next 20 characters in main-memory are processed. This will continue until the entire block is accessed, then the next block is read and the procedure is repeated.

Blocking of logical records maximizes the:

1. efficient use of the disk by decreasing wasted space (interblock space gap),
2. increases the speed at which data is transferred to or from CPU, and
3. handling of blocked files is relatively easy for COBOL programmers.

Drawbacks of Tape

1. Records must be processed in the order in which they reside on the tape. Therefore, accessing a record requires the scanning of all records that precede it. This form of access is called Sequential Access.
2. Operations such as rewinding a tape or back-spacing a certain number of records or blocks increase the performance and flexibility of a magnetic-tape device.

Tape File Organization Format

In addition to data, other items of information required in a tape file are:

Beginning-of-tape (BOT)

It is a reflective strip with adhesive backing. The reflective marker identifies the starting point for tape use and is automatically sensed by the read/write head in both forward and rewind operations.

Header Label

This is a block of data containing identifying information about the tape file. We can use adhesive label but to be on safer side we use a magnetic label, which serves as a means of machine verification of the content of a reel of tape.

It contains:

Field Identification : in terms of file name or a file number

Retention Period : date prior to which the tape can not be over written.

Creation Date : the date on which the file was established.

Reel sequence and number

Trailer Label

Trailer label is last record on the tape. It contains the same information as the header label, but in addition it contains a block count, which is a count of the number of data blocks written on the reel. This block count is used for control purposes.

End-of-tape (EOT)

It is again a reflective strip and serves to stop the tape drive in order to prevent the tape from dethreading. When EOT marker is sensed, the tape drive will not advance forward even if a programming command so directs the computer. It is particular for stopping for further writing.

FLOPPY DISKS

There are two kinds of floppies, 3½" and 5¼" in sizes. These floppies are made of vinyl material and have a plastic coated jacket over them. The vinyl material has a coating of magnetic oxide so that data can be stored on it. Floppy disk can be used both as an input device and an output device meaning that you can both write on it and read from it.

Floppy disk is used for the storage of data which is encoded by electromagnetic means on to tracks on the disk surface. A floppy disk is made of flexible material usually a kind of plastic which has magnetizable particles upon its surface. Floppy disks are supplied within special envelopes which have holes set in them for the drive shaft and read/write heads of the disk drives which are used to operate with the disks. The disks are designed to be handled within the envelope which protects the recording surface.

Floppy disks are used with word processing systems and with PCs and their popularity is related to the ease with which they can be handled and stored off line. They are classed as exchangeable disks. It is also known as diskette.

Types of Floppy Disks

Floppies come in two physical sizes:

5 1/4 inch and

3 1/2 inch.

The size refers to the diameter of the disk, not to the capacity.

The 5 1/4" type is encased in a flexible vinyl envelope with an oval cutout that allows the read/write head to access the disk.

The density of the disk is a measure of the quantity of the disk surface: the higher the density, the more closely the iron-oxide particles are packed and the more data the disk can store. The disk itself is made of soft flexible mylar plastic with a magnetically sensitive iron oxide coating. The coating is present on both sides, even for single-sided disks that are intended to be recorded on only one side. The second side of a single-sided disk may not have its second side finished, polished and tested but it still has the same coating.

These days 5.25 inch disks (1.2 MB capacity) are used primarily in older computers although some people buy optional 5.25" disk drives for their new PCs to be able to read and write to the old disks.

3.5 inch type is encased in a hard plastic shell with a sliding metal cover. When the disk is inserted into the drive, the cover slides back to expose the disk to the read/write head. The term floppy disk refers to the disk inside, not to the square plastic protector.

The 3.5 inch size floppy disk come in three capacities:

1. double density
2. high density and
3. very high density

Floppy Disk Drives

A floppy-disk drive is a device that reads and writes data to and from floppy disks. The drive includes:

1. a spindle that rotates the disk
2. read/write head that can move in and out as the disk spins to position themselves at any spot on the disk surface.
3. drive light
4. eject button

The diskettes, spin at around 300 revolutions per minute (RPM), so the longest it can take to position a desired point under read/write head is the amount of time required for one revolution = 60/300 = 1/5 seconds. The farthest the heads would ever have to move is from the center of the disk to the outside edge. The heads can move from one extreme to the other in even less time about 1/6 seconds. For example, workers carry their files from office computer to home computer and back on a diskette instead of in a briefcase. Students use the campus computers but keep their files on their own diskettes.

But since both operations, the horizontal movement of read/write head and the rotation of disk take place simultaneously, the maximum time to position the heads over a given location on the floppy disk remains the greater of the two times or 1/5 second.

The most common uses of the floppy disks are the following:

Portability

Moving files between computers that are not connected through communications hardware. i.e; copy the data to a floppy disk remove the floppy disk from drive and insert into the drive of another computer.

Loading

Loading new programs onto a system. Although extremely large programs are available on CD-ROM or tape, most programs are sold on floppy disks. You copy the contents of floppy disk to your hard disk.

Backup

Backing up data or programs, the primary copy of which is stored on a hard disk. Backing up is the process of creating a duplicate set of the hard disk's program and data for safekeeping.

How Data is Organized on a Floppy Disk

Before the computer can use floppy disk to store data, they must be magnetically mapped so that the computer can go directly to a specific point on the disk without searching through data. The process of mapping a disk is called formatting or initializing the disk.

Every new floppy disk must be formatted. However, you can buy floppy disks that have been pre-initialized for your particular computer. The first thing a floppy drive does when formatting a disk is to create a set of magnetic concentric circles called tracks, numbered from outer to inner tracks. High-density disks have 80 tracks. The tracks on a disk do not form a continuous spiral like those on a phonograph record; each one is a separate circle.

Each track on a disk is split into smaller parts. Each part would cut across all the disk's track, resulting in short segments called sectors. All the sectors on the tracks are numbered in one long sequence, so that computer can access each small area on the disk with a unique number.

When you refer to the number of sectors a disk has, the unit you use is sectors per track. For example, if a disk has 80 tracks and 18 sectors per track then it has 80x18 = 1440 sectors. The 3.5 inch, 1.44 M B floppy disk has a total of 2880 sectors (80 tracks per side x 2 sides x 18 sectors per track).

On most disks, a sector contains 512 bytes or 0.5 KB. The sector is the smallest unit with which any disk can work. Each bit and byte within a sector can have different values, but the drive can read or write only whole sectors at a time. Even if the computer needs to change just one byte of 512, it rewrites the entire sector.

The Data Area

The part of the disk that remaining free after the boot sector, FAT and directory have been created in the data area.

How to Take Care of Your Floppy Disks

Although diskettes come in protective jackets, users must take at lest ordinary care of them to protect the data contents:

1. Keep floppy disks away from anything that has magnetic charge or that generates magnetic field, including telephone, stereo speakers.
2. Don't slide the cover back on 3.5 inch disks and don't touch the recording medium of any disk.
3. Never force a disk into a disk drive and never remove a disk from a drive when the drive light is on. The light tells you that the drive is working, and removing the disk is likely to damage the data on it.
4. Do not expose disks to excessive heat or humidity.

Measuring Drive Performance

When evaluating the performance of common storage devices, you need to be aware of two common measures:

1. The average access time and
2. The data-transfer rate.

Average Access Time

The average access time of a device is the amount of time it takes the device to position its read/write heads over any spot on the recording medium. Access time is the combination of two factors:

1. the speed at which the disk spins (in RPM) and
2. time the read/write head takes to move the heads from one track to another.

Access time is measured in msec. (1/1000 second), so the maximum access time for floppy disks = 60/30 * 1000/1 = 200 m secs.

Average Data- Transfer Rate

It implies at which rate drive can transfer data, i.e., how long it takes to read or write data. For data-transfer rates, the unit of time is almost always the second, but units of data may be measured in bytes, KB or MB. Disk controllers coordinate the flow of data to and from the computer and disk drive.

They are often connected to the system as an expansion card and can control the flow of data to several drives.

Drive Interface Standards

Another important factor in determining how quickly a drive can read and write data is the type of controller that the drive uses. A disk controller is connected directly to the computer's bus on some computers, the disk controller is an integral part of the computer's main motherboard. On others, the controller is an expansion board that connects to the bus by plugging into one of the computer's expansion slots.

Integrated Drive Electronics (IDE)

The IDE interface places most of the controller's circuitry on the drive itself to provide a simpler interface with the computer. IDE is capable of providing data-transfer rates of about 1 MB per second under ideal conditions.

Enhanced Small Device Interface (ESDI)

It encodes the data on the drive instead of on the controller card. This results in a higher degree of reliability - which in turn allows for higher speeds. ESDI is capable of transferring data at rate of 3 MB per second.

Small Computer System Interface (SCSI)

It takes an approach to interfacing peripheral devices. Because the original concept of SCSI was to provide peripherals access to the computer's bus, one way to think of SCSI is as an extension of the computer's bus. One benefit of SCSI is that bringing the computer's bus directly into the drive improves efficiency greatly. Because a SCSI interface is essentially an extension of a computer's bus, it can accommodate multiple devices - as many as the bus can handle. Most current implementations of SCSI limit the number of devices to seven.

Hard Disks

It is also called as mass-storage device. Like floppy disks, hard disks store data in tracks that are divided into sectors. A hard disk is a stack of metal platters that spin on one spindle, like a stack of rigid floppy disks. Each platter is coated with iron oxide and the entire unit is encased in a sealed chamber to make it free from dust and other contamination.

Hard Disk

Floppy Disks Versus Hard Disk

Unlike floppy disks, where the disk and drive are separate, the hard-disk drive or hard drive is the whole unit. It includes the hard disk, the motor that spins the platters and a set of read/write heads you generally can't remove the hard disk from its drive; the two terms are used interchangeably to mean the whole unit, both disk and drive. Some manufacturers also make removable hard disks that plug into a separate drive unit. A major physical difference between floppy disks and hard disks is that hard disks are rigid. They are usually made of metal (frequently aluminum) instead of flexible mylar or plastic from which a floppy disk is made. When a hard disk spins its rigid construction keeps the platters from flexing as much as a floppy disk and that allows much more precision in pinpointing positions on the disk.

The hard disks are sealed inside an airtight vacuum chamber. This allows the heads of the hard disk to fly much closer to the surface of the disk, also allowing much greater precision. In fact, the heads of hard disks fly so close to the surface of the disk that if a dust particle, a human hair or even a fingerprint were placed on the disk it would bridge the gap between the heads and the disk, causing the heads to crash. A head crash, in which the head touches the disk destroys the data stored in the area of the crash and can destroy a read/write head as well.

Because materials such as hair, fingerprints, and dust or smoke particles are much thicker than the gap between the disk and the read/write head, they can cause the head to crash. The increased surface areas provided by multiple platters is the main reasons that hard disk can store so much more data than floppy disks. Waving a magnet past an electric coil like the one in a drive's read/write head causes a current to flow through the coil. The interesting thing is that the faster you move a magnet, the larger the current it generates in the coil. Conversely, the more current you apply to the magnet the stronger its magnetic field becomes.

Hard disk spins at around 3600 RPM instead of a floppy disk's 300 RPM. Some hard drives spin as fast as 5400 RPM. As the hard disk spins faster, the drive's heads can use a lower- intensity current to polarize a spot on the disk. When the drive head reads data from the surface of the disk the fast speed of the disk amplifies the intensity of the current induced in the read head.

Some hard-disk drives hold as many as 12 disks but both sides of disks are not always used. With hard disk, the number of sides that the disk uses in specified by the number of heads. For example, a particular hard-disk drive might have six disk platters (12 sides) but only 10 heads, indicating that two sides are not used to store data. Often these are the top side of the top disk and the bottom side of bottom disk.

As hard disks are actually a stack of platters, we use new term cylinder to refer to the same track across all the disk sides. Hard disks generally store 512 bytes of data in a sector, but because of their higher tolerance hard disk can have more sectors per track-54, 63 or more.

When reading from or writing to a hard disk, all access arms are moved to the appropriate cylinder. Although the addressing schemes vary considerably between disks, the address normally will include the cylinder (or track), the recording surface, and the sector number. PC users, who never seem to have enough hard disk storage space, may turn to a removable hard disk cartridge. Once full, a removable hard disk cartridge can be replaced with a fresh one. In effect, a removable cartridge is as portable as a diskette, but the disk cartridge holds much more data.

A concept of using several small disks that work together as a unit is called a redundant array of inexpensive disks or simply RAID. The group of connected disks operates as if it were just one large disk, but it speeds up reading and writing by having multiple access paths. The data file for, say automobile factory tools, may be spread across several disks, thus if the computer is used to look up tools for several workers, the computer need not read the data in turn but instead read them at the same time in parallel.

Furthermore, data security is improved because if a disk fails, the disk system can reconstruct data on an extra disk; thus computer operations can continue uninterrupted.

Disk Access Time

Access time is the interval between the instant a computer makes a request for transfer of data from a disk-storage device to RAM and the instant this operation is completed. The access of data from RAM is performed at electronic speeds-approximately the speed of light. But the access of data from disk storage depends on mechanical apparatus. Any mechanical movement significantly increases the access time.

Seek Time

The seek time, the largest portion of the total access time, consists of how long it takes the access arm (mechanical) to move the read/write head to the desired track or cylinder. Some hard disk drives have two sets of access arms, one for reading and writing on the inside tracks and another for the outside tracks.

Two independent sets of access arms significantly reduce the average seek time because they have a shorter distance to move and can move while the other is reading or writing.

Rotational Delay Time

The rotational delay time is the time it takes for the appropriate data to be positioned under the read/write head.

On the average, it would be half the time it takes for one revolution of the disk or about 8 msec for a hard disk spinning at 3600 rpm.

Transmission Time

The transmission time i.e; the time it takes to transmit the data or RAM, is negligible.

Disk Access Time = Seek time + rotational delay time + transmission time

Winchester Disks

A magnetic disk drive which is similar in size to a floppy disk but overcomes speed and storage limitations by closer head alignment and denser recording. The movable read/write head floats above a rotating disk on a cushion of air produced by the rotating surface. When rotation stops, the air cushion is lost and the head comes to rest on the surface of the disk in a landing zone where no data is recorded. Winchester drives are sealed to prevent contamination that can cause head crash. A Winchester is a fixed disk system and is named after the 30-30 Winchester rifle, the original Winchester disk being 30 MB of data on 30 tracks. The disk is coated with a special lubricant which reduces the friction when the heads land.

Standard sizes are 5.25 inch and 8-inch. Storage capacities range around 40 MB to 760 MB. Mostly it is used with microcomputers. A Winchester hard disk contains several disk platters stacked on a single rotating spindle. Data are stored on all recording surfaces. The enclosure of Winchester disk keeps the disk-face surfaces free from contaminants such as dust and cigarette smoke. The rotational movement of a magnetic disk passes all data under or over read/write head, thereby making all data available for access on each revolution of the disk. A fixed disk will have at least one read/write head for each recording surface. The heads are mounted on access arm that moves over the spinning recording surfaces.

Winchester disks normally are permanently installed in the same physical unit as the processor and diskette drives. There are interchangeable hard disk also These interchangeable Winchester disks are inserted and removed in a manner that is similar to the way you insert and remove tapes on a VCR. Only a small percentage of PCs are configured to accept interchangeable Winchester disk.

Virtual Memory Operations Use Disk Drives as Extension of the Computers Memory.

Physical Characteristics of Magnetic Disks

Magnetic disk is a flat circular plate generally made of aluminium and coated with magnetic material like Ferric oxide or chromium oxide. One or both sides of the disk can be used to record data magnetically.

Each surface of the disk is divided into a number of concentric circles called as tracks. Also each track is again divided into a number of sectors (i.e; number of blocks of data) Each sector has an identifying address. Instruction to be stored on a disk by a single instruction must start from the beginning of a sector.

If required, consecutive sectors can be used to store the information, but if the said information does not require an integral number of sectors, the remaining portion of the last sector is left unused. This address consists of the track number and sector number. Usually tracks are assigned consecutive numbers starting with 0 for the outermost track.

If more than one surface is used, the surface number should also be included in the sector address. In some disks, the sectoring can be altered by a system Software. In case of a disk, the information need not necessarily be accessed sequentially. This is why disk drives are often called random-access or direct-access devices. Typically there are several hundred usable tracks on the surface of a magnetic disk. Each track can contain a few thousand character around its circular length.

Each track is separate from the others, and all tracks have the same capacity even though the circles become smaller as we move away from the periphery. The uniformity of capacity is achieved by appropriate adjustment of the density of data representation for each track's dimensions. A major benefit of this uniform capacity approach is that files can be relocated on the disk without changing the number of sectors (or tracks or cylinders) allocated to the file.

Almost all disk unit hold the same amount of data per sector on a small track near the center of a disk as that on a large track near the outside of the disk. The reason for this is that it takes the same amount of time for a sector on a small track to pass the read/write heads as it takes for a sector on a large track. Thus to keep the data transfer rate amount of data per sector on every track. A disk pack of 6 disks has 10 usuable surfaces, because the top and bottom surfaces of the two outer disks are not used since they are not exposed to handling and to the possibility of being "scratched".

A cylinder refers to a set of tracks having the same track number of belonging to same disk pack. For example, track 1 of each disk surface in a disk pack constitutes cylinder 1. Thus if each disk surface has 200 tracks, there are 200 cylinders in such a disk pack. Therefore, unique reference to particular tracks can be made in terms of cylinder and track number. For example, if a disk pack of 10 surfaces is assumed, cylinder 5, track 3 identifies 5th track of the 3rd surface.

For access, a disk pack is mounted on a disk drive, which include a controller, access arms, read/write heads and a mechanism for rotating the pack. The controller manages buffer storage for the unit, handles error detection and correction of control read/write activities. The platters of mounted disk pack spin continuously at a speed of about 3600 rpm. Unlike magnetic tape devices, a rotating disk device does not stop between block accesses.

A widely used disk device is the IBM 3330. A disk pack in this system consists of 11 disks (20 recording surfaces). Each disk surface consists of 400 tracks, with a capacity of about 13,000 bytes per track. Data is transferred from the disk system to central storage and vice versa, at the rate of 806,000 bytes/sec. The time required for the read/write head to reach a given track depends on the distance between the current and the desired portion of the head. Once the right track has been accessed, on the average it takes 8.4 ms to access a specific record on a given track.

How to minimize the seek time

If records of a file stored on disk are to be accessed sequentially, then access time can be minimized by properly allocating disk space to the file. Assume the file requires 10 tracks of space. Rather than allocating 10 tracks on one surface to the file, space should be allocated to tracks on one cylinder, thereby minimizing the arm movement required to access the records.

Recording Data on Disk

Data can be recorded on disk tracks with or without the use of keys. A key is a label that is used to identify a particular record. A key is required whenever the location of the record can't be specified exactly. Layout of the fields on a track in disk storage when data is recorded without the use of keys can be as given below:

BT : beginning of track

G : fields are separated by a gap

HA : home address consists of 4 fields

TC : track condition signals as to whether the track is operative or defective

CY : cylinder number

HD : Head number

EC : Error checking code which tells whether the data is read/write correctly or not.

TDR : Track descriptor record, serves to indicate an alternative track if the given track is defective.

Many disk systems contain spare tracks that are used as alternates whenever a track becomes defective; this avoids the necessity of terminating a job in the middle or re creating an entire file because of difficulty with one or two tracks.

Record

The data are often consists of hundreds of characters, and thus is much longer than the identification and control fields which preceded it on the track. Data is recorded with associated keys. In many disk systems the length of the key is limited to 255 bytes. Key field makes it possible to check the identification of a record in the disk control unit before it is transferred to the central processor, thus conserving central processor time.

CENTRAL PROCESSING UNIT

Central Processing Unit is a computer's brain and is a place where data are manipulated. In a micro-computer, the entire CPU is contained on a tiny chip called a microprocessor. Every CPU has at least three parts:

1. Control Unit
2. Arithmetic-Logic Unit
3. Memory

The parts of the CPU are usually connected by an electronic component referred to as bus.

The Control Unit

Just as the processor is the nucleus of a computer system, the control unit is the nucleus of the processor. The control unit contains circuitry that uses electrical signals to direct the entire computer system to carry out or execute stored program instructions. The instruction set, which is built into the circuitry of the control unit is a list of operations that CPU can perform e.g.; ADD, SUB, DIV, JUMP etc. The control unit does not execute instruction itself, but it tells others what to do.

The function of the control unit is to coordinate all the computer's activities, for this all the instructions and data are sent along wires or bus lines. The bus is the path (circuitry) that connects the CPU with internal and external components. Peripheral hardware is connected to CPU (i.e.; control unit) through the expansion bus.

The control unit has three primary functions:

1. To read and interpret program instructions
2. To direct the operation of internal processor components
3. To control the flow of programs and data in and out of RAM

A program must first be loaded to RAM before it can be executed. During execution, the first in a sequence of program instructions is moved from RAM to the control unit, where it is decoded and interpreted by the **decoder**. The control unit then directs other processor components to carry out the operations necessary to execute the instruction.

The control unit contains high-speed **working storage** areas called registers, which are temporary storage and can store no more than a few bytes (see Figure 9.2). Registers handle instructions and data at a speed about 10 times faster than the register, called the **instruction register**, contains the instruction being executed. Other general-purpose registers store data needed for immediate processing and also store status information. For example, the **program register** (counter) contains the RAM address of the next instruction to be executed.

Registers facilitate the movement of data and instructions between RAM, the control unit, and the arithmetic and logic unit. Registers are not a part of memory; rather they are special additional storage locations that offer the advantage of speed. They work under the direction of the control unit to accept, hold and transfer instructions or data and perform arithmetic or logical comparison at high speed.

Most computer use several types of registers. Inspite of variation in the number of registers in different computers. These are some registers which are common to all computers. These are:

1. An **accumulator**, which collects the result of computations. It also holds the initial data to be operated upon. In many computers there are more than one accumulator.
2. A **general-purpose register**, which is used for several functions e.g.; arithmetic operations.
3. A **program register**, which keeps track of where a given instruction or piece of data is stored in memory. Each storage location in memory is identified by an address.
4. A **decoder**, decoders and interprets the instruction given to computer through input.
5. A **memory address register** (MAR) contains the address of a word currently required.
6. A **memory buffer register** (MBR) is used for storing a word as it is read from memory or just prior to being written into memory.

When the computer runs a program it looks upto the commands contained in the program in the CPUs instruction set and execute them in order. CPUs that are made by different companies (viz., Intel, Cyrix, Motorola) have different instruction sets.

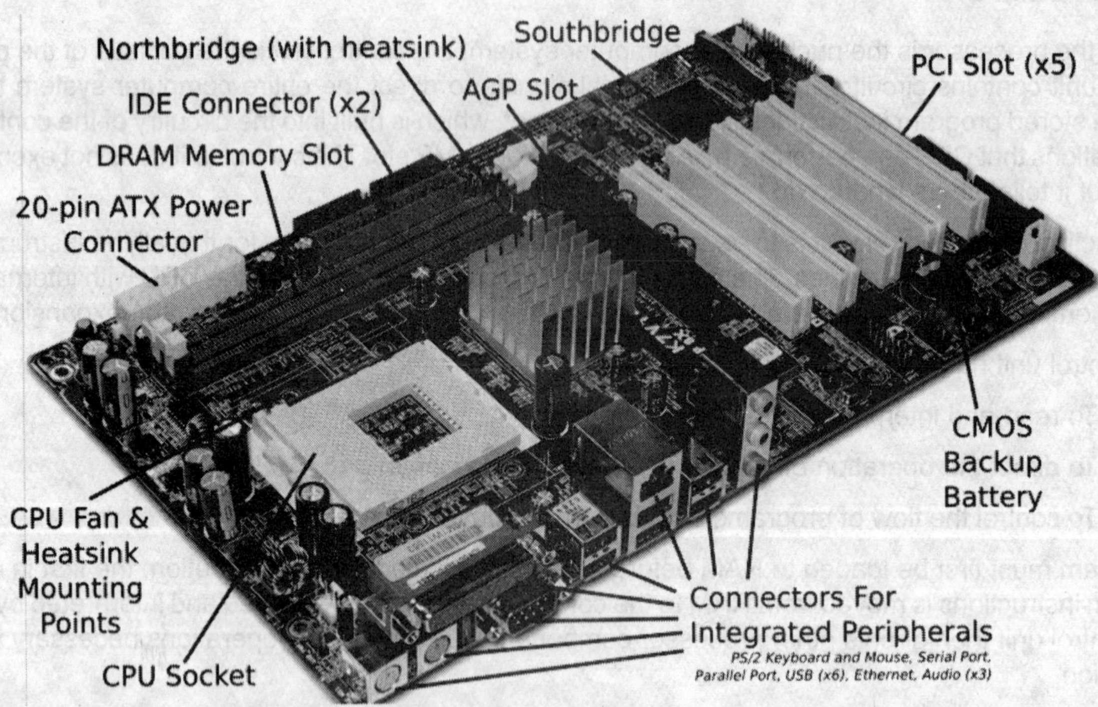

THE ARITHMETIC-LOGIC UNIT:

The arithmetic-logic unit (ALU) contains the electronic circuitry that executes all arithmetic and logical operations.

Arithmetic operations

The ALU unit can perform four kinds of arithmetic operations:

1. Addition,

2. Subtraction,
3. Multiplication, and
4. Division

All the arithmetic a computer performs is, essentially, addition. The computers can add two numbers to obtain a sum. Subtraction is actually negative addition, multiplication is repeated addition, and division is repeated negative addition. For example, a computer will use addition to find solutions of the following problems.

Subtraction	**Multiplication**	**Division**
9 – 3 = n	9 x 3 = n	9 / 3 = n
9 + (–3) = 6	9 + 9 + 9 = 27	9 + (-3) + (-3) + (-3) = 0

In the division computation the computer determines the answer (3) by counting the number of -3s that must be added before 0 is reached. Thus simple **addition** enables the computer to solve complex arithmetic problems. Repetitions of **arithmetic functions** (especially addition) takes very little time, because millions of instructions can be processed every second.

Logical Operations

The ALU unit can also perform logical operations. A logical operation is usually a comparison. So the ALU unit can compare letters, numbers, or special characters. The computer can then take action based on the result of the comparison. Logical operations can test for three conditions:

Equal-to Condition:

In a test for this condition, the ALU compares the values to determine if they are equal.

Less-than Condition:

To test for this condition, the computer compares values to determine if one is less than another.

Greater-than Condition:

In this type of comparison, the computer determines if one value is greater than another.

In fact, a logic unit can usually distinguish six logical relationships:

1. Equal to
2. Less than
3. Greater than
4. less than or equal to
5. Greater than or equal to
6. Less than or greater than (it is same as not equal to)

The symbols that let you define the type of comparison you want the computer to perform are called **relational operators**. The most common relational operators are:

1. the equal sign (=)
2. the less-than symbol (<), and
3. the greater-than symbol (>)

As with arithmetic, the computer executes logical functions at ultrahigh speeds, performing **millions of instructions per second**, or **MIPS**.

MEMORY

The CPU contains the logic and circuitry to run the computer, but one thing it does not have built into it is room to store programs and data.

The CPU does contain **registers** for data and instructions, but these are small areas that can hold only a few bytes at a time. Also the storage in registers are temporary in nature.

In addition to the registers, the CPU needs to have millions of bytes of space where it can store whole programs. The memory we are talking here consists of some chips either on motherboard or on a small circuit board attached to the motherboard. This built-in memory allows the CPU to store and retrieve data very quickly. This built in memory is called as **main memory** (also **primary storage unit**). It holds data and instructions between processing steps and supplies them to the control unit and arithmetic-logic unit during processing.

Primary storage media such as semiconductor storage chips are called **direct access** or **random access** memories (RAM). It means that an element of data or instructions (such as a byte or record) can be directly stored and retrieved by selecting and using any of the locations on the storage media. It also means that each storage position has a unique address and can be individually accessed in approximately the same length of time without having to search through other storage positions. For example, each memory cell on a microelectronics semiconductor RAM chip can be individually sensed or changed in the same length of time.

The **Primary Storage** (main memory) of most modern computers consists of microelectronics **semiconductor storage** circuits. Millions of semiconductor storage circuits can be etched on LSI circuit chips. Memory chips with capacities of 8MB to 512 MB are used in current computers.

Some of the major attractions of semiconductor storage are small size, great speed, shock and temperature resistance, and low cost due to mass production capabilities. One major disadvantage of semiconductor memory is its nature of **volatility**. i.e.; it tends to lose the contents stored when the computer the computer's power is shut off. So uninterrupted electric power must be supplied or the contents of memory will be lost. This implies that a standby electrical power (through battery packs or emergency generators) is required if data are to be saved. Another alternative is to permanently "burn in the data" in semiconductor devices so that they can't be erased by a loss of power.

Each generation is related to memory capabilities. The major trend of primary storage is towards large capacities and use of smaller microelectronics circuits.

There are two types of built-in memory :

1. Non volatile memory and
2. Volatile memory.

Non-volatile memory

In it the memory chip always retain the data they hold even when the computer is turned off, e.g., ROM

ROM

Read-only-memory, as the name specifies there is no way of changing it, i.e., they are nonvolatile and in addition the data in them can not be changed. Putting data permanently into this kind of memory is called "burning in the data."

One of the main reason that a computer needs, ROM is that it helps in knowing what to do when the power is first turned on. It contains a set of startup instructions that check to see that the rest of memory is functioning properly and look for an operating system and hardware devices. So the ROM is used to store the system's startup programs (the BIOS, Basic Input/Output System program). In some portable computers application and even the operating system are stored in ROM. There are other types of ROM viz., PROM, EPROM, EEPROM which can be programmed after manufacture.

PROM (Programmable ROM)

Chips memory cell contains a 1. In order to store data or software on it, the contents of selected cells are changed to 0. For PROM chips this process is irreversible.

EPROM (Erasable PROM)

It is a user programmed semiconductor memory. Here the stored data can be erased by bathing the chips in ultraviolet light. The chip can then be reprogrammed i.e. selected memory cells can be set to zero value.

EPROM chips are found in nearly every PC. They supply the boot-up information to the PC. When an EPROM is in use in the microcomputer, it behaves like a ROM. In order to erase information and re-program that EPROM, it needs to be taken out of the microcomputer.

EEPROM (Electrical Erasable PROM)

Here individual cells can be reprogrammed by reversing the voltage used to create a 0.

EEPROMs are used where the application requires stable storage without power, but where the chip may have to be reprogrammed. EEPROMs (Microcontrollers) are useful in prolonging the use of machine tools. The device can sense the wear and automatically compensate by reprogramming its EEPROM so that frequent adjustments of the machine are not required.

An important application of a ROM is to store stables which do not change, e.g., tables of trigonometric functions. Another application of ROM is for storing short programs for special applications, e.g., a program to control the sequencing of operations of a washing machine may be stored in a ROM and interpreted by the processing unit. EEPROM is often called a Read Mostly Memory (RMM) since it is often used to store data for extended periods of time.

Volatile Memory

In it the memory chip losses its contents. When the computer's power is shut off.

RAM : Random-Access Storage

Memory that can be changed in called RAM. When people talk about computer memory in connection with microcomputers, the usually mean the volatile RAM memory. The purpose of RAM is to hold programs and data. Information can be read off a RAM chip and written to it. When a computer is switched off, any information stored in RAM is lost i.e.; memory is volatile. RAM is also called read/write memory or user memory. It is used to store user program and data.

Data, the raw material from which information is derived, are stored **temporarily** during processing in a section of the computer system called **primary storage**. Primary storage is also called **random-access memory (RAM)**. Whereas data are stored permanently on **secondary storage** devices such as magnetic tape and disk drives.

Unlike magnetic secondary storage devices, such as tape and disk, **RAM** (primary storage) has no moving parts. With no mechanical movement, data can be accessed from RAM at electronic speeds, or close to the speed of light.

Most of today's computers use **CMOS (Complimentary Metal-Oxide Semiconductor)** technology for RAM. But there is a major problem with semiconductor storage. When the electrical current is turned off or interrupted, the data are lost. Scientists are working to perfect a RAM technology that will retain its contents after the electrical interruption. Several "nonvolatile" technology have emerged, namely:

Bubble Memory

If the surface of a non-magnetic material is coated with a thin layer of magnetic material which is magnestised in a small magnetised in the opposite direction away from the surface. There bubbles can be moved around and used to represent the binary digits.

Bubble memories can not replace the main memory (CMOS) because they are too slow. However they can contain a great deal of information in a small space and may be used to replace the magnetic disk eventually, as they have the advantage of no moving parts. Bubble memory is highly reliable, it is not susceptible to environment fluctuations and it can operate on battery power for a considerable length of time.

These qualities make bubble memory well suited for use with industrial robots and in portable computers.

Flash Memory (Flash RAM)

It is a high-density non-volatile technology. These memory chips are non-volatile and are therefore a true replacement for disk storage. The contents of the flash memory can be altered by the computer, and the data can still be retained when the power is turned off. Access to data in flash memory is not as fast as a RAM, but is still many times faster than retrieving data using a disk drive (secondary storage). Because flash memory does not use any moving parts that draw power, it is used when power consumption must be kept to a minimum. This is particularly good for portable computers relying on batteries.

The first common application of flash memory will probably be replacing hard disks in laptop and notebook computers. Next, you will be able to plug your laptop's memory card into your PC to transfer programs and data between them easily.

Flash chips are currently being used in cellular phones and cockpit flight recorders and they are replacing disks in some handheld computers. Flash memory chips are being produced in credit-cardlike packages, which are smaller than a disk drive and require only half the power; that is whey they are being used in notebook computers and handheld personal digital assistants.

Holographic Memory

Engineers are currently developing a new storage medium called holographic memory. Holographic memory will be a 3-D optical medium capable of storing upto 6.5 terabytes of data in a cube the size of a sugar cube.

Charged-coupled Memories

Charged - coupled memory store data as electronic charges within a chip. It uses a large number of charge-coupled devices for data storage and retrieval; whereas charge-coupled devices are semiconductor devices arrayed so that the electric charge at the output of one provides the input stimulus to the next. It is suitable for applications where memory is accessed serially. Charge-coupled memories suffered the same fate as the bubble memory and are now just a footnote in computer history.

Wafer-Scale Integration

When dynamic or static RAM devices are made, hundreds are built at a time on one semiconductor wafer. After the processing of the wafer is completed, it is sliced up who are pushing wafer-scale integration think that they can build cheaper, large-capacity memories by placing an entire wafer into one memory device. They have access times of a few microseconds. If these devices can be built in quantity at low prices, they may replace disks in many applications.

Capacity of RAM

The capacity of RAM is stated in terms of the number of bytes it can store. Memory capacity is usually stated in terms of Kilobytes (KB), which is equivalent to 1024(2^{10}) bytes of storage, and in terms of megabytes (MB) which is 1,048,576 (2^{20}) bytes. Note that 1 KB is about 1000 and 1 MB is about 1000,000, thus the origin of the prefixes kilo (thousand) and mega (million). Occasionally you will see memory capacities of individual chips stated in terms of Kilobits (Kb) and megabits (Mb).

There are several types of memory that can be implemented in a given machine. Dynamic Random Access Memory (DRAM) is the most common low-cost and flexible RAM available. DRAM is now usually implemented using SIMM (Single In-lineModules) packs and SIMM slots. Static RAM (SRAM) is much faster, but also much more expensive. DRAM is usually used in the cache portion of the machine because of speed requirements.

Static Memory is made up of flip-flops and it stores a bit as a voltage.

Dynamic Memory is made up of MOS transistor gates and it stores a bit as a charge.

The advantage of dynamic memory is that a large number of transistor gates can be placed on a memory chip; thus it has high density and is faster than static memory. The disadvantage is that bit information stored gets leaked, so the information needs to be read and written again after every few msec. This is called refreshing the memory.

Function of RAM

RAM provides the processor with temporary storage for programs and data. All programs and data must be transferred to RAM from an input device or from secondary storage before programs can be executed or data can be processed. RAM space is always at a premium; therefore, after a program has been executed, the storage space it occupied is reallocated to another program awaiting execution.

The input message is interprted and the processor initiates action to retrieve the appropriate program and data from secondary storage. This is a nondestructive read process, i.e; the program and data that are read, reside in both RAM (temporarily) and secondary storage (permanently). The data are manipulated according to program instructions and an information is received at output.

A program instruction or a piece of data is stored in a specific RAM location called an address. Addresses permit program instructions and data to be located, accessed and processed. The content of each address is constantly changing as different programs are executed and new data are processed.

Virtual Memory: Imaging RAM

For the execution of a program, all the data and programs needed should be resident in RAM. Therefore, RAM is a critical factor in determining the throughput of a computer. Once RAM is full, no more programs can be executed until a portion of RAM is made available.

Virtual memory is a system software addition to the operating system that effectively expands the capacity of RAM through the use of software and secondary storage. This allows more data and programs to be resident in RAM at any given time.

Factors Affecting Processing Speed

How Registers Affect Speed

The size of the registers (16-bit register or 32-bit register) which is also called the word size indicate the amount of data with which the computer can work. The bigger the size of register, the faster the computer can process a set of data. Registers retain information on a temporary basis. They are not considered part of main memory. Registers have the ability to receive information, hold it temporarily and then pass it on as directed by supervisory control unit.

There are several type of registers:

1. Instruction Register : It holds the instruction which is being executed.
2. Address Register: It holds the storage location address.
3. Accumulator: It collects results.

Memory and Computing Power

More RAM make the computer run faster. The computer does not necessarily have to load an entire program into memory to run it, but the more of the program it can fit into memory, the faster the program will run. The computer loads only the most essential parts into memory. When it needs access to other parts of the program on the disk, it can unload, or swapout non essential parts and swap in program code or data it needs.

Computer's Internal Clock

Every microcomputer has a system clock made up of quartz crystal. The molecules in the crystal vibrate millions of times per second which is constant. The system uses the vibration of the crystal (quartz) in the system clock to time its processing operations. The clock speed is measured in hertz. Pentium CPU today have clock speed from 75 MHz to 200 MHz.

Bus

The system bus carries bits between CPU and only one peripheral at a time. In computer terminology bus refers to the paths between the components of a computer.

There are three main buses:

Data Bus

is an electrical path that connects the CPU, memory and other devices on the motherboard. In real sense bus is a group of parallel lines. The number of lines in the bus affects the speed at which data can travel between hardware components since each wire can transfer one bit at a time a 16-wire bus can move 16-bits at a time which is 2 bytes. Similarly a 32-bit bus can transfer 4-bytes at a time. In computer industry a data bus with 16-bit wide is called as Industry Standard Architecture (ISA) bus. A 32-bit bus is known as Extended Industry Standard Architecture (EISA) bus

Address Bus

It connects only the CPU and memory and helps in locating memory address faster. The number of lines in it determines the maximum number of memory addresses. Today most CPUs have 32-bit address buses that can address 4GB (over 4 billion bytes) of memory.

Control Bus

It controls the direction, flow, origin and destination of data. It comprises of various single lines that carry synchronization signals. Control bus are individual lines that provide a pulse to indicate an CPU operation. The CPU generates specific control signals for every operation it performs. These signals are used to identify a device type with which the CPU intends to communicate.

Cache Memory

A cache is similar to RAM except that it is extremely faster compared to normal memory. The cache speeds up processing storing frequently used data or instructions in its high-speed memory. Whenever the CPU requests information from RAM, the cache controller intercepts the request and searches its own memory for the requested information.

If the information is not there the CPU retrieves the required data from the memory (RAM) and also sends a copy back to the cache. The next time the CPU needs the same information, the cache finds that information and quickly sends it to the CPU leaving RAM out of the loop.

The small amount of data that a CPU needs at any time is placed in a very high-speed memory the cache. Also the computer system must be able to quickly move unnecessary data out of fast memory and replace it with new data. Cache memory can be created at many levels in the computer system. A cache can be created in the CPU itself, between the CPU and the main memory and in the hard disk.

A simpler way to store small amounts of data temporarily is to put it in a buffer. A buffer differs from a cache in that it must be read from randomly. Further as it does not use sophisticated methods of storing data it can not access its data as quickly as a cache can.

Math Coprocessor

When the computer has to do a lot of floating-point arithmetic (viz; in spreadsheet, drawing programs or CAD programs) the presence of a math coprocessor either built into the CPU (viz; 486 DX-2 or Pentium) or added on the motherboard (viz; in 286, 386 - in these 287 and 387 chip are acting as math coprocessor) can speed up processing considerably. So math coprocessor is a chip or part of a chip that is specially designed to handle complicated mathematical operations.

Flash Memory

A long-standing speed problem has been the rate of accessing data from a secondary storage device such as a disk, a rate significantly slower than internal computer speeds. To overcome this, flash memory (non-volatile RAM) can be used. Since data and instructions will be ever-closer to the microprocessor, conversion to flash memory chips would have a pivotal impact on a computer's processing speed.

RISC: More Is Not Always Better

An important aspect of computer system is the design of the instruction set for the processor; because it determines the way, machine language programs are constructed. Early computers had small and simple instruction sets; this was because of the high cost of hardware. With the invention of integrated circuits, computer instruction set tend to increase both in number and complexity. For example, the most common microprocessors found in small computers today viz; 80x86 and 680x0 families uses large (from 100 to 200) instruction sets.

A computer with a large number of instructions is classified as a complex instruction set computer (CISC).

CISC Characteristics

The main reason for provision of a complex instruction set is due to the requirement of the simplification of compilation, and the requirement in the improvement of the overall computer performance. The task of a compiler is to generate a sequence of machine instructions for each high level language statement. The task is simplified if there are machine instructions that implement the statements directly.

The essential goal of a CISC architecture is to attempt to provide a single machine instruction for each statement in a high level language.

Examples of CISC architecture are:

IBM 370 and VAX

Another characteristics of CISC architecture is the incorporation of variable-length instruction formats.

RISC Characteristics

A newer theory in the design of microprocessor holds that, if the instruction set is kept small and simple each instruction will execute much faster, allowing the processor to complete more instructions during a given period. This design results in a faster and less expensive processors. CPUs designed around this methodology are called reduced instruction set computers (RISC). The major characteristics of a RISC methodology are:

1. Relatively few instructions
2. Memory access limited to load and store instructions
3. All operations done within the registers of the CPU
4. Fixed length, easily decoded instruction format

RISC technology is used extensively in mid-size computers such as the IBM RS/6000 and high-end UNIX workstations such as those built by Hewlett Packard & Sun Microsystem.

RISC CPUs are also used extensively in printers and other intelligent devices that have their own internal CPUs.

RISC technology are designed and manufactured by the same companies that produce CISC technology.

In 1989, Intel introduced i860 RISC Chip of 64-bit, which contains more than 1 million transistors. Newer RISC chip include the Intel i960, the Motorola 88100. Sun Microsystems are also produced a RISC chip known as SPARC, which it uses in its UNIX workstations.

Parallel Processing

Computer manufacturers have relied on the single processor design architecture since the late 1940s. In this environment, the processor addresses the programming problem sequentially, from beginning to end, i.e., the processor gets an instruction from memory, acts on it, returns processed data to memory, and then repeats the process. The problem with the conventional computer is that the single electronic pathway, the bus line, acts like a narrow outlet which impedes smooth data flow. Because of this computers are restricted to handling one piece of data at a time, so they are not efficient for application, such as simulating the air flow around an entire aeroplane in flight.

Today designers are doing research on computers that will be able to break programming problem into pieces. Work on each of these pieces will then be executed simultaneously in separate processors, all of which are part of the same computer. The concept of using multiple processors in the same computer in known as parallel processing. By dividing the workload among several special-function processors, the system throughput can be increased. In parallel processing, one main processor (a host mainframe) examines the programming problem and determines what portions, if any, of the problem can be solved in pieces. Those pieces that can be addressed separately are routed to other processors and solved. The individual pieces are then reassembled in the main processor for further computation, output, or storage. The net result of parallel processing is better efficient output.

Computers using parallel processing are:

1. IBM 3090 which has two to four processors
2. Cray XMP4 has four processors

At the other end of the spectrum, dual processor version of PCs are available today. Unfortunately, the DOS operating system can't make use of the added power of an additional processors. Whereas some UNIX developers have developed software that takes advantage of the additional processor.

Data Representation in Memory

Binary Codes for Data

George Boole held that all logical conditions could be described as either true or false. Computer circuitry is an application of this theory. When electricity is present, circuits on paths through the computer's processing components may be either open or closed to the electrical pulses. Bit patterns or combinations of these ON/OFF bits, are how data and programs are processed and stored.

An "ON" or "OFF" electronic state is represented by a bit. The presence or absence of a bit is referred to as ON-BIT and OFF-BIT, respectively. In the binary numbering system and in written text, the ON-BIT is 1 and the OFF-BIT is a 0.

The vacuum tubes, transistors, and integrated circuits that characterize the generations of computers all enable them to distinguish between ON and OFF and, therefore, use binary logic. Physically, these states are achieved in a number of ways. For example, in primary memory the two electronic states are represented by the direction of the current flow. Another approach is to turn the circuit itself ON and OFF. In secondary memory the two states are made possible by the magnetic arrangement of the surface coating on magnetic tapes and disks.

This bits representation may be fine for computers to understand, but human beings are more comfortable with letters, decimal numbers and colours that we put to a computer system must be translated into 1s and 0s for processing and storage. The computer translates the bits back into letters, decimal numbers and colours on output. This translation is performed so that we can recognize and understand the output.

Bits, Bytes and Words

Bits

Each 0 or 1 in binary system is called a bit (for binary digit).

Bytes

Since single bits by themselves can't store all the numbers, letters and special characters (such as $ and &) that a computer must process, the bits are put together in a group called a byte. There are usually 8-bits in a byte. Each byte usually represents one character of data - a letter, digit, or special character.

Computer manufacturers express the capacity of memory and storage in terms of the number of bytes it can hold. The number of bytes can be expressed as kilobytes. It is equivalent to 1024 (2^{10}) bytes and is written in abbreviated form as KB.

Memory capacity may also be expressed in terms of megabytes. It is equivalent to 1,048,576 (2^{20}) bytes and is written in abbreviated form as MB. Memory capacity may also be expressed in terms of gigabits. It is equivalent to 1,073,741,824(2^{30}) bytes and is written in abbreviated form as GB. Memory in older PC may hold only 640 KB; in newer machines, memory may hold anywhere from 1 MB to 64 MB and more. Mainframe memories can hold gigabytes (GB).

Words

A computer word, typically the size of a register, is defined as the number of bits that constitute a common unit of data, as defined by the computer system. Word is a basic unit of data in a computer memory. It consists of a predetermined number of characters or bits to be processed as an entity. The size of a word is called word length which is a measure of the number of digits it contains. For example, a 16-bit word will be able to hold numbers in the range - 2^{15} to +2^{15} - 1.

The length of a word varies by computer. In many digital computers a fixed word length are 8-bits (for very early PC), 16-bits (for traditional minicomputers and some PCs), 32-bits (for full-size mainframe computers, some minicomputers, and some PCs), and 64- bits (for supercomputers). A recent microprocessor, Intel's pentium, intended for both PCs and larger machines, is a 64-bit chip. Generally the word-length of modern microcomputer is normally 32-bit, i.e; the system's bus, which connects the processor, RAM, and the system's peripherals, can move 32-bits at a time.

Encoding Schemes: Combining Bits to Form Bytes

All input, whether a keystroke from a keyboard or a scan from a scanner, is converted to zeros and ones. Keystrokes can be alphanumeric symbol or a control character which represent, special instruction for cursor movement, tabulation, carriage, return, and so on. A scanner converts a photograph into a computer-usable format by organizing the image into rows and columns of dots whose location and colour are represented in binary code. Music is converted to bit combinations to indicate the pitch and duration of individual notes. Different combinations of bits represent textual, graphical, and audio data.

Now the question arises that which particular set of bits is equivalent to which character. In theory we could make up our own definitions, declaring certain bit patterns to represent certain characters. Since we need to communicate with the computer and with each other, it is appropriate that we use a common scheme for data representation, i.e; there must be agreement on which groups of bits represent which characters. So bits are combined according to a standard encoding scheme for data representation, i.e; there must be agreement on which groups of bits represent which characters. So bits are combined according to a standard encoding scheme to represent letters (S, U, K, H and so on), numbers (5, 7, 9 etc.). In practice, several standard binary codes exist to represent textual data. Typically, computers use codes that assign either 7 or 8 bits per byte. Codes vary according to the type of computer system used.

Standard Codes for Data:

1. ASCII and
2. EBCDIC

ASCII (American National Standard Code for Information Interchange)

Most smaller computers use a 7-bit code called the ASCII (pronounced "as-kee"). ASCII was used originally by the communication industry for transmission over telegraph lines.

This code has been adopted as the standard for many computers, particularly PCs. With ASCII, users can transmit data from one computer to another, even if the machines have different internal coding systems. Even software also exists to convert data to an ASCII file for storage on disk.

The 7-bit ASCII code can represent upto 128 characters (2^7). Although the English language has considerably fewer than 128 printable characters, the extra bit configurations are needed to represent a variety of common and not-so-common special characters viz; - (hyphen); @ (at); ~ (tilde).

ASCII is a 7-bit code, but the microcomputer byte can store 8- bits. There are 256(2^8) possible bit configurations in an 8-bit byte. Hardware and software vendors use the extra 128 bit configurations to represent control characters or non character images to complement their hardware or software product.

For example, the IBM-PC version of extended ASCII contains the characters of many foreign languages [viz; Â (umlaut) and Ë (acute)] and a wide variety of graphic images that can be combined on a text screen to produce larger images.

EBCDIC (Extended Binary Coded Decimal Interchange Code)

Larger computers (viz; mainframe) use an 8-bit code called EBCDIC (pronounced "ed-shidik"). Whereas ASCII is used most commonly with PCs and data communication, EBCDIC is used primarily for internal data handling by larger computers.

8-bit code EBCDIC has 256 different combinations. These coding systems adequately cover all the written characters traditionally used in English and other Indo-European languages, however, they do not take into consideration other languages, such as Japanese and Chinese, that employ thousands of characters. A new 16-bit system called Unicode support 65,536 different binary combinations. Unicode is designed as a way for computers to process and store text in every written language.

COMPUTER OUTPUT

The success of business today can depend to a large extent on how meaningful and timely the information a computer can produce i.e., the output. So the two most important requirements of computer output are that it is meaningful and convenient to use.

Categorization of Output

There are two basic categories of computer-produced output:

1. output for immediate use by people and
2. output that is stored in computer usable form for later use by the computer

Output can be of two forms Hardcopy and Softcopy

Hardcopy

Information output on to paper, often produced at the same time that information is output in machine-readable form or produced as a transient display on a visual display unit (VDU). Hardcopy is a permanent copy of a display image generated on an output device such as printer or plotter and which can be carried away.

Softcopy

Information that is displayed on a screen, given by voice, or stored in a form that can't be read directly by a person as on magnetic tape, disk or microfilm.

Examples of Softcopy and Hardcopy

Graphic output such as bar graphs and pie charts can be output in hardcopy and softcopy form. So can animation which can be viewed on a computer screen (softcopy) or output in computer usable form on disk (hardcopy). Voice Output is of softcopy form.

Paper is one of the most widely used hardcopy output media. Individually placing one sheet of paper takes a lot of time, so they are all available in continuous form. Paper product come in a variety of forms such as

1. Plain Computer paper (8 1/2" x 11")
2. Lined Computer paper (11" x 14 1/2")
3. Preprinted paper

Let us now read about various Output devices in details.

PRINTERS

They are hardcopy output devices and can be divided into two distinct categories:

1. Impact Printers
2. Non-impact Printers

Impact Printers

A printer in which printing is the result of mechanically striking the printing medium. An impact printer makes contact with the paper to produce an image. The impact may be produced by a print hammer character, like that of a typewriter key striking a ribbon against the paper or by a print hammer hitting paper and ribbon against a character.

An impact printer must be used if printing a multiple copy report so that the duplicate copies will receive the imprint.

Impact printers are of following types:

Solid Font

A complete character, such as on a typewriter key, strikes a carbon ribbon or other inked surface against paper to produce an image of the character. The solid-font characters are mounted on one of several types of printing heads such as a ball, wheel or cup.

Advantage

1. The advantage of a solid-font over non-solid is that they give the best quality formed character images.

Disadvantage

2. Solid-font print heads are usually slower than other types.

Dot Matrix

It is made of separate pinlike (needles) hammers that strike the ribbon against the paper in computer-determined patterns of dots. This type of printer is usually faster than solid-font type, but the image quality is not as good. All of printers print the characters in ASCII character set. This is a set of 128 printable and special control characters. Print speeds are critically important in computer environments because of the volume of output involved. On the basis of speed printers can further be classified as:

Serial or Character Printers

It is the slowest printer. The two major types of character-at-a- time impact printer are:

1. Dot-matrix printers and
2. Daisy wheel printer

DOT-MATRIX PRINTER

In it the individual characters are formed by a matrix of wires or styluses. Dot-matrix printers are also called serial printers. The images are formed by a print head that is composed of a series of little print hammers that look like the heads of pins. The print head usually has nine pins or 24 pines. The bottom 2 pins are used to form the descenders of lower case letters viz., p, q, g and y. Many expensive dot-matrix printers do not provide descenders, but print quality is improved when they are used.

However, high-quality dot-matrix printers have print heads with as many as 2 pins which allows much more precise image to be produced - about 360 dpi (dots per (square) inch). Dot matrix printers can be either 80 column printers depending on the maximum number of characters that can be printed in a line. Some of dot-matrix printers in India include EPSON EX-1000 EPSON LQ 1050 etc. The size of the matrix in a dot-matrix printer varies from manufacturer to manufacturer. Typical grid sizes are 5x7 dots, 7x9 dots and 9x13 dots. The larger the grid size, the more dots in the matrix and the higher the print resolution or clarity of the printed character.

Some dot-matrix printers use a heat process to create characters. These thermal printers use print wires that "burn" dots into the print page. The resulting characters are about the same print quality as inked characters, but some thermal printers require special heat-sensitive paper that many people find "greasy". The print resolution of dot-matrix printer is usually not as clear as that of typewriter because dot-matrix printers depend upon the human eye to connect the dots and recognizable symbols.

One way to make dot-matrix characters clearer is with a double pass. In the first-pass the dot-matrix printer types the character as usual. This is sometimes called as draft-quality printing. In the second-pass, the paper in the carriage is advanced slightly and the printers "fills in between the dots". The resultant characters come closer to resembling complete typewriter characters and output clarity is thereby enhanced. On dot-matrix printers this is called as correspondence-quality printing because it closely resembles the printing of a typewritten letter.

Features common to most dot-matrix printers include boldface, underline, subscript and superscript and compressed print (narrowed letters). Optional features include proportional spacing (using more or less space, depending on the width of the character) and italics. Dot matrix printers are very versatile since the character set can be changed by software or firmware such as a PROM for different styles, alphabets or graphic symbols. Dot-matrix printers are comparatively inexpensive and one of the fastest types of character-at-a-time printers available. The speed ranges from 50 cps to 400 cps (character per second).

Their abilities to use different type fonts, different line densities and different types of paper are also important.

Drawbacks

1. Their speed limitation is slow as compared to line printers.
2. Their print resolutions are inferior to the daisywheel printers.
3. These printers may not be able to print graphic objects adequately but can handle applications such as accounting, personnel and payroll very well.

Daisywheel Printers

A serial impact printer in which the printing element is a plastic hub that has a large number of flexible radial spokes, each spoke having one or more different raised printing characters, the wheel is rotated as it is moved horizontally step by step under computer control, and stops when a desired character is in a desired print position so a hammer can drive that character against an inked ribbon.

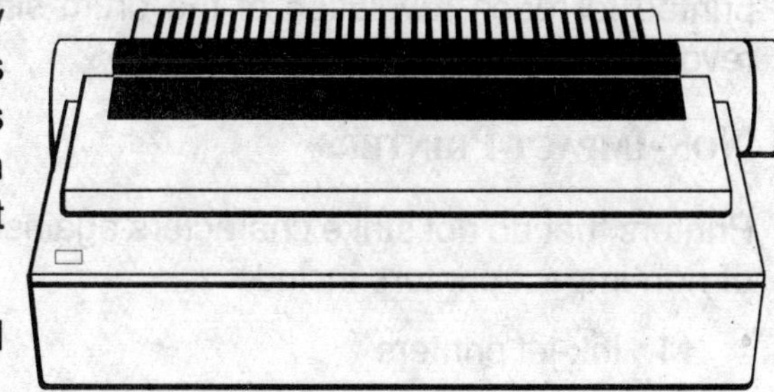

Daisy Wheel Printers are slower than dot-matrix printers, but they produce a high-resolution output. This high-resolution output is often called letter quality printing because it is suitable for business letters and memos. You can print in as may type fonts or foreign languages on a daisywheel printer as there are print wheels to fit your particular model of machine.

It is also called as a smart printer because of its bi-directional printing and built-in microprocessor control features.

Disadvantages

1. They are noisy
2. They are still too slow for many large volume output situations.
3. To change the typeface style, machine has to be stopped and then the print wheel is changed.
4. They cannot produce graphic output.

Line Printers

It prints an entire line in a single operation without necessarily printing one character at a time. These are generally electro-mechanical devices which print complete lines of print, up to 160 characters in width, at speeds about 300 to 2000 lines per minute. Line printers are used primarily in the mini/mainframe processing environment.

Examples of line-at-a-time impact printers are:

1. Chain Printers
2. Band Printers and
3. Drum Printers

Chain Printer

It is a high-speed printer in which the type are carried by the links of a revolving chain. As the characters on the print chain revolve in a horizontal loop, a desired character eventually aligns in a given column. At this instant, the hammer strikes the paper forcing the page into the inked ribbon and the ribbon against the character thus creating the desired symbol on the print page. The chain is cycled continuously until a complete print line has been formed. The print page is then advanced one line and the process is repeated.

Band Printers

On a band printer, several similar sets of fully formed characters are embossed on a horizontal band that is continuously moving in front of the print hammers. In band printer, the paper is momentarily stopped and, as the desired character passes over a given column, the hammer activates, pressing the ribbon against the paper to form the image.

It is a line printer that uses band of type characters as its printing mechanism.

Drum printers or (barrel Printers)

A printer in which all the characters for printing are placed round the surface of a cylinder (the barrel) the entire character set being placed round the cylinder at each print position. Print hammers opposite each print position can be activated by the computer striking the paper and bringing it in contact with a continuous ink ribbon between the paper and the surface of the barrel. The barrel rotates at high speed, the appropriate character being selected as it reaches a position immediately opposite the print hammers. A complete line of output is printed for each revolution of the drum since all the characters in each set pass their print stations during revolution.

Non-Impact Printers

Printers that do not strike characters against ribbon or paper when they print, are non-impact printers. Example of non-impact printers include

1. Ink-jet printers
2. Laser printers

These printers makes much less noise than impact printers.

If you are using a non-impact printer, do not try to print on multiple-part carbon forms: because no impact is being made on the paper you will end up with no copies.

A drum printer uses 80 or more character sets embossed on a cylindrical drum. A separate hammer for each character set forces the print page into an inked ribbon and the character when the character aligns at the print position.

Advantages of Non-impact Printers

1. They are faster and quieter
2. They have got the ability to change typefaces automatically and their ability to produce high-quality graphics.

Ink-jet Printers

It uses a technique of projecting droplets of ink at paper to form the required image. Ink-jet printer create an image directly on paper by spraying ink through as many as 64 tiny nozzles. It provides a print resolution of around 360 dots per inch.

Advantages

1. Many of ink-jet printers can also be programmed to print unusual symbols e.g; Japanese or Chinese characters.
2. It provide an excellent middle ground between dot-matrix and laser printers.
3. Multiple-nozzle print heads enables them to print in several colours.

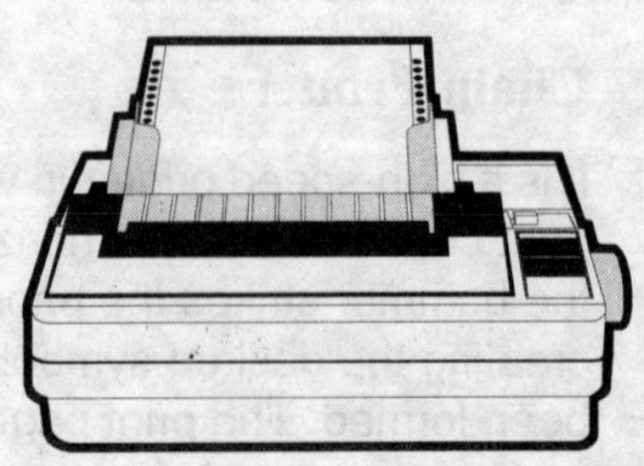

Disadvantages

1. They can only create one character at a time and therefore can not match the print speed of line printers.
2. They are expensive

LASER PRINTERS

The physical properties of LASERS (Light Amplification by Stimulate Emission of Radiation) allows for the very precise positioning of narrow beam of light, transferring a high energy source to a very small area. This property is used to control printing, i.e., laser printers, to read information from bar codes and to read and write information in optical storage devices.

Laser printer is a non-impact printer that creates, by means of a laser beam directed on a photosensitive surface, a latent image which is then made visible by a toner and transferred and fixed on paper. A separate computer is built into the printer to interpret the data that it receives from the computer and to control the laser. Just as electron gun in a graphic monitor can target any pixel, the laser in a laser printer can aim at any point on a drum creating an electrical charge.

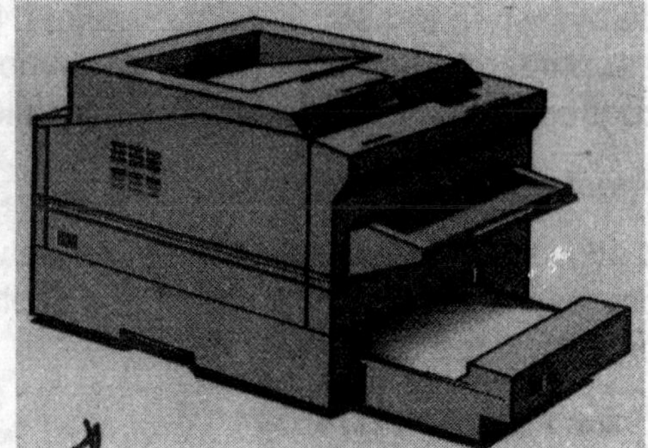

Just as electron gun in a graphic monitor can target any pixel, the laser in a laser printer can aim at any point on a drum creating an electrical charge. Toner which is a composed of tiny particles of oppositely charged ink, sticks to the drum in the places the laser has charged. Thus, with pressure and heat, the toner is transferred off the drum to paper. Also laser printers contain special memory to store the images they print.

The resolution of laser printers is 600 DPI both horizontally and vertically; some high-end models have resolution of 1200 DPI.

Advantages

1. Very high speed
2. Low noise level
3. Very high image quality
4. Excellent graphics capabilities
5. A variety of type sizes and styles
6. Uses standard, inexpensive copy paper which is loaded into a paper tray.

THERMAL PRINTERS

The thermal printers (a non-impact) is an alternative to the other serial printers. Heat elements produce dot-matrix images on heat- sensitive paper. Some fax machines use technique similar to thermal printers to produce documents on heat-sensitive paper. Output on thermal paper fades quickly when exposed to light, but the hardware is often inexpensive.

Advantages

1. The advantages include compact size, limited noise, and low purchase price.

Disadvantages

1. The major disadvantage is the cost of the heat-sensitive paper.

A thermal printer uses heated dot-matrix wires to print output on specially treated paper.

ELECTROSTATIC PRINTERS

Electrostatic printers are devices in which the parts of paper which are to be printed are electrostatically charged, and attract a fine dust which is then fused to the paper by the application of heat. An electrostatic printer may be used in some instances as a plotter.

Some properties associated with printers.

Spooling and Printer Buffers

The term spooling is derived from the expression Simultaneous Peripheral Operation On Line. Spooling is a temporary storage of input and output on high-speed input-output devices, which helps in reducing processing delays when transferring data between peripheral equipment and the processors of a computer. The speed of the printers is incredibly slow as compared with the processing speed of the computers to which they are connected. Which makes CPU to sit idle during printing process. To overcome this, two approaches are used

Spooler Program

It allows the processor to alternate between processing a user's ongoing activity and controlling the printing process. Of course disk space or a dedicated block of primary storage must be available to store the text to be printed by the spooler.

Printer Buffer Hardware

It is an additional storage device that can accept text to be printed as fast as the computer can send it. The buffer then slowly releases the test data to match the printer's speed while the computer is free to do other things.

GRAPHICS OUTPUT DEVICES

Business people have found that sophisticated and colourful graphics add an aura of professionalism to any report or presentation. This demand for presentation graphics has created a need for corresponding output devices.

Computer-generated graphic images can be re-created on paper and transparency acetates with printers and plotters. Graphic images also can be captured on 35-mm slides, or they can be displayed on a monitor or projected onto a large screen. The main popular graphic output device is the plotter, which can draw hard-copy graphics output in the form of maps, bar charts, engineering drawings and even two or three-dimensional illustration. Plotters often come with a set of four pens in four different colours. Most plotters also offer shading features.

PLOTTERS

It is an output unit that directly produces a hardcopy record of data on a removable medium, in the form of a two-dimensional graphic representation. Plotters are designed to produce large drawings or images such as construction plans for buildings or blueprints for mechanical objects.

There are two major types of pen plotters:

1. Flatbed plotters
2. Drum plotters

FLATBED PLOTTERS

It uses a bed or tray to hold paper in a fixed position. A movable pen is usually held by a single arm that can move the pen both horizontally and vertically. The computer instructs the flatbed plotter by directing the pen to x-y position on the page.

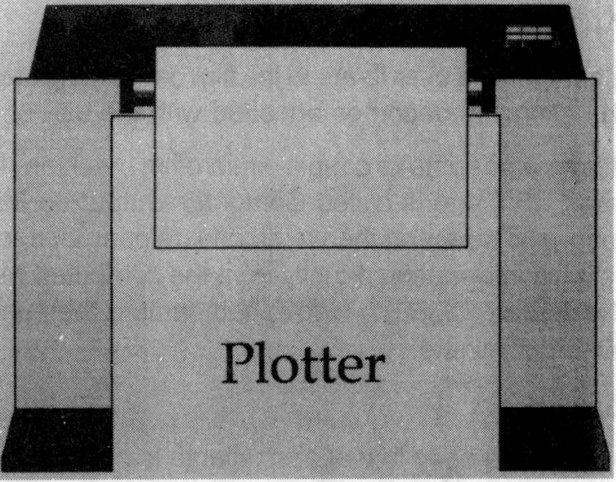

Drawback

1. It limits picture sizes to the page dimensions of their tray.
2. Slow output device : can take hours to complete a complex drawing.

Drum Plotter

It has a single arm that can only move across the drum horizontally. The drum itself moves the paper forward or backward to enable the pen to draw in any vertical direction. Any type of diagonal line is drawn by combining a horizontal movement of the pen arm with a vertical page movement via the drum.

Drum plotters are used to produce continuous output, such as plotting earthquake activity, or for long graphic output, such as the structural view of a 'skyscraper'.

Working of Plotter

A plotter uses a robotic arm to draw with coloured pens on a sheet of paper. The instructions that a plotter receives from a computer consists of a colour and beginning and ending coordinates for a line.

With that information, the plotter picks up the appropriate pen, positions it at the beginning coordinates, drops the pen down to the surface of the paper and draws to the ending coordinates. Plotter draw curves by creating a sequence of very short straight lines. There is one major type of plotter that does not use pens i.e.; Electrostatic plotter

Electrostatic plotters use electrostatic charges to create images out of very small dots on specially treated paper. The paper is run through a developer to allow the image to appear Electrostatic plotters are faster than pen plotters and can produce images of very high resolution.

Computer Output Microfilm (COM) System

Microfilm means "miniature film". It requires only 2 percent of the space required by paper documents. Computerized microfilming can be accomplished in these ways:

1. a photographic process
2. microfiche plate process
3. non-photographic techniques

Photographic Process

It is the oldest method, which develops a permanent microfilm slide negative. In this technique information on a source document is reduced in size, much like an object's picture is reduced in size through a camera lens.

Microfiche Plate Process

Microfilm can also be created with high speed cameras using rolls of microfilm or alternatively. On film plates called microfiche. The high-speed camera takes the photographs of the information displayed on the CRT.

This process is very fast 10 to 20 times faster than high speed printers. The photographs can be taken at speeds up to 32000 lines per minute.

Non Photographic Techniques

It enables the user to avoid the film developing stage entirely. In one technique a silver-plated film is exposed and the microfilm becomes encoded with the use of an electron-beam recorder.

It is now possible to couple a microfilm machine directly to a computer to record output information. The process uses CRT and is called Computer Output on Microfilm (COM). In this process computer output is read onto magnetic tape and then in an off line operation, entered on film by a micro film recorder. The recorder can also receive information directly from the computer. Most recorders project the characters of output information onto the screen of CRT. A high speed camera then photographs the displayed information at speeds of up to 32000 lines per minute.

Advantages

1. It is easy to use and reliable to operate
2. The film used in microfiliming is inexpensive, compared to paper copying costs per page. COM equipment can produce on a printer. But the real advantage of COM is the elimination of cumbersome volumes of printed output.
3. It reduces the amount of physical storage required for archival documents.

Disadvantages

1. It is permanent and therefore nonreusable
2. Once encoded in a particular sequence, can not be changed.
3. It can not be read without the assistance of a special reader device.

Microfilm output is used for distribution of airline schedules, automotive parts catalogues, medical X-rays, and list of books in print. It also is ideal for storing back issues of newspapers and magazines as well as keeping archival records for hospitals, businesses, and universities. Recently the CD-R (Compact Disk-Recordable) has been used instead of COM for storing certain types of permanent output.

Audio-Response: Voice Output

There are two types of voice-response units:

1. the first type, uses a reproduction of a human voice and other sounds, and
2. the second type, uses a speech synthesizer.

Like monitors, audio-response units provide a temporary, soft- copy output.

The first type of audio-response unit selects output from user- recorded words, phrases, music alarms, or anything you might record on audiotape. In these recorded audio-response units, the actual analog recordings of sounds are converted into digital data, then permanently stored on a memory chip. When output, a particular sound is converted back into analog before being routed to a speaker.

These chips are mass-produced for specific applications, viz., smoke detectors, microwave ovens, elevators, alarm clocks, automobile warning system, video games, telephones and banking, to mention only a few.

Audio Response

It is an output device that provides a spoken response to digital inquiries from a telephone or other device. The response is composed from a prerecorded vocabulary of words and can be transmitted over telecommunication lines to the location from which the inquiry originated. Audio response can be used in some situations where traditional display screen output is inappropriate. It is certainly more helpful to hear a warning that you are speeding than to take your eyes off the road to check a display.

Audio response includes

Automobiles: Drivers are warned of open doors or low oil levels.

Telephones: When you try to call a telephone number that has been changed, you hear : "The number you have dialled has been changed to 300279". The first part of this response is a conventional recording, but the new number is given in the voice of the computer's audio response unit.

Audio inquiry: Many organizations use audio response systems to respond to human inquiry that are transmitted over telephone lines to a central computer. All the sounds needed to process the possible inquiries are pre-recorded on a storage medium. Each sound is given a specific code. When inquiries are received, the processor follows a set of rules to create a reply message in a coded form. This is then transferred to an audio-response unit which assembles the sounds in the proper sequence and transmits the audio message back to the station requesting the information.

Banking: Bank customers use touch-tone telephones to obtain their account balances.

Advantages:

1. Used in telephone inquiries.
2. It does not require complete attention of the user i.e.; a user can do other thing while listening the response from audio response unit.
3. Convenient to the blind.

Disadvantages:

1. No permanent record of output is produced.
2. It forces users in some area to listen carefully because there may be no automatic way to obtain repeated messages.

SPEECH SYNTHESIZERS

Speech Synthesizers, which convert the raw data into electronically produced speech, are more popular in the microcomputer environment. A speech synthesizer is capable of producing at least 64 unique sounds. Even with its limitations, the number of speech synthesizer application is growing. For example, a person who is visually impaired can use the speech synthesizer to translate printed words into spoken words.

In another application, speech synthesizers are used by people unable to communicate through speech.

THE MONITOR

These are perhaps the most important output devices because they are the output devices that people interact with most intensively.

Two basic types of monitors are used with microcomputers.

The first is the typical monitor that you see on a desktop computer, which looks like a TV screen and work in same way. This type uses a large vacuum tube called a Cathode Ray Tube (CRT).

The second type, known as a flat panel monitor is commonly used with notebook computers. Most of these employ Liquid Crystal Displays (LCDs) to render images.

Either of these types can be

Monochrome: Displaying only one colour against a contrasting background

Colour The most common technique for forming a characters on video screen in the dot matrix consisting of 35 dots as shown below

A screen usually displays between 500 to 2000 characters.

Some of the terms associated with Monitors.

Refresh Cathode-Ray Tubes

The monochromatic CRTs used for graphics displays are essentially the same as those used in black and white home television sets. A beam of electrons (cathode rays) emitted by an electron gun, passes through focussing and deflection systems that direct the beam toward specific positions on the phosphor coated screen. The screen phosphor coating is organized into a grid of dots called pixels (picture elements). The phosphor then emits a small spot of light at each position contacted by the electron beam. Because the light emitted by the phosphor fades very rapidly some method is needed for maintaining the screen picture.

Refresh Rate

One way to keep the phosphor glowing is to redraw the picture repeatedly by quickly directing the electron beam back over the same points. This type of display is called a refresh CRT. Refresh rate is typically 60 per second for raster displays. As refresh rate decreases, flickers develop because the eye can no longer integrate the individual light impulses coming from a pixel. The refresh rate above which the picture stops flickering and fuses into steady state is called Critical Fusion Frequency.

The primary component of an electron gun in a CRT are the heated metal cathode and a control grid. Heat is supplied to the cathode by directing a current through a coil of wire, called the filament, inside the cylindrical cathode structure. This causes electrons to be "boiled off" the hot cathode surface. In the vacuum inside CRT the free, negatively charged electrons are then accelerated towards the phosphor coating by a high voltage. The control-grid voltage determines how many electrons are actually in the electron beam. The more negative the control-grid voltage is, the fewer the electrons that pass through the grid. This phenomenon allows the spot's intensity to be controlled, because the light output of the phosphor decreases as the number of electrons in the beam decrease.

The focusing system concentrates the electron beam so that the beam converges to a small point when it hits the phosphor coating. It is not enough for the electron beam to move parallel to one another. They would diverge because the electron repulsion, so the focusing system must make them converge to counteract the divergence. Focusing is accomplished with either electric or magnetic fields. Electrostatic focusing is commonly used in TV and computer graphics monitors. The electron beam are made to pass through a positively charged metal cylinder that forms the electrostatic lens. The electrostatic lens focuses the electron beam at the center of the screen.

Additional focusing hardware is used in high-precision systems to keep the beam in focus at all screen positions. As the beam moves to the outer edges of the screen, displayed images become blurred. To compensate for this the system can adjust the focusing according to the screen position of the beam. As with focusing, deflection of the electron beam can be controlled either with electric fields or with magnetic fields. Cathode-ray tubes are now commonly constructed with magnetic deflection coils mounted on the outside of the CRT envelope.

Spots of light are produced on the screen by the transfer of CRT beam energy to the phosphor. When the electrons in the beam collide with the phosphor coating, they are stopped and their kinetic energy is absorbed by the phosphor. Part of the beam energy is converted into heat energy and the remainder causes electrons in the phosphor atoms to move up to higher quantum energy levels. When the excited phosphor electrons begins to return to the ground state they emit light at frequencies (i.e., colour) predicted by quantum theory. The frequency of light emitted is proportional to the energy difference between the excited state and the ground state.

Persistence

Different kinds of phosphors are available for use in a CRT. Besides colour a major difference between phosphors is their persistence: how long they continue to emit light after the CRT beam is removed. Persistence is defined as the time it takes the emitted light from the screen to decay to one-tenth of its original intensity. Lower-persistence phosphors requires higher refresh rates to maintain a picture on the screen without flicker. Eliminate flicker for 99% of viewers of very high-intensity images requires refresh rates of 80 to 90 Hz.

For example, a phosphor with low persistence is useful for animation. A phosphor with high persistence is useful for complex, static pictures. Monitors are usually constructed with a persistence in the range from 10 to 60 sec.

Resolution

The maximum number of points that can be displayed without overlap on a CRT is referred to as the resolution i.e; number of points per centimeter that can be plotted horizontally and vertically. The resolution of a CRT is dependent on the type of phosphor, the intensity to be displayed and focussing and deflection systems. Typical resolution of high-quality systems are 1280 by 1024 or 1024x768 pixels. The physical size of a graphics monitor is given as the length of the screen diagonal, with sizes varying from about 12" to 27" or more.

Raster-Scan Display

It is based on TV technology. In a raster-scan system, the electron beam is swept across the screen, one row at a time from top to bottom. As the electron beam moves across each row, the beam intensity is turned on and off to create a pattern of illuminated spots. Picture definition is stored in a memory area called the refresh buffer or frame buffer.

This memory area (refresh buffer) holds the intensity values for all the screen points. Stored intensity values are then retrieved from the refresh buffer and pointed on the screen one row (scan line) at a time. Each screen point is referred to as a pixel or pel (picture element). Home TV sets, monitors and printers are examples of systems using raster-scan methods.

Black and White System

In a simple black and white system each screen point is either on or off, so only one bit per pixel is needed to control the intensity of screen positions. For a bilevel system a bit value of 1 indicates that electron beam is turned on at that position and a value of 0 indicates that the beam intensity is to be off. Additional bits are needed when intensity and colour variations can be displayed upto 24 bits per pel are included in high quality systems, which can require several megabytes of storage (3MB) for the frame buffer, depending on the resolution of (1024x1024) the system.

Refreshing on raster-scan displays is carried out at the rate of 60 to 80 frames per second, although some systems are designed for higher refresh rates. Sometimes refresh rates are described in units of cycles per second or Hertz (Hz), where a cycle corresponds to one frame. Using these units, we would describe a refresh rate of 80 frames per second is simply 80 Hz. At the end of each scan line the electron beam returns to the left side of the screen to begin displaying the next scan line.

The return to the left of the screen after refreshing each scan line is called the horizontal retrace of the electron beam. And at the end of each frame (1/80 of sec). The electron beam returns vertical retrace to the top corner of the screen to begin the next frame.

Interlacing

Interlacing scan lines on a rasterscan display. First, all points on the even-numbered (solid) scan lines are displayed; then all points along the odd-numbered (dashed) lines are displayed. On some raster-scan systems, each frame is displayed in two passes using a interlaced refresh procedure. In the first pass, the beam sweeps across every alternate scan line from top to bottom. Then after the vertical retrace the vertical retrace the beam sweeps out the remaining scan lines.

This procedure allows us to see the entire screen displayed in one-half the time it would have to taken to sweep across all the lines at once from top to bottom. Interlacing is primarily used with slower refreshing rates.

With interlacing, each of the two passes can be accomplished in 1/80th of a second, which brings the refresh rate nearer to 80 frames per second. This is an effective technique for avoiding flicker, providing that adjacent scan lines contain similar display information.

Raster-Scan Systems

Interactive raster graphics systems typically employ several processing units. In addition to CPU, display controller (or video controller) is used to control operation of the display device. Here the frame buffer can be anywhere in the system memory, and the video controller accesses the frame buffer to refresh the screen.

Video Controller

Here a fixed area of the system memory is reserved for the frame buffer and video controller is given direct access to the frame- buffer memory. Frame-buffer locations and the corresponding screen positions are referenced in Cartesian Coordinates. For many graphic monitors the coordinate origin is defined at the lower left screen and in some upper left screen.

Operations performed by Video Controller:

1. It provides refreshing operations
2. It can retrieve pixel intensities from different memory areas on different refresh cycles.
3. It provides transformations, i.e., during refresh cycles helps the area on the screen in reducing, enlarging, moving from one location to another.
4. It helps in controlling the CRT beam intensity.

Raster-Scan Display Processor

It is also called as Graphics Controller or Display Coprocessor. It sets free the CPU from the graphic chores. It helps in digitizing a picture definition given in an application program into a set of pixel-intensity values for storage in the frame buffer. This digitization process is called scan conversion.

Random-Scan Displays

Under this technique a CRT has the electron beam, which is directed only to the parts of the screen where a picture is to be drawn. Random-Scan monitors draws a picture one line at a time and for this reason are also referred to as Vector displays or Stroke-writing displays or Calligraphic displays.

Random-scan systems are designed for line-drawing applications and can not display realistic shade scenes.

Colour CRT Monitor

A CRT monitor displays colour pictures by using a combination of phosphors that emit different-coloured light. By combining the emitted light from the different phosphors a range of colours can be generated. The two basic techniques for producing colour displays with a CRT are:

1. Beam-penetration method and
2. Shadow-mask method

Beam-Penetraction Method

It is used with random-scan monitors. Two layers of phosphor, usually red and green are coated onto the inside of the CRT screen and the displayed colour depends on how far the electron beam penetrates into the phosphor layers. A beam of slow electrons excites only the outer red layer.

A beam of very fast electrons penetrates through the red layer and excites the inner green layer. At intermediate speeds combinations of red and green light are emitted to show two additional colours orange and yellow.

At intermediate speed combinations of red and green light are emitted to show two additional colours orange and yellow. The speed of electrons and hence the screen colours at any point is controlled by the beam-acceleration voltage.

Shadow-Mask Methods

These methods are commonly used in raster-scan systems (including colour TV) because they produce a much wider range of colours than the beam penetration method. It has 3-phosphor colour dots at each pixel position. One phosphor dot emits red light, another emits a green light and the third emits a blue light. This type of CRT has three electron guns one for each colour.

The 3-electron beams are deflected and focused as a group onto the shadow mask, which contains a series of holes aligned with the phosphor dot patterns. When the three beams pass through a hole in the shadow mask they activate a dot triangle which appears as a small colour spot on the screen.

We obtain colour variations in a shadow-mask CRT by varying the intensity levels of the three electrons beams. By turning off the red and green guns, we get only the colour coming from the blue phosphor. The colour we see depends on the amount of excitation of the three phosphorus. When all the three phosphors are activated by equal intensity of beam we g e t grey or white colour. Colour CRTs in graphics systems are designed as RGB monitors. These monitors use shadow-mask methods & take the intensity level for each electron gun (red, green & blue) directly from the computer system without any intermediate processing.

Flat-Panel Displays

These are thinner than CRTs and are used in small TV monitors, calculators, pocket Video games, laptop computers, armrest viewing of movies on airlines etc. We can separate flat-panel displays into two categories:

1. emissive displays
2. non-emissive displays

The emissive displays are devices that convert electrical energy into light e.g; light-emitting diodes. Non-emissive displays use optical effects to convert sunlight or light from some other source into graphic patterns. For example; Liquid-crystal device.

Liquid-Crystal Displays (LCDs)

A digital display that consists of two sheets of glass separated by a sealed-in normally transparent liquid crystal material. The outer surface of each glass sheet has a transparent conductive coating such as tin oxide or indium oxide.

These non-emissive devices produce a picture by passing polarized light from the surrounding or from an internal light source through a liquid-crystal material that can be aligned to either block or transmit the light. A voltage applied between front and back electrode coatings disrupts the orderly arrangement of the molecules darkening the liquid enough to form visible characters even though no light is generated.

Advantages :

1. Low power consumption and cost

2. Small size

Disadvantages

1. LCD do not emit light so the image has very little contrast
2. Resolution is poor
3. Screen is susceptible to glare so the optimum viewing angle is very narrow

Electroluminescent Display

Electroluminescent (EL) screen emits light at each pixel by electrical activation of phosphors or by passing an electrical current through a semiconductor material such as gallium arsenide.

Electroluminescence: It is a process in which emission of light is not due to heating effects alone, but results from application of an electric field to a material, usually solid.

EL display provides very high image resolution and excellent graphics capability; it also generates its own light (called an active display) unlike LCD, which only reflects light.

Plasma Display

A visual display which creates an image by causing a series of gas filled cells to illuminated by means of an electric current. Each cell represents a picture element. It is an oldest flat screen technology. It uses neon gas and electrodes above and below the g as. Depending on the mixture of gases the colour displayed ranges from orange to red.

Advantages

1. Resolution is good
2. Glare is less
3. Flickering is absent
4. Images are brighter than CRT

Disadvantages:

1. Uses lot of power
2. The technology is costly
3. Only a single colour is available (reddish orange)

TERMINALS

Terminals that use video screens are commonly called Visual Display Terminals or VDTs. The most common visual display terminals use Cathode Ray Tube (CRTs). Other technologies include Liquid Crystal Displays (LCDs), Electroluminescent (EL) displays and Plasma displays. The cathode ray tubes used in CRT terminals are similar to those used in TV and depend upon an electron gun aimed at a silvered screen.

Terminals: Input and Output

A Terminal consists of an input device, an output device, and a communications link to the main computer. Most commonly a terminal has a keyboard for an input device and a screen for an output device. The number and variety of special-function terminals is growing rapidly. Special function terminals are designed for a specific application, viz., convenience banking. You probably are familiar with the automatic teller machine (ATM) and its input/output capabilities. A badge reader (magnetic stripe) and keypad enable input to the system. A monitor and printer (for printing transaction receipts) provide output.

Some ATMs use voice response as a backup to the monitor to alert people when to perform certain actions e.g; take their receipts. The magnetic stripe on the ATM card contains identification and security information that, when read, is sent to the bank's computer system. The ATM responds with instructions via its monitor. The customer enters an identification number and data via a keypad.

Nongraphics Terminals

These are much like typewriters and can only display letters, numbers and other typed characters in fixed columns on its screen. The patterns of pixels used to represent the standard characters displayed on a monitor in character-mapped displays are drawn from prerecorded templates (guides) stored in a video display ROM chip. e.g; When a user's sends a request to display a letter S at a specific location the template for that pixel pattern is looked up in the video display ROM chip. The electron gun then uses this pattern when it fires at the phosphors in the appropriate character box.

Graphic Terminals

A cathode-ray-tube or type of computer terminal capable of producing some form of line drawing, graphs, charts etc. based on data being processed by or stored in computer. Nongraphics terminals can not be used for extensive graphics because of the limited number of templates available. To create the variety of images necessary to produce graphics, the computer needs to be able to direct each electron beam individually at each pixel on the screen.

In a video display with bit-mapped (also called all-points addressable or dot-addressable) graphics capability the entire screen is a single character box. Bit-mapped graphics-capable monitors require an ample supply of main memory to store all the image specifications before electron gun firing can begin. In real sense bit-mapping means that corresponding bit in computer memory is turned on or off so as to make the pixel on the screen appear light or dark. The greater the density of pixels on the screen, the higher the resolution of the picture image.

It is a device usually with a keyboard and display device, capable of sending and receiving information. The terms terminal, and workstation are often used interchangeably. However a terminal may not have a human operator (e.g; in a network system data can enter or leave a terminal without human interference). A workstation is a terminal at which a human operator performs an application.

The terminal typically consists of a Video Display Unit (VDU), a keyboard, and communication link (LAN OR WAN) to hook the terminal with the main computer system. Terminal is used for inputting data to and retrieving data from a remotely located main system. VDUs are the most common form of terminal - the information is displayed on the screen as it is typed. The majority of computer terminals used in online computer systems are visual display terminals. These are called "soft-copy terminals" because they output information to screen.

Terminals can be "dumb" "smart" or "intelligent"

Dumb Terminal

It can do nothing except communicate data to and from a central processing unit. It is also called as fixed function terminal or non-programmable terminal. So a dumb terminal can not do any processing of its own and is used only for data input (by keyboard) and retrieval (display in the data on monitor). For example, a railway/ airline reservation clerk might use a dumb terminal at customer counter for reserving or cancelling seats by sending information to main serve which does processing for dumb terminal.

Smart Terminal

It can input and retrieve data and can do limited processing of its own viz., editing or verifying the data. A smart terminal can not be used for programming. They are designed with a microprocessor chip that contains the circuit needed to perform arithmetic logic and control functions.

Intelligent Terminal

It has inbuilt microprocessors that are user-programmable. They can process small jobs without the need to interact with the mainframe. In addition to keyboard, monitor and communication link, it also includes a processing unit, storage capabilities and software.

Uses of Terminals

A Financial Transaction Terminal is used to store and retrieve customer status (in terms of credit or debit) from central computer. Under smart terminal we have Automated Teller Machine (ATM), which has special keys that allow the teller to identify which type of account is being used (saving etc.) and to enter the account number. So Consumer Transaction Facility (CTF) or Automatic Teller Machine (ATM) is a stand alone finance device used to handle transaction for banking customer.

Also banks have dumb terminals which are mainly used by bank tellers to retrieve a customer's account balance when he withdraws or deposits money. A point-of-sale terminal is a smart terminal is used to enter sales and inventory data at the point of sale and sends it to server. This type of terminal usually display the product identification number, its description and the price.

Workstation have number of intelligent terminals. These terminals usually include a full-sized keyboard with special function keys.

Advantages of Terminals

1. They are relatively inexpensive.
2. Terminals are usually connected on line to a mainframe. This enables users to enter data directly into a processing system, thereby increasing the timeliness of data input and eliminating the need for intermediary storage media viz., floppy disks.
3. User's ability to correct errors or to alter data that has already been typed.
4. Its ability to enter data to computer system from remote sites.
5. Terminals extend the use of the computer to various places of work. They are widely used for such tasks as control, entering orders, updating accounts and seat reservations. They can be sited at various points on a factory floor to record and receive information on different stages of an industrial process.

Disadvantages of Terminals

1. Terminal dependency on the main server. If the main server goes down the connected terminals are useless.
2. Long hour work at visual display terminals are unhealthy i.e.; can cause strain in eyes, pain in wrist and back.
3. Terminals can not store data or create backup copies of data input, thereby forcing the user to rekey the original input data if it is lost.

Punched Cards and Card Readers

Used in the older generation of computers, now obsolete, it was made of card board and had holes in it to pass the current to pass on the information to the computer. Used with Card Punch machine and Card Reader for inputting data, you could store data or programs on punched cards to be read later. Thus, these could also be used as part of an output device. Punched Card was the one of the most commonly used media for communicating data and instructions to the computer in India before 1980. A punched card is a rigid piece of paper containing rows and columns of numbers. IBM card is called standardized card which has 80 columns and is of the size 7 1/2 inches x 3 1/4 inches x 0.007 inch. The columns are numbered 1-80 from left to right. One of its corner is usually trimmed to help to maintain proper positioning during processing. The top row in a card is called the 12-punch row; next is called 11th row and then next 10 rows are numbered consecutively from 0 to 9. The top 2 rows are called as Zone Punch Rows and the bottom 10 rows are called as Digit Punch Rows.

These cards are put into a keypunch machine. As the operator keys in the data to be stored, the keypunch machine places holes in the card to represent the data. The pattern of punched holes used to represent characters on the card is called the Hollerith code, named after its inventor, Herman Hollerith. Each column of the punched card can record a single character as a set of holes punched in the vertical column. Thus a single can hold a maximum of 80 characters. The holes punched in the cards are interpreted to a card reader that translates the punched information into a machine-readable code, then sends it to the CPU for processing.

The punched-card system was one of the first methods used to input data. It has been almost totally replaced by newer, more efficient input devices.

Key Punching Machine

Punching of data on the card is called Key Punch and key punching is accomplished by means of a key punching machine which looks like a Typewriter. The most common type of key punch machines were IBM 026 and IBM 029. These machines have the following components:

1. Keyboard
2. Card Hopper
3. Punching Station
4. Card Stacker
5. column indicator
6. Back-space key
7. Program control unit
8. Program drum
9. Reading section
10. Switches
11. Printing mechanism, etc.

Card Reader

Card Reader was used as the primary input device in most of the early day computers. A card reader connected to the computer and is required to initiate the following steps:

1. Put the punched cards in the read hopper of the card reader.
2. Command is given from computer to read the punched holes.
3. Punched holes are read at points for verification of data being read.
4. The punched holes are converted into signals and transmitted to the computer for storage.
5. Card is then submitted in the output stack.

There are two types of card readers depending upon the mechanism used for sensing the punched holes.

Photoelectric Card Reader

In photoelectric type card reader, light passing through the punched holes are detected by photoelectric cells. These are faster and accurate in comparison to another type of card reader.

Wire Brush Card Reader

In brush type card reader, a card is passed between a wire brush and a metal roller. If there exists punch, the brush makes electric contact with the roller and thus sends signals to the computer.

CD-ROM TECHNOLOGY

This is not doubt the latest and the best medium for storing data. Though they look very similar to music CDs, so to differentiate from them, the computer ones are called CD-ROMs. They are round in shape and are about 5" in diameter. Till recently they used to be Read Only but now writeable CDs are also available with the relevant drives to write on them. With capacity to write data of about 600 floppies, it has become very popular over the recent times.

In the form of videodisks or compact disks (CDs), optical disks represent a new trend in small, high-capacity storage of images and sound. A single optical disks stores nearly 1 GB of data on one side. To put this storage capacity into perspective, an optical disk can hold 800 television quality images or 60 minutes of high fidelity music.

The explosive growth in storage needs has driven the computer industry to provide cheaper, more versatile storage devices with greater capacity. New storage technologies using optical disks exceed the storage capacities currently available with magnetic disks of the same size. Optical storage techniques used by computers are basically the same as those used to record music on compact disks.

Optical disks differ from magnetic disk storage by the way data is stored and read from the storage media. A laser beam is used to write and read data on these reflective disks, so they are also known as laser disks. In this technology a laser hits a layer of metallic material spread over the surface of a disk. When data is being entered heat from the laser produces tiny spots on the disk surface. To read the data, the laser scans the disk, and a lens picks up different light reflections from the various spots.

Optical disks are becoming a very inviting option for users. They are less sensitive to environmental fluctuations, and they provide more direct-access storage at a cost than is much less per megabyte of storage than the magnetic disk alternative.

Optical disk technology is still emerging and has yet to stabilize; however at present there are three different types of optical disks in common use:

- read-only
- recordable, and
- erasable

READ-ONLY DISKS: CD-ROM

Introduced in 1980 for stereo buffs, the extraordinarily successful compact disk, is a an optical disk designed to enhance the reproduction of recorded music. To make a CD recording, the analog sounds of music are translated into their digital equivalents and stored on a 5.25 inches optical disk. In effect, anything that can be digitized can be stored on optical disk: data, text, voice, still pictures, music, graphics, and video.

CD-ROM (Compact disk-read only memory) a spinoff of audio CD technology, are created at a mastering facility, just as audio CDs are created at a recording studio. The master copy is duplicated or "pressed" at the distribute large amounts of data, such as an online encyclopedia or multimedia presentations. Computer programs and associated user manuals are often distributed on CD-ROMs video sequences and library references are also recorded for educational applications. Since CD-ROMs have the capacity to hold lots of high-quality images, this type of storage is well suited for structural drawings used by architects and engineers.

Unlike an audio CD player, however a CD-ROM drive is nearly devoid of buttons and LCD readouts, excepts for a button to load and unload a disk and few lights to tell you when the drive is reading a disk or playing music. The drive is controlled by a software in your PC that sends instructions to controller circuitry that is either a part of the computer's motherboard or on a separate board installed in an expansion slot.

Over the year CD-ROM drive performance has improved as the hardware technology provided faster access speeds. The original single-speed 150 KBps CD-ROM drives are now considerable obsolete. Double-speed 2x(300 KBps) and quad-speed 4x(600 Kbps) CD-ROM drives currently offer the best performance for the price, with access speeds at 300 msec or less. Faster drives viz., 6x and 8x (1.2 MBps) are on the drawing board multimedia disks the most demanding CD-ROMs of all, are written only for 2x or 4x drives. So going faster won't increase the performance of video and audio until multimedia software titles are written specifically for the faster CD-ROM drives.

Working of Optical Disks

Optical storage techniques make use of the pinpoint precision possible with laser beams. Lasers beam is coherent in nature. For example, light energy is perfectly aligned in the same direction, which helps in focusing laser on an extremely tiny area.

Optical storage devices focus a laser beam on the recording medium, which is a spinning disk, same as phonograph record. Some areas of the disk reflect the laser light into a sensor (called as lands), whereas others scatter the light (called as pits). As the disk rotates past the laser and sensor, a spot that reflects the laser beam into the sensor is interprted as a 1 and the absence of reflection as a 0.

A laser can read an optical disks surface, where pitted areas represent binary 0's and landed areas represent binary 1s.

CD-ROM: (Compact disk-Read-only Memory)

CD-ROM uses the same technology that is used in music CDs. If we have a sound board and speakers connected to our computer, we can play CDs with our PC. Because of the high precision and data density possible with CD-ROM a single CD can typically hold up to 660 MB of data. Its diameter is 5.25 inches (12 cm disk).

Because of CDs high capacities and the fact that no one can change the data on CDs some companies regard CDs as the distribution medium of choice. A CD is a thin layer of aluminum sandwiched between two layers of plastic. The aluminum has a spiral track that contains millions of tiny pits (1s). As the CD spins a laser beam shines on the track.

To manage the enormous data files on CD=ROMs we use special indexing methods.

The indexes on CD-ROMs contain information on how to find virtually every single word on the CD-ROM.

Computers with CD-ROMs can display graphics with quality as high as those we see on television.

Advantages

1. Instead of using 15 to 20 diskettes an entire suite of programs and data could reside on a single CD-ROM.
2. CD-ROM are not vulnerable to magnetic fields which can destroy the data on a diskette.
3. Optical media are extremely durable and reliable under normal use. Because the surface of the disk

(sealed in its plastic coating) is never touched by anything but light and because the medium itself is virtually unaffected by moisture on temperature conditions.

4. One reason optical technology is so reliable is that the read head is several millimeters away from the disk surface.

Data Transfer Speed in Various CD Drives			
Transfer Speed	Megabytes/s	Megabits/s	Mebibits/s
1x	0.15	1.2	1.1444
2x	0.3	2.4	2.2888
4x	0.6	4.8	4.5776
8x	1.2	9.6	9.1553
10x	1.5	12.0	11.4441
12x	1.8	14.4	13.7329
20x	3.0	24.0	22.8882
32x	4.8	38.4	36.6211
36x	5.4	43.2	41.1987
40x	6.0	48.0	45.7764
48x	7.2	57.6	54.9316
50x	7.5	60.0	57.2205
52x	7.8	62.4	59.5093

However there are two main reasons that prevent CD drives from totally displacing hard devices:

One reason is that CD drives are still slow. A drive that meets the multimedia PC2 standard for performance only has to move 900 KB of data per second. A good hard drive, by comparison, transfers 10 MB of data per second.

Whereas on time scale the internal hard drive can find the data your application asks for in 10 msec, and on the other side CD-ROM drive takes upto 300 msec for the same task.

The other reason is that you can not write to portions of a writable CD-ROM that already have data written to them. You can add to data that was written to the disk in an earlier session but you can't delete or change what is already there.

Recordable Disk: Write Once, Read Many (WORM)

As with the CD, once data have been etched into the surface of a WORM disk they can not be changed. WORM is an ideal medium for making a permanent record of data, i.e; it can be a feasible alternative to magnetic tape for archival storage.

For example, many banks use WORM disks to store a record of each day's transactions. The transactions are written to an optical disk and become a permanent record that can be read but never altered.

Another popular application of WORM disks is in information systems, that require the merging of text and images that do not change for a period of time. A good example is an "electronic catalog".

A customer can pursue a retailer's electronic catalog on a VDT, or perhaps a PC, and see the item while he reads about it and, with a few keystrokes the customer can order the item as well.

Erasable Disks: Magneto-Optical Disks

A hybrid disk, called magneto-optical (MO), combines the best features of magnetic and optical disk technologies. A magneto-optical disk has the high-volume capacity of an optical disk but can be written over as a magnetic disk. The disk surface is coated with plastic and embedded with magnetically sensitive metallic crystals.

To write data, laser beam melts a tiny spot on the plastic surface and a magnet aligns the crystal before the plastic cools. The crystal are placed in such a way that some reflect lights and others do not. Later on, when the data is read by a laser beam, only the crystals that reflect light are picked up.

Disadvantages

1. Magneto-optical disks are too expensive and do not offer anywhere near the kind of reliability that users have come to expect of magnetic media.

2. The access time in magneto-optical disks are relatively slow, about the same as a low-end, Winchester disk.
3. As optical disk technology matures to offer reliable, cost-effective, read/write operation, it eventually may dominate secondary storage in the future as magnetic disks and tape to today.

PENTIUM V ARCHITECTURE

Processor is the main component inside the main system unit. This is the biggest electronic circuit board inside the computer system, on which many other board are attached. The boards that attach to the motherboard are known as daughterboard or expansion board.

The motherboard contains following :

1. **Processor Support:** The motherboard dictates directly your choice of processor for use in the system.
2. **Peripheral Support:** The motherboard determines, what types of peripherals you can use in your PC.
3. **Performance:** The motherboard is a major determining factor in system's performance, the motherboard determines what types of processors, memory, system buses, and hard disk interface speed your system can have, and these components dictate directly your system's performance.
4. **Upgradability:** The capabilities of motherboard dictate to what extent you will be able to upgrade your machine.
5. **Organization:** The way that the motherboard is designed and laid out dictates how the entire computer is going to be organized.
6. **Control:** The motherboard contains the chipset and BIOS program, which control most of the data flow within the computer.
7. **Communication:** All communication between the PC and its peripherals, other PCs, and user, goes through the motherboard.

ADVANCEMENTS IN MOTHERBOARD TECHNOLOGY

Intel NetBurst microarchitecture delivers a number of innovative features including Hyper-Threading Technology, hyper-pipelined technology, 1066, 800, 533 or 400 MHz system bus, and Execution Trace Cache. It also provides a number of enhanced feature such as Advanced Trnaster Cache, Advanced Dynamic Execution, enhanced floating-point and multimedia unit, and Streaming SIMD Extension, enhanced floating-point and multimedia unit, and Streaming SIMD Extensions 2 (SSE2). Further enhancements in the 90 nm process-based Pentium 4 processor include Steaming SIMD Extension 3 (SSE3).

Many of these innovations and advances were made possible with improvements in processor technology, process technology, and circuit design and could not previously be implemented in high-volume, manufacturable solutions. The features and resulting benefits of the microarchitecture are defined below:

Hyper-Threading Technology

Hyper-Threading Technology (HT Technology) is a ground breaking technology to improve processor performance. It allows software programs to "see" two processors and work more efficiently.

This new technology enables the processor to execute two series, or threads, of instructions at the same time, thereby improving performance and system responsiveness. Hyper-Threading Technology requires a computer system with an Intel Pentium 4 processor supporting HT Technology and a HT Technology enabled chipset, BIOS and operating system.

Hyper-Pipelined Technology

The hyper-pipelined technology of the Intel NetBurst microarchitecutre increases the pipeline depth delivering increased performance, frequency and scalability of the processor.

Intel Enhanced Memory 64 Technology (Intel EM64T)

Intel EM64T provides an enhancement to the Intel's 32-bit architecture by enabling the desktop processor platform to access larger amounts of memory. With appropriate 64-bit supporting hardware and software, platforms based on an Intel processor supporting Intel EM64T can enable use of extended virtual and physical memory. EM64T requires a computer system with a processor, chipset, BIOS, operating system, device drivers and applications enabled for Intel EM64T, Processor will not operate (including 32-bit operation) without an Intel EM64T enabled BIOS.

Integrated 2MB Level 3 Cache on Intel Pentium 4 Processor Extreme Edition 3.46 GHz

The 2-MB L3 cache is available only with the Pentium 4 processor Extreme Edition. The additional third level of cache is located on the processor die and is designed specifically to meet the computer needs of high-end gamers and other power users. The Integrated L3 cache is available in 2 MB and when coupled with either the 1066 MHz or 800 MHz system bus provides a high bandwidth path to memory. The efficient design of the integrated L3 cache provides a faster path to large data sets stored in cache on the processor. This results in reduced average memory latency and increased throughput for larger workloads.

Integrated 2MB Level 2 Cache on Intel Pentium 4 Processor Extreme Edition 3.73 GHz and 6xx

The 2-MB Advanced Transfer Cache (on-die, full speed Level 2 cache) with 8-way associative and Error Correcting Code (ESS) can improve overall performance by allowing the processor to have faster access to a larger amount of the most often used data.

Advanced Dynamic Execution

The Advance Dynamic Execution engine is a very deep, out-of-order speculative execution engine that keeps the execution units executing instructions. It also includes an enhanced branch prediction algorithm that has the net effect of reducing the number of branch mispredictions.

Chipsets for the Pentium and Beyond

Pentium chipsets (referred to as fifth-generation chipsets) were more closely tied to the design of the processor than were the 486 chipsets. When Intel created the Pentium processor, it also developed the PCI bus and a chipset to support and integrate the capabilities of these two developments. This PCIset, as it became known, was developed as an exact match for the Pentium processor. Intel chipsets are designated in numbered series: the 420 for 486 chipsets, the 430 for Pentium chipsets, the 440 series for Pentium II and the 450 series for Pentium Pr chipsets (along with the 400FX). The newer 460 and 800 series chipsets just being announced are designed to support the IA-64 (Intel Architecture – 64 bits) processors, such as the Itanium, now emerging.

Here are some of the more common Intel Pentium and above chipsets:

430LX (Mercury): The 430LX was the first Pentium chipset developed to support the 60MHz and 66MHz 5V processors. The Mercury chipset included the PCI bus and supported up to 128MB of RAM. This chipset was made absolute by the chipsets that supported the 90MHz and 100MHz 3.3V processors.

430NX (Neptune): The 430NX was developed to support Intel's second generation Pentium chips. It supported Pentium processors running at 90MHz to 133MHz. Some of the improvements offered over he 430LX chipset are support for dual processors, 512MB of RAM and 512KB of L2 cache.

430FX (Triton I): This was first of the Triton chipsets. It featured support for EDO RAM pipelined burst and synchronous cache, Plug-and-Play and PCI level 2.0 compliance. However, it only supported 128MB of RAM (down from the 512MB supported by the Neptune chipset) and did not have dual processor capabilities.

430MX (Mobile Triton): This is a version of the 430FX designed for laptop, notebook and other portable PCs.

430HX (Triton II): This chipset supported EDO RAM and concurrent PCI buses and was designed for use in business-level servers. It was the next generation of the 430NX and included support for 512MB of RAM and L2 cache.

430VX (Triton III): This chipset was developed to support the home PC market. It featured support for USB, SDRAM and PCI interfaces.

430TX: With this chipset, Intel dropped the Triton label for its chipsets. The 430TX was adaptable for both desktop and mobile use and provided CPI, USB, DMMA and other interfaces.

440LX: Designed for the Pentium II, this AGPset chipset provides support for the LS-120 "superdisk," Ultra DMA, AGP, USB, SDRAM, ECC RAM and the PC97 power management specification. Figure 5-5 shows this chipset.

440LXR: A low-end version of the 440LX chipset.

440BX: Another Pentium II chipset that supports 100MHz bus, dual processors, FireWire and up to 1GB of RAM.

440GX: This chipset is designed for midrange workstations and supports dual CPU and up to 2GB of SDRAM along with dual AGP interfaces. This is an AGPset.

440FX (Natoma): This chipset supported both the Pentium II and the Pentium Pro processors with USB, EDO RAM, ECC memory, dual processors and PCI.

450GX (Orion server): The 450GX chipset and the 450KX share the same basic design. However, the GX version is optimized for the Pentium Pro and supports four processors and 8GB of RAM but FPM memory only.

450KX (Orion workstation): The workstation version of the Orion chipset supports dual processors and 1GB of RAM.

450NX: This is a high-powered chipset designed for Xeon workstations and servers. It supports up to four CPUs, 2MB of L2 cache, 8GB of EDO memory & two 32-bit or one 64-bit PCI interface.

460GX (Merced): This chipset supports very high-end servers and workstations with supports for four CPUs and other high-performance features. You will see this chipset linked to the new high powered Itanium processor.

810: This chipset is designed for value-priced PCs. It includes support for integrated 3-D graphics (AGP) with MPEG-2, 100MHz system bus, two USB ports and the Intel Accelerated Hub, which features a 266MB per second bus speed between memory and peripherals.

810e: This chipset is an extended version of the 810 chipset based on the 440BX chipset and intended for home market and office PCs. Its features are the same as the 9\810 chipset, with added support for 133MHz system bus and the ATA-66 interface.

815: The Intel 815 chipset is specifically designed to work with the Pentium III processor, but it also provides backward compatibility to other Intel processors.

820: Another extension of the 810 chipset designed to support high-end desktops and workstations.

850: The Intel 850 chipset was designed in tandem with the Pentium 4 processor and supports, among many high-performance innovations and features, a 400 MHz system bus that provides over 3 times the bandwidth of previous chipset and processor technologies.

Itanium Processor

Itanium is the brand name for 64-bit Intel Microprocessors that implement the Intel Itanium architecture (formerly called IA-64). Intel has released two processor families using the brand: Itanium and Itanium 2. The processors are marketed for use in enterprise servers and high-performance computing systems. The architecture originated at Hewlett-Packard (HP) which was then later developed by HP and Intel together. Itanium's architecture differs dramatically from the x86 and x86-64 architectures used in other Intel processors. The architecture is based on explicit instruction-level parallelism, with the compiler making the decisions about which instructions to execute in parallel. This approach allows the processor to execute up to six instructions per clock cycle. By contrast with other superscalar architectures, Itanium does not need elaborate hardware to keep track of instruction dependencies during parallel execution.

Intel Itanium processor

Central processing unit

Itanium processor

Produced:	From June 2001 to June 2002
Manufacturer:	Intel
CPU Speeds:	733 MHz to 800 MHz
FSB Speeds:	266 MT/s to 266 MT/s
Instruction Set:	**Itanium**
Socket:	PAC418
Core Name:	Merced

After a protracted development process, the first Itanium was released in 2001, and subsequently more powerful Itanium processors have been released periodically. HP produces most Itanium-based systems, but several other manufacturers have also developed systems based on Itanium. As of 2007 Itanium is the fourth-most deployed microprocessor architecture for enterprise-class systems, behind x86-64, IBM POWER, and SPARC. After a schedule slip of several years, Intel released its newest Itanium 2, codenamed Montecito, in July 2006.

Itanium processor: 2001–2002

By the time Itanium was released in June, 2001, it was no longer superior to contemporaneous RISC and CISC processors. Itanium competed at the low-end (primarily 4-CPU and smaller systems) with servers based on x86 processors, and at the high end with IBM's POWER architecture and Sun Microsystems' SPARC architecture. Intel repositioned Itanium to focus on high-end business and HPC computing, attempting to duplicate x86's successful "horizontal" (i.e., single architecture, multiple systems vendors) market. Its success was limited to replacing PA-RISC and Alpha in HP systems and MIPS in SGI's HPC systems. POWER and SPARC remained strong, while the 32-bit x86 architecture grew into the enterprise space. With economies of scale fueled by its enormous installed base, x86 was the preeminent "horizontal" architecture in enterprise computing. HP and Intel recognized that Itanium was not competitive and replaced it with Itanium 2 a year later, as they had planned. Only a few thousand of the original Itaniums were sold, due to limited availability caused by poor yields, relatively poor performance, and high cost. However, these machines were useful for software development for the Itanium 2 processors that followed. IBM delivered a supercomputer based on this processor.

Itanium 2 processors: 2002–present

The Itanium 2 was released in 2002, and was marketed for enterprise servers rather than for the whole gamut of high-end computing. The initial Itanium 2 was codenamed McKinley. McKinley used a 180 nm process, but it relieved many of the performance problems of the original Itanium. In 2003, AMD released the Opteron, which implemented its x86-64 64-bit architecture.

Opteron gained rapid acceptance in the enterprise server space because it provided an easy upgrade from x86. Intel responded by implementing x86-64 in its Xeon microprocessors in 2004. Intel released a new Itanium 2 family member, codenamed Madison, in 2003. Madison used a 130 nm process and was the basis of all new Itaniums until Montecito was released in June 2006.

In March, 2005, Intel announced that it was working on a new Itanium device, codenamed Tukwila, to be released in 2007. Tukwila would have four processors and would replace the Itanium bus with a new Common System Interface, which would also be used by a new Xeon. Intel later said that Tukwila would be delivered in late 2008.

In November 2005, the major Itanium server manufacturers joined with Intel and a number of software vendors to form the Itanium Solutions Alliance to promote the architecture and accelerate software porting. The Alliance announced that its members would invest $10 Billion in Itanium solutions by the end of the decade. As of June 2007, Intel has released seven additional versions of the Itanium 2, and another is expected in late 2007.

Xeon Processors Family

The Xeon brand refers to Intel's x86 multiprocessing CPUs targeted at server and workstation computers. The brand has been maintained over several generations of x86 and x86-64 processors. Older models added the Xeon moniker to the end of the name of their corresponding desktop processor, but more recent models used the name Xeon on its own. The Xeon CPUs generally have more cache than their desktop counterparts in addition to multiprocessing capabilities. Intel's non-x86 IA-64 processors are called Itanium, not Xeon.

Pentium II Xeon

The first Xeon processor was released in 1998 as the Pentium II Xeon (codenamed "Drake") as the replacement of the Pentium Pro. It was based on the 0.25 μm, P6 microarchitecture "Deschutes" Pentium II (sharing its 80523 product code) and used either a 440GX (a dual-processor workstation chipset) or 450NX (quad-processor, or oct with additional logic) chipset, and differed from the desktop Pentium II in that its off-die L2 cache ran at full speed. It also used a larger slot known as slot 2. Cache sizes were 512 KiB, 1 MiB and 2 MiB, and it used a 100 MT/s bus.

Pentium III Xeon

In 1999, the Pentium II Xeon was replaced by the Pentium III Xeon. The initial version, "Tanner", was just like its predecessor except for the addition of Streaming SIMD Extensions (SSE) and a few cache controller enhancements found in the "Katmai" Pentium III. The second version, "Cascades", was based on the "Coppermine" Pentium III core. It was more controversial in that while it had a 133 MT/s bus it only had a 256 KiB on-die L2 cache — in other words, it was the same as the desktop Pentium III whose Slot 1 versions were also capable of dual-processor operation but not quad-processor operation. To improve this situation, Intel released another version, officially also named "Cascades", but often referred to as "Cascades 2 MB". That came in two variants: with 1 MiB or 2 MiB of L2 cache. Its bus speed was fixed at 100 MT/s, though in practice the cache was able to offset this. Product codes for Tanner and Cascades mirrored that of Katmai and Coppermine; 80525 and 80526 respectively.

Xeon & Xeon MP (32-bit)

In mid-2001, the Xeon was introduced ("Pentium" was dropped from the name). The initial variant that used the new NetBurst architecture, "Foster", was slightly different from the desktop Pentium 4 ("Willamette"). It was a decent chip for workstations, but for server applications it was almost always outperformed by the older Cascade 2 MiB core and AMD's Athlon MP. Combined with the need to use expensive Rambus Dynamic RAM, the Foster's sales were somewhat unimpressive.

At most two Foster processors could be accommodated in an SMP system built with a mainstream chipset, so a second version (Foster MP) was introduced with a 1 MiB L3 cache and Jackson Hyper-Threading. This improved performance slightly, but not enough to lift it out of third place. It was also priced much higher than the dual-processor (DP) versions.

In 2002 Intel released a 130 nm version of the Xeon, codenamed "Prestonia". It supported Intel's new Hyper-Threading technology and had a 512 KiB L2 cache. This was based on the "Northwood" Pentium 4 core. A new server chipset, E7500 (which allowed the use of dual-channel DDR SDRAM) was released to support this processor in servers, and soon the bus speed was boosted to 533 MT/s (accompanied by new chipsets: the E7501 for servers and the E7505 for workstations). The new Xeon performed much better than its predecessor and noticeably better than Athlon MP. The support of new features in the E75xx series also gave it a key advantage over the Pentium III Xeon and Athlon MP (both stuck with rather old chipsets), and it quickly became the top-selling server/workstation processor. The Xeon MP version of the Prestonia was the "Gallatin", which had an L3 cache of 1 MiB or 2 MiB. It also performed much better than Foster MP, and was popular in servers. Later, Intel's experience with the 130 nm process allowed it to port Xeon to the Gallatin core and also create a Xeon MP with 4 MiB cache.

Foster shared the 80528 product code with Willamette; Prestonia and Gallatin Xeons were designated 80532, like Northwood.

Xeon & Xeon MP (64-bit)

Due to a lack of success with Intel's Itanium and Itanium 2 processors, the 90 nm version of the Pentium 4 ("Prescott") was built with support for 64-bit instructions (called Intel 64, Intel's implementation of x86-64), and a Xeon version codenamed "Nocona" was released in 2004. Released with it were the E7525 (workstation), E7520 and E7320 (both server) chipsets, which added support for PCI Express, DDR-II and Serial ATA. The Xeon was noticeably slower than AMD's Opteron, although it could be faster in situations where Hyper-Threading came into play. A slightly updated core called "Irwindale" was released in early 2005, with twice the L2 cache of Nocona and able to reduce its clockspeeds during low processor demand. However, independent tests showed that AMD's Opteron still outperformed Irwindale.

64-bit Xeon MPs were introduced in April 2005. The cheaper "Cranford" was an MP version of Nocona, while the more expensive "Potomac" was a Cranford with 8 MiB of L3 cache. All these Prescott-derived Xeons have the product code 80546.

SUMMARY

1. Input device is used to input data into computer.
2. Output device is used to get result from the computer.
3. Keyboard has 101 keys.
4. Alpha keys are there for typing alphabets A to Z.
5. Numeric keys are there for typing numerals 0 to 9.
6. Function keys are used in programming.
7. Arrow keys are used for moving the cursor on the screen.
8. Special keys are used for special purposes.
9. Numeric pad has other keys too besides the numeric ones.
10. Mouse is basically a pointing device.
11. There are three basic types of Mouse: Mechanical Mouse; Optomechanical Mouse and Optical Mouse.
12. Joystick is used for playing games.
13. There are two types of optical recognition input devices: Optical Character Recognition (OCR) and Optical Mark Reading (OMR).
14. A scanner reads text, photographs and graphics from paper which are then converted into bit patterns for processing, storage or output.
15. A digital camera can store many more pictures than an ordinary camera.
16. MICR is a technology related to the recording of information on document by means of magnetized ink characters.
17. A light pen is a small pen-shaped wand, which contains light sensors.
18. Trackball is a pointing device that works like an upside-down mouse.

19. Voice recognizers accept the spoken word through a microphone and convert it into binary code.
20. Monitor is like a TV and is used to display output.
21. The printers can be divided into two distinct categories: Impact Printers and Non-impact Printers.
22. Dot matrix printers use hammers to print characters.
23. Line printer prints an entire line in a single operation without necessarily printing one character at a time.
24. Laser printer is a non-impact printer that creates a laser beam transfers the same on the paper for printing.
25. Card Readers were used in earlier computers but not now.
26. Web cameras are used for sending and receiving pictures on the Internet.
27. Dumb terminals have only keyboard and monitors.
28. Smart terminals have microprocessors too.
29. Intellignet terminals have everything except big storage capacity.
30. Data can be stored on the micro films too.
31. The CD-ROM has two sections namely Mechanical Section and the Electronics Section.
32. The main CD subassembly called a drive engine, which uses to hold eject, spin, and read the disk.
33. A CD drive ideally requires a linear motor to act much like the voice coil motor used to position hard-drive R/W heads.
34. CDs are recorded as a single, continuous spiral track running from the spindle to the lead out area.
35. A CD-ROM frame is composed of 24 synchronization bits, 14 control bits, 24 of the 14-bit data symbols you saw previously, and eight complete 14-bit Error-Correction (EC) symbols.
36. CD-ROM (Compact disk-read only memory) are created at a mastering facility.
37. A magneto-optical disk has the high-volume capacity of an optical disk but can be written over as a magnetic disk.
28. DVD stand stands for digital video disc or digital versatile disc, is the next generation of optical disc storage technology.
29. Motherboard is the main component inside the main system unit.
30. It is used for the following: Processor Support, Peripheral Support, Performace, Upgradability, Organization, Contol and Communication.
31. Itanium is the brand name for 64-bit Intel Microprocessors that implement the Intel Itanium architecture (formerly called IA-64).
32. The Itanium 2 was released in 2002, and was marketed for enterprise servers rather than for the whole gamut of high-end computing.
33. The first Xeon processor was released in 1998 as the Pentium II Xeon (codenamed "Drake") as the replacement of the Pentium Pro.
34. In computer science, a cache is a collection of data duplicating original values stored elsewhere or computed earlier, where the original data is expensive to fetch (due to slow access time) or to compute, relative to the cost of reading the cache.
35. The Athlon 64 X2 is the first dual-core desktop CPU manufactured by AMD.

MULTIPLE CHOICE QUESTIONS

1. For seeing the output, you use:
   (a) Monitor (b) Keyboard (c) Mouse
2. In programming, you use the following keys:
   (a) Arrow keys (b) Function keys (c) Alpha keys
3. Keyboard has ________ number of keys.
   (a) 100 (b) 88 (c) 101
4. With CD you can:
   (a) Read (b) Write (c) Both
5. Printer is an _________ device.
   (a) Input (b) Output (c) Both
6. Mouse is a _________ device.
   (a) Input (b) Output (c) Both

7. A scanner scans
   (a) Pictures (b) Text (c) Both
8. Laser printer is an ________ device.
   (a) Input (b) Output (c) Both
9. With digital camera, you can store:
   (a) text (b) pictures
10. In MICR, C stands for:
   (a) Colour (b) Code (c) Character
11. Trackball has a
   (a) ball (b) track (c) football
12. Cards for Card Reader were made from
   (a) Plastic (b) Paper (c) Rubber
13. Dumb terminals have terminals and
   (a) mouse (b) speakers (c) keyboard
14. Dot matrix printers uses ______ for printing
   (a) hammers (b) slugs (c) mouse
15. DVD stands for:
   (a) Direct Video Disc (b) Data Video Disc (c) Digital Video Disc
16. CD-ROM stand for:
   (a) Current Disk Read Only Memory (b) Compact Disk Read Only Memory (c) Close Disk Read Only Memory
17. CD ROM storage is .... MB.
   (a) 650 (b) 702 (c) 750
18. WORM stands for:
   (a) Write Once, Read Many (b) Write Once, Read Maybe (c) Write Over, Read Many

REVIEW QUESTIONS

1. What are the Input Devices?
2. What is the main function of Input Devices?
3. What are the characteristics of Input Devices?
4. What are the advantages and disadvantages of Input Devices?
5. What do you understand by Direct Input Devices and Manual Input Devices.
6. What is Keyboard? Explains its main features of Keyboard.
7. Explain different types of keys in a Keyboard?
8. What is the role of special keys in the Keyboard?
9. Write short note on the following:
   DVORAK Keyboard AZERTY Keyboard Concept Keyboard
10. What is the main function of Mouse?
11. Write down the different types of Mouse?
12. Write down the steps to use the Mouse?
13. How Mouse Works?
14. Write down the use of button of the mouse and also how it is connected to the computer?
15. Write down the advantages and disadvantages of mouse.
16. What is Joystick and how it works?
17. What is Optical Recognition?
18. What are the advantages and disadvantages of Optical Mark Reading (OMR)?
19. What are the drawbacks of Optical Mark Reading (OMR)?

20. What is a Scanner?
21. Define different types of Scanners?
22. What is a Digital Camera?
23. What are the uses of Digital Camera?
24. What is MICR (Magnetic-Ink Character Recognition)?
25. Write down the advantages and disadvantages of MICR (Magnetic-Ink Character Recognition).
26. Write short note on the following"
    E13B Font CMC7 Font
27. What is a Light Pen? How does it work?
28. What are the drawbacks of Light Pen?
29. What is a Trackball? What are the uses of Trackball?
30. What is a Touch Screen?
31. What is the use of Touch Pad?
32. What do you understand by Digitizer?
33. What are the advantages and disadvantages of Digitizer?
34. What is Voice Recognisers?
35. Write down the steps for to illustrate how voice recognition works.
36. What are the drawbacks of Voice Recogniser?
37. What is Voice Input device?
38. What are Output Devices?
39. Categorise the Input Devices?
40. Write Short note on the following:
    Hard Copy Soft Copy Solid Font
41. What is the difference between Hard Copy and Soft Copy
42. What is a Printer? Define different kind of printers?
43. Write down the advantages and disadvantages of Solid Font.
44. What is a Dot Matrix Printer? Write down the drawbacks of a Dot Matrix Printer.
45. Write down the characteristics of Daisywheel Printers.
46. Write down the drawbacks of Daisywheel Printers.
47. What are Line Printers? Explain with examples.
48. What is Non-Impact Printers? Explain with examples.
49. What are the advantages and disadvantages of Ink-jet Printers?
50. What is a Laser printer? What are the characteristics of Laser printer?
51. What are the Thermal Printers? Write down the advantages and disadvantages of Thermal Printers.
52. What are Electrostatic Printers?
53. What do you understand by Graphics Output Devices?
54. What are Plotters? Write down different type of plotters.
55. Write down the advantages and disadvantages of different kind of Plotters.
56. Explain the working of a Plotter.
57. What is Computer Output Microfilm (COM) System?
58. How Computer Output Microfilm (COM) System works?
59. What are the advantages and disadvantages of Output Microfilm (COM) System.
60. What is Audio Response? Where Audio Response is used? Explain with appropriate example.
61. What are the advantages and disadvantages of Audio Response?
62. What is Speech Synthesizers?
63. What is Monitor? What are the terms associated with Monitor?
64. What is Colour CRT Monitor? What are the basic techniques used for producing colour displays with a CRT?

65. What is Liquid-Crystal Displays (LCDs)? Write down the advantages and disadvantages of Liquid-Crystal Displays (LCDs).
66. What do you understand by Electroluminescent Display.
67. What is Plasma Display? Write down the advantages and disadvantages of Plasma Display.
68. What are the Terminals? Explain different types of Terminals.
69. What are the uses of Terminals?
70. What are the advantages and disadvantages of Terminals?
71. What is the main function of Punched Cards and Card Readers?
72. What is Key Punching Machine? Write down the main components of Punching Machine.
73. What are the Input, Output and Storage Devices?
74. How Magnetic Media Works?
75. Write short notes on the following:

Magnetic bubble	Hard disks	Magnetic tapes
Bits and Characters	Fields	Records
Files	Database	Tape Density
Magnetic Tape Units	Tape Records	Blocks
Interblock Gaps	Buffer	Header Label
Trailer Label	Backup	Hard Disks
Rotational Delay Time		

76. What do you under by File Organization? Explain different types of File Organization.
77. What do you understand by Magnetic Tape? What are the Physical Characteristics of a Magnetic tape?
78. How Data is represented on a Magnetic Tape?
79. Explain different types of Buffers.
80. What do you understand by Parity and Error Control?
81. What are the drawbacks of tapes?
82. What is a Floppy disk? Define different types of Floppy disk.
83. What is a Floppy disk drive? Define different types of Floppy disk drive.
84. What are the uses of Floppy disk?
85. How Data is Organized on a Floppy Disk?
86. How do you take care of your Floppy Disks?
87. What is Average Access Time and Average Access Time?
88. Differentiate between Hard Disks and Floppy disk
89. What do you understand by Winchester Disks?
90. What are the Physical Characteristics of Magnetic Disks?
91. How is the data is recorded on Hard Disk?
92. What is CD-ROM? Define different types of CD-ROMs.
93. What are the advantages and disadvantages of CD-ROMs?
94. What do you understand by Erasable Disks? What are the drawbacks of Erasable Disks?

ANSWERS

Multiple Choice Questions

1. a	2. b	3. c	4. c
5. b	6. a	7. c	8. b
9. b	10 c	11. a	12. b
13. c	14. a	15. c	16. b
17. c	18. a		

CHAPTER 4

Number Systems

Learning Objectives

After going through this chapter, you should appreciate the following:

- Data Representation
- Number System
- Decimal System
- Binary Numbering System
- Binary Calculations
- Octal System
- Hexadecimal System
- Redix Conversion
- Arithmetic Operations of Octal Numbers.
- Arithmetic Operations of Hexadecimal Numbers
- Floating Point Numbers
- Encoding Systems
- Information Processing

DATA REPRESENTATION

The smallest piece of data that can be recognized and used by the computer is the bit, a binary digit, a bit is a single binary value 1 or 0. A grouping of eight bits is a byte. The byte is the basic unit for measuring the size of memory; although with today's memory sizes, it is more common to hear term kilobyte (KB) or megabyte (MB)

1 Kilobyte = 1024 bytes

1 Megabyte = 1024 x 1024 bytes = 1,048,576 bytes

NUMBER SYSTEM

Symbols could be combined to represent specific quantities, but the order of their combination followed no consistent rules. None of the early symbolic systems included all the concepts necessary for straight forward mathematical computation. Separate symbols were needed for each possible digit value (included zero) and other symbols were needed to separate the whole part of the number from the fractional part.

DECIMAL SYSTEM

The decimal system is important because it is universally used to represent quantities outside a digital system. This means that there be will situations where decimal values have to be converted to binary values before they are entered into digital system, e.g., computer. Likewise, there will be situations where the binary values at the outputs of a digital circuit have to be converted to decimal values for presentation to the outside world.

In addition to decimal and binary number system, two other number systems find wide spread applications in digital systems. The octal (base 8) and hexadecimal (base 16) number systems are used to provide a convenient and efficient means for representing large binary numbers. In digital system, three or four of these number systems may be in use at the same time, so that an understanding of the system operation requires the ability to convert from one number system to another. You would learn about these conversions later in the chapter.

Decimal numbers are the numbers in everyday use and also known as Denary numbers or numbers to base 10, because 10 is the base of the decimal number system.

The system of writing numbers in which successive digit positions are represented by successive powers of radix 10 and in which lowest integral weight is 1.

For example, $187.3 = 1 \times 10^3 + 8 \times 10^2 + 7 \times 10^0 + 3 \times 10^{-1}$

This is called **expanded notation** for the integer. Decimal numbers system uses ten different digits 0, 1, 2, 3, 4, 5, 6, 7, 8, 9.

The base or radix of a number system is defined as the number of digits it uses to represent numbers in the system. Since the decimal number system uses ten digit so its radix is 10. The decimal number system is also called as base 10 number system.

In computers decimal numbers are usually represented by binary digits arranged in group of four, each group corresponding to a digit of a decimal number. The decimal system is a positional value system in which the value of the digit depends on its position. All positional number system have the highest numerical symbol having a value one less than the base or radix, e.g., in decimal system the base of it is 10 and its symbols vary from 0 to 9.

For Example:

Explain the weight of each digit of the number 18730.

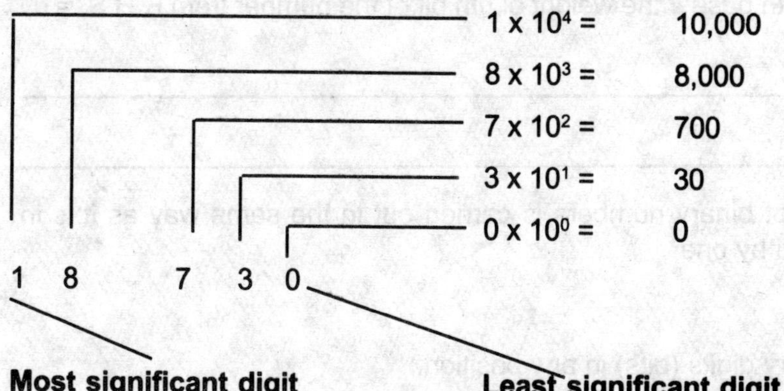

The weight of each digit of a decimal number depends on its relative position within the number. In a positional representation system, the factor by which the value represented by a character in a digit place is multiplied to obtain its additive contribution in the representation of a number.

The weight of the 1st digit of the number from the R.H.S. = 1st digit X 10^0

The weight of second digit of the number from the R.H.S. = 2nd digit X 10^1

and so on.

Its general form that is weights/significance of the nth digit of the number from R.H.S.

= nth digit x 10^{n-1}

= nth digit x $(\text{radix})^{n-1}$

BINARY NUMBERING SYSTEM

The turning point in the history of number system occurred in 1666 A.D. when Leibniz generalized treatise on positional number system. Thirteen years later Leibniz defined the binary number system which today is so important that every beginner in computer science has to learn this number system.

Many of the electronic components of a computer are bistable in nature, i.e., they can be in either of two states ON or OFF. Reliable recording and reading on a magnetic surface is achieved when the surface is magnetized in either clockwise or anticlockwise directions.

Thus all data to be stored and processed in computers are transformed as strings of two symbols 0 and 1, which are also the symbols for digits of the binary number system. It is an example of positional numeration system.

Programmers usually use data and other information in the form of decimal digits, alphabets and special symbols. This information is converted to binary codes within the computer because a digital computer operates on binary bits only.

Binary number system has a base or radix of 2. Its two digits are denoted by 0 & 1 and are called bits. There is no digit in the binary number system to represent 2 or 3 etc. Therefore, using positional technique

2 is written as 10

3 is written as 11

4 is written as 100

and so on.

The weight of each binary bit of a binary number depends on its relative position within the number, i.e., the weight of a digit in any positional number system depends on its relative position within the number and the base of the number system in binary number system with base 2 the weight of nth bit of the number from R.H.S. = n^{th} bit x 2^{n-1}

BINARY CALCULATIONS

Addition, subtraction, multiplication and division of binary numbers is carried out in the same way as it is in decimal system. Let us take these operations one by one.

Binary Addition

Only four cases can occur in adding the two binary digits (bits) in any position.

They are

0 + 0 = 0

0 + 1 = 1

1 + 0 = 1

1 + 1 = 10 = 0 + carry of 1 into next position

1 + 1 + = 11 = 1 +, carry of 1 into next position

The last case occurs when the two bits in a certain position are 1 and there is a carry from the previous position. When we add two binary numbers we write the numbers one below the other with their LSB, aligned, e.g.,

Full Adder				
X	Y	Z	SUM	CARRY
0	0	0	0	0
0	0	1	1	0
0	1	0	1	0
0	1	1	0	1
1	0	0	1	0
1	0	1	0	1
1	1	0	0	1
1	1	1	1	1

When we add, we start with least significant bit depending upon the values of x,y and z of the bits to be added we will have a sum and may have a carry to the next stage of addition. There are 8 possible combinations of x, y, and z.

Example Calculate the binary sum of 110010 and 101101.

Solution

110010

101101

1011111

Example Calculate the sum of 1010, 1100, 1110, 101

Solution

11

111 : Carry

1010

1100

1110

101

101001

or

1010

1100

10110

+01110

100100

+000101

101001

Example Calculate the sum of 11011.01 and 10.1101

Solution First write the binary numbers such that they are vertically aligned and then add

11.1 : carry

11011.0100

10.1101

11110.0001

It is not necessary to consider the addition of more than two binary numbers at a time because in all digital systems the circuitry that actually performs the addition can handle only two numbers at a time. When more than two numbers are to be added the first two are added together and then their sum is added to the third number and so on.

Most modern computers perform operations, viz., subtraction, multiplication and division by actually using only binary addition as their basic operation.

Binary Subtraction

Rules for subtraction of binary numbers are as follows:

0 – 0 = 0

1 – 0 = 1

1 – 1 = 0

0 – 1 = 1 with one borrow

Examples

(i) Subtracting 101111 from 110101

Binary	Decimal
110101	53
101111	47
000110	6

110_2 is equivalent to 6 in decimal system.

(ii) Subtracting 1101 from 10110

```
 10110
– 1101
------
  1001
```

Binary Multiplication

Rules for multiplication of binary numbers are as follows:

0 x 0 = 0

0 x 1 = 0

1 x 1 = 1

Examples

(i) Multiplying 0110 with 1101

```
    10110
     1101
    -----
    10110
   00000x
  10110xx
 10110xxx
---------
100011110
```

In order to check, let us see the decimal equivalent of these binary numbers.

22 x 13 = 286 which is 100011110_2.

(ii) Multiplying 111 with 101

```
   111
   101
   ---
   111
  000x
 111xx
------
100011
```

Binary Division

Division for binary numbers can be carried out by following same rules as those applcable to decimal system.

Examples

(i) Dividing 100011_2 by 101

```
101 ) 100011 ( 111
      101
      ---
       111
       101
       ---
        101
        101
        ---
          0 or 35 ÷ 5 = 7
```

(ii) Dividing 11110_2 by 110_2.

```
101 ) 11110 ( 101
      101
      ---
        110
        110
        ---
          0
```

OCTAL SYSTEM

The **Octal** number system uses exactly eight symbols 0, 1, 2, 3, 4, 5, 6 and 7, i.e., it has a base or radix 8. Since $8 = 2^3$, therefore, each octal digit has a unique 3 bit binary representation. The use of octal as a shorthand for binary is common in printed output of main storage and in some cases in programming. IBM XT and some earlier micro computers used octal numbers for Input/Output operations but now this number system has been superseded by the hexadecimal system as its base 16 corresponds to half cycle.

Base 10 (Decimal)	Base 2 (Binary)	Base 8 (Octal)
0	0000	0
1	0001	1
2	0010	2
3	0011	3
4	0100	4
5	0101	5
6	0110	6
7	0111	7
8	1000	10
9	1001	11
10	1010	12
11	1011	13
12	1100	14
13	1101	15
14	1110	16
15	1111	17

Note here that $(10)_8$ is pronounced as one zero and not ten. The weights assigned to the digit of an octal system are powers of 8.

HEXADECIMAL SYSTEM

Think about a situation, when you actually have to work with the computer in binary. It would be so time consuming to encode instructions and to decode output that it would hardly be worth the trouble. For this reason, it made sense to devise a method to represent all the ones and zeros that make up binary numbers in a form that is easier to read, write and understand.

The base 16 number system, which is also called hexadecimal or hex, uses 16 symbols to represent numbers. Since there are only ten different numerals in the decimal number system (0 through 9), hex uses letters instead of numerals to stand the values greater than nine, i.e., 0, 1, 2, 3, 4, 5, 6, 7, 8, 9, A, B, C, D, E and F. In hexadecimal system A, B, C, D, E and F represents 10, 11, 12, 13, 14 and 15. Hexadecimal numbers are more convenient for people to recognize and interpret than the long strings of binary numbers.

It is synonymous with Sexadecimal

Since $16 = 2^4$, each hexadecimal digit has a unique 4-bit representation. Therefore, since a byte is made up of eight bits, any byte can be represented by exactly two hex digits.

For example, consider binary number

$(00101101)_2 = (45)_{10}$

When you split this number into two groups of 4-bits, it becomes

0010 1101

2 D = $(2\,D)_{16}$

REDIX CONVERSION

Now, we come to the conversions of various systems from one to another.

Conversion of Decimal System to other Systems

Integers

Decimal system may be converted to other systems by using the following two methods.

(a) Remainder Method: This is the most common method for carrying out conversions from decimal system to other systems. It involves the following steps.

1. Dividing the given number of decimal system by the radix R of the proposed system. From this, we will get a quotient Q_1 and a remainder R_1.
2. Dividing the quotient Q_1 by the radix R again to get quotient Q_2 and remainder R_2.
3. Dividing the quotient Q_2 by the radix R again to get quotient Q_3 and a remainder R_3.

This process of division of the successive quotients by the radix R of the proposed system should be repeated until the quotients become less than the radix R. Thus, the required number can be obtained by writing the last quotients first and then remainders in the reverse order, i.e.,

$Q_n\, R_n\, R_{n-1}\, R_{n-2}$ .... $R_2\, R_1$

(b) Power Method: This method involves the following steps:

1. Subtacting the highest number which is obtained by raising the radix to the power of the proposed system. R_1 be the remainder.
2. Subtracting the next highest number from this remainder R_1.
3. This procedure should be repeated until the remainder is zero.
4. Write the multiplication factors in the sequential order in such a way that the powers which have been used should be multiplied by 1 and the the ones missing should be multiplied by zero.

Fractions

The integer part of the fraction can be converted to othe systems following the Remainder method or Power Method. The fraction part can be converted to other systems by following these steps.

1. Finding out the readix of the system to which fraction has to be converted.
2. Multiplying fraction with radix. Let the fraction part of this product be F_1 and I_1 resulting integer.
3. Multiplying the resulting fraction part F1 with the radix again, we will get F2 and I_2.
4. The required fraction number in the required system with radix R would be:

   $I_1 I_2 I_3 ...... I_n$.

Examples

(i) Decimal to Binary (Integers)

(a) Using the Remainder Method.

1. 300_{10}

2	300	
2	150	0
2	75	0
2	37	1
2	18	1
2	9	0
2	4	1
2	2	0
2	1	0
	0	1

$300_{10} = 100101100_2$

2. 300_{10}

2	1024	
2	512	0
2	256	0
2	128	0
2	64	0
2	32	0
2	16	0
2	8	0
2	4	0
2	2	0
2	1	0
	0	1

$1024_{10} = 10000000000_2$

(b) Using Power Method.

1. 300_{10}

Radix of binary system = 2.

Powers of radix which are less than 300:

2^8	2^7	2^6	2^5	2^4	2^3	2^2	2^1	2^0
256	128	64	32	16	8	4	2	1

$$\begin{array}{rl} 300 & \\ -256 & 2^8 = 1 \times 2^8 \\ \hline 44 & \\ -32 & 2^5 = 1 \times 2^5 \\ \hline 12 & \\ -8 & 2^3 = 1 \times 2^3 \\ \hline 4 & \\ -4 & 2^2 = 1 \times 2^2 \\ \hline 0 & \end{array}$$

1×2^8	0×2^7	0×2^6	1×2^5	0×2^4	1×2^3	1×2^2	0×2^1	0×2^0
1	0	0	1	0	1	1	0	0

$300_{10} = 100101100_2$.

2. 1024_{10}

Radix of binary system = 2.

Powers of radix which are less than 1024:

2^{10}	2^9	2^8	2^7	2^6	2^5	2^4	2^3	2^2	2^1	2^0
1024	512	256	128	64	32	16	8	4	2	1

$$\begin{array}{rl} 1024 & \\ -1024 & 2^{10} = 1 \times 2^{10} \\ \hline 0 & \end{array}$$

Conversion from Decimal to Binary (Fraction)

External to computer we use decimal numbers whereas internally we use binary representation, so we have to convert decimal numbers to binary. Also it is sometimes convenient to use a number in a base different from the base currently being used, i.e., to change the number from one base to another.

In a decimal number the value of the

1st digit from R.H.S. = $10^0 = 1$

2nd digit from R.H.S. = $10^1 = 10$

3rd digit from R.H.S. = $10^2 = 100$

Similarly in a binary number the value of the

1st digit from R.H.S. = $2^0 = 1$

2nd digit from R.H.S. = $2^1 = 2$

3rd digit from R.H.S. = $2^2 = 4$

.... and so on.

The process, often called the remainder method, is basically a series of repeated divisions by the number of the base to which you are converting (in our case base is 2). There are two points to remember:

Keep dividing until you reach a zero quotient

Use the remainder in reverse order.

Under the process of conversion we determine which multiples of 2 are present in a given decimal number. Consider the following examples.

Example

$(187)_{10}$ =

2	187		
2	93	1	Least significant bit. (L.S.B.)
2	46	1	
2	23	0	
2	11	1	
2	5	1	
2	2	1	
2	1	0	
	0	1	Most significant bit. (M.S.B.)

$(187)_{10} = (10111011)_2$

Another Example

$(330)_{10}$

2	330		
2	165	0	Least significant bit. (L.S.B.)
2	82	1	
2	41	0	
2	20	1	
2	10	0	
2	5	0	
2	2	1	
2	1	0	
	0	1	Most significant bit. (M.S.B.)

$(330)_{10} = (101001010)_2$

The binary equivalent of the decimal number is given by the sequence of remainders obtained during division. L.S.B. of the binary number is the 1st remainder obtained and M.S.B. is the last remainder.

Conversion of Decimal to Octal (Integers)

This conversion uses a simpler process but more complicated arithmetic. This process which is often called the remainder method, is basically a series of repeated division by the number of the base, i.e., 8 to which you are converting. To obtain the octal equivalent of a decimal number, the decimal number and its successive quotients are repeatedly divided by 8, till a zero quotient is obtained. There are two points to remember:

- Keep dividing until you reach a zero quotient
- Use the remainder in the reverse order.

Example Convert 4823 to base 8

Solution

Division	Quotient	Remainder
4823/8	602	7
602/8	75	2
75/8	9	3
9/8	1	1
1/8	0	1

Thus $(4823)_{10} = (11327)_8$

Conversion of Decimal to Octal (Fraction)

1. Converting $(634.640625)_{10}$ to Octal equivalent.

   Integer part = 634 . Using Remainder Method

8	634	
8	79	2
8	9	7
8	1	1
	0	1

$634_{10} = 1172_8$.

Fraction part = .640625

	F	I
0.640625 x 8	5.125	5
0.125 x 8	1.0	1

$0.640625_{10} = 51_8$.

$634.640625_{10} = 1172.51_8$.

Conversion of Decimal to Hexadecimal (Integer)

1. Converting 7551_{10} to its hexadecimal equivalenet.

Using Remainder Method

16	7551		
16	471	15	15 = F
16	29	7	
16	1	13	13 = D
	0	1	

$7551_{10} = 1D7F_{16}$.

Conversion of Decimal to Hexadecimal (Fraction)

1. Converting 3370.75_{10} to hexadecimal equivalent.

   Integer part = 3370. Using Remiander Method

16	3370		
16	210	10	10 = A
16	13	2	
	0	13	13 = D

$3370_{10} = D2A_{16}$.

Fraction part = .75

	F	I
0.75 x 16	12.0	12

0.75 = .C

$3370.75_{10} = D2A.C_{16}$.

Conversion of Binary System to Other Systems

Conversion from Binary to Decimal (Integer)

In this process we first mark the bit position and then we give the weight of each bit to the number depending on its position. The sum of the weight of all bits gives the equivalent decimal number. Also we know that the weight of nth bit of the number from R.H.S. in binary system = nth bit x 2^{n-1}. For example consider the following binary numbers.

Example: Convert $(10111011)_2$ to decimal.

Bit Position

	8	7	6	5	4	3	2	1
	1	0	1	1	1	0	1	1
Weight of each bit	2^7	2^6	2^5	2^4	2^3	2^2	2^1	2^0

Sum of weight of all bits

$= 1 \times 2^7 + 0 \times 2^6 + 1 \times 2^5 + 1 \times 2^4 + 1 \times 2^3 + 0 \times 2^2 + 1 \times 2^1 + 1 \times 2^0$

$= 128 + 0 + 32 + 16 + 8 + 0 + 2 + 1$

$= (187)_{10}$

Another Example: Convert $(101001010)_2$ to decimal

Bit Position

	9	8	7	6	5	4	3	2	1
	1	0	1	0	0	1	0	1	0
Weight of each bit	2^8	2^7	2^6	2^5	2^4	2^3	2^2	2^1	2^0

Therefore, decimal number = sum of weight of all bits

$= 1 \times 2^8 + 0 \times 2^7 + 1 \times 2^6 + 0 \times 2^5 + 0 \times 2^4 + 1 \times 2^3 + 0 \times 2^2 + 1 \times 2^1 + 0 \times 2^0$

$= 256 + 0 + 64 + 0 + 0 + 0 + 8 + 0 + 2 + 0$

$= (330)_{10}$

Conversion from Binary to Decimal (Fraction)

For converting a fraction of any system with radix R to the decimal system, the following steps should be taken:

1. Multiplying the digits after the point R–1, R–2, R–3 ...... respectively.
2. Simplifying the resulting fractions and adding them together to get the required fraction of the decimal system.

Example

Obtain the decimal/equivalent of $(10101.1010)_2$

Taking the integer part

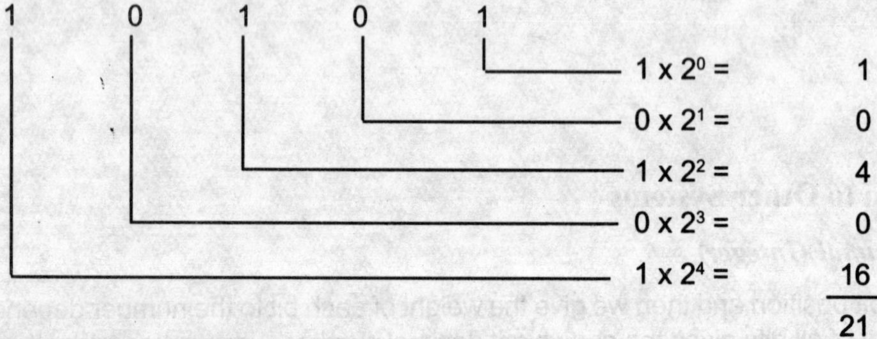

Changing a Binary to Octal (Integer)

A binary number can be quickly converted to its octal equivalent by grouping together successively 3-bits of the binary number starting from the least significant bit. Each group is then replaced by its equivalent octal digit.

The number of digits is reduced by one third in the octal designation, For example,

$(1111\ 1111\ 1111)_2 = (7777)_8$

If the number of bits in the integer part is not a multiple of 3, we insert leading zeros, as leading zeros have no significance for the integer part. Consider the following example.

Example Convert $(0111110111000000)_2$ to base 8

Solution 0111 1101 1100 0000

We can leave the 0 in MSB because it has no significance. Now we replace each group by its equivalent Octal digit.

111 110 111 000 000

7 6 7 0 0

i.e., $(76700)_8$

Changing a Binary to Octal (Fraction)

For fraction also, we will first conver binary number to its decimal equivalent and then convert the resulting decimal number into octal form.

Example: Convert 1111111101.111111 into octal form.

Integer =1111111101. Multiplying each binary digits with its position weights, we get

Fraction = .111111

$1 \times 2^{-1} + 1 \times 2^{-2} + 1 \times 2^{-3} + 1 \times 2^{-4} + 1 \times 2^{-5} + 1 \times 2^{-6}$

10th	9th	8th	7th	6th	5th	4th	3th	2th	1th	Position
2^9	2^8	2^7	2^6	2^5	2^4	2^3	2^2	2^1	2^0	Weights
1	1	1	1	1	1	1	1	1	0	

$1 \times 2^0 = 1$
$1 \times 2^1 = 0$
$1 \times 2^2 = 4$
$1 \times 2^3 = 8$
$1 \times 2^4 = 16$
$1 \times 2^5 = 0$
$1 \times 2^6 = 0$
$1 \times 2^7 = 128$
$1 \times 2^8 = 256$
$1 \times 2^9 = 512$

1021

$$\frac{1}{2} + \frac{1}{4} + \frac{1}{8} + \frac{1}{16} + \frac{1}{32} + \frac{1}{64} = \frac{63}{64} = .9843$$

$(1111111101.111111)_2 = (1021.9843)_{10}$

Now, we can convert this decimal number into octal form.

Integer = 1021

8	1021	
8	127	5
8	15	7
8	1	7
	0	1

$1021_{10} = 1775_8$

Fraction = .9843

	F	I
.9843 x 8 =	7.8744	7
.8744 x 8 =	6.9952	6
.9952 x 8 =	7.9616	7
.9616 x 8 =	7.6928	7
.6928 x 8 =	5.5424	5
.5425 x 8 =	4.3392	4
.3392 x 8 =	2.7136	2
		:
		:

$(1111111101.111111)_2 = (1021.9843)_{10} = (1775.7677.......)_8$

Changing a Binary to Hexadecimal (Integer)

A binary number can be quickly converted to its hexadecimal equivalent by grouping together successively 4-bits of the binary number starting from the rightmost bit. Each group is then replaced by its equivalent hexadecimal digit.

If the number of bits in the integer part is not a multiple of 4, we insert leading zeros, as leading 0s have no significance for the integer part. The number of digits is reduced by one fourth in the hexadecimal designation.

Example $(1111\ 1111\ 1111)_2 = (FFF)_{16}$

We follow the following steps for converting binary number to hex number.

Step 1 Form the 4-bit binary blocks.

Step 2 Replace each group by its equivalent hex digit.

Example $(0111\ 1101\ 1100\ 0000)_2$ to base 16

Solution 0111 1101 1100 0000

7 D C 0 = 7DC0H

Changing a Binary to Hexadecimal (Fraction)

Exampl: Convert 1101.1111 to hexadecimal form

Integer = 1011

$1101_2 = 13_{10} = D$

Fraction = .1111

.1111 = .F

$(1101.1111)_2 = (D.F)_{16}$

Conversion of Octal System to Other Systems

Conversion of Octal to Decimal (Integer)

For converting octal to decimal, each octal digit should be multiplied by its position weights.

Example: Convert 454_8 to decimal form

3rd	2nd	1st	Position
$8^2 = 64$	$8^1 = 8$	$8^0 = 1$	Weights
4	5	4	

$4 \times 8^0 = 4$

$5 \times 8^1 = 40$

$4 \times 8^2 = 256$

300

Conversion of Octal to Decimal (Fraction)

To convert a number in octal system, to its equivalent in decimal system form we follow the following steps:

Step 1 Determine the positional value of each digit. It depends on the position of the digit and the base (i.e. 8) of the number system.

Step 2 Multiply the obtained positional values by the digit in the corresponding positions.

Step 3 Sum the product obtained in above step.

Example Convert $(200)_8$ to base 10.

Step 1 Find positional values

Position Number (from R.H.S.)	**Position Value**
1	$8^0 = 1$
2	$8^1 = 8$
3	$8^2 = 64$

Step 2 Multiply position value by corresponding digits

Position Number (from R.H.S.)	Position Value	Digit (in decimal)	Product = Digit x Position Value
1	1	0	0 x 1 = 0
2	8	0	0 x 8 = 0
3	64	2	2 x 64 = 128

Step 3 Sum of the product obtained above 0 + 0 + 128 = 128

Therefore, $(200)_8 = (128)_{10}$

Conversion of Octal to Binary (Integer)

A simple relationship exists between octal and binary, because $8 = 2^3$. As 8 is power of 2, there is a one to one correspondence between an octal digit and its binary equivalent. We need only 3 bits to represent a octal digit (i.e. from 0 to 7)

An octal number can be quickly converted to its binary equivalent by simply converting each octal number in 3 bits. Consider the following examples.

Example 1 $(764)_8$ can be represented in binary form by writing each digit in 3 bits form i.e.

7/111 6/110 4/100

We have to follow the following steps for conversion of octal number to binary number.

Step 1 Convert the octal digit to 3-bit binary form.

Step 2 Combine all the groups of 3- bits blocks written from the leftmost to the rightmost, which gives the number.

Leading zeros—zeros added to the front of the number may be needed in each grouping of digits to fill out each to 3-digits.

Example 2 Convert $(745)_8$ to base 2.

Step 1 Convert the octal digit to its 3-bit equivalent form

$7_8 = 111$

$4_8 = 100$

$5_8 = 101$

Step 2 Combine all the groups of 3-bits

$745_8 = (111100101)_2$

Example 3 Convert $(60310)_8$ to base 2.

Step 1 Convert the octal digit to its 3-bit equivalent form

$6_8 = 110$

$0_8 = 000$

$3_8 = 011$

$1_8 = 001$

$0_8 = 000$

Step 2 Combine all the groups of 3-bits

$(60310)_8 = (110000011001000)_2$

Conversion of Octal to Binary (Fraction)

For converting octal to binary form, it should first be converted into decimal and the resulting decimal should be converted to binary.

Example: Converting 134_8 to its binary form.

$134_8 = 92_{10}$

2	92	
2	46	0
2	23	0
2	11	1
2	5	1
2	2	1
2	1	0
	0	1

$134_8 = 92_{10} = 1011100_2$

Conversion of Hexadecimal System to Other Systems

Conversion of Hexadecimal to Decimal

To convert a number in hexadecimal system to its equivalent in decimal form we follow the following steps.

- Determine the positional value of each digit. It depends on the position of the digit and the base (i.e. 16) of the number system.
- Multiply the obtained positional values by the face value (i.e. digit) in the corresponding position.
- Sum the product obtained in above step. The total is the value in decimal.

Example 1 To find decimal equivalent of $(C14A)_{16}$ or Convert C14AH to base 10.

Step 1 To find positional values

Position Number from Right Hand Side	Position Value
1	$16^0 = 1$
2	$16^1 = 16$
3	$16^2 = 256$
4	$16^3 = 4096$

Step 2 Multiply position values by corresponding digits

Position Number	Position Value	Digit	Product = Digit x Position Value
1	1	$A_{16} = 10_{10}$	10 x 1 = 10
2	16	4	4 x 16 = 64
3	256	1	1 x 256 = 256
4	4096	$C_{16} = 12$	12 x 4096 = 49152

Step 3 Sum of the product obtained in above step.

Position Number	Position Value	Digit	Product = Digit x Position Value	Sum of Products
1	1	10	10	10 + 64 +
2	16	4	64	256 +
3	256	1	256	49152
4	4096	12	49152	=49482

Therefore, C14AH = $(49482)_{10}$

Example 2 Convert ABCX to base 10.

Step 1 Find positional values

Position Number (from R.H.S.)	Position Value
1	$16^0 = 0$
2	$16^1 = 16$
3	$16^2 = 256$

Step 2 Multiply position value by corresponding digits

Position Number (from R.H.S.)	Position Value	Digit (in Decimal)	Product = Digit x Position Value
1	1	C = 12	12 x 1 = 12
2	16	B = 11	11 x 16 = 176
3	256	A = 10	10 x 256 = 2560

Step 3 Sum of the product obtained above

12 + 176 + 2560 = 2748

Therefore, ABCX = 2748

Conversion of Hexadecimal to Binary

Conversion Table		
Decimal Number	**Hexadecimal Number**	**Binary Number**
0	0	0000
1	1	0001
2	2	0010
3	3	0011
4	4	0100
5	5	0101
6	6	0110
7	7	0111
8	8	1000
9	9	1001
10	A	1010
11	B	1011
12	C	1100
13	D	1101
14	E	1110
15	F	1111

A simple relationship exists between hexadecimal and binary because $16 = 2^4$. To do conversion it is merely necessary to remember binary equivalent for the sixteen hexadecimal symbols. As 16 is a power of 2, there is a one-to-one correspondence between a hexadecimal digit and its binary equivalent. We need only four bits to represent a hexadecimal digit (see the conversion table). A hexadecimal number can be quickly converted to its binary equivalent by simply converting each hex number in 4-bits. Consider the following examples.

Example 1 DACH can be represented in binary form by writing each digit (D = 13, A = 10, C = 12) in four bit form i.e.

D(13)	A(10)	C(12)
1101	1010	1100

In short we can say that we have to follow the following steps for conversion of hexadecimal number to binary numbers.

Step 1 Convert the decimal equivalent of each hex digit to 4 bit binary form.

Step 2 Combine all the groups of 4-bit blocks written from the leftmost to the rightmost which gives the number. Leading Zeros—Zeros added to the front of the number may be needed in each grouping of digits to fill out each to 4 digits.

Example 2 Convert $(A046)_{16}$ to base 2.

Step 1 Convert the decimal equivalent of each hex digit to 4 bits.

$A_{16} = 10_{10} = 1010$

$0_{16} = 0_{10} = 0000$

$4_{16} = 4_{10} = 0100$

$6_{16} = 6_{10} = 0110$

Step 2 Combine all the groups of 4 bits.

$A046B_{16} = (1010\ 0000\ 0100\ 0110)_2$

Example 3 Convert BACOX to base 2.

Step 1 Convert the decimal equivalent of each hex digit to 4 bits.

$B_{16} = 11_{10} = 1011$

$A_{16} = 10_{10} = 1010$

$C_{16} = 12_{10} = 1100$

$0_{16} = 0_{10} = 0000$

Step 2 Combine all the groups of 4-bits

$BACOX = (1011\ 1010\ 1100\ 0000)_2$

ARITHMETIC OPERATIONS OF OCTAL NUMBERS

Octal Addition

Addition of octal numbers is done in much the same way as decimal addition as long as you remember that the largest octal digit is 7 instead of 9. The following procedure is suggested for octal addition:

- Add two octal digits in decimal.
- If the sum is 7 or less it can be directly expressed as a octal digit.
- If the sum is greater than 7, subtract 8 and carry a 1 to the next digit position.

Example 1 Add octal numbers 57 and 14.

5	7	
1	4	
7	11	Decimal Sum
	-8	Modification
7	3	Octal Sum

Adding the least significant digits (7 and 4) produces 11 which is greater than 7, so subtract 8 to get 3; write down the 3 and carry a 1 into the next position. This carry is added to 5 and 1 to produce a sum of $(7)_{10}$ which is then converted to octal $(7)_8$.

Example 2 Add $(754)_8$ and $(376)_8$.

Solution

1	1	1		
	7	5	4	
	3	7	6	
	11	13	10	Decimal Sum
	-8	-8	-8	Modification
1	3	5	2	Octal Sum

- The sum of 4 and 6 is considered as $6 + 4 = 10_{10}$. Since this is greater than 7, subtract 8 to get 2 and a carry 1 into the second position.
- Add this carry to add 5 to 7, i.e., 1 + 5 + 7 = 13, which is again greater than 7, subtract 8 to get 5 and a carry 1 into the third position.
- Add this carry to add 7 and 3, i.e., 1 + 7 + 3 = 11, which is again greater than 7, subtract 8 to get 3 and a carry 1 into the 4 position.

Octal Subtraction

In octal subtraction we use the same method as we have adopted in binary numbers. The 2's complement of the octal subtahend will be taken and then added to minuend. Carry out of the most significant digit (MSD) position will be disregarded.

Example Subtract $(436)_8$ from $(742)_8$

Step 1 We find 2's complement of octal number $(436)_8$. The way is to convert it to binary, take the 2's complement of the binary equivalent and than convert it back to octal. This process is illustrated below.

4	3	6	
100	011	110	Binary Number
011	100	010	2's Complement
3	4	2	Octal Number

Step 2 $(742)_8 - (436)_8$

$= (742)_8 +$ 2's complement of $(436)_8$

$= (742)_8 + (342)_8$

	1	1		
	7	4	2	
	3	4	2	
1	11	8	4	Decimal number
-	-8	-8	-	Modification
1	3	0	4	Octal number

ARITHMETIC OPERATIONS OF HEXADECIMAL NUMBERS

Hexadecimal Addition

Addition of hex numbers is done in much the same way as decimal addition as long as you remember that the largest hexadecimal digit is F instead of 9.

The following procedure is suggested for hexadecimal addition.

- Add the two hexadecimal digits in decimal, mentally inserting the decimal equivalent for those digits larger than 9.
- If the sum is 15 or less, it can be directly, expressed as a hexadecimal digit.
- If the sum is greater than 15, subtract 16 and carry a 1 to the next digit position.

Since the base here exceeds 10, we need mentally to change each hexadecimal letter digit to its decimal form when finding the decimal sum and each decimal difference greater than 9 to its hexadecimal form when modifying the decimal sum.

For example, we must remember that

A = 10,

B = 11,

C = 12,

D = 13,

E = 14 and

F = 15

Consider the following examples:

Example 1 Add the hex number 59 and 43.

Solution	5	9	
	4	3	
	9	12	Decimal Sum
	-	-	Modification
	9	C	Hex Sum

Adding the least significant digits (9 and 3) produces 12, which is C in hex. There is no carry into the next digit position. Adding the 5 and 4 produces 9.

Example 2 Add the hex number 59 and 4C.

Solution	1		
	5	9	
	4	C	
	10	21	Decimal Sum
	-	(-16)	Modification
	A	5	Hex Sum

Start by adding 9 and C, mentally substituting decimal 12 for C. This produces a decimal sum of 21. Since 21 is greater than 16, so subtract 16 to get 5, write down the 5 and carry a 1 into the next position. This carry is added to 5 and 4 to produce a sum of $(10)_{10}$, which is then converted to hexadecimal A.

Example 3 Add the hex numbers 3EF to D2D.

Solution				
	1	1	1	
	3	E	F	
	D	2	D	
1	17	17	28	Decimal Sum
1	-16	-16	-16	Modification
1	1	1	12	Decimal Form
1	1	1	C	Hex Form

- The sum of F and D is considered as 15 + 13 = 28_{10}. Since this is greater than 16, subtract 16 to get 12, which is hexadecimal C, and a carry 1 into the second position.
- Add this carry to add E and 2 i.e. 1 + 14 + 2 = 17, which is again greater than 16, subtract 16 to get 1, which is hexadecimal 1, and a carry 1 into the third position.
- Add this carry 1 to add 3 and D i.e. 1 + 3 + 13 = 17, which is again greater than 16, subtract 16 to get 1, which is hexadecimal 1, and a carry 1 into the 4th position, where there is not digit to be added.

Hexadecimal Subtraction

In hex subtraction we use the same method as we have adopted in binary numbers. The 2's complement of the hex subtrahend will be taken and then added to the minuend, and carry out of the MSD position will be disregarded. Consider the following example.

Example Subtract $(73A)_{16}$ from $(94B)_{16}$.

Solution There is a simple way to find the 2's complement of a hex number. We convert it to binary, take the 2's complement of the binary equivalent, and then convert it back to hex. This process is illustrated below.

7	3	A	Hex Number
0111	0011	1010	Binary Number
1000	1100	0110	2's Complement
8	C	6	Hex Number

$(94B)_{16}$ - $(73A)_{16}$ = 1

9	4	B	
8	C	6	
18	17	17	Decimal Sum
-16	-16	-16	Modification
2	1	1	Decimal form
2	1	1	Hex form = $(211)_{16}$

FLOATING POINT NUMBERS

Floating point number is also a method of representing data. In this method, a real number is expressed as a combination of mantissa and exponent.

The mantissa is kept as less than 1 and greater than or equal to 0.1, and the exponent is the power of 10 which multiplies the mantissa.

Let us take an example to make it more clear.

94.75×10^5 is represented as 0.9475E7

where E7 is used for 10^7

Here, Mantissa = 0.9475

Exponent = 7

While storing the numbers, the leading digit in the mantissa is always made non-zero by approximately shifting it and adjusting the value of the exponent, i.e.,

.004642 ---> 0.4642×10^{-2} -----> $0.4642E^{-2}$

This shifting of the mantissa to the left till its most significant digits is non-zero, is called normalization. It is done to preserve the maximum number of usuful digits.

Addition

For adding two numbers in normalized floating point notation, the exponents of the two numbers must be made equal and the mantissa shifted appropriately.

Subtraction

The process can be treated as adition of one positive number to one negative number.

Multiplication

For multiplication of two floating numbers, first their mantissa are multiplied and the exponents are added.

Division

For division of two floating numbers, their mantissa are divided and the exponent of the denominator is subtracted from the numerator exponent. The quotient mantissa is then normalized.

ENCODING SYSTEMS

BCD Approach

Binary Coded Decimal, Digital computers all used some form of binary numbers for their internal operations, whereas humans use decimal numbers. To understand and thereby work with computers there is a need for conversion from one system to another. A method of encoding which is a mix of decimal and binary systems has evolved. This is known as Binary Coded Decimal (BCD). The following example illustrates this difference.

124 = 0001 0010 0100 BCD

124 = 01111100 Binary

ASCII and EBCDIC

Pronounced "ass-key." It is a binary code for data that is used in communications, mostly in minicomputers and all personal computers. ASCII is a 7-bit code providing 128 possible character combinations, the first 32 of which are used for printing and transmission control. Since the common storage unit is an 8-bit byte (256 combinations) and ASCII uses only 128, the extra bit is used to hold a parity bit or special symbols. For example, the PC uses the additional values for foreign language and graphics symbols.

Extended Binary Coded Decimal Interchange Code Pronounced "eb-see-dick." IBM character code originating with System/360, used in its mainframes and most of its midrange computers. It is an 8-bit code (256 combinations) that stores one alphanumeric character or two decimal digits within a byte, EBCDIC and ASCII are the two codes most widely used to represent data.

INFORMATION PROCESSING

Irish logician and mathematician Georgebooble, developed a special language of digital circuits for exressing logic ciruit functions as well as analysing and designing logic circuis. This algebra also provides an economical way of describing he circuitary used in digital computers. It is the mathematical foundation of switching theory and logic design. Boolean algebra is a set of rules, laws and theorems by which logical operations can be mathematically expressed.

Boolean Posulates: A Boolean agebra is an algebra (B ; ., +, ' ; 0, 1) consisting of a set B, which consists of at least two elements 0 and 1) together with three operations, the AND (Boolean product) operation, the OR (Boolean sum) operation +, and the NOT (complement) operation defined on the set, such that for any objects/ elements x, y and z of B, x, ε, B denotes that x is an element of the set B, and y ∉ Bdenotes that y is not an element of B.

x, y	the product of x and y	x + y	the sum of x and y
x'	the complement of x are in B		

Here + and . are binary operators and ' (not) is a unary operator. To satisfy the Boolean posulates, there are at least two elements x, y ε B such that $x \neq y$. The posulates of a mathematical system form the asumptions form which it is possible to deduce the reles, theorems and properties of the system. For Boolean algebra, the following posulates hold.

Postulate 1: 'Closure' : A set B is closed with respect to a binary operator, if for every pair of elements of B, the binary operator specifies a rule for obtaining a unique element of B. For example: the set of natural numbers N = (1, 2, 3, 4, ...) is closed with respect to the binary operator plus (+) by the rules of arithemtic addition, since for any x, y, ε N we obtain a unique z ε N by the operation x + y = xz.

The set of natural numbers is not closed with respect to the binary operator minus (–) by the rules of arithmetic subtraction because 2 – 3 = –1 and 2, 3, ε N while (–1) ∉ N.

Postulate 2 : 'Commutative Law' : The binary operator + and . on a set B are said to be commutative whenever (a) x.y = y.x (b) x + y = y + x for all x, y ε B.

Postulate 3 : 'Associative Law' : A binary operators . and + on a set are said to be associative whenever

(a) (x,y).z = x.(y.z)

(b) (x + y) + z = x + (y + z) for all x, y, z, ε B

Postulate 4 : 'Distributive Laws' : A binary operator . in a set B, is said to be distributive over + whenever.

(a) x. (y + z) = x.y + x.z for all x, y, z ε B and + is distributive over . when

(b) x + (yz) = (x + y) . (x + z)

Postulate 5 : 'Absorptive Law' : The binary operators . and + on a set B, are said to be absorptive whenever

(a) x. (x + y) = x (b) x + (x.y) = x

Postulate 6 : Inverse : A set B having the identity element e with respect to a binary operator . is said to have an inverse whenever for every x ε B, there exists an element y ε B such that, x.y = ε

Postulate 7 : Union Law : Zero (null, smallest) and one (universal, largest) elements

There exists a unique element (the one element) 1 e B such that for each element x ε B, x.1 = 1.x = x

There exists a unique element (the zero element) 0 e B such that for each element x ε B, x + 0 = 0 + x = x

Postulate 8 : Complementary : For each x ε B there exists a unique element x' ε B, called the complement of x, such that x.x.' = 0 and x + x' = 1.

SUMMARY

1. To a computer, everything is a number.
2. Various number systems are used in computers.
3. Most common are the Binary (base 2) system and Hexadecimal (base 16) systems.
4. What we use mostly in mathematics is the Decimal system (base 10).
5. Octal system (base 8) is also common.
6. Decimal numbers use digits from 0 to 9.
7. All digits here are expressed in 10 to the power of the digits.
8. Binary system is based on 1s and 0s.
9. All numbers in binary are expressed as 0s and 1s.
10. Binary system's digits are denoted by 0 and 1 and are called bits.
11. You can convert numbers from one base to another.
12. For converting numbers from Decimal to Binary, we process a series of divisions.
13. For converting from Binary to Decimal, each bit position is marked and given the weight.
14. In Octal number system the digits are used from 0 to 8.
15. In Hexadecimal system numbers used are 0 to 9, A, B, C, D, E and F.
16. When you convert a decimal number to a binary number, every decimal digit is shown as equivalent binary coded number.
17. Most commonly used code for representing numbers in computers are ASCII codes.

MULTIPLE CHOICE QUESTIONS

1. Computer uses which number system.
   (a) Decimal (b) Binary (c) Octal
2. Hexadecimal system has a base of:
   (a) 2 (b) 8 (c) 16
3. Decimal system uses the numbers from 0 to:
   (a) 8 (b) 9 (c) 16
4. Decimal systems have the base:
   (a) 8 (b) 10 (c) 16
5. A Binary system number can be represented as 0 and:
   (a) 1 (b) 8 (c) 16
6. Binary system numbers are usually:
   (a) short (b) long (c) zeros

7. Octal number system uses numbers from 0 to:

   (a) 8 (b) 16 (c) F

8. Hexadecimal number system uses numbers from 0 to:

   (a) 8 (b) 16 (c) F

REVIEW QUESTIONS

1. Why is the binary number system used for computers?
2. Determine the decimal equivalent of the following binary numbers:

   (a) 1001111 (b) 11100 (c) 110011

3. Convert the following binary number number to decimal and octal forms:

   (a) 11011010 (b) 100100101001 (c) 10010011001

   (d) 101100110 (e) 11100111 (f) 101010101

4. Which are the various number systems in use?
5. What is the base of Decimal system?
6. What is the base of Binary system?
7. Find the decimal equivalent of the following octal numbers.

   (a) 6607 (b) 7576

8. How would you convert a Decimal number to its Binary counterpar?
9. How would you convert a Binary number to its Decimal counterpart?
10. How is a Binary fraction represented?
11. Which steps are used in Decimal number addition?
12. How is Binary addition done?
13. How is Binary subtraction done?
14. What is an Octal system?
15. How would you convert an Octal number to Decimal number?
16. How would you convert an Octal number to Binary number?
17. How would you convert an Octal number to Hexadecimal number?
18. How would you convert an Binary number to Octal number?
19. How would you convert a Decimal number to Octal number?
20. How is an Octal addition done?
21. How is an Octal subtraction done?
22. What is hexadecimal system?
23. How is a Hexadecimal number converted to Decimal number?
24. How is a Hexadecimal number converted to Decimal number?
25. How is an Hexadecimal number converted to Octal number?
26. How is a Binary number converted to Hexadecimal number?
27. How is a Decimal number converted to Hexadecimal number?
28. How is Hexadecimal number additon done?
29. How is Hexadecimal number subtraction done?
30. What is the usefulness of Octal and Hexadecimal system?

ANSWERS

Multiple Choice Questions

1. b 2. c 3. b 4. b
5. a 6. b 7. a 8. b

CHAPTER 5

Data Communication and Networks

Learning Objectives

After going through this chapter, you should appreciate the following:

- Data Communications
- Local Area Networks
- Electronic Mail
- Electronic Data Interchange
- Wide Area Networks
- Client/Server Computing and Database
- An Overview of TCP/IP

DATA COMMUNICATIONS

It is not that the Personal Computers are for personal use only. They can be used for sharing of information too with others having similar type of equipments. Logically it sometimes is fisible to have a number of PCs then having a bigger computer which can give the same thoughput as the number of PCs. But, overall it becomes a expensive proposition and sometimes is not fisible, specially for individuals and small businesses or small companies.

Another problem arises for those who are physically placed at a distance. They would need to send messages and receive messages, or use the same data at, or share program at, many different locations. One answer to this problem is to keep separate data files at each location, but this approach is very costly and potentially a dangerous solution. It is very expensive to maintain these redundant files of data and difficult to ensure the continuing accuracy of data at any one location. The solution of both, the need for more power and the ability to receive, send messages and share data, are found in data communication technology.

Communicating Data

When you send data from one location to another using any electronic means, it is called Data communication. Linking one computer to another permits the power and resources of that computer to be tapped. It also makes possible the updating and sharing of data at different location. Computer that are located in the same room office building, can communicate data through a direct cable link. For example, in a multiuser system, a single processing unit is linked by several dumb terminals through direct cables. Since multi-user systems link inexpensive terminals instead of the more expensive personal computers used with other systems, multi-user systems provide cost savings for small companies purchasing a complete system or adding users to a system currently in operation. In general, multi-user systems are most appropriate for companies requiring a shared data base for extensive data input and output. Computer located far away from the processor use a special form of data communication – telecommunication or telegraph. For example, teller and point-of-sale terminals are spotted in location away from computers: airlines, car-rentals, railway reservation systems and hotel reservation systems have thousands of terminals located many miles from the processors. In these cases, the process of using communication facilities such as the telephone system and microwave relays to send data between computers is a form of data communication, sometimes referred to as telecommunication, or tele-processing.

Dr. George Stibitz was the first to link computer and computing devices and send data way back in 1940. He used telegraph lines to send data files from Dartmouth College in New Hampshire, USA to a Bell Laboratories calculator in New York City, USA. An early large-scale business application was the Sabre passenger reservation system, developed in late 1950s and early 1960s by American Airlines. Hundreds of terminals were linked to the central processing unit. Communication usage has grown steadily since then.

Now-a-days minis and larger machines are in constant communication with outlying terminals. With available attachments, computers can use telecommunications channels to link up with information retrieval services, banks and electronic bulletin boards. An electronic-mail message can be sent from one place to another and an answer can be returned by electronic mail as soon as it is received. This service eliminates the hassle of continually trying to return a call, or long mail delays.

Data Transmission Techniques

Telephone lines are used for sending human voice. They were never planned to send Data. So to send data through telephone lines you have to convert the data into the format which can be read by telephone lines. These are called analog signals. For data communication between computers to take place over a telephone line, the digital pulses of the data to be transmitted must be converted to an analog signal before they are transmitted.

After its journey over the telephone lines, the analog signal must be re-converted to digital pulses so that it can be used by the receiving computer. The process of converting digital pulses to an analog signal is called modulation. And the process of re-converting an analog signal to digital pulses is called demodulation. The device that accomplishes modulation-demodulation process is called a modem.

There are 3 basic types of modems used in microcomputers.

Acoustic Coupler Modem

This is used to provide the necessary interface. The acoustic coupler is attached to a portable terminal and a standard telephone handset fits into rubber cups located on the coupler. The acoustic coupler modem sends data through the mouthpiece and receives data through the earpiece of the handset. The digital pulses produced by the terminal are converted into audible tones that are picked up by the handset receiver. The signals from these tones are then sent to the processor location where another modem converts them back to digital pulses.

External Direct-Connect Modem

It is external to the computer and connects directly to computer via RS-232 serial interface cable and to the telephone line via a modular phone jack. An external direct-connect modem may be equipped with microprocessors, storage chips and specialized communication chips. Such intelligent modem is programmed to automatically perform dialing, disconnecting functions, check the operating status using status lights and speakers, self test to verify the modem's ability to correctly transmit data, respond to commands from a communication program and change the speed at which data are transmitted.

Internal Direct-Connect Modem

It has all the needed communication circuitry on a plug-in board that fits into one of the expansion slots inside the computer. Internal direct connect modem also links directly to the telephone line via a modular phone jack.

These modems have many of the same special features as the external direct connect modems.

Communcation Channels

It is actually the media through which data is transmitted from one place to another. There are 3 types of communication channels.

Wire Cable

These are the most popular and widely used channels to transmit data from one location to another. This is so because it is cheaper and easier to use. Wire cable includes telegraph lines, telephone lines and coaxial cables. An advantage of wire cable is that the technology used to transmit data over wire cables is standardized, thus reducing the compatibility problems.

A disadvantage of wire cable is that it is subject to electrical interference making it less reliable than other types of communication channels. Another disadvantage is that wire cable must transmit data in analog form. Therefore, digital data must be converted to an analog signal before they reach the wire cable. This conversion not only needs special hardware, i.e., modem but also slows down the transmission of digital data.

Various items used are:

Telephone Lines

Telephone lines may be used to transmit computer data using the modems. The lines themselves may be either leased or switched.

Leased Lines

A leased line is a telephone line that is leased for the express purpose of maintaining a communication channel between two computers. The line is not shared with any other users and is available at all times for data communication between the computers. A leased line is similar to a telephone connection that is always open. Both computers are always listening for a signal to start the communication. Leased lines are used in computer networks where computers or terminals in the network must be in constant contact with one another. For example, leased lines are used in a network employing point-of-sale terminals, as the terminals must be in constant contact with the main computer. Leased lines are often conditioned to limit the level of noise on the line. Conditioned leased lines are usually necessary to carry on high speed data communication. Security requirements often require that leased lines be shielded from outside interference and unauthorized snooping.

Switched Lines

A switched line can be used for either voice or data communication and is switched from user to user, as requirements dictate. When switched lines are used, one computer must establish contact with the other by dialing a telephone number. After the transmission has been completed, the connection between the computers is broken, just as if a telephone receiver were hung up.

Twisted Pair Cable

Twisted pair [YP] is a common scheme for using copper wire as telecommunication cable. Because copper is such a good conductor of electrons, copper wires do not constrain electromagnetic signals well. When two copper wires conduct electric signals in close proximity, a certain amount of electromagnetic interference occurs. This type of interference is called cross-talk. In addition, because of the electromagnetic range used, TP transmits and receives unwanted signals from other sources. Twisting the copper wires reduces cross-talk and signal emissions. Each intertwined strand conducts a current whose emitted waves are cancelled out by the other wire's emissions. Twisted pairs are formed by two insulated 22 to 26 gauge copper wires that are twisted about each other. When one or more twisted pairs are combined within a common jacket, they form a twisted pair cable.

The two types of TP cables are:

Unshielded Twisted Pair Cable

This type of cable is composed of a set of twisted pairs with a simple plastic encasement. You may be familiar with UTP because it is commonly used in telephone systems. It is widely available and has been largely standardized. The Electrical Industries Association (EIA) popularized a category labeling scheme for five different qualities of twisted pair cable.

Category 3 and Category 5 UTP are commonly used in computer networking. While Category 3 is suitable for most contemporary computer networks, Category 5 included some enhancements, such as more twists per foot and a higher grade insulator, to improve the transmission media performance. Category 5 installations also require compatible equipment and more exacting installation techniques. Due to its voice telecommunication heritage, computer network UTP is often installed in the same manner as most telephone installations. A user device contains a port which accommodates a modular RJ-45 (4-pair) or RJ-11 (2-pair) telephone connector. The cost of UTP is extremely low compared to other transmission media. It continues to be mass produced for telecommunications and has become a popular computer network medium.

Some network integrators use existing spare wires from telephone cables to significantly reduce the already low implementation costs. However, this practice is not recommended if the existing UTP cable is lower than Category 3, if the cable drops exceed 100 meters, or if significant crosstalk is already present between the voice wires. UTP installation equipment is also inexpensive, easy to use and widely available.

Installation techniques are so simple that the cable can be adequately installed with very little training. Because voice telecommunication connection techniques have been optimized for easy moves, adds and changes, UTP is easily managed and reconfigured. Using current and emerging techniques, UTP may support data transfer rates from 1 to 100 Mbps at distances up to 100 m. Ten Mbps is the most common transmission rate in use today. All copper wire suffers from rapid attenuation when used as a communication medium. UTP is no exception.

Current technology restricts the effective range of UTP to hundreds of meters.

The copper cable used in UTP is very susceptible to EMI. Although the twists greatly reduce crosstalk, a certain amount of interference exists between pairs of wires.

Also, signals on the pairs are easily influenced by outside emitters of electromagnetic waves. External devices can also be used to intercept signals that are emitted from the pairs, breaching the security of a network.

Shielded Twisted Pair Cable

Though most of the cable is unshielded, but some forms of Shielded Twisted Pair (STP) is also used at some places. STP is insulated cable which included bundled pairs wrapped in a foil shielding. Various transmission media specifications from Apple Computer and IBM use STP cable. STP is more difficult to install than UTP.

Like coaxial cable, an electric ground, created by special connectors and installation techniques, must be provided for the shield. However, STP is more difficult to install than coaxial cable. If you use standardized and pre-configured cables, it makes installation simple. Bulk STP is moderately expensive. It currently costs more than UTP but is less expensive than thick coaxial or fiber optic cable. With the reduction of outside interference, STP can use higher frequencies and more bandwidth-efficient signaling techniques.

It is capable of greater transmission speeds, up to 500 Mbps at 100 m, but has not been widely implemented at data rates higher than 155 Mbps. The most common transmission rate is 16 Mbps. The biggest difference between UTP and STP is the reduction of interference and EMI emissions provided by STP's shielding. However, STP still suffers from relatively low immunity from interference. STP suffers from attenuation at a rate similar to UTP. Current technology also restricts the effective range of STP to hundreds of meters.

Coaxial Cables

This type of cable come in protective cover which shields the cable from physical dangers as well as from electromagnetic interference. Within the cover, the various cables are shielded from interference with one another. Coaxial cables are used in communication networks that require many simultaneous communication links. Each coaxial cable can provide more than 5000 links. The initial installation of coaxial cable is relatively simple. However, current installation techniques usually use a single strand of cable, which may become difficult to manage and reconfigure.

Local drops may be connected to the base cable to make device connections easier. Using current technologies, coax supports data transfer rates between twisted pair and fiber optic cable, although the typical data rate in use today is 10 Mbps. Much greater data rates are available. However, these higher rates are only infrequently used in computer networking. It is important to note that coaxial cable's bandwidth potential increases with the diameter of the inner conductor.

The cost of coaxial cable increases with the diameter and composition of the conductor. The cost of thin coaxial cable is relatively low (less than STP or Category 5 UTP). Thick coaxial cable is moderately expensive (more than STP or Category 5 UTP). Both are more expansive than Category 3 UTP (all comparisons are made in reference to bulk cable with no connectors).

As a copper wire media, coaxial cable suffers from high attenuation, but at a much lower rate than either variety of twisted pair. Using current LAN technology, the effective range of coaxial cable is in the low thousands of meters. While copper wire generally is a poor resistor to EMI, the shielding provided by coaxial cable greatly reduces its effects.

There are two types of coaxial cables: baseband and broadband.

A baseband coaxial cable transmits a single signal at a time at very high speed, while a broadband coaxial cable can transmit many simultaneous signals using different frequencies. A baseband cable transmits a single stream of digital data at a very high communication rate (millions of bits per second) but must be amplified every 1000 feet or so. It is mainly used for local area networks. A baseband coaxial cable can carry only an analog signal, so it must be used in conjunction with a modem. It is more complex to use in a network.

Fiber Optics

They are very reliable communication channels and they transmit data in digital form. They use light impulses that travel through clear flexible tubing (tiny threads of glass or plastic). A single glass fiber is thinner than the size of a human hair and it can transmit all the characters in dozens of books of the same size of this one across the country in a single second. It would take about 21 hours to send the same information over a copper telephone line. Since thousands of these fibers can be fit in the same amount of space required for one wire cable, the future cost of broad band transmission capability should be within the reach of small organizations and individuals.

Fiber optics can transmit data at very high speed with no errors. Unlike wire cables, fiber optic cables are not subject to electrical interference. They do, however, require repeaters to read and boost the signal strength because light pulses will lose signal strength over long distances. Optical fibers support extremely high bandwidths because they are limited by the high-frequency photon properties of light rather than by lower frequency properties of electrical systems.

Current technologies allow data rates from 100 Mbps to over 2 Gbps, at distances from 2 to 25 km. The data rate of a given fiber optic system is dependent upon the fiber composition (glass or plastic), the mode and the wavelength of the light transmitted. The most common LAN installations include glass multi-mode fiber and 850 nm wavelength LEDs. This configuration can sustain a transmission rate of 100 Mbps at distances of approximately 20 km. Historically, bulk fiber and connectors have been relatively expensive compared to copper wire, but these costs are falling rapidly.

However, the extreme cost of installation far outpaces the cost of materials. The nature of fiber optic cable poses installation problems. Every fiber junction, splice, or connection must be made with extreme care to ensure that the light path is unobstructed. Installers must be careful not to excessively stretch or bend the fiber. Fiber optic cables have extremely low attenuation rates. The amount of attenuation varies depending upon the operating wavelength, but effective ranges are usually measured in kilometers. Therefore, fiber optic cable attenuates much less than any copper wire transmission medium. Due to the use of the light spectrum, fiber optic cables do not leak signals and are immune to electromagnetic interference and eavesdropping. Also, the light spectrum does not require electrical grounds, so fiber optic cables do not suffer from potential shifts to the electrical ground not do they produce sparks. These characteristics make fiber ideal for hazardous, high voltage, or eavesdropping sensitive environments.

Microwave

This is also a type of analog communication channel. Microwave signals are transmitted through the atmosphere rather than through wire cables, similar to the way radio and television signals are transmitted. Microwave signals must be transmitted in a straight line, they do not bend around corners or around the curve of the earth. Transmitter stations redirect and boost the signals. The data may be beamed to a communications satellite that acts as a reflector by accepting signals from one point on earth and returning the same signals to some other point on earth.

The satellite appears from the earth to be stationary target for the microwave signals because its precisely positioned 22,300 miles above the equator with an orbit speed that matches the earth's rotation. Dozens of satellites are now in orbit to handle international and domestic data, voice and video communications.

Compared to wire cable, microwave has a much lower error rate, making it more reliable. Also, because there are no physical links between the sending and receiving systems communication links can be made over large distance and rough terrains. The only disadvantage is the high cost of ground stations and satellites to support a microwave network.

Bandwidth Channels

The bandwidth, or grade, of a communication channel determines the rate or speed that data can be transmitted over a channel. The term **bandwidth** is often shortened to **band**.

There are 3 bands for communication channels.

Narrow-band

The narrow-band channel is used where data volume is relatively low and which transmits data at a rate between 40 to 100 bits per second (bps). Telegraph lines are an example of narrow-band channels and their transmission rate is slow.

Voice-band

The voice-band channels are able to speed up the transmission rate between 110 to 9600 bits per second. Telephone lines are an example of voice-band channels. In many cases, a terminal operator at a remote location uses the regular dial-up telephone switching network, calls a number at the control processor location and enters the data. For large volumes of data, it is cheaper for an organization to acquire its own dedicated or leased line which can be used for both voice and data transmissions.

Broad-band

The broad-band channels are used where data volumes are large and which transmit data at rate upto several megabits per second. Microwaves, coaxial cables, fiber optics and communications satellites are examples of broad-band channels.

Data Transmission

The 2 forms of data transmission are discussed below.

Analog Data Transmission

Here the transmission of data is in a continuous wave form. The telephone system, for instance, is designed for analog data transmission.

Waves are measured using one or more of the following 3 characteristics.

Amplitude

You can consider the amplitude of a wave as the signal strength compared to some reference value (measured in volts). Analog signals are based upon amplitude, or strength, shifts which vary constantly from positive to negative values. Amplitude is commonly expressed in volts when measuring electrical potential, amps when measuring electrical current, watts when measuring electrical power, and decibels when measuring the ratio between the power of two signals.

Frequency

The frequency of a wave is the time it takes for a wave to complete one cycle. In other words, if a signal takes one second to make a transition from high amplitude to low and back to high, the frequency of the wave is one second. Frequency is typically measured in hertz[Hz], or cycles per second.

Phase

The phase of a signal refers to the relative state of the wave when timing began. Two signals cross at a slightly different time. Signal phase is measured in degrees. As with digital signals, analog signals can be modulated on encoded to represent binary data.

Current State

The most common analog current state strategies use different signal amplitudes or frequencies to represent data. These are two type of analog signal encoding schemes:

Amplitude-shift keying (ASK)

Amplitude-shift keying encodes binary data by varying the signal's amplitude between two or more levels. For example, a binary 0 might be one volt and a binary 1 might be three volts.

Frequency-shift keying (FSK)

Frequency-shift keying encodes binary data by varying the signal's frequency between two or more values.

For example, a binary 0 would be one frequency or group of frequencies and a binary 1 would be some other frequency or group of frequencies.

Network devices, using current state analog signaling, periodically measure the signal's amplitude, frequency, or both simultaneously.

State Transition

Transitions from one analog phase to another can also encode data on an analog signal. This method of analog signaling is called Phase-Shift Keying (PSK). This encodes binary data by varying the phase of the signal to indicate a value. For example, a 180 degree phase shift could represent 1 and no shift could indicate 0. Network devices periodically measure the analog signal to determine if a phase change has occurred.

Digital Data Transmission

It is the transmission of data using distinct **ON** and **OFF** electrical states. Computer circuitry represents data as a pattern of **ON** or **OFF** electrical states. These two states are represented by a 1 or **ON** and 0 for **OFF**. Digital data communication is faster and more efficient than analog. All the data communication between the computers is in digital form as the computers understand and work only in digital forms.

However, telephone system, an analog data transmission system, is used for a great percentage of data communication because it is the largest and the most widely used communication system in the world. The modem, sometimes referred as interface element, is used to bridge the gap between digital and analog data transmission, or to allow the digital data to be transmitted/received over from the telephone lines.

Buffers and Protocols

Before data are transmitted, a set of traffic rules and procedures, called protocol, must be established. The same protocol must be followed by all devices participating in the communication session. These rules may vary depending on the devices being used. Prearranged signals defining the protocol to be followed when transmitting and receiving data are sent between computers in an exchange called handshaking. Data communication between computers takes place independently of the CPU through the use of buffers at both the receiving and sending ends.

A buffer is a section of RAM which holds the data being transmitted or received. When the sending computer's buffer is almost empty, the CPU is interrupted and asked to refill the buffer. At the receiving end, the receiving buffer interrupts the CPU when it is full and the data are moved to their ultimate destination such as screen, printer or disk.

If the buffer size is large or the communication rate is slow, the buffer may be manipulated without interrupting the transmission of data. If the buffer size is smaller the communication rate is high, the sending and receiving modems use a protocol or prearranged sequence of signals, to interrupt the transmission while the buffer is filled or emptied. When the receiving computer's buffer is full, the receiving modem sends a signal to inform the sending computer to stop. When the buffer has been emptied, the receiving modem sends another signal to inform the sending computer to resume sending.

Error Detection

A number of methods have been used to detect errors while transmitting data. The most popular method for detecting errors is inserting a parity bit alongside the data bits for a character. When the receiving modem detects an incorrect parity bit, it can request the sending modem to retransmit the character.

Serial and Parallel Interface

A parallel interface is the one that uses eight wires to transmit all 8 bits in a byte at the same time. Therefore, parallel interfaces are faster and more expensive than serial interfaces. An interface connection is often called a port. The program instructions used by the computer to communicate with other devices is called driver program. In other words, most data are organised into 8 bit bytes. In some computers, data are further organised into multibyte words. Sometimes data are transmitted, a byte or a word at a time. This is done by using many wires, with one wire carrying each bit, which is known as parallel communication.

Unlike parallel interface, in a serial interface, the 8 bit bytes are lined up into a single stream for bits for transmission to a peripheral device. That is, a serial interface transmits only one bit at a time and hence it is slow. Parallel communication is used primarily for transferring data between devices at the same site. For example, communication between a computer and a printer is mot often parallel, so that an entire byte can be transferred in one operation. Communication between computers is almost always serial.

Rate of Data Transmission

The speed at which data travel over a communication channel is called the communication rate. It is also known as the transmission speed. The rate at which the data are transferred is the baud rate. Baud rate is the number of time per second that the signal being transmitted changes (modulation or demodulation). Baud is often equated with bits per send (bps), however, this comparison is not entirely accurate because a signal does not always carry one bit.

Although higher speeds are possible, typical data transmission speeds are 300, 1200, 2400, 4800 and 9600 bps. Modems used with microcomputers typically use 300, 1200 or 2400 bps. Larger computer systems used for communication in business typically transmit data at speeds of 4800 bps or higher using high-speed modems.

Methods of Data Transmission

There are 3 main methods of data transmission.

Asynchronous Transmission

Here one character is transmitted at a time. The transfer of data is controlled by start bits and stop bits. Each character is surrounded by bits that signal the beginning and end of the character. These characters allow the receiving terminal to synchronize itself with the receipt of data on a character-by-character basis. Asynchronous transmission is often used for low-speed transmission of data in conjunction with narrow-band and few slower speed (less than 1200 bps) voice band channels where the transmitting device operates manually or intermittently. It is least expensive of the two methods. Because the bit strings are relatively short, timing errors between the two device's clocks will not cause the receiving device to mistake the start of a frame.

This type of transmission is often used when characters are generated at random intervals, such as when a user types at a terminal. The start and stop bits not only indicate when a receiver should measure for the presence of bits, but also indicate the beginning and end of the data stream.

Synchronous Transmission

This transmission of data is a method in which blocks of characters are transmitted in timed sequences. Rather than using start and stop bits around each character, each block of characters is marked with synchronization characters. The receiving device accepts data until it detects a special ending character or a predetermined number of characters at which time the device knows the message has come to an end.

Synchronous transmission commonly uses the faster (greater than 1200 bps) voice-band and broad-band channels and is usually used when data-transfer requirements exceed several thousand bits per second. It is much faster than asynchronous transmission. Synchronous transmission is used in direct computer-to-computer communication for large computer systems because of the high data-transfer speeds required. The special characters used by asynchronous (start/stop bits) and synchronous (synchronization characters) transmission to alert the modem when data are being send and when the transmissions are finished are called message characters.

Synchronized transmissions resist timing errors much better than a synchronized transmission because both the transmitter and receiver use the same clock. To maintain framing when no data is being transmitted, synchronous transmission systems use fill bits. The sender can then maintain the integrity of the transmission timing. As with asynchronous transmission, synchronous transmission can perform error detection.

A method known as Cyclic Redundancy Check (CRC) is often used the CRC process subjects the block of data to an algorithm. The result of the computation (called the CRC) is appended to the block of data prior to transmission. On the receiving side, the same algorithm is used and the results are compared with the CRC field. Any difference is assumed to mean frame damage occurred during transmission. CRC is less vulnerable to multiple bit errors than asynchronous error-detection methods.

Isochronous Transmission

These methods use a constant fixed-frequency transmission clock to create set time slots. A clock signal is generated by a designated network device and is passed to all other devices on the network. Using the prescribed media access rules, the network devices monitor the network for free space within the slots and insert data as needed.

Multiple frames can be inserted into each slot until the slot is full. By using this method, a clock signal is not provided for every frame like asynchronous, or provided by the sender at the beginning of a string like synchronous. Rather the clock is provided at a constant rate by a single device for all other devices on the network.

Communication Channel Configurations

The two main communication channel configurations are as follows:

Point-to-point

In a point-to-point channel configuration, a device is connected directly to another devices by a dedicated communication channel. This communication channel configuration can be inefficient and costly if a terminal is not active enough to keep the line busy.

Multi-point

In the multi-point channel configuration, three or more devices, e.g., a terminal or computer, are connected to the same line. Compared to point-to-point configuration, multipoint channel configuration is more efficient and less costly because it reduces the amount of intercabling needed.

Communication Processors

A number of communication processors are used by network designers to achieve their goals. They increase the efficiency of a communication channel. These processors are used for a number of purposes, some of which are as follows:

Multiplexing

It is the process of combining the transmission, character by character, from several devices into a single data stream that can be transmitted over a single communication channel. A multiplexer is a device that produces multiplexing. It is also used at the receiving end to separate the transmissions and send them back in their original order for processing. A multiplexer allows the communication channels to transmit much more data, at any one time, than what a single device can send. Multiplexers are more efficient and less expensive. The equipment that multiplexes and demultiplexes is sometimes called a multiplexer or mux.

The following methods are used by multiplexers to allow multiple devices to communicate concurrently.

Frequency-Division Multiplexing

It uses separate frequencies to establish multiple channels within a broadband medium. To do this, the mux creates special broadband carrier signals that operate on different frequencies. Data signals are added to the carrier signals and are removed, at the opposite end of the media segment, by another mux. FDM is used in broadband LANs to separate different direction traffic on the cable and to provide special services like dedicated connections between machines.

Time-Division Multiplexing

These systems divide a single channel into short time slots. Bits, blocks of bits, bytes, or frames can be placed into each time interval is not exceeded. Time division is a multiplexing technique that you can use on baseband systems. You can also use it on an individual channel of a broadband FDM system. Conventional TDM systems are sometimes called synchronous TDM because the time-divisions are fixed when the muxes are set up. The time slots are always of the same length and are assigned in the same order.

Statistical Time-Division Multiplexing

Conventional synchronous TDM systems waste bandwidth if many of the time slots are left unused. Statistical time-division multiplexing (StatTDM) solves this problem by dynamically allocating time slots to active devices on a first-come, first-served or priority basis. A control field identifies the owners of each slot's data so that the receiving mux can appropriately split out all the individual signals.

Concentration

Very often, it is required to connect more devices (or terminals) to a computer so that the communication channel can handle all at once. Concentration is the process of connecting and serving these devices. A concentrator is hardware that provides concentration. The data are stored in the buffer of concentrator for later transmission, when the number of devices transmitting exceeds the capacity of the communication channel. However, today's micro-processor equipped multiplexers perform much like concentrators. Compared to concentrators, multiplexers are less expensive.

Message Switching

The message switcher receives and analyzes data messages from points in the network, determines the destination and the proper routing and then forwards the messages to other network locations. If needed, a message can be stored till an outgoing line is available.

Front-end Processing

The front-end processor is a computer, which is usually located at a central computer site. It handles all the data communication control functions while the Central Processing Unit (CPU) of the front-end processor handles all the communication tasks. Its purpose is to relieve the main computer – called a host computer – of a number of the functions required to interact with and control the communications network. The two processors interact only when data need to be passed between them.

A typical front-end processor might control scores of communication channels of varying types and speeds coming from a number of diverse remote terminals. The functions of communication processors differ from one network to another and there may be an overlapping of functions. A message switching processor, for example, may also function as a remote concentrator; a front-end processor may perform message-switching function; and, in less complete networks, the host computer may perform most or all of the functions of the front-end processor.

TRANSMISSION MODES

Data transmission may occur in one of the following 3 modes.

Simplex Mode

In this mode, data can be transmitted in one direction. A device using the simplex mode of transmission can either send or receive data, but it cannot do both. Simplex mode (circuits) are seldom used because a return path is generally needed to send acknowledgment, control or error signals.

Half-duplex Mode

Here, data can be transmitted back and forth between two stations, but data can only go in one of the directions at any point of time. An example is a citizens band radio where the user must either talk or listen, but cannot do both at the same time.

Full-duplex Mode

The full-duplex mode allows a device to receive and send data simultaneously. A full-duplex mode is faster, since it avoids the delay that occurs in a half-duplex circuit each time the direction of transmission is changed.

COMMUNICATION PROCEDURES

All communication between computers are managed by data communication software. The precise procedures used depend on the particular software, but the following account outlines the general procedures.

Communication Between Two Microcomputers

A small business that uses microcomputers has accumulated information that it wants to send to a customer who also uses microcomputers.

The procedure used to send the information is as follows:

1. Both the business and the customer start the communication program, which gives them a menu of options.
2. Both the business and the customer choose the same options, including the number of start and stop bits, the type of parity checking, the communication rate, full-duplex or half-duplex transmission and so on.
3. The communication link is established. The users decide who will originate the telephone call and the originator enters the telephone number. The communication program then instructs the modem to detail the number and reports to the users if a connection has been made.
4. After the connection has been made, the users can have an on-line conversation. They can type messages back and forth to each other and can record their conversation.
5. When the business is ready to transfer the information, it sets its computer to send; the customer sets

its computer to receive. The business starts, the transfer. The communication program takes over by reading the information from the disk and sending it through the communication link. The receiving computer stores the incoming information on a disk. The transfer proceeds without any further human attention.

6. When the transfer has been completed, the business and the customer say "goodbye" and terminate the connection.

Communication Between Microcomputer and Larger Computer

The procedure for communication between a microcomputer and a minicomputer or mainframe is similar. The only difference is that the larger computer have safeguards that limit access to files and facilities to authorized users. The most common safeguards are the user identification number and the user password. After the communication link has been established, the receiving computer asks for the user's identification number.

This number is assigned to the microcomputer user by the operators of the larger computer. When requested to do so, the microcomputer user types in the user identification number. The receiving computer checks that the identification number is valid. It then asks for the user's password.

A password is a confidential sequence of characters that allows access to the system.

An example of a password is:

S12$T11

The password is required for the user to obtain access to the larger computer. It also determines exactly which files and facilities the microcomputer user is allowed to read. If the typed password is valid, the microcomputer user is allowed access to the large system.

Going On-Line

Before you establish a communication link, you must adjust various settings to match those of the computer you want to connect with. Called communication parameters, these settings vary with different types of computers and programs. Fortunately, most communication programs let you store and retrieve the parameters that apply to various remote systems. When you connect to a remote system such as an on-line information service, you will probably be asked to reply to one or more on-screen questions.

Generally, you will need to provide some kind of identification, such as your name, an account number and a password. This brief dialogue between you and the remote system is often called a logon procedure. Some remote systems compare your identification with a list of paid subscribers. Obviously, if you are not on the list, you would not be able to access the service.

Other systems use the logon procedure as a security measure, protecting valuable records from tampering. In either case, the remote system maintains a record or log of every caller. Many communication programs support automated logon procedures. When you log on for the first time, the program "records" your entries for later use.

Subsequently, when you access the remote system, these entries are automatically supplied in response to prompts from the remote system. Many communication software packages let you dial, connect and log on to a remote system at the touch of a single function key. Once you have gone through the formalities, the remote system usually welcome you with a greeting and waits for your net command.

At this point, your communication software has turned your computer into a simple video terminal, allowing you to use the remote system's software as if you were connected directly to the system.

File Transfer

Transferring files to and from your disk drive is one of the most common communication applications. These files may be bulletins, electronic mail messages, airline information or even computer programs. In addition to matching communication parameters, file transfer requires that both systems in a communication link agree on a common protocol.

A protocol consists of the technical details that regulate data transmission between computers. Fortunately, you need only a rough idea of how a protocol works in order to use one. The simplest to understand is the text or ASCII protocol. This method sends a file as one uninterrupted stream of ASCII characters.

While this protocol offers transmission of maximum characters in the shortest possible time, it is also the one most likely to produce errors, especially over noisy telephone lines. To combat flaws in file transfer, most protocols offer error correction. Specific methods vary from protocol to protocol, but the basic error correction scheme is the same; breaking up a file into small blocks and then comparing the received blocks to those that were sent to make sure they are identical.

Each block includes an extra character mathematically derived from the ASCII values of the characters it contains. If the receiving computer comes up with a different value for that character after it receives a block, it assumes an error has occurred and requests that block again. While this procedure reduces throughput, error checking and correction virtually assure error free file transfer.

Common error correction programs now include more advanced session level protocols that check for errors throughout an entire communication session, not just during file transfer.

Choosing Parameters

Before loggin on, you must make sure that you and the remote system are using the same communication parameters – the various settings that regulate the means of communication. To clarify this point, baud rate, parity, stop bits and echo are further discussed. Baud rate refers to the rate or "speed" of data transfer. In common parlance, this means the number of bits per second (bps) sent or received.

Technically, baud rate refers to the rate of the phase-shifting method a modem uses to transmit information – which is not necessarily the same as the bps rate. However, most modem manufacturers use baud rate to describe bps and this corruption of the technical term is now commonplace. Since transmitting one character usually takes 10 bits, dividing the baud rate by 10 will give you a rough approximation of how many characters per second are being transferred. Which baud rate you use depends on the capabilities of your modem, as well as the equipment used by the remote system.

Most modems for personal computers transfer data at 300, 1200 or 2400 baud. Whatever baud rate your modem supports, it has to be seen that the rate for your modem and the remote system must be identical. Sometimes a remote system will have different phone access numbers for different baud rates. In general, you should communicate at the highest baud rate possible, since this reduces the amount of connect time you are charged for.

However, some commercial information systems charge premium rates for communication at higher baud rates. Even so, the time saved makes using higher baud rates more economical when transferring large files. Parity refers to a scheme using a single bit along with each character to test for accurate data transfer. The most popular configuration for PC communications uses seven bits for data and the eighth bit for even parity. Using even parity during data transfer means that the eight bit always makes the 1 and 0 bits within a character add up to an even number. If the receiving computer detects an odd number, it either requests re-transmission or ignores the character completely.

Sometimes, however, eight bits are used for data and an additional bit is used for parity, resulting in other common setting; eight bits and no parity. Other parity schemes, such as odd number, space and mark are also used, but they are rather uncommon in PC communications. Stop bits refer to the variable number of bits used to mark the end of each character transferred. Often, you may see parity, the number of data bits and the number of stop bits in one reference. "E-7-1" for example, means even parity, seven data bits and one stop bit.

One stop bit is used almost universally in personal computer communication and many communication programs automatically use this setting unless you specify otherwise. Echo refers to a remote system's practice of sending back the characters you transmit, giving you on-screen verification that the characters have been received.

Mainframe computers and commercial information services often use this procedure, while most PC link-ups omit echo. When you are on-line, it is easy to determine whether to turn the echo function on or off. If you see no characters on the screen as you type, turn echo on; if the characters you type appear in duplicate, turn echo off. Most communication programs let you adjust the echo setting while you are engaged in a communication session.

Logging Off

When you have finished a session with a remote system, you need to formally log off. Usually, the system displays a message on screen confirming that log off procedures have been properly completed. Standard log off commands include log out, Bye, Quit, Off and Exit. If you disconnect without formally logging off the system, the remote system may be fooled into believing that you are still connected. When you are using a commercial service that charges by the minute for connect time, this can be quite an expensive mistake. Therefore, it is a good idea to watch for the remote system's log off confirmation on screen.

Applications of Data Communication

The applications of data communication fall into one of 4 categories.

Electronic Mail

A business depends on the efficient exchange of information between different parts of the business and between the business and the outside world. Much of this exchange has been traditionally carried out through paper documents, delivered by secretary, mail or messenger service. With the growing use of personal computers, a more efficient alternative has emerged, i.e., electronic mail. Electronic mail is usually used to exchange messages and data files. Each user is assigned an electronic mailbox.

Using the appropriate command, the user can scan a list of messages in the mailbox, display the contents of a particular message, send a message to another user and so forth. To send a message, it is not necessary for the recipient to be present at the computer. The message resides in the mailbox until it is read. The sender may restrict delivery of the message to authorised readers by using a password. That is, the recipient must "sign" for the message by typing his or her identifying password. Many other features of standard mail delivery are implemented in electronic mail systems.

For example, mail can be forwarded, stored for delayed delivery and sent to anyone at a particular phone number. In addition, electronic mail systems implement many new features. An electronic mail system can deliver copies of a message to all individuals listed in a certain file. It also allows merging of standard data (from a data file) with a particular message. Now-a-days, several companies have started subscription to electronic mail services. These services are accessed through a modem and allow users to communicate with other subscribers to the service. The service may also accept a message and transmit it to its destination city. There the message is printed out and delivered with the next day's mail. This technique can be used to communicate with people who are not subscribers to the network.

Using External Databases

The most important applications of data communication is the ability to access external databases. There are literally thousands of databases containing information on almost every conceivable subject. Users can subscribe to many of these databases at a cost of the initial fee and a charge for the amount of time spent accessing the database. Users can locate information in an index or can just browse through the database as they would brows through books at a public library.

The types of information available through services vary greatly, as can be seen in the following examples. The Dow Jones News Services provide current news, current stock and commodity prices and securities research data. The stock prices are very nearly the same up-to-the-minute prices that are simultaneously crossing the tape at the major stock exchange. This allows users to use the service for the data on which they base trading decisions. A number of subscription services supply on-line transactions. For example, a number of banks now allow subscribers to bank through a communication link to a personal computer. Some services even allow users to pay bills in this way. Personal computers may also be used to execute stock trades through several on-line brokerage systems. Transaction-oriented services are in their infancy. In the years to come, they will certainly grow in number and sophistication. A number of multiple-listing real estate services offer on-line options.

This allows a broker to find all homes meeting particular criteria, price range, neighbourhood, size and so on, to match client demands. Also in the real estate field, services supply on-line listings of currently available mortgage money, interest rates and restrictive terms. These services allow a prospective home buyer to shop the entire country to obtain the best mortgage terms.

Sharing Data Files

Probably no single data communication application is as important to a large business as is the link between its micro-computers and its mainframe computers. In the last few years, businesses have purchased millions of personal computers to increase their employees productivity. The initial applications of personal computers were stand alone activities, such as word processing and the use of spreadsheets.

To increase productivity further, businesses are taking the additional step of making data stored in mainframe computers available to microcomputer users. The savings including financial ones can be huge. With data communication and networking, the tasks of data collection, analysis, decision making, report writing and data distribution can be integrated into a single, efficient system. In effect, the entire office (or even the entire company) becomes one large communication network.

Bulletin Board Systems

A bulletin board is a communication system that allows users to call in and either leave or retrieve messages. It is similar to an electronic mail system, but there are no private mailboxes, only a single large mailbox. The messages may be directed to all users of the bulletin board or only to particular users. But all messages can be read by all users. Some computer equipment manufactures maintain bulletin boards that users may call to determine the status of company products, corrections to programs and the like. Users may report problems, ask for literature or place orders. Some computer user groups maintain bulletin boards for notifying members of meetings and other group activities. Other bulletin boards are maintained by individuals are meeting places for like-minded people.

Communication Processing

Communication processing is the collective term for all the activities that help to ensure the successful entry, transmission and delivery of information. Just as data processing involves taking raw data and adding value by changing the inherent information content, communication processing adds value to the raw message by ensuring that the message arrives at its destination in a timely manner, in the proper form, at the proper speed, in the proper language and without errors.

The basic responsibilities of communication processing can be divided into three major areas: editoriai, conversion and arbitration. Editorial functions include formatting of the message, editing the data and controlling errors. Conversion functions include translating transmission speed and code. Arbitration functions involve network control and message routing. Communication processing can be performed in any intelligent device, using the storage and processing capabilities of that device. In the microcomputer based of LAN, most communication processing occurs within the micro-computer itself. Within a network, communication processing is implemented as protocols, the rules that govern the transmission of information.

The following are sample communication processing services:

- Accommodating different video display characteristics such as screen size, line strength and paging.
- Translating data into the standard network format and subsequently re-translating the data to meet the requirements of the receiving station.
- Controlling the sequence in which messages are sent.
- Assembling and transmitting messages on the basis of time interval, order received, receipt of particular character or other characteristics.
- Alerting users to error conditions and possible problems.

Packets

It is neither practical nor advantageous to transmit long messages as a single entity. Therefore, for the purpose of data transmission, particularly in local area networks, messages are broken down into segments, called packets. Each packet normally contains five parts.

- A start frame, identifying the beginning of the packet.
- A header, containing information for maintaining control of the packet and the network.
- An information field, containing a segment of the total text information or data to be communicated.
- An error control field, permitting the system to verify packet integrity.
- An end frame, signifying the end of the packet.

The control information contained in the header includes the source address, which identifies where the packet originated; the destination address, to which the segment is to be delivered; the packed sequence number, which helps insure that the packets can be reassembled in proper order; and a control block, which helps prevent duplication, loss or looping (in which a packet is routed back and forth in an endless circle) of the packet.

Additional information to insure proper operation of the network under various overload or impaired operating conditions also may be included. Overhead is the additional information that must be transmitted through the network in order to facilitate the proper transmission and delivery of messages. It is created by the system's need to maintain control of all transactions. A percentage of overall network capacity is dedicated to this control information. Overhead information exists on the network in two basic forms; data appended to each user packet, such as the control and error-checking fields named above. The amount of data appended to a basic message varies from one system to another and itself contained acknowledgment and control packets, which are transmitted from one device to another. These packets keep the system advised of the status of the components.

Communication Software

Most computer applications, including data communication, require both appropriate hardware and software. Specialised data communication software is required to set up a communication link between two computers and to transmit data. Data communication software performs a number of jobs. One is to send data at the proper speed; if the receiving and sending computers do not agree on the communication rate, the receiving computer will not be able to understand the communication. Another job is to monitor signals from the receiving computer that indicate any transmission errors. The communication program you choose plays a key role in data exchange between computers. If you are on the receiving end, communication software lets you decide whether you want to save data to disk, send it to a printer or simply let it scroll off the screen.

When you transmit data, most programs let you choose between sending it form a disk file or typing it directly from the keyboard. Software for communication also stores telephone numbers, modem commands and other critical settings. Usually, these parameters reside in a dialing directory, so you do not have to re-enter them each time you want to hook up with a remote system. A well-designed communication program makes it easy to select a remote system from the directory and begin connection procedures. Many communication programs direct modems to dial, hang up and answer incoming calls automatically. While it is modem that actually performs these tasks, the software provides the appropriate instructions. For example, when the program sends the modem a dial command and a phone number. The modem automatically goes off-hook (the same as lifting a telephone handset), waits for a dial tone and proceeds to generate click pulses or tones that dial the number.

Most modems provide an audible indication that dialing is in progress, followed by a signal that a connection has been made. You will hear the modem beeping out tones like fast fingers on a touch-tone phone. Then, if all goes well, you should hear the remote system's line ring and the remote modem "pick up" the call. The remote modem then generates a high-pitched answer tone, to which your modem responds with a burst of tones of its own. This opening interchange is called handshaking.

Once two modems are locked on to each other, most communication programs display a 'Connect' message on screen. In the foregoing paragraphs, we listed the rudimentary features of a communication program but a typical one has many additional features. Some programs allow users to redial a number repeatedly (if the line is busy, for example) until a connection is made and others allow users to take remote control of the computer at the other end. That is, the program user can control the other computer from his own keyboard. This allows communication with no one in attendance at the other end. Some programs allow users to dial a sequence of numbers one after the other. These are sometimes used to generate recorded advertising calls.

Micro-to-Mainframe Link

Micro-computers can also be connected to large systems in a micro-to-mainframe link to share data and computing power. As the number of micro-computers used in business increases, this connection is being seen more and more. Line micro-to-micro communication, micro-to-mainframe communication can be accomplished via modem and telephone lines or by hard wiring. However, the connection is not as simple because large systems use different formats for communication and they handle data differently internally. To complicate the problem, the communication and data formats used among the various large systems also differ. Specialized hardware designed for the particular type of computer being used is usually needed to make the data compatible.

For a micro-computer to communicate with a large system, three facts must be known:

1. Type of mainframe to be communicated with;
2. Mainframe's specific data format; and
3. Mainframe's specific communication protocols.

Communication Challeges

The use of data communication is not without its challenges. Data sent over communication channels are subject to various kinds of interference which may alter or destroy some of that data. In addition to ensuring the security of the data, privacy of the data must often be protected. However, unauthorized access to data files can be limited by the use of passwords and access codes. To prevent highly sensitive data from being accessed and used from the communication channels, the data are often encrypted, or scrambled, based on some code before they are sent. Then they are unscrambled using that same code after they are received.

Suppliers of Data Communication Services

Various kind of Data Communication Carriers are:

Common Carriers

To handle large public telephone and telegraph networks, services of common carriers are availed. A common carrier is an organisation that is licensed and regulated by the government to transmit the data communication property of others at regulated rates. There are thousands of licensed common carriers of data communication.

Specialized Common Carriers

In addition to these common carriers that offer a wide range of facilities, there are specialized common carriers whose public networks are often restricted to a more limited number of services. MCI communication corporation is an example of satellite using organizations.

Value Added Carriers

A value added carrier is an organization that leases communication channels from the common carriers (it may not have its own transmission facilities) and adds extra services over and above what the common carriers provide. For example, Tymnet and Telenet both have computer networks that receive customer data coming in over telephone lines. These data are temporarily stored and organized into 'packets' of characters. These packets are then routed and transmitted at high speed over the final data destination. At these offices, data in the packets are reassembled into the complete message for transmission to the final destination. The transmission cost of value-added network (VAN) is less than directly utilizing common carrier channels. Telenet and Tymnet are sometimes referred to as packet-switching networks.

Micro-to-Micro Link

Microcomputers are often connected for data communication in a micro-to-micro link so that microcomputer users with incompatible data formats can share data. For instance, data on an Apple IIc disk cannot be used by an IBM PC/XT drive because the data are not saved on the disk in a format that the IBM can read. However, that data, provided they are in a standard format such as ASCII, can be sent via modem and telephone line to the IBM, saved on the disk by the IBM and used in that format. The reverse, sending data from the IBM to the Apple computer, is also possible. If the two computers are located near each other, another option is to connect directly (hard wire) using a null modem cable. The null modem cable uses a different pin configuration from a modem cable and eliminates the need for a modem by directly matching the data transmit pin from one computer to the data receive pin on the other computer.

The advantages of hard wiring are:

- It allows incompatible computers to transfer data.
- It eliminates the need for modems at each computer.
- It allows data transfer to take place at speeds upto 9600 bps.

However, there are no error dedication capabilities with hard wiring. A small business that uses microcomputers has accumulated information that it wants to send to a customer who also uses microcomputers. The precise procedures used depend on the particular software, but the following account outlines the general procedures:

1. The business and the computer both start the communication program, which gives them a menu of options.
2. The business and computer both, choose the same options, including the number of start and stop bits, the type of parity checking, the communication rate, full-duplex or half-duplex transmission and so on.
3. The communication configuration is made. The users decide who will originate the telephone call and the originator enters the telephone number. The communication program then instructs the modem to dial the number and reports to the users if a connection has been established.
4. When the connection has been established, the users can have an on-line conversation. They can type messages back and forth to each other and can record or capture their conversation.

5. At the business end, if the computer is ready to transfer the information, it sets its computer to send; the customer set its computer to receive. The business starts the transfer. The communication program takes over by reading the information from the disk and sending it through the communication link. The receiving computer stores the incoming information on a disk. When the transfer of a file has been completed, the business and customer sides computers saying "good-bye" and then terminate the connection.

LOCAL AREA NETWORKS

Networking is a concept, where 2 or more than 2 computers are joined together to share information. This can be in the form of data or programs. These computers can be within a walking distance or in the same building of the office or in the same city or even across the cities.

But, why is this needed. Have you ever found yourself rushing from one computer to another in your office or home, attending to several different jobs at various locations? Or do you often find yourself moving files that need printing form a PC that you happen to be working on the PC that is connected to the printer? All of these situations can be made easier by allowing the various machines to communicate with each other – by networking the PCs.

The distance between the computers is narrowed down by the telephone lines. The information from the computer is converted to the media understandable by the communication lines and then transferred from one place to another.

With networking you can not only share data and programs, but can also share the resources like printers, scanners, etc. In PC technology, such a collection of computers, all located within a few thousand feet of each other, is called Local Area Networking.

Networking Basics

Networking several computers together allows data to be transmitted form one machine to another in rapid and easily managed data streams. This sharing of data allows many of the resources that are located on a single machine to effectively become available to all other machines on the network.

These resources can be physically located on the machine, e.g., as files on the hard disk, or connected logically to the machine. An example of a logically connected resource would be a printer that is connected to a PC, but which is then available over the network to other machines on that network.

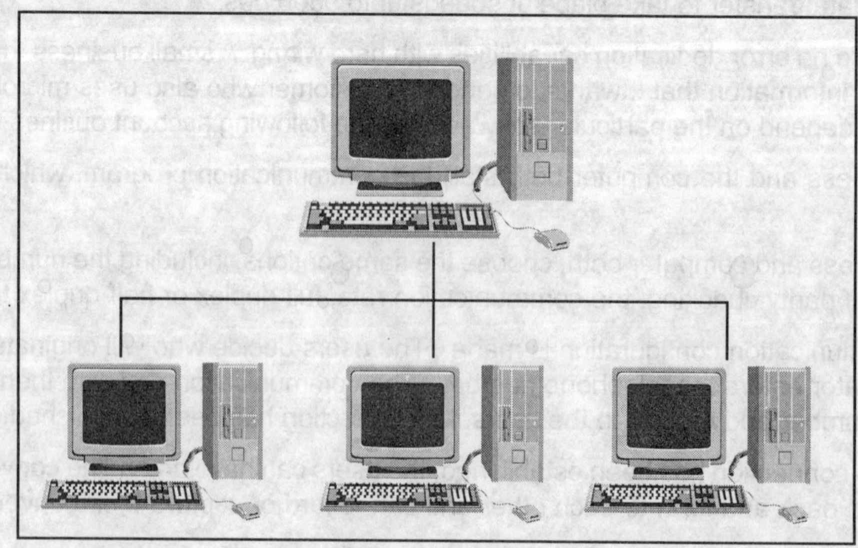

An alternative situation would be where access to the Internet is available to all the PCs on a network through a special communication device attached to the network. Access to all external and internal resources are thus made available to PC users on the network.

A network server provides network services to a user workstation (server) on the network. Services can range from sharing database and files, printers; communications or other network resources. Thus, the network servers are also called file servers, print servers, communication servers, etc. They can be dedicated to the task of providing network services.

They are then called dedicated network servers. Otherwise, they may be called non dedicated servers. A typical networking is shown on the last page.

Another factor which also favours the networking is the cost factor.

Cost Reduction

If you have 2-3 computers attached in a single networking system, you may go in for a single printer which can be used by all of them. The same goes for other devices like Scanner, Plotter, etc. This results in lots of costs.

The main advantages of Networking can be clubbed as follows:

Resource Sharing

There are two main types of networking systems. The type used for larger networks is known as the Client/ Server model. This model involves using a powerful computer that runs a Network Operating System and acts as the 'server'. The Network Operating System then runs the server, supplying network services to the other 'client' computers.

These services might include the management of file transfers, running printing jobs, or even running applications across the network. For example, a word processing software package running on a PC is actually being 'served' form the server across the network, rather than being loaded onto the PC's local hard disk.

The problem with the Client/Server model is that it requires specialised hardware, software and to a large extent skilled networking techniques to configure and maintain the network. All of this can become expensive.

The second model, the Peer-to Peer system or resource Sharing is fortunately a lot easier to implement and maintain and it is this model that we will use in this book.

Resource Sharing is incorporated into Windows 98 and allows all network users access to all resources such as the hard drives, directories, printers or CD-ROM drives that are available on the network. It also allows access to external resources across the network via special intermediary devices.

Resource Sharing involved each computer on the network taking on equal an equal part in the networking process and is ideally suited to smaller networks.

Security

Being able to have complete access to all resources on the network is not always desirable. It is often the case that certain resources may need to be restricted to certain users.

Resources Sharing within Windows allows for this and incorporates the ability to protect access to particular resources with passwords. These passwords can then be stored within the windows 98 configuration files so that access to protected resources is automatically assigned once the user has gained access to the network; the relevant passwords is therefore only entered once during the network login procedure. This function can also be disabled so that a password is required every single time the user attempts to access a protected resource.

Password access can also be configured to allow the user to read but not to change a particular resource or to allow full access, including the ability to write to a resource (which would be necessary for sending jobs to a printer).

Each individual resource can also be configured separately so that different passwords and access rights can be assigned for different resources

Types of Networking

The three basic types of networks are:

1. Local Area Networks or LAN
2. Metropolitan Area Network or MAN
3. Wide Area Network or WAN

Let us see them in details.

Local Area Network

A local area network (LAN) is two or more computers directly linked within a small well-defined area such as a room, building, or group of closely placed buildings. A LAN may be made up of only microcomputers or any combination of microcomputers and large systems.

A LAN usually consists of the following:

1. Two or more computers
2. Peripheral devices such as printers and hard-disk drives
3. Software to control the operation of the computers or other devices connected to the LAN
4. Special cables, usually coaxial or fibre optic, to connect the computers and other devices
5. A plug-in board to handle the data transmissions.

Some computers require that all the computers be of a certain brand, while others allow a variety of brands to be connected. The number of computers in a LAN varies from smaller LANs that typically connect 2 to 25 computers, to large LANs that can connect as many as 10,000 computers.

The length of the cable connecting a computer to a LAN also varies depending on the LAN. Most LANs allow cables of about 1,000 feet, but some allow cables of several miles to be used. The data transfer speeds range from several thousand bits per second to around 10 million bits per second. The programs that control the LANs also vary in the features they offer. Some programs allow the user of more than on operating system; others allow only one. On some LANs file access is limited to one user at a time; on others, more than one user can access a file simultaneously.

Hardware for LAN

The following are the major hardware components/devices for establishing LAN:

1. Transmission Channel
2. Network Interface Unit or NIU
3. Servers
4. Workstations

Transmission Channel for LAN

Generally four types of channels are used for data transmission in a LAN. These are:

1. Twisted Pair Cables
2. Coaxial Cables
3. Fibre Optic Cables
4. Radio Waves

Interface for LAN

Network interface units connect each devices in the LAN network to shared transmission device. It contain the rules or logic to access the LAN. NIU is also used to implement LAN protocols and for device attachments. Its function depends on the type of topologies (to be told later in the this chapter), used in LAN.

Server and Workstations

One of the major benefits of implementation of LAN is sharing expensive resources such as storage devices, printers, etc. This is achieved through providing servers on the LAN. It is dedicated computer that controls one or more resources. This contains both hardware and software interface for LAN. Three major categories of services used in LANs are:

1. File Server
2. Printer Server
3. Modem Server

In networking, file server is used to share storage for files. Besides providing storage space for files in a LAN environment, it is used for taking periodical backup, and also to provide gateway to other servers with and between LANs. Similarly printer server is used to handle printing works of all workstation connected in the network. In LAN environment also modem is required to get connected to other network or simply to use a telephone. A modem server is used to share this expensive resource by all connected workstations in a network ring.

Software for LAN

LAN operating system is required to operate on the LAN system. It has basically two aspects:

1. Server Software
2. Workstation Software

LAN operating system facilitates :

1. Sharing of expensive resources, e.g., printer, storage space, etc.
2. Security for data
3. Connection to other network

There are various types of LAN operating system. Some popular LAN operating systems are :

— Novel Netware

— Ethernet

— Corvus

— ArcNet

— LAN Server

— Omni Net

— PC Net
— IBM PC LAN
— Etherlink Plus, etc.

Wide Area Networks or WAN

A wide area network is two or more computers that are geographically dispersed, linked by communication facilities such as telephone system or microwave relays. This type of network is usually limited to use by large corporations and government agencies because of the high cost involved in building and maintaining them. A WAN is a network that links separate geographical locations and this network can be a public system or any of the various packet switched services provided by the public telecommunication agencies.

The main difference between a WAN and LAN is under the complete control of the owner, whereas the WAN needs the involvement of another authority like telecom department. LANs are successful and capable of handling very high data transfer rates at low cost because of the small area covered. Besides LANs have a lower error rate than WANs.

Transmission Channel for WAN

Generally 3 types of channels are used for data transmission in a WAN. These are:

1. Radio Waves
2. Micro Waves
3. Communication Satellites

Hardware Requirements for WAN

There are mainly 4 hardware devices which are required to establish linkage between geographically separated computers. These are:

1. Bridges
2. Routers
3. Gateways
4. X.25 Standard Interface

These are explained below.

Bridges

These are used to connect two LANs that use the identical protocols over a wide area. The bridge acts as an address filter which picks up packets from one LAN that are intended for a destination on another LAN and passes these packets on the network. The amount of processing required at the bridge is minimal because all the devices use the same protocols. In case the distance between two LANs is very large then the user is required to employ two identical bridges at either end of the communication link.

Routers

It is a special type of device that can be used to connect networks that may not be similar. Such type of devices provide connectivity between two LANs and two WANs over large geographical distances. These devices operate at the Network Layer of the OSI model. These devices participate in a routing protocol to access the network topology, and on the basis of this information routers compute the best route from a sender to the receiver.

Gateways

These are used to connect two dissimilar LANs. The terms Gateways and Routers are used interchangeably, though there is discriminating difference between the two. A router operates at the network layer whereas a gateway operates on the application layer of the OSI model. A gateway is required to convert data packets from one protocol format to another before forwarding it, as it connects two dissimilar networks.

X.25 Standard Interface

X.25 is a protocol for interfacing to a Public Packet Switched Network. It is not a protocol used for implementing a network. Two systems that support X.25 can't necessarily be connected back-to-back. They can only be connected through a DCE in a Public Packet Switched. International Telegraph and Telephone Consultative Committee (ITTCC) developed X.25 as the standard interface between the Data Terminal Equipment (DTE) and Data Circuit Terminating Equipment (DCTE). This recommendation has been widely accepted as the industry standard for public packet switched networks.

Types of Wide Area Networks

There are mainly two types of WAN:

Public Networks

These are those networks which are installed and run by the telecommunication authorities and are made available to any organization or individual who go for their subscription.

Private Networks

The basic technique used in all forms of private WAN is to use private circuits to link the locations to be served by the network. Between these fixed points the owner of the network has complete freedom to use the circuits in any way they want. They can use the circuits to carry large quantities of data or for high speed transmissions. Private wide area networks can be built using whatever standard technology is available.

Topology

There are ways in which you can connect the various computers for networking. This physical arrangement is called Topology. Different types of topologies are:

The Ring Topology

As the name suggests all the server/nodes are joined together to form a ring. There is no central server in this case. A ring may be unidirectional or bi-directional. A unidirectional ring moves data in one direction only; a bi-directional ring moves data in both directions, but only one direction at a time. In a unidirectional ring, if one computer breaks down, special software is required to keep the network functional. When one node malfunction in a bi-directional ring, a message can usually be sent in the opposite direction still allowing the node to communicate with all the other active nodes in the network.

Advantages of the Ring Network

1. **Short cable length:** the amount of cabling involved in a ring topology is comparable to that of a bus and is small relative to that of a star. This means that less connections will be needed, which will in turn increase network reliability.
2. **No wiring closet space required:** Since there is only one cable connecting each node to its immediate neighbours, it is not necessary to allocate space in the building for wiring closets.
3. **Suitable for optical fibers:** Optical fibers offer the possibility of very high speed transmission. Because

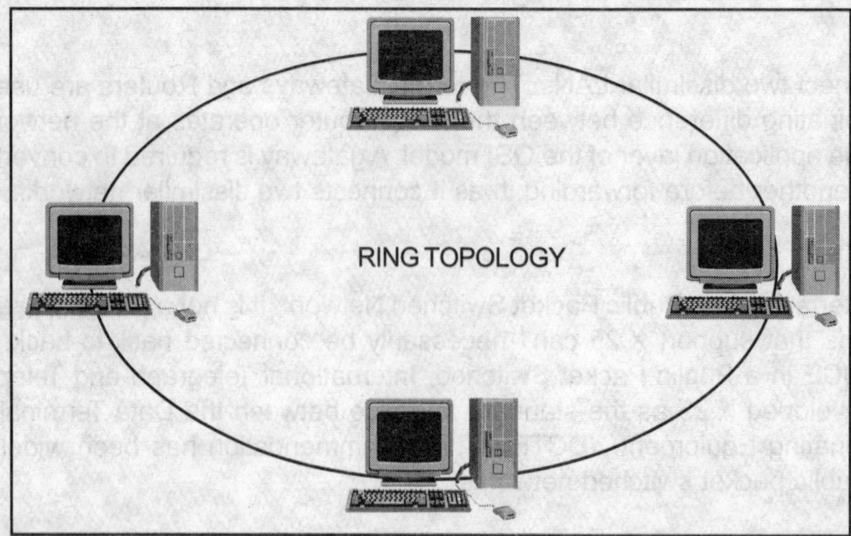

traffic on a ring travels in one direction, it is easy to use optical fibers as a medium of transmission. Also, since a ring is made up of nodes connected by short segments of transmission medium, there is a possibility of mixing the types used for different parts of the network. Thus, a manufacturing company's network could use copper cables in the office area and optical fibers in the factory areas, where electrical interference may be a problem.

Disadvantages of the Ring Network

1. **Node failure causes network failure:** the transmission of data on a ring goes through every connected node on the ring before returning to the sender. If one node fails to pass data through itself, the entire network has failed and no traffic can flow until the defective node has been removed from the ring.
2. **Difficult to diagnose faults:** The fact that failure of one node will affect all other has serious implications for fault diagnosis. It may be necessary to examine a series of adjacent nodes to determine the faulty one. This operation may also require diagnostic facilities to be built into each node.
3. **Network reconfiguration is difficult:** The all or nothing nature of the ring topology can cause problems when one decides to extend or modify the geographical scope of the network. It is not possible to shut down a small section of the ring while keeping the majority of it working normally.
4. **Topology affects the access protocol:** Each node on a ring has a responsibility to pass on data that it receives. This means that the access protocol must take this into account. Before a node can transmit its own data, it must ensure that the medium is available for use.

The Bus Topology

In this case all the server/nodes share a common bus of connecting cables. Every computer can communicate directly with every other computer or device in the network. Each node is given an address.

To access a particular, a user just needs to know its address. This topology is frequently used with local area networks. Going through a hierarchy of nodes is not necessary.

Advantages of the Bus Network

1. **Short cable length and simple wiring layout:** Because there is a single common data path connecting all nodes, the bus topology allows a very short cable length to be used. This decreases the installation cost and also leads to a simple, easy to maintain, wiring layout.
2. **Resilient architecture:** The bus architecture has an inherent simplicity that makes it very reliable from

a hardware point of view. There is a single cable through which all data passes and to which all nodes are connected.

3. **East to extend:** Additional nodes can be connected to an existing bus network at any point along its length. More extensive additions can be achieved by adding extra segments connected by a type of signal amplifier known as a repeater.

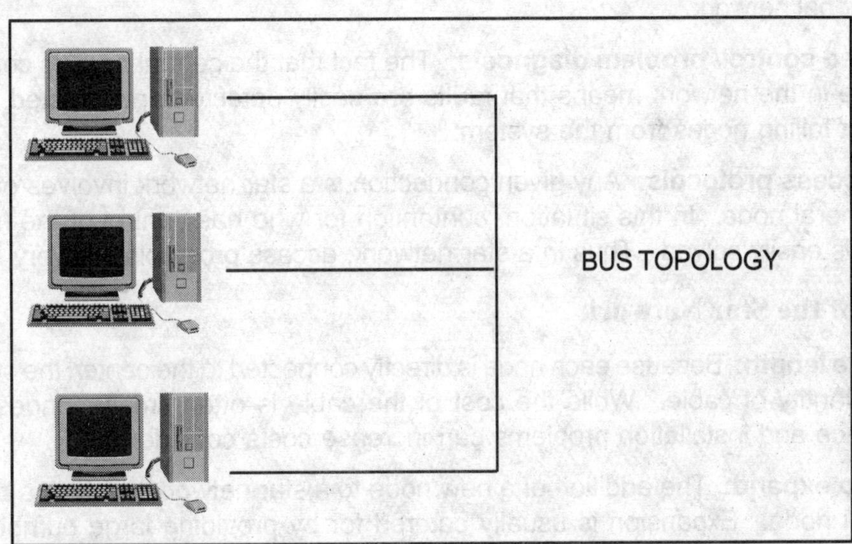

Disadvantages of the Bus Network

1. **Fault diagnosis is difficult:** Although the simplicity of the bus topology means that there is very little that can go wrong, fault detention is not a simple matter. In most LANs based on a bus, control of the network is not centralized in any particular node. This means that detection of a fault may be performed from many points in the network.
2. **Fault isolation is difficult:** In the star topology, a defective node can easily be isolated from the network by removing its connection at the center. If a node is faulty on a bus, it must be rectified at the point where the node is connected to the network. Once the fault has been located the node can simply be removed. In the case where the fault is the network medium itself, an entire segment of the bus must be disconnected.
3. **Repeater configuration:** When a bus-type network has its backbone extended using repeaters, reconfiguration may be necessary. This may involve tailoring cable lengths, adjusting terminators, etc.
4. **Nodes must be intelligent:** Each node on the network is directly connected to the central bus. This means that some way of deciding who can use the network at any given time must be performed in each node. It tends to increase the cost of the nodes irrespective of whether this is performed in hardware of software

The Star Topology

In this case all the computers and the main server form a star like shape. All the computers are connected to a single main host. All communication first goes through the centralized computer allowing it to control the operation, work load, and resource allocation of the other computers in the network. For example, a bank with branch offices would typically use a star network to control and coordinate those branches. The advantage is relative simplicity, but a problem exists with the single-point vulnerability of the network. If the central computer breaks down, none of the other computers can communicate with each other.

Advantages of the Star Network

1. **Ease of service:** The star topology has a number of concentration points, i.e. at the central node or at intermediate wiring closets. These provide easy access for service of reconfiguration of the network.
2. **One device per connection:** Connection points in any network are inherently prone to failure. In the star topology, failure of a single connection typically involves disconnecting one node from an otherwise fully functional network.
3. **Centralized control/ problem diagnosis:** The fact that the central node is connected directly to every other node in the network means that faults are easily detected and isolated. It is a simple matter to disconnect failing nodes from the system.
4. **Simple access protocols:** Any given connection is a star network involves only the central node and one peripheral node. In this situation, contention for who has control of the medium for transmission purposes is easily solved. Thus in a star network, access protocols are very simple.

Disadvantages of the Star Network

1. **Long cable length:** Because each node is directly connected to the center, the star topology necessitates a large quantity of cable. While the cost of the cable is often small, congestion in cable ducts and maintenance and installation problems can increase costs considerably.
2. **Difficult to expand:** The addition of a new node to a star network involves a connection all the way to the central node. Expansion is usually catered for by providing large numbers of redundant cables during the initial wiring. However, problems can arise if a longer cable length is needed or an unanticipated concentration of nodes is required.
3. **Central node dependency:** If the central node in a star network fails, the entire network is rendered inoperable. This introduces heavy reliability and redundancy constraints on this node.

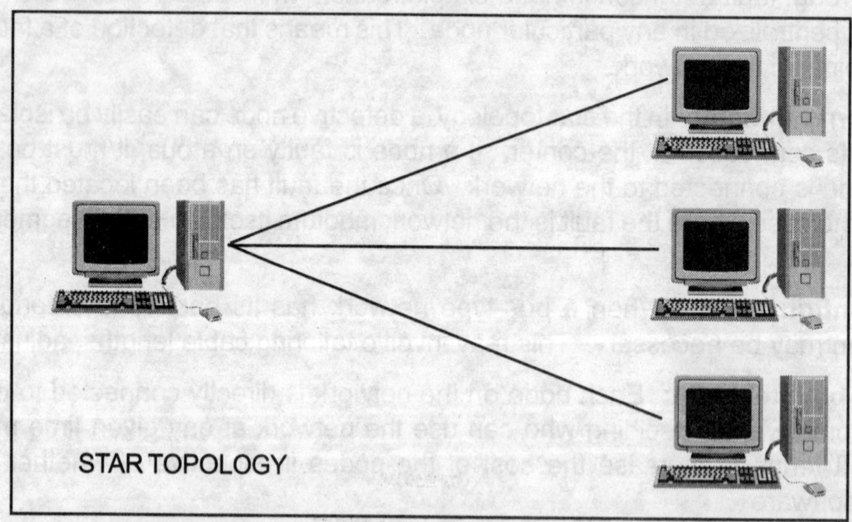

STAR TOPOLOGY

Mesh Topology

A network topology featuring a direct path between two nodes. The backbone of this topology looks like this, where most major cities have a direct connection to most major cities.

Advantages and Disadvantages of the Mesh Network

- **Units affected by media failure:** Mesh topologies resist media failure better than other topologies. Implementations that include more than two devices will always have multiple paths to send signals from one device to another. If one path fails, the transmission signals can be routed around the failed link. Theoretically, no units are affected by media failure. However, if all paths normally use the maximum capacity of each link, some performance degradation will occur are signals are routed around a failed link.

- **Ease of installation:** Mesh networks are relatively difficult to install because each device must be linked directly to all other devices. As the number of devices increases, the difficulty of installation increases geometrically.
- **Ease of troubleshooting:** Mesh topologies are easy to troubleshoot because each medium link is independent of all others. You can easily identify faults and can isolate the affected link.
- **Ease of reconfiguration:** Mesh topologies are difficult to reconfigure for the same reasons that they are difficult to install.

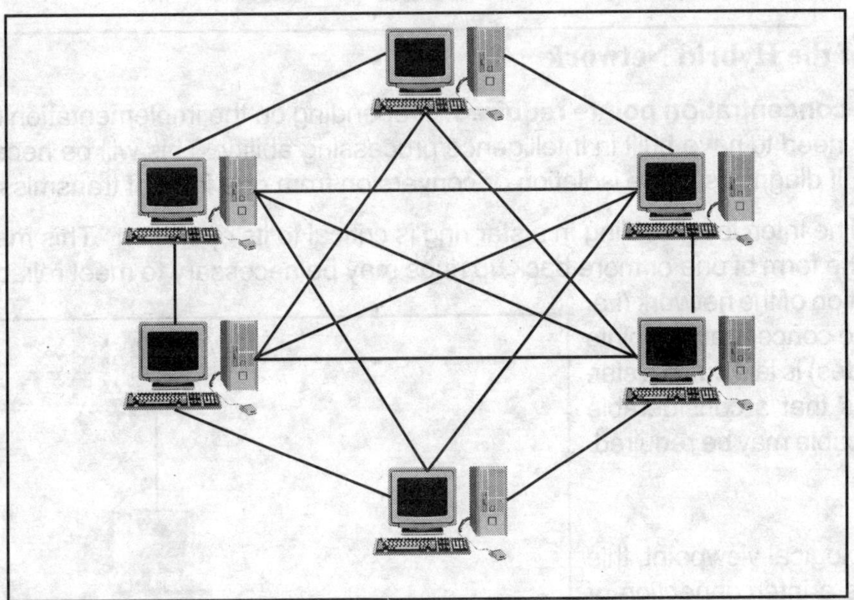

Hybrid Topology

A combination of two or more network topologies. The resultant is a hybrid network. Although the backbone is mostly a mesh network, each local loop is a star network with the central office at each hub.

Advantages of the Hybrid Network

1. **Fault diagnoses and isolation:** The presence of concentration points in the network greatly eases fault diagnosis. If a fault is detected on the network, the initial problems to find out which concentration point in the ring is to blame. The fact that this ring is quite small in relation to the total size of the network makes this problem more manageable. The offending concentration point can be isolated easily, leaving the network in a fully functional state while further fault diagnosis is carried out.
2. **Ease of expansion:** The modular construction of a star-ring network means that new sections may be easily added. When designing the network originally, each concentration can have extra, unused lobes which can be called upon later, if needed. The next growth step involved adding a new concentration point and wiring it into the ring.
3. **Cabling:** The concentration points in a star-ring are connected via a single cable. This simplifies wiring between areas in an installation and cuts down on the congestion of cable ducts. Also, the wiring practices involved are very similar to that of telephone system installation. These techniques are well understood by building engineers and lend themselves well to the prewiring of buildings.

Disadvantages of the Hybrid Network

1. **Intelligent concentration points required:** Depending on the implementation used, the concentration points may need to have built in intelligence/processing ability. This will be necessary if it is to assist in network fault diagnosis, node isolation or conversion from one form of transmission medium to another.
2. **Cabling:** The intercloset cabling in a star ring is critical to its operation. This may mean that redundant cabling in the form of one or more back up rings may be necessary to meet reliability requirements. The largest section of the network (i.e. between the concentration points and the nodes) is laid out in a star. This means that a considerable amount of cable may be required.

Tree Topology

From a purely topological viewpoint, this network resembles a interconnection of star networks. Individual peripheral nodes must transmit to and receive from one other node only, toward a central node. An advantage of a tree structure is that functional groupings can be created.

For example, one branch could contain all the general ledger terminals, another branch all the accounts receivable terminals, and so on. If one branch stops functioning, the other branches in a tree network are not affected. However, data movement through this network can be slow.

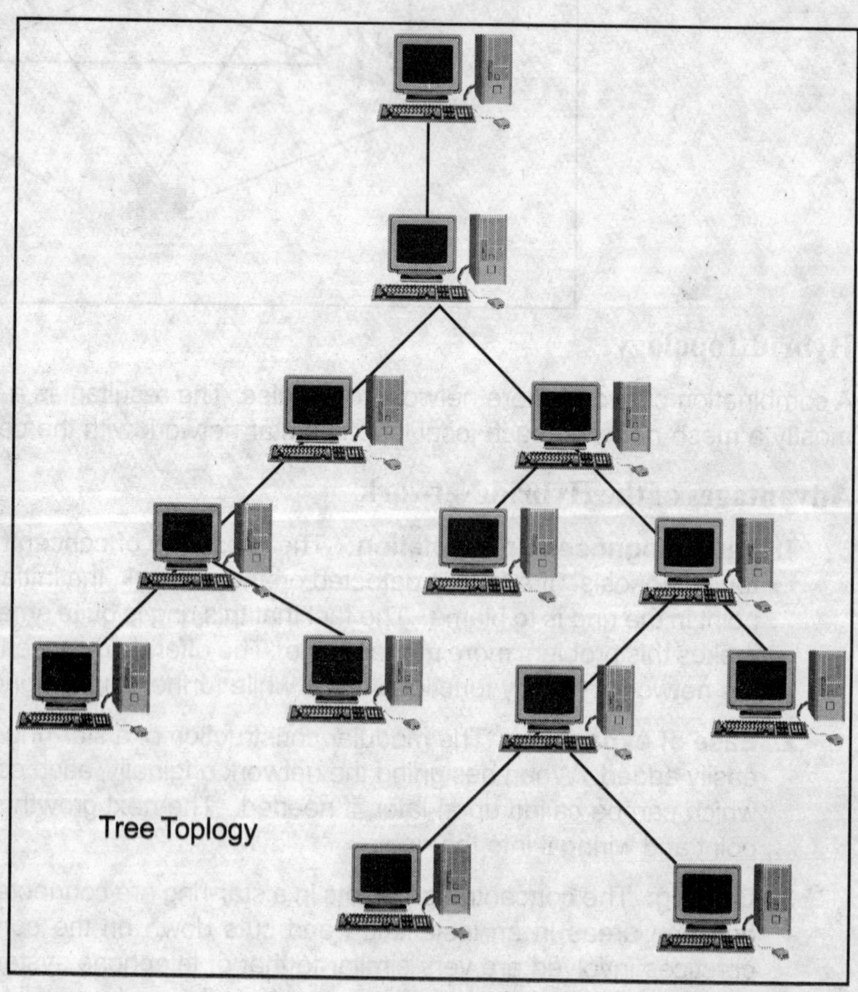

Tree Toplogy

Advantages of the Tree Network

1. **Easy to extend:** Because the tree is of its very nature, divided into subunits, it is easier to add new nodes or branches to it.

2. **Fault isolation:** It is possible to disconnect whole branches of the network from the main structure. This makes it easier to isolate a defective node.

Disadvantages of the Tree Network

1. **Dependant on the root:** If the "headend" device fails to operate, the entire network is rendered inoperable. In this respect, the tree suffers from the same reliability problems as the star.

APPLICATIONS OF NETWORKING

In business, government organizations, universities and many other organizations networks of all types of computers provide tremendous benefits. Four of the most compelling benefits are as follows:

SIMULTANEOUS ACCESS

In business computing, most office workers use the same software package. With a network, business can save a lot by purchasing special network versions of the most commonly used software rather than buying separate copies for each machine. When employees need to use the software, they simply load it from a shared storage device into their own desktop computer. Since a single network copy of the software can serve the needs of large number of users simultaneously, all the employees also save the storage space that the software program would occupy on his computer's disk drive. The same is true of data that multiple employees need access to at the same time. Another major area of computer network advantage is access to remote databases.

SHARED PERIPHERAL DEVICES

The best incentive for small businesses from computers networking is sharing of peripheral devices, especially expensive ones such as laser printer and scanners.

EASIER BACKUP

In business, data can be extremely valuable, so making sure that employees backup their data is critical. One way to address this problem is to keep all valuable data on a shared storage device that employees access through a network. That way, one person can be charged with making regular backup of the data on the shared storage device.

ELECTRONIC MAIL

Computer networking has helped in increasing the speed of the message transfer tremendously. With the help of e-mail, messages can be transferred through computer network within a short span of time. User can send written message without worrying about whether the other user is currently using his/her computer or not. Over centralized networks, the message is delivered almost instantaneously. E-mail cross time zones, can reach many people with the same message, reduces the paper flood and does not interrupt meetings the way a ringing phone does.

VOICE MAIL

It releases workers from the tyranny of the telephone. In it, if the person being called does not answer, the called is given instructions to dictate a message to the system. The voice mail computer system stores the message in the recipient's Voice mailbox. Later when the recipient dials the mailbox, the system delivers the message. A voice mail system translates the word of a message into digital impulses, which it then stores on disk, just as any other data. Later this message is reconverted to audio form.

The Ethernet Protocol

Ethernet is the most popular protocol used for LAN communications. In essence it uses a digital 'packet' that can contain any other digital information. Every computer that uses this protocol contains an Ethernet Network Interface Card (NIC) that has a unique address code embedded into a microchip on the NIC. This address is used by the protocol to identify each individual computer. This allows every electronic packet that is sent from one machine to another to contain the destination address for which the packet is intended.

Every computer on the network 'listens' for packets that contain its own address. When a packet is placed on a network, that packet is broadcast to and received by every other computer on the network but only the computer which corresponds to the destination address is allowed to claim that packet and receive the digital information contained within it. Only a single packet is allowed onto the network at any one time, but the process operates at such a high speed that effectively the packet is delivered to the destination within milliseconds, allowing the next packet access to the network almost immediately.

The Ethernet protocol also provides a means of preventing two computers from trying to place packets onto the network at the same time. When a NIC tries to place a packet onto the network, it first 'listens' to see if there is already a packet being transmitted to and from other machines, If so, then it is forced to wait for a random amount of time (milliseconds), before trying again. This continues until a 'gap' is found and then the packet can be successfully transmitted onto the network. The Ethernet protocol provides a means of delivering data from any PC on the network to any other on the same network at a theoretical rate of up to 10 Mega bits per second. Ethernet can also be used to connect remotely located PCs, but this requires special communications links to be set up over specialised equipment.

Fast Ethernet

It is a new standard of the Ethernet protocol, based on the existing 10 Mhz standard, but designed to operate at the much faster data rate of 100 Mhz. Mhz stands for megahertz or a million cycles per second and represents the operating frequency of the protocol. The terms 'Mhz' and 'Mega bits per second' are often used interchangeably, but this is only true where one cycle represents one bit (a bit being a unit of data). For many protocols, this direct relationship holds true, but it is not always the case and so the terms should be used with caution.

The TCP/IP Protocol

TCP/IP is actually two protocols. These two protocols are almost invariably use together, hence the term TCP/IP has come to be accepted as describing a single system. We will be using this assumption here. TCP/IP is the networks protocol that is used throughout the Internet. It was originally developed in American academic institutions as a means of communicating between university computer systems, first locally and then nationally across America and internationally between universities, that formed the basis of what is now know as the Internet.

It is the capability for being used over existing telephone systems that gives TCP/IP (and hence the Internet) its enormous potential for worldwide data communication. Ethernet is designed to run over relatively short distances at a very high data rate, but the physical limitations of the public phone systems mean that this high data rate cannot normally be sustained, except perhaps over the larger truck routes between countries and major cities. TCP/IP however is independent of the various data rates associated with different communication media and so can be used over both very slow and very high speed systems. Like Ethernet, the TCP/IP protocol uses an addressing system to determine the intended destinations for a data packet, but unlike Ethernet TCP/IP also includes a source address in the data packet. This system of addresses is used to route the data packet across the Internet, very much like the address on a envelope is used to route a letter across the various national postal systems.

However, unlike Ethernet, each packet is not broadcast cross the entire network, but is routed individually using the addressing system to a single destination. This system is known as 'packet switching'.

Packet Switching

When one computer communicates with another using the TCP/IP protocol, it breaks the information it needs to send into 'chunks' small enough for the TCP/IP packet to be handle and then attaches a destination address and a source address. The packet is then sent out across the Internet, containing all of the information it needs to navigate its way to a remote destination. It is a feature of the Internet that each individual packet can then take one of many different routes via the thousands of intermediate computer systems across the world to reach its final destination. Each computer along the way reads the destination address of he packet and routes it according to certain sets of rules to the next computer system on the Internet. This fragmenting of information and use of many alternative routes means that the receiving computer may well receive the packets in a different order to that in which they were sent. It must therefore have some means of making sure that it reads the incoming packets in the correct order.

The job of the 'TCP' part of TCP/IP is to ensure that each packet reaches its destination intact and that the packets are numbered effectively so that the receiving computer can put the incoming packets back into the correct order. It is the 'IP' part TCP/IP that looks after the addressing. Because TCP/IP packets contain a source address as well as a destination address, the receiving computer system also has a way or replying automatically to the sender by simply reading the source address and then generating another TCP/IP packet using this source address as the destination address for the new packet.

Another feature that is very useful part of the TCP/IP protocol is that because each packet is essentially self-sufficient in its journey across the Internet, many packets from different sources can share a single communication channel, allowing perhaps hundreds of thousands of channels to share a single cable at the same time.

BASIC ELEMENTS IN NETWORKING

All networks require the following three elements:

1. **Network Services**: At least two individuals who have something to share.
2. **Transmission Media**: A method or pathway for contacting each other.
3. **Protocols**: Rules so that two or more individuals can communicate.

NETWORK SERVICES

Network services are provided by numerous combinations of computer hardware and software. Depending upon the task, network services require data, input/output resources and processing power to accomplish their goals.

In the computer industry, the following 3 types of service providers and requestor are as follows:

Servers: Servers are only allowed to provide services.

Clients: Clients are only allowed to request services from others.

Peers: Peers may do both concurrently.

Computer networks are often classified as one of the following two types:

Peer-to-peer

Server-centric

Peer-to-Peer Networks

This type of networks allow any entity to both request and provide network services. Peer-to-peer network software is designed so that peers perform the same or similar functions for each other.

Server-Centric Networks

This network involves strictly defined roles. By definition, a server-centric network places restrictions upon which entity may make requests or service them. Currently, the most popular personal computer networks are server-centric.

TRANSMISSION MEDIA

It is the pathway by which networked entities use to contact each other. Computer transmission media includes cable and wireless technologies that allow networked devices to contact each other. Transmission media cannot guarantee that other network devices will understand a message. It can, however, guarantee a message delivery path.

PROTOCOLS

A protocol can be one rule or a complete set of rules and standards that allow different devices to hold conversations. For example, human communication would be impossible without language, grammar and cultural rules. The following is an example of set of rules and standards in which network service requesters and service providers can communicate:

- How is the transmission media physically set up?
- How do network entities contact one another?
- How do network entities know how much data can be transmitted?
- How are network entities guaranteed that a message has been received correctly?
- How is a message passed to the intended recipient(s)?
- How are bits transmitted on the media?
- How do network entities, with disparate languages, communicate?
- How do network entities know when to transmit data?

When you formally agree that you will both use the same language in future communications, you have established a communication protocol.

VALUE ADDED NETWORKS

Another type of network is the value added network. This is an established data communication network that owns a leases communication facilities and computers to manage communication. The facilities may include microwave antennas and communication satellites. The owners design and maintain the value added network. They then rent the network simultaneously to many subscribers, who link their own equipment tot he facilities. Using value added network saves organizations the time and cost of designing and maintaining their own networks. The concept of value added common carriers was important in the development of computer networking.

A value added carrier leases communications facilities from conventional common carriers and uses these in conjunction with computers to build a network which offers new types of communications services and tariffs. These are called Value Added Networks (VANs). Graphnet offered services for delivery of documents, often in facsimile form. Telenet built a network for the interconnection of data processing machines, like the ARPA network although the software and hardware mechanisms eventually became substantially different from ARPANET. Telnet delivers packets of data between computers or terminals in a fraction of a second and charges by the packet. TYMNET offering similar services evolved from a private time sharing network to a value added common carrier. In 1971 the United States Office of Telecommunications Policy recommended a policy of first tier second tier common carriers.

The first tier carriers construct and own telecommunications links and lease channels to their customer. They typically own 50% to 100% of the channel miles in service and lease the remainder from another carrier. The second tier carriers are the value added carriers. They add equipment including multiplexers and computers, to channels leased from first tier carriers and sell services that they create in this way, including message delivery services, computer networks and possibly information retrieval services and computer timesharing devices. It seems likely that second markets will develop in may telecommunications areas. The second tier carrier may minimize investment in terminals by letting the customer provide these. Legislation in favour of second tier carriers has increased the diversity and competitiveness of the telecommunications industry in those countries where it has been passed.

In most countries, such legislation does not yet exist. Telecommunication systems use computer in different ways. Some use them for switching; some for sorting messages which are transmitted; some for processing the data transmitted. At one extreme the computer merely switches the circuits; at the other the circuits are merely linked into a data processing system. The term "computer utility" became used for describing public access to computer networks and in 1966 the United States Federal Communications Commission (FCC) initiated a lengthy inquiry to determine whether public computing services should be regulated. Hybrid communication services must be completely tariffed and regulated by the FCC. Common carriers may not offer data processing services (hybrid or otherwise) except through a separate corporation with separate facilities, officers and accounting. AT&T has been excluded from offering any such unregulated services under an earlier consent decree. Most countries do not have these legislative problems because the state telecommunications authority rigorously enforces its absolute monopoly over all telecommunications, no matter how bad its service may be.

Public Networks

During the mid 1970's the need for building a public data network was realised by the telecommunication administration of various countries, with two specified objectives. One was to provide better services to the computer community and the other was to earn revenue which was enormous. This is the revenue from the switches, concentrators, multiplexers polling equipment, line control equipment, etc., - the various devices used in the interconnection of machines.

Common carriers operate (this term includes the telecommunication administrations of countries with government-controlled telecommunications – the PTT's) the equipment for switching and routing telephone calls; it seemed natural that they should operate the new equipment for switching routing data. One computers were used for switching the desire grew to use them for other functions also. AT&T developed its plans for ACS (Advanced Communications Service) in which the nodes would not only switch data but provide a variety of functions which need processing and storage. The British Post Office created its Viewdata scheme (subsequently called Prestel) for operating public data bank accessible with television sets in homes or offices, initially via the telephone network.

Private Networks

Some networks are designed specifically for and used completely by individual organizations. They are called private networks. The communication equipment that forms the network is purchased or leased in the name of the organization. The first WAN to be designed and developed was the private network, ARPANET, a United States network. The objective was to make the interesting and unique computer facilities available in some computer centers accessible to a large community of users. It has grown from a four-site experimental network to a nationwide communication system interconnecting more than fifty universities and research centers. A few computer networks link computer centers in multiple locations. To operate these multicorporate networks, a separate service organization is usually set up and that organization will take care of creating and operating the network. A leading example is the SWIFT electronic fund transfer network that passes financial transactions between banks. SWIFT (Society for Worldwide Interbank Financial Transactions) is a non-profit organization set up and wholly owned by the banks connected to it. The objective of this network is to replace mail, cable and telex and work for 24 hours a day and 7 days a week. It handles over a million transactions per day. It is used to send money, messages and bank statements at high speed between banks and the transaction time is drastically reduced.

SWIFT connects about 3000 financial institutions in more than 600 countries. Citibank Corp. in New York, was the first one to opt for the system and over 40 banks in India have joined the network. The computer based terminals of these banks are hooked with SWIFT's access center in Bombay, which is maintained by CMC Ltd. From here, messages are relayed to the overseas communication center of VSNL and then transmitted to SWIFT's international receiving centers based in London or Singapore, depending on the location of the receiver, through VSNL's GPSS services. The software needed for the operations has been supplied by SWIFT terminal services, a wholly owned subsidiary of SWIFT and the hardware is being supplied by Tata Unisys, Digital Equipment (India) Ltd. The participating banks finance the system and a tariff structure has been built based on the message, connection charge and annual charge.

Common Network Services

The following common network services are available:

File Services

The network file services improve the efficient storage and retrieval of computer data, they are one of the primary services offered on computer networks. The following file service functions are :

- File transfer – Rapidly move files from place to place.
- File storage and data migration – Use storage hardware efficiently.
- File update synchronization – Manage multiple copies of the same file.
- File archiving – Back up critical data

File Transfer

Before computer networks were widely implemented, users physically moved storage media from computer to computer. This inefficient practice has been called "sneaker-net" (because users hand carried data from machine to machine). Organizationally, it is relatively expensive and time consuming to employ people to move computer storage media. The network file service file transfer refers to any service that saves, retrieves, or moves files for a network client. This service allows you to handle data much more efficiently. The major advantage of Computer Networks is, file transfers can be performed with relative ease regardless of file size, distance and often even the local operating systems. This service increases the organization's efficienty, as well as it also provided access to data and information that were previously inaccessible. File services may also coordinate access rights because of the increased information access that the file transfer service provides. An organization may allow network transfer of sensitive information, but only by authorized individuals. During file transfer, network file services often use passwords to control access to systems and files. They use data encryption schemes to encode data so that it can only been read by appropriate individuals.

File Storage and Data Migration

The rapidly increasing amount of computerized data has caused the development of numerous online, nearline and offline storage devices. Hard disk drive, tape jukebox and removable storage is an example of online storage, nearline storage and offline storage respectively. Computers store data on a variety of magnetic and optic disks, diskettes and tapes. Each storage medium exhibits characteristics that make it suitable for a specific use. Because the efficient use of each storage device requires continuous management of multiple devices, network application are well suited to control data storage activities on different storage systems. In addition, if you are working with high end equipment, such as magnetic tape banks or optical libraries, you can use the network's economy of scale to justify the equipment purchase, operation and maintenance. Using file storage and data migration functions, all networked computers can take advantage of the data storage device that is appropriate for their access time, reliability and longevity needs. As data ages and becomes less used, it can be moved from expensive online hard disk drives to less expensive and longer life offline storage media. Moving data from one storage media or location to another is call data migration. Through data migration, you can set up file services to move files based on age, user, size or various other criteria.

File Update Synchronization

File update synchronization is a service that compares the time and date corresponding files were saved and determines which is most current. It may also keep track of who has a specific file and if intermediary changes have been made. Using this information, it automatically updates all file locations with latest version. For examples, mobile computers are not always connected or available to the network. If you are a mobile computer user and you want access to a file that is on a network file server, you would normally save a copy of the file to your computer' shard drive. However, someone else may access and change the original file in the meantime. If that person does make changes, your copy now contains out of date information. Somehow you need to recognize when changes have occurred and take the appropriate action.

File Archiving

Many organizations create duplicate copies of important data on magnetic tape or some other offline storage media in case of emergency. This practice is called file archiving or file backup. The original file can be kept in addition to the backup copy, or it can be removed from online storage media so that the offline media contains the only copy. When file storage devices are interconnected on a network, file archiving becomes much easier. Computer operators use the network to traverse great distances, saving the organization time and money.

Print Services

These are network applications that control and manage access to printers and fax equipment. Print services accept print job request, interpret print job formats and printer configurations, manage print queues and interact with networkable printers and fax equipment for network clients.

The following are print service functions:

- Provide multiple access from limited interfaces – Reduce the number of printers your organization needs.
- Eliminate distance constraints – place printers wherever is most convenient.
- Handle simultaneous requests – Queue print jobs to reduce the time your computer spends sending a print job.
- Share specialized equipment – share specialized printers efficiently.
- Network fax service – Computerize the transmission and reception of fax images.

Providing Multiple Access from Limited Interfaces

Reducing the total number of printers can save your organization a substantial amount of money having fewer printers reduces the number of devices to buy, maintain and manage.

Most modern printer provide multiple ports or interfaces. However, the number of interfaces is finite and relatively small. Typically, only two or three computers may be directly connected to each printer. On the other hand, a network connection requires only one interface. Through this interface, many computers may send data to the printer.

Therefore, print services allow numerous clients to be serviced by a single printer. Managing access to printers, or other devices with limited interfaces, is a major use of modern computer networks.

Eliminating Distance Constraints

Printer ports are often based on cable interface specification that limit the distance between the printer and attached computers. Network cable systems and devices allow longer distances for cable specifications. Organizations can use the network to place printers in strategic locations throughout a building or campus.

Handling Simultaneous Request (Queuing)

Print servers can often handle simultaneous request for print services. When two users try to send data to a printer at the same time, both applications compete for the printer's limited ability to accept and store print request. Queuing solves this bottleneck problem. A print queue is the part of the print server which captures and stores computer print jobs. Depending upon each implementation's specific features, print queues can hold, prioritize, and manage print jobs. When printing with network printing services, your application sends print requests and data to what it believes is a printer. These requests are actually routed to a print queue. The print requests remain in the queue until the desired printer is available. Print queuing increases the efficiency of network print services by organizing the interaction between printers and their clients. In addition, because multiple clients may send data simultaneously to the print queue at full network speeds, each may complete print request rapidly and return to other tasks.

Sharing Specialized Equipment

Some printer are designed for specific use, such as high speed output, large format paper, or color printing. Specialized equipment may be expensive or may not be frequently used by end users. The economies of scale produced by networking each device with numerous clients can reduce the effective cost per user and optimize printer use.

Network Fax Service

Network fax allows users to send and receive faxes using special network hardware and software. This service is becoming increasingly popular because it reduces the time and paper handling normally involved in traditional fax transmissions. Traditional fax machines use computer modem, scanner and printer technologies to send a digital document image to remote locations. Network fax systems use the same computer technologies and computer networks to better integrate fax service with the rest of the network's print and message services.

Message Services

Message services include storing, accessing and delivering text, binary, graphic, digitized video and audio data. Message services are similar to file services. However, unlike file services, message services deal actively with the communication interactions between computer users, user applications, network applications, or documents. Instead of simply storing data files, message services transport data from point to point.

The following are the message services functions:

- Electronic Mail
- Integrated electronic mail and voice mail
- Object oriented applications
- Workgroup applications

Electronic Mail

A business depends on the efficient exchange of information between different parts of the business and between the business and the outside word. Much of this exchange has been traditi0onally carried out through paper documents, delivered by secretary, mail or messenger service. With the growing use of personal computers, a more efficient alternative has emerged, i.e., electronic mail. Electronic mail is usually used to exchange messages and data files. Each user is assigned an electronic mailbox.

Using the appropriate command, the user can scan a list of messages in the mailbox, display the contents of a particular message, send a message to another user and so forth. To send a message, it is not necessary for the recipient to be present at the computer. The message resides in the mailbox until it is read. The sender may restrict delivery of the message to authorized readers by using a password. That is, the recipient must "sign" for the message by typing his or her identifying password. Many other features of standard mail delivery are implemented in electronic mail systems. For example, mail can be forwarded, stored for delayed delivery and sent to anyone at a particular phone number. In addition, electronic mail systems implement many new features. An electronic mail system can deliver copies of a message to all individuals listed in a certain file. It also allow merging of standard data (from a data file) with a particular message. Now-a-days, several companies have started subscription to electronic mail services. These services are accessed through a modem and allow users to communicate with other subscribers to the service. The service may also accept a message and transmit it to its destination city. There the message is printed out and delivered with the next day's mail. This technique can be used to communicate with people who are not subscribers to the network.

Integrated Electronic Mail and Voice Mail

Message services that integrate E-Mail and voice mail are also being developed. Voice mail is a service offered by specialized computer hardware and software that answers telephone calls and records audio messaged. Because voice mail systems are simply specialized computers, thy can be incorporated into computer networks. Computer network and voice mail vendors are currently developing ways to make voice mail system cooperate on computer networks. Eventually, user could retrieve messages from whatever type of device is convenient.

Object Oriented Applications

Object oriented application are computer programs that combine smaller applications to accomplish complex tasks. Message services often facilitate communications between objects on a computer network. Messaging application accomplish this by acting as the object's agent, so every object does not meet to contact every other object. The object simply communicates with an agent from the local messaging service. The agent then become responsible for communicating the message to the destination object.

Workgroup Applications

Message service have also been used to create a new class of applications called workgroup applications. The following are common types of workgroup applications:

Workflow management

Workflow management application intelligently forms, route notices and documents among network clients. These service providers are designed to handle multiuser distributed business processes. For example, assume that you want to convert a payroll process using workflow management. The old manual process required that employees fill out a paper based time card. The time card was then signed by a manager and sent to the payroll department. Upon receipt payroll employees entered the information from the time card, calculated the employee's pay and benefits and generated a check. At each point along the path, an auditor verified that the steps were completed correctly and that errors did not occur. In addition, all of these steps had to take place hurriedly to meet employee expectations and government regulations. Message services are ultimately responsible for making workflow routing and delivery decisions. Workflow management can improve this process by intelligently routing electronic forms to each individual. The form can contain data provided previously by other users that is customized to represent the formats required by each individual. In addition, data can now be moved, stored, manipulated, verified and presented to each user much faster than similar manual processes.

Linked object documents

The computer industry is moving towards the linked object model for creating compound documents. Linked object documents, similar to object oriented applications, incorporate independent data objects into larger structures. For example, a single electronic document could contain text, spreadsheets, graphics, voice and video elements which are linked to other files, objects, or parts. Although this technology is still in development, network message services may act as agents on behalf of the data objects that comprise linked object documents. Conceptually each object includes the intelligent required to pass messages between a document element and its originating application of file. A single document serves as the integrator of the various pieces.

Application Services

Application services are network services that run software for network clients. They are different from file services because they allow computers to share processing power, not just share data. The two other aspects normally associated with application services are:

Specialization of Servers

The greatest benefit of application serves is that they can employ specialized equipment to increase speed, data integrity and security. However, how much processing should be handled by a server and how much is left to the client? Application servers have more computing power than user workstations and they often use special operating systems that have been optimized to perform a specific operation. For example, a personal computer user wants to perform a complex mathematical calculation to create a graph. Using a personal computer (PC), the calculation would take an extremely long time. To accomplish the task more rapidly, the PC sends out the math portion of the calculation to be processed by a mainframe computer. The mainframe quickly processes the request and sends back the results. The PC is only required to collect the resulting data set and generate the graph. What would normally take a very long time can now be accomplished much more rapidly.

Scalability and Growth

Network application services can also provide organizations with relatively inexpensive upgrade paths. If more computing power is required, only the network application server is upgraded. For example, assume that you use an extremely complex modeling application and that the application server software currently runs on a minicomputer. As your company grows, the minicomputer becomes overworked and response time gets worse and worse. To improve response times you simply move the application software to a faster computer, or add another server. You can improve the processing power of your computer while leaving other client and server computer totally unaffected.

Database Services

Network database services provide server based database storage and retrieval that allow network clients to control data manipulation and presentation. A special term has been created to describe database applications that allow clients to request data from these specialized servers: client server databases. Client server database applications divide and optimize the tasks involved in requesting and providing data. Depending upon the design goal, the client is given a portion of the tasks involved in formulating the request and processing the response, while database servers typically evaluate incoming requests and return data.

Network database provide the following services:

- Optimize the computers which store, search and retrieve database records.
- Control where data is stored geographically
- Organize data logically between organizational departments.
- Provide data security.
- Reduce database client access time.

The following aspects of network database services are:

Coordinating Distributed Data

Large organizations often segregate tasks and information between multiple departments. When data access is shared, concerns arise about who controls what data and where it should be stored. Network database services employ a tactic called distributed data to achieve seamless data sharing. They divide control over the pieces of the database among the various departments' computer systems. The database management system is responsible for making the database appear as one logical unit while coordinating changes that occur on various computer systems.

Replication

Data from local databases may typically be retrieved much more rapidly than from remote databases. Therefore, users prefer to work on local data. However, when more than two copies of a database exist, organizations run the risk of making decisions based upon out-of-data or incorrect information. Replication creates and synchronizes multiple copies of a database over the network. Presently, the leading database software uses two different methods to perform replication. One method uses a master database, which is the repository of all additions and changes. The database management system is responsible for making sure that the changes recorded in the master are sent to all copies of the database. The second method gives several local databases responsibility for recording adds and changes. In addition, the local portion of the management system must then coordinate adds and changes with all the other copies.

ELECTRONIC MAIL

Since the facility of e-Mail provided by Internet, people have more or less stopped using the post. It has been in fact, named as Snail mail, or the mail which moves at the snail speed. Whereas electronic mail is fast and moves over from one computer to another electronically at an amazing speed. Most of the Internet users are very happy with this facility. In fact, you can send not only the text, but pictures and graphics too.

Most of the offices are sending their mail through computers. No more fussy papers or carbons. In fact, no need to file them too. All is stored in computers and can be accessed whenever needed. All you need is to open an e-mail account and start mailing your letters even if you do not have a computer. You can send the mail using your account number from any Cyber cafe too.

So to work with e-mail you must have an account of your own. For this, as already mentioned in the earlier chapter, each popular search engine allows you to open an e-mail account. Here, in our case, I am using the account opening process of Hotmail.com.

Opening of E-mail account

The following are the popular sites which allow you to open an e-mail account:

Yahoo	http://www.mail.yahoo.com
Hotmail	http://www.hotmail.com
Rediff	http://www.deiff.com
Mailcity	http://www.mailcity.com

Besides these most of your ISPs would allow you to open an account. Please remember that these e-mail services are all free and the sites do not charge any amount for using the same.

The following dialog boxes would show you how to create your own e-mail account with hotmail.

E-mail organization

With reference to the e-mail program named Outlook Express, the messages in the software can be roughly organized in the following folders:

Inbox	For all incoming messages

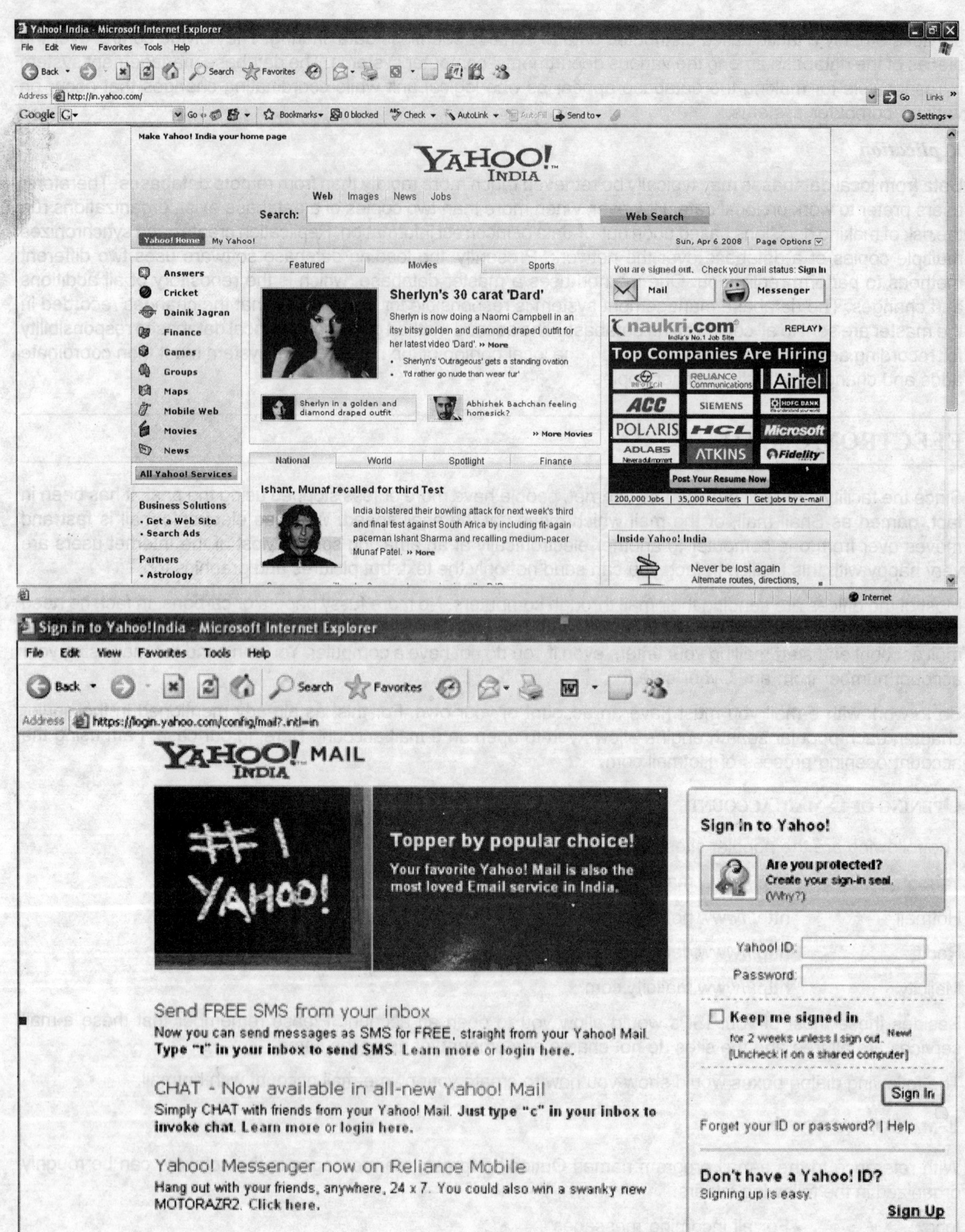
Yahoo! India - Microsoft Internet Explorer
Make Yahoo! India your home page
YAHOO! INDIA
Web Images News Jobs
Search:
Web Search
Sherlyn's 30 carat 'Dard'
Sherlyn is now doing a Naomi Campbell in an itsy bitsy golden and diamond draped outfit for her latest video 'Dard'. » More
Ishant, Munaf recalled for third Test
India bolstered their bowling attack for next week's third and final test against South Africa by including fit-again paceman Ishant Sharma and recalling medium-pacer Munaf Patel. » More
Top Companies Are Hiring
Post Your Resume Now
Sign in to Yahoo!India - Microsoft Internet Explorer
YAHOO! INDIA MAIL
Topper by popular choice!
Your favorite Yahoo! Mail is also the most loved Email service in India.
Send FREE SMS from your inbox
Now you can send messages as SMS for FREE, straight from your Yahoo! Mail. Type "t" in your inbox to send SMS. Learn more or login here.
CHAT - Now available in all-new Yahoo! Mail
Simply CHAT with friends from your Yahoo! Mail. Just type "c" in your inbox to invoke chat. Learn more or login here.
Yahoo! Messenger now on Reliance Mobile
Hang out with your friends, anywhere, 24 x 7. You could also win a swanky new MOTORAZR2. Click here.
Sign in to Yahoo!
Are you protected? Create your sign-in seal. (Why?)
Yahoo! ID:
Password:
Keep me signed in
for 2 weeks unless I sign out. New!
[Uncheck if on a shared computer]
Sign In
Forget your ID or password? | Help
Don't have a Yahoo! ID?
Signing up is easy.
Sign Up

Yahoo! Registration - Microsoft Internet Explorer

File Edit View Favorites Tools Help

Back Search Favorites

Address https://edit.india.yahoo.com/registration?.intl=in&new=1&.done=http%3A//mail.yahoo.com&.src=ym&.v=0&.u=d28ua7h3vjlk8&partner=&.partner=&pk

YAHOO! INDIA

Yahoo

Hi there!

Already have an ID or e-mail addr

Forgot your password or Yahoo! ID

We'll get you set up on Yahoo! in three easy steps! Just answer a few simple questions, select an ID and password, and you'll be all set.

I prefer content from Yahoo! India

1. Tell us about yourself...

My Name

Gender - Select One -

Birthday - Select Month -

I live in India

Postal Code

2. Select an ID and password

Yahoo! ID and Email @ yahoo.co.in

Password

Re-type Password

3. In case you forget your ID or password...

Alternative e-mail

Security Question - Select One -

Your Answer

Just a couple of more details...

Marketing Preferences Contact me occasionally about special offers, promotions and Yahoo! features. More informatio here.

Type the code shown

Try a different image

4Gb76p67

Do you agree? I have read and agree to the Yahoo! Terms of Service and Yahoo! Privacy Policy, and to receive important communications electronically from Yahoo!

For your convenience, these documents will be e-mailed to your Yahoo! Mail account.

Create My Account Cancel

Outbox	For all messages queued for sending
Sent Items	For all messages previously sent
Deleted items	For all messages marked for deletion
Drafts	For all messages which are pending completion

All these can be seen in the figure on the next page.

Before we start reading and sending the e-mails, we must understand few e-mail terms which are quite useful in reading and sending messages.

Using Abbreviations

An abbreviation would save both time and space. It is important that the abbreviations used by you are understood equally well by the receiver of your e-Mail. So I give here a list of abbrevations which have by now become the universally accepted abbrevations around the world.

Full Word/Term/Phrase	***Abbreviation***
By The Way	BTW
Frequently Asked Questions	FAQ
Friend of a friend	FOAF
For what it is worth	FWTW
For Your Information	FYI
In My Humble Opinion	IMHO
In My Opinion	IMO
In my opinion	IMO
In other words	IOW
In Regard To	IRT
Later	LR
Laughing out loud	LOL
Member of the appropriate sex	MOTAS
Member of the opposite sex	MOTOS
On The Other Hand	OTOH
Refer to/Regarding	RE:
Rolling on the floor and laughing	ROFTAL
Significant other	SO
You	U
With respect to	WRT

Using Smilies

There are lots of ways that you can convey your messages across. Not, only in terms of abbrevations but in terms of small similies too. These are also like abbrevations are finding their way into most of the computers around the world. A smiley is a sequence of characters on your computer's keyboard. For example, the colon represents the eyes, the dash represents the nose and the right parenthesis represents the mouth.

Given below a list of the most common smileys.

Emotions	***Meaning***
8:-)	Little girl
X-(	Mad
&-L	Makes me cry
:-(*)	Makes me sick
:-S	Makes no sense
:-{	Moustache
:-#	My lips are seaed
8-O	Omigod!
:^)	Personality
:-C	Real unhappy
:-)^<	Big boy
(:-)	Big face
:-D	Said with a smile
:-)8<	Big girl
:-@	Screening
:-V	Shouting
:-(<	Standing firm
:-0	Talkative
H-)	Cross-eyed
:-@!	Cursing
:-E	Disappointed
(:-(	Very unhappy
:-6	Eating something spicy
]-I	Wearing sunglasses
:")	Embrassed
'-)	Winking
L-O	Yawning

As you become proficient in e-Mailing, you will be able to learn many more of these fascinating emoticons, which exist in thousands.

Parts of E-mail Text

Like a formal letter e-mail also is divided into various sections. In a good business letter, you would have, date, the name and address of the person to whom the letter is addressed, salutation, text matter, sender's name, etc. Most of these you would find here too but with some difference. Lets see what an e-mail is supposed to have.

Headers

It is very important that your header must be loud and clear for it can be seen and read from a distance too.

To

The To: field contains the e-mail address of the person to whom you are sending the e-mail. If you are sending e-mail to someone in your own domain, you do not need to include @ domain.

From

In most of the cases, you would not be typing this, since it would be taken from the system. It in fact includes your e-mail address.

Subject

The Subject: field should contain a very short description (20-30 characters) of what your message is about. This field can also be called Subject of the Message: or simply message. It is not compulsary to have a subject.

Cc

You can send the copy of the same e-mail to another person. For this you have to mention the e-mail address of the second receipt. The software would take care that the same message is sent to the second recepient too.

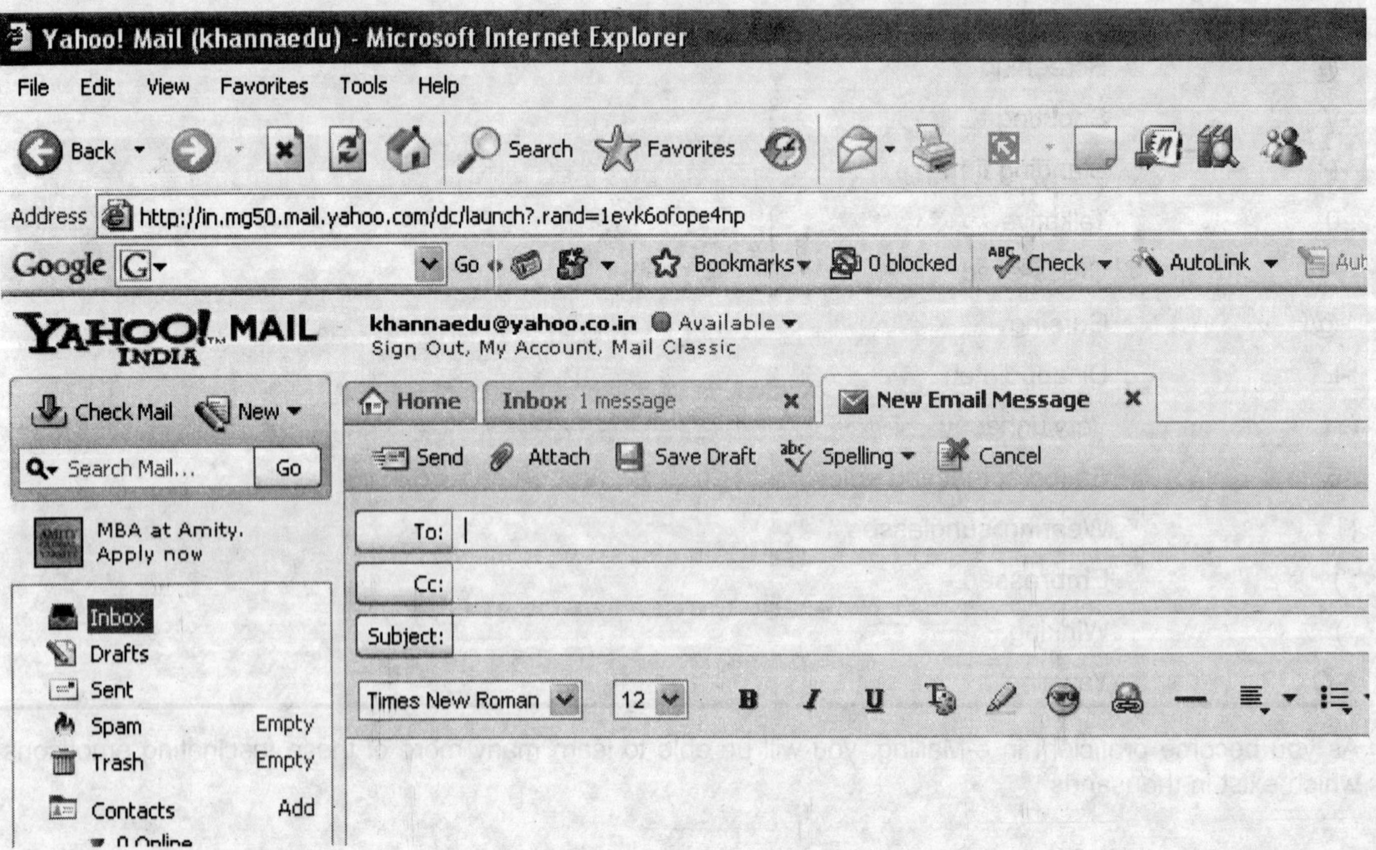

Bcc

It is the short form of Blind Carbon Copy, which gives you a way of copying and transmitting an e-Mail message to another person, without the first person (the main addressee), knowing about it.

Attachments

Using this option you can attach a file created in other software along with this e-mail. In most of the cases while applying for a job, the letter is typed in the e-mail text and the bio-data which is mostly in some word processing mode, attached to it.

Date

Date and time are usually taken from the system. You need not type it.

Body

The body of an e-Mail message is simply the text that you want to send to the other person.

Working with Messages

The first thing that you would do on opening the software would be receive the messages. For this you will have to click on Send/Receive button.

You can also set Outlook to automatically check for messages at regular intervals, or you can have Outlook check for message whenever you want.

1. Click the Send/Receive button on the Standard toolbar, as shown below.
2. The Intenet connection will be made depending upon the type of connection you have. Its progress will be shown to you in the dialog box in the lower right corner of the window.
3. When messages arrive, Outlook asks you whether you want to start reading them. Click Yes in the Microsoft Outlook dialog box to starting reading messages, or click No to read them later.

Reading a Message

Once the messages have been received in the Inbox, they will be appended to the other ones, i.e., in the last. The last few messages are always new. There are various type of messages which are there in the mailbox.

The messages in the Inbox can have the following symbols attached to them.

- Unread message
- High importance message
- Low importance message
- Message that has been read
- Message with attachment
- Message that has been forwarded
- Message that has been replied to
- Meeting for which response is requested
- Follow-up flag

All these have a symbol attached to them.

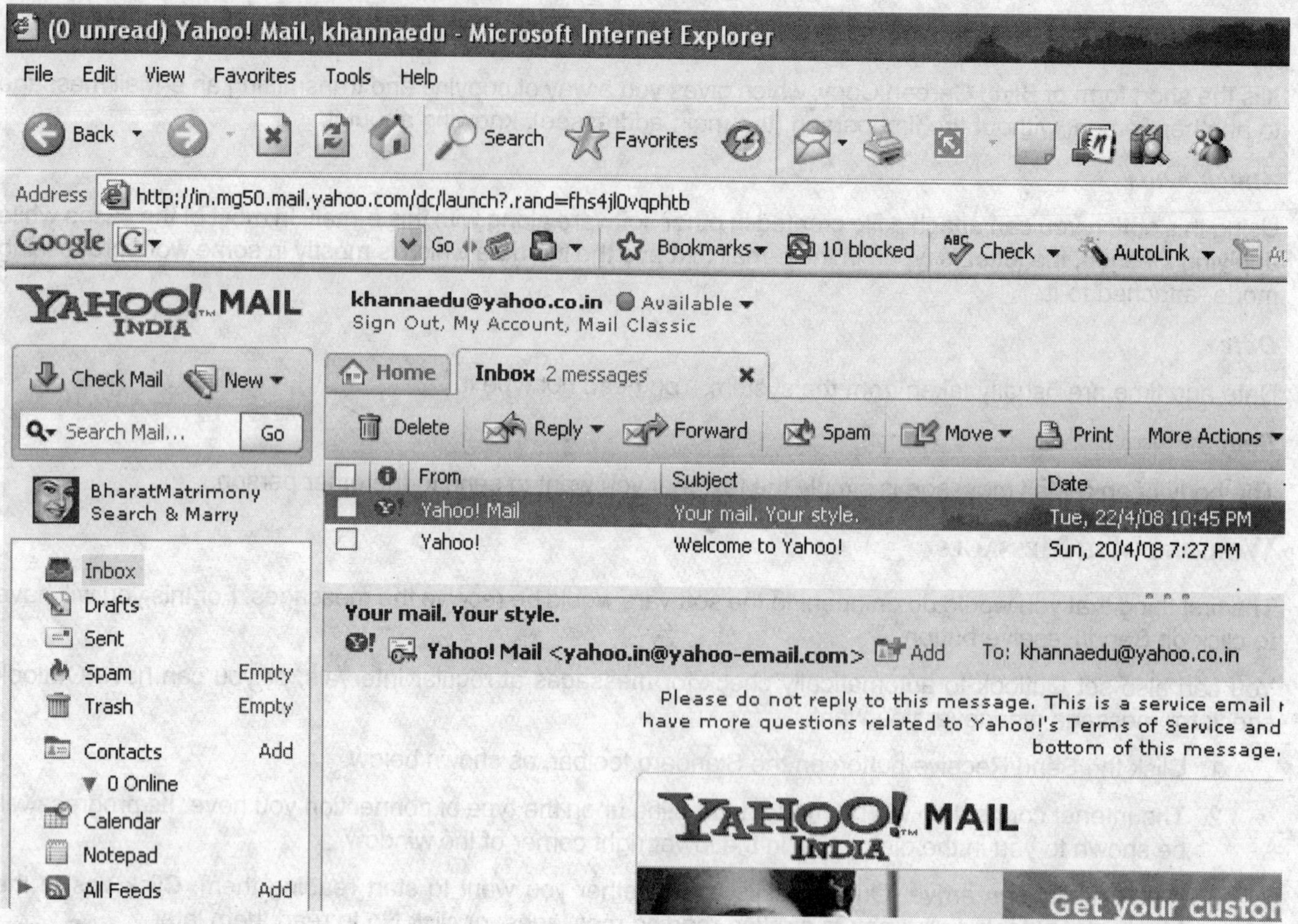

Reading the Message

1. Double-click a message in the Inbox list.

   Or

   Select the message to open and press Ctrl + O

   Or

   Select the message to open and from the File menu, choose Open. Then choose Selected Items from the submenu.

Each message opens in a separate window.

Replying to a Message

Once read, a message can either be replied or trashed.

To reply to a message:

1. With a message selected in the Inbox window or with the message open, click the Reply button on the Standard toolbar. The reply has the sender in the To box and the original subject in the Subject box preceded by RE.
2. In the text area, type your reply. The reply appears above the original message.

Replying in a Phased Manner

You can reply in phases. You can type half a reply now, save it and then complete it later. In this case, since the reply is half baked, it is stored in drafts folder.

For this do the following:

1. Click Save on the Standard toolbar.

   Or

   From the File menu, choose Save.

2. Close the window.
3. Outlook places the reply in the Drafts folder. You can open it there to continue working on it.
4. To reply to all of them, click the Reply to All button on the Standard toolbar.
5. You can still edit a message that is waiting in the Outbox. Just double-click the message, make your changes, and then click Send again.

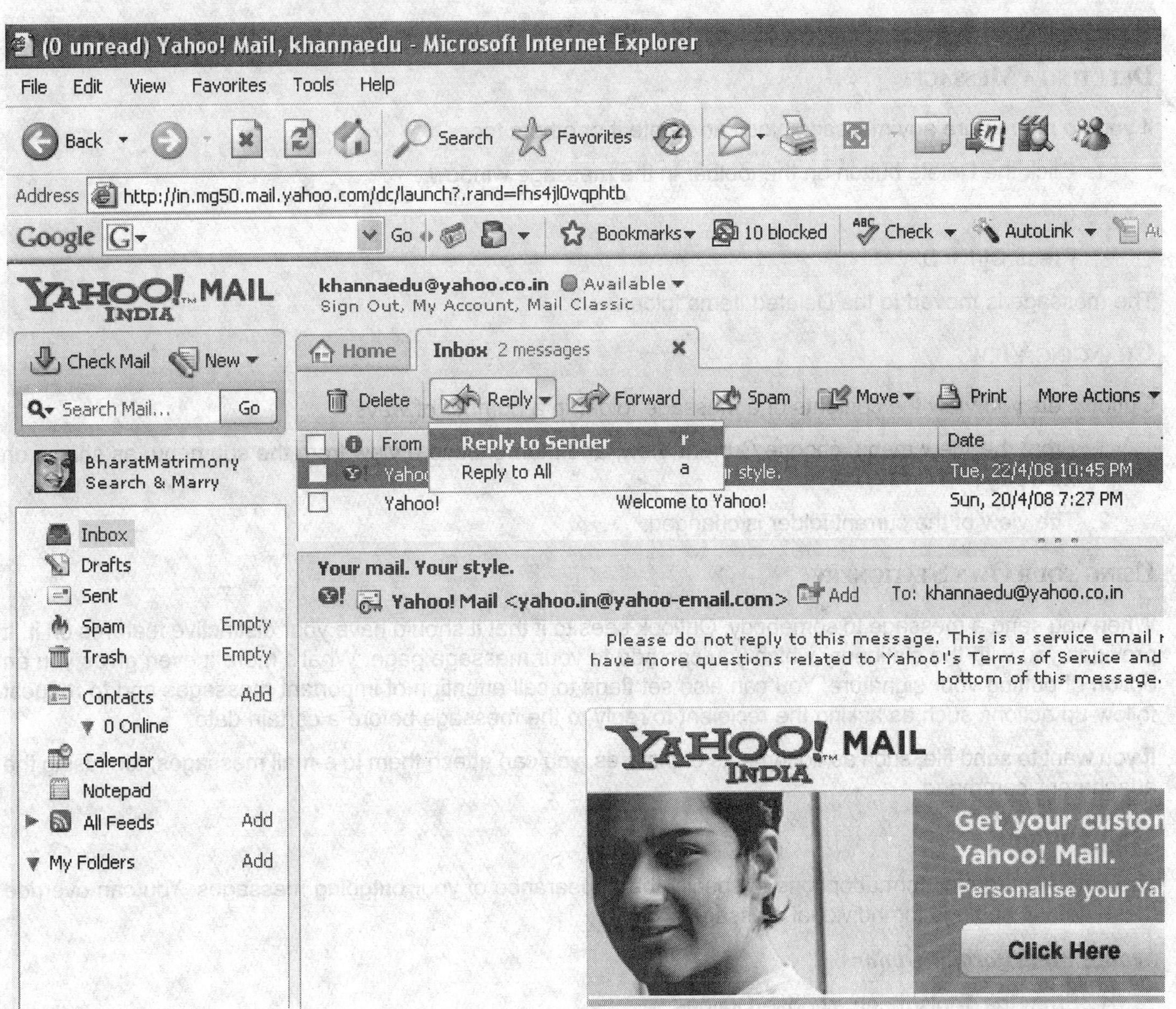

Forwarding a Message

The message received from A can be sent to B by using Forward option. You can also add your own comments to it before sending it.

1. With a message selected in the Inbox window or with the message open, click the Forward button on the Standard toolbar.

   The new message shows the original subject in the Subject box preceded by FW, as shown here.

2. Type the recipient's e-mail address in the To box.

   Or

   To select an address from the Address Book, click the To button, select one or more names in the Select Names dialog box, click the To button in the dialog box, and click Ok.

3. Type comments which you want to add in the space above the message.
4. Click Send on the Standard toolbar to move the message to the Outlook folder.
5. If a message has files attached, the files are forwarded as well.

Deleting a Message

If you do not require any message, you can delete it or others too.

1. Click the Delete button on the toolbar in the message window.

   Or

   Press Ctrl + D

The message is moved to the Deleted Items folder.

Changing View

Outlook lets you view the contents of a message folder in a number of ways.

1. From the View menu, choose Current View, and then choose a view from the submenu, as shown on next page.
2. The view of the current folder is changed.

Using your Own Stationery

When you send a message to somebody, Outlook sees to it that it should have your distinctive features on it. It provides you with the stationery which you can add to your message page. What's more it even gives you an option of putting your signature. You can also set flags to call attention of important messages and to request follow-up actions such as asking the recipient to reply to the message before a certain date.

If you want to send file, such as documents or pictures, you can attach them to e-mail messages, too, using the attachment command.

Mail Options

You can use the mail format options to specify the appearance of your outgoing messages. You can override these default settings for individual messages.

Setting Mail Format Options

1. From the Tools menu, choose Options.

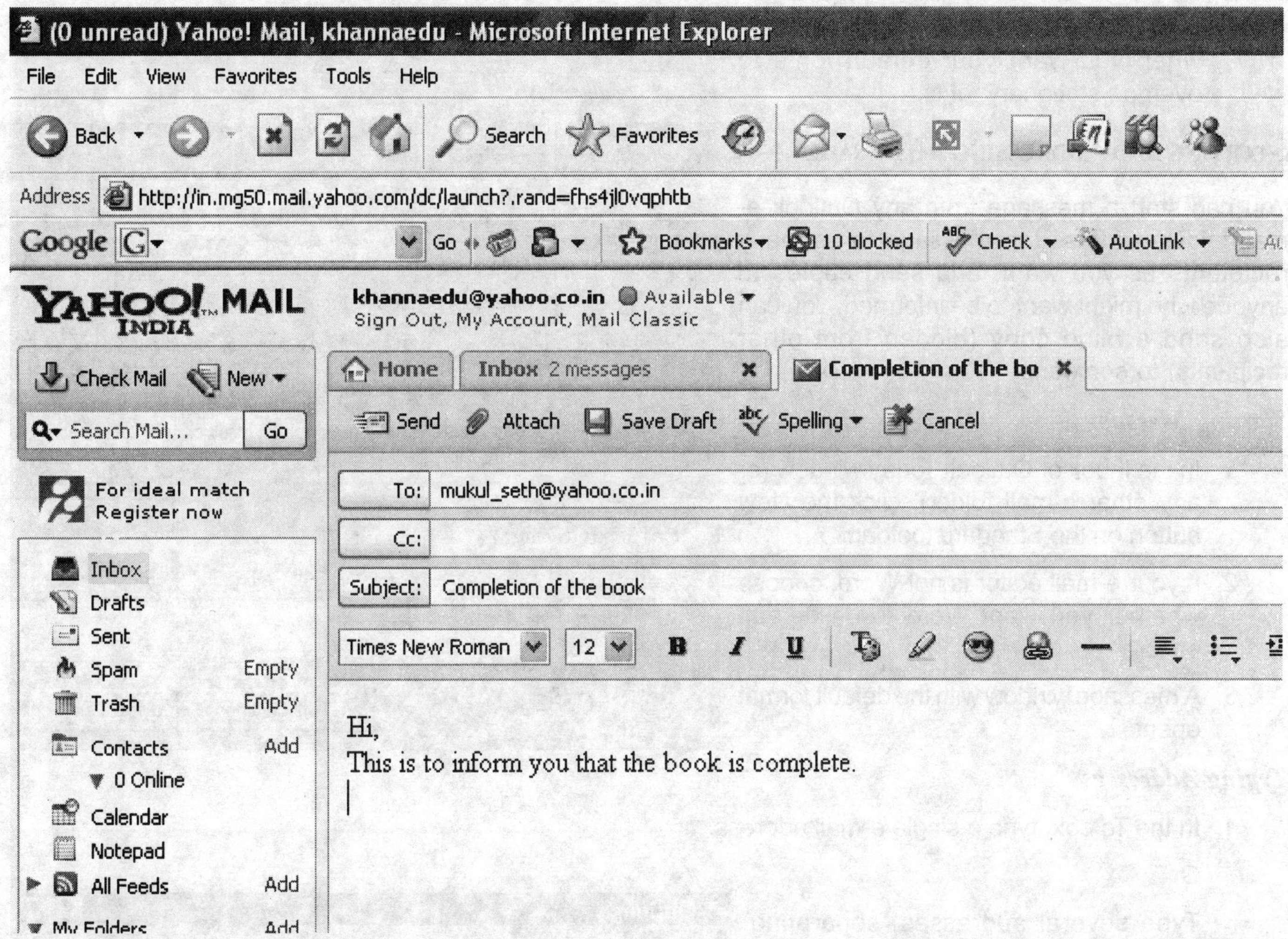

2. On the Send tab of the Options dialog box, choose a format from the Send in this Message Format drop-down list.

   Choose HTML to send the message in the format used for Web pages, which allows text formatting. Most popular mail programs can display HTML e-mail messages.

   Choose Microsoft Outlook Rich Text if you know that your recipient uses Outlook too. This setting allows you to use boldfacing and other formatting in the message.

3. Click Ok when you have finished.

Choosing Default Fonts

1. On the Mail Format tab of the Options dialog box, choose the Plain Text or Microsoft Outlook Rich Text format option.
2. Click the Fonts button.
3. In the Fonts dialog box, choose the default fonts for messages you type.
4. Click Ok to return to the Options dialog box.
5. Click Ok when you have finished setting options.
6. If you choose HTML or Microsoft Outlook Rich Text as the mail format, a formatting toolbar appears in a new message window. You can use the buttons on this toolbar to set text formatting for the message text.

7. In the Fonts dialog box, you can indicate when you want your default fonts to override stationery fonts.

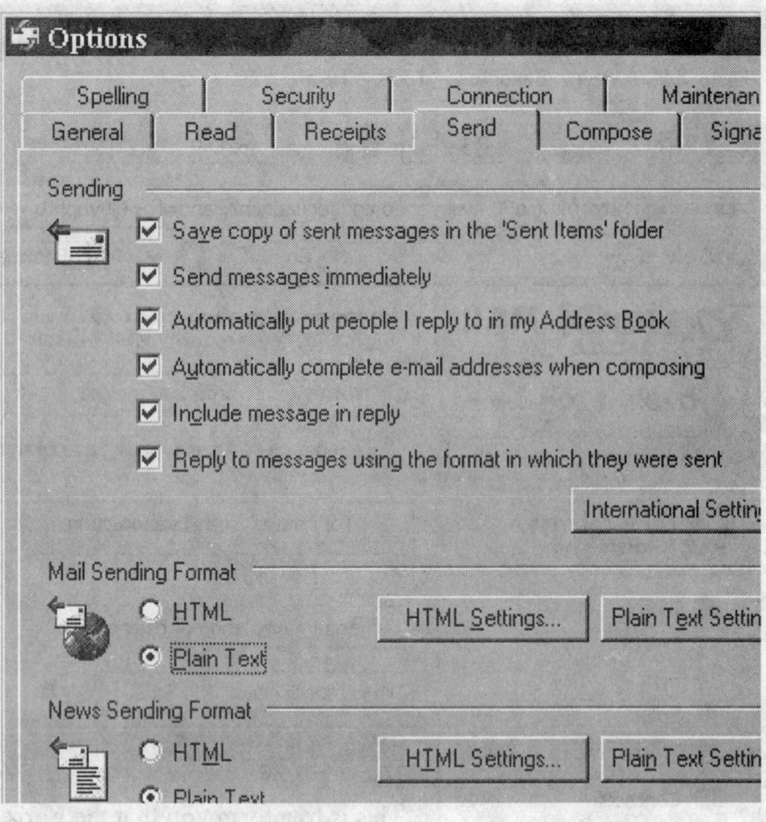

Starting and Addressing a Message

You can start a message from any Outlook e-mail folder, address the message to as many recipients as you want, and send copies to anyone who might want to be informed. You can also send a blind copy (hidden from other recipients) to someone.

Starting Message

1. In the Inbox or Outlook Today window (or any other e-mail folder), click the New button on the Standard toolbar.
2. If your e-mail editor is not Word, choose whether you want Word to be default editor.
3. A message window with the default format opens.

Typing Addresses

1. In the To box, type a single e-mail address.

   Or

   Type several addresses, separating them by commas or semicolons.

Using Address Book

1. Click the To or the Cc button to choose from the Address Book.
2. Choose a name in the Select Names dialog box and click the To, Cc, or Bcc button to add the name.
3. When you have finished adding names, click Ok to return to the new message.
4. If you want others to receive a copy of this message, you can add e-mail addresses in the Cc box as well.
5. To verify that you have typed an e-mail address properly, click the Check Name button on the Standard toolbar. Outlook checks the address against the Address Book and warns you if no match is found.
6. If you want to display the Bcc field, choose Bcc field from the View menu.

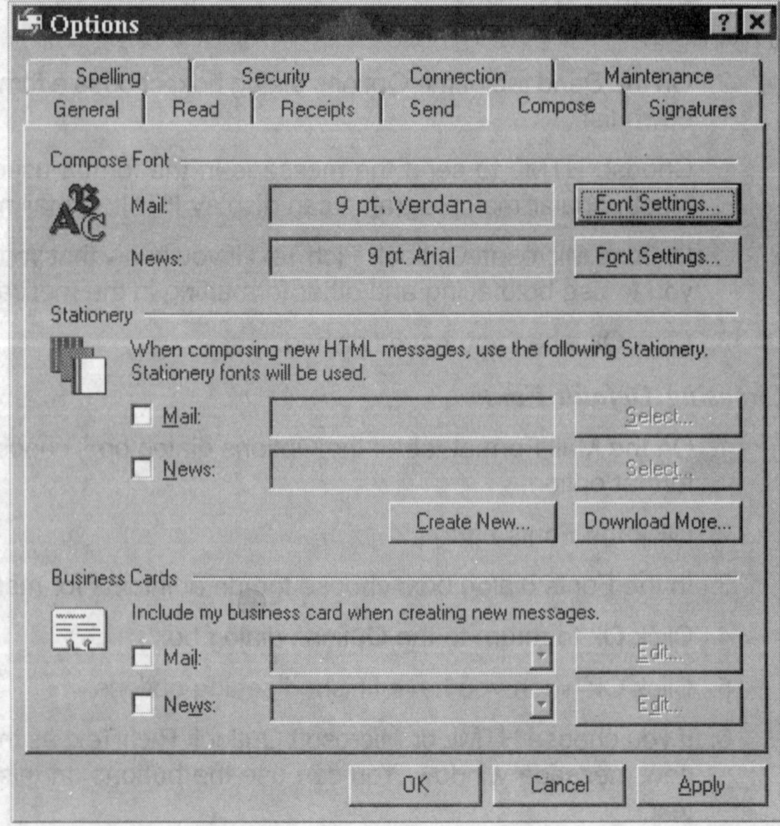

7. For help finding a name, click the Find button in the Select Names dialog box to open the Find People dialog box.
8. To open the Address Book quickly, click the Address Book button on the Standard toolbar.

Creating Stationery

For e-mail in HTML format, you can choose predesigned stationery, which includes a background; graphical elements such as bullets, pictures, and horizontal lines; text fonts; and colours that blend with the background design. If Word is specified as your e-mail editor and HTML is selected format, the first time you create a new message you can choose a theme.

Choosing Default Outlook Stationery:

1. From the Tools menu, choose Options.
2. On the Send tab of the Options dialog box, choose HTML as the format.
3. Click at Create New.
4. This would lead you to a Stationery Picker Wizard, which will guide you to select the stationery of your choice.
5. On this and next pages, you will see the various options of the wizard and their selection.
6. You can use the same options or can have some of your own.

More Stationery Options:

1. In the Options dialog box, choose Download More.
2. From the net, this would give you more options of stationery to choose from.

Attaching a File or an Item to a Message

You can attach files to your message, and you also attach or include as text the items in your Outlook folders.

Attaching a File

1. From the Insert menu, choose Attachment or Picture whichever the case maybe.

   Or

   Click the Insert File button on the Standard toolbar.
2. In the Insert File dialog box, select the file you want to attach and click Insert.

The file icon appears at the bottom of the message. The recipient can view the attachment by double-clicking its icon.

ELECTRONIC DATA INTERCHANGE

Electronic Data Interchange (EDI) refers to the structured transmission of data between organizations by electronic means. It is used to transfer electronic documents from one computer system to another, i.e., from one trading partner to another trading partner. It is more than mere E-mail; for instance, organizations might replace bills of lading and even checks with appropriate EDI messages. It also refers specifically to a family of standards, including the X12 series. However, EDI also exhibits its pre-Internet roots, and the standards tend to focus on ASCII (American Standard Code for Information Interchange)-formatted single messages rather than the whole sequence of conditions and exchanges that make up an inter-organization business process.

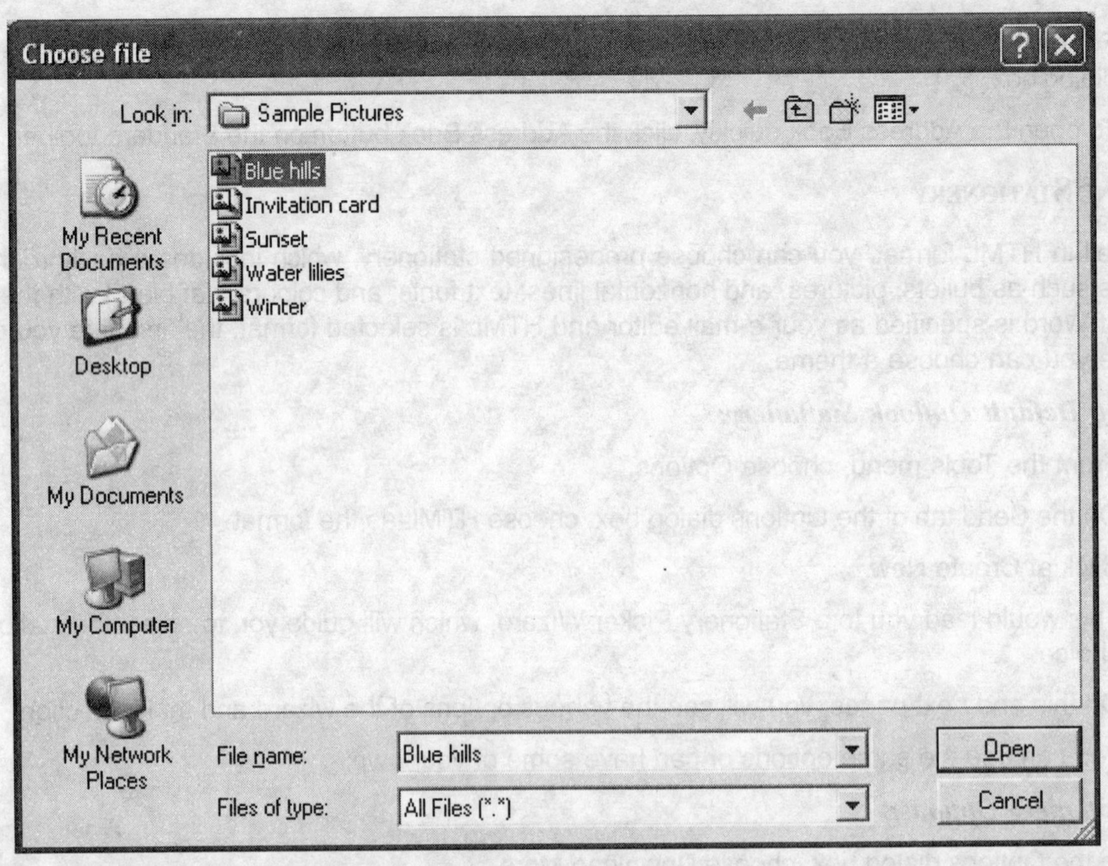
Choose file
Look in:
Sample Pictures
Blue hills
Invitation card
Sunset
Water lilies
Winter
My Recent Documents
Desktop
My Documents
My Computer
My Network Places
File name:
Blue hills
Files of type:
All Files (*.*)
Open
Cancel

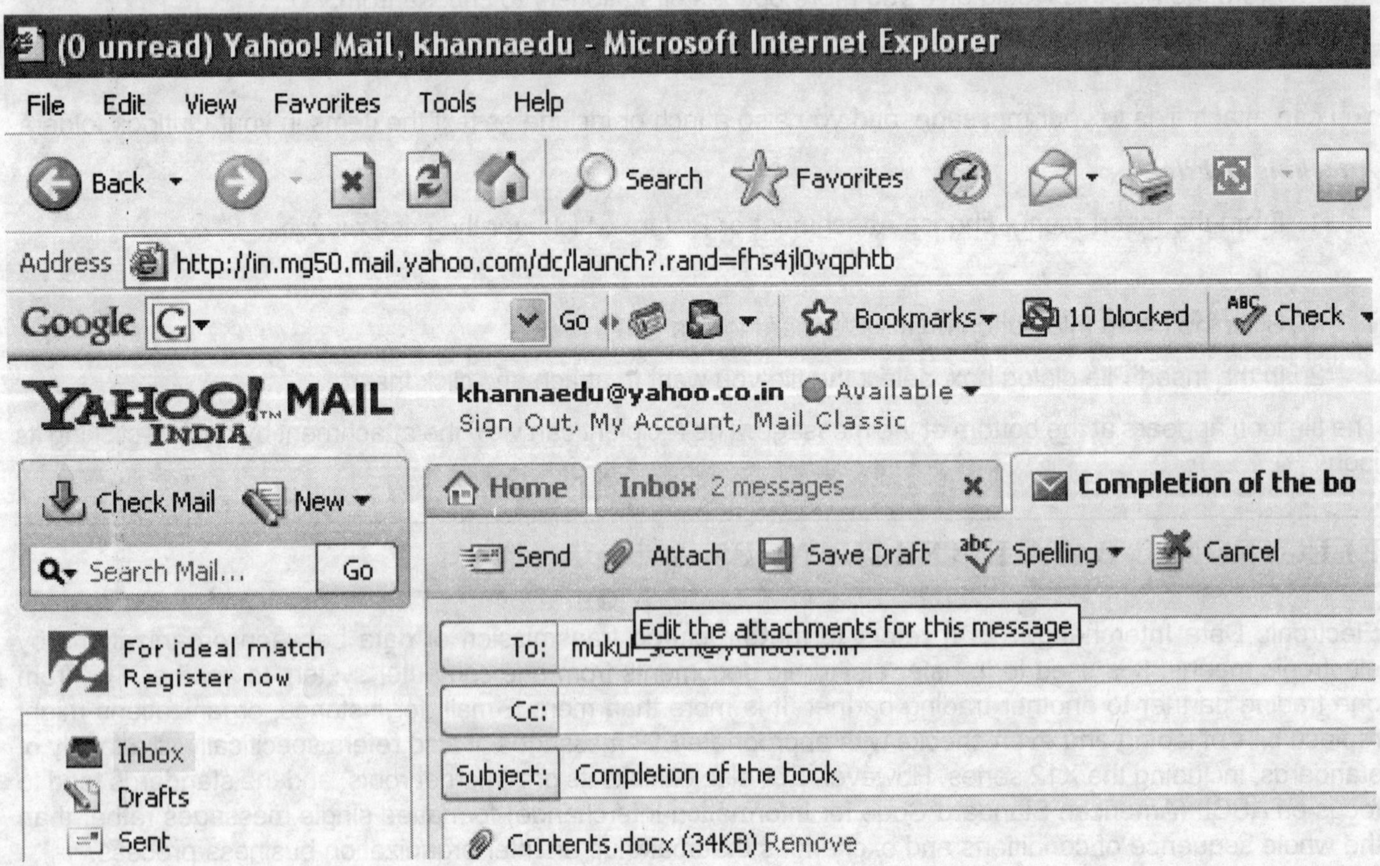

(0 unread) Yahoo! Mail, khannaedu - Microsoft Internet Explorer
File Edit View Favorites Tools Help
Back
Search
Favorites
Address
http://in.mg50.mail.yahoo.com/dc/launch?.rand=fhs4jl0vqphtb
Google
Go
Bookmarks
10 blocked
Check
YAHOO! MAIL INDIA
khannaedu@yahoo.co.in
Available
Sign Out, My Account, Mail Classic
Check Mail
New
Search Mail...
Go
Home
Inbox 2 messages
Completion of the bo
Send
Attach
Save Draft
Spelling
Cancel
Edit the attachments for this message
For ideal match
Register now
To:
Cc:
Subject:
Completion of the book
Inbox
Drafts
Sent
Contents.docx (34KB) Remove

The National Institute of Standards and Technology in a 1996 publication defines Electronic Data Interchange as "the computer-to-computer interchange of strictly formatted messages that represent documents other than monetary instruments. EDI implies a sequence of messages between two parties, either of whom may serve as originator or recipient. The formatted data representing the documents may be transmitted from originator to recipient via telecommunications or physically transported on electronic storage media.". It goes on further to say that "In EDI, the usual processing of received messages is by computer only. Human intervention in the processing of a received message is typically intended only for error conditions, for quality review, and for special situations. For example, the transmission of binary or textual data is not EDI as defined here unless the data are treated as one or more data elements of an EDI message and are not normally intended for human interpretation as part of online data processing."

EDI can be formally defined as 'The transfer of structured data, by agreed message standards, from one computer system to another without human intervention'. Most other definitions used are variations on this theme. Even in this era of technologies such as XML web services, the Internet and the World Wide Web, EDI is still the data format used by the vast majority of electronic commerce transactions in the world.

Standards

Generally speaking, EDI is considered to be a technical representation of a business conversation between two entities, either internal or external. Note, there is a perception that "EDI" constitutes the entire electronic data interchange paradigm, including the transmission, message flow, document format, and software used to interpret the documents. EDI is considered to describe the rigorously standardized format of electronic documents.

The EDI standards were designed to be independent of communication and software technologies. EDI can be transmitted using any methodology agreed to by the sender and recipient. This includes a variety of technologies, including modem (asynchronous, and bisynchronous), FTP, Email, HTTP, AS1, AS2, etc. It is important to differentiate between the EDI documents and the methods for transmitting them. When they compared the bisynchronous protocol 2400 bit/s modems, CLEO devices, and value-added networks used to transmit EDI documents to transmitting via the Internet, some people equated the non-Internet technologies with EDI and predicted erroneously that EDI itself would be replaced along with the non-Internet technologies. These non-internet transmission methods are being replaced by Internet Protocols such as FTP, telnet, and E-mail, but the EDI documents themselves still remain.

As more trading partners use the Internet for transmission, standards have emerged. In 2002, the IETF published RFC 3335, offering a standardized, secure method of transferring EDI data via e-mail. On July 12, 2005, an IETF working group ratified RFC4130 for MIME-based HTTP EDIINT (aka. AS2) transfers, and is preparing a similar RFC for FTP transfers (aka. AS3). While some EDI transmission has moved to these newer protocols, the providers of the value-added networks remain active.

EDI documents generally contain the same information that would normally be found in a paper document used for the same organizational function. For example an EDI 940 ship-from-warehouse order is used by a manufacturer to tell a warehouse to ship product to a retailer. It typically has a ship to address, bill to address, a list of product numbers (usually a UPC code) and quantities. It may have other information if the parties agree to include it. However, EDI is not confined to just business data related to trade but encompasses all fields such as medicine (e.g., patient records and laboratory results), transport (e.g., container and modal information), engineering and construction, etc. In some cases, EDI will be used to create a new business information flow (that was not a paper flow before). This is the case in the Advanced Shipment Notification (856) which was designed to inform the receiver of a shipment, the goods to be received and how the goods are packaged.

There are four major sets of EDI standards:

- The UN-recommended UN/EDIFACT is the only international standard and is predominant outside of North America.
- The US standard ANSI ASC X12 (X12) is predominant in North America.

- The TRADACOMS standard developed by the ANA (Article Numbering Association) is predominant in the UK retail industry.
- The ODETTE standard used within the European automotive industry

All of these standards first appeared in the early to mid 1980s. The standards prescribe the formats, character sets, and data elements used in the exchange of business documents and forms. The complete X12 Document List includes all major business documents, including purchase orders (called "ORDERS" in UN/EDIFACT and an "850" in X12) and invoices (called "INVOIC" in UN/EDIFACT and an "810" in X12).

The EDI standard says which pieces of information are mandatory for a particular document, which pieces are optional and give the rules for the structure of the document. The standards are like building codes. Just as two kitchens can be built "to code" but look completely different, two EDI documents can follow the same standard and contain different sets of information. For example a food company may indicate a product's expiration date while a clothing manufacturer would choose to send color and size information.

Specifications

Organizations that send or receive documents between each other are referred to as "trading partners" in EDI terminology. The trading partners agree on the specific information to be transmitted and how it should be used. This is done in human readable specifications (also called Message Implementation Guidelines). While the standards are analogous to building codes, the specifications are analogous to blue prints. (The specification may also be called a mapping but the term mapping is typically reserved for specific machine readable instructions given to the translation software.) Larger trading "hubs" have existing Message Implementation Guidelines which mirror their business processes for processing EDI and they are usually unwilling to modify their EDI business practices to meet the needs of their trading partners. Often in a large company these EDI guidelines will be written to be generic enough to be used by different branches or divisions and therefore will contain information not needed for a particular business document exchange. For other large companies, they may create separate EDI guidelines for each branch/division.

Transmission

Trading partners are free to use any method for the transmission of documents. In the past one of the more popular methods was the usage of a bisync modem to communicate through a value added network (VAN). Some organizations have used direct modem to modem connections and bulletin board systems (BBS), and recently there has been a move towards using some of the many Internet protocols for transmission, but most EDI is still transmitted using a VAN. In the healthcare industry, a VAN is referred to as a "clearinghouse".

Value Added Networks

In the most basic form, a VAN (value added network) acts as a regional post office. They receive transactions, examine the 'from' and the 'to' information, and route the transaction to the final recipient. VANs provide a number of additional services, e.g. retransmitting documents, providing third party audit information, acting as a gateway for different transmission methods, and handling telecommunications support. Because of these and other services VANs provide, businesses frequently use a VAN even when both trading partners are using Internet-based protocols. Healthcare clearinghouses perform many of the same functions as a VAN, but have additional legal restrictions that govern protected healthcare information.

VANs also provide an advantage with certificate replacement in AS2 transmissions. Because each node in a traditionally business-related AS2 transmission usually involves a security certificate, routing a large number of partners through a VAN can make certificate replacement much easier.

Internet/AS2

Until recently, the Internet transmission was handled by nonstandard methods between trading partners usually involving FTP or email attachments. There are also standards for embedding EDI documents into XML. Many organizations are migrating to this protocol to reduce costs. For example, Wal-Mart is now requiring its trading partners to switch to the AS2 protocol (Wal-Mart EDI Requirement).

AS2 (Applicability Statement 2) is the draft specification standard by which vendor applications communicate EDI or other business-to-business data (such as XML) over the Internet using HTTP, a standard used by the World Wide Web. AS2 provides security for the transport payload through digital signatures and data encryption, and ensures reliable, non-repudiable delivery through the use of receipts.

EDI via the Internet (Web EDI)

The Internet, as with VAN providers, uses its own communications protocols to ensure that EDI documents are transmitted securely. The most popular protocols are File Transfer Protocol Secure (FTPS), Hyper Text Transport Protocol Secure (HTTPS), and AS2.

The Internet has provided a means for any company, no matter how small or where they are located in the world, to become part of a major supply chain initiative hosted by a global retailer or manufacturing company. Many companies around the world have shifted production of labour intensive parts to low-cost, emerging regions such as China and Eastern Europe. Web-based EDI, or webEDI, allows a company to interact with its suppliers in these regions without the worrying of implementing a complex EDI infrastructure.

In its simplest form, webEDI enables small to medium-sized businesses to receive, turn around, create and manage electronic documents using just a web browser. This service seamlessly transforms your data into EDI format and transmits it to your trading partner. Simple pre-populated forms enable businesses to communicate and comply with their trading partners' requirements using built-in business rules. Using a friendly web-based interface, EDI transactions can be received, edited and sent as easily as an email. You will also be able to receive EDI documents and send EDI invoices and shipping documents with no software to install. All you require is an Internet connection. WebEDI has the added advantages that it is accessible anywhere in the world and you do not need a dedicated IT person to manage any software installation.

Even though VANs offer a very secure and reliable service to companies wishing to trade electronically, the Internet is making EDI more available to all. This is especially important in the emerging markets where IT awareness and infrastructure are very limited. WebEDI is traditionally based around the "hub and spoke"'model, with major trading partners or Application Service Providers (ASPs) being the hubs and smaller partners being the spokes.

Hubs or ASPs implement EDI using email or virtual mailboxes

- Trading partners can send EDI messages directly to a web-enabled EDI messaging site, via the hub. EDI messages are simply sent using a web browser
- Systems that are currently being developed will enable EDI messages to be displayed in a web browser and directed via open standard XML, directly into the user's accounts system
- WebEDI-based users can interact with VANs without incurring the costs of setting up a dedicated VAN connection

EDI Outsourcing

Operating an EDI program is becoming increasingly complex as companies face a wider range of requirements from trading partners. Many companies have chosen to outsource their EDI needs to an integration service provider that offers the people, processes, and technology to operate a robust EDI program.

- People - Skilled people with both technical and business expertise who can support and deliver a B2B program that meets current and future business objectives
- Processes - Best-practice processes for implementing or extending the use of B2B e-commerce in an organization, managing a B2B program on an ongoing basis, and quickly and easily bringing new trading partners onto a B2B network

- Technology - The comprehensive infrastructure needed to exchange EDI transactions with partners, translate business documents between any of the many EDI e-commerce standards now in use, and provide reporting and visibility into B2B processes and networks

Interpreting data

Often missing from the EDI specifications (referred to as EDI Implementation Guidelines) are real world descriptions of how the information should be interpreted by the business receiving it. For example, suppose candy is packaged in a large box that contains 5 display boxes and each display box contains 24 boxes of candy packaged for the consumer. If an EDI document says to ship 10 boxes of candy it may not be clear whether to ship 10 consumer packaged boxes, 240 consumer packaged boxes or 1200 consumer packaged boxes. It is not enough for two parties to agree to use a particular qualifier indicating case, pack, box or each; they must also agree on what that particular qualifier means.

EDI translation software provides the interface between internal systems and the EDI format sent/received. For an "inbound" document the EDI solution will receive the file (either via a Value Added Network or directly using protocols such as FTP or AS2), take the received EDI file (commonly referred to as a "mailbag"), validate that the trading partner who is sending the file is a valid trading partner, that the structure of the file meets the EDI standards and that the individual fields of information conforms to the agreed upon standards. Typically the translator will either create a file of either fixed length, variable length or XML tagged format or "print" the received EDI document (for non-integrated EDI environments). The next step is to convert/transform the file that the translator creates into a format that can be imported into a company's back-end business systems or ERP. This can be accomplished by using a custom program, an integrated proprietary "mapper" or to use an integrated standards based graphical "mapper" using a standard data transformation language such as XSLT. The final step is to import the transformed file (or database) into the company's back-end enterprise resource planning (ERP).

For an "outbound" document the process for integrated EDI is to export a file (or read a database) from a company's back-end ERP, transform the file to the appropriate format for the translator. The translation software will then "validate" the EDI file sent to ensure that it meets the standard agreed upon by the trading partners, convert the file into "EDI" format (adding in the appropriate identifiers and control structures) and send the file to the trading partner (using the appropriate communications protocol).

Another critical component of any EDI translation software is a complete "audit" of all the steps to move business documents between trading partners. The audit ensures that any transaction (which in reality is a business document) can be tracked to ensure that they are not lost. In case of a retailer sending a Purchase Order to a supplier, if the Purchase Order is "lost" anywhere in the business process, the effect is devastating to both businesses. To the supplier, they do not fulfill the order as they have not received it thereby losing business and damaging the business relationship with their retail client. For the retailer, they have a stock outage and the effect is lost sales, reduced customer service and ultimately lower profits.

In EDI terminology "inbound" and "outbound" refer to the direction of transmission of an EDI document in relation to a particular system, not the direction of merchandise, money or other things represented by the document. For example, an EDI document that tells a warehouse to perform an outbound shipment is an inbound document in relation to the warehouse computer system. It is an outbound document in relation to the manufacturer or dealer that transmitted the document.

Advantages of using EDI over paper systems

EDI and other similar technologies save a company money by providing an alternative to, or replacing information flows that require a great deal of human interaction and materials such as paper documents, meetings, faxes, etc. Even when paper documents are maintained in parallel with EDI exchange, e.g. printed shipping manifests, electronic exchange and the use of data from that exchange reduces the handling costs of sorting, distributing, organizing, and searching paper documents. EDI and similar technologies allow a company to take advantage of the benefits of storing and manipulating data electronically without the cost of manual entry. Another advantage of EDI is reduced errors, such as shipping and billing errors, because EDI eliminates the need to rekey documents on the destination side. One very important advantage of EDI over paper documents is the speed in which the trading partner receives and incorporates the information into their system thus greatly reducing cycle times. For this reason, EDI can be an important component of just-in-time production systems.

According to the 2008 Aberdeen report "A Comparison of Supplier Enablement around the Word", only 34% of purchase orders are transmitted electronically in North America. In EMEA, 36% of orders are transmitted electronically and in APAC, 41% of orders are transmitted electronically. They also report that the average paper requisition to order costs a company $37.45 in North America, $42.90 in EMEA and $23.90 in APAC. With an EDI requisition to order costs are reduced to $23.83 in North America, $34.05 in EMEA and 14.78 in APAC.

Barriers to implementation

There are a few barriers to adopting electronic data interchange. One of the most significant barriers is the accompanying business process change. Existing business processes built around slow paper handling may not be suited for EDI and would require changes to accommodate automated processing of business documents. For example, a business may receive the bulk of their goods by 1 or 2 day shipping and all of their invoices by mail. The existing process may therefore assume that goods are typically received before the invoice. With EDI, the invoice will typically be sent when the goods ship and will therefore require a process that handles large numbers of invoices whose corresponding goods have not yet been received.

Another significant barrier is the cost in time and money in the initial set-up. The preliminary expenses and time that arise from the implementation, customization and training can be costly and therefore may discourage some businesses. The key is to determine what method of integration is right for your company which will determine the cost of implementation. For a business that only receives one P.O. per year from a client, fully integrated EDI may not make economic sense. In this case, businesses may implement inexpensive "rip and read" solutions or use outsourced EDI solutions provided by EDI "Service Bureaus". For other businesses, the implementation of an integrated EDI solution may be necessary as increases in trading volumes brought on by EDI force them to re-implement their order processing business processes.

The key hindrance to a successful implementation of EDI is the perception many businesses have of the nature of EDI. Many view EDI from the technical perspective that EDI is a data format; it would be more accurate to take the business view that EDI is a system for exchanging business documents with external entities, and integrating the data from those documents into the company's internal systems. Successful implementations of EDI take into account the effect externally generated information will have on their internal systems and validate the business information received. For example, allowing a supplier to update a retailer's Accounts Payables system without appropriate checks and balances would be a recipe for disaster. Businesses new to the implementation of EDI should take pains to avoid such pitfalls.

Increased efficiency and cost savings drive the adoption of EDI for most trading partners. But even if a company would not choose to use EDI on their own, pressures from larger trading partners (called hubs) often force smaller trading partners to use EDI. An example of this is Wal-Mart`s insistence on using EDI with all of its trading partners; any partner not willing to use EDI with Wal-Mart will not be able to do business with the company.

Examples of Disadvantages of EDI

United States Health Care Systems

The United States health care system consists of thousands of different companies and other entities. In 1996, the Health Insurance Portability and Accountability Act (HIPAA) was enacted. In short, it set down standard transaction sets for specific EDI transactions and mandated electronic support for every insurance company in the United States for these transactions. While the benefits of EDI are numerous and only increase with increased volume, the drawbacks, though not directly related to EDI itself, include managerial problems in the support, maintenance and implementation of EDI transactions.

Though an EDI standard exists for health care transactions, the standard allows for variation between implementation, which gives way to the existence of Companion Guides, detailing each company's variation[3].

Each entity may have a different method of delivery, ranging from dial-up BBS systems[4]; mailing hard media such as a CD-ROM or tape backup; or FTP. Some entities may elect not to support different methods of delivery depending on a trading partner's expected volume.

Due to varying implementation on nearly all points of EDI including contact, registration, submission and testing of transactions between different entities in US health care, the existence of EDI clearinghouses has sprung up. An EDI clearinghouse is one entity agreeing to act as a middle-man between multiple entities and their end-clients, such as between medical providers and insurance companies they accept coverage from. They may act as a value-added network and attempt to conform their different supported entities to one submission standard. One such example is Emdeon. An EDI clearinghouse will not cover all health care entities, though they may cover a large portion, and they may not cover all HIPAA-mandated transactions for all of their supported entities.

Because of the above points, one single computer application cannot handle all health care entities. Though this may not be necessary, it can lead to an obvious management headache as a company attempts to register itself with various EDI partners.

This all comes at a massive cost in time and management as a company may attempt to support a broad range of transactions with a broad range of entities. This example is an extension of the lack of strict standards across implementations, transactions and methods.

WIDE AREA NETWORKS

Wide Area Network (WAN) is a computer network that covers a broad area (i.e., any network whose communications links cross metropolitan, regional, or national boundaries. This is in contrast with personal area networks (PANs), local area networks (LANs), campus area networks (CANs), or metropolitan area networks (MANs) which are usually limited to a room, building, campus or specific metropolitan area (e.g., a city) respectively. The largest and most well-known example of a WAN is the Internet.

WANs are used to connect LANs and other types of networks together, so that users and computers in one location can communicate with users and computers in other locations. Many WANs are built for one particular organization and are private. Others, built by Internet service providers, provide connections from an organization's LAN to the Internet. WANs are often built using leased lines. At each end of the leased line, a router connects to the LAN on one side and a hub within the WAN on the other. Leased lines can be very expensive. Instead of using leased lines, WANs can also be built using less costly circuit switching or packet switching methods. Network protocols including TCP/IP deliver transport and addressing functions. Protocols including Packet over SONET/SDH, MPLS, ATM and Frame relay are often used by service providers to deliver the links that are used in WANs. X.25 was an important early WAN protocol, and is often considered to be the "grandfather" of Frame Relay as many of the underlying protocols and functions of X.25 are still in use today (with upgrades) by Frame Relay.

Academic research into wide area networks can be broken down into three areas: Mathematical models, network emulation and network simulation.

Performance improvements are sometimes delivered via WAFS or WAN optimization.

Several options are available for WAN connectivity:

Option:	Description	Advantages	Disadvantages	Bandwidth range	Sample protocols used
Leased line	Point-to-Point connection between two computers or Local Area Networks (LANs)	Most secure	Expensive		PPP, HDLC, SDLC, HNAS
Circuit switching	A dedicated circuit path is created between end points. Best example is dialup connections	Less Expensive	Call Setup	28 - 144 kbps	PPP, ISDN
Packet switching	Devices transport packets via a shared single point-to-point or point-to-multipoint link across a carrier internetwork. Variable length packets are transmitted over Permanent Virtual Circuits (PVC) or Switched Virtual Circuits	Shared media across link		(SVC)	X.25 Frame-Relay
Cell relay	Similar to packet switching, but uses fixed length cells instead of variable length packets. Data is divided into fixed-length cells and then transported across virtual circuits	Best for simultaneous use of voice and data		Overhead can be considerable	ATM

Transmission rate usually range from 1200 bps to 6 Mbps, although some connections such as ATM and Leased lines can reach speeds greater than 156 Mbps. Typical communication links used in WANs are telephone lines, microwave links & satellite channels.

Recently with the proliferation of low cost of Internet connectivity many companies and organizations have turned to VPN to interconnect their networks, creating a WAN in that way. Companies such as Cisco, New Edge Networks and Check Point offer solutions to create VPN networks.

CLIENT/SERVER COMPUTING AND DATABASE

There has been lot of talks about Client/Server computing. But, before we go further at seeing what it does, let us first understand what this Client Server Computing is.

Client/Server

What is Client/Server? Frankly even I do not have a definite definition for it. It is not that I do not have one definition, in fact, there is no definite definition of Client Server. Maximum you can say is that this type of computing allows you to serve clients. This can be said in terms of networking that clients and servers are separate logical entities that work together over a network to accomplish a task. In any case client/server systems have the following distinguishing characteristics:

Asymmetrical protocols

There is many-to one relationship between clients and server. Clients always initiate the dialog by requesting a service. Servers are passively awaiting request from the clients.

Encapsulation of services

The server is a "specialist." A message tells a server what services are requested; it is then unto the server to determine how to get the job done.

Services can be upgraded without affecting the clients as long as the published message interface is not changed.

server data is centrally maintained. Which results in cheaper maintenance and the guarding of shared data integrity? At the same time, the clients remain personal and independent.

Message-based-Exchanges

Clients and servers are loosely coupled systems that interact though a message-passing mechanism. The message is the delivery mechanism for the service requests and replies.

Mix-and-match

The idea client/server software is independent of hardware or operating system software platforms. You should be able to mix-and-match client and server platforms.

Scalability

Client/server systems can be scaled horizontally or vertically. Horizontally scaling means adding or removing client workstations with only a slight performance impact. Vertical scaling means migrating to a larger and faster server machine or multiservers.

Service

Client/server is primarily a relationship between processes running on separate machines. The server is a provider of services. The client is a consumer of services. In essence, client/ server a clean separation of function based on the idea of service.

Shared resources

A server can service many clients at the same time and regulate their access to shared resources.

Transparency of location

The server is a process that can reside on the same machine as the client or on a different machine across a network. Client/server software usually masks the location of the server from the client by redirecting the service calls when needed. A program can be a client, a server, or both.

The client/server characteristics described here allow intelligence to be easily distributed across a network. These features also provide a framework for the design of loosely coupled, network based applications.

WHAT IS REAL CLIENT/SERVER?

As mentioned above that there is fixed definition of Client Server. Similarly there is fixed configuration for a client server computer system. Vendors often use client/server as if the term can only be applied to their specific packages. For example, file server vendors swear they first invented the term and databases server vendor is known in some circles solely as the client/server vendors. The idea of splitting an application along client/server lines has been used over the last ten years to create various forms of Local Area Network (LAN) software solutions. Typically, these solutions sell as shrink-wrapped software packages and many are sold by more than one vendor.

Each of these solutions, however, is distinguished by the nature of the service it provides to its clients, as shown in the following sections.

FILE SERVERS

Computers which allow the files to be shared across the network are called file servers. They provide controlled access to files and usually have some method of determining which user have access to which files and other system resources. But, how it is done. Well, the main source for this is software.

The particular machine that is used for a file server might be a standard PC of any type, a minicomputer, or specialized proprietary computer designed specifically as a file server. In any case, it is the software running in that machine that defines it as a file server. The primary purpose of the file server software is to synchronize access to shared resources. This means the server software in cooperation with applications programs, makes sure that users have simultaneous file access where appropriate, while preventing simultaneous access where it is inappropriate. File server can also provide various levels of security and access control, allowing a system manager to designate who has access to what resources.

In this area there are vast differences in capabilities among various file server systems, the efficiency and sophistication of a file server's data management and retrieval vary widely from one network operating system to another. High-speed disk access techniques use a disk caching (keeping recently requested data blocks in server memory) and use of proprietary disk file structures are among the methods used to increase data retrieval speed.

Servers can be divided into the following categories:

Dedicated Servers

They function strictly as servers and are not available as user workstations. Dedicated servers generally provide better performance and system integrity than non-dedicated servers.

Generic Servers

These are usually industry standard mini or microcomputers. For PC LANs, 80386 and 80486 based personal computers are commonly used as file servers. Generic servers often offer greater flexibility than proprietary servers.

Non-Dedicated Servers

They function as user workstations as well as file servers. Although most manufacturers provide for non-dedicated servers, performance and system integrity issues can make this a risky approach. Users and application can easily lock up a non-dedicated server. Non-dedicated servers can sometimes provide hardware cost savings, but these savings are often quickly offset by the increased requires to resolve problems. Non-dedicated servers almost always compromise system reliability.

Proprietary Servers

These machines are designed specifically to be used as network severs for particular vendor's LAN system. They often provide high performance than generic servers because of features tailored to a server's needs. To their disadvantage, they usually operate only with a specific vendor's LAN hardware and operating system and are usually more expensive than their generic counterparts. Novell, Banyan and 3 Com have provided proprietary servers in the past, but have move towards generic platforms.

Super Servers

They are computers designed specifically to be network servers, but which are not specific one vendor's LAN operating system. Super servers usually provide certain enhancements, such as multiple processors, fault-tolerant or high-performance disk systems. Compaq, NetFrame, Dell, Tricord and Evered, among others, all provide machines that fall into this category.

Various File Servers

File Service can be provided as task running under another operating system. Microsoft takes this approach with LAN Manager, which runs as a task under OS/2 and Novell takes this approach with NetWare VMS for DEC VAXes and portable NetWare for Unix computers. With this approach performance is generally sacrificed to obtain the benefits of connectivity between dissimilar systems.

Batch-Processing Servers

Batch processing servers allow time consuming tasks, such as reports to be off-loaded from a user's machine to an idle LAN workstations, allowing the user to continue working while the batch processing handles the off loaded tasks. Third- party products, such as Campbell Software's Bobware Job Server provide this capability.

Central File-Server Systems

Most high-end LAN systems use a central file server approach. One or more computers on the LAN are specifically designed as file servers and generally run operating systems specifically designed or the file service tasks. Although hardware costs for central-server systems are usually higher than peer-to-peer systems, the added performance, security, system integrity and ease of maintenance more than make up for the increased cost, especially in larger systems.

Communication Servers

These provide connection between client computers on a LAN and off-LAN services or provide access to LAN resources from off-LAN systems. For example, communication servers provide LAN users with terminal emulation and access to time-sharing computers, connections to remote systems, or dial-in access from remote PCs. Like file and print servers, communication servers can be dedicated or non-dedicated, depending on the particular communication server product. Communications service can also be a task on a network file server (again, depending on the particular product). Although communications services can be integrated into the file server operating system (Banyan VINES uses this approach), usually they are not.

Communication servers include the following:

- Host Gateways allow multiple LAN clients to access a time-sharing computer via a single connection to the LAN.
- Asynchronous communication servers allows multiple LAN users to share a pool of dial-out modems or asynchronous connection to host computers.
- Remote access servers allow remote PCs or terminals to access LAN resources via dial up phone lines or leased lines.

Database Servers

These can be divided into 3 primary components: Development tools, User interface and Database engine. The database engine does all the selecting, sorting and updating. Currently, most DBMS combine the interface software to run on each user's PC (the client) and running the database engine in a separate machine (the database server) shared by all users. This approach can increase databases performances as well as overall LAN performance because only selected records are transmitted to the user's PC, not large blocks of files.

However, because the database engine must handle multiple requests, the database server itself can become a bottleneck when a larger number of requests are pending. Database servers offer real potential for remote database access and distributed databases. Because the database server only returns selected database record(s) to the client machine (instead of large blocks of data), remote access over relatively slow telephone lines can provide acceptable performance.

In addition, a client computer can make requests of multiple servers regardless of physical location.

Facsimile Servers

FAX servers (or gateways) give multiple LAN workstations the ability to send and receive FAXes through a single network connection. The FAX server can be workstation with an installed FAX board and special software or a specialized device designed for fax service.

Groupware Servers

Groupware addresses the management of semi-structured information such as text, image, mail, bulletin boards and the flow of work. These client/server systems place people in direct contact with other people. Lotus Notes is the leading example of such a system, although a number of other applications-including document management, imaging multiparty applications and workflow-are addressing some of the same needs.

Specialized groupware software can be built on top of the vendor's canned set of client/server APIs. In most cases, applications are created using a scripting language and form-based interfaces provided by the vendor. The communication middleware between the client and the server is vendor-specific. Eventually, the Internet will become the middle ware of choice for GroupWare.

Object Server

With an object server, the client/server application is written as a set of communicating object. Client object communicates with server objects using an Object Request Broker (ORB). The client invokes a method on a remote object. The ORB locates an instance of that object server class, invokes the requested method, and returns the result to the client object. Server objects must provide support for concurrency and sharing. The ORB brings it all together. After years of incubation, some "real life" commercial ORBs are now in production. Examples of commercial ORBs that comply with the Object Management Group's CORBA standard include Digital's ObjectBroker, IBM's SOM 3.0, Sun's NEO, HP's ORB plus, Expersoft's PowerBroker, Iona's Orbix, and PostModern's BlackWidow.

Peer- to-Peer LANs

An alternative to the central server approach is the peer-to-peer approach. In a peer-to-peer LAN each user can offer his or her disks, printers and other resources for use by others. This means that any workstations can become a server. Because a special server machine is not required, peer to peer LANs can be more cost effective, but central server LANs provide for easier manageability, easier backup and greater security.

In addition, peer-to-peer LANs usually rely on the workstation operating systems to provide network services and this usually means lower performance than central-servers LANs.

Print-Servers

These provide shared access to printers. Most LAN operating systems provide print service. Print service can run on a file server or on one or more separate print server machines. Non-file server print servers can be dedicated to the task of print service, or they can be non-dedicated workstations. These disadvantages of using workstations, as print servers are similar to the disadvantages of using file servers as workstations.

The workstation may run a little slower when print services are being used, a user could shut down the server without warning, or an application could lock up the server. The consequences of a lock-up or shut-down on a print server, however, are usually less severe than the consequences of locking up a file server. The time involved in dealing with these problems, however, can be costly.

Transaction Servers

With transaction servers, the client invokes remote procedures that reside on the server with an SQL database engine. These remote procedures on the server execute a group of SQL statements. The network exchange consists of a single request/reply message (as opposed to the database server's approach of one request/ reply message for each SQL statement in a transaction).

The SQL statement either all succeed or fail as a unit. These grouped SQL statements are called transactions. With a transaction server, you create the client/server application by writing the code for both the client and server components. The client component usually includes a Graphical User Interface (GUI). The server components usually consists of SQL transactions against a database.

This application called online transaction processing or OLTP. They tend to be mission–critical application that requires a 1-3 second response time 100% of the time. OLTP applications also require tight controls over the security and integrity of the databases. Two forms of OLTP are there: TP lite, based on the stored procedures provided by database vendors; and TP Heavy, based on the TP monitors provided by OLTP vendors.

Web Servers

The World Wide Web is the first truly intergalactic client/server application. This new model of client/server consists of thin, portable, "universal" clients that talk to superfat servers. In its simplest incarnation, a Web server returns documents when clients ask for them by name.

The clients and severs communicate using an RPC-like protocol called HTTP. This protocol defines a simple set of commands: parameters are passed as strings, with no provision for typed data.

The Web is being extended to provide more interactive forms of client/server computing. In addition, the Web and distributed objects are starting to come together. Java is the first manifestation of this new Object Web.

Fat Servers

Client/server applications can also be differentiated by how the distributed application is split between the client and the server. The fat server model places more function on the server. The fat client model does the reverse. Groupware, transaction and web servers are examples of fat servers; database and file servers are example of fat clients. Distributed objects can be either. Fat clients are the more traditional forms of client/server. The bulk of the application runs on the client side of the equation. In both the file server and database server models, the clients know how the data is organized and stored on the server side.

Fat clients are used for decision support and personal software. They provide flexibility and opportunities for creating front-end tools that let end users create their own applications. Fat server application is easier to manage and deploy on the network because most of the code runs on the servers. Fat servers try to minimize network interchange by creating more abstract levels of service. Transaction and object servers, for example, encapsulate the database. Instead of exporting raw data, they export the procedures (or method in object-oriented terminology) that operates on that data.

The client in the fat server model provides the GUI and interacts with the server through remote procedures calls (or methods invocations). Each client/server model has its uses. In many cases, the models complement each other, and it is not unusual to have them coexist in one application. For example, a GroupWare imaging application could require an "all-in-one" server that combines file, database, and transaction and object services. Fat servers, used for mission critical application, represents the new growth area for PC based client/server computing.

2 Tier Versus Vs 3 Tier

Fat clients and Fat servers are also called 2 Tier and 3 Tier client/server architectures. It's all about how you split the client/server application into functional units that you can then assign to either the client or to one or more servers. The most typical functional units are the user interface, the business logic and the more servers.

The most typical functional units are the user interface, the business logic and the shared data. There many possible variations of multi-tier architectures depending on how you split the application and the middleware you use to communicate between the tiers. In 2-tier client/server systems, the application logic is either buried inside the user interface on the client or within the database on the server (or both).

In 3-tier client/server systems, the application logic (or process) lives in the middle-tier; it is separated from the data and user interface. Processes become first-class citizens; they can be managed and deployed separately from the GUI and the database. In theory, 3-tier client/server systems are more scalable, robust and flexible. In addition, they can integrate data from multiple sources.

Examples of 3-tier client/server systems are TP Monitors, distributed objects and the web. Examples of 2-tier client/server systems are file servers and database server with stored procedures.

FUTURISTIC CLIENT/SERVER

Client/server applications are on a threshold to be brought in by:

1. The exponential increase of low-cost bandwidth on Wide Area Network-for example, the internet and CompuServe; and
2. A new generation of network enabled, multi-threaded desktop operating systems-for example, OS/2 Warp Connect and Windows 95.

This new threshold marks the beginning of a transition from Ethernet client/server to intergalactic client/server that will result in the irrelevance of proximity. The center of gravity is shifting from single-server, 2- tier, LAN-based departmental client/server to a post-scarcity form of client/server where every machine on the global "information highway " can be both a client and a server.

The following table contrasts these two eras of client/server computing.

Table Web client/server Versus Traditional Client/Server

Application characteristics	*Intergalactic Era Client/Server*	*Ethernet era Client/Server*
Number of clients per application	Millions	Less than 1000
Number of servers per application	100,000+	1 or 2
Geography	Global	Campus based
Server-to server interactions	Yes	No
Middleware	ORBs on top of Internet	SQL and stored procedures
Client/server architecture	3-tier (or n-tier)	2 tier
Transactional updates	pervasive	very infrequent
Multi media content	High	Low
Mobile agents	Yes	No
Client front-ends documents, and shippable places	OOUIs, compound	GUI
Time-frame	1997-2000	1985 till present

What do we need?

Some key technologies are needed at the client/server application level to make all this happen, including:

Intelligent Middleware

The distributed environment must provide the semblence of a single system-image across potentially millions of hybrid client/server machines. The middle ware must create this Houdini-sized illusion by making all servers on the global network appear to behave like a single computer system. Users and programs should be able to dynamically joint and leave the network and then discover each other. You should be able to use the same naming conventions to locate any resource on the network.

Intelligent Self-managing Entities

With the introduction of new multithread, high volume, network ready desktop operating systems, we anticipate a world where millions of machines can be both client and servers. However, we can't afford to ship a system administrator with every operating system. To avoid doing this, we need distributed software that knows how to manage and configure itself and protect itself against threats.

Rich Data Management

This includes active multimedia compound documents that you can move, store, view and edit in-place anywhere on the network. Again, most nodes on the network should provide compound document technology-for example, OLE or OpenDoc-for doing mobile document management. Of course, this environment must also be able to support existing record-based structured data including SQL databases.

Rich Transaction Processing

In addition to supporting the venerable flat transaction, the new environment requires nested transactions that can span across multiple servers, long lived transaction that execute over long periods of time as they travel from server to server and queued transaction that can be used in secure business dealings. Most nodes on the network should be able to participate in a secured transaction; superserver nodes will handle the massive transaction loads.

Roaming Agents

The new environment will be populated with electronic agents of all types. Consumers will have personal agents that look after their interests: businesses will deploy agents to sell their wares on the network; and sniffer agents will be sitting on the network, at all the times, collecting information to do system management or simply looking for trends. Agent technology includes cross-platform scripting engines, workflow and Java-like mobile code environment that allow agents to live on any machine on the network.

WHICH SERVER GOES WHERE?

You have a lot of flexibility in determining where server functions provide. File service, for example, can be handled by a dedicated machine, buy a non-dedicated workstations, or by a task running under an operating system such as UNIX or DEC's VMS. Print services, database services and other services can all is handled in similar fashion.

How do you determine which service goes there? Here are some factors to consider:

CPU load factor and resource requirement

Consider the CPU usage, RAM (random access memory) requirements etc. that services require. Putting multiple services on one machine may have adverse performance consequences. Also, even with single services, you must make sure that the server machine is adequate to the task. An old AT-286 might be fine as a print server, for example, but it will probably be inadequate as a mainframe gateway or a communications server.

Connectivity

Using a Unix-based computers or a DEC VAX as a NetWare file server is not going to provide the highest performance, but can provide PC users with easy, transparent access to minicomputer resources.

Cost

When making cost decisions consider the cost of lower performance, down time and troubleshooting should problems occur with multiple service that are installed on a single server.

Reliability

Consider the reliability of a service (and related hardware) if you are planning to add that service to an existing server. An unreliable service can cause another service to crash, or require the server to be shut down so a problem can be fixed. If a communications service needs to be shut down for resetting, for example, it would affect any other services running in the same machine. It is, at the very least, inconvenient to have to power down a file server that everyone relies on to reset a service used by a few.

What is a LAN Database?

Not too many years ago, the only Database Management System (DBMSs) that existed ran large mainframe computers. In that environment, needs were usually thoroughly assessed before any software was purchased or code was written. In today's PC environment, however, users often do the bulk of database designing and programming themselves. This approach, while perhaps workable on a stand-along PC, can be a problem in the LAN environment, where different levels of users may need access to a same data. LANs have extended the usefulness of database software by allowing a whole department or company to have access to a same data concurrently.

However, a DBMS designed to be used by an occasional users for simple list management would probably be completely unusable for someone trying to create a complex inventory and invoicing application. Similarly, a DBMS optimized for free-form query of data stored in table form may not be the best program for some entry and transaction processing systems. Before deciding what database system will fit your needs, you need to examine what your needs really are and in what direction they are likely to go. You should realize that the system you design includes the computer system, but must be designed in the context of the larger system that constitutes the office. System design identifies the work that an office as a whole must accomplish, the people who will participate and what each will do and the tools trey will use and the precise steps to be taken by whom, when where and with what. The system you design will change the work flow in your department or company, so the stakes can be high. For example, you will be choosing the degree of centralization for your system.

Some advantages of a more centralized system are that it can be easier for all users to access all data (the "big picture") and it can be easier for you to enforce data standards and security and the hardware costs can be less. On the other hand, a more distributed system encourages people to manage the information relevant to their jobs themselves. This helps avoid keeping information for its own sake. Distributed systems give remote users more immediate access to the computer as a dynamic tool of use to them in accomplishing work, rather than as a system for reporting work that is already done. A system approach that fails miserably in one office might work perfectly well in another.

Factors that influence the success of the approach include the fit of the software to the users needs, the degree of training and support and the fit between the company's management style and the system's style. For example, a system that enables salespeople in the field to use the computer for managing their contact schedules, writing orders and communicating with customers directly will work well only if management supports that degree of independence. If communication with customers (mail contact invoicing and the like) is mainly conducted by the central office, the salesperson "ownership" and maintenance of customer names and addresses can impede customer communication.

If sales and tightly controlled by the central company, this software system will frustrate salespeople and management alike and will eventually go unused. The system implementer rarely gets to start from scratch, nor design in a vacuum. Usually a system is being designed in reaction to the failures of the current setup.

System designers often fail to take into account user attitudes shaped by previous systems, but the strength of strong negative assessments of certain programs or styles may preclude otherwise acceptable solutions. The section, which follows, reviews the kinds of database software from which you can choose and issues surrounding their implementation and use.

DATABASE SERVICE AND SERVER-BASED APPLICATIONS

Software for DBMSs is undergoing rapid evolution in the industry. Database service and server-based applications are currently hot topics of discussion. Many writers and industry analysts assume that database service is inherently better and faster for shared database access than file service and that file server-based servers are better than other approaches. Currently, the standard approach to retrieving data from a networked database is file service.

With file service, a database program running on a workstation PC requests blocks of files from the file server. With most database files, for example, only the file blocks that contain the requested data records and associated indexes, if any, are downloaded. In most cases that portion of the database is then locked to other users. The workstation PC can modify and/or update the specific locked records, then upload the file blocks containing them back to the server, at which time they will be unlocked to other users. With file service, database processing takes place at the workstation. Database server systems split up the job of database processing: each user's workstation PC runs the "front end" or user interface software, while another machine on a network processes the database requests. This "back end" processor is called a database engine or database server.

With this approach, only individual records are transmitted from the database server to a workstation. Because individual records are being sent to and from the workstation, traffic on the network may be lessened. On the face of it, it sounds as if database service should be faster and more efficient for database processing than file service; yet this may not always be the case.

A database server can be implemented in several ways:

1. It can be a separate, secondary process on a network file server.
2. It can be a Value-Added Process (VAP) on a file server, working as part of the LAN operating system.
3. It can employ a co-processor in a LAN file server.
4. It can use a dedicated PC on the LAN.
5. It can be a separate background process on a designated LAN workstation.
6. It can employ a co-processor in a LAN workstation.

All of these approaches can be considered server-based applications and each has its own advantages and disadvantages. Remember, server-based does not necessarily mean file server-based, although that is still the current prevalent usage of the term.

Database Service as a Second Task on a File Server

This is the approach that is currently receiving the most attention by the press. The CPU of the server divides its attention between its file server function and its database server function. For example, Microsoft's network operating system LAN Manager runs the database service as a secondary, separate process on the network file server (that should be using the OS/2 PC operating system). The basic idea is that the file server machine is the "logical" place for database service to take place.

What is not often considered sufficiently in this implementation is the degradation on overall performance that can result. With a slow network, a fast server and little traffic, this approach may not worsen performance at all. But on a fast, busy network, sharing the server CPU between the file service and database service can create a performance bottleneck at the server, while workstation processors lie idle.

Database Service as a Value-Added Server Process

A Value Added Process (VAP) is an extension to the file server software. A VAP performs tasks whose results are then integrated with the file server work. Although tighter integration of tasks cold result in less overheads, this approach can have the same potential bottleneck performance problems described above when the database service is performed directly by the file server resources.

Application Co-processor in the File Server

With this approach, a separate processor board is installed in the file server. Workstation database requests are routed to the co-processor. This eases the load on the main processor while eliminating the LAN traffic that would ensue if database requests had to be sent across the cable to individual workstations for processing. All other things being equal, using an application co-processor in a file server probably provides the best performance of the database server designs available.

It does not use file server CPU time or data processing, it does not add to traffic on the LAN cable and it minimizes the time files or records are locked by workstation requests.

Dedicated Database Server

By using a dedicated database server (that is, a second PC separate from the file server and used only for database processing), you can reduce traffic on the LAN cable and free workstations from lengthy database processing. You can store database files on the hard disk of the database server PC or on the file server. (For security and backup reasons, it can be desirable to store the files on the file server.

In that case, the database server has to update the files on the file server, which increases LAN traffic that was supposed to be avoided).

Background Database Server on a Workstation

Under OS/2, you can use a workstation PC as a database server, where the server functions are performed as background tasks. This would have most of the attributes of a dedicated database server, but would provide lower performance due to the sharing of the workstation CPU, bus and network interface.

Application Co-processor in a Workstation

A co-processor in a workstation PC would probably have about the same overall effect on performance as a separate database server. Because the expansion bus and network interface are being shared, performance of the host workstation could be affected in a heavy traffic situation. One additional performance factor to consider is the database server itself.

Multiple requests and updates must be queued by the database server, while update processing with file service is provided by the workstation PC. With a busy system, the database server itself can become a bottleneck, while DBMSs that do not employ a database server distribute the workload to each user's workstation. A serious potential problem with distributed database processing is that each of the workstations has the power to corrupt the entire database.

With database service, since all database processing being handled by a single dedicated CPU, there is less chance of file corruption. System integrity is another factor to consider, especially with applications and/or co-processors running in the file server, What if a server-based application "hands up" the server?

Applications have been known to hang single PCs and they could also hang a file server running a server-based application. One primary advantage of the database server approach is that a "client" workstation can access multiple database servers, so that physically separate database can be treated by the user as one logical distributed database.

A user can request data without necessarily knowing or caring where the data is physically located; the database software locates and delivers the requested data. With this distributed database approach, available databases could include a PC database server on the local LAN, a mini-or mainframe computer on the local LAN or accessed through a gateway or bridge, or a remote database accessed through a remote gateway or bridge.

Because you care generally not moving vast amounts of data across a LAN when accessing a database server, low-speed remote LAN bridges (say, 19.2 Kb/sec. or lower) may become more viable.

With database servers, you are only sending requests and retrieving records, not massaging large blocks of data at the client PC. Distributed databases enable you to remain central control and empower remote uses and offices. While many database server systems have been announced, few are actually available for PC LANs and very few benchmark tests have been published.

Most of the forthcoming database server systems are based on Structured Query Language (SQL) is an ANSI standard for data retrieval based on IBM's design and specifications. Most announced SQL servers are based on the ANSI standard. Even after the SQL, database servers reach the market, it will take time to create or modify applications to make use of them. In the long run, standardization on SQL servers will probably mean interchangeability of various vendors' DBMS front ends and applications generators with various database servers. The big advantage of this approach is that user can get many different views of the same data, using familiar front-end DBMS interfaces, like Lotus1-2-3, Paradox, Data Flex, Database and dBase. Initially, however, DBMS vendors may have to choose sides, as each database engine developer attempts to lock front end developers into their "enhanced" standard SQL severs.

This would in turn force users to choose the SQL server that runs their favorite interface and that SQL server might not run other interfaces that they need. Eventually, however, front-end developers will provide their interfaces for all the SQL severs that survive the initial market struggle. They will have to in order to survive themselves. Some DBMS vendors have already announced alliances with particular SQL database server vendors.

For example, Borland's Paradox, Micro Database Systems' MDBS III and Ashton-Tate's (taken over by Borland) dBase IV will front-end the Ashton Tate/Sybase/Microsoft SQL Sever for LAN Manager. Paradox and WorldTech's dBXL will work with Oracle's database server, while dBXL and Gupta Technology's SQL Windows and Oracle's front end will work with Novell's Netware SQL. On the downside, expect the first generation of SQL database servers to be slow performers. There will inevitably be problems to solve, incompatibilities and unexpected bottlenecks.

As SQL database servers are optimized, performance will improve. Like the database, servers may well use specialized operating software (and possibly even specialized hardware) optimized for database service. As the technology matures, however, SQL (or whatever it may evolve into) and database servers will come into their own.

Faster hardware, including machines optimized for database service, more sophisticated server software and optimized applications, could all contribute to the process. Much of the commentary about SQL database servers by the press and by vendors is speculative. It is too early to tell which products will prevail and what their practical shortcoming will be, since so few have actually been released.

LAN Operating Systems

The focus of the book is on SQL Server, that is, PC Workstations connected to servers running some of the Operating Systems, such as OS/2 UNIX and Windows NT. The overwhelming choice for client workstations today is Windows. In the LAN environment there exist a few network operating systems: Novell's, Netware, LAN Manager, Windows NT, BANYAN VINES DIGITAL Network Architecture (DNA). AppleTalk, etc. Depending on your client and server operating system and the Network environment.

Appropriate networking software needs to be loaded on both ends in order for them to communicate. This section introduces several leading protocol stacks for computer networking. To gain a rudimentary understanding of any protocol, try to relate it to the OSI Reference Model and identify the general methods the protocol uses.

You can apply this approach when evaluating real-world computer networking scenarios, industry publications and any other source of information in networking technologies. You should understand that the OSI Reference Model is not tangible. However, computer networks actually require design specifications from which they are built. These specifications are called protocols. A protocol is a statement of formalized rules, conventions and standards.

You will also use the terms protocol suite to indicate a group of specifications that are meant to be used together and protocol stack as the suite that is ordered in a logical hierarchy. Typically, protocols are created by computer networking standards organizations and vendors. Once a protocol has been established, the hardware and software vendors implement it in their various products. Protocols and protocol implementations do not always fit well into the conceptual framework that the OSI Reference Model provide.

Some protocols specify functions corresponding to more than one layer while skipping part or all of another. In many cases this mismatch is not intentional. Many protocols were already in use and quite popular before the OSI Reference Model was developed. Note that the Network communications may be possible when using these non-OSI standard protocols, however it is often more difficult for the corresponding devices to communicate with those of other protocols.

Organizations that attempted to interconnect devices which use differing protocols have driven the industry towards open systems. There is much disagreement as to what entails an open system, but the OSI model remains the most unifying model of network communications. Some vendors have attempted to retrofit their protocols to the OSI model or options of it since not all of the protocols cover the entire seven-layer model. Others have tried to prove the merit of their own protocols and justify their models as being open. As a result, today's protocols demonstrate several degrees of conformance to the OSI model.

Still, the OSI Reference Model serves as a valuable tool for comparing disparate protocols, which are attempting to perform similar functions. The Internet protocol suite specifies functions corresponding to OSI model layers above the Data Link layer. The lower-layer protocols are intentionally open to allow the use of various protocols. The suite was designed to allow the Internet protocols to work with diverse data link and physical technologies. This has been one of the keys to the Internet protocols' success. Similarly, Netware suite specified functions corresponding to OSI layers above the Physical Layer. The lower layer protocols are open to allow the use of various protocols.

The Digital Network Architecture (DNA), Apple Talk and Systems Network Architecture (SNA) functions on all the layers of OSI model, which is one of the major disadvantage of not getting success.

NETWARE (IPX/SPX)

Today, Netware is the most popular and widely used LAN operating system available in the market. Created by Novell, Inc, and introduced to the marketplace in the early 1980s, the NetWare architecture resembles that of an early network system developed in the 1960s by Xerox at its Palo Alto Research Center (PARC). The Xerox Network System (XNS) is the basis for many past and present PC networking systems, including those from 3Com, Ungermann-Bass, and Banyan. The complete NetWare system provides file, print, message, application and database services. It is based on a server-centric network architecture through which remote network devices appear local to the user.

Another Novell product-Personal NetWare-provides similar functionality through a peer-to-peer network architecture. Since its introduction, the marketplace acceptance of NetWare has steadily grown. NetWare's success is at least partially attributable to its flexibility. NetWare runs with a number of different transport protocol stacks, links technologies and computer platforms. NetWare also supports communications with a number of today's most popular local operating systems, including DOS, Macintosh, OS/2 Windows NT, UNIX and VMS. Because of the tremendous variety of protocols and programming interfaces associated with NetWare, mapping NetWare and related technologies to the OSI Reference Model is not trivial.

Although the NetWare protocols are modular and layered, NetWare's architects concentrated on providing a high level of functionality without strict adherence to any existing standard model. Therefore, the protocol suite dose not fit nearly into ISO's seven layers. However, since all computer networks must address similar topics and methods, the NetWare protocols can be assigned or grouped. Multiple Link Interface Driver (MLD) is Novell's name for a network for interface board driver.

Specifically, each MLID is a piece of software (typically created by the board's manufacturer) that complies with Novell's Open Data-Link Interface (ODI) architecture. An MLID is not directly linked to an individual protocol stack so that it can be concurrently bound to various stacks. The Media Access for MLID are contention, token passing and polling. Link Support Layer (LSL) is the interface between an MLID and the various upper-layer protocol stacks. The LSL interprets each packet's protocol identification field and passes the packet to the appropriate protocol stack. Internetwork Packet eXchange Protocol (IPX) is a connectionless (datagram) Network layer protocol derived from XNS's Internetwork Datagram Protocol (IDP). As a network layer protocol, IPX addresses and routes packets form one location to another on an IPX Internetwork. To do so, IPX performs logical network addressing and Internetwork routing functions. It relies upon the underlying hardware's physical device address for node addressing and upper-layer service addresses (called sockets) to address the ultimate packet destination within the node. In addition, IPX makes route selections based on network reachability information compiled by RIP (Routing Information Protocol). Router Information Protocol (RIP) was also derived from XNS. RIP is a distance-vector route discovery protocol, which uses a hop count to determine cost.

Although RIP is implemented as a service, it is directly based on IPX and performs Network layer functions. NetWare Link Service Protocol (NLSP) is a link-state route discovery protocol modeled after a routing protocol, developed by an ISO standards organization, called Intermediate. System-to-Intermediate System (IS-IS). Due to its inherent link-state features, NLSP supports the highly fault-tolerant mesh, a hybrid mesh networks. Sequenced Packet exchange Protocol (SPX) is an extension of IPX that provides for connection oriented Transport layer packet delivery.

Derived from the Xerox Sequenced Packet Protocol, SPX enhances the IPX protocol by providing reliable delivery. SPX virtual circuits are referred to as connections and have specific connection identifiers (connection IDs), which are placed in the SPX header. Multiple connection IDs can be attached to a single upper-layer process. SPX ensures reliable delivery by retransmitting information that is not received correctly. NetWare Core Protocols (NCP) Many NetWare server application functions (for example, file service, print service, name management, file locking and synchronization) are made available to users through the NetWare Core Protocols (NCP).

NCP is comprised of numerous function calls that support network services. NetWare client software runs on the workstation to provide transparent file and printer access to service clients through NCP function calls. Service Advertising Protocol (SAP) NetWare servers use SAP to advertise their services. Each server running SAP may identify itself and its services each minute by broadcasting a Service Identification Packet. A SAP user can also determine the servers' identities and services on the Internetwork using a Service Query Packet.

By referencing the IPX header information, SAP implementations identify the service addresses required to initiate a session.

Digital Network Architecture(DNA)

Digital Network ArchitectureTM (DNA) is a network architecture created by Digital Equipment Corporation (DEC). Originally announced in 1974, DNA is now in its fifth iteration. Products that implement DNA are referred to as DECnet products.

Although the name DECnet is commonly used to identify this protocol stack, this section specifically discusses DNA as network architecture without dwelling on the specific products classified as DECnet. DNA has evolved over the years to reflect changes in computer networking. It is complex and complete, spanning all seven layers of the OSI Reference Model.

DNA supports both DEC proprietary protocols and standards-based protocols. Most recently, DNA has been focused on supporting ISO standards that are based on the OSI Reference Model. For this reason, DNA can be mapped relatively well to the OSI Reference Model. With DNA Phase V, the DNA architecture becomes two-headed above the Transport layer. Even at and below the Transport layer old DNA and new OSI protocols are supported, but they are reasonably well integrated.

DNA Protocol Summary

Ethernet Version 2 was first co-developed by Digital, Intel and Xerox as Version 1 of the Ethernet Specification, a 10 Mbps Physical and Data Link Layer protocol. It was based on the existing 3 Mbps Xerox Research Ethernet and has since been revised and documented in Ethernet Version 2. Ethernet Version 2 uses CSMA/CD and Manchester encoding and was originally developed using coaxial cable.

The Ethernet v.2 specification provided the design basis for and is very similar to the IEEE/ISO 802.X/8802.X protocol family. However, the Ethernet V.2 frame format is slightly different from the IEEE/ISO frame format. High-level Data Link Control (HDLC) is a Data Link layer protocol which supports both asynchronous and synchronous transmission synchronization using Physical layer modem protocols.

HDLC defines both the format of data frames as well as the command syntax to establish frame transfer. Using the defined commands, HDLC can also achieve LLC-level flow control. Digital Data Communications Message Protocol (DDCMP) was the original DNA Data Link protocol designed in 1974 for WAN links. Like HDLC, DDCMP can operate with synchronous or asynchronous transmissions. It can also be used with full-or half-duplex point-to-point or multi-point configurations. DDCMP uses commands and acknowledgments to provide connection-oriented error control, LLC-level flow control and message sequencing services (DDCMP literature uses the term message for Data Link layer frames).

Connectionless-Mode Network Service (CLNS) is supported at the Network layer DNA. DNA supports both connectionless (OSI CLNS) and connection-oriented network services (OSI CONS). However, DNA Phase V typically uses CLNS. CLNS is supported through the following three ISO protocols:

- ISO 10589, Intermediate System to Intermediate System Intra-Domain Routing Exchange Protocol for Use in Conjunction with the Protocol for Providing the Connectionless-Mode Network Service, which defines the mechanisms for moving data packets between routers (or routing nodes).
- ISO 8473, Protocol for Providing the Connectionless-mode Network Service, which controls data transmission tasks between two end systems
- ISO 9542, End System to Intermediate System Routing Exchange Protocol for Providing the Connectionless-Mode network Service, which is used to perform routing functions.

Since these protocols provide connectionless service, they are limited to performing address, switching, route discovery, and route selection tasks.

Connection-Mode Network Service (CONS) is supported by DNA through the following protocols:

- ISO 8208, X.25 Packet-level Protocol for Data Terminal Equipment is the ISO version of X.25.
- ISO 8878, Use of X.25 to Provide the OSI Connection-Mode Network Service is simply additional protocol required to enable standard X.25 implementations to provide full connection-oriented services.

ISO 8073, Connection Oriented Transport Protocol Specification is used by provider a reliable connection at the Transport layer. Implementation of this protocol determines the level of flow, error and packet sequence control provided by the network.

Network Services Protocol (NSP) was designed by DEC for DNA and has been a part of DNA since its announcement in the mid-1970s. NSP offers a connection-oriented, flow controlled service through normal or expedited full-duplex subchannels. To achieve end-to-end flow control, the Network layer reports congestion to the transmitting NSP, which reduces the number of outstanding messages it will tolerate using either the guaranteed rate or window flow control method. Session Control provides an interface between applications and the Transport layer protocols. It assumes responsibility for the Session and Presentation functions for non-OSI complaint DNA implementations.

It is a proprietary architecture which performs the following functions:

- Address/name resolution
- Protocol stack selection
- Transport connection management
- Connection identifier addressing

ISO 8327, Session Protocol Specification, implements the service definition found in ISO 8326, Session Service Definition. ISO 8327 provides negotiated connection establishment and release as well as half-duplex data transfer.

In addition, the protocol can use one or more Transport layer connections for each session. It organizes data transfers by synchronizing the transfer of packets through major and minor synchronization tokens. Using tokens, a session's dialog can be reset to any synchronization point.

For example, if someone were reading this paragraph to you and you didn't hear or understand what was read, you could ask them to return to the first line of "ISO 8327, Session Protocol Specification." Using the subsection title as a token, both of you know exactly where your dialog would resume. ISO 8824, Abstract Syntax Notation One – ASN.1 with ISO 8825, Specification of Basic Encoding Rules for ASN.1 – BER is a standard character code set that disparate entitles may use as a mutually agreeable code. ASN.1 can perform character code translation. The BER protocol defines the rules to be used when translating to and from ASN.1 notation. It describes the length and location of character code type descriptions. Naming Service and X.500 Directory is the portion of DNA that performs address/name resolution.

X.500 is a directory service recommendation. Some differences exist between these two architectures, but DEC has stated that it intends to eventually convert the naming service to comply with the OSI Directory. ISO 8571 File Transfer, Access and Management – FTAM and DATA Access Protocol (DAP) is a standard protocol for file services. It may be implemented differently by every vendor who chooses to develop an FTAM application; a DECnet FTAM application may look completely different from other applications.

However, the FTAM protocol does specify that each implementation must support some combination of specific document types and service classes. The document types include textual, binary and hierarchical files and service classes include file transfer and file management tasks. DNA provides file transfer through the Data Access Protocol (DAP). DAP offers the usual file system operations, including file retrieval, storage, creation, deletion and renaming. It supports heterogeneous file systems and allows multiple accesses to the same remote file.

Unlike some other file access protocols, DAP allow access to indexed files such as those used for database applications. MAILbus Product Family and X.400 Message Handling System, while not technically protocols, provides the architectural specifications for DECnet message services. MAILbus is a family of proprietary E-mail services developed by DEC. MAILbus products use the X.400 recommendation to interact with their X400 implementations on an Internetwork. Network Virtual Terminal Service (NVTS) By using NVTS, data can be translated from the local terminal format to the network format before it is transmitted to a networked host.

The host then translates the data into its own format. The network command terminal format ensures that heterogeneous systems can communicate.

AppleTalk

Apple Computer, Inc. began development of the AppleTalk protocol suite in 1983. AppleTalk was created as the network architecture for Apple Macintosh computers. Today, AppleTalk provides connectivity for a variety of computer systems including IBM PCs running MS-DOS, IBM mainframes, Digital Equipment VAX and various UNIX computers.

To integrate the Macintosh into enterprise networks, Apple expanded the capabilities of the original AppleTalk with AppleTalk Phase 2. Introduced in 1989, AppleTalk Phase 2 increases the potential size and complexity of AppleTalk networks. Phase 2 allows AppleTalk and other protocol suites to coexist on large, complex networks. The AppleTalk protocol suite was developed after the OSI Reference Model was conceived.

Some of the key architects of AppleTalk mention that the layered approach to designing these network protocols was inspired by the prior use of layered models for "describing various concepts (in particular, operating systems) of stand-alone computers". For these reasons, the AppleTalk protocol stack can be mapped reasonably well to the ODI Reference Model. Local Talk, EtherTalk and TokenTalk ink Access Protocols (LLAP, ELAP and TLAP) are Apple's successful integration of Physical and Data Link layer technologies into AppleTalk.

To maintain consistent naming conventions, Apple refers to AppleTalk protocols over Ethernet as EtherTalk and AppleTalk protocols over token-Ring as Token Talk. The LocalTalk Link Access Protocol is an Apple specific CSMA/CA protocol for shielded twisted pair transmission media. It is best suited for small workgroups because LocalTalk segments are limited to a distance of 300 meters, maximum of 32 devices and a data rate of 230.4 Kbps.

One of the unique features of LocalTalk devices is that they can automatically assign themselves an address. At startup, each device negotiates with the other active devices to determine an acceptable physical device address. EtherTalk (also called ELAP) and TokenTalk (TLAP) are simply implementations of AppleTalk protocols that use the Ethernet and Token-Ring protocols. AppleTalk Address Resolution Protocol (AARP)- Since both ELAP and TLAP use predefined physical device addresses, AARP is used by AppleTalk addresses to the ELAP and TLAP predefined physical addresses.

AARP allows the upper layers of the AppleTalk stack to work with a variety of Data Link layer protocols. Datagram Delivery Protocol (DDP) is AppleTalk's primary Network layer protocol. DDP provides connectionless service between two sockets. Routing Table maintenance Protocol (RTMP) performs route discovery functions to create and maintain AppleTalk routing tables.

It uses a distance vector routing algorithm that is similar to the RIP routing protocol. Zone Information Protocol (ZIP) uses the concept of zones to logically organize service provider names on large Internet works, where the number of service providers can get quite large. However, most users are only interested in some subset of all the service providers. Zones can limit the number of service providers that are presented to the user at one time. ZIP is used by routers to perform the following functions:

- Coordinate relationships between zone and network names.
- Assign service providers to zones.

Name Binding Protocol (NBP): AppleTalk uses names to identify what this course refers to as an entity. However, computer network devices typically rely upon numbers for identification. AppleTalk, in particular, allows the assigned addresses to change as each device joins the network. To make AppleTalk user friendly, the architects decided to use NBP to map AppleTalk names to these dynamic addresses.

AppleTalk Transaction Protocol (ATP) is an acknowledged connectionless transaction-based transport protocol. ATP acknowledges information delivery and initiates retransmission when data is unacknowledged for a given time period. Unlike most transport protocols, however, ATP is based on the concept of a transaction rather than on simply moving a stream of data across a reliable connection. ATP also divides and combines data packets that are too large for the underlying protocols, provides error control for lost packets and performs segment sequencing to the extent that packets are numbered and messages can be buffered until lost packets are retransmitted. AppleTalk Session Protocol (ASP) is standard OSI Session layer protocol designed to optimize file service functions. ASP establishes, maintains and releases connections or sessions.

ASP allows multiple sessions to be established with one service provider; however, each session must be established or requested by the service requester. ASP is a client of ATP and works with ATP to provide a full-fledged transport service to service requesters and providers.

Printer Access Protocol (PAP) is a very similar to ASP. It is also an OSI Session layer protocol. PAP is actually a much more generic protocol than its name implies. It can be used for connections between workstations and any type of server (print, file and so on). However, it was designed to optimize print service functions.

The following are subtle differences between PAP and ASP:

1. PAP allows either the service requester or service provider to initiate a session.
2. ASP can use multiple ATP transactions to reduce overhead on large date transfers.

AppleTalk Data Stream Protocol (ADSP) is AppleTalk's latest Session layer protocol. ADSP is considered a Session layer protocol since it can establish and release logical relationships between two sockets.

ADSP also performs segment sequencing and sliding window flow control Transport layer functions. ADSP provide a full-duplex, flow-controlled, connection-oriented service that runs on DDP. Unlike ATP, ADSP is not transaction based. It uses a connection identifier and bite stream rather than transactions. Because of this and other differences, ADSP is better suited for low bandwidth channels than ATP-ASP, (or ATP-PAP) implementations.

AppleTalk Filing Protocol (AFP) facilitates the file sharing by translating native local file system commands into an acceptable format for network file service. To accomplish this goal, AFP performs command syntax translation and provides a mechanism for other applications to perform file syntax translation. In addition, AFP verifies and encrypts login names and passwords for file access security.

AppleShare AppleTalk's three primary applications are AppleShare File Server, AppleShare Print Server and AppleShare PC.

AppleShare File Server uses AFP services to access remote files. It provides a way for users to store and access files on network servers. AppleShare File Server registers users and maps them to volumes and directories. Through this application, users log in to servers and access their resources.

AppleShare Print Server uses NBP and PAP to send information to prints on an AppleTalk Network. AppleShare Print Server calls use NBP's name lookup service to find the address of the currently selected AppleTalk printer. PAP then opens a connection to that printer. Information is spooled and maintained by AppleShare Print Server. The AppleShare Print Server interacts with the printer to send files when the printer is ready to print them.

Access to AppleShare file servers is not limited to Apple computer users. Computers running MS-DOS can also use AppleShare file services as long as they run **AppleShare PC**. AppleShare PC provides access to files in the AppleTalk file system and allows MS-DOS computers to print to AppleTalk-compatible printers. AppleShare PC supports a variety of third-party Ethernet and token ring interface cards.

Systems Network Architecture(SNA)

IBM has also announced the Systems Application Architecture (SAA) in 1987. SAA's Common Communication Support (CCS) incorporated only specific portions of SNA. SNA LU 6.2 and PU 2.1 are the strategic architectural components that IBM is promoting for the future. However, due to a large installed base, traditional SNA components and architectures should persist for many years. Systems Network Architecture (SNA) is IBM's proprietary networking architecture. As architecture, SNA does not define a single stack of protocols.

Instead, SNA describes the general characteristics of computer hardware and software required for interconnection. It was a primary basis for the OSI Reference Model, which was established roughly a decade later and is one of the oldest network architectures still in existence. In its initial 1974 release, SNA supported only hierarchically organized networks, with hosts, communications controllers, cluster controllers and terminals.

The original architecture was altered by IBM in 1984 to support distributed processing, internetworking, network management and many other advance features. The new peer-to-peer SNA architecture is called Advanced Peer-to-Peer Networking (APPN).

APPN exploits the computer processing power distributed throughout the network in the form of mainframe, minicomputer and PC systems. Because of its prominent use during the OSI model's formation, the relationship between SNA and the OSI Reference Model can be mapped fairly well.

However, SNA is truly Architecture or a model, not a protocol stack as are the other suites described in this section. Therefore, this section performs the following:

- Compares the two models
- Describes basic architectural components
- Identifies topic methods of select protocols, key products, and marketing terms.

The SNA layers are briefly described as follows:

Physical Control is concerned with electrical, mechanical and procedural characteristics of the physical media and interfaces to the physical media. It is directly analogous to the OSI Physical layer; SNA does not define any specific protocols for this layer. IBM assumed that this layer would be implemented with various international standards. However, IBM has developed its own implementations such as Token-Ring.

Data Link Control is also quite similar to the OSI Data Link layer. SNA defines the SDLC protocol for implementation of communication links where master/primaries communicate with slaves/secondaries and IBM Token-Ring on peer-to-peer networks.

Path Control includes many of the functions of the OSI Network layer, such as routing and datagram fragmentation and reassembly. The Path Control layer also describes some OSI Data Link layer functions, such as flow control.

Transmission Control provides a reliable end-to-end connection service and is therefore quite similar to the OSI Transport layer. The Transmission Control layer also provides encryption and decryption services, a function performed by the OSI Presentation layer.

Data Flow Control roughly corresponds to the OSI Session layer. The Data Flow Control layer control request and response processing, determines whose turn it is to talk, groups messages and interrupts data flow on request.

Presentation Services specifies data transmission algorithms, which is also the principal duty of the OSI Presentation layer. The Presentation Services layer also coordinates resource sharing and synchronizes operations.

NAU Services is analogous to OSI's Application layer which provides application services in the form of programs that implement distributed processing or management services. A good example of a transaction service is SNADS (SNA Distribution Services), which provides a distribution system for use by SNA applications.

SNA was designed to integrate IBM and IBM-compatible products; the architecture was based upon specific units called nodes. The following definitions describe the node types used in SNA:

Host nodes (type 5) include mainframes and midrange systems. A host node controls a domain, which includes one or more subareas, each with subordinate nodes and peripherals. Domains consist of the physical and logical units, links and all associated resources that a host has the ability to control. Subareas are portions of SNA networks-consisting of a communication controller, physical units and logical units. SNA networks typically include multiple host nodes and allow a terminal in one host domain to access applications in another host domain.

Communication controller nodes (type 4), also called front-end processors, are hardware devices that route and control the flow of data in a hierarchical structure. A communications controller can be directly attached via a high-speed data channel to the host or remotely attached via a data link to another communications controller.

Peripheral nodes (type 2) include the many different client devices in a hierarchical structure. Cluster controllers, terminals and printers are examples of peripheral nodes,

To interconnect these nodes, SNA relies upon the following concepts:

(1) Physical units

(2) Logical units

(3) Control points

Physical Units (PU's): Physical units are combinations of hardware, firmware and software that manage and monitor the resources of a node. Several of the PUs was previously described as node types. The following is brief description of the PU types:

- Type 1.0 PUs are terminal nodes.
- Type 2.0 PUs are terminals, printers, cluster controllers, or other peripherals which can only communicate with a mainframe.
- Type 2.1 PU devices are typically minis, cluster controllers, gateway devices and occasionally workstations that can communicate with a mainframe or another type 2.1 device.
- Type 4.0 PUs are communication controllers that link host mainframes and cluster controllers or other type 2 devices.
- Type 5.0 PUs are host computers

Logical Units: Logical units are the "entitles" of the network that provide the means to establish a connection with another logical unit and exchange information. They allow people and applications to access the network and the functions provided by VTAM. The following is a list of LU types:

- Type 0 LUs are general purpose LUs used in program-to-program connections.
- Type 1 LUs batch-type terminals, card readers, and printers (such as 3770 and 3270).
- Type 2 LUs are terminals (such as 3270).
- Type 3 LUs are batch-type terminals, card readers, and printers (such as 3270 printers).
- Type 4 LUs were used in old peer-to-peer connections (such as 6670 and 6670 connections and 5250 printers).
- Type 6.0 and 6.1 LUs are used in CICS to CICS or IMS connections between mainframes.
- Type 6.2 LUs are used in new peer-to-peer connections.
- Type 7 LUs are 5270 display stations.

Control Points: Control Points are used to manage and control data flow on the network. Control points are found in type 5.0 and 2.1 PUs. Type 5.0 PUs operate a System Services Control Point (SSCP) which is the software program and central location point within an SNA network that manages configuration, coordinates requests, and provides session services for users on the network. Multiple SSCPs can divide the network into domains of control, with each SSCP having a hierarchical control relationship to the Physical units and logical units with its domain.

Type 2.1 PUs offer a control point which provides similar services, but on a smaller scale. These control points operate in conjunction with other type 2.1 PU control, points to provide peer-to-peer functionality.

Token-Ring is IBM's LAN specification that was used as a model for IEEE 802.5 with the caveat that Token-Ring specifies a physical start topology. Token-Ring uses a token-passing media access method to provide data rate of 4 and 16 Mbps. The specification defines specific cable and connector types.

Synchronous Data Link Control (SDLC) typically uses specific hardware to interface with dedicated, eased or dialup telephone lines. It can support point-to-point or multi-point and half-duplex or full-duplex connections. SDLC generates its own specific control messages in addition to adding data link level headers to packets received from higher layers.

Network Control Program (NCP) is an IBM product that resides in and controls resources connected to a communication control. It was designed to operate front-end processors and perform data link and limited network layer functions. Now, NCP provides routing and gateway functionality in SNA networks.

Virtual Telecommunications Access Method (VTAM) is another IBM product that controls communication and the flow of data in SNA network. It provides single domain, multiple domain and interconnected network capability. VTAM works with NCP to control network resources. Often VTAM and SSCP are considered synonymous terms. However, VTAM is the program product while SSCP is the main software program in VTAM.

Customer Information Control System (CICS) supports transaction processing applications by generalizing input and output commands for use on a network. Software developers use CICS commands to build applications that carry out transactions on local and remote systems. CICS provides terminal-to-application communication, distributed file access, security, multitasking, storage management, transaction tracking and recovery, transaction reversal and a graceful restart facility.

Advanced Peer-to-Peer Networking (APPC) is a network-and transport-level architecture tat allows SNA to operate networks using only type 2.1 PUs.

Information Management System (IMS) is a similar transaction processing product. It is actually composed of two products: the IMS Transaction Manager and the IMS Database Manager. Using these products, IMS allows multiple applications to share IMS Database Manager databases, provides message switching capabilities and facilities the scheduling of priority transactions.

Advanced Program-to-Program Communication (APPC) is actually a term for the SNA extension that added LU 6.2. This version of SNA was the first to allow peer-to-peer communication between logical units that did not involve a mainframe host.

Distributed Data Management (DDM) provides transparent remote file access to SNA service requestors. It performs this function similar as OS Call Interception, "The OSI Application Layer." DDM receives file requests from applications and executes them though the local OS or through a DDM server across the network.

SNA Distribution Services (SNADS) is an application-level service that initiates store-and-for-ward transfers or "distribution" of messages and documents.

Documents Interchange Architecture (DIA) defines the functions required for exchanging documents between different computer systems. DIA coordinates file services such as the storing and retrieving of documents and file transfer.

LAN Manager and Windows NT

Today, Windows NT is the most popular and widely-used LAN operating system available in the market. Created by Microsoft Inc, and introduced to the marketplace in 1996. The difference between all Network Operating Systems lies in their architecture. As discussed earlier, NetWare uses a proprietary implementation of Xerox Network system (XNS) called SPX/IPX as the underlying transport protocol. On top of that, it provides Netware

Core Protocol (NCP) for access to network services. NCP spans the session and presentation OSI layers. Hence in Netware environments the file server is reserved for running Netware and providing network services.

Netware is both the NOS and the OS in this case; it does its own file management, task scheduling, I/O and so on. This means you cannot run standard applications written for Windows NT and OS/2 on a traditional Netware file server. The solution is to have a dedicated Windows NT or OS/2 application sever computer on the Netware LAN. A LAN Manager server, however, runs on top of OS/2. In this case, NOS uses all of the underlying facilities of OS/2 for file management, process management, scheduling and so on.

LAN manager itself resides at the OSI presentation layer and is implemented on top of the NetBIOS session protocol stack, an interface defined by IBM. This insulated it form underlying transport protocols and hardware considerations. Therefore, other transport stacks, such as TCP/IP, or other access protocols such as token-ring, can be substituted without affecting any LAN Manager services. Microsoft's Windows NT is client-server operating system that includes all of the key features of OS/2 and includes built-in networking based on LAN Manager. In this sense it acts as both the OS and NOS.

In fact the networking functionality in Windows NT is very similar to LAN Manager and LAN Manager and Windows NT workstations and servers can co-exist and interoperate with each other. This discussion will not dwelve deeper into the architectural differences between these network operating systems. Most NOSs are moving in the direction of providing transport protocol and hardware independence, while retaining control of the network operating system and its features.

In case of LAN Manager and Windows NT, for example this means the adherence to two standards:

(1) Each transport must provide a NetBIOS interface at the session layer.

(2) Each transport is written to conform to a specific interface based on the network driver interface specifications (NDIS) at the data link layer.

In this way, different transport stacks and network drivers (for network adapter cards) can be substituted, without affecting functionality. For example, LAN Manager supports the TCP/IP and ISO TP4 transport stacks, while there are already network drivers for all of the popular access protocols and hardware.

SQL Server Platforms

SQL Server is a high-performance SQL-based, relational database server that is based on client/server architecture. Client applications formulate queries in SQL and ship them via the LAN to the SQL Server where they are processed. SQL Server processes the SQL request and returns to the application only the required data in response to the request. SQL Server is available for several different platforms. They include SQL Server for OS/2 and SQL Server for Windows NT (available today from Microsoft) and SQL Server NLM and SQL Server for UNIX (available from Sybase). In each case the target OS on which SQL Server runs is different and based on the network environment, the transport protocols and IPC mechanisms supported vary. For SQL Server for OS/2, the IPC mechanism required is named pipes. Thus, SQL Server will run on any LAN as long as the NOS supports named pipes. Currently, support exists for OS/2-based LANs (such as IBM's LAN Server) and for Novell's NetWare and Banyan Vines. Novell and Banyan provide named pipes support in the form of an OS/2 requestor that basically allows a machine running OS/2 on the LAN to run SQL Server on the machine. The named pipes interface frees applications developers from having to write low-level NOS calls to enable IPC between client applications and SQL Server. As discussed earlier, SQL Server for Windows NT has built-in support for multiple IPC mechanism (named pipes, sockets and SPX) running on top of multiple transport protocol stacks and in fact can activated them simultaneously.

Thus SQL Server for Windows NT server can co-exist in a wide variety of network environments (including networks based on Windows NT Advanced Server) and supports a wide range of client workstations including DOS, OS/2, Windows, Windows NT, UNIX and Macintosh. SQL Server NLM (Netware Loadable Module) is an implementation of SQL Server for NetWare servers. It could run concurrently with the file server or may be run on a dedicated computer. The NLM version supports communication through native SPX/IPX and hence would be a natural choice for all NetWare environments, since additional protocols would not have to be loaded on the client side. SQL Server is available form Sybase for most of the leading UNIX platforms. These include variants for UNIX available from Sub (Solaris), HP (HP-UX), DEC (Ultrix), IBM (AIX) and SCO UNIX. In fact, it was first developed by Sybase for UNIX and VMS minicomputer environments using TCP/IP and DECNET protocols. The basic client/server architecture of the SQL Server, however, is still the same on all the platforms.

The important point is that client/server architecture offers a scalable and open platform. With client support for different protocols stacks and IPC mechanism, you can have a truly heterogeneous solution that allows different client workstations to talk to SQL Servers running under different sever and network environments.

SQL RDBMS Servers

Novell NetWare SQL

Novell is offering Netware SQL as their back-end database "engine" for NetWare 2.1 and above. Netware SQL runs on a file server or Netware External Bridge as a VAP. The workstation runs only the front-end application and the NetWare SQL Requestor, which takes the front-end application requests, translates them into SQL requests and transmits the SQL requests to the database server for processing. NetWare SQL relies on NetWare's System Fault Tolerance (SFT) for error recovery, but it continues transaction recovery and record locking within itself. NetWare SQL uses the NetWare record manager to access the database files.

The NetWare Btrieve server program consists of two VAPs. BSERVER, which directly accesses database files on the server and BROUTER, which routes requests to other servers. When there are multiple database servers on the network, BROUTER determines which server the data is on and routes the request there.

BSERVER user NetWare's Transaction Tracking System (TTS) to provide file roll-back and recovery. NetWare XQL is Novell's application program interface to SQL. XQL provides access to the SQL database through ANSI-standard SQL statements and other lower-level function calls. Using XQL, a C, BASIC, Pascal, or COBOL application can pass requests to the NetWare SQL database. Third-party front-end programs for NetWare SQL include WorldTech's dBXL and Quicksilver, Gupta Technologies' SQL Windows, Revelation Technologies' Revelation, Borland's Paradox and others. Novell itself provides a "blueprint" driver for Lotus 1-2-3 users.

Fox Software FoxServer

Fox Software, has a Microsoft company, provides a version of Novell's NetWare SQL called FoxServer. It incorporates dBase language functions into NetWare SQL. This means that front-end applications can use SQL, XQL, Btrieve and/or dBASE commands to directly access the database server.

Ashton-Tate/Microsoft SQL Server

Another example of SQL server software is Borland/Microsoft SQL Server, developed jointly by Microsoft, Borland and Sybase as their database engine for OS/2 servers. SQL server can run as tasks in an OS/2-based file server, or on a separate machine running OS/2. Network operating systems supported by SQL Server include Novell NetWare, IBM LAN Server and networks based on Microsoft LAN Manager. SQL Server is compatible with Sybase's minicomputer-based SQL server. SQL Server provides on-line, write-ahead transaction logging. This means that transactions are written to a log file before the database is updated. In the event of a system failure, database changes can be recovered from the transaction log. SQL Server incorporates a set of extensions (nearly all SQL databases have their own nonstandard extensions) called TRANSACT-SQL that can store commonly used group of commands at the database server and execute them with a procedure call. This means that a "client" workstation can send a single command to the server to execute complex transactions.

Among others, products that will "front-end" SQL Server include Borland's Paradox, Revelation Technologies' Revelation, Borland Dbase IV and Word Tech's dBXL and Quicksilver.

Gupta SQL Base

Gupta Technologies is a pioneer in SQL database servers. Gupta shipped the first SQL database server for PC LANs. Its SQL back-end engine offerings are SQLBase and SQLBase for OS/2, both of which work on any NetBIOS compatible LAN. Gupta produces a powerful, event-oriented application program developer called SQL Windows. SQL Windows is a Microsoft Windows-based application generator that supports graphics, menus, dialogue boxes, and mice. Although SQL Windows only works with SQLBase now, Gupta plans to allow it to interface with other SQL DBMSs including ORACLE, Novel's NetWare SQL, Lotus's forthcoming DBMS product (based on Gupta's software and Microsoft's SQL Server). SQL Windows currently run under DOS Windows and will eventually run under the OS/2 Presentation Manager, Since SQL Windows does not (yet) have a built-in report writer, Gupta has licensed SQL, a report writer produced by SQ Software originally intended to enhance the report writing capabilities of the ORACLE DBMS. Gupta also supplies versions of WorldTech's DBXL and Quicksilver dBASE-like products that will access the SQL-Base server. SQL Network is a series of products that provides connectivity between Gupta's SQL products and IBM's mainframe-based DB2. SQL Network uses IBM's Application Program-to-Program Communications (APPC) to provide this connectivity.

Oracle

Oracle Corporation, one of the largest independent vendors of DBMS software, currently provides a XENIX-based SQL database server for use with PC LANs. This means that PCs on NetWare LANs and others must use network interface cards that support NetWare and the TCP/IP protocol concurrently, or a TCP/IP gateway to access the database server. Users on MS-Net and LAN Manager-based LANs and others must be similar methods. A primary advantage of ORACLE is the fact that it currently runs in a wide range of operating environments on microcomputers, minicomputers and mainframes. Like Gupta Technologies, ORACLE supplies versions of World Tech's DBXL and Quicksilver dBASE-like products that will access its SQL database server.

AN OVERVIEW OF TCP/IP

So far, we have discussed about networking and its cables and hardware/software. But one another thing very important is the protocols. In fact, there are lots of protocols in the market which makes it very confusing. Not only that even the software has various versions to add to the confusion. So in this chapter we try to solve some of the doubts of the protocols.

Ethernet, for instance, boasts a vast number of protocol suites such as DDCMP, LAT, MOP, XNS, SNS, TCP/IP, VRP, NRP and a slew of other three-letter acronyms for various protocols that will solve all the problems a customer could possibly have. Within the scheme of protocols, however, some still seem to rear their ugly heads, no matter how hard the industry tries to put them down or get rid of them.

One suite, **Transmission Control Protocol/Internet Protocol (TCP/IP)**, is such an occurrence. Every other vendor of networks will claim that their protocol is better and that (TCP/IP) is going away. Some will point to the decisions made by the US department of defense (DOD) to eventually migrate to internationally recognized and standardized communications hardware and protocols, obviating the need for TCP/IP and eventually replacing it.

Some view TCP/IP as a workhorse whose time has come to be put out to pasture. Then there are the zealots—those that think that the only communications protocol suite for use in the world is TCP/IP and all other are fluff. These folks are dangerous because they not only are vocal about TCP/IP; many times they are UNIX zealots as well. Some where in the middle of the camps are those who do not know what to do with TCP/IP or, worse, do not even really understand its significance to networks.

Unfortunately, these individuals are usually the managers of such diverse camps of attitudes and must make decisions on whether to use TCP/IP on a project or not. Although it is the ISO open systems protocols which have received most recent publicity, there are other well-established protocols sets, particularly on Ethernet, which have a large share of the current LAN market. Some argue that these protocols offers a better alternative to the largely untried and potentially cumbersome ISO set, but most manufacturers indicate a willingness to adopt ISO protocols at some point of time in future. The non ISO protocol described in this chapter illustrate different approach from the ISO protocol set to open system working . TCP/IP, is a vendor –independent wide are network protocol set, which has been widely used on LANs for peer-to-peer communication.

Here, we all examine the TCP and IP networking protocols and some implementation that have become de-facto standards in the military area as well as academic and UNIX areas. In recent years, knowledge of the capabilities of Transmission Control Protocols/Internet Protocol (TCP/IP) has spread far in the globe. IT managers in all types of organization have begun to research its suitability as an internetworking.

TCP/IP seems to be a ready-made solution to the commercial information systems requirements of intercommunication and interoperation. In US, government officials and research communities and many UNIX aficionados are already well versed in the vocabulary and configuration issues of this set of protocols. But for the newcomers to TCP/IP, the existing sources of information are, in many cases, written by developers apparently for developers.

Most information is primarily technical with detailed description of the bits, flags and fields of the protocols. But less information is given about the practical problems of implementing TCP/IP from scratch. For example, in a commercial rather than a technical or research environment; here the skills and constraints may be very different. The information needed does exist, but one has to read a considerable quantity of material before finding what one needs.

What is TCP/IP?

A comprehensive set of 'ready-made' communication protocols called TCP/IP became widely available and well known only when Berkeley Software Distribution released Berkeley UNIX 4.2 BSD in September 1983. This was not a coincidence; its inclusion in this release was funded by the US government TCP/IP protocols are based on standards originally developed for the US government and US research community. With the release of UNIX 4.2BSD, these communication standards emerged from the confines of the US Departments of defense and the US University and research networks; TCP/IP became the way to interconnect UNIX system. Berkeley UNIX 4.2 BSD and subsequent releases spread quickly throughout the US University and commercial communities.

With UNIX achieving wide popularity as an 'open system' the frame of TCP/IP has continued to spread. But TCP/IP is not and never has been, narrowly confined to UNIX. It was developed to allow free interchange of data among all machines, independent of type, manufacturer, hardware or operating system. In the late 1980s, TCP/IP received a further boost to its fortunes when Sun Microsystems published the specification for Open Network Computing (ONC), often called the Network File System (NFS). NFS adds important functions to TCP/IP and is now very widely available and regarded as an integral part of the TCP/IP protocol suite.

It is particularly valuable for the commercial implementer because of the simple user interfaces that it provides. TCP/IP was developed to satisfy the need to interconnect various projects that included computer networks and also allow for the addition of dissimilar machines to the networks in a systematic and standardized manner. While it is quite true that smaller defense projects may not have warranted the use of TCP/IP for project aspect, edicts from various DOD concerns such as the Undersecretary of Defense for Research and Development forced many government contractors and in-house developed projects to use the suite to conform with DOD requirements. The suite of protocols commonly referred to as TCP/IP (US Military Standards 1778 and 1777) was developed by the United States Department of Defense for its A.R.P.A (Advanced Research Project Agency) network. This is a very large scale wide area network linking many major commercial, university and military establishments.

The relevance of TCP/IP to LANs is two–fold. First, as it is a data gram based protocol, it is well suited to LAN access method, particularly Ethernet. Secondly, it is particularly popular within the UNIX community, giving it a large user base, many of whom wish to use LANs. Cost effective implementations of TCP/IP are now available for all types and sizes of machines from the largest a mainframe to personal computers and workstations. This has brought TCP/IP and its capabilities to the attention of a very wide audience.

Computer managers and users in commercial organizations throughout the world have begun to implement TCP/IP as a way of solving the problems of networking between machines of different manufacture. TCP/IP provided all the facilities for two computer systems to exchange information (intercommunication), interpret it properly and present it in a format which can be understood by the local machine and its users (interoperation). NFS gives a simple and locally-familiar representation of a set of remote and possibly unfamiliar computer filing system; like the original components of the TCP/IP suite, NFS is now available for many different computers.

How TCP/IP Works?

Most networks provide some sort of connection mechanism to get from point A to point B. Other networks worry about how to get from node A on network X to node B on network Y. If a program wishes to send information from itself on node A to another node on the same network, TCP will provide the packet sequencing, error control and other services that are required to allow reliable end-to-end communications.

This does not mean that IP is required. In fact, some implementations of TCP connect directly to the network services layer and bypass IP altogether. If, however, a program on node A on an Ethernet wished to connect to a destination program on node B on an X.25 network, an internet routing function would be necessary to get data packets sent properly between the two dissimilar network services.

IP would take the packet from TCP, pass it through a gateway that would provide conversion services and then send the packet to the IP layer at the remote node for delivery to the remote TCP layer and subsequently, the destination program. A good comparison would be as follows:

(a) Program A on node ALPHA wishes to connect to program B on node BET on the same network. Program A would send a data packet to TCP with the proper destination address. TCP would then encapsulate the data with the proper header and checksums in accordance with whatever services the program requested and pass the TCP packet to the IP layer. IP would then determine, from network directory information, that the remote node is on the same network as itself and simply pass the packet through to the network services layer for local network routing and delivery.

(b) Program A on node ALPHA on network X wishes to connect to program B on node BETA on network Y. In this situation, data would be handled as in case (a) above, but IP would determine that the destination is not on the local network. As a result, the IP layer in node ALPHA would determine the best route to get to the remote node and send the TCP packet to the next IP node in the path to get to the remote. IP does not care which program the source wants to connect to; all it cares about is which node to send the packets to.

IP nodes in the path from node ALPHA to node BETA will examine the packet to determine the destination and will forward the packet to the proper IP until it reaches the destination network IP. That IP determines that the node is on its local network and the packet is handed to the network services layer for the network on which BETA resides for delivery to node BETA. Once the packet is received at the final destination IP, it is passed up to the TCP layer, which breaks out the packet header to figure out which program on the destination node is to receive the data.

First, however, the packet header is examined carefully to insure that it has arrived in the proper sequence and that there are no special handling issues that need to be serviced. Once TCP is satisfied that everything is reasonable, the data is delivered to the destination program. While all of this seems pretty straightforward, there are some implementation issues that make this entire complex. Since TCP and IP allow many service options such as message priority, security classification, data segmentation at the TCP level, packet segmentation at the IP level and other issues that some network architectures, such as DECnet, need not concern themselves with, there can be some considerable overhead associated with packet processing.

As a result, TCP/IP performance varies significantly from network hardware to network hardware as well as from machine implementation to machine implementation. Now that we have examined the generalized delivery model, let us look at some of the specifics.

What is TCP supposed to do?

One of the base problems that TCP was built to address is the issue of connection from a particular program on a particular node on a particular network to a remote program destination that may or may not be on the same network as the originator. As such a method of addressing nodes needed to be developed that identified a particular program on a particular node in a particular network. A possible solution is to develop hard addresses for all entities on a particular network.

While this solves the problem, it is inflexible and usually does not provide an upwardly flexible network architecture. Another problem is that some networks have their own proprietary (and sometimes bizarre) addressing scheme that must be considered as TCP/IP are above the local network addressing scheme mechanism in the network architecture and will need to use the local mechanism on packet delivery.

To solve the problem, TCP/IP uses a three-layer addressing mechanism that allows for delivery of packets across dissimilar network architectures. To begin with, each program (called a PROCESS in TCP) has a unique one-up address on each machine. That unique local program address is combined with a particular node address to form something called a port. The port address is further combined with the local network address, forming a new entity called a socket. There can be many, many sockets on a TCP/IP network but each socket identifies, exactly, one specific application on a specific node on a specific network.

Through this mechanism, IP will get the packets to the proper node and TCP will deliver the packet to the proper program on that node. Some nodes provide a standard process type (such as type 23 for remote log-ins) that are "known" to other network entities and that provide certain standard services. Through this mechanism TCP provides a multiplexing capability that is essential in the efficient use of the network resource.

From One Socket to Another

As with any network, two sockets that wish to connect to each other must have a mechanism by which this happens. TCP provides this in various ways. One of the more common ways connections are established is via an ACTIVE/PASSIVE network OPEN. A PASSIVE OPEN is when a receptive socket declares itself to be open and available for incoming connections (this would typically be the mode used by something like a database server). A PASSIVE OPEN, however, may be set up in various ways. First, the PASISVE OPEN may be set up to be FULLY SPECIFIED, which means that the socket issuing the PASSIVE OPEN tells the network exactly which socket may connect to it, including security levels allowed and other related details.

Another type of PASSIVE OEPN is the UNSPECIFIED PASSIVE OPEN in which the socket will accept any connection request from any remote socket provided that the remote system requesting connection meets prescribed security and other criteria. In both types of network OPENS, it is pertinent to point out that the socket OPENing the network may also declare timeout values for all data received from the originator of the connection.

This allows for the expeditious handling of data as well as providing a means by which "old" messages are handled in a reasonable fashion and messages requiring special handling (in terms of time) are processed correctly. Another type of OPEN is the ACTIVE OPEN. Unlike the PASSIVE OPEN, the ACTIVE OPEN aggressively seeks a connection to a particular socket. An ACTIVE OPEN will only be successful if there is a cooperating and corresponding PASSIVE OPEN or other ACTIVE OPEN from the destination socket. Once a connection has been established between two sockets, data may be transferred between the sockets.

TCP provides several mechanism for data transfer, but the two most popular are segmented data transfer and

PUSH mode. Segmented data transfer allows TCP to end user data in chunks across the network. As such, TCP may send the data in such a manner that allows for the best efficiency for the network being used. This means that even if the user has transferred 25 blocks of use data to TCP, TCP may not send it all at once, opting to segment the data in such a manner as to provide optimal flow of data on the network. While this technique is great for data flow issues and network congestion issues, it can be troublesome for transfers in which the data needs to get to the remote system NOW! In such cases, the user may specify the PUSH flag.

A PUSH request forces TCP to end whatever has been passed from the user to TCP right away with no consideration for optimal flow control. In addition to the PUSH flag, the user may specify the urgency of the data being transferred to keep the remote system on its toes. How much data is allowed to be sent from one socket to another is a function of the network and programs involved. Since TCP was developed with multiple network architectures in mind, it allows some level of link negotiation on connection and data transfer that provides for maximum buffer sizes (somewhat dynamically) and maximum buffer allocation.

TCP Sequencing

To insure that everything gets to where it is going and in the proper order, TCP provides packet sequencing services as well as error detection functions utilizing a 16-bit checksum in the TCP header area. It is also interesting to note that TCP presumes the IP layer to be unreliable and therefore, includes a 96-biy pseudoheader in front of the actual TCP packet header that includes the source address, destination address, protocol being used and segment size.

Through the use of the pseudoheader, TCP protects itself from IP delivering the packet to the wrong place (or not at all) by misinterpreting TCP header fields. The checksum in the TCP header also includes the pseudoheader bits to insure that everything is clean when it hits the remote side. After the connection is established and all data has been transferred, the link may be shut down via user request. This is the clean way. It is very possible that the link may also be abruptly aborted due to link from or some catastrophic failure of the network or socket-to-socket linkage.

TCP provides mechanisms to handle both situations. A CLSOE primitive issuance tells TCP that the user is finished with the network link and to close down the link gracefully by sending all remaining data in local buffers and notifying the remote socket that the sending user wishes to CLOSE the link. The remote TCP socket notifies the user that a CLOSE has been issued. The user may then send any remaining data and issue a CLOSE to the sender. When the sender received the CLSOE acknowledgement from the receiver, it sends a TERMINATE to the user and notifies the remote TCP that a TERMINATE has been issued.

The remote TCP socket sends a TERMINATE to the remote user and the links is closed completely. If a network link abort occurs, for whatever reason, the ABORT primitive is sent to the remote TCP, which tells the remote user that a TERMINATE has occurred. No more data of any kind is transmitted on the link and the link is closed immediately on both sides. Obviously, a link termination of the ABORT kind is not desirable, as data may be lost and other integrity issues may be involved.

TCP Needs Not an IP

It is important to understand that TCP need not be connected to an IP, although that is frequently the case. TCP provides the essential network connection and data transfer features which a sure would require to connect with a particular program on a remote system. Some companies use TCP as the protocol of choice when setting up simple direct-connect network connections (where the remote node is hard-wired to the originating node) or when performing tasks such as downline system loading.

In any case TCP is a powerful and full-featured protocol that provides reasonable network services for user data. Many times, however, just getting the data from one socket to another may involve the connection to various types of network technologies.

A TCP packet coming in from an asynchronous link may need to be routed on to an Ethernet to reach its ultimate destination, Because of the need to connect and properly route data through to its proper network and destination socket, the IP layer was developed.

What is an IP?

IP is a datagram service. It basically provides rudimentary internetwork routing, services without any regard to the destination program, TCP formats, error control, packet sequencing etc. Its function in life is to get the packet to the right network and eventually, to the right node. Further, IP allows for expedited routing of packets that need to get to a destination quicker than other, routine packets. In many respects, with the exception of routing priority, IP functionality is similar to Ethernet packet handling. If a packet arrives that is damaged (there is an IP checksum), the packet is discarded.

What is in the data field of the packet is of no interest to IP. IP could be sending a TCP packet or some other protocol for all it cares. As long as the proper SEND (user sending to the network) primitive fields have been filled in, IP will send the packet on its merry way. When the packet reaches the remote node and the checksum figures out OK, IP sends the packet to TCP (or whatever the receptor protocol is) via DELIVER directive and all is well with the universe. If the packet gets trashed in the process of being delivered, so be it. If the packets arrive out of sequence, that is not IP's problem. If a packet is missing, again, IP does not care. IP gets the data packet (usually a TCP packet) form point A on network X to point B on network Y. That is all, nothing more.

Gateways and IP

To provide the internetwork routing function, IP makes use of special nodes called gateways. A gateway, in IP terms, is a machine that allows two dissimilar networks to be connected to each other. The two networks may or may not be the same type (Ethernet, X.25, token ring, etc.), as IP operates above the hardware itself and is only interested in the virtual connection function, not the physical path or hardware used. As such, there may be a need to segment large messages from the upper software layers into sizes that are applicable to the remote network's allowances.

To do this, IP will segment large messages into proper-sized chunks (such as when going from 1500 byte Ethernet packets to 128 byte X.25 packets) for the destination network and reassemble them at the remote destination IP layer before delivery to the user. If a packet gets destroyed in the segmented message and the remote IP detects the packet loss, the entire segment is killed off by the remote IP. Obviously, TCP would detect that a segment is missing and request a retransmission from the remote TCP for any missing packets.

TCP has the option of forcing IP NOT to segment packets, but this is usually not implemented as it can cause routing problems where differing network technologies are concerned. IP also provides for proper security classification of packets being sent to a remote site. If an intermediary gateway or network is not at the same security level as the transmitted packet, the packet will not be sent through that network. As a result, some strange routing of data may occur sometimes as IP must contend with the problem of expeditious routing but also the problem of security-oriented routing. Finally, IP has some different terminology than that typically used in a network. In many networks, the concept of a "hop" is the routing of a data packet through a node on its way to its final destination point.

In IP, a hop is when a data packet goes through a gateway to another network. Therefore, it is quite possible that a packet may wander through various nodes in a local network before it actually gets to the remote network gateway, depending, of course, upon previously discussed variables. If the packet does not incur a route through a gateway, it, in IP terms, has not incurred a hop. If it transverses through two gateways, it would be considered to have incurred two hops on its path to the final destination. Hops, therefore, are not referred to in the same manner as many other popular communications architectures. As can be seen, TCP and IP are not the same and may actually be implemented totally independent of each other for separate uses. More often than not, however, they are both included in many offerings from various vendors.

TCP/IP Applications

In any network architecture, the protocols and transmission methods are not enough. Users frequently want and need utilities that implement the protocols in the network architecture to allow file transfer, program communication, virtual terminal support and electronic mail. Most TCP/IP implementations are the same and a few standard applications exist.

File Transfer

File Transfer facilities are usually provided for by a mechanism known as the File Transfer Protocol (FTP). FTP is a simple featured file-moving utility that allows a record-oriented (one record at a time) transfer, a block transfer (which moves chunks of a file), or an image transfer (which does not look in any way at the file contents). Further, FTP knows about EBCDIC and ASCII (also NVT-ASCII) and may provide some rudimentary conversion facilities BEFORE a transfer begins.

As file systems are very complex and the need for file transfer between systems is growing, FTP has evolved in some cases to special implementations that know how to convert specific file formats between certain types of machine architectures. This conversion facility is not within the defined scope of FTP, but some vendors include the conversion features anyway. To transfer a file, the user invokes the host. FTP utility, specifies file name, type (if necessary), remote destination and off it goes. One interesting feature on some FTP implementation is the recovery facility.

Networks, as most are well aware, will fail from time to time. In the case of failure, any transfers in process will usually have to be restarted from scratch. If the file is being transferred with FTP in block mode, it may be possible to resume the transfer at a later time by specifying which block was the last transmitted. FTP would then continue to send the file as if nothing had happened.

This feature is not available on all FTP would then continue to send the file as if nothing had happened. This feature is not available on all FTP implementations and has some host and remote system software considerations involved with it, but, all in all, it is a useful feature to have when transferring very large files.

Telnet

Another popular utility is known as TELNET. TELNET is a virtual terminal facility that allows a user to connect to a remote system as if the user's terminal were hard-wired to that remote system. As with file systems, virtual terminals may need to emulate a wide variety of terminals, which may be impractical on larger, complex networks. As such, TELNET provides a basic protocol handling facility and a negotiation facility that allows for the inclusion of different types of terminal protocols and signaling mechanisms. There are four ways of using Telnet. The terminal could be a simple 'dumb' terminal connected to a TCP/IP terminal server with a standard communications interface (V.24/V.28 or EIA232). Equally, that simple terminal could be a workstation or PC running a terminal emulator and connected to the same terminal server in the same way.

A minicomputer can run Telnet software which provides the terminal server capability from within the minicomputer. Alternatively, a PC or other workstation could run a version of TCP/IP and a terminal emulator and connect directly to a LAN. The Telnet service was one of the first to be provided in a standard way by the TCP/IP architecture. It delivers a similar service to that provide by the switching statistical multiplexers of the early to mid-1980s which provided many companies with their first example of flexible access to information. Telnet allows terminal or workstation users to gain access to a host system and to display host data on their screens.

It is a remote terminal service; any terminal user must know how to operate the host system or host application from a terminal of that type. No attempt is made to map the user interface environments from one system to the other. The Telnet service is most commonly used with ASCII asynchronous terminals such as the ANSI standard terminal or the DEC VT series. Most manufacturers of other terminal types have registered them with the Internet assigned Numbers Authority (IANA) so that they can be identified to the Telnet protocol. That does not mean that a particular implementation of workstation Telnet will necessarily match the host software.

Any-to-any protocol conversion is not necessarily a feature; systems which match must be carefully chosen. The advantage of the Telnet terminal server is that it provides a low cost connection. But the interface often operates in asynchronous character-by-character mode; the terminal is strictly limited in its capabilities with little possibility of upgrading the service in the future. Asynchronous interfaces can involve large management overheads. Cabling for the terminals may require only three wires, but for some terminal types and uses, it could be more. A structured cabling system with centrally located terminal servers can reduce management costs.

At each interface, a number of parameters must be configured—speed, parity, flow control method and type of terminal, to ensure the correct control sequences are used. Unless a single standard for these parameters can be enforced throughout the organization, any apparent cost savings can be quickly allowed up in increased management costs. This is particularly so in the larger installation, where the unit costs of supporting large numbers of terminal servers may not reduce with increasing size. Where terminal servers can be remotely configured from a central network management system, support costs may be more easily contained.

Trivial File Transfer Protocol

The **Trivial File Transfer Protocol** (TFTP) is a simple program with minimal facilities, designed to be implemented in permanent memory (PROM), so that diskless computers may perform their initial loading of an operating system. It is often used in conjunction with the boot protocol. It is not usual for it to be used for other purposes. TFTP lacks the security features of FTP and it is normal to disable the TFTP server on hosts which do not provide a BOOTP service.

Simple Mail Transfer Protocol (SMTP)

A final utility that is somewhat popular is the Simple Mail Transfer Protocol or SMTP as it is more affectionately known. SMTP provides a mechanism by which a user can specify a destination address (or addresses if to more than one remote user), a particular path to follow (if desired) and a message. Like other electronic mail systems, SMTP provides for return receipts, forwarding of mail, and other similar features. The only odd issue has to do with the problem of the term "simple". Having used SMTP for some years now, it is not intuitive and the routing issues can get strange. Yet, it is a useful utility and heavily used in the defense area.

Some of the organizational issues of SMTP arise because of the association of a person with a particular computer. Those computers are the .MDBO/ mail servers. MDNM/of SMTP and they must always be available to receive mail. An individual workstation or PC is unlikely to make a satisfactory mail server as its availability cannot be guaranteed. A mail server is more likely to be a part-time task carried out by another server machine. Building on SMTP protocol, some manufacturers have introduced the mail relay or mail store, which receives and stores mail on behalf of workstation users until they access the store using an SMTP client on their workstation.

A workstation can be a satisfactory generator of SMP mail, but it is a poor and inattentive recipient. Staff who travel must be able to access the mail system they are registered on, for that is where their mailbox resides. Alternatively, a method of mail forwarding can be devised, but such features are beyond the SMTP itself and are implementation dependent. If mail users change location permanently, their mail addresses may change. They will have to advise all their correspondents for that change.

TCP/IP standards do not include a directory service to relate people to mail addresses or for that matter to relate application servers to network addresses. Worldwide research into directory services has concentrated on perfecting and implementing the CCITT X.500 recommendations which are accepted as part of OSI. Indeed, the US Internet is said to be the biggest trial of X.500 directory services in the world. Several RFCs describe how X.500 is to be used on the Internet and the adaption needed to operate over TCP/IP protocols.

Network File System

The Network File System (NFS), as it is still commonly known, or Open Network Computing (ONC), as its creator Sun Microsystems Inc, now calls it, is one of the more recent standard additions to the TCP/IP protocol suite. ONC was developed by Sun Microsystems Inc. for its high performance UNIX workstations and later released to the 'public domain' as three RFCs which describe the major protocol components. Recognizing the importance of the IBM PC, SUN also developed NFS software for the IBM PC, the PC-NFS client. This allows PCs to use UNIX workstations as remote file and print servers.

NFS client and server software is now available for most computer systems. NFS provides user services familiar to any user of a proprietary resource-sharing LAN such as NetWare, LAN Manager or Banyan VINES. Files directories and peripherals on a remote NFS server are mapped to 'virtual' drives directories peripherals on the local system. For most purposes these virtual drives and printers area indistinguishable from and are used identically to local resources. On a UNIX system each remote directory appears as an additional directory of the main local directory structure. For a PC, with PC-NFS, the remote directories appear as additional disk drives. From the perspective of the commercial information system manager, this is ideal, for unlike other TCP/IP applications described below, most business users need no new training to use NFS; they merely have a access to more information with bigger disks and better printers. But NFS can go beyond simple resource sharing. It provides the mechanism for true distributed computing, where processing power, not just data, is shared among networked machines.

These client/server applications can reduce the load on busy networks significantly. The major management issues of NES can be hidden from the users. These issues centre on the security and mapping of user identifiers and access rights between different operating system. NFS works in conjunction with the Network Information Services (NIS), a distributed database system for NFS security which provides for centralized management of a highly distributed system.

Technically, the tools have been provided by Sun; the administration of a large user population still requires careful organization, with the correct clerical procedures in place to ensure that security meets the requirements of the organization. It must not be so lax as to compromise data integrity and not so tight that no one can get work done. NFS uses the UDP transport protocol. Remote disk data transfer rates can be reduced significantly by delay, particularly in wide area links.

There is at least one implementation providing the same services as NFS, which uses TCP transport. An alternative solution is to buy more servers and place them close to the users. Where the main NFS activity is resource sharing, poor configuration options in the workstations can have a dramatic effect on network traffic. The use of print spoolers, temporary files backup files, PC batch files and the format of the 'path' statement can all influence the traffic, a workstation generates on the network. To make NFS completely invisible to end users, each workstation should have a script or batch file which executes the NFS 'mount' commands to make the remote resources locally available.

The details of the command line can be totally hidden. In the past, memory requirements for PC network software have left too little of the available 640k to run some of the more demanding PC applications. Some implementations of PC-NFS require in excess of 130 kbytes to load a LAN card driver, the TCP/IP core software and the NFS client application. By reducing the number of file systems which may be mounted and by tuning other parameters, this figure can be reduced by a few kilobytes.

As 80386 processors with large amounts of memory and the MS DOS 5.0 operating system replace older configurations and software, the PC memory will become less of a restriction. Where replacement cannot be considered, careful memory sizing will be required for NFS systems.

TCP/IP Implementations

Some vendors of TCP/IP have made a cozy living out of providing their wares to defense contractors and UNIX/Ultrix shops that need to connect and communicate with their compatriots supporting TCP/IP. How the vendors have implemented TCP and IP varies greatly, which also means that features and performance vary significantly. Some vendors, such as Excelan, have chosen to implement much of the protocol suite in a controller card, effectively offloading the host from the duties of running TCP and IP programs and utilities and yet providing the necessary connectivity.

This is nice as it offloads the host and makes the overall system more cost effective and less bogged down in the network mire. Other companies, such as Wollongong, have chosen to implement TCP/IP in software on the host. This degrades the host system, sometimes severely, but has the advantage of being able to function as a true IP node, allowing connection to various network technologies simultaneously. Each implementation has its benefits and drawbacks. Which one is best for a particular system depends heavily upon cost factors, system loading expectations and how many different kinds of networks a site may be connected to.

Some vendors have begun to introduce TCP/IP routers that allow IP services to different types of networks by connecting the networks through a dedicated IP router (sometimes referred to as an IMP) and allowing TCP messages to be created by a particular network protocol, translated into TCP and sent to a destination node on either the same or another network. Such routing and translation trickery is beginning to become more and more prevalent in environments where TCP and other types of networking software exist. In the quest to TCP/IP, the bottom line is how long can it last? A few years ago it would have been said that it was a safe bet that usage of TCP/IP would last a company for some years to come. Now that the DOD no longer requires the absolute use of TCP/IP, opting, instead, to go with OSI, such is not a safe bet for all sites.

There are enough TCP sites installed that it would be foolish and expensive to haul off and convert all sites to something else. It is also prudent to remember that the number of networked machines that will appear in near future will far eclipse anything currently installed in such a way as to make protocols such as TCP/IP become a minority. Much has to do with who is buying what as to how long it will last. However, TCP/IP will be around for a while, if to do nothing else than support current systems.

As those systems cut over to OSI, however, fewer and fewer nodes will be seen running TCP or IP in favour of OSI. What would we do if we had to buy today? Buy TCP/IP, of course. Why? Because it works and it is now. It would server very nicely for the short term (2-4 years) and give the OSI packages sometime to mature before diving in headlong. A nice side benefit is that the OSI transport service and TCP's capabilities are very similar, as are the OSI network layer routing service and the IP services. Further, TCP/IP prescribes standardized network hardware, so OSI-compliant hardware is given in many TCP/IP environments, allowing a nice migration path to OSI at a future date. If one installs OSI-compliant hardware, then conversion to OSI from TCP/IP is not as traumatic as it could be.

TCP/IP Communication Architecture

An interconnected set of lines and terminals allowing processing to take in one or several locations is usually viewed as a network. A network may have several hosts interacting with multiples of terminals. To bring structure to this view of a network, the concept of network Architecture is proposed; this is a structured hardware and software design that supports the interconnection of a number of physical and logical components. A network architecture is a way to define the set of rules to which these interconnecting elements must conform. It is not however, a definition of how the internal design is made or how the functions in the network operate or how a rule is actually implemented.

A network architecture is a statement of what services need to be provided to enable the network to follow one set of rules. In the past several years the International Organization for Standardization (ISO) has developed a model of network architecture. The goal of this model is to promote the interconnecting of networks of all types. The underlying principle exploited by the OSI model is layering. The idea is to create network architecture with several layers where each layer provides certain unique functions which are not provided by any of the other layer is strictly defined.

Based on some standard structuring techniques, the OSI model defines seven distinct layers. Each layer need only interact with the adjacent layers and has no knowledge about any other layers. Information flows down through the layers of the sending host and then up through the layers of the receiving host. Because the layers are isolated from each other by strict interfaces, information that is added by a layer in the sending host will only be used by the matching layer in the receiving host. In this sense the matching layers of the sending and receiving hosts communicate with each other in a peer-to-peer relationship. Each layer adds value to the services provided by the set of lower layers in such a manner that the highest layer is offered the set of services needed to run an application distributed over several networks.

Each layer provides services to the layer above and requests services from the layer below. Thus, the total network problem is divided into a set of smaller problems. Intermediate networks that merely relay information from one network to another will only need to implement some of the lower three layers to act as transferal agents. In the standard which describes the reference model, OSI standard developers state that they will exclude any details which would be implementation dependent. The result is that while the standards have been kept 'pure', many details which would aid they would aid development of viable OSI products are excluded from the standards themselves. While some would argue that OSI is more rigorous in its standardization that TCP/IP, the OSI development process seems to have become enmeshed in procedures weighed down by the difficulties of obtaining consensus in large committees and dogged by supplier politics.

By confining OSI standards to abstract definitions in a complex vocabulary, defined just for the purpose and then charging considerable sums for copies of those standards, ISO committees have, undoubtedly, if unintentionally, slowed the OSI development process and the delivery of useful conforming products. With a more restricted geographic and technical scope, TCP/IP developers adopted a pragmatic approach. TCP/IP standardization was based on the Request For Comments (RFC), a flexible and fast standardization process using electronic mail to publish and exchange comments and ideas and to update drafts.

Developers often outlined parts of a standard in a familiar computer language, usually 'C' which, while not intended to be implemented directly, gave a very good starting point for an initial implementation. TCP/IP standards are freely available on-line from a number of computer systems, originally without full drawings or graphics, but today with all the quality of a laser-printed, desktop-published document as Postscript files. For manufacturers of communications and computing products, the contrast with OSI could not be more stark; it is just so much easier to obtain TCP/IP information than OSI.

Standards were produced more quickly and they are written in a readable and comprehensible form by developers for developers. The US government demanded TCP/IP for all systems, thereby ensuring every US government computer supplier provided it. They also funded universities to implement the standards. In the USA, such publicly funded work enters the public domain and if not of a military nature, is freely available to all citizens.

While it may not be used directly for commercial purposes, having a working example in 'C' source code certainly assists future developments by commercial suppliers! Neither OSI nor TCP/IP has been developed in isolation. There has been a considerable interchange of ideas and techniques, particularly evident in the changes in OSI since the mid-1980s with the development of the connectionless OSI suite. Nor have the OSI standards been ignored by suppliers. As with TCP/IP in the USA, universities have been busy developing OSI implementations and governments have, since the mid-1980s, required OSI-conforming products.

But this activity has not as yet created a general market demand and the same level of fully developed OSI computing products, except perhaps with the notable exception of X.25 network equipment. The 'pump priming' of TCP/IP has been more successful and has ensured, thereby, that it has moved ahead much faster than OSI. Governments and commercial organizations worldwide have waited patiently for OSI to become available and to reap the benefits of the promised flexibility of an international standard for computer communications and inter operation.

In short, the development of OSI has lagged considerably behind TCP/IP despite support from a number of governments (including since 1985, the US government and Department of Defense). When it comes to breaking down communications barriers between different computer suppliers, information systems managers in commercial companies now see TCP/IP as a fully functional, proven and low-cost alternative to open systems interconnection. OSI is still immature and almost unavailable.

This may change in near future but the explosive interest in TCP/IP will, on the one hand, delay OSI implementation and on the other, encourage it as larger organizations come up against some of the known fundamental limitations of TCP/IP. As with much of the specialist vocabulary which surrounds computers and telecommunications networks, the term TCP/IP will conjure up different concepts to different readers. TCP/IP is used as shorthand for a large set of standards with many different features and functions. The letters 'TCP/IP' stand for two communications protocols, Transmission Control Protocol (TCP) and Internet Protocol (IP).

These were developed during the late 1970s and early 1980s as the key communications protocols for the US 'Internet', the collected set of interconnected communications networks (originally comprising ARPAnet, but now including UFSnet, and NYSERnet and the Department of Defense Network among many others). Today these support the US government. Department of Defense, US military and the university, education and commercial organizations conduct research on behalf of those bodies. (Use of the US Internet for commercial traffic between commercial organizations is not allowed.) TCP and IP, are but two of the building blocks required for a complete communications 'architecture', but the term 'TCP/IP' is most often used as a **shorthand** term of the whole communications 'architecture' specified originally by the US Department of Defense.

This architecture is a much bigger set of standards than just TCP and IP. We shall also use 'TCP/IP' to mean the complete architecture, except where this will cause confusion. **Communication architectures** have been developed by computer manufacturers since the mid 1970s. An architecture describes three facets of communications in an abstract way which is independent of particular hardware or technology. The three aspects are:

(1) Data exchange (intercommunications)

(2) Data interpretation (interoperation)

(3) System management

Like the OSI reference model, communications architectures are described in layers; each layer providing its own functions but using the functions of the layer below. This layering decouples the functions of one layer from another making layered architectures flexible; their designers can respond to changes in technology and in application software without a major upheaval for existing users. The implementation and existing installations can be extended, as new, often faster techniques and technologies become available. It is important to realize that the standards do not specify the interfaces seen by computer users.

Though suppliers often base their implementations on a competitor's successful product, one must expect that user interfaces will differ, in major or minor ways, from supplier to supplier. For TCP/IP, the architectural standards and the operational US Internet are controlled by the Internet Activities Board (IAB). The IAB devolves its responsibilities for development, operations and management to a number of subcommittees and working groups which it controls and to other commercial companies specializing in communications and computing research and consultancy.

TCP/IP The Complete Suite

The TCP and IP, explain only the communication aspects, the movement of data across a set of interconnected physical networks. The complete architecture must include standard mechanisms for interpreting and converting data for the common tasks that users of computers have come to expect. As these tasks sit on top of and depend on the communications protocols, they are sometimes called the **Upper Layer Protocols (ULPs).**

- Generally, computer users have needed three major functions:
- File Transfer
- Terminal access (virtual terminal protocols)
- Mail preparation and transfer

In commercial environments other tasks have become equally important.

- Resource sharing (for example: files, printers, plotters)
- Diskless workstations
- Transaction processing
- Management
- Directory services
- Security

Those familiar with the resource-sharing Local Area Network (LAN) (such as Microsoft LAN Manager and Novell NetWare) must have seen the power of remote or distributed file and disk sharing and of peripheral sharing; and of peripheral sharing; for some companies, diskless workstations have a number of advantages. In a complete, modern architecture, standard protocols are needed for all these new distributed systems as well as for the proven minicomputer and mainframe-based architectures. The TCP/IP protocol suite addresses these issues comprehensively. The standards are not static but are being added to at a steady rate.

Current activities relate to new facilities in directory services at the application layer and improvements in routing and addressing mechanism at the lower layers.

Upper Layer Protocols

Beginning with the well-known application layer protocols, File Transfer Protocol (FTP), Telnet (TCP/IPs virtual terminal protocol), and Simple Mail Transfer Protocol (SMTP), NFS adds a disk/file system resource-sharing capability, LPR deals with printing, the BOOT Protocol (BOOTP) provides the basis for diskless workstation operation and Simple Network Management Protocol (SNMP) is the Internet Standard for management.

Lower Layer Protocols

IP is not the lowest level of the layered architecture. TCP/IP does not explain new standards for low-level communications but TCP/IP standards include descriptions of how IP operates over the commonly available long-distance and local physical communications networks. These descriptions include many proprietary networks as well as CCITT and other international standard transmission mechanisms. For long-distance operation over public telecommunications circuits, the standards include point-to-point leased and dial up, synchronous and asynchronous links and X.25 connections.

For local communications. Ethernet Version 2 (as specified by DEC, Intel and Xerox) is by far the most widely used. ISO/IEEE networks (ISO 8802.3, 8802.4, 8802.5) and FDDI (ISO 9314) are also specified as are proprietary networks such as ARCNET.

TCP/IP Protocol Set Structure

The TCP/IP suite is not a single protocol. Rather, it is four-layer communication architecture that provides some reasonable network features, such as end-to-end communications, unreliable communications line fault handling, packet sequencing, internetwork routing and specialized functions unique to DOD communications needs such as standardized message priorities. The bottom layer, network services, provides for communication to network hardware. Network hardware used in the various networks throughout the DOD typically reflects the usage of FIPS (Federal Information Processing Standard) compliant network hardware (such as IEEE 802 series of LANs and other technologies such as X.25). The layer above the network services layer is referred to as the Internet protocol (IP) layer.

The IP layer is responsible for providing a datagram service that routes data packets between dissimilar network architectures (such as between Ethernet and say, X.25). IP has a few interesting qualities, one of which is the issue of data reliability. As a datagram service, IP does not guarantee delivery of data. Basically, if the data gets there, great. If not, that's OK too. Data concurrency, sequencing, and delivery guarantee is the job of the TCP protocol. TCP provides for error control, retransmission, packet sequencing and many other capabilities.

It is very complex and provides most of the features of the connection to other applications on other systems. To understand properly what TCP/IP is all about, it is important to understand that: (a) it is not OSI in implementation (although some argue that there are substantial similarities) and (b) it is a unique network architecture that provides what are considered traditional network services in a manner that can be overhead intensive in some implementations. The structure of the TCP/IP protocol set is shown in Figure 13.1.8, alongwith the approximately equivalent ISO model layers. It can be seen that this is essentially a four layer model, although the layers are not as clear cut as in the ISO model and the model has been drawn from analysis of what is used, rather than being defined first and then the protocols specified.

The TCP/IP philosophy is the antithesis of the ISO philosophy. In ISO protocols, everything appears to be put into the protocol, but parts are made optional. In TCP/IP, the protocols are kept very simple. If more functionality is required, then another protocol is added to deal with the situation.

The main protocols are as follows:

IP The Internet Protocol, which provides a connectionless datagram 'network' layer.

ICMP The Internet Control Message Protocol is an example of the bolt-on approach mentioned above. It adds functionality to the IP protocol and can be considered as an extension to that protocol.

UDP The User Datagram Protocol provides the rough equivalent of the ISO connectionless transport service.

TCP The Transmission Control Protocol is a connection oriented, reliable, end-to-end transport protocol.

The protocols which run above TCP include TELNET, a terminal access protocol and a file transfer protocol FTP. The four main protocols are now examined further as a contrast to the ISO approach.

Internet Protocol

There is a second difference in philosophy between ISO and the TCP/IP approach, which revolves around the word 'network'. In the TCP/IP model, a network is an individual packet switched network which may be a LAN or a WAN, but is generally under the control of one organization.

These networks connect to each other by gateways, and the resulting collection of such networks is called a catenet (from concatenation). The internet protocol provides for the transmission of datagrams between systems over the whole catenet. It specifically allows for the fragmentation and reassembly of the datagrams at the gateways, as the underlying networks may demand different packet sizes.

The Internet Protocol (US Military Standard 1771) is a very simple protocol, with no mechanism for end-to-end data reliability, flow control or sequencing. The header is quite complex, the fields being as follows:

Version

The version number of IP. There have been several new releases, which (given the size of ARPANET) must co-exist for some time.

IHL

The IP header length. Because of the options field, the header is not a fixed length. This field shows where the data starts.

Type of

This field allows for a priority system to be imposed, plus service indication of the desired, but not guaranteed, reliability required.

Length

The total length of the IP packet. Although there is a theoretical maximum of 64 Kbytes, most networks operate with much smaller packets, though all must accept at least 576 bytes.

ID/flags/offset

These fields enable a gateway to split up the datagram into smaller segments. The ID field ensures that the receiver can place together the fragments from the correct datagrams, as fragments from many datagrams may arrive in any order. The offset tells how far down the datagram this fragment is and the flags can be used to mark the datagram as non-fragmentable.

Time to live

This is a count which limits the lifetime of a datagram on the catenet. Each time it passes through a gateway, the count is decremented by one. If it reaches zero, the gateway does not forward it. This prevents permanently circulating datagrams.

Protocol

This indicates which higher level protocol is being carried, e.g. TCP or UDP

Checksum

This checksum covers the header only. It is up to the higher layers to detect transmission errors in the data.

Source/dest address

To assist the gateways to route datagrams by the most efficient path, each IP address is structured into a Network Number and a local address. There are three classes of network providing different numbers of locally administered addresses.

Options

The final part of the header is a variable number of optional fields, which are used to enforce security or network management.

Padding

This field is used to align the header to the next 32-bit boundary.

Because there is not facility for error reporting in IP, for example, the sender of a datagram is not informed if the intended recipient is available, an extra protocol is used particularly to help gateways between networks. This is called the Internet Control Message Protocol (ICMP) which, although it is carried over IP, is considered to be an integral part of it. It does not help in making IP reliable, however, it merely reports errors without trying to recover from them. Examples of ICMP messages include TIME EXCEEDED when the lifetime of a datagram expires and DESTINATION UNREACHABLE when a gateway or network has failed.

The gateways also exchange routing information using another extra protocol, called the gateway-to-gateway protocol. This enables the gateways to have up-to-date information on the loading on certain routes, so that bottlenecks can be avoided.

User Datagram Protocol

The User Datagram Protocol (UDP) provides a connectionless transport service to applications. Unlike the ISO protocols, which are layer independent, it assumes that IP is running below and implementations must have access to incoming IP headers. The UDP header, is very simple and can be considered as an extension of the IP header to permit multiple services to be addressed within the same IP network address.

Transimission Control Protocol

TCP (US Military Standard 1781) provides a highly reliable, connection oriented, end-to-end transport service between processes in end systems connected to the catenet. TCP only assumes that the layer below offers an unreliable datagram service and thus could run over any such protocols. In practice, however, it is invariably linked to IP. TCP provides the types of facility associated with the ISO Class 4 transport service, including error recovery, sequencing of packets, flow control by the windowing method and the support of multiplexed connections from the layer above. The operational procedures are similar to the ISO connection oriented protocols, such as LLC Type 2. The fields in the header are as follows:

Source/dest ports

These fields identify multiple streams to the layer above

Sequence/ack number

These are used for the windowing acknowledgement technique.

Data Offset

This is the number of 32-bit words in the TCP header which like the IP header has a variable length options field.

Flag bits

There are several bits used as status indicators to show, for example, the resetting of the connection.

Window

This field is used by the receiver to set the window size.

Checksum

Again this covers only the header.

Urgent pointer

The sender can indicate that an urgent datagram is coming and urges the receiver to handle it as quickly as possible.

Options

This variable-sized field contains some negotiation parameters to set the size of the TCP packets, for example.

Padding

To align to the next 32-bit boundary.

The procedures used by the TCP protocol are too complex to describe here. It can be seen however, that the catenet style of networking has benefit for linking LANs— hence the widespread use of TCP/IP on LANs. It should not be assumed, however, that TCP/IP networks are immune from the compatibility problems discussed earlier for ISO networks. Differences in interpretation of the protocols can drastically reduce interoperability and there are reports of deficiencies in many of the protocols. One interesting recent development, however, is an experimental implementation of the ISO transport service on top of TCP, which means that ISO applications could be carried over IP catenets. TCP/IP can also co-exist with ISO and other protocols on a LAN and it can be expected that the production of protocol converters should ease the transition between TCP/IP and ISO for many users.

Internet Architecture

Two networks can only be connected by a computer that attaches to both of them. A physical attachment does not provide the interconnection we have in mind, because such a connection does not guarantee that the computer will cooperate with other machines that wish to communicate. To have a viable internet, we need computers that are willing to shuffle packets from one network to another.

Computers which interconnect two networks and pass packets from one to the other are called internet gateways or internet routers. The idea of a gateway seems simple, but it is important because it provides a way to interconnect networks, not just machines. Note that in a TCP/IP Internet, computers called gateways provide all interconnections among physical networks. You might suspect that gateways, which must know how to route packets to their destination are large machines with enough primary or secondary memory to hold information about every machine in the internet to which they attach. However, gateways used with TCP/IP internets are usually minicomputers; they often have little or no disk storage and limited main memories. The concept of building a small internet gateway is gateways route packets based on destination network, not on distinction host. If routing is based on networks, the amount of information that a gateway needs to keep is proportional to the number of networks in the internet, not the number of machines. Note that TCP/IP is designed to provide a universal interconnection among machines independent of the particular networks to which they attach.

Thus, we want the user to view an internet as a single, virtual network to which all machines connect despite their physical connections. In addition to gateways that interconnect physical networks, internet access software is needed on each host to allow application programs to use the internet as if it were a single, real physical network. The advantage of providing interconnection at the network level now becomes clear. Because application programs that communicate over the internet do not know the details of underlying connections, they can be run without change on any machine. Because the details of each machine's physical network connections are hidden in the internet software, only that software needs to change when new physical connections appear or old ones disappear. It is possible to optimize routing by altering physical connections without event recompiling application programs. A second advantage of having communication at the network level is more subtle: users do not have to understand or remember how network connect or what traffic they carry.

Application programs can be written that operate independent of underlying physical connectivity. In fact, network managers are free to change interior parts of the underlying internet architecture without changing application software in most of the computers attached to the internet. It may be necessary for traffic traveling from one machine to another to pass across several intermediate networks. Thus, networks participating in the internet are analogous to highways in the US interstate system: each net agrees to handle transit traffic in exchange for the right to send traffic throughout the internet.

Typical users are unaffected and unaware of extra traffic on their local network. It is important to understand a fundamental concept: from the internet point of view, any communication system capable of transferring packets counts as a single network, independent of its delay and throughput characteristics, maximum packet size, or geographic scale. Note that the TCP/IP internet protocols treat all network equally. A local area network like an Ethernet, a wide area network like the NSFNET backbone, or a point-to-point link between two machines each count as one network.

TCP/IP Network Planning

The aim of TCP/IP network planning and design is to provide a communications infrastructure that meets the requirements of the organization with readily available equipment and skills. It must provide the correct level of performance for different functions within the organization, at different places and at acceptable costs. In setting up a local and wide are structure for TCP/IP, the first task of the designer is to consider what each of these terms means for that situation. Each case is unique but the overall size of the organization and its network requirement will determine the complexity of the problems to be solved.

Growth Rate

Whatever aspect of human communications you consider, it could be said that a measurement of success is often that the size and usage grows rapidly. As a result of experience in road network planning, this has become known as the 'motorway (or highway) effect'. If a system is useful, people change their travel habits and use the system in new ways that the planners never envisaged.

Traffic grows to fill the space available. In an organization a successful network has been seen to grow at a rate which was totally unexpected and to expand rapidly to cover the company. It is advisable to consider the initial size of the network while planning a TCP/IP installation and have some indication of maximum size and growth rate.

This measure of size has two dimensions:

(i) The total number of attached ports, that is, computer and router connections to the network

(ii) The geographic coverage.

It is important to consider what ways the network could grow—by addition of devices on the same network or by connection to other TCP/IP installations. In the first case, all the issues are under the control of one organization; in the second, they may not be. The problems to be solved will be different in each case. Today's computer applications and systems are distributed on workstations and PCs throughout the sites and buildings where the computer users sit. Some types of change cannot be centrally managed and must be carried out at each machine. These changes are always difficult and labour-intensive and hence costly. As far as possible, they must be predicted and eliminated.

These considerations can affect the detailed planning process the LAN and WAN links, the planning of the address space and of the bridges and routers which interconnect LANs and sites. Planners will wish to determine solutions to the following questions. How many cable systems will there be? How should the address plan for the network evolve? Is there a requirement for the Domain Name Service? Is responsibility split with one person or body? If it is split, is the division by function, by location, or by technology? Is there a need to split application management from communications management? Is there a need to split communications management into more than one subfunction?

Existing Standards

To avoid duplication of effort and perhaps more importantly to avoid choosing incompatible solutions to the same TCP/IP options and problems, it is quite important to determine if there are any other existing TCP/IP implementations in the organization. Some systems may hide their use of TCP/IP; the banyan VINES resource-sharing LAN or any communications management system which uses the simple network management protocol are current examples.

If other examples do exist and will share the same cables or TCP/IP equipment at any time, the developments must be coordinated. In some situations there may already be a central authority for TCP/IP implementation which has set local standards for the use of TCP/IP.

These standards should relate to:

- Addressing conventions
- Host-naming conventions
- Local area network
- Choice of equipment
- Choice of network software
- Configuration and management of the network
- Configuration and management of the applications

It is easier if these standards can be used rather than starting from scratch.

Traffic Flows and Capacity

While planning the network layout and capacity it is important to know the volume of information which will be carried. At the simplest level, high-performance routes in the network must follow the high traffic flows in the organization. Faults on those major arterial routes will affect more users, so they, if any, may need to be protected against failure. Judging future traffic flows is always one of the most difficult estimates in installing new TCP/IP systems.

One of the great successes of modern software development techniques is to provide an effective barrier between the application developer and the underlying network. But it leaves the network planners with a major problem. Some people can relate the use of an application to the traffic it will generate. Given the continued growth in workstation performance, existing LAN implementations already seem slow. For many commercial environments, a single physical LAN can support only 20 to 50 workstations and one or two file servers before the network must be partitioned with bridges or routers.

The need for 100 Mbps Fiber Distributed Data Interface (FDDI) or even higher network speeds (1 Gbps—10 Gbps) is evident, particularly for backbone networks and image systems, but the costs of such a system are not yet within the budgets of most network operators. In the absence of such speeds, planners must ration the limited resource of normal speed LANs.

They must understand how particular applications use the network and what the traffic flow between different user groups and applications processor are at different times of the day and business year.

Key questions are as follows:

- What will be the total volume of data on different parts of the network at the busiest time of the day? Is this traffic seasonal?
- How will the traffic grow with time, taking into account the changing and improving user perception of the network services and the increase in number of attached devices and a move towards more demanding applications?
- How is the traffic distributed among adjacent machines and to more remote machines?

The only way of obtaining such information is to measure the operation of real applications and extrapolate the results. Armed with the traffic information and its growth, it is time to consider the network structure.

Partitioning the Network

Bridges and **routers** partition the network and improve performance for workstations on the same cable. The majority of network traffic should be local to the group of users and a small percentage (15-30%) should cross the bridges into a backbone network which interconnects different user groups. If this traffic split cannot be achieved, then the bridge is not used in the optimum way. Splitting a network into small pools of users interconnected by routers and bridges is always a poor substitute for that single, reliable, large, high-speed network, for at any time a high proportion of the traffic is less than optimum.

By adding bridges and routers to a network the cost per user, the administrative and the technical difficulties all increase and the reliability and performance between some remote portions of the network can fall to unacceptable levels. So why do it? In local area networks it is justified by the **containment of traffic** to physical networks which that traffic must traverse; this reduces the load on the local LAN segment and there is a dramatic improvement in performance for local traffic to local file servers. For long-distance wide-area interconnection, there must be a convertor between different link layer technologies. The prime purpose of a bridge in a LAN is to prevent traffic flowing where it does not need to, rather than to allow traffic to flow where it will. In many networks, it is only secondary function of the bridge to provide communications where none existed by translating to a different type of cable and extending the cable length limits of the basic LAN specification.

In network partitioning, routers have few advantages and few disadvantages over bridges. They have a more positive role to play. Routers relay only what they are specifically told to relay. They are part of the IP protocol and are designed to interconnect network technologies of different performance.

Routers are particularly useful at matching the high speeds of LANs to the much lower speeds of intersite communications circuits that are now available. On the other hand they have a higher cost and lower performance and need more careful management than bridges.

Using Bridges

Bridges filter traffic by Media Access Control (MAC) address. They must examine each frame received on each port and build a table of frame source addresses with the port on which the frame was received. When the bridge learns that a source and destination are on the same port, it will not pass traffic for that destination to any other cable.

- The important performance factors of bridges are described as follows:
- Filtering rate – the ability to examine frames for possible relaying.
- Forwarding rate – the ability to relay frames which have to be relayed
- 'Routing' algorithm that allows bridges to be connected redundantly in parallel and in loops but prevents frames circulating round the loops.
- Transit delay—normally related to forwarding rate.
- Filter table size
- Variations in performance with filter table occupancy.

Bridges Filtering Rate

Bridges can filter at the theoretical maximum rate for Ethernet of 14880 frames per second. Even in busy operational networks the offered traffic will not be this demanding, for this figure is based on all minimum-sized frames. The true demand depends on the type of TCP/IP services in use. Networks used mainly for character-by-character TCP/IP Telnet terminal server traffic have a much higher number of small frames than those used for file transfer and NFS.

The importance of a bridge operating at this theoretical maximum figure is not that it can examine the number of frames per second but that there is no limitation to the number of successive short frames that can be captured by the bridge, since it can capture at the maximum possible rate. The frame rates on Token Ring systems are theoretically much higher than on Ethernet (20,000 fps on 4 Mbps and 80,000 fps on 16 Mbps Token Ring) but the overheads of TCP/IP mean that the absolute maximum practical frame rates are approximately 7700 and 31,000, respectively.

Bridges for TCP/IP traffic could be chosen accordingly. For multi-port hub bridges, one must ensure that each bridge port can examine all frames on every port simultaneously and that the specification does not just give some aggregate figure.

Limited Horizon

A TCP/IP application working through a bridge has a limited horizon. A bridge isolates two cable segments so that systems have no knowledge of the traffic on the other cable, that is, on the other side of the bridge. A bridge is more likely to be unable to relay all traffic, not because it does not have the power, but because the output cable is continuously busy. Frames will queue in the bridge but bridges eventually throw away any frames that are older than about one second.

Most low-level protocols – those which carry data over bridges – do not have any error correction or flow control. End stations may retransmit these lost frames from higher level software but, in an extreme case, this may just add to the network congestion that caused the problem in the first place. It is up to the network manager to design the network so that traffic is distributed correctly and does not concentrate on one work area or in one bridge.

Using a high-speed FDDI or Token Ring backbone or a hub bridge may complicate the design of the network. Traffic flows can become more critical, for they may arrive on the high-speed backbone successfully but focus on one work area where a number of key resources are located. High-performance resources, such as ONC (NFS) servers, should either be directly attached to the backbone or must be distributed on a number of feeder work area LANs.

Broadcasts, Broadcast Stroms and Multicast Frames

TCP/IP protocols use two techniques which impact on the performance of a bridged network. They use **broadcast** and **multicast frames** for discovering the locations of resources and for communicating between systems which cooperate to provide a common service. Multicast frames take capacity on the cable but are not processed by every station.

They become a problem only on slower wide area bridge links. 'Slow' is a relative term; for today's LANs, 'slow' could be 256 kbps, 128 kbps or less. Broadcast frames are much more detrimental to performance. They are generated by ARP, RARP, BOOTP and RIP. Every system on an Ethernet or Token Ring network must process every broadcast frame. If the number of broadcast frames increases, the performance of every system will degrade noticeably. A frame takes some time to process, independent of its size.

Each broadcast frame can reduce the performance of a PC by almost one normal data frame of 1000 to 1450 bytes. PCs slow down noticeably with 10 to 15 broadcast packets per second. Bridges relay broadcast frames everywhere. To try to filter broadcasts is to destroy the possibility of any-to-any communication. So networks which are interlinked only with bridges reach a size where the percentage of broadcast traffic from all the devices is unacceptable. Unless the broadcast traffic can be reduce, it becomes impossible to manage the network or to grow it further successfully. It has been known for in-house application programmers who do not appreciate the potential harmful effects to write applications using broadcasts.

On more than one occasion a complete LAN including powerful minicomputers, has been brought to a standstill by a **broadcast storm** of about 100 packets per second. Broadcast storms are sometimes attributed to Ethernet design limitations; it is often not realized that the broadcast storm is usually caused by a combination of bad software design and a poor bridged network structure of any type of LAN.

Bridging to a Backbone

As an aid to structuring the distribution of data between work areas it is common practice to use a **backbone** LAN to carry the transit traffic. This backbone may be built with the same technology as the work area, though often on a more robust cable (Thick Ethernet, 10Base5, rather than Thin Ethernet, 10Base2, or Unshielded Twisted Pair, 10BaseT), or it may use a different technology (16 Mbps Token Ring or 100 Mbps FDDI). This topology places a minimum of two bridges in series between any two work areas.

Unless application processor or file servers are directly attached to the backbone, the performance for demanding file transfer applications is affected by this double hop. This is most noticeable if the backbone is no faster than the work areas. Those applications using TCP as their transport layer will need an increase in window size; applications which use UDP protocols with a small datagram size may suffer badly.

Hub Bridges

Hub and **multiport bridges** replaces the backbone network with a single internal high-speed bus of greater speed than any LAN.

This reduces the double hop effect but requires more extensive cabling and potentially reduces the backbone to a single point of failure.

Identifying a Network Connection

Connections to a TCP/IP network are often known to each other and to users in three different ways, which identify the same connection to the network but at different levels of TCP/IP.

- As names: in the **fully qualified host** and **domain** name

  Vax1.icds.com.in

- Using the domain name scheme is often not considered early enough in the planning of commercial networks; users of larger networks will find it invaluable.
- As a group of four numbers separated by full stops. This is the IP or network address used by the IP layer of TCP/IP.

  164.120.9.61

- On a shared LAN by its network interface card address the 48-bit MAC address. (Medium Access Control address often called the physical address)

  02 60 8C 12 34 56

The three levels of address is required, since they all refer to the same connection to the TCP/IP Internet. The reason is that while at any one time these addresses identify the same location, over a period of time, each may change for different reasons. The three types of address allow a degree of flexibility where none would exist if the functions were not separated:

- The host and domain name should remain unchanged for the longest time, it is completely determined by the system designers and managers, though it will often change if there is a major change in machine location.
- The IP address may change due to network growth and reconfiguration, for instance, if a machine is moved from one location in a building to another.
- The MAC address may change for similar growth or performance reasons, or because the network card is replaced following a card failure. The shortest lived address is likely to be the MAC address.

The fully qualified domain name is for 'human consumption' and consists of a set of identifiers, separated by full stops, which describe a computer in a hierarchical relationship to all others. For example:

machine.departmet.site.organization.org_type.country

Introducing flexibility brings with it the possibility of error and communications failure if the flexible functions are not managed and controlled correctly.

Planning the IP Address Scheme

To plan an IP addressing scheme you must have the following information:

(i) The maximum number of host ports that your organization could ever wish to interconnect. The whole of your organization is not just your particular department, but the whole organizational structure, if necessary worldwide, which may at any time be interconnected.

(ii) An understanding of the number of devices at each location and in each building on each site. Assume one address per member of staff in those buildings and leave some 25% spare.

(iii) An understanding of the different departments, their geographic locations and the likelihood that they will need to communicate. An estimate of the amount of information that is exchanged is useful but it has a very short-lived value.

(iv) A knowledge of any other current users of TCP/IP and any standardization decisions that have been taken already

In a small organization of a few hundred people, getting this information is straightforward in comparison to a large corporation; but it is the large corporation that must have accurate figures and which must derive centralized standards that are adhered to everywhere.

Internet Protocol

The Internet Protocol (IP) may be described as the network layer protocol of TCP/IP. IP is operated and interpreted by each intermediate relay in an interconnected set of LANs and WANs which is using the TCP/IP protocol suite co communicate.

Such a collection is often called an **internetwork** and the intermediate relays are routers. IP provides a best efforts delivery service based on a technique called **datagram transmission;** 'best efforts' and 'datagram' because no attempt is made by IP to recover any errors which may occur in transmission.

IP supports routing and relaying of information between communicating hosts or end devices according to the Type or quality Of Service (TOS) they require. IP allows routing errors to be trapped and reported and their effects on system performance to be minimized. IP does not make assumptions about the underlying network of physical cables. LAN hardware (Ethernet, Token Ring or FDDI) or the point-to-point wide area links (PTT circuits).

IP Addressing

The IP address is one component in the Internet protocol. The IP address is a number that uniquely identifies the connection of a host computer or end system as OSI would call it, to a physical network as it communicates with other computers or end systems. Hosts with more than one connection have a different IP address for each one.

IP routers also have their own IP addresses for they can be the source and destination of IP datagrams. The purpose of the IP address is twofold: to identify each connection to the internetwork in a way that is independent of the underlying physical network (LAN or WAN) technology and to collect a group of connections together to simplify routing. Internetwork routers use IP addresses to make routing decisions. IP addresses must be unique in the communicating internetwork. If not, communications will fail erratically.

Since TCP/IP protocols do not directly provide any technical means by which IP addresses can be automatically made unique, it is up to network managers to configure and manage them correctly by traditional manual methods aided by database and network management technology.

MAC Addresses

Where TCP/IP systems are connected to a shared cable such as an Ethernet or Token Ring LAN, communication between stations must take place using MAC addresses, normally built into the network adapter card. Since the IP address is configured independently of the MAC address, it remains unchanged even if the network card fails and is replaced. Every Ethernet or token Ring card comes with a preconfigured 48-bit MAC address, its universally managed address. LAN standards also allow locally managed addresses; network cards can be loaded with a 48-bit address chosen by the network manager.

Locally managed addresses are not normally used in TCP/IP systems. AS IP addressed in TCP/IP must be controlled and managed, there is little value in adding a second layer of management by also configuring and controlling MAC addresses. But the issue of MAC address management does not disappear completely from the TCP/IP story; some of the facilities of TCP/IP such as the Boot Protocol, BOOTP, use the MAC address as a fixed reference point for obtaining other information. If you wish to use these features, you must at least have a record of the MAC address of each computer for which the facility will be used.

These addresses appear as a reference point in look-up tables in information servers. But as discussed above, the MAC address can change if the network card is replaced. In a large network, keeping an up-to-date record of MAC addresses and ensuring that all servers have the correct record can be time-consuming. Few advanced star wiring systems have management facilities that can record the MAC address attached to each user drop cable.

Such systems make it easier to record the location of particular MAC addresses.

CHARACTERISTICS OF THE IP ADDRESS

The IP address is a 32-bit number which must be unique in internetwork. Devices which must have an IP address include every connection of each application processor and of each network router. As mentioned previously, computers with more than one network connection have a different IP address for each connection.

In TCP/IP literature, such computers are referred to as **multihomed.** These connections are usually on different networks. This is the reason for sizing the network-by-network connections rather than the number of computers, though these numbers will often be very similar. Unlike some other network addressing schemes, the IP address does not necessarily convey any information about geographic location.

Given an IP address you can only deduce a management authority; that authority could manage one corporate network which in itself has global coverage and meshes with many other global networks. This has interesting implications for routing between two worldwide networks. In other way, the IP addressing scheme is not hierarchical unlike the telephone or telex network or for that matter the CCITT X.121 addressing scheme for the X.25 interface to public packet switched networks. The 32-bit IP address has two components a **network number** or network identifier and a **host number** or host identifier.

Some 'class bits' can be extracted from the network number, but trying to examine these on their own can lead to confusion. It is safer always to think of the network number as containing the class bits.

It is the network number which identifies the controlling organization and the port number which identifies the particular connection within the authority of that organization. The term 'host number' is historic and this name could cause confusion for, as we have seen, a multihomed host has more than one IP address and hence more than one host number.

For reasons that will become apparent later, it would be unusual for two ports on the same machine to have the same network number.

Class bits + Network number	**Host number**

The terms **net id.** and **host id**. are in common usage for network number and host number. IP addresses are divided into five address classes (A to E). It is important to understand that these divisions were conceived to ease the management of addresses by the Internet Activities Board (IAB); they have less immediate significance for the network manager. The first three classes, A, B, C, are available for normal allocation and for host-to-host communications.

Class D and class E addresses are not for general use; class D is reserved for special use by IAB designated protocols and class E is reserved for future use. One use of class D addresses is by routers, so network managers may encounter them while monitoring router protocols. There are no practical distinctions in the way in which computer systems with class A, class B or class C addresses use those addresses.

With some noted exceptions, which are discussed further below, any address from any class is equivalent for communications purposes. In principle, any host can communicate equally well using an address is the number of network numbers and the number of host connections which each network number can support.

The limitations of each class are described as follows:

Network class	Max. number of network numbers	Max. number of hosts on Each network number
A	126	16 777 214
B	16 382	65 534
C	2 097 150	254
D	Not applicable—reserved for multicast systems	
E	Reserved for IAB use	

Network Numbers and Host Numbers

The choice of network numbers is most important. Network connections with the same network number should communicate directly on the same physical LAN.

Network connections with different network numbers do not communicate directly; they must use the services of a router.

This router either is directly connected between the two LANs to which the hosts connect or it in turn knows of a router which can relay the message towards its ultimate destination.

These factors determine the basic rules for choosing network numbers and host numbers. They may alternatively be stated as:

- Computers separated only by bridges or repeaters will have the same network number
- Computers or workstations separated by routers have different network numbers.

For the network implementor, the most important factor is the choice of IP address for a particular host is affected by the presence of routers. The positioning of routers is determined by the exact geography of the underlying physical networks which connect computers, floors, buildings, sites and countries into a complete internetwork.

It is also heavily influenced by organizational needs, traffic flows and traffic volume. The layout will change as the network grows and matures. If a bridge is replaced by a router, the network number on one side of the new router must change. A TCP/IP addressing scheme evolves as the needs of users are better understood during the design process.

Adding a TCP/IP addressing scheme to a LAN must take into account the existing layout of that LAN. One factor is key. Network planners must attempt to design an addressing scheme that can remain substantially unchanged in a changing environment.

This can be achieved using subnetwork addressing. The convention is the address is written down, or described to software, in **dotted decimal notation.** Each eight bits of the address (each **octet)** is converted to a decimal number in the range 0 to 255 and separated by a dot (.).

While the US standards initially specified 'dotted decimal notation' some computer staff are more at home with hexadecimal notation. **Dotted hexadecimal** (and UNIX or C-style hexadecimal) and **octal** notations are sometimes used and will be accepted by some (though by no means all) implementations.

Occasionally it is useful, it somewhat long-winded, to represent these numbers in binary. Leading zeros in each octet, which have no significance, need not be included. 128.1.0.9 is valid and more usual than 128.001.000.009, though this is also perfectly acceptable; however, 128.1.0.9 or 128...9 are not valid.

Table: Distinguishing the class of address

Address Class	*Class bits*	*Number of network bits*	*First usable value*	*Last usable*	*Remark*
A	0	7	1	126	Value 0 and 127 are reserved
B	10	14	128.1	191.254	
C	110	21	192.0.1	223.255.254	
D	1110	—	224.0.0.0	239.255.255.254	Not available for general use
E	1111	—	240.0.0.0	255.255.255.254	Not available for general use

Distinguishing the Class of Address

The five classes of address have already been mentioned. The class of address is determined by certain bits in the first eight bits, that is, in the first decimal number of the four. The magnitude of the first number that defines the class of the address is given in the table.

There are two important features of this system:

(i) The division between one class and the next is always at an octet boundary. This simplifies finding the boundaries between the classes of address, since each decimal number represents one octet.

(ii) When the network number is written down the 'class bits' are always included in the first octet, to ensure that the class of address and hence the true network number are unambiguous.

It is important that users of TCP/IP, planners and implementors would be fully familiar with the different classes of address and the limitations that they place on network growth. Many people new to the subject at first find the technique of dotted decimal notation a little eccentric.

But it should become second nature to recognize the class of address, the network number and the host id. As compared to other network addressing schemes the TCP/IP addressing range is quite limited. Current work in the IAB is investigating the options for extending the address range.

IAB and Network Number Registration

The address in an internetwork must be unique, there has to be a registry which ensures that such a policy can be enforced. TCP/IP was developed for use on the US Internet. This collection of networks is managed by many different authorities, with the IAB as overall design authority. In this environment of devolved management, the network number has two functions.

First, since each IP address on the whole set of interconnected networks must be unique, the network number is used to identify one addressing authority, often called an autonomous system, responsible for issuing unique connection ids in that part of the address space. The second function is to support routing. The IAB ensures that IP addresses on the Internet are unique, by registering and issuing network numbers to organizations that have reasons to connect to the Internet.

Such organizations don't choose their own network number, it is issued to them. They agree to undertake certain network management responsibilities when they request an official IAB address allocation. They must then issue host Ids so that they are unique within their own network number address space. If they fail to issue unique host numbers, only the services of that organization will be affected. The IAB has devolved the clerical tasks of registering and issuing IP network numbers to the Internet Registry, part of the Internet assigned Numbers Authority (IANA) which controls all numbers in the TCP/IP protocol suite, which must be managed if correct operation is to be guaranteed.

Configuring the IP Address

Every computer, workstation, personal computer, network router and network management station which 'speaks IP' must have a different IP address for each of its connections. The IP address is entered through the normal configuration management processes. IP addresses are usually represented and entered in dotted decimal notation; occasionally dotted hexadecimal notation is accepted.

The address is usually stored in non-volatile memory, either RAM or on a disk file when available. Diskless workstations often have no nonvolatile storage. They obtain their IP address across the network at start-up time using BOOTP or RARP. Visiting each device to change the IP address is time-consuming, particularly in dispersed networks. BOOTP provides a mechanism for centralizing the distribution of IP addresses and other useful TCP/IP parameters, even for machines which do have storage. The key to distributing the correct IP address and other information via BOOTP is the MAC address of the interface card. It is then essential to record accurately the MAC address used by each machine on the network that uses the BOOTP service. This is excellent policy for fault diagnosis and security in any case, though it is often neglected. In an operational network, IP addresses become recorded in distributed tables and in software in machines.

While this is bad practice, it is unavoidable. Frequent wholesale changes to IP addresses must not occur, so preplanning is essential. Such changes are labour-intensive because of the widespread distribution of addresses; the change introduces errors and has unpredictable consequences for the integrity of operational applications and for the time taken to restore any-to-any communications.

Reserved IP Addresses

Certain IP network numbers and host numbers are reserved for the use of particular aspects of TCP/IP communication. Not all these protocols are regularly used. Once you configure a connection with a reserved IP address, the faults caused are likely to be obscure, apparently intermittent and difficult to isolate. No all host software checks that the IP address it is requested to use is invalid. The following addresses are reserved:

- Network number 127.X.X.X, where X.X.X is any set of numbers. This is used for a local software loopback test.
- A network number of all 0s is classless and means 'my current network which I do not know the number of –sometimes referred to as 'this network'
- A network number of all 1s.
- Host number 0 is reserved to refer to a particular network number. For example, 192.0.0.1 is the first class C network address which could be allocated.
- Host number 'all 1s' is reserved to broadcast to all hosts on a specific network; it can only be used as a destination address.
- The full address 0.0.0.0 is reserved. It is used in two ways: as a source address when the host does not know its genuine address, for example during bootstrapping of a diskless workstation and by routers in a list of addresses to advertise the default route, the route to all networks which are not explicitly listed.
- The full address 255.255.255.255 is reserved as a destination address to mean 'broadcast to all hosts on my network'. 0.0.0.0 as a destination is an obsolete form of 255.255.255.255.

IP Addresses with Routers an Dial-up Devices

Few older router implementations need a point-to-point wide area PTT or dial-up link between two LANs should be identified with its own unique IP network number with only two connections attached. In the larger network that is wasteful of the limited resource of IP network numbers. Check with your router manufacturer that the most modern techniques, which conserve network and subnetwork numbers, are used in their implementation.

SUMMARY

1. PCs can be used for sharing of information too with others having similar type of equipments.
2. When you send data from one location to another using any electronic means, it is called Data communication.
3. Telephone lines may be used to transmit computer data using the modems.
4. A leased line is a telephone line that is leased for the express purpose of maintaining a communication channel between two computers.
5. A switched line can be used for either voice or data communication and is switched from user to user, as requirements dictate.
6. Twisted pair [YP] is a common scheme for using copper wire as telecommunication cable.
7. Coaxial cables come in protective cover which shields the cable from physical dangers as well as from electromagnetic interference.
8. Fiber optics can transmit data at very high speed with no errors.
9. Microwave signals are transmitted through the atmosphere rather than through wire cables, similar to the way radio and television signals are transmitted.
10. The narrow-band channel is used where data volume is relatively low and which transmits data at a rate between 40 to 100 bits per second (bps).
11. The voice-band channels are able to speed up the transmission rate between 110 to 9600 bits per second.
12. The broad-band channels are used where data volumes are large and which transmit data at rate upto several megabits per second.
13. The broad-band channels are used where data volumes are large and which transmit data at rate upto several megabits per second.
14. Amplitude-shift keying encodes binary data by varying the signal's amplitude between two or more levels.
15. Frequency-shift keying encodes binary data by varying the signal's frequency between two or more values.
16. A parallel interface is the one that uses eight wires to transmit all 8 bits in a byte at the same time.
17. In a point-to-point channel configuration, a device is connected directly to another devices by a dedicated communication channel.
18. In the multi-point channel configuration, three or more devices, e.g., a terminal or computer, are connected to the same line.
19. In Half-duplex mode, data can be transmitted back and forth between two stations, but data can only go in one of the directions at any point of time.
20. The full-duplex mode allows a device to receive and send data simultaneously.
21. Transferring files to and from your disk drive is one of the most common communication applications.
22. A protocol consists of the technical details that regulate data transmission between computers.
23. The most important applications of data communication is the ability to access external databases.
24. A bulletin board is a communication system that allows users to call in and either leave or retrieve messages.
25. For the purpose of data transmission, particularly in local area networks, messages are broken down into segments, called packets.
26. Most computer applications, including data communication, require both appropriate hardware and software.
27. Micro-computers can also be connected to large systems in a micro-to-mainframe link to share data and computing power.
28. A value added carrier is an organization that leases communication channels from the common carriers (it may not have its own transmission facilities) and adds extra services over and above what the common carriers provide.
29. Microcomputers are often connected for data communication in a micro-to-micro link so that microcomputer users with incompatible data formats can share data.
30. Networking is a concept, where 2 or more than 2 computers are joined together to share information.
31. Password access can be configured to allow the user to read but not to change a particular resource or to allow full access, including the ability to write to a resource (which would be necessary for sending jobs to a printer).
32. A local area network (LAN) is two or more computers directly linked within a small well-defined area such as a room, building, or group of closely placed buildings.

33. A wide area network is two or more computers that are geographically dispersed, linked by communication facilities such as telephone system or microwave relays.
34. There are ways in which you can connect the various computers for networking. This physical arrangement is called Topology.
35. In Ring Topology all the server/nodes are joined together to form a ring.
36. In Bus Topology all the server/nodes share a common bus of connecting cables.
37. In Star Topology all the computers and the main server form a star like shape.
38. Mesh Topology features a direct path between two nodes.
39. Hybrid is a combination of two or more network topologies.
40. Ethernet is the most popular protocol used for LAN communications.
41. When one computer communicates with another using the TCP/IP protocol, it breaks the information it needs to send into 'chunks' small enough for the TCP/IP packet to be handle and then attaches a destination address and a source address.
42. Value Added Network is an established data communication network that owns a leases communication facilities and computers to manage communication.
43. File update synchronization is a service that compares the time and date corresponding files were saved and determines which is most current.
44. Print services accept print job request, interpret print job formats and printer configurations, manage print queues and interact with networkable printers and fax equipment for network clients.
45. Print servers can often handle simultaneous request for print services.
46. Message services include storing, accessing and delivering text, binary, graphic, digitized video and audio data.
47. Workflow management application intelligently forms, route notices and documents among network clients.
48. Application services are network services that run software for network clients.
49. Network database services provide server based database storage and retrieval that allow network clients to control data manipulation and presentation.
50. Like a formal letter e-mail also is divided into various sections.
51. The message received from A can be sent to B by using Forward option.
52. If you do not require any message, you can delete it or others too.
53. Electronic Data Interchange (EDI) refers to the structured transmission of data between organizations by electronic means.
54. The EDI standards were designed to be independent of communication and software technologies.
55. VANs provide a number of additional services, e.g., retransmitting documents, providing third party audit information, acting as a gateway for different transmission methods, and handling telecommunications support.
56. One of the most significant barriers is the accompanying business process change.
57. Client/server systems can be scaled horizontally or vertically. Horizontally scaling means adding or removing client workstations with only a slight performance impact. Vertical scaling means migrating to a larger and faster server machine or multiservers.
58. Computers which allow the files to be shared across the network are called file servers.
59. Groupware addresses the management of semi-structured information such as text, image, mail, bulletin boards and the flow of work.
60. With an object server, the client/server application is written as a set of communicating object.
61. Client/server applications can also be differentiated by how the distributed application is split between the client and the server.
62. Fat clients and Fat servers are also called 2 Tier and 3 Tier client/server architectures.
63. With file service, a database program running on a workstation PC requests blocks of files from the file server.
64. A Value Added Process (VAP) is an extension to the file server software.
65. By using a dedicated database server, you can reduce traffic on the LAN cable and free workstations from lengthy database processing.
66. Appropriate networking software needs to be loaded on both ends in order for them to communicate.

67. Physical units are combinations of hardware, firmware and software that manage and monitor the resources of a node.
68. Logical units are the "entitles" of the network that provide the means to establish a connection with another logical unit and exchange information.
69. SQL Server is a high-performance SQL-based, relational database server that is based on client/server architecture.
70. Oracle Corporation, one of the largest independent vendors of DBMS software, currently provides a XENIX-based SQL database server for use with PC LANs.
71. The relevance of TCP/IP to LANs is two–fold. First, as it is a data gram based protocol, it is well suited to LAN access method, particularly Ethernet. Secondly, it is particularly popular within the UNIX community, giving it a large user base, many of whom wish to use LANs.
72. Most networks provide some sort of connection mechanism to get from point A to point B.
73. IP is a datagram service. It basically provides rudimentary internetwork routing, services without any regard to the destination program, TCP formats, error control, packet sequencing etc.
74. File Transfer facilities are usually provided for by a mechanism known as the File Transfer Protocol (FTP).
75. TELNET is a virtual terminal facility that allows a user to connect to a remote system as if the user's terminal were hard-wired to that remote system.
76. The TCP and IP, explain only the communication aspects, the movement of data across a set of interconnected physical networks.

MULTIPLE CHOICE QUESTIONS

1. Which of the following is not a transmission medium?
   (a) telephone lines (b) coaxial cable **(c) modem**
2. Which of the fofllowing type of channels moves data relatively slowly?
   (a) narrowband channel (b) wideband channel (c) voiceband channel
3. Which of the following communication modes support two-way traffic but in only one direction at a time?
   (a) simplex **(b) half duplex** (c) three quarter duplex
4. Most data communications involving telegraph lines are:
   (a) simplex lines (b) wideband channels **(c) narrowband channels**
5. A distributed data processing configuration which all activities must pass through a centrally located computer is called a:
   (a) ring network **(b) spider network** (c) hierarchical network
6. The device which performs modulation and demodulation is called :
   (a) modem (b) fibre optics (c) satellite
7. Which of the following communication lines is best suited to interactive processing applications?
   (a) narrow band channels (b) simplex lines **(c) full duplex lines**
8. A communication device that combines transmission from server I/O devices into on line is a:
   (a) concentrator (b) modifier **(c) multiplexer**
9. A required characteristic of an on-line real-time system is:
   (a) more than one CPU (b) offline processing **(c) no delay in processing**
10. Communication circuits that transmit data in both directions but not at the same time are operating in:
    (a) a simplex mode (b) **a half duplex mode** (c) a full duplex mode

REVIEW QUESTIONS

1. What is client server computing?
2. Define the terms:
   Asymmetrical Protocols / Encapsulation of Services
   Integrity / Message-based-Exchanges

Mix-and-Match
Service
Transparency of location

Scalability
Shared resources

3. What is the Client Server?
4. What are file servers?
5. Define the followings:

Dedicated Servers
Non-Dedicated Servers
Proprietary Servers
Super Servers
Value File Servers
Batch processing servers
Central File Server Systems
Communication Servers
Database Servers
Facsimile Servers
Groupware Servers
Object Server
Peer-to-Peer LAN
Print Servers
Transaction Servers
WEB Servers
FAT Servers

8. What do you understand by 2 Tier and 3 Tier?
9. Write a short note on Futuristic Client/Server?
10. What technological do you need for client server application?
11. What is a LAN database?
12. Describe the various options available in the form of software for server based database?
13. In how many ways a database server can be implemented?
14. How does a database server effect the file server?
15. Define the term Dedicated Database Server.
16. How can you have a background database server on a workstation?
17. Write a short note on Application Coprocessor in Workstation.
18. Which are the prominent software developers who have gone in for SQL database server?
19. What do you mean by LAN Operating Systems?
20. Write a short note on NETWARE.
21. Describe Digital Network Architecture.
22. Describe DNA Protocol Summary.
23. What functions does the proprietary architecture perform?
24. Write a short note on AppleTalk.
25. Define the following topics:

Name Binding Protocol
AppleTalk Transaction Protocol
Printer Access Protocol
AppleTalk Data Stream Protocol
AppleTalk Filing Protocol
AppleShare File Server
AppleShare Print Server

26. Describe Systems Network Architecture
27. Define SNA layers specially the following:

Physical Control
Data Link Control
Path Control
Transmission Control
Data Flow Control
Presentation Services
NAU Services
Physical Units
Logical Units
Control Points
Token-Ring
Synchronous Data Link Control
Network Control Program
Virtual Telecommuncations Access Method
Customer Information Control System
Advanced Peer-to-Peer Networking

Information Management System
Advanced Program-to-Program Communication
Distributed Data Management
SNA Distribution Services
Documents Interchange Architecture

28. Describe LAN manager interaction with Windows NT.
29. Describe the various SQL server platforms.
30. Write short note on following servers:
    Novell Netware SQL
    Fox Software FoxServer
    Microsoft SQL Server
    Gupta SQL Base
    Oracle
31. What is TCP/IP?
32. What are protocols?
33. Describe the working of TCP/IP.
34. What is the function of TCP?
35. What is an IP?
36. What is the difference between TCP and IP?
37. Write a short note on Gateways and IP.
38. Describe the following:
    File Transfer
    TELNET
39. What do you understand by the following:
    Trival File Transfer Protocol
    Simple Mail Transfer Protocol
40. Write a short note on:
    Network File System
    TCP/IP Implementations
41. Describe in details the TCP/IP Communication Architecture.
42. Which 3 aspects does an architecture looks for in a communications protocol?
43. Write short notes on:
    Upper Layer Protocols
    Lower Layer Protocols
44. Describe TCP/IP Protocol Set Structure.
45. Describe Internet Protocol.
46. Describe the following terms in respect of Internet Protocol:
    Version
    IHL
    Type of
    Length
    ID/Flags/Offset
    Time to live
    Protocol
    Checksum
    Source/dest address
    Options
    Padding
47. Describe the following terms with respect to Transmission Control Protocol:
    Source/dest ports
    Sequence/ack number
    Data Offset
    Flag bits
    Window
    Checksum
    Urgent pointer
    Options
    Padding
48. Write a short note on Internet Architecture.
49. Describe what all goes into TCP/IP Network Planning
50. What are Bridges and how are they used?
51. Define the terms:
    Bridges Filtering Rate
    Broadcasts
    Broadcast Stroms
    Multicast Frames

Bridging to a Backbone Hub Bridges

52. How would you identify a network connection?
53. What all goes into planning the IP address scheme?
54. Write short notes on:

    Internet Protocol IP Addressing

    MAC Address
55. What are the characteristics of the IP Address?
56. What are Network Numbers and Host Numbers?
57. How would you configure the IP Address?
58. What do you understand by reserved IP Address?

ANSWERS

Multiple Choice Questions

1. c	2. a	3. b	4. c
5. b	6. a	7. c	8. c
9. c	10. b		

CHAPTER 6

System Software

Learning Objectives

After going through this chapter, you should appreciate the following:

- **System Software**

Operating System	Definition of Operating Systems
Types of Operating Systems	Importance of Operating Systems
Memory Organization	Linking, Loading and Executing Control Program
Functions of Operating System	Process Management Functions

- **Microsoft Disk Operating System (DOS)**

File Structure in DOS	Storage of Files
Creating and Changing Directory	DOS commands

- **Windows XP**

System Requirements	Step-by-Step Installation
Exploring Windows XP Desktop	Exploring the Taskbar
My Computer	Recycle Bin
My Documents	Introduction to Control Panel
Accessing Control Panel	Appearance and Themes
Printers and Other Hardware	Network and Internet Connections
User Accounts	Add or Remove Programs
Date, Time, Language and ...	Sound, Speech and Audio Devices
Accessibility Options	Performance and Maintenance

- **Compilers**

  Assembler — Loader

- **Open Systems**
- **UNIX/XENIX**

  Development of UNIX

- **UNIX Design**

Programmer's Interfaces	Users Interfaces
Process Management	Memory Management
File System	

- **LINUX**

Linux Commands and Filters	Shell
Linux file structure	Vi Editor
System Administration	

SYSTEM SOFTWARE

By System Software, we mean the *Software* which runs the *System*. Here the System means the *Computer* and Software means the *Computer Program*. In each and every computer, a system software is a **must**. Otherwise it will not run. Now, *why it is needed* and *what it does*? Well, it is needed to direct the various parts of the computer to work accordingly. It does the work of controlling the hardware parts of the computer so that they can perform better. Thus, we can say that:

System software – a set of programs that organise, utilise and control hardware in a Computer System.

Let us now go back and understand what computer software is. Computer software is a set of programs, which enables a computer to perform specific tasks. This is opposite to what hardware does. There are many types of software.

Remember: Software is always written as Software and not as Softwares.

Let us now see the various types of software.

Types of Software

Computer software systems divide software systems into three major classes: System software, Programming software and Application software.

Each one of them is further divided into various other types of software.

System Software

System software helps run the computer hardware and computer system. It includes operating systems, device drivers, diagnostic tools, servers, windows systems, utilities and more. The purpose of systems software is to:

- Extract the applications programmer as much as possible from the details of the particular computer complex being used.
- Utilize the memory and other hardware features and such accessory devices as communications, printers, readers, displays, keyboards, etc.

Programming Software

Programming software usually provides tools to assist a programmer in writing computer programs and software using different programming languages in a more convenient way. The tools include text editors, compilers, interpreters, linkers, debuggers, and so on. These programs are then bundled into a package called Software. It creates link between the various programs of the software, so that the user has not to bother about jumping from one program to another, they have already been done so.

Programming Software are used to write programs.

Application Software

Application software allows users to accomplish one or more specific (non-computer related) tasks. Typical applications include industrial automation, business software, educational software, medical software, databases, and computer games. Businesses are probably the biggest users of application software, but almost every field of human activity now uses some form of application software.

Application Software are used to create applications.

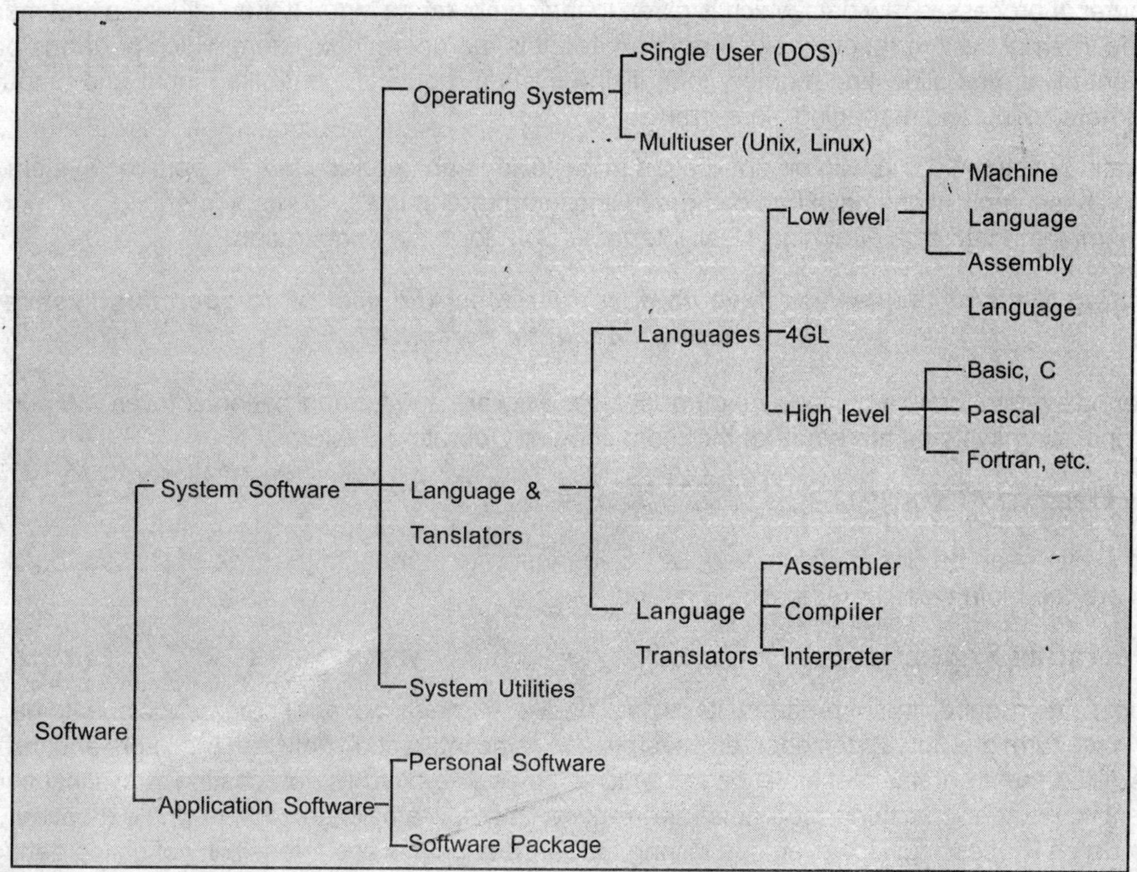

Operating System

An Operating System (OS) is a set of computer programs that manage the hardware and software resources of a computer. An operating system processes raw system and user input and responds by allocating and managing tasks and internal system resources as a service to users and programs of the system. At the foundation of all system software, an operating system performs basic tasks such as controlling and allocating memory, prioritizing system requests, controlling input and output devices, facilitating networking and managing file systems.

Operating Systems themselves have no user interfaces.

Most operating systems come with an application that provides an interface to the OS managed resources. These applications have had command line interpreters as a basic user interface, but more recently have been implemented as a graphical user interface (GUI) for ease of operation. Operating Systems themselves have no user interfaces; the user of an OS is an application, not a person. The operating system forms a platform for other system software and for application software. Windows, Linux, and Mac OS are some of the most popular OS's.

Operating systems (OS) provide a set of functions needed and used by most application-programs on a computer, and the necessary linkages for the control and synchronization of the computer's hardware. On the first computers, without an operating system, every program needed the full hardware specification to run correctly and perform standard tasks, and its own drivers for peripheral devices like printers and card-readers. The growing complexity of hardware and application-programs eventually made operating systems a necessity.

Definition of Operating Systems

An operating system (OS) is a set of computer programs that manages the hardware and software resources of a computer. It processes raw data which is given to the computer as input. It then allocates and manages the tasks of the internal system resources of the computer. It is the operating system which performs basic tasks such as controlling and allocating memory, prioritizing system requests, controlling input and output devices, facilitating networking and managing file systems.

Most operating systems come with an application that provides an interface to the operating system managed resources. These applications have had command line interpreters as a basic user interface, but more recently have been implemented as a Graphical User Interface (GUI) for ease of operation.

Operating Systems themselves have no user interfaces; the user of an operating system is an application, not a person.

The operating system forms a platform for other system software and for application software. Windows, Linux, and Mac operating systems are some of the most popular Operating Systems.

Types of Operating Systems

Operating system can be classified into various categories, with respect to the type of processing, it supports. Following are the main types of Operating System:

Batch Operating System

Batch processing requires that a program, its related data and relevant control commands should be submitted together, in the form of a Job. Batch operating system allows no interaction between the users and the executing programs. Thus the programs that have long execution times (like payrolls, forecasting, statistical analysis and large scientific number-crunching programs) and require little operator interaction during execution, were well served by Batch Processing. However, due to long turn-around delays and infeasibility of online debugging, the Batch Processing was not at all suitable for software development.

Batch operating system allows no interaction between the users and the executing programs.

The typical features of a batch operating system are:

1. **Scheduling**. The scheduling of jobs was normally in the order of their arrival, i.e., First Come First Served (FCFS). This criteria provides a fair deal to the jobs, but suffers from long average turn-around time and average waiting time, since some short jobs may have to wait for unduly long periods to get executed, if some long jobs are already queued ahead of the short jobs. To overcome this limitation, another criteria known as Shortest Job Next, was evolved, which offered preference to pending shorter jobs over the long jobs. This offered much better average turn around time and average waiting time of the pending jobs.
2. **Memory Management**. Memory used to be divided into two permanent partitions—one permanently occupied by the resident portion of the operating system and the other dynamically used to load the transient programs for execution. When a transient program terminates, it vacates the memory partition occupied by it and the same is assigned to other waiting transient program.
3. **I/O Management**. Since, only one program is used to be under execution at a time, there was no contention for the allocation of I/O Devices. So, a simple program-controlled I/O approach was good enough to access the I/O Devices.
4. **File Management**. Since, these used to only one program accessing the files at a time, there was no need of providing concurrency control.

   Thus, in a nutshell the Batch operating system was limited to a Loader and some simple Device Drivers.

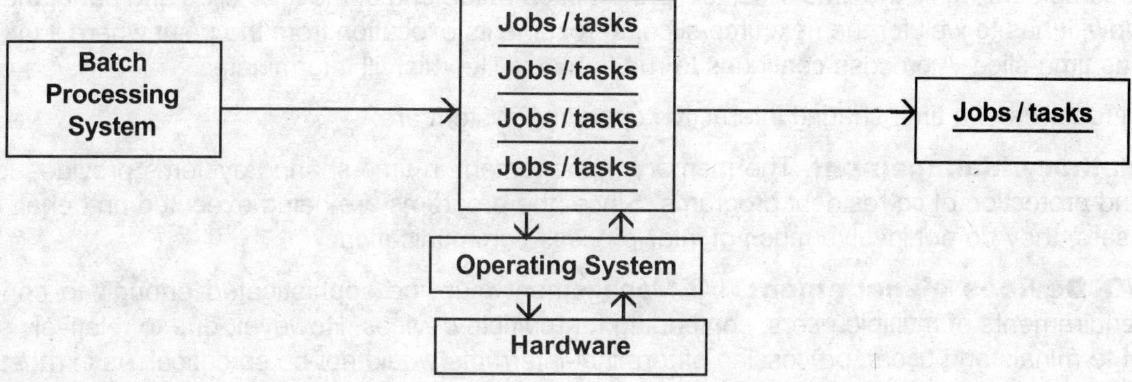

Multi-programming Operating System

A multi-programming oprating system permits multiple programs to be loaded into the memory and execute the programs concurrently. A program in execution is called a "Process" or a "Task".

The concurrent execution of programs has a significant potential for improving the utilization of system resources and thus enhancing the system throughout, as compared to batch and serial processing.

This potential is exploited by multi-programming operating system, which multiplexes the computer resources amongst a multitude of concurrent programs. A program in execution is called a Process. When a running process requests one I/O, it goes to "Wait" state. Then another Ready process (i.e., one of the processes from the "Ready" queue) is scheduled to "Run". So, when a process goes for I/O, the CPU is not left idling. When the I/O requested by a Waiting process is completed, it is transferred from "Waiting" to "Ready" state and wait to be scheduled, as per the predecided scheduled criteria.

Time-sharing Interactive Operating System

The time-sharing interactive operating systems belong to the era of a large mainframe systems, that were made available to a large number of users for accessing concurrently in an interactive mode. Each user used to interact with the system through a separate Video Terminal. A programmer could enter its source code using sophisticated editors, compile the source code, link the object code and run the executable code interactively. At any stage, the user could interact with the execution of its program. Debugging could be performed online. This reduced the time needed for program development, drastically. The operating system served the interactive users, in a round-robin fashion, allowing a fixed time-slice for each user to have control of the CPU. Since, the operators were interacting through slow I/O devices, each user had a feel as if the CPU was available solely to itself. So, the computation capacity of the CPU is multiplexed evenly, amongst the interactive users.

At any stage, the user could interact with the execution of its program. Debugging could be performed online.

So, time-sharing systems were large multi-programmed multi-user systems, designed for program development. One of the major requirements of such a system is good terminal response. It should give an illusion to each user as if the entire computer resources are available to itself, solely. It should provide an equitable share of common resources to each user. For example, when the system is overloaded, the program with higher processing requirements is made to wait longer.

Most time-sharing systems use time-sliced, non pre-emptive scheduling. It has FCFS Queue; and a program requiring service is put at the end of the queue. When the process reaches the front of the queue, it is despatched.

If it is not completed within the time slice, it is pre-emptied at the end of the time-slice and put at the end of the queue. Now, it has to wait for the next time-slice, to resume its execution from the point where it left at the end of previous time-slice. A process continues to run in bursts like this, till it terminates.

The main features of a time-sharing interactive operating system are:

1. **Memory Management**. The memory management in time-sharing systems provides for isolation and protection of co-resident programs. Since, the programs are being executed on behalf of different users, they do not involve much of inter-process communication.
2. **I/O Devices Management**. I/O Management must be sophisticated enough to cope with the requirements of multiple users, contending for multiple devices. However, due to relatively slow speed of terminals and users, processing of terminal-interrupts would not be so critical. As in most multi-user environments, allocation and de-allocation of devices must be handled in a manner so as to provide the system integrity, while attempting to optimize the system performance.
3. **File Management**. Since multiple users will be sharing access to multiple files, the file management must provide protection and access control.

Real Time Operating System

It refers to the environment of embedded systems, with a very rigid requirement to complete the processing of input data, in a pre-specified time. The input data, in such systems, is invariably received from real-world sensors. The outputs may be used to control some real-world processes.

For example, an Adir Defence system, receiving information about aircraft movements from radars and control weapons for the elimination of hostile aircraft. For such an application, it can be well appreciated that the processing of data inputs, within specified time limits, is absolutely critical.

So, the real time systems are used in environments, where a large number of events, mostly external to the computer system, must be accepted and processed to a highly time-bound manner (with specified deadlines).

Such applications include process control in indusry (like steel, petro-chemical plants, thermal plants and nuclear plants, etc.), military systems for processing of sensor information and weapon control, telephone switching equipment, flight control, real-time simulations, etc.

1. **Scheduling**. A primary objective of a real-time system is to provide quick response to external events, so as to meet the specified deadlines of processing. Such systems have to be multi-tasking (may not be multi-user). The scheduling is normally priority-based pre-emptive, in which the processes handling the priority process become ready to run, it pre-empts a lower priority running process. User convenience and resource optimization are of secondary concern. Such systems may be expected to handle thousands of interrupts per second, with a stringent requirement of not missing even a single event.
2. **Memory Management**. The memory management is relatively less demanding, since the process population is more or less static and memory is so designed that most of the processes will always be memory resident, in order to provide a quick response. In fact, the programs are normally ROM resident. But, the processes have closer interaction. This requires features that enable sharing of memory, amongst processes and at the same time provide protection from each other.
3. **I/O Devices Management**. Time critical device management is one of the major requirements of real time systems. The external events and data have to be accepted and processed, in a highly time-bound manner. This is implemented using interrupt mechanism. The system calls allow the users to connect the devices and access Interrupt Service Routines (ISRs) directly, so as to achieve a good response time.
4. **File Management**. The file management is not very critical, since most of the real-time databases will be memory-resident. Some embedded systems may have program and static data on ROM and

may not need any online secondary devices at run-time. The dynamic databases are maintained in ROM. If at all any files are to be accessed, as in the case of large real-time systems, the primary objective is fast access.

Category of Real Time Operating Systems

1. **Hard Real Time Operating System**. In Hard Real Time Systems, all critical tasks have to be completed stricly within the specified time limits. Not meeting the deadlines can be catastrophic; like an embedded system controlling the operation of a refinery. In such systems, all code and data must be in RAM/ROM. All kernel delays must be bounded. So, the Operating System should not have any unnecessary frills. Interrupt mechanism must be optimized, so as to respond to the real world inputs, with minimal delays.
2. **Soft Real Time Operating System**. This is less restrictive type of real time system. If the input data is not processed within specifed time intervals, the results may not be catastrophic, but the output may lose its utility. For example, in a system monitoring flight path of an aircraft, the delayed information will have no utility. In such systems, tasks are divided into two categories—Real Time Tasks and Non-Real Time Tasks. The Real-Time Tasks are accorded priority over the other tasks. Any output from such systems would be useful, only if it is produced within a specified time after receiving the corresponding inputs. So, the kernel delays must be bounded. The soft real time systems are not suitable for industrial and defence use, since the delays are not uncertain.

Combination Operating System

Different types of operating systems are optimized or geared up to serve the needs of specific environments. However, sometimes an environment may be a hybrid of such environments, for example the same computer may be used as software development platform and as a target machine in a real-time environment. For this reason, the commercial operating systems like UNIX, VMS, etc., are designed to provide a large set of services, catering to the need of various environments. If batch and interactive jobs are being run simultaneously, lower priority is assigned to batch jobs. In fact, the batch jobs may be used as filter, executed only when system resources are idling. The processes, handling real-time interrupts to receive real-world events and inputs, will be assigned higher priority. Such systems would normally employ time-sliced, priority-based pre-emptive scheduling. A combination operating system will be one which caters for the needs of a wide spectrum of target environments. For obvious reasons, such operating systems will not be optimized for a specific environment.

If batch and interactive jobs are being run simultaneously, lower priority is assigned to batch jobs.

Distributed Operating System

A distributed operating system caters for a distributed environment, wherein a collection of autonomous computer systems, capable of communicating and cooperating with each other through network, are connected to each other through a Local Area Network/Wide Area Network. A distributed operating system governs the operation of such a distributed system and provides a virtual machine abstraction to its users. Key objective of distributed operating system is transparency, i.e., the resource distribution must be hidden from the users and the application programs, unless they need to determine this information, in which case the information is provided through system services, provided the user has authorization for the same. The distributed operating system provides means for system-side sharing of resources like computational capacity, I/O and files, etc.

A distributed operating system governs the operation of such a distributed system and provides a virtual machine abstraction to its users.

Thus, it should also cater for the following services:

1. **Global sharing of resources**
2. **Distribution of computations:** Computation can be partitioned into a number of Sub Computations that can run concurrently, then a distributed system may allow us to distribute the computation among the various sites - to run that computation concurrently.
3. **Enabling processes to access remote resources**: If a number of different sites are connected to one another, then a user at one site may be able to use the resource available at another. For example — a user at site A may be using a laser printer available only at site B. Meanwhile a user at B may access a file that resides at A.
4. **Enabling processes to communicate with remote processes**: There are many instances in which programs need to exchange data with one another on one system. When many sites are connected to one another by a communication network, the process at different sites have the opportunity to exchange information. Users may initiate file transfer or communicate with one another via electronic mail.
5. **Reliability**: If one site fails in a distributed system, the remaining sites can potentially continue operating.

IMPORTANCE OF OPERATING SYSTEMS

As we know the importance of operating system in a computer system. It is there to run the computer and that too without any fault. For this we look at the various needs, goals, services and characteristics of the operating system.

Needs of Operating Systems

Initially the computers were introduced as bare machines. The programs in them were developed by manually by translating sequence of instructions into binary or some other code where base is usually an integer power of 2. Then the instructions and data were entered into computer by means of console switches or through a hexadecimal keyboard. Then address of first instruction was loaded into program as a counter to start execution of the program.

Results were obtained by examining the contents of the relevant registers and memory locations. Input/output devices were controlled by the executing program itself. There was no concept of any supporting system software at all. User had to do mostly all of sub-controlling jobs manually or through program. The need was of a user who knew each and everything about machine. A general/naive user was not at all able to work on computer.

At that time the following needs gave birth to the system software and development of operating system.

1. **For fast and automatic working:** As the manual entry and working in absence of system software result into the slow speed of processing so a need of such a software was felt which could do most of the intermediate job automatically so that user has to be least bothered about machines working, resulting into fast and automatic working of the machine. The operating system automates the sequencing of operations involved in program execution.
2. **For better utilization of system Resources:** The bare machine approach was not very efficient. With this approach, running of computer system may require frequent manual loading of programs and data. This results in low utilization of system resources. To overcome this problem operating systems with multiuser environment were developed. In absence of operating system even with the help of editors, debuggers and loaders the program development process was very slow.
3. To realize the resource utilization potential of batch processing, a mounted batch of jobs must be executed automatically, without slow human intervention and their results into the development of operating system.
4. To provide a human interface which could present a communication mode for both of them, the operating system was developed.

5. To match the speed of fast processors and comparatively slow I/O devices the need of operating system was felt.

Goals of Operating Systems

Any operating system should meet the following major goals:

1. Optimize the use of computer resources so as to maximize its throughput.

$$\text{Throughput} = \frac{\text{The number of jobs completed}}{\text{The total time required to complete the jobs}}$$

2. Create a user-friendly computing environment for accessing the computer resources.

To fulfill these two goals operating system started from command mode and travelled upto graphical user interfaces, i.e., the operating system progressed and became more and more friendly. To facilitate the use of hardware resources researchers developed different types of operating systems which also consider the user and time requirements. Various types of operating systems are developed over 45 years and they are discussed earlier.

Services of Operating System

An operating system provides an environment for the execution of user programs. Operating System provides certain services to the programs and to the users of those programs for the accessing of system resources. Some of the common services are:

Program Execution

The main purpose of operating system is to provide an efficient and convenient environment for the execution of programs. So, an operating system must provide various functions for loading of a program into RAM and execute it. Each executing program must terminate, either normally or abnormally.

I/O Operations

A running program would need I/O operations for reading-in of input data and for outputting of results. This I/O may be from/to a file or from/to an I/O device. For each device, some special functions may be necessary (such as rewind a tape, clear screen, etc). All these operations are managed by an operating system.

File Manipulations

Each executing program would need to create, delete and manipulate files, which is managed by the operating system.

Communications

Operating system manages inter-process communication between the processes, executing on the same computer or running on different computers in a distributed/multi-processor environment. An operating system would provide mechanisms for the inter-process communications like mailboxes, shared memory, etc.

Error Detection and Recovery

Errors may occur during execution of a program; like divide by zero, memory access violation, etc. The operating system should provide for detection of such errors (or exceptions) and handle recovery (called Exception Handling).

Resource Allocation

When multiple users are logged onto the system or multiple jobs are runing concurrently, resources would need to be shared amongst them. The operating system would decide on the allocation of resources; like the CPU scheduling algorithm will determine the control of CPU amongst the concurrent processes. Similarly, there will be routines for the allocation and de-allocation of other resources like memory, I/O devices, files, etc.

Accounting

It relates to the accounting of resources used by each user in a multi-user environment. Resource usage statistics may be useful in planning the futuristic requirements of an enterprise.

System Protection

This is also a service provided to ensure that the users and user processes are protected from each other. For example, when a process is having an exclusive access to a device allocated to it, no other process would be granted access to that device during that period. Also, no process would be permitted to access a memory location in a segment not assigned to that process. This service ensures that a process can execute safety.

Characteristics of an Operating System

Characteristics of an Operating System can be discussed under the following heads.

Process Management

Every program running on a computer, be it background services or applications, is a process. As long as it is used to build computers, only one process per CPU can be run at a time. Older microcomputer operating systems such as MS-DOS did not attempt to bypass this limit, with the exception of interrupt processing, and only one process could be run under them (although DOS itself featured TSR as a very partial and not too easy to use solution).

Mainframe operating systems had multitasking capabilities since the early 1960s. Modern operating systems enable concurrent execution of many processes at once via multitasking even with one CPU. Process management is an operating system's way of dealing with running multiple processes. Since most computers contain one processor with one core, multitasking is done by simply switching processes quickly. Depending on the operating system, as more processes run, either each time slice will become smaller or there will be a longer delay before each process is given a chance to run.

Modern operating systems enable concurrent execution of many processes at once via multitasking even with one CPU.

Process management involves computing and distributing CPU time as well as other resources. Most operating systems allow a process to be assigned a priority which affects its allocation of CPU time. Interactive operating systems also employ some level of feedback in which the task, with which the user is working, receives higher priority. Interrupt driven processes will normally run at a very high priority. In many systems there is a background process, such as the System Idle Process in Windows, which will run when no other process is waiting for the CPU.

Memory Management

Current computer architectures arrange the computer's memory in a hierarchical manner, starting from the fastest registers, CPU cache, random access memory and disk storage. An operating system's memory manager coordinates the use of these various types of memory by tracking which one is available, which is to be allocated or de-allocated and how to move data between them. This activity, usually referred to as virtual memory management, increases the amount of memory available for each process by making the disk storage seem like main memory.

There is a speed penalty associated with using disks or other slower storage as memory – if running processes require significantly more RAM than is available, the system may start thrashing. This can happen either because one process requires a large amount of RAM or because two or more processes compete for a larger amount of memory than is available. This then leads to constant transfer of each process's data to slower storage.

An operating system's memory manager coordinates the use of these various types of memory by tracking which one is available.

Another important part of memory management is managing virtual addresses. If multiple processes are in memory at once, they must be prevented from interfering with each other's memory (unless there is an explicit request to utilise shared memory). This is achieved by having separate address spaces.

Each process sees the whole virtual address space, typically from address 0 up to the maximum size of virtual memory, as uniquely assigned to it. The operating system maintains a page table that matches virtual addresses to physical addresses. These memory allocations are tracked so that when a process terminates, all memory used by that process can be made available for other processes.

The operating system can also write inactive memory pages to secondary storage. This process is called "**paging**" or "**swapping**" – the terminology varies between operating systems. It is also typical for operating systems to employ otherwise unused physical memory as a page cache; requests for data from a slower device can be retained in memory to improve performance.

The operating system can also pre-load the in-memory cache with data that may be requested by the user in the near future; SuperFetch is an example of this.

Disk and file systems

All operating systems include support for a variety of file systems. Modern file systems comprise a hierarchy of directories. While the idea is conceptually similar across all general-purpose file systems, some differences in implementation exist. Two noticeable examples of this are the character used to separate directories, and case sensitivity. Unix demarcates its path components with a slash (/), a convention followed by operating systems that emulated it or at least its concept of hierarchical directories, such as Linux, Amiga OS and Mac OS X. MS-DOS also emulated this feature, but had already also adopted the CP/M convention of using slashes for additional options to commands, so instead used the backslash (\) as its component separator. Microsoft Windows continues with this convention; Japanese editions of Windows use ¥, and Korean editions use © .

Unix and Unix-like operating allow for any character in file names other than the slash, and names are case sensitive. Microsoft Windows file names are not case sensitive. File systems may provide journaling, which provides safe recovery in the event of a system crash. A journaled file system writes information twice: first to the journal, which is a log of file system operations, then to its proper place in the ordinary file system.

In the event of a crash, the system can recover to a consistent state by replaying a portion of the journal. In contrast, non-journaled file systems typically need to be examined in their entirety by a utility such as fsck or chkdsk. Soft updates is an alternative to journalling that avoids the redundant writes by carefully ordering the update operations. Log-structured file systems and ZFS also differ from traditional journaled file systems, in that they avoid inconsistencies by always writing new copies of the data, eschewing in-place updates.

A journaled file system writes information twice: first to the journal, which is a log of file system operations, then to its proper place in the ordinary file system.

Many Linux distributions support some or all of ext2, ext3, ReiserFS, Reiser4, GFS, GFS2, OCFS, OCFS2, and NILFS. Linux also has full support for XFS and JFS, along with the FAT file systems, and NTFS. Microsoft Windows includes support for FAT12, FAT16, FAT32, and NTFS. The NTFS file system is the most efficient and reliable of the four Windows file systems, and as of Windows Vista, is the only file system which the operating system can be installed on. Windows Embedded CE 6.0 introduced ExFAT, a file system suitable for flash drives.

Common to all these (and other) operating systems is support for file systems typically found on removable media. FAT12 is the file system most commonly found on floppy discs. ISO 9660 and Universal Disk Format are two common formats that target Compact Discs and DVDs, respectively. Mount Rainier is a newer extension to UDF supported by Linux 2.6 kernels and Windows-Vista that facilitates rewriting to DVDs in the same fashion as what has been possible with floppy disks.

Networking

Most current operating systems are capable of using the TCP/IP networking protocols. This means that one system can appear on a network of the other and share resources such as files, printers, and scanners using either wired or wireless connections. Many operating systems also support one or more vendor-specific legacy networking protocols as well, for example, SNA on IBM systems, DECnet on systems from Digital Equipment Corporation, and Microsoft-specific protocols on Windows. Specific protocols for specific tasks may also be supported such as NFS for file access.

Security

Many operating systems include some level of security. Security is based on the two ideas that:

- The operating system provides access to a number of resources, directly or indirectly, such as files on a local disk, privileged system calls, personal information about users, and the services offered by the programs running on the system;
- The operating system is capable of distinguishing between some requesters of these resources who are authorized (allowed) to access the resource, and others who are not authorized (forbidden). While some systems may simply distinguish between "privileged" and "non-privileged", systems commonly have a form of requester identity, such as a user name. Requesters, in turn, are divided into two categories:
  - Internal security: an already running program. On some systems, a program once it is running has no limitations, but commonly the program has an identity which it keeps and is used to check all of its requests for resources.
  - External security: a new request from outside the computer, such as a login at a connected console or some kind of network connection. To establish identity there may be a process of authentication. Often a username must be quoted, and each username may have a password. Other methods of authentication, such as magnetic cards or biometric data, might be used instead. In some cases, especially connections from the network, resources may be accessed with no authentication at all.

In addition to the allow/disallow model of security, a system with a high level of security will also offer auditing options. These would allow tracking of requests for access to resources (such as, "who has been reading this file?").

Security of operating systems has long been a concern because of highly sensitive data held on computers, both of a commercial and military nature. The United States Government Department of Defense (DoD) created the Trusted Computer System Evaluation Criteria (TCSEC) which is a standard that sets basic requirements for assessing the effectiveness of security. This became of vital importance to operating system makers, because the TCSEC was used to evaluate, classify and select computer systems being considered for the processing, storage and retrieval of sensitive or classified information.

Internal Security

Internal security can be thought of as protecting the computer's resources from the programs concurrently running on the system. Most operating systems set programs running natively on the computer's processor, so the problem arises of how to stop these programs doing the same task and having the same privileges as the operating system (which is after all just a program too). Processors used for general purpose operating systems generally have a hardware concept of privilege. Generally less privileged programs are automatically blocked from using certain hardware instructions, such as those to read or write from external devices like disks. Instead, they have to ask the privileged program (operating system kernel) to read or write. The operating system, therefore, gets the chance to check the program's identity and allow or refuse the request.

An alternative strategy, and the only sandbox strategy available in systems that do not meet the Popek and Goldberg virtualization requirements, is the operating system not running user programs as native code, but instead either emulates a processor or provides a host for a p-code based system such as Java.

Internal security is especially relevant for multi-user systems; it allows each user of the system to have private files that the other users cannot tamper with or read. Internal security is also vital if auditing is to be of any use, since a program can potentially bypass the operating system, inclusive of bypassing auditing.

External Security

Typically an operating system offers (or hosts) various services to other network computers and users. These services are usually provided through ports or numbered access points beyond the operating systems network address. Services include offerings such as file sharing, print services, email, web sites, and file transfer protocols (FTP), most of which can have compromised security.

At the front line of security are software known as firewalls. At the operating system level, there are a number of software firewalls available. Most modern operating systems include a software firewall, which is enabled by default. A software firewall can be configured to allow or deny network traffic to or from a service or application running on the operating system.

Therefore, one can install and be running an insecure service, such as Telnet or FTP, and not have to be threatened by a security breach because the firewall would deny all traffic trying to connect to the service on that port.

Graphical User Interfaces

Today, most modern operating systems contain Graphical User Interfaces (GUIs, pronounced goo-eez). A few older operating systems tightly integrated the GUI to the kernel—for example, the original implementations of Microsoft Windows and Mac OS. More modern operating systems are modular, separating the graphics subsystem from the kernel (as is now done in Linux, Mac OS X, and to a limited extent in Windows).

Many operating systems allow the user to install or create any user interface they desire. The X Window System in conjunction with GNOME or KDE is a commonly found setup on most Unix and Unix derivative (BSD, Linux, Minix) systems.

Graphical user interfaces tend to evolve over time. For example, Windows has modified its user interface almost every time a new major version of Windows is released, and the Mac OS GUI changed dramatically with the introduction of Mac OS X in 2001.

Device Drivers

A device driver is a specific type of computer software developed to allow interaction with hardware devices. Typically this constitutes an interface for communicating with the device, through the specific computer bus or communications subsystem that the hardware is connected to, providing commands to and/or receiving data from the device, and on the other end, the requisite interfaces to the operating system and software applications. It is a specialized hardware-dependent computer program which is also operating system specific that enables another program, typically an operating system or applications software package or computer program running under the operating system kernel, to interact transparently with a hardware device, and usually provides the requisite interrupt handling necessary for any necessary asynchronous time-dependent hardware interfacing needs.

The key design goal of device drivers is abstraction. Every model of hardware (even within the same class of device) is different. Newer models are also released by manufacturers that provide more reliable or better performance and these newer models are often controlled differently. Computers and their operating systems cannot be expected to know how to control every device, both now and in the future. To solve this problem, OSes essentially dictate how every type of device should be controlled. The function of the device driver is then to translate these OS mandated function calls into device specific calls. In theory a new device, which is controlled in a new manner, should function correctly if a suitable driver is available. This new driver will ensure that the device appears to operate as usual from the operating systems' point of view for any person.

Memory Organization

For a program to be executed, it must be mapped to absolute addresses and loaded into memory. As the program executes, it accesses program instructions and data from memory by generating these absolute addresses. When a program terminates, the memory space occupied by this program is declared available and the next program can be loaded and executed in the memory simultaneously. The operating system is responsible for the following functions related to memory management:

- Keeping track of which segment of memory is in use and by whom.
- Deciding which processes are to be loaded into memory when space becomes available.
- Allocation and de-allocation of dynamic memory.
- Swapping-in and swapping-out of processes.

Linking, Loading and Executing Control Program

A computer program exists in a source code form, viewable as a programming language; as a tokenised form, ready to be interpreted; or in machine code form, ready to be executed. A computer program is loaded into memory (usually by the operating system) and then executed ("run"), instruction by instruction, until termination, either with success or through software or hardware error.

Before a computer can execute any sort of program (including the operating system, itself a program), the computer hardware must be initialized. This initialization is done in modern PCs by a piece of software stored on programmable memory chips installed by the manufacturer, called the BIOS. The BIOS will attempt to initialize the boot sequence, making the computer ready for higher-level program execution.

Assembler/compiler produces an object code which may not be good for execution, especially when a large program is made up of serveral subroutines and each subroutine has been translated individually. Now the object subroutines must be combined together to form a complete run unit (also known as load module) and the software that combines these object subroutines into one load module is known as linkage editor or linker.

Before a computer can execute any sort of program the computer hardware must be initialized.

If our program consists of library routines then the linking of the program with library functions is also essential. Remember that in some computer systems, the translator performs the task of linking as well as translation. If our source program is a single entity or if all the source subroutines are provided to the translator together as a single entity then the output of a translator is a load module rather than an object program. This object program/ load module is placed on some secondary storage such as disk. During the initialization of the execution process, this load module is loaded into main memory of the computer system and the system software that does this loading from secondary memory to primary memory is known as loader.

Additionally, the loader also performs the functions of relocation.

The concept of relocation is expalined as: let a program A calls a standard subroutines SQRT then SQRT must be linked with a program A, now the question arises: where to load both programs, program A and SQRT. One possible solution of this is to load these two according to the addresses assigned by the operating system, when they are translated. Let program A occupies 200 to 298, while SQRT occupies 100 to 170 then the vacated space between program A and SQRT may get wasted or if A occupies 100 to 198 and SQRT occupies 100 to 170 then overlapping can create an erroneous result.

Thus, a typical direct linking loader performs four functions:

Allocation, Linking, Relocation and Loading.

Sometimes, linking and loading is performed by a single system software, known as the linking loader. A typical direct linking loader loads a program in two passes:

1. The first pass allocates space for the subroutines and defines the values of the external symbols.
2. The second pass actually loads the text and uses the global external symbol table, produced by pass 1, to relate and link the subroutines/address constants.

Functions of Operating System

The main functions of the operating system are defined below::

Input/Output Operations

The Operating System is responsible for handling various types of inputs, e.g., input from keyboard, input from mouse, etc., and various types of outputs in the appropriate manner. For instance, if the input is coming from mouse, then it requires different types of handling as compared to input coming from keyboard. Similarly, if an output is targeted for printer, then it requires different types of handling as compared to output targeted for monitor.

Handling File System

This task involves the making of decisions regarding the storage of files, i.e., where and how a particular file is to be stored, may be on floppy disk or hard disk.

Execution of Program

The Operating System is responsible for executing various programs whether user programs or system programs, i.e., special programs required for the machine functioning.

Allocation of Resources

This task aims at proper use of resources available. For example, if multiple files are to be printed then "who and in which order this task will take place?" will be decided by the operating system.

Detection of Errors

The Operating System is also responsible for detecting any type of error that occurs and then properly handling it.

Information and Resource Protection

The Operating System is responsible for ensuring that the information and resources available on machine are used in the correct way. The Operating System foils the attempts to use them incorrectly.

These services ensure that your computer works smoothly.

The functions offered by different operating systems differ from one operating system to another, but more or less they provide the same type of services.

Current Operating System Scene

Modern operating systems usually feature a Graphical user interface (GUI) which uses a pointing device such as a mouse or stylus for input in addition to the keyboard. Older models and Operating Systems, not designed for direct-human interaction (such as web-servers), generally use a Command line interface (or CLI) typically with only the keyboard for input. Both models are centered around a "shell" which accepts and processes commands from the user (e.g., clicking on a button, or a typed command at a prompt).

The choice of operating system may be dependent on the hardware architecture, specifically the CPU, with only Linux and BSD running on almost any CPU. Windows NT 3.1, which is no longer supported, was ported to the DEC Alpha and MIPS Magnum. Since the mid-1990s, the most commonly used operating systems have been the Microsoft Windows family, Linux, and other Unix-like operating systems, most notably Mac OS X. Mainframe computers and embedded systems use a variety of different operating systems, many with no direct connection to Windows or Unix. QNX and VxWorks are two common embedded operating systems, the latter being used in network infrastructure hardware equipment.

Operating system is usually Hardware dependent.

Personal computers

- IBM PC compatible - Microsoft Windows, Unix variants, and Linux variants.
- Apple Macintosh - Mac OS X (a Unix variant), Windows (on x86 Macintosh machines only), Linux and BSD.

Mainframe Computers

The earliest operating systems were developed for mainframe computer architectures in the 1960s. The enormous investment in software for these systems caused most of the original computer manufacturers to continue to develop hardware and operating systems that are compatible with those early operating systems. Those early systems pioneered many of the features of modern operating systems. Mainframe operating systems that are still supported include:

- Burroughs MCP— B5000,1961 to Unisys Clearpath/MCP, present.
- IBM OS/360 — IBM System/360, 1964 to IBM zSeries, present
- UNIVAC EXEC 8 — UNIVAC 1108, 1964, to Unisys Clearpath IX, present.

Modern mainframes typically also run Linux or Unix variants. A "Datacenter" variant of Windows Server 2003 is also available for some mainframe systems.

Embedded systems

Embedded systems use a variety of dedicated operating systems. In some cases, the "operating system" software is directly linked to the application to produce a monolithic special-purpose program. In the simplest embedded systems, there is no distinction between the operating system and the application. Embedded systems that have certain time requirements are known as Real-time operating systems.

In embedded systems, there is no difference between the operating system and the application.

Unix-like operating systems

The Unix-like family is a diverse group of operating systems, with several major sub-categories including System V, BSD, and Linux. The name "UNIX" is a trademark of The Open Group which licenses it for use with any operating system that has been shown to conform to their definitions. "Unix-like" is commonly used to refer to the large set of operating systems which resemble the original Unix.

Unix systems run on a wide variety of machine architectures. They are used heavily as server systems in business, as well as workstations in academic and engineering environments. Free software Unix variants, such as Linux and BSD, are popular in these areas. Unix and Unix-like systems have not reached significant market share in the consumer and corporate desktop market, although there is some growth in this area, notably by the Ubuntu Linux distribution. Linux on the desktop is also popular in the developer and hobbyist operating system development communities.

Various variants of Unix operating software are available.

Some Unix variants like HP's HP-UX and IBM's AIX are designed to run only on that vendor's hardware. Others, such as Solaris, can run on multiple types of hardware, including x86 servers and PCs. Apple's Mac OS X, a hybrid kernel-based BSD variant derived from NeXTSTEP, Mach, and FreeBSD, has replaced Apple's earlier (non-Unix) Mac OS.

Open source

Over the past several years, the trend in the Unix and Unix-like space has been to open source operating systems. Many areas previously dominated by UNIX have seen significant in-roads by Linux; Solaris source code is now the basis of the Open Solaris project.

The team at Bell Labs that designed and developed Unix went on to develop Plan 9 and Inferno, which were designed for modern distributed environments. They had graphics built-in, unlike Unix counterparts that added it to the design later. Plan 9 did not become popular because, unlike many Unix distributions, it was not originally free. It has since been released under Free Software and Open Source Lucent Public License, and has an expanding community of developers. Inferno was sold to Vita Nuova and has been released under a GPL/MIT license.

Microsoft Windows

The Microsoft Windows family of operating systems originated as a graphical layer on top of the older MS-DOS environment for the IBM PC. Modern versions are based on the newer Windows NT core that first took shape in OS/2 and borrowed from VMS. Windows runs on 32-bit and 64-bit Intel and AMD processors, although earlier versions also ran on the DEC Alpha, MIPS, Fairchild Clipper and PowerPC architectures.

As of May-2007, Microsoft Windows held a near-monopoly of 92.68% of the worldwide desktop market share, although some predict this to dwindle due to Microsoft's restrictive licensing, (CD-Key) registration, and customer practices causing an increased interest in open source operating systems. Windows is also used on low-end and mid-range servers, supporting applications such as web servers and database servers. In recent years, Microsoft has spent significant marketing and R&D money to demonstrate that Windows is capable of running any enterprise application, which has resulted in consistent price/performance records and significant acceptance in the enterprise market.

The most widely used version of the Microsoft Windows family is Microsoft Windows XP, released on October 25, 2001. The latest release of Windows XP is Windows XP Service Pack 2, released on August 6, 2004.

In November 2006, after more than five years of development work, Microsoft released Windows Vista, a major new version of Microsoft Windows which contains a large number of new features and architectural changes. Chief amongst these are a new user interface and visual style called Windows Aero, a number of new security features such as User Account Control, and new multimedia applications such as Windows DVD Maker.

Windows Vista is the latest version of Windows Operating Software.

Mac OS X

Mac OS X is a line of proprietary, graphical operating systems developed, marketed, and sold by Apple Inc., the latest of which is pre-loaded on all currently shipping Macintosh computers. Mac OS X is the successor to the original Mac OS, which had been Apple's primary operating system since 1984. Unlike its predecessor, Mac OS X is a Unix-like operating system built on technology that had been developed at NeXT through the second half of the 1980s and up until Apple purchased the company in early 1997.

The operating system was first released in 1999 as Mac OS X Server 1.0, with a desktop-oriented version (Mac OS X v10.0) following in March 2001. Since then, four more distinct "end-user" and "server" editions of Mac OS X have been released, the most recent being Mac OS X v10.4, which was first made available in April 2005. Releases of Mac OS X are named after big cats; Mac OS X v10.4 is usually referred to by Apple and users as "Tiger". In October 2007, Apple will release Mac OS X 10.5, nicknamed "Leopard".

The server edition, Mac OS X Server, is architecturally identical to its desktop counterpart but usually runs on Apple's line of Macintosh server hardware. Mac OS X Server includes workgroup management and administration software tools that provide simplified access to key network services, including a mail transfer agent, a Samba server, an LDAP server, a domain name server, and others.

Mac OS runs on Macintosh type of Apple Computers.

TRON Project

TRON is an open real-time operating system kernel design, and is an acronym for "The Real-time Operating System Nucleus". The project was begun by Prof. Dr. Ken Sakamura of the University of Tokyo in 1984, Japan. The project's goal is to create an ideal computer architecture and network, to provide for all of society's needs.

As of 2003, the TRON system (or more specifically the ITRON derivative) is one of the world's most used operating systems, being present in millions of electronic devices. The operating system is mainly used by Japanese companies, although interest in its use is growing worldwide. However, it has been said that there is much misinformation in the English speaking world about TRON due to majority of the documentation being in Japanese.

Hobby operating system development

Operating system development, or OSDev for short, as a hobby has a large cult following. As such, operating systems, such as Linux, have derived from hobby operating system projects. The design and implementation of an operating system requires skill and determination, and the term can cover anything from a basic "Hello World" boot loader, to a fully featured kernel, user desktop, and office suite.

Other Operating Systems

Mainframe operating systems, such as IBM's z/OS, and embedded operating systems such as VxWorks, eCos, and Palm OS, are usually unrelated to Unix and Windows, except for Windows CE, Windows NT Embedded 4.0 and Windows XP Embedded which are descendants of Windows, and several *BSDs, and Linux distributions tailored for embedded systems. OpenVMS from Hewlett-Packard (formerly DEC), is still under active development.

Older operating systems which are still used in niche markets include OS/2 from IBM; Mac OS, the non-Unix precursor to Apple's Mac OS X; BeOS; XTS-300. Popular prior to the Dot COM era, operating systems such as AmigaOS and RISC OS continue to be developed as minority platforms for enthusiast communities and specialist applications.

Research and development of new operating systems continues. GNU Hurd is designed to be backwards compatible with Unix, but with enhanced functionality and a microkernel architecture. Similarly, a project at Microsoft Research to develop an operating system with better memory protection based on the .Net managed code model.

Process Management Functions

Operating systems have generally evolved to support programmers who want to write distributed computation.

The evolution of networks enabled computers to communicate at relatively high speeds. This caused the device management part of operating systems to be updated to better handle networks. Remote files on the other hand caused the existing operating system to redesign and reimplement the file managers to support distributed computation.

To achieve device, file and memory management transparency, the general technique was to create client and server components of each manager at the local and remote computers. This suggests that distributed process managers could have "agents" operating on each machine involved in the computation.

As is to be expected, most of the early development in distributing the process manager has been experimental.

Scheduling

There are two general types of scheduling used in distributed environments:

Explicit scheduling

The application programmer takes responsibility for determining where the process or threads should be executed.

Transparent scheduling

The application process begins to execute as a single thread in a process on one computer. Then, when new schedulable units of computation are created and made ready to run, the scheduler on the local machine interacts with schedulers on other machines to determine the best place to execute a unit.

The client-server model can be used to build an explicit scheduling mechanism. The servers are started on the network at explicit locations. The clients start independently at arbitrary places in the network, using the servers. In this case, a client or server unit of computation is treated as an ordinary process within the computer in which it executes. In the default, the computer's multiprogramming scheduling policy is used to provide service to that part of the computation.

A client or server unit of computation is treated as an ordinary process within the computer in which it executes.

In transparent scheduling, the application can create schedulable units of computation to be executed in the distributed environment without considering which machine will actually be used to execute any particular unit. The schedulers on the machines in the network are designed to communicate with one another using their own specialized protocol. In this way, when a schedulable unit of computation is made ready to run, the unit is transferred to a selected machine and then executed in that machine.

Normally, once the unit has been assigned to a particular machine, it will complete its execution on that machine. It will share the CPU with other units according to the local multiprogramming scheduler's policy. Transparency is a primary motivating factor for the operating system to support network-transparent threads or objects.

Job Scheduler

A job scheduler is an enterprise software application that is in charge of unattended background executions, commonly known for historical reasons as batch processing. They may also be known as Distributed Resource Management Systems (DRMS) or Distributed Resource Managers (DRM). Today's job schedulers typically provide a graphical user interface and a single point of control for definition and monitoring of background executions in a distributed network of computers.

Increasingly job schedulers are required to orchestrate the integration of real-time business activities with traditional background IT processing, across different operating system platforms and business application environments.

Basic features expected of job scheduler software are:

- Interfaces to define workflows and/or job dependencies
- Automatic submission of executions
- Interfaces to monitor the executions
- Priorities and/or queues to control the execution order of unrelated jobs.

If software from a completely different area includes all or some of those features, this software is considered to have job scheduling capabilities. Most operating system platforms such as Unix and Windows provide basic job scheduling capabilities, for example Cron. Many programs such as DBMS, backup, ERPs, and BPM also include relevant job scheduling capabilities.

Operating system (OS) or point program supplied job scheduling will not usually provide the ability to schedule beyond a single OS instance or outside the remit of the specific program. Organizations needing to automate highly complex related and un-related IT workload will also be expecting more advanced features from a job scheduler, such as:

- Real-time scheduling based on external, un-predictable events
- Automatic restart and recovery in event of failures
- Alerting and notification to operations personnel
- Generation of incident reports
- Audit trails for regulatory compliance purposes.

These advanced capabilities can be written by in-house developers but are more often provided by solutions from suppliers that specialize in systems management software.

Main Concepts

There are many concepts that are central to almost every job scheduler implementation and that are widely recognized with minimal variations:

- Jobs
- Dependencies
- Job Streams
- Users

Beyond the basic, single OS instance scheduling tools there are two major architectures that exist for Job Scheduling software.

- **Master/Agent architecture** — the historic architecture for Job scheduling software. The Job Scheduling software is installed on a single machine (Master) while on production machines only a very small component (Agent) is installed that awaits commands from the Master, executes them, and returns the exit code back to the Master.
- **Cooperative architecture** — a decentralized model where each machine is capable of helping with scheduling and can offload locally scheduled jobs to other cooperating machines. This enables dynamic workload balancing to maximize hardware resource utilization and high availability to ensure service delivery.

Scheduling

Various schemes are used to decide which particular job to run.

Parameters that might be considered include:

- Job priority
- Compute resource availability
- License key if job is using licensed software
- Execution time allocated to user
- Number of simultaneous jobs allowed for a user
- Estimated execution time
- Elapsed execution time
- Availability of peripheral devices
- Occurrence of prescribed events.

Benefits of a Job Scheduler

Scheduling out to the field can maximize the performance of the field worker.

Some benefits of using a DRM system include:

- Field workers complete more jobs per day
- Create a flexible field team
- Improve worker utilization, equipment utilization and vehicle utilization
- Field operations become transparent
- All field worker jobs become measurable over time and service level agreements can be achieved.

Process Scheduler

The following are the major tasks that have been identified in various research and development efforts for the general process management requirements to support distributed computation.

Creation/destruction

When a computation starts, normally a single process decides at runtime what other processes should be created and used in the computation. The process manager must provide facilities to allow the process to create and destroy, child threads and processes on other machines.

Scheduling

In some distributed environments, the location where a process executes is determined by the scheduler rather than the process. When a thread becomes ready in such an environment, the scheduler looks around the network for an appropriate place to execute the thread, attempting to automatically overlap execution.

Synchronization

The classic synchronization mechanism relies on the existence of shared memory to coordinate process activity. In a network, the operating system generally has to provide an alternative synchronization mechanism based on messages, rather than rely on shared memory.

Deadlock Management

Deadlock detection algorithm rely on the knowledge of the allocation state of the system's resources to determine whether a deadlock exists. In a network, the set of resources includes all resources on every machine. Furthermore, detecting the status of all machines at given moment has proved to be very difficult; that is, distributed deadlock detection is a difficult issue to resolve in a network environment.

Process Synchronization

Process synchronization refers to the coordination of simultaneous threads or processes to complete a task in order to get correct runtime order and avoid unexpected race conditions. There are many types of synchronization:

- barrier
- lock/semaphore
- thread join
- mutex
- non-blocking synchronization
- synchronous communication operations.

A synchronization point is the location, in a process or collection of threads or processes, where the synchronization occurs. The interaction of synchronization points is one of the objects of study in the theory of concurrent computing.

Barrier

In parallel computing, a barrier is a type of synchronization method. A barrier for a group of threads or processes in the source code means any thread/process must stop at this point and cannot proceed until all other threads/processes reach this barrier.

Many collective routines and directive-based parallel languages impose implicit barriers. For example, a parallel do loop in Fortran with OpenMP will not be allowed to continue on any thread until the last iteration is completed. This is in case the program relies on the result of the loop immediately after its completion. In message passing, any global communication (such as reduction or scatter) may imply a barrier.

Lock

In computer science, a lock is a synchronization mechanism for enforcing limits on access to a resource in an environment where there are many threads of execution. Locks are one way of enforcing concurrency control policies.

Types of Locks

Generally, locks are advisory locks, where each thread cooperates by acquiring the lock before accessing the corresponding data. Some systems also implement mandatory locks, where attempting unauthorized access to a locked resource will force an exception in the entity attempting to make the access.

A (binary) semaphore is the simplest type of lock. In terms of access to the data, no distinction is made between shared (read only) or exclusive (read and write) modes. Other schemes provide for a shared mode, where several threads can acquire a shared lock for read-only access to the data. Other modes such as exclusive, intend-to-exclude and intend-to-upgrade are also widely implemented.

Independent of the type of lock chosen above, locks can be classified by what happens when the lock strategy prevents progress of a thread. Most locking designs block the execution of the process requesting the lock until it is allowed to access the locked resource. A spinlock is a lock where the thread simply waits ("spins") until the lock becomes available. It is very efficient if threads are only likely to be blocked for a short period of time, as it avoids the overhead of operating system process re-scheduling. It is wasteful if the lock is held for a long period of time.

Most locking designs block the execution of the process requesting the lock until it is allowed to access the locked resource.

Semaphore

A semaphore is a protected variable (or abstract data type) and constitutes the classic method for restricting access to shared resources (e.g., storage) in a multiprogramming environment. It was invented by Edsger Dijkstra and first used in the THE operating system.

The value of the semaphore is initialized to the number of equivalent shared resources it is implemented to control. In the special case where there is a single equivalent shared resource, the semaphore is called a binary semaphore. The general case semaphore is often called a counting semaphore.

Semaphores are the classic solution to the dining philosophers problem, although they do not prevent all deadlocks.

Thread Join

A thread in computer science is short for a thread of execution. Threads are a way for a program to fork (or split) itself into two or more simultaneously (or pseudo-simultaneously) running tasks. Threads and processes differ from one operating system to another, but in general, the way that a thread is created and shares its resources is different from the way a process does.

Threads are a way for a program to split itself into two or more simultaneously running tasks.

Multiple threads can be executed in parallel on many computer systems. This multithreading generally occurs by time slicing (similar to time-division multiplexing), wherein a single processor switches between different threads, in which case the processing is not literally simultaneous, for the single processor is really doing only one thing at a time. This switching can happen so fast as to give the illusion of simultaneity to an end user. For instance, most PCs today only contain one processor core, but you can run multiple programs at once, such as typing in a document editor while listening to music in an audio playback program; though the user experiences these things as simultaneous, in truth, the processor quickly switches back and forth between these separate processes. On a multiprocessor or multi-core system, now coming into general use, threading can be achieved via multiprocessing, wherein different threads and processes can run literally simultaneously on different processors or cores.

Many modern operating systems directly support both time-sliced and multiprocessor threading with a process scheduler. The operating system kernel allows programmers to manipulate threads via the system call interface. Some implementations are called a kernel thread, whereas a lightweight process is a specific type of kernel thread that shares the same state and information.

Absent that, programs can still implement threading by using timers, signals, or other methods to interrupt their own execution and hence perform a sort of ad-hoc time-slicing. These are sometimes called user-space threads.

Threads compared with processes

Threads are distinguished from traditional multitasking operating system processes in that processes are typically independent, carry considerable state information, have separate address spaces, and interact only through system-provided inter-process communication mechanisms.

Multiple threads, on the other hand, typically share the state information of a single process, and share memory and other resources directly.

Context switching between threads in the same process is typically faster than context switching between processes. Systems like Windows NT and OS/2 are said to have "cheap" threads and "expensive" processes; in other operating systems there is not so great a difference.

Multithreading is a popular programming and execution model that allows multiple threads to exist within the context of a single process, sharing the process' resources but able to execute independently. The threaded programming model provides developers with a useful abstraction of concurrent execution. However, perhaps the most interesting application of the technology is when it is applied to a single process to enable parallel execution on a multiprocessor system.

This advantage of a multithreaded program allows it to operate faster on computer systems that have multiple CPUs, CPUs with multiple cores, or across a cluster of machines. This is because the threads of the program naturally lend themselves to truly concurrent execution. In such a case, the programmer needs to be careful to avoid race conditions, and other non-intuitive behaviours.

In order for data to be correctly manipulated, threads will often need to rendezvous in time in order to process the data in the correct order.

Threads may also require atomic operations (often implemented using semaphores) in order to prevent common data from being simultaneously modified, or read while in the process of being modified. Careless use of such primitives can lead to deadlocks.

Operating systems generally implement threads in one of two ways: pre-emptive multithreading, or cooperative multithreading. Pre-emptive multithreading is generally considered the superior implementation, as it allows the operating system to determine when a context switch should occur.

Cooperative multithreading, on the other hand, relies on the threads themselves to relinquish control once they are at a stopping point. This can create problems if a thread is waiting for a resource to become available. The disadvantage to pre-emptive multithreading is that the system may make a context switch at an inappropriate time, causing priority inversion or other bad effects which may be avoided by cooperative multithreading.

Traditional mainstream computing hardware did not have much support for multithreading as switching between threads was generally already quicker than full process context switches. Processors in embedded systems, which have higher requirements for real-time behaviours, might support multithreading by decreasing the thread switch time, perhaps by allocating a dedicated register file for each thread instead of saving/restoring a common register file. In the late 1990s, the idea of executing instructions from multiple threads simultaneously has become known as simultaneous multithreading.

This feature was introduced in Intel's Pentium 4 processor, with the name Hyper-threading.

Mutual exclusion

Mutual exclusion (often abbreviated to mutex) algorithms are used in concurrent programming to avoid the simultaneous use of a common resource, such as a global variable, by pieces of computer code called critical sections.

Examples of such resources are fine-grained flags, counters or queues, used to communicate between code that runs concurrently, such as an application and its interrupt handlers. The problem is acute because a thread can be stopped or started at any time.

To illustrate: suppose a section of code is mutating a piece of data over several program steps, when another thread, perhaps triggered by some unpredictable event, starts executing. If this second thread reads from the same piece of data, the data, in the process of being overwritten, is in an inconsistent and unpredictable state. If the second thread tries overwriting that data, the ensuing state will probably be unrecoverable. These critical sections of code accessing shared data must, therefore, be protected, so that other processes which read from or write to the chunk of data are excluded from running.

A mutex is also a common name for a program object that negotiates mutual exclusion among threads, also called a lock.

Non-blocking synchronization

In computer science, non-blocking synchronization ensures that threads competing for a shared resource do not have their execution indefinitely postponed by mutual exclusion. Literature up to the turn of the century used "non-blocking" synonymously with lock-free: an algorithm with guaranteed system-wide progress. However, since 2003, the term has been weakened to only prevent progress-blocking interactions with a pre-emptive scheduler.

In modern usage, therefore, an algorithm is non-blocking if the suspension of one or more threads will not stop the potential progress of the remaining threads.

They are designed to avoid requiring a critical section. Often, these algorithms allow multiple processes to make progress on a problem without ever blocking each other. For some operations, these algorithms provide an alternative to locking mechanisms.

Synchronous Communication Operations

A distinctly different (but related) concept is that of data synchronization. This refers to the need to keep multiple copies of a set of data coherent with one another.

Examples include:

- File synchronization, such as syncing a hand-held MP3 player to a desktop computer.
- Cluster file systems, which are file systems that maintain data or indexes in a coherent fashion across a whole computing cluster.
- Cache coherency, maintaining multiple copies of data in sync across multiple caches.
- RAID, where data is written in a redundant fashion across multiple disks, so that the loss of any one disk does not lead to a loss of data.
- Database replication, where copies of data on a database are kept in sync, despite possible large geographical separation.
- Journalling, a technique used by many modern file systems to make sure that file metadata are updated on a disk in a coherent, consistent manner.

MICROSOFT DISK OPERATING SYSTEM (DOS)

DOS translates the commands that we enter through the keyboard into signals that can be interpreted by the computer. The CPU (Central Processing Unit) processes the raw data as per the commands we feed (Input) into the computer and returns the results (gives the Output).

The results are displayed on the Monitor in our language. The results can also be printed on a printer. Directed by the instruction that we type, the DOS operates and controls the operating system. With DOS we can do the following:

- Create new files
- Delete old files
- Rename existing files
- List all the files in the hard disk or floppy
- Enhance the storage capacity of the disk
- Format new floppy or hard disk for usage

- Reorganize the storage files on the disk
- Make back up files on the hard disk or to the floppy disks
- Scan for viruses.

Type of DOS Commands

There are 2 types of DOS commands, mainly, Internal and External commands.

Internel Commands

These commands can be given from the DOS prompt, irrespective of the fact the command is there in the DOS directory or not. These can be said to be the in-built commands of DOS. All these commands are contained in file of DOS, i.e., COMMAND.COM.

For example, the following commands are internal commands:

Chdir It changes the current directory, shortname is CD.

Cls It clears the screen.

Copy It is used for copying files, read more about it later in the chapter.

Copy con It is used to create a quick batch file.

Ctty This command is used to redirect the keyboard and screen to the serial port.

External Commands

These commands are such that they have to be present in the hard disk to be used.

Some of external commands are given below:

Append It lets programs open data files as if they were in the current directory.

Assign It is used to reassign drives when programs work only with specific drives.

Attrib It changes file attributes, which are settings in every DOS file.

Backup/Restore It lets you backup your hard disk onto as many floppies as required. Restore command can be used to use backedup files.

Chkdsk It checks disk status, memory status, files and flags unidentifiable files.

Comp It compares two files for identical content and reports up to 10 mismatches.

File Structure in DOS

All the data in the computer is stored in terms of Files. Each file is unique and is identified by name, date and time of creation, number of bytes, etc. The name of the file usually in the form of 8 + 3 digits (also called 8.3 rule) which is recognised by DOS. The 8 digits are reserved for the first name and the next 3 for the extension, which signifies the type of the file.

A typical filename in DOS can be represented as:

```
MSM.COM
```

where

MSM is the first name

. is always there

COM represents the last name or popularly called extension.

STORAGE OF FILES

Files are stored in the hard disk just as we store packets in godown. A hard disk is divided into various subdirectories like rooms in a house. When you start your PC, the first directory that you see is the root directory. The root directory can be compared to a house. Within a subdirectory, you can have another subdirectory and files. You can create and delete these directories yourself. Related files are kept in the same directory.

Seeing the File

If you want to see the files or subdirectories available in a particular directory, you use the DIR command. Simple DIR command produces the display shown below.

All the files in this directory will be listed along with the information like name, extension, number of bytes, data and time of creation. At the end, the total number of files in the directory is given along with the total number of bytes used. The total number of bytes remaining free in the hard disk is also given.

```
USER     DEF            11  12-17-02 11:14a USER.DEF
AUTOEXEC 001            26  12-06-02 12:38p AUTOEXEC.001
PR_ADDC  DBF           872  12-13-02  7:23p pr_addc.DBF
PR_ADDC  CDX         9,216  12-13-02  7:23p pr_addc.CDX
MTNL_G~1 DBF           360  12-13-02  7:23p mtnl_groupc.DBF
OUT      TXT           132  12-18-02  3:59p out.txt
C&CGOLD        <DIR>        01-26-03 12:52a c&cgold
        26 file(s)         281,630 bytes
        13 dir(s)           189.29 MB free

C:\>
```

Another way of using the DIR command is DIR/P, which is shown next .

```
 Directory of C:\

USERS    TXT            90  01-05-02  5:46p USERS.TXT
FRUNLOG  TXT         1,012  04-20-99  9:59a FRUNLOG.TXT
AUTOEXEC BAT            35  12-11-02  1:23p AUTOEXEC.BAT
CONFIG   SYS            10  11-14-02  9:05a CONFIG.SYS
WINDOWS        <DIR>        04-20-99  9:46a WINDOWS
PROGRA~1       <DIR>        11-13-01 11:31a Program Files
SETUPXLG TXT         1,104  06-01-02  2:31p SETUPXLG.TXT
INFERNO  LOG            67  08-17-01  8:20p inferno.log
PM65           <DIR>        08-18-01 10:53a PM65
KPCMS          <DIR>        08-18-01 10:54a KPCMS
ACROBAT3       <DIR>        08-18-01 10:54a Acrobat3
PSFONTS        <DIR>        08-18-01 10:54a psfonts
SCANDISK LOG         2,393  02-21-03 10:50a SCANDISK.LOG
ADOBEAPP       <DIR>        08-18-01  8:58p ADOBEAPP
WINZIP         <DIR>        08-18-01 11:34a WinZip
WINDOW~1 BMK            63  08-21-01  6:30p WINDOWSWinHlp32.BMK
NCDTREE        <DIR>        09-12-01  7:58p NCDTREE
LOGFILE  TXT           108  09-30-01 12:36a LOGFILE.TXT
TRACE    LOG             0  11-06-01  2:07p TRACE.LOG
Press any key to continue . . .
```

The /P added to DIR, stands for pagewise. Suppose there are a large number of files and subdirectories within a directory. Now when you use DIR command, you will find that most of the file names scroll past the screen and only the last few entries are displayed. This may result in your not seeing the required file which may appear in the first lot. For this you should be able to stop and continue at will, the scrolling of the listing to look for a particular file. The following command gives you that option:

Once the screen has been filled up, the listing on the screen will stop with this message at the bottom:

```
Press any key to continue . . .
```

When you do press any key, the monitor will again display the next screen and stop. You can repeat this till all the files in the directory have been displayed.

Another option is DIR/W.

```
C:\>dir/w/p

 Volume in drive C has no label
 Volume Serial Number is 2919-10EC
 Directory of C:\

USERS.TXT       FRUNLOG.TXT     AUTOEXEC.BAT    CONFIG.SYS      [WINDOWS]
[PROGRA~1]      SETUPXLG.TXT    INFERNO.LOG     [PM65]          [KPCMS]
[ACROBAT3]      [PSFONTS]       SCANDISK.LOG    [ADOBEAPP]      [WINZIP]
WINDOW~1.BMK    [NCDTREE]       LOGFILE.TXT     TRACE.LOG       WINZIP.LOG
STUB.LOG        [MYDOCU~1]      ADOBEWEB.LOG    NETLOG.TXT      COMMAND.COM
FRONTPG.LOG     [SCANJET]       AILOG.TXT       [SIERRA]        TMP.INI
CONFIG.000      AUTOEXEC.000    USER.DEF        AUTOEXEC.001    PR_ADDC.DBF
PR_ADDC.CDX     MTNL_G~1.DBF    OUT.TXT         [C&CGOLD]
       26 file(s)        281,630 bytes
       13 dir(s)          189.27 MB free
```

The /W stands for widthwise display. This command is used when you want to see only the names of the files and are not interested in any detail. This results in the appearance of file names on the screen in groups of 3-4. Usually, all the files are listed together on the screen. If, however, the files still don't fit together on the screen, you can give the command DIR/W/P. Then the following will be displayed:

Creating and Changing Directory

To create a new directory, you have to assign a name to it. This should, as far as possible, signify the type of data or programs you are going to store into it. The command is given as following:

```
MD  SACHIN
```

This will create a new directory by the name of SACHIN. In the beginning, it is blank. Your cursor will remain at the position of its start.

Supposing you want to enter this or any other directory, then the command will be:

Change Directory

This command can be given as following:

```
C:\>CD  SACHIN
C:\>SACHIN>
```

This means that you have entered the directory called SACHIN. However, if you are in any other directory and want to enter the SACHIN directory from there, the command becomes:

```
C:>CD\
```

The backslash (\) means that you are entering a different directory. Actually (\) means more than that. If you type CD\ at the DOS prompt of any subdirectory, your cursor reaches the root directory. This is a quick way to go to the root directory, skipping several levels of subdirectories. If you write only CD then it will show the current directory.

```
C:\>cd windows

C:\WINDOWS>
```

Directory Structure of DOS

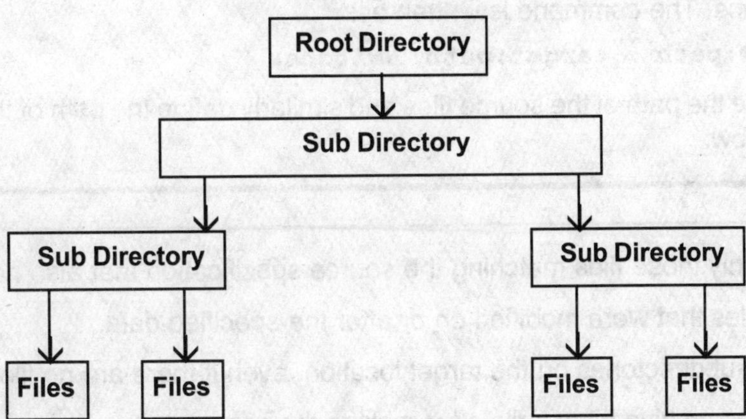

Remove Directory

Sometimes, it is possible that you have finished using a software and do not want to keep it or have finished with a project and taken the backup too and don't want to burden your hard disk by keeping it. In this case you would like to remove the directory all together. This would help in having more space for working. This command has to be given from outside the directory which you want to remove. So, if you are in the directory, go out from it and then give the remove directory command. You can use either RD or RMDIR. The command is given as:

```
RD SACHIN
```

Before, you do this, however, you must make sure that you have removed all the files in the directory by using the DEL command. If you have not done so, this command will give you the message that the directory is not empty and cannot be deleted.

DOS COMMANDS

Now you will be introduced to various DOS commands, mainly copy, delete, rename, etc.

Copying a File

It is used to copy file or files from one directory to another or to shift to another drive. The command given is:

```
Copy sachin.doc a:sachin.doc
```

Here the file sachin.doc would be copied to drive A with the same name, i.e., sachin.doc. If you want to change the name, that is also possible. Then after the a: type the new name.

Another way of using the copy command is by using the wild card option, i.e., *. This is how it is used:

```
Copy *.doc a:
```

The above command will copy all files ending with doc to the floppy drive a. Let us use * at both the places, for example:

```
Copy *.* a:
```

This will copy all files irrespective of their names or extensions to drive a.

You can, if you want, copy files starting with an alphabet. For example:

```
Copy b*.doc a:
```

will copy all doc files starting with b.

Xcopy

This command is an extended command of copy. Here you can copy any number of files from any place in the hard disk to another place. The command is written as:

```
Xcopy source:path  target:path switches
```

where you have to define the path of the source files and similarly define the path of the target. Various switches used here are listed below:

Switch	*Action*
/A	Copies only those files matching the source specification that also have their archive bit set.
/D:date	Copies files that were modified on or after the specified data.
/E	Creates subdirectories on the target location, even if there are no files in them.
/M	Resets the archive bit in a file after making the copy.
/P	Issues a prompt asking you to confirm the copy of each source file.
/S	Copies files matching the source specification that are found in sub directories nested below the source subdirectory.
/V	Performs a verification check against the image of the file in memory.
/W	Causes XCOPY to pause before making copies allowing you an opportunity to change disks in the source drive if necessary.

For example,

```
Xcopy c:\sachin\*.doc a:
```

This command will copy all the doc files from the sachin subdirectory to the drive a.

Backup

There are times when you need to backup files to another drive to save the disk space area. The command is used as:

```
MSBACKUP file(s) /switches
```

where file(s) are the files which have to be backedup. Following switch options are available:

Switch	*Action*
/BW	Starts MSBACKUP in black-and-white for monitors that have trouble displaying the screen colours.
/TD	Back up all files named in the specification file that have changed since the last full backup.
/TF	Backs up all files named in the specification.
/TI	Backs up all files named in the specification file that have changed since the last full backup.

Deleting a File

By deleting the name of a file, you remove it completely, including its contents. So be very sure that you are not going to need the file again before giving the delete command. You can delete a file by giving its full name. For example, when you give the following command:

```
DEL  SACHIN.DOC
```

This would delete the file called sachin.doc.

Date and Time

These commands are used to display system time and date. By simply typing Date and Time, you can see the system date and time. What's more you can change them too, by retyping the Date and Time in the same format as displayed. Date is usually displayed in the format of Day and mm-dd-yyyy, where dd, mm and yy have the usual notations. Time is shown in terms of hours, minutes, seconds, etc. You can opt to display the time in 12-hour or 24-hour format.

```
C:\>time
Current time is  1:44:33.97p
Enter new time: _
```

```
C:\>date
Current date is Mon 04-21-2003
Enter new date (mm-dd-yy):
```

Prompt

If you do not like the usual C:\ format, you can change it by various other options available under DOS. The various switch options are:

Switch	*Action*
PROMPT	This option is used to get the default setting.
String	Specifies the text that you want to display as your system prompt.
$$	$(dollar sign)
$_	Carriage return/linefeed.
$B	| (bar or pipe symbol)
$D	Current date
$e	Escape code (you cannot use E instead)
$G	> (greater than symbol)
$H	Backspace (erases the preceding character)
$L	< (less than symbol)
$N	Current drive
$P	Current drive name and path name
$Q	= (equal sign)
$T	Current time
$V	System DOS version number.

Renaming a File

Sometimes, you may not like the name that you gave to a file. You may want to give it a new name without distributing the contents of the file. For this, you use the Rename command as following:

```
REN SACHIN.DOC GOLDEN.DOC
```

This will result in changing the name of the file from sachin.doc to golden.doc. Remember to put a space in between the two file names.

Restore

Once you backup the file, you must restore them too. The command for this is:

```
Restore source drive: target drive: /switches
```

where source drive has the files which have been backed up. Various switch options are:

Switch	*Action*
/A:mm-dd-yy	Restores only those files that were modified on or after the specified date, where mm is the month, dd is the day and yy is the year.
/B:mm-dd-yy	Restores only those files that were modified on or before the specified date, namely mm-dd-yy.
/D	Displays file name(s) on the backup disk but does not restore them.
/E:hh-mm-ss	Restores those files modified at or earlier than the specified time, where hh is the hour (in 24 hour format), mm is the minutes after the hour, and ss is the seconds.
/L:hh: mm: ss:	Restores only those files that were modified at or after the specified time.
/M	Restores files that were modified since the last backup was made.
/N	Restores files that were deleted since the last backup.
/P	Prompts to confirm the restoration of files that were changed since the last backup or marked as read-only files.
/S	Restores files in sub directories nested below the specified target subdirectory.

Changing the Attrib

Each file in DOS has various attributes attached to it. These attributes decide the fate of the file. Among them are read-only, hide, etc. So you can change the attribute of a file using the command called Attib, and the options attached to it. The command is:

```
Attrib modes path /switches
```

where path is the path of the file whose attributes you want to change. Various switches in use are:

Switch	*Action*
+A	Changes file setting to archived.
–A	Changes file settings to not archived.
+H	Changes specified file(s) to hidden, which means the file(s) will not be visible to most DOS operations.
–H	Makes hidden files visible again.

+R Changes specified file(s) to read-only which means the file(s) cannot be overwritten or erased.

–R Changes specified file(s) to read write which means, the file may be overwritten or erased.

+S Marks specified file(s) as DOS system file(s).

–S Removes DOS system-file setting.

/S Used with the file names that contain wildcard character or subdirectory names without file names. This option will include matching files in sub directories nested below the current subdirectory.

Type

This command is used to see the contents of a text file. The command is:

```
Type filename
```

where filename is the name of the file whose contents you have to see. Since this shows the plain listing of the files, it is advised that you use this command mainly for plain text files and not for formatted document files.

You can use | More to see all the contents of the file.

```
C:\>type out.txt
Num cars in race = 4
Num cars in race = 4
Num cars in race = 4
Num cars in race = 4
Num cars in race = 4
Num cars in race = 4
```

This is not the end of the DOS commands, there are more. The commands given here are just to give you an idea of the type of commands available under DOS. You can get the complete list of commands of DOS by typing

```
?
```

at the DOS prompt.

WINDOWS XP

Windows XP is a new Windows that represents a major shift in personal computing. Windows XP gives users the freedom to experience the digital world by building on the momentum of the internet and digital media with improvements that increase dependability and productivity for home users (Windows XP Home Edition) and businesses of all sizes (Windows XP Professional). Windows XP puts the exciting experiences of the digital age at user's fingertips by uniting PCs, devices and services with enhanced reliability, security and performance.

What does Windows XP stand for?

The XP stands for experience. The name Windows XP represents Microsoft's focus on enabling end-to-end experience, unlocking the power of the PC and empowering users to make the most of their computer experience in the simplest way possible. With Windows XP Microsoft is extending the power of the PC to devices, web services and applications that enable the broadest set of experiences.

Difference between Home Edition & Professional Edition

Windows XP Home Edition is designed to deliver the power and reliability of Windows 2000 to the home user, while improving on the best of Windows Me and providing application compatibility for users moving from either

Windows 2000 or Windows Me/98/98 SE. Windows XP Professional is a superset of Windows XP Home Edition and offers numerous additional technologies and features including roaming profiles, remote desktop, domain account support and dual processor support. Windows XP Professional meets the requirements for C2 security certification and includes Encrypting File Systems (EFS).

System Requirements for Windows XP

Following is the recommended configuration for loading Windows XP in your computer.

Hardware: PC with 300 MHz or higher processor clock speed recommended; 233 MHz is minimum required.

Memory: 128 MB of RAM or higher recommended (64 MB minimum supported; may limit performance and some features).

Hard Disk: 1.5 GB of available hard disk space.

CD-ROM: CD-ROM drive.

Input Device: Keyboard and Mouse or compatible pointing device

Multimedia: **For sound**: Sound card and speakers or headphones. **For DVD video playback**: DVD drive and DVD decoder card or DVD decoder software & 8 MB of video RAM. For Windows Movie Maker: Video capture feature requires appropriate digital or analog video capture device & 400 MHz or higher processor for digital video camera capture.

Step-by-Step Installation

As all the operating systems go, Windows XP is very smart. For many configurations, you can just boot up, put the CD in the drive, and start running Setup. The system will install without a hiccup.

Setup will then perform a more thorough check of your system, including looking for installed components of Windows and making sure that you have enough hard drive space to complete the installation.

After copying all the files required for setting up of Windows XP, the Setup Wizard will restart your computer and finish up. Your system might not restart by itself. Wait five minutes or so, and if nothing appears to be happening, hit the Reset button on your computer. This won't harm your installation and is not a sign of installation failure. After the restart, Windows XP still has a few chores. It will detect and set up plug-and-play devices and possibly other hardware whose settings could not be taken over from Windows XP. This may involve restarting again.

Then Setup will run though a series of other tasks, including setting up the **Control Panel** and putting your programs on the **Start Menu**. The last one, updating system settings, may take quite a while. Finally, there will be another restart, and you will see the **Welcome to Windows** screen and will take you through a beautiful video highlighting the various new features of Windows XP.

One distinct feature of Windows XP is the user name with password, without which this version would not work. In earlier versions you could bypass it by using Esc key. So make sure you give the user name and password very carefully.

Once installed the Windows XP screen would look like the one shown on the next page. With your Windows XP fully installed, you can go ahead and start working.

As was in the earlier version of Windows, Windows XP too has a familiar desktop from where you can launch your programs using their shortcuts.

A Windows XP desktop is shown on the next page with all the relative icons. You may or may not have the same desktop on computer. But, it will be quite similar.

Exploring Windows XP Desktop

On the desktop, there are few icons which are a must for all the desktops being used by Windows XP and there are few which are optional and are created by the users according to their likings.

Among the permanent ones are: **My Computer**, **Recycle Bin**, **My Documents**, etc.

Before we go into details of all these and see how they help us in working, we explore the other parts of the desktop. At the bottom most left corner of the desktop is the **Start** button. By pressing it you can launch the following options: (A typical set of options as available on pressing Start button are shown next).

For those of you who have used earlier versions of Windows, this would look very different from the earlier ones. The main difference being that it is in 2 cols.

Various options on the Start button, as shown on the next page, are:

Internet: It opens up Internet Explorer version 6.0 for you to access Internet.

e-mail: If opens up Outlook Express for you to send and receive e-mail.

Shortcut to Cricket: A program loaded by me.

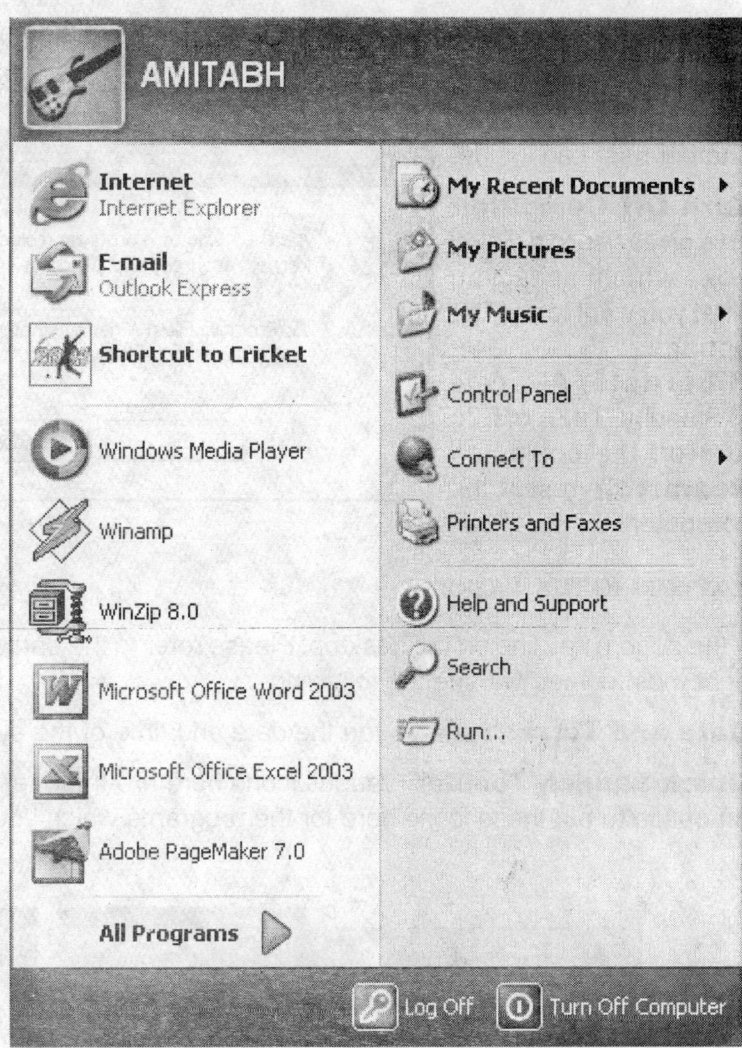

Recently used programs: Windows XP shows here the recently used programs so that you can access them easily. The ones shown here are: Windows Media Player, Winamp, WinZip 8.0, Microsoft Office Word 2003, Microsoft Office Excel 2003 and Adobe PageMaker 7.0.

All Programs: It gives you access to all programs loaded in your computer. You can start these programs by just clicking at them.

My Recent Documents: It gives you access to the last 15 documents opened.

My Pictures: It gives you the list of pictures stored by you in your computer.

My Music: It gives you the list of music files stored in the computer.

Control Panel: You can access to Control Panel from here.

Connect To: It provides access to connecting you to your own connection or show all the connections available in the computer.

Printers and Faxes: It shows you the various printers and faxes connected to your computer.

Help & Support: It opens the extensive Windows XP Help system and gives you access to the Troubleshooting.

Search: This allows you to search for a file or folder.

Run: Allows you to run a particular program using a dialog box.

Log Off..: It logs off the system quickly so that you can log back with a different user profile or so that another user can log on.

Turn Off Computer: This gives rise to a dialog box, which asks you what you want to do. The options are: **Hibernate**: Alternate to Standby. **Turn off**: To turn off the computer. **Restart**: To restart the computer

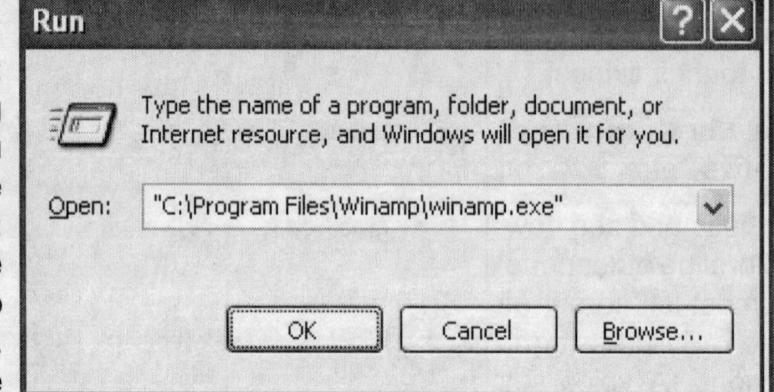

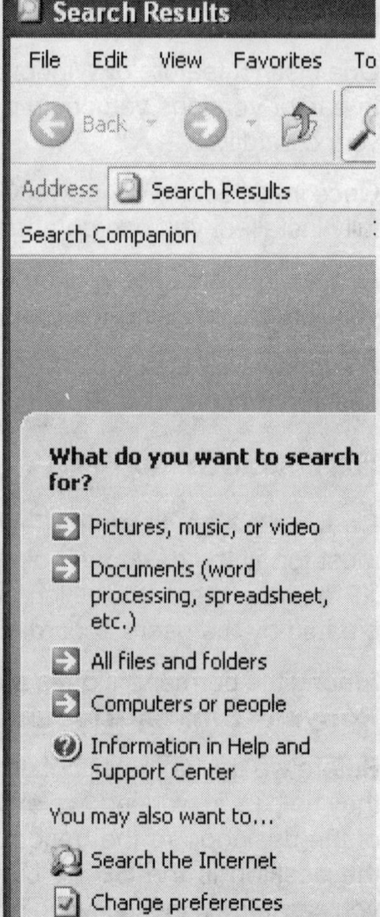

Exploring the Taskbar

It the bottom key line on the desktop. Please refer to the earlier figure of desktop for the details. Starting with the right most corner, we see the following:

Date and Time : It shows you the date and time of the system.

Quick Launch Toolbar: Various icons here are the ones used for launching different programs. You have an option to put these icons here for the programs which you often use.

Running Tasks: When you have a program running in your system, its name will be reflected here on this taskbar to show that this program is open.

Now we come to the various options of the desktop.

My Computer

It helps you browse the contents of your computer, open folders, open documents and run your favourite applications. As shown here, it is divided into 3 sections, System Tasks, Other Places, Details. You click at any icon on the right hand side of the dialog box and then choose the option on the left hand side. Details will give you the detail of the item selected. System tasks will allow you to perform a task. You can access other places by clicking at any one of them. On the right hand side, you have the users first. Then the hard drives and then removable ones like Floppy and CD drive. By clicking at any one of them, you can see the details of the files in it. Contents of the hard disk C are shown here.

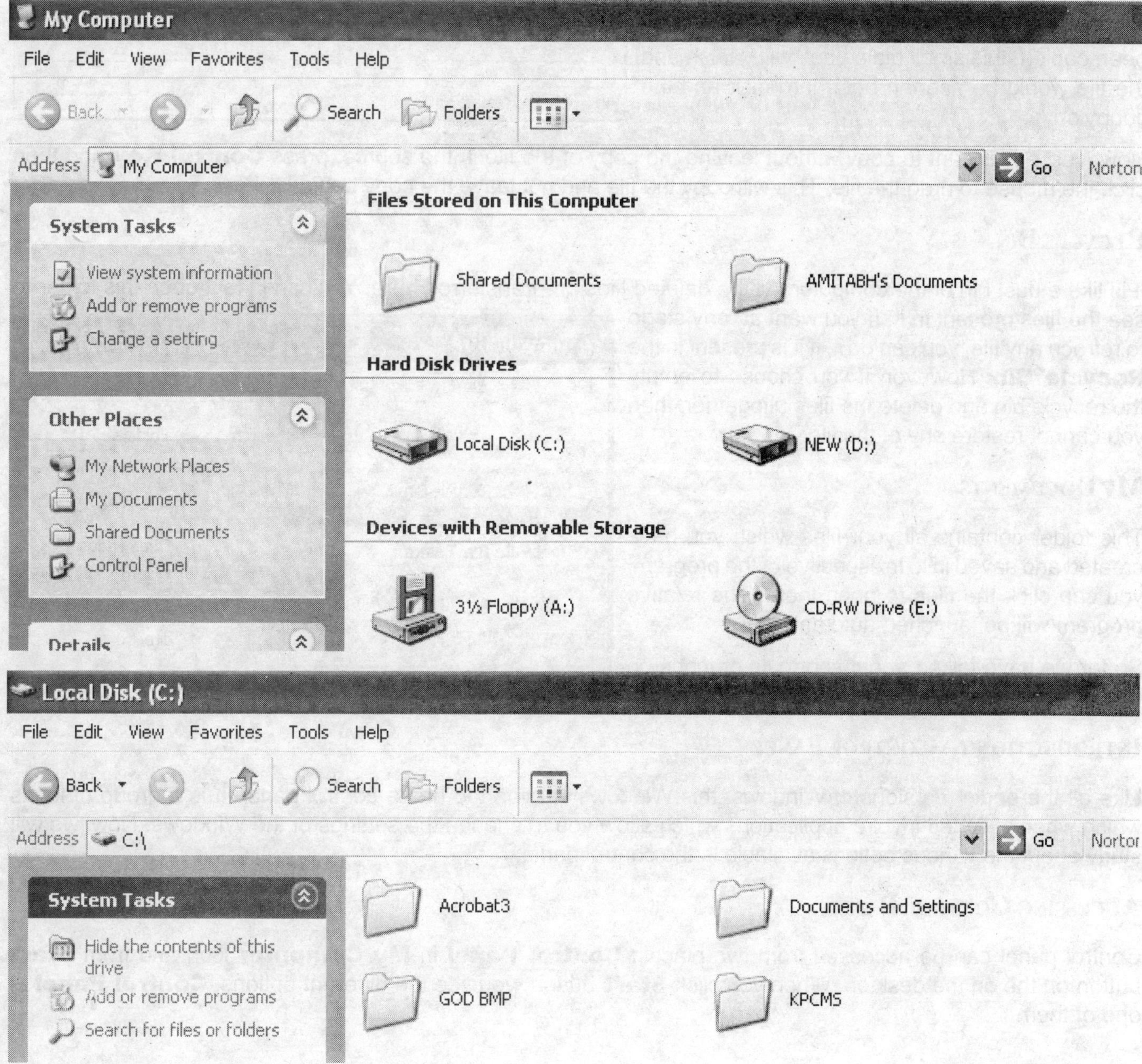

The buttons on the top are useful for going and coming back to the various folders. Seeing the various views of the files, etc.

Now let us see how **My Computer** is used for copying of files.

Copying of Files

Supposing you have to copy a file from floppy disk to the hard disk. As in the previous case click at the icon of floppy drive A to get the open folder. Also open the folder of hard disk and the particular folder where you want the file to be copied. You will have to click the icon of **My Computer** again for this.

Now that both the folders of hard disk and floppy drive are open and you can see the file icon, which you want to copy to the hard disk. Just click this and drag it to drop in the folder of the hard disk. You will see the copying start. Once the file has been copied, this small dialog box will vanish and the file would be seen in both hard disk and the floppy drive.

However, if you want to copy without leaving the copy of the file in the source, press **Control Key** and then click the mouse to drag the file. This will copy the file and not leave the copy behind.

Recycle Bin

It is like a dust bin of the computer. All the deleted files are transferred here. You can in fact open this folder to see the files present in it. If you want at any stage to retrace any file, you can do it, if it is present in the **Recycle Bin**. However, if you choose to empty the recycle bin and delete the files altogether, then you cannot restore any of the file.

My Documents

This folder contains all your files which you have created and saved in it. Irrespective of the program, you can click the files to open them. The relative program will be launched automatically.

So far we have talked about shortcuts or icons on the desktop. But, we have not told you how they are created.

Introduction to Control Panel

Like all the earlier versions of Windows, this Windows version too has a control panel. It is a group of icons which when selected invoke applications which allow you to change the settings of the Windows. Now, we will study about the various options available in the control panel.

Accessing Control Panel

Control panel can be accessed from two places: **Control Panel** in **My Computer** icon and from **Start** button on the on the desktop. When you click **Start** button, you see the different options. **Control Panel** is one of them.

Appearance and Themes

Here the options are listed in the form of tasks and icons. You can work either way.

Changing Theme

Windows XP's display is based upon the various themes which you select for displaying information and icons on your desktop. You select a theme, the displays associated with it change automatically. There are various themes to choose from. Each theme has its versions of displaying in various colours.

Changing Desktop Background

Like the earlier task, here also you can choose to display how your desktop background would look like. In my case I have chosen home, as shown on the next page.

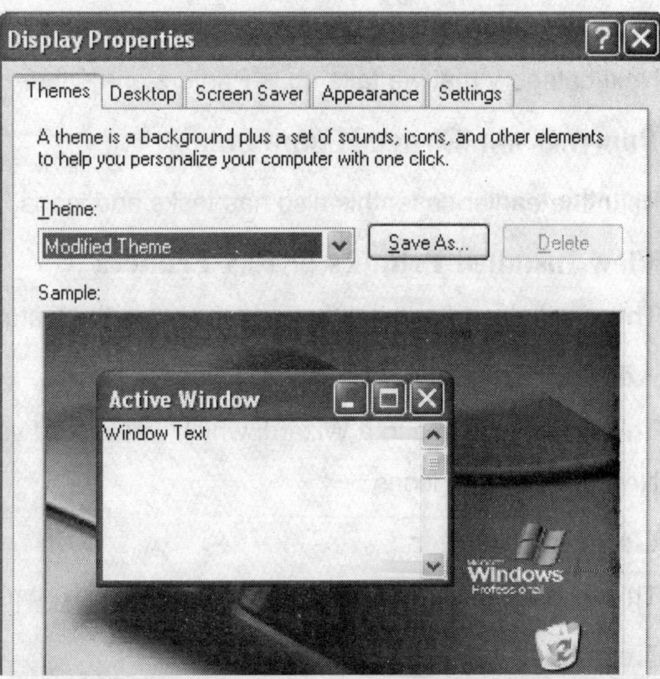

Choosing a Screen Saver

Screen saver allows you to save your screen from burning out specially in the case where you leave the screen without doing anything. There are various options which can be set to work after a gap certain minutes, which you can set.

Changing Screen Resolution

You can set the resolution of your screen display from here. It also shows the name of the monitor which you are using.

In case of any problem you can click at Troubleshooting and change the display to suit the screen.

Advanced features allow you to go deep into the features and change the monitor display.

This ends the tasks, now we can go for the icons.

Display

By clicking at it, you can get the display settings of the monitor in one go. You will get the monitor dialog box, which allows you to set the various settings, according to your liking.

Folder Options

As you can see from the dialog box here, it has 5 panels, each one of them having its own set of settings. Well as the name suggests, all of these setting are concerning the folders and files.

General allows you to set options, as shown here.

View takes care of the settings regarding viewing of the folders.

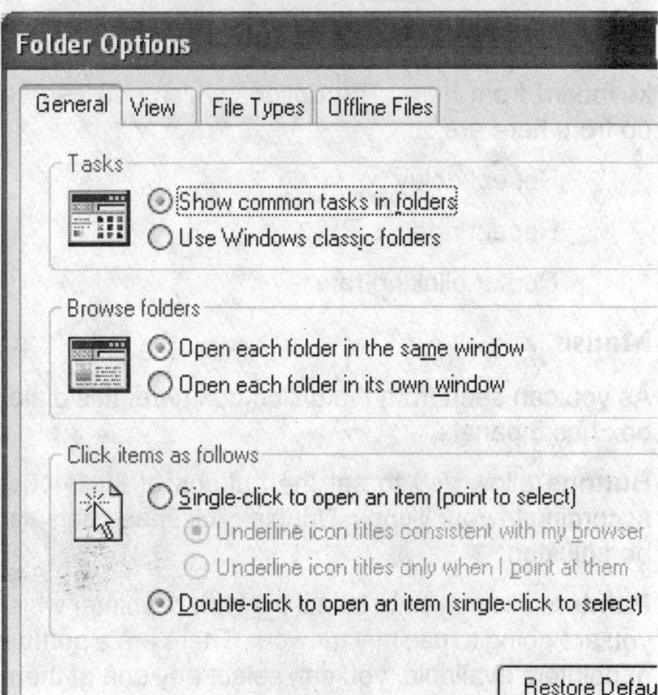

File Types let you set the type of files you are going to use.

Offline files allow you to work with files which are under networking which is not connected.

Taskbar and Start Menu

You now know what the taskbar is. Using this dialog box, you can set how to display various items on the taskbar.

This is as far as the tasks and icons are concerned. Under the troubleshooters we have Sound and Display. Both of these lead to Microsoft Help and Support Centre. You can find out the solution of your problem from here. But, in case the problem does not vanish, you can always call the engineer.

See also suggests you the name of the folder which you can see in support of those given here.

Next category that we take up is Printers and Other Hardwares.

PRINTERS AND OTHER HARDWARE

As in the earlier case, this also has tasks and icons. Let us see them one by one.

View Installed Printers or Fax Printers

This gives rise to a dialog box which shows the installed printers.

Add a Printer

This would give rise to a Wizard, which would lead you to add a printer in a easy way.

Now we come to icons.

Game Controller

This icon when clicked gives rise to a dialog box, which allows you to set a game controller.

Keyboard

There is no doubt that keyboard is very important part of the computer. You can set the various options of keyboard from here. The options which you can set up from here are:

- Repeat delay
- Repeat rate
- Cursor blinking rate

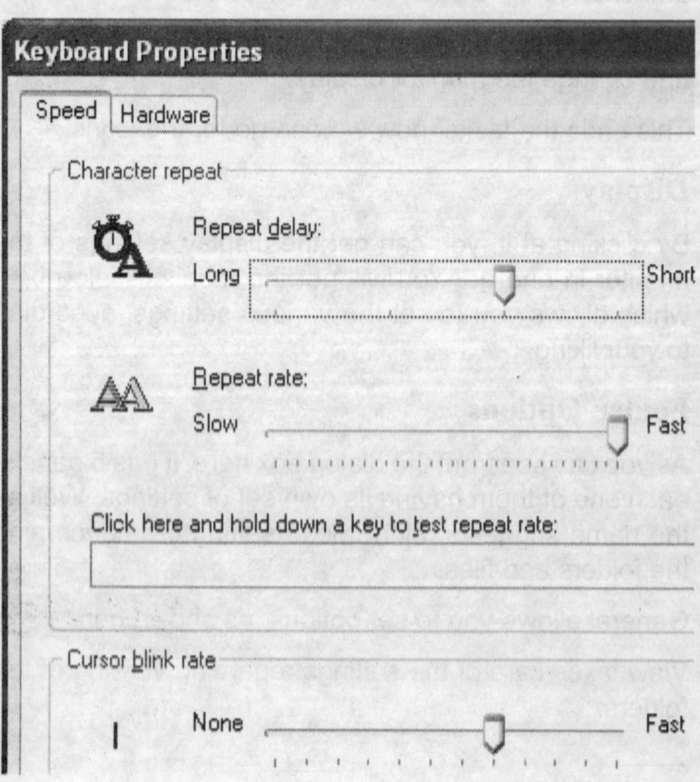

Mouse

As you can seen from the dialog box here, this dialog box has 5 panels.

Buttons allow you to set the buttons of the mouse according to your likings. Double click speed can also be adjusted.

Pointers allows you to select the type of pointer which you are going to use in your work. There are a number of pointers available, you can select any one of them.

Pointer Options allows you to set the motion of the mouse, snapping of the mouse, and visibility of mouse at the time of the selection. You can set the options according to your liking.

Wheel allow you to set the option of number of wheels in your mouse.

Hardware displays the name of the mouse attached to your printer.

Phone and Modem Options

There are 3 panels in it. One of them, Modem shows you the modem attached to the computer. If not, it will allow you to install a modem through a wizard. Dialing Rules allow you to set the various dialing rules for the phone numbers which you are going to dial. Advanced would show the various advanced features installed in your computer.

Printers and Faxes

It shows the various printers connected to you computer and an option to installed a new one.

Scanners and Cameras

It shows the scanners and cameras attached to your computer and an option to installed one if not there.

Next in line is the option of Network and Internet Connections

NETWORK AND INTERNET CONNECTIONS

This has various tasks and icons as shown below.

Set up or change your Internet Connection

This option allows you to open either by single click or by double click. Choose the way you want it.

Similarly, you can use the options in the View and File Types panels.

Create a connection to the network at your workplace

This will introduce you to a wizard which will take you through the process of connecting to a network.

Set up or change your home or small office network

This would also take you to a wizard of setting up of the network for your home or small office.

Internet Options

As shown here, you can change the various settings of the internet from here.

The options here in the form of panels are: General, Security, Privacy, Content, Connections, Programs and Advanced.

Make changes according to the information required by you.

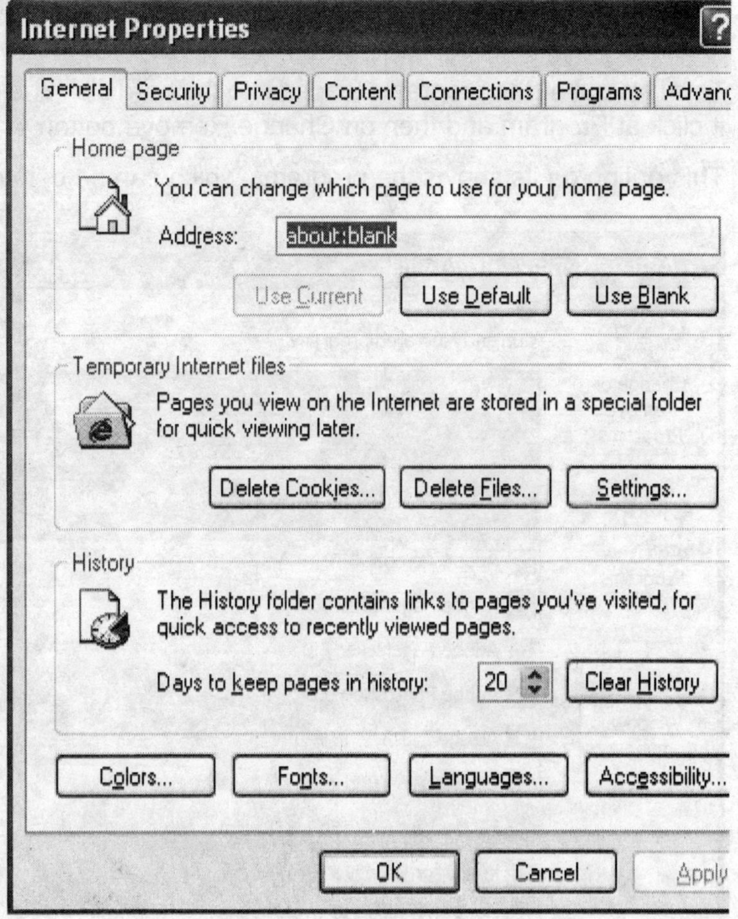

Network Connections

This shows the network connection you have made.

This section also provides for Troubleshooting mainly relating to networking and internet.

User Accounts

I had mentioned earlier that Windows XP is run on individual basis. You can have your own account and have your own password. All these changes will have to be made here.

Change an Account

This allows you to change the information of individual accounts already listed.

Clicking at individual account would lead you to another dialog box which asks you which of the following you want to do:

Change my name

Change my password

Remove my password

Change my picture

Change my account type

Set up my account to use a .NET Passport.

Next is Add or Remove Programs

Add or Remove Programs

Using this option you can Add or Remove programs from the hard disk. The program files should never be deleted from the directory itself using delete command. This leaves the program information in Windows Registery and does not remove all the files.

This lists out all the programs loaded into the hard disk, their size and the date of last used. If you want to update it click at Program and then on Change/Remove button.

This option on its shows the programs which can be deleted, which cannot be, as shown on next page.

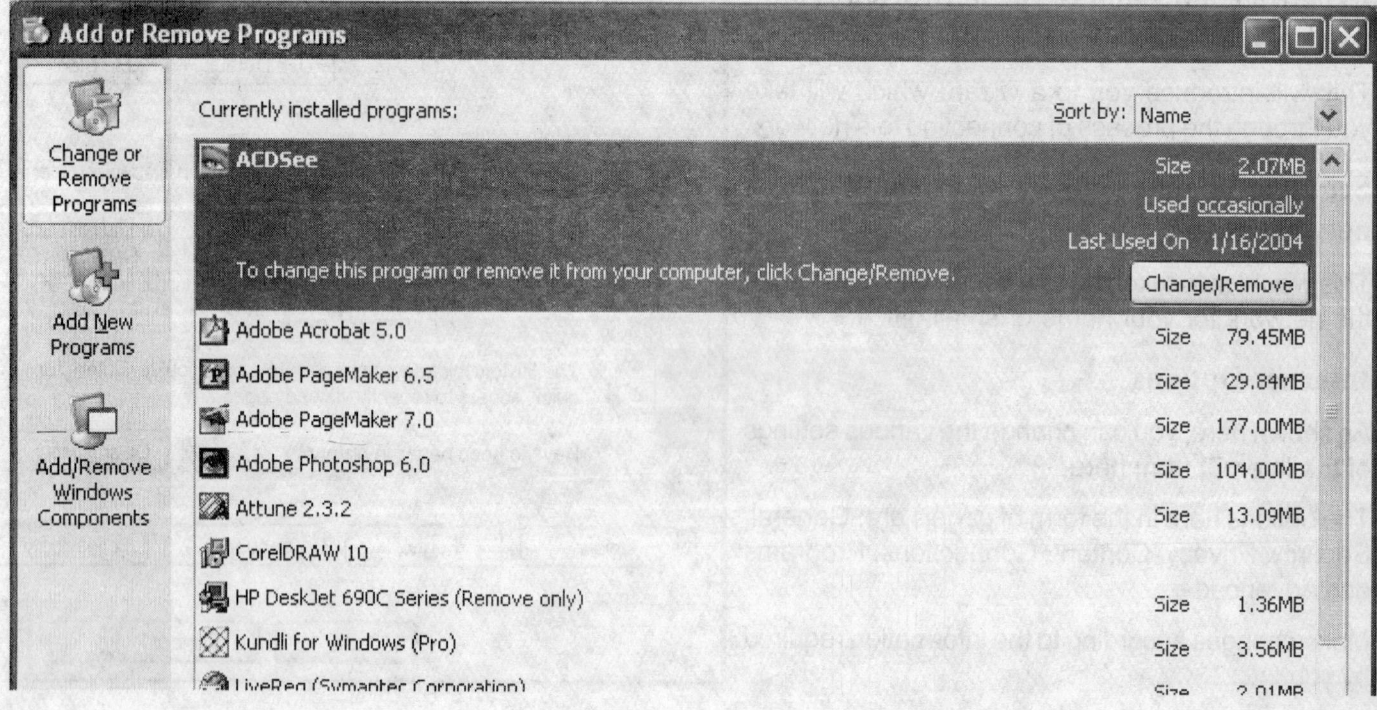

Date, Time, Language and Regional Options

This option allows you to change Date, Time and other information which you have fed in the computer at the time of installing Windows or otherwise.

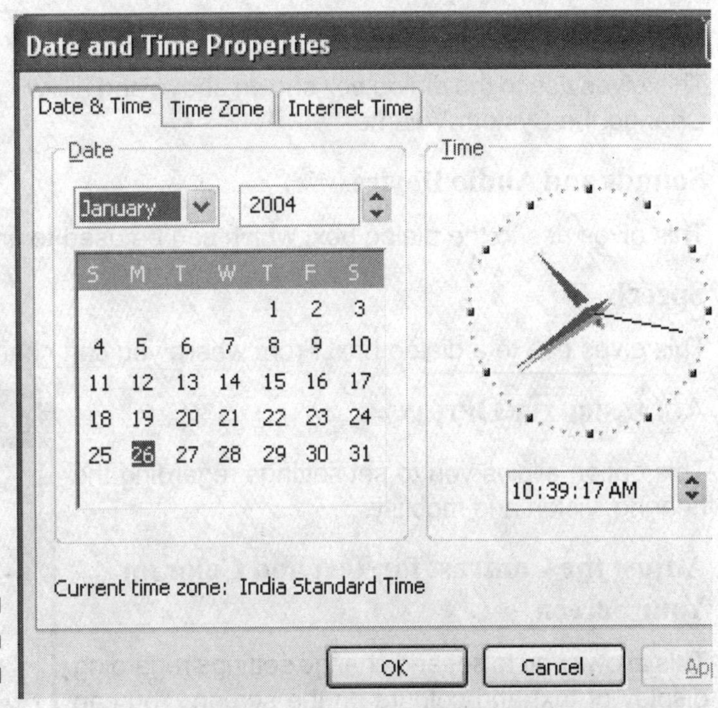

Change the Date and Time

There are 3 panels in it.

Date & Time shows and allows you to set time, date and year

Time Zone allows you to set the time zone in which you are working.

Internet Time allows you to synchronize time with the Internet time.

Change the format of Numbers, Date and Times

There are 3 panels here. Regional Options, Languages and Advanced.

Regional Options allow you to change the way you display numbers, currency, time, date, etc. You can change their format from here. Languages allow you install additional language in which you want to work.

Advanced allows you to work in your native language in which the computer allows. There are various languages which are listed for which the conversion codes are available, select one in which you want to work.

Add Other Languages

This gives rise to the Language panel of the above option.

Date and Time

Clicking on this icon would lead to the dialog box of Date and Time from which you make various changes.

Regional and Language Options

This gives rise to the dialog box of Regional options which allows you to change the number formats, etc., and languages.

Sound, Speech and Audio Devices

This option allows you to change the sound, speech and audio devices attached to the computer.

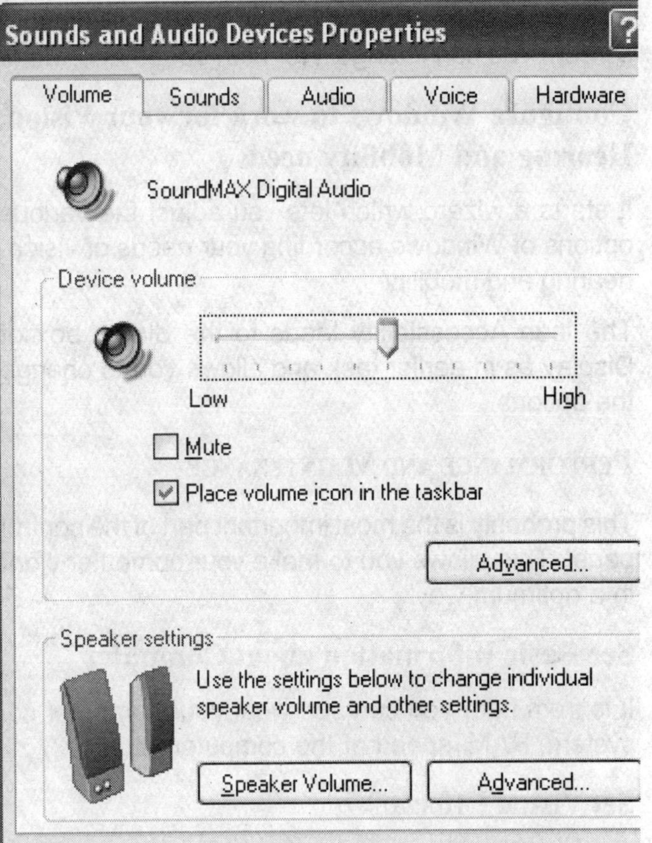

Adjust the System Volume

This gives rise to the following dialog box which allows you to set the volume of the sound device attached to your computer. You can also make settings of your speakers from here.

Change the Sound Scheme

Using this panel you can set sound for each activity of your working under Windows. For example while closing a program, a sound will be heard and while opening a software a different sound will be heard.

Change the Speaker Setting

This gives rise to the dialog box shown above and allows you to make the speaker settings, as mentioned under Change the System Volume.

Sounds and Audio Devices

This gives rise to the dialog box, which can be used to fine tune the sound in your system.

Speech

This gives rise to a dialog box. From where you can change the options of your microphone, language, etc.

ACCESSIBILITY OPTIONS

This option allows you to set settings regarding the hearing, vision and mobility.

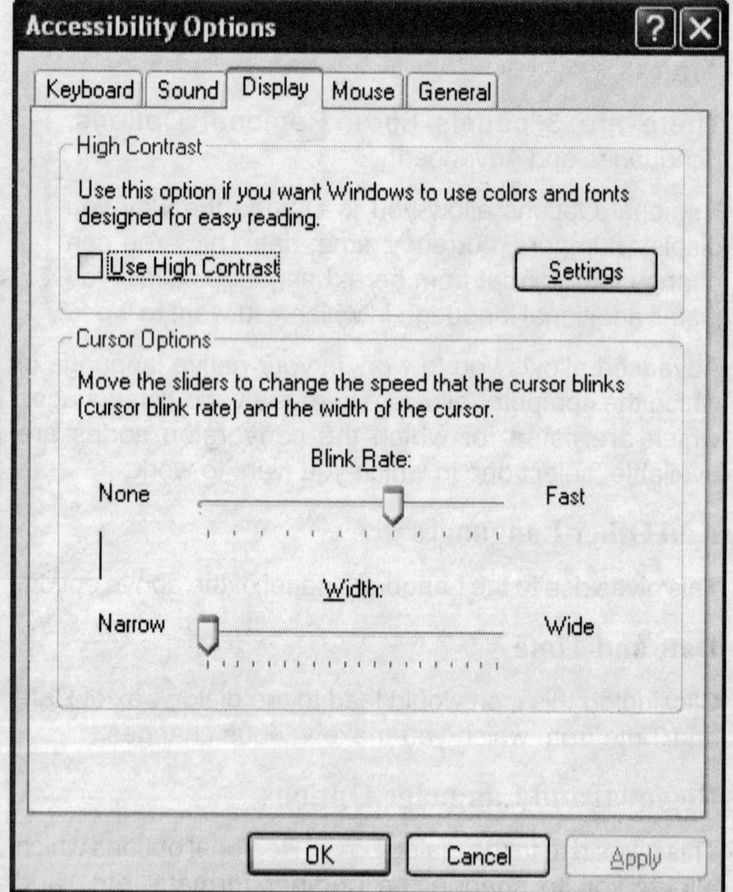

Adjust the Contrast for Text and Color on Your Screen

This allows you to set and change settings regarding display of text and colours on the screen. You can also change the blinking rate of the cursor on your screen. You can change it for both speed and width.

Configure Windows to work for your Vision, Hearing and Mobility needs

It starts a wizard which lets you adjust the various options of Windows according your needs of vision, hearing and mobility.

The icon Accessibility leads to the dialog box of Display as in earlier task and allows you to change the options.

PERFORMANCE AND MAINTENANCE

This probably is the most important part of the control panel. This allows you to make your computer work in a optimum way.

See Basic Information about Computer

It is from here you can see what your computer configuration is. It gives the complete details of the operating system, RAM, speed of the computer, etc.

Set Visual Effects

This panel gives you options for setting up various visual effects. If you have any doubt, just leave it as it is.

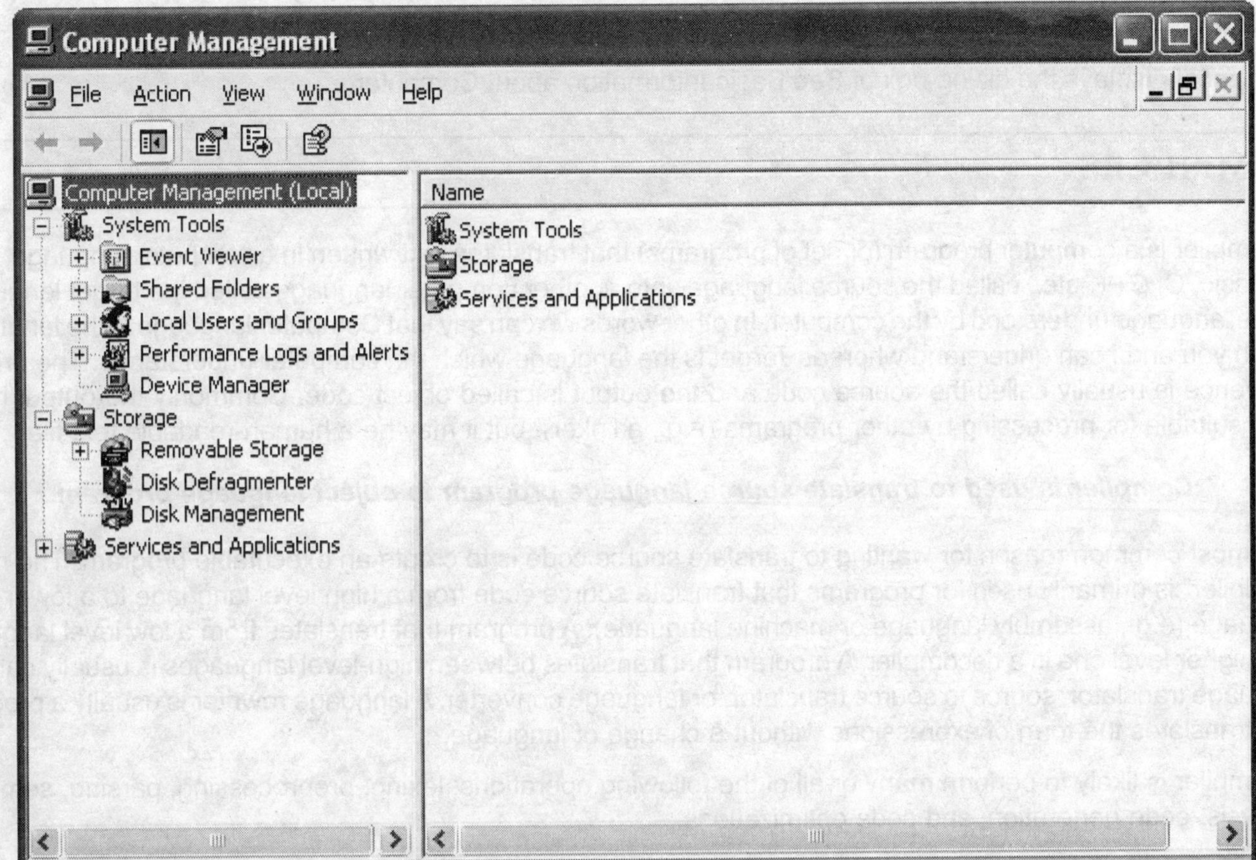

Free up Space on Your Hard Disk

Using this option you can delete the unwanted files from your hard disk to make more space for working.

Backup Your Data

This leads to a wizard which allows you to back up your data from hard disk to a removable drive.

Rearrange Items on Your Hard Disk to run Programs Faster

Defragmater is a method by which all the used and free hard disk is segregated to make the working of programs easier. Though, it takes little time but is worth running it from time to time to make more breathing space for programs.

Administrative Tools

As can be see from the figure on the next page, it has various tools for setting up various items of the hard disk. One of the them Computer Management is shown here.

Power Options

If you are working on a lap top then this option is for you. You can set in terms of minutes when to put off monitor, hard disk when not in use, to save power.

Scheduled Tasks

You can schedule to run some jobs for you on a regular basis. For example, you may like Anti-virus program to run every Sunday. Disk Fragmenter to run every 1st of the month, etc. This panel allows you to set these schedule tasks.

System

This panel displays the dialog box of See Basic Information about Computer.

COMPILERS

A compiler is a computer program (or set of programs) that translates text written in a computer language, such as Basic, C, C++, etc., called the source language, into another computer language called the target language, or the language understood by the computer. In other words we can say that Computer language is the language, which you and I can understand whereas Target is the language which the computer understands. The original sequence is usually called the source code and the output is called object code. Commonly the output has a form suitable for processing by other programs (e.g., a linker), but it may be a human-readable text file.

Compiler is used to translate source language program to object language program.

The most common reason for wanting to translate source code is to create an executable program. The name "compiler" is primarily used for programs that translate source code from a high level language to a lower level language (e.g., assembly language or machine language). A program that translates from a low level language to a higher level one is a decompiler. A program that translates between high-level languages is usually called a language translator, source to source translator, or language converter. A language rewriter is usually a program that translates the form of expressions without a change of language.

A compiler is likely to perform many or all of the following operations: lexing, preprocessing, parsing, semantic analysis, code generation, and code optimizations.

Types of Compilers

There are many ways to classify compilers according to the input and output, internal structure, and runtime behaviour, etc. For example,

- A program that translates from a low level language to a higher level one is a decompiler.
- A program that translates between high-level languages is usually called a language translator, source to source translator, language converter, or language rewriter.

One-pass versus Multi-pass Compilers

Classifying compilers by number of passes has its background in the hardware resource limitations of computers. Compiling involves performing lots of work and early computers did not have enough memory to contain one program that did all of this work. So compilers were split up into smaller programs each of which made a pass over the source (or some representation of it) performing some of the required analysis and translations.

The ability to compile in a single pass is often seen as a benefit because it simplifies the job of writing a compiler and one pass compilers are generally faster than multi-pass compilers. Many languages were designed so that they could be compiled in a single pass (e.g., Pascal).

In some cases the design of a language feature may require a compiler to perform more than one pass over the source. For instance, consider a declaration appearing on line 20 of the source which affects the translation of a statement appearing on line 10. In this case, the first pass needs to gather information about declarations appearing after statements that they affect, with the actual translation happening during a subsequent pass.

The disadvantage of compiling in a single pass is that it is not possible to perform many of the sophisticated optimizations needed to generate high quality code. It can be difficult to count exactly how many passes an optimizing compiler makes. For instance, different phases of optimization may analyse one expression many times but only analyse another expression once.

By compiling in passes you save the compilation time.

Splitting a compiler up into small programs is a technique used by researchers interested in producing provably correct compilers. Proving the correctness of a set of small programs often requiring less effort than proving the correctness of a larger, single, equivalent program.

While the typical multi-pass compiler outputs machine code from its final pass, there are several other types:

- A "source-to-source compiler" is a type of compiler that takes a high level language as its input and outputs a high level language.
- Stage compiler that compiles to assembly language of a theoretical machine.
- Just-in-time compiler, used by Smalltalk and Java systems, and also by Microsoft .Net's Common Intermediate Language (CIL).
- Applications are delivered in bytecode, which is compiled to native machine code just prior to execution.

Compiled versus Interpreted Languages

Many people divide higher-level programming languages into compiled languages and interpreted languages. However, there is rarely anything about a language that requires it to be compiled or interpreted. Compilers and interpreters are implementations of languages, not languages themselves. The categorization usually reflects the most popular or widespread implementations of a language — for instance, BASIC is thought of as an interpreted language, and C a compiled one, despite the existence of BASIC compilers and C interpreters.

There are exceptions; some language specifications spell out that implementations must include a compilation facility (eg, Common Lisp), while other languages have features that are very easy to implement in an interpreter, but make writing a compiler much harder; e.g. APL, SNOBOL4, and many scripting languages are capable of constructing arbitrary source code at runtime with regular string operations, and then executing that code by passing it to a special evaluation function. To implement these features in a compiled language, programs must usually be shipped with a runtime environment that includes the compiler itself.

Compilers and interpreters are implementations of languages, not languages themselves.

Compiler output

One classification of compilers is by the platform on which their generated code executes. This is known as the target platform.

A native or hosted compiler is one whose output is intended to directly run on the same type of computer and operating system that the compiler itself runs on. The output of a cross compiler is designed to run on a different platform. Cross compilers are often used when developing software for embedded systems that are not intended to support a software development environment.

The output of a compiler that produces code for a virtual machine (VM) may or may not be executed on the same platform as the compiler that produced it. For this reason such compilers are not usually classified as native or cross compilers.

Hardware compilation

The output of some compilers may target hardware at a very low level, for example a Field Programmable Gate Array (FPGA) or structured Application-specific integrated circuit (ASIC). Such compilers are said to be hardware compilers or synthesis tools because the programs they compile effectively control the final configuration of the hardware and how it operates; the output of the compilation are not instructions that are executed in sequence - only an interconnection of transistors or lookup tables. For example, XST is the Xilinx Synthesis Tool used for configuring FPGAs. Similar tools are available from Altera, Synplicity, Synopsys and other vendors.

Compiler design

In the early days, the approach taken to compiler design used to be directly affected by the complexity of the processing, the experience of the person(s) designing it, and the resources available.

A compiler for a relatively simple language written by one person might be a single, monolithic piece of software. When the source language is large and complex, and high quality output is required the design may be split into a number of relatively independent phases. Having separate phases means development can be parceled up into small parts and given to different people. It also becomes much easier to replace a single phase by an improved one, or to insert new phases later (eg, additional optimizations).

The division of the compilation processes into phases was championed by the Production Quality Compiler-Compiler Project (PQCC) at Carnegie Mellon University. This project introduced the terms front end, middle end, and back end. All but the smallest of compilers have more than two phases. However, these phases are usually regarded as being part of the front end or the back end. The point at where these two ends meet is always open to debate. The front end is generally considered to be where syntactic and semantic processing takes place, along with translation to a lower level of representation (than source code).

The middle end is usually designed to perform optimizations on a form other than the source code or machine code. This source code/machine code independence is intended to enable generic optimizations to be shared between versions of the compiler supporting different languages and target processors.

The back end takes the output from the middle. It may perform more analysis, transformations and optimizations that are for a particular computer. Then, it generates code for a particular processor and OS.

This front-end/middle/back-end approach makes it possible to combine front ends for different languages with back ends for different CPUs. Practical examples of this approach are the GNU Compiler Collection, LLVM, and the Amsterdam Compiler Kit, which have multiple front-ends, shared analysis and multiple back-ends.

Front end

The front end analyzes the source code to build an internal representation of the program, called the intermediate representation or IR. It also manages the symbol table, a data structure mapping each symbol in the source code to associated information such as location, type and scope. This is done over several phases, which includes some of the following:

Line reconstruction. Languages which strop their keywords or allow arbitrary spaces within identifiers require a phase before parsing, which converts the input character sequence to a canonical form ready for the parser. The top-down, recursive-descent, table-driven parsers used in the 1960s typically read the source one character at a time and did not require a separate tokenizing phase. Atlas Autocode, and Imp (and some implementations of Algol and Coral66) are examples of stropped languages whose compilers would have a Line Reconstruction phase. Lexical analysis breaks the source code text into small pieces called tokens. Each token is a single atomic unit of the language, for instance a keyword, identifier or symbol name. The token syntax is typically a regular language, so a finite state automaton constructed from a regular expression can be used to recognize it. This phase is also called lexing or scanning, and the software doing lexical analysis is called a lexical analyzer or scanner.

Preprocessing. Some languages, e.g., C, require a preprocessing phase which supports macro substitution and conditional compilation. Typically the preprocessing phase occurs before syntactic or semantic analysis; e.g. in the case of C, the preprocessor manipulates lexical tokens rather than syntactic forms. However, some languages such as Scheme support macro substitutions based on syntactic forms.

Syntax analysis involves parsing the token sequence to identify the syntactic structure of the program. This phase typically builds a parse tree, which replaces the linear sequence of tokens with a tree structure built according to the rules of a formal grammar which define the language's syntax. The parse tree is often analyzed, augmented, and transformed by later phases in the compiler.

Semantic analysis is the phase in which the compiler adds semantic information to the parse tree and builds the symbol table. This phase performs semantic checks such as type checking (checking for type errors), or object binding (associating variable and function references with their definitions), or definite assignment (requiring all local variables to be initialized before use), rejecting incorrect programs or issuing warnings. Semantic analysis usually requires a complete parse tree, meaning that this phase logically follows the parsing phase, and logically precedes the code generation phase, though it is often possible to fold multiple phases into one pass over the code in a compiler implementation.

Back end

The term back end is sometimes confused with code generator because of the overlapped functionality of generating assembly code. Some literature uses middle end to distinguish the generic analysis and optimization phases in the back end from the machine-dependent code generators.

The main phases of the back end include the following:

Analysis: This is the gathering of program information from the intermediate representation derived from the input. Typical analyses are data flow analysis to build use-define chains, dependence analysis, alias analysis, pointer analysis, escape analysis etc. Accurate analysis is the basis for any compiler optimization. The call graph and control flow graph are usually also built during the analysis phase.

Optimization: the intermediate language representation is transformed into functionally equivalent but faster (or smaller) forms. Popular optimizations are inline expansion, dead code elimination, constant propagation, loop transformation, register allocation or even automatic parallelization.

Code generation: the transformed intermediate language is translated into the output language, usually the native machine language of the system. This involves resource and storage decisions, such as deciding which variables to fit into registers and memory and the selection and scheduling of appropriate machine instructions along with their associated addressing modes (see also Sethi-Ullman algorithm).

Compiler analysis is the prerequisite for any compiler optimization, and they tightly work together. For example, dependence analysis is crucial for loop transformation.

In addition, the scope of compiler analysis and optimizations vary greatly, from as small as a basic block to the procedure/function level, or even over the whole program (interprocedural optimization). Obviously, a compiler can potentially do a better job using a broader view. But that broad view is not free: large scope analysis and optimizations are very costly in terms of compilation time and memory space; this is especially true for interprocedural analysis and optimizations.

Interprocedural analysis and optimizations are common in modern commercial compilers from HP, IBM, SGI, Intel, Microsoft, and Sun Microsystems. The open source GCC was criticized for a long time for lacking powerful interprocedural optimizations, but it is changing in this respect. Another open source compiler with full analysis and optimization infrastructure is Open64, which is used by many organizations for research and commercial purposes.

Due to the extra time and space needed for compiler analysis and optimizations, some compilers skip them by default. Users have to use compilation options to explicitly tell the compiler which optimizations should be enabled.

ASSEMBLER

Typically a modern assembler creates object code by translating assembly instruction mnemonics into opcodes, and by resolving symbolic names for memory locations and other entities. The use of symbolic references is a key feature of assemblers, saving tedious calculations and manual address updates after program modifications. Most assemblers also include macro facilities for performing textual substitution — e.g., to generate common short sequences of instructions to run inline, instead of in a subroutine.

Assemblers are generally simpler to write than compilers for high-level languages, and have been available since the 1950s. Modern assemblers, especially for RISC based architectures, such as MIPS, Sun SPARC and HP PA-RISC, optimize instruction scheduling to exploit the CPU pipeline efficiently.

More sophisticated high-level assemblers provide language abstractions such as:

- Advanced control structures
- High-level procedure/function declarations and invocations
- High-level abstract data types, including structures/records, unions, classes, and sets
- Sophisticated macro processing
- Object-Oriented features as encapsulation, polymorphism, inheritance, interfaces.

Loader

In computing, a loader is the part of an operating system that is responsible for loading programs from executables (i.e., executable files) into memory, preparing them for execution and then executing them. The loader is usually a part of the operating system's kernel and is usually loaded at system boot time and stays in memory until the system is rebooted, shut down, or powered off.

Loader is part of the operating system.

Some operating systems that have a pageable kernel may have the loader in the pageable part of memory and thus the loader sometimes may be swapped out of memory. All operating systems that support program loading have loaders. Some embedded operating systems in highly specialized computers run only one program and have no program loading capabilities and thus no loaders, for example embedded systems in cars or stereo equipment.

Linker or Link Editor

In computer science, a linker or link editor is a program that takes one or more objects generated by compilers and assembles them into a single executable program. In IBM mainframe environments such as OS/360 this program is known as a linkage editor. The objects are program modules containing machine code and information for the linker. This information comes mainly in the form of symbol definitions, which come in two varieties:

- Defined or exported symbols are functions or variables that are present in the module represented by the object, and which should be available for use by other modules.
- Undefined or imported symbols are functions or variables that are called or referenced by this object, but not internally defined.

In short, the linker's job is to resolve references to undefined symbols by finding out which other object defines a symbol in question, and replacing placeholders with the symbol's address.

Linkers can take objects from a collection called a library. Some linkers do not include the whole library in the output; they only include its symbols that are referenced from other object files or libraries. Libraries for diverse purposes exist, and one or more system libraries are usually linked in by default. The linker also takes care of arranging the objects in a program's address space. This may involve relocating code that assumes a specific base address to another base. Since a compiler seldom knows where an object will reside, it often assumes a fixed base location (for example, zero). Relocating machine code may involve re-targeting of absolute jumps, loads and stores.

The executable output by the linker may need another relocation pass when it is finally loaded into memory (just before execution). On hardware offering virtual memory this is usually omitted, though—every program is put into its own address space, so there is no conflict even if all programs are loaded at the same base address.

OPEN SYSTEMS

Open systems are computer systems that provide some combination of interoperability, portability, and open software standards. It can also mean specific installations that are configured to allow unrestricted access by people and/or other computers; this article does not discuss that meaning. The term was popularized in the early 1980s, mainly to describe systems based on Unix, especially in contrast to the more entrenched mainframes and minicomputers in use at that time. Unlike older legacy systems, the newer generation of Unix systems featured standardized programming interfaces and peripheral interconnects; third party development of hardware and software was encouraged, a significant departure from the norm of the time, which saw companies such as Amdahl and Hitachi going to court for the right to sell systems and peripherals that were compatible with IBM's mainframes.

The definition of "open system" can be said to have become more formalized in the 1990s with the emergence of independently administered software standards such as The Open Group's Single UNIX Specification.

Although computer users today are used to a high degree of both hardware and software interoperability, in the 20th century the open systems concept could be promoted by Unix vendors as a significant differentiator. IBM and other companies resisted the trend for decades, exemplified by a now-famous warning in 1991 by an IBM account executive that one should be "careful about getting locked into open systems".

However, in the first part of the 21st century many of these same legacy system vendors, particularly IBM and Hewlett-Packard, began to adopt Linux as part of their overall sales strategy, with "open source" marketed as trumping "open system". Consequently an IBM mainframe with Linux on zSeries is marketed as being more of an open system than commodity computers using closed-source Microsoft Windows—or even those using Unix, despite its open systems heritage. In response, more companies are opening the source code to their products, with a notable example being Sun Microsystems and their creation of the OpenOffice.org and OpenSolaris projects, based on their formerly closed-source Star Office and Solaris software products.

Open source is an approach to the design, development, and distribution of software, offering practical accessibility to a software's source code. Some consider open source as one of various possible design approaches, while others consider it a critical strategic element of their operations. Before open source became widely adopted, developers and producers used a variety of phrases to describe the concept; the term open source gained popularity with the rise of the Internet, which provided access to diverse production models, communication paths, and interactive communities.

Software development costs in organizations have been touted as being approximately 15% of total costs. This indicates that the value of one over another development methodology is more of a marketing decision (which customers and pricing models) as much as it is about the design of software. The open source model of operation and decision making allows concurrent input of different agendas, approaches and priorities, and differs from the more closed, centralized models of development. The principles and practices are commonly applied to the peer production development of source code for software that is made available for public collaboration. The result of this peer-based collaboration is usually released as open-source software, however, open source methods are increasingly being applied in other fields of endeavor, such as biotechnology.

Open Source history

Very similar to open standards, researchers with access to the Advanced Research Projects Agency Network (ARPANET) used a process called Request for Comments to develop telecommunication network protocols. Characterized by contemporary open source work, this 1960s' collaborative process led to the birth of the Internet in 1969. There are earlier instances of open source and free software such as IBM's source releases of its operating systems and other programs in the 1950s, 60s, and the SHARE user group that formed to facilitate the exchange of software.

The decision by some people in the free software movement to use the label "open source" came out of a strategy session held at Palo Alto, California, in reaction to Netscape's January 1998 announcement of a source code release for Navigator. The group of individuals at the session included Christine Peterson who suggested "open source", Todd Anderson, Larry Augustin, Jon Hall, Sam Ockman, Michael Tiemann and Eric S. Raymond. They used the opportunity before the release of Navigator's source code to free themselves of the ideological and confrontational connotations of the term free software. Netscape licensed and released its code as open source under the Netscape Public License and subsequently under the Mozilla Public License.

The term was given a big boost at an event organized in April 1998 by technology publisher Tim O'Reilly. Originally titled the "Freeware Summit" and later known as the "Open Source Summit", the event brought together the leaders of many of the most important free and open source projects, including Linus Torvalds, Larry Wall, Brian Behlendorf, Eric Allman, Guido van Rossum, Michael Tiemann, Paul Vixie, Jamie Zawinski of Netscape, and Eric Raymond. At that meeting, the confusion caused by the name "free software" was brought up. Tiemann argued for "sourceware" as a new term, while Raymond argued for "open source." The assembled developers took a vote, and the winner was announced at a press conference that evening. Five days later, Raymond made the first public call to the free software community to adopt the new term.The Open Source Initiative was formed shortly thereafter.

The Open Source Initiative (OSI) formed in February 1998 by Raymond and Perens. With about 20 years of evidence from case histories of closed and open development already provided by the Internet, the OSI continued to present the 'open source' case to commercial businesses. They sought to bring a higher profile to the practical benefits of freely available source code, and wanted to bring major software businesses and other high-tech industries into open source.

The Open Source Definition

The Open Source Definition is used by the Open Source Initiative to determine whether a software license can be considered open source. The definition was based on the Debian Free Software Guidelines, written and adapted primarily by Bruce Perens.[9][10] Perens did not base his writing on the "four freedoms" of Free Software from the Free Software Foundation, which were only widely available later.

Perens' principles

Under Perens' definition, open source describes a broad general type of software license that makes source code available to the general public with relaxed or non-existent copyright restrictions. The principles, as stated, say absolutely nothing about trademark or patent use and require absolutely no cooperation to ensure that any common audit or release regime applies to any derived works. It is an explicit "feature" of open source that it may put no restrictions on the use or distribution by any organization or user. It forbids this, in principle, to guarantee continued access to derived works even by the major original contributors.

Proliferation of the term

While the term applied originally only to the source code of software,[12] it is now being applied to many other areas such as open source ecology,[13] a movement to decentralize technologies so that any human can use them. However, it is often misapplied to other areas which have different and competing principles, which overlap only partially.

Non-software use

The principles of open source have been adapted for many other forms of user generated content and technology, including open source hardware. Supporters of the open content movement advocate some restrictions of use, requirements to share changes, and attribution to other authors of the work.

This "culture" or ideology takes the view that the principles apply more generally to facilitate concurrent input of different agendas, approaches and priorities, in contrast with more centralized models of development such as those typically used in commercial companies. Advocates of the open source principles often point to Wikipedia as an example, but Wikipedia has in fact often restricted certain types of use or user, and the GFDL license it has historically used makes specific requirements of all users, which technically violates the open source principles.

Business models

There are a number of commonly recognized barriers to the adoption of open source software by enterprises. These barriers include the perception that open source licenses are viral, lack of formal support and training, the velocity of change, and a lack of a long term roadmap. The majority of these barriers are risk-related. From the other side, not all proprietary projects disclose exact future plans, not all open source licenses are equally viral and many serious OSS projects (especially operating systems) actually make money from paid support and documentation.

A commonly employed Business Strategy of Commercial Open Source Software Firms is the Dual-License Strategy, as demonstrated by Ingres, MySQL, Alfresco, and others.

Widely used open source products

Open source software (OSS) projects are built and maintained by a network of volunteer programmers. Prime examples of open source products are the Apache HTTP Server, and the internet browser Mozilla Firefox. One of the most successful open source products is the GNU/Linux operating system, an open source Unix-like operating system.

Society and culture

Open source culture is the creative practice of appropriation and free sharing of found and created content. Examples include collage, found footage film, music, and appropriation art. Open source culture is one in which fixations, works entitled to copyright protection, are made generally available. Participants in the culture can modify those products and redistribute them back into the community or other organizations.

The rise of open-source culture in the 20th century resulted from a growing tension between creative practices that involve appropriation, and therefore require access to content that is often copyrighted, and increasingly restrictive intellectual property laws and policies governing access to copyrighted content. The two main ways in which intellectual property laws became more restrictive in the 20th century were extensions to the term of copyright (particularly in the United States) and penalties, such as those articulated in the Digital Millennium Copyright Act (DMCA), placed on attempts to circumvent anti-piracy technologies.

Although artistic appropriation is often permitted under fair use doctrines, the complexity and ambiguity of these doctrines creates an atmosphere of uncertainty among cultural practitioners. Also, the protective actions of copyright owners create what some call a "chilling effect" among cultural practitioners. In the late 20th century, cultural practitioners began to adopt the intellectual property licensing techniques of free software and open-source software to make their work more freely available to others, including the Creative Commons.

The idea of an "open source" culture runs parallel to "Free Culture," but is substantively different. Free culture is a term derived from the free software movement, and in contrast to that vision of culture, proponents of Open Source Culture (OSC) maintain that some intellectual property law needs to exist to protect cultural producers. Yet they propose a more nuanced position than corporations have traditionally sought. Instead of seeing intellectual property law as an expression of instrumental rules intended to uphold either natural rights or desirable outcomes, an argument for OSC takes into account diverse goods (as in "the Good life") and ends.

One way of achieving the goal of making the fixations of cultural work generally available is to maximally utilize technology and digital media. In keeping with Moore's law's prediction about processors, the cost of digital media and storage plummeted in the late 20th Century. Consequently, the marginal cost of digitally duplicating anything capable of being transmitted via digital media dropped to near zero. Combined with an explosive growth in personal computer and technology ownership, the result is an increase in general population's access to digital media. This phenomenon facilitated growth in open source culture because it allowed for rapid and inexpensive duplication and distribution of culture. Where the access to the majority of culture produced prior to the advent of digital media was limited by other constraints of proprietary and potentially "open" mediums, digital media is the latest technology with the potential to increase access to cultural products. Artists and users who choose to distribute their work digitally face none of the physical limitations that traditional cultural producers have been typically faced with. Accordingly, the audience of an open source culture faces little physical cost in acquiring digital media.

Open source culture precedes Richard Stallman's codification of the concept with the creation of the Free Software Foundation. As the public began to communicate through Bulletin Board Systems (BBS) like FidoNet, places like Sourcery Systems BBS were dedicated to providing source code to Public Domain, Shareware and Freeware programs.

Essentially born out of a desire for increased general access to digital media, the Internet is open source culture's most valuable asset. It is questionable whether the goals of an open source culture could be achieved without the Internet. The global network not only fosters an environment where culture can be generally accessible, but also allows for easy and inexpensive redistribution of culture back into various communities. Some reasons for this are as follows.

First, the Internet allows even greater access to inexpensive digital media and storage. Instead of users being limited to their own facilities and resources, they are granted access to a vast network of facilities and resources, some for free. Sites such as Archive.org offer up free web space for anyone willing to license their work under a Creative Commons license. The resulting cultural product is then available to download for free (generally accessible) to anyone with an Internet connection.

Second, users are granted unprecedented access to each other. Older analog technologies such as the telephone or television have limitations on the kind of interaction users can have. In the case of television there is little, if any interaction between users participating on the network. And in the case of the telephone, users rarely interact with any more than a couple of their known peers. On the Internet, however, users have the potential to access and meet millions of their peers. This aspect of the Internet facilitates the modification of culture as users are able to collaborate and communicate with each other across international and cultural boundaries. The speed in which digital media travels on the Internet in turn facilitates the redistribution of culture.

Through various technologies such as peer-to-peer networks and blogs, cultural producers can take advantage of vast social networks in order to distribute their products. As opposed to traditional media distribution, redistributing digital media on the Internet can be virtually costless. Technologies such as BitTorrent and Gnutella take advantage of various characteristics of the Internet protocol (TCP/IP) in an attempt to totally decentralize file distribution.

Government

Open politics (sometimes known as Open source politics) — is a term used to describe a political process that uses Internet technologies such as blogs, email and polling to provide for a rapid feedback mechanism between political organizations and their supporters. There is also an alternative conception of the term Open source politics which relates to the development of public policy under a set of rules and processes similar to the Open Source Software movement.

Open source governance — is similar to open source politics, but it applies more to the democratic process and promotes the freedom of information.

Ethics

Open Source ethics is split into two strands:

Open Source Ethics as an Ethical School - Charles Ess and David Berry are researching whether ethics can learn anything from an open source approach. Ess famously even defined the AoIR Research Guidelines as an example of open source ethics.

Open Source Ethics as a Professional Body of Rules - This is based principally on the computer ethics school, studying the questions of ethics and professionalism in the computer industry in general and software development in particular.

Media

Open source journalism — referred to the standard journalistic techniques of news gathering and fact checking, and reflected a similar term that was in use from 1992 in military intelligence circles, open source intelligence. It is now commonly used to describe forms of innovative publishing of online journalism, rather than the sourcing of news stories by a professional journalist. In the Dec 25, 2006 issue of TIME magazine this is referred to as user created content and listed alongside more traditional open source projects such as OpenSolaris and Linux.

Weblogs, or blogs, are another significant platform for open source culture. Blogs consist of periodic, reverse chronologically ordered posts, using a technology that makes webpages easily updatable with no understanding of design, code, or file transfer required. While corporations, political campaigns and other formal institutions have begun using these tools to distribute information, many blogs are used by individuals for personal expression, political organizing, and socializing. Some, such as LiveJournal or WordPress, utilize open source software that is open to the public and can be modified by users to fit their own tastes. Whether the code is open or not, this format represents a nimble tool for people to borrow and re-present culture; whereas traditional websites made the illegal reproduction of culture difficult to regulate, the mutability of blogs makes "open sourcing" even more uncontrollable since it allows a larger portion of the population to replicate material more quickly in the public sphere.

Messageboards are another platform for open source culture. Messageboards (also known as discussion boards or forums), are places online where people with similar interests can congregate and post messages for the community to read and respond to. Messageboards sometimes have moderators who enforce community standards of etiquette such as banning users who are spammers. Other common board features are private messages (where users can send messages to one another) as well as chat (a way to have a real time conversation online) and image uploading. Some messageboards use phpBB, which is a free open source package. Where blogs are more about individual expression and tend to revolve around their authors, messageboards are about creating a conversation amongst its users where information can be shared freely and quickly. Messageboards are a way to remove intermediaries from everyday life - for instance, instead of relying on commercials and other forms of advertising, one can ask other users for frank reviews of a product, movie or CD. By removing the cultural middlemen, messageboards help speed the flow of information and exchange of ideas.

OpenDocument is an open document file format for saving and exchanging editable office documents such as text documents (including memos, reports, and books), spreadsheets, charts, and presentations. Organizations and individuals that store their data in an open format such as OpenDocument avoid being locked in to a single software vendor, leaving them free to switch software if their current vendor goes out of business, raises their prices, changes their software, or changes their licensing terms to something less favorable.

Open source movie production is either an open call system in which a changing crew and cast collaborate in movie production, a system in which the end result is made available for re-use by others or in which exclusively open source products are used in the production. The 2006 movie Elephants Dream is said to be the "world's first open movie", created entirely using open source technology.

An open source documentary film has a production process allowing the open contributions of archival material, footage, and other filmic elements, both in unedited and edited form. By doing so, on-line contributors become part of the process of creating the film, helping to influence the editorial and visual material to be used in the documentary, as well as its thematic development. The first open source documentary film to go into production "The American Revolution" [19]," which will examine the role that WBCN-FM in Boston played in the cultural, social and political changes locally and nationally from 1968 to 1974, is being produced by Lichtenstein Creative Media and the non-profit The Fund for Independent Media. Open Source Cinema is a website to create Basement Tapes, a feature documentary about copyright in the digital age, co-produced by the National Film Board of Canada. Open Source Filmmaking refers to a form of filmmaking that takes a method of idea formation from open source software, but in this case the 'source' for a film maker is raw unedited footage rather than programming code. It can also refer to a method of filmmaking where the process of creation is 'open' i.e. a disparate group of contributors, at different times contribute to the final piece.

Open-IPTV is IPTV that is not limited to one recording studio, production studio, or cast. Open-IPTV uses the Internet or other means to pool efforts and resources together to create an online community that all contributes to a show.

Education

Within the academic community, there is discussion about expanding what could be called the "intellectual commons" (analogous to the Creative Commons). Proponents of this view have hailed the Connexions Project at Rice University, OpenCourseWare project at MIT, Eugene Thacker's article on "Open Source DNA", the "Open Source Cultural Database" and Wikipedia as examples of applying open source outside the realm of computer software.

Open source curricula are instructional resources whose digital source can be freely used, distributed and modified.

Another strand to the academic community is in the area of research. Many funded research projects produce software as part of their work. There is an increasing interest in making the outputs of such projects available under an open source license. In the UK the Joint Information Systems Committee (JISC) has developed a policy on open source software. JISC also funds a development service called OSS Watch which acts as an advisory service for higher and further education institutions wishing to use, contribute to and develop open source software.

Innovation Communities

The principle of sharing predates the open source movement; for example, the free sharing of information has been institutionalized in the scientific enterprise since at least the 19th century. Open source principles have always been part of the scientific community. The sociologist Robert K. Merton described the four basic elements of the community - universalism (an international perspective), communism (sharing information), disinterestedness (removing one's personal views from the scientific inquiry) and organized skepticism (requirements of proof and review) that accurately describe the scientific community today. These principles are, in part, complemented by US law's focus on protecting expression and method but not the ideas themselves. There is also a tradition of publishing research results to the scientific community instead of keeping all such knowledge proprietary.

One of the recent initiatives in scientific publishing has been open access - the idea that research should be published in such a way that it is free and available to the public. There are currently many open access journals where the information is available for free online, however most journals do charge a fee (either to users or libraries for access). The Budapest Open Access Initiative is an international effort with the goal of making all research articles available for free on the Internet. The National Institutes of Health has recently proposed a policy on "Enhanced Public Access to NIH Research Information." This policy would provide a free, searchable resource of NIH-funded results to the public and with other international repositories six months after its initial publication. The NIH's move is an important one because there is significant amount of public funding in scientific research. Many of the questions have yet to be answered - the balancing of profit vs. public access, and ensuring that desirable standards and incentives do not diminish with a shift to open access.

Farmavita.Net - Community of Pharmaceuticals Executives have recently proposed new business model of Open Source Pharmaceuticals [20]. The project is targeted to development and sharing of know-how for manufacture of essential and life saving medicines. It is mainly dedicated to the countries with less developed economies where local pharmaceutical research and development resources are insufficient for national needs. It will be limited to generic (off-patent) medicines with established use. By the definition, medicinal product have a "well-established use" if is used for at least 15 years, with recognized efficacy and an acceptable level of safety. In that event, the expensive clinical test and trial results could be replaced by appropriate scientific literature.

Certification

In order to build higher user confidence, certification is mandatory. Certification could be applied to the simplest component that can be used by developers to build the simplest module to a whole software system. There have been numerous institutions involving in this area of the open source software including The International Institute of Software Technology / United Nations University (http://www.iist.unu.edu). UNU/IIST is a non-profit research and education institution of The United Nations. It is currently involved in a project known as "The Global Desktop Project". This project aims to build a desktop interface that every end-user is able to understand and interact with, thus crossing the language and cultural barriers. It is drawing huge attention from parties involved in areas ranging from application development to localization. Furthermore, this project will improve developing nations' access to information systems. UNU/IIST aims to achieve this without any compromise in the quality of the software. It believes a global standard can be maintained by introducing certifications and is currently organizing conferences in order to explore frontiers in the field (http://opencert.iist.unu.edu).

Open Source Software

Open source software (OSS) is defined as computer software for which the source code and certain other rights normally reserved for copyright holders are provided under a software license that meets the Open Source Definition or that is in the public domain. This permits users to use, change, and improve the software, and to redistribute it in modified or unmodified forms. It is very often developed in a public, collaborative manner. Open source software is the most prominent example of open source development and often compared to user-generated content. The term open source software originated as part of a marketing campaign for free software. A report by Standish Group states that adoption of open source software models has resulted in savings of about $60 billion per year to consumers.

The Open Source Definition is used by the Open Source Initiative to determine whether or not a software license can be considered open source.

Open source doesn't just mean access to the source code.

The distribution terms of open-source software must comply with the following criteria:

1. Free Redistribution: The license shall not restrict any party from selling or giving away the software as a component of an aggregate software distribution containing programs from several different sources. The license shall not require a royalty or other fee for such sale.

2. Source Code: The program must include source code, and must allow distribution in source code as well as compiled form. Where some form of a product is not distributed with source code, there must be a well-publicized means of obtaining the source code for no more than a reasonable reproduction cost preferably, downloading via the Internet without charge. The source code must be the preferred form in which a programmer would modify the program. Deliberately obfuscated source code is not allowed. Intermediate forms such as the output of a preprocessor or translator are not allowed.

3. Derived Works: The license must allow modifications and derived works, and must allow them to be distributed under the same terms as the license of the original software.

4. Integrity of The Author's Source Code: The license may restrict source-code from being distributed in modified form only if the license allows the distribution of "patch files" with the source code for the purpose of modifying the program at build time. The license must explicitly permit distribution of software built from modified source code. The license may require derived works to carry a different name or version number from the original software.
5. No Discrimination Against Persons or Groups: The license must not discriminate against any person or group of persons.
6. No Discrimination Against Fields of Endeavor: The license must not restrict anyone from making use of the program in a specific field of endeavor. For example, it may not restrict the program from being used in a business, or from being used for genetic research.
7. Distribution of License: The rights attached to the program must apply to all to whom the program is redistributed without the need for execution of an additional license by those parties.
8. License Must Not Be Specific to a Product: The rights attached to the program must not depend on the program's being part of a particular software distribution. If the program is extracted from that distribution and used or distributed within the terms of the program's license, all parties to whom the program is redistributed should have the same rights as those that are granted in conjunction with the original software distribution.
9. License Must Not Restrict Other Software: The license must not place restrictions on other software that is distributed along with the licensed software. For example, the license must not insist that all other programs distributed on the same medium must be open-source software.
10. License Must Be Technology-Neutral: No provision of the license may be predicated on any individual technology or style of interface.

Early releases

The first version of the software should be released as early as possible so as to increase one's chances of finding co-developers early.

Frequent integration

New code should be integrated as often as possible so as to avoid the overhead of fixing a large number of bugs at the end of the project life cycle. Some open source projects have nightly builds where integration is done automatically on a daily basis.

Several versions

There should be at least two versions of the software. There should be a buggier version with more features and a more stable version with fewer features. The buggy version (also called the development version) is for users who want the immediate use of the latest features, and are willing to accept the risk of using code that is not yet thoroughly tested. The users can then act as co-developers, reporting bugs and providing bug fixes.

High modularization

The general structure of the software should be modular allowing for parallel development.

Dynamic decision making structure

There is a need for a decision making structure, whether formal or informal, that makes strategic decisions depending on changing user requirements and other factors. Cf. Extreme programming.

Most well known OSS products follow the Bazaar model as suggested by Eric Raymond. These include projects such as the Linux kernel, Firefox, Apache, the GNU Compiler Collection, and Perl to mention a few.

Licensing

A license defines the rights and obligations that a licensor grants to a licensee. Open Source licenses grant licensees the right to copy, modify and redistribute source code (or content). These licenses may also impose obligations (e.g., modifications to the code that are distributed must be made available in source code form, an author attribution must be placed in a program/ documentation using that Open Source, etc.).

Authors initially derive a right to grant a license to their work based on the legal theory that upon creation of a work the author owns the copyright in that work. What the author/licensor is granting when they grant a license to copy, modify and redistribute their work is the right to use the author's copyrights. The author still retains ownership of those copyrights, the licensee simply is allowed to use those rights, as granted in the license, so long as they maintain the obligations of the license. The author does have the option to sell/assign, versus license, their exclusive right to the copyrights to their work; where upon the new owner/assignee controls the copyrights. The ownership of the copyright (the "rights") is separate and distinct from the ownership of the work (the "thing") - a person can own a copy of a piece of code (or a copy of a book) without the rights to copy, modify or redistribute copies of it.

When an author contributes code to an Open Source project (e.g., Apache.org) they do so under an explicit license (e.g., the Apache Contributor License Agreement) or an implicit license (e.g., the Open Source license under which the project is already licensing code). Some Open Source projects do not take contributed code under a license, but actually require (joint) assignment of the author's copyright in order to accept code contributions into the project (e.g., OpenOffice.org and its Joint Copyright Assignment agreement).

Placing code (or content) in the public domain is a way of waiving an author's (or owner's) copyrights in that work. No license is granted, and none is needed, to copy, modify or redistribute a work in the public domain.

Examples of free software license / open source licenses include Apache License, BSD license, GNU General Public License, GNU Lesser General Public License, MIT License, Eclipse Public License and Mozilla Public License.

The proliferation of open source licenses is one of the few negative aspects of the open source movement because it is often difficult to understand the legal implications of the differences between licenses.

An important legal milestone for the open source / free software movement was passed in 2008, when the US federal appeals court ruled that free software licences definitely do set legally binding conditions on the use of copyrighted work, and they are therefore enforceable under existing copyright law. As a result, if end-users do violate the licensing conditions, their license disappears, meaning they are infringing copyright.

Open source vs. Closed source

The debate over open source vs. closed source (alternatively called proprietary software) is sometimes heated.

One source of conflict is related to economics: Making money through traditional methods, such as sale of the use of individual copies and patent royalty payment (generally called licensing), is more difficult and in many ways against the very concept of open source software.

Some closed-source advocates see open source software as damaging to the market of commercial software. This is one of the many reasons, as mentioned above, that the term free software was replaced with open source — because many company executives could not believe in a product that did not participate economically in a free-market or mixed-market economy.

The counter to this argument is the use of open source software to fuel the market for a separate product or service. For example:

Providing support and installation services; similar to IT Security groups, Linux Distributions, and Systems companies.

Using the software as a stepping stone to sell a higher-end product or service; e.g., OpenOffice.org vs. StarOffice.

Cost avoidance / cost sharing: many developers need a product, so it makes sense to share development costs (X Window System and the Apache web server)

Since Open Source software is open, all of the defects and security flaws are easily found. Closed-source advocates argue that this makes it easier for a malicious person to discover security flaws. Further, that there is no incentive for an open-source product to be patched. Open-source advocates argue that this makes it easier also for a patch to be found and that the closed-source argument is security through obscurity, which this form of security will eventually fail, often without anyone knowing of the failure. Further, that just because there is not an immediate financial incentive to patch a product, does not mean there is not any incentive to patch a product. Further, if the patch is that significant to the user, having the source code, the user can technically patch the problem themselves. These arguments are hard to prove. However, most studies show that open-source software does have a higher flaw discovery, quicker flaw discovery, and quicker turn around on patches.

Open source software vs. Free software

The main difference is that by choosing one term over the other (i.e. either "open source" or "free software") you let others know about what your goals are.

"As one person put it, 'Open source is a development methodology; free software is a social movement.'"

Critics have said that the term "open source" fosters an ambiguity of a different kind such that it confuses the mere availability of the source with the freedom to use, modify, and redistribute it. Developers have used the alternative terms Free/open source Software (FOSS), or Free/Libre/open source Software (FLOSS), consequently, to describe open source software which is also free software.

The term "Open Source" was originally intended to be trademarkable; however, the term was deemed too descriptive, so no trademark exists. The OSI would prefer that people treat Open Source as if it were a trademark, and use it only to describe software licensed under an OSI approved license.

OSI Certified is a trademark licensed only to people who are distributing software licensed under a license listed on the Open Source Initiative's list.

Open source software and free software are different terms for software which comes with certain rights, or freedoms, for the user. They describe two approaches and philosophies towards free software. Open source and free software (or software libre) both describe software which is free from onerous licensing restrictions. It may be used, copied, studied, modified and redistributed without restriction. Free software is not the same as freeware, software available at zero price.

The definition of open source software was written to be almost identical to the free software definition. There are very few cases of software that is free software but is not open source software, and vice versa. The difference in the terms is where they place the emphasis. "Free software" is defined in terms of giving the user freedom. This reflects the goal of the free software movement. "Open source" highlights that the source code is viewable to all and proponents of the term usually emphasize the quality of the software and how this is caused by the development models which are possible and popular among free and open source software projects.

Free software licenses are not written exclusively by the FSF. The FSF and the OSI both list licenses which meet their respective definitions of free software. open source software and free software share an almost identical set of licenses.[citation needed] One exception is an early version of the Apple Public Source License, which was accepted by the OSI but rejected by the FSF because it did not allow private modified versions; this restriction was removed in later version of the license. There are now new versions that are approved by both the OSI and the FSF.

The Open Source Initiative believes that more people will be convinced by the experience of freedom.The FSF believes that more people will be convinced by the concept of freedom. The FSF believes that knowledge of the concept is an essential requirement, insists on the use of the term free, and separates itself from the open source movement. The Open Source Initiative believes that free has three meanings: free as in beer, free as in freedom, and free as in unsellable. The problem with the term "open source" is that it says nothing about the freedom to modify and redistribute, so it is used by people who think that source access without freedom to modify and redistribute is a sufficient definition. This possibility for misuse is the case for most of the licences that make up Microsoft's "shared source" initiative.

Open source vs. Source-available

Although the OSI definition of "open source software" is widely accepted, a small number of people and organizations use the term to refer to software where the source is available for viewing, but which may not legally be modified or redistributed. Such software is more often referred to as source-available, or as shared source, a term coined by Microsoft.

Michael Tiemann, president of OSI, had criticized companies such as SugarCRM for promoting their software as "open source" when in fact it did not have an OSI-approved license. In SugarCRM's case, it was because the software is so-called "badgeware" since it specified a "badge" that must be displayed in the user interface (SugarCRM has since switched to GPLv3. Another example is Scilab, which calls itself "the open source platform for numerical computation" but has a license that forbids commercial redistribution of modified versions. Because OSI does not have a registered trademark for the term "open source", its legal ability to prevent such usage of the term is limited, but Tiemann advocates using public opinion from OSI, customers, and community members to pressure such organizations to change their license or to use a different term.

Pros and cons

Software experts and researchers on open source software have identified several advantages and disadvantages. The main advantage for business is that open source is a good way for business to achieve greater penetration of the market. Companies that offer open source software are able to establish an industry standard and, thus, gain competitive advantage. It has also helped build developer loyalty as developers feel empowered and have a sense of ownership of the end product. Moreover less costs of marketing and logistical services are needed for OSS. It also helps companies to keep abreast of all technology developments. It is a good tool to promote a companies' image, including its commercial products. The OSS development approach has helped produce reliable, high quality software quickly and inexpensively. Besides, it offers the potential for a more flexible technology and quicker innovation. It is said to be more reliable since it typically has thousands of independent programmers testing and fixing bugs of the software. It is flexible because modular systems allow programmers to build custom interfaces, or add new abilities to it and it is innovative since open source programs are the product of collaboration among a large number of different programmers. The mix of divergent perspectives, corporate objectives, and personal goals speeds up innovation. Moreover free software can be developed in accord with purely technical requirements. It does not require to think about commercial pressure that often degrades the quality of the software. Commercial pressures make traditional software developers pay more attention to customers' requirements than to security requirements, since such features are somewhat invisible to the customer.

It is sometimes said that the open source development process may not be well defined and the stages in the development process, such as system testing and documentation may be ignored. However this is only true for small (mostly single programmer) projects. Larger, successful projects do define and enforce at least some rules as they need them to make the teamwork possible. In the most complex projects these rules may be as strict as reviewing even minor change by two independent developers.

Not all OSS initiatives have been successful, for example, SourceXchange and Eazel. Software experts and researchers who are not convinced by open source's ability to produce quality systems identify the unclear process, the late defect discovery and the lack of any empirical evidence as the most important problems (collected data concerning productivity and quality). It is also difficult to design a commercially sound business model around the open source paradigm. Consequently, only technical requirements may be satisfied and not the ones of the market. In terms of security, open source may allow hackers to know about the weaknesses or loopholes of the software more easily than closed-source software. It is depended of control mechanisms in order to create effective performance of autonomous agents who participate in virtual organizations.

UNIX/XENIX

UNIX is an operating system, just as you have Microsoft DOS and Microsoft Windows. In this chapter we will discuss the 4.3BSD version of UNIX. We will also go through a brief history of UNIX, and then present the system's user and programmer interfaces. Lastly, we will discuss the internal data structures and algorithms used by the UNIX kernel to support the user-programmer interface.

UNIX is also an Operating System.

Development of UNIX

Dennis Ritchie and Ken Thompson are the people behind its development. The first version of UNIX was developed in 1969 by Ken Thompson of the Research Group at Bell Laboratories to use on otherwise idle PDP-7. He was soon joined by Dennis Ritchie. Thompson, Ritchie, and other members of the Research Group produced the early versions of UNIX. Ritchie had previously worked on the MULTICS project, and MULTICS had a strong influence on the newer operating system.

Even the name *UNIX* is quite similar to *MULTICS.* The basic organization of the file system, the idea of the command interpreter (the shell) as a user process, the use of a separate process for each command, the original line editing characters (# to erase the last character and @ to erase the entire line), and numerous other features came directly from MULTICS.

Ideas from various other operating Systems, such as from MIT's CTSS and the XDS-940 system, were also used. Ritchie and Thompson worked quietly on UNIX for many years. Their work on the 1st version allowed them to move it to a PDP-11/20, for a 2nd version. A 3rd version resulted from their rewriting most of the operating system in the system-programming language C, instead of the previously used assembly line C was developed at Bell Laboratories to support it.

UNIX was also moved to larger PDP-11 models, such as the 11/45 and, 11/70, Multiprogramming and other enhancements were added when it was rewritten in C and moved to systems (such as the 11/45) that had hardware support for multiprogramming. As UNIX developed, it became widely used within Bell Laboratories and gradually spread to a few universities. The first version widely available outside Bell Laboratories was Version 6, released in 1976. In 1978, Version 7 was distributed. This UNIX system ran on, the PDP-11/70 and the Interdata 8/32, and is the ancestor of most modern UNIX systems. In particular, it was soon ported to other PDP-11 models and to the VAX computer line. The version available on the VAX was known as 32V. Research has continued since then.

After the distribution of Version 7 in 1978, the UNIX Support Group (USG) assumed administrative control and responsibility from the Research Group for distributions of UNIX within AT&T, the parent organization for Bell Laboratories.

UNIX was becoming a product, rather than simply a research tool. The Research Group has continued to develop their own version of UNIX, however, to support their own internal computing. Next came Version 8, which included a facility called the *stream I/O system* that allows flexible configuration of kernel IPC modules. It also contained RFS, a remote file system similar to Sun's NFS.

Next came Versions 9 and 10 (the latter version, released in 1989, is available only within Bell Laboratories).

USG mainly provided support for UNIX within AT&T. The first external distribution from USG was System III, in 1982. System III incorporated features of Version 7, and 32V, and also of several UNIX systems developed by groups other than Research. Features of UNIXIRT, a real-time UNIX' system, as well as numerous portions of the Programmer's Work Bench (PWB) software tools package were included in System IH. USG released System V in 1983; it is largely derived from System III. The divestiture of the various, Bell operating compares from AT&T has left AT&T in a position to market System V aggressively, USG was restructured as the UNIX System Development Laboratory (USDL), which released UNIX System V Release 2 (V.2) in 1984.

UNIX System V Release 2, Version 4 (V2.4) added a new implementation of virtual memory with copy-on-write paging and shared memory USDL was in turn replaced by AT&T Information Systems (ATTIS), which distributed System V Release 3 (V.3) in 1987. It adapts the V8 implementation of the stream I/O system and makes it available as *STREAMS.* It also includes RFS, an NFS-like remote file system.

The small size, modularity; and clean design of early UMX Systems led to UNIX-based work at numerous other computer-science organizations, such as at Rand, BBN, the University of Illinois, Harvard, Purdue, and even DEC. The most influential of the non-Bell Laboratories and non-AT&T UNIX development groups, however, has been the University of California at Berkeley.

The first Berkeley VAX UNIX work was the addition in 1978 of virtual memory, demand paging, and page replacement to 32V; this work was done by Bill Joy and Ozalp Babaoglu to produce 3BSD UNIX. This version was the first implementation of any of these facilities on any UNIX system. The large virtual-memory space of 3BSD allowed the development of very large programs, such as Berkeley's own Franz LISP.

The memory-management work convinced the Defence Advanced Research Projects Agency (DARPA) to fund Berkeley for the development of a standard UNIX system for government use; 4BSD UNIX was the result. The 4BSD work for DARPA was guided by a steering committee that included many notable people from the UNIX and networking communities.

One of the goals of this project was to provide support for the DARPA Internet networking protocols (TCP/IP).

This support was provided in a general manner. It is possible in 4.2BSD to communicate uniformly among diverse network facilities, including local area networks (such as Ethernets and token rings) and wide-area networks (such as NSFNET). This implementation was the most important reason for the current popularity of these protocols. It was used as the basis for the implementations of many vendors of UNIX computer systems, and even other operating systems. It permitted the Internet to grow from 60 connected networks in 1984 to more than 8000 networks and an estimated 10 million users in 1993 and since then it is growing tremendously. In addition, Berkeley adapted many features from contemporary operating systems to improve the design and implementation of UNIX.

Many of the terminal line-editing functions of the TENEX (TOPS-20) operating system were provided by a new terminal driver. A new user interface (the C Shell), a new text editor (ex/vi), compilers for Pascal and LISP, and many new systems programs were written at Berkeley. For 4.2BSD, certain efficiency improvements were inspired by the VMS operating system. UNIX software from Berkeley is released in *Berkeley Software Distributions.* It is convenient to refer to the Berkeley VAX UNIX systems following 3BSD as 4BSD, although there were actually several specific releases, most notably 4.1BSD and 4.2BSD. The generic numbers BSD and 4BSD are used for the PDP-11 and VAX distributions of Berkeley UNIX. 4.2BSD, first distributed in 1983, was the culmination of the original Berkeley DARPA UNIX project. 2.9BSD is the equivalent version for PDP-11 systems.

In 1986, 4.3BSD was released. It was so similar to 4.2BSD that its manuals described 4.2BSD more comprehensively than the 4.2BSD manuals did. It did include numerous internal changes, however, including bug fixes and performance improvements. Some new facilities also were added, including support for the Xerox Network System protocols. 4.3BSD Tahoe was the next version, released in 1988. It included various new developments, such as improved networking congestion control and TCP/IP performance.

Also, disk configurations were separated from the device drivers, and are now read off the disks themselves. Expanded time-zone support is also included. 4.3BSD Tahoe was actually developed on and for the CCI Tahoe system (Computer Console, Inc., Power 6 computer), rather than for the usual VAX base. The corresponding PDP-11 release is 2.10.1BSD, which is distributed by the USENIX Association, which also publishes the 4.3BSD manuals. The 4.32BSD Reno release saw the inclusion of an implementation of ISO/OSI networking. The last Berkeley release, 4ABSD, was finalized in June of 1993. It includes new X25 networking support, and POSIX standard compliance. It also has a radically new file system organization, with a new virtual file system interface and support for *stackabie* file systems, allowing file systems to be layered on top of each other for easy inclusion of new features. An implementation of NFS is also included in the release, as is a new log-based file system.

The 4.4BSD virtual memory system is derived from Mach. Several other changes, such as enhanced security and improved kernel structure, are also included. With the release of version 4.4, Berkeley has halted its research efforts. 4BSD was the operating system of choice for VAXes from its initial release (1979) until the release of Ultrix, DEC's BSD implementation. 4BSD is still the best choice for many research and networking installations. Many organizations would buy a 32V license and order 4BSD from Berkeley without even bothering to get a 32V tape.

The current set of UNIX operating systems is not limited to those by Bell Laboratories, which is currently owned by Lucent Technology, and Berkeley.

However, Sun Microsystems helped popularize the BSD flavour of UNIX by shipping it on their workstations. As UNIX has grown in popularity it has been moved to many different computers and computer systems. A wide variety of UNIX, and UNIX-like, operating systems have been created. DEC supports its UNIX (called Ultrix) on its workstations and is replacing Ultrix with another UNIX derived operating system, OSF/1; Microsoft rewrote UNIX for the Intel 8088 family and called it XENIX, and its new Windows/NT operating system is heavily influenced by UNIX; IBM has UNIX (AIX) on its PCs, workstations, and mainframes. In fact, UNIX is available on almost all general-purpose computers; it runs on personal computers, workstations, minicomputers, mainframes, and supercomputers, from Apple Macintosh IIs to Cray IIs.

Because of its wide availability it is used in environments ranging from academic to military to manufacturing process control. Most of these Systems are based on Version 7, System III, 4.2BSD, or System V. The wide popularity of UNIX with computer vendors has made UNIX the most portable of operating systems, and has made it possible for users to expect a UNIX environment independent of any specific computer manufacturer.

But the large number of implementations of the system has led to remarkable variation in the programming and user interfaces distributed by the vendors. For true vendor independence, application-program developers need consistent interfaces. Such interfaces would allow all "UNIX" applications to run on all UNIX systems, which is certainly not the current situation. This issue has become important as UNIX has become the preferred program-development platform for applications ranging from databases to graphics and networking, and has led to a strong market demand for UNIX standards.

There are several standardization projects underway, starting with the */usr/group 1984 Standard* sponsored by the UniForum industry user's group. Since then, many official standards bodies have continued the effort, including IEEE and ISO (the POSIX standard). The X/Open Group international consortium completed XPG3, a Common Application Environment, which subsumes the IEEE interface standard. Unfortunately, XPG3 is based on a draft of the ANSI C standard, rather than the final specification, and therefore, needs to be redone.

In 1989, the ANSI standards body standardized the C programming language, producing an ANSI C specification that vendors were quick to adopt. As these projects continue, the variant flavours of UNIX will converge and there will be one programming interface to UNIX, allowing UNIX to become even more popular. There are in fact two separate sets of powerful UNIX vendors working on this problem: the AT&T-guided UNIX International (UI) and the Open Software Foundation (OSF) have both agreed to follow the POSIX standard.

Recently, many of the vendors involved in those two groups have agreed on further standardization (the COSE agreement) on the Motif window environment, and ONC+ (which includes Sun RPC and NFS) and DCE network facilities (which includes AFS and an RPC package). AT&T replaced its ATTIS group in 1989 with the UNIX Software Organization (USO), which shipped the first merged UNIX, System V Release 4.

This system combines features from System V, 4.3BSD, and Sun's SunOS, including long file names, the Berkeley file system, virtual memory management, symbolic links, multiple access groups, job control, and reliable signals; it also conforms to the published POSIX standard, POSIX.1. After USO produced SVR4, it became an independent AT&T subsidiary named Unix System Laboratories (USL); in 1993, it was purchased by Novell, Inc.

The UNIX system has grown from a personal project of two Bell Laboratories employees to an operating system being defined by multinational standardization bodies. Yet this system is still of interest to academia. We believe that UNIX has become and will remain an important part of operating-system theory and practice. UNIX is an excellent vehicle for academic study. For example, the Tunis operating system, the Xinu operating system, and the Mmix operating system are based on the concepts of UNIX, but were developed explicitly for classroom study.

There is a plethora of ongoing UNIX-related research systems, including Mach, Chorus, Comandos, and Roisin. The original developers, Ritchie and Thompson, were honoured in 1983 by the Association for Computing Machinery Turing award for their work on UNIX. The specific UNIX version used in this chapter is the VAX version of 4.3BSD. This system is used because it implements many interesting operating-system concepts, such as demand paging with clustering, and networking.

It has also been influential in other UNIX systems, in standards, and in networking developments. The VAX implementation is used because 4.3BSD was developed on the VAX and that machine still represents a convenient point of reference, despite the recent proliferation of implementations on other hardware (such as the Motorola 68040 and 88000, the Intel i486, the Sun SPARC, DEC Alpha, HP Precision, and the MIPS R4000 CPUs).

UNIX DESIGN

The main principle of UNIX is time-sharing. The standard user interface (the shell) is simple and can be replaced by another, if desired. The file system is a multilevel tree, which allows users to create their own subdirectories. Each user data file is simply a sequence of bytes. Disk files and I/O devices are treated as similarly as possible. Thus, device dependencies and peculiarities are kept in the kernel as much as possible; even in the kernel, most of them are confined to the device drivers. UNIX supports multiple processes.

Each user data file is simply a sequence of bytes.

A process can easily create new processes. CPU scheduling is a simple priority algorithm. 4.3BSD uses demand paging as a mechanism to support memory-management and CPU-scheduling decisions. Swapping is used if a system is suffering from excess paging. Because UNIX was originated first by one programmer, Ken Thompson, and then by another, Dennis Ritchie, as a system for their own convenience, it was small enough to understand. Most of the algorithms were selected for *simplicity;* not for speed or sophistication.

The intent was to have the kernel and libraries provide a small set of facilities that was sufficiently powerful to allow a person to build a more complex system if one were needed. UNIX's clean design has resulted in many imitations and modifications. Although the designers of UNIX had a significant amount of knowledge about other operating systems, UNIX had no elaborate design spelled out before its implementation. This flexibility appears to have been one of the key factors in the development of the system.

Architecture of UNIX Operating System

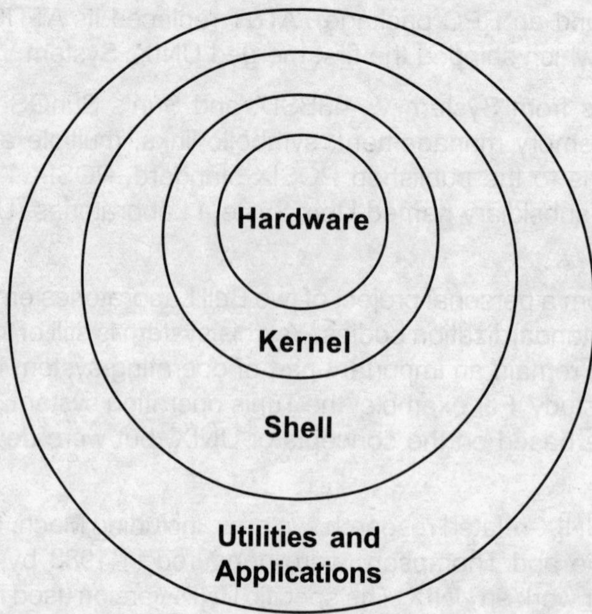

Unix is powerful, effective, multiuser and multitasking operating system. It is composed of

i) Kernel

ii) Shell

iii) Utilities and applications

Some design principles were involved, however, even though they were not made explicit at the outset. The UNIX system was designed by programmers for programmers. Thus, it has always been interactive; and facilities for program development have always been a high priority. Such facilities include the program make (which can be used to check to see which of a collection of source files for a program need to be compiled, and then to do the compiling) and the Source Code Control System (SCCS) which is used to keep successive versions of files available without having to store the entire contents of each step.

The operating system is written mostly in C, which was developed to support UNIX, since neither Thompson nor Ritchie enjoyed programming in assembly language.

The avoidance of assembly language was also necessary because of the uncertainty about the machine or machines on which UNIX would be run. It has greatly simplified the problems of moving UNIX from one hardware system to another. From the beginning, UNIX development Systems have had all the UNIX sources available on-line, and the developers have used the systems under development as their primary systems. This pattern of development has greatly facilitated the discovery of deficiencies and their fixes, as well as of new possibilities and their implementations.

It has also encouraged the plethora of UNIX variants existing today, but the benefits have outweighed the disadvantages: if something is broken, it can be fixed at a local site: there is no need to wait for the next release of the system. Such fixes, as well as new facilities, may be incorporated into later distributions. The size constraints of the PDP-11 (and earlier computers used for UNIX) have forced a certain elegance. Where other systems have elaborate algorithms for dealing with pathological conditions, UNIX just does a controlled crash called panic. Instead of attempting to cure such conditions, UNIX tries to prevent them.

Where other Systems would use brute force or macro-expansion, UNIX mostly has had to develop more subtle, or at least simpler approaches. These early strengths of UNIX produced much of its popularity, which in turn produced new demands that challenged those strengths. UNIX was used for tasks such as networking, graphics, and real-time operation, which did not always fit into its original text-oriented model. Thus, changes were made to certain internal facilities and new programming interfaces were added.

These new facilities, and others—particularly window interfaces—required large amounts of code to support them, radically increasing the size of the system. For instance, networking and windowing both doubled the size of the system. This pattern in turn pointed out the continued strength of UNIX —whenever a new development occurred in the industry, UNIX could usually absorb it, but still remain UNIX.

Programmer's Interfaces

Most computer systems, consist of two separable parts: *the kernel* and *the systems programs*. Even UNIX consists of these. We can view the UNIX operating system as being layered. Everything below the system-call interface and above the physical hardware is the kernel. The kernel provides the file system, CPU scheduling, memory management, and other operating system functions through system calls. Systems programs use the kernel-supported system calls to provide useful functions, such as compilation and file manipulation.

System calls define the programmer interface to UNIX; the set of systems programs commonly available defines the user interface. The programmer and user interface define the context that the kernel must support. System calls in VAX 4.2BSD are made by a trap to location 40 of the VAX interrupt vectors. Parameters are passed to the kernel on the hardware stack; the kernel returns values in registers R0 and R1. Register R0 may also return an error code. The carry bit distinguishes a normal return from an error return. This level of detail is seldom seen by a UNIX programmer fortunately.

Most systems programs are written in C, and the UNIX Programmer's Manual presents all system calls as C functions.

A system program written in C for 4.3BSD on the VAX can generally be moved to another 4.3BSD system and simply recompiled, even though the two systems may be quite different. The details of system calls are known only to the compiler. This feature is a major reason for the portability of UNIX programs.

System calls for UNIX can be roughly grouped into three categories: file manipulation, process control, and information manipulation. Earlier, we had seen a fourth category device manipulation, but since devices in UNIX are treated as (special) files, the same system calls support both files and devices (although there is an extra system call for setting device parameters).

Manipulation of Files

A *file* consists of a sequence of bytes. Different programs expect various levels of structure, but the kernel does not impose a structure on files. For instance, the convention for text files is lines of ASCII characters separated by a single newline character (which is the linefeed character in ASCII), but the kernel knows nothing of this convention. Files are organized in tree-structured directories.

Directories are themselves files that contain information on how to find other files. A path name to a file is a text string that identifies a file by specifying a path through the directory structure to the file. Syntactically, it consists of individual file-name elements separated by the slash character. For example, in */usr/local/font*, the first slash indicates the root of the directory tree, called the root directory. The next element, *usr*, is a subdirectory of the root, local is a subdirectory of usr, and font is a file or directory in the directory local. Whether font is an ordinary file or a directory cannot be deterred from the path-name syntax.

The UNIX file system has both: *absolute path names and relative path names.*

Absolute path names start at the root of the file system and are distinguished by a slash at the beginning of the path name; */usr/local/font* is an absolute path name. Relative path names start at the *current directory,* which is an attribute of the process accessing the path name. Thus, *local/font* indicates a file or directory named font in the directory *local* in the current directory, which might or might not be /usr. A file may be known by more than one name in one or more directories.

Such multiple names are known as *links,* and all links are treated equally by the operating system. 4.3BSD also supports *symbolic links,* which are files containing the path name of another file. The two kinds of links are also known as *hard links* and *soft links.* Soft (symbol) links, unlike hard links, may point to directories and may cross file-system boundaries. The file name "." in a directory is a hard link to the directory itself. The file name ".." is a hard link to the parent directory.

Thus, if the current directory is */user/jlp/programs,* then *../bin/wdf* refers to */user/jlp/bin/wdf.* Hardware devices have names in the file system. These *device special files* or *special* files are known to the kernel as device interfaces, but are nonetheless accessed by the user by much the same system calls as are other files. The root (/) normally contains a small number of directories as well as, say, */vmunix,* the binary boot image of the operating system; */dev* contains the device special files, such as */dev/console, /dev/lp*0, */dev/mt*0, and so on; */bin* contains the binaries of the essential UNIX systems programs.

Other binaries may be in */usr/bin* (for applications systems programs, such as text formatters), */us/ucb* (for systems programs written by Berkeley rather than by AT&T), or */usr/local/bin* (for systems programs written at the local site). Library files—such as the C, Pascal, and FORTRAN subroutine libraries—are kept in */lib* (or */usr/lib* or */usr/local/lib).* The files of users themselves are stored in a separate directory for users, typically in */user.* Thus, the user directory for *carol* would normally be in */user/carol.*

For a large system, these directories may be further grouped to ease administration, creating a file, structure with */user/prof/avi* and */user/staff/carol.* Administrative files and programs, such as the password file, are kept in */etc.* Temporary files can be put in */tmp,* which is normally erased during system boot, or in */usr/tmp.* Each of these directories may have considerably more structure. For example, the font-description tables for the troff formatter for the Merganthaler 202 typesetter are kept in */usr/lib/troff/dev*202. All the conventions concerning the location of specific files and directories have been defined by programmers and their programs; the operating system kernel needs only */etc/init,* which is used to initialize terminal processes, to be operatable. System calls for basic file manipulation are **create**, **open**, **read**, **write**, **close**, **unlink**, and **trunc**.

Temporary files can be put in* /tmp, *which is normally erased during system boot.

The **create** system call, given a path name, creates an (empty) file (or truncates an existing one). An existing file is opened by the **open** system call, which takes a path name and a mode (such as read, write, or read-write) and returns a small integer, called a *file descriptor.* A file descriptor may then be passed to a **read** or **write** system call (along with a buffer address and the number of bytes to transfer) to perform data transfers to or from the file. A file is closed when its file descriptor is passed to the **close** system call. The **trunc** call reduces the length of a file to 0.

A file descriptor is an index into a small table of open files for this process. Descriptors start at 0 and seldom get higher than 6 or 7 for typical programs, depending on the maximum number of simultaneously open files. Each **read** or **write** updates the current offset into the file, which is associated with the file-table entry and is used to determine the position in the file for the next **read** or **write**.

The **lseek** system call allows the position to be reset explicitly. It also allows the creation of separate files. The **dup** and **dup2** system calls can be used to produce a new file descriptor that is a copy of an existing one. The **fcntl** system call can also do that, and in addition can examine or set various parameters of an open file. For example, it can make each succeeding **write** to an open file append to the end of that file.

There is an additional system call, **ioctl**, for manipulating device parameters. It can set the baud rate of a serial port, or rewind a tape, for instance. Information about the file (such as its size, protection modes, owner, and so on) can be obtained by the **stat** system call. Several system calls allow some of this information to be changed: **rename** (change file name), **chmod** (change the protection mode), and **chown** (change the owner and group).

Many of these system calls have variants that apply to file descriptors instead of file names. The **link** system call makes a hard link for an existing file, creating a new name for an existing file. A link is removed by the **unlink** system call; if it is the last link, the file is deleted. The **symlink** system call makes a symbolic link. Directories are made by the **mkdir** system call and are deleted by **rmdir**. The current directory is changed by **cd**.

Although it is possible to use the standard file calls on directories, it is inadvisable to do so, since directories have an internal structure that must be preserved. Instead, another set of system calls is provided to open a directory, to step through each file entry within the directory to close the directory and to perform other functions; these are **opendir**, **readdir**, **closedir**, and others.

Process Control

We know that a process is program in execution. They are identified by their *process* identifier; which is an integer. A new process is created by the **fork** system call. The new process consists of a copy of the address space of the original process (the same program and the same variables with the same values).

Parent process program

```
# include <sys /wait.h>
# define NULL 0
int main (void) {
   If (fork() = = 0) { /* This is the child process */
      execve ("child", NULL, NULL);
      exit (0); /* Should never get here, terminate */
   }
/* Parent code here */
Printf ("Process [%d]: Parent in execution . . . /n", getpid());
Sleep(2)
If (wait (NULL) >0) /* Child terminating */
   child /n";
getpid ());
Printif ("Process [%d]; Parent terminating ... /n" getpid());
}
```

Both processes (the parent and the child) continue execution at the instruction after the **fork** with one difference. The return code for the **fork** is zero for the new (child) process, whereas the (nonzero) process identifier of the child is returned to the parent. Typically, the **execve** system call is used after a fork by one of the two processes to replace that process virtual memory space with a new program.

The **execve** system call loads a binary file into memory (destroying the memory image of the program containing the **execve** system call) and starts its execution. A process may terminate by using the **exit** system call, and its parent process may wait for that event by using the wait system call. If the child process crashes, the system simulates the **exit** call. The **wait** system call provides the process id of a terminated child so that the parent can tell which of possibly many children terminated.

A second system call, **wait3**, is similar to **wait** but also allows the parent to collect performance statistics about the child. Between the time the child exits, and the time the parent completes one of the **wait** system calls, the child is *defunct.* A defunct process can do nothing, but exists merely so that the parent can collect its status information. If the parent process of a defunct process exits before a child, the defunct process is inherited by the *init* process (which in turn **waits** on it) and becomes a *zombie* process.

The simplest form of communication between processes is by *pipes,* which may be created before the **fork**, and whose endpoints are then set up between the **fork** and the **execve**. A pipe is essentially a queue of bytes between two processes. The pipe is accessed by a file descriptor, like an ordinary file.

One process writes into the pipe, and the other reads from the pipe. The size of the original pipe system was fixed by the system. With 4.3BSD, pipes are implemented on top of the socket system, which has variable-sized buffers. Reading from an empty pipe or writing into a full pipe causes the process to be blocked until the state of the pipe changes. Special arrangements are needed for a pipe to be placed between a parent and child (so only one is reading and one is writing).

All user processes are descendants of one original process, called *init.* Each terminal port available for interactive use has a *getty* process forked for it by *init.* The getty process initializes terminal line parameters and waits for a user's *login name,* which it passes through an **execve** as an argument to a *login* process. The *login* process collects the user's password, encrypts the password, and compares the result to an encrypted string taken from the file */etc/passwd.*

If the comparison is successful, the user is allowed to log in. The *login* process executes a *shell;* or command interpreter, after setting the numeric *user identifier* of the process to that of the user logging in. (The shell and the user identifier are found in */etc/passwd* by the user's login name.)

It is with this shell that the user ordinarily communicates for the rest of the login session; the shell itself forks subprocesses for the commands the user tells it to execute. The user identifier is used by the kernel to determine the user's permissions for certain system calls, especially those involving file accesses. There is also a *group identifier,* which is used to provide similar privileges to a collection of users.

In 4.3BSD a process may be in several groups simultaneously. The *login* process puts the shell in all the groups permitted to the user by the files */etc/passwd* and */etc/group.* There are actually two user identifiers used by the kernel: the *effective user identifier* is the identifier used to determine file access permissions. If the file of a program being loaded by an **execve** has the **setuid** bit set in its mode, the effective user identifier of the process is set to the user identifier of the owner of the file, whereas the *real user identifier* is left as it was.

This scheme allows certain processes to have more than ordinary privileges while still being executable by ordinary users. The **setuid** idea was patented by Dennis Ritchie and is one of the distinctive features of UNIX. There is a similar **setuid** bit for groups. A process may determine its real and effective user identifier with the **getuid** and **geteuid** calls, respectively. The **getgid** and **getegid** calls determine the process identifier and group identifier, respectively. The rest of a process' groups may be found with the **getgroups** system call.

Signals

We know there are interrupts in various software for various conditions. Similarly in UNIX we have signals. There are 20 different signals, each corresponding to a distinct condition. A signal may be generated by a keyboard interrupt, by an error in a process (such as a bad memory reference), or by a number of asynchronous events (such as timers or job-control signals from the shell).

Almost any signal may also be generated by the **kill** system call. The *interrupt* signal, SIGINT, is used to stop a command before that command completes. It is usually produced by the ^C character (ASCII 3). As of 4.2BSD, the important keyboard characters are defined by a table for each terminal and can be redefined easily. The *quit* signal, SIGQUIT, is usually produced by the ^bs character (ASCII 28). The *quit* signal both stops the currently executing program and dumps its current memory image to a file named *core* in the current directory. The core file can be used by debuggers. SIGILL is produced by an illegal instruction and SIGSEGV by an attempt to address memory outside of the legal virtual-memory space of a process. Arrangements can be made either for most signals to be ignored (to have no effect), or for a routine in the user process (a signal handler) to be called.

A signal handler may safely do one of two things before returning from catching a signal: call the **exit** system call, or modify a global variable. There is one signal (the *kill* signal, number 9, SIGKILL) that cannot be ignored or caught by a signal handler. SIGKILL is used, for example, to kill a runaway process that is ignoring other signals such as SIGINT or SIGQUIT. Signals can be lost: If another signal of the same kind is sent before a previous signal has been accepted by the process to which it is directed, the first signal will be overwritten and only the last signal will be seen by the process.

In other words, a call to the signal handler tells a process that there has been at least one occurrence of the signal. Also, there is no relative priority among UNIX signals. If two different signals are sent to the same process at the same time, it is indeterminate which one the process will receive first. Signals were originally intended to deal with exceptional events. As is true of the use of most other features in UNIX, however, signal use has steadily expanded. 4.1BSD introduced job control, which uses signals to start and stop subprocesses on demand.

This facility allows one shell to control multiple processes: starting, stopping, and backgrounding them as the user wishes. 4.3BSD added the SIGWINCH signal, invented by Sun Microsystems, for informing a process that the window in which output is being displayed has changed size. Signals are also used to deliver urgent data from network connections. Users also wanted more reliable signals, and a bug fix in an inherent race condition in the old signals implementation.

Thus, 4.21BSD also brought with it a race-free, reliable, separately implemented signal capability. It allows individual signals to be blocked during critical sections, and has a new system call to let a process sleep until interrupted. It is similar to hardware-interrupt functionality. This capability is now part of the POSIX standard.

Process Groups

One or more related processes group together to achieve a common result. For example, processes may create, and communicate over, pipes. Such a set of processes is termed *a process group,* or a *job.* Signals may be *sent* to all processes *in a* group. A process usually inherits its process group from its parent, but the **setpgrp** system call allows a process to change its group.

Process groups are used by the C shell to control the operation of multiple jobs.

Only one process group may use a terminal device for I/O at any time. This *fireground* job has the attention of the user on that terminal while all other non-attached jobs *(background* jobs) perform their function without user interaction. Access to the terminal is controlled by process group signals.

Each job has a *controlling terminal* (again, inherited from its parent). If the process group of the controlling terminal matches the group of a process, that process is in the foreground, and is allowed to perform I/O. If a non-matching (background) process attempts the same, a SIGTTIN or SIGITOU signal is sent to its process group. This signal usually results in the process group freezing until it is foregrounded by the user, at which point it receives a SIGCONT signal indicating that the process can perform the I/O. Similarly, a SIGSTOP may be sent to the foreground process group to freeze it.

Manipulation of Information

System calls exist to set and return both an interval timer (**getitimer/setitimer**) and the current time (**gettimeofday/settimeofday**) in microseconds. In addition, processes can ask for their process identifier (**getpid**), their group identifier (**getgid**), the name of the machine on which they are executing (**gethostname**), and many other values.

Library Routines

Those of you who are familiar with C programming, must be aware of the library and header files. UNIX also has its own set of library routines and header files. The header files provide the definition of complex data structures used in system calls. In addition, a large library of functions provides additional program support. For example, the UNIX I/O system calls provide for the reading and writing of blocks of bytes. Some applications may want to read and write only 1 byte at a time.

Although it would be possible to read and write 1 byte at a time, that would require a system call for each byte—a very high overhead. Instead, a set of standard library routines (the standard I/O package accessed through the header file <*stdio.h*>) provides another interface, which reads and writes several thousand bytes at a time using local buffers, and transfers between these buffers (in user memory) when I/O is desired. Formatted I/O is also supported by the standard I/O package.

Additional library support is provided for mathematical functions, network access, data conversion, and so on. The 4.3BSD kernel supports over 150 system calls; the C program library has over 300 library functions. Although the library functions eventually result in system calls where necessary (for example, the *getchar* library routine will result in a **read** system call if the file buffer is empty). It *is* generally unnecessary for the programmer to distinguish between the basic set of kernel system calls and the additional functions provided by library functions.

Users Interfaces

While using UNIX, both users and programmers make use of the system programs and routines which are available in UNIX for execution. These programs make the necessary system calls to support their function, but the system calls themselves are contained within the program and do not need to be obvious to the user.

The common systems programs can be grouped into several categories; most of them are file or directory oriented.

For example, the system programs to manipulate directories are *mkdir* to create a new directory, *rmdir* to remove a directory, *cd* to change the current directory to another, and *pwd* to print the absolute path name of the current (working) directory. The *ls* program lists the names of the files in the current directory. Any of 18 options can ask that properties of the files be displayed also. For example, the *-l* option asks for a long listing, showing the file name, owner, protection, date and time of creation, and size. The cp program creates a new file that is a copy of an existing file. The mv program moves a file from one place to another in the directory tree.

In most cases, this move simply requires a renaming of the file; if necessary, however, the file is copied to the new location and the old copy is deleted. A file is deleted by the *rm* program (which makes an **unlink** system call). To display a file on the terminal, a user can run cat. The cat program takes a list of files and concatenates them, copying the result to the standard output, commonly the terminal. On a high-speed cathode-ray tube (CRT) display, of course, the file may speed by too fast to be read. The *more* program displays the file one screen at a time, pausing until the user types a character to continue to the next screen.

The *head* program displays just the first few lines of a file; *tail* shows the last few lines. These are the basic systems programs widely used in UNIX. In addition, there are a number of editors *(ed, sed, emacs, vi,* and so on), compilers (C, Pascal, FORTRAN, and so on), and text formatters (troff, TEX, scribe, and so on). There are also programs for sorting (*sort*) and comparing files (*cmp, diff*), looking for patterns (*grep*, *awk),* sending mail to other users *(mail),* and many other activities.

Commands and Shells

Command interpreter is used to execute system programs and the programs written by the users, which is a user process like any other process. It is called a *shell,* as it surrounds the kernel of the operating system. Users can write their own shell, and there are, in fact, several shells in general use.

The* Bourne shell, *written by Steve Bourne, is probably the most widely used—or, at least, it is the most widely available.

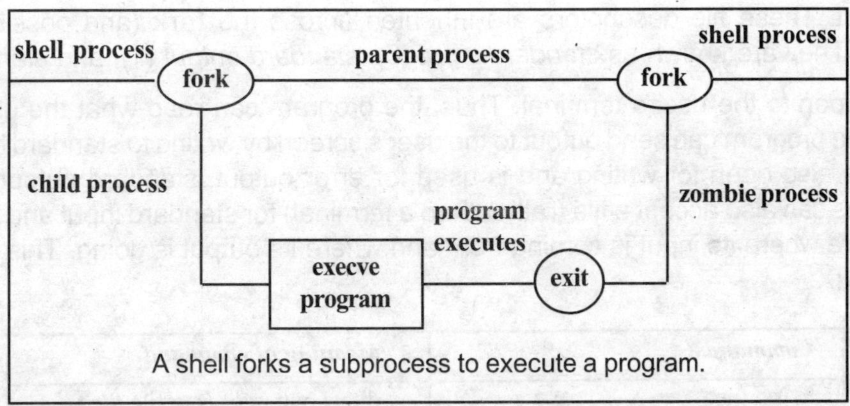

A shell forks a subprocess to execute a program.

The C *shell,* mostly the work of Bill Joy, a founder of Sun Microsystems, is the most popular on BSD Systems. The Korn shell, by Dave Korn, has become popular because it combines the features of the Bourne shell and the C shell. The common shells share much of their command-language syntax. UNIX is normally an interactive system. The shell indicates its readiness to accept another command by typing a prompt, and the user types a command on a single line.

For instance, in the line

% *ls – l*

the percent sign is the usual C shell prompt, and the *ls – l* (typed by the user) is the (long) list-directory command. Commands can take arguments, which the user types after the command name on the same line, separated by white space (spaces or tabs). Although there are a few commands built into the shells (such as *cd),* a typical command is an executable binary object file. A list of several directories, the *search path,* is kept by the shell.

For each command, each of the directories in the search path is searched, in order, for a file of the same name. If a file is found, it is loaded and executed. The search path can be set by the user. The directories */bin* and */usr/bin* are almost always in the search path, and a typical search path on a BSD system might be

(. */home/prof/avi/bin /usr/local/bin /usr/ucb /bin /usr/bin*)

The ls command's object file is */bin/ls,* and the shell itself is */bin/sh* (the Bourne shell) or */bin/csh* (the C shell). Execution of a command is done by a **fork** system call followed by an **execve** of the object file. The shell usually then does a **wait** to suspend its own execution until the command completes, as shown below. There is a simple syntax (an ampersand [&] at the end of the command line) to indicate that the shell should not wait for the completion of the command.

A command left running in this manner while the shell continues to interpret further commands is said to be a *background* command, or to be running in the background. Processes for which the shell *does* wait are said to run in the *foreground.* The C shell in 4.3BSD systems provides a facility called *job control* (partially implemented in the kernel), as mentioned previously. Job control allows processes to be moved between the foreground and the background. The processes can be stopped and restarted on various conditions, such as a background job wanting input from the user's terminal. This scheme allows most of the control of processes provided by windowing or layering interfaces, but requires no special hardware.

Job control is also useful in window systems, such as the X Window System developed at MIT. Each window is treated as a terminal, allowing multiple processes to be in the foreground (one per window) at any one time. Of course, background processes may exist on any of the windows. The Korn shell also supports job control, and it is likely that job control (and process groups) will be standard in future versions of UNIX.

Standard I/O

Processes can open files as they like, but most processes expect 3 file descriptors (numbers 0, 1, and 2) to be open when they start. These file descriptors are inherited across the **fork** (and possibly the **execvc**) that created the process. They are known as *standard input* (0), *standard output* (1), and *standard error* (2).

All 3 are frequently open to the user's terminal. Thus, the program can read what the user types by reading standard input, and the program can send output to the user's screen by writing to standard output. The standard-error file descriptor is also open for writing and is used for error output; standard output is used for ordinary output. Most programs can also accept a file (rather than a terminal) for standard input and standard output. The program does not care where its input is coming from and where its output is going. This is one of the elegant design features of UNIX.

Command	*Meaning of command*
% ls > filea	direct output of *ls* to file *filea*
% pr < filea > fileb	input from *filea* and output to *fileb*
% lpr < fileb	input from *fileb*
% % make program >& errs	save both standard output and standard error in file

Standard I/O redirection.

The common shells have a simple syntax for changing what files are open for the standard I/O streams of a process. Changing a standard file is called *I/O redirection*. The syntax for I/O redirection is shown below. In this example, the *ls* command produces a listing of the names of files in the current directory, the *pr* command formats that list into pages suitable for a printer, and the *lpr* command spools the formatted output to a printer, such as */dev/lp0*.

The subsequent command forces all output and all error messages to be redirected to a file. Without the ampersand, error messages appear on the terminal.

Pipelines, Filters, and Shell Scripts

The first three commands of earlier example, could have been coalesced into the one command

% *ls* | *pr* | *lpr*

Each vertical bar tells the shell to arrange for the output of the preceding command to be passed as input to the following command. A pipe is used to carry the data from one process to the other. One process writes into one end of the pipe, and another process reads from the other end. In the example, the write end of one pipe would be set up by the shell to be the standard output of *ls,* and the read end of the pipe would be the standard input of *pr*; there would be another pipe between *pr* and *lpr.*

A command such as *pr* that passes its standard input to its standard output, performing some processing on it is called a *filter.* Many UNIX commands can be used as filters. Complicated functions can be pieced together as pipelines of common commands. Also, common functions, such as output formatting, do not need to be built into numerous commands, because the output of almost any program can be piped through *pr* (or some other appropriate filter).

Both of the common UNIX shells are also programming languages, with shell variables and the usual higher-level programming language control constructs (loops, conditionals). The execution of a command is analogous to a subroutine call. A file of shell commands, a *shell script,* can be executed like any other command, with the appropriate shell being invoked automatically to read it.

Shell programming *thus can be used to combine ordinary programs conveniently for sophisticated applications without the necessity of any programming in conventional languages.*

This external user view is commonly thought of as the definition of UNIX, yet it is the most easily changed definition. Writing a new shell with a quite different syntax and semantics would greatly change the user view while not changing the kernel or even the programmer interface. Several menu-driven and iconic interfaces for UNIX now exist, and the X Window System is rapidly becoming a standard.

The heart of UNIX is, of course, the kernel. This kernel is much more difficult to change than is the user interface, because all programs depend on the system calls that it provides to remain consistent. Of course, new system calls can be added to increase functionality but programs must then be modified to use the new calls.

PROCESS MANAGEMENT

Designers of the operating systems have to come across many problems. Among them the major one is the design problem for representation of processes. One substantial difference between UNIX and many other systems is the ease with which multiple processes can be created and manipulated. These processes are represented in UNIX by various control blocks.

There are no system control blocks accessible in the virtual address space of a user process; control blocks associated with a process are stored in the kernel. The information in these control blocks is used by the kernel for process control and CPU scheduling.

Process Control Blocks

The most basic data structure associated with processes is the *process structure.* A process structure contains everything that the system needs to know about a process when the process is swapped out, such as its unique process identifier, scheduling information (such as the priority of the process), and pointers to other control blocks. There is an array of process structures whose length is defined at system linking time.

The process structures of ready processes are kept linked together by the scheduler in a doubly linked list (the ready queue), and there are pointers from each process structure to the process' parent, to its youngest living child, and to various other relatives of interest, such as a list of processes sharing the same program code (text). The *virtual address space* of a user process is divided into text (program code), data, and stack segments.

The data and stack segments are always in the same address space, but may grow separately, and usually in opposite directions: most frequently, the stack grows down as the data grows up toward it. The text segment is sometimes (as on an Intel 8086 with separate instruction and data space) in an address space different from the data and stack, and is usually read-only. The debugger puts a text segment in read-write mode to be able to allow insertion of breakpoints.

Every process with shareable text (almost all, under 4.3BSD) has a pointer from its process structure to a *text structure.* The text structure records how many processes are using the text segment, including a pointer into a list of their process structures, and where the page table for the text segment can be found on disk when it is swapped. The text structure itself is always resident in main memory: an array of such structures is allocated at system link time. The text, data, and stack segments for the processes may be swapped. When the segments are swapped in, they are paged. The *page tables* record information on the mapping from the process' virtual memory to physical memory. The process structure contains pointers to the page table, for use when the process is resident in main memory, or the address of the process on the swap device, when the process is swapped.

There is no special separate page table for a shared text segment; every process sharing the text segment has entries for its pages in the process page table. Information about the process that is needed only when the process is resident (that is, not swapped out) is kept in the *user structure* (or *U structure),* rather than in the process structure. The U structure is mapped read-only into user virtual address space, so user processes can read its contents. It is writeable by the kernel. On the VAX, a copy of the VAX PCB is kept here for saving the process' general registers, stack pointer, program counter, and page-table base registers when the process is not running.

There is space to keep system-call parameters and return values. All user and group identifiers associated with the process (not just the effective user identifier kept in the process structure) are kept here. Signals, timers, and quotas have data structures here. Of more obvious relevance to the ordinary user, the current directory and the table of open files are maintained in the user structure.

Every process has both a user and a system phase. Most ordinary work is done in user *mode,* but, when a system call is made, it is performed in *system mode.* The system and user phases of a process never execute simultaneously. When a process is executing in system mode, a *kernel stack* for that process is used, rather than the user stack belonging to that process. The kernel stack for the process immediately follows the user structure: The kernel stack and the user structure together compose the *system data segment* for the process. The kernel has its own stack for use when it is not doing work on behalf of a process (for instance, for interrupt handling).

The system and user phases of a process never execute simultaneously.

The **fork** system call allocates a new process structure (with a new process identifier) for the child process, and copies the user structure. There is ordinarily no need for a new text structure, as the processes share their text; the appropriate counters and lists are merely updated. A new page table is constructed, and new main memory is allocated for the data and stack segments of the child process. The copying of the user structure preserves open file descriptors, user and group identifiers, signal handling, and most similar properties of a process.

The **vfork** system call does *not* copy the data and stack to the new process; rather, the new process simply shares the page table of the old one. A new user structure and a new process structure are still created. A common use of this system call is by a shell to execute a command and to wait for its completion. The parent process uses **vfork** to produce the child process. Because the child process wishes to use an **execve** immediately to change its virtual address space completely, there is no need for a complete copy of the parent process.

Files may be closed in one process without affecting the other process, since the kernel data structures involved depend on the user structure, which is not shared.

Such data structures as are necessary for manipulating pipes may be kept in registers between the **vfork** and the **execve**. Files may be closed in one process without affecting the other process, since the kernel data structures involved depend on the user structure, which is not shared. The parent is suspended when it calls **vfork** until the child either calls **execve** or terminates, so that the parent will not change memory that the child needs. When the parent process is large, **vfork** can produce substantial savings in system CPU time.

However, it is a fairly dangerous system call, since any memory change occurs in both processes until the **execve** occurs. An alternative is to share all pages by duplicating the page table, but to mark the entries of both page tables as *copy-on-write*. The hardware protection bits are set to trap any attempt to write in these shared pages. If such a trap occurs, a new frame is allocated and the shared page is copied to the new frame. The page tables are adjusted to show that this page is no longer shared (and therefore, no longer needs to be write-protected), and execution can resume.

An **execve** system call creates no new process or user structure; rather, the text and data of the process are replaced. Open files are preserved (although there is a way to specify that certain file descriptors are to be closed on an **execve**). Most signal-handling properties are preserved, but arrangements to call a specific user routine on a signal are cancelled, for obvious reasons. The process identifier and most other properties of the process are unchanged.

Scheduling of CPU

Processes in UNIX are given small CPU time slices by a priority algorithm that reduces to round-robin scheduling for CPU-bound jobs. Every process has a *scheduling priority* associated with it; larger numbers indicate lower priority. Processes doing disk I/O or other important tasks have priorities less than "pzero" and cannot be killed by signals.

Ordinary user processes have positive priorities and thus are all less likely to be run than are any system process, although user processes can set precedence over one another through the *nice* command. The more CPU time a process accumulates, the lower (more positive) its priority becomes, and vice versa, so there is negative feedback in CPU scheduling and it is difficult for a single process to take all the CPU time. Process aging is employed to prevent starvation.

Older UNIX Systems used a 1-second quantum for the round-robin scheduling. 4.3BSD reschedules processes every 0.1 second and recomputes priorities every second. The round-robin scheduling is accomplished by the *timeout* mechanism, which tells the clock interrupt driver to call a kernel subroutine after a specified interval; the subroutine to be called in this case causes the rescheduling and then resubmits a *timeout* to call itself again.

The priority recomputation is also timed by a subroutine that resubmits a *timeout* for itself. There is no preemption of one process by another in the kernel. A process may relinquish the CPU because it is waiting on I/O or because its time slice has expired. When a process chooses to relinquish the CPU, it goes to sleep on an event. The kernel primitive used for this purpose is called *sleep* (not to be confused with the user-level library routine of the same name).

It takes an argument, which is by convention the address of a kernel data structure related to an event that the process wants to occur before: that process is awakened. When the event occurs, the system process that knows about it calls *wakeup* with the address corresponding to the event, and *all* processes that had done a *sleep* on the same address are put in the ready queue to be run. For example, a process waiting for disk I/O to complete will *sleep* on the address of the buffer header corresponding to the data being transferred.

When the interrupt routine for the disk driver notes that the transfer is complete, it calls *wakeup* on the buffer header. The interrupt uses the kernel stack for whatever process happened to be running at the time, and the *wakeup* is done from that system process. The process that actually does run is chosen by the scheduler. *Sleep* takes a second argument, which is the scheduling priority to be used for this purpose. This priority argument, if less than "pzero," also prevents the process from being awakened prematurely by some exceptional event, such as a *signal.*

When a signal is generated, it is left pending until the system half of the affected process next runs. This event usually happens soon, since the signal normally causes the process to be awakened if the process has been waiting for some other condition. There is no memory associated with events, and the caller of the routine that does a *sleep* on an event must be prepared to deal with a premature return, including the possibility that the reason for waiting has vanished.

There are *race conditions* involved in the event mechanism. If a process decides (because of checking a flag in memory, for instance) to sleep on an event, and the event occurs before the process can execute the primitive that does the actual sleep on the event, the process sleeping may then sleep forever. We prevent this situation by raising the hardware processor priority during the critical section so that no interrupts can occur, and thus only the process desiring the event can run until it is sleeping. Hardware processor priority is used in this manner to protect critical regions throughout the kernel, and is the greatest obstacle to porting UNIX to multiple processor machines.

However, this problem has not prevented such ports from being done repeatedly. Many processes such as text editors are I/O bound and usually will be scheduled mainly on the basis of waiting for I/O. Experience suggests that the UNIX scheduler performs best with I/O bound jobs, as can be observed when there are several CPU-bound jobs, such as text formatters or language interpreters, running. What has been referred to here as *CPU scheduling* corresponds closely to the *short-term scheduling*, although the negative-feedback property of the priority scheme provides some long-term scheduling in that it largely determines the long-term *job mix.* Medium-term scheduling is done by 'the swapping mechanism.

Memory Management

We know from the history that UNIX was earlier developed for PDP-11, which has only eight segments in its virtual address space, and each of these are at most 8192 bytes. The larger machines, such as the PDP-11/70, allow separate instruction and address spaces, which effectively double the address space and number of segments, but this address space is still relatively small.

In addition, the kernel was even more severely constrained due to dedication of one data segment to interrupt vectors, another to point at the pre-process system data segment, and yet another for the UNIBUS (system I/O bus) registers. Further, on the smaller PDP-11s, total physical memory was limited to 256K. The total memory resources were insufficient to justify or support complex memory-management algorithms. Thus, UNIX swapped entire process memory images.

Swapping

Prior to the 3BSD UNIX version, computers used swapping exclusively to handle memory contention among processes. If there is too much contention, processes are swapped out until enough memory is available. Also, a few large processes can force many small processes out of memory, and a process larger than nonkernel main memory cannot be run at all.

The system data segment (the *u* structure and kernel stack) and the user data segment (text [if nonshareable], data, and stack) are kept in contiguous main memory for swap-transfer efficiency, so external fragmentation of memory can be a serious problem. Allocation of both main memory and swap space is done *first-fit.* When the size of a process' memory image increases (due to either stack expansion or data expansion), a new piece of memory big enough for the whole image is allocated.

The memory image is copied, the old memory is freed, and the appropriate tables are updated. An attempt is made in some systems to find memory contiguous to the end of the current piece, to avoid some copying. If no single piece of main memory is large enough, the process is swapped out such that it will he swapped back in with the new size. There is no need to swap out a shareable text segment, because it is read-only, and there is no need to read in a shareable text segment for a process when another instance is already in core.

That is one of the main reasons for keeping track of shareable text segments: less swap traffic. The other reason is the reduced amount of main memory required for multiple processes using the same text segment. Decisions regarding which processes to swap in or out are made by the *scheduler process* (also known as the *swapper).* The *scheduler* wakes up at least once every 4 seconds to check for processes to be swapped in or out. A process is more likely to be swapped out if it is idle, has been in main memory a long time, or is large; if no obvious candidates are found, other processes are picked by age.

A process is more likely to be swapped in if it has been swapped out a long time, or is small. There are checks to prevent thrashing, basically by not letting a process be swapped out if it has not been in memory for a certain amount of time. If jobs do not need to be swapped out, the process table is searched for a process deserving to be brought in (determined by how small the process is and how long it has been swapped out). If there is not enough memory available, processes are swapped out until there is.

In 4.3BSD, swap space is allocated in pieces that are multiples of a power of 2 and a minimum size (for example, 32 pages), up to a maximum that is determined by the size of the swap-space partition on the disk. If several logical disk partitions may be used for swapping, they should be the same size, for this reason. The several logical disk partitions should also be on separate disk arms to minimize disk seeks.

Many systems still use the swapping scheme just described. All Berkeley UNIX systems, on the other hand, depend primarily on paging for memory-contention management, and depend only secondarily on swapping. A scheme similar in outline to the traditional one is used to determine which processes get swapped, but the details differ and the influence of swapping is less.

Paging

Berkeley introduced paging to UNIX with 3BSD. VAX 4.2BSD is a demand-paged virtual-memory system. External fragmentation of memory is eliminated by paging. There is, of course, internal fragmentation, but it is negligible with a reasonably small page size.

Swapping can be kept to a minimum because more jobs can be kept in main memory, because paging allows execution with only parts of each process in memory. *Demand paging* is done in a straightforward manner. When a process needs a page and the page *is* not there, a page fault to the kernel occurs, a frame of main memory is allocated, and the proper disk page is read into the frame. There are a few optimizations.

If the page needed is still in the page table for the process, but has been marked invalid by the page-replacement process, it can be marked valid and used without any I/O transfer. Pages can similarly be retrieved from the list of free frames. When most processes are started, many of their pages are prepaged and are put on the free list for recovery by this mechanism.

Arrangements may also be made for a process to have no prepaging on startup, but that is seldom done, as it results in more page-fault overhead, being closer to pure demand paging. If the page has to be fetched from disk, it must be locked in memory for the duration of the transfer.

This locking ensures that the page will not be selected for page replacement. Once the page is fetched and mapped properly, it must remain locked if raw physical I/O is being done on it. The *page-replacement* algorithm is more interesting. The VAX architecture has no hardware memory page-reference bit. This lack of hardware support makes many memory-management algorithms, such as page-fault frequency, unusable. 4.2BSD uses a modification of the *second chance* (clock) algorithm.

The map of all nonkernel main memory (the *core* map or cmap) is swept linearly and repeatedly by a software *clock hand.* When the clock hand reaches a given frame, if the frame is marked as in use by some software condition (for example, physical I/O is in progress using it), or the frame is already free, the frame is left untouched, and the clock hand sweeps to the next frame. Otherwise, the corresponding text or process page-table entry for this frame is located.

If the entry is already invalid, the frame is added to the free list; otherwise, the page-table entry is made invalid but reclaimable (that is, if it does not get paged out by the next time it is wanted, it can just be made valid again). 4.3BSD Tahoe added support for systems which do implement the reference bit. On such systems, one pass of the clock turns the reference bit off, and a second pass places those pages whose reference bits remain off onto the free list for replacement.

Of course, if the page is dirty (the VAX *does* have a dirty bit), it must first be written to disk before being added to the free list. Pageouts are done in clusters to improve performance. There are checks to make sure that the number of valid data pages for a process does not fall too low, and to keep the paging device from being flooded with requests. There is also a mechanism by which a process may limit the amount of main memory it uses. The LRU clock hand scheme is implemented in the *pagedaemon,* which is process 2 (remember that the *scheduler* is process 0, and *init* is process I).

This process spends most of its time sleeping, but a check is done several times per second (scheduled by a *timeout)* to see if action is necessary; if it is, process 2 is awakened. Whenever the number of free frames falls below a threshold, *lotsfree,* the *pagedaemon* is awakened; thus, if there is always a large amount of free memory, the *pagedaemon* imposes no load on the system, because it never runs.

The sweep of the clock hand each time the *pagedaemon* process is awakened (that is, the number of frames scanned, which is usually more than the number paged out), is determined both by the number of frames lacking to reach *lotsfree* and by the number of frames that the *scheduler* has determined are needed for various reasons (the more frames needed, the longer the sweep). If the number of frames free rises to *lotsfree* before the expected sweep is completed, the hand stops and the *pagedaemon* process sleeps.

The parameters that determine the range of the clock-hand sweep are determined at system startup according to the amount of main memory, such that *pagedaernon* does not use more than 10 percent of all CPU time. If the *scheduler* decides that the paging system is overloaded, processes will be swapped out whole until the overload is relieved. This swapping usually happens only if several conditions are met: load average is high, free memory has fallen below a low limit, *minfree;* and the average memory available over recent time is less than a desirable amount, *desfree,* where *lotsftee* > *desfree* > *minfree.*

In other words, only a chronic shortage of memory with several processes trying to run will cause swapping, and even then free memory has to be extremely low at the moment. (An excessive paging rate or a need for memory by the kernel itself may also enter into the calculations, in rare cases.) Processes may be swapped by the *scheduler,* of course, for other reasons (such as simply for not running for a long time). The parameter *lotsfree* is usually one-quarter of the memory in the map that the clock hand sweeps, and *desfree* and *minfree* are usually the same across different systems, but are limited to fractions of available memory.

Every process' text segment is by default shared and read-only.

This scheme is practical with paging, because there is no external fragmentation, and the swap space gained by sharing more than offsets the negligible amount of overhead involved, as the kernel virtual space is large. CPU scheduling, memory swapping, and paging interact the lower the priority of a process, the more likely that its pages will be paged out and the more likely that it will be swapped in its entirety. The age preferences in choosing processes to swap guard against thrashing, but paging does so more effectively.

Ideally, processes will not be swapped out unless they are idle, because each process will need only a small working set of pages in main memory at any one time, and the *pagedaemon* will reclaim unused pages for use by other processes. The amount of memory the process will need is some fraction of that process total virtual size, up to one-half if that process has been swapped out for a long time.

The VAX 512-byte hardware pages are too small for I/O efficiency, so they are clustered in groups of two so that all paging I/O is actually done in 1024-byte chunks. In other words, the effective page size is not necessarily identical to the hardware page size of the machine, although it must be a multiple of the hardware page size.

File System

Like in any other operating system, UNIX also supports files and directories. Directories are just files with a special format, so the representation of a file is the basic UNIX concept.

Blocks and Fragments

Most of the file system is taken up by *data blocks,* which contain whatever the users have put in their files. Let us consider how these data blocks are stored on the disk. The hardware disk sector is usually 512 bytes. A block size larger than 512 bytes is desirable for speed.

However, because UNIX file systems usually contain a very large number of small files, much larger blocks would cause excessive internal fragmentation. That is why the earlier 4.1BSD file system was limited to a 1024-byte (1K) block. The 4.2BSD solution is to use *two* block sizes for files which have no indirect blocks: all the blocks of a file are of a large *block* size (such as 8K), except the last. The last block is an appropriate multiple of a smaller *fragment* size (for example, 1024) to fill out the file. Thus, a file of size 18,000 bytes would have two 8K blocks and one 2K fragment (which would not be filled completely). The *block* and *fragment* sizes are set during file-system creation according to the intended use of the file system: If many small files are expected, the fragment size should be small; if repeated transfers of large files are expected, the basic block size should be large. Implementation details force a maximum block-to-fragment ratio of 8:1, and a minimum block size of 4K, so typical choices are 4096:512 for the former case and 8192:1024 for the latter.

Suppose data are written to a file in transfer sizes of 1K bytes, and the block and fragment sizes of the file system are 4K and 512 bytes. The file system will allocate a 1K fragment to contain the data from the first transfer. The next transfer will cause a new 2K fragment to be allocated. The data from the original fragment must be copied into this new fragment, followed by the second 1K transfer. The allocation routines do attempt to find the required space on the disk immediately following the existing fragment so that no copying is necessary, but, if they cannot do so, up to seven copies may be required before the fragment becomes a block. Provisions have been made for programs to discover the block size for a file so that transfers of that size can be made, to avoid fragment recopying.

Inodes

The name *inode* (pronounced *EYE node)* is derived from "index nodes" and was originally spelled "i-node"; the hyphen fell out of use over the years. The term is also sometimes spelled "I node." A file is represented by an *inode*. An inode is a record that stores most of the information about a specific file on the disk.

The inode contains the user and group identifiers of the file, the times of the last file modification and access, a count of the number of hard links (directory entries) to the file, and the type of the file (plain file, directory, symbolic link, character device, block device, or socket). In addition, the inode contains 15 pointers to the disk blocks containing the data contents of the file. The first 12 of these pointers point to *direct blocks;* that is, they contain addresses of blocks that contain data of the file. Thus, the data for small files (no more than 12 blocks) can be referenced immediately, because a copy of the mode is kept in main memory while a file is open.

If the block size is 4K, then up to 48K of data may be accessed directly from the inode. The next three pointers in the inode point to *indirect blocks.* If the file is large enough to use indirect blocks, the indirect blocks are each of the major block size; the fragment size applies to only data blocks. The first indirect block pointer is the address of a *single indirect block.* The single indirect block is an index block, containing not data, but rather the addresses of blocks that do contain data. Then, there is a *double-indirect-block pointer,* the address of a block that contains the addresses of blocks that contain pointers to the actual data blocks. The last pointer would contain the address of a *triple indirect block;* however, there is no need for it. The minimum block size for a file system in 4.2BSD is 4K, so files with as many as 232 bytes will use only double, not triple, in direction.

That is, as each block pointer takes 4 bytes, we have 49,152 bytes accessible in direct blocks, 4,194,304 bytes accessible by a single indirection, and 4,294,967,296 bytes reachable through double indirection, for a total of 4,299,210,752 bytes, which is larger than 232 bytes. The number 232 is significant because the file offset in the file structure in main memory is kept in a 32-bit word. Files, therefore, cannot be larger than 232 bytes.

Since file pointers are signed integers (for seeking backward and forward in a file), the actual maximum file size is 232-1 bytes. Two gigabytes is large enough for most purposes.

Directories

There is no distinction between plain files and directories at this level of implementation; directory contents are kept in data blocks, and directories are represented by an inode in the same way as plain files. Only the mode type field distinguishes between plain files and directories. Plain files are not assumed to have a structure, however, whereas directories have a specific structure.

In Version 7, file names were limited to 14 characters, so directories were a list of 16-byte entries: 2 bytes for an inode number and 14 bytes for a file name. In 4.2BSD, file names are of variable length, up to 255 bytes, so directory entries are also of variable length. Each entry contains first the length of the entry, then the file name and the inode number. This variable-length entry makes the directory management and search routines more complex, but greatly improves the ability of users to choose meaningful names for their files and directories, with no practical limit on the length of the name. The first two names in every directory are "." and "..". New directory entries are added to the directory in the first space available, generally after the existing files. A linear search is used.

The user refers to a file by a path name, whereas the file system uses the inode as its definition of a file. Thus, the kernel has to map the supplied user path name to an inode. The directories are used for this mapping. First, a starting directory is determined. If the first character of the path name is "/", the starting directory is the root directory. If the path name starts with any character other than a slash, the starting directory is the current directory of the current process. The starting directory is checked for proper file type and access permissions, and an error is returned if necessary. The inode of the starting directory is always available. The next element of the path name, up to the next "/", or to the end of the path name, is a file name. The starting directory is searched for this name, and an error is returned if the name is not found.

If there is yet another element in the path name, the current inode must refer to a directory, and an error is returned if it does not, or if access is denied. This directory is searched as was the previous one. This process continues until the end of the path name is reached and the desired inode is returned. This step-by-step process is needed because at any directory a mount point may be encountered, causing the translation to move to a different directory structure for continuation. Hard links are simply directory entries like any other. We handle symbolic links for the most part by starting the search over with the path name taken from the contents of the symbolic link. We prevent infinite loops by counting the number of symbolic links encountered during a path-name search and returning an error when a limit is exceeded. Nondisk files (such as devices) do not have data blocks allocated on the disk.

The kernel notices these file types and calls appropriate drivers to handle I/O for them. Once the inode is found by, for instance, the **open** system call, a file *structure* is allocated to point to the inode. The file descriptor given to the user refers to this file structure. 4.3BSD added a *directory name cache* to hold recent directory-to-inode translations. This improvement greatly increased file system performance.

LINUX

Bill Gates is no doubt the richest man in the World. He made his money by selling commercial software, specially operating software like MS-DOS and Windows. Compare this with the Linux which is nothing short of a phenomenon. It is an operating software which has no financial strings attached to it. It can be just downloaded freely from the net. Imagine if the producers of this software too would have insisted on selling it commercially they would have been in league with Bill Gates. But, they choose not to do so.

Linux is available free.

It is not that since Linux is available cheaply it would be cheap in performance too. In fact, it lacks no punch as far as its competitors in operating system from Microsoft, Apple, Novell and IBM. It is also handling more demanding applications, it is also a serious contender against rival Unix-derivative operating systems such as Solaris, HP-UX and SCO-Unix for larger businesses.

History of Linux

Linux was created as an offshoot of Unix. It has more similarities to UNIX than to any other operating systems. As an operating system, Unix continues to be widely used in commercial environment, as well as in the educational world, although it is also often found running on today's client-server intranet networks too. While versions of Unix have long been available for PCs, they never had the grace or power of the operating systems available for minicomputers, mainframes and today's servers.

In addition, the early commercial versions of Unix were costly, sometimes costing more than the PC hardware they were destined to run on. This lack of accessibility ultimately gave birth to Linux as a means to make a Unix-like operating system available on a widespread basis. Richard Stallmand and the Free Software Foundation (FSF) began work on this alternative operative system in the mid-1980s. By the end of that decade, they had developed functional alternatives to every major Unix component except the kernel. Linux Torvalds at the University of Helsinki in Finland developed the original Linux kernel in 1991.

The combined work became the Linux as you know today. Torvalds originally intended to develop Linux as a hobby. Early versions of Linux didn't have consumers in mind; instead, they provided the barest bones of functionality to allow Unix programmers the apparent joy or programming the kernel. As the core of the operating system, the kernel keeps everything running smoothly – without a stale, powerful kernel, you don't have an operating system. But as programmers integrated the work of the FSF with the Torvalds kernel, the base software for a complete operating system emerged. It became clear to those involved that Linux was evolving the state where it could respectably be called an operating system.

In March 1992, version 1.0 of the kernel came into being, marking the first official release of Linux. At this point, Linux ran most of the common Unix tools from compilers to networking software to X Windows. Linux continues to evolve as the pre-eminent Unix-clone operating system for PCs. Hardware support is now broad, including the most popular and common peripherals; performance is strong, giving many PCs power comparable to that of mind range workstations such as Sun Microsystems' SPARC systems.

Earlier, Linux ran most of the common Unix tools from compilers to networking software to X Windows.

Linux is even now ported to the PowerPC and Compaq Alpha platforms, among others. Although technically today's Linux is not Unix because it fails to quality for the brand name, Linux is functionally equivalent to Unix in almost every important way.

Linux Overview

Linux is used in two ways: specifically to refer to the kernel itself—the heart of any version of Linux—and more generally to refer to any collection that run on the kernel, usually referred to as a distribution. The kernel's job is to provide the basic environment in which applications can run, including the basic interfaces with hardware and the systems for managing tasks and currently running programs. In the specific sense, there is only one current version of Linux at any one time the current revision of the kernel. Torvalds keeps the kernel as the domain in the world of Linux development, leaving all the applications and services that sit on top of the kernel to any of the thousands of other Linux developers in the world.

In the general meaning of the term Linux, referring to cohesive collections of applications that run on top of the Linux kernel, there are numerous versions of Linux. Each distribution has its own unique characteristics, including different installation methods, different collections of features and different upgrade paths. But since all distributions are fundamentally Linux, in almost every case an application that works with a current version of one distribution will work with a current version of another distribution. The interesting thing about this dichotomous use of the term "Linux" is that it exactly parallels the same confused usage of the term "operating system".

For consumers, an operating system has come to mean a large collection of applications centered around a kernel. This is what Windows 95, 98, Me, NT and 2000 are. This is what the Macintosh OS is. In a purist, technical sense, an operating system is a much smaller core kernel that provides those basic system functions needed to develop any application. In both ways, Linux is an operating system.

One of the features of the Linux kernel that sets it apart from other consumer operating systems designed to run on desktop PCs is that it is both multitasking and multiuser.

A Multitasking Operating System

You are probably familiar with the term multitasking, even if you are not really sure what it means. When desktop computing graduated from Windows 3.1 to Windows 95, the multitasking capabilities of the then-new Windows 95 were among its biggest claims to fame. To say that a system can multitask is to say that it can appear to be running more than one application, or process, at a time. For example, the system can print a document, copy a file and dial into the Internet while the user is comfortably typing in a word processing program.

Even with these background tasks happening, the foreground word processor should not freeze up or be unusable. This is the wonder of multitasking: It allows a computer with a single processor to appear to be performing multiple tasks simultaneously. Of course, a single CPU can execute only a single instruction at a time – that is, only one action can be taking place at any one time. Multitasking creates the appearances of simultaneous activity by switching rapidly between tasks as the demands of those processes dictate. When multitasking works well, a user running a word processor, while several other things happen, will not be aware of the extra work the computer is doing.

Linux allows a computer with a single processor to appear to be performing multiple tasks simultaneously.

All processes will seem to be running smoothly and the computer will be responsive. Historically, Unix systems have been much better than Windows at multitasking; Unix is able to run large number of simultaneous applications in a way that made it an ideal fit for large corporate servers and high-powered work stations.

Today, only Windows 2000 and its predecessor Widows NT 4.0 can really claim to offer a similar robust multitasking implementation. Even Windows 95/98/Me, despite all of this fanfare, has trouble effectively handling large number of simultaneous processes. To take things further, Linux, like Windows NT and Windows 2000, offers support for computer with multiple processors, such as dual-Pentium III systems.

These systems can in fact perform two actions at exactly the same time. Combining multitasking with multiple processors greatly increase the number of simultaneous applications a computer can run smoothly.

A Multiuser Operating System

Even more important than being a multitasking operating system, Linux—like all versions of Unix and Unix clones – is a multiuser operating system. All consumer versions of Windows and the Mac OS are single-user systems. In other words, only one user can be logged in and running applications at any one time in these operating systems. By comparison, Linux allows multiple simultaneous users, fully leveraging the multitasking capabilities of the operating system. The great advantage of this is that Linux can be developed as an applications server. From their desktop computers or terminals, users can log into a Linux server across a LAN and actually run applications on the server instead of on their desktop PCs.

Linux allows multiple simultaneous users, fully leveraging the multitasking capabilities of the operating system.

Linux Releases

A number of companies and groups have released the Linux packages. Some of them are listed here.

Red Hat Linux Releases:

Red Hat 7.1

Red Hat 7.2

Red Hat 7.3

Red Hat 8.0

Red Hat 8.1

Red Hat 9.0

Standard Versions

Linux 1.0

Linux 1.1

Linux Netwosix 1.2

Linux 2.0

SUSE Linux Releases:

SUSE Linux Desktop

SUSE Linux Enterprise Server 9

SUSE Linux Open Exchange Server 4.1

SUSE Linux Standard Server (UK)

SUSE Linux Standard Server (International)

SUSE Linux 8.0

SUSE Linux 8.1

SUSE Linux 9.1

SUSE Linux Professional 9.2

Caldera Linux Releases

Open Linux

Debian Linux Releases:

Debian GNU/Linux 3.0 code named Woody

Debian GNU/Linux 2.2 code named Potato

Debian GNU/Linux 2.1 code named Slink

Debian GNU/Linux 2.0 code named Hamm

Digital Dave Releases:

KNOPPIX 3.6

Mandrake Linux 10.1 Beta 2

Other Linux Releases:

Slackware Linux 10.0

Simply MEPIS 2004.04

Gentoo 2004.1

Gentoo 2004.3

United Linux 1.2

VA Linux Releases—NAS Server

Open Linux

Given all the capabilities promised by Linux, you might think that the operating system is expensive. On the contrary, the Linux kernel and most of the applications written for Linux are available for free on the Internet, often with no restriction on the copying and redistribution of the software. To begin with, the Linux kernel is distributed under the GNU General Public License (GPL). This special software licence, developed by Stallman's Free Software Foundation, promotes the open distribution and more importantly open development of software.

Unlike the software licenses common with most commercial software, the GNU license allows anyone to redistribute software, even for a fee, so long as in the redistribution, the terms of the GNU license are still in force. In other words, anyone can take GNU software, alter it if they wish and redistribute it, but they can't stop someone who buys GNU-licensed software from them from turning around and redistributing it again. Most of Linux is available under the GNU General Public License.

Linux kernel is distributed under the GNU General Public License (GPL).

This makes it possible for many different vendors to produce both free and commercially available Linux distributions. This approach to free software is not the same as public domain software. With GNU products, the software developers retain the copyright to the software and may choose in the future to stop distributing that software under the GNU license. What is special about the GNU license is that it encourages iterative development of applications by many people, each making changes that they consider important or necessary and then redistributing the software. This process is enabled by the fact that all GNU-licensed software must be distributed with its complete source code.

Unlike commercial software, where the original code is unavailable and hence unalterable, GNU software not only makes it possible to alter and customize software but actually encourages interested and capable users to do so. In fact, this model has been so successful in the development of Linux and applications for Linux that Netscape has adopted it for its Web browser product lines. Using basic BNU principles, Netscape makes its Web browser freely available and allows anyone to license the source code for its Web browser or to redistribute them.

Linux Commands and Filters

Some of the Linux commands and filters are:

Mkdir

Creates one or more directories.

```
mkdir [-p] [-m mode] [—parents] [—mode=mode] directory …
```

where the variables are:

-m/— mode mode: Sets the mode for the created directory using the same symbolic notation as the chmod command. If this is not specified, the default mode is assigned to the directory.

-p/—parents: Ensures that the parents of the specified directory exist and creates any missing parent directories needed.

CD

Changes the current directory. If you type cd without specifying an argument, this command changes to the current user's home directory.

```
cd [directory | path name]
```

where the variables are:

directory: is the name of the directory.

path name: path name of the directory

mdir

Displays the contents of a directory on an MS-DOS file system such as a floppy disk. If specific files are indicated, then only those files are listed. Similar to the DOS DIR command.

```
mdir [-w] msdosdirectory
    mdir [-a] [-f] [-w] msdosfile [msdosfile ...]
```

where the variables are:

-a: Lists hidden files as well as regular files.

-f: Displays files without listing total free space at the end of the listing

-w: Displays files in wide output.

ls

Displays a listing of files and directories. If no file or directory is specified, then the current directory's contents are displayed. By default, contents are sorted alphabetically.

```
ls [-acdlrRsStuX] [—all] [—time=ctime] [—time=status] [—directory] [—format-
        long] [—format=verbose] [—reverse] [— recursive] [—size] [—sort-size]
        [—sort=time] [—time=atime] [—time-access] [—time-use] [—sort=extension]
        [file |directory ...]
```

where the variables are:

-a/—all: Lists all files in the directory, including those that start with ".".

-c/—time=ctime,—time=status: Sorts entries by the change time of the files.

-d/—directory: Lists directory names only, without showing directory contents. By default, directory contents are listed.

-l/—format-long/—format=verbose: Lists files in long format, including file type, permissions, owner and size.

-r/—reverse: Displays files in reverse order.

-R/—recursive: Lists the content of all subdirectories recursively.

-s/—size: Displays the size of files, in kilobytes.

-S/—sort=size: Sorts entries by the file starting with the largest file.

-t/—sort=time: Sorts entries by timestamp starting with the newest files.

-u/—time=atime/—time=access/—time=use: Sorts entries by the last access time.

-X/—sort=extension: Sorts files by the file extension in alphabetical order.

who

Displays a list of the uses currently logged into the system. If you type who without an option, you will see the user's name, the terminal they are using, and the time they logged on.

```
who [option]
```

If you use -H or -heading as options, you will get column headings. -help will give you the list of available options.

whoami

Displays the username of the user currently logged in to this terminal session or it identifies the user who invoked the command.

```
whoami
```

cat

Combines one or more files and displays them on the standard output. If no files are given, then the standard input is written to the standard output.

```
cat [—benstvAET] [—number] [—number-nonblank] [squeese-blank] [—show-
        nonprinting] [-show-ends] [—show-tabs] [—show-all] [file...]
```

where the variables are:

-A/—show-all: Displays a $ at the end of each line, tab characters as ^I and control characters preceded by a^. This is the same as the combination of –v, -T and –E.

-b/—number-nonblank: Causes all non-blank lines to appear numbered. Numbering starts at 1.

-e: Displays a $ at the end of each line and control characters preceded by a ^. This is the same as the combination of –v and –E.

-E/—show-ends: Displays a $ at the end of each line.

—n/—number: Causes al lines to appear numbered. Numbering starts at 1.

-s/—squeeze-blank: Replaces sequences of multiple blank lines with single blank lines when displayed.

-t: Displays tab characters as ^I and control characters preceded by a^. This is the same as the combination of –v and -T.

-T/—show-tabs: Displays tab characters as ^I.

-v/—show-nonprinting: Displays control character preceded by a^.

more

Displays one or more files screen-by-screen and allows for searching and jumping to an arbitrary location in the file.

```
more [-dlfs] [-number] [+number] [file ...]
```

where the variables are:

-number: Sets the number of lines per screen.

+number: Specifies the line to start on when displaying.

-d: Prompts the user at the end of each screen.

-f: Causes long lines not to be folded and to be counted as a single line.

-l: Prevents Ctrl+L from being treated as a form feed.

-s: Squeezes multiple blank lines into a single blank line.

For details of the commands that can be used when viewing files, consult the more man page.

tail

Print the last ten lines of each file to the standard output. You can specify more than one filename in a space-separated list or by using a shell pattern. The command prints the name of each file before the text. If you remove the filename, the command accepts input from the standard input.

```
tail [option] [filename]
```

where the options can be:

-retry: Keep trying to open the file.

-c, -bytes=n: Output the last n bytes

-f, -follow: Ouput appended data the file grows

-help: Shows the available options

-n, -lines=n: Output the last n lines instead of the last 10 lines

-pid=pid: Terminates after pid terminates

-q, -quiet, -silent: Suppress the display to filenames

-s, -sleep-interval=n, Sleep n seconds after iterations

-v, -verbose Always show filenames

-version Show the version number

head

Displays the first part of one or more files. By default, unless otherwise specified, the first 10 lines of each file are displayed. If no filenames are provided, then needs data from the standard input and displays the first section of the data, following the same rules as for files.

```
head [-c number[bkm] [-n number] [-qv] [—bytes number[bkm]] [—lines number]
      [—quiet] [—silent] [file ...]
```

where the variables are:

-c/—bytes number: Displays the specified number of bytes from the start of each file. Optionally, the number can be followed by b for 512-byte blocks, k for kilobytes and m for megabytes.

-n/—lines number: Displays the specified number of lines from the start of each file.

-q/—quiet/—silent: Prevents printing of filename headers when multiple files are being processed.

concept of mv

Renames and moves files. When a directory is the last argument, move all other specified files into that directory.

```
mv [-bfiu] [—backup] [—force] [—interactive] [—update] [source destinations |
      source ... directory]
```

where the variables are:

-b/—backup: Makes a backup of files that are about to be overwritten by the move without prompting.

-f/—force: removes existing files that are about to be overwritten by the move without prompting.

-i/—interactive: Prompts before overwriting any existing files.

-u/—update: Does not overwrite an existing file if it has the same or newer modification time.

chmod

Changes the access permissions of one or more files or directories.

```
chmod [-Rcfv] [—recursive] [—changes] [—silent] [—quiet] [—verbose] mode file
      ...
```

where the variables are:

-c/—changes: Displays the names of only those files whose permissions are being changed.

-f/—silent/—quiet: Suppresses display or error messages when a file's permissions cannot be changed.

-R/—recursive: Recursively changes the permissions of all files in all subdirectories of any directory that has its permissions changed.

-v/—verbose: Displays the results of all permission changes.

Modes can be specified in two ways: symbolically and numerically. When done symbolically, modes take the form [ugoa] [[+-=] [rwxXstugo …]. The first element ([ugoa]) represents the users whose permissions are being affected (u=user who owns the file or directory, g=all members of the group that owns the file or directory, o=anyone who is not the owner or in the owner group, a=all users). The + symbol means that the specified modes should be added to already specified permissions, the – symbol means the specified modes should be removed from existing permissions and the = symbol means that the specified modes should replace existing permissions. There are many different permissions that can be specified in the third element of the mode, including r for read permissions, w for write permissions and x for execute permissions.

Full details of symbolic and numeric modes appear in the chmod man page.

grep

Searches files for lines matching a specified pattern and displays the lines.

```
grep [-bCcEFGiLinux] [-number] [-e pattern] [-f file] [-basic-regexp] [—byte-
        offset] [—exended-regexp] [—fixed-strings] [—byte-offset] [—context]
        [—count] [—regex[=pattern] [—file=file] [—ignore=case] [—files-without-
        match] [—files-with-match] [—line-number] [—revert-match] [—word-regexp]
        [—line—regexp] [pattern] file [file …]
```

where the variables are:

-number: Displays matching lines with the specified number of lines of leading and trailing context.

-b/—byte-offset: Prints the byte offset of the match before each line.

-c/—count: Instead of displaying matching lines, simply outputs a count of the total number of lines matching the expressions (when combined with –v, displays the total count of non-matching lines).

-C/—context: Displays matching lines with two lines of leading and trailing context (this is the same as -2).

-e pattern/—regexp=pattern: Uses the specified pattern rather than one provided as an argument.

-E/—extended-regexp: Treats the pattern as an extended regular expression (similar to egrep).

-f file/—file=file: Uses the pattern found in the specified file rather than one supplied as an argument.

-F/—fixed-strings: Treats the pattern as a list of new line separated strings, one of which must match. This is the same as fgrep.

-G/—basic-regexp: Treats the pattern as a basic regular expression.

-i/—ignore=case: Ignores case in both the pattern and the files being searched.

-l/—files-with-matches: Instead of displaying each matched line, simply displays the name of each file that contains at least one match for the pattern.

-L/—files-with-match: Instead of displaying each matched line, simply displays the name of each file that contains no matches for the patterns.

-n/—line-number: Prefixes each output line with its line number in the file.

-v/—revert-match: Displays non-matching lines instead of matching lines.

-w/—word-regexp: Displays only those lines with matches for the pattern that are complete words.

-x/—line-regexp: Displays only those lines with matches for the pattern that are complete lines.

The syntax of regular expressions used by grep can be found in the grep man page.

wc

Prints the number of bytes (characters), words and lines in one or more documents. When multiple filenames are provided, each file will be counted and displayed separately and then a cumulative total will be displayed. If no files are specified, then the standard input is counted.

```
wc [-clw] [—byte]s [—chars] [—lines] [—words] [file ...]
```

where the variables are:

-c/—bytes/—chars: Displays only the number of bytes.

-l/—lines: Displays only the number of lines.

-w/—words: Displays only the number of words.

The results are displayed in this order: characters, words, lines. The values are separated by spaces.

comm

The comm command in Linux is a utility that is used to compare two files. It shows common lines in one column and differing lines in separate columns for left and right files. This functionally is similar to diff.

One notable difference between comm and diff is that comm will not try to indicate that a line has "changed" between the two files; lines are either shown in the "from file #1", "from file #2", or "in both" columns. This feature can be especially useful if one wishes two lines to be considered different even if they only have subtle differences.

comm also has options to suppress any of the three columns which is useful for a scripting.

split

split is a Unix utility most commonly used to split a file into one or more smaller files.

The command-syntax is:

```
split (optional parameters) (input filename) (output filename)
```

The default behaviour of split is to generate output files of up to 1000 lines. The files are named by appending aa, ab, ac, etc. to output filename. If output filename is not given, the default filename of x is used, for example, xaa, xab, etc. When a hyphen (-) is used instead of input filename, data is derived from standard input.

To join the files back together again use the cat command

```
cat xaa xab xac > filename
```

or

```
cat xa[a-c] > filename
```

Additional program options permit a maximum character count (instead of a line count), a maximum line length, how many incrementing characters in generated filenames, and whether to use letters or digits.

sort

Sorts the lines contained in one or more text files and displays the results. If no files are indicated, data is taken from the standard input and sorted. The resulting sorted data is displayed to the standard output.

```
sort [-cu] [-t separator] [-o file] [-T temdier] [-bdfMnr] [+POS1 [-POS2]] [-
     k POS1[,POS2]] [file ...]
```

where the variables are:

-b: Ignores leading blanks in lines when trying to find sort keys.

-c: Checks whether the input data is sorted and prints an error message if it isn't. No sorting actually takes place.

-d: Ignores all characters except letters, digits and blanks in the sorting process.

-f: Converts lowercase letters to uppercase letters during the sorting process.

-k POS1[,PS2]: Specifies the field to use as the sorting key. The field will start at POS1 and run up until POS2 or the end of the line. Fields and character positions are specified starting at zero.

-M: Sorts months. That is, any strings that starts with zero or more blank followed by three letters are converted to uppercase and sorted as if they were abbreviated month names.

-n: Compares strings numerically, which assumes that strings start with zero or more blanks followed by an optional sign and then number.

-o file: Outputs the results to the specified file instead of the standard output.

+POS1 [-POS2]: Specifies the field to use as the sorting key. The field will start at POS1 and run up until POS2 or the end of the line. Fields and character positions are specified starting at zero.

-r: Reverse the sort order.

-t separator: Indicates that the specified separator should serve as the field separator for finding sort keys on each line.

-u: When two lines compare as equal, only output the first.

diff

In Linux, diff is a file comparison utility that outputs the differences between two files. The program displays the changes made per line for text files. Modern implementations also support binary files. The output is called a diff or more commonly a patch since the output can be applied with the program patch. The output of similar file comparison utilities are also called a "diff". Like the use of the word "grep" for describing the act of searching, the word diff is used in jargon as a verb for calculating any difference.

kill

Sends a kill signal to one or more running processes.

```
kill [-s signal| -p] pid …
kill -l
```

where the variables are:

-l: Displays a list of signal names.

-p: Prints the process ID of a specified process rather than sending it a signal.

-s signal: Sends the specified signal to the specified processes.

-pid: Specifies either the ID of a process or its name. When specifying processes by name, all processes with the specified name will receive the signal.

write

Write is the Linux facility to forward the contents of a file to a user. This command allows to send a message to another user, currently on the system.

```
writer user [tty] [<file name>]
```

Communication continues from one terminal to another, unit <ctrl + D> is pressed. <EOT> or <EOF> on the other user's screen indicating the end of transmission or end of the file.

wall

Wall has similar function as the write command. However, the main difference is that wall delivers the message to all the users logged on the system. Once the user is given the message from standard input, command reads the message from standard input (keyboard) and proceeds to write it simultaneously on every user's terminal.

merge

This command combines the features of mail and news, which are listed next.

mail

Sends and receives e-mails. The user will be prompted for the test of the message unless it is provided through the standard input. Also, other information such as the subject can be provided as a flat when sending messages or the program can prompt for the information. If no options or arguments are specified, the current user's mailbox is opened for reading.

```
mail [-s subject] [-c address …] [-b address ….] address
    mail -f [mailbox]
    mail - u [user]
```

where the variables are:

ib address …: Indicates a list of addresses that should receive blind carbon copies of outgoing messages.

-c address …: Indicates a list of addresses that should receive a carbon copy of outgoing messages.

-f [mailbox]: Reads mail from your inbox or the mailbox specified.

-s subject: Specifies the subject line of outgoing messages.

-u user: Opens the specified user's inbox for reading.

The mechanics of using mail to read messages is discussed in the mail man page.

news

Write and wall commands are used to give the message to all users who are currently logged onto the system. By using news command, the messages or news can be sent to all users even if they are not logged in.

```
news [option]
```

SHELL

It is a utility of Linux. Each distributor has its own version of Shell. Well, you need not to bother about the distributor but work with the shell.

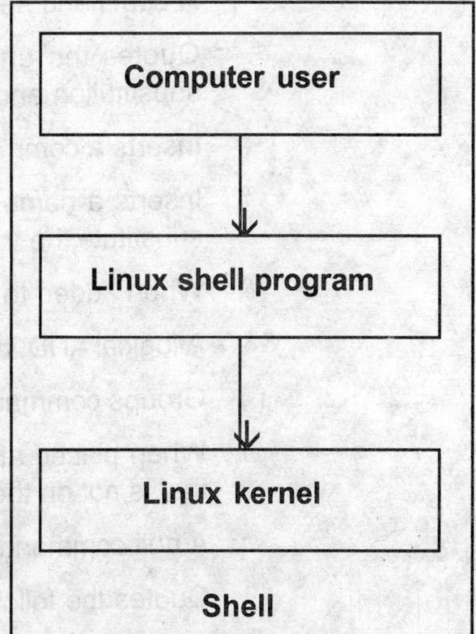

Various features of the Shell are:

Interactive Processing

Shell issues the prompts to user to give a command, by which user can communicate with the Linux system.

Input/Output Redirection

Linux is restricted to accept the data from standard I/O lines. When a user issues a command through keyboard, the shell is responsible to redirect the data into standard input file. Kernal places the output of these commands into standard output file. Shell also redirects the output data to printer or screen from standard output file.

Piping Facility

Another Linux utility is called as pipe utility by which simple functions can be connected together and form the more complex functions. By using this facility the output of one command is to be sent as input of another command.

Background Processing

Shell gives the control to the Kernal for execution of jobs such that Kernal executes the non-interactive and time consuming jobs in the background.

Selection criteria with special characters

Shell provides special characters called as “meta characters” to the user. By using these meta characters user can specify a pattern or selection criteria to select one or more files.

Shell Variables

Shell allows the user to control the environment, by setting of these variables.

Shell Script

Shell script is a set of commands and treated as a Linux program file. This feature allows the user to use the shell as a programming language.

The Command Line Special Characters and File Arguments

Listed here are the Special Characters and File Arguments which are supported by Linux.

Special Characters

Character — Purpose

“ — Quotes all the enclosed text, remove the meaning of special character contained in the text.

| — A command sequence.

“ ” — Quotes the enclosed text with the exception of variable expansion and command substitution and removes the special meaning spaces.

— Inserts a comment; hash ignores the rest of the line.

$ — Inserts a name variable. It is also used for command and arithmetic substitution, i.e., substitute the value of a variable.

& — When added to a command name, executes a command in the background.

&& — A logical AND in a command sequence.

( ) — Groups commands for execution by a subshell. It is also used to identify a function.

/ — When placed at the beginning of a line, executes a command in the working directory that is not on the current path.

: — A null command.

\ — Quɔtes the following character.

‘ ’ — Indicates a command substitution, execute the substitue command & use the results as the argument of the command line.

{ } — Groups commands. It enables you to generate several output patterns from a single entry.

| Redirects the command output to a second command.

|| A logical OR in a command sequence.

< Takes input from a file rather than from the keyboard.

<< Uses the standard input but only up to the specified text.

> Redirects the command output to a file.

>> Appends the command output to a file.

% Indicates a job number.

> ! The exclamation symbol after the redirect symbol indicates the overwriting of a file if it already exists.

File Arguments

Argument	Meaning
*	Stands for zero or any character in the file name.
?	Stands for any one character in a shell pattern.
[characters]	Match only one character given in the brackets.
[character1-character2]	Match one character from the range of characters given in the bracket.
[!characters]	Match one character i.e., not given in bracket.
[!character1-character2]	Match one character, i.e., not in the range of given character in bracket.

Standard Input/Output and Redirection

By using the input/output redirection feature of shell, the standard input and output files can be re-assigned with the help of shell's special symbols.

Command Form	Meaning
command > filename	Directs output from command to the file specified by filename.
filename < command	Use filename as the input for command.
command >> filename	Append output from command to the file specified by filename; create the file, if necessary.
command <> filename	Use filename as both the input and the output for command.
command << text	Use the standard input for command, but only up to the specified text.

Pipes

In computing, a pipeline is a set of data processing elements connected in series, so that the output of one element is the input of the next one. The elements of a pipeline are often executed in parallel or in time-sliced fashion; in that case, some amount of buffer storage is often inserted between elements.

Computer-related pipelines include:

- Instruction pipelines, such as the classic RISC pipeline, which are used in processors to allow the parallel execution of two or more consecutive instructions from a nominally sequential stream; the processing elements are the logical circuits that implement the various stages of an instruction (address decoding and arithmetic, register fetching, cache lookup, etc.).
- Graphics pipelines, found in most graphics cards, which consist of multiple arithmetic units, or complete CPUs, that implement the various stages of common rendering operations (perspective projection,

window clipping, colour and light calculation, rendering, etc.).

- Software pipelines, consisting of multiple processes arranged so that the output stream of one process is automatically and promptly fed as the input stream of the next one. Unix pipelines are the classical implementation of this concept.

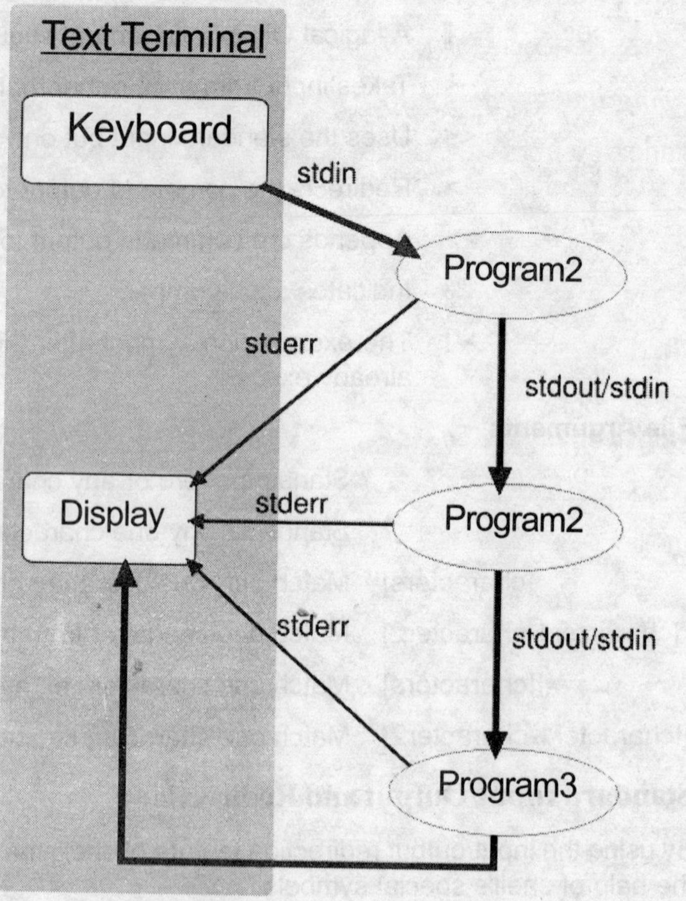

The syntax for pipe is:

```
<command>  |  <command>
```

All the commands in a pipeline execute at the same time. Linux handles the data flow from one command to the next. Intermediate outputs in a pipeline are discarded later, when all the commands in the pipeline are executed.

Example:

Let us give the command as:

$ who > usr, lst

wc-1 usr, lst

The output would be given as 4.

Now, use the pipe method and give the following command.

$ who | wc-1

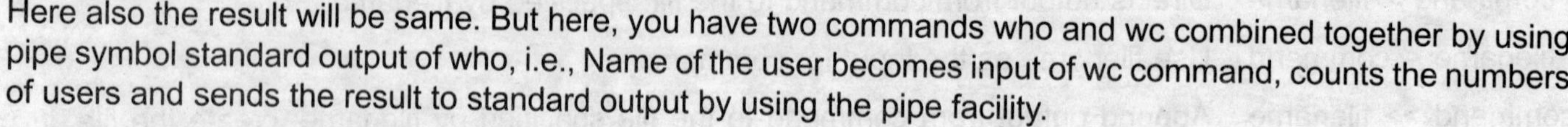

Here also the result will be same. But here, you have two commands who and wc combined together by using pipe symbol standard output of who, i.e., Name of the user becomes input of wc command, counts the numbers of users and sends the result to standard output by using the pipe facility.

Advantages of using pipe facility are:

1. Processing becomes fast.
2. Intermediate files are automatically removed after the execution of pipeline.
3. No more disk space is used as the intermediate files are automatically removed.

Redirecting and Piping with Standard Errors

When user enters a command through standard input, shell accepts it and during processing if any error occurs, Linux displays this error message on the standard output, i.e., screen or printer. This error can be due to any reason.

Redirecting with Standard Errors

Error message can be redirected to another file or device with the help of the following redirectional symbols.

Redirectional Symbol Usage

2 > Redirects the standard error to a file or device.

2 > > Redirects and appends the standard error to a file or device.

2 > & 1 Redirects the standard error to standard output in the shell.

> & Redirects the standard error to a file or device in the C shell.

Piping the Standard Error

Standard errors can be used as input to another command by using the piping utility of Linux. '1&' symbol is used to pipe the standard error as input to another command.

=> command 1& command

$ cat exam 2 >> errfile |& sort

Shell Scripts

It is a program file which contains all the commands which can be given. By using text editor you can write the set of commands.

It can be executed by Sh or . command.

Shell scripts are writen when:

- You want to execute a sequence of commands.
- You need to repeat the task many times, i.e., looping.
- You need to execute the commands based on some conditions, i.e., testing.
- User requires to access the command line arguments.

Features of shell script:

- Shell script has read and write permission, when it is created. By using the chmod command, the permission of shell scripts can be changed for user, group members and other users.
- Shell script uses the named variables in which values can be stored.
- By typing the values as arguments on the command line data can be passed to shell scripts as variables. Arguments are referenced with operator. The first argument is denoted as $1, second as $2 and so on.
- The sequence of executed commands can be changed by using some conditions.
- One of the several alternative command sequences can be selected for execution.
- A set of commands can be executed repeatedly for a number of times.
- Command substitution can be done with shell script.
- Comment lines are also used in shell script.

Jobs

Job is nothing but a new name for command. But, it is different from processes. When user enters a command, referred as Job, shell accepts the job from standard input and interprets it. After that shell gives the control to Kernel to execute the job, that time the same job is called as process. Therefore, a process is a command or program that is being executed.

In Linux multiple processes can run concurrently. Most of the Linux systems have only one processor. The system can, therefore, work on only one process at a time. Thus, to manage many users, the system has to switch CPU time from one process to the next. To manage all the processes at a time, Linux can run some processes in the background while execute others in the foreground. The following commands are provided by shell to control over jobs:

Commands	Action
&	Executes a job in the background + sign indicates that the job is currently being processed. - sign indicates that the next job is to be executed.
fg % jobnumber	Brings a job out of the background to the foreground or resume an interrupted program.
bg	Place a job running in the foreground into the background.
Ctrl-Z	Interrupts and stops the currently running jobs. The job remains suspended and waiting in the background till a new command is given.
notify %jobnumber	Notifies when a job ends. The system interrupts what you are doing and gives the message about the ending of the job.
kill %jobnumber	Cancels and ends a job running in the background.
kill processnumber	Cancels and ends a process running in the background.
jobs	Lists all the background jobs.
ps	Lists all currently running processes including background jobs.
at time date	Executes a command at a specified time and date. The time can be entered in hours and minutes. Or even as A.M or P.M.

LINUX FILE STRUCTURE

Through DOS we are familiar with pathname. In LINUX too, each directory or file has a pathname. Here it is referred to from the beginning of the root directory. For example, the directory user is referred to as /user; book is referred to as /user/book, where user is the parent directory of book directory.

A pathname can be of two types

- Absolute Pathname
- Relative Pathname

Absolute Pathname

It tells you the complete path of a directory starting from the root, as explained above. For example, absolute pathname of "ittools" directory is /usr/books/laxmi/doe/ittools.

Relative Pathname

It gives location of a directory, relative to the current working directory. For example, suppose your current working directory is /usr/books/laxmi/doe/ittools. Then the relative pathname to the "ittools" directory is ittools. Relative pathnames do not start with a "/".

If you do not start a pathname with "/", LINUX assumes that you are using relative pathname.

The other features of the Linux file system are:

Hierarchical Strucutre

The Linux file structure is like the upside-down of tree.

File Sharing

Number of users can access a file simultaneously.

Structure-less internal structure

Linux file's contents have no internal shortcuts. Linux utility decides that what should be internal structure of the file.

File expansion

Users need not to specify the size of the file, it grows dynamically.

File security

Files can be protected from unauthorised users.

Linux files

There are two important features of Linux files, Naming conventions and File information.

Naming Conventions

Following is what you have to keep in mind while naming the files.

- You can create file names of upto 255 characters in length.
- Linux file names are case sensitive, e.g., subject.DOC,. SUBJECT.doc, subject.doc are three different files.
- Avoid using the illegal characters in the file name. The list of illegal characters follows:

Character	Function
#	Inserts a comment; bash ignores the rest of the line.
&	Inserts a named variable.
* ? [ ] ~ !	Constructs shell patterns.
< >	Redirects input and output.
`	Inserts the output of the specified command.
;	Begins new command on the same line.
( )	Groups commands for execution in a subshell. The grouped commands execute before other commands.
{ }	Groups commands so that they execute before other commands.

- You can use only the letter a–z, A–Z, the numbers 0–9, and underscore (_).
- Avoid using the <space bar>, <Tab> and <Backspace> in filenames for practical reasons.
- Linux does not require the use of suffers called as extensions. Extension is the part of file name mostly of three characters after the period.
- Filenames begining with a period are called hidden files.

File Information

Each Linux file has the following information:

Information	Meaning
Location	Where is the file stored on the disk?
File type	What is the type of file?

Permissions	Who can access the file-owner, group members, or other users?
Number of Linux	How many names of the existing file?
Owner name	Name of the owner of the file.
Grouphone	Group's name of file.
Size	Size of files in bytes
Modification	Date and time of file when was last modified.
Filename	Name of the file.

Command to be given for the information about the file.

file

Determines and displays the type of files.

```
file [-zL] [-f file] file …
```

where the variables are:

- -f file: Reads the list of files to be checked from the specified file. These will be checked before checking files provided as arguments.
- -L: Causes symbolic links to be followed.
- -z: Attempts to look at the type of files inside compressed files.

File Structure

Linux uses the method of hierarchical file structure. The files which it uses are ordinary, directory, character and block device files. It is as said earlier, an upside-down tree structure with the root directory on the top. It can be followed by three types of directories:

System directory

These directories make the Linux system. All system directories have same files and system programs used to specify the features of Linux system.

Home directory

When user logs in system opens the home directory for user to create the number of files. System gives the same name to home directory as the user's log in name called as working directory of user.

User directory

User's home directory containing a number of directories created by user is called as users directory.

Standard Directory Structure

Directory	Purpose
/	The root directory. Stores essential start-up files and serves as the top-level directory for the entire directory structure. It is different from with/root.
/bin	Stratup programs and commands used in signle-user mode.
/boot	Files used to start the system.
/dev	Special files representing system devices and device drivers.
/etc	System-level configuration files and scripts.

/home	The user's home directories
/lib	Shared library files.
/mnt	The mount point for temporary file systems.
/opt	The installation directory for commercial software.
/proc	The virtual file system for kernal and process information.
/root	The home directory for the user. It is different from the root directory (/).
/sbin	Essential system utilities that are used for booting the system.
/tmp	The storage space for temporary files.
/usr	The storage space for files that need to be made available system wise, including user utilities and programs (/usr/bin); documentation (/usr/doc); libraries used by user-installed programs (/usr/lib); software installed by users (/usr/local); man pages (/usr/man); non-essential system administration utilities (/usr/sbin); and other shared items, such as fonts and icons (/usr/share).
/var	Data files of variable length, including spool directories for mail and printing.

Directory Names and Symbols

Example	Description
.	The current or working directory
..	The parent directory
-	The home directory of the current user
/	The root directory (not/root)
../directory	Refers to another directory of the same parent
/home/class/subject/chapter	The absolute path name.

Listing Displaying and Printing Files

Various commands which are used for listing files are: dir, is, and pwd. For displaying are: od, cat, more, comm, diff, tail, split, and less. For printing we use the commands lpr, and lpq. Details of the commands are as follows:

dir

Displays a listing of the files in a specified directory, in alphabetical order unless otherwise specified. By default, displays the contents of the current directory unless another directory is specified.

```
dir [-acCGlnrRStuU[ [-all] [—no-group] [—numeric-uid-gid] [—reverse] [—recursive]
      [file ...]
```

where the variables are:

-a/—all: Shows all entries, including those whose names start with *.*.

-c: Sorts by the creation time of the file and when displaying complete file information (with the –l flag), displays the creation time.

-C: Displays entries in column.

-G/—no-group: Prevents display of group information.

-l: displays files with long listing format.

-n/—nimeric-uid-gid: Lists user IDs and group IDs (UIDs and GIDs) instead of names.

-r/—reverse: Reverses order of entries when sorting.

-R/—recursive: Recursively lists contents of subdirectories.

-S: Sorts files by size.

-t: Sorts by the modification time of the file and when displaying complete file information (with the –l flag), displays the modification time.

-u: sorts by the last access time of the file and when displaying complete file information (with the –l flag), displays the last access time.

-U: Displays entries in their directory order rather than sorted.

pwd

Displays the name of the current directory.

```
pwd
```

Displays the full path name of the current directory. If you have forgotten which directory is current, type pwd and press Enter to see the directory's path name. pwd accepts no input. It has no options and displays a single line of output.

od

Writes filename to the standard output in octal and other formats. When no filename is specified, the utility accepts input from the standard input.

```
od [option] [filename]
```

Various options which can be used are:

Option	To do
–A	Use radix as the file offset. For radix, you can use d for decimal, o for octal, x for hexadecimal, or n for none.
–help	Show the available options.
–j n	Skip n bytes at the start of each file.
–N n	Do not process more than n bytes per file.
–s [n]	Output strings of n graphics characters.
-t type	Use the specified type of output format. The output formats are listed below.
–v, –output	Suppress use of asterisks to mark line suppression.
–w n, –width [=n]	Write n bytes per output line.

Output Types

Name	Description
a	Named character
c	ASCII character or backslash Escape
d [n]	Signed decimal with n bytes per integer
f [n]	Floating point with n bytes per integer
o [n]	Octal with n bytes per integer

u [n]	Unsigned decimal with n bytes per integer
x [n]	Hexadecimal with n bytes per integer.

less

Displays the specified filename on-screen and enables you to page through it easily. You can specify more than one filename in space-separated list or by using a shell pattern. If you omit the filename, the utility accepts input from the standard input.

```
less [option] [filename]
```

Various options which can be used are:

Option	To do
–?, –help	Displays available options.
+ command	Start less with command.
–a	Begin searches after the screen's last line.
–h n	Scroll back no more than n lines.
–I, –ignore-case	Ignore case in searches.
-I, -IGN, E-CASE	Ignore case in searches even when the search expression contains uppercase letters.
–j n	Jump to line number n. The first line of the screen is line 1.
–n, –line-numbers	Suppress the line numbers.
–N, –LINE NUMBERS	Display the line numbers.
–u, –undeline-special	Display back spaces and carriage returns as control characters.
–V, –version	Displays the version number of less.
–w, –hilite-unread	Highlight the first new line after scrolling.
–W, –HILITE-UNREAD	Highlight the first new line after any forward movement.
–x n, –tabs=n	Set tab stops every n spaces. The default is 8.
–y n, –max-f=n, w-scroll=n	Scroll forward no more than n lines.

lpr

Prints filename. Sends a file to the line printer.

```
lpr [option] filename
```

Various options which can be used are:

Option	To do
–# n	Prints n copies.
–C string	Print the specified string as the job classification on the burst page.
–h	Suppress the printing of the burst page.

lpq

Prints one or more files to the specified printer spool. If no files are indicated, then the standard input is sent to the printer spool. If no printer is specified, data will be sent to the default printer.

```
lpt [[-Pprinter] [-#number] [-C class] [-j job] [-I [numcols]] [-hlmrs] [file ...]
```

where the variables are:

-#number: Specifies the number of copies to print of each file. The default is one copy.

-C class: Prints the specified class name instead of the host name on the header page.

-h: Suppresses the printing of a header page.

-I [numcols]: Indicates that output should be indented by the number of blanks specified or by 8 characters if no number is indicated

-j job: Prints the specified job name instead of the filename on the header page.

-l: Allows control characters to be printed while suppressing page breaks.

-m: Sends an e-mail to the user when the print job is finished.

-Pprinter: Prints to the specified printer.

-r: Removes files after printing them.

-s: Creates a symbolic link to the file being printed rather than copying the file to the spool directory. This is useful when printing extremely large files.

Managing Directories

Commands for managing directories are: cd, mkdir, rmdir, mv and chmod.

mkdir

Creates one or more directories.

```
mkdir [-p] [-m mode] [—parents] [—mode=mode] directory ...
```

where the variables are:

-m/— mode mode: Sets the mode for the created directory using the same symbolic notation as the chmod command. If this is not specified, the default mode is assigned to the directory.

-p/—parents: Ensures that the parents of the specified directory exist and creates any missing parent directories needed.

rmdir

Deletes empty directories.

```
rmdir [-p] [—parents] directory ...
```

where the variables are:

-p/—parents: Removes the directory as well as all parents explicitly indicated on the command line as long as deleting the directory causes the parent to become empty.

chmod

Changes the access permissions of one or more files or directories.

```
chmod [-Rcfv] [—recursive] [—changes] [—silent] [—quiet] [—verbose] mode file ...
```

where the variables are:

-c/—changes: Displays the names of only those files whose permissions are being changed.

-f/—silent/—quiet: Suppresses display or error messages when a file's permissions cannot be changed.

-R/—recursive: Recursively changes the permissions of all files in all subdirectories of any directory that has its permissions changed.

-v/—verbose: Displays the results of all permission changes.

Modes can be specified in two ways: symbolically and numerically. When done symbolically, modes take the form [ugoa] [[+-=] [rwxXstugo …]. The first element ([ugoa]) represents the users whose permissions are being affected (u=user who owns the file or directory, g=all members of the group that owns the file or directory, o=anyone who is not the owner or in the owner group, a=all users).

The + symbol means that the specified modes should be added to already specified permissions, the – symbol means the specified modes should be removed from existing permissions and the = symbol means that the specified modes should replace existing permissions. There are many different permissions that can be specified in the third element of the mode, including r for read permissions, w for write permissions and x for execute permissions.

Full details of symbolic and numeric modes appear in the chmod man page.

File and Directory Operations

Various commands used for these operations are: find, cp, mv, rm, and ln.

find

Looks for files below specified paths that match all the criteria indicated by the command-line options and takes any action indicated by those options. If no paths are specified, the search takes place below the current directory.

```
find [path …] [options]
```

where the variables are:

-amin minutes: Looks for files last accessed the specified number of minutes ago.

-anewer file: Looks for files that were accessed more recently than the specified file was modified.

-atime days: Looks for files last accessed the specified number of 24-hour periods ago.

-cmin minutes: Looks for files whose status was last changed the specified number of minutes ago.

-cnewer file: Looks for files whose status was last changed more recently than the specified file was modified.

-ctime days: Looks for files whose status was changed the specified number of 24-hours period ago.

-empty: Looks for empty files or directories.

-exec command \;: Executes the specified command. The string () is replaced by the currently found filename and the command is repeated for each found filename.

-gid gid: Looks for files with the specified numeric GID.

-group group: Looks for files belonging to the named group.

-ilname pattern: Looks for symbolic links whose names match the specified pattern in a case-insensitive manner.

-iname pattern: Looks for files whose names match the specified pattern in a case-insensitive manner.

-ipath pattern: Looks for files whose path matches the specified pattern in a case-insensitive manner.

-lname pattern: Looks for symbolic links whose names match the specified pattern in a case-sensitive manner.

-maxdepth levels: Descends at most the specified numbers of levels below the specified paths.

-mindepth levels: Descends at least the specified numbers of levels below the specified paths.

-mmin minutes: Looks for files that were last modified the specified number of minutes ago.

-mount: Does not descend any directories that are on other file systems than the current one.

-mtime days: Looks for files that were last modified the specified number of 24-hours period previously.

-name pattern: Looks for files whose names match the specified pattern in a case-sensitive manner.

-newer file: Looks for files modified more recently than the specified file.

-nogroup: Looks for files whose numeric GID does not correspond to any existing group.

-nouser: Looks for files whose numeric UID does not correspond to any existing user.

-ok command \;: Executes the specified command for each file found after prompting the user. The string () is replaced by the currently replaced filename.

-path: Looks for files whose path matches the specified pattern in a case sensitive manner.

-perm mode: Looks for files whose permissions exactly match the specified mode. If +mode is used, then matches any of the specified permission bits; if –mode is used, then matches all of the specified permission bits.

-print: Prints the full filename of all found files.

-regex pattern: Looks for files whose names match the specified regular expression.

-size size[bckw]: Looks for files the specified size in the specified units. Units include b(512-byte blocks), c (bytes), k (kilobytes) and w (2-byte words).

-type type: Looks for files that match the specified type. Types include d (directories), f (regular files) and l (symbolic links).

-uid uid: Looks for files with the specified UID.

-user username: Looks for files owned by the specified username of UID.

When providing numeric time information such as minutes days, normally the match must be exact. Preceding the number with a + matches any value greater than the specified number and preceding a value with a – matches any value less than the number.

cp

Copies files and directories.

```
cp [-a] [-archive] [-b] [—backup] [-d] [—no-dereference] [-f] [—force] [-i]
     [—interactive] [l]
 [—link] [-p] [—preserve] [-r] [—recursive] [-s]
 [—symbolic-link] [-u] [—update] source destination
```

where the variables are:

cp [optional] source ...... destination

-a/—archive: Copies files and directories recursively, maintaining symbolic links and preserving ownership and permissions of the original files. This is the same as –dpR.

-b/—backup: Makes backup copies of files before the original files are overwritten.

-d/—no-dereference: Copies links as links rather than copying the files to which the links point.

-f/—force: Forces removal or existing destination files that need to be overwritten.

-i/—interactive: Prompts before overwriting existing destination files.

l/—link: Makes hard links instead of copying files. This applies only to files, not to directories.

-p/—preserve: Preserves the ownership and permission of the original files.

-r/—recursive: Recursively copies directories. That is, for every source directory specified, every file in the directory and all its subdirectories are copied while retaining the matching directory structure.

-s/—symbolic-link: Makes symbolic links instead of copying files. Source files must be specified with full paths.

-u/—update: replaces only those destination files that have older modification times than the corresponding source files.

Care needs to be taken with the –f flat when working as the root user. Making a mistake can cause important system files to be overwritten because the root user generally has write permission for all files and directories.

mv

(Refer to the command reference given at page 166)

rm

Deletes one or more files or directories.

```
rm [firR] [–force] [–interactive] [–recursive] field|directory...
```

where the variables are:

-f/—force: Does not prompt the user for permission to delete files. This is dangerous if used as the root user.

-i/—interactive: Always prompts the user before deleting each file.

-r/R/—recursive: Recursively removes the content of directories.

ln

Makes links between files. When the last argument is a directory, then each of the other source files specified is linked into a file with the same name in the specified directory.

```
ln [bis] [–backup] [–interactive] [–symbolic] source [destination]
  ln [-bis] [–backup] [–interactive] [–symbolic] source ...directory
```

where the variables are:

-b/—backup: Makes the backups of files that are being removed.

-i/—interactive: Prompts when it is necessary to remove a destination file.

-s/—symbolic: Makes symbolic links instead of hard links.

Vi Editor

The Visual Editor (Vi) is an utility for Linux. It has the following features:

1. It is a huge complex program with many commands designed for specialized purposes.
2. The multiple actions can be redone and undone.
3. It has a powerful feature called as 'command history' feature, that means you can not only repeat the last given command but also repeat all previous commands in the current session.

4. It has a 'substitution' feature which is more readable and friendly.
5. It can handle multiple files and buffers.
6. With this, you can split the screen into multiple windows. Each window may be empty or contain a file.
7. With this you can move and copy mutiple text section. A block of text is called as region.

Basic Commands of Vi Editor

Getting Help

:help or F1	Get help with vi commands
Ctrl +]	Go to a tagged subject
Ctrl + t	Go back after jumping to a tagged subject

Scrolling

Ctrl + e or down arrow	Move down one line
Left arrow or h	Move left one character
b	Move left one word
Right arrow or l	Move right one character
w	Move right one word
Home	Move top the beginning of the line
End	Move to the end of the line
Ctrl + y or up arrow or k	Move up one line
z or Ctrl + L	Redraw the screen with the current line at the top of the window
Ctrl + f	Scroll down one page
Ctrl _ d or PgDn	Scroll down one window
Ctrl + u or PgUp	Scroll up one-half window
Ctrl + b	Scroll up one page

Working with Files

:w >> filename	Append to the specified filename
:qall	Close all buffers and exit vi
:q	Close the current buffer and exit vi if no other buffers exist
:e filename	Open the specified filename
:x	Save the current file only if changes have been made and exit
·wq	Save the current file and exit
:x filename	Save the current file to the specified filename only if changes have been made and exit
:w	Save to the current file
:w filename	Save to the specified filename
:n	Edit the next file when two or more files are open

Working with Windows

:sp	Split the screen into two windows
Ctrl _ w, q	Close the current window
Ctrl + w, k	Move to the window above
Ctrl + w, j	Move to the window below
Ctrl + w, =	Make all windows equal height
Ctrl + w, –	Decrease the current window height
Ctrl + w, +	Increase the current window height

Working with Buffers

:buffers	Show all buffers
:bunload buffer	Remove the specified buffer from the memory
:buffer buffer	Go to the specified buffer
:bnext	Go to the next buffer
:bprevious	Go to the previous buffer

Vi Editing Commands

Various commands for editing are:

Starting the Insert Mode

a	Append text after the cursor
A	Append text at the end of the current line
i	Insert text before the cursor
I	Insert text at the beginning of the line
o	Open a line below the current line
O	Open a line above the current line
R	Begin overwriting the text at the cursor
s	Substitute a character
S	Substitute a line
Esc	Exit insert mode

Deleting Text in Insert Mode

Backspace	Delete the previous character
Delete	Delete the current character

Changing Text

cw	Change the current word
cc	Change the current line
p	Insert the last deleted text before the cursor

P	Insert the last deleted text after the cursor
r character	Replace the current character with character
R string	Replace the string beginning at the cursor
s	Substitute the current character
S	Substitute the entire line
–	Change the case of the selected character

Copying and Deleting Text to Buffers

"register name	Create a register named register name (use one character only) to store the next delete or copy operation
Y	Copy the current line into the current register
:reg register name	Show the contents of all the specified registers
:reg	Show the contents of all registers
"register name Y	Delete the current line into register name

Pasting Text

p	Insert the contents of the current register after the cursor
P	Insert the contents of the current register before the cursor
"register name p	Insert the contents of the specified register name after the cursor

Undoing Editing Changes

u	Undo the last change
U	Restore the current change

Redoing Editing Changes

[Ctrl-r]	Repeat the last change

Deleting Text

dd	Delete the current line
D	Delete the remainder of the line
dw	Delete the current word
D}	Delete up to the next paragraph
d^	Delete back to the beginning of the line
d/string	Delete up the next occurrence of the specified string
df pattern	Delete up and including the specified pattern on the current line
dL	Delete up to the last line on the screen
dG	Delete to the end of the file
x	Delete the current character
X	Delete the previous character

Searching for Text

/ string	Search forward for the specified string
? string	Search backward for the specified string
/	Repeat the forward search
?	Repeat the backward search

Advanced Vi Editing Commands

Various commands for editing are:

Command	**Function**
<n> u	Undo the last n number of editing actions
<n> [ctl-r]	Redo the last n number of editing actions
: s	Repeats the last substitution on the current line
: and press up arrow key repeatedly	To recall all previous last line mode commands and select one of the command and press Enter
/and press up arrow key	Same as above function
: r file 1	Reads the file 1 below the current line
: r! date	Reads output of date command after current line
: e file2	Stops editing current file and changes file2
: e! file2	Abandoning changes made to current file and edits the file2.
: e!	Last saved edition of current file is loaded.
: e#	Returns to most recently edited file
ctrl-^	Same as above command.

Commands of Vi with Multiple File Names

: n	Edits next file
: rew	Rewind the file list to start from beginning, i.e., very first file of the file list
: sp	Splits existing windows in two
: new	New blank window is opened
[ctrl-w] [ctrl-w]	To move between two windows
[ctrl-w] +	Increase size of current window
[ctrl-w] –	Reduces size of current window
: on	Removes all other windows except current window
: q	Quit editing from the current window & close it
: qa	Quit from all windows without saving
: xa	Save all windows and quit

Line Editing Commands

Various commands for line editing are:

Keyboard shortcut	To do this
w	Saves file
x filename	Inserts file text
q	Quits editor
q!	Quits without saving
d	Deletes a line or set of lines
mN	Moves a line or set of lines by copying them and then inserting them after line N
coN	Copies a line or set of lines by copying them, and then inserting the copied text after line N
N	Indicates the line number
N, N	Two numbers separated by a comma indicate a range of lines
N-N	Two numbers separated by a dash indicate a range of lines
–N	The minus sign (–) preceding a number offsets to a line before the current line
+N	The plus sign (+) preceding a number offsets to a line after the current line
$	The dollar sign symbol ($) indicates the last line
/string/	Searches forward for the line containing that string
? string ?	A search for the string
g/string/	A set of lines can be searched by a repeated string reference; all lines with a string in it are referenced
.	Matches on any one possible character
*	Matches on repeated characters in a string
[ ]	Matches on classes of characters, a set of characters, in the string
^	Refers to the beginning of a line
/ <	Refers to the start of a word
> /	Refers to the end of a word
s/string/replacement string/	Searches string on a line and replaces it with replacement string
s/string/replacement string/g	Replaces all instances of a string on a line with the replacement string
1, $ s/string/replacement string/g	Replaces all instances of a string in the file with the replacement string

Options in Vi

Various options in Vi are:

Use this option	To do this
+n	Position the cursor on line n
+/pattern	Postition the cursor at the first instance of the specified pattern
–b	Edit the file in binary code
–C	Start editor in vi compatibility mode

-g	Start editor in the GUI mode, if this was enabled when the program was compiled
–m	Prevent modifications to files
–n	Operate without creating a swap file. This makes recovery impossible in case of a system failure during editing
–o [n]	Open one window for each of the specified filenames, or open n windows if n is included
–R	Displays files in read-only mode
–r	To salvage unsaved work lost in a system crash

Abbreviations which can be used instead of the full options. They are listed here.

Abbreviation	**Option**	**Function**
nu	number	Displays line numbers on the screen
no nu	no number	Does not display any line number on the screen
-	all	Displays the settings of all the options
–	show mode	Displays the mode, vi is currently in. Such as INPUT MODE, APPEND MODE, REPLACE MODE, CHAR MODE and so on
sm	showmatch	Shows momentarily the matching bracket to a) and }
ic	ignore case	searches ignore case, (uppercase or lowercase characters) in making matches
–	noignorcase	Ignore case option turns 'off'
ai	auto indent	Automatically indent a new line
aw	auto write	Current file is automatically saved before moving to next one, i.e., switching files in vi editor with : n or [ctrl-^]
–	magic	When searching for strings the characters of regular expression set as special
ts	tab stop	Sets tab on screen
ws	wrapscan	Entire file is scanned for searching the specified string
wm	wrapmargin	Automatically start a new line at a specifed margin.

System Administration

System administration of Linux is very strong. It allows you to work on multiuser environment. It allows all users to share commands, programs, etc. These operations come under System Administration. Various functions of a system administrator are:

1. Changing system states.
2. Add and configure hardware such as terminals, printers, etc.
3. Mounting a file system.
4. Create and Restore system back ups.
5. Switching to super user.
6. Manage two or more operating systems on your system.

7. Keeping a system log.
8. Administration tasks such as add, modify, remove and lock the user accounts.
9. System security maintenance.
10. Maintenance and installation of software packages.
11. Starting and shutting down the systems.

System Management

To accomplish the administrative tasks of the system, every Linux system must have a super user. He has the super powers as far as the system is concerned. He can access to all commands and files. He has all the privileges. He has to manage the security, add or remove the users, create and restore the system backups, schedule the tasks, manage files and directories.

To become a superuser, log into the root user account. Type root at login prompt and enter correct password. Linux provides a shell to superuser to enter administrative commands.

login : root [Enter]

password : [Enter correct password]

a shell prompt appears

System Tasks

Various commands used by the system administrator are: login, logout, rlogin, shutdown.

login

Log into the system.

```
login username
```

The command prompts the user to supply a username and password and establishes a new user session on the current terminal. In addition, the command checks to see whether the user has received a new mail, starts the shell specified for this user in the /etc/passwd file (the default shell is bash), and executes startup shell scripts associated with the user's account.

logout

Exit the current session and displays login. This command should be used in text mode sessions only.

```
logout
```

rlogin

Logs in to a remote host.

```
rlogin [-Kx] [-l username] host
```

where the variables are:

-K: Turns off all Kerberos authentication.

-l username: Indicates that the connection should be logged in under the specified username rather than the user running rlogin.

-x: Turns on DES encryption for all data sent while logged in to the remote system.

shutdown

Shuts down the system, stopping logins and possibly delaying before shutting down and issuing an optional warning message. When a time is specified, the shutdown will occur at the specified time; otherwise it occurs immediately.

```
shutdown [-rkhc] time [warning]
```

where the variables are:

-c: Cancels a running shutdown.

-h: Halts after shutting down.

-k: Sends the warning message but doesn't actually shut down the system.

-r: Reboots after shutting down.

The time can be specified as an absolute time in the form HH:MM or as a number of minutes to wait before shutting down in the form +minutes.

Changing System States

After the boot process begins, a script called init starts automatically which is responsible for changing the system states. init script refers the inittab table to change the states. This inittab table remains in a configuration file /etc/inittab ready by init script. Each state is also called as run level that determines whether the Linux system is in single user mode or multiuser mode and whether the linux system starts with X windows system automatically or user defined, the init program exits in one state at a time. The states or runlevel defined as S or s, 0, 1, 2, 3, 4, 5, 6.

The run levels are defined here.

Run level	Description
S or s	Single user with no background running tasks
0	Halts the system
1	Single user mode (useful for troubleshooting and with background running tasks)
2	Multi-user system (console mode) without Network File System (NFS) support
3	Full multi-user console mode (text only), i.e., Network multiusers
4	User defined
5	Starts X Window System automatically or unused
6	Reboots or immediate shut down

Setting the System Date and Time

date command is used to set the date and time. In Linux user can use Linuxconf or the control panel to set the system date and time. Whenever the system clock is set an entry is made in the \etc\wtmp.

date

Displays or sets the current system date and time.

```
date [-u] [—universal] [MMDDhhmm[CC]YY] [.ss]]
```

where the variables are:

-u/—universal: Displays the time in Greenwich Mean Time (also known as Coordinated Universal Time).

If a date and time are provided as an argument, this is done entirely with numbers where the two-digit elements shown previously represent the following values:

MM:	month
DD:	day of the month
hh:	hour
mm:	minute
CC:	century (first two digits of the year)
YY:	last two digits of the year
ss:	seconds

Keep in mind that only the root user can set the system clock.

Scheduling Automated Processes

To schedule processes run at a certain time or time interval cron utility is used. In most of the versions of Linux it is given by default. System administrator or super user or root user can schedule jobs by giving an instruction. This instruction makes an entry of scheduled job in crontab file. Instructions given by super user have six fields:

Field	Description
1	Minute (0 to 59)
2	Hour (0 to 23)
3	Day of the month (1 to 31)
4	Month (1 to 12 or the first three letters of the month's name)
5	Day (0 to 6, with 0 referring to Sunday, or the first three letters of the day's name)
6	Command to execute at the specified time

Crontab is used as following:

```
crontab [option] [filename]
```

This launches the default text editor with which you can create or edit the user's cron settings. Filename here is an argument.

Installation of a Software Package

Before installing any software, you must check whether your computer hardware is going to support it or not. So before we read about the actual installing, we must know what all is needed both in terms of Hardware and Software for installing Linux.

Hardware Requirements

For an ideal Linux based PC your computer must have the following:

- An IBM Compatible PC with minimum 80386. 80486 is better.
- Any processor from Intel, Sparc, Alpha or AMD
- Minimum 128 MB RAM
- Minimum 2 GB free hard disk space
- Input devices such as keyboard, mouse, etc.
- Controller cards such as SCSI, IDE, etc.
- A Network card such as ISA, PCI or USB etc.

• Sound card compatible to LINUX

Software Requirements

• A partitioning program such as fdisk or disk druid supplied by Red Hat.

• Linux Software package.

Steps before Installation

First you must create an installation disk.

Creating an installation disk

For this do the following:

1. Copy the file **boot.img** from the Red Hat CD-ROM disk to a floppy disk. This file can be found in the / images directory of the CD. The file can be created using either the DOS rewrite command (in a DOS/ Windows system) or the Linux dd command (in an existing LINUX or UNIX system). For example, to create an installation diskette using the dd command, do the following:

(a) Insert and amount the CD-ROM and then insert a blank floppy into the floppy drive of you computer.

(b) Now give the following command

```
# dd if = mnt/cdrom/images/boot.img of = /dev/fd0 bs = 1440k
```

and then press Enter

The above command will copy from the input file ("if) mnt/cdrom/boot.img onto the output file ("of") / dev/fd0. It is assumed that floppy drive is accessible from /dev/fd0. To create an installation diskette using the rewrite program, give the following command. (it is assumed that CD-ROM is accessible as drive D):

```
D:>cd images dousutils\rawrite enter
```

For the source file enter "D:\boot.img" and for destination enter "A:".

The bootable installation disk is now ready and you can use it to install your LINUX system.

Red Hat LINUX can also be installed by booting using any of the following methods using :

- a floppy diskette
- CD-ROM
- hard drive partition to hold the installation software
- DOS command line
- a network using HTTP or FTP protocols.
- an NFS (Network File System) mounted hard drive.

2. This is the most important step, partitioning. For this you must have some knowledge of the hardware. For this you have to look into the following:

- Disk space, required now and may be in future
- Requirement of any other operating system
- Installation of applications software, now and in future
- Data back up needs
- Number of users

3. Refer to the step above, where if you have opted for one or more operating system besides Linux, then step becomes compulsory. All you have to do is to select a boot loader. It is a software that is responsible for booting LINUX along with any other operating system. It can be either LILO (LINUX Loader) or GRUB (Grand Unified Boot loader). Here you must know whether the version of operating system is compatible with the current version of Linux.
4. Now insert the floppy disk (the installation diskette you have created if you are using floppy to boot your system) into a floppy drive and power-on your system. After a few moments, the Red Hat installation program screen will appear.
5. Follow the steps as directed on the screen.

Managing Users

System administrator while performing the tasks mentioned earlier has to perform the following jobs too: Such as add, modify, remove and lock the user accounts. Add modify and remove the group users too. Before logging a user, the system administrator must create an account for the user.

Adding a New User

1. Password file (/etc/password) must be updated. Password file holds the password for the user's account.
2. Group file (/etc/group) must be updated. It holds the group to which the user belongs.
3. The super user must login as a root and add a new account to the password file.
4. A home directory (\home) must be created for the new user, /home contains the location of the user's own home directory.
5. Provide the working environment for the new user. For this, the new account must be provided with shell startup files. These shell start up files (.bash-profile for boune again shell or ..cshrc for tc shell) are held by /etc/skel directory. /etc/shells holds the login shells.

Removing a User Account

System administrator can remove a user account from the system. Actually user account is not deleted, it is deactivated. To remove a user account the following points should be kept in mind:

1. Check whether the user's account has to be removed or not.
2. User's files should be archive.
3. Remove the user's account name from group file (/etc/group), password file /etc/passwd and message file /etc/spool/mail).
4. Removes the user's account home directory with the rmdir command.
5. Now check whether all the user's files have to be removed or not.

To Modify a User Account

To modify a user account usermod command should be used. To modify the permissions and ownership of user's account chmod and chown commands are used.

1. chmod
2. chown

Installing and Managing Devices

Every operating system allows you to install and manage various devices attached to the computer. It is more so since Linux is a multi-user, can support these devices for all the users.

To install a device you need to know the basics

Device file that contains all the information about the specified device. This information used by operating system to tell the device what task is to be performed and how.

Configuration tool that is needed to configure the device on your system. This configuration tool can be provided by Linux conf software or gnome control center.

Kernel support which is necessary for the device to provide the interface between user and system. In most Linux distributions, kernel support is in-built. Otherwise a module can be loaded.

Commands to install and manage the devices are given below:

To create a device file mknod command is used.

mknod

Creates a special file with the specified name and type, where type is p (FIFO), b (block special file), or c (character special file). When this command is used to create a block or character special file, the major and minor device numbers must be supplied. This command is used by system administrators when the system is first set up.

```
mknod (option) name type
```

To manage the printer lpr, lpq, pprm and lpd commands are used. These commands have been discussed earlier.

To install the modules you use the commands: Install, rpm, and make. rpm has been discussed earlier. The other two are given here.

install

Copies the source file to a destination file, or multiple source files to a destination directory, and enables you to specify permissions and ownership.

```
install [option] [source] [destination]
```

Various options used for the command are:

Option	Use
–b, –backup	Make a backup copy of existing destination files that will be deleted by the copying operation.
–d, –directory	Creates needed directories and subdirectories when copying and set the file permissions and ownership to the specified settings or to the default settings.
–h, –help	Display the available options
–g group name	Set the group ownership of the copied files and directories to the specified group name.
–group = group name	You can use the group name or a numeric group ID.
–o owner name	Set the file ownership of the copied files and directories to the specified owner name.
–owner=owner name	You can use the owner name or a numeric owner ID.
–m mode, –mode=mode	Set the permissions of the copied files and directories to the specified mode. You can use octal number or symbolic mode specifications. The default mode is 0755.

make

Compiles a program from source code following the instructions in the specified target. If you omit the target, the command looks for a file named Make.

```
make [option] [source] [destination]
```

To install programs provided in source code form, you can usually complete the installation by using the following instructions:

1. Use the tar utility to extract the files from the source code archive.
2. Switch to the directory that tar created when it extracted the files.
3. Type ./configure and press Enter.
4. Type make and press Enter.
5. Switch to the root user by typing su and pressing Enter.
6. Type make install and press Enter.

Various options used for the command are:

Option	Use
–C directory	Change to the specified directory before reading the make file or undertaking any other actions.
–d	Display debugging information in addition to the usual messages.
–e	If possible, use the current environmental variables rather than those specified in the make file.
–f filename	Use the specified filename as a make file
–i	Ignore errors generated by utilities launched by the make file and continue processing the make file
–I directory	Search the specified directory for including make files.
–j n	Run n jobs simultaneously.
–k	If possible, continue after an error.
–l n	Delay new jobs if the load average exceeds the specified load level (n).
–n	Display but do not execute the commands that would be executed.
–p	Display the rules and variable rules and then execute them.
–q	Check to see whether the targets are up to date, if so exit without making changes
–r	Ignore the built-in implicit rules
–s	Hide program messages
–t	Make the target files as up-to-date without actually altering them.
–v	Display the version number and continue processing

Floppy Disk Management

For managing the floppy you use the commands kuje fdformat and dd.

fdformat

Formats the floppy disk contained in the specified device. fd is used for floppy disk. /devv/fdn block device file consist the drive dependent driver for floppy driven that automatically detects media format and capacity where h = 0 to j, i.e., fd0 fd1 etc.

```
fdformat [option] device
```

Various options which can be used for formatting different types of floppies are:

Device name	Type of disk to be formatted
/dev/fd-D720	Double density, 3.5 inch disk (720K) in drive fd0
/dev/fd0H1440	High-density, 3.5 inch disk (1440K) in drive fd0
/dev/fd0E2880	Extra-density, 3.5 inch disk (2880K) in drive fd0
/devv/fd1D720	Double density, 3.5 inch disk (720K) in drive fd1
/dev/fd1H1440	High-density, 3.5 inch disk (1440K) in drive fd1
/dev/fd1E2880	Extra-density, 3.5 inch disk (2880K) in drive fd1

dd

Copy a file with the conversions specified by one or more options. Use it to specify the input file, and of to specify the output file. To specify block sizes with options that require them, you can use the abbreviations shown in the Block Sizes table, note that the equals signs are mandatory. You can use this utility to create an emergency boot disk.

```
dd [option]
```

Various options which can be used are:

Option	Use
–bs=n	Force the input and output bit streams to read or write n bytes at a time.
cbs=n	Convert n bytes at a time
conv=keywords	Convert the file using the specified keywords expressed in a comma-separated list.
count=n	Copy only n input blocks
–help	Show the available options
ibs=n	Read n bytes at a time
if=filename	Use the specified filename as the input file
obs=n	Write n bytes at a time
of=filename	Use the specified filename as the output file
seek=n	Skip n blocks at the start of output. Use obs to specify the block size
skip=n	Skip n blocks at the start of input. Use ibs to specify the block size
–version	Show the version number.

Block Sizes

Abbreviation	Block size
c	1 byte

w	2 bytes
b	512 bytes
kD	1,000 bytes
k	1,024 bytes
MD	1,000,000 bytes
M	1,048,576 bytes
GD	1,000,000,000 bytes
G	1,097,741,824 bytes

Keywords

Keyword	Use
ascii	Convert from EBCDIC to ASCII
block	Pad neline-terminated records with spaces up to the block size specified by cbs.
ebcdic	Convert from ASCII to alternated EDCDIC
ibm	Convert from ASCII to alternated EBCDIC
lcase	Convert uppercase characters to lowercase
noerror	Continue processing even if an error is generated
notrunc	Skip truncating the output file
ucase	Convert lowercase characters to uppercase characters

File System Administration

File system can be studied under four heads: Boot block, Super block, Inode list and Data area.

Boot block: It contains the Linux kernal and the boot program.

Super block: It contains the general information about the file system.

Inode list: Each file system has fixed number of inodes. Inode list contains the information about which inode is allocated to files or which inode is free.

Data area: It contains the blocks of data in each file or directory.

Various tasks to be preformed by the file system administrator are:

Creating Additional File System

For this the commands used are: mkfs, mde2fs, and hformat. Out of this the command hformat is discussed here, the others have been listed earlier.

hformat

This command is used for formatting. But to use this, you must use the low level formatting command called fdformat first.

Accessing the File System

File system can be accessed by mounting the file system. Mounting means attaching the file system to a specified directory. If you want to access the files from the floppy disk, firstly you have to mount the file system from floppy disk to hard disk of the system. To mount a floppy disk you use the comand umount and mount are used.

umount

Unmount a mounted file system. The file system is specified by either its device name, its directory name or its network path.

```
umount -r device|directory|path …
```

where the variables are:

-r: If unmounted fails, tries to remount the file system in read-only mode.

mount

Mounts a file system to a specified directory.

```
mount -a [-rw] [-t vgstype]
mount [-rw [-o options [,….]] device] dir
mount [-rw] [-t vfstype] [-options] device dir
```

where the variables are:

-a: Mounts all file systems in /etc/fstab. If a type is specified with –t, then only the file systems in /etc/fstab of the specified type will be loaded.

-o: See Note below.

-r: Mounts the file system in read-only mode. This is the same as –o ro.

-t fstype: Indicates the file system type.

-w: Mounts the file system in read-write mode. This is the same as –o rw.

Possible file system types of the –t flag include.

Minix	vfat	ufs
ext	proc	romfs
ext2	nfs	sysv
xiafs	iso9660	xenix
hpfs	smbfs	coherent
msdos	ncpfs	
umsdos	affs	

For a list of options for the –o flag, consult the mount man page, which provides detailed descriptions of the various options available.

Checking the File System

A file system may be damaged while mounting due to hardware failure, human error or program interrupts. Therefore, the system administrator can check the file system's damage and repair it by using fsck and e2fock commands.

fsck

Performs an anlaysis of the specified device and optionally repairs errors. This command is essentially a front end to other utilities, such as e2fsck, that performs the analysis and repairs on the specified type of file system. Never run fsck on a mounted file system. Unmount the file system first.

```
fsck [option] [-t type] [-a] [-r] device
```

Various options which can be used are:

Option	Use
–a	Repair the file system automatically. This option is the same as –p.
–A	Check all file systems listed in /etc/fstab if possible.
–C	Display progress bars if possible.
–N	Show the actions that would be performed without actually executing them.
–r	Repair the file system interactively.
–R	Skip the root file system, which may be mounted as read and written.
–t type	Specify the type of file system. Available types are listed in /proc/filesystems.
–V	Display messages.

e2fsck

Checks the state of a Linux second extended file system. This is the default file system used for Linux partitions.

```
e2fsck [-cfnpy] [-B blocksize] device
```

where the variables are:

-B blocksize: Specifies a specific block size to use in searching for the superblock. By default, the program will search at various different block sizes until it finds the superblock.

-c: Causes the bad blocks program to be run and marks any bad blocks accordingly.

-f: Forces checking of the system that outwardly seem clean.

-n: Opens the file system in read-only state and answers "no" to all prompts to take action.

-p: Forces automatic repairing without prompts.

-y: Assumes an answer of "yes" to all questions.

The device to be checked should be specified using the complete Linux device path, such as /dev/hdal or /dev/sdb3. It is advisable that the file system must not be mounted or, if you need to check the root the file system or a file system that must be mounted, that this be done in single-user mode.

Managing the Disk Space

Linux provides the df (disk free), du (disk used) commands to the system administrator to manage the disk space.

df

Displays free space on one or more mounted disks or partitions. If no files (or directories) are specified, then the free space on all mounted file systems is displayed. If filenames are specified, then the free space for the file system containing each file is displayed.

```
df [-T] [-t fstype] [-x fstype] [—all] [—inodes] [—type=fstyle] [—exclude-
        type=fstype] [—print-type] [filename ...]
```

where the variables are:

-t/— type=fstype: Displays information only for life systems of the specified type.

-T/—print-type: Displays the file system type for each file system reported.

-x/—exclude-type=fstype: Does not report information for life systems of the specified type.

du

displays a report of disk space usage for each specified file or directory as well as all subdirectories or specified directories. By default, displays information for all files and directories in the current directory.

```
du [-abcksx] [-all] [-bytes] [-total] [-kilobytes] [-summarize] [-one-file-
        system] [-file ...]
```

where the variables are:

-a/—all: Displays usage information for files and directories.

-b/—bytes: Displays usage information in bytes.

-c/—total: Displays a total usage figure for all.

-k/—kilobyte: Displays usage information in kilobytes.

-s/—summarize: Displays a total for each argument and does not displays individual information for each file or subdirectory inside a directory.

-x/—one-file-system: Skips directories that are not part of the current file system.

Compressing and Decompressing Files

Linux like any other operating system supports the compressing utilities like zip and unzip.

zip

Creates a ZIP archive from one or more files and directories.

```
zip [-effgmrSu@] [zipfile [file1 file2 ...]]
```

where the variables are:

@: Accepts the list of files to be archived from the standard input.

-e: Encrupts the archive after prompting for a password. The password will be necessary to extract files from the archive.

-f: Replaces entries in an existing archive only if the file is newer than the file currently in the archive.

-F: Tries to fix a damaged archive.

-g: Adds files to an existing archive.

-m: Moves files into the archive, deleting them from their original location once they are in the archive.

-r: Recursively works with directories, adding all files in subdirectories to the archive.

-S: Includes system and hidden files in the archive.

-u: Replaces entries in an existing archive if a file is newer than the file currently in the archive or of the file that does not already exist in the archive.

The zip command offers many other options that have subtle, sometimes useful, impact on the behaviour of the program.

unzip

Manipulates and extracts ZIP archives.

```
unzip [-cflptuz] [-d exdir] file[.zip]
```

where the variables are:

-c: Extracts files to the standard output, printing the name of each file as it is extracted.

-d exdir: Uncompresses the archive to the specified directory instead of the current directory.

-f: Extracts only those files that are newer than already-existing versions of the files.

-l: Displays the contents of the archive without extracting.

-p: Extracts files to the standard output without sending any other data such as filenames.

-t: Tests the integrity of files in the archive.

-u: Extracts files that are newer than already-existing versions of files as well as files that do not already exist in the extract directory.

-z: Displays the archive comment.

This is a powerful program that supports many modifiers.

gzip

Compresses file using Lempel-Ziv encoding. The resulting file generally replaces the original, uncompressed file and will have a .gz extension.

gzip [-cdflrt] [—decompress] [—uncompress] [—stdout] [—to-stdout] [—force] [—list] [—recursivel] [—test] [name ...]

where the variables are:

-c/—stdout/—to-stdout: Writes output to standard output, keeping original file unchanged. By default, gzip replaces the original, uncompressed files with the compressed versions of the files.

-d/—decompress/—uncompress: Decompress the specified files, like gunzip, rather than compressing them.

-f/—force: Forces compression even then a corresponding file already exists and will be overwritten by the compressed file.

-l/—list: Lists files in a compressed file.

-r/—recursive: Compressed recursively, descending the directory structure and compressing all files in subdirectories of directories named on the named line as arguments.

-t/—test: Test the integrity of compressed files.

gunzip

Decompresses file compressed with the gzip command (as well as the compress command and the zip command).

gunzip [-cflrt] [—stdout] [—to-stdout] [—force] [—list] [—recursive] [—test] [name ...]

where the variables are:

-c/—stdout/—to-stdout: Writes output to standard output, keeping original file unchanged. By default, gunzip replaces the original compressed files with the uncompressed versions of the files.

-f/—force: Forces decompression even when a corresponding file already exists and will be overwritten by the decompressed file.

-l/—list: List files in the compressed file without decompressing.

-f/—recursive: Decompresses recursively, descending the directory structure and decompressing all files in subdirectories of directories named on the command line as arguments.

-t/—test: Tests the integrity of compressed files.

Backups

A backup is a copy of the filesystem on the storage media such as Floppy disk or CD ROM. A backup of all the files on the system on the storage media is called as a full backup. Partial backup do not save all files. It saves the particular files based on some conditions. Therefore, on the base of partial backup and full backup some levels are decided in Linux. This Backup level shows that information is backed up. Level iies from 0 to 3.

Level 0 indicates the full backup.

Level 1-3 indicates the partial backup, i.e., save those files that have been changed since the last lower backup.

Various levels have the following meanings:

Levels	Meaning
0	Backups every file in the file system
1	Backups the all changes since 1 day
2	Backups the all changes since 2 days

Various commands used in backup are:

tar

Creates an archive file of one or more files or directories.

```
tar [-crtuxz] [-f tarfile] [—file tarfile] [—create] [—delete] [—preserve] [—append] [—same-owner] [—list] [—update] [—extract] [—get] [—gzip] [—gunzip] [file|directory ...]
```

where the variables are:

-c/—create: Creates a new archive.

—delete: Deletes files from an existing archive.

-f tarfile/—file tarfile: Specifies the name of the archive file being created or read from.

—preserve: Keeps permissions and order of files the same in the archive.

-r/—append: Adds file to an existing archive.

—same-owner: Signifies that extracted files keep their original owners.

-t/—list: Displays a list of an archive's contents.

-u/—update: Only adds files to an existing archive that are newer than the copy in the archive.

-x/—extract/—get: Extracts files from an existing archive.

-z/—gzip/—ungzip: Filters the archive through gzip when archiving and unarchiving.

cpio

Creates archives or extracts files from archives; an aditional mode copies files from one directory tree to another. In contrast to tar, this command uses the standard input and standard output by default; therefore, you must use a file or pipe to provide the program with a list of filenames to work with. Use output redirection to specify where the output should go.

```
cpio -o [option] [<name list>] [>archive]
cpio -l [option] [shell pattern] [<archive]
cpio -p [option] directory < name-list
```

Various options which can be used are:

Option	Use
–A, –append	Append to an existing archive that is a disk file. Use with –O.
–, –make-directories	Create needed directories.
–f, –nonmatching	Copy only those files that do not match any of the specified patterns.
–F, filename, –file=filename	Use the specified filename as the archive.
–I, –extract	Use the copy-in mode
–I filename	Use the specified filename instead of the standard input.
–M string, –message=string	When the end of a media volume is reached, display string to prompt the user to insert the next volume.
–n, –numeric-uid-gid	Show the user and group ownership using numeric IDs.
–no-absolute-filenames	Create all files in the working directory, even if the filenames contain path information
–o, –create	Use the copy-cut mode
–O filename	Use the specified filename instead of the standard output
–quiet	Do not display messages
–r, –rename	Rename files interactively.

SUMMARY

1. System software is a must for every computer.
2. Computer software, is a set of programs, which enables a computer to perform specific tasks.
3. Computer software systems divide software systems into three major classes: System software, Programming software and Application software.
4. Programming software usually provides tools to assist a programmer in writing computer programs.
5. Application software allows users to accomplish one or more specific (non-computer related) tasks.
6. A compiler is a computer program that translates text written in a computer language into another computer language called the target language, or the language understood by the computer.
7. Compiling involves performing lots of work and early computers did not have enough memory to contain one program that did all of this work.
8. Splitting a compiler up into small programs is a technique used by researchers interested in producing provably correct compilers.
9. Many people divide higher-level programming languages into compiled languages and interpreted languages.
10. Typically a modern assembler creates object code by translating assembly instruction mnemonics into opcodes.
11. Loader is the part of an operating system that is responsible for loading programs from executables into memory.
12. A linker or link editor is a program that takes one or more objects generated by compilers and assembles them into a single executable program.
13. An Operating System (OS) is a set of computer programs that manages the hardware and software resources of a computer.
14. Most operating systems come with an application that provides an interface to the OS managed resources.
15. An operating system (OS) is a set of computer programs that manage the hardware and software resources of a computer.
16. Batch processing requires that a program, its related data and relevant control commands should be submitted together, in the form of a Job.
17. A program in execution is called a Process.
18. The time-sharing interactive systems belong to the era of a large mainframe systems, that were made available to a large number of users for accessing concurrently in an interactive mode.
19. The real time systems are used in environments, where a large number of events, mostly external to the computer system, must be accepted and processed in a highly time-bound manner.
21. Different types of operating systems are optimized or geared up to serve the needs of specific environments.
21. A distributed operating system caters for a distributed environment, wherein a collection of autonomous computer systems, capable of communicating and cooperating with each other through network, are connected to each other through a LAN/WAN.
22. Any operating system should meet the following major goals: Optimize the use of computer resources so as to maximize its throughput and Create a user-friendly computing environment for accessing the computer resources.
23. Every program running on a computer, be it background services or applications, is a process.
24. Process management involves computing and distributing CPU time as well as other resources.
25. An operating system's memory manager coordinates the use of these various types of memory by tracking which one is available.
26. All operating systems include support for a variety of file systems.
27. Most current operating systems are capable of using the TCP/IP networking protocols.
28. The operating system provides access to a number of resources, directly or indirectly, such as files on a local disk, privileged system calls, personal information about users, and the services offered by the programs running on the system.
29. Internal security can be thought of as protecting the computer's resources from the programs concurrently running on the system.

30. At the front line of security are hardware devices known as firewalls.
31. Today, most modern operating systems contain Graphical User Interfaces.
32. A device driver is a specific type of computer software developed to allow interaction with hardware devices.
33. For a program to be executed, it must be mapped to absolute addresses and loaded into memory.
34. An operating system (OS) aims at proper use of resources available.
35. The Operating System is also responsible for detecting any type of error that occurs and then properly handling it.
36. Modern operating systems usually feature a Graphical user interface (GUI) which uses a pointing device such as a mouse or stylus for input in addition to the keyboard.
37. Embedded systems use a variety of dedicated operating systems.
38. Unix systems run on a wide variety of machine architectures.
39. The Microsoft Windows family of operating systems originated as a graphical layer on top of the older MS-DOS environment for the IBM PC.
40. Mac OS X is a line of proprietary, graphical operating systems developed, marketed, and sold by Apple Inc.
41. Operating systems have generally evolved to support programmers who want to write distributed computation.
42. The client-server model can be used to build an explicit scheduling mechanism.
43. In transparent scheduling, the application can create schedulable units of computation to be executed in the distributed environment without considering which machine will actually be used to execute any particular unit.
44. A job scheduler is an enterprise software application that is in charge of unattended background executions, commonly known for historical reasons as batch processing.
45. When a computation starts, normally a single process decides at runtime what other processes should be created and used in the computation.
46. In some distributed environments, the location where a process executes is determined by the scheduler rather than the process.
47. Deadlock detection algorithm rely on the knowledge of the allocation state of the system's resources to determine whether a deadlock exists.
48. In parallel computing, a barrier is a type of synchronization method.
49. In computer science, a lock is a synchronization mechanism for enforcing limits on access to a resource in an environment where there are many threads of execution.
50. A semaphore is a protected variable (or abstract data type) and constitutes the classic method for restricting access to shared resources (e.g., storage) in a multiprogramming environment.
51. A thread in computer science is short for a thread of execution.
52. Multithreading is a popular programming and execution model that allows multiple threads to exist within the context of a single process, sharing the process' resources but able to execute independently.
53. Operating systems generally implement threads in one of two ways: pre-emptive multithreading, or cooperative multithreading.
54. Among the popular operating system are Disk Operating System (DOS).
55. DOS has internal and external commands.
56. Internal commands can be given from anywhere.
57. In DOS the filename is of 8 + 3 format.
58. Root directory is the main directory of the hard disk.
59. DIR command gives the listing of files in directory.
60. DIR/P allows you to view the files on screen page by page.
61. DIR/W gives the listing widthwise.
62. MD command allows you to create directory.
63. CD command is used for changing directory.
64. RD command is used for removing directory.

65. A file can be copied on to another drive or another directory.
66. Xcopy command can be used to copy various files.
67. Backup is used to copy several files at a time for storing.
68. An existing file can be deleted too.
69. Using Date and Time commands, you can see the system date and time.
70. Prompt command allows you to change the command prompt.
71. You can give a file a new name by using the REN command.
72. Restore command allows you to restore the backed up files.
73. Attribute command allows you to change the attributes of the file.
74. UNIX is an operating system, just as you have Microsoft DOS and Microsoft Windows.
75. The first version of UNIX was developed in 1969 by Ken Thompson of the Research Group at Bell Laboratories.
76. Multiprogramming and other enhancements were added when it was rewritten in C.
77. A new user interface (the C Shell), a new text editor (ex/vi), compilers for Pascal and LISP, and many new systems programs were written at Berkeley.
78. Sun Microsystems helped popularize the BSD flavour of UNIX by shipping it on their workstations.
79. In 1989, the ANSI standards body standardized the C programming language, producing an ANSI C specification that vendors were quick to adopt.
80. There is a plethora of ongoing UNIX-related research systems, including Mach, Chorus, Comandos, and Roisin.
81. The main principle of UNIX is time-sharing.
82. UNIX was used for tasks such as networking, graphics, and real-time operation, which did not always fit into its original text-oriented model.
83. A *file* consists of a sequence of bytes.
84. The **creat** system call, given a path name, creates an (empty) file (or truncates an existing one).
85. Each **read** or **write** updates the current offset into the file, which is associated with the file-table entry and is used to determine the position in the file for the next **read** or **write**.
86. The **execve** system call loads a binary file into memory (destroying the memory image of the program containing the **execve** system call) and starts its execution.
87. The simplest form of communication between processes is by *pipes,* which may be created before the **fork**, and whose endpoints are then set up between the **fork** and the **execve**. A pipe is essentially a queue of bytes between two processes.
88. We know there are interrupts in various software for various conditions. Similarly in UNIX we have signals.
89. Almost any signal may also be generated by the **kill** system call.
90. System calls exist to set and return both an interval timer (**getitimer/setitimer**) and the current time (**gettimeofday/settimeofday**) in microseconds.
91. UNIX also has its own set of library routines and header files.
92. Command interpreter is used to execute system programs and the programs written by the users, which is a user process like any other process.
93. For each command, each of the directories in the search path is searched, in order, for a file of the same name.
94. A command such as *pr* that passes its standard input to its standard output, performing some processing on it is called a *filter.*
95. One substantial difference between UNIX and many other systems is the ease with which multiple processes can be created and manipulated.
96. Processes in UNIX are given small CPU time slices by a priority algorithm that reduces to round-robin scheduling for CPU-bound jobs.
97. Allocation of both main memory and swap space is done *first-fit.*
98. Swapping can be kept to a minimum because more jobs can be kept in main memory, because paging allows execution with only parts of each process in memory.

99. Linux is an operating system.
100. It is available free.
101. Linux runs on PC machines with minimum of 386 processor.
102. Linux is a complete operating system with Graphical User Interface, X windows system, TCP/IP, Emacs editor and other components usually found in an operating system.
103. Kernal, Shell and File structures are three major components of Linux.
104. Kernal is a master program that runs programs and controls the resources of the computer system.
105. Shell provides an interface to the user. Three types of Linux shell are: Boure Again Shell, TC-Shell and Public Domain Shell.
106. Linux has Hierarchical File structure.
107. Linux is a command line Interpreter.
108. Prompt designates the beginning of the command line.
109. Keyboard and screen are treated as standard input and standard output respectively.
110. dir command lists the files in the current directory.
111. cd changes the current directory
112. is lists the files in the current directory.
113. pwd displays the full path name of the current directory.
114. mkdir creates the specified directory.
115. rmdir removes the directory.
116. cat displays the specified file name on screen.
117. more displays filename on screen page wise.
118. tail prints the last ten lines of the each file on the screen.
119. head displays the first ten lines of filename on screen.
120. chmod changes the permissions of the file name.
121. symbolic and numeric are the two types of modes to set the permissions of the file.
122. mv renames or moves one source file to a destination file.
123. rm removes the specified file.
124. wc displays line, word and character counts for the specified file.
125. sort command sorts the specified file line by line in character order.
126. cmp compares the two specified files.
127. diff locates the differences between two files.
128. com prints the lines in each file as well as those common to both.
129. who displays a list of users currently logged in.
130. whoami identifies the user who invoked the command.
131. ps displays information about processes executing on the system.
132. kill terminates the execution of a background process.
133. write is used to send a message to a user on the system.
134. wall is used to send a message to all users on the system.
135. news is used to send a message to all users who logged or not logged in.
136. mail is used to send the message to all users on the network.
137. grep is a utility to search and select Linux filters.
138. !, #, $, &, &&, ( ), /, ;, " ", { }, || are the special characters of shell.
139. *, ?, < >, are wild card characters.
140. ' ', " ", \ are quotation characters, used to prevent bash from processing special characters.

141. >, <, >>, << are redirectional symbols.
142. '1' is the pipe character.
143. 2 > 2 >> & 1, >& are redirecting symbols for standard errors.
144. 1 & are the piping symbol for standard errors.
145. File descriptions for standard input, standard output and standard errors are 0, 1, 2 respectively.
146. A sequence of Linux commands to perform a specific task is called as shell script.
147. Shell script can be run by sh or . commands.
148. Command given by user is called as job performed by system.
149. A process is a command or program that is being executed.
150. &, notify, fg, bg, ctrl-z, kill, ps are the commands to control the jobs.
151. Linux file structure is a hierarchical tree type structure.
152. File information of Linux contains location, file type, permissions, number of links, owner name, group name, size, modification and file name.
153. Three categories of files are ordinary, directory and device files.
154. Root directory contains three types of directories: System directory, Home directory and User directory.
155. A complete path from root to particular file is called as Absolute path name.
156. In relative path none of the current work in directory is the initial directory.
157. dir, is, pwd, commands are used to list the files.
158. od, cat, more, comm, diff, tail, split, less commands are used to display the files.
159. lpr, lpq, lprm commands are used to print the file.
160. To manage the directories cd, mkdir, rmdir, mv, chmod commands are used.
161. find, cp, mv, rm in commands are used to operate the file and directory.
162. Links to file are of two types: Hard link and Symbolic link.
163. Vi is the editor of Linux.
164. Vi can operate in one of three modes easily, i.e., command mode, input mode and last line mode.
165. Input mode and command mode are used to edit or change the text of the file.
166. Input mode is terminated by using Esc key.
167. To switch from command mode to last line mode ':' is used.
168. Last line mode is used for file handling and substitution.
169. Current line in last line mode is denoted by a '.' dot and last line by '$' dollar symbol.
170. System administrator or super user is an end user who have all the facilities provided by Linux.
171. Super user is the root user.
172. Linux can be initialized in different modes such as single user mode, multiuser mode, user defined mode, text mode, etc.
173. Current system state can be viewed by run level command.
174. Daemon are the background processes.
175. Superuser can schedule the automated processes by using 'crontab' utility.
176. /var/log/mail log directory contains all the transmitted mail messages.
177. Each username and group name have unique UID and GID number respectively.
178. To add, remove and modify the user's account useradd, userdel, and usermod commands are used.
179. To change the permission, ownership and group name chmod, chown, chgrp commands are used.
180. Each device have a special file called as device file.
181. To install a device on the system device file, configuration tool and kernal support is required.
182. In Linux device may be of two types block device and character device.

183. Serial interface device type has suffix $ with device type.
184. Major number of terminal device is 4 and minor number is starting from 64.
185. To create a device file mknod command is used.
186. To install and manage the printers lpadmin, lpr, lpq, lprm, and lpd commands are used.
187. To install the kernal modules install, rpm, make commands are used.
188. To manage the modules ismod, insmod, rmmod, modprobe commands are used.
189. To manage the floppy disk format, fdformat, dd and mount commands are used.
190. File system of Linux has four sections: Bootblock, Superblock, Inode list and Data area.
191. Inode is an index number, contains the information about file and directory.
192. Inode list contains the information about the inode whether they are used or free.
193. System administrator can create, access, check the disk space and repair the file system.
194. To create file system mkfs, mke2fs, hformat commands are used.
195. To access file system mount, unmount commands are used.
196. fsck, e2fsck commands are used to repair the file system damages.
197. df, du and quot commands are used to manage the file systems.
198. zip, unzip, gzip, gunzip, bzip2, bunzip2 commands are used to compress and decompress the files.
199. A backup is a copy of the file system on the storage media.
200. tar, cpio commands are used for backups.
201. Full backup and partial backup can be based on backup level.
202. Backup can be performed to overcome power failure, hardware failure, human errors and software bugs.

MULTIPLE CHOICE QUESTIONS

1. Software which runs the computer is called:
   (a) System Software (b) Application Software (c) Programming Software.
2. Software which is used to run applications is called:
   (a) System Software (b) Application Software (c) Programming Software.
3. Software which is used to write programs is called:
   (a) System Software (b) Application Software (c) Programming Software.
4. Compiler converts Source language program to:
   (a) Object language (b) Programming language (c) Application language.
5. Loader loads the programs from operating system to:
   (a) Hard disk (b) Memory (c) Floppy disk.
6. Operating system manages:
   (a) Hardware (b) Software (c) Both.
7. The computer software, which translates instructions to menmonics, is called:
   (a) Compiler (b) Assembler (c) Loader.
8. The processing system, which did not allow the interference of users, is called:
   (a) Batch Operating System (b) Time Sharing Operating System (c) Real Time Operating System.
9. FCFS means:
   (a) First Compile First Served (b) First Come First Served (c) First Come First Shared.
10. Time sharing systems are:
    (a) Time tested user systems (b) Single user systems (c) Multi programming systems.
11. Unix uses which symbol to demarcate the path:
    (a) / (b) \ (c) :

12. The hardware which blocks the breach of security is called :
(a) Firetable (b) Firewall (c) Firewindow.
13. GUI stands for:
(a) Graphical User Interface (b) Graphical Used Interface (c) Graphical User Interaction.
14. A barrier is :
(a) Scheduling method (b) Synchronization method (c) Self operating method.
15. A thread is a:
(a) Thread in CPU (b) Thread between units (c) Thread of execution.
16. Operating systems generally implement threads in one of two ways: pre-emptive multithreading, or ________ multithreading.
(a) cooperative (b) called (c) covered.
17. A job scheduler is a:
(a) Hardware (b) Software (c) Both.
18. Which command is used to shift the command from one directory to another?
(a) CD (b) MD (c) RD.
19. Which command would you use to create a new directory?
(a) CD (b) MD (c) RD.
20. The main directory of the hard disk is:
(a) Main directory (b) Root directory (c) Final directory.
21. Which command will always transfer to the root directory?
(a) CD\ (b) CD/ (c) CD.
22. For listing the files widthwise, we give the command as?
(a) DIR/P (b) DIR/W (c) DIR.
23. The files in DOS are named in which format ?
(a) 9 + 2 (b) 10 + 1 (c) 8 + 3.
24. A directory whithin a directory is called:
(a) Sub directory (b) Part directory (c) Junior directory.
25. Prompt command is used to change the command prompt from:
(a) c:\ (b) c: (c) c.
26. Backup files can be restored using the command called:
(a) Prompt (b) Restore (c) Cleanup.
27. Time shows the time in hh:mm and ___ format:
(a) ss (b) nn (c) pp.
28. To rename a file, you give the command as:
(a) name (b) REN (c) re.
29. You can change the status of the file using the command:
(a) Status (b) Change (c) Attrib.
30. UNIX was developed at:
(a) Bell Laboratories (b) Microsoft Corporation (c) Adobe Systems.
31. DARPA is :
(a) Defense Agent Research Projects Agency
(b) Defense Advanced Research Projects Agency
(c) Defense Advanced Ready Projects Agency.

32. The command which reduces the size of file to 0 is:
(a) short (b) reduce (c) trunc.

33. To create directory, we use the command:
(a) mkdir (b) mdir (c) dir.

34. To delete directory, we use the command:
(a) mdir (b) rmdir (c) dir.

35. To identify the user of the process, we use the command:
(a) getgo (b) getgod (c) getgid.

36. Linux is a:
(a) single user operating system (b) multiuser operating system (c) hardware.

37. Which is the central part of Linux?
(a) kernal (b) shell (c) file structure.

38. Linux is a:
(a) firmware (b) slackware (c) freeware.

39. Which part of Linux interacts with the users directly?
(a) kernal (b) shell (c) file structure.

40. KDE stands for:
(a) korn desktop environment (b) korn develop environment (c) k desktop environment.

41. Linux is a _____ operating system:
(a) 32-bit (b) 64-bit (c) 16-bit.

42. Which of the following best describes the file structure of Linux:
(a) binary tree structure (b) hierarchical tree structure (c) network tree structure.

43. To pipe the standard error which one special symbol is used:
(a) >& (b) 2> (c) 1.

44. Which one is not the wild card character:
(a) 1 (b) * (c) ?.

45. Find the odd one:
(a) > (b) < (c) 1.

46. File description of standard output is:
(a) 0 (b) 1 (c) 2.

47. Which one is odd:
(a) & (b) % (c) &&.

48. ps stands for:
(a) Process status (b) Program status (c) Place status.

49. To place the several commands in background which one command is used:
(a) && (b) bg (c) &.

50. Which one is odd:
(a) || (b) && (c) !.

51. Which one is not the pipe symbol:
(a) | (b) |& (c) ||.

52. Find the odd one:
(a) System administrator (b) Super user (c) Simple user.

53. Mounting a file system is technique for:
(a) Accessing (b) Creating (c) Checking.

54. S in systems stand for:
   (a) System states (b) Super user (c) Serial interface.
55. crontab utility is used for:
   (a) schedule automated processing
   (b) configuring user's crontab file
   (c) making an entry of scheduled job in crontab file.
56. To give the model type of printers, which options are used:
   (a) -p (b) -v (c) -d.
57. To change the user's account which one command is used:
   (a) chmod (b) ismod (c) usermod.
58. Login shell lies in which one directory:
   (a) /etc/shells (b) \etc\shell (c) \var\shells.
59. For serial ports which description is used:
   (a) ttys (b) S (c) sp.
60. Which one is odd:
   (a) install (b) rpm (c) make.
61. Which one is odd:
   (a) -chmod (b) -insmod (c) rmmod.

REVIEW QUESTIONS

1. What is a System Software?
2. What is Computer software?
3. What is compiler used for?
4. Describe the various types of compilers.
5. What is a Loader?
6. What is an Operating System?
7. What is an operating system?
8. Describe the various types of operating systems.
9. Why do you need an operating system?
10. What are the goals of an operating system?
11. What sort of services are provided by an operating system?
12. What are the characteristics of an operating system?
13. Describe the various functions of an operating system.
14. Describe the various types of scheduling.
15. What do you understand by Job Scheduler?
16. What is Process Scheduler?
17. Describe the various functions of Process Synchronization.
18. What is DOS used for?
19. What is the command to remove all files in a directory?
20. Is it possible to remove the root directory of your hard disk by using the RD command? If yes, how?
21. Type the command to remove a directory. Where must the cursor be to remove a directory or subdirectory?
22. What are the different options of the DIR command?
23. What is the command to display a directory pagewise?

24. What does the symbol \(backslash) stand for?
25. What display does your monitor show when you type CD?
26. What does the command Backup do?
27. How would you restore the backuped files?
28. What is prompt command used for?
29. Describe what do you understand by UNIX?
30. How was UNIX developed?
31. How do you manipulate files in UNIX?
32. Describe how the signals are used in UNIX.
33. How the information is manipulated?
34. Describe the various library routines in UNIX.
35. Describe the various commands and shells in UNIX.
36. Which are the standard input output commands in UNIX.
37. How CPU is scheduled in UNIX?
38. In UNIX, how is memory managed using swapping and paging?
39. Describe UNIX's file system.
40. How Linux was evaluated?
41. What are the various shells available in Linux?
42. Explain various characteristics of Linux.
43. Discuss hardware requirements of Linux.
44. What is the difference between single user and multi-user operating systems?
45. Linux is free, how?
46. Write down the various releases of Linux.
47. How would you install Linux?
48. What is the Booting and shutdown process of Linux?
49. Explain the mkdir and rmdir command.
50. Explain why the -r option of rm is dangerous.
51. Give any three circumstances when a directory file cannot be removed using rm dir command.
52. What are the standard input, output and error files?
53. What is the difference between write and wall command?
54. How news command is different from wall command?
55. Explain the function of the grep command.
56. Explain the modes to set the permission of the specified file.
57. What is the difference between head and tail commands?
58. Name the command that is used to send the message within mail system.
59. Write a command to display a file subject in an alphabetical order and after sorting stored in strsubject.
60. List all currently executing processes whether background or foreground.
61. List all filenames beginning with "b" and having a "s" somewhere in the filename.
61. What do you mean by command-line arguments?
63. What is the difference between job and process?
64. How you can interrupt a running job and move it into foreground?
65. What is the difference between directory = 'pwd' and directory = pwd?
66. What do you mean by piping?
67. How you can redirect the standard errors?

68. What do you mean by shell script?
69. What is command substitution?
70. Which file is the parent of all files?
71. What do you mean by current working directory?
72. Describe the file system of Linux.
73. Describe the standard directory structure of Linux.
74. What is a file?
75. Describe the different categories of file.
76. What do you mean by Link?
77. What are the file and directory operations?
78. Differentiate between lpr, lpq, lprm, pr commands.
79. To manage the directory, which command is used?
80. Give the advanced features of Vi editor of Linux.
81. What are the three ways of quitting from Vi after saving?
82. What are the three modes of Vi editor?
83. What is the difference between : x, : q and zz commands?
84. Write the set options.
85. What is the difference between cursor-based and window-based editors?
86. Write about the advanced editing commands of Vi editor.
87. How can you work with regions in Vi editors.
88. What do you mean by root user?
89. Write the functions of the System Administrator.
90. How can you become a superuser?
91. Write the commands to start and shutdown the system.
92. Write the initialization process of Linux.
93. How the superuser can schedule the automated processes?
94. What do you mean by daeman?
95. How you can install and manage the printers?
96. What do you mean by module?
97. Write about the floppy disk management.
98. How system administrator can administrate the file system?
99. What do you mean by inode?
100. How you can compress and decompress the files?
101. What is backup?
102. Write short notes on the following:

Shell
Operating system
Free ware
command line
symbolic mode
comm and diff
Hierarchical structure
Device directory
Root directory
Hard link
File security
Last line mode
Line editing commands
EXINIT variable
.exrc file
Device files
System log
chmod
cpio
Device types
Linux file system.

ANSWERS

Multiple Choice Questions

1. a	2. b	3. c	4. a
5. b	6. c	7. b.	8. a
9. b	10. c	11. a	12. b.
13. a	14. b	15. c	16. a
17. b.	18. a	19. b	20. b
21. a	22. b	23. c	24. a
25. a	26. b	27. a	28. b
29. c.	30. a	31. b	32. c
33. a	34. b	35. c.	36. b
37. b	38. c	39. b	40. a
41. a	42. b	43. c	44. a
45. c	46. a	47. b	48. a
49. c	50. c	51. b	52. c
53. a	54. b	55. a	56. a
57. c	58. a	59. b	60. c
61. c.			

CHAPTER 7

Applications Software

Learning Objectives

After going through this chapter, you should appreciate the following:

- **Electronic Spreadsheet**

  Sheets

  Moving within a Sheet

  Entering Data

  Editing the Data

  Selecting Cells

  Moving data

  Copying Data

  Drag and Drop Method

  Inserting Rows and Columns

  Inserting and Deleting Cells

  Changing Width of a Column

  Changing Height of a Row

  Formatting Text

  AutoFormat

  Formatting Numbers

  Adding Border to a Range

  Formulae

  Summing of a Row or Column

  Sum Function

  Average Function

  Using Function Wizard
- **Word Processing**

  Some Important Terms of Word Processing

  Things which can be done by Word Processing

  Important Word Processing Programs

  Starting Word

  Microsoft Word Screen
- **Pre-written Sofware Packages**

ELECTRONIC SPREADSHEET

Excel for Windows is a spreadsheet program. A spreadsheet is a graphical representation of rows and columns. Data can be fed into these rows and columns and mathematical and other operations performed on it. An opening screen of Excel is shown here.

Naming Convention

It is not I have named rows from 1 onwards and columns A onwards on my own but they are so numbered by the software itself. These are the standard way of expressing these columns and rows.

If we have to name a large number of cells or columns, for that too we have the convention which asks us to call them with starting cell address and last cell address with colon in between. For example, see the addressed cells here.

Another convention is of the sheets in the worksheet.

SHEETS

These are like pages in a book. Initially there are 16 worksheets in a file. But, you can add more. However, there may be only 6 of them visible on the screen. These sheets are independent but you can transfer data from one sheet to another.

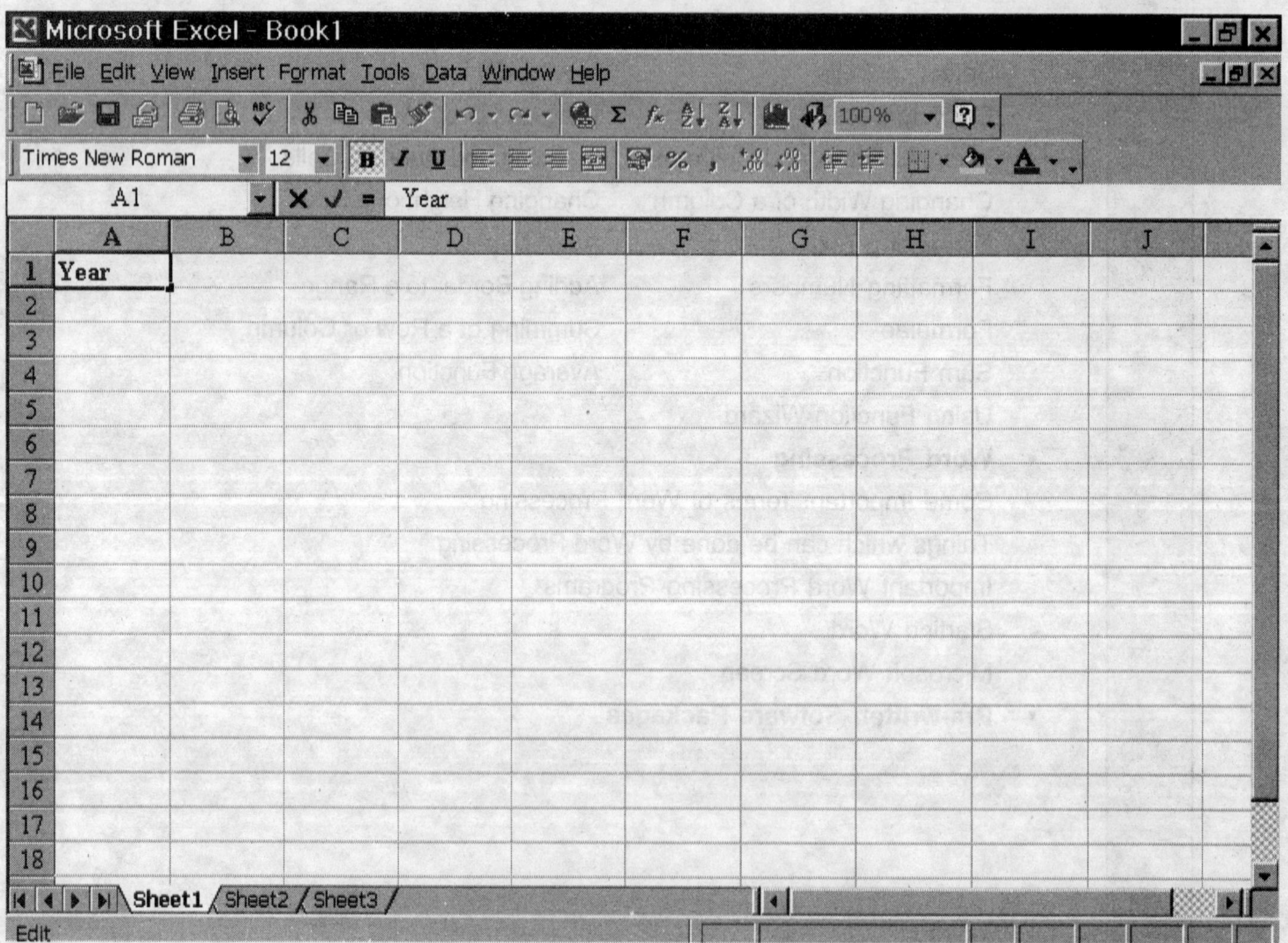

These sheets are very helpful. For example, for a salary spreadsheet, one sheet may belong to one month and there may be a sheet for the total of the year.

Moving within a Sheet

To enter data in a cell, you must first move to that particular cell.

To Move to a Cell

1. Click in the cell.

   Or

   Press the arrow keys to move the cell pointer to the cell.

   Or

   Select the current cell address in the **Name** box and replace it with the address of the cell to which you want to move.

Remember

1. The cell surrounded by the cell pointer is called the active cell.
2. You can use the scroll bars to scroll through the document without changing the active cell.
3. To move within the worksheet, you can use the keyboard shortcuts, given below:

Keyboard Shortcuts for Moving Around the Worksheet

Keyboard Shortcut	*Result*
Arrow key	Moves to the adjacent cell (Up, Down, Left or Right)
Ctrl+Arrow Key	Moves to the edge of the current data region (Up, Down, Left or Right)
Tab	Moves right one cell
Shift + Tab	Moves left one cell
Enter	Moves down one cell
Shift + Enter	Moves up one cell
Home	Moves to the first cell of the row
Ctrl + Home	Moves to cell A1
Ctrl + End	Moves to last cell of last row with data
Page Down	Moves down one screen
Page Up	Moves up one screen
Alt + Page Down	Moves one screen to the right
Alt + Page Up	Moves one screen to the left
Ctrl + Page Down	Moves to the next sheet in the workbook
Ctrl + Page Up	Moves to the previous sheet in the workbook

Entering Data

You can enter text, a number, or a formula into each cell in a worksheet. You enter text to create a label, such as a column heading. You can enter a number to provide information with which you can do calculations.

To Type Data in a Cell

1. Select the cell.
2. Type text, a number, or a formula. A flashing insertion point will appear at the end of whatever you type. You will notice that whatever you type will appear not only in the active cell but also in the Formula bar.
3. Press Enter key to move to the next cell. The cell below will become the new active cell.

Remember

1. You don't have to press Enter after you type the contents of a cell. You can simply press right arrow key to move to the next cell.
2. Excel right aligns the numbers in the cell but left aligns the text.

Editing the Data

The easiest way to change the text or number in a cell is to click the cell and then type right over the contents. But if you have a formula or extensive text in the cell, you might prefer to edit the existing contents to avoid retyping the whole entry.

To edit data in a cell

1. Click the cell and then type over its contents

   Or

   Double click the cell to position an insertion point with the cell contents.
2. Edit the contents as though you were editing text in Word.
3. Press Enter to enter the revised text in the cell.

This is if you have just one cell to edit, But, if you have more than one cell to edit. Then you need to select the various cells.

Selecting Cells

You can select a number of consecutive cells called a range by one of the following methods:

1. Click and drag over the selection.
2. Click in one cell, and then hold down the Shift key and click in the opposite corner of the selection.
3. Click on the Select All button, the gray rectangle where the column and row heading meet, to select the entire worksheet.
4. Click in a column or row heading to select the whole column or row.

Moving data

1. Select a range of cells. The cells will be highlighted.
2. Click on the Cut button. Moving dashes (called a marquee) will appear around your selection.
3. In this case the data does not disappear like text does in a word processor.
4. Click in the cell that will be upper left corner of the new location of the range. The cell will be selected.
5. Click on the Paste button. The data will be pasted in the new location.

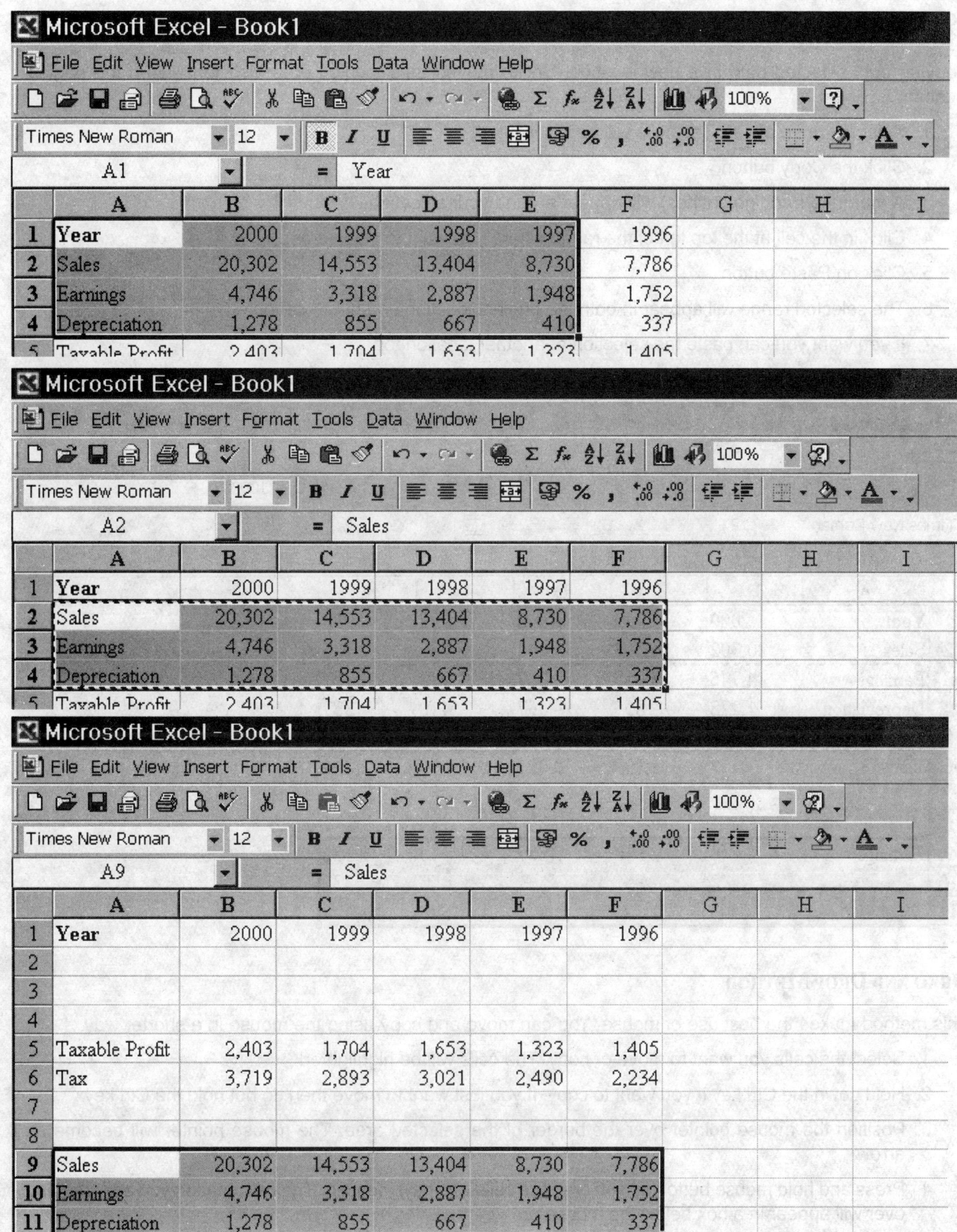
Microsoft Excel - Book1
File Edit View Insert Format Tools Data Window Help
100%
Times New Roman 12
A1 = Year
A B C D E F G H I
1 Year 2000 1999 1998 1997 1996
2 Sales 20,302 14,553 13,404 8,730 7,786
3 Earnings 4,746 3,318 2,887 1,948 1,752
4 Depreciation 1,278 855 667 410 337
5 Taxable Profit 2,403 1,704 1,653 1,323 1,405
Microsoft Excel - Book1
File Edit View Insert Format Tools Data Window Help
100%
Times New Roman 12
A2 = Sales
A B C D E F G H I
1 Year 2000 1999 1998 1997 1996
2 Sales 20,302 14,553 13,404 8,730 7,786
3 Earnings 4,746 3,318 2,887 1,948 1,752
4 Depreciation 1,278 855 667 410 337
5 Taxable Profit 2,403 1,704 1,653 1,323 1,405
Microsoft Excel - Book1
File Edit View Insert Format Tools Data Window Help
100%
Times New Roman 12
A9 = Sales
A B C D E F G H I
1 Year 2000 1999 1998 1997 1996
2
3
4
5 Taxable Profit 2,403 1,704 1,653 1,323 1,405
6 Tax 3,719 2,893 3,021 2,490 2,234
7
8
9 Sales 20,302 14,553 13,404 8,730 7,786
10 Earnings 4,746 3,318 2,887 1,948 1,752
11 Depreciation 1,278 855 667 410 337

COPYING DATA

Copying puts selected data in a new location. Unlike moved data, copied data also remains in the original location.

1. Select a range of cell. The cells will be highlighted.
2. Click the Copy button.
3. A marquee (running dashes) will appear around your selection.
4. Click in the cell at the top left of the range where you want to place a copy.
5. Click on Paste button.
6. The selected range will appear in both the original location and new location.
7. If you want you can paste the selection at another location too.

The next figure show the result of highlighting, copying of the cells range and copying them at a new location.

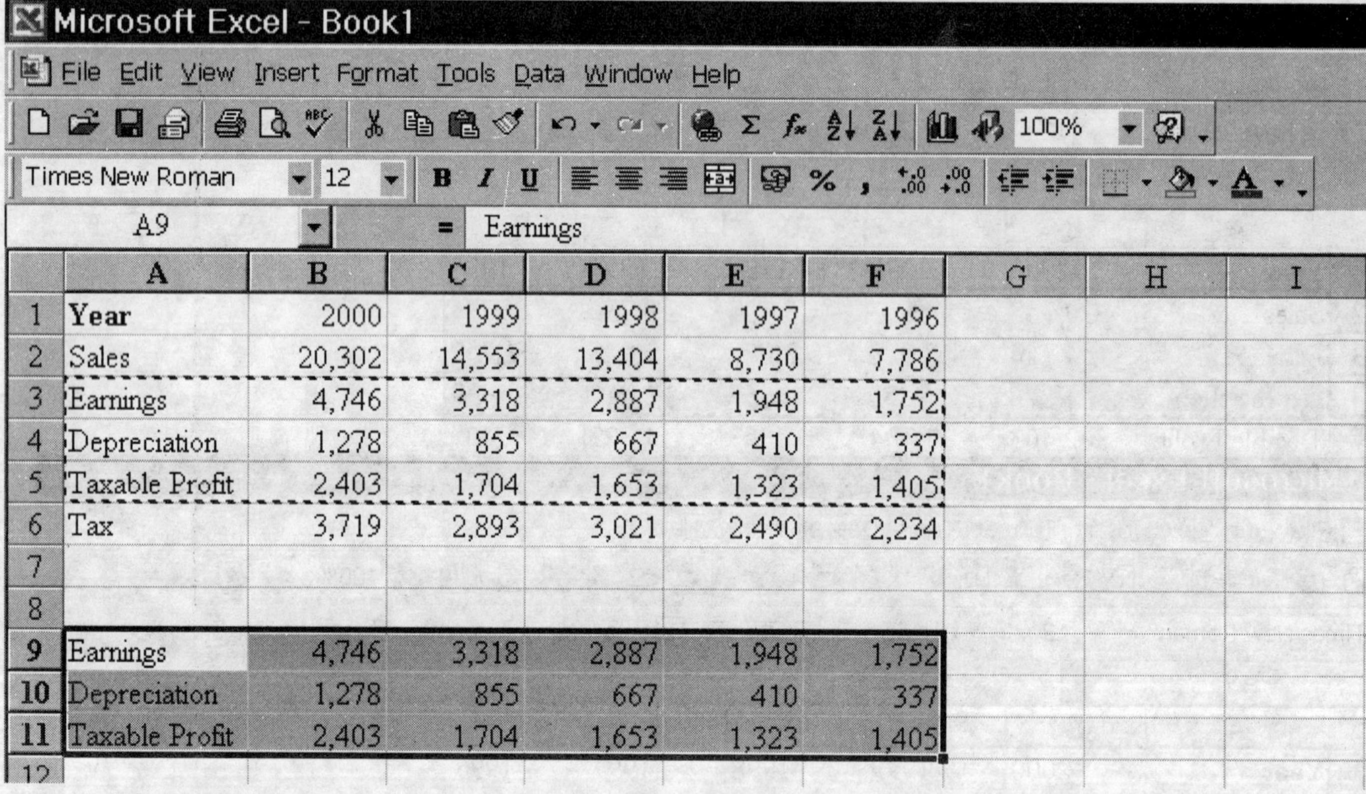

	A	B	C	D	E	F	G	H	I
1	Year	2000	1999	1998	1997	1996			
2	Sales	20,302	14,553	13,404	8,730	7,786			
3	Earnings	4,746	3,318	2,887	1,948	1,752			
4	Depreciation	1,278	855	667	410	337			
5	Taxable Profit	2,403	1,704	1,653	1,323	1,405			
6	Tax	3,719	2,893	3,021	2,490	2,234			
7									
8									
9	Earnings	4,746	3,318	2,887	1,948	1,752			
10	Depreciation	1,278	855	667	410	337			
11	Taxable Profit	2,403	1,704	1,653	1,323	1,405			
12									

DRAG AND DROP METHOD

This method makes the best use of mouse. You can move and copy using the mouse in a shorter way.

1. Select the cells you want to move or copy. The cells will be highlighted.
2. Hold down the Ctrl key if you want to copy. If you just want to move then do not hold the Ctrl key.
3. Position the mouse pointer over the border of the selected area. The mouse pointer will become an arrow.
4. Press and hold mouse button as you drag the cells to a new location. The cell location you are dragging over will appear in a box below the mouse arrow.

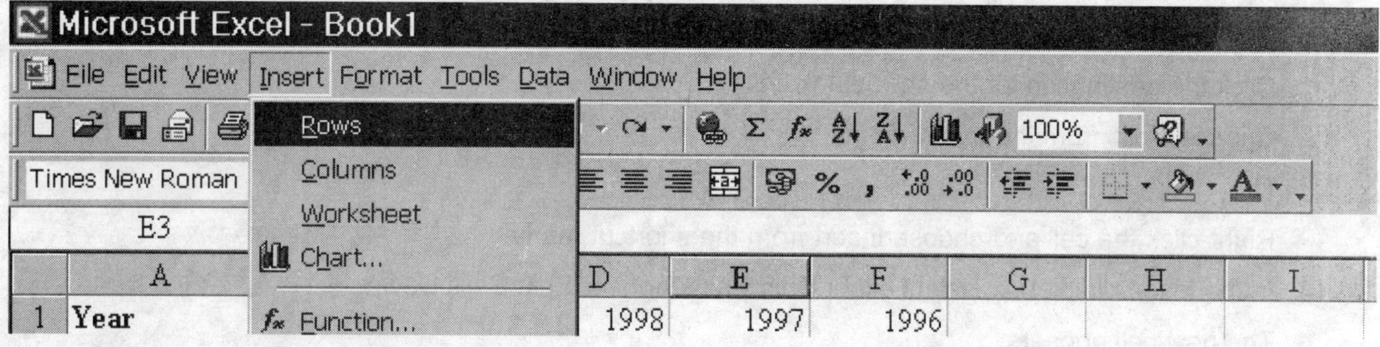

5. Release the mouse button.
6. The cells will be dropped in the new location. This is much quicker than using buttons or menus.

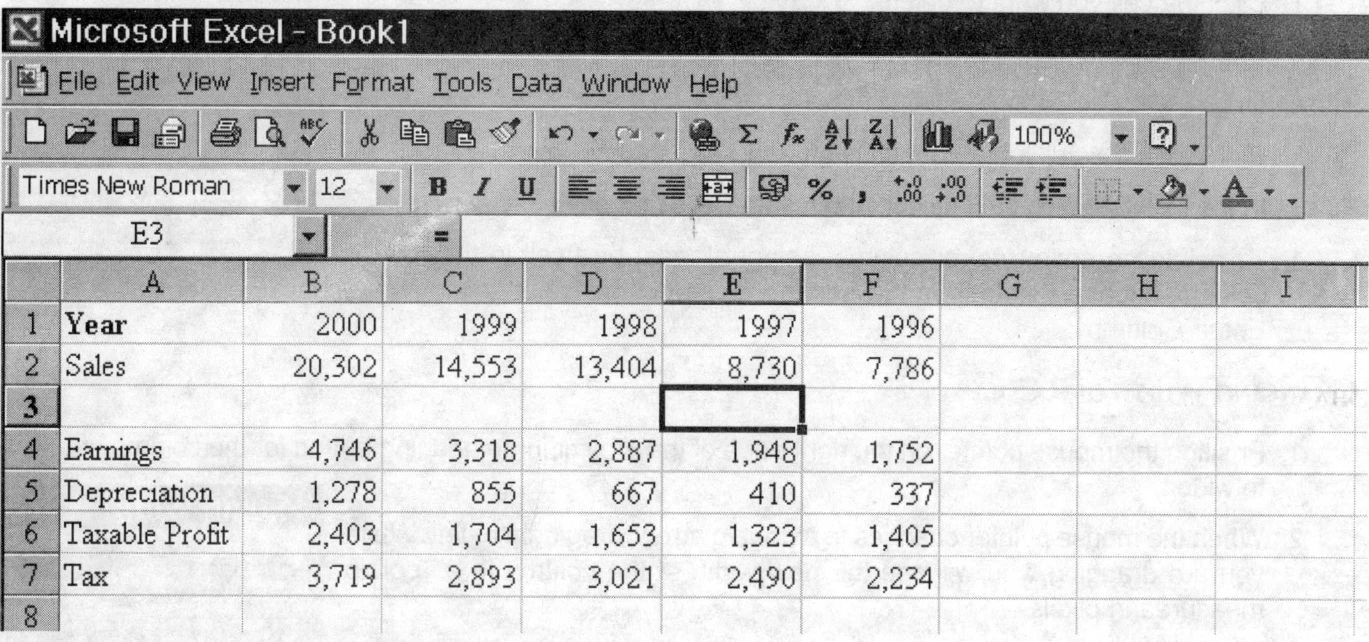

	A	B	C	D	E	F	G	H	I
1	Year	2000	1999	1998	1997	1996			
2	Sales	20,302	14,553	13,404	8,730	7,786			
3									
4	Earnings	4,746	3,318	2,887	1,948	1,752			
5	Depreciation	1,278	855	667	410	337			
6	Taxable Profit	2,403	1,704	1,653	1,323	1,405			
7	Tax	3,719	2,893	3,021	2,490	2,234			
8									

Inserting Rows and Columns

You can insert rows and columns at any time, and Excel adjusts all formulas to accommodate the new rows or columns. If you insert a row, it will appear **above** the selected cell; if you insert a column, it will appear to the **left** of the selected cell.

Insert

Insert
- Shift cells right
- Shift cells down
- Entire row
- Entire column

OK Cancel

To insert a row or a column

1. Click any cell of the row or column in which you had like to insert the new blank row or column.
2. From the Insert menu, choose Rows to insert a row or choose Columns to insert a column, as shown next.
3. A new Row in this case will be inserted, as shown next.

Inserting and Deleting Cells

When you tell Excel to insert or delete a cell within a range of data, Excel needs to know how to move the data that is in adjacent cells. You specify your preferences in the Insert or Delete dialog box.

To Insert a Cell

1. Click the destination for the new, blank cell.
2. Choose Cells from the Insert menu.

   Or

   Right-click the cell and choose Insert from the shortcut menu.
3. In the Insert dialog box, select either Shift Cells Right or Shift Cells Down.
4. The new cell appears.

To Delete a Cell

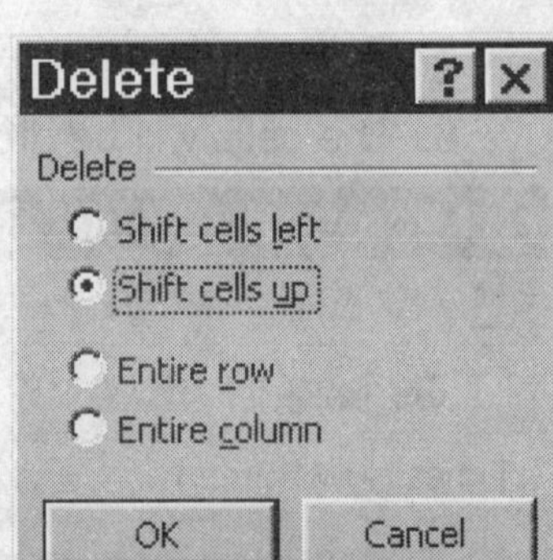

1. Click the cell you want to delete.
2. Choose Delete from the Edit menu.

   Or

   Right-click the cell and choose Delete from the shortcut menu.
3. In the Delete dialog box, select either Shift Cells Left or Shift Cells Up.
4. To delete an entire row or column, select at least one cell in the row or column, choose Delete from the Edit menu, and in the Delete dialog box, choose either Entire Row or Entire Column.

Changing Width of a Column

1. Position the mouse pointer on the right edge of the gray column heading button for the column you want to widen.
2. When the mouse pointer changes to a double arrow, drag right or left. While you are dragging, you will see the new width of the column in a ToolTip measured in pixels.
3. You can also select Column from the Format menu and then choose Width from the submenu to open the Column Width dialog box. In this case, you can specify the exact setting.

Column Width
Column width: 8.38
OK Cancel

Changing Height of a Row

1. Position the mouse pointer on the bottom edge of the gray row heading button for the row whose height you want to change.
2. When the mouse pointer changes to a double arrows, drag up and down.
3. You can also select Row from the Format menu and then choose Height from the submenu to open the Row Height dialog box. In this case, you can specify the exact setting.

Row Height
Row height: 15.75
OK Cancel

Formatting Text

You can use formatting to improve the appearance of your worksheet and to make it easier to locate the information you need.

To format selected text

1. Select the cell or cells containing the text to format.

2. Choose formatting options by clicking the text formatting buttons on the Formatting toolbar.

Or

1. Select the cell or cells containing the text to format.
2. From the Format menu, choose Cells, or right-click and choose Format Cells from the shortcut menu.
3. In the Format Cells dialog box, change the options on the Alignment and Font tabs.
4. Click Ok.

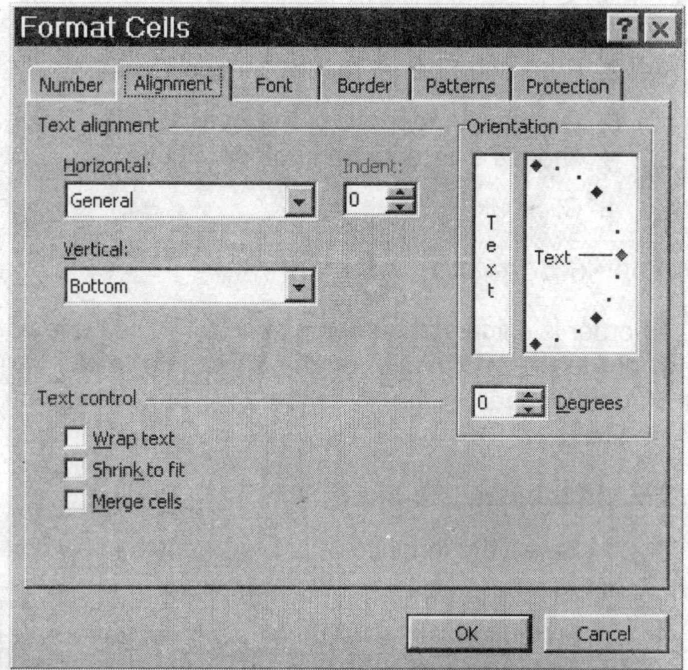

AUTOFORMAT

The fastest and easiest way to make a worksheet presentable is to give an AutoFormat command. **AutoFormat** supplies a complete look for a range of data by changing the font, text alignment, number formatting, borders, patterns, colours, column widths, and row heights. Excel provides a selection of AutoFormats, each with a unique look.

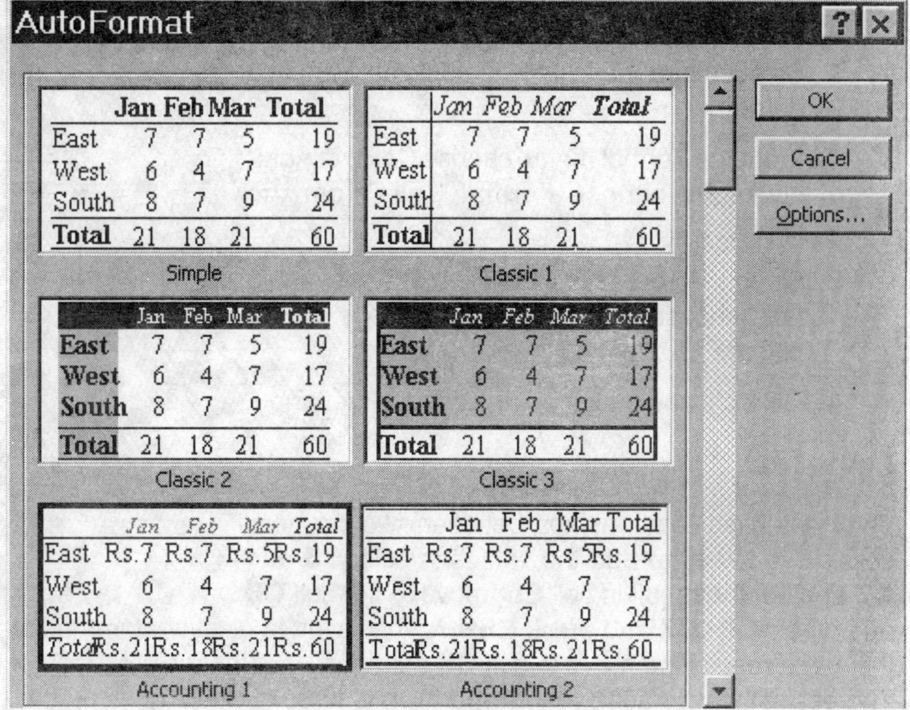

To choose an AutoFormat

1. Click any cell in the range to format.

   Or

   Select the range to format.
2. From the Format menu, choose AutoFormat.
3. In the AutoFormat dialog box, select an AutoFormat from the display.
4. Click Ok.

FORMATTING NUMBERS

Excel makes available to you a variety of number formatting options, some from the Formatting toolbar and others from the Format Cells dialog box.

To format numbers

1. Select the numbers to format.
2. Click the appropriate number formatting button on the Formatting toolbar.

   Or

1. Select the numbers to format.
2. From the Format menu, choose Cells.
3. On the Number tab of the Format Cells dialog box, choose a category and other options.
4. Click Ok.

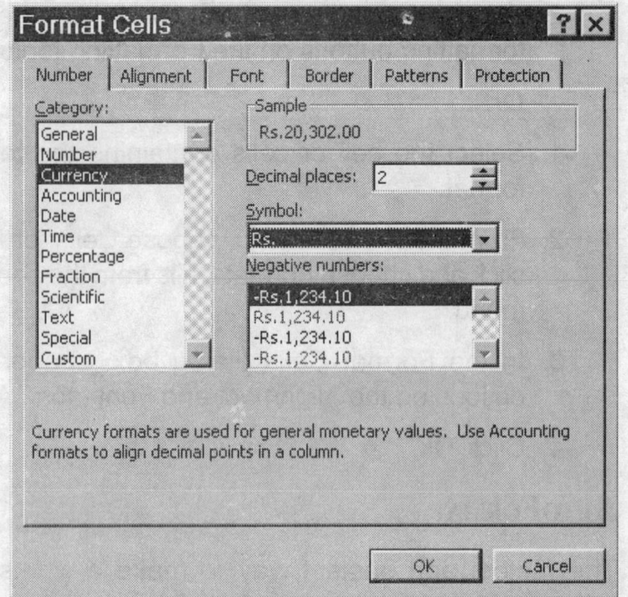

Adding Border to a Range

A border is a line at the edge of a cell. You can use borders to divide the information on the sheet into logical regions. Borders appear on the screen and will print when you print the sheet.

To add a border to a cell

1. Select the range to which you want to apply a border.
2. Click the arrow button next to the Borders button to see the full range of border you want for the range

Or

1. Select the range to which you want to apply a border.
2. From the Format menu, choose Cells, or right-click and choose Format Cells from the shortcut menu.
3. On the Border tab of the Format Cells dialog box, choose a border, a border style, and a colour.
4. Click Ok and the border is added to the range.

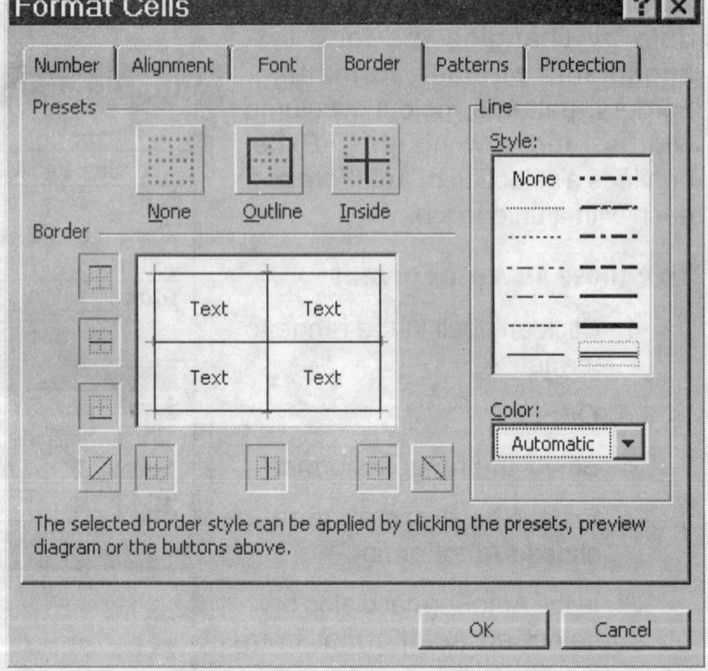

Formulae

They establish relationships between two or more cells. If you want to add the values in cells **C6** and **C7** and put the result in cell **C8**, move to the cell **C8** and type **=C6+C7** and press **Enter**. The result is displayed immediately in cell **C8**. Another way to achieve the same result is to move to cell **C8** and type **+**, point to cell **C6**, type **+**, then point to **C7**, and press **Enter**. The easiest way to achieve this operation is to point to **C8**, pick up the AutoSum button Σ on the toolbar.

Summing of a Row or Column

1. Click in the empty cell below the last entry in the column or to the right of the last entry in the row.
2. Click the AutoSum button on the Standard toolbar.
3. Press Enter to enter the formula that has automatically appeared in the cell.

Remember

1. Excel looks for the range of numbers to sum above the cell you have selected for the total. If it does not find a range of numbers or if it finds text, it looks to the left for a range of numbers.

2. Excel will not skip over an empty cell when it is looking for a range of cells to sum.

3. To quickly enter sums below multiple adjacent columns, select the empty cells at the bottoms of all the columns before clicking the AutoSum button. Excel will insert a sum in each selected cell.

Microsoft Excel - Sample

File Edit View Insert Format Tools Data Window Help

Times New Roman 12 100%

B7 = =SUM(B2:B6)

	A	B	C	D	E	F	G	H
1	**Year**	2000	1999	1998	1997	1996		
2	Sales	Rs.20,302.00	Rs.14,553.00	Rs.13,404.00	Rs.8,730.00	Rs.7,786.00		
3	Earnings	Rs.4,746.00	Rs.3,318.00	Rs.2,887.00	Rs.1,948.00	Rs.1,752.00		
4	Depreciation	Rs.1,278.00	Rs.855.00	Rs.667.00	Rs.410.00	Rs.337.00		
5	Taxable Profit	Rs.2,403.00	Rs.1,704.00	Rs.1,653.00	Rs.1,323.00	Rs.1,405.00		
6	Tax	Rs.3,719.00	Rs.2,893.00	Rs.3,021.00	Rs.2,490.00	Rs.2,234.00		
7		Rs.32,448.00						

SUM FUNCTION

The **Sum** function is perhaps the most commonly used of the Excel functions that carry out mathematical, statistical, financial, date, time, and other calculations.

1. Click the destination cell for the formula.

2. Type an equal sign to start the formula and then type the word SUM and a left parenthesis.

3. Drag down the column of numbers to sum.

4. Press Enter.

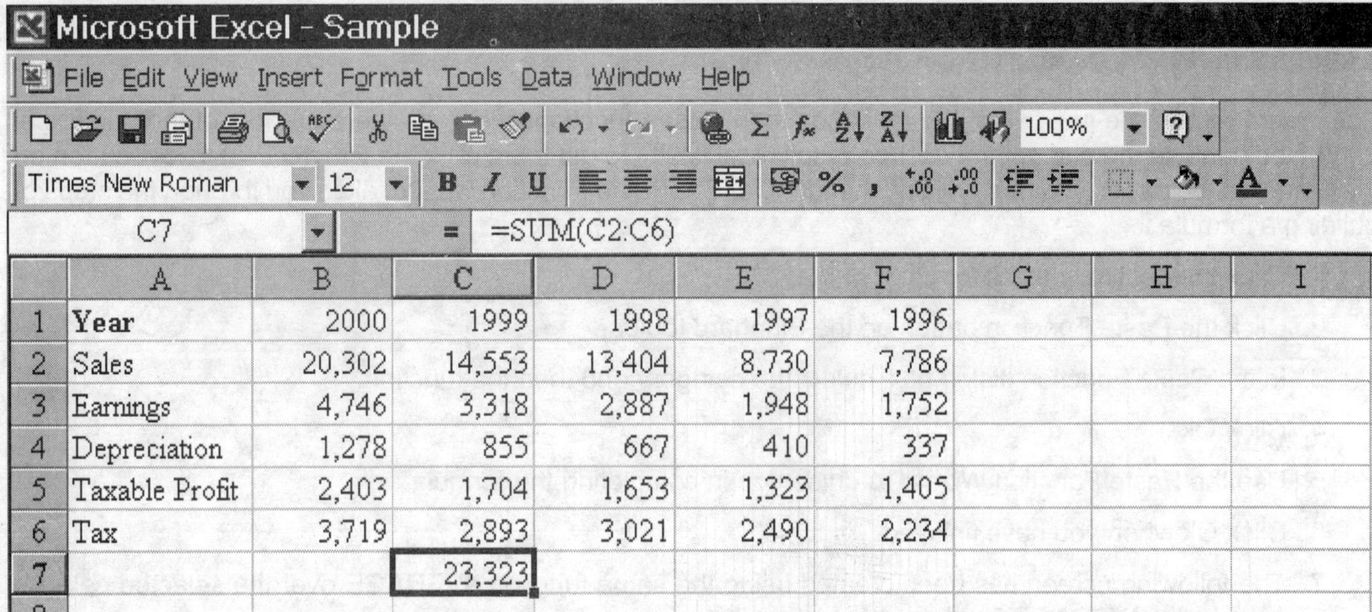

Microsoft Excel - Sample

File Edit View Insert Format Tools Data Window Help

Times New Roman 12 100%

C7 = =SUM(C2:C6)

	A	B	C	D	E	F	G	H	I
1	**Year**	2000	1999	1998	1997	1996			
2	Sales	20,302	14,553	13,404	8,730	7,786			
3	Earnings	4,746	3,318	2,887	1,948	1,752			
4	Depreciation	1,278	855	667	410	337			
5	Taxable Profit	2,403	1,704	1,653	1,323	1,405			
6	Tax	3,719	2,893	3,021	2,490	2,234			
7			23,323						

Remember

1. You do not need to type the close (right) parenthesis before you press Enter—Excel will do it for you.
2. Use this technique instead of AutoSum to sum ranges of cells that contain blanks.

Average Function

You can use the Average function to calculate the average of values in cells.

1. Click the cell where you want to place the average function.
2. Type an equal sign (=) and then type the word AVERAGE and a left parenthesis.
3. Drag across the cells whose values you want to average.
4. Press Enter.

Remember

1. Blank cells in the range are not counted in the average.

Microsoft Excel - Sample

File Edit View Insert Format Tools Data Window Help

Times New Roman 12 100%

D7 = =AVERAGE(D2:D6)

	A	B	C	D	E	F	G	H	I
1	**Year**	2000	1999	1998	1997	1996			
2	Sales	20,302	14,553	13,404	8,730	7,786			
3	Earnings	4,746	3,318	2,887	1,948	1,752			
4	Depreciation	1,278	855	667	410	337			
5	Taxable Profit	2,403	1,704	1,653	1,323	1,405			
6	Tax	3,719	2,893	3,021	2,490	2,234			
7				4,326					

Using Function Wizard

Sum and Average are just two of the most commonly used functions whereas there are lots of them in Excel 2000. You can use them to get the desired results in a flash. To get them click the **Paste Function** button on the Standard toolbar as your are building the formula. The Paste Function wizard takes you through the steps of building a formula.

1. Click the destination cell for the formula.
2. Click the Paste Function button on the Standard toolbar.
3. In the Paste Function dialog box, select the category and then the function.
4. Click Ok.
5. Use the Paste Function Wizard to guide you in completing the formula.
6. Click Ok when you have finished.
7. The following screen has been created using the same function AVERAGE over the selected cells as used in the AVERAGE function.

INTRODUCTION TO WORD PROCESSING

Word processor is a computer program for processing of words, very similar to a food processor (*mixie*) which processes food. Most of the word processors would start from a blank screen assumed to be a blank page with a blinking starting point known as `Cursor`. For all practical purposes it is like a typewriter, but it is much more than that.

You can type the text (even enter graphics) in the word processor, save it under a name to recall it again and again. Spell check it for errors, format it to look good, and then if needed print it too.

This makes it much easier for writing the text since you can make as many mistakes as you like since you can correct them by just pressing a key. This way you save a lot of paper and make the document look more neat and clean.

Some Important Terms of Word Processing

Before we go any further and study word processing, let us understand few basic terms of word processing:

Text	It is the matter which you type.
Document	It is whole text matter which you create, like a letter, or a chapter, etc.
Fonts	In typewriting you have just one type of handwriting. In word processing you can have your text written in many writings, these are called Fonts. Each font has its own way to writing the alphabets (A to Z) and even numerals (0 to 9).
Cursor	It is as said before, the blinking point which tells you where to start typing or what your current position is.
Arrow keys	These keys are on the arrow pads of your keyboard and are shown as: Up-arrow (↑), Down-arrow (↓), Left-arrow (←) and Right-arrow (→).
Space bar	It plays a very important role in word processing. The space between the words is given by this.
Tabs	These are used to set the text into tabular form.
Backspace	This is another important keyboard key which is used to delete the wrongly typed character in your text. You can even use the Del key for this.

Things which can be done by Word Processing

Let us now see what are the things which can be done by Word Processing and cannot be done on the typewriter.

Alignment	You can set your text in any alignment, e.g., Left, Right or Centre. You can even do box setting, i.e., aligned from both sides.
Deleting Mistakes	You can delete word, line, paragraph in a stroke and the rest of the matter will get adjusted automatically.
Line Spacing	You can set line spacing according to your liking from one to nine.
MailMerging	A very important feature of any word processing. This helps you in sending the same text to the different people, all in original format.
Moving the Cursor	You can move your cursor from word to word or from paragraph to paragraph, if needed.
Naming a Document	As mentioned earlier, you can name a document and recall it anytime from hard disk for editing, updating, correcting and even printing.

Overwriting Mistakes You can overwrite your mistakes on the screen itself. No more messing of eraser and spoiling of paper.

Page Breaks You can set a page break at any place within the text so that while printing it will jump to next page.

Page Numbers You can set page numbers according to your liking.

Search and Replace You can search for a particular word in the whole document and replace it with another one. You can even replace all the occurrence of the same word.

Spell Checking Probably the most important part of any word processing. Each word processor comes with a dictionary built inside it. You can check your text with it see whether any word has been wrongly typed.

Important Word Processing Programs

Most of the big time software producers have a word processing program of their own. But, it depends on the operating system which you are using. If you are working under DOS, then there is nothing to beat WordStar. It has been very popular word processing software till more and more users started working under Windows. Then, the preference shifted to Word for Windows. So here we will discuss Word for Windows.

Starting Word

You can start Word by one of the following methods:

From Start Button

Click at Start button to access the various commands. Click on Programs to get the various programs. From here click at the program called Microsoft Word to run Word for Windows, as shown here.

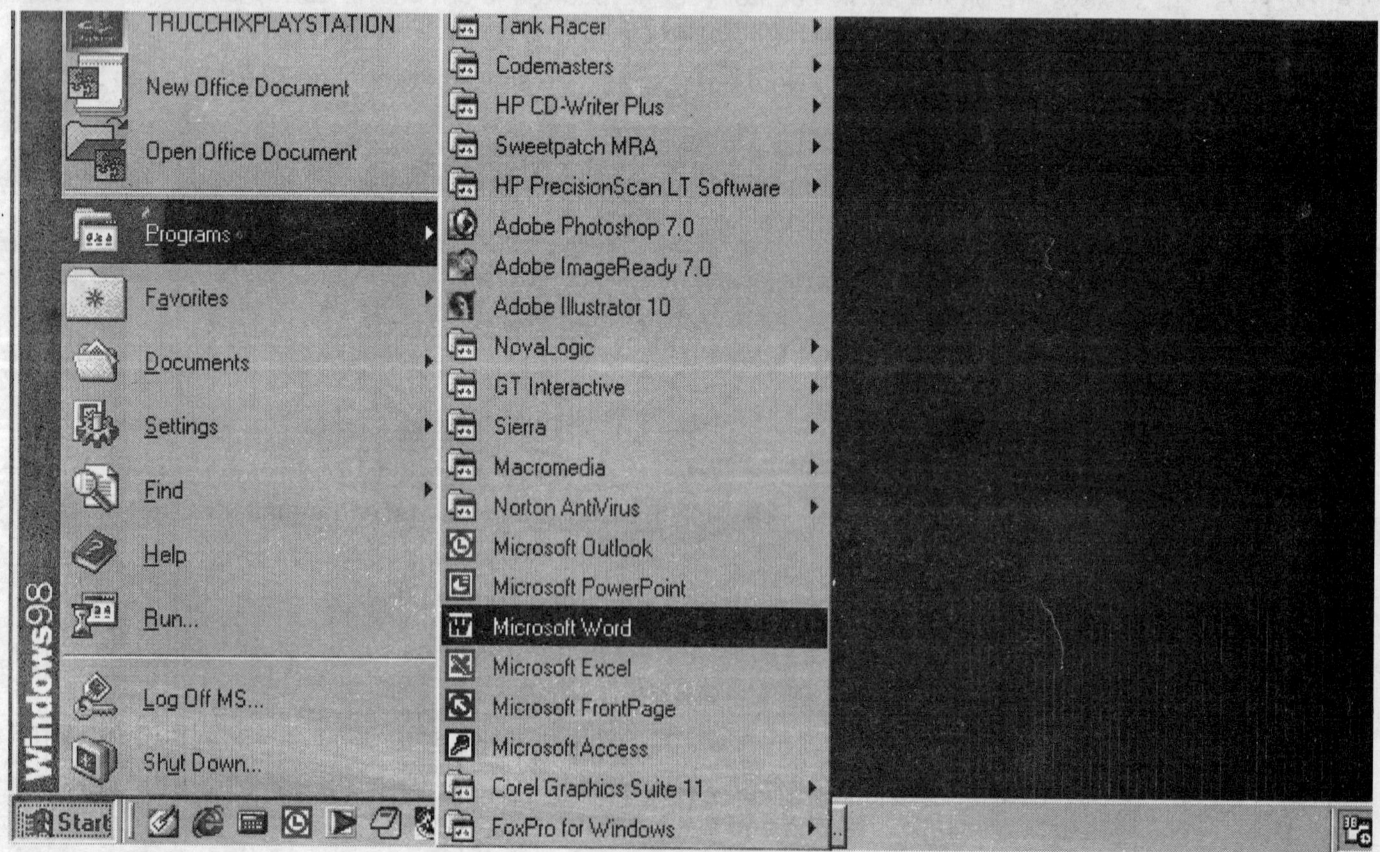

From Icon of Word

You can choose to have an icon of Word on your desktop. This icon can be created by using the feature of Creating Shortcut.

MICROSOFT WORD SCREEN

Once started Word give rise to a blank slate for typing your text. This screen has various items on it. One must know them before actually starting typing and using the commands.

Close button	This would close Word for Windows session.
Drawing toolbar	One of the various toolbars which can be made available on the screen. This particular one is used for making drawings in the document.
Formatting bar	This bar is used to format the text. For example you can set font, font size, alignment, etc., using this bar.
Horizontal scroll bar	Sometimes the width of the text is such that it cannot be displayed on the whole screen. This bar is then used to see the text on the left or right.
Menu bar	Like in other programs Word for Windows also has various commands which can be accessed by clicking at the menu options under these menu heads.
Minimize button	While working, you can minimize your word document to reach desktop for working with another program, maybe.
Restore button	You have the option of working between two different views of the document by toggling this switch.
Ruler	Using this ruler you can see how much of the line you have consumed by typing.

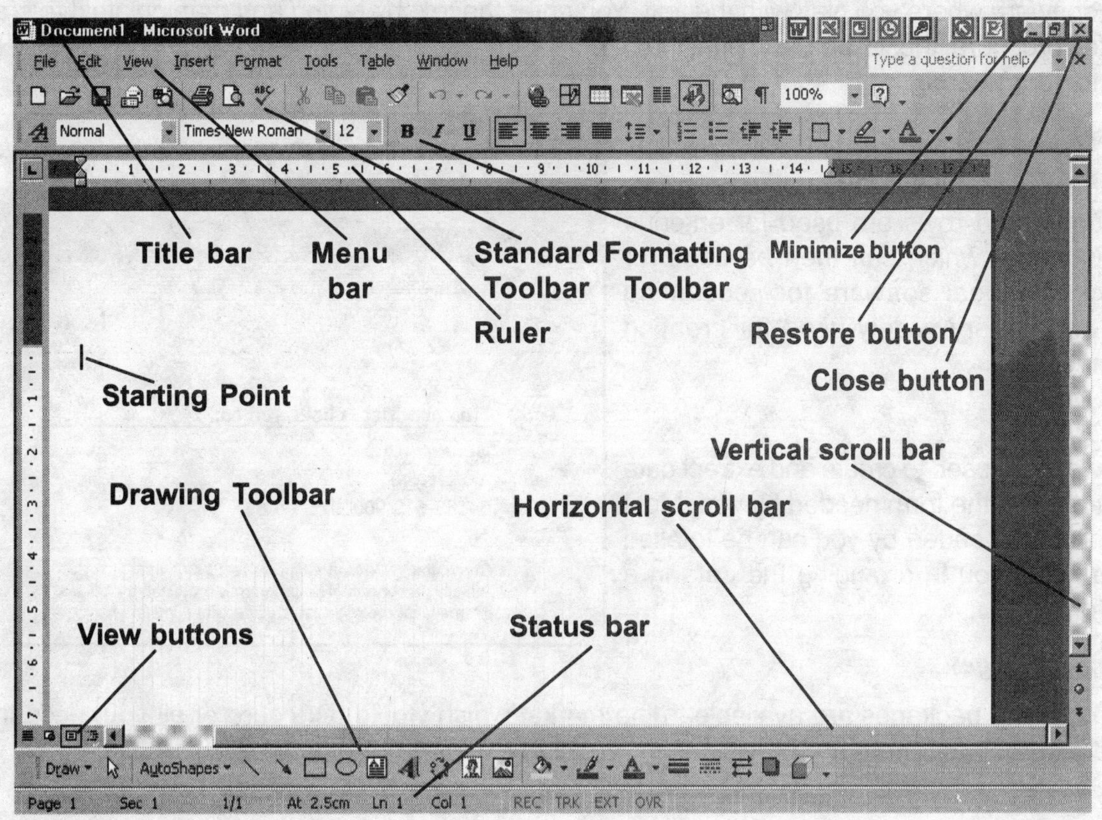

Standard toolbar	There are a number of toolbars which allow you to select various tools for working in Word for Windows. This one is the standard which has all the icons of various file options, etc.
Starting point	This is the starting point of your text on the document. This is the point from where you would start typing.
Status bar	This bar will always show you your current position as far as the text goes. It will tell you your current position with respect to page number, line number, etc.
Title bar	Another permanent feature of Word for Windows which shows you the name of the file on which you are working and at the end has the various buttons like Close, Restore and Minimize.
Vertical scroll bar	For a larger text in the document, you can scroll the vertical bar to see the text at various positions.
View buttons	Word for Windows allows you to work in various views of the document. Using these buttons you can go from one view to another.

PRE-WRITTEN SOFTWARE PACKAGES

It is a set of programs designed for specific uses or applications such as word processing, graphics or spreadsheet analysis. In fact, most of the commercial software fall under this category. Application software can be custom-made but is usually purchased off the shelf.

Popular Software Packages

Word Processors

This is the software where you play with the text. You enter the text by typing and manipulate it to create a good looking letter, brochure, thesis, etc., and print them according to your needs.

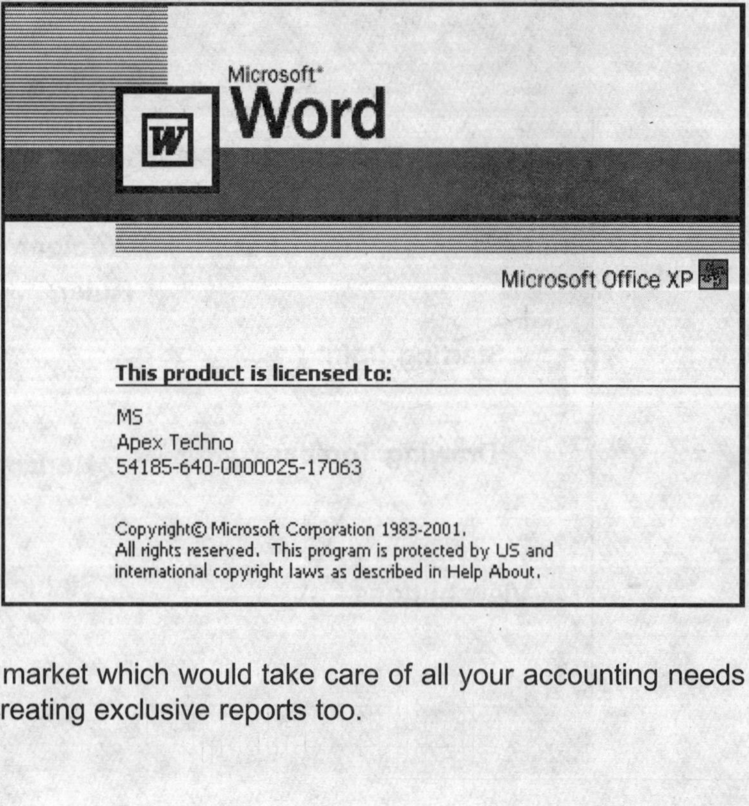

Spreadsheets

A spreadsheet is a matrix of rows and columns. These columns and rows are used for entering text and numbers, which can then be used for calculations. An ideal software for accounting purposes and is very widely used for creating balance sheet, etc.

Database System

These software are used to create and extract data from a database in the form needed by you. Most of the information needed by you can be totalled too. It also helps you in arranging the data in a particular format too.

Microsoft® Word

Microsoft Office XP

This product is licensed to:

MS
Apex Techno
54185-640-0000025-17063

Copyright© Microsoft Corporation 1983-2001.
All rights reserved. This program is protected by US and international copyright laws as described in Help About.

Accounting Packages

Various accounting packages are available in the market which would take care of all your accounting needs from ledgers to reports. There are provisions for creating exclusive reports too.

DTP Packages

Without these packages, this book would not have been possible. It sort of acts as via media between computer and printing press. All the pre-press work can be done using these software. From designing a page with text and graphics to creating complicated art works, everything can be done using them.

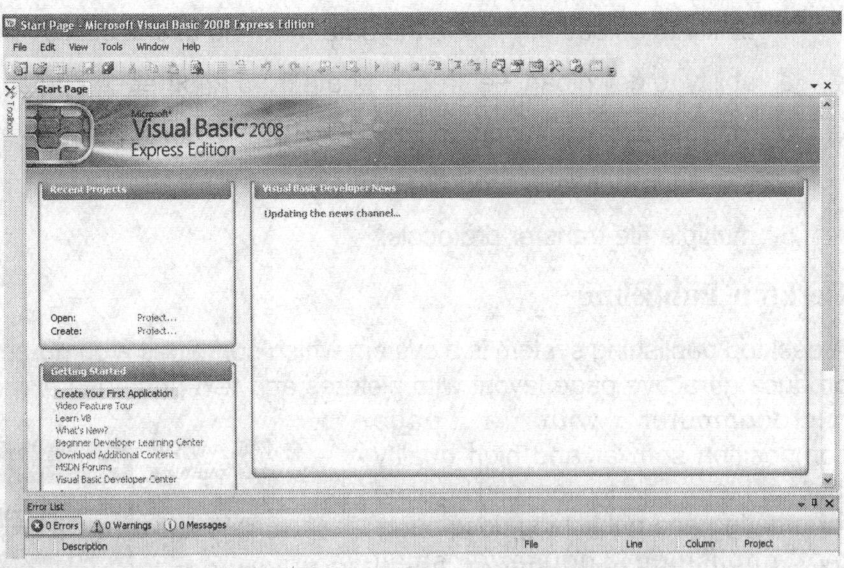

Graphic Packages

These are used for working with pictures and graphics instead of numbers and text. Computer-accessible data can readily be converted to graphic form on the screen as well as on paper using dot-matrix printers, ink-jet printers or plotters.

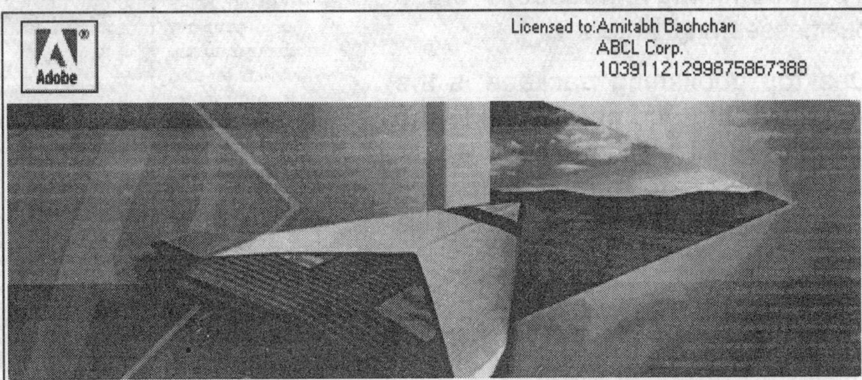

Anti Virus Software

Though viruses are mushrooming at a faster rate than virus vaccines, still there are few very good and reasonable anti-virus software to assist users to keep their computer system virus free.

Data Communication Software

Data communication refers to the means and methods by which data can be transferred between processing locations. Data communication packages are programs that are designed to control commuication between two computers. They allow a user to send and receive data over communication lines. Most of the data that is transmitted and manipulated is text. The data transfer may be between two points or between a network of computers and workstations. Most of the data movement between computers at different sites flow over telephone circuits. The communications packages act as intelligent gatekeepers to speed the flow of data between the sites. The powerful features of a communcation package can be listed as:

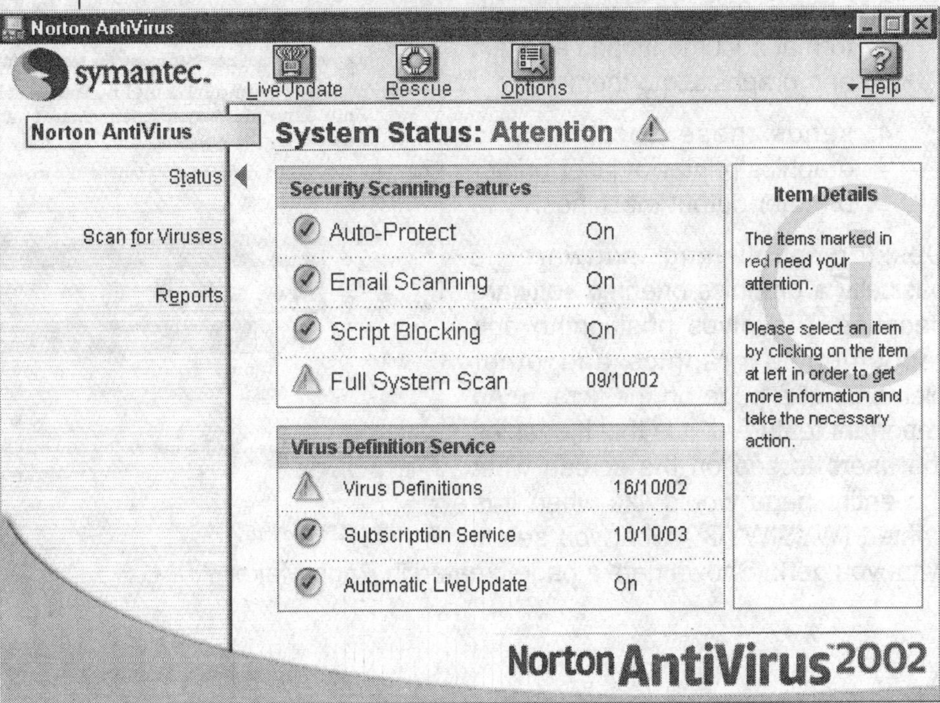

1. ability to upload, i.e., send the data from the user's disk to another computer.
2. ability to download, i.e., receive data from another computer and save them on the user's disk.
3. multiple data-capturing options.
4. switching between program modes
5. multiple file-transfer protocols.

Desktop Publishing

A desktop publishing system is a system which combines a computer and suitable peripherals with software to produce attractive page layout with pictures and text printed in a variety of typefaces. It combines the user of microcomputer with a page composition softwar and high quality laser printers. This system can be used for creating and publishing documents by publishing houses, small businesses and writers.

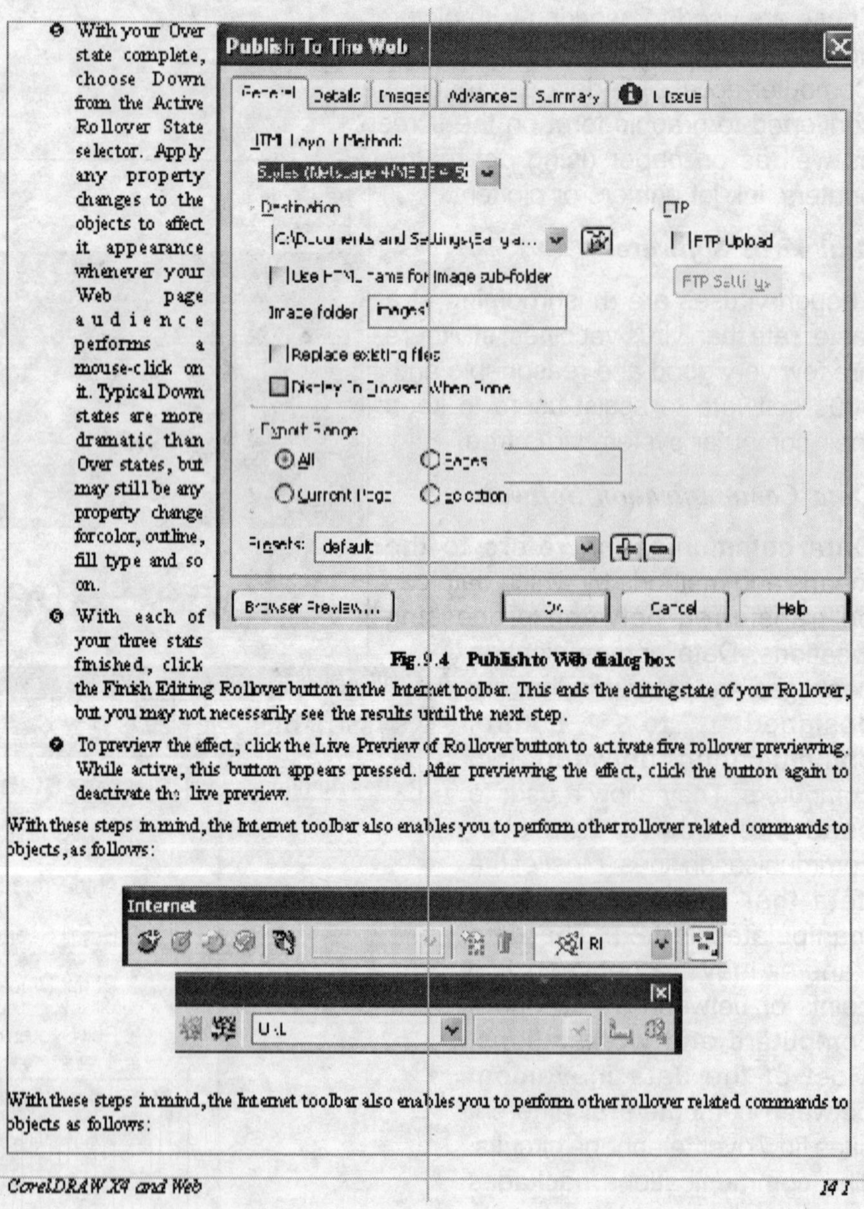

❺ With your Over state complete, choose Down from the Active Rollover State selector. Apply any property changes to the objects to affect it appearance whenever your Web page audience performs a mouse-click on it. Typical Down states are more dramatic than Over states, but may still be any property change for color, outline, fill type and so on.

❻ With each of your three stats finished, click the Finish Editing Rollover button in the Internet toolbar. This ends the editing state of your Rollover, but you may not necessarily see the results until the next step.

Fig. 9.4 Publish to Web dialog box

❼ To preview the effect, click the Live Preview of Rollover button to activate five rollover previewing. While active, this button appears pressed. After previewing the effect, click the button again to deactivate the live preview.

With these steps in mind, the Internet toolbar also enables you to perform other rollover related commands to objects, as follows:

With these steps in mind, the Internet toolbar also enables you to perform other rollover related commands to objects as follows:

CorelDRAW X4 and Web 141

Desktop publishing package is the software that combines text and graphics manipulating capabilities for allowing users to format charts and pictures with text and headlines. This package:

1. accepts digitizer text and picture input.
2. accepts data imported from word processor, page format and graphic files.
3. allows user to create, edit, format documents and add text and graphics into them.
4. sends these documents to graphics printer or laser printer or other output machines.

Desktop publishing software is basically a graphics-oriented software because it involves positioning and repositioning graphics and other elements of a page on the screen. An important feature of it is that it enables the users to see on the screen what the entire page would like when it is printed (WYSIWYG - what you see is what you get). Shown here a page created in Page Maker 7.0.

SUMMARY

1. Excel can be started from the Start button, Microsoft Office Bar or from Windows Explorer.
2. Excel has like other software, Toolbar, Formatting bar, Standard toolbar, etc.
3. Scroll button allows you to scroll through the whole worksheet.
4. Formula bar shows you the formula being applied.
5. Word processing programs allow you to manipulate text consisting of words.
6. In a word processing program, you can change the various aspects of the text.
7. Among the various features of Word Processing are: Alignment, Deleting Mistakes, Line Spacing, MailMerging, Moving the Cursor, Naming a Document, Overwriting Mistakes, Page Breaks, Page Numbers, Search and Replace, Spell Checking.
8. Text is the matter which you type.
9. Document is whole text matter which you create, like a letter, or a chapter, etc.
10. Fonts are the various styles which you can use for your text.
11. Cursor is the blinking point which tells you where to start typing or what your current position is.
12. Space bar is used for giving space between the words.
13. Tabs are used to set the text into tabular form.
14. Backspace is used to delete the wrongly typed character in your text.
15. You can start Microsoft Word from the Start button and Programs.
16. You can also start Word from its icon.
17. Opening screen of Word is like a blank screen.
18. Word processors are used for manipulating text.
19. Spreadsheets are used for calculations.
20. DTP packages are used for text and graphics.
21. Anti virus software are used for virus detection and removal.

MULTIPLE CHOICE QUESTIONS

1. For opening and closing of the file in Excel you can use which bar.
   a. Formatting b. Standard c. Title
2. What are numbered from A to Z, etc?
   a. Rows b. Cells c. Columns
3. You can move around the worksheet using which buttons?
   a. Scroll b. Logic c. Start
4. For making the text bold in the cell, you use B in which bar.
   a. Standard b. Formatting c. Title
5. In word processing, you manipulate _______
   (a) numbers (b) text
6. You can set Left, Right and ______ alignment in word processing.
   (a) Center (b) Justify (c) Both
7. Can you spell check you text in word processing?
   (a) Yes (b) No
8. Can you locate a word in word processing?
   (a) No (b) Yes

REVIEW QUESTIONS

1. Describe the various components of the Excel worksheet window.
2. Describe the method of copying formula.
3. Describe the process of saving a worksheet.
4. Word processing is to mix words.
5. You can spell check your typed text.
6. You cannot use various fonts available under Windows for your text.
7. Spacebar is used for giving space between words.
8. Which are the various popular software packages?

ANSWERS

Multiple Choice Questions

1. b	2. c	3. a	4. b
5. b	6. c	7. a	8. b

CHAPTER 8

Programming Languages

LEARNING OBJECTIVES

After going through this chapter, you should appreciate the following:

- **First Generation of Languages**
- **Second Genration of Languages**
- **Third Generation of Languages**

  High Level Languages
  Business Languages
  Scientific Languages
  Multipurpose Languages
- **Other Procedure Oriented Languages**

  LOGO
  Modula-2
- **Problem Oriented Languages**
- **Object Oriented Languages**

  C++
  Clipper
  dBASE
  FoxBase+
  FoxPro
  MUMPS
  Prolog
- **Fourth Generation Languages**
- **Fifth Generation Languages**

  Application Generators
- **Natural Languages: The Ultimate Programming Language**

INTRODUCTION

To do a useful job a computer normally needs two forms of input, data and a set of instructions. A set of instructions expressed in a way that the computer can understand is called a program. Programs have to be written in languages especially invented for the purpose of instructing computers and enabling the programmer to tell the computer the various operation it must perform in the correct sequence.

We talk to computers within the framework of a particular programming language. At present, there are over 200 programming languages - and these are the ones that are still being used. The selection of a programming language depends on who is involved and the nature of the "conversation". Initially, programming languages were created by the people in universities or in government and were devised for special functions. Some languages endured because they served special purpose in science, engineering and the like.

Programming languages are said to be "lower" or "higher", depending on how close they are to the language the computer itself uses (0s and 1s - low) or to the language people use (more English-like-high). Low-level languages are machine-dependent; that is, they are designed to be run on a particular computer. In contrast high-level languages (e.g. COBOL and BASIC) are machine independent and can be run on a variety of computers.

Through the first four decades of computing, programming languages evolved in generations. The first two generations were low-level and the next two consecutive were high and very-high level generations of programming languages. Whereas the fifth generation languages are called natural languages. The higher-level languages do not necessarily provide us with greater programming capabilities, but they do provide more sophisticated programmer/computer interaction. In short, the higher the level of language, the easier it is understand and use. When programming in one of the first three generations of languages, you have to tell the computer what to do and how to do it. With each new level, fewer instructions are needed to tell the computer to perform a particular task. The ease with which the later generations can be used in certainly appealing, but the earlier languages also have their advantages. All generations of languages are in use today.

For all practical purpose, programmers never write computer instructions in machine language. The programmer writes instructions in a language more suited to human use, which is then translated to machine language. When programs are needed which are very specific to machine efficiency, they are generally written in an assembly language. However, except for operating system programs and some applications that require close coordinations with hardware characteristics, most programming is done in high-level language. Some important type of high-level languages for instructing a computer are procedure-oriented languages (viz, Pascal, C etc.), query languages (viz., SQL), report generators, program generators, analysis and modelling facilities, very high-level languages and natural languages.

FIRST-GENERATION OF LANGUAGES

Machine Language:

Computer recognizes and operates in binary numbers. So to communicate with a computer one must give instructions in binary language, i.e., machine language. This machine language is the lowest level of language, which represents data and program instructions as 1s and 0s which corresponds to the on and off electrical states in the computer.

Each computer has its own set of instructions based on the design of its processor. e.g., 8085 is a microprocessor with 8-bit word length. Its instruction set (or machine language) is designed by using various combinations of these 8-bits. With these 8-bits we can have 256 (28) combinations, but 8085 microprocessor uses only 246 bit patterns and amounting to only 74 different instructions for performing various operations. These 74 different instructions are called its Instruction Set.

This binary language of communication with a predetermined instruction set is called the 8085 machine language. Programs written in assembly language are not transferable from one machine to another, i.e., it is machine-dependent. So each type of computer has its own machine language.

SECOND-GENERATION OF LANGUAGES

Assembly Languages

Since it was difficult for people to communicate with computers in the language of 0's and 1's, the binary instructions were given abbreviated form by using hexadecimal code system. But inspite of it, it was difficult to understand a program written in hexadecimal numbers. This problem led each manufacturer of microprocessor to device a new symbolic code for each instruction, called mnemonic, which form the assembly language. The mnemonic for a particular instruction consists of letters which suggest the operation to be performed by that instruction (e.g., ADD for Addition, MULT for multiplication etc.).

The user employs symbols (letters, numerals or special characters) for the operation part, the address part and other parts of the instruction code. Each symbolic instruction can be translated into one binary coded instruction. This translation is done by a special program called an assembler. Because an assembler translates the symbols, this type of symbolic program is referred to as an assembly language program. This assembler languages ushered in the second generation of programming languages.

Assembly Language Format

A typical language programming statement is divided into four parts called fields.

That are:

- Label
- Operation code (opcode)
- Operands
- Comments

These fields are separated by delimiters for the CP/M assembler as shown below:

Delimiter	***Placement***
Colon	After label (optional)
Space	Between an opcode and operand
Comma	Between two operand
Semicolon	Before the beginning of a comment

The assembler statements have a free-field format, which means that any number of blanks can be left between the fields. Comments are optional but are included for good documentation. Similarly label for an instruction is also optional, but its use greatly facilitate specifying jump locations. For example,

Label	**Opcode**	**Operands**	**Comments**
START	COPY	A,B	;Copy the content of A into B

Rules of writing a symbol in an assembly-language statements are

- the first character should be an alphabet
- other characters should be alphabets or digits and

- total length should not exceed 8-characters.

Although assembly languages represent a step forward, they still have many disadvantages.

These are:

- An assembly language program written for one microprocessor is not transferable to a computer with another microprocessor unless the two microprocessors are compatible in their machine codes. This implies that assembly language is machine-dependent. This computer dependency makes assembly language a low-level language.
- Assembly language is detailed in the extreme, making assembly programming repetitive, tedious and error prone.

Assembly language may be easier to read than machine language, but it is still tedious. Assembly language is most frequently used for writing micro-programs. A micro-program consists of a series of binary codes which carry out the specific actions requested by assembly language statements.

There is a tradeoff implicit between the use of high-level languages and machine oriented assembler languages. The high-level languages obtain human productivity at the expense of extra storage and inefficiencies in execution. The human productivity gains come through languages are less error-prone and at least partly self-documenting. High-level languages are also easier to learn and are not dependent on a particular type of computer, so that the programmer's skills are more transferable. Machine costs have decreased to the extent that high-level languages are almost always preferred.

This example changes Fahrenheit to Celsius:

```
HP 3000
begin
intrinsic read, print binary, ascii;
array buffer (0 : 17);
array string (0 : 3);
byte array b' string (*) = string;
integer ftemp, ctemp, len;
move buffer: = "Enter Fahrenheit";
print (buffer, - 30, %320); len : = read (string, -4);
ftemp: = binary (b' string , len);
ctemp : = (ftemp-32) * 5 / 9;
len : = ascii (ctemp, 1-, b' string);
move buffer : = "Celsius is"
move buffer (14) : = string, (-len) ;
print (buffer, -32, %0) ;
end
```

THIRD-GENERATION OF LANGUAGES

HIGH-LEVEL LANGUAGES

An assembly language is specific to a given machine; so programs written in assembly language are not transferable from one machine to another. To circumvent this limitation, such general purpose languages as BASIC and FORTRAN have been devised. A program written in these languages can be machine-independent. These languages are called high-level languages. A high-level language is a language where a single statement may correspond to several instructions in machine language. Another powerful facility in high-level languages is the use of subroutines which are like complete programs in themselves.

In high-level languages the programs are written in a sequence of statements in a form that people prefer to think in when solving a problem. No matter which high-level language (third or later generations) a program is written in, it must be translated into machine language before it can be executed. System software programs called compilers and interpreters perform this task. There are many compilers for each language and one for each type of computer.

Third-generation programming languages fall into three categories:

- procedure-oriented languages,
- problem oriented languages, and
- object-oriented languages

Procedure-Oriented Languages

Procedure-oriented languages are designed to facilitate the accurate description of procedures, algorithms, or routines belonging to a certain set of procedures. The flexibility of procedure-oriented languages permits programmers to model almost any scientific or business procedure. In it, instructions are cocded, or written, sequentially and processed according to program specifications. Procedure-oriented languages are classified as:

- business languages,
- scientific languages, and
- multipurpose languages

Business languages

Business programming languages are designed to be effective tools for developing business information systems. The strength of business-oriented languages lies in their ability to store, retrieve and manipulate alphanumeric data. COBOL and RPG are two main business languages which are commonly used in business.

COBOL (Common Business Oriented Language)

COBOL, the first business programming language, was developed in 1959 by a U.S. government-appointed committee. It was developed by this committee under the leadership of retired Navy Commodore and mathematician Grace Hopper. The original intention of the developers of COBOL was to make its instructions approximate to English language. Here is a typical COBOL sentence:

```
IF SALARY-CODE IS EQUAL TO 'S'
MULTIPLY SALARY BY HOURLY_RATE
GIVING GROSS-PAY
ELSE PERFORM
SALARIED-EMPLOYEE-ROUTINE.
```

Note that the COBOL sentence contains several instructions and even a period at the end of sentence.

A COBOL program is written in four divisions; these are:

- Identification Division:
- Environment Division;
- Data Division;
- Procedure Division

The Identification Division contains descriptive information that identifies the program being compiled, for example.,

```
IDENTIFICATION
PROGRAM-ID, program-name-sample.
INSTALLATION. COMPANY BAPS ACCOUNTING DEPT.
AUTHOR. AMITABH BACHCHAN.
DATE-WRITTEN. 11-OCTOBER-2000.
DATE-COMPILED. 12-OCTOBER-2000.
SECURITY. CONFIDENTIAL
```

The Environment Division deals with the specification of the computer to be used for operating the object program, including such information as the size of memory, the number of tape decks, printers and other peripheral devices that will be used; a description of the computer to be used for compiling the source program is also given, for example,

```
ENVIRONMENT DIVISION
CONFIGURATION SECTION
SOURCE-COMPUTER
        Computer and model number supplied by manufacturer
OBJECT-COMPUTER
        Computer and model number supplied by manufacturer
INPUT-OUTPUT SECTION
FILE-CONTROL
        Entries which assign file-name to devices.
```

The Data Division is used to allocate identifying names or labels to all units of data on which operations are to be performed. All input and output files are defined and associated with the peripheral units to be used for input and output. Records and fields within the files are described. For example,

```
DATA DIVISION
FILE SECTION
FD STUDENT-FILE
LABEL RECORDS ARE OMITTED.
01 STUDENT-REC.
05 NAME PIC X(20)
05 BOOK-FOLLOWED PIC X(25).
FD TRANSCRIPT-FILE.
```

```
LABEL RECORDS ARE OMITTED
01 TRANSCRIPT-REC.
05 NAME-OUT PIC X(20).
05 BOOK-PURCHASED PIC X(3).
WORKING-STORAGE SECTION
01 ARE-THERE-MORE-RECORDS PIC X(3) VALUE 'YES'.
```

The Procedure Division gives the step-by-step instructions necessary to the problem. These steps are specified by means of instructions expressed in stylized but meaningful English statements which can be recognized by the compiler and translated into a sequence of machine code instructions capable of being used by the computer to solve the problem

RPG (Report Programs Generator)

Another popular business programming language is RPG. RPG, introduced in 1964, has always differed somewhat from other procedure-oriented languages in a way that the programmer specifies certain processing requirements by selecting the desired programming options viz., printing results, summaries etc., for computer files.

Scientific Languages

Scientific languages are designed for the writing of mathematical or scientific programs. These algebraic formula-type languages are specially designed to meet typical scientific processing requirements, such as matrix multiplication, precision calculations, interactive processing, the expression and resolution of mathematical equations, and so on. FORTRAN, ALGOL and APL are three main scientific languages which are commonly used for the writing of mathematical or scientific programs.

FORTRAN (FORmula TRANslation)

FORTRAN, the first procedure-oriented language, was developed in 1955. It was and remains the most popular scientific language. FORTRAN was developed by John Backnus and a team of programmers at IBM. FORTRAN was enhanced and standardized in 1966, and again in 1977 and 1990. The current version is often referred to as FORTRAN-90. Because of its almost exclusive focus on mathematical and engineering applications, FORTRAN has not been widely used with personal computers.

Instead, FORTRAN remains a common language on mainframe systems, especially those used for research and education. A FORTRAN program consists of data items, executable statements and non-executable statements. The program is structured in Segments, which consists of a master segment and optional function segments and subroutines.

Data items in FORTRAN are either variables or constants, and are assigned alphanumeric names by the programmer. Data items in FORTRAN may take the following forms:

Integer; Real; Complex (a complex number in which two real numbers are used to express the real and imaginary parts). Logical; Text (Character information, which is not used for mathematical operations). The actual operations of the programs are expressed by means of 'executable statements'.

These can, take two basic forms:

- 'assign statements' and
- 'control statements'

An assign statement takes the form

Variable = Expression

The expression may be either arithmetic or logical.

Control statements enables the program to branch to other statements and enable loops to be constructed. Branches may also be constructed which are conditional on the results of arithmetic or logical operations, for example,

GO TO 18

This statement is an unconditional branch to statement number 18. While executable statements specify the operations the program is to perform 'non-executable statements' merely provide the compiler with information, for example,

COMPLEX ROOT1, ROOT2, ANS

This statement indicates to the compiler that storage is required for three complex variables with labels as specified. The following example converts Fahrenheit to Celsius:

```
WRITE (6, *) ` Enter Fahrenheit `
READ (5, *) XFAHR
XCENT = (XFAHR-32)*5/9
WRITE (6, *) ` Celsius is `, XCENT
STOP
END
```

ALGOL (ALGOrithmic Languages)

ALGOL was originally known as IAL (international Algebraic Language) and was developed in Europe at the same time as FORTRAN was being developed in United States. It is a problem oriented high level programming language for mathematical and scientific use, in which the source program provides a means of defining algorithms as a series of statements and declarations having a general resemblance to algebraic formulae and English sentences.

An ALGOL program consists of

- data items;
- statements; and
- declarations

Every data item processed in an ALGOL program is termed a variable, and is assigned a general name or identifier by the programmer. Every operation a program is to perform is represented as a statement. Statements may be assignment statements or conditional statements. An assignment statement has the form

Variable : = Arithmetic Expression

Declarations are used in ALGOL to provide the compiler with information about quantities appearing in the remainder of the program.

The following example changes Fahrenheit to Celsius:

```
Fahrenheit
begin
   real fahr;
```

```
    print  (Enter  Fahrenheit");
    read (farh);
    print("Celsius  is",  (fahr-32.0)  *5.0/9.0);
  end
 finish
```

APL (A Programming Language)

APL, introduced in 1968, is a symbolic interactive programming language that is popular with engineers, mathematicians, and scientists. A special keyboard with "shorthand" symbols helps speed the coding process. APL simplifies notations and the handling of arrays. It is primarily an interpreted language, but compilers are available. APL uses unique character symbols and requires special software or ROM chips to enable the computer to display and print them. APL is popular in Europe.

The Following example converts fahrenheit to Celsius:

```
[0]   CONVERT
[1}  'Enter  Fahrenheit
[2]  fahr
[3]  cels 5 x (fahr-32) + 9
[4]  'Celsius  is  ',  (cels)
```

COGO

COGO another higher-language oriented toward civil engineering, enabling one to write a program in a technical vocabulary familiar to engineers and feed it to the computer. COGO is derived from COordinate GeOmetry.

MULTIPURPOSE LANGUAGES

Multipurpose languages are equally effective for both business and scientific applications. They are an outgrowth of the need to simplify the programming environment by providing programmers with one language capable of addressing all programming needs of a company. BASIC, Pascal, PL/I, C and Ada are the major multipurpose languages.

BASIC (Beginners All-purpose Symbolic Instruction Code)

The BASIC language started out largely as a tool for teaching programming to students. BASIC was developed by John Kemeny and Thomas Kurtz at Dartmouth College (in England) in 1964. Kemeny and Kurtz wanted a language that would be suitable for teaching students programming on time sharing computers at Dartmoth.

BASIC is commonly used in both scientific and business applications - and even in developing video games. Because of its simplicity and comparative power, the language is much used on PC's.

The Following BASIC example coberts Fahrenheit to Celsius;

```
10 INPUT "Enter Fahrenheit "; FAHR
20 PRINT "Celsius is",  (FAHR-32)*5/9
```

Pascal

In 1968, a Swiss computer scientist named Niklaus Wirth introduced Pascal. Pascal, named after 17th century

French mathematician Blaise Pascal, has experienced tremendous growth during the last decade. Pascal was intended to overcome the limitations of other programming languages and to demonstrate the proper way to implement a computer language. It is a derivative of ALGOL.

Pascal is highly structured and, as such, is considered an excellent language for learning about structured programming. Pascal's power, flexibility, and self documenting structure have made it the language of choice in many computer science curriculum's and for many developers of system software.

PL/1 (Programming Language 1)

PL/1, a programming language introduced in 1964, was developed with the intention of combining the features of business languages (such as COBOL) and scientific languages (such as ALGOL, FORTRAN). It was developed by IBM for the Model 360 systems. PL/1 aims at combining the problem-solving facility of scientific languages with the data-handling capabilities of commercial languages, in order to meet the needs of increasingly mathematical commercial analysis and increasingly large volumes of data being processed by scientific routines.

C

C was developed in the early 1970s at Bell Labs., by Brian Kerninghan and Dennis Ritchie. Ritchie with Ken Thompson, had also developed the Unix operating system. Kerninghan & Richie developed C from another language called B, which in turn was derived from language called BCPL (a system programming language).

Developers of proprietary packaged software are very interested in C because it is considered more transportable than other languages. That is, it is relatively machine-independent: A C program written for one type of computer can be run on another type with little or no modifications.

The following C example converts fahrenheit to centigrade:

```
main ( )        {
float  fahr;
printf  ("Enter Fahrenheit")  ;
scanf  (" % f", &fahr);
printf  ("Celsius  is  %f\n",(fahr-32)*5/9);
}
```

Ada

Ada, a programming language introduced in 1980, was developed for US Department of Defence specifically for real-time systems and in particular for systems in which computers were used for control. Ada therefore includes facilities for concurrent programming and allows development of very large systems with program development tools specified in an Ada Programming Support Environment (APSE). The language is named after Lord Byron's daughter Augusta Ada Lovelace, who worked with Charles Babbage and is not unjustly described as the first programmer.

Following Ada program, converts Fahrenheit to Celsius:

```
with  Text_IO
procedure  Cobert  is
package  Int_IO  is  new  Text_IO.  Integer_IO  (Integer);
Fahrenheit  :  Integer;
begin
Text_IO.Put_line  ("Enter  Fahrenheit");
```

```
Int_IO.Get(Fahrenheit);Text_IO.Put  ("Celsius  is  ");
Int_IO.Put  (Fahrenheit-32)*  5/9)  ;
Text_IO.New_Line;

end  Convert;
```

OTHER PROCEDURE-ORIENTED LANGUAGES

Many other procedure-oriented languages which are commonly used in business and taught in academic institutions are:

LISP, LOGO, FORTH, Prolog, Modula-2, CONTRAN, CORAL, DETAB, IAL, IPL, JOSS, JOVIAL, NELIAC, QUCKTRAN, SNOBOL, TELCOMP, SIMSCRIPT and so on.

LISP (LISt Processing)

LISP programming language was introduced in 1959. It was designed for manipulating non-numeric data, such as symbols and strings of text, particularly used in artificial intelligence applications. It can also be used to manipulate mathematical and arithmetic logic. It is based on the lambda calculus of mathematical logic.

LISP is used extensively in AI applications, as well as in compiler creation, and is available in both interpreter and complier versions. It automatically handles more program activities than conventional languages, such as dynamic memory management, and lets the programmer concentrate on manipulating the objects.

The language itself can be modified and expanded. Many varieties of LISP have been developed, including versions that perform calculations efficiently. LISt processing , a high level language designed in the late 1950s at Massachusetts Institute of Technology (USA). LISP is used for Artificial Intelligence and other complex applications.

The following Common LISP example converts Fahrenheit to Celsius:

```
(defun convert   ( )
   (format t "Enter Fahrenheit   "  )
   let  ( (fahr       (read)))
   (format  t "Celsius is ~D"

   (truncate(*(- farh 32)  (5/9 )
```

Logo

High-level programming language noted for its ease of use and graphics capabilities. It is a recursive language that contains many list processing functions that are in LISP, although Logo's syntax is more understandable for novices. Logo's graphics language is also called turtle graphics, which allows complex with a minimum of coding. The turtle is a triangular shaped cursor, which is moved on screen with commands that activate the turtle as if you were driving it.

Stemming from a National Science Foundation project, Logo was created by Seymour Papert in the mid 1960s along with colleagues at MIT and members of Bolt Beranek & Newman. Originally developed on large computers, it has been adapted to most personal computers.

The following Object Logo example converts Fahrenheit to Celcius:

```
convert
local (fahr)
print "|Enter Fahrenheit   |
make "fahr ReadWord
print "|Celsius is   |
print (:fahr -32) *5/9

end
```

FORTH

FORTH a high-level programming language, introduced in 1971. Originally it was designed, for the use, by astronomers. FORTH uses postfix notation and was designed primarily for process control applications and now is also used for microprocessor applications. It allows compile-time error checking.

Programs written in FORTH can be run on various types of computers with little or no modifications.

Prolog (PROgramming in LOgic)

Prolog (Programmation Logique) is a high-level application programming language for rule-based on logic programming. It is oriented to action when declared conditions are met. It is used for artificial intelligence applications, particularly expert systems and is based on the first-order predicate calculus of mathematical logic.

MODULA-2 (MODULAR LANGUAGE-2)

Enhanced version of Pascal introduced in 1979 by Swiss professor Nieklaus Wirth, creator of Pascal. It supports separate compilation of modules.

The following example changes Fahrenheit to Celsius:

```
MODULE FahrToCent;
FROM InOut IMPORT ReadReal, writeReal,
WriteString,   WriteLn;
VAR Fahr : REAL;
BEGIN WriteString("Enter Fahrenheit");
ReadReal (Fahr);
WriteLn; WriteString ("Celsius is");
WriteReal ((Fahr-32)*5/9);

END FahrToCent
```

CONTRAN

CONTRAN a computer programming language in which instructions are written at the compiler level, thereby eliminating the need for translation by a compiling routine.

CORAL

CORAL is a high-level language for real-time application.

DETAB (DEcision TABle)

DETAB is a programming language based on COBOL. In it problems can be specified in the form of decision tables.

IAL

IAL (International Algebraic Language) was developed into ALGOL.

JOSS

Joss is a time-sharing language, designed for concurrent use by a number of people, each at its own console typewriter, and for programs of moderate size and running time.

JOVIAL

JOVIAL is Jules' own version of International language. It is a multipurpose procedure-oriented language derived from ALGOL and commonly used in programming command an control procedures.

NELIAC (Navy Electronics Laboratory International Algol Compilers)

NELIAC is an early dialect of ALGOL, which was developed for a specific data-processing application. But unlike ALGOL, it is not primarily concerned with being used for complex scientific and engineering calculations.

QUICKTRAN

QUICKTRAN is a subset of the programming language FORTRAN, design primarily for use with multi-access systems. QUICKTRAN is a time-sharing language developed by IBM for use on an IBM 1050 terminal connected to an IBM 7044 computer.

As a programming system, it provides concurrent computer access to a maximum of 50 remotely located terminals from a centralized data-processing system having tape, drum, and disk storage.

SNOBOL (StriNg-Oriented symBOlic Language)

SONOBL has a significant applications in program compilation and generation of symbolic equations.

PROBLEM-ORIENTED LANGUAGES

Problem-oriented languages are designed for handling problems in certain broad application types related to for example, mathematical, scientific or engineering systems, or to business systems.

Problem-oriented languages do not require the programming detail of procedure-oriented ones. The emphasis of problem-oriented languages is more on input and the desired output than on the procedures on mathematics involved. It enables the user to write statements in a form with which he is familiar, say in mathematical notation or English. It reflects the concepts of a particular application area, for example, SQL for database applications

Problem-Oriented Languages have been designed for scores of applications:

Simulation for example, GPSS (General Purpose Systems Simulator) a programming language based on block diagrams and used for discrete simulation. SLAM Programming Machine Tools, e.g., APT (Automatic Programming Tool) is a computer language used to program numerically controlled machine tools and Analysis of Stress Points in buildings and bridges COGO (COordinate Geometry) programming language is oriented toward civil engineering. It enables civil engineers to write a program in technical vocabulary familiar to them.

OBJECT-ORIENTED LANGUAGES

In procedure-oriented languages the emphasis is on what is done. In Object-Oriented Languages, the emphasis is on the object of the action, thus the object orientation. Object-oriented programming is a method of implementation in which

- programs are organized as cooperative collection of objects
- each of which represents an instance of some class and
- whose classes are all members of a hierarchy of classes united via inheritance relationships. This facilitates programming in that the programmer needs only to address the differences in the objects rather than starting from scratch for each object.

Object-Oriented Languages must support

- encapsulated objects
- the class and instance concepts
- inheritance between classes and
- polymorphism

Peter Wegner classified the programming languages in object-based world as:

Object-based languages, e.g., Ada is an object-based language, because it supports the object concept, whereas it does not support the class concept.

Object-oriented languages, e.g., Smalltalk, C++, Object Pascal, CLOS, Simula, Eiffel and Object-C are object-oriented languages because they support the class and inheritance concepts.

C++

C++ was developed in 1980s at Bell laboratories by Bjarn Stroustrup as an object oriented programming language. This language C++ is considered by many as an extension of the programming language C. The extension of the programming language C to create C++ is obtained by adding concept of classes to C. This is why C++ was initially called "C with classes". The programming language C++ derives it name from the increment operator ++ used in C++, which increments the value of variable by 1. The symbolic name C++ rightly inidcates that this language is enhanced version of C.

In other words C++ may be considered as C language with object oriented features included in it.

A sample C++ program `First.CPP`, can be written as following:

```
#include <iostream.h>

void main(void)
    {
        cout <<  "Let us learn C++";
    }
```

CLIPPER

Application development system from Computer Associates, Originally a dBASE compiler, it has become a complete stand-alone development environment with many unique features. Clipper was developed by Nantucket Corp., which was acquired by CA in 1992.

A sample program in Clipper.

```
USE Student NEW
SET ORDER TO Student
? SET (_SET_SOFTSEEK) // (.F.)
SEEK "RAJ"
? SET (_SET SOFTSEEK)
// Still (.F.)
   IF FOUND ( )
   .
   . <statements>
   .

ENDIF
```

dBASE

Relational DBMS for PCs from Borland. It was the first comprehensive DBMS for personal computers. Originally named Vulcan, DBASE was created by Wayne Ratliff to manage a company football pool. Renamed DBASE II when Hal Lashlee and George Tate formed Ashton-Tate was acquired by Borland in 1991), dBASE became a huge success within a couple of years. It is the most widely used PC database system, and its file formats have become de facto standards.

dBASE III & III PLUS: Introduced in 1984, dBASE II for PCs only. It handles larger databases, has more programming commands and includes a memo field and menu. In 1986, dBASE III PLUS introduced redesigned menus and added new features including the ability to store queries and relational views.

dBASE IV: introduced in 1988, it is a major upgrade of dBASE III PLUS with redesigned menus and report and forms generation screens. It adds a QBE methods for asking questions as well as an SQL language interface. Many new programming commands and features are added, including arrays and windows. Versions of dBASE IV are also available for UNIX on 386s, Sun workstations and VAXs under VMS, and a runtime version is available for the Macintosh.

The following programming language example converts Fahrenheit to Celsius:

```
INPUT "Enter Fahrenheit TO FAHR

? "Celsius is ", (FAHR_32)*5/9
```

FoxBASE+

dBASE III PLUS-compatible DBMS for the Macintosh from Microsoft. Originally developed by Fox Software for the PC, FoxBASE gained a reputation for its high speed and compatibility.

A sample program in FoxBASE+

```
. WAIT
. WAIT 'PRESS ESC TO ABORT'
. WAIT
```

```
. WAIT 'TYPE "Q" TO QUIT,

ANY OTHER KEY TO CONTINUE ... TO OFF
```

FoxPro

dBASE IV-compatible DBMS from Microsoft for PCS. An enhanced version of windowing, SQL and QBE interfaces and :Rushmore" technology for fast queries on large databases.

```
clear @ 5,0 get mittle
read
if updated ( )
use nitalib
replace title with mittle

ENDIF
```

MUMPS

Advanced, high-level programming language and integrated database used for business applications. It has extensive string handling making it suitable for database with vast amounts of free text. MUMPS has unique features including the ability to store both data and program statements in its database. In addition, formulas written in a program can be stored and used by other programs.

The following example converts Fahrenhiet to Celsius;

```
READ "Enter Fahrenheit",FAHR
SET CENT=(FAHR-32)*5/9

WRITE "Celsius is", CENT
```

Prolog

(PROgramming LOGic) Programming language used for developing AI applications (natural language translation, expert systems, abstract problem solving etc.). Developed in France in 1973, it is used throughout Europe and Japan and is gaining popularity in the U.S. similar to LISP, it deals with symbolic representation of objects.

The following example converts Fahrenheit to celsius;

```
convert:-write ('Enter Fahrenheit')'
read (Fahr)'
write ('Celsius is ')'
cent is (5* (Fahr - 32))/9'

write (Cent), nl.
```

FOURTH-GENERATION LANGUAGES (4GLS)

The Fourth-Generation language is any high-level language designed to enable users who are not trained programmers to develop applications. Often it is based on a non-procedural language with relational data base support. The 4GL are essentially shorthand programming languages. An operation that requires hundred of lines in a 3GLs such as COBOL typically requires only five to ten lines in a 4GL.

Prior to 4GLs, the 3GLs were procedural in nature, which required to tell computer how a task is to be done, for example, Add this, compare that, do this if something is true, and so forth - a very specific step-by-step process.

Whereas 4GLs are non-procedural in nature. Here, users define only what they want the computer to do; the user does not provide the details of just how it is to be done. Most of the procedure portion of a 4GL program is generated by the computer and the language software. The characteristics of a 4GL program is generated by the computer and the language software.

The characteristics of a 4GL include English-like instructions, limited mathematical manipulation of data, automatic report formatting, sequencing (sorting) and record selection by criteria. 4GLs can improve productivity by a factor of 5 to 50.

The trend in software development is toward using high-level user-friendly fourth-generation languages (4GLs). There are two types of 4GLs

- Production-Oriented 4GLs and
- User-Oriented 4GLs.

Production-Oriented 4GLs:

Production-Oriented 4GLs are designed primarily for computer professionals. They use 4GLs such as:

- ADR's (Application Definition Records) Ideal,
- Software AG's Natural 2,

which helps in creating information systems. Professional programmers who use 4GLs claim productivity improvements over 3GLs procedure-oriented languages (COBOL, FORTRAN, BASIC & so on) of 200% to 1000%.

User-Oriented 4GLs

This type of 4GL is designed primarily for end users. Users write 4GL programs to query a data base and to create personal or departmental information systems. User-Oriented 4GLs include Information Builders' FOCUS.

Fourth-generation languages are beneficial because:

- They are result-oriented; they emphasize what instead of how.
- They improve productivity because programs are easy to write and change.
- They can be used with a minimum of training by both programmers and nonprogrammers.

The problem with 4GLs is that they are less efficient than third-generation languages. This is because 4GLs require more computer capacity to perform a particular operation.

FIFTH-GENERATION OF LANGUAGES

Application Generators

Application Generators are designed primarily for use by computer professionals to assist them in the development of full-scale information systems. When using application generators (also called code generators) to develop information systems, programmers specify what information processing tasks are to be performed by engaging in an interactive dialogue with the system. This is essentially a fill-in-the-blank process.

The code generators asks a question and the programmer responds by filling in the blank. For example, the application generators might ask the user to categorize the proposed program as data entry, inquiry, report generation, or file maintenance. If the programmer responds "inquiry", then the application generator will ask the programmer to identify appropriate data bases.

Application generators interpret the programmer-supplied information and actually generate the program code or instructions usually in the form of COBOL or PL/1 programs. When using application generators to create an information system, system analysts and programmers describe the data base, then specify screen layouts for file creation and maintenance, data entry, management reports, and menus.

Code generators are currently in the young stage of development. Existing code generators do not have the flexibility of procedure-oriented languages; therefore, the generic reusable code of code generators must occasionally be supplemented with custom code to handle unique situations. When used properly, application generators can quadruple the output of programmers and system analysts.

NATURAL LANGUAGES: THE ULTIMATE PROGRAMMING LANGUAGE

Fifth-generation languages are, as you may guess, even more ill- defined than fourth-generation languages. They are most often called natural languages because of their resemblance to the "natural" spoken English language. Natural languages refers to software that enables computer systems to accept, interpret, and execute instructions in the native, or "natural" language of the end user-typically, English.

The logic behind a natural language is that the programmer or user needs little or no training. The programmer simply writes or perhaps verbalizes, processing specifications without regard for instruction syntax. In theory, people using natural languages are not constrained by the instruction syntax inherent in traditional programming languages.

Natural languages are sometimes referred to as knowledge-based languages, because natural languages are used to interact with a base of knowledge on some subject. The use of a natural language to access a knowledge base is called a knowledge-based system. Most commercial natural languages are designed to provide the front end, or the user interface, for a variety of domain- specific applications.

These applications could involve an interface with the corporate data base, and expert system, or certain micro-based software products, such as electronic spreadsheets.

SUMMARY

1. A set of programs is called Software.
2. There are two types of system software and they are: Operating System; and Language Translators.
3. There are 3 types of translators: Assembler, Interpreter and Compiler.
4. Word processors are used for manipulating text.
5. Spreadsheets are used for calculations.
6. DTP packages are used for text and graphics.
7. Anti virus software are used for virus detection and removal.
8. For communicating with the computer, we use computer language called programming language.
9. The machine language is the only one that computer can understand directly.
10. A program written by a programmer in an assembly language is called a Source Program.
11. LOGO programming allows you to draw pictures on the screen.
12. COBOL is basically used for business applications.
13. PASCAL is a general purpose language.
14. JAVA programming is used on Internet.

MULTIPLE CHOICE QUESTIONS

1. A computer language which is used for drawing pictures on the screen is:
   (a) LOGO (b) COBOL (c) BASIC
2. Computer program which controls the operations of computer is called:
   (a) Assembler (b) Operating System (c) Interpreter
3. A computer program used for Business applications is:
   (a) LOGO (b) COBOL (c) BASIC
4. A software package for creating printing artworks is called:
   (a) Word Processing (b) DTP (b) Spreadsheet
5. Computer understands the ________ language.
   (a) Machine (b) Assembly (c) High level language
6. Computer language used on Internet is
   (a) PASCAL (b) JAVA (c) BASIC

REVIEW QUESTIONS

1. What do you understand by Computer Languages?
2. Define different types of computer languages.
3. Explain the following in detail:
   Machine Language
   Assembly Languages
   High Level Languages
   Data Division
   Procedure Division
   Environment Division
   Identification Division
   COGO
   Multipurpose Languages
4. What is the format for Assembly Language
5. What is Procedure-Oriented Languages? Give some examples.
6. Define Business Languages.
7. What do you understand by Common Business Oriented Language
8. What is Scientific Languages
9. What do you understand by FORmula TRANslation?
10. What is ALGOrithmic Languages?
11. What is A Programming Language (APL)?
12. What do you understand by BASIC?
13. Distinghuish between Software and Application software.
14. What is High Level Language? Give examples.
15. Who has written the BASIC language.
16. What is PASCAL?
17. Who has been developed the C language?
18. What is use of C language? Explain.
19. What are the utilities of ADA? Who has developed the ADA language.
20. What is LOGO?
21. What is FORTH?
22. Explain MODULA-2.
23. Write short note on the following:
    CONTRAN
    CORAL
    DETAB
    IAL

JOSS	JOVIAL
NELIAC	QUICKTRAN
SNOBOL	C++
CLIPPER	

24. What is Problem-Oriented Languages? Explain with examples.
25. What is Object-Oriented Languages? Write some examples.
26. What is the use of DBase.
27. What do you understand by FoxBASE?
28. What are the characteristics of FoxPro.
29. Write down the utilities of MUMPS.
30. What is Prolog?
31. What is Fourth-Generation Languages (4GLs)?
32. What do you understand by Production-Oriented 4GLs?
33. What is characteristics of Fifth-Generation Languages?
34. What do you understand by Application Generators?
35. What are Natural Languages?
36. What are the characteristics of Natural Languages?

ANSWERS

Multiple Choice Questions

1. a	2. b	3. b	4. b
5. a	6. b		

CHAPTER 9

Database Management Systems

LEARNING OBJECTIVES

After going through this chapter, you should appreciate the following:

- **Introduction to RDBMS**
- **Database Systems**

  Database and its purpose
  Characteristics of the Database Approach
  Advantages and disadvantages of database systems

- **Classification of DBMS Users**

  Actors on the Scene
  Database Administrators
  Databse Designers
  End Users
  System Analysts and Application Programmers
  Workers Behind the Scene

INTRODUCTION TO RDBMS

Database means base of the data. It is based on the information given by you. It can be catalogued, stored and used. For all this information, database is used. Any collection of related information grouped together as a single item is a database. A metal filling cabinet containing customer records, a card file of names and phone numbers, and notebook containing a listing of a store inventory, all are databases.

Any collection of related information grouped together as a single item is a database.

However, a file cabinet or a notebook does not itself make a database. Containers, like cabinets, notebooks, or computer programs like FoxPro, are only aids in organizing information.

In Database, data is stored in the form of rows and columns.

Database uses the table format of **rows** and **columns** to store the information, as shown here. A database, or a FoxPro database file, may consist of one such table or several ones.

Name	Address	City	State	Pin	Ph. No.	Cust.No.
R.Dayal	F-19, Sec-20	Noida	UP	201301	8531642	0005
Sachin	G-478, Sakurpur	Delhi	Delhi	110034	2454312	0001
Rahul	12, Asaf Ali Road	Delhi	Delhi	110002	3255582	0002
Saurav	14, Asaf Ali Road	Delhi	Delhi	110002	3266698	0004
Anil	21, Kinari Bazar	Delhi	Delhi	110006	3280816	0006
Yuvraj	345, Surya Nagar	Ghazi	UP	201204	8876543	0003

In the example shown next you will notice that each row contains a name, an address, a phone number and a customer number. *Each row is related to the others because they all contain the same types of information in the same places.*

A mailing list, for example, containing a similar type of data about various people, is a good example of a database.

Rows in a database table are called records, and columns are called fields.

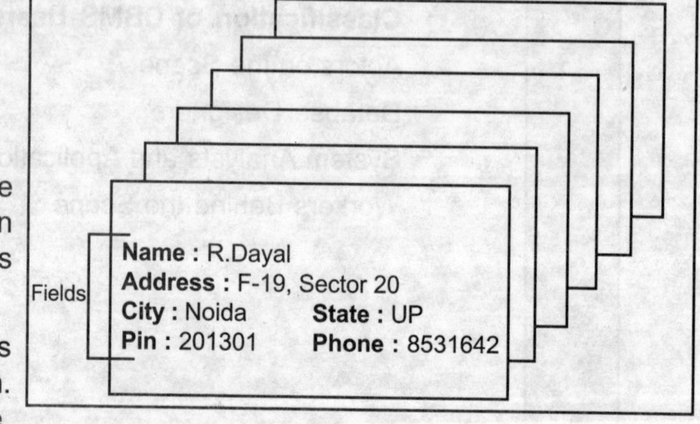

The figure here illustrates this idea by comparing a simple one-table database to an address filling system kept on 3x5 file cards. Each **category** of information on a card is a field.

Fields can contain any type of information, as long as each field always contains the same type of information. In the card box, each record contains six fields: a name, address, city, PIN code, and phone number. Since every card in the box has the same type of information, the card box is a database.

A computerized database provides speed, compactness and flexibility. It is also easier to locate a particular record in computerized database.

Databases and database technology are having a major impact on the growing use of Computers. It is fair to say that databases play a critical role in almost all areas where computers are used, including business, electronic commerce, engineering, medicine, law, education, and library science, to name a few.

The preceding definition of database is quite general; for example, we may consider the collection of words that make up this page of text to be related data and hence to constitute a database. However, the common use of the term database is usually more restricted.

A database has the following implicit properties:

- A database represents some aspect of the real world, sometimes called the miniworld or the universe of discourse (UoD). Changes to the miniworld are reflected in the database.
- A database is a logically coherent collection of data with some inherent meaning. A random assortment of data cannot correctly be referred to as a database.
- A database is designed, built, and populated with data for a specific purpose. It has an intended group of users and some preconceived applications in which these users are interested.

We will use the word data as both singular and plural, as is common in database literature; context will determine whether it is singular or plural. In standard English, data is used only for plural; datum is used for singular.

DATABASE SYSTEMS

A database can be of any size and of varying complexity. For example, the list of names and addresses referred to earlier may consist of only a few hundred records, each with a simple structure. On the other hand, the computerized catalog of a large library may contain half a million entries organized under different categories—by primary author's last name, by subject, by book title—with each category organized in alphabetic order.

A library database may contain name of book, author's last name, subject, book title in alphabetical order.

A database of even greater size and complexity is maintained by the *Internal Revenue Service* to keep track of the tax forms filed by taxpayers. If we assume that there are 100 million taxpayers and if each taxpayer files an average of five forms with approximately 400 characters of information per form, we would get a database of $100 \times 10^6 \times 400 \times 5$ characters (bytes) of information. If the revenue department keeps the past three returns for each taxpayer in addition to the current return, we would get a database of 8×10^{11} bytes (800 gigabytes). This huge amount of information must be organized and managed so that users can search for, retrieve, and update the data as needed.

A database may be generated and maintained manually or it may be computerized. For example, a library card catalog is a database that may be created and maintained manually. A computerized database may be created and maintained either by a group of application programs written specifically for that task or by a database management system. Of course, we are only concerned with computerized databases in this book.

A **DataBase Management System** (DBMS) is a collection of programs that enables users to create and maintain a database. The DBMS is hence a general-purpose software system that facilitates the processes of defining, constructing, manipulating, and sharing databases among various users and applications. Defining a database involves specifying the **data types**, **structures**, and **constraints** for the data to be stored in the database.

Definition: ***A DataBase Management System (DBMS) is a collection of programs that enables users to create and maintain a database.***

Constructing the database is the process of storing the data itself on some storage medium that is controlled by the DBMS. Manipulating a database includes such functions as querying the database to retrieve specific data, updating the database to reflect changes in the miniworld, and generating reports from the data. Sharing a database allows multiple users and programs to access the database concurrently.

Other important functions provided by the DBMS include protecting the database and maintaining it over a long period of time. Protection includes both system protection against hardware or software malfunction (or crashes), and security protection against unauthorized or malicious access.

A typical large database may have a life cycle of many years, so the DBMS must be able to maintain the database system by allowing the system to evolve as requirements change over time.

It is not necessary to use general-purpose DBMS software to implement a computerized database. We could write our own set of programs to create and maintain the database, in effect creating our own specific-purpose DBMS software, in either case—whether we use a general-purpose DBMS or not—we usually have to deploy a considerable amount of complex software. In fact, most DBMSs are very complex software systems.

Database and its purpose

Information from the database, stored in the form of a computerized filling system, can be stored and retrieved quite easily. Tasks that would be time-consuming to accomplish manually, are easily done with the aid of a computer. *In principle, a database in a computer is not different from a database recorded on paper and filled in cabinets.* But the computer does the tedious work like maintaining and searching through a database, and it does so quickly. A computerized database that can do all of this is known as a DataBase Management System, or DBMS for short.

Storing massive amounts of information into written directories and filling cabinets can consume a great deal of space and time.

Manual database systems are usually not fool-proof. A telephone book, for example, is fine for finding telephone numbers, but if you have an address and not the name of the person who lives there, the telephone directory becomes useless for finding that person's telephone number. A similar problem plagues conventional office filling systems: if the information is organized by name and you want to find all the clients located in a particular area, you could be in for a tedious search. In addition, storing massive amounts of information into written directories and filling cabinets can consume a great deal of space.

A manual database can also be tedious to modify. For example, inserting a new phone number into a list and rearranging the list. Or, if the phone company were to assign a new area code, someone would have to search for all phone numbers having the old area code, and replace it with the new one. It is very easy to eliminate these type of problems, if you are using the computer for your database. **Advanatages of using the Database** can be listed as following:

- A computerized database provides speed; finding a phone number from among a thousand entries or putting the file in alphabetical order takes just seconds with the database management system.
- A computerized database is compact; a database with thousands of records can be stored on a single floppy CD.
- A computerized database is flexible: it has the ability to examine information from a number of angles, so you can search for a phone number by name, by address, or by pin code and then name.

Of course, these are just few of them.

A manual database can also be tedious to modify.

Characteristics of the Database Approach

Computer programmers who have written programs for other applications know how much a database programming differs from the traditional programming. Here the database programming is quite different from the traditional approach of programming with files. In **traditional file processing**, each user defines and implements the files needed for a specific software application as part of programming the application.

Programming for database is quite different from traditional programming.

For example, for one user, the grade reporting office, may keep a file on students and their grades. Programs to print a student's transcript and to enter new grades into the file are implemented as part of the application. For second user, the accounting office, may keep track of students fees and their payments. Although both users are interested in data about students, each user maintains separate files—and programs to manipulate these files—because each requires some data not available from the other user's files. This redundancy in defining and storing data results in wasted storage space and in redundant efforts to maintain common data up to date. In the database approach, a single system of data is maintained that is defined once and then is accessed by various users. The main characteristics of the database approach versus the file-processing approach are the following:

- Self-describing nature of a database system
- Insulation between programs and data, and data abstraction
- Support of multiple views of the data
- Sharing of data and multiuser transaction processing

Let us study each one of them separately.

Self-Describing Nature of a Database System

A fundamental characteristic of the database approach is that the database system contains not only the database itself but also a complete definition or description of the database structure and constraints. This definition is stored in the DBMS catalog, which contains information such as the structure of each file, the type and storage format of each data item, and various constraints on the data. The information stored in the catalog is called meta-data, and it describes the structure of the primary database.

The catalog is used by the DBMS software and also by database users who need this information about the database structure. A general-purpose DBMS software package is not written for a specific database application, and hence it must refer to the catalog to know the structure of the files in a specific database, such as the type and format of data it will access. The DBMS software must work equally well with any number of database applications—for example, a university database, a banking database, or a company database—as long as the database definition is stored in the catalog.

In traditional file processing, **data definition** is typically part of the application programs themselves. Hence, these programs are constrained to work with only one specific database, whose structure is declared in the application programs. For example, an application program written in C++ may have struct or class declarations, and a COBOL program has Data Division statements to define its files. Whereas file-processing software can access only specific databases, DBMS software can access diverse databases by extracting the database definitions from the catalog and then using these definitions.

In the example, shown next, the DBMS catalog will store the definitions of all the files shown. These definitions are specified by the database designer prior to creating the actual database and are stored in the catalog. Whenever a request is made to access, say, the Name of a STUDENT record, the DBMS software refers to the catalog to determine the structure of the STUDENT file and the position and size of the Name data item within a STUDENT record.

STUDENT file	**Name**	**Number**	**Class**	**Course**
	Sachin	10	1	Phd
	Rahul	44	2	Phd

COURSE file	**Name**	**Number**	**Hours**	**Dept.**
	Visual Basic	VB10	5	Phd

	RDBMS	RD10	4	Phd	
	Computer Sc.	CS10	2	CS	
SECTION file	**Section**	**Course**	**Semester**	**Year**	**Teacher**
	88	VB10	IInd	2005	Tony
	90	RD10	Ist	2005	Greg
	112	CS10	IIIrd	2005	Tom
	120	MIC10	IInd	2005	Bob

GRADE_REPORT	**Number**	**Section**	**Grade**
	10	90	A
	44	88	B

PREREQUISITE	**Course**	**Per. Number**
	VB10	CS10
	RD10	MIC10

By contrast, in a typical file-processing application, the file structure and, in the extreme case, the exact location of Name within a STUDENT record are already coded within each program that accesses this data item.

DBMS software can access diverse databases by extracting the database definitions from the catalog and then using these definitions.

Insulation between Programs and Data, and Data Abstraction

In traditional file processing, the structure of data files is embedded in the application programs, so any changes to the structure of a file may require changing all programs that access this file. By contrast, DBMS access programs do not require such changes in most cases. The structure of data files is stored in the DBMS catalog separately from the access programs. We call this property program-data independence.

For example, a file access program may be written in such a way that it can access only STUDENT records of the structure. If we want to add another piece of data to each STUDENT record, say the BirthDate, such a program will no longer work and must be changed. By contrast, in a DBMS environment, we just need to change the description of STUDENT records in the catalog to reflect the inclusion of the new data item BirthDate; no programs are changed. The next time a DBMS program refers to the catalog, the new structure of STUDENT records will be accessed and used.

Data Item Name	*Starting Position in Record*	*Length in Characters (bytes)*
Name	31	30
StudentNumber	33	8
Class	37	8
Major	39	8

In some types of database systems, such as object-oriented and object-relational systems, users can define operations on data as part of the database definitions. An operation (also called a function or method) is specified in two parts. The interface (or signature) of an operation includes the operation name and the data types of its arguments (or parameters).

The *implementation* (or method) of the operation is specified separately and can be changed without affecting the interface. User application programs can operate on the data by invoking these operations through their names and arguments, regardless of how the operations are implemented. This may be termed program-operation independence.

The characteristic that allows program-data independence and program-operation independence is called data abstraction. A DBMS provides users with a conceptual representation of data that does not include many of the details of how the data is stored or how the operations are implemented. Informally, a data model is a type of data abstraction that is used to provide this conceptual representation.

The data model uses logical concepts, such as objects, their properties, and their interrelationships, that may be easier for most users to understand than computer storage concepts. Hence, the data model hides storage and implementation details that are not of interest to most database users.

The characteristic that allows program-data independence and program-operation independence is called data abstraction.

The internal implementation of a file may be defined by its record length—the number of characters (bytes) in each record—and each data item may be specified by its starting byte within a record and its length in bytes. The STUDENT record would thus be represented. But a typical database user is not concerned with the location of each data item within a record or its length; rather, the concern is that when a reference is made to Name of STUDENT, the correct value is returned. A *conceptual representation* of the STUDENT records is shown earlier. Many other details of file storage organization—such as the access paths specified on a file—can be hidden from database users by the DBMS.

In the database approach, the detailed structure and organization of each file are stored in the catalog. Database users and application programs refer to the conceptual representation of the files, and the DBMS extracts the details of file storage from the catalog when these are needed by the DBMS file access modules. Many data models can be used to provide this data abstraction to database users.

In object-oriented and object-relational databases, the abstraction process includes not only the data structure but also the operations on the data. These operations provide an abstraction of miniworld activities commonly understood by the users. For example, an operation CALCULATE_GPA can be applied to a STUDENT object to calculate the grade point average. Such operations can be invoked by the user queries or application programs without having to know the details of how the operations are implemented. In that sense, an abstraction of the miniworld activity is made available to the user as an abstract operation.

TRANSCRIPT	**Name**	**Transcript**				
		Number	Grade	Semester	Year	Section
		VB10	C	Fall	99	119
	Smith					
		VB10	B	Fall	99	112
		RD10	A	Fall	98	85
		MIC10	A	Fall	98	92
	Brown					
		RD10	B	Spring	99	102

		MIC10	A	Fall	99	135
PREREQUISITES	CName	CNumber		Pre.		
				RD10		
		Database	DB10	VB10		
		Computer Sc.	MIC10	MIC20		

Support of Multiple Views of the Data

A database typically has many users, each of whom may require a different perspective or view of the database. A view may be a subset of the database or it may contain virtual data that is derived from the database files but is not explicitly stored. Some users may not need to be aware of whether the data they refer to is stored or derived. A multiuser DBMS whose users have a variety of distinct applications must provide facilities for defining multiple views. For example, one user of the database may be interested only in accessing and printing the transcript of each student; the view for this user is shown in the above table(a). A second user, who is interested only in checking that students have taken all the pre-requisites of each course for which they register, may require the view shown in the table above(b).

Some users may not need to be aware of whether the data they refer to is stored or derived.

Sharing of Data and Multiuser Transaction Processing

A **multiuser DBMS**, as its name implies, must allow multiple users to access the database at the same time. This is essential if the data for multiple applications is to be integrated and maintained in a single database. The DBMS must include concurrency control software to ensure that several users trying to update the same data can do so in a controlled manner and the result of the updates is correct. For example, when several reservation clerks try to assign a seat on an airline flight, the DBMS should ensure that each seat can be accessed by only one clerk at a time for assignment to a passenger. These types of applications are generally called OnLine Transaction Processing (OLTP) applications. A fundamental role of multiuser DBMS software is to ensure that concurrent transactions operate correctly.

The concept of a transaction has become central to many database applications. A transaction is an executing program or process that includes one or more database accesses, such as reading or updating of database records. Each transaction is supposed to execute a logically correct database access if executed in its entirety without interference from other transactions. The DBMS must enforce several transaction properties. The isolation property ensures that each transaction appears to execute in isolation from other transactions, even though hundreds of transactions may be executing concurrently. The atomicity property ensures that either all the database operations in a transaction are executed or none are.

Each transaction is supposed to execute a logically correct database access if executed in its entirety without interference from other transactions.

The preceding characteristics are most important in distinguishing a DBMS from traditional file-processing software.

Advantages and disadvantages of database systems

It is not that the DBMS has only advantages, there are disadvantages too. Here we list few of them.

Advantages

Database Administrator must utilize these capabilities to accomplish a variety of objectives related to the design, administration, and use of a large multiuser database.

Controlling Redundancy

In traditional software development utilizing file processing, every user group maintains its own files for handling its data-pricing applications. For example, consider the UNIVERSITY database example here, two groups of users might be the course registration personnel and the accounting office. In the traditional approach, each group independently keeps files on students. The accounting office also keeps data on registration and related billing information, whereas the registration office keeps track of student courses and grades. Much of the data is stored twice: once in the files of each user group. Additional user groups may further duplicate some or all of the same data in their own files.

In the traditional approach, each group independently keeps files on all students.

This redundancy in storing the same data multiple times leads to several problems.

First, there is the need to perform a single logical update—such as entering data on a new student—multiple times: once for each file where student data is recorded. This leads to duplication of effort.

Second, storage space is wasted when the same data is stored repeatedly, and this problem may be serious for large databases.

Third, files that represent the same data may become inconsistent. This may happen because an update is applied to some of the files but not to others. Even if an update—such as adding a new student—is applied to all the appropriate files, the data concerning the student may still be inconsistent because the updates are applied independently by each user group.

For example, one user group may enter a student's birthdate erroneously as JAN-19-1984, whereas the other user groups may enter the correct value of JAN-29-1984. In the database approach, the views of different user groups are integrated during database design. Ideally, we should have a database design that stores each logical data item—such as a student's name or birth date—in only one place in the database.

This ensures consistency, and it saves storage space. However, in practice, it is sometimes necessary to use controlled redundancy for improving the performance of queries. For example, we may store StudentName and CourseNumber redundantly in a GRADE_ REPORT file because whenever we retrieve a GRADE_REPORT record, we want to retrieve the student name and course number along with the grade, student number, and section identifier. By placing all the data together, we do not have to search multiple files to collect this data.

In such cases, the DBMS should have the capability to control this redundancy so as to prohibit inconsistencies among the files. This may be done by automatically checking that the StudentName-StudentNumber values in any GRADE_REPORT record match one of the Name-StudentNumber values of a STUDENT record. Similarly, the SectionIdentifier-CourseNumber values in GRADE_REPORT can be checked against SECTION records. Such checks can be specified to the DBMS during database design and automatically enforced by the DBMS whenever the GRADE_REPORT file is updated. A GRADE_REPORT record that is inconsistent with the STUDENT file, which may be entered erroneously if the redundancy is not controlled.

(a) Consistent data

GRADE_REPORT	Student Number	Student Name	Section Identifier	Course Number	Grade
	17	Sachin	112	MATH2410	B
	17	Sachin	119	CS1310	C
	8	Balmeet	85	MATH2410	A
	8	Balmeet	92	CS1310	A

	8	Balmeet	102	CS3320	B
	8	Balmeet	135	CS3380	A

(b) Inconsistent record.

GRADE_REPORT	Student Number	Student Name	Section Identifier	Course Number	Grade
	17	Balmeet	112	MATH2410	B

Restricting Unauthorized Access

When multiple users share a large database, it is likely that most users will not be authorized to access all information in the database. For example, financial data is often considered confidential, and hence only authorized persons are allowed to access such data. In addition, some users may be permitted only to retrieve data, whereas others are allowed both to retrieve and to update. Hence, the type of access operation—**retrieval** or **update**—must also be controlled.

Typically, users or user groups are given account numbers protected by passwords, which they can use to gain access to the database. A DBMS should provide a security and authorization subsystem, which the DBA uses to create accounts and to specify account restrictions. The DBMS should then enforce these restrictions automatically.

Notice that we can apply similar controls to the DBMS software. For example, only the DBA's staff may be allowed to use certain privileged software, such as the software for creating new accounts. Similarly, parametric users may be allowed to access the database only through the canned transactions developed for their use.

A DBMS should provide a security and authorization subsystem, which the DBA uses to create accounts and to specify account restrictions.

Providing Persistent Storage for Program Objects

Databases can be used to provide persistent storage for program objects and data structures. This is one of the main reasons for object-oriented database systems, programming languages typically have complex data structures, such as record types in Pascal or class definitions in C+ + or Java.

The values of program variables are discarded once a program terminates, unless the programmer explicitly stores them in permanent files, which often involves converting these complex structures into a format suitable for file storage. When the need arises to read this data once more, the programmer must convert from the file format to the program variable structure. Object-oriented database systems are compatible with programming languages such as C++ and Java, and the DBMS software automatically performs any necessary conversions.

Hence, a complex object in C++ can be stored permanently in an object-oriented DBMS. Such an object is said to be persistent, since it survives the termination of program execution and can later be directly retrieved by another C++ program.

Object-oriented database systems are compatible with programming languages such as C++ and Java, and the DBMS software automatically performs any necessary conversions.

The persistent storage of program objects and data structures is an important function of database systems. Traditional database systems often suffered from the so called impedance mismatch problem, since the data structures provided by the DBMS were incompatible with the programming language's data structures. Object-oriented database systems typically offer data structure compatibility with one or more object-oriented programming languages.

Providing Storage Structures for Efficient Query Processing

Database system must provide capabilities for efficiently executing queries and updates. Because the database is typically stored on disk, the DBMS must provide specialized data structures to speed up disk search for the desired records. Auxiliary files called indexes are used for this purpose. Indexes are typically based on tree data structures or hash data structures, suitably modified for disk search. In order to process the database records needed by a particular query, those records must be copied from disk to memory. Hence, the DBMS often has a buffering module that maintains parts of the database in main memory buffers. In other cases, the DBMS may use the operating system to do the buffering of disk data.

The **query processing** and **optimization module** of the DBMS is responsible for choosing an efficient query execution plan for each query based on the existing storage structures. The choice of which indexes to create and maintain is part of physical database design and tuning, which is one of the responsibilities of the DBA staff.

DBMS often has a buffering module that maintains parts of the database in main memory buffers.

Backup and Recovery

A DBMS must provide facilities for recovering from hardware or software failures. The *backup and recovery subsystem* of the DBMS is responsible for recovery. For example, if the computer system fails in the middle of a complex update transaction, the recovery subsystem is responsible for making sure that the database is restored to the state it was in before the transaction started executing.

Alternatively, the recovery subsystem could ensure that the transaction is resumed from the point at which it was interrupted so that its full effect is recorded in the database.

Multiple User Interfaces

Because many types of users with varying levels of technical knowledge use a database, a DBMS should provide a variety of user interfaces. These include query languages for casual users, programming language interfaces for application programmers, forms and command codes for parametric users, and menu-driven interfaces and natural language interfaces for stand-alone users. Both forms-style interfaces and menu-driven interfaces are commonly known as **Graphical User Interfaces** (GUIs). Many specialized languages and environments exist for specifying GUIs. Capabilities for providing Web GUI interfaces to a database—or Web-enabling a data able—are also quite common.

Both forms-style interfaces and menu-driven interfaces are commonly known as Graphical User Interfaces (GUIs).

Complex Relationships among Data

A database may include numerous varieties of data that are interrelated in many ways. The record for Balmeet in the STUDENT file is related to four records in the GRADE_ REPORT file. Similarly, each section record is related to one course record as well as to a number of GRADE_REPORT records——one for each student who completed that section. A DBMS must have the capability to represent a variety of complex relationships among the data as well as to retrieve and update related data easily and efficiently.

Integrity Constraints

Most database applications have certain integrity constraints that must hold for the data. A DBMS should provide capabilities for defining and enforcing these constraints. The simplest type of integrity constraint involves specifying a data type for each data item. For example, we may specify that the value of the Class data item within each STUDENT record must be an integer between 1 and 5 and that the value of Name must be a using of no more than 30 alphabetic characters. A more complex type of constraint that frequently occurs involves specifying that a record in one file must be rented to records in other files.

For example, we can specify that "every section record must be related to a course record." Another type of constraint specifies uniqueness on data item values, such as "every course record must have a unique value for CourseNumber."

These constraints are derived from the meaning or semantics of the data and of the miniworld it represents. It is the database designers' responsibility to identify, integrity constraints during database design. Some constraints can be specified to the DBMS and automatically enforced. Other constraints may have to be checked by update programs or at the time of data entry.

A data item may be entered erroneously and still satisfy the specified integrity constraints. For example, if a student receives a grade of A but a grade of C is entered in the database, the DBMS cannot discover this error automatically, because C is a valid value for the Grade data type. Such data entry errors can only be discovered manually (when the student receives the grade and complains) and corrected later by updating the database. However, a grade of Z can be rejected automatically by the DBMS, because Z is not a valid value for the Grade data type.

Some constraints can be specified to the DBMS and automatically enforced.

Inferencing and Actions Using Rules

Some database systems provide capabilities for defining deduction roles for inferencing new information from the stored database facts. Such systems are called **deductive database systems**. For example, there may be complex rules in the miniworld application for determining when a student is on probation.

These can be specified declaratively as rules, which when compiled and maintained by the DBMS can determine all students on probation. In a traditional DBMS, an explicit procedural program code would have to be written to support such applications. But if the miniworld rules change, it is generally more convenient to change the declared deduction rules than to recode procedural programs. More powerful functionality is provided by active database systems, which provide active rules that can automatically initiate actions when certain events and conditions occur.

Additional Advantages of Using the Database Approach

Now we look at the more advantages of using the database approach.

Potential for Enforcing Standards

The database approach permits the DBA to define and enforce standards among database users in a large organization. This facilitates communication and cooperation among various departments, projects, and users within the organization. Standards can be defined for names and formats of data elements, display formats, report structures, terminology, and so on. The DBA can enforce standards in a centralized database environment more easily than in an environment where each user group has control of its own files and software.

Reduced Application Development Time

A prime selling feature of the database approach is that developing a new application—such as the retrieval of certain data from the database for printing a new report—takes very little time. Designing and implementing a new database from scratch may take more time than writing a single specialized file application. However, once a database is up and running, substantially less time is generally required to create new applications using DBMS facilities. Development time using a DBMS is estimated to be one-sixth to one-fourth of that for a traditional file system.

Flexibility

It may be necessary to change the structure of a database as requirements change. For example, a new user group may emerge that needs information not currently in the database. In response, it may be necessary to add a file to the database or to extend the data elements in an existing file. Modern DBMSs allow certain types of evolutionary changes to the structure of the database without affecting the stored data and the existing application programs.

Availability of Up-to-Date Information

A DBMS makes the database available to all users. As soon as one user's update is applied to the database, all other users can immediately see this update. This availability of up-to-date information is essential for many transaction processing application, such as reservation systems or banking databases, and it is made possible by the concurrency control and recovery subsystems of a DBMS.

Economies of Scale

The DBMS approach permits consolidation of data and applications, thus reducing the amount of wasteful overlap between activities of data-processing personnel in different projects or departments. This enables the whole organization to invest in more powerful processors, storage devices, or communication gear, rather than having each department purchase its own (weaker) equipment. This reduces overall costs of operation and management.

Disadvantages

In spite of the advantages of using a DBMS, there are a few situations in which such a system may involve unnecessary overhead costs that would not be incurred in traditional file processing. The overhead costs of using a DBMS are due to the following:

- High initial investment in hardware, software, and training.
- The generality that a DBMS provides for defining and processing data.
- Overhead for providing security, concurrency control, recovery, and integrity.
- Additional problems may arise if the database designers and DBA do not properly design the database or if the database systems applications are not implemented properly.

Hence, it may be more desirable to use regular files under the following circumstances:

- The database and applications are simple, well defined, and not expected to change.
- There are stringent real-time requirements for some programs that may not be met because of DBMS overhead.
- Multiple-user access to data is not required.

CLASSIFICATION OF DBMS USERS

A database user can be anyone, who knowingly or unknowingly may be using it. A clerk in a bank may be using the bank's database which is stored at the head-office which is located may be thousand miles away. A programmer may be using it at the same time at the head office for some other programming use. Let us look at the various users in details.

Actors on the Scene

For a small personal database, such as the list of addresses discussed, one person typically defines, constructs, and manipulates the database, and there is no sharing. However, many persons are involved in the design, use, and maintenance of a large database with hundreds of users. Let us identify the people whose jobs involve the day-to-day use of a large database; we call them the "*actors on the scene*." He may be the clerk at the bank.

We consider people who may be called "*workers behind the scene*"—those who work to maintain the database system environment but who are not actively interested in the database itself. He may be the programmer at the head office.

Users who use the database on day-to-day basis are called Actors on the Scene.

Database Administrators

In any organization where many persons use the same resources, there is a need for a chief administrator to oversee and manage these resources. In a database environment, the primary resource is the database itself, and the secondary resource is the DBMS and related software. Administering these resources is the responsibility of the DataBase Administrator (DBA).

The DBA is responsible for authorizing access to the database, for coordinating and monitoring its use, and for acquiring software and hardware resources as needed. The DBA is accountable for problems such as breach of security or poor system response time. In large organizations, the DBA is assisted by a staff that helps carry out these functions.

DBA is responsible for authorizing access to the database, for coordinating and monitoring its use.

Database Designers

Database designers are responsible for identifying the data to be stored in the database and for choosing appropriate structures to represent and store this data. Where tasks are mostly undertaken before the database is actually implemented and populated with data, it is the responsibility of database designers to communicate with all prospective database users in order to understand their requirements, and to come up with a design that meets these requirements.

In many cases, the designers are on the staff of the DBA and may be assigned other staff responsibilities after the database design is completed. Database designers typically interact with each potential group of users and develop views of the database that meet the data and processing requirements of these groups. Each view is then analyzed and integrated with the views of other user groups. The final database design must be capable of supporting the requirements of all user groups.

Database designers typically interact with each potential group of users and develop views of the database that meet the data and processing requirements of these groups

End Users

End users are the people whose jobs require access to the database for querying, updating, and generating reports; the database primarily exists for their use. There are several categories of end users:

- **Casual end users** occasionally access the database, but they may need different information each time, They use a sophisticated database query language to specify their requests and are typically middle or high-level managers or other occasional browsers.
- **Naive or parametric end users** make up a sizable portion of database end users. Their main job function revolves around constantly querying and updating the database, using standard types of queries and updates—called canned transactions—that have been carefully programmed and tested. The tasks that such users perform are varied:
  - Bank tellers check account balances and post withdrawals and deposits.
  - Reservation clerks for airlines, hotels, and car rental companies check availability for a given request and make reservations.

- Clerks at receiving stations for courier mail enter package identifications via bar codes and descriptive information through buttons to update a central database of received and in transit packages.

- **Sophisticated end users** include engineers, scientists, business analysts, and others who thoroughly familiarize themselves with the facilities of the DBMS so as to implement their applications to meet their complex requirements.
- **Stand-alone users** maintain personal databases by using ready-made program packages that provide easy-to-use menu-based or graphics-based interfaces. An example is the user of a tax package that stores a variety of personal financial data for tax purposes.

A typical DBMS provides multiple facilities to access a database.

Naive end users need to learn very little about file facilities provided by the DBMS; they have to understand only the user interfaces of the standard transactions designed and implemented for their use.

Casual users learn only a few facilities that they may use repeatedly.

Sophisticated users try to learn most of the DBMS facilities in order to achieve their complex requirements. Stand-alone users typically become very proficient in using a specific software package.

System Analysts and Application Programmers

System analysts determine the requirements of end users, especially naive and parametric end users, and develop specifications for canned transactions that meet these requirements. Application programmers implement these specifications as programs; then they test, debug, document, and maintain these canned transactions. Such analysts and programmers—commonly referred to as software engineers should be familiar with the full range of capabilities provided by the DBMS to accomplish their tasks.

System Analysts and Application Programmers are also called Software Engineers.

Workers Behind the Scene

In addition to those who design, use, and administer a database, others are associated with the design, development, and operation of the DBMS software and system environment. These persons are typically not interested in the database itself. We call them the "*workers behind the scene*," and they include the following categories.

- DBMS system designers and implementers are persons who design and implement the DBMS modules and interfaces as a software package. A DBMS is a very complex software system that consists of many components, or modules, including modules for implementing the catalog, processing query language, processing the interface, accessing and buffering data, controlling concurrency, and handling data recovery and security. The DBMS must interface with other system software, such as the operating system and compilers for various programming languages.
- Tool developers include persons who design and implement tools—the software packages that facilitate database system design and use and that help improve performance. Tools are optional packages that are often purchased separately. They include packages for database design, performance monitoring, natural language or graphical interfaces, prototyping, simulation, and test data generation, In many cases, independent software vendors develop and market these tools.
- Operators and maintenance personnel are the system administration personnel who are responsible for the actual running and maintenance of the hardware and software environment for the database system.

Although these categories of workers behind the scene are instrumental in making the database system available to end users, they typically do not use the database for their own purposes.

SUMMARY

1. Any collection of related information grouped together as a single item is a database.
2. Database uses the table format of rows and columns to store the information.
3. Fields can contain any type of information, as long as each field always contains the same type of information.
4. A database is a logically coherent collection of data with some inherent meaning.
5. A database may be generated and maintained manually or it may be computerized.
6. A DataBase Management System (DBMS) is a collection of programs that enables users to create and maintain a database.
7. Manipulating a database includes such functions as querying the database to retrieve specific data, updating the database to reflect changes in the miniworld, and generating reports from the data.
8. Information from the database, stored in the form of a computerized filling system, can be stored and retrieved quite easily.
9. Manual database systems are usually not fool-proof.
10. A manual database can also be tedious to modify.
11. A computerized database is flexible.
12. In the database approach, a single system of data is maintained that is defined once and then is accessed by various users.
13. A fundamental characteristic of the database approach is that the database system contains not only the database itself but also a complete definition or description of the database structure and constraints.
14. The DBMS software must work equally well with any number of database applications.
15. DBMS access programs do not require such changes in most cases.
16. The characteristic that allows program-data independence and program-operation independence is called data abstraction.
17. In the database approach, the detailed structure and organization of each file are stored in the catalog.
18. In object-oriented and object-relational databases, the abstraction process includes not only the data structure but also the operations on the data.
19. A view may be a subset of the database or it may contain virtual data that is derived from the database files but is not explicitly stored.
20. A multiuser DBMS, as its name implies, must allow multiple users to access the database at the same time.
21. A transaction is an executing program or process that includes one or more database accesses, such as reading or updating of database records.
22. In traditional software development utilizing file processing, every user group maintains its own files for handling its data-pricing applications.
23. DBMS should have the capability to control this redundancy so as to prohibit inconsistencies among the files.
24. When multiple users share a large database, it is likely that most users will not be authorized to access all information in the database.
25. Databases can be used to provide persistent storage for program objects and data structures.
26. Traditional database systems often suffered from the so called impedance mismatch problem.
27. In spite of the advantages of using a DBMS, there are a few situations in which such a system may involve unnecessary overhead costs that would not be incurred in traditional file processing.
28. Many persons are involved in the design, use, and maintenance of a large database with hundreds of users.
29. Database designers are responsible for identifying the data to be stored in the database and for choosing appropriate structures to represent and store this data.
30. End users are the people whose jobs require access to the database for querying, updating, and generating reports.

31. Naive end users need to learn very little about file facilities provided by the DBMS.
32. Casual users learn only a few facilities that they may use repeatedly.
33. Sophisticated users try to learn most of the DBMS facilities in order to achieve their complex requirements.
34. System analysts determine the requirements of end users, especially naive and parametric end users, and develop specifications for canned transactions that meet these requirements.
35. DBMS system designers and implementers are persons who design and implement the DBMS modules and interfaces as a software package.
36. In addition to those who design, use, and administer a database, others are associated with the design, development, and operation of the DBMS software and system environment. These persons are typically called "workers behind the scene,"

MULTIPLE CHOICE QUESTIONS

1. A system where you deal with more than one databases, which are linked to each other is called _________ :
   (a) Relational Database System (b) Database System (c) Database
2. Data is _________ information :
   (a) raw (b) polished (c) computer output
3. Data administrator grants you the permission to use database :
   (a) True (b) False
4. A database is a collection of ________ data :
   (a) meaningful (b) not required data (c) programs
5. Data in the database can be :
   (a) retrieved (b) updated (c) both
6. The characteristic that allows program-data independence and program-operation independence is called ___________ :
   (a) data administration (b) database (c) data abstraction
7. In the database approach, the detailed structure and organization of each file are stored in the ___________ :
   (a) box (b) catalog (c) magazine
8. Traditional database systems often suffered from the so called impedance _______ problem :
   (a) mismatch (b) match (c) no match
9. _________ are the people whose jobs require access to the database :
   (a) System Analysts (b) End users (c) Programmers
10. ___________ determine the requirements of end users :
   (a) Programmers (b) Users (c) System Analysts

REVIEW QUESTIONS

1. Which is RDBMS?
2. Write a short note on Database Approach.
3. What do you understand by Multiple Views of the database?
4. What is meant by sharing of Data and Multiuser Transaction Processing?
5. What are the advantages of using RDBMS?
6. Who is Database Administrator?

7. What work is performed by Database Designers?
8. Who are Application Programmers?

ANSWERS

Multiple Choice Questions

1. a	2. a	3. a	4. a
5. c	6. c	7. b	8. a
9. b	10. c		

CHAPTER 10

Introduction to Software Testing

LEARNING OBJECTIVES

After going through this chapter, you should appreciate the following:

- **Why do we test Software?**
- **Developers ar not Good Testers**
- **What is Defect?**
- **What is Quality Software?**

  The Two Software Quality Gaps

  What is a Defect to a Software Tester
- **Why does a development process produce defects?**

  What does it mean for a process to be in or out of control?

  Do testers need to know SPC?
- **Reducing the frequency of defects in software development**

  The five levels of maturity
- **The multiple roles of the software tester**
- **People relationships**

  Scope of Testing

  When should testing occcur

  Requirements

  Design

  Program (Build/Construction)

  Test process

  Installation

  Maintenance

WHY DO WE TEST SOFTWARE?

The simple answer as to why we test software is that developers are unable to build defect-free software. If the development processes were perfect, meaning no defects were produced, testing would not be necessary. The example of the manufacturing process producing boxes of cereal is perfect, as is the case for most food manufacturing companies, testing each box of cereal is unnecessary.

Making software is a significantly different process than making a box of cereal. Cereal manufacturers may produce 50,000 identical boxes of cereal a day, while each software process is unique. This uniqueness introduces defects, and thus making testing software necessary.

As we introduce the skill categories of the Common Body of Knowledge (CBOK) for software testers, it is helpful to understand these six concepts, which explain why we test software:

- Developers are not good testers
- What is a defect?
- Why does a development process produce defects?
- Reducing the frequency of defects in software development
- An effective development process that minimizes defects
- How is quality defined?

DEVELOPERS ARE NOT GOOD TESTERS

Testing by the individual who developed the work has not proven to be a substitute to building and following a detailed test plan. The disadvantages of a person checking their own work using their own documentation are as follows:

- Misunderstandings will not be detected, because the checker will assume that what the other individual heard from him was correct.
- Improper use of the development process may not be detected because the individual may not understand the process.
- The individual may be "blinded" into accepting erroneous system specifications and coding because he falls into the same trap during testing that led to the introduction of the defect in the first place.
- Information services people are optimistic in their ability to do defect-free work and thus sometimes underestimate the need for extensive testing.
- Without a formal division between development and test, an individual may be tempted to improve the system structure and documentation, rather than allocate that time and effort to the test.

WHAT IS A DEFECT?

A defect is an undesirable state. In order to know what a defect is we must first define a desirable state. For example, if we believe a desirable state for a corporation is that a phone call is answered by a person, then if it is not answered by a person that would be considered an undesirable state.

The term quality is used to define a desirable state. A defect is defined as the lack of that desirable state. In order to fully understand what a defect is we must understand quality.

WHAT IS QUALITY SOFTWARE?

There are two important definitions of quality software:

IT's view of quality software means meeting requirements.

User's of software view of quality software means fit for use.

These two definitions are not inconsistent. Meeting requirements is IT's definition of quality; it means that the person building the software builds it in accordance with requirements. The fit for use definition is a user's definition of software quality; it means that the software produced by IT meets the user's need regardless of the software requirements.

The Two Software Quality Gaps

In most IT groups, there are two gaps as illustrated in the following figure, the different views of software quality between the user and IT.

The first gap is the IT gap. It is the gap between what is specified to be delivered, meaning the documented requirements and internal IT standards, and what is actually built. The second gap is between what IT actually delivers compared to what the user wants.

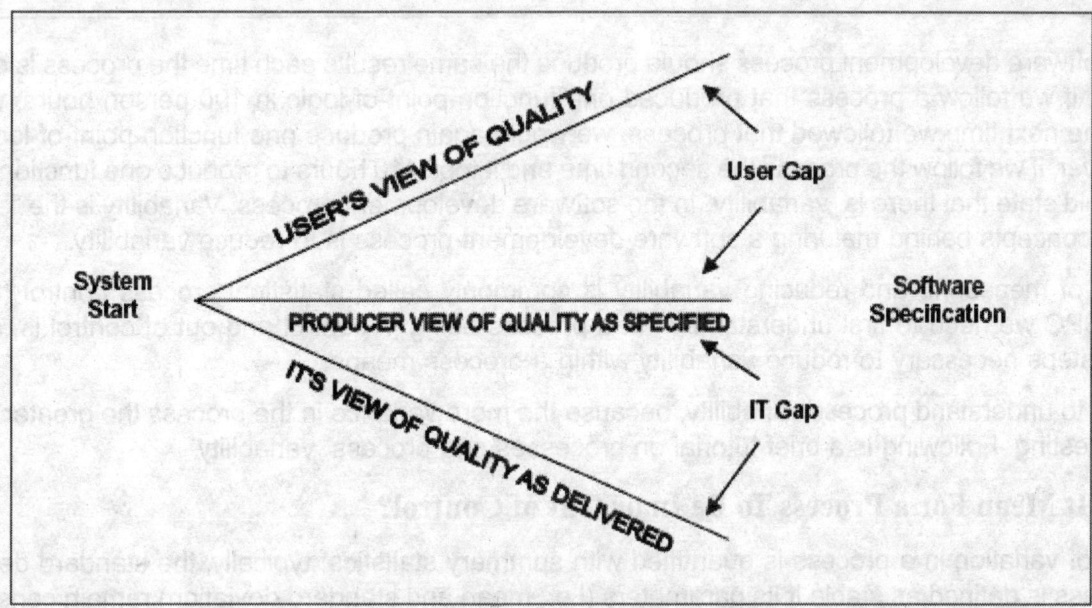

A potential role of software testing becomes helping to close the two gaps. The IT quality function must first improve the processes to the point where IT can produce the software according to requirements received and its own internal standards. The objective of the quality function closing IT's gap is to enable an IT function to provide its user consistency in what it can produce. At QAI, we call this the "McDonald's effect." This means that when you go into any McDonald's in the world, a Big Mac should taste the same. It doesn't mean that you as a customer like the Big Mac or that it meets your needs, but rather, that McDonald's has now produced consistency in its delivered product.

To close the user's gap, the IT quality function must understand the true needs of the user. This can be done by the following:

- Customer surveys

- JAD (joint application development) sessions – the IT and user come together and negotiate and agree upon requirements
- More user involvement while building information products

It is accomplished through changing the processes to close the user gap so that there is consistency, and producing software and services that the user needs. Software testing professionals can participate in closing these "quality" gaps.

What is a Defect to a Software Tester?

The goal or mission for the software tester needs to be defined. For manual testing, the only concern is whether or not the implementation software meets the requirements as specified by the IT organization. From a business perspective this is too narrow a view. Testers need to ensure that software not only meets the requirements, but is in fact usable by the customer.

If both types of defects are incorporated into the software testing charter, testing must be viewed as a life cycle activity. The fact that software may not meet the customer's needs requires testing during the definition of requirements and software system architecture. That process will be described later in this skill category as "verification."

WHY DOES A DEVELOPMENT PROCESS PRODUCE DEFECTS?

Ideally, the software development process should produce the same results each time the process is executed. For example, if we follow a process that produced one function-point-of-logic in 100 person hours, we would expect that the next time we followed that process, we would again produce one function-point-of-logic in 100 hours. However, if we follow the process the second time and it took 110 hours to produce one function-point-of-logic, we would state that there is "variability" in the software development process. Variability is the "enemy" of quality – the concepts behind maturing a software development process is to reduce variability.

The concept of measuring and reducing variability is commonly called statistical process control (SPC). To understand SPC we need to first understand what a process being in control and out of control is, and what some of the steps necessary to reduce variability within a process means.

Testers need to understand process variability, because the more variance in the process the greater the need for software testing. Following is a brief tutorial on processes and process variability.

What Does It Mean For a Process To Be In or Out of Control?

The amount of variation in a process is quantified with summary statistics; typically, the standard deviation is used. A process is defined as stable if its parameters (i.e., mean and standard deviation) remain constant over time; it is then said to be in a state of statistical control. The following figure illustrates a stable process. Such a process is predictable, i.e., we can predict, within known limits and with a stated degree of belief, future process values. Accepted practice uses a prediction interval three standard deviation distances in width around the population mean ($\mu \pm 3d$) in establishing the control limits.

Continuous process improvement through the use of quantitative methods and employee involvement sets quality management apart from other attempts to improve productivity. Continuous process improvement is accomplished by activating teams and providing them with quantitative methods such as SPC techniques and supporting them as they apply these tools. We will further discuss the concept of variation, common and special causes of variation, and QAI's Continuous Improvement Strategy.

The natural change occurring in organizational life moves systems and processes towards increasing variation. Statistical methods help us collect and present data in ways that facilitate the evaluation of current theories and

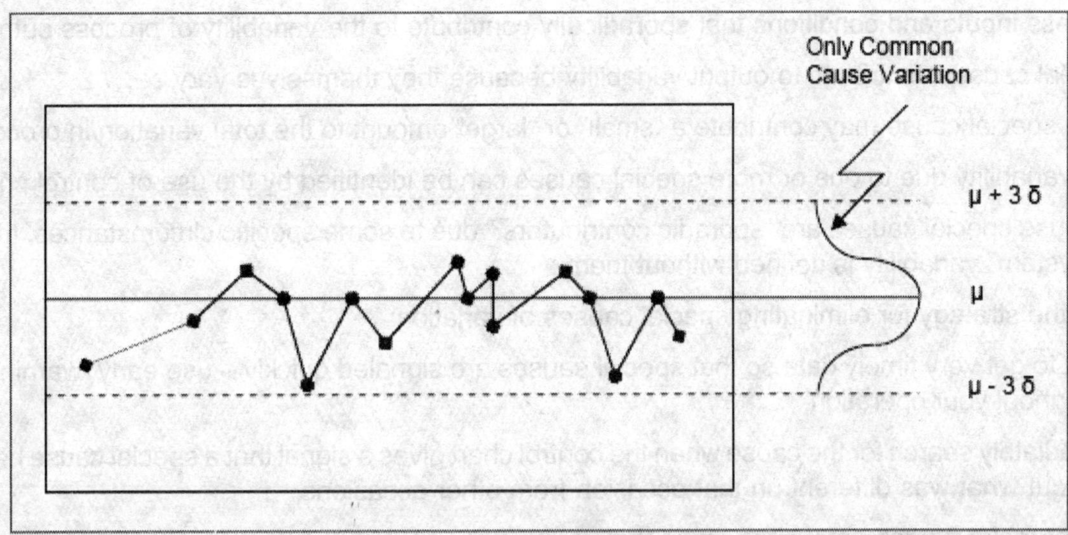

the formation of new theories. These tools are the only methods available for quantifying variation. Since the key to quality is process consistency, variation (the lack of consistency) must be understood before any process can be improved. Statistical methods are the only way to objectively measure variability. There is no other way!

Variation is present in all processes. The following table lists some sources of variation for administrative processes.

Measurement Components Counting Sampling	**Material Components** Forms Suppliers
Machine Components Office equipment Computers Software	**Method Components** Procedures Policies Accounting practices
People Components Training Experience Attitude Aptitude	**Environment Components** Temperature Humidity Noise Level Lighting

The cumulative effect of sources of variation in a production process is shown in the table. One of the challenges in implementing quality management is to get those working in the process thinking in terms of sources of variation. How much of the observed variation can be attributed to measurements, material, machines, methods, people and the environment?

Consistency in all the processes from conception through delivery of a product or service is the cornerstone of quality. Paradoxically, the route to quality is not just the application of SPC and the resulting control charts. Managers must change the way they manage. They must use statistical methods in making improvements to management processes as well as all other processes in the organization.

Special causes of variation are not typically present in the process. They occur because of special or unique circumstances. If special causes of variation exist, the process is unstable or unpredictable. Special causes must be eliminated to bring a process into a state of statistical control. A state of statistical control is established when all special causes of variation have been eliminated.

The special causes of variation can be summarized as follows:

- Process inputs and conditions that sporadically contribute to the variability of process outputs.
- Special causes contribute to output variability because they themselves vary.
- Each special cause may contribute a "small" or "large" amount to the total variation in process outputs.
- The variability due to one or more special causes can be identified by the use of control charts.
- Because special causes are "sporadic contributors," due to some specific circumstances, the "process" or "system" variability is defined without them.

Following is the strategy for eliminating special causes of variation:

- Work to get very timely data so that special causes are signaled quickly – use early warning indicators throughout your operation.
- Immediately search for the cause when the control chart gives a signal that a special cause has occurred. Find out what was different on that occasion from other occasions.
- Do not make fundamental changes in that process.
- Instead, seek ways to change some higher-level systems to prevent that special cause from recurring. Or, if results are good, retrain that lesson.

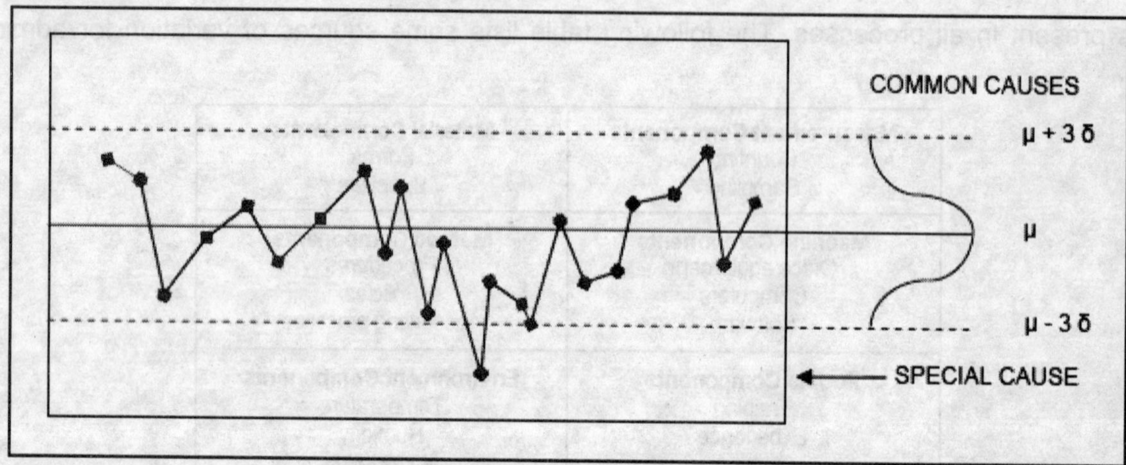

Common causes of variation are typically due to a large number of small random sources of variation. The sum of these sources of variation determines the magnitude of the process's inherent variation due to common causes; the process's control limits and current process capability can then be determined. The following figure illustrates an out of control process.

Common causes of variation can be listed as:

- Process inputs and conditions that regularly contribute to the variability of process outputs.
- Common causes contribute to output variability because they themselves vary.
- Each common cause typically contributes a small portion to the total variation in process outputs.
- The aggregate variability due to common causes has a "nonsystematic," random- looking appearance.
- Because common causes are "regular contributors," the "process" or "system" variability is defined in terms of them.

Strategy for reducing common causes of variation can be as follows:

- Talk to lots of people including local employees, other managers, and staff from various functions.

- Improve measurement processes if measuring contributes too much to the observed variation.
- Identify and rank categories of problems by Pareto analysis (a ranking from high to low of any occurrences by frequency).
- Stratify and desegregate your observations to compare performance of subprocesses.
- Investigate cause-and-effect relations. Run experiments (one factor and multifactor).

'hose working in the process (employees) have the lead responsibility for the reduction of special causes of ariation. Those working on the process (management) are responsible for leading the effort to reduce common ause variation. These higher-level improvements to the process usually require process or system changes. : is now widely recognized that at least 85% of problems in any organization are system problems and the esponsibility of management to solve. Some sources are now quoting 94%. The concept of statistical control llows us to determine which problems are in the process (due to common causes of variation) and which are xternal to the process (due to special causes of variation).

ringing a process into a state of statistical control is not really improving the process; it is just bringing it back ɔ its typical operation. Reducing variation due to common causes is process improvement and the real essence f continuous process improvement.

s previously mentioned, variation due to special causes must be identified and removed to create a stable rocess. However, a stable process may not be an acceptable process. If its variation, due to common causes esults in operation of the process beyond specifications, the process is called "incapable." The process must e improved, i.e., variation due to common cause must be reduced or the process retargeted or both. The next gure illustrates the transition of a process from incapable to capable.

eming defines tampering as "action taken on a stable system in response to variation within statistical control, ı an effort to compensate for this variation – the results of which will inevitably increase the variation and will

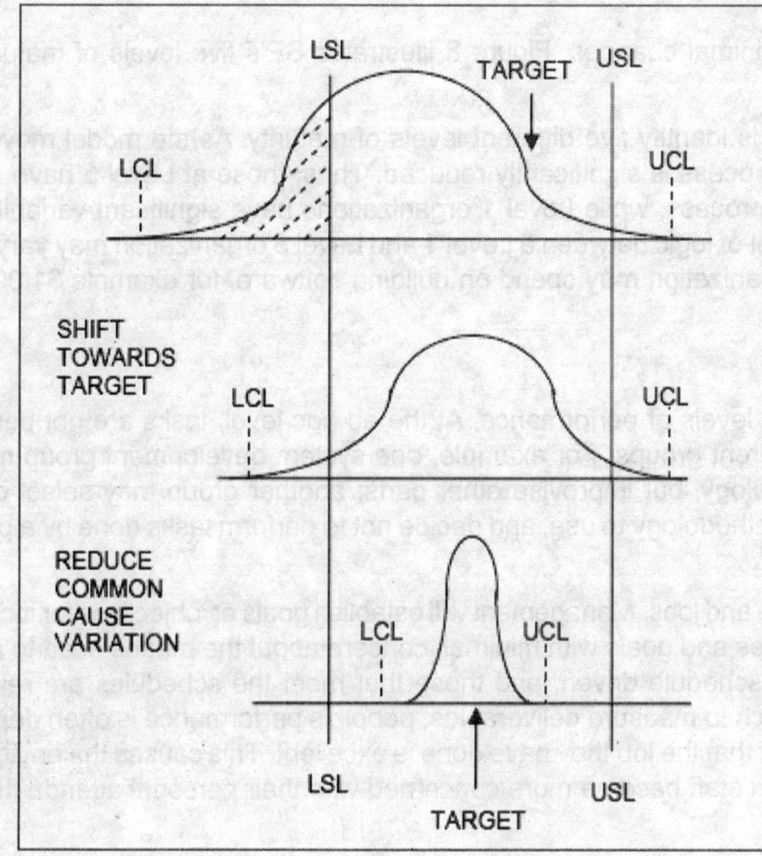

increase cost from here on out." Tampering is any adjustment to a process (typically by operator or machine) in response to variation due to common causes (i.e., that variation between the control limits). By definition process variation (due to common causes) is expected and is not a reason for adjusting or changing the process (tampering). Management that does not understand variation, time and time again asks for an explanation or corrective action when confronted with variation due to common causes.

Do Testers Need to Know SPC?

Testing is a measurement process. It attempts to measure the implemented software against either or both specifications and user needs. Statistical process control is a measurement tool.

The more you know about the process used to develop software, the more effective the testing process will become. For example, if you know that the requirements process has significant variability, meaning there is a high probability that the requirements as defined are not correct, you should then focus testing efforts on determining the "correctness" of the requirements as viewed by the customer. Software testing does not add a lot of value to the business if all they are doing is validating that incorrect requirements are implemented correctly.

REDUCING THE FREQUENCY OF DEFECTS IN SOFTWARE DEVELOPMENT

In the early days of computing, experience showed that some software development processes were much more effective than other software development processes. As one of the major purchasers of customized software, the Department of Defense (DOD) undertook a study to identify the criteria that made software development more effective. This research was conducted by Carnegie Mellon University's Software Engineering Institute (SEI). The end result was an algorithm that enabled the DOD to identify the more effective and efficient software development. This algorithm is now known as the capability maturity model.

The Five Levels of Maturity

QAI follows SEI's maturity model with minimal changes. Figure 8 illustrates SE's five levels of maturity in a quality management environment.

What the capability maturity model does is identify five different levels of maturity. As the model moves from Level 1 to Level 5, the variability in the process is significantly reduced. Thus, those at Level 5 have minimal variability in their software development process, while Level 1 organizations have significant variability. The cost differences to produce a function point of logic between a Level 1 and Level 5 organization may vary by 100 times. In other words, what a Level 1 organization may spend on building software, for example $1,000, may only cost $10 for a Level 5 organization.

Level 1 – Ad Hoc

Ad hoc means unstructured, inconsistent levels of performance. At the ad hoc level, tasks are not performed the same way by different people or different groups. For example, one system development group may use part of the system development methodology, but improvise other parts; another group may select different parts of the same system development methodology to use, and decide not to perform tasks done by a previous group.

At this level, management manages people and jobs. Management will establish goals or objectives for individuals and teams, and manage to those objectives and goals with minimal concern about the means used to achieve the goals. This level is normally heavily schedule driven, and those that meet the schedules are rewarded. Since there are not standards against which to measure deliverables, people's performance is often dependent upon their ability to convince management that the job they have done is excellent. This causes the environment to be very political. Both management and staff become more concerned with their personal agenda than with meeting their organization's mission.

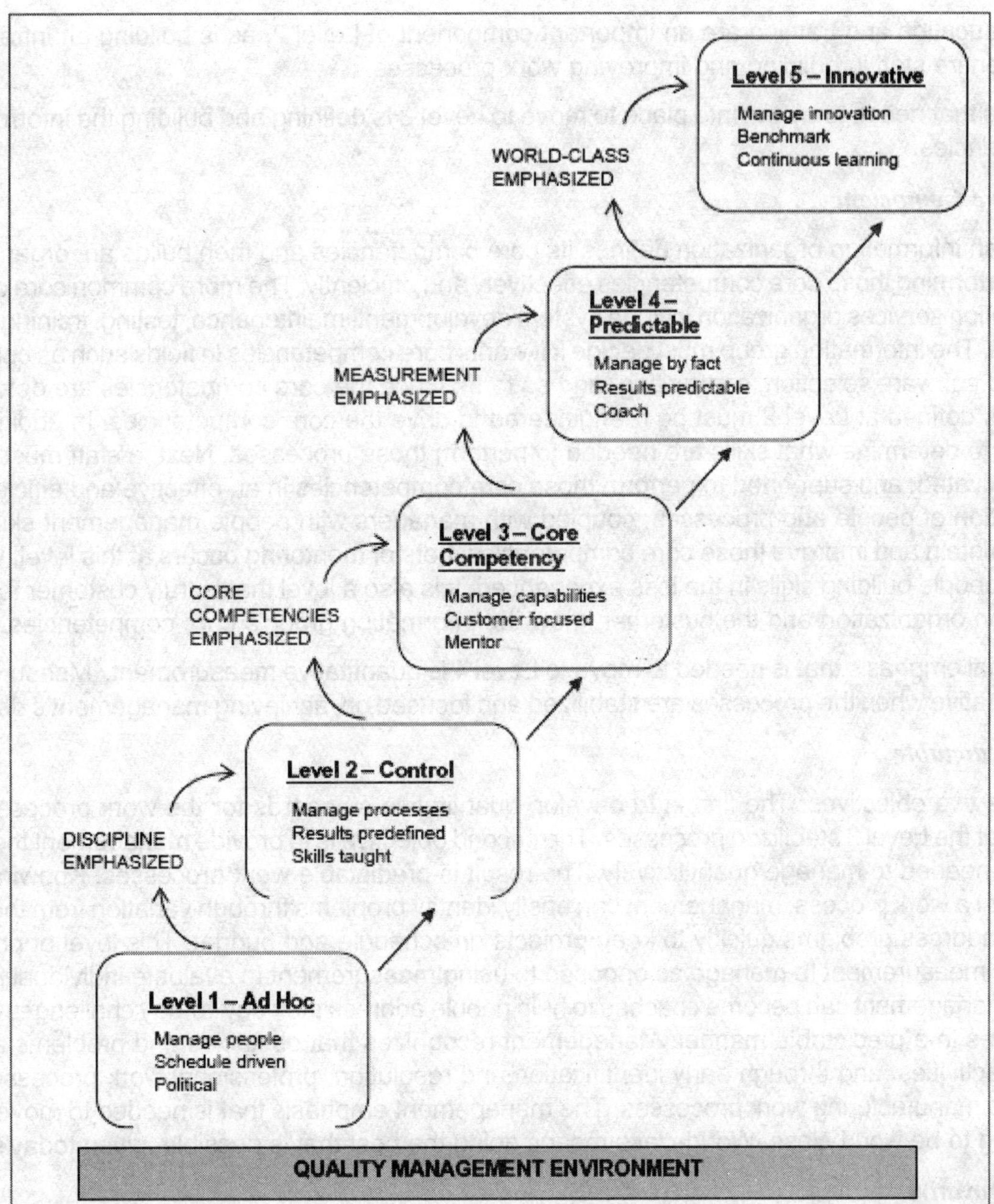

The emphasis needed to move from Level 1 to Level 2 is discipline and control. The emphasis is on getting the work processes defined, training the people in the work processes, implementing sufficient controls to assure compliance to the work processes, and producing products that meet predefined standards.

Level 2 – Control

There are two major objectives to be achieved at Level 2. The first is to instill discipline in the culture of the information organization so that through the infrastructure, training, and leadership of management individuals will want to follow defined processes. The second objective is to reduce variability in the processes by defining them to a level that permits relatively constant outputs. At this level, processes are defined with minimal regard to skills needed to perform the process AND with minimal regard to the impact on other processes. At Level 2, the work processes are defined; management manages those processes, and uses validation and verification techniques to check compliance to work procedures and product standards. Having the results predefined through a set of standards enables management to measure people's performance against meeting those standards. Education and training are an important component of Level 2, as is building an infrastructure tha involves the entire staff in building and improving work processes.

The emphasis that needs to be put into place to move to Level 3 is defining and building the information group's core competencies.

Level 3 – Core Competency

At this level, an information organization defines its core competencies and then builds an organization that is capable of performing those core competencies effectively and efficiently. The more common core competencies for an information services organization include system development, maintenance, testing, training, outsourcing and operation. The information group must decide if it wants core competencies in fields such as communication hardware and software selection, contracting, and so forth. Once the core competencies are determined, then the processes defined at Level 2 must be reengineered to drive the core competencies. In addition, the tasks are analyzed to determine what skills are needed to perform those processes. Next, a staff must be retrained recruited, motivated, and supported to perform those core competencies in an effective and efficient manner. I is the integration of people and processes, coupled with managers with people management skills, which are needed to maintain and improve those core competencies. Lots of mentoring occurs at this level, with the more experienced people building skills in the less experienced. It is also a level that is truly customer focused – both the information organization and the customer know the information group's core competencies.

The managerial emphasis that is needed to move to Level 4 is quantitative measurement. Measurement is only a practical initiative when the processes are stabilized and focused on achieving management's desired results

Level 4 – Predictable

This level has two objectives. The first is to develop quantitative standards for the work processes based on performance of the Level 3 stabilized processes. The second objective is to provide management the dashboards and skill sets needed to manage quantitatively. The result is predictable work processes. Knowing the normal performance of a work process, management can easily identify problems through variation from the quantitative standards to address problems quickly to keep projects on schedule and budget. This level of predictability is one that uses measurement to manage as opposed to using measurement to evaluate individual performance. At this level, management can become coaches to help people address their day-to-day challenges in performing work processes in a predictable manner. Management recognizes that obstacles and problems are normal in professional activities, and through early identification and resolution, professional work processes can be as predictable as manufacturing work processes. The management emphasis that is needed to move to Level 5 is one of desiring to be world-class. World-class means doing the best that is possible, given today's technology.

Level 5 – Innovative

At Level 5, the information organization wants to be a true leader in the industry. At this level, the organization is looking to measure itself against the industry through benchmarking, and then define innovative ways to achieve higher levels of performance. Innovative approaches can be achieved through benchmarking other industries, applying new technology in an innovative way, reengineering the way work is done, and by constantly studying the literature and using experts to identify potential innovations. This level is one in which continuous learning occurs, both in individuals and the organization.

Testers Need to Understand Process Maturity

Software testers face a much greater challenge testing software developed by maturity Level 1, than they do by testing software developed by higher maturity levels. Some have categorized Level 1 organizations as "Sign and Fix" organizations. At this level, testing and rework will consume more than 50% of the total software development effort. As software development processes mature, two things happen: more testing occurs during the building of software and the amount of testing required is reduced.

THE MULTIPLE ROLES OF THE SOFTWARE TESTER

The roles established for software testers vary from organization to organization. Many factors affect the tester's role. The major factors are:

- People relationships
- Scope of testing
- When should testing occur
- How should testing be performed
- Testing constraints

Each of these factors will be discussed individually to explain how the role of testing in an IT organization is determined.

PEOPLE RELATIONSHIPS

With the introduction of the CSTE certification, testing is finally being recognized as a profession with a specialized skill set and qualifications. Organizations are finally becoming convinced that testers truly can not test in quality at the end of the development process and that the traditional waterfall methodology has lead to many of the issues surrounding testing today. We now understand that testing has typically not been well defined and leaving it as the last activity in the development process was not the best approach.

The word "testing" conjures up a variety of meanings depending upon an individual's frame of reference. Some people view testing as a method or process by which they add value to the development cycle; they can even enjoy the challenges and creativity of testing. Other people feel that testing tries a person's patience, fairness, ambition, credibility, and capability. Testing can actually affect a person's mental and emotional health if you consider the office politics and interpersonal conflicts that are often times present.

Some attitudes that have shaped a negative view of testing and testers are:

- Testers hold up implementation.
- Giving testers less time to test will reduce the chance that they will find defects.
- Letting the testers find problems is an appropriate way to debug.
- Defects found in production are the fault of the testers.
- Testers do not need training; only programmers need training.

Although testing is a process, it is very much a dynamic one in that the process will change somewhat with each application under test. There are several variables that affect the testing process including: the development process itself, software risk, customer/user participation, the testing process, a tester's skill set, use of tools, testing budget and resource constraints, management support, and morale and motivation of the testers. It is obvious that the people side of software testing has long been ignored for the more process-related issues of test planning, test tools, defect tracking, and so on.

Top ten people challenges have been identified as:

- Training in testing
- Relationship building with developers
- Using tools

- Getting managers to understand testing
- Communicating with users about testing
- Making the necessary time for testing
- Testing "over the wall" software
- Trying to hit a moving target
- Fighting a lose-lose situation
- Having to say "no"

Testers should perform a self-assessment to identify their own strengths and weaknesses as they relate to technical and people-oriented skills. They should also learn how to improve the identified weaknesses, and build a master plan of action for future improvement.

Essential testing skills include test planning, using test tools (automated and manual), executing tests, managing defects, risk analysis, test measurement, designing a test environment, and designing effective test cases. Additionally, a solid vocabulary of testing is essential. A tester needs to understand what to test, who performs what type of test, when testing should be performed, how to actually perform the test, and when to stop testing.

Scope of Testing

The scope of testing is the extensiveness of the test process. A narrow scope may be limited to determining whether or not the software specifications were correctly implemented. The scope broadens as more responsibilities are assigned to software testers.

Among the broader scope of software testing are these responsibilities:

1. Software testing can compensate for the fact that the software development process does not identify the true needs of the user, and thus test to determine whether or not the user's needs have been met regardless of the specifications.
2. Finding defects early in the software development process when they can be corrected at significantly less cost than detected later in the software development process.
3. Removing defects of all types prior to software going into a production state when it is significantly cheaper than during operation.
4. Identifying weaknesses in the software development process so that those processes can be improved and thus mature the software development process. Mature processes produce software more effectively and efficiently.

In defining the scope of software testing each IT organization must answer the question, "Why are we testing?"

When Should Testing Occur?

The traditional view of the development life cycle places testing prior to operation and maintenance as illustrated in the following table. All too often, testing after coding is the only verification technique used to determine the adequacy of the system. When testing is constrained to a single phase and confined to the later stages of development, severe consequences can develop. It is not unusual to hear of testing consuming 50 percent of the development budget. All errors are costly, but the later in the life cycle that the error discovered is made, the more costly the error. An error discovered in the latter parts of the life cycle must be paid for four different times. The first cost is developing the program erroneously, which may include writing the wrong specifications, coding the system wrong, and documenting the system improperly. Second, the system must be tested to detect the error. Third, the wrong specifications and coding must be removed and the proper specifications, coding, and documentation added. Fourth, the system must be retested to determine that it is now correct.

Table—Life Cycle Verification Activities

Life Cycle Phase	*Verification Activities*
Requirements	- Determine verification approach - Determine adequacy of design - Generate functional test data - Determine consistency of design with requirements
Design	- Determine adequacy of design - Generate structural and functional test data - Determine consistency with design
Program (build/construction)	- Determine adequacy of implementation - Generate structural and functional test data for programs
Test	- Test application system
Installation	- Place tested system into production
Maintenance	- Modify and retest

If lower cost and higher quality systems are the information services goals, verification must not be isolated to a single phase in the development process, but rather, incorporated into each phase of development. One of the most prevalent and costly mistakes on systems development projects today is to defer the activity of detecting and correcting problems until late in the project. A major justification for an early verification activity is that many costly errors are made before coding begins.

Studies have shown that the majority of system errors occur in the design phase. These numerous studies show that approximately two-thirds of all detected system errors can be attributed to errors made during the design phase. This means that almost two-thirds of the errors must be specified and coded into programs before they can be detected. The recommended testing process is presented in Table 5 as a life cycle chart showing the verification activities for each phase. The success of conducting verification throughout the development cycle depends upon the existence of clearly defined and stated products at each development stage. The more formal and precise the statement of the development product, the more amenable it is to the analysis required to support verification. Many of the new system development methodologies encourage firm products even in the early development stages.

The recommended test process involves testing in every phase of the life cycle. During the requirements phase, the emphasis is upon validation to determine that the defined requirements meet the needs of the organization. During the design and program phases, the emphasis is on verification to ensure that the design and programs accomplish the defined requirements. During the test and installation phases, the emphasis is on inspection to determine that the implemented system meets the system specification. During the maintenance phases, the system will be retested to determine that the changes work and that the unchanged portion continues to work.

The following activities should be performed at each phase of the life cycle:

- Analyze the structures produced at this phase for internal testability and adequacy.
- Generate test sets based on the structure at this phase.

In addition, the following should be performed during design and programming:

- Determine that the structures are consistent with structures produced during previous phases.
- Refine or redefine test sets generated earlier.

Throughout the entire life cycle, neither development nor verification is a straight-line activity.

Modifications or corrections to a structure at one phase will require modifications or reverification of structures produced during previous phases.

Requirements

The verification activities that accompany the problem definition and requirements analysis phase of software development are extremely significant. The adequacy of the requirements must be thoroughly analyzed and initial test cases generated with the expected (correct) responses. Developing scenarios of expected system use helps to determine the test data and anticipated results. These tests form the core of the final test set. Generating these tests and the expected behavior of the system clarifies the requirements and helps guarantee that they are testable. Vague or requirements that are not testable leave the validity of the delivered product in doubt. Late discovery of requirements inadequacy can be very costly. A determination of the criticality of software quality attributes and the importance of validation should be made at this stage. Both product requirements and validation requirements should be established.

Design

Organization of the verification effort and test management activities should be closely integrated with preliminary design. The general testing strategy – including test methods and test evaluation criteria – is formulated, and a test plan is produced. If the project size or criticality warrants, an independent test team is organized. In addition, a test schedule with observable milestones is constructed. At this same time, the framework for quality assurance and test documentation should be established.

During detailed design, validation support tools should be acquired or developed and the test procedures themselves should be produced. Test data to exercise the functions introduced during the design process, as well as test cases based upon the structure of the system, should be generated. Thus, as the software development proceeds, a more effective set of test cases is built.

In addition to test organization and the generation of test cases, the design itself should be analyzed and examined for errors. Simulation can be used to verify properties of the system structures and subsystem interaction; the developers to verify the flow and logical structure of the system, while the test team should perform design inspections using design walkthroughs. Missing cases, faulty logic, module interface mismatches, data structure inconsistencies, erroneous I/O assumptions, and user interface inadequacies, are items of concern. The detailed design must prove to be internally coherent, complete, and consistent with the preliminary design and requirements.

Program (Build/Construction)

Actual testing occurs during the construction stage of development. Many testing tools and techniques exist for this stage of system development. Code walkthrough and code inspection are effective manual techniques. Static analysis techniques detect errors by analyzing program characteristics such as data flow and language construct usage. For programs of significant size, automated tools are required to perform this analysis. Dynamic analysis, performed as the code actually executes, is used to determine test coverage through various instrumentation techniques. Formal verification or proof techniques are used to provide further quality assurance.

Test Process

During the test process, careful control and management of test information is critical. Test sets, test results, and test reports should be catalogued and stored in a database. For all but very small systems, automated tools are required to do an adequate job – the bookkeeping chores alone become too large to handle manually. A test driver, test data generation aids, test coverage tools, test results management aids, and report generators are usually required.

Installation

The process of placing tested programs into production is an important phase normally executed within a narrow time span. Testing during this phase must ensure that the correct versions of the program are placed into production; that data if changed or added is correct; and that all involved parties know their new duties and can perform them correctly.

Maintenance

Over 50% of the life cycle costs of a software system are spent on maintenance. As the system is used, it is modified either to correct errors or to augment the original system. After each modification the system must be retested. Such retesting activity is termed regression testing. The goal of regression testing is to minimize the cost of system revalidation. Usually only those portions of the system impacted by the modifications are retested. However, changes at any level may necessitate retesting, re-verifying and updating documentation at all levels below it. For example, a design change requires design re-verification, unit retesting and subsystem retesting.

Test cases generated during system development are reused or used after appropriate modifications. The quality of the test documentation generated during system development and modified during maintenance will affect the cost of regression testing. If test data cases have been catalogued and preserved, duplication of effort will be minimized.

SUMMARY

1. The simple answer as to why we test software is that developers are unable to build defect-free software.
2. Testing by the individual who developed the work has not proven to be a substitute to building and following a detailed test plan.
3. A defect is an undesirable state. In order to know what a defect is we must first define a desirable state.
4. The term quality is used to define a desirable state.
5. IT gap is the gap between what is specified to be delivered, meaning the documented requirements and internal IT standards, and what is actually built.
6. The second gap is between what IT actually delivers compared to what the user wants.
7. The goal or mission for the software tester needs to be defined.
8. Ideally, the software development process should produce the same results each time the process is executed.
9. The amount of variation in a process is quantified with summary statistics; typically, the standard deviation is used.
10. One of the challenges in implementing quality management is to get those working in the process thinking in terms of sources of variation.
11. Common causes of variation are typically due to a large number of small random sources of variation.
12. Bringing a process into a state of statistical control is not really improving the process; it is just bringing it back to its typical operation.
13. Testing is a measurement process. It attempts to measure the implemented software against either or both specifications and user needs. Statistical process control (SPC) is a measurement tool.
14. At the ad hoc level (level 1), tasks are not performed the same way by different people or different groups.
15. There are two major objectives to be achieved at Level 2. The first is to instill discipline in the culture of the information organization so that through the infrastructure, training, and leadership of management individuals will want to follow defined processes. The second objective is to reduce variability in the processes by defining them to a level that permits relatively constant outputs.
16. At level 3, an information organization defines its core competencies and then builds an organization that is capable of performing those core competencies effectively and efficiently.
17. Level 4 has two objectives. The first is to develop quantitative standards for the work processes based on performance

of the Level 3 stabilized processes. The second objective is to provide management the dashboards and skill sets needed to manage quantitatively.

18. At Level 5, the information organization wants to be a true leader in the industry. At this level, the organization is looking to measure itself against the industry through benchmarking, and then define innovative ways to achieve higher levels of performance.

MULTIPLE CHOICE QUESTIONS

1. WBS is:
   (a) Work Breakdown Structure (b) Work Break Structure (c) Work Breakdown Situation
2. CBOK is:
   (a) Common Bay of Knowledge (b) Common Body of Knowledge (c) Called Body of Knowledge
3. SPC is:
   (a) Statistical Process Counter (b) Statistical Proven Control (c) Statistical Process Control

REVIEW QUESTIONS

1. Why do we test software?
2. What is a quality software?
3. How can we reduce the frequency of defects?
4. How would you deveop the Test Plan?
5. What sort of constraints are there?
6. Why are defects hard to find?
7. Describe the testing process.
8. Describing the various levels of testing.

ANSWERS

Multiple Choice Questions

1. a 2. b 3. c

CHAPTER 11

Introduction to System Analysis

LEARNING OBJECTIVES

After going through this chapter, you should appreciate the following:

- **The need for system analysis**
  System objectives
  System boundaries
  System importance
  Nature of the system
  Role of the system as an interface
  Participation of users
  Assessment of feasibility
- **System Analysis of the Existing System**
  Procedure of analysing the existing system
- **System Analysis of a New Requirement**
- **System Development Model**
  The system development methods
- **Computer System Design**
  Output design
  Input design
  Processing design
  Data specifications
  Procedure design

INTRODUCTION

During the course of fulfilling the role of system development, a number of different situations arise, which must be understood to facilitate decisions on the approach, strategy, technology and development. The role of the designer may either be to develop a smaller system or a complex large system. It may also be to design an integrated system, covering all the business systems, requiring their operations on the heterogeneous platform of hardware and software. At times, the system designer is faced with the problem of developing the additional systems and integrating them with the systems which are in operation already.

The third possibility is to change the entire system suitable to meet the current business information needs. The system in use may be old in terms of technology, design and lacks flexibility requiring a higher maintenance cost. The systems developed in the seventies and eighties, were designed for the mainframe computer systems with the assumption that the information needs do not change often and once the same are discussed and known from the users point of view they are final. Most of such systems catered to the standard operational needs of the business.

The information required for strategic management, competitive strategy built, customer, servicing and changing the information needs of the changing dynamics of the business, could not be delivered faster to the users. Due to the use of deficient information technology and the system development approach not focusing on the design, the nature and type of the systems were more of a data processing nature and less of data analysis type. The late eighties and nineties, however, have seen the exposition of the information technology and now it is offering a number of functions, facilities and features which has created a challenge to the System Designer and developer.

The distance between the two users or the sources of data is not a problem now. The speed and the response is no longer an issue in the advance hardware-software configurations. The communication is possible within the company, across the cities and countries. It is not necessary that the database should be near to its owner and the user. The distributed database and the access to it from anywhere is possible. The user in the business organisation has become more literate in terms of knowledge use of information technology and its application in the management of business. With the computer being more reliably used for building the knowledge bases and also for designing the support systems, the problems of meeting the changing information needs is solved by keeping the databases and the knowledge bases at the back-end.

Also the users are equipped to derive their information needs by using the front-end development tools of data and the information processing. With the fast changing business management practices all over the world, the systems that sought to serve them are also changing faster. At the same time, what is needed is a robust design, easy to change, with the changed components being minimal, user-friendly and easy to learn and hardware software independent. For the integrity of the information in all respects, the system should have less human intervention, the data input should be once at a valid source and shareable on the selective basis. The systems designed now in the competitive world are intelligent, action triggering, self-controlled, demanding the users attention in extreme cases. There are a variety of systems where system analysis would be required. The needs can be symbolically be represented in terms of the type or the kind of systems.

The systems can be classified as shown in the following table.

The role of the system analyst to fulfil this requirement is different as compared to the role played by him in the seventies and eighties. The system analyst now has to play the role of a business analyst, technology expert and a consultant, giving a solution to the business needs of the information requirement. The nature of the solution is not of a micro level but of a macro level. The information systems users are more in the middle and the top management and less in the lower level of the organisation as their role is taken over by the system itself.

The system analysis and design, therefore, has become more complex, as most of the systems are open

Data processing systems	The data already exists but needs processing to achieve certain results. The focus is on computing.
Transaction processing system	Processing of transaction using some stored data and business rules. The focus is on the transaction execution
Functional systems	The production, sales, purchase and finance systems, where several transactions and stored data is used to produce certain information. The focus is on the Operation Management
Integrated systems	More than one system is processed together to produce an updated status and business results, where the systems are networked and interfaced. The focus is on process management across the business functions
Enterprise management	It is set of systems functioning in the respective areas, playing a local service role, as well as providing service inputs to other systems in the organisation. The focus is on decision support for strategic management to achieve enterprise goals and mission

systems and probabilistic in nature as a against the closed, deterministic systems experienced in the seventies and eighties.

THE NEED FOR SYSTEM ANALYSIS

When you are asked to computerise a system, as a requirement of the data processing or the information need, it is necessary to analyse the system from different angles. While satisfying such need, the analysis of the system is the basic necessity for an efficient system design.

The need for analysis stems for following points of view.

System Objective

It is necessary to define the system objective(s). Many a times, it is observed that the systems are historically in operation and have lost their main purpose of achievement of the objectives. The users of the system and the personnel involved are not in a position to define the objective(s). Since you are going to develop a computer based system, it is necessary to redefine or reset the objective(s). Since you are going to develop a computer based system, it is necessary to redefine or reset the objective(s) as a reference point in context of the current business requirement.

System Boundaries

It is necessary to establish the system boundaries which would define the scope and the coverage of the system. This helps to sort out and understand the functional boundaries of the system, the department boundaries in the system and the people involved in the system. It also helps to identify the inputs and the outputs of the various subsystems, covering the entire system.

System Importance

It is necessary to understand the important of the system in the organisation. This would throw more light on its utility and would help the designer to decide the design features of the system. It would be possible then to position to the system in relation to the other systems for deciding the design strategy and development.

Nature of the System

The analysis of the system will help the system designer to conclude whether the system is the closed type or an open and deterministic or a probabilistic. Such an understanding of the system is necessary, prior to design the process to ensure the necessary design architecture.

Role of the System as an Interface

The system, many a times, acts as an interface to the other systems. Hence through such an interface, it activates or promotes some changes in the other systems. It is necessary to understand the existing role of the system, as an interface, to safeguard the interests of the other systems. Any modifications or changes made should not affect the functioning or the objectives of the other systems.

Participation of Users

The strategic purpose of the analysis of the system is to seek the acceptance of the people to a new development. System analysis process provides a sense of participation to the people. This helps in breaking the resistance to the new development and it also ensures the commitment to the new system.

Understanding of Resource Needs

The analysis of the system helps in defining the resources requirements in terms of hardware and software. Hence, if any additional resources are required, this would mean an investment. The management likes to evaluate the investment from the point of view of return on such investment. If the return on the investment is not attractive, the management may drop the project.

Assessment of Feasibility

The analysis of the system helps to establish the feasibility from different angles. The system should satisfy the technical, economic and operational feasibility.

Many times, the systems are feasible from the technical and economic point of view; but they may be infeasible form the operational point of view.

The assessment of feasibility will save the investment and the system designer's time. It would also save the embarrassment to the system designer as he is viewed as the key figure in such projects.

One can approach the system analysis and design exercise in a systematic manner in steps, as shown in the table shown next.

SYSTEM ANALYSIS OF THE EXISTNG SYSTEM

When the objectives of the information system are finalised, as the first step towards development, it is necessary to analysis the existing system.

Such an analysis the helps in achieving the following:

- Understanding the existing system.
- Understanding the objectives achieved by the existing system.
- Evaluating he system for computerisation and its placement in the total MIS design.
- Knowing whether the system is feasible technically and optionally.
- Are the information needs fully justified?
- If so, is the cost of the system design justified to increase the value of the information.

Steps	Elaboration	Explanation
Need for nformation	Define the nature of information. Also who wants and who uses.	Identity the users and application of the information for achieving the objectives.
Define the system	Decide the nature, type of the system and its scope	Helps to determine the system ownership, its benefits and complexity.
Feasibility	Technical success	Hardware and software availability and capacity, for implementation.
	Economic viability	Study the investment and benefits. Assess the improvement in value of the information. Determine the return on investment.
	Operational effectiveness	Examine whether the system will perform as desired in terms of time and results. Are the users ready to use the system?
Detailing the requirements	Identity in precise terms, the strategic, functional and operational information needs.	Study the sources of generating the information. Establish I/O linkages. Modify the existing system to satisfy the needs.
Conceptual system design	Determine the inputs, process and outputs and design a conceptional model.	Conceptualisation is necessary to understand the system process.
Detailing the system design	Draw the document flow charts and the dataflow diagrams, the data and system hierarchy diagrams, the data, information versus its users mapping table.	Helps in bringing a clarity in the dataflow. The responsibility centres and the process centres are identified.
Structuring the system design	Break the system into its hierarchical structure	Helps in understanding the dataflow from one level to the other and the processes carried out at each level.
Conceptual model of computer system	Define step by step the usage of files, processes and interface. Define the data structures and the validation procedures.	Help to put down the data processing flow in the computerised system. Draw the computer system charts.
Break the system in programme modules	Make a physical conversion of the system into the programme structures in a logical order.	Modules will be data entry, data validation, data processing, reporting and storing.
Develop the test data for checking the system ability	Test the modules and the integrity of the system in terms of input versus output. Plan white box and black box testing.	Confirms whether the system design is satisfactory. Suggests the modifications.
Install the system	Install on the hardware	Install, test and run the system before the user is exposed in a live mode.
Implementation	Train the personnel. Run the system in parallel. Prepare a system manual.	Helps to identify the problems and provide solutions.
Review and maintenance	Review the system through audit tail and test data, also confirm whether the objective is fulfilled. Carry out the modifications, if any.	Helps to maintain the system quality and the quality of information through modification, if necessary.

Procedure of Analysing the Existing System

System analyst while analysing the existing system should:

1. Carry out the analysis of the system at a place where the system is functioning. This step will ensure that the analyst is accepted as one of those operating the system.
2. Note down the key personnel in the system besides the head of the department. The key personnel are those who contribute towards the system operations.
3. Spend some time with the operating personnel and observe the system to understand the finer details of the system.
4. Define the scope of the system and its objective. The scope will cover the boundaries of the system. Further, should identify the problems faced in the system. Further, should identify the problems faced in the system which cause difficulties in achieving the objectives.
5. Collect all the documents which are raised in the system. These documents carry data from one point to another. The documents could be printed or handwritten. While collecting the documents, the analyst should note down who raises the document, the purpose it achieves and the manner in which it is distributed.
6. Collect separately the outputs such as statements, reports, memos, etc. made in the system to throw more light on the information it generates. If these reports and the statements are sent to other departments, make a note of it. Also fine out if any register or notebook is maintained at various points, which act as data storage and reference. Note down against each such document, its use.
7. Make a list of rules, formulae, guidelines, policies, etc., which are used in running the system.
8. Note down the check points and the controls used in the system to ensure that the dataflow is complete, processing of the data is correct and the analysis is precise.
9. Study the flow of data in the system in units, summary and aggregates from document to document and from one stage to the other.
10. Make a small system note as a base document and seek an appointment with each head of the department to discuss the system. In the discussion, ensure that your system view and understanding is the same as that of the head of the department. Ascertain from his whether he has any other objectives which the system should achieve.
11. Examine whether the achievement of the system's objectives is feasible in the present system. This means, examining whether adequate data exists, whether it can be processed by the rules, methods, model, already there to generate information. If so, will the information be correct, precise and complete. Further, can it be processed on time to be useful to the user or the decision maker?
12. If there are problems in the feasibility of implementation, then examine whether the present system can be modified by introduction of documents, controls, procedures and systems. If this is not possible, redefine the scope of the system and objectives in the light of the study.
13. Draw a revised system flow chart to indicate how the system runs the major steps of processing the information. This chart should include all the modification which had been suggested and accepted.
14. Discuss the flow chart with the personnel operating the system so that they understand the system. Impress upon that they should run the system as per the flow chart and resist any deviations there from that would cause a disturbances in the system. Explain the modified system in such a way that the user would appreciate the changes.
15. Make a list of the outputs (statements, reports) containing information. Get the contents of the reports approved by the head of the department.

16. Analyse the requirements of the information and reports from the utility point of view. More the information, higher is the cost of its generation. Decide the utility based on the value of information.
17. Compare the costs of the old and the new system and benefits offered.
18. Obtain approval of the new system from the users and the top management.
19. Write a system manual for use of the people in the department and for reference to the other users of the system.

SYSTEM ANALYSIS OF A NEW REQUIREMENT

It is not always necessary that the analysts are required to conduct the analysis of the existing system. In a number of cases when legacy systems have outlived utility or a new business environment requires a totally radically approach, the analyst is called for redesigning the process, practices and procedures. Today's business world of a company is beyond the four walls of the organisation. The vendors and the customers are being treated as trusted business partners of the organisation. This change in the management philosophy calls for a change in the information management function in the organisation. It cuts across all the facets of processing the data and the information, right from the input to the output and its distribution.

The conventional confidential access to the information and the practice of authorising a person to make decisions has undergone a substantial change. The decision centres in the organisation have been diffused and a substantial delegation of decision making has taken place at the lower level. The characteristic change in the organisation is that it is being looked as a process organisation as against a functional organisation. The work culture is changing from the single hierarchical command control principal to the working through work groups principle. These work groups are empowered to make decisions with an access to support the information. In such changed environment, the information system architecture, the design and processes and the hardware-software configuration should be restructured to meet the changed requirement of information.

The trend is towards building a system which is potentially flexible adaptable to the new technology, easy to use and which enables the user to meet his own needs through his knowledge and expertise. The system analyst, in such a virgin situation of policy change, has to think globally taking into consideration the technology, the user and the business it serves. He is required to make analysis to evolve the system and the technology strategy and configuration them to work for executing the business strategy through the information support. The system analyst work has to choose between the client server versus the Host-slave processing strategy. He has to make a choice between the different variants of Unix OS, Windows NT and so on. He has to choose the language platform and select a variety of packages and put them together to achieve the information support goal. He will also be confronted with techno-commercial issues arising out of the multiple vendors dealing with different technologies.

Putting all the system components together to achieve the information processing strategy success is quite a complex job requiring a vision and a foresight.

Hence, the system Analysis and Design, in such situations, is an exercise at a macro level with a top-down approach in understanding the requirement.

The information system development cycle for a new application consists of the five major stages:

1. Definition of the system and its objective
2. Development of the system (Analysis-Design-Programming)
3. Installation of the system
4. Operations of the system
5. Review and evaluation

The details of this system development cycle are given in the following table.

Stages in development cycle	Steps in each stage	Purpose
Definition of the system and its objective	Define the system and its elements. Determine the system boundaries andscope. Set the objectives for the system in line with the business objectives.	The stage assures clarity to the users of the system and the System Designer. The terms of reference are also set.
Development of the system	The system analysis of the existing business systems and changes therein.	More clear understanding of real life situations, problems and weaknesses.
	System analysis of similar systems.	
	Decision making needs are identified and corresponding inforamtion needs are defined.	This step ensures that the inforamtion requirements are defined as a support to decision making.
	A feasibility of system is examined.	The technical, economic and operational feasibility is ascertained before a major effort is spent on the system.
	A conceptual design of the system	The post feasibility understanding of the system for users and designer.
	An initial prototype of the system.	The step ensures the supply of the basic information needs. It helps to refine and revise the inforamtion needs and then the conceptual design.
	Strucutred break-up of the system in the smaller subsystems/processes in hierarchical order for development.	Helps to understand the system functioning and brings a clarity in the input and outputs of each subsystem.
	Design a computer system - output design, input design, processing design, procedure design. Flo charting the system and documentation. this includes a database design architecture and application development design.	Ensures step by step approach to a computer system design and provides clarity to the user and designer through documentation.
Installation of the system and testing.	The system is tested and installed on the hardware for implementation. Switching over to computer system after through operational testing.	The step ensures that the operational problems are resolved and the user gets live experience of the system. Modifications, if any, are carrid out. Checks and controls are ensured through testing and he parallel runs.
Operations of the system.	The system is operated in full course and existing systems (if any) discontinued.	The user confidence is built and hte designer simultaneously evaluates the performance of the computer system.
Review and Evaluation	A review is taken whether the system objectives are being met with and what are the problems in the smooth running. Steps are taken to resolve them.	This is an audit by the designer for improvement through test data and audit trail.

Following the system development cycle approach is the best bet for the successful completion of any system project. The main advantage of the approach is that the process helps the analyst to conceive, develop, design and implement the system. Following procedure provides the basis for management and control of the project as each step in the process is a well defined task. The most important step in the process is the definition and the objectives of the system. Unless the user and the designer agree on this point, it will be risky to proceed further. The system analysis is the second most important step in the cycle. The designers who spend more time on this step succeed in completing the project effectively.

About 30% of the time should be spent in the first two phases and about 10% of the time in the post implementation review and evaluation. The photo typing step is a critical step where the user understand the system in the initial stage and helps to try out the ideas in the system leading to the purpose design of the information system. The life cycle procedure is a tool for the system leading to the process design of the information system. The life cycle procedure is a tool for the system designer. Its meticulous following is a safe method to accomplish the system objectives.

SYSTEM DEVELOPMENT MODEL

In order to design a good system, traditionally, the developers have used the Waterfall model as shown on the next page. As waterfall flows form the top to the bottom, the system model shows the development process from the top to the bottom in steps. As water does not rise from a lower level to a higher level, it is presumes that once a step in the model is over, it is not required to go back. This model fits well when the changes into the requirement specifications are not required frequently. The minor changes can be taken care of through a maintenance process or through small design changes. The waterfall model applies well to the basic rule based data and information processing systems in accounting materials, production and personnel. However, some systems are more dynamic and require changes in specifications more often to continue to be useful. These modifications are termed as the versions of the basic model.

One of the popular model developed by Boehm is a Spiral model as shown on the next page. A spiral model fits well, when we are developing large systems, where the specifications cannot be ascertained in one stroke completely and correctly. Some of them get surfaced when the system is put to use after its testing. The continuous revision of these steps in the system development is very common and then the designers call them as versions.

The new version provides an additional functionality, features and facilities to the user and addresses the issues of the users of the users of the system viz. performance, response, security and so on, irrespective of which development model is used in developing the system. The user wants the system to be user friendly, reliable and effective and one which gives correct results, while the developer wants, the system easy to modify, easy to understand, portable and compatible to other systems.

The definition of a good system varies with the system's environment. In some systems the performance is the key measure of a good system while in other cases the ability to change fast is a key measure of a good system case. In some cases the user friendliness could be a measure of good system. In all the cases, however, the correctness of the result is a common measure, making them reliable and dependable for the business operations.

The speed and response are the performance measures in case of large volume transaction based system designed for real time applications. The flexible design is a measure of performance where the system needs continuous modifications to meet the revised requirements of the specifications. When it comes to a complex system the user friendliness and the ease of applications become the measures of a good system. In other words, a good system design considers the environment and the user and incorporates all the needs and expectations so that its utility is the highest.

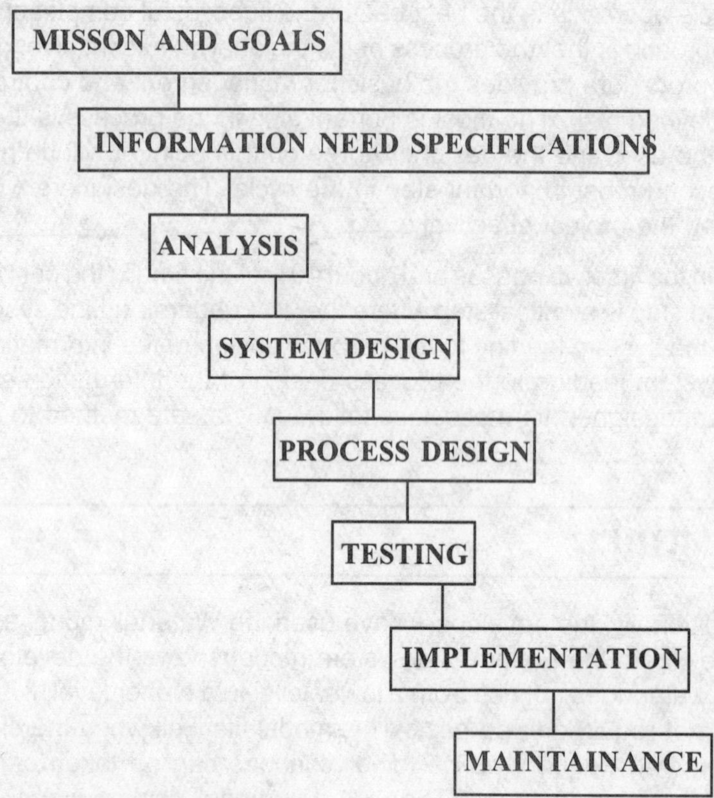

The System Development Methods

The traditional software development methods are the Structured Systems analysis and Design (SSAD) by Ross; the Requirement Driven Design by Alford and the Structured Analysis and Structure Design (SASD) by Yourdon. All these methods deal with the functions and data separately. The modern methodology is object-oriented, where the functions and the data are viewed together as an object. Traditional methods consider the function and the data independent of each other. The function provides the behaviour or operation which will use the data to perform. The data set so produced will hold information on the latest status of the transaction or function.

These methods operate on the data model which has a structure, definition and application. The same data when used in different functions will produce different results and information. A system developed with the SSAD and the similar approaches are difficult to maintain. The reason is that for each function and its behaviour the data structure is defined. The functionality behaves correctly under the conditions of the rigid data definition and structure. However, in real life, the data format changes, calling for a change in the programmes to increases due to first checking the data condition and then moving the control to an appropriate command set for its processing. The SSAD is, therefore, easy to understand but difficult to maintain.

The user of the system does not think in terms of the data and its definition but thinks in terms of the functionality or process producing a result. In the SSAD approach, therefore, the user must have two views on the system to understand. The first view on the data and the second on its functionality. The two views create a problem of understanding the system correctly. The Object Oriented Technology (OOT) approach differs from the SSAD approach. The difference is that the OOT views the system and then models it in terms of an item called the Object, where the function and the data are defined at its lowest level where changes rarely occur.

The OOT views the functions and the data as one integrated entity. It reflects the requirements directly into the objects. In the SSAD approach, the requirement is fulfilled through defining and associating the data for each function. While in the OOT approach the requirement is fulfilled, through the object(s) processing, where the object itself is based on the behaviour. If a new requirement arises the new object(s) view is taken and the model is modified in that portion only leaving the rest of the design and the programme structure as it is.

In the OOT approach the change boil down to the lowest level in most of the cases. A good object model of the system does not require any changes at a Class or super Class level. They are, generally, at the instance level. For example, in invoice preparation, new functionality is required to calculate the invoice amount. In SSAD this would need a condition definition for recognition, then the changes in the data and process flow, further defining the output of the new requirement. In OOT the same situation would be handled by creating an instance where only the computing behaviour is different from the others. The instance is created by using the principle of inheritance. Hence the change in the system and the programme progress is only at the lowest level and is local, not running across the total model of the system. In short, for a given business functionality the objects are defined in different categories and the system design is built through the objects and it is processed through object processing. Hence, in a business organisation to conduct a business, it requires the customer orders, purchase indents, material indents, work orders, purchase orders, receipts, issues payments, usage the analysis is made of the business operations and it is modelled into objects.

For example, the object class ORDER will handle all kinds of orders, viz., the customer orders, purchase orders, pay orders, appointment orders and so on. The objects are constructed for the documents, transactions and operations. The method which uses the objects in modelling the processing is called as the object oriented methodology. Whether it is a Waterfall model or a Spiral model of system development or whether it is the SSAD or the SASD approach or whether it is the object oriented technology of system development the following steps of the development common.

- Requirement analysis
- Requirement Definition
- System design
  - Input Design
  - Process Design
  - Output Design
- System Development
  - Structuring the modules
  - Developing
- Unit testing
- Integration of the modules
- System Testing
- Implementation
- Maintenance

The requirement analysis is carried out from the top downwards in the organisation hierarchy, linking the goals and the objectives of the business organisation, with the strategy mix decided to achieve them. In this phase the information needs of the individuals, groups and functions are analysed from a decision making or a support point of view. Such information needs would fully satisfy the operations and management information needs. Once the needs are justified, the next step is to define them in clearer terms for the purpose of development.

The requirement definition bring clarity in the content and its application in various ways in the organisation. The third step is to design a physical and a logical system through which the output are designed. The processes which would give the output are determined and the data which would be required by these processes is finalised in terms of definition, source and quality. And further, the collection, creation, validation and storage of the input data is also decided. The fourth step is to break the system design into modules in the hierarchical top-down structure to facilitate the development effort as well as is implementation. Once the modules are developed, the unit testing is carried out to confirm data transaction and outputs validity and accuracy.

In this testing, the transaction level processes are checked to confirm the input-process-output relation and the data storage and the transaction level updating. When the unit testing is over and the module level processing is confirmed, the modules are put together to generate the information as determined in the requirement definition. The process of putting the modules together is a process of integration. The system so developed is tested as a whole for several aspects such as information, quality, performance, utility, user acceptance and so on. Once the system testing is complete, the system is implemented at site, on the hardware and software platform.

The implementation step has its own procedure starting from the installation of the hardware and the software, training the users and then shifting to a fully designed system. While implementing the system some minor modifications/adjustments, may be required for the ease of acceptance by the user. Even after complete installation, the system may require modifications or changes in terms of functions and features over a period of time. The process of introducing these new requirements without disturbing the time tested basic system is called maintenance. Such changes are required swiftly and hence they are required to be carried out very easily. The system is designed keeping this natural requirement in post implementation period. A good system design and its implementation has high user acceptance because it helps solve the problems in business performance and meets the information needs, within a sensible time scale, with an assured quality and security of information.

COMPUTER SYSTEM DESIGN

After analysing the system by way of structured analysis, the next task of the designer is to design a computer system. The computer system design consists of five major steps, viz., designing the output, the input, the processing, the data specifications and the procedure specifications.

Output Design

The output design should be able to communicate information to the users in the organisation effectively. The information, as an output, can be printed, displayed or stored. If it is necessary to print the information, as a report, then the designer has to decide the format of the report. If it is to be displayed, then the designer has to provide a screen format. The output design requires to determine the reports, the screens, the contents of the reports and the screen and the layout of the contents. While designing the report and the screen formats the designer should pay attention to the concepts of information presentation so that the utility of the system is not reduced because of a noise, an information overload, an incomplete coverage an inadequate references etc.

The attention should also be given to the security of information through access control. The designer should decide an appropriate balance between the print reports and the display screens. The layout of the report, whether it is printed or displayed, must satisfy some basic features. Each report should have an appropriate title with a period reference, date of processing and a system title. The pages should be numbered, with the title repeated and at the end of the processing it should provide the statistics such as the number of records, items, etc. The layout should be such that the readability will be from left to right and from top to bottom.

Each column and row should have meaningful titles. The layout should provide sub-totals and grand totals with reference to the unit such as class, group or family. It should sub-totals and grand totals with reference to the unit such as class, group or family. It should provide suitable blank spaces to enhance readability. If any abbreviations are used, the expanded forms should be given alongside. As far as possible, the abbreviations should be universal and common to all reports to avoid confusion. A good layout improves the utility of the information reports by highlighting the areas of concern where the attention of the management and its response is required immediately. In many cases the design of pre-printed forms is an easy solution for a good layout. The use of the pre-printed stationery saves the printing time and enforces a standardisation in the information layout. With the use of the pre-printed stationery, the main user can blank out certain columns and rows or certain results to avoid an exposure to the unwanted users. This saves the duplicate printing and the additional programming effort required for it.

Input Design

In this phase the designer's task is to identify those data items that will be an input to the system. The designer finds a linkage to the input data from the output. Once the items are identified, it is necessary to find the documents from where these data will be taken. A document containing several data items will be treated as a record in the system. For example, if the sales information is an output of the system then it can be represented as shown below. It shows the path to find the documents and records.

To obtain the sales information, the system must consider the Order Acceptance, the Invoice and the debit Note records containing the related data items.

The guidelines for selecting the data item from the document and grouping them into a record are as follows:

1. Only the data items which have a current and prospective use should be included. The others should be ignored.
2. The data items from a document should be grouped together and arranged in logical order of its use in processing. For example, a document number of a product code should be at the beginning of the record.
3. The grouping of the data items should be in line with its application and not in line with their placement in the report format. For example, the invoice amount, the discount, the taxes, the duties etc. should be grouped together.

Processing Design

After the output and the input design, the designer has to develop a process design which will specify the various steps that will convert input data into outputs.

The process design deals with the following two types of processes, viz. computing decision making.

1. Computation process for the net value of invoice:

   Quantity x Rate = Amount

   Amount + 10% (Amount) = Gross amount

   Gross Amount + 6% (Gross Amount) = Net value

2. Decision making for choice of the invoice processing:

   If the customer is of a type 'Industry' then follow the invoice process – A.

   If the customer is of a type 'Distributor' then minor follow the invoice process – B

   If the customer is of a type 'OEM' then follow the invoice process – C and so on.

As a part of the process design, the designer has to decide the source of the data items, viz., the documents and the files. Since the files will be used for storage of the record and for retrieval, their organisation becomes an important factor. The designer classifies the files as master file(s) and transaction files and also decides their use in system in a logical sequence. The files can be organised in a number of ways. The organisation of the files relates to the storage of data items and its recording layout on the magnetic media.

The files can be organised either in random ordered fashion or in indexed sequential fashion. Each file organisation has its own advantages related to access and processing. A data processing situation dictates the type of the organisation. In database environment data and records are arranged in a table form.

Data Specifications

Having identified data items at atomic level and configuring them into a set to form a record of an input entity, it is necessary to design specification for each data item. These specifications of the items will be followed uniformally at all places wherever they are used. The specification is expressed in terms of length of an item in terms of characters, its nature in terms of numeric or alpha or alpha numeric known as picture. A data item may have some value and hence it would have some conditions and validity. For example, date is an item having eight characters, presented in numeric value with two spaces after date and two spaces after a month, followed by a year mentioned in four numeric characters.

The date will not have null value and has no upper value. The order of date presentation is day, month and year. The specifications are used for error checking, control and processing. A data item before it is accepted as in input is checked against specifications. If there is a violation, it is corrected through a formal process of editing before acceptance.

Procedure Design

This phase specifies how the computer system will function from data entry to the output stage. The procedure indicates the logic of data processing and the flow of system control from one step to the other. Since the process design is complete, each process will be a step in the procedure design of the computer system. Each of such processes will be implemented through a computer programme. The procedure design steps will be shown in the computer system flow chart. In all the system design procedures, there are broad steps which are required to complete the design procedure.

These steps are shown in the table shown next.

Steps	Explanation	Comment
Data Entry of the transactions, masterdata	A simple data entry as per the input desing specification.	Provides the data entry programmes for all the documents considered in the system.
Data validation	The data entry is validated as per the input picture specification and control specification.	Shows the errors of presence and absence of the data entity and any violation of given specifications.
Transaction validation	Validates the transactions for its type and for its internal consistency	Shows the wrong type of transactions entering in the system and the mistake in hte documentation or in the transaction.
Edit and update	The errors and new data to be updated to complete the records.	Helps to correct the data at all the levels.
Data processing	Shows at each stage the process and the acitvities such as sort, merge, collate and compute. It also shows the use of files and creation of new files and its further use in the system.	Helps to understand the step by step development of system processing.
Output processing	Shows whether the output is printed, displayed and stored. Shows the device on which the output is processed.	Helps to understand how the output is produced.

A flow chart of the system using all the specifications of process design and procedure design guides the designer the analyst and the programmer in developing the system. It provides and logical overview of the system. The guidelines for drawing the system flow chart are as under:

1. Identify the start and the end of the system.
2. Identify the inputs, in terms of the data and the documents entering in the system, in their logical order. Determine the transaction and the master files in the system.
3. Identify the output at each stage and decide the media for processing and storage.

SUMMARY

1. The distance between the two users or the sources of data is not a problem now.
2. The role of the system analyst to fulfil this requirement is different as compared to the role played by him in the seventies and eighties.
3. When you are asked to computerise a system, as a requirement of the data processing or the information need, it is necessary to analyse the system from different angles.
4. It is necessary to define the system objective(s).
5. It is necessary to establish the system boundaries which would define the scope and the coverage of the system.
6. It is necessary to understand the important of the system in the organisation.
7. The analysis of the system will help the system designer to conclude whether the system is the closed type or an open and deterministic or a probabilistic.
8. The analysis of the system helps in defining the resources requirements in terms of hardware and software.
9. When the objectives of the information system are finalised, as the first step towards development, it is necessary to analysis the existing system.
10. The trend is towards building a system which is potentially flexible adaptable to the new technology, easy to use and which enables the user to meet his own needs through his knowledge and expertise.
11. Following the system development cycle approach is the best bet for the successful completion of any system project.
12. In order to design a good system, traditionally, the developers have used the Waterfall model.
13. The user of the system does not think in terms of the data and its definition but thinks in terms of the functionality or process producing a result.
14. Even after complete installation, the system may require modifications or changes in terms of functions and features over a period of time.
15. The output design should be able to communicate information to the users in the organisation effectively.
16. To obtain the sales information, the system must consider the Order Acceptance, the Invoice and the debit Note records containing the related data items.
17. After the output and the input design, the designer has to develop a process design which will specify the various steps that will convert input data into outputs.
18. Procedure design phase specifies how the computer system will function from data entry to the output stage.

MULTIPLE CHOICE QUESTIONS

1. WBS is:
   (a) Work Breakdown Structure (b) Work Break Structure (c) Work Breakdown Situation
2. CBOK is:
   (a) Common Bay of Knowledge (b) Common Body of Knowledge (c) Called Body of Knowledge
3. SPC is:
   (a) Statistical Process Counter (b) Statistical Proven Control (c) Statistical Process Control

REVIEW QUESTIONS

1. Which tools are available for system study and analysis?
2. What is the difference between the study and analysis?
3. What is the purpose of system flow chart?
4. What is data mapping and how it is done?
5. How is systems analysis approach different in new system requirement as against existing one?
6. What is SSAD?
7. Explain the mechanics of structure analysis.
8. Why is input design important? Can it always be linked to output design?
9. Using DFD symbols draw a dataflow diagram for issuing a purchase order for a standard inventory item.
10. Explain the following terms:
    Data Design   Process Design
    Output Design

ANSWERS

Multiple Choice Questions

1. a   2. b   3. c

CHAPTER 12

Program Development Cycle

LEARNING OBJECTIVES

After going through this chapter, you should appreciate the following:

- **Introduction**

  General concepts | Modular approach
  Stylistic guidelines | Documentation
  Program maintainance | Running and debugging program
  Testing

- **Problem solving methodlogy and techniques**

  Understanding of the Problem
  Identifying Minimum number of Inputs
  Step by Step Solution for the Problem
  Breaking Down Solution into Simple Steps
  Identification of Arithmetic and Logical Operations required for Solution
  Using Control Structure | Statements
  Compound Statement (Block) | Selection Statements
  The If Statement of C++ | Nested Ifs
  The If-else-If Ladder | The ? : Alternative to If
  The Switch Statement

- **Iteration Statements**

  The for loop | The while loop
  The do-while loop | Nested loops

INTRODUCTION

A good programmer is an asset to the company. But, nobody is born to write programs. A good programmer is not born but is developed by his own actions. These actions make him a good programmer. There is a methology which he has to follow to become a good programmer. In this chapter I will discuss this methology, and how it is used while writing programs irrespective of the language he is using.

Programming is a team effort. What can a good programmer do if the inputs to him are given wrong. He has to coordinate between the various users and data providers to cater to their needs and write a good program which would produce the results the user is looking forward to. A manager for example, is not concerned how the problem is solved or how the data is obtained. He is only interested in results which the program is supposed to provide.

For writing any program the programmer has to keep lots of things in mind. Few of them have been mentioned above, the others including problem definition, program design, coding, debugging, testing, documentation, maintenance and redesign. Let us start with the general concepts used for writing any program.

General Concepts

Program writing is definitely a technique. One has to master it by experience. One should always start with writing small and simple programs and then graduate to complex and complicated programs. Whatever he may write, it should be written in a manner which is understood by others. God forbid if he is not around the others should be able to run and modify it. Here the documentation parts becomes very necessary. I will talk about it little later but first let us see what a good program should have.

A good program should have the following characteristics:

1. Readability
2. Efficiency
3. Reliability
4. Meaningfulness
5. Portability
6. User-friendly.

Let us read about them in little details.

Readability

As mentioned above the program should be such that it can be read and understood by others. This makes it easy to modify by others.

Efficiency

While writing the program the programmer must take care of the following:

Processing

He should make sure that the program takes the minimum processing time.

Memory

Mimimum utalization of memory and hard disk space should be used.

Time

The programmer should be able to produce the program in time frame given.

Realiability

It goes beyond saying that the program should be reliable and must be in a position to produce good and accurate results. It should take care that the various checks are provided to overcome wrong data and machine malfunctions.

Meaningfullness

The program should give the meaningful outputs.

Portability

With the advent of PCs the compatability of one computer with another has been taken care of. But, still there is a possibility that the program may be required to run on a machine which is alien to the program. In this case the program should be such that it needs minimum efforts to be modified to suit the new environments.

User-friendly

A program should be user-friendly.

Modular approach

This is mainly applicable in the case of bigger programs. Instead of running a big program altogether, the program is divided into small parts and they are run independently. These parts are self sufficient and can be run alone. These parts are called subroutines or modules. Take for example the case of DOS which in itself a independent software but it has small modules such as COPY, MOVE, FORMAT, etc., all of them are independent of each other. In FORMAT also, there are modules to handle different type of floppies and each one of them can be run alone.

A module can be further divided into sub modules, as in the case of FORMAT above. All these small modules join together and can be called as superior module. A superior module should be capable of calling sub-modules in programming with the help of calling statement. Modular Programming does not use GOTO statement for the purpose of calling a sub-module by a module. This is so since after executing the modules, the control has to come back whereas in the case of GOTO the control goes out of hand.

There are different ways of using the modular programming. They are:

1. Sequence structure
2. Decision/Selection structure
3. Loop structure

Let us read about them in details.

Sequence Structure

In this case the execution of modules takes place in sequence. The following statements s1, s2, ... were written in sequence and they are executed in sequence too.

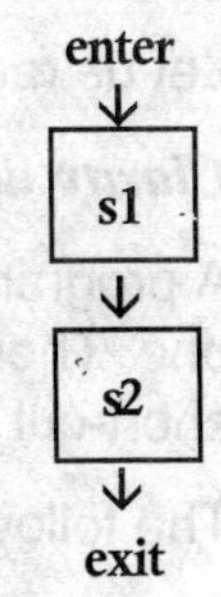

Decision/Selection Structure

Here a course of action is dependent upon one of the two courses.

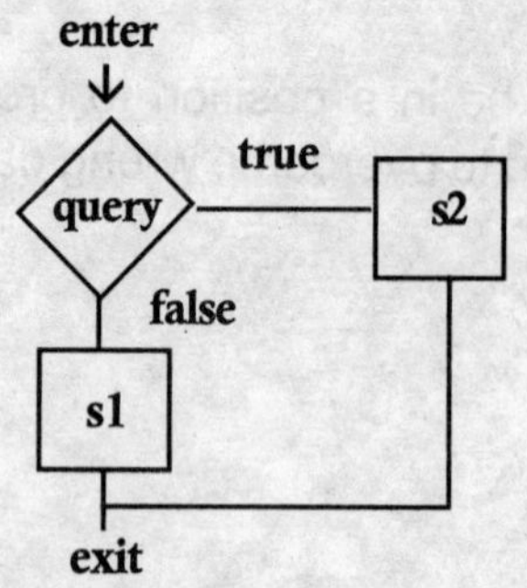

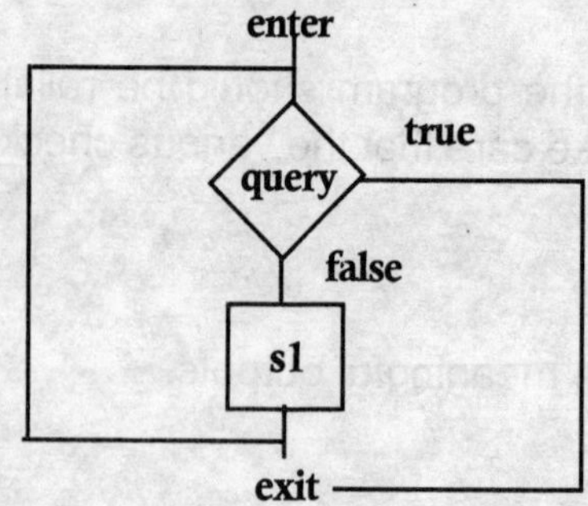

Looping

It is used when you have to repeat a structure different times. It is thus called looping. A while-loop structure is generally used in programming.

Advantages of Modular Programming

- easy to understand
- easier to test a program
- easy modification
- speedy execution
- easier development of the modules

Disadvantages of Moduler Programming

- occupy more memory space
- testing every module is a time consuming process
- difficult combination of modules due to different design of modules.

Stylistic Guidelines

A company may employ different set of programmers for its working. Each one of them has his own way of working. It may happen that one programmer may not be able to read the program written by another. So to overcome this problem, what the company does is that it sets its own guidelines, which are given to each programmer and they are asked to work under those guidelines. But, how the company sets these guidelines. Most of these guidelines are based upon following set of norms:

1. Clarity/Simplicity of Expressions
2. Names and Functions
3. Use of comments
4. Use of Indentation

Let us read about them in details.

Clarity and Simplicity of Expressions

A programmer capabilities are judged by the program/software he develops. Program should not be confusing one. There may be different ways to solve the given problem but the good program is that which solves it with short-cut but simple methods.

The following example show how a good program should look like.

```
//Demonstration of get() and put() functions
#include<iostream.h>
main()
{
    char char_val;              //Holds incoming intial
    char fname, lname;          //Holds converted first and last initials;
    cout <<"Enter your first name initials: ";
    cin.get(char_val);
    fname = char_val;
    cin.get(char_val);                  //Ignore new line
    cout <<"Enter your second name initials: ";
    cin.get(char_val);
    lname = char_val;
    cin.get(char_val);                  //Ignore new line
    cout <<"Your name initials are : ";
    cout.put(fname);
    cout.put(lname);
    return 0;
}
```

Names

Naming of the variables and constants are also very important. Somebody would put names of the cricketers and the other would put the name of the film stars. But, as usual it is upto to the company who along with the other guidelines decide what name to be given in the program.

Look at the following example.

```
// Program to find number of blanks, tabs and newline in the given input.
    #include<iostream>
    #include<stdio.h>
    main()
    {
        int nb, nt, nl;
        char c;
        nb = nt = nl =0;
        while ((c = getchar()) != EOF)
        {
            if (c == `1')
                ++nb;
            if (c == `t')
                ++nt;
            if (c == `\n')
                ++nl;
        }
        cout <<"\n\tNumber of blanks space => " <<nb;
        cout <<"\n\tNumber of tabs => " <<nt;

        cout <<"\n\tNumber of newline => " <<nl;
```

In this case the variables are given as the short forms of the headings, such as nt for number of tabs and nl for number of newlines. This can be decided in advance so that for a new person to look at this program and immediately he should understand what it written.

Functions

Functions play an important role while writing the programs. Function should be clear and be written in the program with their objectives.

Consider the following example:

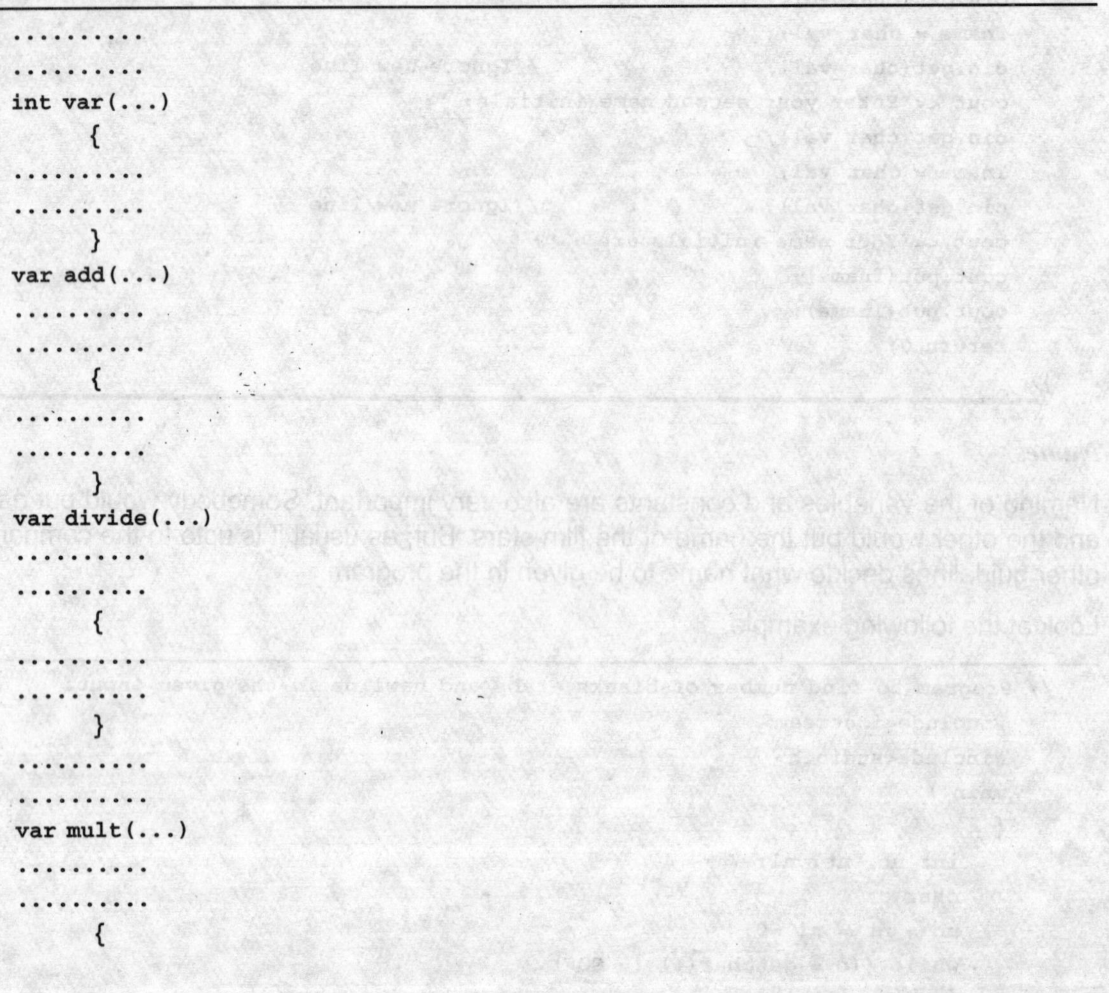

```
..........
..........
int var(...)
      {
..........
..........
      }
var add(...)
..........
..........
      {
..........
..........
      }
var divide(...)
..........
..........
      {
..........
..........
      }
..........
..........
var mult(...)
..........
..........
      {
..........
```

Comments

These are the comments which you write in the program as some sort of instructions for the operator or user of the program. These lines are not executable lines. Sometimes they are also written in between the executable lines too but are defined that these are comments and are not to be executed. Usually you would put comments at the following places:

1. In the beginning of the program
2. In the beginning of the functions

Efforts should be made that comments are at appropriate place and the meaning of various modules is clear. Commercial programs are large in nature and consist of many variables and constants at different places. To make a program modifiable comments are a must. These comments would always be welcomed by the modifier becuase then he would know what is happening where.

In the following program you would see that the comments have been made in the beginning and in between too.

```
//To see how the initialization of an array works.
#include<iostream.h>
main()
{
    char s_name[] = Mount St. Mary School;
    float scores[5] = {50 60 40 45 55};
    float average = 0.0;
    int ctr;
    //Calculate the total of scores
    for (ctr = 0; ctr < 5; ctr++)
    {
        average = average + scores[ctr];
    }
    //Calculate the average
    avg = average / (float)5;
    cout <<"at "<s_name<<", your class average is" <<average <<"\n";
    return 0;
}
```

In this case the comments have been made using // at the beginning of the line.

Indentation

These are used to show each instruction line independently. This way you can make the documentation of the program proper. It also helps in understanding the program better. Indentation improves the quality of the program. Usually indentation is used in the case of sub heading, headings, etc. Similary in the programs these are used to show the different levels of program execution.

In indenting the following rules should be remembered:

1. There should be one instruction in one line.
2. The statement in each level is to be indented to the right by a few spaces by setting a tab.

Documentation

Documentation of a program is a must. One should file all the relative papers relating to that particular program in a file. You never know what would be needed at which time. It may be possible that your results shows something which has not been asked for. If you have the input documentation paper, you can always prove that this was asked for.

Documentation is the proper record of the program. It is definitely needed when the program is to be modified or even if some problem occurs.

Documentation can be divided into 2 parts:

Externel Documentation and

Internal Documentation

Let us read about them in details.

External Documentation

It contains program specifications (given by the bosses at the time of writing the program), development history (notes made on the way), proper design of the process of the program including the steps properly explained with the help of flow chart symbols. In totally it is the document which can be called as the User document.

With the help of this you can generate few other documents, if need be. They are:

User's guide

Reference manual

Operators guide

Among the above, I think the user's guide is very important.

User's Guide

It highlights the type of inputs and outputs which the program generates. This helps in planning for their proper disbursement, e.g., which department which report is to be given, etc.

Operators Guide

It contains all the instructions that the operator has to follow while executing the program. It could be:

1. How and when to use the compiler
2. Executing the compiled program
3. What type of errors expected and how to handle them
4. Where to get the input data required by the program
5. How to disburse the output.

Reference Manual

It contains all the instructions about the system specifications of the program, which may include the type of computer used, operating system used, etc. It also has the complete coding of the program.

Program Maintainance

Everything needs maintainance. Be it be man or machine. This may be needed even after the program has been thoroughly tested and run. On an average an employee, specially a programmer, works for an organization not more than 2 years. And the life of a program is much more than that. This is exactly what happened in the year 2000.

All those problems related to last 2 digits of the year could not have been compounded if the original programmer were still available and the machines used for the same. Alas, both the options were not available. What saved the companies were the documentations and their proper maintainance. So the logic and flow was known, only the environment had to be changed.

Lets see why the changes in the programs are required :

Newly discovered bugs

Errors that have not been detected during the original testing phase may be discovered during the actual program operation.

Changes

The original problem changes because of new laws, user needs or new consumer demands. The program must be modified to reflect these changes.

Expansion

The original program must be expanded to provide additional information that had not been anticipated. It can be possible that 1 consolidated program may be needed instead of 2.

Equipment

The program must be rewritten to take advantage of a new computer or compiler. The costs involved in program maintenance are usually grossly underestimated by most programmers. It has been studied that in a typical programming environment, over 50 percent of the time is dedicated to maintaining existing programs which means that less than 50 percent of the time is devoted to designing and coding new programs.

Environment Changes

Most of the programming techniques, styles, methods and approaches briefed earlier have been designed for precisely that purpose. In reviewing these techniques, we can now appreciate why they are so critical.

Clarity and Readability

Program listing is the primary piece of technical documentation. The clarity of the listing significantly affects the time it takes to implement a program change.

Portability and Generality

Software tends to last longer than hardware. Therefore, a program written with portability in mind will create less havoc when the inevitable new computer arrives. Likewise, when the user needs change, the truly general program will require little or no programmer time to adapt to the new specifications.

Structured Code

The most common maintenance operation is tracking down bugs that when unnoticed during the testing phase. A program implemented as a series of single entry-single exit blocks will facilitate debugging.

Modularity

When a change can be localized to a single module, it makes maintenance much easier. We do not need to worry about the effects of that change "rippling" throughout other modules in the system.

Running and Debugging programs/Program Testing

When the program has been written, it has to be tested. For testing it may be possible that the original data is not available. So you have to make use of the test data which may not contain all the possible options which may be there in the original data. So while testing one has to prepare a data which has all the possible errors which one can expect. Testing of the program can be done in the following steps:

1. Choosing input data whose result (output) is for testing.
2. Testing of modules or submodules.
3. Choose input data which can activate all parts of the program so that any deficiency in any of the parts be judged correctly.
4. Testing whatever program can produce suitable error-message so that the error may be located easily in any of the parts.

Debugging

Checking the program for errors and correcting them is called Debugging. It is not that you will be able to write a program which runs in the first go. You may need to run the program a number of times to find out the various types of errors and correcting them. These errors may occur in the beginning, in the middle or even at the end of the execution. Or even the results produced may have some errors in it. These errors can happen due to the following:

1. Incorrect coding
2. Faults in design
3. Run time errors.
4. Designing errors

These errors may occur together in a program or one at a time. One has to run the program to find out the type of errors. There are various tools available which help you in debugging the program. They are:

Simulators

A simulator is a computer program that simulates the execution of programs on another computer.

Logic analyzers

A logic analyzer is a test instrument that is the digital bus oriented version of the oscilloscope. It detects the states of digital signals during each clock cycle and stores them in the memory. It then displays the information on a CRT, much as an oscilloscope does.

Breakpoints

A breakpoint is a place in a program at which execution can be halted, in order to examine the current contents of registers, memory locations and I/O ports.

Trace routines

A trace is a program that prints information concerning the status of the processor at specified intervals. Most simulator programs and some microcomputer development systems have trace facilities.

Memory dumps

A memory dump is a listing of the current contents of a section of the memory. Most simulator programs, microcomputer development systems and monitors can produce memory dumps.

Software interrupts

The software interrupts or trap instruction is frequently used for debugging purposes. The instruction usually saves the current value of the program counter and then branches to a specified memory location.

That memory location can be the starting point of a debugging program that lists of displays status information – breakpoints may be inserted with trap instructions.

Each program has its own unique errors. Nevertheless, some errors are sufficiently common to deserve mention. They include:

1. Failure to initialize variables, particularly counters and pointers. Registers, flags and memory locations should not be assumed to contain zero at the start of the program.
2. Failure to handle trivial cases, such as an array or table with no elements or only one element.
3. Inverting conditions, such as jumping on zero instead of on not zero.
4. Reversing the order of operands, such as moving X to Y when Y to X was meant.
5. Jumping on conditions that have been changed, since they were set to the desired values.
6. Failure to handle fall-through conditions, such as an entry that is never found in a table or a condition that is never met. Such a failure can cause an endless loop.

7. Confusing addresses and values. Memory location 100 does not necessarily contain the number 100.
8. Confusing numbers and characters. ASCII zero or EBCDIC zero is not the same as number zero.
9. Ignoring the direction of noncumulative operations.
10. Ignoring overflow when doing signed arithmetic.

Syntax Errors

Every language whether English, Hindi or otherwise has fixed grammatical rules and these are called syntax rules. Violation of any grammatical rules can cause syntax errors. Similary each programming language has its own fixed rules and syntaxes which have to used properly. If not used in the way they are required to, the syntax error would occur. Syntax errors are also called as compilation errors.

Some common reasons for the syntax errors.

1. Wrong use of statements like, if-else, while, do-while, for.
2. Wrong use of variables and constants or use of those variables which have not been declared in the program.
3. Missing semi-colon.
4. Wrong punctuation.
5. Misspelt keywords.
6. Missing braces.

For example, you may have used two mathematical expressions together in a statement or may have forgotton to add semi colon (;) at the end of the statement. These errors can be detected with the help of compilers which tell the programmer to use the appropriate word in place of wrong usuage.

Run-Time Errors

These errors occur only when the program is run. So you may call them execution errors. The common Run-Time errors are as shown below:

- Dividing a number of zero
- Array indices out of bounds
- Arithmetical Errors like square root of negative number
- Range Errors
- Other Input Errors

Logical Errors;

After removing run time errors and syntax errors, we can execute the program to obtain the result. If the results obtained are correct then it is a scuccessful programming. But sometimes the program does not produce the desired results even if there is no run time or syntax error. The errors which occur at this stage are called logical errors. The computer is not capable of recognizing these errors because it cannot present logic on its own. These are hidden errors made by the programmer and the computer flashes no error message for these mistakes.

Testing

This stage is the validation of the program. Testing ensures that the program performs correctly the required tasks. Program testing and program debugging are closely related. Testing is essentially a later stage of debugging in which the program is validated by trying it on a suitable set of test cases. Some of the test cases will certainly be the ones used in debugging – the all-zeros case, the various special cases and other obvious cases that must be checked. Program testing is, however, more than a simple matter of exercising the program a few times. Exhaustive testing of all possible cases is the best alternative, but this process is usually impractical. Formal validation methods exist, but are only applicable to very simple programs.

Thus, program testing requires a choice of test cases. The situation is further complicated by the fact that many microcomputer programs depend on realtime inputs that are difficult to control or simulate; the microprocessor must interact in a precise manner with a large and complex system. How can the necessary data be generated and presented to the microcomputer?

Several tools are available to help with this task. Clearly, the debugging tools mentioned earlier will be useful. Among the rules that can aid in program testing are the following:

1. Make the test plan part of the program design. Testing should be one of the factors in the problem definition, program design and coding stages.
2. Check all trivial and special cases. Often the simplest can lead to the most annoying and mysterious errors.
3. Select test data on a random basis. Doing so will eliminate any inadvertent bias caused by the programmer selecting test data. Random number tables are widely available and most computers have random number generators.
4. Plan and document software testing just like hardware testing. Obviously, testing can never prove that no errors exist; so good software design, like good hardware design, is an essential part of the testing process.
5. Use the maximum and minimum values of all variables as test data. Extreme values are often use source of special errors.
6. Use statistical methods in planning and evaluating complex tasks. Methods are available for selecting data and evaluating the significance of results. Optimization of techniques may suggest good choices for system parameters and efficient sets of test data.

There are two goals in preparing a test plan. First, a popularly detailed test plan demonstrates that the program specifications are understood completely. Second, the test plan is used during program testing of the program is prepared and documented, indicating the number of tests needed and the purpose of each test. In addition, all input test data is defined in detail and all excepted results, including reporting, are determined and documented.

Program testing includes physically running the tests specified in the test plan as well as correcting errors found in the code during the testing. This step is complete when the test results have been reviewed and approved by the project leader. To build a more consistent history of the time expended to complete each step, the life of the coding step can be defined. The time used in making coding changes needed to correct errors that were detected during the testing step, is recorded as test time. This eliminates the question of where to record those hours and facilitates consistent recording of time throughout the programming staff. Similarly, it is not allowed to record time in any step that has been previously completed. However, if a flaw is detected, that forces redesign of all or part of a program, this time can be reported in the earlier phases.

In order to test a program properly, test plan development has to be undertaken at some point in the program development process. It has been experienced that performing this step before any logic is constructed ensures that a usable and exhaustive plan for proving the correctness of a program is available when the coding of the program has been completed. This will most likely provide a more sensible approach to testing all facets of a program with as few test runs as possible. If the development of a test plan is postponed until after the program is coded, it will tend to test only those parts of the program which the programmer has become most concerned with or interested in.

PROBLEM SOLVING METHODOLOGY AND TECHNIQUES

It is impossible to solve a problem by using a computer, without a clear understanding and identification of the problem. Inadequate recognition of a problem is the key element responsible for poor performance of computers. This step is generally difficult and the programmer should invest a significant portion of his time in problem identification. If he does not spend enough time at this state, he may find that his well-written program fails to solve the real problem.

Understanding of the Problem

Depending on the complexity of the problem, the result of a careful analysis may be simply a testing of the factors with which the program must deal, or it may be a formal written statement of the problem, supported by a description of all the considerations necessary to solve the problem. This step is the process of becoming familiar with the problem that will be solved with a computer program. It starts when the programmer is assigned the task.

This step includes the reviewing of the design document that was prepared for the program, as well as any system-wide information that would be helpful. The process ends when all the programmer's questions have been resolved and the requirements of the program are understood. Problem definition may, thus, include many factors. Input/Output, time constraints, processing requirements, accuracy, memory limitations, error handling and interfaces with other programs or tables must all be considered.

Identifying Minimum number of Inputs required for Output

In any problem soloving exercise, the computer center receives information from various departments and sends the processed output to various other departments. In most of the cases, the computer center does not have control over the input of the data. Each department which sends the data for processing has to ensure that the data sent is free from errors. But can the computer center make its own checks, yes, they can provide various checks in the data. For example, they can make sure that the number of days worked in never beyond 31, the age of the employee is never less than 18, the basic salary is not less than DA, etc. But still if any error occurs, it is the fault of input and not the processing.

Human factor is also important here. Since the date and time of receiving data is fixed, the department sending the data is under pressure for the same. This results in wrong filling up of the data sheet. This results in wrong results. These data sheets are the results of the various sittings which the computer center has had with both the users and input providers.

Step by Step Solution for the Problem

An often used rule is that a programmer working on a large software project, will write two to ten fully corrected lines of program per day. Since the writing of even ten lines hardly takes just a few minutes, coding is clearly not the most time-consuming stage of software development. So what he does he chalks out the various steps in which the program has to be written. The solution of the problem lies in good steps.

A program writing can be divided into several stages:

1. Program Definition
2. Program Design
3. Coding
4. Debugging
5. Testing

6. Documentation

7. Maintenance

Some of them have been discussed earlier.

Once these steps have been marked down the next step becomes easier.

Breaking Down Solution into Simple Steps

This step is considered complete when a clean compile walkthrough has been held and the program coding has been approved. These steps would not only result in good program but would give satisfactory results.

Stylistic Guidelines

This section presents stylistic guidelines on programming style that will be useful, regardless of the particular language or processor involved.

Using meaningful names and labels

Meaningful names and labels can be helpful in documentation and maintenance as well as in debugging and integrating programs. The names should be as simple and straight forward as possible – PRNTR for the system printer, TTY for a teletypewriter, MAX for a teletypewrite. MAX for the maximum value, START for the beginning of the program. The use of meaningful names will save the programmer endless time and confusion in the various stages of programming.

Clarity and Simplicity of Expressions

Expressions play a key role in the programming. It must be clearly understood by the programmers as far as possible used the standard functions in expressions to improve the readability. There should not be any compromise with the clarity of expressions.

Keep short modules

Divide long modules into sections. Not only will a shorter module be easier to debug and correct, but it is also more likely to be useful in subsequent programs, since its function will be a small one and is more likely to recur. One or two pages of code (50 to 75 lines) is the maximum size for a module. Modules can be implemented as macros or simply copied into the program in order to avoid a massive number of calls and returns.

Keep names and labels distinct

Distinctive names and labels reduce confusion. The use of number 0, 1 and 2 and letter O, I and Z should be kept to a minimum. Certainly the programmer should not, for example, use both MINI and MIN1 as identifiers; the chance for error is too great. Names that, for one reason or another, continually confuse the programmer should be changed; there are always enough errors in programs without inviting additional ones.

Make modules fairly general

Obviously a module that is too specific (for example, one which sorts precisely 30 elements or searches for the letter S) will find little repeated use. Greater generality can often be achieved with little or no extra code; a sort that will handle any number of elements will bono harder to write than one that handles a specific number. General that requires considerable extra code and ingenuity, such as writing a code conversion routine to handle both ASCII and EBCDIC characters, is not worthwhile.

Simple ways to achieve generality have already been mentioned – the use of names instead of specific addresses of data, the collection of definitions at the start of the routine and the use of meaningful names that suggest the purposes or identities of items. All these techniques can produce a program that can be used frequently and easily modified.

Emphasise simplicity and comprehensibility

The first objective of programming is to write a program that works. Saving a few microseconds or few memory locations is seldom important; the code can be optimized later.

Avoid obscure constructions

Examples include the use of offsets from the program counter in computers that have many multiple-word instructions, the use of complex expressions that depend on the order in which operations are performed or operators that are seldom used and complex conditional assemblies. Even if the programmer knows the effects of an obscure construction at that moment, surely a few days or a few months time will return it to obscurity.

Avoid jumps when possible

Jumps make programs difficult to follow and debug. Repeating an instruction is often faster and clearer than jumping to a particular instruction. Programs with a series of jumps should be rewritten before the debugging stage.

Place definitions in groups at the start of the program

Definitions that are grouped at the start of the program can be easily located, checked and changed when necessary. Definitions that are scattered throughout the program can greatly hinder debugging and decomentation.

Use names instead of specific addresses or data

The use of names instead of specific memory addresses, constant, masks, I/O device numbers, or numerical factors, can not only suggest the actual purpose or meaning of the particular address or data but can also make the program easier to change.

Use Comments and Identification

Comments provide the internal documentation of a program. It makes the program easy to understand. The comments, should be included: at the beginning of the program which summarises the purpose of the program, at the beginning of the procedures and functions and to clarify the global and local variables.

Indentation makes program more clear to understand. The statements should be indented in such a manner that nesting of groups of control statement can be matched (i.e. if ....else). The braces pair (.....) should be written in the same column to help in proper matching.

Identification of Arithmetic and Logical Operations required for Solution

Each step of the job has to be properly defined and put on paper. As the steps are performed the logic of each step is very precisely defined. It is usually required by the System Analysts to check and verify these steps while testing with the actual data. I remember in the case of IBM, each job was divided into steps and each step was numbered. When a operator would perform any step, he would record the time taken in that step. At the end of the job, the time taken by each step is compared with the time mentioned in the flow chart. If there is lots of discrepency, the system analyst is taken to task.

These steps are written and bounded in the form of a folder with all flow charts, data inputs, expected outputs and their disposals are all there.

Using Control Structure

Programs not only store data but they also manipulate data in terms of consolidation, rearranging, modifying data. To perform their manipulative miracles, programs need tools for performing repetitive actions and for making decisions. C++ of course provides such tools by providing statements to attain so. Such statements are called program control statements that control the flow of control of a program.

Statements

Statements are the instructions given to the computer to perform any kind of action, be it data movements, be it making decisions or be it repeating actions. Statements form the smallest executable unit within a C++ program. Statements are terminated with a semicolon ;. The simplest statement is the empty, or null statement. It takes the following form:

```
; // It Is a null statement
```

A null statement is useful in those instances where the syntax of the language requires the presence of a statement but where the logic of the program does not. We will see it in loops and their bodies.

Compound Statement (Block)

A compound statement in C++ is a sequence of statements enclosed by a pair of braces ({ }). For instance,

```
{
    statement 1 ;
    statement 2 ;
    :
    :
}
```

represents a compound statement. A compound statement is equivalently called a block. A com- pound statement or a block is treated as a single unit and may appear anywhere in the program where a single statement may appear.

Selection Statements

Normally, the statements are executed sequentially as written in the program. This is known as the normal flow of control. But sometimes, the operational flow of control of a program has to be altered depending upon a condition. The statements that allow you to do so, are known as selection statements. C++ provides two types of selection statements: if and switch. In addition, in certain circumstances ? : operator can be used as an alternative to if statement. The selection statements are also called conditional statements or decision statements.

The If Statement of C++

An if statement tests a particular condition; if the condition evaluates to true, a course-of- action is followed i.e. a statement or set-of-statements is executed. Otherwise (if the condition evaluates to false), the course-of-action is ignored. The syntax (general form) of the if statement is as shown below:

```
if ( expression)
statement;
```

where a statement may consist of a single statement, a compound statement, or nothing (in case of empty statement). The expression must be enclosed in parentheses. If the expression evaluates to true i.e. a nonzero value, the statement is executed, otherwise ignored. For instance, the following code fragment

```
if(ch=='')
    spaces ++ ;
```

checks whether the character variable ch stores a space or not; If it does, the number of spaces are incremented by 1.

The following code fragment also makes use of an if statement :

```
int A, B, C;
cin > > A > > B ;
if (A > 10 && B < 15)
{  C = (A - B) * (A + B) ;
   cout << "The result is"
       << C << "\n" ;

}
```

The above example uses a compound statement (or a block) in the body of if.

What if there is another course of action to be followed if the expression evaluates to false. There is another form of if that allows for this kind of either-or condition by providing an else clause. The syntax of the if-else statement is the following ;

```
if (expression)
    statement1 ;
else

    statement2;
```

If the expression evaluates to true, i.e., a nonzero value, the statement1 is executed, otherwise, statement2 is executed. The statementl and statement2 can be a single statement, or a compound statement, or a null statement.

Remember, in an if-else statement, only the code associated with if (i.e., statement-1) or the code associated with else (i.e., statement-2) executes, never both.

Nested Ifs

A nested if is an if that has another if in its ifs body or in its else's body. The nested if can have one of the following three forms:

```
1. If (expressionl)
   {
      :
      if  (expression 2)
          statement 1;
      [else
          statement-2;]
      :
   }
   else
      body-of-else
```

```
2. If  (express/on 1)
      body-of-if;
   else
   {
      :
          if  (expression 2)
              statement-1;
          {   else
```

```
            statement-2;]
      :
   }
```

```
3. If  (expression 1)
   {
      :
        if  (expression 2)
            statement-1;
        [else
            statement-2;]
      :
   }
   else
      {
        :
        If  (expression 3)
            statement-3;
        [else
            statement-4;]
              :
      }
```

In an if statement, either there can be if statement(s) in its body-of-if or in its body-of-else or in both.

The part in [ ] means, it is optional. The inner ifs can themselves be nested ifs, but the inner if must terminate before an outer if.

The If-else-If Ladder

A common programming construct in C++ is the if-else-if ladder, which is often also called the if-else-if staircase because of its appearance. It takes the following general form:

```
if (expression 1) statement 1;
else
    if (expression 2) statement 2;
    else
        if (expression 3) statement 3 ;
          :
          :
        else statement 4 ;
```

Although it is technically correct to have indentation in the if-else-if ladder as shown above, however, it generally leads to overly deep indentation. For this reason, the if-else-if ladder is generally indented like this:

```
if (expression 1)
    statement 1;
else if (expression 2)
    statement 2;
else if (expression 3)
    statement 3;
    :
    :
```

```
else

    statement;
```

The ? : Alternative to If

C++ has an operator that can be used as an alternative to if statement. You are familiar with this operator, the conditional operator ? : This operator can be used to replace if-else statements of the following, general form:

```
If (expression1)
    expression2;
else

    expresslon3;
```

The above form of if can be alternatively written using ? : as follows:

```
expression1 ? expression2: expression3;
```

It works in the same way as the above given form of if does i.e. expression1 is evaluated, if it is true, expression2 gets executed (i.e. its value becomes the value of entire expression) otherwise expression3 gets executed (i.e. its value now becomes the value of the entire expression). For instance, the following if statement

```
int c;
    if (a > b)
        c=a;
    else
        c= b;
```

can be alternatively written as

```
int c= a > b ? a: b;
```

The Switch Statement

C++ provides a multiple-branch selection statement known as switch. This selection statement successively tests the value of an expression against a list of integer or character constants. When a match is found, the statements associated with that constant are executed. The syntax of switch statement is as follows:

```
switch (expression)
{
case constant1 : statement sequence 1 ;
                 break ;
case. constant2 : statement sequence 2 ;
                 break ;
case constant3: statement sequence 3 ;
                 break ;
                 :
case constant n-1 : statement sequence n-1;
                 break;
[ default : statement sequence n ;]

}
```

The expression is evaluated and its values are matched against the values of the constant specified in the case statements. When a match is found, the statement sequence associated with that case is executed until the break statement or the end of switch statement is reached. The default statement gets executed when no match is found. The default statement is optional and, if it is missing, no action takes place if all matches fail.

A case statement cannot exist by itself, outside a switch.

When a break statement is encountered in a switch statement, program execution jumps to the line of code following the switch statement i.e. outside the body of switch statement.

ITERATION STATEMENTS

The iteration statements allow a set of instructions to be performed separately until a certain condition is fulfilled. The iteration statements are also called loops or looping statements. C++ provides three kinds of loops: for loop, while loop, and do-while loop.

The for Loop

The for loop is the easiest to understand of the C++ loops. All its loop-control elements are gathered in one place (on the top of the loop), while in the other loop construction of C++, they are scattered about the program. The general-form (syntax) of the for loop statement is

```
for (initialization expression(s); test- expression; update expression(s))
    body-of-the-loop;
```

The following example program illustrates the use of for statement.

Program using for loop to print numbers from 1 to 10.

```
# include <iostream.h>
int main ( )
{ int i; // declaring variable /
  for (i=1; j<=10; ++/)
      cout << "\n"<< i ;
  return 0 ;
}
```

The above program prints values from 1 to 10. The variable i is initialised with value 1 (initialisation expression :i = 1) ; as long as the value of i is less than or equal to 10 (test expression : i <= 10) the loop prints the value of i on a separate line ; and at the end of each iteration, the value of i is incremented. by 1 (update expression ++ i).

The three elements : initialization expression, test expression and update expression, generally govern the working of a loop and thus, are known as loop control elements. In a for loop, there can be multiple initialization and update expressions. But these multiple expressions must be separated by commas. There must be semicolons before and after test-expression. Also, the three loop control elements are optional in a for loop but the two semicolons must appear even if any (or all) of these expressions is missing.

The While Loop

The second loop available in C++ is the while loop. The while loop is an entry-controlled loop.

The syntax of a while loop is

```
while ( expression)
      loop-body
```

where the loop-body may contain a single statement, a compound statement or an empty statement. The loop iterates while the expression evaluates to true. When the expression becomes false, the program control passes to the line after the loop-body code.

In a while loop, a loop control variable should be initialised before the loop begins as an uninitialized variable can be used in an expression. The loop variable should be updated inside the body-of the-while. Following example program illustrates the working of while loop.

Program to calculate the factorial of an integer.

```
# include <iostream.h>
int main ( )
{.int i, num, fact= 1;
   cout << "Enter integer :" ;
   cin >> num; // num gets its first value
   i = num;
   while (num) //while num is true, i.e., non zero
   {
       fact .* = num;
       - - num;     // update the value of num
   }               // end of while's loop-body
   cout    << "The factorial of" << i
           << "is" << fact <<"\n";
   return 0;
 }
```

The above program inputs an integer num. Then as long as num is nonzero (according to while (num)) the loop-body iterates, i.e., fact is multiplied with num and the result is stored back in fact, followed by the decrement of num. Again the test-expression (num) is evaluated: If it is true, the loop is repeated otherwise terminated.

The do-while Loop

Unlike the for and while loops, the do-while is an exit-controlled loop i.e. it evaluates its test-expression at the bottom of the loop after executing its loop-body statements. This means that a do-while loop always executes at least once. In the other two loops for and while, the test-expression is evaluated at the beginning of the loop i.e. before executing the loop-body.

If the test-expression evaluates to false for the first time itself, the loop is never executed. But in some situations, it is wanted that the loop-body is executed at least once, no matter what the initial state of the test-expression is. In such cases, the do-while loop is the obvious choice. The syntax of the do-while loop is:

```
   do     {
                statement1;
          }
    while ( test-expression) ;
```

The braces { } are not necessary when the loop-body contains a single statement. The following do-while loop prints all upper-case letters:

```
char ch = 'A';
do      {
            cout << "/n" << ch;
            ch ++ ;
```

```
        }   while (ch <='Z');
```

The above loop prints characters from 'A' onwards until the condition ch <= 'Z' becomes false. The most common use of the do-while loop is in menu selection routine, where the menu is flashed at least once. Then depending upon the user's response it is either repeated or terminated.

Nested Loops

A loop may contain another loop in its body. This form of a loop is called nested loop. But in a nested loop, the inner loop must terminate before the outer loop. The following is an example of a nested loop:

```
        :
for ( i = 1 ; i < 5 ; ++1) (
        cout << .'\n" ;
        for (j = 1; j <=i; ++j)
        cout << ."*";
}
        :
```

The above prints the following output

```
*
**
***
****
```

The inner for loop is executed for each value of i. The variable i takes values 1, 2, 3 and 4. The inner loop is executed once for i = 1 (according to condition j < = I, i.e., 1 < = 1 means once), twice for i = 2, thrice for i = 3 and four times i = 4. Generally, for loop is appropriate when you know in advance how many times the loop will be executed. The other two loops while and do-while loops are more suitable to the situation, where it is not known before-hand when the loop will terminate. The while should be preferred when you may not want to execute the loop body even once, and the do-while loop should he preferred when you're sure you want to execute the loop body at least once.

SUMMARY

1. A good programmer is not born but is developed by his own actions.
2. What can a good programmer do if the inputs to him are given wrong.
3. One should always start with writing small and simple programs and then graduate to complex and complicated programs.
4. A good program should have the following characteristics: Readability, Efficiency, Reliability, Meaningfulness, Portability and User-friendly.
5. Instead of running a big program altogether, the program is divided into small parts and they are run independently.
6. There are different ways of using the modular programming. They are: Sequence structure, Decision/Selection structure and Loop structure
7. Most of the guidelines for writing good programs are based upon following set of norms: Clarity/Simplicity of Expressions, Names and Functions, Use of comments and Use of Indentation
8. Comments are which you write in the program as some sort of instructions for the operator or user of the program.
9. Operator guide contains all the instructions that the operator has to follow while executing the program.
10. User guide highlights the type of inputs and outputs which the program generates.
11. Reference manual contains all the instructions about the system specifications of the program

12. Each program needs maintainance.
13. Program testing is a must before running for final use.
14. Debugging is method of checking errors in the program.
15. Syntax errors are those which occur due to wrong use of language.
16. Run time errors occur at the time of execution.
17. Logic errors are not pointed at the time of execution.
18. Testing ensures that the program performs correctly the required tasks.
19. It is impossible to solve a problem by using a computer, without a clear understanding and identification of the problem.
20. Depending on the complexity of the problem, the result of a careful analysis may be simply a testing of the factors with which the program must deal.
21. A program writing can be divided into several stages: Program Definition, Program Design, Coding, Debugging, Testing, Documentation and Maintenance
22. Meaningful names and labels can be helpful in documentation and maintenance as well as in debugging and integrating programs.
23. The use of number 0, 1 and 2 and letter O, I and Z in a program should be kept to a minimum.
24. The first objective of programming is to write a program that works.
25. Jumps make programs difficult to follow and debug.
26. Comments provide the internal documentation of a program. It makes the program easy to understand.

MULTIPLE CHOICE QUESTIONS

1. In a program, a number has been divided by zero. It is a .
   (a) Logical error (b) Syntax error (c) Run time error
2. Comments are written :
   (a) In the begging of the program (b) At the end of the program (c) Anywhere in the program
3. Syntax errors include :
   (a) wrong use of statements
   (b) wrong use of manipulators
   (c) wrong use of braces/any missing brace
4. Modular programming does not include the property which :
   (a) easy to understand
   (b) eases the process of modification
   (c) eases the process of testing the program
5. Syntax errors inlcude :
   (a) misspelt keywords (b) missing braces (c) missing commas
6. Which are the errors, in spite of which, the program will compile and run?
   (a) Logical errors (b) Syntax errors (c) Run time errors
7. Instructions for the operator are there in :
   (a) User manual (b) Operators guide (c) Reference manual
8. Checking and removing errors is called :
   (a) Checking (b) Removing (c) Debugging

REVIEW QUESTIONS

1. Which are the general concepts of a program?
2. What do you understand by the modular approach of the program?
3. Describe the various types of modular approach.

4. Describe the various type of guidelines which you will keep in mind while writing the program.
5. Describe the various type of documents that are prepared for the program.
6. What steps would you take for maintainance of the program.
7. What sort of errors you get while running the program?
8. How would you test the program?
9. Describe what do you mean by understanding of the problem.
10. How would you break down the problem in steps before actually solving it?

ANSWERS

Multiple Choice Questions

1. c	2. c	3. a, b, c	4. b
5. a, b, c	6. a	7. b	8. c

CHAPTER 13

Computer Engineering and Graphics

LEARNING OBJECTIVES

After going through this chapter, you should appreciate the following:

- **Introduction**
- **How the Interactive Graphics Display Works?**
- **Graphics packages**
  - Printing and drawing programs
  - Desgn programs
  - Business and analytical programs
- **Point Plotting Techniques**
- **Coordinate Systems**
- **Line Drawing Algorithms**
- **Line Drawing Displays**
  - Line drawing images
  - Continous tone images
- **Graphic Display Devices**
- **Inherit Memory Devices**
- **Matrix Representations**
- **Modelling Three Dimensional Graphics**
- **Computer Aided Design**
- **Rules for Graphics Software Design**
- **The General CAD Systems**
  - Graphic functions
  - Utility functions
  - Filing facilities
  - Editors
- **Software Design and Organization**
  - Organisation of Program and Data
  - System modules
- **Data Storage**
- **The CAD/CAM System**
- **The CAD Software**
- **The CAM Software**

INTRODUCTION

Computers and graphics have always gone hand in hand since the need for graphic was always felt when it was felt that computer was no longer there for doing calculations only. For this even the calculator would have been enough. Since the development of Microsoft Windows and the graphical interface used by Apple Computers, it was graphics all over the place. The most important example of this being Video Games which you play on your computers or even the ones which you play in those so called video parlours.

Computer graphics can be divided into two parts:

(i) Non-interactive or passive computer graphics

(ii) Interactive computer graphics

In non-interactive computer graphics, the observer has no control over the image. For example, such pictures may be generated on paper or film with the help of computer controlled plotter, the titles shown on TV and other forms of computer art. These are the examples, where the observer has no control over the image, only he can watch the pictures.

In interactive computer graphics, the observer has control over the image by providing him with an input device. It involves two-way communication between the computer and the user.

Interactive computer graphics affects our lives in a number of indirect ways.

For example,

(i) It helps to train the pilots of our airplanes. These pilots spend lot of time for their training not in a real aircraft but on the ground at the controls of a flight simulator. Flight simulator have many advantages over real aircraft for training purposes, including safety, fuel saving and ability to familiarize the trainee.

(ii) Architects can explore alternative solutions to design problem at an interactive graphics.

(iii) The molecular biologist can display pictures or molecules and gain insight into their structure.

(iv) The electronics industries are even more dependent on the interactive computer graphics to carry out tasks that would otherwise be prohibitively expensive to perform i.e. typical integrated electronic circuit used in a computer is so complex that it would take weeks to draw it by hand. By using an interactive computer graphics, the integrated electronic circuit can be drawn in a much shorter time, easier and less expensive.

HOW THE INTERACTIVE GRAPHICS DISPLAY WORKS?

To display a diagram, it should be drawn either on the paper in case of plotter or on the computer screen. Commonly, all such drawings surfaces are two dimensional in nature. It is possible to give special effects of three dimensional drawing by using various techniques. The modern graphics display is extremely simple in construction. It consist of three components:

(i) A digital memory or frame buffer, in which the displayed image is stored as a matrix of intensity values.

(ii) A television monitor i.e. a home TV set without turning and receiving electronics.

(iii) Simple interface i.e. display controller, that passes the contents of the frame buffer to the monitor.

The image must be passed repeatedly to the monitor to maintain a steady picture on the screen. Inside the frame buffer the image is stored in terms of binary digital numbers, which represents a rectangular array of picture element or pixels. A 16 x 16 array of black and white pixels can be represented by the binary values stored in the 32 eight bit bytes. In simple case, we wish to store only black and white images, black pixels can be represented by 1s and white pixels by 0s in the frame buffer. The display controller reads each successive byte of data from the frame buffer and converts it's 0s as 1s into the corresponding vide signal. This signal is then fed to the TV monitor to produce a black and white picture on the screen. Several games have been programmed in this manner.

GRAPHICS PACKAGES

Graphics packages can be divided into three categories:

Painting and Drawing Programs

These types of packages are used by small businesses to create forms, logos and letterheads. With input devices like mouse, light pen and graphics tablet or digitizer, thee programs let users choose from many different pointers or brushes, sizes and shapes to paint an image, draw and fill shapes and change color and texture. For example, MacPaint and Paint brush are examples of paint and draw programs.

Design Programs

The Design programs help designers, engineers, draftman, etc., to complete the tasks associated with hand drafting of designs easily and more efficiently. The user may go further than two-dimensional drawings by creating three-dimensional objects that can be rotated and viewed from any angle. Computer-Aided Design (CAD) is an example of a design program. Some packages also provide simulation capabilities like, a skyscraper design might be mathematically tested with a program.

Business and Analytical Programs

The business and analytical program transforms numerical data into pictorial representations I.e. charts and graphs, which show the relationships among the data. Typical graphs that can be produced include bar, pie, line, stacked-bar, three dimensional and surface graph. These are sometimes referred as presentation-graphics programs, though they do not provide high-quality presentation graphics (graphics which are suitable for a normal presentation). Many of the graphics programs incorporated in spreadsheets are adequate for informal use, but they are not appropriate in a formal presentation. Many of the stand-alone programs like PC Story board, Grafix partner and Lotus 1-2-3 can enhance charts and graphs generated by other programs.

POINT PLOTTING TECHNIQUES

The frame buffer (in which the displayed image is stored as a matrix of intensity values) is an example of a point plotting display device. Inside the frame buffer the image is stored as a pattern of binary digital numbers, which represents a rectangular array of picture elements or pixels.

To construct a picture on a point plotting display we have to build the picture out of many hundreds of pixels, each generated by a separate command from the computer. To display a line, curve, text characters etc., we have a pattern or matrix of closely spaced pixels. For example, an enlarged picture of lines and text characters constructed on a point plotting display.

COORDINATE SYSTEMS

The point plotting techniques are based on the use of a Cartesian Coordinate System. Points are represented by their x and y coordinates, the value of x increases from left to right and y form bottom to top.

LINE DRAWING ALGORITHMS

Straight line segments are used to a great extent in generating pictures like bar charts, block diagrams, graph, engineering drawings, architectural plans, etc. Since the straight line drawing is very important and so useful, it is worth taking care that they are well drawn.

The following steps would be taken to generate accurate computer lines.

Step 1: Lines should appear straight. For example, point-plotting techniques are admirably suited to the generation of lines parallel at 45" to the x and y axes.

Step 2: Lines should terminate accurately. For example, if the lines are not plotted accurately, they may terminate at the wrong place. The effect is often seen as a small gap between the endpoint of one line and the starting point of the next.

Step 3: Line should have constant density. For example, to maintain constant density, dots should be equally spaced.

LINE DRAWING DISPLAYS

The computer generated pictures can be divided into two categories:

Line drawing images

The line drawings images are easier to create because the information required to represent them is less and the algorithms for their generation are simpler.

Continuous-tone images

In continuous-tone images in fact would not be displayed at all until the advent in the late 1960's of the frame – buffer display and algorithms for generating these images are still be developed.

GRAPHIC DISPLAY DEVICES

The quality of the displayed image is very important in most of the applications of the computer graphics. The Cathode Ray Tube (CRT) is the only available device, which is capable of converting the computer's electrical signals into visible images at high speeds. The face of CRT is more or less flat and is coated on the inside with phosphor, which glows when the electron beam strikes it. At the narrow end of a sealed conical glass tube is an electron gun that emits a high velocity, finely focused beam of electrons. A beam of electrons i.e. cathode rays is emitted by an electron gun and is passé though focusing and deflection systems that direct the beam on the specified point on the phosphor coated screen. A yoke is mounted on the outside of the tube at the base of the neck; it deflects the electron beam to different parts of the tube when currents pass through the coils. As phosphor light fades rapidly, the electron beam is repeated quickly to draw the picture.

INHERENT MEMORY DEVICES

The most popular widely used devices Direct-View Storage Tube (DVST), which includes the plasma and the laser-scan display. When the display picture is complex, refresh line drawing displays based on the Cathode Ray Tube have the disadvantages of high cost and tendency to flicker. These two problems led to develop the display device with inherent image storage capability.

MATRIX REPRESENTATIONS

The use of concatenated transformation has so many advantages. However the rules for concatenating transformation equations are quite complex. They are much easier it we use matrices to define transformations. We can represent it more compactly than a sequence and we can generally compute the transformation with fewer arithmetic operations than if we were to apply each of the transformations in the sequence one after the other. The two-dimensional transformations can be represented in a uniform way by a 3 x 3 order matrix.

MODELLING THREE DIMENSIONAL GRAPHICS

Many graphics packages involve the display of three-dimensional objects and scenes. However, computer-aided design systems allow the users to manipulate models of machined components, automobile bodies and air craft parts. Similarly, simulation systems present a continuously moving picture of a three-dimensional world to the pilot of a ship or aircraft. These packages differ from two dimensional packages not only in terms of added dimension but they also require concern for realism in the display of objects.

The need for modelling and image-generation techniques stems from requirements imposed by applications. To communicate information to a computer user, the application program generates an image, which must show the information clearly, without ambiguity and with a little extraneous information as possible.

The following packages/applications illustrate the range of imaging requirements.

(a) **Computer – aided design (CAD):** Computer-generated images are useful in designing automobiles, ships, airplanes, oil refineries, mechanical parts, etc. These applications must offer enough realism for the designer to evaluate a design, the airframe designer must visualize the shape of a wing to judge aerodynamic properties etc.

(b) **Molecular modelling**: Chemists prefer to build three-dimensional models of molecules in order to understand their behaviour. These models are obtained indirectly, by observing the three dimensional electron density in a crystal and then inferring where atoms of the molecule must lie. The model is built interactively by adding atoms one at a time, orienting bonds according to the electron – density information. Realism is not an important objective in generating images of atoms in molecules.

(c) **Simulation**: Realism is an important objective in some simulation applications, including moving images. A day light flight simulator, uses computer generated images of the vie from the cockpit to generate very realistic pictures. Pilots seem to depend for depth perception on subtle visual cues, such as skid marks on a harbour; a complex harbour scene, including other ships in motion etc. Not all simulation applications demand such realistic images.

(d) **Animation**: Sequence of pictures that educate or explain may require images of three dimensional objects. Although animation uses graphics as much for art as for realism, it depends heavily on motion to substitute for realism on an individual image. Inexpensive animation communicates depth information with "2 ½ dimensional images – opaque images painted on a few transparencies that slide relative to each other. This allows one image to appear closer to the observer than another.

The following techniques are sued to generate the images:

(a) **Parallel projections**: Fundamental to the production of two dimensional display of a three – dimensional scene is the notion of projection. In the case of parallel projection, a point on the screen is identified with a point in three-dimensional scene by a line perpendicular to the screen. An architect often draws three such parallel projections to illustrate a house, a plan view and two evaluations views. This simple technique depends on the ability of the user to reconstruct the scene from the multiple projections. So far, many types of projection techniques have been developed, mainly to ease the draftsman's task of generating images. Few of these techniques, like orthogonal projection, are relatively easy. When a computer is available to perform the calculations, the simplicity of the projection technique is not as critical as graphics applications tend to use more complicated but more realistic projections.

(b) **Perspective projection**: The perspective projection technique is the most common one, familiar to us. The image formed by the eye and by lenses on photographic file are perspective projections. The perspective projection conveys depth information by making the distant object smaller than near ones. In perspective projection, the lines of projection do not remain parallel. They all converge at a single point called the centre of projection. The projected image on the screen is obtained by the points of intersection of the converging lines with the plane of the screen.

(c) **Intensity cues**: one depth cue that is not expensive to implement in hardware is a modulation of the intensity of lines with depth. Lines far away appear fainter than those near the viewer. As the complexity of the image increases, the effectiveness of the cue usually decreases. In addition, if the range of depths of near by liens is small, the intensities or widths may not vary enough to the noticeable.

(d) **Stereoscopic views**: A dramatic depth cue is provided by generating, two stereoscopic images. One image is shown to the left eye is generated from a view appropriate to the location of the eye, while the other is generated analogously for the right eye. Some people can fuse two separate stereo without the aid of any separation mechanism.

COMPUTER AIDED DESIGN

Computer aided design (CAD) is a technique in which man and machine are blended into a problem solving team, intimately coupling the best characteristics of each. The result of this combination works better than either man or machine would work alone and by using a multi-discipline approach it offers the advantage of integrated team-work.

CAD implies by definition that the computer is not used when the designer is most effective and vice versa. This being so, it is therefore useful to examine some individual characteristics of man and computer in order to identify which processes can best be separately performed by each and where one can aid the other. Table 91.1 compares the capabilities of man and computer for a range of tasks. It can be seen that in most cases the two are complementary, that for some tasks man is far superior to the computer and that in others the computer excels. It is, therefore, the marriage of the characteristics of each which is so important in CAD. These characteristics affect the design of a CAD system in the following areas:

(a) DESIGN CONSTRUCTION LOGIC – the method of constructing the design.

(b) INFORMATION HANDLING – the storing and communication of design information.

(c) MODIFICATION – the handling of errors and design changes.

(d) ANALYSIS – the examination of the design and factors influencing it.

Let us now consider these four areas which are of such significance in CAD.

(a) **Design construction logic**: The use of experience combined with judgement is a necessary ingredient of the design process. The design construction must therefore be controlled by the designer. This means that the designer must have the flexibility to work on various parts of the design at any time and in any sequence and be able to follow his own intuitive design logic rather than a styled computer logic. The computer cannot cope with any significant learning. This must be left to the designer, who can learn from past designs. The computer can, however, provide rapid recall of old designs for reference. Thus, in some ways the designer can pass on his experience to the computer and other designers can then have access to it.

(b) **Information handling**: Information is required from the specification before the design solution stage can proceed. Similarly, when the design solution is complete, information must in turn be output to enable the design to be manufactured. The initial specification must be input to the designer in order that selected parts can be communicated to the computer in a form it can understand and use. The first role of the computer is to check the information for human errors, which must then be corrected by the intervention of the designer. The human brain is able to store information in an intuitively ordered manner, but its storage capacity is limited and the information is not all retained as time passes. By contrast, computers have no ability to organize data intuitively but have large permanent storage capacities. Information storage should therefore be carried out by the computer under the direction of the designer. The output of manufacturing information, from the solution stage of the design process, usually involves the production of drawings. This is a slow and mundane process when carried out manually but is quite suitable for execution by the computer. It is therefore, desirable to allow the computer to generate as much production information as possible, so freeing the designer form repetitious work at all stages of the design process.

(c) **Modification**: Design descriptive information must frequently be modified to make correction or errors, to make design changes and to produce new designs from previous ones. The computer has the ability to detect those design errors which are systematically definable; whereas man can exercise an intuitive approach to error detection. For example, the computer can calculate the torque capacity of a shaft, whilst a designer can tell from experience and judgement that the shaft is too small. The automatic correction of errors is generally difficult for a computer. It should therefore be left to the designer to monitor corrections or errors and may other design changes which may be needed.

(d) **Analysis**: A computer is very good at performing those analytical calculations of a numerical analysis nature which man finds time-consuming and tedious. As much as possible of the numerical analysis involved in the design should be done by the computer, leaving the designer free to make decisions based on the results of this and his own intuitive analysis.

It can be seen from the discussion so far that there exists a clear division between the functions of man and computer in CAD.

The computer has three main functions:

1. To serve as an extension to the memory of the designer.
2. To enhance the analytical and logical power of the designer.
3. To relieve the designer from routine repetitious tasks.

The designer is left to perform the following activities:

1. Control of the design process in information distribution.
2. Application of creativity, ingenuity and experience.
3. Organisation of design information

RULES FOR GRAPHICS SOFTWARE DESIGN

The main difficulty in constructing such a package is to give adequate consideration to the many issues that affect the usefulness of the package. Some of the more important of these issues are:

Simplicity: Features that are too complex for the application programmer to understand will not be used. It is often difficult for the graphics package designer to detect potentially difficult aspects of his design. These aspects do, however, become more obvious when the user's manual is written. One way to avoid these difficult features is to tray to write the user's manual before implementing the system. Anything difficult to explain will almost certainly be difficult to use.

Consistency: A consistent graphics system is one that behaves in a generally predictable manner. Function names, calling sequences, error handling and coordinate systems all should follow simple and consistent pattern without exceptions. The application programmer is then able to build up a conceptual model of how the package functions. Again, inconsistencies often show up when the user's manual is written as small-print passages – sentences here and there, often overlooked by the reader, that warn of anomalies in the system.

Completeness: There should be no irritating omissions in the set of functions provided by the system: missing functions will have to be supplied by the applications programmer, who may not have the necessary access to the computer's resources to be able to write them. Completeness does not imply comprehensiveness: i.e. the system need not provide every imaginable graphics facility. The system designer must try to design a reasonably small set of functions that can conveniently handle a wide range of applications.

Robustness: Application programmers are capable of extraordinary misuse of graphics systems, either through misunderstanding or through the mischievous enjoyment of trying everything once. The system should accept such treatment with a minimum of complaint. Trivial errors of omission or thing seriously wrong, the system should report the error in the most helpful manner possible. Only in extreme circumstances should errors cause termination of execution since this will generally cause the user to lose valuable results.

Performance: Graphics – system performance is often limited by such factors as operating system response and display characteristics, factors beyond the system designer's control. There is nothing much to be done here by the graphics – system designer except to minimize the effect by omitting highly dynamic graphic functions that demand fast response or expensive hardware. Apart from this, the system designer should try to maintain consistent performance, so that application programs provide an equally consistent speed of response. It should be possible for the application programmer to achieve this consistency without resorting to special tricks. A really good graphics system offers no special advantages to those who understand the system's internal workings.

Economy: It is always frustrating to write an application program only to find that it is too bulky or too expensive to use. Graphics systems should be small and economical, so that adding graphics to an existing application program can always be considered.

These issues provide us with a number of ground rules of graphics software system design. Abiding by these rules is not always easy but is almost always worthwhile.

THE GENERAL CAD SYSTEMS

The general CAD system was developed by considering a wide range of possible users of system. The following were considered in detail:

1. Mechanical engineering design.
2. Building design.
3. Structural engineering design.
4. Electronic circuit design.
5. Animation and graphic design.

It was postulated that four basic processes involving graphic occurred to various degrees in each field, namely:

(a) **Pure analysis** – standard design and analysis processes.

(b) **Pure draughting** – production of a drawing or picture by the manual creation and manipulation of lines, arcs, etc.

(c) **Drawing by analysis** – the production of a picture or part of a picture directly from analysis, for example, production of cam profiles.

(d) **Analysis of drawings** – evaluation of the properties of an item described graphically, for example, the production of a quantity list by analysis of a builder's plan drawing.

For the system to be able to support pure analysis it must contain facilities for the running of analysis programs of unlimited length and for the storage and rapid retrieval of large amounts of data. It was considered important that the user should be able to communicate directly and graphically with analysis programs. Graphics facilities were provided which were considered to be sufficient for a general design draughting system. However, the range of graphical construction techniques is so large in practice that the system contained only as many facilities as could practically be incorporated in the draughting system, leaving other more specialized techniques to be developed by the applications programmer.

For both the production of drawing items by analysis and the analysis of drawings, it is essential that there is a simple efficient link between data produced by the draughting system and analysis programs. It is also essential that graphic data can be annotated in a way which is recognized by analysis programs but which does not affect the draughting system. It was thought that for most practical applications the general draughting system would be incorporated in a much larger specific applications system.

For this reason the draughting system was as simple as possible consistent with reasonable running efficiency, so that it could be incorporated into an applications system with the minimum of effort. The facilities embodies in the general CAD system are now described. These facilities are aimed at allowing the user to input graphical information into the computer and file it. Initial data entry is made by digitizing rough sketches. The system also permits the user to access the data, manipulate it, process it, output in hard-copy form or re-file it for permanent storage.

Graphic Functions

The input of graphics of CAD takes place in one of a number of symbol modes. The symbol mode used is selectable from a menu command. The mode provided in the basic system includes:

- Line Mode
- Arc Mode
- Circle Mode
- Alphanumeric Mode
- Dimension Mode
- Rectangle Mode

Messages displayed on the screen inform the user of the significance of points digitized in each mode; for example. When the user selects arc mode the message START POINT appears on the screen. Digitizing the arc's start point causes CENTRE POINT to be displayed, a further point causes END POINT and digitizing the end point will cause an arc to be displayed and the message START POINT to reappear. Up to 40 symbol modes can be present in an application system. They may include ellipses, polygons etc.

Utility Functions

A number of functions are incorporated in GCADS to make it easier for the user to operate. These include the following:

- Windowing
- Drive mode
- Angular measurement
- Grid round-off

The windowing process allows the user to specify an area of the drawing he is constructing and to expand it to fill the screen. This enables the detail work to be carried out on a small area of a drawing at a large scale. Drive mode enables the user to specify angles and lengths of lines accurately without digitizing them. The display of X, Y coordinate positions is produced on the coordinate display unit. By specifying grid factor the user can, in effect, reduce the resolution of the digitizing area. Thus specifying a 300 mm grid means that only which are on a 300 mm grid from the drawing original can be digitized. The grid factor is in real units: that is, in table coordinates multiplied by the drawing input scale.

Filing Facilities

Files are assigned to a number which is digitized from the menu. A file is brought into use by the menu command FILE TO WORK SPACE followed by digitizing the required file number. Data is files away by the command WORK SPACE TO FILE followed by the file number to which the data is to be assigned. Other facilities exist for transferring files to and from more permanent names files stores.

Editors

A number of powerful editors are incorporated into GCADS. These include:

Point editor – allows point to be moved independently, providing the ability stretch lines.

Line editor – provides an efficient means of locating and deleting lines.

Macro and symbol editors – macros and symbols to be located and deleted (Macros are standard components or items that are in regular use)

SOFTWARE DESIGN AND ORGANISATION

The system described is based on a single-user system, although multiple-user systems are now emerging. The essential features of the software are very similar in single-and multi-user systems.

Organisation of Program and Data

Operating System

The software for the GCADS system was written to operate under DECs PDP II DOS (Disc Operating System). This occupies approximately the lowest 4000 words of core and contains many more facilities than the needed by GCADS. A considerable saving in core storage could therefore be made by either rewriting DOS to contain only the facilities needed or by cutting these facilities from the existing DOS system. This was not done, for two very important reasons:

1. Changing DOS would severely limit the scope of analysis programs which may be added to GCADs in the future.
2. As the price of core storage is decreasing and the cost of software increasing, it becomes cost-ineffective to spend large amounts of programming time endeavouring to economise on storage especially if this leads to restrictions in writing future programs.

Core Utilization

The core storage available in the PDP-II for program was divided into two areas called the resident and overlay areas. An overlay is a program resident on the disc which can be brought into core for use by the CPU and then returned to disc. This technique permits the use of many or even large programs to be seen in a computer with small core storage capacity. All user programs and system operations are called as overlays and operate in the overlay area. The resident area is used to handle overlay calling and to provide small areas of data storage for the communication of vital information between overlays. The resident area was kept as small as possible in order to allow the maximum amount of space for overlays.

Overlay Handling and Storage

Since all system and user functions were to be called as overlays, the overlaying system had to be very fast. The system provided by DOS was not fast or versatile enough, so an independent high-speed overlaying system was written by Hamlyn. This was later modified by Thompson for greater efficiency and simpler operation. An important requirement of the overlaying system was that overlays should be called just like subroutines; that is, each overlay does not have to specify which overlay is to be called next. This facility was provided by incorporating an overlay execution stack into the overlaying routines. This allows overlay calls to be stacked up ready for execution. A return from over overlay causes the next on the stack to be executed.

By stacking not only the overlay number but also additional overlay segment variable, overlays can be segmented giving, in effect multiple entry point overlays. Overlays are stored on an overlay file on disc. This consists of a number of contiguous disc blocks with a directory occupying the first three. The overlay library program OVAL writes overlays, which may be of any length, into the best fitting contiguous space in the overlay file and updates the overlay directory. It is also able to produce directory listings of the overlay file, eliminate the free space between overlays, delete overlays and return free space available.

Disc Data Filing

For the operation of the basic system and user analysis packages it was considered essential that GCADS should contain a range of filing facilities varying in speed and complexity. Three types of file were specified.

(1) Workfiles – high speed, random access, image format.

(2) Semi-permanent files – medium speed, sequential access, binary format.

(3) Permanent files – low speed, sequential access, ASCII format.

Each type of file can be written to or read from via Fortran calls to subroutines.

Workfiles are a set of 14 fixed length contiguously blocked files on disc. They can be written to at random without reference to the disc directory being necessary and are therefore ideal for the temporary storage of volumes of data too large to be held in core.

Semi-permanent files are a set of 128 variable length random access file which are program deletable. It is intended that these should be used for the storage of workfile over periods of days or weeks. Permanent files may be of any number on any medium: paper tape, magnetic tape, etc. They are intended as archival storage media for completed projects.

System modules

The software system consists of a number of system modules. The functions of the major modules will now be described.

Setup Module

This module is called before any others when the system is run. It sets the following principal parameters:

1. Table origin - The origin point of the table's coordinates (bottom left-hand corner).
2. Input origin - The origin point of the drawing or drawing area, to the tables x, y axis, defined by digitizing two points representing a horizontal line.
3. Input scale - The scale at which graphic information is to be input.
4.. Grid factor - Defines the lowest resolvable increment allowed.
5. Text size - The standard size for text added to a drawing.

Any of these parameters may be rest at a later stage by menu command.

User Operations Monitor (UOM)

When the setup routines are completed, the UOM overlay is called. This is the heart of the system and contains the interrupt, menu level and symbol handlers a well as the background loop.

Background Loop

The background loop has the following duties:

(1) Read the table coordinates.

(2) Convert them to real drawings coordinates: that is, subtract the drawing origin de-skew, scale and grid.

(3) Apply CONTROL and TRAILING ORIGIN adjustments if in the appropriate mode, then convert to try 3-D coordinates.

(4) Display the background messages.

(5) Display pen coordinates on the coordinate display.

(6) Display a cursor on the screen related to the pen position.

(7) Look for a pen button interrupt.

Background messages are stored in an array in the resident common data area called MESSAGE. Five messages may be displayed, the first two being reserved for system use and the rest for user programs. A user program can request a message to be displayed in background by writing the message to an appropriate part of the MESSAGE array.

Interrupt Handler

The digitizing pen has eight buttons. When one of these is pressed it is detected by the background loop and control passed to the interrupt handler in order to access certain facilities. Buttons 2, 3, 6 and 7 perform the most commonly used functions which are break line, set 3-D trailing coordinate, control and find. Button commands 2, 3, 6 and 7 are serviced by the UOM. When button 1 is pressed the program determines whether or not the pen is on the menu. If it is, then control is passed to the menu handler; if not, then a check is made to see if the system is in line mode. If it is, then the interrupt is serviced by the UOM; if not, then a return from the UOM is made to the next stacked overlay (which will be a symbol of processor overlay). Button 4 is used to enlarge a portion of drawing on the screen or plotting surface. It causes the display module to be stacked and the button 4 processing overlay to be called and executed. When button 8 is pressed the user is invited to specify manually the next 3-D coordinate either as an absolute coordinate or as an offset from the last specified coordinate.

Menu handler

The GCADS menu consists of a 65 x 5 matrix of 15 mm squares located along the bottom edge of the digitizer and further 2 x 5 squares located along the left-hand edge.

The overall menu is subdivided into a number of sections as follows:

(a) System commands consisting of

 (i) Display and manipulation of data

 (ii) Date specification

 (iii) Numeric Input and calculator

 (iv) Answer

 (v) Joystick

 (vi) Macros

(b) User commands

(c) Files

(d) Symbols

(e) Macro library

The user commands are similar in nature to the system commands except that they are written for user applications. For example, if the draughting system was used in conjunction with analysis programs then the analysis programs would be called from the user command area. The commands are along the lower edge of the digitizer for ease of access. To permit flexibility in the arrangement of commands on the menu there is a mapping routine which translate the position of a square on the menu to a position on an abstract software menu. The arrangement of the software menu is fixed, as its square number is an important parameter in the execution of menu commands. An identical technique is used to allow flexibility in the arrangement of symbol squares. When a menu commands is given, the menu square number is mapped onto the software menu and from the square number of this menu, the menu handler determines which overlay is to be called to service the command.

Commands are grouped by types, hence these functions are interlaced with ordinary commands. When macro or symbol squares are digitized the appropriate handler is brought into operation.

Level Handler

Levels are used to divide up drawing data, so that a file can be broken up into a series of sub-files Sixteen level are provided in GCADS and the level system is controlled direct from the menu. A set of 16 bits from what will be referred to as a level sieve. All operations on drawing data are carried out after it has passed through the sieve. Each bit in the sieve represents a level. If the bit is zero, the operation is not carried out on that level of data and vice-versa. Therefore individual levels can be selected for displaying by setting the appropriate bits in the sieve. When a display level is specified the sieve bit corresponding to that level is set. The command SET INPUT LEVEL enables the user to select a new data level. Menu commands exist to open or close all holes in the sieve.

Symbol Handler

all graphic items which are not straight lines are handled as symbols. Each symbol is processed by a number of symbol overlay segments called

- Symbol initialiser segment
- Symbol point processor segment
- Symbol display segment

When a symbol square is digitized the symbol initialiser overlay segment is stacked. When subsequently, a point is digitized by using button 1, the initialiser is entered. This has the job of storing the digitized point, stacking the symbol point processors and returning to the UOM. Subsequent points digitized will cause the symbol's point processors to be executed until the symbol is complete, when the symbol display segment will be entered to display the symbol on the screen. Symbol overlays can be written by applications programmers and can serve as construction techniques as well as a means of entering non-standard graphic items, such as ellipses or rectangles.

File handler

Workfile 1, generally referred to as the WORSPACE holes data for the current drawing before it is transferred to one of the 128 semi-permanent files available in the system. These 128 files are accessed by number and the user has the ability to write onto a file, recall an old file to the workspace, display the contents of a file on the VDU or delete a file. If the user tries to write over a file that is already assigned, the previous contents are lost, so for security of important data it is possible to protect a file so that it cannot be overwritten until the protect state is removed. In addition, a user directory is available in which an appropriate description of the contents of the file can be stored. This directory is merely for convenience and is not essential to the operation of the basic file handler.

Macro Handler

A further set of 128 files is available for strong macros. For speed of operation these are accessed by a block of squares on the left-hand edge of the menu. Unlike files, the 3-D macros have to be specially prepared before being filed in order that they may be recalled with the maximum efficiency. During drawing input, a macro may be recalled simply by digitizing over the appropriate square. In addition the macro directory contains a codeword which may also be used for recalling the required macro. The macro handler displays the macro in perspective in the top right-hand corner of the screen and marks the reference points the user must digitize to place it in 3-D space. From these points the handler works out the required scale factors, rotations and translations and places the macro accordingly. In some examples, such as, valves, the macro may be defined by a set of reference tables depending on, for example, the pipeline diameter. In this case it is possible to store such a table; the macro handler will extract the relevant data for the selected macro and manipulate it accordingly, using the digitized reference points merely for orientation.

Display and Plot Modules

The function of these modules is to display or plot the data in the workspace. Symbols are stored with various identification markers and module contains a section to display any of the symbols available. This is considerably faster than the existing system of stacking the relevant symbol overlay to the display section.

DATA STORAGE

One of the first decision made in designing GCADS concerned the type of structure and format to be used for the storage of drawing data. Several types of data storage structures were examines and some test programs were written.

In early systems data was stored as a list of codes in the order in which they were entered. This meant that many points having two or more lines connected to them appeared in the data more than once. It seemed likely, therefore, that storage space could be saved by storing points separately from their interconnections, with one file to store point coordinates and another to store interconnection data. A test program for this data system was written with lines as the only graphic items. The system worked well if the point file was small enough to be largely core resident.

However, when a significant part of the point file was stored on disc, the system became slow because of the number of disc access needed to retrieve points. Another disadvantages of separate storage is that double buffering of data is virtually impossible. This means that it is possible to save time by reading the next block while process the current block, as the data is not accessed sequentially.

When searching for points the separate storage method is obviously the faster, as only the point file has to be searched. It was concluded that separate point storage, although it produced reductions in data volume was

(a) slow for large volumes of data.

(b) complicated and difficult for applications programs to handle.

(c) inflexible, as different data types were difficult to add.

It also depended upon a number of points being used several times. This often will not be the case. It was therefore decided that data should be stored in a list type structure. Another method of economising on data volume is to store macros (repeated sequence of data) once only. This means that macros would be stored on a drawing macro file and referenced by a code in the data list specifying not only the macro used but its scale rotation, position etc.

This system is similar to the separate point storage system. It does not, however, suffer form the same time problems as separate point storage, as macros are usually quite large and in any case they require a disc read each time they are accessed.

The advantages of this system are:

(1) Editing the contents of a macro when it has been positioned on a drawing becomes difficult.

(2) Display time is slightly increased as a transformation has to be applied to the macro before it is displayed.

(3) Finding a point within a macro requires a complicated searching routine.

For these reasons it was decided that in the general CAD system macros should not be stored separate, although it is recognized that applications where many standard items are used could use such a system to great advantage.

THE CAD/CAM SYSTEM

The use of computer system in the engineering industry is widespread for both the design and manufacture of components. The fields of manufacture and design are invariably separate, but it is a natural step to decrease the gap between the drawing board and the manufactured item. Also, if manufacture and design are more linked, it is inevitable that the amount of efforts required to proceed through design to manufacture will be reduced. The way to achieve this is to effort required to proceed through design to manufacture will be reduced. The way to achieve this is to ensure that work carried out in the design process is not needlessly repeated during manufacture. It designs are produced by means of CAD techniques, so that the geometry is in a computerised form, this data can be presented to the manufacturing department instead of, or with the drawings. The success of this procedure depends on the type of manufacturing techniques available and the machines used. Many companies are turning to computer-aided manufacturing (CAM) techniques, mainly in the form of numerically controlled (NC) machines, in order to provide greater flexibility in batch production. At present, integrated CAD/CAM systems are mainly used in problems involving surface definition, particularly in the aircraft industry.

These problems are often very complex and they produce such large quantities of data for both design and manufacture that computerised methods are essential. Less sophisticated industries than the aircraft industry are using NC machines and are becoming interested in CAD/CAM systems. It is in this wider context that research at Imperial College has been conducted. The aim of this work has been to integrate CAD and CAM by linking the existing computer aided draughting facilities with a manufacturing suite of programs geared to NC machine technology. When an item has to be manufactured the first decision to be made is whether to use

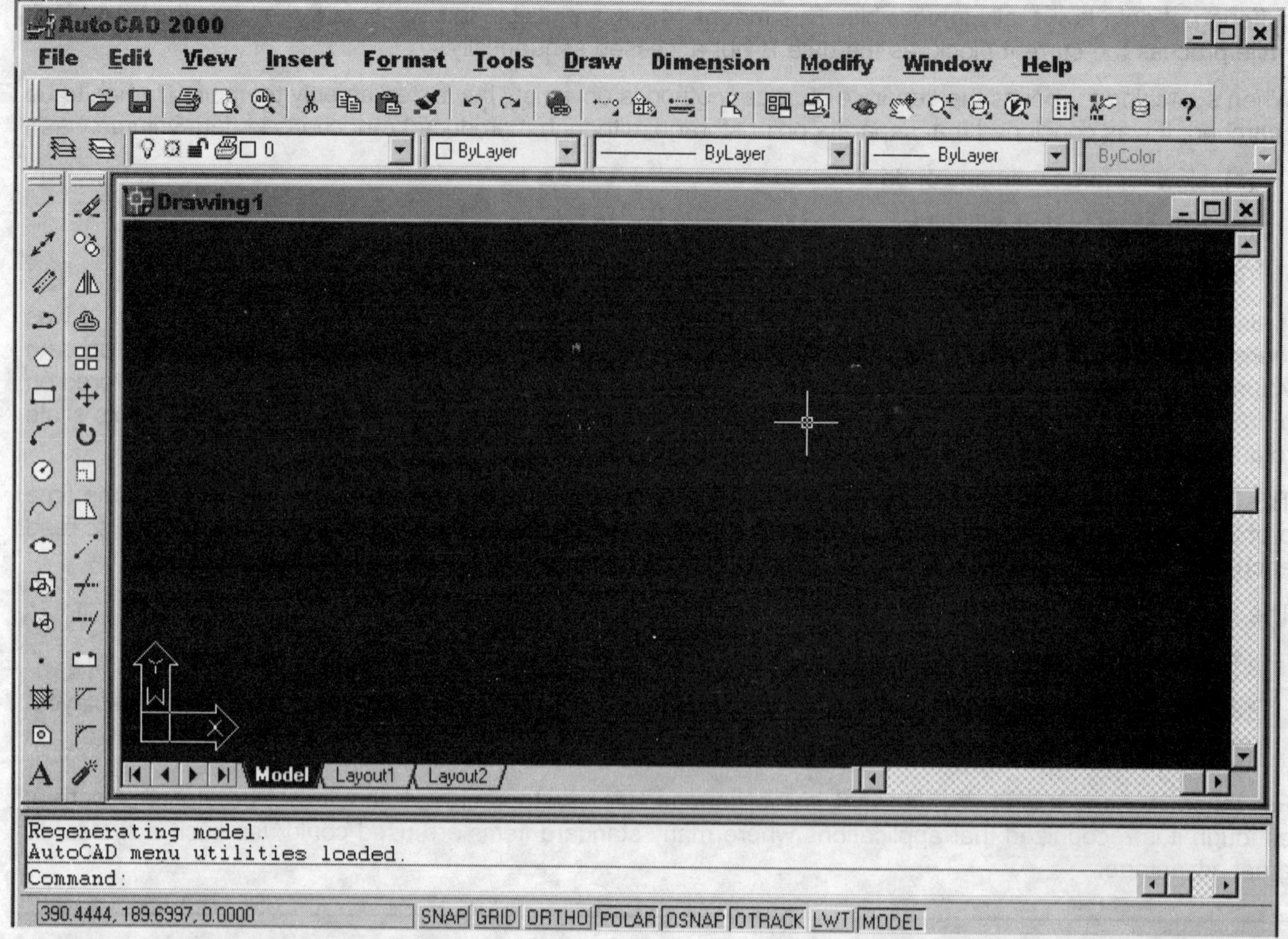

numerical control or more conventional methods. If the object is to be produced in sufficient quantities or is complex, then numerical control methods may be used.

In the case of NC, a part-programmer will be given an engineering drawing of the required object and will produce a part program manuscript. This involves the coding of the geometry of the item (a repetition of work carried out during the design process) followed by the coding of statements of describe the tool motions required to carry out machining. The manuscript, when complete, will be processed by an NC processor and if no errors are found, a control tape will be produced. The coming and testing of the part-program is time-consuming and expensive. In the case of a large batch this initial time and expense can be justified.

However, for a one-off job or small-batch production this may not be so. The integrated CAD/CAM system developed at Imperial College by Craig is based on the similarity of the output form the design process (defining the geometry of the design) and the input for the manufacturing process. This means that the design and manufacturing software can be completely separate but can share a common data base. The design process is made as interactive as possible to give the designer maximum flexibility; but once the design is frozen, the software for the manufacturing process will take the design data with the minimum of man interaction and will produce a part program from submission to the APT system. The term APT stands for Automatically Programmed Tools and refers to both a language and a computer program.

The APT language describes the sequence of operations to be performed by an NC machine. The APT part-program is a series of instructions in pidgin English which describes the tool and its motions. The part-program is input to the main APT program which runs on a large computer. The program converts the simple instructions of the part-program into a set of numerical commands by performing the necessary computation. These commands are then processed by a part-processor program which converts the numerical commands into a form suitable for a particularly machine. The final-form numerical commands are produced on punched tape, the control (CL) tape. The CAD part is based on the GCADS system, consisting of a minicomputer with a digitizer and Tektronix display. Hard copy is via a flat-bed plotter. The manufacturing part of the system is based on a NOVA minicomputer controlling a MECOV triple-axis mill.

The NOVA is linked to an IBM 370 mainframe where the APT processor resides. At present a part-program generated by the CAD system for APT is output onto punched paper tape. It is then read onto a file on the disc of the NOVA. It is then transferred to the IBM 370 for processing and post-processing. The data is then sent back to the NOVA for implementation on the MECOV mill. It is possible to terminate operations on the mill at any time during the execution of a block of instructions and to insert new instructions. It must be emphasized that there are a number of pointer around the system where users can interact with the software. Some of these interactions will be of a management nature in operating the system. Only the CAD work station and machine tool are shown in the CAD/CAM system. It is not difficult to have more work works stations on the CAD system or more machine tools on the NOVA.

At present, data transfer between the CAD system and NC system is via punched paper tape, it is planned to eliminate this system and replace it with a direct link.

THE CAD SOFTWARE

The system software is based on the general draughting system. The interface between design and manufacture is a file known as the workspace file. It is based on fixed length records; each record consists of coordinates (x, y, z) and the numbers which qualify the coordinate. These numbers are packed into one integer word by the computer and where necessary a further record can be used to describe a coordinate. We are concerned with solids which can be represented graphically in a number of ways. Orthogonal projection is the well-established method of engineering drawing, with at least two views which are plane areas (more views may make the visualization simpler).

It is relatively simple to obtain three-dimensional coordinates from such drawings. The input facilities of the system obviate the need for the drawings to be of standard engineering drawing office quality: rough sketches will suffice. We have seen how the two-dimensional surface of the digitizer is divided into areas corresponding to an X-Y, Y-Z or Z-X plane in order to digitize in three dimensions. It is possible to use more than three planes, but usually only three are needed. It is necessary to digitize the same coordinate in two planes in order to obtain a three-dimensional coordinate.

However, the training origin facility obviates the need to do this in many cases, since if a series of points lie on one plane, say at a particular z level, then the x, y coordinates can be digitized until a new z coordinate is necessary. This approach makes the digitizing of cross-section and contour data a very simple process. All the standard draughting facilities such as FIND, DRIVE and CONTROL 90 give the user the power necessary to handle 3-D digitizing. In many cases, it is useful to digitize with respect to a reference grid which may be used as a reference skeleton of the object to be defined. A three dimensional grid is set up in the following way.

A grid origin is defined by digitizing a point in a two-dimensional view; then grid increments are set up independently in any of the orthogonal directions. For example, the cursor may be constrained to move on a particular grid in the X and Y direction, whereas its movement could be left entirely arbitrary in the Z direction. The grid points can be displayed on the storage tube and ten grid files are available for storage and retrieval of commonly used grid configurations. Points are entered off the grid by using DRIVE mode and it is also possible to disable the grid temporarily to input some arbitrary points and then to enable it again. When the user wishes to define a component which is clearly 2 ½ dimensional, the all that is necessary is to digitize one of the required plane faces of he component and enter DOUBLING mode.

The required plane is indicated to the program and the thickness is defined. The program automatically generates the data for the solid and stores it in workspace file. Components which have one or more axes of symmetry can be generated by using the mirroring facilities of the system which allow data to be mirrored about any plane defined by the user. Some of the more difficult work in manufacture is the machining of curved surfaces. Consequently the specification of curved surfaces in CAD is important.

Curves on a surfaces can be defined in two ways. The first method produces an approximation to a curved to a curved surface and is performed by using a method called continuous digitizing. Here the user traces the outline of the curve with the digitizing cursor and data points are stored automatically by the computer at short intervals along the curve. This is a speedy way of producing contour and cross-section data, but it is only as accurate as the user's skill in tracing the curve. If data points are known only at sparse intervals along a required curve, the second method should be used. Here, the points on the curve are defined by the user, either by digitizing or using DRIVE mode and a cubic spline is passed through the points, using CURVEFIT. This techniques ensures that a curve is fitted to the specified points so that continuity of curvature and slope is maintained at all spanes. There are surfaces such as moulds for castings which do not easily and themselves to definition in mathematical terms. The worse cases could be sculpted surfaces of an artistic nature.

There surfaces tend to be described by a series of sections together with contours where necessary. A set of programs modules has been developed to cope with such surfaces; it will produce, from the input data a surface which is smooth and which contains all the data points. The techniques is based on the use of the facilities already described. The method of obtaining a surface requires the specification of a number of sections from given data.

There are three methods available for specifying sections. In the first method the user is asked to specify two points on a line. This line is then used to interest with the data in the X-Y plane of the drawing and to return the x, y and z coordinates of the intersection point sin an ordered form. In the second method two points on a line are defined and a third point is digitized to indicate the bounds on a sweep. The program finds the intersection for a series of lines parallel to the one digitized within the bounds of the sweep. In the third method a centre is defined, a number of lines at various angles are passed through this centre and the intersections are found and stored as before. When a sufficient number of cross-sections have been defined, the spline blending modules are initiated. The lines as defined previously are then tested fro intersection in the X-Y plane.

When intersections are found between two lines, a cubic spline is generated by the set of points on each line and the Z coordinate at the point of intersection is found for each line. These ordinates are averaged and are taken as being points on the two lines; they are added to the data describing those sections. Unsatisfactory points are eliminated at this stage. When this process has ended, the output is the raw data plus a set of cubic splines which intersect in three dimensions with the raw data and themselves. The next stage is to generate a set of splines in the X and Y direction which contain the raw data and the generated splines. The final output is the raw data (as input) plus a family of splines which can readily be used to machine the surface.

THE CAM SOFTWARE

The CAM program modules are entered after the definition and acceptance of the component designed by the user. In the design process it was deemed essential that the user should be in complete control of the machine and input was made as flexible as possible. In the manufacturing area the NC modules play the leading part and operate on the workspace data. Interaction between the user and machine is still necessary but is minimized since the user only supplies information to the modules after the request from them. The CAM programs initially inspect the workspace data and attempt to split the data up into various machining sections.

For example, to produce a sculpted facia panel it would be necessary to machine the basic shape of the panel, which could probably the rectangular and hen to machine the sculpted surface as a secondary operation. This discrimination of data by the NC programs is aided by the fact that it is possible to determine which of the CAD modules was used to generate the data in the workspace. Where the machine is unable to discriminate between surfaces, the user is called upon the interact and help to specify the surfaces more clearly. When the basic machining processes have been decided, the component is inspected to determine whether any rough cutting is necessary to remove access material generating the accurate machining commands.

This is determined to a large extent on whether the mould (or model) is to be moulded form a solid billet or casting. This information is provided by the user. At present the user is requested to supply all information concerning cutter sizes, feed rates and spindle speeds; but it is hoped that the user will soon have the option of specifying these or allowing the machine to calculate suitable ones. The information supplies by the user and the data in the workspace allow the computer to automatically generate a file which is a digital representation of the part-program manuscript.

In this file certain numbers are used which correspond to APT geometry words and points in the workspace are referred to by a numerical label corresponding to their record number. On completion of this process any or all the tool movements over the components can be displayed on the storage tube or drawings can be produced. All these displays are based on the data in the file which is created by the CAM programs. APT can be programmed in two basic ways.

The most commonly used and the one used by the CAM programs where possible, is to describe the tool motion over a component in terms of the relationship of the tool to three surfaces, the part drive and check surfaces. Where this is inconvenient, as when producing tool movements from the data defining the artistic surfaces, the CAM programs use Apt in the straight point-to-point fashion in which the tool head is moved from one discrete point to another.

SUMMARY

1. Computers and graphics have always gone hand in hand since the need for graphic was always felt when it was felt that computer was no longer there for doing calculations only.
2. To display a diagram, it should be drawn either on the paper in case of plotter or on the computer screen.
3. The Design programs help designers, engineers, draftman, etc., to complete the tasks associated with hand drafting of designs easily and more efficiently.
4. The business and analytical program transforms numerical data into pictorial representations I.e. charts and graphs, which show the relationships among the data.
5. The frame buffer (in which the displayed image is stored as a matrix of intensity values) is an example of a point plotting display device.
6. Straight line segments are used to a great extent in generating pictures like bar charts, block diagrams, graph, engineering drawings, architectural plans, etc.
7. The quality of the displayed image is very important in most of the applications of the computer graphics.
8. The most popular widely used devices Direct-View Storage Tube (DVST), which includes the plasma and the laser-scan display.
9. Many graphics packages involve the display of three-dimensional objects and scenes.
10. Computer aided design (CAD) is a technique in which man and machine are blended into a problem solving team, intimately coupling the best characteristics of each.
11. The input of graphics of CAD takes place in one of a number of symbol modes.
12. The digitizing pen has eight buttons. When one of these is pressed it is detected by the background loop and control passed to the interrupt handler in order to access certain facilities.
13. The use of computer system in the engineering industry is widespread for both the design and manufacture of components.
14. The CAM program modules are entered after the definition and acceptance of the component designed by the user.

MULTIPLE CHOICE QUESTIONS

1. Graphics packages can be divided into three categoes, namely, Painting and Drawing Programs, Design Programs and ______________________.
   (a) Business and Analytic Programs (b) Business and Analysis Programs (c) Business and Analytic Projects
2. CAD is:
   (a) Colour Aided Design (b) Computer Aided Design (c) Computer Aided Data
3. CAM is:
   (a) Colour Aided Manufacturing (b) Computer Aided Method (c) Computer Aided Manufacturing

REVIEW QUESTIONS

1. Explain Computer Graphics
2. How the Interactive Graphics Display Works?
3. What are the categories of Graphics Packages?
4. What is Point Plotting Techniques?
5. Define Coordinate Systems.
6. What is Drawing Algorithms?
7. Define Line Drawing Displays.
8. What are Graphic Display Devices?
9. Explain Modelling Three Dimensional Graphics.
10. What is Computer Aided Design?
11. What are the basic areas of Computer Aided Design?
12. What are the Rules for Graphics Software Design?
13. What is the usage of Computer Aided Design?
14. What is the basic processes involved in graphics?
15. Explain the following in Computer Aided Design:

    Graphic Functions — Utility Functions
    Filing Facilities — Editors
    Core Utilization — Overlay Handling and Storage
    Disc Data Filing — Background Loop
16. What is System Modules and also explain Setup Module.
17. What is User Operations Monitor (UOM)
18. Write short note on the following"

    Interrupt Handler — Menu Handler
    Level Handler — Symbol Handler
    File Handler — Macro Handler
19. What is Data Storage?
20. What do you understand by CAD and CAM system?
21. What is CAD Software?
22. What CAM Software?
23. Differentiate between the CAD and CAM systems?

ANSWERS

Multiple Choice Questions

1. a 2. b 3. c

CHAPTER 14

Computers in Management

Learning Objectives

After going through this chapter, you should appreciate the following:

- Why Information Systems Are Important?
- Some Basic Definitions
- Information Systems and Society
- Information Systems and Organizations
- What Managerial End Users Need to Know?
- Technological versus Behavioural Aspects
- Fundamental Information System Concepts
- System Concepts
- Information System Concepts
- Processing of Data into Information
- Software Resources
- Management Information System (MIS): Concept
- MIS : Definition
- Role of the Management Information System
- Impact of the Management Information System
- Management Information System and Computer
- Management Information System and Academics
- MIS and the User
- Role and Importance of Management
- Approaches to Management
- Functions of the Manager
- Managers and the Environment
- Management as a Control System
- Management by Exception
- MIS: A Support to the Management
- Applications of MIS
- Personal Management
- Financial Management
- Production Management
- Materials Management
- Marketing Management
- Conventional Office System
- Modern Office System
- Office Automation Technology
- Application of Office Automation
- IT for Office Automation
- Decision Support Systems
- PROBLEMS IN BUILDING DECISION SUPPORT SYSTEMS
- EXAMPLES OF DECISION SUPPORT SYSTEMS
- Expert systems and aritificial Intelligence
- Regular Versus AI Programming
- Major Areas of AI
- Expert Systems
- Components of an Expert System
- FACT FINDING AND INFORMATION GATHERING
- FEASIBILITY AND COST-BENEFIT ANALYSIS

WHY INFORMATION SYSTEMS ARE IMPORTANT?

Why study information systems? That's the same as asking why anyone should study accounting, finance operations management, marketing, human resource management or any other major business function. Information systems have become a vital component of successful business firms and other organizations.

They thus constitute an essential field of study in Business Administration and Management. That's why most business majors must take a course or two in information systems. Since you probably intend to be a manager, entrepreneur, or business professional, it is just as important to have a basic understanding of information system as it is to understand the basics of accounting, marketing, or other functional areas in business.

SOME BASIC DEFINITIONS

Before going any further, we should define some key terms so we can communicate effectively. We will keep our definitions simple here, waiting until later chapters to explain these more extensively.

Information

Information is data (for example, raw facts or observations) that have been put into a meaningful and useful context. This gives the information value for specific persons and meets their particular information needs. Thus, information is a basic resource that individuals and organizations must have to survive and succeed in today's society. That's why information systems are so important.

Information System

A set of people, procedures, and resources that collects, transforms, and disseminates in an organization. Today's organizations rely on many types of information systems (IS). they include simple manual (paper-and-pencil) information systems and informal (word-of-mouth) information systems. In this text, we will concentrate on computer-based information systems that use hardware, software, and people resources to transform data resources into information products for end users.

Management information system

Many people use this term as a synonym for information system. Others use it to describe an information system that provides information in the form of standardized reports and displays to managers. In this text we'll use management information systems (MIS) to describe a broad class of information systems that are designed to provide information needed for effective decision making by managers.

This makes MIS a popular term in the field of information systems. Thus, the term is used by many organizations as the title of their computer services departments or the name of business information systems they develop, and by many universities as the title of their departments and academic programs in information systems.

End user

Anyone who uses an information system or the information it produces. This usually applies to most people in an organization, as distinguished from the smaller numer of people who are information system specialists, such as systems analysts or professional computer programmers.

Type of management user	***Characteristics***
Hands-on end user	Operates the system, Direct interaction through systems equipment
Indirect end user	Uses reports or information produced by system but does not operate equipment.

User manager	Oversees investment in development or use of the system. Has organizational responsibility for control of system activities.
Senior management	Incorporates competitive and strategic uses of information systems with corporate plans and strategies. Evaluates organization's exposure to risk from information systems failure.

Managerial end user

A manager, entrepreneur, or managerial-level professional who personally uses information systems. Also, the manager of a department or other organizational unit that relies on information systems.

INFORMATION SYSTEMS AND SOCIETY

Information is a basic resource in today's society. We are living in an information society whose economy is heavily dependent on the creation, management, and distribution of information resources. We no longer live in an agricultural society, composed primarily of farmers, or even an industrial society, where a majority of the work force consists of factory workers. Instead, the work force today consists mainly of workers in service occupations or knowledge workers, that is, people who spend most of their workday creating, using, and distributing information.

The category of knowledge workers includes executives, managers, and supervisors; professionals such as accountants, engineers, scientists, stockbrokers, and teachers; and staff personnel such as secretaries and clerical office personnel. these people all make their living using information and clerical office personnel. These people all make their living using information system to create, distribute, manage, and use information resources, which are the used to help them manage the human, financial, material, energy, and other resources involved in their work responsibilities.

Information, then, is a valuable commodity to knowledge workers, their organizations, and society. A major challenge for the information society is to manage its information resources to benefit all members of society. This means, for example, using information systems to find more efficient ways of using the world's limited supplies of material, energy, and other resources. For these reasons, information systems play a vital role in our society, dependent as it is on the effective use and management of information resources.

INFORMATION SYSTEMS AND ORGANIZATIONS

Information and information systems are also valuable organizational resources that must be properly managed for an organization to succeed. That's because organizations are faced with continual changes in the size, complexity, and scope of their operations. For example, business firms are continually battling with their competitors to provide better products and services to a variety of customers at many locations with a minimum number of employees.

Organizations rely on information systems to provide the many types of information necessary for their efficient operations and effective management. This information must be reasonably accurate, timely, and tailored to the needs of managers and end users. It must also help organization gain strategic advantages over their competitors.

Thus, information systems can play a vital role in the success of modern organizations. However, information systems that do not properly support an organizations' strategic objectives, corporate culture, or employee needs can seriously damage that organization systems is thus a major organizational challenge. For managerial end users, information system represent:

- A major part of the resources of an organization and its cost of doing business, thus posing a major resource management challenge.

- An important factor affecting operational efficiency, employee productivity and morale, and customer service and satisfaction.
- A major source of information and support needed to promote effective decision making by managers.
- An important ingredient in developing competitive products and services that give an organization a strategic advantage in the marketplace.
- A vital, dynamic, and challenging career opportunity for millions of men and women.

WHAT MANAGERIAL END USERS NEED TO KNOW?

Information systems technology involves relatively simple concepts that quickly expand into complex details. The (necessary) jargon that comes with the description of the myriad components that have to be linked together to provide a service can numb the mind. If, though, the discussion stays at the level of simple ideas, it quickly becomes simplistic, and the relevant details become so divorced from the concepts that the whole picture loses focus. The gap makes it hard for technicians and managers to understand each other.

It makes no sense for managers to try to learn the nuts and bolts of the technology. The field is too fast-moving for even specialists to maintain their expertise. What managers need is the same level of basic understanding that anyone involved in business has to have about accounting. They should have a sense of the major categories and terms, analogous to debits, credits, depreciation, and so on.

They must be able to interpret an information systems plan in the same way that they read a financial statement. That level of knowledge in no way qualifies them as experts but helps them use experts effectively and allows them to take part in discussions of planning and not be scared off because they do not feet qualified to hold an opinion.

The preceding quotation by MIS scholar Peter Keen emphasizes that managerial end users need to know how information systems can be employed successfully in a competitive business environment. Business firms and other organizations need people who can help them manage their information resources.

Knowledgeable managerial end users can play a major role in information resources management (IRM). That is, they can manage information system personnel, and effectively for the benefit of the entire organization. However, what exactly does a managerial end user need to know about information systems? The answers are as diverse and dynamic as the area itself. Like other areas in Management and Business Administration, the field of Information Systems is based on a variety of other academic disciplines and encompasses a great amount of technological and behavioural knowledge.

The field is constantly changing and expanding as dramatic technological developments and behavioural knowledge. The field is constantly changing and expanding as dramatic technological developments and behavioural research findings push back the frontiers of this dynamic discipline.

TECHNOLOGICAL VERSUS BEHAVIOURAL ASPECTS

Computer Science, Engineering, and Mathematics are disciplines that contribute to the technological aspects of information systems. It is these disciplines, along with the Information Systems discipline, whose research drives developments in computer hardware, software, telecommunications, and other information-processing technologies. Areas such as Psychology, Sociology, and Political Science, on the other hand, contribute to the behavioural aspects of information systems. The research findings of these disciplines and the discipline of Information system shed light on the effective use and management of technology by individuals and organizations. Their focus is on adjusting technology to support individual and organizational goals, and helping individuals and organizations take advantage of the benefits of information systems technology.

Both of these aspects, the technological and the behavioural, are important for managerial end users. Although computer-based information systems are heavily dependent on information-processing technologies, they are designed, operated, and used by people in a variety of organizational settings. Thus, for managerial end users, the success of an information system should be measured not only by its technical efficiency, but also by its effectiveness in meeting end user and organizational goals.

A Framework for Managerial End Users

It is easy to feel overwhelmed by the complex technologies, abstract behavioural concepts, and specialized applications involved in the field of information systems. However, most people do not have to absorb all of this knowledge.

Foundation Concepts

What are information systems, and why are they important to end users and their organizations? In order to answer this question, you need to have a knowledge of the generic components and properties of information systems, which requires an understanding of some basic concepts in general systems theory and information processing. However, you should also appreciate the vital roles played by information systems in businesses and other organizations. In this context, you should learn some fundamental behavioural and technical concepts that will help you understand how information systems can play important operational, managerial, and strategic roles in organizations.

Development

How should managerial end users or information specialists develop information systems solutions to business problems? To answer this question, you should learn some basic problem-solving and developmental concepts. You should understand how methodologies such as the systems approach, the systems development life cycle, and prototyping can be used to construct information systems applications that successfully meet end user and organizational needs.

Technology

What should managerial end users know about the technologies used in computer based information systems? The answer to this question is that they should have an understanding of major concepts, developments, and management issues in information technology (IT), that is, hardware, software, telecommunications, database management, and other information-processing technologies. Technology is so dynamic in this field that a factual knowledge that concentrates on detailed characteristics and capabilities would soon be outdated. Instead, you should focus on generic capabilities, major developmental trends, and management challenges in the use of information systems technology.

Applications

In what ways can information systems assist end users and organizations in accomplishing their work activities and meeting their strategic objectives? Answering this question requires a knowledge of the major applications of information systems for end user activities and the operations, management, and strategic advantage of organizations. You should gain a basic understanding of information systems concepts and applications in areas such as end user computing, office automation, transaction processing, information reporting, decision support, executive support, and artificial intelligence.

Management

How should managerial end users meet the major challenge of managing the information systems of their organizations? Answering this question requires understanding the major challenges and methods involved in managing the resources, technologies, and activities of information systems. Developing and using information systems can be as difficult and costly as it is beneficial to a firm. Thus, you should understand concepts such as information resource management and information systems planning, implementation, and control.

FUNDAMENTAL INFORMATION SYSTEM CONCEPTS

Systems concepts underline the field of information systems. Other disciplines may use the term "system" as an important concept or as a convenient way of describing the phenomena they must deal with. However, a knowledge of systems concepts is vital to a proper understanding of the development, technology, applications, and management of information systems. This section introduces you to generic systems concepts as they apply to organizations, information processing, and information systems. This should provide you with a "systems viewpoint," which will help you understand and apply the information system concepts contained in this text.

SYSTEM CONCEPTS

What is a system? A system can be simply defined as a group of interrelated or interacting elements forming a unified whole. Many examples of systems can be found in the physical and biological sciences, in modern technology, and in human society. Thus, we can talk of the physical system of the sun and its planets, the biological system of the human body, the technological system of an oil refinery, and the socioeconomic system of a business organization. However, the following generic concept of a system is widely used in the information systems discipline.

- A system is a group of interrelated components working together toward a common goal by accepting inputs and producing outputs in an organized transformation process.
- Such a system (sometimes called a "dynamic system") has three basic interacting components or functions:
- Input involves capturing and assembling elements that enter the system to be processed. For example, raw materials, energy, data, and human effort must be secured and organized for processing.
- Processing involves transformation processes that convert input into out put. Examples are a manufacturing process, the human breathing process, and data calculations.
- Output involves transferring elements that have been produced by the transformation process to their ultimate destination. For example, finished products, human services, and management information must be transmitted to their human users.

Examples

A manufacturing system accepts raw materials as inputs and produces finished goods as output. An information system can be viewed as a system that accepts data resources as input and process them into information products as output.

Feedback and Control

The systems concept can be made even more useful by including two additional components: feedback and control. A system with feedback and control components is sometimes called a "called a "cybernetic" system, that is a self-monitoring, self-regulating system.

Input	***Processing***	***Output***
A Manufacturing System	Raw Material	Manufacturing Process
Finished Products		

An Information System	Input of Data Resources Information	Processing Data into Output of Information Products

Feedback is data about the performance of a system.

Control is a major system function that monitors and evaluates feedback to determine whether the system is moving toward the achievement of its goal. It then makes any necessary adjustments to the input and processing components of the system to ensure that proper output is produced. Feedback is frequently included as part of the concept of the control function because of the essential role feedback plays in control. This emphasizes that the feedback and control functions perform an important supportive role. They assure that other system components property transform inputs into outputs so the system can achieve its goal.

Control of System Performance

A system performing properly generates positive feedback, which signals the control function to maintain the system's current course toward its goal. A system whose performance is deteriorating—deviating from the attainment of its goal—generates negative feedback. In the real world, the performance of most systems tends to deteriorate over time. This characteristic is called entropy—the tendency of a system to lose its homeostasis, that is, a relatively stable state of equilibrium. The Control function strives to reverse the entropy and maintain the equilibrium of a system through a variety of corrective actions. It monitors feedback and attempts to reduce deviations by the system from previously established standards of acceptable performance. Control is accomplished by (1) detecting feedback with sensors of some kind, (2) measuring the size, quantity, direction, or intensity of the feedback, (3) comparing the results to the established standards of proper performance, (4) transmitting control signals that initiate corrective actions to adjust the activities of other system components, and (5) bringing system performance "under control," that is, back within an acceptable range of performance that leads to the attainment of system goals.

Examples

A familiar example of a self-monitoring, self-regulation system is the thermostat-controlled heating system found in many homes, which automatically monitors and regulates itself to maintain a desired temperature. Another example is the human body, which can be regarded as a cybernetic system that automatically monitors and adjusts many of its functions, such as temperature, heartbeat, and breathing.

Other System Characteristics

Several systems may share the same environment. Some of these systems may be connected to one another by means of a shared boundary, or interface.

Example

Organizations such as businesses and government agencies are subsystems of society, which is their environment. Society contains a multitude of such systems, including individuals and their social, political, and economic institutions. Organizations themselves consist of many subsystems, such as departments, divisions, and other work groups. Organizations are open systems, since they interface and interact with since they possess the ability to modify themselves to meet the demands of a changing environment.

A Business as a System

You should be able to visualize any organization as a system. A business consists of the following interrelated system components:

Input.	Economic resources such as people, money, material, machines, land, facilities, energy, and information are acquired by a business from its environment and used in its system activities.
Processing.	Organizational processes such as marketing, manufacturing, and finance transform input into

output. Other organizational processes are engineering, research and development, legal services, and so on.

Output. Products and services, payments to employees and suppliers, dividends, contributions, taxes, and information are all outputs produced by a business and exchanged with or transferred to its environment.

Feedback. A primary role of information systems is serving as the feedback component of an organizational system. They provide information to management concerning the performance of the organization.

Control. Management is the control component of an organizational system. Managers control the operations of a business so that its performance meets organizational goals such as profitability, market share, and social responsibility. Feedback about organizational performance is compared to standards of performance established by management. Managers then make decisions to adjust performance to meet organizational goals.

A business must maintain appropriate relationships with other economic, political, and social systems in its environment. This group includes its stakeholders, such as customers, suppliers, competitors, stockholders, labour unions, financial institutions, governmental agencies, and the community, all of which have a "stake" in the proper and successful operation of the business. Information system can help a business shape its relationships with each of these stakeholders. A business is a system where economic resources (input) are transformed by various organizational processes (processing) into goods and services (output). Information systems provide information (feedback) on the operations of the system to management for the direction and maintenance of the system (control), as it exchanges inputs and outputs with its environment.

Information Processing Concepts

It is important to understand information systems in the context of their use in information processing, which is also called data processing. We can define data or information processing as the processing of data to make it usable and meaningful, thus transforming it into information. Let's take a closer look at the concepts involved.

Data versus Information

The word data is the plural of datum, though data is commonly used to represent both singular and plural forms. Data is commonly defined as raw facts or observations, typically about physical phenomena or business transactions. For example, a spacecraft launch or the sale of an automobile would generate a lot of data describing those events. More specifically, data are objective measurements of the attributes (the characteristics) of entities (such as people, places, things, and events). These measurements are usually represented by symbols such as numbers and words, or by codes composed of a mixture of numerical, alphabetical, and other characters. However, data commonly takes a variety of forms, including numeric data, text, voice, and images.

Data → Processing Data into Information → Information

The terms data and information are often used interchangeably. However, it is helpful to view data as raw material resources that are processed into finished information products. Information can then be defined as data that has been converted into a meaningful and useful context for specific end users. Of course, data may not require processing in order to constitute information for a particular end user. However, data is usually not useful until subjected to a "value-added" process, where (1) its form is aggregated, manipulated, and organized, (2) its content is analyzed and evaluated, and (3) it is placed in a proper context for a human user. Thus, you should view information as processed data placed in a context that gives it value for specific end users.

Example

Names, quantities, and dollar amounts recorded on sales forms represent data about sales transactions. However, a sales manager may not regard these as information. Only after such facts are properly organized and manipulated can meaningful sales information be furnished, specifying, for example, the amount of sales by product type, sales territory, or salesperson.

INFORMATION SYSTEM CONCEPTS

Earlier we said that an information system is a set of people, procedures, and resources that collects, transforms, and disseminated information in an organization. In this section, we have said that an information system is a system that accepts data resources as input and processes them into information products as output. How does an information system accomplish this? What system components and activities are involved?

An Information System Model

An information system uses the resources of hardware (machines and media), software (programs and procedures), and people (specialists and end users) to perform input, processing, output, storage, and control activities that convert data resources into information products.

Information systems

Hardware Resources

An information system model, Information systems use hardware (machines and media), software (programs and procedures), and people (specialists and end users) resources to perform input, processing, output, storage, and control activities that transform data resources into information products. This information system model will help you tie together many of the facts and concepts involved in the study of computer-based information systems. It emphasizes three major concepts:

Hardware (machines and media), **software** (programs and procedures), and **people** (specialists and end users) are the primary resources needed to accomplish information processing activities in information systems. Data Resources are transformed into a variety of information products by the information processing activities of information system. Information processing consists of the basic system activities of input, processing, output, storage, and control.

Information System Activities

Let's take a closer look now at each of the basic information processing activities that occur in information systems. Then we will discuss the resources needed to accomplish them. Data about business transactions and other events must be captured and prepared for processing by the basic data entry activities of recording and editing, End users typically record data about transactions on some type of physical medium such as a paper form, or enter it directly into a computer system. This usually includes a variety of editing activities to assure they have recorded data correctly. Once entered, data may be transferred onto a machine-readable medium such as magnetic disk or tape, until needed for processing.

For example, data about sales transactions can be recorded on source document such as paper sales order forms. (A source document is the original formal record of a transaction.) Alternately, sales data could be captured by salespersons using computer keyboards or optical scanning devices who are visually prompted to enter data correctly by video displays. This provides them with a more convenient and efficient user interface, that is, methods of end user input and output with a computer system. Methods such as optical scanning and displays of menus, prompts, and fill-in-the blanks formats make it easier for end users to enter data correctly, into an information system.

PROCESSING OF DATA INTO INFORMATION

Data is typically manipulated by such activities as calculating, comparing, sorting, classifying, and summarizing.

These activities organize, analyze, and manipulate data, thus converting it into information for end users. The quality of any data stored in an information system must also be maintained by a continual process of correcting and updating activities. For example, data received about a purchase can be (1) added to a running total of sales results, (2) compared to a standard to determine eligibility for a sales discount, (3) sorted in numerical order based on product identification numbers, (4) classified into product categories (such as food and nonfood items), (5) summarized to provide a sales manager with information about various product categories, and, finally, (6) used to update sales records.

Output of Information Products

Information in various forms is transmitted to end users and made available to them in the output activity. The goal of information systems is the production of appropriate information products for end users. Common information products are video displays, paper documents, and audio responses that provide us with messages, forms, reports, listings, graphics displays, and so on. We use these information products to improve our personal and professional performances as we work in organizations and live in society.

Storage of Data, Model, and Knowledge Resources

Storage is a basic system component of information systems. Storage is the information system activity in which data and information are retained in an organized manner for later use. For example, just as written text material is organized into words, sentences, paragraphs, and documents, stored data is commonly organized into fields, records, files, and databases. This facilitates its later use in processing or its retrieval as output when needed by users of a system.

Data and information are vital organizational resources that can be stored in information systems in the following forms:

Databases, which hold processed and organized data

Model bases, which hold conceptual, mathematical, and logical models that express business relationships, computational routines, or analytical techniques. Knowledge bases, which hold knowledge in a variety of forms such as facts and rules of inference about various subjects.

For example, sales data is accumulated and stored in a sales database for subsequent processing, which yields daily, weekly, and monthly sales analysis reports for management. Decision support systems, on the other hand, rely on model bases for decision rules and analytic techniques that help managers make decisions, while expert systems use knowledge bases to develop inferences about specific subjects and give end users expert advice.

Common data elements

This is a common method of organizing stored data in information systems.

Name field

A field is a grouping of characters that represent a characterstic of a person, place, thing, or event. For example, an employee's name field.

Payroll Record

A record is a collection of interrelated fields. For example, an employee's payroll record might consist of a name field, a social security number field, a department field, and a salary field.

Payroll file

A file is a collection of interrelated records. For example, a payroll file might consist of the payroll records of all employees of a firm.

Personnel Database

A database is an integrated collection of interrelated records or files. For example, the personnel database of a business might contain payroll, personnel action, and employee skills files.

Control of System Performance

An information system should produce feedback about its input, processing, output, and storage activities. This feedback must be monitored and evaluated to determine if the system is meeting established performance standards. Then appropriate system activities must be adjusted so that proper information products are produced for end users. For example, a manager may discover that subtotals of sales amounts in a sales report do not add up to total sales. Then input or processing procedures will have to be changed to accumulate correctly all sales transactions captured and processed by the sales information system.

Information System Resources

An information system includes four major resources: hardware, software, people, and data. Let's briefly discuss some basic concepts and examples of how these resource contribute to the information processing activities of information systems.

Hardware Resources

The concept of hardware resources includes all physical devices and materials used in information processing. Specifical devices and materials used in information processing. Specifically, it includes not only machines, such as computers and calculators, but also all data media—that is, all tangible objects on which data is recorded; based information systems are:

Large mainframe computers, minicomoputers, and microcomputer systems.

Computer workstations, which use a keyboard for input of data, a video screen or printer for output of information, and magnetic or optical disks for storage. Telecommunications processors, and other devices interconnected by a variety of telecommunications media to provide computing power throughout an organization.

SOFTWARE RESOURCES

The concept of software resources includes all sets of information-processing instructions. This generic concept of software includes not only the sets of operating instructions called programs, which direct and control computer hardware, but also the sets of information-processing instructions needed by people, which are called procedures. The following are examples of software:

System software, such as an operating system program, which manages and supports the operations of a computer system. Application software, which are programs that direct processing for a particular use of computers by end users. Examples are an inventory program, a payroll program, and a word processing program. Procedures, which are operating instructions for the people who will use an information system. Examples are instructions for filling out a paper form or using a software package.

People Resources

People are required for the operation of all information systems. These people resources include specialists and end users. Specialists are people who develop and operate information systems. They include systems analysts, programmers, computer operators, and other managerial, technical, and clerical personnel.

Basically, systems analysts design information systems based on the information requirements of end users; programmers prepare computer programs based on the specifications of systems analysts; and computer operators operate large computer systems.

Data Resources

Data is more than the raw material of information system. The concept of data resources has been broadened by managers and information systems professionals. They realize that data and information constitute a valuable organizational resource. Thus, data and information stored in databases, model bases, and knowledge bases are now considered to be part of the data resources or information resources of an organization.

Data can take many forms, including traditional alphanumeric data, composed of numbers and alphabetical and special characters that describe business transactions and other events and entities. Text data, consisting of sentences and paragraphs used in written communications, and image data, such as graphic shapes and figures, are also important forms of data. However, data frequently takes the form of video data, data presented for viewing by a variety of video display devices; audio data, the human voice and other sounds; tactile data, generated by touch-sensitive materials; and sensor data, provided by a variety of sensors used in the control of physical processes.

Data resources are typically recorded and stored on several types of data media, including paper, magnetic, optical, film, and electronic media. Examples are paper documents, magnetic disks, magnetic tape, optical disks, microfilm, and electronic circuit chips.

Sales Manager

Sales Analysis Displays

Sales Analysis Reports

Sales Databases and Programs

Recognizing Information Systems

There are many kinds of information systems in the real world. Some are simple manual information systems, where people use tools such as pencils and paper, even machines such as calculators and typewriters, to convert data into information. Others are computer-based information systems that use one or more types of computers and a variety of computer devices to process data automatically. These are frequently called electronic data processing (EDP) system. However, whether they are manual or computer-based, you should be able to use an information system model and other system concepts to help you understand the information systems you encounter in the real world.

MANAGEMENT INFORMATION SYSTEM (MIS): CONCEPT

The concept of the MIS has evolved over a period of time comprising many different facets of the organizational functions. MIS is a necessity of all the organizations.

The initial concept of MIS was to process data from the organization and present it in the form of reports at regular intervals. The system was largely capable of handling the data from collection to processing. It was more impersonal, requiring each individual to pick and choose the processed data nd use it for his requirements. This concept was further modified when a distinction was made between data and information. The information is a product of an analysis of data. This concept is similar to a raw material and the finished product. What is needed is an information and not a mass of data. However, the data can be analysed in a number of ways, producing different shades and specifications of the information as a product. It was, therefore, demanded that the system concept should be an individual-oriented, as each individual may have a different orientation towards the information. This concept was further modified, that the system should present information in such a form and format that it creates an impact on its user, provoking a decision, an action or an investigation. It was later realized that even through such an impact was a welcome modification; some sort of selective approach was necessary in the analysis and reporting. Hence, the concept of exception reporting was imbibed in MIS. The norm for an exception was necessary to evolve in the organization. The concept remained valid till and to the extent that the norm for an exception remained true and effective. Since the environment turns competitive and is over changing fixation of the norm for an exception becomes a futile exercise at least for the people in the higher echelons of the organization. The concept was then evolved that the system should be capable of handling a needbased exception reporting. This need may be either of an individual or a group of people. This called for keeping all data together in such a form that it can be accessed by anybody and can be processed to suit his needs. The concept is that the data is one but it can be viewed by different individuals in different ways. This gave rise to the concept of DATABASE and the MIS based on the DATABASE proved much more effective.

Over a period of time, when these conceptual developments were taking place, the concept of the end user computing using multiple databases emerged. This concept brought a fundamental change in MIS. The change was, decentralisation of the system and the user of the information becoming independent of computer professionals. When this became a reality the concept of MIS changed to a decision making system. The job in a computer department is to manage the information resource and leave the task of information processing to the user. The concept of MIS in today's world is a system which handles the databases, provides computing facilities to the end and gives a variety of decision making tools to the user of the system.

The concept of MIS gives high regard to the individual and his ability to use the information. An MIS gives information through data analysis. While analyzing the data, it relies on many academic disciplines. These include the theories, principles and concepts from the Management Science, Management Sciences, Management Accounting, Operations Research, Organizational behavior, Engineering, Computer Science, Psychology and Human Behavior, making the MIS more effective and useful. These academic disciplines are used in designing the MIS, evolving the decision support tools for modeling and decision-making.

The foundation of MIS is the principles of management and its practices. MIS uses the concept of management control in its design and relies heavily on the fact that the decision maker or the manager is a human being and is a human processor of information. A Management Information System can be evolved for a specific objective if it is evolved after systematic planning and design. It calls for an analysis of a business, management views and policies, organization culture and the management style. The information should be generated in this setting and must be useful in managing the business. This is possible only when it is conceptualized as a system with an appropriate design. The MIS, therefore, relies heavily on the systems theory. The systems theory offers solutions to handle the complex situations of the input and output flows. It uses theories of communication which helps to evolve a system design capable of handling data inputs, process and outputs with the least possible noise or distortion in transmitting the information from a source to a destination.

It uses the principles of System design, viz., an open system or a closed system. An open system of the MIS offers an ability of continuous adjustment or correction in the system in line with the environmental changes in which the MIS operates. Such a design helps to keep the MIS tuned with the business management needs of the organization. The concept, therefore, is a blend of principles, theories and practices of the Management Information and System giving rise to single product known as Management Information System (MIS).

The physical view of the MIS can be as an assembly of several subsystems based on the databases in the organization. These subsystems range from data collection, transaction processing and validating, processing, analyzing and storing the information in databases. The subsystems could be at a functional level or a corporate level. The information is evolved through them for a functional or a departmental management and it provides the information for the management of business at the corporate level. The MIS is a product of a multi-disciplinary approach to the business management. It is a product which needs to be kept under a constant review and modification to meet the corporate needs of the information. It is a prescribed product design for the organization. The MIS differs in two organizations involved in the same business. The MIS is for the people in the organisation. Since the people in two different organizations are different, the design of MIS would also differ. The MIS model may be the same but it differs greatly in the contents.

The MIS, therefore, is a dynamic concept subject to change, time and again, with a change in the business management process. It continuously interacts with the internal and the external environment of the business and provides a corrective mechanism in the system so that the changed needs of information are met with effectively. The MIS, therefore, is a dynamic design, the primary objective of which is to provide the information for decision making and it is developed considering the organisational fabric, giving due regard to the people in the organisation, the management functions and the managerial control.

The MIS model of the organisation changes over a time as the business passes through several phases of developmental growth cycle. It supports the management o he business in each phase by giving the information which is crucial in that phase. Every business has critical success factors in each phase of growth cycle and the MIS model gives more information on the critical success factors for decision making.

MIS : DEFINITION

The Management Information System (MIS) is a concept of the last decade or two. It has been understood and described in a number of ways. It is also popularly known as the Information and Decision System, the Computer-based Information System.

The MIS has more than one definition, some of which are given below.

1. The MIS is defined as a system which provides information support for decision making in the organisation.
2. The MIS is defined as an integrated system of man and machine for providing the information to support the operations, the management and the decision making function in the organisation.
3. The MIS is defined as a system based on the database of the organisation evolved for the purpose of providing information to the people in the organisation.
4. The MIS is defined as a Computer-based Information System.

Through there are a number of definitions, all of them converge on one single point, i.e., the MIS is a system to support the decision making function in the organisation. The difference lies in defining the elements of the MIS. However, in today's world, the MIS is a computerized business processing system generating information for the people in the organisation to meet the information needs for decision making to achieve the corporate objectives of the organisation.

The difficulty in handling this multiple requirement of the people is due to a couple of reasons. The information is a processed product to fulfill an imprecise need of the people. It take time to search the data and may require a difficult processing path. It has a time value and unless processed on time and communicated, it has no value. The scope and the quantum of information is individual-department and it is difficult to conceive the information as a well-defined product for the entire organisation. Since the people are instrumental in any business transaction, a human error is possible in conducting the same. Since a human error is difficult to control, the difficulty arises in ensuring a hundred percent quality assurance of information in terms of completeness, accuracy, validity, timeliness and meeting the decision making needs.

In order to get a better grip on the activity of information processing, it is necessary to have a formal system which should take care of the following points:

- Handling of a voluminous data.
- Confirmation of the validity of data and transaction.
- Complex processing of data and multidimensional analysis.
- Quick search and retrieval.
- Mass storage

- Communication of the information system to the user on time.
- Fulfilling the changing needs of the information.

The management information system uses computers and communication technology to deal with these points of supreme importance.

ROLE OF THE MANAGEMENT INFORMATION SYSTEM

The role of the MIS in an organisation can be compared to the role of heart in the body. The information is the blood and MIS is the heart. In the body the heart plays the role of supplying pure blood to all the elements of the body including the brain. The heart works faster and supplies more blood when needed. It regulates and controls the incoming impure blood when needed. It regulates and control the incoming impure blood, processes it and sends it to the destination in the quantity needed. It fulfills the needs of blood supply to human body in normal course and also in crisis.

The MIS plays exactly the same role in the organisation. The system ensure that an appropriate data is collected from the various sources, processed and sent further to all the needy destinations. The system is expected to fulfill the information needs of an individual, a group of individuals, the management functionaries: the managers and the top management.

The MIS satisfies the diverse needs through a variety of systems such as Query Systems, analysis Systems, Modelling System and Decision Support Systems. The MIS helps in Strategic Planning, Management Control, Operational Control and Transaction Processing.

The MIS helps the clerical personnel in the transaction processing and answers their queries on the data pertaining to the transaction, the status of a particular record and references on a variety of documents. The MIS helps the junior management personnel by providing he operational data for planning, scheduling and control and helps them further in decision making at the operations level to correct an out of control situation. The MIS helps the middle management in short term planning, target setting and controlling the business functions. It is supported by the use of management tools of planning and control. The MIS helps the top management in goal setting, strategic planning and evolving the business plans and their implementation.

The MIS plays the role of information generation, communication, problem identification and helps in the process of decision making. The MIS, therefore, plays a vital role in the management, administration and operations of an organisation.

IMPACT OF THE MANAGEMENT INFORMATION SYSTEM

Since the MIS plays a very important role in the organisation, it creates an impact on the organisation's functions, performance and productivity.

The impact of MIS on the functions is in its management. With a good MIS support, the management of marketing, finance, production and personnel becomes more efficient. The tracking and monitoring of the functional targets becomes easy. The functional managers are informed about the progress, achievements and shortfalls in the activity and the targets. The manager is kept alert by providing certain information indicating the probable trends in the various aspects of business. This helps in forecasting and long-term perspective planning. The manager's attention is brought to a situation which is exceptional in nature, including him to take an action or a decision in the matter. A disciplined information reporting system creates database and knowledge base for all people in the organisation. The information is available in such a form that it can be used straight away or by blending and analysis, saving the manager's valuable time.

The MIS creates another impact in the organisation which relate to the understanding of the business itself. The MIS begins with the definition of a data entity and its attributes. It uses a dictionary of data, entity and attributes, respectively, designed for information generation in the organisation. Since all the information systems use the dictionary, there is common understanding of terms and terminology in the organisation bringing clarity in the communication and a similar understanding of an even in the organisation.

The MIS calls for a systemization of the business operations for an effective system design. This leads to streamlining of the operations which complicate the system design. It improves the administration of the business by bringing a discipline in its operations as everybody is required to follow and use systems and procedures. This process brings a high degree of professionalism in the business operations.

Since the goals and objectives of the MIS are the products of business goals and objectives, it helps indirectly to pull the entire organisation in one direction towards the corporate goals and objectives by providing the relevant information to the people in the organism.

A well designed system with a focus on the manager makes an impact on the managerial efficiency. The fund of information motivates an enlightened manager to use a variety of tools of the management. It helps him to resort to such exercises as experimentation and modeling. The use of computers enables him to use the tools and techniques which are impossible to use manually. The ready-made packages make this task simpler. The impact is on the managerial ability to perform. It improves the decision making ability considerably.

Since the MIS works on the basic systems such as transaction processing and databases, the drudgery of the clerical work is transferred to the computerized system, relieving he human mind for better work. It will be observed that a lot of manpower is engaged in this activity in the organisation. If you study the individual's time utilization and its application, you will find that seventy percent of the time is spent in recording, searching, processing and communicating. This is a very large overhead in the organisation. The MIS has a direct impact on this overhead. It creates an information-based work culture in the organisation.

MANAGEMENT INFORMATION SYSTEM AND COMPUTER

Translating the real concept of the MIS into reality is technically, an infeasible proposition unless computers are used. the MIS relies heavily on the hardware and software capacity of the computer and its ability to store, process, retrieve and communicate with no serious limitations.

he variety of the hardware having distinct capabilities makes it possible to design the MIS for a specific situation. For example, if the organisation needs a large database and very little processing, a computer system is available for such a requirement. Suppose the organisation has multiple business locations at long distances and if the need is to bring the data at one place, process and then send the information to various locations, it is possible to have a computer system with a distributed data processing capability. If the distance is today long, then the computer system can be hooked through a satellite communication system.

The ability of the hardware to store data and process it at a very fast rate helps to deal with the data volumes, its storage and access effectively. The ability of the computer to sort and merge helps to organize the data in a particular manner and process it for complex lengthy computations. Since the computer is capable of digital, graphic, word, image, voice and text processing, it is exploited to generate information and present it in the form which is easy to understand for the information user.

The ability of a computer system to provide security of data brings a confidence in the management in the storage of data on a magnetic media in an impersonal mode. The computer system provides the facilities such as READ ONLY where you cannot delete or UPDATE. It provides an access to the selected information through a password and layered access facilities. The confidential nature of the data and information can be maintained in a computer system. With this ability, the MIS becomes a safe application in the organisation.

The software, an integral part of a computer system, further enhances the hardware capability. The software is available to handle the procedural and nonprocedural data processing. For example, if you want to use a formula to calculate a certain result, an efficient language is available to handle the situation. If you are required to use a formula but have to resort every time to a new procedure, the nonprocedural languages are available.

The software is available to transfer the data from one computer system to another. Hence, you can compute the results at one place and transfer them to a computer located at another place for some other use. The computer system being able to configure to the specific needs helps to design a flexible MIS.

The advancement in computers and the communication technology has made the distance, speed, volume and complex computing an easy task. Hence, designing the MIS for a specific need and simultaneously designing a flexible and open system becomes possible, thereby saving a lot o drudgery of development and maintenance of the system. The concept of user friendly systems and the end user computing is possible, making information processing a personalized function. However, the application of the management principles and practices in today's complex business world is possible only when the MIS is based on a computer system support.

MANAGEMENT INFORMATION SYSTEM AND ACADEMICS

The management information systems draws a lot of support from other academic disciplines too. The foundation of MIS is the management theory. it uses the principles and practices of management while designing the system and gives due regard to the theory of organisational behavior.

It considers the human mind as a processor of information. While designing he report format and forming communication channels, MIS takes into account the behaviour of the manager as an individual and in a group. it gives due regard to the personal factors such as bias, thinking with a fixed frame of reference, risk aversion, strengths and weaknesses.

Another area of academics is operational research. The operational research is used for developing the models of management problem and they are then incorporate in the MIS as decision support systems. The inventory control, queuing theory and resource programming are used in the MIS as decision support systems. The network theory is used for planning and controlling large projects. The application of PERT/CPM to a project planning is now easily possible through the MIS support.

In the area of accounting applications, it uses the accounting principles to ensure that the data is correct and valid. It uses the principles of double entry bookkeeping for balancing the accounts. It uses the accounting methodology for generating a trial balance, balance sheet and other books of accounts.

The MIS uses the communication theory in a significant manner. The principle of feedback is used while designing analysis and reporting systems. While designing the report format, attention is paid to avoid noise and distortions in the communication process. The MIS further relies heavily on the decision theory and the decision methodology. It uses different mathematical techniques to handle the situation of decision making under risk and uncertainty. It uses the method of decision-making under certainty directly for decision making and action.

The MIS is based on database and uses the database for generating information. Te three types of data structures, viz., hierarchical, network and relational database have roots in the mathematics and the set theory.

The MIS becomes rich in content and more useful when it becomes more and more a decision-making or decision-support system. This is possible when it builds decision making systems in MIS which in turn is possible if it draws tools, techniques, methods, rules and principles from pure science and application science and use them as an integral part of the system. The MIS draws data from its own source and uses it in the application of a variety of tools and techniques to solve the management problems in business. The MIS uses knowledge from management, business management, mathematics, accounting, psychology, communication theory, operations research and probability theory for building processors, methods and decision-support systems in designing business applications.

MIS AND THE USER

Every person in the organisation is a user of the MIS. The people in the organisation operate at all levels in the hierarchy. A typical user is a clerk, an assistant, an officer, an executive or a manager. Each of them has a specific task and a role to play in the management of business. The MIS caters to the needs of all persons.

The main task of a clerk is to search the data, make a statement and submit it to the higher level. A clerk can use the MIS for a quick search and reporting the same to higher level. An assistant has the task of collecting and organizing the data and conducting a redimentary analysis of it. The MIS offers the user tools to perform these tasks. An officer has a role of integrating the data from different systems and disciplines to analyse it and make a critical comment if anything adverse is found.

The MIS offers the methods and facilities to integrate the data and report the same in a proper format. An executive plays the role of a decision maker. He is in a position of responsibility and accountability; a position of a planner and a decision maker. He is responsible for achieving the targets and goals of the organisation. The MIS provides facilities to analyse the data and offers the decision support systems to perform the task of execution. The MIS provides an action-oriented information.

The manager has a position of responsibility and accountability for the business results. His management role expands beyond his management function. He is a strategist and a long-term planner. He is a person with a foresight, an analytical ability and is expected to use these abilities in the functions of top management. The MIS provides information in a structured or unstructured format for him to react. The MIS caters to his constant changing needs of information. The user of the MIS is expected to be a rational person and the design of the MIS is based on this assumption.

However, in reality the impact created on individuals by MIS is difficult to explain. The nature of the impact in a few cases is negative. However, this negative impact can be handled with proper training and counseling.

It is observed that at lower level, there is a sense of insecurity. As the MIS takes away the drudgery of search, collection, writing and reporting the data, the work vacuum, so created, is not easily filled, thus creating a sense of insecurity. To some extent the importance of the person is also lost, giving rise to a fear of non-recognition in the organization.

At the level of an officer and an executive, the MIS does the job of data manipulation and integration. It analyses the data in a predetermined manner. This means that the knowledge of business is transferred from an individual to the MIS and is made available to all in the organisation. This change arising out of the MIS creates a sense of being neglected for knowledge, information and advice. The psychological impact is larger if the person is not able to cope with this change by expanding or enriching the job and the position held by him. The manager, holding a position in the top or middle management, suffers from fear of challenge and exposure. The MIS makes his competitors more effective as they have access to the information and have an ability to interpret. This leads to a situation where he is afraid that his position, decision and defence will be challenged and may be proved wrong sometimes. The risk of adverse exposure to the higher management also increases. The effects so far pointed out are all negative and they are seen only a few cases.

The positive effects on the individuals at all levels are that they have become more effective operators. The time and energy which was spent earlier in unproductive work is now applied for a productive work. Some are able to use their analytical skills and knowledge with the information support for improving their position in the organisation. Managers, having improved their decision-making ability, are able to handle the complex situations with relative ease. Some are benefited by improving their performance and being held in high esteem by the higher management.

The enterprising managers are able to use the systems and the models for trying out a number of alternatives in a given problem situation. The impact of the MIS on people of the organisation is phenomenal as it has made same body of people collectively more effective and productive. The recent major technological advances in communication such as Multimedia, Imaging, Graphical User Interfaces (GUI), etc., and the ability to access the data stored at different locations on the variety hardware of platforms would make MIS more attractive and efficient proposition. An intelligent user of information can demonstrate the ability of decision making, since his manipulative capability is considerably increased, with the information now being available on his desktop.

Through the MIS, the information can be used as a strategic weapon to counter the threats to business, make businesses more competitive, bring about the oranisational transformation through integration. A good MIS also makes an organisation seamless by removing all the communication barriers.

ROLE AND IMPORTANCE OF MANAGEMENT

Management as defined by Mary Follett is the art of getting things done through people. A manager is defined as a person who achieves the organisation's goals by motivating others to perform – not by performing himself. Whether management is an art or a science is a very subjective question. But it can be said without doubt that modern management in the environment of technology is becoming more of a science than an art. We define management for the purpose of Management Information Systems as the process of planning, organizing, staffing, coordinating and controlling the efforts of the members of the organisation to achieve common stated goals of the organisation.

In the process of management, a manager uses human skills, material resource and scientific methods to perform all the activities leading to the achievement of goals. The management process involves a continuous resolution of conflicts of one kind or the other which affects the achievement of goals. In the management of any activity, a manger comes across human conflict, conflict of goals, conflict between alternative resources, conflict of time, conflict of approach or method and the conflict of choice. The manager uses a variety of tools, techniques and skills while executing the management process of planning, organizing, staffing coordinating and controlling. An effective way of handling this process is to treat the organisation as a system. The result-oriented management approaches the problem of management through the systems view of the organisation.

The key concepts of the systems theory used in the management are as follows:

1. A system is a comprehensive assembly of parts becoming an organisation to achieve the stated goals.
2. A system is called OPEN if it has an interaction with the environment, and CLOSED if it does not have an interaction with the environment.
3. A system is defined, described and understood by the boundaries within which it performs.
4. The systems are subject to entropy, i.e. the tendency to "run-down". Closed systems suffer from entropy as they are cut off from the environment, while open systems interact with the environment and draw upon the support of resources to maintain a given condition.
5. Systems try to remain in an equilibrium or a steady state by taking resource to corrective action. This is possible when the system has its own feedback, i.e. an informational input about the state of the system.

The advantage of viewing the management as a system is that it enables us to see the critical variables, constraints and their interaction with one another. It forces the manager to look at the situation in such a way that due regard is given to the consequences arising out of interaction with the related elements or subjects. The process of management explained earlier consists of steps which are relationally linked and locked with each other.

In the context of the MIS, the systems approach to management is the most efficient one. The understanding of the basic principles of management theory evolved by the scholars Henri Fayol, Chester Barnard and Alvin Brown is very much essential. The application of management principles in an environment, recognizing the specific situation, is the accepted practice of management. Deviating from the principle to honor the situation and at the same time not diluting the management principle is the managerial skill. The manager must have a knowledge of management theory and principles as well as the skill to use them in a particular environment.

APPROACHES TO MANAGEMENT

Federik W Taylor is recognized as the father of scientific management. His principles can be summarized as follows:

1. Replace the rules of thumb with scientific rules.
2. Obtain a harmony in group action.
3. Achieve cooperation of human beings, rather than chaotic individualism.
4. Work for a maximum output.
5. Develop all workers to the fullest possible potential for their own highest possible prosperity.

Carl George Barth, Henry L Gantt, Frank and Lillian Gilberth are the disciples of Taylor, who promoted the thought of the scientific management.

The French industrialist Henri Fayol promoted the theory of operational management. Fayol is of the view that all the activities of an industrial or a business undertaking can be broken into operational functions such as technical, commercial, financial, security accounting and so on. He evolved the principles of operational management. These are also given in the following table.

Principles of Operational Management

Principle	***Comments***
Division of work	Efficient handling of work
Authority and responsibility	Pinpoints accountability
Discipline	Adherence to rules, regulations, norms and priorities
Unity of command	Single source direction to avoid confusion.
Unity of direction	Efforts should be directed towards one objective.
Subordination of individual to corporate interest	Ignore the individual interests for overall betterment of the organisation.
Remuneration	Should be fair for maximum satisfaction.
Centralisation	Authority should be centralized just enough for control. Overecentralisation is unproductive.
Scalar chains	Chain of authority vested into the people should not be short-circuited.
Order	Orderly arrangement of men, material and other resources is necessary.
Equity	Subordinates should be dealt with kindliness and justice to elicit loyalty and devotion.
Stability of tenure	It is necessary to ensure that the turnover of people is controlled for stability.
Initiative	The initiative of subordinates should be encouraged, sacrificing personal vanity of the superior.

Fayol regarded the elements of management as planning, organizing, commanding, coordinating and controlling. He believed that the operational management would succeed through the elements of management. Durin the same period when Taylor, Fayol and others were concentrating on the scientific management, another group of scholars was concentrating on industrial psychology and social theory as the basis for the scientific management.

Robert, Owen, Routree, Lyndall Urwick are credited to evolve the management with a focus on the personnel management can be improved through the social factors as morale and satisfactory relation between the members of work group and an effective management is possible only if only behaviour and group behaviour is managed through the interpersonal skills, viz., motivating, counseling, leading ad communicating.

Harthorne's studies brought out the theory that man is a "Social Animal" operating in the socio-technical system and therefore, the emphasis in effective management is on behavioural sciences. Chester Barnard advocated the theory of systems as an approach to the management. Barnard said that due to the physical and biological limitations of individuals, they cooperate in the work environment. The cooperation increases with effective and efficient incentives.

The further said that the cooperation is more effective if the members of the group communicate with one another, are willing to contribute to group action and have a conscious common purpose. He further said that a group of people in the system work as an organisation. An effective management is possible if the organisation is looked upon as a system of functions, a system of incentives, a system of authority and a direction and a system of logical decision making. The emergence of the modern management thought is credited to the social scientists, the behavioural scientists, the systems scientists and the practicing managers.

FUNCTIONS OF THE MANAGER

An individual who gets the things done is a Manager. It is necessary to distinguish between the tasks and the functions. While managing, a manager may perform the activities such as accounting, selling, manufacturing, purchasing etc. These activities are called as tasks and not as functions.

The activities that are performed through the managerial functions are Planning, Organising, Staffing, Directing, Coordinating and Controlling.

- Planning is a process of determining the goals and objectives and evolving strategies, policies, programmes and procedures for the achievement of these goals. The essence of the process is decision making as there are a number of alternatives in each of these factors.
- Organisation involves evolving the structure of the people working in the organisation and their roles. It specifies an authority structure and assigns activities to the people backed by the delegation of authority. Building a meaningful effective structure of authority and the relationship is known as organizing.
- Staffing involves manning the position in the organisation structure. It requires defining the manpower needs per position or centre of activity. It requires appropriate selection of the person ensuring that they together will achieve the goals and objectives of the organisation.
- Directing is a complex task of implementing the process of management. In the process, the manager is required to guide, clarify and solve the problems of the people and their activities. It is necessary to motivate the people to work for the goal with an interest and a confidence.
- Coordinating is the function which brings a harmony and smoothness in the various group activities and individual efforts directed towards the accomplishment of goals. It is a process of synchronizing individual actions and the efforts which may differ because of the differences in the personal goals and the common goals, the differences in the interpretation of methods and directions. it is, therefore, necessary to undertake centrally a process of coordinating and reconciling the differences in the approach, timing, efforts and interests towards a common goal. This task is to be carried out by the authority placed at a higher level in the organisation structure.
- Controlling is a process of measurement of an output, comparing it with the goals, the objectives and

the target, and taking corrective actions, if the output is falling short of the stated norms. Controlling ensures an achievement of the plan. The essence of the control lines in good planning. It helps to evaluaee the performance, highlights abnormal deviations, guides a manager to take specific corrective actions. This may call for a change of plan, a realloation of resources, a modification of methods, procedures and even the organisation structure. The control is central to the managerial function.

The manager's main function, therefore, is planning and control of the business functions and operations. While performing these functions, he resorts to the scientific approach to the management.

MANAGERS AND THE ENVIRONMENT

All mangers, whether they are managing a business, a school, a hospital, a Government Department, or any enterprise, work in an environment in which the organisation operates. There are a number of forces which are generated in the environment, which have an impact on the managerial performance. These forces may be from within or from outside the organisation. They affect, directly or indirectly, the process of the managerment and a manager is required to meet these forces effectively.

While to some extent the internal environment is controllable, the external environment is beyond his control. Since it is proven that the external environment also has an impact on the business manager's performance, it is necessary to know and understand the environment. For the purpose of discussion, the external environment is classified into 5 classes as the enconomic, the technological, the social, the political and the ethical environment.

Economic Environment

The economic environment comprises capital, labour, price changes, productivity, fiscal and monetary policy and customers.

Capital

It is required to run the organisation. The enterprise needs a long-term and a short term capital. The capital required can be either from the internal sources or borrowed from the financial institutions. When a capital is borrowed, it is borrowed at an interest. The organisation is forced to borrow for various reasons and the interest charged by the lending financial institution forms the cost of the capital. Hence management of the capital is an important aspect of the business.

Labour

The next important cost of a business is the cost of labour. The cost of labour is determined every two to three hears by a union agreement. The settlement of an agreement is based on the cost of living index, the industry wage standards, the availability of labour, etc. These aspects are external to the organisation and a manager has no control on them.

Price Changes

Price changes occur in the economy for various reasons. The change occur because of decrease in the demand and supply, the changes in the consumer behaviour, in the consumption pattern and the money supply and so on. The price changes affect the cost of raw material and labour and on these changes a manager has no control.

Productivity

Productivity is a result of the capital, labour and technology. Many a times an organisation's business is taken over by better technology. The costs are affected by the technology changes affecting the productivity. The manager has to respond quickly to the technological changes to save the business.

Fiscal and Monetary Policy

The Government announces fiscal policies and controls them. The organisation's profit position is affected by these policies. These policies affect the credit terms, the prices of the inputs and the money supply affecting the cash position of the organisation. A manager has a very little leverage to deal with these policy changes.

Customers

The customers rule the business, especially when the business operates in a buyer's market. In a competitive world, it is very difficult to predict the customer behaviour. The changes in the demands occur with growth and technology. The customer does not show consistent preference to the product. The change in the business orientation to suit the changes in the consumer demand is a difficult task for the manager. It is not always possible to predict these changes well in advance in order to take any managerial action to meet the changed situation.

Technological Environment

The technology has a major impact on the business. It affects the business prospects, cuts down the profits and forces the management to change the course of the business operates. It requires changes in the product design and promotes new concepts. It generates new business opportunities. Any change in technology changes the work culture, the methods and the systems. It affects the speed of the operations and gives a boost to the productivity of the production systems. Examples of technological changes are seen in aviation, electronics, energy, communication, consumer goods industry, optics, medicines and manufacturing.

Social Environment

The social environment is built around the attitudes, the desires, the expectations, the degree of intelligence and education, the beliefs and customs, the religion, the caste and creed of the people. The social environment is built in centuries and hence it is deeply rooted in the society. The social environment has an important impact on the business and the organisation productivity.

Social factors create an attitude towards the work, generate the product choices and manipulate the consumer behaviour. It is well known that it took a lot of time to convince the farmers in India about the use of fertilisers. It is recognised that rural marketing is different from the urban marketing. In spite of the technological advances, frozen foods are not finding consumer preferences. Introduction of computers in the service industry is still a difficult proposition. A number of such examples can be cited to prove that the social environment affects business and makes the manager's task very difficult and challenging.

Political Environment

The political factor is the most important factor which affects the business in India environment. The unstable political environment brings stagnancy in the business development. The change sin ruling part bring economic policy changes, affecting the business. The sectoral preferences, such as an agricultural versus an industrial, an educational versus a basic research, an investment in the service sector versus a core sector come about with change in the ruling political party and its policies. Such changes have a long-term impact on business performance. The manager has to deal with such changes effectively.

Ethical Environment (Systems of a Moral Behaviour)

Some business problems arise due to failing on the ethical grounds. The government has enacted many laws and regulations to bring about harmonious operations in business. However, some aspects of the business operations are left as ethics, called the business ethics. The business ethics emerge from the professional conduct, the business norms and codes on confidentiality, the payment and documentation, the adherence to generally accepted standards of accounting and auditing. Business ethics is a set of norms which are universally accepted as a business behaviour.

All these factors discussed so far, are beyond the control of the manager. At best he can predict, assess, evaluate and take such actions which will help him to control the situation.

MANAGEMENT AS A CONTROL SYSTEM

Planning, organising, staffing, coordinating, directing and controlling are the various steps in a management process. All the steps prior to a control are necessary but are not necessarily self-assuring the results unless it is followed by a strong control mechanism. The management experts have viewed these steps as 'Management Control System'. They postulate the hypothesis that unless a control is exercised on the process, the goals will not be achieved. They advocate a system of effective control to ensure the achievement of the business objectives. A definition of control is the process through which managers assure that actual activities conform to the planned activities, leading to the achievement of the stated common goals.

The control process measures a progress towards those goals and enables the manager to detect the deviations from the original plan in time to take corrective actions before it is too late. Robert J Mockler defines and points out the essential elements of the control process. The basic steps of the control process are given in the figure given next. The management is a systematic effort to set the performance standards in line with the performances objectives, to design the information feedback systems, to compare the actual performance with these predetermined standards, to identify the deviations from the standards, to measure its significance and to take corrective action in case of significant deviations. This systematic effort is undertaken through the management control system.

The control system is essential to meet the environmental changes discussed earlier, to meet the complexity of today's business, to correct the mistakes made by the people and effectively monitor the delegation process. A reliable and effective control system has the following features.

Early Warning Mechanism

This is a mechanism of predicting the possibility of achieving the goals and the standards before it is too late and allowing the manager to take corrective actions.

Performance Standard

The performance standard must be measurable and acceptable to all the organisation. The system should have meaningful standards relating to the work areas, responsibility and managerial functions and so on. For example, the top management would have standards relating to the business performance, such as production, sales, inventory, quality, etc. The operational management would have standards relating to the shift production, rejections, down time, utilisation of resources and sale in a typical market segment and so on. The chain of standards, when achieved, will ensure an achievement the goals of the organisation.

Strategic Controls

In every business there are strategic areas of control known as the critical success factors. The system should recognise them and have controls instituted on them.

Feedback

The control system would be effective, if it continuously monitors the performance and sends the information to the control centre for action. It should not only highlight the progress but also the deviations.

Accurate and Timely

The feedback should be accurate in terms of results and should be communicated on time for corrective action.

Realistic

The system should be realistic so that the cost of control is far less than the benefits. The standards are realistic and are believed as achievable. Sufficient incentive and reward are to be provided to motivate the people.

The information Flow

The system should have the information flow aligned with the organisation structure and the decision makers should ensure that the right people get the right information for action and decision making.

Exception Principle

The system should selectively approve some significant deviations from the performance standards on the principle of management by exception.

A standard is meaningful when it is achievable and provides a challenge to the achieve.

A management control system has a set of objectives, standards to measure, a feedback mechanism and an action centre as elements of the system. They need to be properly evolved and instituted in the organisation with due recognition to the internal and the external environment.

The system as a whole should be flexible to be changed with ease so that the impact of changed environment is handled effectively.

MANAGEMENT BY EXCEPTION

Pareto's principle of 80:20 is applicable to the management of enterprise. Several terms have been coined on this principle such as management by objectives, management by results, management of strategic areas. At the root of the management methodology is the management by exception. When the management operates under time constraint, each manager has to allocate specific time for the several demands made on his time. It is, therefore, necessary for him to attend to the situation where his attention is necessary. Such attention would lead to an action, a decision or a wait-and-see approach. If all the situations are considered in a routine manner, it consumes time and tends to be neglected over a period of time. An efficient manager tries for selective attention to manage within the available time resource. The principle evolved, therefore, is of the management by exception. The exception is decided on the impact a situation would make on the performance, the process and the standards set in the management control system.

The exception is defined as a significant deviation from the performance or the process and the standard. The deviation could be abnormal on a positive or on a negative side of the standard. The deviation could be predictive or could be arising out of random causes in the business operations. It is, therefore, necessary to assess whether the deviation is sporadic or consistently coming in, calling for managerial attention. The manager is interested in knowing the significant deviation by the yardsticks of consistency and not out of random causes. The significant deviations are exceptional in nature and require to be attended to immediately. A manager is further interested in knowing the reasons behind the exceptional nature of the situation. It is possible to trace the reasons of deviation and it is possible to take a corrective action.

The significant deviation can occur on account of wrong performance standards and wrong management process. Many a times the standards are set very low and they need to be looked into to avoid the misuse of resources. If the standards are set too high, then the people fail to achieve them on account of demotivating factor of the high standards.

A wrong management process refers to a variety of decisions a manager has taken in the planning, organising, staffing, directing and controlling a given management task. These decisions relate to the choice and the allocation of resources, the methods of using resources, the application of the tools and the techniques, the use of manpower by way of staffing and the manner in which the efforts are coordinating in the organisation. For an efficient and an effective management, without loss of time, it is, therefore, necessary to report the significant deviations to the right persons in the organisation. In this regard a manager himself has to provide the conditions of exceptions in the control system so that they are highlighted and informed. The management by exception commands grip on the management process. The managerial effort gets directed towards the goal with the purpose of achievement.

MIS: A SUPPORT TO THE MANAGEMENT

The management process is executed through a variety of decisions taken at each step of planning, organising, staffing, directing, coordinating and control. As discussed in Chapter 1, the MIS aids decision making. If the management is able to spell out the decisions required to be taken, the MIS can be designed suitably. The decisions required to be taken in these steps are tabulated in the following table.

Steps in management	***Decision***
Planning	A selection from various alternatives – strategies, resources, methods, etc.
Organisation	A selection of a combination out of several combinations of the goals, people, resources, method and authority
Staffing	Providing a proper manpower complement
Directing	Choosing a method from the various methods of directing the efforts in the organistion.
Coordinating	Choice of the tools and the techniques for coordinating the efforts to optimum results.
Controlling	A selection of the exceptional conditions and the decision guidelines.

The objective of the MIS is to provide information for a decision support in the process of management. It should help in such a way that the business goals are achieved in the most efficient manner. Since the decision making is not restricted to a particular level, the MIS is expected to support all the levels of the management in conducting the business operating. Unless the MIS becomes a management aid, it is not useful to the organisation.

APPLICATIONS OF MIS

This seciton is an introduction to the business applications of Management Information System. It gives an overview of the application and does not give small details which may be specific to a typical organisation. The approach development is on the basis of database and not conventional file system. The MIS model of an application, considers transaction processing as a basis. The online transaction processing system develops data for DBMS and the application development is based on such database.

For each application, inputs, which are processed by online transaction processing (OLTP) systems are determined. The system designer develops the applications with the objective of accounting the transaction based results and providing the reports on the same. The second objective is to provide a Query system for assessment of the status on record, result or document. The system provides on the spot screen display showing a status, such as stock of an item, balance of an account, position of purchase order and so on. Third objective is to provide a system of analysis of processed data revealing certain business trends or results. It is supposed to give certain analytical assessment of the even which will throw light on the validity of decisions, policy and rules. It is also supposed to provide certain guidelines and norms for strategic and tactical planning.

The analytical information provides support for decision making in the Decision Support System (DSS). The analysis system provides fund of information at all level for planning and execution of business operations. The fourth objective is to provide control information to ensure that the business runs as per the plan, progress in a set direction and achieves the goals.

The control information is generated by using the standards, norms, targets and budgets. The actual results are compared with these entities and exceptions are highlighted. Whenever possible, the information is provided on the basis of feed forward control, i.e., providing early signal of probable adverse conditions or results. The designer of business application focuses the development on the aspect of accounting, querying, analysis and control.

The report generation is decided on the basis of certain business information needs. These needs are Statutory compliance, Knowledge update, operation management, decision analysis Control and Action. The reports are designed for screen display or for print. The contents of the reports are decided as per users of the information. The frequency, duration and coverage of the report is decided as per the user requirements.

A typical information system begins with OLTP System, uses RDBMS for creation of Database, 4 GL for application development and SQL for querying and report generation. It uses programme for complex data processing and report generation. It uses business models accounting and commercial principles for processing the information leading to business results. The information system is designed on the principle of open system design, providing flexibility and friendliness to the users of the system.

A typical information system primarily serves the needs at function levels such as Personnel Finance, Production, Materials, Marketing and Corporate Business Management. These systems when integrated provide cross functional information to management highlighting the business implications of the decisions taken on one area of the business or the other integrated systems provide data and information for business planning at the middle management level and for strategic planning at the top management level.

PERSONAL MANAGEMENT

Personnel management function has the primary objective or providing suitable manpower in number and with certain ability, skills and knowledge, as the business organisation demands from time to time. Its goal is to control personnel cost through continuous increase in manpower productivity by resorting to the following technique.

- Human Resource Development through training and upgrading the skills.
- Motivation through leadership and job enrichment.
- Promotion and rewards through performance appraisal.
- Grievance handling.
- Structuring the organisation.

Input Transaction Documents

The various forms or documents which serve as inputs for the personnel department are listed as follows:

1. Personnel application form
2. Appointment letter
3. Attendance and leave record
4. Biodata, self and family
5. Appraisal form
6. Production/Productivity data on the jobs.
7. Wage/Salary agreement
8. Record of complaints, grievances, accidents

9. Industry data on wage/salary structure
10. Industry data on manpower, skills, qualifications
11. Record of source of manpower – University, Institutions, Companies
12. Record on manpower application trend in view of mechanisation, automation and computerisation

Applications

The viewers of the database are personnel managers, heads of the human resource development department and top management.

Accounting

Following entities are accounted in the personnel management system.

1. Attendance
2. Manpower
3. Leave
4. Salary/Wages, statutory deductions
5. Loans and deductions
6. Accidents
7. Production data
8. Skills
9. Bio Data
10. Family data

Query

Personnel management has queries as to the following:

1. Who is who?
2. Strength of a section, department, division.
3. Number of persons with a particular skill.
4. Attendance, leave and absenteeism record of all employees.
5. Salary/Wage of employees.
6. Designations and number of persons holding these designations.
7. Personal records of the employees.

The queries are processed with employee number, skill code, department/division code as keys.

Analysis

1. Analysis of attendance by a class of employee.
2. Leave analysis by a group of employees.
3. Trend in the leave record.
4. Analysis of accidents and types thereof.
5. Analysis of salary/wages structure.

6. Analysis of overtime.

Control

1. Probable absence versus workload.
2. Projection of personnel cost against manpower increase.
3. Assessment of accident records against safety measures taken.
4. Personnel cost versus Industry cost and its projection.
5. Projection of manpower needs and evolving recruitment and training programmes.

Reports

The reports of the system will be used mainly by the Personnel Department and the Top Management. Following is the list of reports of different categories.

Statutory reports

There are some statutory reports which are to be prepared by the personnel department of almost all the organisation. These are as follows:

1. Attendance record (muster).
2. Strength of the employees by category – permanent, trainees and apprentices.
3. Provident Fund, ESI Reports, Ledgers and Returns.
4. Accident Reports
5, Income Tax Form 16, 24A.
6. Strength of employees to Director General of Technical Development (DGTD).

These reports are submitted to the Provident Fund Authorities, ESI Authorities, Income Tax Department, Directorate of Industrial Safety and Health and Labour Department.

Knowledge updates

1. Daily attendance report.
2. Employee strength.
3. Joining and transfers of the employees.
4. Personnel cost by department, job, product.
5. Periodical statement showing personnel cost by salary/wages, overtime.

Operation update

1. Daily attendance to plan the workload.
2. Overtime versus work completed.
3. Projected absenteeism and distribution of workload.
4. Cot of personnel by jobs or work completed.

Decision analysis

1. Analysis of attendance for season, festival and skills, scheduling of the job accordingly.
2. Overtime analysis by department, employees and job to decide the strength of personnel.

3. Analysis of accidents and deciding on safety measures and training.
4. Cost analysis by personnel versus jobs as skills and planning for new recruitement.

Action reports

1. Recruitment and additional manpower or subcontracting of jobs.
2. Acceptance of orders on the basis of workload.
3. Reduction, transfer and reorganisation of employees to control costs.
4. Preparation of training and development programmes with specific needs.

Most of these reports are used by people in operation management. The information needs at the top management emerge when issues of controlling the wage bill, entering into new agreement/s, etc. come up. Most of the application development is standard and rule based, requiring very little modifications.

FINANCIAL MANAGEMENT

Financial management function has a primary objective of meeting the financial needs of the business, from time to time, by way of providing working capital and long-term loans to run the business with the goal of containing the cost of capital at the minimum. The second objective of financial management is to meet the statutory compliance by way of declaring the audited and fulfil the obligations to the shareholders. In meeting these objectives Financial Management uses a variety of tools and techniques as under.

1. Break Even Analysis
2. Cost Analysis
3. Crash Flow Projections
4. Ratio Analysis
5. Capital Budgeting and ROI Analysis
6. Financial Modelling
7. Management Accounting
8. Expense Analysis, Auditing and Control.

Input Transaction Document

1. Payment: To suppliers, authorities, employees, shareholders, financial institutions and other others.
2. Receipts: From customers, authorities, employees, financial institution and others.
3. Data from Stock Exchange on the shares prices, consolidated financial results of the other Companies, etc.
4. Data from stock Exchange on the shares prices, consolidated financial results of the other Companies etc.

Transactions are payments and receipts and they are documented through journal vouchers, bills, debit notes, credit notes, receipts and transfer documents. The payments and receipts are for a variety of purpose and they are documented in typical formats suiting the respective business organisations.

Applications

In financial management major application is the Financial Accounting System, which accounts for the financial transactions of the company and produces financial results fro the company. It produces balance sheet for the company where the performance of the company is published in standard format prescribed by the government. There are companies where fixed deposits and share accounting are also part of financial functions. The system is made so comprehensive that it not only collects financial data but also collects data on different matters such as job, department, division and so on.

Due to versatility of the financial management system, it becomes a repository of financial data which can be used in the other systems of the organisation. It forms a basis for certain reports which are required by the top management. The viewers of the financial database are, finance managers, cost controllers, auditors, materials managers, marketing managers, company secretaries and the top management.

Accounting

The system accounts for all money transactions which have taken place, directly or indirectly and which affect the company. The memory transactions may affect several aspects of the business such as Sales, Production, Purchase, Travel, Shareholding etc.

The financial management system accounts for the following:

1. Sales
2. Purchase
3. Salary/Wages
4. Inventory
5. Expenses
6. Capital Purhcases
7. Fixed Deposits
8. Sharehoders' Funds
9. Income Tax
10. Sales Tax
11. Excise Duty
12. Customs Duty
13. Octroi and other Local Taxes
14. Consumption
15. Budgets
16. Fixed Assets

The system accounts for such main heads and then accounts for its subsidiary heads. For example, it accounts for sales and gives sales ledger and sales register. It accounts for purchase and give creditors ledger. It accounts for all payments to employees and gives personnel entertainment, miscellaneous purchase and produces a subsidiary ledger.

Financial management accounting system provides facility to perform multidimensional accounting of financial transactions. It provides a lot of data and information which forms a valid database for other applications in the business.

Query

The query system throws light on the debit or credit balance of an account. It shows the details of transactions which have resulted into that balance. The queries are normally put to ascertain the business results by its subsidiary. For example, the query could be on sales with respect to the customer. The query could be on sales of the product.

The query is processed for the following with the respective codes as keys.

1. Main account
2. Subsidiary account
3. Location (Factory, Branch, etc.)
4. Document (Bills, Credit note, Debit note, Receipt, etc.)

The query processes the transactions and shows the current status of the reference such as Account, Document, etc.

Decision analysis

Financial management calls for a number of decisions, based on the analysis of the financial status of the company. The decisions fall in all areas of financial management. The decisions are, borrowing of short-term working capital, source of finance, analysis of debtors and creditors and revision of credit terms, capital budgeting and selection of investment alternatives, etc.

The applications which support the above decisions are:

1. Cash flow analysis
2. Sources and uses of funds
3. Debtors analysis and aging
4. Creditors analysis and aging
5. Budget analysis
6. Ratio analysis and management norms
7. Capital budgeting and ranking of investment alternatives
8. Cist analysis of various production inputs and alternatives

Control

The cost of running a business increases, when the business does not progress on a planned basis. The lags and leads in activities, delays in completion of tasks and non-performance of certain business functions give rise to additional costs eating away the margin in the business. The control is exercised, based on the exception funds in the business operations. Some exceptions are mentioned as follows:

1. Accounts receivables, outstanding beyond the acceptable norms.
2. Advance to creditors and non realisation of obligations.
3. Valuation of non-moving inventory for disposal.
4. Analysis of non-moving accounts and legal actions.
5. Shortage of funds in excess of planned and rescheduling of activities, priorities.
6. Cost overruns beyond the norms and action on alternatives.
7. Performance analysis of lines of business showing adverse performance leading to the decision – whether to continue or discontinue the line of business.

The control applications lead to decision or revision of business terms, going for alternative source of finance, review of certain activities to cut down the expenses, reallocation of resources, revision of schedules, plans and priorities.

Financial control takes longer time to show the effect and hence they are to be carried out well in advance before the crisis crops up. Most of the control applications are based on the principle of feed forward control where failure is sensed earlier and action is desired immediately.

Reports

A major portion of a financial management system is devoted to statutory compliance and operations update. The top management heavily relies on the reports source form the financial management system. The information emerging from the financial management system.

The information emerging from the financial management system, is found reliable, as the basic data, is thoroughly checked, audited and validated through a computer system. Many companies rely on he financial management system for management information.

Statutory compliance

1. Tax Returns
2. Registers: Sales Tax, Excise, Tax deducted at source.
3. Declaration of certain results, to the financial institutions.
4. Declaration of financial results to the public every six months.
5. Declaration of annual results to the Board, Shareholders and Public within a stipulated time.

Knowledge updates

1. Monthly Trial Balance, Balance Sheet and Profit and Loss Account.
2. Stock Valuation.
3. Accounts receivables and aging
4. Accounts payables and aging
5. Expenses on major accounts.
6. Cash position.
7. Payments and receipts which are statutory obligations.
8. Sales, Purchase of assets by certain classification.
9. Overall business achievements in major lines of business.

Operations update

1. Filling of statutory returns and reports.
2. Statutory payments such as Advance Tax, Sales Tax, Octroi, Excise Duty, etc.
3. Transactions executed and accounted in the system.
4. Report on finished goods, despatches and invoicing.
5. Reports on material receipts and payments to the suppliers.
6. Obligatory payments such as rents, insurance premium, membership fees, interest and dividend.

If operations updates are satisfactory, the management can infer that business transactions are taking place in order.

Decision analysis

1. Break even Analysis for cost and price decision.
2. Return on Investment Analysis for choice of investment.
3. Trend Analysis on price of selected commodities which play a crucial role in business performance leading to decisions of alternative material, supplier, change in product design, etc.
4. Cash flow, sources and uses of funds, leading to control on expenses and selection of alternative source of financing.
5. Analysis of current and fixed assets in terms of use and decision on alternate use or disposal.
6. Analysis of current liabilities and decision on liquidation on priority basis.
7. Analysis of overdue receivables and decision on the revision of terms or commercial and legal, actions.

Action update

Though decision analysis indicates the areas of decisions, action is taken in exceptional cases. Exception reports on implementation of the decision and its impact on the business are listed as follows:

1. Overdue receivables
   - Legal action
   - Termination of business association.
2. Non supply of goods and services but advance paid.
   - Legal Action
   - Revision of terms
   - Termination of business association.
3. Payments to creditors, where penalties are involved.
4. Poor usage of fixed assets and disposal.
5. Non-moving inventory of, say, more than two years and its disposal.
6. Evolving new systems and procedures to control expenses and implementation.

PRODUCTION MANAGEMENT

The objective of Production Management (PM) functions is, to provide manufacturing services to the organisation. This involves the manufacture of products of a certain specified quality and within certain costs in a stipulated time fulfilling the promises given to the customer.

The production management function is supported by other functions, viz., Production Planning and Control, Industrial Engineering, Maintenance and Quality Control. It has a very strong interface with Materials Management function. The organisation of the Production Management differs according to the type of production, i.e., Jobshop or continuous. It also varies with the production policy of the organisation, viz., where the production is initialised against a customer order or for stock. The system and methodology differs with respect to the manufacturing technology the organisation has adopted.

The functional goals of the production management are fuller utilisation of the manufacturing capacity, minimal rejections, maximum uptime of plant and equipment and meeting the delivery promises. The function assumes key importance, when business strength is in technology and manufacturing and the market for product and services exists. The function is pegged with the responsibility of managing high investment in plant, equipment and machinery. It also has to control the large labour force at its disposal.

Input Transaction Documents

The production management is conducted through innumerable transactions. They relates to planning, issuing and controlling the various tasks involved in the course of production. The details are listed as under:

1. Production programme
2. Production schedule
3. Process planning sheet
4. Job card
5. Job status advice
6. Quality assurance rating form
7. Finished goods advice
8. Breakdown advice
9. Material requirement
10. Material requisition
11. Customer order

The production management also uses standards and norms extensively developed over a period of time as inputs in the system. These are generally known as production rate, available capacity, labour complement, material usage standards, rejection norms, etc.

The transaction documents mentioned above are indicative and may be more or les different, depending upon the type of production, nature of production and industry. The input data in each transaction would also vary from industry to industry as would the production methodology adopted by the organisation. The systems and procedures used by the organisation in performing the production function also vary respectively.

Applications

The production management is performed through production planning and control, bill of material processing, drawings and process planning, scheduling and monitoring systems as support systems.

Accounting

Production management accounts for a number of entities in a systematic manner to fulfil the needs of production management function in various tasks and activities. The entities are as follows:

1. Quality of production with respect to a time period.
2. Material requirement and its usage.
3. Rejection quantity at each intermediate stage and at the final stage.
4. Breakdown incidence.
5. Labour complement with respect to a period.
6. Use of power, fuel and consumables.

7. Machine and facilities utilisation
8. Labour hours.

Accounting of the above entities is essential to build up the information base to develop norms and standards for use in planning. It also provides day to day or period by period update on the events, activities and tasks that the production management is expected to perform.

Query

The queries in the production management relate to seeking of status of job or information on fixed entities such as machine or worker or process data.

1. Status of the job or order in terms of stage and level of completion.
2. Production programme and jobs schedules.
3. Load status on machine, group of machines.
4. Status on availability of material.
5. Standard information on machines, tools, specifications.
6. Standard information on skills and capacities of each worker.
7. Standard information on products and processes.

Decision analysis

The production management is required to make a number of decisions both for long-term and short-term period. The typical decisions are:

1. Make or buy
2. Make or subcontract
3. Use of alternative material
4. Use of alternative process
5. Evolving optimum product mix/job mix
6. Rescheduling the loading of jobs
7. Planning and scheduling of jobs
8. Selection of production facilities
9. Selection of alternative maintenance policies.

These decision analysis applications help to make policy decisions on techno-economic basis. The decision implications are on cost, productivity, efficiency, proper utilisation of the manufacturing facility and usage of material and physical resources.

Control

These application are developed to control production programme, production capacity and quality of production. The other issues with which the production management has to deal are utilisation of the production capacity and labour force. It has to ensure that plant, machines and equipment, having high investment are fully utilised. There are always some jobs, which have to be pushed through the production programme by way of scheduling and loading the jobs on the machines. These are the areas where control of the production management is essential.

The exceptions which need to be highlighted are:

1. Excessive product rejection on account of material and/or process.
2. Hold up of key jobs beyond a certain limit.
3. Excessive work in process inventory.
4. Continued breakdown of the manufacturing facility beyond a certain period.
5. Utilisation of key facilities below a limit.
6. Continuous significant deviation from standards or norms of production rate.
7. Backlog of a large number of orders and failure to meet promised delivery date.

Reports and Screen Display

Statutory compliance

There are very few areas in production management which require information for reporting to authorities under the category of statutory compliance. There are some industries, which require to keep the account of raw material and finished goods and submit the report to the Government. The industries which are classified under Director General of Technical Development (DGTD) are required to inform certain data on production and production hours to DGTD.

Knowledge update

For the purpose of evolving standards and norms on the various aspects of he production function, analysed information is built up in the system for subsequent use, for example, the data on the down-time of production facilities, a typical reason for rejection, output of various job versus machines and so on.

The information is kept up-to-date enabling the managers in the production function to plan the production properly by using these standards. The data on job completion time helps to give correct delivery promises to the customers. The data on breakdowns, causes of breakdowns and the down-time helps to assess the correct available capacity for production. The data on absenteeism helps to assess the available labour hours by skills and trade.

Accounting, decision analysis and control applications provide a lot of valuable key data which build the knowledge base for use in the production management.

Operations updates

These reports provide information on day to day events. The statistics, such as the production per day, the rejections by process or job, the machine breakdowns the jobs completed and handed over for inspection and so on is collected and reported to the concerned operating personnel as the latest update.

The reporting of highlights – planned versus actual – on every important aspects of production function. The Decision Support Systems (DSS) are extensively used to enable the management to take decisions. The programming models, simulation techniques, material requirement planning systems, artificial intelligence and knowledge based systems, planning and scheduling systems provide continues analysis on many issues which affect the production function.

The analysis through DSS helps to make decisions, such as optimum product mix, alternate loading pattern, alternate assignment of jobs and machines, use of alternate material, tools and process. Some of the decisions change old practices, conventions and decision rules. The fall in the category of strategic and tactical decisions.

Action update

These reports provide information update on the post implementation scenario of decisions. The reports inform whether the decision has resulted into expected performance as designed. The information provides knowledge whether the implemented decision is proper or not. It provides an early opportunity to the management to correct its own decision if the action taken by the management.

For example, a new process is evolved and implemented. The information on quantity produced, quantity rejected, quality level achieved and its comparison with the earlier process gives sufficient guidelines to confirm whether decision to switch over to a new process is correct or not. Once the action update confirms that the decision is correct, its reporting will be discontinued.

MATERIALS MANAGEMENT

The objective of Materials Management (MM) is to provide material for production, maintenance and services at economical prices, in an appropriate quantity and quality with least stockouts and with no extra cost of carrying the inventory.

The function of materials management is important, as it is the single largest function, which takes away large capital as working capital. Secondly, it is important from the point of view of controlling the material cost and the cost of carrying inventory.

Apart from providing material to production, maintenance and services, it has a responsibility of searching new substitutes to reduce the cost of material, reduction of inventory and disposal of non-moving and slow-moving inventory. The function deals with suppliers of all kinds and has to evolve systems and procedures suitable to manage the function and reduce paperwork.

The managerial task revolves around a number of aspects such as balancing the cost or procuring with the cost of carrying inventory, the cost of stockouts with the cost of production hold up, the price with the quality, performance with price. The function is also controlled by corporate management, through audits and checks, to ensure the procurement of material is done at an economic price.

Input Transaction Documents

The materials management has the following transactions, which need to be covered in the system.

1. Purchase requisition.
2. Purchase order.
3. Receipt of goods.
4. Return of goods to supplier.
5. Issue for production.
6. Return from production
7. Certification of bill for payment.

Apart from these basic transactions, the materials management draws data from quotations, tenders and from documents in Excise, Sales Tax, Octroi. It also depends on the data from external sources such as Industrial Associations, Trade Journals, Research Laboratories and so on. The nature of documents is non-standards through it may become tedious and lengthy. A typical purchase transaction will be executed only if it is processed through, at least, ten to twelve documents. The materials Management deals with a variety of supplier, small, medium, Government and foreign suppliers, each having typical requirement of selling the goods, which the materials management has to fulfil. Owing to the variety and complexity of transactions, its processing is a completed task, demanding high level scrutiny, checks and controls and accounting which is time consuming and monotonous. The materials management function has to interface with finance and production while executing the functional responsibility.

Applications

The materials management function is conducted through several administrative and management systems, each having different purpose and focus. It has the following systems:

1. Forecasting and planning
2. Procurement
3. Purchase ordering
4. Goods receipt
5. Inspection
6. Issuing the material
7. Processing the returns
8. Bill passing and control

Through these systems, different functional needs of accounting, query, analysis, decision making and controls are fulfilled.

Accounting

The materials management function account for a number of things, as shown below:

1. Purchase quantity
2 Issue quantity
3 Stocks
4. Goods returns
5 Rejections
6. Performance
7. Value of purchase
8. Average or standard rate of accounting

The systems are Purchase ordering and accounting. Accounting of stocks and purchase, Consumption, Stocks and Performance of supplier.

Accounting is a major basic function of the material management, which provides a lot of valuable data to other systems within materials management and also to other functional systems, viz. finance and production.

Query

Queries in the materials management largely centre around price, supplier, stock and pending aspects of purchase, returns and payments. The query may be on one key or on several keys together. The query may be on an item seeking the latest purchase price or it may be on an item seeking a price in a particular purchase order placed on a particular supplier.

The query could be a processed one seeking information on, say the number of stockouts in the last six months of a particular item. Or it could be on the items in case of which the stock is zero and supply is not due in the current month. The query applications are designed as processing routines which are often put in the system. The others are handled through SQL by the users of the system.

Decision analysis

As materials is the single largest component of the cost, in nay manufacturing organisation, a majority of the decisions centre around the cost of purchase and the cost of materials consumed.

The first major decision in the function is price of an item. The prices vary from supplier to supplier and the supplier differ from each other on a number of accounts. The price is a commercial decision influenced by reliability of supply, quality of material and dependability. The materials management is required to make multidimensional analysis to decide on price.

A DSS can be developed around the parameters requiring analysis. The second major decision the materials management has to take, is stocking of items. The stocking decision means, whether to stock or not, if to stock, what are the inventory levels, viz., minimum stock, maximum stock, reorder level, economic order quantity and so on.

The third major decision the materials management has to take, is on the system of controlling the item. There are three systems of control, viz., Fixed Order Quantity (FOQ) and Reorder Level (ROL) System, Periodic review System, with varying order quantity and fixed period ordering with quantity not more than a fixed quantity. Several inventory control systems are available under the category of static and dynamic inventory models with finer variations suitable for varying requirements.

To make these decisions, inventory is analysed in a number of ways, viz., A-B-C analysis, Production Holding and other, imports and indigenous and so on. The analysis of inventory indicate the importance and critically of an item to decide on Inventory Control Policy. The decision analysis applications are developed to aid planning and control decisions in the Materials Management.

Control

The performance of the materials management function, is evaluated on four accounts, viz., capital blocked in the inventory, number of stockouts affecting the production activity, reliability and dependability of suppliers and cost of purchase. The management stipulates certain norms on these accounts which become the reference for control.

Inventory is valued every month to indicate whether capital blocked is above and budget. The stockouts are counted and compared with the norm. The delivery promise and quality of material supplied is rated to arrive at performance index of the supplier and compared with the norm. Lastly, the purchase cost is computed with purchase price plus taxes and duties and compared with the purchase budget.

In all these comparisons, whenever adverse results are seen, the system selects items and suppliers, based on some criteria, for specific action or decision. The decisions may be to find a substitute item or another supplier. It could be that the system of inventory control is changed for the item. It may be a possibility that inventory control parameters need a revision.

There are a number of cases where inventory turns out to be non-moving or non-usable and needs to be disposed off. These could be a decision on the source of supply, where instead of imports, indigenous supply could be economical. There could be a decision on the choice of supplier based on terms and conditions of supply, payment of advance, credit terms and delivery. The control applications help in making and implementing the decisions.

Reports and Display

There are many reports and screen displays in the Materials Management System. They are largely based on accounting applications and decision analysis systems. They are produced at regular intervals, say monthly or quarterly. The report screens are developed to answer adhoc queries on various aspects of the materials management function, viz., price, stock specifications, supplier, pending positions and valuations.

Statutory compliance

Reporting the value of inventory in balance sheet of the company is a statutory compliance. Maintenance of registers and filling returns in the areas of Sales Tax, Octroi, Excise Duty and Customs Duty is a statutory obligation.

The essential reports are:

1. Stock ledger
2. Valued stock statement
3. Octroi register
4. MODVAT register
5. Excise duty returns registers such as RG1, RT12, etc.
6. Customs bond register
7. Returns on tax deducted at source

All statutory obligations are to be fulfilled and invariably each one of them has a date of submission. The source of these registers are required to be kept up-to-date, as they are subject to surprise scrutiny by the concerned authorities. Hence, processing of data correctly on a regular basis is an absolute necessity. The data source for these outputs is accounting applications developed to account receipts, issues, consumptions, returns and payments to suppliers.

Knowledge update

A materials manager to build up the knowledge on a couple of aspects of the function. These aspects are:

1. Price fluctuations and trend
2. Information on alternative materials with specification and test results
3. New suppliers and source of supplies
4. Current incidence of taxes and duties
5. Value of inventory computed at standard price
6. Performance of suppliers
7. Stockouts
8. Value on non-moving inventory
9. Materials required for the next planning period.

The reports on the knowledge base are as under:

1. Reports on price trends of high value and high purchase rate items
2. Compiled reports from trade journals on new material and source
3. Statements showing basic price, taxes, duties on items of high consumption value
4. Stock ledger with value
5. Value of stockouts versus total inventory
6. Value of non-moving inventory versus total inventory
7. report on the material requirement for the next planning period in quantity and value

Operations update

Operations updates are useful for day to day functioning of operating departments, viz., Purchase, Stores and Workshop. It is necessary to know the arrival of material, whether inspected and taken in stock. The second update is on the issue of material for consumption. The third update is on the purchase action against a purchase requisition. These updates are provided either through screen on through report. These reports are:

1. Daily Goods Received Register
2. Statement showing items in short supply or stockouts
3. Reports on purchase requisitions received but not converted into purchase orders
4. Statement on supplies due but not yet received
5. Statement on payment due to suppliers but not yet paid
6. Statement on supplies received and rejected

The operations update help to perform day to day routine operations at the junior management level in purchase, stores and workshops.

Decision analysis

The reports of decision applications are primarily exceptional in nature. For example, exception report on stockout or short supply will call for the decision of advance procurement, the information on purchase orders placed but delivery is not due. It will show the effect on the production programme and probable change in the programme or alternative choice of material to overcome the short supply.

The decision analysis report identifies the problem and provides logical relational linkage into other systems where solution can be found. The exception reports will centre around the following parameters:

1. Stockouts
2. Cost f Purchase and Overrun
3. Value of Inventory and Analysis
4. Excessive delay in purchase action
5. Excessive delay in inspection
6. Reliability of suppliers
7. Vendor Performance
8. Material Performance
9. Floor Rejections

These reports will lead to such decisions as emergency procurement, revision of price and terms of supplies, disposal of inventory, cutting down the procedures of purchase and the inspection by streamlining the activities and switching over to a new supplier.

Action update

The action update comes through a control system which indicates whether the decision is implemented or not. Many a times decision is taken and delegated for action at a lower level. It is necessary to know whether action is taken and what is the impact. This will be selective reporting. For example, it stockout is noticed, action is taken to purchase by raising a new purchase order. The update is necessary to know whether the material under new purchase order has arrived or not. The action updates, therefore, will centre around the parameters which are mentioned in decision analysis applications.

MARKETING MANAGEMENT

The marketing management function deals with satisfying the consumer. The scope of function starts form identifying the need of consumer, evolving product concept, designing the product, positioning the product in the market and selling at appropriate price. In the process of performing the marketing function, activities such as market research, consumer survey, advertising, sales promotion campaign, stocking of products, developing dealer distributor network from the major tasks.

The function has a very strong interface with the production and finance department. It relies heavily on production for uninterrupted supply of goods, appropriate stock replenishments and inventory at various locations. The major source of finance in the organisation is sales and marketing has a responsibility to obtain the orders from customers and fulfil them.

The control of sales from the point of view of sales income is a major task of marketing management. Forecasting of sales, evolving marketing strategies, pricing, product designing and launching are some of the key responsibilities of marketing management. Retaining market share, penetrating into new markets, assessing consumer responses to a new market launch are the challenging tasks of the marketing management. In a competitive environment, the function assumes key role in the organisation. The major responsibility of the function then remains to evolve competitive strategies in all the branches of marketing management.

Input transaction Documents

The most important input transaction documents used in the marketing management function include:

1. Customer order
2. Order acceptance
3. Delivery note
4. Invoice, credit note, debit note

As a support to these transactions, data is borrowed from company literature such as price lists, product literature, etc. Marketing function needs a host of other information which is not transaction based. It draws heavily from sources such as market survey and market research studies conducted by the company. It further relies on external sources such as product journals, industry association publications, etc. for industry data.

These transactions may take place at various locations but their assimilation has to take place to conclude the marketing result. The number and the nature of transactions would vary depending upon the product, industry, marketing organisation and infrastructure of production and warehouses.

Applications

Accounting

There are several highly process-oriented accounting applications of the marketing management. The main accounting entity is sales in terms of quantity and value. The detailed entities are as follows:

1. Product Sale
2. Product Family
3. Sales Value
4. Sales Tax
5. Dealer
6. Distributor

7. Customer
8. Excise Duty
9. Zone
10. Area
11. Inventory
12. Receivables
13. Market Segment
14. Exports Market
15. Returns
16. Complaints

Accounting applications build a lot of basic data for the organisation, which meets the needs of statutory compliance and operations update.

Query

The queries in the marketing management are on customer, product, price, stock sale and certain cumulative statistics pertaining to sales. The query may be on order pending position followed by whether stock exists for allocation to the order. If the customer order is to be fulfilled by manufacturing, then whether manufacturing order is issued and if so, what is its status.

The query could be on assessment of sales performance on single dimension or multi dimensions by comparison between two Product Groups, Customer Groups, Zones and Areas. The query could be on the performance of overall sales in relations to the budget.

In marketing function, a lot of importance is given to handling of customer complaints. The queries are raised on its satisfactory disposal. Many times, queries are on basic data such as product specifications, price and discounts, quality, names and addresses of customer, dealers and distributors.

Decision analysis

In day to day functioning, the decisions required to be taken are no pricing allocation of stocks to orders, acceptance of order, discounts and commission, deciding sales terms and so on. In some of these decision areas, decisions are rule-based and can be supported by decision support systems.

The complex decisions are price increase or decrease, deciding on a new product, packaging, distribution channels, product positioning. These decisions have far reaching effects on the marketing performance. They fall in the category of strategic and tactical decisions.

Applications are developed to support these decision building models such as the break even model, risk analysis model, distribution model, network model, product launch model etc. The form he basis for analysis the decision alternatives and their impact on marketing performance, prospects and growth.

The organisation in consumer industry have applications which are designed to collect consumer information of preference, behaviour, response to advertising campaigns, etc. This data is collected on a routine basis to build up independent database on consumer profiles, product rating and buying decisions. Some organisations collect this data from the point of sale, dealers and distributors. The database then is used for various top management and middle management decisions in business planning and execution.

Control

In marketing management, there are a number of factors, which need to be controlled for achieving business goals. These factors are Sales versus Budget, Marketing Cost versus Budgeted Cost, Product Sale versus target fixed for Market Segments – Distributor, Dealer, Branch and Marketing persons, planned sales programme versus actual sales versus competitor's sales.

The applications are developed to report on these comparisons. However, a release routine is added in each application to bring out abnormal variations between actual versus expected. This helps to take specific decision and action in the area of shortcoming or failure.

Some control applications help to correct ongoing operational performance. Some applications help to reset the direction or trend in the development towards desired goals or objectives. Some applications help to take decisions on the strategic subjects such as product positioning, pricing, choice of market segment, design and so on.

The control application in marketing are designed with a very narrow focus for pinpointed attention, decision and action. It requires considerable understanding of behaviour of the consumer, market, product and competition. Many times corrective action is required in areas other than marketing. Marketing decisions take long time to respond and their implications are difficult to judge in short durations. The control applications required by the top and the middle management in marketing are non-standard, industry specific and are linked to business philosophy, policy and strategy.

Reports

Statutory compliance

In marketing management, statutory compliance is mainly related to taxes and duties and filling the returns to appropriate government authorities. The main reports are sales tax register and returns and excise duty returns. In some industries like alcohol, tobacco, gold etc., the organisation is required to keep the information in a format prescribed by the government and file the returns in a prescribed format. These documents are to be kept up-to-date and are subject to surprise checks by government auditors and inspectors.

Knowledge updated

These reports are based on summaries of various entities such as orders, value, sales, stocks, budgets with reference to the past, current and future projections. They are produced regularly at equal intervals with classification on various accounts and are distributed to the concerned agencies.

The knowledge update reports are as under:

1. Product sales ledger
2. Sales summaries
3. Accounts receivables
4. Orders received and accepted
5. Sales analysis
6. Aging of receivables
7. Contribution analysis
8. Market analysis
9. Competition analysis

Most of these reports are generated as functional information and they are not related to an individual's needs. It is expected that these reports will be used by all concerned by picking up relevant information suited to them. These reports have a fixed general format and they are produced in a summarised fashion in line with organisation structure, i.e. the reports will be made by Branch, Zone and Area.

There are eleven factors, viz., Customer, Class of Customer, Market Segment, Product, Product Family, Sales Representative, Branch Area and Zone, Dealer and Distributor, which are sued for classification and summaries in these reports. Such factorial analysis gives valuable information and builds marketing knowledge helping to evolve the strategic in marketing.

Operations update

These reports inform the details of the marketing operations ranging from orders received, processed, accepted, executed, despatched, billed and money recovered. These report are processed by way of daily transaction processing and making statistical summaries for quick update. They are not analysis reports but reports informing facts on day to day operations. These are made for Junior Management personnel in marketing and related functional areas such as stores and accounts.

A typical report will indicate daily order received and orders invoiced. Some more typical reports are as follows:

1. Order book
2. Despatch report
3. Inventory
4. Invoice
5. Customer complaints
6. Complaints disposed

These reports are produced with reference to a date and cumulative since beginning of the year. No high order data processing is involved. Transactions during a day are processed in document sequence and grand summaries are taken on a daily basis, such as daily sales, despatches, inventory and invoice. These reports provide guidance to the operating personnel as to how they are performing. No external information is connected and processed along with this statistical data.

Decision analysis

Decision analysis reports convey whether the desired/expected results are realised or not. These reports tie up the specific decision to its results. For example, a decision is taken to launch an advertising campaign in two segments to test the efficiency of the campaign. A report analysis pre and post-sales of the campaign will indicate a good advertisement.

In marketing function, a number of such decision situations are present, where analysis of sales is necessary, to confirm whether the choice of the alternative is correct or not. The analysis may be with reference to price, choice of market, packaging, design and so on. Market research analysis reports fall in this category. These reports are unstructured and are decision specific.

There is another class of reports, which are generated using models. For example, risk analysis model throws light on the market share, given the probable conditions of the company and its competitor in price, market, design and so on. New product introduction, Break Even analysis, Product Market Mix, Marketing Mix are the examples of decision analysis models helping the marketing management to take a correct decision.

Action update

The action update reports will lead to such decisions as price reduction, withdrawal of product from the market, changing the product position, allocating more budget for expenses, inventory and personnel resources. Some of the action update reports are:

Sale versus Budget

Expenses versus Sales

Sales Growth versus Sales Objective

Sales versus Market Segment versus Budget

Stocks versus Budgeted Stock Levels

Complaints versus Number of Complaints Serviced

Corporate Overview

The top management, in all organisations, is kept informed of the on goings through various MIS reports, in each function and informal channels such as Notes, Inter-office Memos, Minutes of the Meetings and so on. However, this reporting on business performance is not very systematic and it is in infrequent and irregular overview. This reporting does not throw light on the inter-functional implications. The management does not get a clear picture of the totality.

For example, sales versus raw material inventory, production versus finished goods inventor, invoicing versus receivables and its aging, purchase liability versus payable and its aging, uses of fund and its resources, sales versus market segments versus products, product family, machine shop loading versus utilisation of the capacity etc.

The management does not receive information which helps to make comparative analysis between the current and the past. It also not receive information on the projection in totality. The top management always like to have an overview of the business at equal time intervals to bring visibility in the business operations.

Such reporting is normally done monthly, on a fixed date, on key parameters of the business. It uses budgets, norms, ratios, targets as a reference for comparison. It provides same information for the corresponding period in the previous years. It also provides the information on the next planned period in each case of reporting parameters.

Along with statistical, comparative analytical information is reported in graphics to create visual impact on the management. The graphics further give some idea of the trend and direction a parameter is setting in. The trend information evokes response to correct the policy, guidelines and strategic decisions that the management has already taken. It forces a critical review of the business operations, leading to corrective action if necessary. It identifies helps to make such a review easily and conveniently. Many organisations review key business parameters along with reporting on special projects or subjects. For example, management would like to have a separate report on special projects or subjects. For example, management would like to have a separate report on new product performance, progress on certain design and development of a new product or an even in the industry, introduction of new product by the competitor, policy change and its implications on the business and so on.

The overview report gives information on key entities of the business highlighting the performance for the current month, cumulative up to the month, cumulative budget, the variable between budget and actual. The entities handled are the following.

•

This overview is built on the basis of information provided by the functional systems. It gives information at equal intervals enabling the management to take critical view of the performance. It provides trend information on these key entities and simultaneously shows if there are any conflicting trends among the entities. It also shows the financial health of the company by relating assets and liabilities. It highlights major expense heads which are controllable. The overview report indicates the assessment of the business performance in the current year and the trend of business direction in future.

In addition to such reports, there is a practice in a number of companies to collect regularly the information from external sources, which are critical to the business of the organisation. This includes competition, policy, projections and forecasts, developments, which may affect business such as new product, process, technology. Such information is used to develop business models for strategic growth, planning and control. The decisions on new product, diversifications or starting Strategic Business Unit (SBU) are taken after mixing external information with internal information from within the company.

The information so collected from internal and external sources is used to develop business development models for testing and stimulating different conditions of business. Such models help in developing corporate plans on implementation of product, process, technology and investment strategy.

CONVENTIONAL OFFICE SYSTEM

The concept of office is not new, it is traditional and historical. However, over the years, the look of the office has changed from the traditional to modern, paper – based to paperless and manual to automated. A conventional office system is one where the work related to information handling is carried out in a manual traditional manner with a lot of paper work.

There have been three primary goals of an office in the past.

- Arranging or records in the form of file cabinets.
- Sorting and searching or records for future purposes.
- Executing the tasks on day to day basis i.e. issue memos, dispatch letters, calculation, documenting, interacting with people and communicating over long distance.

To carry out above three tasks, the following personnel has traditionally been used:

- An officer – to supervise and control the office work.
- A Clerk – to maintain the records of work.
- A typist – to type write the office activities.

Depending upon the nature of work and size of office, above personnel may be in multiplicity.

The traditional and conventional office has the following limitations.

- It is slow in operations or functions.
- It is carrying bulky paper files.
- It is tedious to perform manual activities.
- It incurs high postal and transportation costs.
- It has lot of data duplicacy and redundancy.
- It is big in size for maintaining paper records.
- It is difficult to edit the documents repeatedly.

MODERN OFFICE SYSTEM

Due to advent of information technology, the traditional office has moved to modern office. A modern office is paperless, automated and sophisticated office. An office system of today consists of computer system such as word processing, electronic communication, digital scheduling, etc. An automated office handles and manages the document electronically through the office software packages, desktop publishing systems, document imaging, digital filling, personal digital assistant, e-mails, voice mails, video conferencing etc. Let us briefly discuss the components of an automated office.

Computer : A computer system is a key component of an office with which electronic data processing can be carried out.

Laser Printer: A quality printer to give rise to hard copies of the document on paper to fulfill the requirements of other organizations like government, banks etc.

Word Processing : This is a very important software to edit the information contents like repots, letters, notes, resume etc. The contents can be edited in different styles, formats, and fonts.

Document imaging : A system that transforms a paper document and images into electronic or digital form using scanner and OCR is called document imaging system.

Desktop Publishing : A technology that is capable of generating professionally elegant and quality documents combining the outputs from word processors and graphics and special lay-out features.

Video conferencing : An arrangement of visual and audio communication amongst two or more people sitting at remote places so that a person can talk to another while seeing the face on computer screen.

e-Mails and voicemails : A very popular arrangement of transmitting the messages consisting of character and voices over a long distance instantlu.

Fax : A device capable of transmitting a printed message after scanning and receiving the same on the other similar device.

OFFICE AUTOMATION TECHNOLOGY

An office automation technology works on a document – centric approach. In this approach, emphasis is on integrating various operations to be done on document from multiple perspectives. An office automation technology is an integration of hardware and software. The hardware component of office automation system comprises of

- Personal Computer
- Scanner Device
- Mike and speaker
- Laser printer
- CD/DVD Write System
- Modem for Emailing
- Network Interface for LAN

The software component comprises of

- Office Software
- Web Browsers
- Email and Voice Mail software
- Graphical User Interface (GUI)
- Operating Systems
- Expert Systems & Decision Support System (DSS)

Out of above software elements, the office software is most widely used and it has got the following parts.

- Word Software for Document Editing.

- Spreadsheet for Heterogeneous Document Making.
- Database Application for Data Management.
- Presentation Software for Seminar Preparation.
- Recording Software for Personal Data Management such as Diary.

Microsoft office (MS Office) is a commercial software package available to support above activities. The components of Ms Office are : MS Word for word processing, MS Excel for spreadsheet work, MS Access for database activities, MS Power Point for making presentations and MS Outlook for information handling like personal diary.

APPLICATION OF OFFICE AUTOMATION

There are at least four levels of modern processing in an office of an organization.

These are :

- Office Information System (OIS).
- Transaction Processing System (TPS)
- Management Information System (MIS)
- Decision Support System (DSS)

Office Information System (OIS) deals with execution of day to day task of the office. This includes preparation of documents, movement of files, archival of records, etc. An example is personnel office is an organization.

Transaction Processing System (TPS) deals with the transactions of data items such as journey tickets, bills. The examples are railway reservation system and electronic billing system in a super market.

Management Information System (MIS) deals with system and procedures designed to senior management of an organization in making decisions. Example could be spreadsheets and graphics software.

Decision Support System (DSS) deals with systems that support the decision making using flexible access to data items for the end use. Spreadsheets are used to develop decision support system.

IT FOR OFFICE AUTOMATION

Office automation can be carried out using various types of information technology. Following are the fields of information technology that support implementation of office automation system.

- User Interface Technology
- Database Technology
- Network Technology
- Web Technology
- Multimedia Technology
- Communication Technology

User Interface Technology is meant for efficient, effective and convenient interaction with the computer systems and related technologies. Smart keyboard,s speech I/O, penbased interface, virtual reality etc. fall under this category.

Database Technology is meant for reliable, efficient and better archival of information the storage devices. Oracle, Sybase, access etc. fall under this category.

Network Technology is meant for resource sharing in a modern office for economy and better productivity. Windows NT server and Linux like operating systems, fall under this category

Web technology is meant for access of information over the internet. Web browsers, portals, websties, search engines fall under this category.

Multimedia Technology is meant for publishing the newspapers and animation on the computer screen for advertisement and cartoon movies etc. 3-D studio fall under this category.

Communication Technology is meant for transfer of messages with attachments over a long distance. eMail and SMS fall under this category.

DECISION SUPPORT SYSTEMS

Decision support systems constitute a class of computer-based information systems including knowledge-based systems that support decision-making activities. Management is largely concerned with making decisions and any action originates from such decisions. Most decisions are made with two kinds of information — internal and external. Internal information normally comes from processed data from the organizational data bank or from the personal data bank. External information is obtained from sources external to the individual making decisions and the organization.

LEVELS OF DECISION MAKING

The well-known three-tiered management pyramid - transactional planning at the lower end, operational planning at the middle level and policy planning of the top level — all need to use computers for different purposes. People at the transactional planning level collect routine data generated within the organization and process it in a well-defined, structured and static fashion to be converted to routine reports. At the transaction level, one is bothered only about what happens on a particular time-frame.

The middle level management does operational planning by retrieving data collected by the lower level people, mostly on an exception basis rather than on routine basis. They operate on the information obtained by processing the data already collected. People at this level normally think of why and how things have happened. This can be categorized as semi-struc-tured decision-making of the routine management type.

Low

The top level management, largely depends on external data — knowledge in the field, intuition and judgement. People at this level think mostly in terms of 'what if situations. The top management extracts very little organizational data and relies more on external and personal data. The time-utilization, type of information and information sources for the three levels in the management hierarchy in any organization is shown in Figure 14.5.1. Figure 14.5.2 represents the inter-relation-ship between the various levels of management and the internal and external data bases, through a flowchart.

STRATEGIC LEVEL DECISIONS

Decision support is still largely a concept, the reason being the lack of commercially available systems for the purpose. It may be worthwhile to compare the usage of computers for EDP, MIS and DSS in terms of various factors the technology, applications or environment, (see Table 14.5.1). While MIS can be defined as computer-aided, decision-making based on information of a routine nature generated from a large pool of data through sophisticated processing. DSS can be defined as computer-aided selection of information in combination with the knowledge of the persons using it, to arrive at decisions. While EDP and MIS are hardware, data and accounting oriented; DSS is more opportunity, decision and function oriented. DSS lays more emphasis on utilizing information to improve human effectiveness. Therefore, the objective of DSS is not to replace judgement but'to support it in such a manner that the strengths of both man and machine processes are utilized to the fullest.

	DP	MIS	DSS
Data Volume	Large	Medium	Low
Processing	High	Average	Small
Type of Process	Routine	Unique to Orgn.	Unique to individual
Equipments	Conventional	Interactive	Humane

Mode of Process	Batch	On-Line	Real -Time
Input/Output	Card, Print, Devices	Terminal, Mouse	Speech, Touch
Location of Data	Centralized	Distributed	Individual
Symbolic Opn.	None	Medium	Large
Applications	Program	Query	Menu
People	Replace	Retrain	Little Chance
Management Impact	Lower	Middle	Higher
Man Vs. Machine "	M/C Supreme	Cooperate	Man Supreme
Time-Frame	Past	Past/Present	Present/Future
Typical State	Passive/Reactive	Reactive/ Active	Active/Creative
Identifies With	Problem	Solution	Opportunity

TYPES OF DECISIONS

Researchers have introduced the concept of decision support by extending computer support to a class of organizational problems that elude EDP, MIS and OR/MS approaches. They have characterised this class of problems by grouping organizational problems into structured, semistructured and unstructured categories as shown in the next table.

Organizational Problems and Management Activity

Type of Decision/Task	Operational Control	Management Control	Strategic Planning	Support Needed
Structure	Inventory Reordering	Linear Programming for manufacturing	Plant Location	Clerical, EDP, OR/ MS Models
Semi -Structured	Bond Trading	Setting Marketing Budgets for consumer Products	Capital Acquisition Analysis	DSS
Unstructured	Selecting a cover for TIME Magazine	Hiring Managers Development	R&D Portfolio	Human Intuition

The basis for differentiating between structured and unstructured decision situations is the amount of judgement and *ad hoc* evaluation as well as insights into problem definition the human decision maker must provide. Complex decision situations require a rich, subtle vocabulary to specify appropriate states and inter-relationships of decision elements. A decision situation that is verbalisable is understood well enough to be described accurately using words with precise meanings. At the other extreme, decision situations that are not well understood tend to be described in more general terms whose meanings, like the understanding, are fuzzy. States and inter-relationships of elements are glossed over instead of being specified in precise expressions.

1. Structured Decisions

Structured decisions are those for which a set of rules and procedures for the decision making process can be determined and utilised in subsequent decision situations. This implies that the decision model is essentially closed, because the outcomes and contingencies must all be known. Although structured decisions' imply that the decision situations occur repetitively under the same sets of conditions, this is not necessarily true. The frequency is not the determining factor, the degree to which the contingencies and outcomes can be known in advance, and thus planned for, is the key. Payroll, production, accounts receivable, budget analysis, are examples of structured tasks.

These largely involve situations where no choice, or very little choice or alternative, is possible. The decision situation here is largely self-evident once the facts and numbers are known. Managers make these decisions chiefly in areas of operations, rarely in cases of strategic planning. It is in dealing with the more highly structured decisions where MIS has been used mostly in recent years.

2. Unstructured Decisions

Unstructured decisions are those for which preplanned rules and procedures cannot be completely specified. This implies an open decision model, because all possible outcomes and contingencies cannot be determined. This classification includes a very wide range of decision situations, from a one-time decision to terminate an organisation to regular decisions on changing schedules for production based on the changing economy. Even though decisions must be made regularly to deal with a recurring problem, the conditions are so different each time that no structured rules can be specified,.

These involve no data reference source. They represent decisions based entirely on a manager's intuition and judgment. These kinds of decisions are involved mostly in the area of company strategic planning, not often in areas of management operations and control. Line managers face unstructured decisions chiefly in dealing with people - workers, other managers, bosses, and so on.

3. Semi-structured Decisions

The binary classification structured and unstructured is insufficient to business decision situations. It may not be possible to specify all conditions surrounding a decision situation, but it may be possible to specify a general set of guidelines to assist a decision maker. Such decision situations may be considered semi-structured, depending on the level of detail to which the process can be prespecified.

These involve both data and a manager's intuition and judgment and are the kind most commonly faced by line managers. Examples: In operations control, decisions on expediting; in management controls, decisions on master scheduling; in strategic planning, decisions on optimum plant size and location. DSS can greatly assist line managers in making these kinds of decisions; MIS can help but little.

Thus, at one extreme is algorithmic, or completely structured decision making, and at the other extreme is heuristic, or completely unstructured, decision making and there exists a continuum between the two extremes based upon the degree of structure.

The vast majority of an organisation's business decisions lie somewhere between these extremes - some more or less structured, and some more or less unstructured, than others. For those decision situations that are somewhat more structured, routines and guidelines can be set up to assist the decision makers. For somewhat less structured decision situations, standards and policies may be used, but a decision maker must determine that a problem or opportunity exists, ascertain the possible.

What are Decision Support Systems?

Decision support systems being fairly new are defined in several ways. The following definition of DSSs is widely accepted in the DSS literature:

Decision support systems are interactive computer-based systems that provide the user with easy access to decision models and data in order to support semi structured and unstructured decision-tasks.

The key aspects of DSSs follow directly from this definition and this definition can be made clearer if we look at some characteristics of DSS.

1. Decision making supported by DSS must be in a semistructured or unstructured environment. In every decision-making situation, there are many factors to consider, conflict about the factors, insufficient information, com-plexity, and lack of clarity. While a computer cannot make an actual decision, it can help managers by analyzing the measurable factor. The decision makers then evaluate the other factors.

2. This sort of decision making occurs at all levels of management. Others in a company besides the chief executive officers can benefit from the use of DSS.

3. A DSS should be able to help groups make decisions, rather than just individuals working on independent tasks. Decisions may be developed by many decision makers and then passed along to others as the company's new policy.

4. The DSS should assist in all stages of decision making - including identifying problems, analyzing alternatives, and choosing a solution. How can a computer support all of these stages? Figure 14.5.5 shows the steps in the decision-making process and how a computer can assist at the particular stage by providing a certain type ot information.

5. A DSS should be flexible, fitting the style of a particular manager, and adaptable, accommodating changes in the environment. It is very important for different types of managers to be able to work with the DSS. If a particular manager places the greatest emphasis on mathematical comparisons, the DSS should be able to make such comparisons. If a manager wants to spend more time identifying a problem, the DSS should have powerful report-writing, query, or graphics abilities.

6. The DSS should be easy to use. A user should not be required te be a computer programmer to generate reports, answers to queries, or graphics. It must be convenient for the user to use the DSS. Otherwise, the DSS probably would not be used.

7. DSSs are information systems whose focus is on decision making. In this sense they differ from EDP and MIS which focus on Data and Information respectively.

8. They rely on the man and the machine working together for solving decision problems. In this sense they differ from EDP systems which focus on automating routine processes, and MIS whose main objective is to provide information that can be useful to management.

9. They are support tools under the control of managers. They do not attempt to automate decision making, predefine objectives, or impose solutions.

10. Their functional capabilities are oriented more towards supporting decision-making activities rather than solving decision problems.

11. They provide an environment where a decision maker can effectively apply various kinds of management science methods and quantitative analysis techniques that would otherwise be too cumbersome to use.

12. Their impact is on decisions where the manager's judgement is essential and there is sufficient structure for computers and analytical aids to be of value.

13. They emphasize flexibility and adaptability to accommodate changes in decision-making.

14. Though DSSs can be used for structured problems, they are more suited for semi-structured problems.

15. DSSs are usually ad hoc systems, i.e., designed for specific non-recurring decision problems.

16. DSSs are generally user-friendly systems. They emphasize easy to use and interactive user interfaces.

17. They tend to be extensible, and evolve over time.

18. They provide extensive data management and model management facilities.

19. DSSs are used as much for dec is ion-making as for communicating decisions, and for training purposes.

The focus of much of the work in this field during the early seventies was on articulating these characteristics; establishing DSSs as a class of organizational information system; and clarifying the relationships between DSS, EDP and MIS. The emergence of expert .systems (ES) has recreated similar situation now. Clarifying the similarities and differences between ES and DSS, and developing ways of integrating them is a major thrust in the field today. The following table provides a summary of the key differences between DSS and ES.

Key Differences Between Expert Systems and DSSs

	Expert Systems	*Decision Support Systems*
Objective	Enhance human decision making. Replicate experts. Replace human-decision makers.	Enhance human decision making. Provide intellectual support
Philosophy	Capture and Transfer of Expertise	Amplify a decision maker's capabilities by providing resources and facilities
Control	The system dominates. It determines the problem-solving process	The human dominates. Human determines the overall problem-solving process.
Machine	The machine is more knowledgeable than the user. Carries problem solving capabilities Plays a high level cognitive role	Shared experties and labor. Supplements human expertise capabilities.
Human	Less knowledgeable than the machine. Supports the machine's problem solving process by answering questions. Plays a lower level cognitive role	Shared expertise and roles. Human may not be the expert but quite capable of solving problems on his own.
Domain	Narrow and Deep domains. Decisions are determined by the natural laws of the domain and are less subjective.	Complex, broad and shallow domains. Decisions are subjective and influenced by the personal context of the decision maker.

Type of Decision Support Systems

Decision support systems can be either data-oriented or model-oriented. Data-oriented systems specialize in retrieving or analyzing data. Model-oriented systems provide powerful facilities for using models for simulation of business situations and suggestion of possible choices. The functions performed by the two types of systems are listed in seven basic types of systems that perform different DSS functions. These basic systems are discussed briefly so as to have an idea of the types of functions that can be performed by DSS.

1. File drawer systems give users immediate access to data in a database. A manager who wants information on inventory levels of certain items, for example, could use a file drawer system.
2. Data analysis systems allow managers to work with the data in a single data file. Managers use this type of system to analyze a budget or evaluate alternative investment opportunities.
3. Analysis information systems give managers access to many databases and small models. An example is a sales analysis system, which would give a manager access to the files containing data on detailed sales, customer information, and sales forecasts.
4. Accounting models help managers see the effects of various activities on the company's income statements, balance sheets, and other accounting statements.
5. Representational models help managers predict the results of alternative decisions by analyzing the decisions along with financial data.

6. Optimization models tell managers the optimal solution to a problem. The solution is based on mathematical data about costs, sales volume, sales revenues, and other financial factors that have been entered into mathematical equations. An example is a system that indicates how many of each of a company's products to manufacture to achieve the greatest profit for that company.
7. Suggestion models suggest decisions for fairly routine problems faced by the company. For example, a suggestion model may calculate postal rates for packages of certain weights and dimensions.

The ideal DSS would offer all of these functions. Most of the systems in current use tend to offer only a few of the functions, but newer, more powerful systems offering all of them have been introduced lately. It is becoming more and more common to see organizations building DSS that contain all the functions they need to solve their specific problems. This leads us to the questions of how a DSS is built, which is discussed in the next section.

BUILDING DECISION SUPPORT SYSTEMS

When building a DSS, designers must consider many factors, .including what technology is available and what the DSS will be used for. In this section, we first look at the software used in DSS, then at the components of DSS, and finally at the roles of the people involved with the DSS.

1. DSS Software

Three types of software are used in a DSS.

1. The specific DSS is the system that actually accomplishes the work. It is similar to application software; a specific DSS is what the user needs to perform the tasks described earlier.
2. A DSS generator is general DSS-type software that can be adapted to be used in different situations. The generator can manipulate models and data that relate to a particular problem. Without learning how to write computer programs, users of DSS generators may enter and manipulate these models and data to come up with their own solutions. This is the area of greatest promise in DSS, as it would give managers the ability to use computers directly to help them solve specific problems.
3. DSS tools are used to build both specific DSS and DSS generators. The tools include programming languages, data manipulation software, special graphics software, and so on.

2. DSS Components

Each DSS is different, as it is built to meet the needs of the users. But several general components are found in every DSS: a user, working with computer hardware and software; a software system that includes both data- and model-handling programs; a database that contains internal and external information from all areas in the company; and a model base that contains strategic, tactical, and operational models, as well as tools to build additional models. These components are shown in Figure 14.5.7. The new elements in DSS are the model base and the'modcl base management system (MBMS). These are similar to a database and a database management system, except that the system manages models instead of data.

The data and model approach is the most popular approach for developing practical DSSs. It recognizes two kinds of critical resources: data and models. Data fulfills the basic information needs of the decision maker, and models provide various analytical schemes for analyzing the decision problem, making conclusions from the data, and studying the consequences of potential decisions. The architecture recognizes three major subsystems:

1. Data Base Management System (DBMS)
2. Model Base Management System (MBMS)
3. Dialog Generation and Management System (DGMS)

In a DSS environment, the data base subsystem should provide the following capabilities.

1. Managing a wide variety of data with full range of traditional data management functions such as data base creation and updating, data dictionary, and query processing,
2. Interfacing with a wide variety of external data sources.
3. Integrating data from a variety of data sources through data capture and extraction processes.
4. Portraying logical data structures in user usable terms.
5. Handling temporary and *ad hoc* data bases for experimentation purposes.
6. Interfacing with the model management system.

Themodel management subsystem is unique to DSSs. It should provide the following capabilities:

1. Creating new models
2. Cataloging and maintaining a repertoire of models
3. Interfacing with the data base system.
4. Ability to run model simulations on different sets of data.
5. Providing primitive model building blocks with which complex models can be configured.
6. Ability to manage the model base with management functions analogous to data base management functions.

The Dialog subsystem provides the DSS much of its power, flexibility and useability characteristics. Its capabilities should include:

1. Handling a variety of dialog styles according to users needs.
2. Shifting between dialogue styles as needed.
3. Accommodating a variety of user interface devices and mechanisms.
4. Presenting results in a variety of formats and media.
5. Providing a high-bandwidth communication between the user and the system. For example, graphics and windows.
6. Providing help facilities to assist the user in the use of the system.

Models are built by defining relationships between data items. The relationships most often appear in the form of equations. For example, in a financial DSS, a user may define the following relationships:

Sales = units sold x price per unit

Cost of sales = manufacturing costs - inventory increase

Fixed costs = Rs. 20,000

Gross profit = sales - cost of sales

Net income = gross margin - fixed costs

After these relationships are defined, the model base management software allows a user to ask the DSS questions like:

1. What happens if the price is decreased by 10 per cent?
2. What happens if sales volume is 20 per cent higher than anticipated?
3. How many units must be sold in order to break even?

4. What will our profit be in say seven years, if inflation is 10 per cent per year?

This type of use of models is a critical component of DSS. Without the model base, the computer could produce only traditional reports and information.

In summary, this architecture provides a clear and viable approach for developing practical DSSs. The approach is easy to relate to as it is a natural extension of the EDP and MIS systems. Because it provided concrete directions for action, it has also significantly influenced the research thoughts in the field. It was instrumental in identifying and promoting data management, model management and dialogue management as priority areas of research in the DSS field.

3. People and the DSS

A number of people are involved in running and using the DSS. The manager is the user — the person who has to make the decision. The intermediary helps the user work with the DSS and may even make suggestions. The DSS builder designs the specific DSS from the DSS generator or the DSS tools: the builder should be familiar with both the type of problem to be solved and computer technology. The technical supporter provides new functions, data, and models for the system when they are available; he must be thoroughly familar \\ith computer technology but needs in know only a little about the types of problems being solved. Finally, nV toolsmith develops new tools, models, or software and works to improve the efficiency of the system.

PROBLEMS IN BUILDING DECISION SUPPORT SYSTEMS

If the decision support system concept is so promising, at least two legitimate questions can be raised.

1. Why are there very few decision support systems?
2. Why do computer system design methods still emphasise the data processing and management information system approach to developing a computer-based information system?

The answer to the first question is historical. During earlier development of decision support systems, each organisation invested a great deal of time, money and effort to develop its system. The realisation that costs necessary to develop a decision support system on a cyclic trial-and-error basis arc considerable has served to prohibit a similar effort in all but those organisations with ample resources.

The second question has two answers. First, many system design methodologies emphasise building new systems as extensions to existing systems. The new system must first set about correcting any deficiencies in the existing systems; then new functions can be addressed. Design of a decision support system requires a major reorientation, emphasising support for what decision makers do when they make decisions. What current systems do should not be considered as valuable and necessary solely because it already exists.

The second answer to the question is more basic: existing methods for designing systems so as to provide direct support for decision makers have proved inadequate. They do not adequately address the definition of decision support system requirements. Existing systems arc devised by designers and implementers based upon their perceptions of what is needed to assist the decision making process. The discrepancy, between what the systems provide and what is needed may be because of two reasons.

First, the decision makers seldom know what information they need, because they lack an adequate model of each decision situation they encounter. As a result decision makers are unable to specify verbally their requirements, even to themselves, let alone to system designers and implementers. Second, there is inadequate communication of decision maker's requirements to designers and implementers. Thus, the designers are likely to utilise their own interpretation of the terms to specify requirements. Whether the resulting system outputs match the requirements or not becomes a matter of probability.

Because of the dlscrepancy between what is needed and what is provided by the systems, decision makers must expend time and effort to acquire information and decision support they need but cannot get from their system. They supplement the computer-based system with their own private information systems. The result is additional costs, in terms of lost time and on the part of decision makers to operate these private information systems. At the same time there are reduced benefits from the existing system.

Impact of Decision Support Systems

The impact of a DSS can be hard to measure, since they support managers and aim at helping to improve effectiveness. They facilitate but do not cause the improvement; managers do that. In general, therefore. DSS cannot be justified in terms of costs and benefits. The benefits are often qualitative and not easily measured.

The real stimulus to DSS development has to be the manager's own assessmentof value. If the DSS supports a key decision or task in which improved effectiveness is important, and is designed in terms of the manager's needs and activities, it is likely that the potential value of the system will justify the investment, if there is no perceived value, any cost will be seen as disproportionate.

Fortunately, the costs of DSS are often relatively small. By focusing on a specific decision, starting with a simple DSS that evolves with experience, it is generally possible to deliver a system for under US$15,000 in a few months. However, there may be a prior investment of many months getting to understand the decision process. Understanding the process to be supported is essential and the direct technical costs of a DSS may be far easier to handle.

The benefits of a DSS can be hard to quantify, but not necessarily to recognise. It can change communication patterns, the way the manager views his job and spends his time, and even the type of individual to be hired for the position. The more effective the DSS, the more likely it is to stimulate changes.

Why Do Managers Need Decision Support Systems?

There has always been a need for the types of information that a DSS produces, Decision-support systems have become popular primarily because ol" the hardware and software tools that make them possible. The declining cost of computer hardware has made computer processing and computer storage relatively inexpensive. Second, the advent of data base management systems in the 1970s provided means for storage and management of large amounts of detailed data. These data are now relatively easy to retrieve for use in a dec! si on-support system. Third, there has been a large increase in the number of software packages that incorporate the functions of a DSS. These packages can be used directly to implement DSS applications. And finally, many college graduates trained in analytic techniques are now reaching the middle and upper levels of management where most semistructured and unstructured decisions are made. These individuals know how to use the tools that decision-support systems provide.

EXAMPLES OF DECISION SUPPORT SYSTEMS

Studying some DSS applications in detail can be very useful for gaining a concrete understanding of how the concept translates into practice. A number of decision support systems have been set up and are functioning in various companies that have been described in detail in published books or papers. Some typical examples of DSSs in use are presented here. Note that the systems vary greatly from organizaion to organization, as they were all set up to perform specific functions for those organ izauons.

Successful applications of decision support systems include portfolio management, merger and acquisition analy^s, ski-area design, design of police force beats, redesign of school districts, market planning, corporate planning, manpower planning, policy analysis in state government, R & D management, product planning, media selection, energy management and budgeting.

1. **AIMS (An Analytical Information Management System).** American Airlines developed this system to

support planning, finance, marketing, and operations functions. The system manages a large amount of historical data on the entire airline industry and provides managers with the ability lo access, analyze, compute, and display historical future data interactively. The system is used to facilitate studies and forecasts of load factors, market share, aircraft utilization, productivity measurement, and revenue/ yield, among other things.

2. **EIS (Executive Information System).** Boeing Computer Services has developed this system as one of the services on their time-sharing network, depicted as a set of six interrelated subsystems; report writing graphics; financial applications; forecasting and statistics; modeling, "what if," and simulation; and database management.
3. **GADS (Geo-data Analysis and Display System).** This interactive graphics system assists users in solving problems where the relevant data can be related to geographical areas. It has been used by local governments in solving problems of police personnel deployment, land use planning, and school redistricting. GADS consists of a variety of analysis and display functions that users can invoke in any order, thus following their own problem- solving process.
4. **GODDKSS (Goal-Directed Decision Structuring System).** It is based on a novel, goal-directed structure for representing decision problems. The structure allows the user to slate relations among aspects, effects, conditions, and goals, in addition to actions and stales, which are the basic components of the traditional decision-tree approach. The program interacts with the user in an English-like dialogue, starting with the staled objectives and proceeding to unravel the more detailed means by which these objectives can be realized. Al any point in time, the program focuses the user's attention on the issues that are most crucial to the problem at hand. The struciure is more compatible with the way people encode knowledge about problems and actions.
5. **GPLAN (Generalized Planning System).** This system was developed at Purdue University. It is tailored to support decision making in any of a variety of areas, such as inventory management and water quality planning. Besides generality,there were other intentions for GPLAN: an easy-to-use language system, a flexible knowledge system, and a problem-processing system that could automatically interface a model with some data to perform a desired analysis. The language system was designed for use by persons who are not programmers. It is English-like in appearance, and with it a user can direct both data retrieval and computation nonprocedurally.
6. **PAMPS (Plan Analysis and Modelling System).** Getty Oil developed this system for use in supporting capital investment decision making. It allows managers to interrogate and analyze historical data with an English-like language, displaying the result in tabular or graphic form. The system also provides access to a large repertory of financial routine and models for generating future plans which are analyzed and displayed to aid in data decision making.

EXPERT SYSTEMS AND ARITIFICIAL INTELLIGENCE

These days. scientists are looking for technological breakthrough to propel us into the fifth generation of computers. Many people argue that the development of **artificial intelligence** will mark the beginning of a **fifth generation** of computers. Meanwhile, scientific research is being done on several fronts, all with the purpose of:

- increasing speed, memory and power of computers;
- teaching them to think like humans;
- making them easier to user;
- finding practical applications for the existing technology.

Computers can calculate many times faster than humans; computerized robots can work longer hours and data banks can remember much more than the human mind.

Arificial Intelligence

!t is no doubt that this is the most interesting and active area of computer science. But what is artificial intelligence, anyway? It runs out that there is more than one answer to this question. One common definition states that artificial intelligence (AI) is the area of computer science that deals with the ways in which computers can be made to perform cognitive functions ascribed to humans. Although it gives us a general notion about AI, this definition is actually rather vague. It does not say what functions are performed, to what degree they are performed or how these functions are carried out.

In fact, there are at least three different views on what the term artificial intelligence means.

1. AI is the embodiment of human intellectual capabilities within a computer. This view is called Strong AI.
2. AI is a set of computer programs that produce output that would be considered to reflect intelligence if it were generated by humans.
3. AI is the study of mental faculties through the user of mental models implemented on a computer. This view is called Weak AI.

The capacities ascribed to computers in the first of these definitions are by no means universally acknowledged and those who do hope to program human intellectual capabilities into a computer no longer believe that task will be an easy one. Intelligence itself has not yet been completely defined, let alone programmed. The second, middle-of-the road definition is really a relative standard because as time passes, we tend to expect over more sophisticated output from computer programs.

Thus what looked intelligent many years ago may look commonplace and mechanical today. In fact, as certain AI problems become better understood, they often cease to be classified as AI problems (examples are problems solved by symbolic mathematics systems). The last view of AI which really promise nothing but a study is perhaps the most realistic and the most honest. Most experts think that the next breakthrough will be artificial intelligence (AI) – the ability of machines to think and reason like humans which in turn, the futurists predict, will change the way we use computers.

Uses for these thinking machines will be found that were never before thought possible. What it will take to accomplish this technological leap is more computer speed, more power and more memory than ever before. These factors will be essential to accommodate the sophisticated programming that AI requires.

REGULAR VERSUS AI PROGRAMMING

Let's compare regular programming and AI programming in terms of these three segments.

Regular Programming

Input A sequence of alphanumeric symbols that is presented and stored according to a given set of previously stipulated rules and that utilizes a limited set of communication media, such as a keyboard, magnetic disk or magnetic tape.

Processing Manipulation of the stored symbols by a set of previously defined algorithms. (An algorithm is a set of step-by-step instructions that completely and unambiguously specify how to solve the problem in a finite length of time).

Output A sequence of alphanumeric or graphic symbols, possibly in a give set of colors that represents the result of the processing and that is placed on such a medium as a CRT screen, paper or magnetic disk or tape.

Regular programming tends to be relatively inflexible in terms of the type and order of input and output. Both numeric processing and character processing are done on an item-by-item basis. If special data structures are needed, they must normally be specified during development of the computer program. The easiest programs to write are those that involve well-defined processes with very little variation. AI programming, on the other hand, often mimics the more creative and less well-defined functions that people perform. These include functions that are related to the five senses.

MAJOR AREAS OF AI

Although research in artificial intelligence started in the mid 1950s. It is still in its early stages of development. Progress is slow. Specifically, the areas of artificial intelligence that are being pursued are:

(i) Expert Systems
(ii) Advanced Robotics
(iii) Natural-Language Processing
(iv) Voice Synthesis
(v) Voice Recognition
(vi) Computer Vision
(vii) Symbolic and Numeric Processing
(viii) Knowledge Representation
(ix) Pattern Watching
(x) Search
(xi) Logic Inference
(xii) Problem Solving
(xiii) Learning
(xiv) Social and Ethical Issues

It is not possible to go into details of each one of them, but let us first see the most important usage of AI, i.e., Expert systems.

EXPERT SYSTEMS

As said above it is one of the first and the most practical applications derived form the research on artificial intelligence. Artificial intelligence (AI) is that area of computer science in which scientists are striving to build machines to think and reason in a fashion similar to humans. An expert system is software, based on certain concepts of AI that acts as a consultant or an expert, in a specific field or discipline to help solve a problem or help make a decision. Expert systems are also referred to as knowledge-based systems.

Expert systems attempt to supply attempt to supply both the knowledge and reasoning of human beings. They are expert in only one field, topic or discipline; they can help solve only a narrowly defined problem. The user provides data about a problem through a keyboard and the computer responds with an answer and explanation based on facts and rules that have earlier been extracted from human experts and stored in the computer. An expert system cannot entirely duplicate a human expert's judgement or make the final decision; but it can offer opinions, suggests possible diagnoses and suggests various solutions to a problem. These programs are usually as a supplemental source of advice.

Because of their usefulness, expert systems are one of the first results of AI research to become a viable commercial product. Oil companies use expert systems to analyse geological data, while physicians use them to help diagnose and treat illnesses, People in other types of diagnostic fields, professional assistance and emergency management also take advantage of expert systems. Until recently, most expert systems were designed for use only a large computers because the programming demanded so much power and memory. Now, many expert systems can be used with microcomputers; however, these programs are still very expensive. Early work was done using PROLOG (Programming in Logic), LISP (List Processing) and other specialized programming languages. Now the trend is towards designing these systems for microcomputers and with popular programming languages such as FORTRAN and C.

Conventional Programs Versus Expert Systems

An expert system differs from a traditional program that is used to solve a problem (application software). In traditional software, there is the program and there are the data that the program is given to work on. In expert systems, however, the program is called the inference engine and the data base has been replaced with a knowledge base. Traditional computer programs are composed of a detailed set of sequentially organized instructions to be followed that comprise an algorithm for the processing steps. The computer can do nothing else but strictly follow the sequence of the instructions. Using heuristic programming, an expert system can group instructions in any order and allows different reactions to each situation it encounters. The exact processing activities are determined by the data that the entered during a consultation, not by the sequence of processing statement.

Heuristic programming is a key feature of expert systems. The main difference between expert systems and traditional programs is the inclusion of heuristics, the rules of thumb about the problem. Heuristic programming is an attempt to emulate human intuition, judgement and common sense. This type of program allows the computer to recall earlier results and include them in its programming. That newly gained knowledge is then added to its knowledge base and becomes a basis for the next problem and its solution. Here, the computer has learned form its own experience and mistakes, so when it encounters anew problem, it will recall earlier results and consider them.

Difference Between Expert System and Conventional Programming

- Use of inference engine rather than program
- Use of knowledge base rather than data base
- Processing determined by data entered rather than by the sequence of program instructions.

The following are the other expert systems and tools listed in alphabetic order which are the most successful applications of AI.

COMPONENTS OF AN EXPERT SYSTEM

In reviewing these relatively successful expert systems, we have glossed over their structure and behaviour to concentrate on their performance, seeing that all have attained at least respectable levels of expertise in their problem domains. While this portends well for the economic future of the expert systems business, we will concern ourselves more with the actual design of the programs. The first thing to determine when attempting to implement an expert system or indeed any piece of software, is what capabilities it should have. It used to be enough for an AI program such as an expert system to exhibit innovative or interesting behaviour that had not been seen previously in computers.

But by now the field has matured considerably and users are coming to demand more features form expert systems than a simple question-and-answer session followed by a recommendation or diagnosis. Today, it is generally agreed that a true expert system must be capable of performing three basic services; not only problem solving but also interactive explanation and knowledge acquisition (learning). Like all software, it should be fast, easy to maintain and user-friendly. Most systems interact with the operator through either an English language dialog or a Macintosh-style window and mouse environment. At the very least, the user's inputs should be prompted with a list of applicable possibilities.

An expert system consists of:

(a) A knowledge base on a specific topic

(b) An inference engine

the program that can probe that base to suggest solutions to a proble,

Knowledge Base

The knowledge base is the stored collection of facts on a particular subject and the hundreds or thousands of if-then (situation/action) rules by which the facts relate. The base includes maxims provided by a group of experts in that field and thousands of facts and rules of thumb (heuristics), as well as judgements, intuitions and experiences. The knowledge base differs from a traditional data base. A data base is a collection of related or unrelated facts. A knowledge base, on the other hand includes not only facts about a particular subject, but also instructions on how to use the facts and on how they related, i.e. the if-then rules that connect the pieces of data and draw conclusions. For example, an extremely simplified if then rule for a family physician might be: If patient complains of general aches and pains and if patient's age is greater than eighteen, then prescribe aspirin. Usually, if the knowledge can be expressed clearly in word, it can be presented in an if-then rule.

To create a knowledge base, special designers called knowledge engineers spend months working with the human experts to extract and structure the facts, rules and knowledge. After the knowledge base is developed, then the program (interface engine) will be able to probe that base.

Inference Engine

The human expert has to be able to make inferences from pieces of evidence. The expert system also has to a way to make inferences. An inference engine is the reusable program that allows the computer to intelligently apply the facts and information to a particular problem. It retrieves and manipulates the facts and rules, deciding in which order to make connections, associations and inferences. An inference engine decides how to link the mental associations that a human expert makes instinctively when confronted with a problem and the order in which these decisions are made.

It also has the capability of explaining its reasonings and conclusions to the user. In order to deliver this performance, expert systems are normally organized into four modules: the knowledge base, the working memory, the inference engine and some user interface and support software for other miscellaneous functions. The inference engine is the heart of the expert system embodying the main control structures and algorithms. Normally, the inference engine operates in a continuous two-step cycle that first settles upon an inference to draw and then executes it. The knowledge base stores the system's total, permanent knowledge of its application domain, while the working memory serves as a temporary cache for information specific to the problem currently being solved.

Shells

Sometimes an expert system takes the form of an empty shell in which the user company supplies additional facts. Remember EMYCIN, the shell from MYCIN? It is the expert system with a structure for its knowledge base but it does not contain the knowledge base itself. It includes an inference engine that works well with a variety of different fields and it prompts the user with questions until enough information is accumulated to fill the knowledge base. With a shell, knowledge engineers or sometimes the intended users themselves, can build a knowledge base and create an expert system for specific applications. Shell packages are becoming a popular way for developing expert systems for microcomputers.

Creating an Expert System

The creation of an expert system is an involved process that requires careful planning. The trend among those who need an ES is to acquire an expert systems tool (shell) instead of writing the inference engine and other code "from scratch". The following are the major steps involved in the creation of a knowledge-based expert system when an ES shell is used.

1. Select a domain and a particular task.

   Choose a task that someone (an expert) can do well.

   The performance of the task should be related to both breadth and depth of knowledge.

   The facts and rules should be stable.

   The recommendations should be well defined.

2. Select the ES shell for implementation.

   Decide what type of inference control is needed.

   Decide what type of pattern-matching capability is needed.

   Decide whether certainly factors are necessary

   Begin constructing a prototype system.

3. Acquire initial knowledge about the domain and task.

   Identify the knowledge expert(s).

   Select particular problems associated with each task.

   Obtain, record and cross-check factual knowledge from both reference material and experts.

   Obtain and record task-related rules form the expert(s) and confirm them to the degree possible.

   Prepare a set of test cases.

4. Encode the knowledge, using the appropriate representation.

   Fractional knowledge

   Inference knowledge

   Control knowledge

5. Execute and test the knowledge.

   Evaluate the test cases.

   Be alert for problems with consistency and completeness.

6. Refine the current knowledge and acquire additional knowledge.

   Revise the rules as necessary.

   Modify any facts that need revision.

   Argument the system with information on additional domain tasks and test again.

   Repeat as often as necessary.

7. Complete any necessary interface code

   Demonstrate the system.

Make the system user-friendly.

8. Document the system

   Provide on-line and hard-copy documentation as necessary.

   Document the consultation portion especially well.

   Document the knowledge portion to the degree necessary.

If the expert system is to be coded from scratch, then many more concerns must be addressed. They are related primarily to the design and coding of the inference engine and the explanation subsystem. Coding from scratch can be a substantial undertaking.

Working of an Expert System

Several methods are used to structure knowledge in an expert system so that the inference engine can make its conclusions, but the most common one is with the set of if-then rules. Systems developed with this approach are called rule-based systems. In a rule-based system, the computer moves through the symbols that describes the current situation, looking for patterns that correspond to the "if" sides of its stored rules. When the program finds such a pattern, the relevant rule is triggered. The program then takes an action, such as presenting the user with a conclusion or applying a succeeding chain of rules. Generally, here is how it works when a user consults an expert system. The system interviews (asks questions of) the user and gets the facts about the problem at hand. During the interview questions appear on the computer display screen and the user responds by keying in answers of important data.

Some systems, in order to simplify the user/program interaction, use a natural language; then the computer and the user communicate in a human language (e.g. English) rather than cryptic programming commands. The system keeps the user posted on its "analysis". The user guides the program to choose among sets of options, with each decision opening the gate to another group of choices. Then, utilizing the user's responses, the system searches like knowledge base. The organized information in the knowledge base is probed and intereted by the interference engine which perform deductive reasoning, making inferences on the knowledge.

It systematically searches through the various paths for a solution without becoming lost in the vast number of possibilities. Eventually, the program comes up with the advice and communicates it to the user. Sometimes, it will needed to ask the user more questions to get additional information on which to base its advice. The system also explains its reasoning process and its conclusions. Now, let's briefly go through the process using MYCIN which analyzes bacterial blood infections and recommends proper treatment.

On the basis of symptoms presented to it by the user physician, the program first make a reasonable guess regarding the patient's condition. That input includes data about the patient's history – lab test results, symptoms and other observations. The physician also answers any questions the program asks. The program then determines how well its "first reasonable guess" diagnosis fits the know facts about the behavior of the microorganism suspected to be involved. Once the system has identified the cause of the infection, it reviews all the antibiotics in its knowledge base and makes a recommendation as to which one should be administered to the patient.

Capabilities of an Expert System

An expert system also utilizes other capabilities. For example

1. It is often necessary to be able to easily to remove (retract) given facts or even remove (excise) given rules from consideration during a consultation. Most expert systems provide this capability.
2. It is useful to be able to assign priorities to the firing of rules. This can be accomplished by giving each rule a priority number that the inference engine checks.

3. Some expert systems permit combined forward and backward reasoning (an example is opportunistic reasoning).
4. Certain systems permit the rules to invoke subprograms written in another language (such as LISP, C or FORTRAN) to perform complex operations. One example of this is knowledge-based simulation where in knowledge-based system invokes a discrete or continuous simulation system.
5. Some advanced expert systems combine facts with frames as well as rules and thereby incorporate the capability of inheritance, wherein there is a network of data structures and the offspring automatically inherit properties of the parents.
6. As we have seen, one weakness of expert systems is their lack of so called deep knowledge. Without the type of knowledge, the expert system cannot respond to a question or statement where there is no matching fact or rule. Efforts are under way to build fundamental models to help solve this problem.
7. Learning subsystems are currently being investigated as a way to simplify the task of the knowledge base builder and the knowledge engineer so that the knowledge base can be dynamically updated with reliable information.

A typical expert system, shell or tool has many capabilities. The number and quality of he features also affect the cost of the system, so therefore selecting a system, the user should have a good idea what capabilities she or he needs.

Applications and Examples of Expert Systems

After DENDRAL, CADUCEUS and MYCIN proved their usefulness, other expert systems started to appear in a variety of fields. Today, expert systems are used in the areas of: Ecology, Industry, Medical, Education, Marketing and Date Processing and others.

The RCS (River Conservation Status) System

South Africa's river systems vary from practically pristine natural systems to heavily exploited and degraded drainage ditches. The Olifants river system of the southwestern cape flows through a mountainous catchment of unique vegetation and includes in its fauna eight fish species endemic to the system. In contrast, 150 km further south, the Black River flows in a concrete canal through Cape Town, with effluent from the cities main sewage works contributing up to 90% of the flow. Other main drainage system for the highly populated, industrialized and mining rich Witwatersrand area which then flows through the Kruger National Park.

FISHFARMET System

The lack of aquaculture expertise has been defined as one of the major constraints on the development of aquaculture in southern Africa. It was decided to develop an expert system to assist potential aquaculturists in assessing the aquaculture potential of various fish species in relation to particular sites and culture methods. Computers have played an increasingly important role in aquaculture in recent years, but their use has been limited to data storage (to aid in pond management) and the monitoring of oxygen levels and water flow. As far as known, FISHFARMET represents the first use of expert system techniques as a means of assessing aquaculture potential. Great emphasis has been placed on user friendliness of the system.

PISCES

PISCES is an expert system which is designed to assist legislators, conservationists and resource managers in determining the advisability of introducing alien (exotic) fish species into local waters. In a country which is attempting to move from third world to fish world status there is tremendous development pressure on the natural environment. Part of this pressure is exerted by the introduction of exotic species. Southern Africa has already experienced the negative effects which such introductions sometimes precipitate. It is important therefore, not to allow the importation of foreign species to become totally out of control. At the same time it is recognised that a compromise is necessary between the needs for the conservation of our natural environment and the needs for the development of the region. It is therefore important that the introduction of exotic species be strictly controlled within well defined lines.

EMEX

An Expert System for Market Analysis and Forecasting. The aim of the EMEX system is to guide the user through the stages of the model building task. Its role is that of an assistant. It is important that the user, as the expert in the market being modeled, exercises judgement over the results and suggestions that the system makes. The combination of the system's model building expertise and the user's market expertise together can provide a very powerful insight into the operation of the market. Ease of use is an important consideration for such a package.

The user and the system interact via a series of forms and menus. There are facilities to allows the user to browse through the details of the current consultation, to c hange previously entered information and at all times a help system can offer advice relevant to the current context.

APES

An Expert System for Nutrition Education. Interaction with a knowledge base can be good for your health! This was the starting point for an attempt at constructing an environment for exploration by pupils, students, teachers and experts. Part of this environment is an expert system which is being developed to provide advice on the nutritional properties of food and the needs of a healthy diet. This requires an underlying knowledge base which itself includes a very large bank of data. A powerful learning environment or microworld is then capable of interrogation, amendment and of supporting computer aided learning (CAL) applications and short programs. Such short programs might be written by the student or teacher to represent a cooling process or composition of a diet for analysis.

The DIABETICS Expert System

The expert system DIABETICS is used for tutoring and teaching medical students, general practitioners and medical related staff on diabetes diagnosis and management. Major complications of diabetes are dealt with as well as treatment using insulin administration. The basic idea of the system is to present the user with a general tool for experimenting with a large number of patient cases by the choice of symptom and history from a menu driven interface. It is a system based on production rules and can be an effective decision making tool in such complex area of medicine as diabetes.

Advanced Robotics

Robot systems can be considered an embodiment of AI. A robot has the potential of incorporating every aspect of AI: sensory input: elaborate internal processing and output which may consist of written or spoken information; dexterous manipulation of objects: physical movement: or all of these activities. Robotics is the area of study dealing with the design, construction and operation of robots. Robots are still used mainly for simple, repetitious tasks on factory assembly lines. However, they have become sophisticated enough for important and dangerous jobs, such as bomb disposal, ocean exploration, outer-space probes, coal mining excavation and cleanup of a chemical or nuclear accident.

Denning Mobile Robotics in Woburn, Massachusetts, makes robot that function as prison guards. These four-foot tall robots detect human movement through sensors. If a prisoner is detected in an unauthorized area, the robot alerts authorities and tells the prisoner to return to the cell. MIT, Standard University and Carnegie-Mellon University are among several institutions and private companies that are heavily involved in robotics research.

They are:

(a) making robots intelligent by using the latest in AI research, i.e. giving them the ability to make decision
(b) giving them highly sensitive tactile capabilities;
(c) providing them with a capacity to see in great detail;
(d) designing them with dependable stabilizing systems.

Applications and Examples of Robotics System

The following is a brief summary of a few robot applications that go beyond industrial robotics.

Cleaning: A robotic device could be used for such cleaning activities as sweeping, scrubbing and polishing floor. Depending on its design, the robot could require assistance in emptying its cleaning containers or it could automatically connect itself with an external device to perform these functions. The primary AI activities would be related to the movement pattern around a floor that the robot would have to follow in order to perform its assigned task successfully. Ideally, such a robot would not require any external devices to determine its position. It would also need an obstacle avoidance system so that it would not damage furniture or tumble down stairways. Various sensors could be used to help accomplish this.

Pharmacy: A robotic device could dispense pills, liquids and other pharmaceuticals. If the prescriptions were in typed from and the required medicines were available, it would be a relatively simple matter for a robot to go a particular location, verify that the medicine stored at that location was the correct medicine and then dispense the needed amount. Verification might be accomplished by the robot's reading a UPC (Universal Product Code) label on the container and checking this information by inspection of its contents (for size, shape, color and so on). If the medicines were not available, the robot might find a generic equivalent. If a patient's medical history was in database, the robot could check it also. Once the prescription was filled, the robot could print the appropriate labels and affix them to the medicine container. In addition to the convenience of having a 24-hour pharmacist on duty, this system would supply an additional level of security which is especially important in the handling of controlled drugs. AI programming would be involved more in verification that the medicine was correct than in the robot's movements. An expert system could be used to help perform the verification. An ES could also be used to deal with the dispensing of generic medicines or other substitutions. It almost without saying that such system would need to have a high degree or reliability.

Surgery: Performing surgery upon a human demands the utmost skill and knowledge. Good surgeons need many years of practice and they are often in relatively short supply. Different surgeons specialize in operating on different parts of the body, such as the skin, limbs, heart or brain. As surgery has advanced over the years, sophisticated electronic equipment has come into use to aid the surgeon. Some of this equipment is used before an operation to assist in diagnosis and to locate areas that require surgery. Examples include X-ray devices and CAT, PET and MRI scans. Other equipment, such as laser, may be used during the operation itself. By integrating information form various scanning devices and utilizing precision cutting and fusing instruments, robots could perform certain types of surgery on immobilized patients. They are reliable, consistent and subject to neither fatigue nor emotion. Oversight of the operation by a human surgeon can help ensure that the step-by-step surgical process goes as smoothly as possible. This type of robotic procedure can reduce patient trauma and limit the time the surgeon must spent at the operating table. The AI techniques that are required include various types of pattern recognition, as well as use of the surgical instruments themselves. Obviously, all the hardware and software must exhibit very high reliability.

Space: When astronauts perform activities outside their space vehicle or space station, they need a great deal of protection from the environment hazards of outer space. Some of the EVA (extravehicular activity) tasks that must be performed during space missions could profitably be done by robots. The robots could stay outside much longer and they would required little (if any) protection. A robot with good vision and radiation sensors, say, could perform routine and continuous monitoring to help ensure that the integrity if the space module. The robot could easily tap into a data base in order to obtain information about the module's components. With appropriate tools, it could even make repairs outside the module. This would not reduce the hazards for the human astronauts but would also leads to increased productivity, because the people about could devote more time on scientific tasks. The AI activities would involve vision and other sensor processing for the monitoring phase of robot activity. Expert systems and more advanced problem-solving techniques would be used during fault diagnosis and repair. Natural language processing would greatly facilitate the communication process.

These are just a few of applications to which robots are suited. Some other sare

Fire fighting	Underground mining
Cleanup to toxic spills	undersea exploration
Nuclear power activities	Security service
Aiding handicapped people	Environment waste disposal

In all of these areas, the tasks proposed for robots that have one or more of the following characteristics:

1. There is a shortage of qualified people to perform the application.
2. The application requires close attention to detail.
3. The application is hazardous, tedious or impossible for people to perform.

There is always some fear of job displacement when any type of automation is discussed and this is especially true of robotics. However, the user of robots has the potential of improving employment conditions for everyone.

Voice Recognition

Most systems with voice recognition capability recognize only a few words. The computer must be "trained" to a recognize the user user's voice; then it accepts data or instructions by having commands spoken into the computer's microphone. However, the speaker must pause after each word.

There are other difficulties:

(a) many words sound like other words:

(b) different people pronounce the same word differently;

(c) one word can have multiple meanings;

(d) the tone in which something is said, such as a sarcastic remark, carries more meaning than the actual words do.

Any programming that improves upon these limiting factors will have to be able to interpret all the characteristics that make up conversation, such inflections, sentence structures and speeds. Kurzwell's VoiceWritter and IBM's Talkwriter are devices to transform human speech into printed text. Voice recognition capability may ultimately be the method for giving computers instructions or robots commands. Computers that can recognize and react properly to the human voice will make computers and other machines assessable to people who can't enter data or text in traditional ways.

Voice Synthesis

Machines that talk to you – have the capability of voice synthesis – are not new. They respond to an inquiry in a simulated human voice. You may have heard the Coca-Cola vending machine say, "Thank you" or used a computerized bank teller that told your account balance in a human-like voice or witnessed the talking cash registers in supermarkets. A typical audio-response system speaks fewer than 200 words and is limited in its ability combine them into sentences. As sophisticated as these devices now seem, the are primitive compared to what inventors visualize. The machines that Apple Computer Inc., is working on will speak while doing other tasks. They will read numbers aloud as they are entered into an electronic spreadsheet or repeat words as children type them.

Computer Vision

Imagine for a moment that we are interested in creating a robot to simulate a human being. We have some of the basic information we need to endow it with commonsense knowledge, capabilities for natural language communication, expert problem-solving, rudimentary planning and a little entertainment from game planning. But so are we can only talk to our machine through its keyboard and display screen. The logical next step is perception, the ability to receive input form the external world in its own media: sights, sounds, smells and so on.

While "odor processing" (if it even deserves study) may be beyond today's AI and engineering techniques, both speech and image understanding have been extensively pursued since the late 1960s. Commercial applications that have evolved since then include voice-activated word processors, optical text scanning and robots that sort containers, for example. But despite the enormous industrial potential of these technologies, perception seems to have an even more natural and uniquely human aura than such purely cognitive abilities as planning and problem solving.

Applications of Computer Vision

Here we will discuss their applications. The first is the visual interpretation of blocks-world which illustrates the advantage that top-down processing offers with a restricted domain containing geometric objects. The second application is related to the first and involves what is usually called parts inspection. The third is one of the more successful vision programs; it is known as ACRONYM.

ACRONYM

ACRONYM is based on the work that Rodney A. Brooks and Thomas O.Binford did at Stanford University around 1981. It is domain-independent but model-driven. This means that a user describes (models) the objects and their relationships in any domain of interest. ACRONYM then tries to identify and classify instances of the modeled objects. It also attempts to determine the 3-D location, shape and orientation of the objects on the basis of a given 2-D image. ACRONYM finds edges and constructs 2-D ribbons that describe the major features of the object. The system uses generalized-cylinder representations for the 3-D shapes. And it contains an algebric-reasoning system to deal with equations and inequalities and has a geometrical-reasoning system to deal with information about coordinates.

One domain for which ACRONYM has been successfully used is in aircraft recognition based on aerial photography. It uses generalized cylinder representations for certain aircraft 9such as, Boeing 747 and Lockheed L-1011s) to model the geometrical structures. The image of an aircraft can often be reduced to a long tapered ribbon (the fuselage) with smaller ribbons (the wings) coming off this main ribbon at certain angles. Algebraic inequalities and equations are then used to indicate the constraints on such items as fuselage radius fuselage length and wing angeles for each class of aircraft. ACRONYM then tries to identify all of the aircraft found in a given image.

Symbolic and Numeric Processing

The idea that AI involves a combination of symbolic and numeric processing is the major theme of this text. Symbolic processing involves the manipulation, within the computer, of symbols such as lists of words and characters. More recently, the languages Prolog and Smalltalk have been influencing AI work, but LISP is still the primary language for manipulating symbols. LISP also supports numeric processing (though other languages can often do so more efficiently). This type of processing frequently stresses computation with vectors and arrays of numbers.

Knowledge Based System

A knowledge base management system (KBMS) manages the knowledge in a given domain of interests and exhibits reasoning power to the level of a human expert in this domain. Artificial Intelligence (AI) application, knowledge representation requires data structures with rich semantics that go beyond the simple structure of the relational model. AI is the part of computer science with designing intelligent computer systems, that is systems that exhibit the characteristics we associate with intelligence in human behaviour. Furthermore, operations in a knowledge base are more complex than those in traditional database. When a rule is added, the system must check for contradictions and redundancy. Such operations cannot be represented directly by relational operations and the complexity of checking increases rapidly as the size of knowledge base grows.

Knowledge can be defined as the body of facts and principles accumulated by human-kind or the act, fact or state of knowing. It is having a familiarity with language, concepts, procedures, rules, ideas, abstractions, places, customs, facts and associations, coupled with an ability to use these notions effectively in modelling different aspects of the world. Without this ability, the facts and concepts are meaningless and therefore, worthless. The meaning of knowledge is closely related to the meaning of intelligence. Intelligence requires the possession of and access to knowledge. And a characteristic of intelligent people is that they possess much knowledge. In computers, knowledge is also stored as symbolic structures, but in the form of collection of magnetic spots and voltage states. State-of-the-art storage in computers is in the range of 1012 bits with capacities doubling about every three to four years. The gap between human and computer storage capacities is narrowing rapidly.

Unfortunately, there is a still a wide gap between representation schemes and efficiencies. AI has given new meaning and importance of knowledge. Now, for the first time, it is possible to package specialised knowledge and sell it with a system that can use it to reason and draw conclusions. The potential of this important development is only now beginning to be realised. Imagine being able to purchase an untiring, reliable advisor that gives high level professional advice in specialised areas, such as manufacturing techniques, sound financial strategies, ways to improve one's health, top marketing sectors and strategies, optimal farming plans and many other important mattes. We are not far from the practical realisation of this and those who create and market such systems will have more than just an economic advantage over the rest of the world.

Knowledge base systems get their power form the expert knowledge that has been coded into facts, rules, heuristics and procedures. The knowledge is stored in a knowledge base separate from the control and inferencing components. This makes it possible to add new knowledge or refine existing knowledge without recompiling the control and inferencing programs. This greatly simplifies the construction and maintenance of knowledge base systems. A knowledge base management system (KBMS) is used to manage and manipulate shared knowledge. A knowledge base system's manipulation facility includes a reasoning facility, usually including aspects of one or more of the following forms of reasoning:

(i) Deductive

(ii) Inductive or

(iii) Abudctive

(i) Deductive reasoning implies that a new fact can be inferred from a given set of facts or knowledge using known rules of inference. For example, a given proposition can be found to be true or false in light of existing knowledge in the form of other propositions can be found to be true or false believed to be either true or false.

(ii) Inductive reasoning is used to prove something by first proving a base fact and then the increment step; having proved these, we can prove a generalised fact.

(iii) Abductive reasoning is used in generating a hypothesis to explain observations. Like deductive reasoning, it points to possible inferences form relate concepts; however, unlike deductive reasoning, the number of inferences could be more than one. The likelihood of knowing which of these inferences corresponds to the current state of the system can be gleaned from the explanations generated by the system. These explanations can facilitate choosing among these alternatives and arriving at the final conclusions.

Above all, a knowledge base system may incorporate an explanation facility by which user can verify whether the reasoning used by the system is consistent and complete. The reasoning facility also offers a form of tutoring to the uninitiated user. The so-called expert systems and the associated expert system generation facilities are one form of knowledge base systems that have emerged from research labs and are being marketed commercially. Since a KBMS includes reasoning capacity, there is a clear benefit in incorporating this reasoning power in database application programs in languages such as COBOL and Pascal.

There is no consensus on the difference between a knowledge base system and a database system. In a DBMS, the starting point is a data model to represent the data and the interrelationships between them, similarly, the starting point of KBMS is a knowledge representation scheme. The requirements for any knowledge representation scheme should provide some mechanism to organise knowledge in appropriate hierarchies or categories, thus allowing easy access to associated concepts. In addition, since knowledge can be expressed as rules and exceptions to rules, exception-handling features must be represent in the knowledge stored in the system must be insulated form changes in usage in its physical or logical structure. The concept is similar to the data independence concept used in a DBMS. To data, little headway has been made in this aspect of KBMS. One difference between the DBMS and KBMS that has been proposed is that the knowledge base system handles a rather small amount of knowledge, whereas a DBMS efficiently handles large amounts of shared data.

Pattern Matching

Pattern matching is related to both symbolic and numeric AI processing and was one of the first general approaches used to aid in the solution of problems. In AI, the pattern may be anything from a symbol or a sequence of symbols to an n-dimensional array or other structure that is to be compared or matches to incoming information. The concept of the search is widely employed in all types of problem solving situation and has been used in operations researches and artificial intelligence for years. Many diverse problems can be partially or completely solved by search methods is the only way to solve certain problems. Here are a few examples of problems that can be solved by search methods.

- Finding a certain object within a collection of objects.
- Finding a preferred answer or best answer to a problem.
- Finding a sequence of operations by which to solve a puzzle.
- Finding the winning strategy in a game.
- Finding the maximum, minimum or zero of a mathematical function.

Logic and Inference

The early philosophers used logic to engage in formal reasoning about the world. Today, logical relations are used in AI programs as a representation mechanism for describing what it must know in order to make consistent and logically correct decisions. Logical operations can be used to derive new facts from old and logic is used directly in expert systems and automatic theorem proving applications. Some of the earliest AI programs were based on the use of deductive logic. Because pure deductive logic is symbolic in nature, it is amendable to LISP implementation. The area of logic and inference involves primarily symbolic processing and includes some of the earliest activities within AI. These activities involved theorem providing. It is through logic and inference that known facts are used to derive new facts. This area emphasizes the more formal, provable reasoning strategies; it has significant applications in mathematical proofs, of the correctness of programs, certain of automated programs and expert systems.

Problem Solving

Problem solving is the process of identifying a problem recognising its major characteristics, formulating a solution plan, dividing the problem into smaller (and more readily manageable) parts, assigning those parts to be solved, solving each part and finally combining the individual solutions into the solution of the original problem. This symbolic process relies heavily on knowledge structuring and search methods. In a sense, general-purpose problem solving is what AI itself is all about. Planning activities are also a major components of robotics.

Applications of Probe Solving

Now, we briefly describe some of the better-known systems for problem solving and planning: GPS, STRIPS and PLANNER.

General Problem Solve (GPS)

When Newell and Simon were working on Logic theorist (LT) to prove theorems in logic, they got the idea of trying to develop a program that would solve problems in general. Both were especially interested in the way humans solve problems and how this process could be captured and modelled on the computer. They derived general rules by observing and analysing methods that human subjects use in the performance of problem-solving tasks. This system was first developed in 1957 at Carnegie Mellon and evolved over about ten years. The original GPS used a modified depth-first search and means-ends analysis. Later versions placed less emphasis on the psychological theory behind GPS and more emphasis on ways to improve its problem-solving ability. Over the years, it solved problems in predicate calculus (as LT did). The Tower of Hanoi problem with four disks and various puzzles and symbolic integration problems. GPS defined a class of problems in terms of the following elements.

1. A set of objects associated with this problem class (examples include formulas, puzzle configurations and geometric figures).
2. A list of operations to transform the objects (examples include arithmetic transformations, legal moves and mappings).
3. A map of determine the difference between objects (examples include numeric, symbolic and positional differences)
4. An operator-difference table from which to select an operator in order to reduce the current difference.
5. An initial state and a goal state that is defined by the particular problem to be solved.

Stanford Research Institute Problem Solver (STRIPS)

STRIPS was developed in 1971 at the Stanford Research Institute Richard Fikes and Nils Nilson. It was used to control to a robot called "Shankey". Shankey was a self-propelled robot designed to move around in a restricted environment and to perform simple actions in response to commands presented in a constrained natural language. These activities included moving through rooms with connecting doorways and manipulating boxes. Problem solving was called for when a goal such as moving a box into a given room was specified. STRIPS was used to create a plan. It drew on some of the concepts behind GPS and incorporated other ingenious ideas to improve the planning process.

Shankey had four main system (1) a sensory system that used a television camera for image recognition and a tough bar to indicate when the robot encountered an object (2) a movement system that enabled it to move about he rooms (3) a communications link between the robot and an external computer to provide instructions and receive feedback (4) the computer itself which translated the natural language commands, instructed the robot on what to do next and utilised the sensory information returned form the robot. Unlike the GPS program which only produced a sequence of steps by which to solve a problem. STRIPS was used with a mechanism that actually carried out these plans.

Planner

Planner was an AI planning language developed by Carl Hewitt in the early 1970s to aid in problem solving situations. Statements are presented in the form of theorems about how to achieve certain goals. In addition to this kind of declarative knowledge, procedural knowledge about how to perform certain functions could also be incorporated. The design of PLANNER allowed for the use of high-level control structures as well as high-level knowledge structures. Perhaps the best-known use of the PLANNER design was the MIT implementation called Micro-Planner. Terry Winograd used Micro-Planner for SHRDLU program which simulated a robot moving objects about in the blocks-world system in order to produce a given block arrangement.

Learning

The activity of learning may be the most important activity in AI. The modeling can be done with the traditional performance paradigm. It can also be accomplished via the brain paradigm which has received renewed emphasis since the development of neural networks. AI learning is largely automatic learning during the use of the associated system, rather than learning through a revised knowledge base or an improved program. That is, the learning is not due to reprogramming; it is brought about by a program's reaction to its input. The extra processing requirements of learning may require additional types of computing hardware.

Social and Ethical Issues

There are many social and ethical issues that have arisen since the development of the electronic computer. Most of these have taken shape since the proliferation of microcomputers and the dawn of these computers ability to communicate with one another. Most of these issues are not peculiar to AI programs and data but rather apply to computing in general. The people who will be responsible for creating and using computer programs and data need to think carefully about social and ethical issues and to discuss them seriously. There are many forms of computer crime, wherein the computer is used as a means of commiting an illegal act. It is a crime, for instance, to access a computer file that contains confidential information. Such a file could contain data describing someone's personal medical or credit history, data describing the design of a new invention, data indicating someone's current account balance at a bank or some other sensitive information. We will return later to the issue of computers and privacy. Sometimes the people who are responsible for maintaining confidential information do not take the proper precautions to protect these data from unauthorised access and possible alteration. And unfortunately, some computer non professionals treat a computer's security system as a challenge and try to break into it for the same reason Sir Edmund Hillary gave for scaling Mount Everest: because it's there. Breaking into a protected computer file is essentially the same as breaking into a locked the cabinet, even though the threat of immediate discovery and physical apprehension may not be the same. One common form that this illegal intrusion takes is the unauthorised copying of protected software.

Because AI is frequently viewed as part of computer science, similar standards hold for Ai professionals. However, unique issues also arise in AI that do not normally appear in computer science activities. We have seen that AI typically involves several domains, not just computer science. Hence issues more commonly encountered in other domains (such as psychology or physiology) may also have to be addressed. As Whitby points out, AI is no longer restricted to research institutions; it is now associated with manor commercial products. Because AI professionals face a unique set of problems, they are in the best position to develop their own professionals standards. In particular, because of the trust that (rightly or wrongly) is often placed in AI systems, it is especially important for the AI programmer to write clear code, document thoroughly and correctly, test exhaustively and ensure the integrity of the AI program and the data upon which it operates.

FACT FINDING AND INFORMATION GATHERING

Introduction

The most critical phase of managing system projects is planning. To launch a system investigation, we need a master plan detailing the steps to be taken, the people to be questioned, and the outcome expected. The initial investigation has the objective of determining whether the user's request has potential merit. The major steps are defining user requirements, studying the present system to verify the problem, and defining the performance expected by the candidate system to meet user requirements. When the initial investigation is completed, the user receives a system proposal summarizing the findings and recommendations of the analyst.

A key part of feasibility analysts is gathering information about the present system. The analyst must know what information to gather, where to find it, how to collect it, and what to make of it. The proper use of tools for gathering information is the key to successful analysis. The tools are the traditional interview, questionnaire, and on-site observation. We need to know, for example, how to structure an interview, what makes up a questionnaire, and what to look for in on-site observations. These tools, when learned, help analysts assess the effectiveness of the present system and provide the groundwork for recommending a candidate system.

System Investigation

The terms "systems analysis" and "systems design" are often encountered; "systems investigation" includes these as well as other activities. A systems investigation is a project undertaken to improve a specific aspect of the information system; its essence is working with people to devise systems that help people work better. A systems investigation, sometimes called a "systems development project", relies on an extensive body of methodology and a well-defined set of tools and techniques in order to analyze, design, and implement an information system or a portion of an information system.

Why Study Systems Investigations?

The student who takes a position in a small or medium-sized company may be one of the most qualified managers in the company in the information systems area and, for this reason, is likely to be asked to participate deeply in a systems investigation. Even in large companies, the opportunity to participate in a systems investigation often is presented to junior managers whose formal education has been recently completed and who have studied systems development and implemen-tation. The new manager should seek such an opportunity because participation is likely to provide invaluable experience. With the information systems knowledge acquired to this point in the text, the student is in a position to participate knowledgeably in systems investigations: the major ingredient lacking is a knowledge of the processes, tools, and techniques involved in systems investigations.

How can junior managers become involved in systems investigations? There are at least five ways and discussed below.

1. As a systems user. All positions inside an organization utilize information, much of which is provided by a formal information system. Users of information systems can become actively involved in specifying their information needs — they need not wait for invitations. A user should understand the nature of information systems in order to recognize possible improvements to these systems.

2. As a user representative. Often, a department of an organization formally designates one member to serve as the liaison with the organisation's information systems department. Liaison activity includes meeting with user representatives of other departments, communicating the department's information needs to systems analysts, and explaining changes proposed by the analysts to other members of the department. Serving as a liaison provides a young manager an opportunity to gain insight into the organization's information systems and the structure of systems project.

3. As a systems investigation participant. A new manager may be assigned temporarily to a particular systems investigation project, perhaps on a task force that utilizes the manager's specialized expertise. This temporary assignment can provide valuable experience.

4. In a supervisory or advisory position. As a manager acquires experience with the organization, the manager may be given a supervisory assignment in a systems investigation. For example, the manager could be made a member or an alternate member of a systems steering committee or the team leader of a systems task force.

5. As a trained systems analyst. A young manager may choose to spend a period of time in systems development work. A career path may include 1 to 3 years spent as a systems analyst, perhaps as part of a management training program. Positions as systems analysts or other systems specialists may be within the central computer group or a part of a user department. Because of the proliferation of microcomputer data centers within operating departments, an increased number of systems positions have become available with user groups.

Even if participation is restricted to communication with the organization's systems analyst, a young manager's knowledge of information systems and systems investigations provides an understanding of the analyst's activities. This knowledge also aids in understanding the entire organization's activities.

A note of caution should be sounded at this time: A systems investigation is a complex activity with many variables, and there is ample scope to permit a wide variety of serious blunders. However, if the student applies the principles and follows the steps outlined in this chapter and the following ones, many of the more common and more serious mistakes may be avoided; the text also notes several areas of systems investigations in which caution is warranted.

The Life Cycle of an Information System

The Concept

The concept of the life cycle of a system is central to systems investigations. Every system moves through several phases of a life cycle during its development, after which it functions with only minor maintenance for a period of years. The system gradually deteriorates to the point where it ceases to function effectively, and a new life cycle begins with the development of a new system.

The life-cycle concept is related to another important concept, that of professional information systems development teams. Large and medium-sized organizations usually have full-time systems investigation specialists including programmers and analysts. Typically, for all but minor systems investigations, a team will be formed at the time the preliminary study phase begins. The team is likely to be expanded for the systems analysis phase and to be altered in composition somewhat for the systems design phase. Then the team, probably again altered in its composition, implements the newly designed system. As each team member completes assigned responsibilities, that member either is assigned additional responsibilities for the project or is assigned to another systems investigation. Thus, the project teams are dynamic - they are continuously forming and re-forming to participate in different aspects of the systems investigations or in other systems investigations. There is a continuous cycling of professional systems personnel through a series of systems investigations.

It is useful to outline briefly each of the phases of the systems investigation;

1. The preliminary study phase. During this phase, a problem with an existing information system or an opportunity to usefully develop a new system is discovered, and a limited amount of initial investigation takes place to see whether a systems project is warranted.

2. The systems analysis phase. During the analysis phase, a problem or opportunity associated with the system is identified, the strengths and weaknesses of the old system are examined, and what a new system could accomplish is determined.

3. The systems design phase. During the design phase, a new system or computer application is designed to satisfy the needs that have been determined during the analysis phase. During this pha;,e, both hardware studies and software systems design are completed.

4. The implementation phase. This phase involves the programming, equipment installation, and other activities related to implementing a newly designed system.

5. The systems maturity and maintenance phase. This phase involves the continuous operation of the system after installation. Usually, the system achieves peak performance, and then its cost effectiveness gradually declines as its environment changes, as its operating costs change, or as its equipment becomes worn or obsolete. Near the end of this phase, the system is deemed to be no longer performing satisfactorily and is replaced.

A brief postaudit is part of the systems maturity and maintenance phase. To determine whether the investigation was conducted efficiently and to establish the extent to which the organization has received the expected benefits, a postaudit team reviews the systems investigation processes and as well as the functioning of the new system.

Because the activities of the various phases typically overlap, they may not be readily distinguishable from one another during a systems investigation. Personnel training, for example, is a pan of the implementation phase, but the lead time for training personnel to accept and use certain types of systems is lengthy, and this activity often begins long before the systems design is complete. Despite this intermixing of phases it is useful to distinguish between them, these distinctions facilitate a better understanding of the systems investigation processes. Additionally, most systems project planning and control activities are formally associated with phases, and thus it is necessary to understand these phases in order to participate usefully in the planning and control of systems investigations.

The general principles of systems investigations are similar for all types and sizes of systems projects, although the application of these principles may require different procedures, analysis, and other methods for different projects. The systems investigation activities are scaled down considerably for small projects, and for a small project the process may be quite informal.

To simplify the discussion, the assumption is made throughout that the systems investigation involves the development of a new system rather than the revision of an existing one, although the general principles are equally applicable in both situations. Here we are concerned with formal systems investigations dealing with computer information systems. However, the student should keep in mind that the principles as well as many of the tools and techniques discussed are equally relevant to noncomputerized information systems.

The People Involved in a System Investigation

Systems investigations involve people interacting with people. While technical tools are important, the most critical ingredient in systems investigations is the ability of people to work with other people. People in several categories become involved in systems investigations.

Syslems analysts Programmers

Computer systems managers Users of information systems User representatives Systems consultants Vendor representatives Managers of the organisation Internal auditors

Systems Analysts

Systems analysts are professional systems personnel who work with users to analyze existing systems and design new **ones.** Analysts determine what information the new or revised system must provide; how the information should be captured, processed, and reported; and what programs and equipment will be needed to satisfy the requirements of the organization. Because systems analysts bear a major responsibility for the design of the information system, they possess a wide variety of systems investigation expertise. Many analysts have specialized experience and training in programming, accounting systems, telecommunications and networking, or equipment selection methods. Some systems analysts understand the computer aspects of operations thoroughly, but lack an adequate understanding of the activities of middle and senior level managers and have difficulty designing systems for higher level management purposes. Some analysis also view systems development as requiring primarily technical expertise rather than an ability to work well with people, which severely limits their effectiveness. Business school graduates are less likely than more technically trained analysts to have these two deficiencies. System analysts often have been programmers, but many also have had experience and training in specialized functional areas, such as accounting, engineering, marketing, and finance.

Programmers

If systems investigations involve the development of computer programs, programmers are used. There are two general types of programmers: applications programmers and systems programmers. Applications programmers prepare computer programs to satisfy user departments' requirements for information. They write detailed programs to accomplish the data processing specified by (he analysts[1] flowcharts and narrative descriptions. In many organizations, the programmers also serve as systems analysis, and the distinction between the two is not maintained.

Syslems programmers, the second type of programmers, often have more technical knowledge of computer systems than any of the other computer systems personnel. Systems programmers write or modify the programs that enable the computer system to control itself and to process applications programs. For example, systems programmers may modify the computer's operating systems, modify a data base management system, or develop various utility programs for the computer, such as sort routines, and edit (error-detection and error-correction) routines. Systems programmers usually do not interact extensively in their work with users, systems analysts, or applications programmers.

Computer Systems Managers

A variety of kinds of managers exist within the computer area. In a medium-scale data processing department there usually is at least a programming manager, an input-output and data entry control manager, a hardware selection manager, a computer operations manager, a project manager, and a data base administrator if there is a data base, as well as other types of managers and a bevy of assistant managers. Most of these managers have previously served as technical personnel in the areas they manage.

Users of Information Systems

"End-users" are the personnel of the organization units for which the information systems and applications programs are designed and implemented. Users provide data to the data processing system and utilize the information provided by the system. Users may include blue-collar workers on the shop floor, clerical employees of all kinds, group leaders and supervisors; middle level managers, technical and professional specialists, and senior managers. Working with systems analysts during the investigation, users ascertain what data must be made available for processing, and they determine their own information needs; this interaction is necessary to design a system that will satisfy the organization's needs.

User Representatives

User representatives, as managers within a user department who officially represent user groups, work closely with systems analysts, help define users' needs, and represent the interest of users in other ways. Their tasks include bringing systems problems to the attention of systems analysts and working with analysts to ensure that existing systems function effectively. The appointment is usually part-time, although user representatives may work full-time on a particular project for a limited period. Junior managers who are knowledgeable about information systems are likely to assume this role.

Systems Consultants

In many systems investigations, the participants include one or more outside consultants with specialized expertise. Sometimes an external consultant can operate effectively as a systems analyst for the organization; however, consultants generally should not design and install a system without the cooperation and extensive participation of the concerned user group. If user groups are not adequately involved, systems installed by a consultant probably will not satisfy their needs and perhaps will not be used at all. In small organizations, without an extensive systems staff, consultants are often asked to play a broad role that may encompass organizing and managing the systems project and helping select equipment. In larger organizations, consultants are likely to be employed for more specialized tasks, such as evaluating the relative technical merits of alternative computer or software systems. Even large organizations with highly sophisticated systems personnel frequently employ outside consultants.

Vendor Representatives

Employed by hardware and software sales companies, vendor representatives sell their companies products and offer advice to clients about the selection of hardware or software. As a general rule, vendor representatives can be relied upon to reflect the perspective of their employers and do not provide an unbiased analysis of an organization's needs. Vendor representatives may be called "customer service representatives" or have a similar title, and vendor technical personnel are often called "customer engineers".

Managers of the Organization

Whether the systems are intended to provide information directly to the managers or not, the organization's managers cooperate, facilitating the required resource allocations, ensuring that systems investigations are well controlled and produce effective information systems, and formally accepting the systems developed.

Internal Auditors

The internal auditors of the organization should participate at numerous points in systems investigations. Their major contribution is to ensure that the completed system embodies adequate internal controls and that the system and its output can be audited. Internal auditors may also participate as members of the postaudit team after the conclusion of the systems investigation.

People Problems in Systems Investigations

When a systems investigation fails to produce a useful system, the failure is usually due to problems involving the people related to the new system; these are called "people problems". All the groups and all the individuals involved with the systems investigation have vested personal interests and psychological needs that affect their acceptance and use of a new system. Individuals may desire to contribute to the organization or to feel wanted by, or important to, the organization; they have feelings about replacing the existing system, as well as perspectives on the problems and the advantages of both the old and the new systems. Frequently they experience fears about job security and concern about the impact of a new system on their jobs.

A systems investigation is a project that involves people working together toward the common goal of improving the information system. While technical expertise is, of course, important, even more important to a systems investigation are diplomacy, tact, persuasiveness, sensitivity to people's needs and concerns, and training in interviewing techniques. Some of the people problems most likely to be encountered are listed in Figure 14.7.6 and discussed below; these problems are due to personality trails that to some degree prevent a system from being properly developed or properly used after development.

1. Commitment to the old information system. Users of the existing information system who do not wish to leam to use a new system may oppose it because they are committed to the old system. Sometimes these users are external to the organization, such as customers who are billed by the system or who interact with it in other ways and resist its being changed. Other such users are peopu in a department who were instrumental in designing and implementing the old system and who fee! loyal to it.

2. Resistance to change. Everyone resi?"? change; to an extent, we are all creatures of habit. Because the usual purpose of a systems investigation is to bring about change, it is not surprising that many people are unwilling to cooperate wholeheartedly with it. This resistance to chang. must be overcome by using diplomacy. Everyone,, including managers who make decisions about the new system, must be shown the advantages of the new system. Often resistance to change erodes

3. Embarrassment. Because people are embarrassed by a lack of knowledge about computer systems or by an inability to specify their information needs fully, tbey may avoid participation in the systems investigation. This reluctance can be reduced in diplomatic ways. For example, senior managers whose participation is needed but who could be embarrassed by their lack of systems knowledge often can participate as members of the systems steering committee in ways that permit them to conceal their ignorance while learning about systems.

4. Fear of being a scapegoat. Many systems investigation participants believe that the organization will seek a scapegoat for problems associated with the existing system or for the possible inability to initiate a satisfactory new system. These persons desire to avoid the systems investigation entirely so that they cannot be blamed for anything. Ironically, if they refuse to become involved, a measure of any blame for an inadequate new system can be assigned to them. The advantages of cooperating with the systems investigation must be shown to them.

5. Fear of job loss. As employees are well aware, new systems frequently eliminate jobs or substantially alter a job's content. Concern about the possibility of losing a job is one of the strongest possible motivations for not cooperating with a systems investigation or not accepting a new system after its installation. Here, the organization's track record is decisive; if in the past when jobs were eliminated, the employees who beld them were given training that qualified them for equally good or (probably) better jobs elsewhere in the organization, most employees' fears of job loss will be eliminated.

6. Lack of interest among key personnel. Often it is difficult to capture the interest of key personnel. Many managers are quite busy and are disinclined to give their attention to a systems project; even if the new system will serve them. In particular, managers at the higher levels of organizations have schedules that seldom permit more than a few minutes for a discussion with a systems analyst, and their lofty positions given them the ability to remain aloof from a systems investigation if they choose to. To appreciate the position of senior managers, reflect for a moment on the difficulty of getting students involved in student political clubs and student business associations. Many worthy activities compete for students' time and attention, and getting them deeply involved is difficult; the same is true in the business world. Senior managers usually are already the busiest people in the organization, and yet their active assistance is necessary. They -can directly contribute to the systems investigation, they allocate the resources, and they motivate subordinates to cooperate as members of a systems steering committee.

7. Analysts' lack of personnel skills. The education of systems analysts, programmers, and designers often con-centrates on technical subjects; little or no attention may be given to psychology, personnel relations, or interview techniques. As a result, in their dealings with other participants in the systems investigation, these systems specialists often are insensitive to people problems. This insensitivity is itself a people problem, which is compounded by another problem; because the mental processes of technicians tend to be different from those of managers; communication between analysts and managers is a serious problem, even if the systems specialists try to be sensitive to other people. Systems specialists should be given special human relations training.

8. Conflicting interests. Animosity between individuals, groups, or departments often prevents cooperation on a systems problem. Individuals or groups may prefer different solutions to a particular systems problem. One very large company, for example, had acquired a medium-sized company and had imposed upon it the corporate chart of accounts. However, the personnel of the acquired company preferred the chart previously used. Discontent led to a systems investiga-tion that was intended to establish a new chart of accounts. Five years later, the two groups finally compromised, although neither group was entirely satisfied with the new chart of accounts. In this case, as often happens with such conflicts, the systems analysts' negotiating skills were more important than their technical expertise.

9. Territorial instincts. Often, a group within an organization that generates data may believe that this data "belongs" to it. The data provides the group with power and influence in the organization, and group members do not wish to share the information, even if that would be in the best interests of the entire organization. Such territorial instincts are not easily overcome, but good personnel skills of systems personnel are useful. Also, including a representative of the dissident group on the systems steering committee may convince the group to share "their" information. If the organization has a data base, the data base administrator is given the authority to resolve this people problem by fiat, if necessary.

10. Expressing a position too early. Frequently, participants (including systems specialists) take initial positions for or against the existing system or a possible new system. Someone who has publicly expressed a position becomes reluctant to change that position at a later time. Participants then find themselves "locked in" to positions that are undesirable in the light of subsequent developments. Systems investigation participants should be asked to take a noncommittal, "wait-and-see" stance during the early stages of a project.

Avoiding People Problems

Many people problems can be avoided. One good practice is for analysts to consult with everyone who should be involved in the systems investigation. If someone who should participate at some point is excluded initially, even as a matter of convenience or expediency, that person will be less inclined to cooperate later. Another good practice is 10 pay careful attention to any objections to a new system; systems personnel should undertake sincere discussions with the persons voicing the objections.

Systems personnel often err in not recognizing the participants' vested interests in the old system. For example, a new system usually requires that managers discard old work routines or techniques. If systems analysts consider the perspectives of participants, many vested interests can be identified and accommodated. Often a new system can be designed to permit personnel to continue their old work routines, with no reduction in the efficiency of the new system.

A common error of a systems specialist is that of claiming the major share of credit for the new system. However, many people participate in the systems investigation, and each deserves an appropriate share of the credit. When appreciation is expressed and proper credit is given, participants accept the new system and cooperate in other systems investigations at a later time.

Another common error is not assuring personnel that their futures are secure even if jobs are eliminated. Few systems investigations result in employees' being terminated, and most displaced personnel are assigned better positions than they had before. Inadequate training of employees for the new system positions can also cause problems. If users understand the advantages of the new system and are properly trained in its use, the system usually will be effectively implemented.

A final problem is improper interviewing techniques, which often cause the alienation of participants in the systems investigation process. Interviewing is the most important systems analysis technique. Interviewing is also useful for many activities other than systems investigations and students should accept any opportunity to learn the principles of good interviewing. For example, a knowledge of interviewing is useful when seeking employment, and it is useful for public accountants who must interview clients to gain information during an audit.

General Principles of Systems Investigations

Several general principles of systems investigation are of paramount importance to the successful completion of a project and are examined briefly below.

1. Involve managers in the project In all systems projects, managers of the user organization should be involved, and in major systems projects, senior managers as well as managers at other levels in multiple areas of the organization should be involved. Senior managers must understand the systems projects in order to allocate resources, make decisions about the overall direction of the information systems, and motivate subordinates to develop and utilize new systems. Lower-level managers are often in a good position to urge that their subordinates cooperate with systems projects. Whenever a systems project has the potential to influence multiple areas of the organization, representatives from all areas should participate, even during the project planning stages.

2. Involve users in the project. The necessity to involve users in systems projects appears self-evident, and yet systems specialists often attempt to develop new systems with no or with minimal user participation. The perspective of systems users is absolutely essential to the decision concerning whether to keep the existing system or design a new one. Users who provide information to, or receive information from, the system are in the best position to know about the availability of information and to know the required capabilities of a new system.

A system that is designed without extensive interaction with users usually becomes an unpleasant surprise to them and is not likely to be utilized. Users generally react negatively to any system that has been designed without their involvement. Additionally,^ystems developed in isolation from users usually are not adequately designed.

3. Plan the project within the context of long-range systems planning. Without adequate long-range planning for the entire information system, individual projects are unlikely to serve the overall interests of the organization satisfactorily. Each proposed project must be evaluated in terms of the goals of the entire organization.

4. Maintain a balanced systems project portfolio. A systems development group in u company of even moderate size generally has several systems investigation projects in process simultaneously. These projects make up its "portfolio", which is much like an investment portfolio. An investment portfolio achieves an optimum balance between high- and low-risk investments; in like manner, a systems project portfolio attempts to balance high- and low-risk projects. This balance is achieved by including both state-of-the-art and routine, easily accomplished projects, as well as projects of both short and long duration. Only a limited number of highly risky projects should be included in the portfolio at any one time. Risky projects are those with a low probability of being completed on schedule, within budget, and with the hoped-for benefits. Too many risky projects in a systems portfolio can result in a high rate of unsuccessful projects. The consequence is a reduction of confidence in the systems group on the part of management and users, low morale in the systems group, and, frequently, the termination of systems analysts or EDP managers who are blamed for the rash of unsuccessful projects.

5. Take into account the evolution of systems. The scale and complexity of projects should be suitable to the level of sophistication of the organization. During the early stages of the evolution of an organization's information systems, systems personnel rarely have the expertise to design and successfully implement sophisticated systems. Even if ultrasophis-ticated systems could be successfully designed and implemented, management and clerical personnel probably could not accept the radical changes in operations and gain full benefit from the sophisticated systems. For example, an organization that does not have most major data processing applications computerized would be unwise to attempt to incorporate all its applications into a computerized data base.

6. Establish a project management system. Formal project management systems that provide regular progress reports can be adapted to fit even small systems projects; project management systems enable projects to be managed in a systematic, controlled manner. The probability of successful implementation of a new system increases dramatically if a project management system is utilized. However, the degree of organization for project management should be tailored to the cost and value of the project. Overorganization of a small project is not cost-effective.

7. Establish the objectives and scope of a proposed system early. If the objectives and scope of a new system are formally established at about the time the project is begun, all effort is focused explicitly on achieving the objectives. Unfocused effort is likely to be frittered away on tangential activities of little value to the organization. By some estimates, as much as 40 percent of the systems development efforts in many organizations are wasted on false starts and unnecessary tasks; this can be reduced by means of a proper and timely definition of the objectives and scope of systems projects. When a systems steering committee exists, it should play a decisive role in establishing the objectives and scope of a proposed system.

8. Identify the proper problem. Failure to identify the most important problem is one of the most common mistakes in systems investigations. Often, for example, the problem is not a systems problem but instead is a people problem. Perhaps the users do not understand how to use the existing system and require more training, or perhaps they are resisting the system for some reason. Small organizations often identify the problem as the lack of a computer, when in fact a computer would not improve operations at all; the real problem often is that the existing manual systems are not properly designed or have degenerated over time. Another common mistake is made when an existing computer is unable to complete the data processing chores; the problem is defined as a lack of adequate computer capacity, when, in reality, the problem is the inefficient utilization of the existing computer.

Political problems, for example,' can be caused by feuding factions. Each faction may have different expectations of the information system, or one group in the organization may refuse to **make** its information available to another group, with the consequence that the second group requests that a new (and redundant) system be developed to provide information that already exists. In these cases negotiation, rather than a new system, is the preferred solution.

Another type of problem may be vendor-related. Often more cost-effective hardware and software or better service is available from another vendor, but misplaced loyalty, an unwarranted reluctance to deal with more than one vendor, or other reasons prevent an organization from seeking another vendor even if the present one does not provide fully satisfactory products or services.

Particularly in small organizations, the quality of data processing service may be low because of high rates of employee turnover or absenteeism. Although the difficulty may be diagnosed as a systems problem, such as inadequate computer capacity, it is a personnel problem. Another frequently misdiagnosed problem relates to the way the information systems are organized. Frequent delays in receiving reports, for example, may be interpreted as the consequence of inadequate systems capacity. In fact, the problem could be as simple as improper scheduling, a need for a night shift in data processing, or a need for a decentralized or distributed system to replace one that has adequate capacity but is too centralized.

9. Establish a reasonable completion schedule. Systems personnel are notorious for proposing schedules that are wildly optimistic. Often this is an indication of their eagerness to please, or their optimism may be a simple matter of underestimation of the effort involved. Frequently, too, an optimistic schedule is a consequence of overzealousness in seeking the approval for a new project. Systems development personnel must be apprised of the consequences to the organization and to themselves of setting unreasonable completion estimates for projects. On the other hand, open-ended projects without deadlines also should be avoided. AH projects should have a project schedule stated in hours, days, or weeks, along with a completion date. Proper scheduling allocates a specific amount of personnel resources to each project. Without careful control, projects sometimes continue indefinitely and consume inordinate amounts of resources.

10. Use a performance evaluation system. Before the project begins, systems and management personnel should determine the criteria that will measure the success of the new system after its implementation, and these criteria should be embodied in a performance evaluation system. Performance evaluation also should encompass evaluation of the efficiency of the systems project. Additionally, the postaudit procedures should be established in advance. When the project personnel understand that the ultimate success of the system will be measured by preestablished criteria, they will commit themselves to meeting these criteria.

11. Make creeping commitments. All decisions made during a systems investigation should remain tentative as long as possible so that they can be gracefully altered if necessary. The organization should "creep" toward a final commitment to the project and toward each resource commitment to it. When a creeping commitment approach is used, if new information is uncovered or if subsequent analyses challenge previous decisions, as is often the case, the previous decisions can be reviewed and altered with a minimum expenditure of resources. Also, there are psychological considerations. First, when decisions that are later altered are initially stated as being tentative rather than final, personnel arc not as likely to lose face, feel defeated or demoralized, or believe that the organization is wishy-washy in its commilrnent to a project. Additionally, if a decision appears final, personnel may not remain alert for alternatives that may be preferable, with the consequence that the organization is less likely to finally receive the system it needs.

12. Start with a broad investigation and then become increasingly detailed. Systems investigations should begin with the "big picture" of how the activity relates to the entile organization and with a consideration of broad alternatives; this may be termed "macro" analysis and design and is called "successive refinement" or "iterative refinement" by some experts. Successive analyses and designs become increasingly focused and detailed, each operating within the context established by the preceding decisions and activities: this is referred to as "micro" analysis and design. In the design phase, especially, several iterations of design, each more detailed than the preceding one, may be required before the final, fully detailed micro design is established.

13. Ensure conformance to standards. Every systems investigation initiated should conform to the organization's prcestablished information systems standards. If" a standards program is not in existence, an initial investment of resources should be made to develop common programming, data definition, documentation procedure, and other systems standards. Increasingly, the development of a data dictionary is the approach adopted to establish many of the information systems standards; this approach can be usefully adopted even if a data base is not intended. Requiring that all new or revised systems conform to these standards will pay high dividends. Conformity promotes efficiency in systems maintenance and develop-ment, and it facilitates the subsequent introduction of distributed data processing systems, the integration of existing applications (such as by a data base), and the implementation of computer models and decision support systems. The development of a standards program is itself an important systems project.

14. Use a structured approach. Systems investigations should use a structured methodology, consisting of a series of steps within each phase, each done more or less in sequence. This provides a discernible structure to the project. This structure also serves to increase the systematic nature of the activity and thereby reduces the extent of wasted effort. In general, the more structured the systems investigation, the lower the proportion of wasted effort. A large proportion of wasted effort occurs when tasks are done out of sequence and when prior completion of the preceding task in sequence would have demonstrated that the task done was not needed or should have been completed differently.

15. Establish priorities for projects. There often appears to be an infinite number of possible systems projects. In the typical organization there is a formal backlog of about 3 years; that is, there, is a list of projects requested which have not yet been initialed and which, because of resource shortages, are not expected to be initiated for 3 years. Additionally, many projects which are needed now but which may not be needed in 3 or 4 years, when they can be completed, are not on the list. In this environment, a system of prioritization should be used to ensure that the most critical systems projects are undertaken first. Typically, priorities are established by systems steering committee; after each project is given a "hearing" to determine its merits, it is assigned a priority level.

A Final Word on Systems Investigation Principles

From the preceding discussion of principles it can be seen that systems investigations are complex and that systems work is both an art and a science. Dealing with people is in good measure an art, and the science is represented by an extensive body of systems development theory and a series of principles for the application of mat theory. To be a proficient analyst requires both study and experience in the application of the ait and science aspects of systems investigations.

Initial Investigation

The first step in the system development life cycle is the identification of a need. This is a user's request to change, improve, or enhance an existing system. Because there is likely to be a stream of such requests, standard procedures must be established to deal with them. The *initial investigation* is now way of handling this. The objective is to determine whether the request is valid and feasible before a recommendation is reached to do nothing, improve or modify the existing system, or build a new one.

The user's request form specifies the following:

1. User-assigned title of work requested.
2. Nature of work requested (problem definition).

3. Date request was submitted.
4. Date job should be completed.
5. Job objective(s)—purpose of job requested.
6. Expected benefits to be derived from proposed change.
7. Input/output description—quantity (number of copies or pages) and frequency (daily, weekly, etc.) of inputs and outputs of proposed change.
8. Requester's signature, title, department, and phone number.
9. Signature, title, department, and phone number of person approving the request.

The user request identifies the need for change and authorizes the initial investigation. It may undergo several modifications before it becomes a written commitment. Once the request is approved, the following activities are carried out: background investigation, fact-finding and analysis, and presentation of results—called project proposal. The proposal, when approved, initiates a detailed user-oriented specification of system performance and analysis of the feasibility of the candidate system. A feasibility study focuses on identifying and evaluating alternative candidate systems with a recommendation of the best system for the job.

Needs Identification

The success of a system depends largely on how accurately a problem is defined, thoroughly investigated, and properly carried out through the choice of solution. User need identification and analysis are concerned with what the user *needs* rather than what he/she *wants.* Not until the problem has been identified, defined, and evaluated should the analyst think about solutions and whether the problem is worth solving. This step is intended to help the user and the analyst understand the real problem-rather than its symptoms.

The user or the analyst may identify the need for a candidate system or for enhancements in the existing system. For example, the cashier {chief operations officer) of a bank may become concerned about the long customer lines in the lobby or about the number of tellers who are "over" or "short" when they balance their cash. Similarly, an analyst who is familiar with the operation may point out a bottleneck and suggest improvements. Often problems come into focus after a joint meeting between the user and the analyst. In cither case, the user initiates ai. investigation by filling out a request form for information. The request provides for statements of objectives and expected benefits. The objectives of the problem situation must be understood within the framework of the organization's MIS objective, us discussed earlier under system planning. If objectives are misunderstood, it is easy to solve the wrong problem. In Table next. It illustrates that the successful design of a system requires a clear knowledge of what the system is intended to do.

Objectives of Decision Situations

Objective Question	*Typical Objective*	*Real Objective*
What is the objective of a city library?	To impart wisdom of the ages to the uneducated	Majority of books checked out are for enjoyment rather than fact-finding
Why do most people buy furniture?	To furnish new homes, apartments; to sit on, eat on, etc.	Marketing informs us that people discard old furniture not because it is nonfunctional but because it does not look good anymore.
What is the objective of a two-car garage?	To store two automobiles and protect them from the elements	Families desire to park one car only and save room to store more important equipment (or junk)
What is the objective of an inventory control system?	To ensure prompt availability of needed material	Isn't locating a key factor? Aren't costs a primary consideration?

Determining the User's Information Requirements

Shared, complete, and accurate information requirements are essential in building computer-based information systems. Unfortunately, determining the information each user needs is a particularly difficult task. In fact, it is recognized as one of the most difficult tasks in system development. The Association for Computing Machinery (ACM) Curriculum Committee on Computing Education for Management recognized this by suggesting two distinct job titles for systems development: "information analyst" and "systems designer" rather than the more general term "systems analyst."[2] The information analyst determines the needs of the user and the information flow that will satisfy those needs. The usual approach is to ask the user what information is currently available and what other information is required. Interaction between the analyst and the user usually leads to an agreement about what information will be provided by the candidate system.

There are several reasons why it is difficult to determine user requirements:

1. System requirements change and user requirements must be modified to account for these changes.
2. The articulation of requirements is difficult, except for experienced users. Functions and processes are not easily described,
3. Heavy user involvement and motivation are difficult. Reinforcement for their work is usually not realized until the implementation phase—too long to wait.
4. The pattern of interaction between users and analysts in designing information requirements is complex.

Users and analysts traditionally do not share a common orientation toward problem definition. For example, in the analyst's view, the problem definition must be translatable into a system design expressed quantitatively in terms of outputs, inputs, processes, and data structures. This is an ideal way to develop a good system when all features are known, under the best of situations, and within time constraints. In contrast, the user seems to be satisfied with a qualitative definition that specifies the system in generalities. Flexibility is a key consideration. System specifications must change with their needs, as must the system after implementation.

Based on these contrasting views, users who try to define their information requirements with the analyst's views find themselves in a predicament. According to Scharer, they defined themselves by producing strategies that will satisfy the analyst.

1. In the *kitchen sink* strategy the user throws everything into the requirement definition—overstatement of needs such as an overabundance of reports, exception processing, and the like. This approach usually reflects the user's lack of experience in the area.
2. The *smoking* strategy sets up a smoke screen by requesting several system features when only one or two are needed. The extra requests are used as bargaining power. This strategy usually reflects the user's experience in knowing what he/she wants. Requests have to be reduced to one that is realistic, manageable, and achievable.
3. The *same thing* strategy indicates the user's laziness, lack of knowledge, or both. "Give me the same thing but in a better format through the computer" is a typical statement. Here the analyst has little chance of succeeding because only the user can fully discover the real needs and problems.

Humans have problems spceit'ying information requirements. "Asking" the user what is needed of a candidate system docs not often yield accurate and complete requirements. According to Davis, humans have these limitations.

1. *Humans as information processors.* The human brain has both high-capacity, long-term memory and limited-capacity (but fast), short-term memory. The limits of short-term memory affect the information requirements obtained, because the user who is interviewed has a limited number of requirements that he/she defines as important. This limits processing responses. He/she may have selectively emphasized a few items of information and recorded them in long-term memory as being the most important. They may be the only ones that are recalled during the interview.

2. *Human bias in data selection and use.* Humans are generally biased in their selection and use of data. Their behavior becomes a representation of the bias. For example, users are influenced more by recent events than by past events. Thus, an information need that was discovered recently tends to carry greater weight than a need experienced in the distant past. This is called the *recency effect.* In another bias, users tend to use only information that is available in the form in which ii is displayed. This means that the requirements provided by the user are biased by currently available information.

3. *Human problem-solving behavior.* Humans have a limited capacity for rational thinking. According to Simon, they must simplify it in order to deal with it. Coined as the concept of *bounded rationality,* it means that rationality for determining information requirements is "bounded" by a simplified model (as well as by limited training, prejudice, and attitude of user) that may not reflect the real situation.[7] Bounded rationality is often reflected in the behavior of systems analysts. A successful analyst uses a general model to search for information requirements. It includes me consideration of ogranizational and policy issues in arriving at realistic requirements. The poorly rated analyst does not consider these issues, but focuses on the immediate (short-term) requirements facing the user.

Preliminary Investigation Steps

To conduct a successful preliminary investigation, you should perform the five steps described below. These steps apply regardless of the size of the project.

Step 1 Obtain an authorization to proceed

Step 2 Identify the necessary information

Step 3 Perform fact-finding to gather the necessary information.

* Obtain and analyze organization charts for those departments undergoing study to determine who should be interviewed.
* Conduct interviews to obtain information.
* Review current system documentation.
* Observe current operations to obtain information.
* If necessary, conduct a brief survey.

Step 4 Analyze the information.

Step 5 Present your results and recommendations to management.

Step 1: Obtain Authorization to Proceed

A systems project often produces significant changes in company operations. Employees may be curious, concerned, or actually opposed to these changes. It is not surprising to encounter some user resistance during a preliminary investigation. Employee attitudes and reactions are important and must be considered. In addition, a preliminary investigation often involves managers who are not direct users of the system. As a systems analyst, you will have to explain the potential benefits of the study to them and seek their cooperation and support.

Before beginning the preliminary investigation, you should obtain clear authorization from management. The authorization could be a memo or an e-mail message to all affected departments. The main thin is to let people know about your involvement and role. Often, a good first step is to arrange an initial meeting with key managers and IS personnel to explain the project, describe your responsibilities, and invite questions, comments, and suggestions. This starts an important dialog with users that will continue throughout the entire SDLC.

Step 2: Identify the Necessary information

You should prepare a list of the specific information you want to obtain during the preliminary investigation.

1. understand the problem
2. define the project scope and constraints
3. identify the benefits
4. estimate the time and costs
5. report to management.

Understand the Problem

The first objective in the preliminary investigation is to understand the true nature of the problem and the reason for the systems request. In many cases, the stated problem in the systems request is not the real problem, but only a symptom. For example, a request for additional hardware to speed up processing actually could be the result of weak systems design or improper scheduling. Similarly, a request for analysis of customer complaints might suggest a quality control problem in the manufacturing plant.

When interacting with users, you should be careful in your use of the word *problem,* because generally it has a negative meaning. When you ask users about *problems,* some will stress current system limitations rather than desirable new features or enhancements. Instead of focusing on difficulties, you should question users about additional capability they would like to have. Remember, every problem is also an opportunity. Using this approach, you highlight ways to improve the user's job, you get a better understanding of operations, and you build better, more positive relationships with users.

A clear statement of the problem also helps define the scope of the preliminary investigation. A systems analyst should not recommend a complete study of the entire system when a less costly approach could be just as effective in solving the problem.

Define the Project Scope and Constraints

The second objective in the preliminary investigation is to define the scope of the project. Project scope means the range or extent of the project. Project scope helps to establish the boundaries of the systems request, because it requires a precise statement of the problem. For example, a statement, payroll is nor being produced accurately, is very general, compared to the statement, overtime pay is not being calculated correctly for production workers. Similarly, a statement that the scope of the systems project is, to modify the accounts receivable system to allow online customer inquiries, is significantly different from a statement that the project scope is, to provide additional information about customer account

Determining who is affected by the problem and the solution is an important part of defining project scope. You first must understand all the business functions involved, and the groups affected by the problem.

The scope of the project also limits the solutions that you can impose. If you set no limits, you might be tempted to investigate unrelated systems, and a project scheduled for completion in several weeks could take months or even years to complete. Along with defining the scope of the project, you need to identify any constraints on the system. A constraint is a condition, restriction, or requirement that the system must satisfy. A constraint can involve hardware, software, time, policy, law, or cost. System constraints also define project scope. For example, if the system must operate with existing hardware, this is a constraint that affects potential solutions. Other examples of constraints are: the order entry system must accept input from 15 remote sites, the human resources information system must produce statistics on hiring practices, and the new Web site must be operational by March 1.

When evaluating constraints, you should identify their characteristics as follows:

1. *Present vs. future,* Is the constraint something that must be met as soon as the system is developed or modified? Or is the constraint necessary at some future time?
2. *Internal vs. external.* Is the constraint due to requirement within the organization or is it imposed by some external force, such as government regulations?

3. *Mandatory vs. desirable.* Is the constraint mandatory? Is it absolutely essential that the constraint be met or is it merely desirable? If desirable, how important is the constraint?

One common mistake is to list all constraints as mandatory, which results in increased development time and costs. Present, external, and mandatory constraints usually are fixed and must be met by the system when it is developed or modified. Constraints that are future, internal, or desirable often can be postponed. Regardless of the type, all constraints should be.identified as early as possible to avoid future problems and surprises.

You must clearly define the project's scope and constraints to avoid misunderstandings that can happen when a manager assumes that the system will contain a certain feature and supports the project, but later finds that the feature is not included. A clear definition of project scope and constraints reduces this problem.

Identify the Benefits

The third objective of the preliminary investigation is to identify the tangible and intangible benefits that are expected to result from the systems request. These benefits, along with the cost estimates you provide, will be used by management in deciding whether to pursue the project beyond the preliminary investigation phase.

Tangible benefits are those that can be stated in terms of dollars. Tangible benefits result from a decrease in expenses, an increase in revenues, or both. Examples of tangible benefits include a new scheduling system that reduces overtime, an online package tracking system that improves service and decreases the need for clerical staff, and a sophisticated inventory control system that cuts excess inventory and eliminates production delays.

Intangible benefits are difficult to measure in dollars, but also should be identified. Several examples are a proposed system that eliminates repetitive clerical tasks and improves employee job satisfaction, a system improvement that supplies more information for marketing decisions, and a new design for customer statements that enhances the company's image.

Estimate the Time and Casts

The fourth objective of the preliminary investigation is to develop specific time and cost estimates for the next phase of the SDLC, which is the systems analysis phase. In making your estimates, you should consider the following issues:

1. What information must you obtain, and how much information will you need to gather and analyze?
2. What sources of information will you use, and what difficulties will you encounter in obtaining the information?
3. Will you conduct interviews? How many people will you interview, and how much time will you need to meet with the people and summarize their responses?
4. Will you conduct a survey? Who will be involved? How much lime will it take people to complete it? How much time will it take to prepare it and tabulate the results?
5. How much will it cost to analyze the information gathered and to prepare a report with findings and alternative solutions?

In addition to accurate estimates for the systems analysis phase, you also should provide ballpark estimates of the money and time required for all subsequent project phases. These estimates can be stated in broad ranges, such as $35,000 to $50,000, or decision based on total costs and benefits.

Report to Management

The final task in the preliminary investigation is to prepare a report to management. The report includes an evaluation of the systems request, an estimate of costs and benefits, and your recommendation. The Systems Analyst's Toolkit can help you achieve effective written and oral communications.

With this list of requirements, you can prepare a schedule of your activities during the preliminary investigation phase.

Step 3: Perform Fact-Finding to Gather the Required Information

Depending on the project, this step can involve just one of the following techniques or all of them. Fact-finding might take an hour or as long as a month—whatever you need to get the job done. Some major techniques that you can use during fact finding are analyzing organization charts, conducting interviews, reviewing current system documentation, observing current operations, and conducting user surveys. .

Analyze Organization Charts. In many instances you will not know the organizational structure of the departments involved in the study. You should obtain organization charts to understand how the department functions and identify individuals you might want to interview. Organization charts often can be obtained from the company's human resources department. If such charts are not available, you should obtain the necessary information directly from department personnel and then construct your own charts. When organization charts are available, you should verify their accuracy. Keep in mind that organization chart? show the formal structure of a group but not its informal alignment, which also is important. You can draw organization charts by hand, or you can use a software package to create them.

Conduct Interviews. The primary method of obtaining information during the preliminary investigation is the interview. Remember that the purpose of the interview, and of the preliminary investigation itself, is to uncover facts about the existing system. The purpose of the interview is not to convince others that a new system is needed. Your primary role in an interview is to ask effective questions and listen carefully. If you plan to talk to several people about the same topic, you should prepare a standard set of questions for all interviews. Also be sure to include opened questions such as, "What else do you think I should know about the system"

When conducting interviews during the preliminary investigation, you should interview managers and supervisors who have a broad knowledge of the system and can give you an overview of the system. Depending on the situation, you might include other personnel to obtain information about how the system functions on a day-to-day basis.

Review Current Documentation, Although interviews are an extremely important method of obtaining information, you also may want to investigate the current system documentation. The documentation might not be up to date, so you should check with users to confirm that you are receiving accurate and complete information.

Observe Current Operations to Obtain Information. Another fact-finding method is to observe the current system in operation. You might see how workers carry out typical tasks. You might choose to trace or follow the actual paths taken by input source documents or output reports. In addition to observing operations, you might want to sample the inputs or outputs of the system. Using simple statistical techniques, you can obtain valuable information about the nature and frequency of the problem.

Conduct a Brief Survey of People who use the System. Interviews can be time-consuming. Sometimes you need a small amount of information, but you need it from a larger group. In this case, you should consider a brief survey that people can complete quickly and return to you.

Step 4: Analyze the Information

After gathering the data that you listed in Step 2, you are ready to analyze the information, identify alternatives with costs and benefits, and recommend a course of action. At this stage, you have several alternatives. You might find that no further action is necessary, or that some other solution, such as additional training, is needed. If the problem and its solution are both minor, you might recommend proceeding directly to the systems implementation phase. Most often, however, your recommendation will be to proceed to the next phase of the SDLC. which is systems analysis.

Step 5: Present Your Results and Recommendations to Management

After conducting a preliminary investigation, you^must submit a report to a systems review committee or top management. The report should include what you found concerning the operation of the system, the problems that you observed, and your recommendations for future action. Your report will be presented in written form, and you also might be asked to give an oral presentation. The format of the preliminary investigation report varies from one company to another. A typical report includes the following seven sections:

1. *Introduction.* The first section is an overview of the report. The introduction contains a brief description of the system, the name of the person or group who performed the investigation, and the name of the person or group who initiated the investigation.
2. *Systems request summary.* The summary describes the basis of the systems request.
3. *Findings.* The findings section contains the results of your preliminary investigation, including a description of the scope of the proposed project and the main conclusions you reached.
4. *Recommendations.* Next, the report contains the recommendations for further action by the IS department. Members of management make the final decisions on future action, and they do not always follow the recommendations of the information systems department. In most cases, however, those recommendations are important factors.
5. *Time & cost estimates.* One factor that will influence management's decision is the cost of the information systems department's involvement. You must include an estimate of time and cost if you recommend further action. Your goal is to make management aware of all costs whenever any systems activity takes place.
6. *Expected benefits.* -The next section contains the anticipated tangible and intangible benefits of implementing the recommendations. Whenever asked to spend money and commit resources, management must be informed of the results it can expect from the expenditures.
7. *Appendix.* The report should include an appendix if you need to attach supporting information. For example, you might list the interviews you conducted, the documentation you reviewed, and other sources of information you obtained. You do not need detailed reports of the interviews or other lengthy documentation. It is critical, however, that you retain these documents to support your findings and to serve as sources for future reference.

Other Fact-Finding Techniques

Document Review

During the requirements determination or fact-finding process, you should review the existing system documentation to understand how the system is supposed to work. Remember that system documentation is sometimes out of date. Forms can change or be discontinued; documented procedures often are modified or eliminated. You should obtain copies of actual forms and operating documents currently in use. You also should review blank copies of forms, as well as samples of actual completed forms. You usually can obtain document samples during interviews with the people who perform that procedure. If the system uses a software package, you should review the documentation for that software.

Observation

The **observation** of current operating procedures is another fact-finding technique. Sometimes, you can understand a system better by observing it in operation. Seeing the system in action gives you additional perspective and a better understanding of the system and its procedures. Personal observation also allows to verify statements made in interviews and determine whether procedures really operate as they are described. Through observation, you might discover that neither the system documentation nor the interview statements are accurate.

Personal observation also can provide important advantages in later SDLC phases. For example, recommendations often are better accepted when they are based on personal observation of actual operations.

Observation also can provide the knowledge needed to test or install future changes and can help build relationships with the operating staff who will be using the new or modified system.

Plan your observations in advance by preparing a checklist of specific tasks you want to observe and questions you want to ask. Consider the following issues when you prepare your list.

1. Ask sufficient questions to ensure that you have a complete understanding of the present system operation. A primary goat is to identify the methods of handling situations that are *not* covered by standard operating procedures. For example, what happens in a payroll system if an employee loses a time card? What is the procedure if an employee starts a shift five minutes late but then works ten minutes overtime? Often, the rules for exceptions such as these are not written or formalized. Therefore, you must try to document any procedures for handling exceptions.
2. Observe all the steps in a processing cycle and not the output from each procedural step.
3. Examine each pertinent form, record, and report. Determine the purpose each item of information serves.
4. Consider each person who works with the system and the following questions: What information is received from other people? What information is generated by this person's work? What tools are used in the process? To whom is the information passed? What questions do the people ask each other? How quickly must each step be completed? How much concentration does each step require? How often do interruptions occur? How often must a worker take a break from a concentrated activity?
5. Talk to the people who receive current reports to see whether the reports are complete, timely, accurate, and in a useful form. Ask whether information can be eliminated or improved and whether people would like to receive additional information.

As you observe people at work, remain aware of a factor called the Hawthorne Effect. The name comes from a study performed in the Hawthorne plant of the Western Electric Company in the 1920s. The purpose of the study was to determine how various changes in the work environment affect employee productivity. The surprising result was that productivity improved during observation whether the conditions were made *better* or *worse*. The conclusion was that productivity seemed to improve whenever the workers key they were being observed.

Thus, as you observe workers, remember that normal operations might not always run as smoothly as your observations indicate. Operations also might run less smoothly because workers might be nervous during the observation. If possible, meet with workers and their supervisors to discuss your plans and objectives to help establish a good working relationship. In some situations, you might even be able to participate in the work yourself to gain a personal understanding of the task or the environment.

Other Systems Development Techniques

introduction

Although structured analysis and design is still the most common method of systems development, many companies use other techniques to develop information systems, such as joint application development (JAD) and rapid application development (RAD), which are team-based approaches, or object-oriented (O-O) systems development, which defines a system in terms of objects, rather than traditional data and processes. These methods are not mutually exclusive. Instead, they are important techniques and strategies that are available to the systems analyst.

Joint Application Development (JAD)

Joint application development (JAD) is a popular systems development technique developed by IBM. As you learned at the beginning of this chapter, in a traditional structured analysis process the IS staff collects information from many users and managers, and then develops the requirements for a new system. In contrast, using the JAD approach, the company creates a task force of users, managers, and IS professionals that works together to gather information, discuss business needs, and define the new system requirements.

The JAD team usually meets over a period of days or weeks, in a special conference room or at an off-site location. The objective is to analyze the existing system, work on potential solutions, and agree on requirements for the new system. The group usually has a project leader and one or more members who document and record the results and decisions. The JAD process involves intensive effort by all team members. Because of the wide range of input and constant interaction among the participants, many companies believe that a JAD group produces the best possible definition of the new system.

Compared to traditional methods, JAD is more expensive and can be cumbersome if the group is too large compared to the size of the project. Many companies find, however, that JAD allows key users to participate effectively in the requirements determination process. When successfully used, JAD can result in a more accurate statement of system requirements, a better understanding of common goals, and a stronger commitment to the success of the new system.

Rapid application development (RAD) is a technique that reduces the time needed to design new information systems. Like JAD, RAD also uses a team approach, but goes further. While JAD typically focuses on the task of requirements determination, RAD involves a mini-SDLC that parallels the traditional SDLC phases. The creator of RAD, James Martin, proposed four RAD phases: requirements planning, user design, construction, and cutover. The objective of the RAD approach is to save development time and expense by using a project group to perform a wide range of systems development tasks. To be successful, RAD requires an IS development team that works closely and interactively with a small group of important users and managers, who actively participate. RAD also involves systems development tools including prototyping and computer-aided software engineering (CASE) tools.

When successfully implemented, the RAD process results in a more continuous design process, rather than clearly segmented SDLC phases. The development team can make any necessary modifications quickly, as the design evolves. Like JAD, rapid application development combines the knowledge and skills of users, managers, and IS professionals. Unlike JAD, the RAD process dots not stop at requirements determination, but continues through system design and implementation. Many companies feel that RAD techniques can reduce new system costs substantially because the development team has the resources, skills, and management support needed to handle the project in a compressed time frame.

The RAD method has advantages and disadvantages compared to the traditional SDLC. The primary advantage is that systems can be developed more quickly with significant cost savings. A disadvantage is that RAD stresses the mechanics of the system itself, and does not place enough emphasis on the company's strategic business needs. The risk is that a system might work well in the short term, but the corporate and long-term objectives for the system might not be met. In addition, another potential disadvantage is that the accelerated time cycle might allow less time to develop quality, consistency, and design standards. RAD can be an attractive alternative, however, if an organization understands these possible-risks.

Object Oriented Systems Development

As the sophistication and capabilities of new computer hardware have grown by leaps and bounds, it has become evident that new software development techniques are needed. Users anxiously await more software that harnesses the capabilities of sophisticated hardware such as the Macintosh II and the PS/2 family of computers. In addition, users' expectations of software quality have increased. They are no longer satisfied with applications that are not user-friendly or that have numerous bugs that must be worked around.

A recent approach to software development, called object-oriented programming, attempts to completely alter tradition-al software development methods, and many computer professionals believe it has the potential for satisfying some of the enormous demand for more sophisticated software. Object-oriented programming requires a new way of programming, one more closely related to how we actually think.

We typically regard the computer as a machine and data as the raw material that the computer processes. The programmer is the technician who controls the machine. The program lists all the steps the computer must take to obtain the needed output from the input. However, an object-oriented program defines the data and the set of operations that can act on that data as one unit called an object. The object is thought of as an actor with a specific set of skills. The programmer is the director of the show. The programmer no longer has to tell each actor exactly what steps to take but instead simply explains the ultimate task to be performed.

Critical to understanding object-oriented programming is the concept of inheritance. Objects can be defined and then used to build a hierarchy of descendant objects, each of which inherits access to methods used by the ancestors' objects. Objects can be reused. Even when a new object is needed, an old one can usually be modified to meet the new needs. The new object inherits the characteristics of the old object.

For example, a horse is a subclass of mammals. It "inherits" the characteristics of a mammal (body hair, live birth, nursing its young and so on). However, it also has characteristics that distinguish from other mammals, such as its size and shape, the way it moves, and the kinds of sounds it makes. When a programmer creates a new object, it is necessary only to add its new features; the inherited ones are already there.

To see how this makes the programmer's job easier, assume you were writing a space-war game. Both sides - the Federation and the Ferengi - have space ships, but of slightly different types. In addition, each side has non-fighting ships, such as space shuttles and cargo barges. The object ship has certain characteristics: X-Y coordinates, shields, warp speeds, and loyalty (Federation or Ferengi). The object fighting ship has everything ship has, plus photon torpedoes. The object shuttlecraft has everything ship has except shields and warp speeds.

Many programmers agree that object-oriented programming can greatly reduce the time needed to implement new software. In addition, because new software builds heavily on existing objects, the code is more likely to be reusable and error-free. Several object-oriented languages are currently available. The first commercially available language was Xerox's Smalltalk. Other languages include C++ (an object-oriented version of C), and Borland's Turbo Pascal, Version 5.5. The next few years will determine whether the full potential of object-oriented programming is as great as many computer profes-sionals believe. If it is, we should see tremendous improvements in the speed of software development and the quality of the final product.

FEASIBILITY AND COST-BENEFIT ANALYSIS

Many organizations assign responsibility for evaluating systems requests to a group of key managers and users, who form a **systems review committee,** which also is called a **steering committee, computer resources committee, or a computer policy committee.** The objective is to use the combined judgement and experience of several managers to evaluate systems projects.

Instead of a committee, in some companies, one person is responsible for systems development and maintenance decisions; this often is the case in smaller companies, or firms where only one individual has information technology skills. In this situation, the systems person must consult closely with users and managers throughout the company to ensure that business and operational needs are considered carefully.

In most organizations, the IS department receives more systems requests than it can handle, and the systems review committee must evaluate the requests and set priorities. Suppose the committee receives four requests; a request from the marketing group to analyze current customer spending habits and forecast future trends, a request from the technical support group for a cellular link so service representatives can download technical data instantly, a request from the accounting department to redesign customer statements and allow them to be accessed via the Internet, and a request from the production staff for an inventory control system that can exchange data with major suppliers directly.

With a limited staff, which of these projects should be considered for further study? What criteria should be applied? How should the committee decide the priorities? To answer these questions, the committee must assess the feasibility of each systems request.

System Performance Definition

A system's required performance is defined by describing its outputs in a user-acceptable format and at a higher level of detail than what was described in the initial investigation. This involves three steps:

1. Statement of constraints
2. Identification of specific system objectives
3. Description of outputs

This phase builds on the previous phase in that much of the work may already have been done.

Statement of Constraints

Constraints are factors that limit the solution of the problem. Some constraints are identified during the initial investigation and are discussed with the user. There are general constraints that might have a bearing on the required performance of a candidate system. Let's consider our safe deposit billing system to illustrate these points. We described the current billing system and how the department handles billing and customer payments. The result of the fact-finding phase of the initial investigation revealed the following general constraints:

1. The president views safe deposit billing as a low priority. He has a false impression that computers are not needed as long as customers can have access to their boxes.
2. The senior vice president is worried that a billing system might require the transfer of safe deposit staff to other departments. Considering Florida's level of unemployment and the cost of retraining, a candidate system has to do more than produce reports,
3. The accounting department has been pushing for installing a computer-based general ledger application for months. The vice president of operations, bogged down with auditing and operations problems, continued to shelve the request.
4. Management has a limited knowledge of computers, although it has several applications on the computer: checking and savings, installment loans, commercial loans, and trusts. The president, in his early sixties and interested in "the bottom line" of the financial statement, is traditionally reluctant to spend money on computers.
5. Safe deposit, while doing belter than breaking even, is not projected to grow as fast as it did in the early 1980s. The community's recent success in controlling burglaries had an adverse impact on the demand for box rentals in general.
6. If an online system is to be installed, it must interface v/ith the existing checking/savings application to allow for the automatic payment of box rentals.
7. A proposed design must be compatible with the bank's Burroughs computer system.

Identification of Specific System Objectives

Once the constraints are spelled out, the analyst proceeds to identify the system's specific performance objectives. They are deirved from the general objectives specified in the project directive at the end of the initial investigation. The steps are to state the system's benefits and then translate them into measurable objectives. In our scenario, the candidate system's anticipated benefits are as follows:

1. Improved collection schedule
2. Cost reduction
3. Physical space reduction
4. Improved customer service

Each benefits is analyzed and translated into measurable objectives.

1. Collection is improved by billing 30 days in advance of the box renewal date, and one more notice is sent within two weeks. It also improves the accounts receivables payment "float".
2. Cost reduction is realized by reducing the payroll by two employees. The new online billing system requires less than two hours of labor per day, compared with axis hours under the current system.
3. Physical space requirements are reduced by placing the microcomputer in the place of one of the four existing desks. The remaining desks are removed, allowing an extra cubicle for customer use.
4. Customer service is improved by placing master cards and box rental information online, thus reducing the waiting time of entry from 3 minutes to 30 seconds.

These objectives are effective in comparing the performance of the candidate system with that of the current system. The information-oriented flowchart, input/output analysis sheet, and data flow diagram produced in the initial investigation lead to the conclusions that (1) the current system is inefficient and (2) a new online, terminal-oriented system would be the solution. This conclusion was reflected in the general project directive submitted to the user for approval. This information is used as a basis for preparing specific objectives for the candidate system:

1. To establish a billing system with six five-day cycles per month.
2. To mail customers no later than the close of the billing cycle and no later than 25 days prior to the box renewal date.
3. To mail customers a reminder two weeks after the initial statement for box renewal.
4. To speed collections and reduce the "float" by 40 percent.
5. To example the availability of boxes by size, rental fees, and location.
6. To evaluate the ratio of rented to available boxes at all times.
7. To produce periodic reports to management on the performance of the safe deposit department.

Description of Outputs

A final step in system performance definition is describing the outputs required by the user. An actual sketch of the format and contents of the reports (layout) as well as a specification of the media used, their frequency, and the size and number of copies required are prepared at this point. Specifying exactly what the output will look like leads to an estimate of the computer storage requirements that form the basis for the file design to be undertaken in the design phase of the life cycle. The analyst is now ready to evaluate the feasibility of candidate systems to produce these outputs.

Feasibility Study

Many feasibility studies are disillusioning for both users and analysts. First, the study often presupposes that when the feasibility document is being prepared, the analyst is in a position to evaluate solutions. Second, most studies tend to overlook the confusion inherent in system development—the constraints and the assumed attitudes. If the feasibility study is to serve as a decision document, it must answer three key questions:

1. Is there a new and better way to do the job that will benefit the user?
2. What are the costs and savings of the alternative(s)?
3. What is recommended?

The most successful system projects are not necessarily the biggest or most visible in a business but rather those that truly meet user expectations. More projects fail because of inflated expectations than for any other reason.

Feasibility Analysis

The system analysis phase also involves a **feasibility study,** which determines whether the system is feasible within the sociotechnical framework of the organization. The feasibility study carefully examines technical, economic, operational, scheduling, legal, and strategic factors.

Technical feasibility analysis determines whether the proposed system can be developed and implemented using existing technologies or whether new technologies are required. Hardware, software, and network requirements for the new system are also determined in this step.

Economic feasibility analysis evaluates the financial aspects of the project by performing a cost-benefit analysis and assessing both the tangible and the intangible benefits of the system. If an organization does not have the resources to develop a new system, then regardless of how useful or innovative the system is, it cannot be done. Establishing economic feasibility is such a difficult task, and is often so badly done, that poor project estimates are cited as one of the top reasons for system failures. (See Figure 14.8.1}

***Operational** feasibility* analysis determines whether there will be any problems in implementing the system in its operational environment, looks at issues such as integrating the new system with existing systems in the organization, and assesses how the system fits with the strategic business plan and the strategic information plan of the organization.

Schedule feasibility studies address the time it will take to complete the project. In this step, decision makers must take into account available resources, such as manpower, time, money, and equipment. It also helps to identify any additional resources that may be required to complete the project on time. Although this may sound like a simple task, determining project completion time is often very difficult. This is one of the primary reasons why so many software projects are behind schedule.

Legal feasibility studies take into account factors such as copyrights, patents, and federal regulations, if any. As the number of lawsuits in the computer industry increases, organizations are being more cautious about the legal implications of system development. In the case of life-threatening systems, legal feasibility can become a deciding factor.

Finally, *strategic feasibility* analysis looks into factors such as the ability of the system to increase market share, give the company a competitive edge in the marketplace, enhance the productivity of knowledge workers, and achieve other strategic goals of the company. "Will the system make the organization more competitive?" "Can competitors easily imitate the system and diminish its long-term benefits?" "Will the organization be at a competitive *disadvantage* if it does *not* develop this system?" These are some issues addressed during this phase.

Feasibility analysis is done in the system analysis phase. This table summarizes the different areas of feasibility analysis and the issues to be addressed. Some guidelines that companies use during this phase are also shown

Build Knowledge	
Process	Define technology and business issues
Goal	Formulate preliminary goals
Timetable	Can take months
Players	Affected business unit and its IS liaison
Determine Feasibility	
Technology	Are current products sufficient?
Skills	Does present staff have them?

Time and cost	Are projections workable?
Risk factor	Is the potential downside acceptable?
Players	Affected business unit and its IS liaison
Test Practicality	
Pilot	Build a prototype of the system
Experiments	Test various tools and technologies
Involvement	Make development interactive
Reviews	Keep business users abreast of progress
Players	Application developers, affected business unit and its IS liaison, central IS
Prove Profitability	
Analysis	Do a traditional cost-benefit analysis
Benefits	Predict intangible benefits
Players	Affected business unit and its IS liaison, central IS
Commercialization	
Deployment	Utilize the finished application or system

Steps in Feasibility Analysis

Feasibility analysis involves eight steps:

1. Form a project team and appoint a project leader.
2. Prepare system flowcharts.
3. Enumerate potential candidate systems.
4. Describe and identify characteristics of candidate systems.
5. Determine and evaluate performance and cost effectiveness of each candidate system.
6. Weight system performance and cost data.
7. Select the best candidate system.
8. Prepare and report final project directive to management.

Form a Project Team and Appoint a Project Leader

The concept behind a project team is that future system users should be involved in its design and implementation. Their knowledge and experience in the operations area are essential to the success of the system. For small projects, the analyst and an assistant usually suffice; however, more complex studies require a project team. The team consists of analysts and user staff—enough collective expertise to devise a solution to the problem. In many cases, an outside consultant and an information specialist join the team until the job is completed.

Projects are planned to occupy a specific time period, ranging from several weeks to months. The senior systems analyst is generally appointed as project leader. He/she is usually the most experienced analyst in the team. The appointment is temporary, lasting as long as the project. Regular meetings take place to keep up the momentum and accomplish the mission—selection of the best candidate system. A record is kept of the progress made in each meeting.

Regarding the safe deposit case, since the whole user area consists of five employees, the analyst handled most of the work.

Prepare System Flowcharts

The next step in the feasibility study is to prepare generalized system flowcharts for the system. Information-oriented charts and data flow diagrams prepared in the initial investigation are also reviewed at this time. The charts bring up the importance of inputs, outputs, and data flow among key points in the existing system. All other flowcharts needed for detailed evaluation are completed at this point.

Enumerate Potential Candidate Systems

This step identifies the candidate systems that are capable of producing the outputs included in the generalized flowcharts. This requires a transformation from logical to physical system models. Another aspect of this step is consideration of the hardware that can handle the total system requirements. In the safe deposit case, it was found that, virtually any microcomputer system with more than 128K-byte memory an dual disk drive will do the job. It was also learned that a microcomputer can be designed to interface with the bank's mainframe. In this design, actual processing is handled by the microcomputer, whereas information such as payments and credits are transmitted to the main computer files for proper adjustment through the customer's checking account. The question here is: Which microcomputer (IBM, Apple, Digital, etc.) should be selected? This is taken up in step 6 of the study.

An important aspect of hardware is processing and main memory. There are a large number of computers with differing processing sizes, main memory capabilities, and software support. The project team may contact vendors for information on the processing capabilities of the system available.

Determine and Evaluate Performance and Cost Effectiveness of Each Candidate System

Each candidate system's performance is evaluated against the system performance requirements set prior to the feasibility study. Whatever the criteria, there has to be as close a match as practicable, although trade-offs are often necessary to select the best system. In the safe deposit case, the criteria chosen in advance were accqracy, growth potential, response time less than five seconds, expandable main and auxiliary storage, and user-friendly software. Often these characteristics do not lend themselves to quantitative measures. They are usually evaluated in qualitative terms (excellent, good, etc.) based on the subjective judgement of the project team.

The cost encompasses both designing and installing the system. It includes user training, updating the physical facilities, and documenting. System performance criteria are evaluated against the cost of each system to determine which system is likely to be the most cost effective and also meets the performance requirements. The safe deposit problem is easy. The

Weight System Performance and Cost Data

In some cases, the performance and cost data for each candidate system show which system is the best choice. The outcome terminates the feasibility study. Many times, however, the situation is not so clear-cut. The performance/cost evaluation matrix does not clearly identify the best system, so the next step is to weight the importance of each criterion by applying a rating figure. Then the candidate system with the highest total score is selected.

The procedure for weighting candidate systems is simple:

1. Assign a weighting factor to each evaluation criterion based on the criterion's effect on the success of the system. For example, if the usability criterion is twice as important as the accuracy factor, usability is assigned weight 4 and accuracy is assigned weight 2.

2. Assign a quantitative rating to each criterion's qualitative rating. For example, ratings (poor, fair, good, very good, excellent) may be assigned respective values (1, 2, 3, 4, 5).
3. Multiply the weight assigned to each category by the relative rating to determine the score.
4. Sum the score column for each candidate system.

Select the Best Candidate System

The system with the highest total score is judged the best system. This assumes the weighting factors are fair and the rating of each evaluation criterion is accurate. According to our safe deposit example in Table 14.8.5, the IBM PC is the best system for the job. Growth potential was the criterion that had the greatest effect on the total score. The HP 100 and the Apple III were given lower ratings than the IBM PC because they were not judged to grow as easily and quickly. Additionally, user training was judged superior for the PC than for other candidate systems.

Most feasibility studies select from more candidate systems than we used in our safe deposit example. The criteria chosen and the constraints are also more complex. In any case, management should not make the selection without having the experience to do so. Management cooperation and comments, however, are encouraged.

Feasibility Report

The culmination of the feasibility study is a feasibility report directed to management; it evaluates the impact of the proposed changes on the area(s) in question. The report is a formal document for management use, brief enough and sufficiently nontechnical to be understandable, vet detailed enoueh to orovide the basis for svsteni design.

There is no standard format for preparing feasibility reports. Analysts usually decide on a format that suits the particular user and system. Most reports, however, begin with a summary of findings and recommendations, followed by documented details. Starting with summary information highlights the essence of the report, giving management the option of reviewing the details later. The report contains the following sections:

1. Cover letter formally presents the report and briefly indicates to management the nature, general findings, and recommendations to be considered.
2. Table of contents specifies the location of the various parts of the report. Management quickly refers to the sections that concern them.
3. Overview is a narrative explanation of the purpose and scope of the project, the reason for undertaking the feasibility study, and the department(s) involved or affected by the candidate system. Also included are the names of the persons who conducted the study, when it began, and other information that explains the circumstances surrounding the study.
4. Detailed findings outline the methods used in the present system. The system's effectiveness and efficiency as well as operation costs are emphasized. The section also provides a description of the objectives and general procedures of the candidate system. A discussion of output reports, costs, and benefits gives management a feel for the pros and cons of the candidate system.
5. Economic justification details point-by-point cost comparisons and preliminary cost estimates for the development and operation of the candidate system. A return on investment (RO1) analysis of the project is also included.
6. Recommendations and conclusions suggest to management the most beneficial and cost-effective system. They are written only as a recommendation, not a command. Following the recommendations, any conclusion from the study may be included.

7. Appendixes document all memos and data compiled during the investigation. They are placed at the end. of the report for reference.

Disapproval of the feasibility report is rare if it has been conducted properly. When a feasibility team has maintained good rapport with the user and his/her staff it makes the recommendations easier to approve. Technically, the report is only a recommendation, but it is an authoritative one. Management has the final say. Its approval is required before system design is initiated.

Oral Presentation

The feasibility report is a good written presentation documenting the activities involving the candidate system. The pivotal step, however, is selling the proposed change. Invariably the project leader or analyst is expected to give an oral presentation to the end user. Although it is not as polished as the written report, the oral presentation has several important objectives. The most critical requirements for the analyst who gives the oral presentation are (1) communication skills and knowledge about the candidate system that can be translated into language understandable to the user, and (2) the ability to answer questions, clarify issues, maintain credibility, and pick up on any new ideas or suggestions.

The substance and form of the presentation depend largely on the purposes sought. Figure 14.8.2 suggests a general outline. The presentation may aim at informing, confirming, or persuading.

1. Informing. This simply means communicating the decisions already reached on system recommendations and the resulting action plans to those who will participate in the implementation. No detailed findings or conclusions are included.
2. Confirming. A presentation with this purpose verifies facts and recommendations already discussed and agreed upon. Unlike the persuading approach, no supportive evidence is presented to sell the proposed change, nor is there elaborate reasoning behind recommendations and conclusions. Although the presentation is not detailed, it should be complete. Confirming is itself part of the process of securing approval. It should reaffirm the benefits of the candidate system and provide a clear statement of results to be achieved.
3. Persuading. This is a presentation pitched toward selling ideas—attempts to convince executives in take action on recommendations for implementing a candidate system.

Regardless of the purpose sought, the effectiveness of the oral presentation depends on how successful the project team has been in gaining the confidence of frontline personnel during the initial investigation. How the recommendations are presented also has an impact. Here are some pointers on how to give an oral presentation:

1. Rehearse and test your ideas before the presentation. Show that you are in command. Appear relaxed.
2. Final recommendations are more easily accepted if they are presented as ideas for discussion, even though they seem to be settled and final.
3. The presentation should be brief, factual, and interesting. Clarity and persuasiveness are critical. Skill is needed to generate enthusiasm and interest throughout the presentation.
4. Use good organization. Distribute relevant material to the user and other parties in advance.
5. Visual aids (graphs, charts) are effective if they are simple, meaningful, and imaginative. An effective graph should teach or tell what is to be communicated.
6. Most important, present the report in an appropriate physical environment where the acoustics, seating pattern, visual

The most important element to consider is the length of the presentation. The duration often depends on the complexity of the project, the interest of the user group, and the competence of the project team. A study that has companywide applications and took months to complete would require hours or longer to present. The user group that was involved at the outset would likely permit a lengthy presentation, although familiarity with the project often dictates a brief presentation. Unfortunately, many oral presentations tend to be a rehash of the written document, with little flare or excitement. Also, when the analyst or the project leader has a good reputation and success record from previous projects, the end user may request only a brief presentation.

Cost/Benefit Analysis Cost and Benefit Categories

In developing cost estimates for a system, we need to consider several cost elements. Among them are hardware, personnel, facility, operating, and supply costs.

1. Hardware Costs relate to the actual purchase or lease of the computer and peripherals (for example, printer, disk drive, tape unit). Determining the actual cost of hardware is generally more difficult when the system is shared by various users than for a dedicated stand-alone system. In some cases, the best way to control for this cost is to treat it as an operating cost.
2. Personnel costs include EDP salaries and benefits (health insurance, vacation time, sick pay, etc.) as well as pay for those involved in developing the system. Costs incurred during the development of a system are one-time costs and are labeled developmental costs. Once the system is installed, the costs of operating and maintaining the system become recurring costs.
3. Facility costs are expenses incurred in the preparation of the physical site where the application or the computer will be in operation. This includes wiring, flooring, acoustics, lighting, and air conditioning. These costs are treated as one-time costs and are incorporated into the overall cost estimate of the candidate system.
4. Operating costs include all costs associated with the day-to-day operation of the system; the amount depends on the number of shifts, the nature of the applications, and the caliber of the operating staff. There are various ways of covering operating costs. One approach is to treat operating costs as overhead. Another approach is to charge each authorized user for the amount of processing they request from the system. The amount charged is based on computer time, staff lime, and volume of the output produced. In any case, some accounting is necessary to determine how operating costs should be handled.
5. Supply costs are variable costs that increase with increased use of paper, ribbons, disks, and the like. They should be estimated and included in the overall cost of the system.

A system is also expected to provide benefits. The first task is to identify each benefit and then assign a monetary value to it for cost/benefit analysis. Benefits may be tangible and intangible, direct or indirect, as we shall see later.

The two major benefits are improving performance and minimizing the cost of processing. The performance category emphasizes improvement in the accuracy of or access to information and easier access to the system by authorized users. Minimizing costs through an efficient system-error control or reduction of staff-is a benefit that should be measured and included in cost/benefit analysis.

Procedure for Cost/Benefit Determination

There is a difference between .expenditure and investment. We spend to get what we need, but we invest to realize a return on the investment. Building a computer-based system is an investment. Costs are incurred throughout its life cycle. Benefits are realized in the form of reduced operating costs, improved corporate image, staff efficiency, or revenues. To what extent benefits outweigh costs is the function of cost/benefit analysis.

Cost/benefit analysis is a procedure that gives picture of the various costs, benefits, and rules associated with a system. The determination of costs and benefits entails the following steps:

1. Identify the costs and benefits pertaining to a given projecL
2. Categorize the various costs and benefits for analysis.

3. Select a method of evaluation.
4. Interpret the results of the analysis.
5. Take action.

Costs and Benefits Identification

Certain costs and benefits are more easily identifiable than others. For example, direct costs, such as the price of a hard disk, are easily identified from company invoice payments or canceled checks. Direct benefits often relate one-to-one to direct costs, especially savings from reducing costs in the activity in question. Other direct costs and benefits, however, may not be well defined, since they represent estimated costs or benefits that have some uncertainty. An example of such costs is reserve for bad debt. It is a discerned real cost, although its exact amount is not so immediate.

A category of costs or benefits that is not easily discernible is opportunity costs and opportunity benefits. These are the costs or benefits forgone by selecting one alternative over another. They do not show in the organization's accounts and' therefore are not easy to identify.

MULTIPLE CHOICE QUESTIONS

1. Which of the following is not a basic configuration used in a data communication network?
   a. computer/peripheral-device configuration
   b. computer-to-computer communication
   c. computer to front-end processor communication
   d. communication through a data switch
2. In data transmission, the bit coding scheme used to represent a byte is typically:
   a. EBCDIC b. ASCII c. SNA
   d. Hexadecimal e. None of the above.
3. Which of the following is true of parallel transmission?
   a. It involves the simulaneous transmission of eight bits.
   b. The speed is quoted in bits per second.
   c. It is slower than serial transmission.
   d. Most microcomputers communicate with other computers in this mode.
   e. All of the above are true.
4. Which of the following is not a device used in data communication?
   a. modem b. multiplexor c. statistical multiplexor
   d. front-end processor e. all of the above are used in data communication
5. Data are allowed to be transmitted in only one direction in a:
   a. simplex channel b. dumb channel c. half-duplex channel
   d. full-duplex channel
6. Which of the following is not a common configuration used in a DDP system?
   a. star b. ring c. tree
   d. real time e. bus
7. Duplicate copies of the data base are stored at all locations under?
   a. partitioning b. polling c. replication
   d. data sharing e. none of the above.

8. Which of the following is not an advantage of decentralized processing over centralized processing.?
   a. reduced data communication costs
   b. improved system reliability
   c. increased employee productivity
   d. increased computer system control
   e. all of the above are advantages.
9. The front-end processor is dedicated to perform which of the following function(s)?
   a. polling b. synchronization c. error checking
   d. two of the above. e. all of the above.
10. Which of the following is not true of office automation?
   a. It enhances office productivity.
   b. Human factors should be considered in im-plementing office automation.
   c. It will increase informal communications between employees.
   d. Software should be designed to be user-friendly.
   e. All of the above are true.
11. Which of the following is not one if the major components of a decision-support system?
   a. language system b. knowledge system c. expert system
   d. problem-processing system.
12. A decision-support system is intended to produce information to support which type of decisions?
   a. well-structured b. unstructured c. anticipated
   d. routine e. none of the above.
13. The major function of the language system is:
   a. to perform various processing tasks
   b. to provide artificial-intelligence capabilities to the DSS
   c. to provide data to the DSS
   d. to enable the users to interact with the DSS
   e. none of the above.
14. Which of the following is not true of non-procedural languages?
   a. They can be English-like.
   b. They can take user-friendly forms
   c. BASIC is an example of a nonprocedural lan-guage.
   d. They allow the user to simply specify the characteristics of a problems and to leave the determination of the logical steps to the DSS.
   e. All of the above are true.
15. A central purpose of most decision-support-systems is
   a. to build a model of the decision-making problem
   b. to design a data-base management system '
   c. to build an expert system
   d. to determine the key decisions in the problem area
   e. none of the above.
16. Which of the following should he done in the design process of building a decision support system?
   a. defining the objective for the decision-support effort
   b. designing the language interface
   c. defining the normative models which can provide information for the key decisions.

d. two of the above.

e. all three of the above.

17. Information concerning the probability distribution of a profit rate can be generated by using:

a. electronic spreadsheet b. artificial intelligence c. time-series analysis

d. management science techniques e. sensitivity analysis

18. Which of the following is not a primary reason for the popularity of decision support systems?

a. declining cost of computer hardware

b. advent of data-base management systems

c. increased number of programmers

d. management trained in analytic techniques

e. increased number of software packages,

19. To be successful in implementing DSS, organisa-tions should have the following characteristics except:

a. a well-controlled data-processing system

b. willingness to commit dollars and personnel to the project.

c. education and training by the organization

d. powerful central computer groups to initiate and manage system projects

e. all of the above are important

20. Which of the following is not a key component of the evaluation process in building a DSS?

a. criteria for evaluation

b. means of measuring system-development time spent on the project

c. means of monitoring the progress of the DSS

d. formal review process

e. all of the above arc key components.

21. Which of the following is not a level of information handling;

a. Decision Support System (DSS)

b. Operations Assistance System

c. Transaction Processing System (TPS)

22. At the shop-floor management level which of the following levels of Information Handling is needed:

a. D S S b. O AS c. EPS

d. T P S

23. Which of the following is not an important prin-ciple for evaluating the raw data for decision-making:

a. selection b. pattern c. leverage

d. overview.

24. An MIS provides :

a. past information b. present information c. future information

d. all of the above e. none of the above

25. An information system that responds immedi-ately to the needs of the physical system is called a(n):

a. inline system b. on-line system c. offline system

d. real-line system e. none of the above

REVIEW QUESTIONS

1. Why is Information System needed?

2. Define the following:

Information | Information System
Management Information System | End User
Managerial End User

3. Write a short note on Information System and Society.
4. How does the Information System effect the Organisations?
5. What information does the Information System provides to Managerial End Users?
6. Write a short not on Technological and Behavioural Aspects.
7. With respect to above define the following:

Framework for Managerial End Users | Foundation Concepts
Development | Technology
Applications | Management

8. Write a short note on System concepts.
9. How can the System Performance can be controlled?
10. Which are the various Information Processing concepts?
11. What do you understand by Information System Activities?
12. How is the Data processed into Information?
13. What sort of storage is required for storing the information?
14. What sort of Software resources are needed for Information Systems?
15. What sort of help databases give to the information systems?
16. Write a short note on concept of Management Information System.
17. Give the various definitions of MIS.
18. Which point the Information system should take care of?
19. What is the role of Management Information System?
20. How impact does the Information System have?
21. How does the Computer effect the Management Information System?
22. What academic disciples effect MIS?
23. How does MIS effect the user?
24. What role does the management play in MIS?
25. What are the approaches to the Management?
26. What functions does the manager serve?
27. What are effects of environment on MIS?
28. What sort of controls does MIS have?
29. Write a short note on Management by Exception.
30. What sort of support does the MIS give to the Management?
31. How is MIS used in Personal Mangement?
32. What sort of input documents are required ?
33. What sort of output reports generated by MIS?
34. How is MIS used in Financial Mangement?
35. What sort of input documents are required ?
36. What sort of output reports generated by MIS?
37. How is MIS used in Production Mangement?
38. What sort of input documents are required ?
39. What sort of output reports generated by MIS?
40. How is MIS used in Materials Mangement?

41. What sort of input documents are required ?
42. What sort of output reports generated by MIS?
43. How is MIS used in Marketing Mangement?
44. What sort of input documents are required ?
45. What sort of output reports generated by MIS?
46. What is an office? What are the activities done in an office?
47. Explain the terms office automation and office automation technology.
48. Distinguish between conventional office and modern office.
49. What are the limitations of conventional office?
50. What are the elements and the features of a modern office?
51. What are the components of an office software?
52. What are the hardware elements of a modern office?
53. What are four levels of processing in an automated office?
54. Explain the terms –OIS, TPS, MIS and DSS.
55. Mention various types of IT in an office environment of today.
56. What do you understand by Artificial Intelligence?
57. What are the different views about Artificial Intelligence?
58. Differenciate between Regular and Artificial Intelligence Programming.
59. What are the major areas of Artificial Intelligence?
60. Differenciate between Programs and Expert Systems.
61. Write down the basic components of an Expert System.
62. How do you create an Expert System
63. Define the working of an Expert System
64. What are the basic capabilities of Expert System.
65. Explain the Applications with examples of Expert Systems.
66. What is Robotics?
67. Explain the Applications with examples of Robotics Systems.
68. Explain Voice Recognition.
69. What is Voice Synthesis.
70. Explain the Knowledge Based System.
71. What is Pattern Matching?
72. What is Problem Solving and write down Applications of Probe Solving.
73. Explain General Problem Solve (GPS).
74. What are the Social and Ethical Issues of Artificial Intelligence?
75. Explain the following
    (a) Regular Programming
    (b) Expert systems
76. Elaborate on the top-down approach to system planning—what it means, its uses, and its implications for system development.
77. What important information does the user's request form provide? Why is it so important in the initial investigation? Explain in detail.
78. Why is it difficult to determine user requirements?
79. List and briefly describe the seven basic sections of the preliminary investigation report.
80. What is the purpose of the preliminary investigation?

81. How would one conduct an on-site observation? Lay out a plan and specify the pros and cons of this tool.
82. What is considered in evaluating forms? Explain.
83. How is the informant useful in systems analysis? Explain.
84. What is object-oriented systems development, and how does it differ from traditional approaches to structured analysis?
85. What are some major advantages and potential disadvantages of object-oriented systems development?

ANSWERS

Multiple Choice Questions

1. c	2. b	3. a	4. e
5. a	6. d	7. c	8. d
9. e	10. c	11. d	12. b
13. d	14. c	15. a	16. b
17. d	18. c	19. d	20. b
21. b	22. d	23. c	24. d
25. d			

CHAPTER 15

Information Systems for Business

Learning Objectives

After going through this chapter, you should appreciate the following:

- **Introduction to Digital Business**
- **Types of Information Systems for Business**
- **New Forms of Business**
- **Strategic Information Systems**
- **Information Resources Management**
- **Financial and Accounting Information Systems (FAIS)**

  Types of Financial and Accounting Information System
- **Integrated Financial and Accounting Systems**
- **Marketing Information Systems**

  Developing Marketing Information Systems

  Benefits of Marketing Information Systems
- **Manufacturing Information Systems**

  Developing a Manufacturing Information System

  Benefits of Manufacturing Information Systems
- **Human Resource Information Systems**

  Some Guidelines for selecting an HRIS

  How to Pick an HR System

INTRODUCTION TO DIGITAL BUSINESS

A business is defined as a mutual activity of two or more organizations were all organizations earn a profit. This is also called win-win activity. The ultimate benefit of business arrives to the end user. A business must be carried out in a methodical and systematic manner in which the work is organized, coordinated and focused to produce a useful service or a quality product. A traditional business approach has been a hierarchical, centralized and structured arrangement pf specialists that depended upon a standard set of operating procedure to deliver a product or a service. The modern business approach is less hierarchical, decentralized, flexible arrangement of generalist and customer centric. The modern business has an important feature that is customer's requirement and satisfaction. The advent of information technology has made it possible to meet the expectations of a customer. The use of information technology has also led to the modern form of business called digital business. A digital business focuses upon where all stack holder right from the manufacture to customer are digitally or electronically connected and mediated to input their wisdom for betterment of the product and / or the service. The core business process or activities are accomplished through the computer networking and database technologies. Digital business can sense and respond quickly, flexible and conveniently to the surroundings and environments as compared to the traditional business. Digital business also extend the opportunity for global business to the people as being connected electronically over the globe. Due to globalization, the spirit of healthy competition is also developed amongst the business makers.

TYPES OF INFORMATION SYSTEMS FOR BUSINESS

As already mentioned, the digital businesses are different from the conventional and traditional businesses in many ways, the use of IT has made the provision of super specializing the business arrangements so as to enable more opportunities for gaining benefits and productivity. There are different and specialized information systems that help and support the business for better profitability. They are explained here in brief.

- Supply Chain Management (SCM) Systems: These systems are meant to automate the relationship between the suppliers and the business firm to optimize the planning, sourcing, manufacturing, quality testing and delivery of the products and the services.
- Customer Relationship Management (CRM) Systems : These systems are the systems that lead to the development of a coherent and integrated perspective of all the possible relationships the business firm maintains with its customers.
- Enterprise Systems : The enterprise systems allow an integrated enterprise-wide informations system within the boundaries to coordinate and to convene the internal process. The activities include the data management right from the inventory upto the information about the customers in addition to manufacturing, sales, finance and human resources.
- Knowledge Management (KM) Systems : The KM systems are meant for the long term productivity of the business in terms of capturing recording of expertise, knowledge and wisdom of people involved.

All these information systems support the business activity in carrying out the following important function.

- Manufacturing and production
- Sales and marketing
- Quality control and testing
- Finance and accounting
- Human Resources
- History and future trends.

NEW FORMS OF BUSINESS

The advances in IT and new philosophies of information systems find extensive uses in business organization, the business methods are taking new form. There are many new form that have come up. We shall discuss only the important ones.

- Digital Market : A digital market is an collaborative information system that is created by the information technologies and meant for linking the buyers and sellers.
- Electronic commerce : The availability of the Internet for the exchange of transactions between the buyers and the sellers has lead to the growth of commerce electronically. Electronic commerce (ore – Commerce) is a form of computerized transactions between seller and buyers. eCommerce involves use of internet, network and web technologies. These days eCommerce portals are available on the net. Electronic commerce has different types known are B2B, B2C and C2C.
- B2B e-Commerce : It is business to business (B2B) transaction of commerce amongst business in terms of sales of goods and services. It gives a transaction from a business organization to another business organization. Example Intel sells the chip Pentium IV to the manufacturers of PCs.
- B2C e-Commerce : It involves retailing of products and services to individual shop keeper who then sell the product to the end user. Book publishers selling the books to the book stores is business to customer (B2C) e-Commerce.
- C2C e-Commerce : It is the direct commercial transaction from customer-to-customer. Auctioning and bidding are the examples of C2C e-Commerce.

Apart from B2B, B2C and C2C, there is one more form of e-Commerce known as m-Commerce (Standing for mobile commerce). It is done on online devices like cell phones, PDAs, wireless LANs and Laptops.

STRATEGIC INFORMATION SYSTEMS

Strategic Information systems are special types of information system which support the change of goal, operation, products, services or environmental relationships of organization. Due to strategic information systems, a competitive edge over the other organizations is gained. Computers play a vital role in implementing strategic information system. Following are the example situations where strategies information systems are executed on computer based environments.

- Cardinal and cardiac health care
- Distribution of pharma products
- Compressed gas management in pipes and cylinders
- Rescheduling of transportation during bad road conditions.
- Control during law and order situation.
- eGovernance system for policy management.

Strategic information systems also allow the management from one level of sociotechnical system to another to impact the thinking pattern and life style. Strategic system benefit the society in terms of

- Newer products are released early
- Costs are reduced
- Quality of products in enhanced

- Customers are made aware of the product
- Services are improved for customer satisfaction
- Value addition in socio-economic terms
- Speed up in the market changes.

INFORMATION RESOURCES MANAGEMENT

In this era of IT, information resources are gaining up their importance. From design to implementation to use of information systems, there are several resources which are coming across in the context. We can categorize the information resources into three main categories.

- Domain Resources i.e. Business related
- Technology Resources i.e. System related
- Human Resources i.e. People related

In the modern context, these resources have to be managed in an effective, efficient and systematic manner. We can further classify the above three categories as under.

- Domain Resources: These resources are the main sources of information and data related to the business i.e. market trend customer need, use of the product, social impact, business profits, customer relationship, supply and demand etc. Such information resources are handled and managed using the documents like survey forms, publicity leaflets, order form, invoicing, service form etc.
- Technology Resources : These resources are system related and they include computers, fax machine, photocopy machines, telephone personal digital assistants, laptops, presentation equipment etc. Such resources are managed and managed by system administrator personnels. Software systems also fall in this category.
- Human Resources : Human resources are crucial for information handling. Therefore they are most important as information resources. The actions are brought in by them. There are various levels at which the human information resources exist.
  - Decision making level, i.e., management
  - Executive level, i.e., knowledge worker
  - Operational level, i.e., data workers
  - Brokers level, i.e., internet and portals

All these information resources are integratedly managed to meet and fulfil the requirement of an information driven organization. Information resources management involves following activities :

- Allocation & reallocation
- Scheduling & rescheduling
- Monitoring and control
- Load Balancing and optimization
- Documentation and Reporting

FINANCIAL AND ACCOUNTING INFORMATION SYSTEMS (FAIS)

A Financial and accounting information system (FAIS) is a system that provides information related to the accounting and financial activities in an organization. The FAIS includes a number of subsystems, such as budgeting, cash and asset management, capital budgeting, portfolio analysis, general ledger, accounts receivable, inventory control, and payroll systems. Other systems include record keeping, account analysis, cash management, financial analysis, leasing options, insurance underwriting, insurance claims processing, and investment management. Financial institutions, such as banks, use specialized FAIS, such as commercial loan analyzers, credit approval systems, commercial account rating systems, credit application systems, automated teller control, and securities trading. Other institutions and companies may have their own specialised FAIS subsystems. Regardless of the type and number of subsystems, financial and accounting subsystems work together to create, record, generate, and disseminate financial and accounting information vital to good decision making.

Types of Financial and Accounting Information System

A FAIS is a collection of subsystems that perform different functions, including general ledger, asset management, order entry, accounts receivable, accounts payable, inventory control, and payroll systems. Since most of these terms are fairly self- explanatory, this section provides only a brief-description of each system.

General ledger systems generate the company's income statements and balance sheets and are responsible for managing new and old accounts in the company. Asset management systems maintain an inventory of the company's long term assets and ensure that accounting practices for company assets comply with regulatory standards. The output of this system often becomes input to the general ledger system. Order entry systems capture and manage different kinds of data relating to a transaction, such as number of units sold, customer billing, credit history, sales tax, and inventory levels. The output of this system is input to a number of other systems, such as accounts receivable and inventory management. Accounts receivable and accounts payable capture and process data, such as creditor and customer billing information, payments received and owed, credit terms, account balances, and payment schedules. The inventory control system captures, processes, and managers all data related to the company's inventory, such as items in inventory, inventory levels and costs, accounting practices related to inventory maintenance, stock balance, and data on lost, damaged, or returned goods. Finally, payroll systems capture and process data related to wages and salaries, including federal and state taxes, other payroll deductions, employee benefits, overtime, and related data.

These systems are designed to support most operational decisions. There are other kinds of FAIS to support tactical and strategic decision making in the organization, such as the following.

- Cash management systems: Systems that ensure that organization has enough cash to conduct normal business, to receive the best possible return on its short-term cash deposits, and to leverage its cash flow to achieve good ratings in financial markets.
- Capital budgeting systems: Systems that ensure the acquisition and disposal of capital assets, such as land, buildings, and so on.
- Investment management systems: Systems that ensure that the organization gets the best possible returns on its long-term investments.

INTEGRATED FINANCIAL AND ACCOUNTING SYSTEMS

FAIS are often integrated with other functional systems in the organization to facilitate data sharing and team sharing and team decision making. After all, financial decisions are not made in a vacuum; they often involve marketing, manufacturing, and human resources, so a free flow of information among these functional units is vital for good decision making.

For global and multinational companies, integrated financial and accounting systems are simply a necessity. For example, a multinational corporation with operations in the U.S., Canada, Europe, and Asia relies on its integrated financial system to monitor the overall financial health of the organization and keep managers abreast of important firiancial events. Although each overseas business unit operates as a separate company with its own policies, procedures, and systems, a common financial reporting system links the company's domestic offices with its international offices. The system ensures that every application, regardless of where it originated, complies with the accounting rules and principles of the U.S.

Another example of an integrated financial system is that of Allergan's A few years ago, Allergan, a maker of pharmaceuticals and ophthalmic products, had two nonintegrated, cumbersome, financial reporting systems: one for interna-tional operations and one for domestic operations. Financial data from Allergan's 40 international subsidiaries had to be re-entered manually into different systems: the company's general-ledger system for currency translation and consolidation, and the company's domestic accounting system for generating financial reports for the entire company.

In early 1992, the company installed a PC-based financial software package that allows data to be sent electronically from the international subsidiaries to the domestic general-ledger system; from there, it is uploaded to the company's central database. Users can now produce customized reports faster and with fewer inconsistencies, thus enhancing organizational decision making. "Information is now transmitted with the speed of a phone call; everyone can pull up the system and see the same set of numbers with just a few keystrokes."

MARKETING INFORMATION SYSTEMS

Marketing systems have evolved through different phases, from a focus on information on key market indicators from a single source, on aperiodic basis (say, weekly, monthly or biannually), to systems designed to gather different kinds of marketing data from multiple sources, both internal and external, more frequently. Today, the goal of marketing systems is to gain instantaneous access to global market information, from internal and external sources, with the primary goal of retaining existing customers and attracting new ones.

A marketing information system is a system that meets the information needs of an organization in sales, distribution, advertising, market analysis, market intelligence, product research, service management, customer nroflle anrt other marketing functions. Organizations that have customer-oriented marketing information systems are inevitably leaders in their fields. L.L. Bean, Federal Express, and MCI are all companies that rose to the top because of their relentless customer focus and their ability to gather, access, analyze, and disseminate up-to-the minute, customer-related information. This gives marketing managers the ability to be flexible and responsive to evolving market forces.

Market information systems are primarily cystomer-oriented information systems that work toward realizing the strategic sales plan and the marketing plan of an organization. A system that is dedicated exclusively to the marketing functions of an organization is called a dedicated marketing information system. However, not all organizations have dedicated marketing information systems and small businesses frequently rely on reports from their transaction processing systems for marketing information.

Marketing systems, unlike other functional systems, cannot be standardised for all companies. Every company has its own way in which it generates leads and prospects, prepares bids, fills orders, and delivers goods to its customers. Therefore, marketing systems must be tailored to match the marketing policies, procedures, and practices of each company. However, every marketing system is guided by, and in turn guides, the strategic marketing plan of the organization, and hence should be developed based on the mission, goals, and objectives stated in the strategic marketing plan.

A very popular marketing information system is one that automates the sales and marketing function. Such systems capture valuable customer information, and hence can improve productivity, enhance customer service, and create better sales and marketing strategies. Campbell Soup, for example, has maintained a leadership position in the highly competitive soup market because it gathers extensive market data and uses it to respond quickly to changing market forces and customer needs. The marketing system helps the company closely monitor and quickly respond to marketing information—such as stock on hand, merchandising opportunities, effectiveness of latest promotion, advertising strategies and so on—that its 900 retail sales reps and 300 account sales reps gather from grocery stores, distribution centres, and customer headquarters. Campbell's representatives gather detailed information through hand-held terminals. The information is then transmitted to the mainframe located at corporate headquarters where the data is then used in sophisticated market analysis and forecasting models. The results are then transmitted back to laptop computers that each sales rep carries. Before the new system was installed, it took the company 6 to 8 weeks to respond to market dynamics. Today, it can do so in less than a day.

In fact, these systems are so powerful that frequently companies that use them realize a 10% to 20% increase in sales each year and a relatively quick return on their investment in software and services. So for a sales centre with $8 million annual sales, a sales automation system is likely to increase sales to about S8.8 million.

Developing Marketing Information Systems

The first step in developing a marketing system is creating a database of internal and external marketing data, a time-consuming process that requires creative thinking. The database should go beyond simply providing infonnation about customers to providing information about noncustomers and the reasons why they have stayed away from the organization. The database should also measure customers' willingness to use new technologies. Safeway Stores, a 1,100-store supermarket chain, introduced an automated point-of- sale system that would allow shoppers to check out their own groceries. When a six-month trial at one of Safeway's busiest stores showed that only 15% of the store's customers used the technoiogy, further investment in the technology-was abandoned, thus saving the company hundreds of thousands of dollars.

The database should also provide answers to the following queries:

- What is the best way to capture data at the point of sale?
- How can we ensure that marketing operations are run smoothly and efficiency?
- What are the goods and services that our customers want?
- How do customers define customer service?
- What kinds of services are important to customers?
- Are customers interested in and willing to use information technology?
- How much are customers willing to pay for higher-quality service?
- What impact would higher-quality customer service have on the profits of the company?
- How can we attract and retain customers?

Benefits of Marketing Information Systems

A good marketing system provides employees with information that helps companies capture niche markets in highly competitive industries. For example, MusicWriter, a company that sells music-related products, captured the market in sheet music through the innovative use of CD-ROM. Its market analysis showed that there was a fairly good market for sheet music, a market that retailers and publishers had chosen to ignore. MusicWriter set up a kiosk called NoteStation in 165 music stores throughout the U.S., Canada, and the United Kingdom. Each NoteStation is equipped with CD-ROMs that store sheet music for 4,000 compositions in all 12 keys. Customers make their choices using touch screen PCs located in the kiosk. As soon as a credit card payment is approved, a printer in the kiosk prints the music.

Another company that benefits from its superior marketing system is the retail chain Ikea North America. The company's market data showed that customers preferred self-service and lower prices over customized service and higher prices. The company found a niche in the highly competitive grocery industry and continues to reap the benefits of its good market analysis.

Marketing information systems have a deep and direct influence on the quality of customer service. In fact, poor customer service can often be traced to poor information systems. Take a look at these facts.

- A whopping 90% of a customer's contact with a company is through the customer service department.
- A dissatisfied customer generally tells three or four people about a bad experience that he or she has had with a company.
- A satisfied customer tells at most one other person about a good experience.
- Recruiting customers costs five times as much as retaining customers.

In spite of these facts, companies are 60% more likely to focus on winning new customers than on keeping existing ones. Hence, marketing information systems play a critical role in helping an organization achieve its goals.

MANUFACTURING INFORMATION SYSTEMS

The world of manufacturing is undergoing significant and rapid changes; today's manufacturing environment looks quite different from the shop floor of a decade ago. In the last few years, mechanical manufacturing has given way to automation, and in the coming years computers and information technologies are expected to play an even bigger role in changing the manufacturing landscape.

A manufacturing information system is a system that supports the manufacturing functions of purchasing, receiving, quality control, inventory management, material requirements planning, capacity planning, production scheduling, and plant design. The term manufacturing information system actually applies to both manufacturing and service environments. Hence the term manufacturing should be viewed within the broad context of delivering both goods and services, since a manufacturer of automobile parts and a travel agency are both likely to have manufacturing information systems. Production systems, a subset of manufacturing information systems, are directly associated with the production of goods and services. While manufacturing system is an umbrella term that covers all activities related to manufacturing and services, production systems specifically address information needs related to acquiring and managing raw materials, scheduling equipment, manpower planning, repair and maintenance, and other activities directly related to production.

Developing a Manufacturing Information System

It is difficult to discuss manufacturing information systems without discussing MRP and MRP II. MRP stands for material requirements planning, a category of software that achieved prominence in the 1970s, which automates the process of production planning. MRP II (manufacturing resource planning) is the next generation of MRP systems; it integrates all the resources required to make a product: personnel, machines and equipment, plant capacity, pricing, distribution, and cost accounting.

Benefits of Manufacturing Information Systems

Clearly, manufacturing goods and services is the primary function of a business. The information generated from the shop floor (or service floor) drives the rest of the organization, so companies that have well-integrated manufacturing information systems are bound to reap significant benefits. For example, the quality of its manufacturing information systems helped Red Devil, supplier to stores such as Home Depot and Ace Hardware, reduce operating costs and inventory levels. When Red Devil changed over from its mainframe to an NCR 3455 UNIX server running manufacturing software in client-server mode, software costs immediately dropped by 80% and hardware costs by 70%. MIS costs, which were 2.2% of sales, fell to 1.37% of sales, and MIS personnel were reduced by 27%. A whopping $2 million in inventory was slashed when users began to trust the output of system and stopped "padding" inventory. Red Devil's ultimate goal? "Software that anticipates when Home Deport is likely to generate the order, so we can start production ahead of time.

HUMAN RESOURCE INFORMATION SYSTEMS

Human resource information systems (HRIS) support the planning, control, coordination, administration, and management of the human resource assets in an organization. They provide managers with information, policies, and procedures concerning recruiting, layoffs, employee evaluation, promotion, termination, transfer, salary equity monitoring, job descriptions and responsibilities, training, affirmative action, and equal employment opportunities. Since they also provide vital information on matters such as payroll, federal and state taxes, health benefits, child care, grievance procedures, and other personal information that affects employees' personal and professional lives, it is imperative that these systems be highly responsive to employee needs.

Human resource systems, unlike accounting and financial information systems, were slow to be computerized. In the 1960s, HRIS were primarily record keeping systems that were developed, managed, and maintained by IS professionals with little or no input from the personnel department. But by the early 1980s, many organizations began to realize the importance of HRIS. In the early 1980s, almost 60%i of the nation's largest 150 banks and nearly 40% of the Fortune 500 firms invested in some kind of personnel information system, largely because of the Johnson and Nixon administrations' legislation on equal employment, benefits, and workplace conditions. It is estimated that by the year 2000, HRIS will be a necessary for major corporations if they are to keep up with increasing government regulations and respond to personal information queries about employees. Table 15.2 provides some guidelines on selecting an HRIS.

Although many people believe that HRIS systems can be used only to enhance HR decisions, in fact they can be used to cut costs, increase efficiency, and achieve a competitive edge in the marketplace. For example, finance and human resource managers at NCR jointly developed a HRIS that determines how hiring and training decisions made by the personnel department can increase sales revenues. Also, the system links the performance of an individual to items such as past training, educational background, and work history, so that managers can be better equipped to make such decisions.

To keep the cost of employee relocation down and ensure smooth transfers, Mobil Oil uses an HRIS to select the best relocation site. Armstrong. World's HRIS enabled the company to self-insure and to better control health care costs.

Some Guidelines for selecting an HRIS

How to Pick an HR System	
Get advice	Help from a reputable HR consulting firm minimizes the risk. These specialists have been through the process before.
Test the payroll	High-volume transaction processing is the toughest job for client-server systems. Ask prospective human resources vendors to run your payroll for you.
Play the numbers	Don't ignore the benefits of outside service bureaus—especially in the area of payroll. Tax, retirement, and other legal conditions change. If you've got more than 500 employees, run a cost-benefits analysis.
Get it in writing	Don't be afraid to ask your vendor for a guarantee. At least two HR suppliers, Ross Systems and ADP, offer "Statements of Commitment."
Train, train, train	Provide plenty of project staffing and technology education for your HR staff on the new system.

Be prepared	^ merger or acquisition can affect your business at any time. A firm might need to add 5,000 employees to benefits and payroll systems within 30 days.
Act like traditional IS	Today's human resources departments must worry about security and data integrity, taking over that responsibility in some cases from information systems departments.

QUALITY INFORMATION SYSTEMS

Total Quality Management (TQM) has been embraced, with religious fervor, by some organizations and discarded by others as a passing fad. Some use TQM to achieve and hold leadership positions in the marketplace: others have been frustrated by their limited success with it. Regardless of the rate of success or failure of TQM, this simple and elegant idea continues to haunt corporations all over the world. In a recent survey of 455 senior managers, 87% of them viewed quality as the key factor for achieving competitive success. Quality information systems are standalone systems or embedded systems that help an organization to achieve its quality goals.

Benefits of Quality Information Systems

The goal of many corporations all over the world is to produce high-quality goods and services; information is essential to achieve this goal—accurate, timely, and reliable information. For example, a few years ago, the $100 million structural products division of Coors Ceramics, Golden, Colorado, was in trouble because its 15-year-old information system was outdated. The system took as long as 2 days to process an order and salespeople couldn't track the status of customer orders. Managers often fudged numbers so that goods could be delivered on time, often resulting in higher finished-goods inventories and an increase in overhead costs. The system also tracked shipping only on a weekly basis. Therefore if a customer wanted an order Monday and Coors shipped it Saturday, the system logged that order as "on time". When customers called to complain, the salesperson got no valid data from the system other than a cheerful "on time" report.

Coors realized that lack of information was one of the primary reasons why its quality was slipping and identified three goals for the new information system; increase customer satisfaction, reduce lead times, and reduce operating costs. The new client- server system runs on a UNIX-based IBM RS/6000, which provides integrated manufacturing, distribution, field service and financial applications. The system tracks inventory and shipments and provides managers with detailed informa-tion on the status of customer orders. The system provides managers with complete and comprehensive information on customers, including order placement, production or shipment status, and payment reports. The new system has helped the company to reduce the product cycle from 10 to 14 weeks to 6 to 10 weeks. On-time shipments have improved to more than 95% and Coors salespeople can be confident that "on time" means that it was delivered on time, not just within a week.

Achieving quality also involves being able to develop strategic alliances wit suppliers and customers, and information is again essential to this process. Nypro, a precision injection molder in Clinton, Massachusetts, tripled its sales to $200 million in just 6 years by using information systems to build strategic alliances with its suppliers by sharing company-related information with them. This had led to the creation of management teams, comprising members from both Nypro and its suppliers, who freely exchange the information necessary to produce high-quality goods.

Some Auto Companies believes that information is essential to building high-quality automobiles and developed a quality information management system (QIMS) to achieve its quality goals. The system tightly integrates information generated on the shop floor, for instance about defective automobiles, so that decision makers can take immediate action to correct the situation. Managers have changed from data gatherers to quality enforcers, since now they can take proactive action to keep the company on the quality track.

GEOGRAPHICAL INFORMATION SYSTEMS

Several years ago, telecommunications carrier GTE tracked the process of its fiber-optic network by poking pins into maps handed out by a car rental agency. Today, Geographical Information Systems (GIS) provide a much more sophisticated way for companies such as GTE to gather a wide range of information and display it on computer-generated maps. Geography plays an important role in many business decisions, since 85% of corporate data involve geographical elements, such as customer addresses and supplier locations. Also a number of business decisions, such as store locations, sales territories, sales promotions, and regulatory compliance rely heavily on geographical data. Awareness of this has led many software vendors, such as Lotus," to embed mapping technology in their products so that users can produce maps easily.

Although the term geographical Information Systems may conjure up images of software tools for geography majors, they are in fact among the most powerful and versatile tools for the business community and can be used in many different ways in the various functional areas of a business. A geographical information system is a computer-based system that stores and manipulates data that are viewed from a geographical point of reference. A GIS has four main capabilities: data input, data storage and retrieval, data manipulation and analysis, and data output. (Although there are many manual geographical information systems, this section focuses on computer-based systems). Note that a GIS should not be confused with cartographic systems, which merely store and generate computer based maps. A GIS is much more versatile and powerful than a cartographic system, since it can create information by integrating different data, sometimes from different sources, and display the data in different ways to the end- user.

SUMMARY

1. A business is defined as a mutual activity of two or more organizations were all organizations earn a profit.
2. The advent of information technology has made it possible to meet the expectations of a customer.
3. Strategic Information systems are special types of information system which support the change of goal, operation, products, services or environmental relationships of organization.
4. In this era of IT, information resources are gaining up their importance. From design to implementation to use of information systems, there are several resources which are coming across in the context.
5. A Financial and accounting information system (FAIS) is a system that provides information related to the accounting and financial activities in an organization.
6. FAIS are often integrated with other functional systems in the organization to facilitate data sharing and team sharing and team decision making.
7. Marketing systems have evolved through different phases, from a focus on information on key market indicators from a single source, on aperiodic basis (say, weekly, monthly or biannually), to systems designed to gather different kinds of marketing data from multiple sources, both internal and external, more frequently.
8. The first step in developing a marketing system is creating a database of internal and external marketing data, a time-consuming process that requires creative thinking.
9. The world of manufacturing is undergoing significant and rapid changes; today's manufacturing environment looks quite different from the shop floor of a decade ago.
10. Human resource information systems (HRIS) support the planning, control, coordination, administration, and management of the human resource assets in an organization.
11. Quality information systems are standalone systems or embedded systems that help an organization to achieve its quality goals.
12. Geographical Information Systems (GIS) provide a much more sophisticated way for companies such as GTE to gather a wide range of information and display it on computer-generated maps.

MULTIPLE CHOICE QUESTIONS

1. SCM stands for:
   (a) Supply Chain Managment Systems
   (b) Supply Chain Managed Systems
   (c) Serious Chain Managment Systems
2. CRM stands for :
   (a) Container Relationship Management Systems
   (b) Customer Relationship Management Systems
   (c) Customer Relationship Manager Systems
3. KM is:
   (a) Knowlall Management Systems (b) Knowledge Manager Systems (c) Knowledge Management Systems

REVIEW QUESTIONS

1. What is a business? What is a digital business?
2. What are the features of a digital business?
3. What are advantages of digital business?
4. What are four different types of Is for modern business?
5. What are functions of an information system in a business?
6. Explain the terms digital market, B2B, B2C, C2C and m-Commerce.
7. What is strategic information system? What are the common situations where it is frequently required?
8. How do strategic systems benefit society?
9. What are various information resources? Give a classified account of resources.
10. Give few examples of digital business, in the real life.
11. What are some of the benefits of information systems to an organization? Identify at least three intangible benefits of IS.
12. Describe agile manufacturing. What are the four key characteristics of agile manufacturing? Why is agile manufacturing sometimes called the "great equalizer"?
13. Why should manufacturing information systems be integrated with other systems in the organization? Describe MRP and MRP II.
14. What is the difference between manufacturing information systems and production system's? Can you give an example of a production system?
15. Briefly describe the five types of functional information systems. Is any one system more important than the other? Discuss.
16. What do we mean by a dedicated marketing information system? What are some of its subsystem? Do all organizations have dedicated marketing systems?
17. What are some subsystems of financial and accounting information systems? Describe any one subsystem of financial and accounting information systems.
18. What are the three competitive strategies of a firm? Why should a firm's competitive strategies be taken into account
19. Describe a GIS; identify some uses of GIS. What are some types of decision that rely on geographical data?
20. What is meant by vendor-managed inventory? Identify two advantages and two disadvantages of vendor- managed inventory.

ANSWERS

Multiple Choice Questions

1. a 2. b 3. c

CHAPTER 16

Inter Personnel Skills and Communications

Learning Objectives

After going through this chapter, you should appreciate the following:

- **Introduction to Digital Business**
- **Types of Information Systems for Business**
- **New Forms of Business**
- **Strategic Information Systems**
- **Information Resources Management**
- **Financial and Accounting Information Systems (FAIS)**
  - Types of Financial and Accounting Information System
- **Integrated Financial and Accounting Systems**
- **Marketing Information Systems**
  - Developing Marketing Information Systems
  - Benefits of Marketing Information Systems
- **Manufacturing Information Systems**
  - Developing a Manufacturing Information System
  - Benefits of Manufacturing Information Systems
- **Human Resource Information Systems**
  - Some Guidelines for selecting an HRIS
  - How to Pick an HR System

INTRODUCTION

A successful systems analyst must have good written and oral communications skills to perform his or her job effectively. Never underestimate the importance of effective communications whether you are using a memo, e-mail, or an oral presentation to convey your ideas. The following guidelines will help you prepare and deliver effective presentations. Remember, however, that nothing increases your ability to communicate belter than practicing these skills.

GUIDELINES FOR SUCCESSFUL COMMUNICATIONS

When you are planning your communications, concentrate on making sure that your communication answers the questions of why, who, what, when, and how.

1. Know why you are communicating, and what you want to accomplish. Ask yourself the question, Is this communication necessary, and what specific results am I seeking? Your entire communication strategy depends on the results that you need.
2. Know who your targets are. The information needs of managers depend on their organizational and knowledge levels. When communicating with management, sometimes a fine line exists between saying enough and saying too much. Each situation is different, so you must use good judgment. You should plan a communication strategy and be alert for feedback from your audience.
3. Know what is expected of you, and when to go into detail. This is directly related to knowing who your targets are and the organizational and knowledge levels of your audience. For example, a vice president might expect less detail and more focus on how a project supports the company's strategic business goals. You must design your communications just as carefully as your systems project. For example, will the recipients expect you to address a specilic issue or topic? Will they expect cost estimates or charts? Design your communications based on the answers to these questions.
4. Know how to communicate effectively. Use the Toolkit and your own experiences and observations of successful and unsuccessful techniques used by others to become a better communicator.

Most importantly, know your subject. Before any presentation, consider what others expect you to know and what questions they will ask. No matter how well you prepare, you will not have an answer for every question. Remember that it is better to say, "I don't know, but I'll find out" rather than to guess.

WRITTEN COMMUNICATIONS

Good writing is important because others often judge you by your writing. Tf you make a mistake while speaking, your audience probably will forget it. Your written errors, however, might be around for a long time. Grammatical, typographical, and spelling errors distract readers from your message.

If you have not taken a writing course, you should consider doing so. If you have a choice of courses, select one that focuses on business writing. Any writing class, however, is worth the effort. Bookstores and libraries have many excellent books on communicating effectively. As you prepare written documents, keep in mind the following suggestions.

1. Know your audience If you are writing for nontechnical readers, use terms that readers will understand.
2. Use active voice whenever possible For example, Tom designed the system, is better than. The system was designed by Tom,

3. Keep your writing concise
4. Use one paragraph to convey a single idea
5. Use the right style. Use a conversational tone in informal documents and a business tone in formal documents
6. Use lists When you must enumerate a number of subtopics related to the same topic, lists are an organized way to present them
7. Use short, easy-to-understand words. Your objective is not to impress your audience with the size of your vocabulary
8. Check your work. Look for grammatical and typographical mistakes and correct them
9. Avoid repeating the same word too often Use a thesaurus to locate synonyms for frequently repeated words. Many word processing programs include a thesaurus and other tools to help you write better.
10. Check your spelling You can use the spell checker in your word processing program to check your spelling, but remember that a spell checker identifies only those words that do not appear in the program's dictionary. You should proofread your documents. The spell checker will not identify instances when you use the word, their, instead of the word, there.

Memos, Letters, and E-mail

Most companies have a standard format for internal letters and memos. When you are preparing documents, you can use a word processor to create templates with specific layouts, fonts, and margin settings. Templates will give your work a consistent look and make your job easier. Some word processing programs even provide a feature that allows you to fill in the blanks as you work.

Many companies now use e-mail as a standard form of written correspondence. E-mail usually is less formal than other written communication, but you still must follow the rules of good grammar, spelling, and clear writing. Although many authors use a more conversational style for e-mail, you should remember that e-mail messages often are forwarded to other recipients or groups, and so they are as important as any other form of written communication. If you regularly exchange messages with a specific group of users, most e-mail programs allow you to create a distribution list that includes the members and their e-mail addresses.

Reports

You must prepare many reports during the SDLC, including the preliminary investigation report, the system requirements document at the end of the systems analysis phase, the system design specification at the end of the system design phase, and the final report to management when the system goes into operation. You also might submit other reports such as status reports, activity reports, proposals, and departmental business plans.

You can use a basic format for all your reports and make modifications as needed. Depending on the type of report and the subject matter, the written document can include the following elements: cover letter, title page, table of contents, summary, findings and conclusions, alternatives, recommendations, and an appendix.

A cover letter usually is addressed to the systems review committee or to management. Use the cover letter to identify the attached report and set a data, time, and place for the oral presentation. You also can request that the recipients read the report in advance of the presentation.

The introduction usually includes a title page, table of contents, and brief description of the proposal. The title page should be clean and neat and contain the name of the proposal, the subject, the date,, and the names of the development team members. If the project already has a recognized name or acronym, use it. Include a table of contents when the report is long or includes many exhibits. Many word processing programs include a tool that can generate a table of contents automatically.

The summary is used to summarize the entire project, including your recommendations, in several paragraphs. Generally, the summary should not exceed 200 words or one page.

Use the findings section to describe the major conclusions that you or the team reached during the systems analysis phase. The findings section can be detailed or summarized, depending on the project. You must explain the logical design of the new system in a way that nontechnical managers can understand clearly. With a management audience, the most important task is to explain how the proposed system supports the company's business needs.

The recommendations section presents the best system alternative, with a brief explanation that does not disparage anyone who favors a different alternative. The essential factors of economic, technical, and operation feasibility should be mentioned in your recommendation.

The alternatives section can be a separate section, or part of the recommendations section. The alternatives section identifies various strategies and alternatives. Tn the alternatives section, you should list the advantages and disadvantages of each major system alternative. In this section, you should include the cost-benefit results, with a clear description of the economic analysis techniques that were used. You can use tables or graphs to support and clarify your alternatives when necessary.

When you have a large number of supporting documents such as questionnaires or sampling results, you should put these items in an appendix. Make sure you include only relevant information, and provide references for interested readers.

ORAL COMMUNICATION

An oral presentation is required at the end of the preliminary investigation and again at the conclusion of the systems analysis phase. You might need to give more than one presentation in some situations to present technical material to members of the IS department or to present an overview for top managers. When preparing an oral presentation, keep in mind the following suggestions: define the audience, define the objectives for your presentation, organize the presentation, define any technical terms you will use, prepare your presentation aids, and practice your material.

Define the Audience

Before you develop a detailed plan for a management presentation, you must define the audience. For vice presidents and senior managers, you should provide less detail and a strategic overview.

Define the Objectives

When you communicate, you should focus on your objectives. In the management presentation for the systems analysis phase, your goals are to:

* Inform management of the status of the current system
* Describe your findings concerning the current system problems
* Explain the alternative solutions that you developed
* Provide detailed cost and time estimates for the alternative solutions
* Recommend the best alternative and explain the reasons for your selection

Organize the Presentation

Plan your presentation in three stages: the introduction, the information, and the summation. First, you should introduce yourself and describe your objectives. During the presentation, make sure that you discuss topics in a logical order. Be as specific as possible when presenting facts—your listeners want to hear your views about what is wrong, how it can be fixed, and how much it will cost. In your conclusion, briefly summarize the main points, and then ask for questions.

Define Any Technical Terms

You should avoid specialized or technical terminology whenever possible. If your audience might be unfamiliar with a term that you plan to use, either define the term or find another way to say it so your material will be understood.

Prepare Presentation Aids

Studies show that 75 percent of everything learndd is acquired visually, so you should use helpful, appropriate visual aids to help the audience follow the logic of your presentation and hold their attention. Visual aids also can direct audience attention away from you, which is helpful if you are nervous when you give the presentation. You can use a visual aid with an outline of topics that will help you stay on track.

Visual aids can help you display a graphical summary of performance trends, a series of cost-benefit examples, or a bulleted list of important points. You can use whiteboards, flip charts, overhead transparencies, slides, films, and videotapes to enhance your presentation. When preparing your visual aids, make sure that the content is clear, readable, and easy to understand. Verify ahead of time that the visual material can be seen from anywhere in the room. Remember that equipment can fail unexpectedly, so be prepared with an alternate plan.

When you create a slide show, you should concentrate on preparing the content of your presentation first, and then focus on visual aids. You should select special effects carefully—too many graphics, colors, or audio and special effects will distract the audience.

Practice

The most important part of your preparation is practice. You should rehearse several times to be sure that the presentation flows smoothly and the timing is correct. Practicing will make you more comfortable and build your confidence.

Do not be tempted to write a script. If you read your presentation, you will be unable to interact with your audience and adjust your content based on their reactions. Instead, prepare an outline of your presentation and practice from the outline. Then, when you deliver the actual presentation, you will not have to struggle to remember the exact words you planned to say, and you will be able to establish a good rapport with your audience.

The Presentation

When you give the presentation, the following points will help you succeed.

Sell Yourself and Your Credibility To be successful in a presentation, you must sell yourself and your credibility. A brilliant presentation will not convince top managers that the system should be approved if they are not sold on the person who gave the presentation. On the other hand, many systems projects are approved because the systems analyst did an excellent sales job.

Your presentation must show confidence about the subject and your recommendations. You should avoid any conflicts with the people attending the presentation. If anyone directs critical remarks to you, address the criticisms honestly and directly. You will have a successful presentation only if you know the material thoroughly, prepare properly, and sell yourself and your credibility effectively.

Control the Presentation During the presentation, you must control the discussion, maintain the pace of the presentation, and stay focused on the agenda — especially when answering questions. Although you might be more familiar with the subject material, you must not appear to be taking a superior attitude toward your listeners.

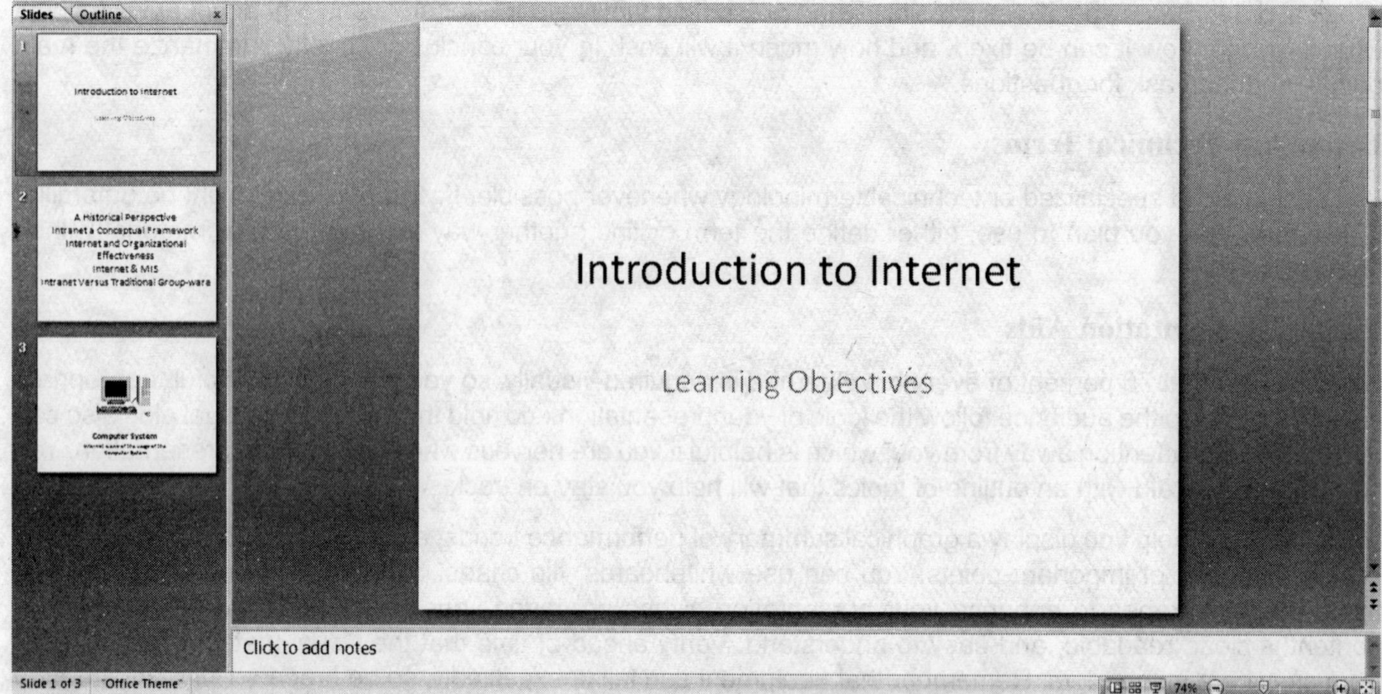

Maintain eye contact with the audience and use some humor, but do not insert irrelevant jokes or make a joke at someone else's expense.

Answer Questions Appropriately Let your audience know whether you would prefer to take questions as you go along or have a question and answer session at the end. Sometimes the question can be quite difficult. You must listen carefully and respond with a straightforward answer. Try to anticipate the questions your audience will ask so you can prepare your responses ahead of time.

When answering a difficult or confusing question, repeat the question in your own words to make sure that you understand it. For example, you can say, "If I understand your question, you are asking whether...". This will help avoid confusion and give you a moment to think on your feet. To make sure that you gave a clear answer, you can say, "Have I answered your question"? Allow follow-up questions when necessary.

Use Good Speaking Techniques The delivery of your presentation is just as important as its content. You can strengthen your delivery by speaking clearly and confidently and projecting a relaxed approach. You also must control the pace of your delivery. If you speak too fast, you will lose the audience and if the pace is too slow, people lose their concentration and the presentation will not be effective.

Many speakers are nervous when facing an audience. If this is a problem for you, keep the following suggestions in mind.

1. **Control your environment** If you are most nervous when the audience is looking at you, use visual aids to direct their attention away from you. If your hands are shaking, do not hold your notes. If you are delivering a computer slide show, use the keyboard to advance to the next slide instead of using the mouse. Concentrate on using a strong, clear voice. If your nervousness distracts you, take a deep breath and remind yourself that you really do know your subject.
2. **Turn your nervousness to your advantage** Many people do their best work when they are under a little stress. Think of your nervousness as normal pressure.
3. **Avoid meaningless filler words and phrases** Using words and phrases such as okay, all right, you know, like, urn, and ah are distracting and serve no purpose,
4. **Practice! Practice! Practice!** Some people are naturally gifted speakers, but most people need lots of

practice. You must work hard at practicing your presentation and building your confidence. Many schools offer a speech or public speaking course that is an excellent way of practicing your skills.

Your success as a systems analyst depends on your ability to communicate effectively. You must know why you are communicating, what you want to accomplish, who your targets are, what is expected of you — and when to go into detail. You must know your subject and how to use good written and oral communications techniques.

You will be judged by your written work, so it must be free of grammatical, spelling, and punctuation errors. Your letters and memos should be written clearly and the writing style should match the situation. Many companies have standard formats for letters and memos, and you can use word processing templates to achieve consistency.

You will prepare various reports during the SDLC and the format will vary depending on the nature of the report. Your reports should have a cover memo and might include a title page, table of contents, summary or abstract, description of alternatives, your recommendations, and an appendix.

In addition to written communications, you must communicate effectively in person. You might be required to deliver several presentations to different audiences at different times during the SDLC. Presentations are an important form of oral communication and you should follow specific guidelines in preparing your presentation. You prepare by defining your audience, identifying your objectives, and organizing the presentation itself. You also need to define technical terms and prepare visual aids to help your audience understand the material. Most importantly, you must practice your delivery to gain confidence and strengthen your presentation skills.

When you give the presentation, you are selling your ideas and your credibility. You must control the discussion, build a good rapport with the audience, answer all questions clearly and directly, and try to use good speaking techniques. Again, the best way to become a better speaker is to practice.

SUMMARY

1. A successful systems analyst must have good written and oral communications skills to perform his or her job effectively.
2. Good writing is important because others often judge you by your writing.
3. Most companies have a standard format for internal letters and memos.
4. A cover letter usually is addressed to the systems review committee or to management.
5. An oral presentation is required at the end of the preliminary investigation and again at the conclusion of the systems analysis phase.
6. Plan your presentation in three stages: the introduction, the information, and the summation.
7. Visual aids can help you display a graphical summary of performance trends, a series of cost-benefit examples, or a bulleted list of important points.
8. The most important part of your preparation is practice. You should rehearse several times to be sure that the presentation flows smoothly and the timing is correct.
9. During the presentation, you must control the discussion, maintain the pace of the presentation, and stay focused on the agenda.
10. You can strengthen your delivery by speaking clearly and confidently and projecting a relaxed approach.
11. Your success as a systems analyst depends on your ability to communicate effectively.
12. The recommendations section presents the best system alternative, with a brief explanation that does not disparage anyone who favors a different alternative.

REVIEW QUESTIONS

1. Why is practice so important when preparing a presentation?
2. Name three specific activities you can do if you get nervous during a presentation.
3. What should you do during the delivery of your presentation to improve the success of the presentation?
4. When you organize your presentation, what three main stages do you plan?
5. Why are visual aids important? Give at least three examples of different types of visual aids, with a specific example of how you would use each type in an actual presentation. You can use the SWL case or make up your own scenario.
6. What is the role of e-mail communication? What techniques can you use to become an effective e-mail communicator?
7. What are the main sections of a written report to management, and what is the purpose of each section?
8. What are live things you can do to prepare an effective oral presentation?
9. Mention five specific techniques you can use to improve your written documents.
10. Describe the who, what, when, where, and why of communications. Explain each term and give an example.

CHAPTER 17

Computer System Management

Learning Objectives

After going through this chapter, you should appreciate the following:

- **Managing the Computer Function**
- **Personnel Structure**
- **Patterns of Organization**
- **Successful EDP Functions**
- **Computer Centre Site Preparation**

SPACE	FLOORING
LOADING CONSIDERATIONS	CEILING
ROOM LAYOUT	AIR CONDITIONING
DUST-FREE	CLEANLINESS
SITING	ACCESS
SECURITY	SAFETY
POWER AND LIGHTING	USER CONTACTS
STAFF FACILITIES	PLANNING

- **Uninterruptible Power Supply (UPS)**
- **Computer Virus and Elimination**
- **History of Virus**
- **Virus Prevention and Elimination**

MANAGING THE COMPUTER FUNCTION

Perhaps no other scientific endeavour has penetrated so much in so many areas of human activity and that too in such a short time as the electronic marvel of this century, the computer. Computers are now being used in most areas of science, technology and management. With the information explosion taking place all over the world, computers are becoming a necessity rather than a luxury in most organizations. With the development of modern management sciences, computers are now being used as tools for strategic and tactical planning and decision-making using tools like productivity softwares and Decision Support Systems. Large scale use and dependence on computer systems demands a successful introduction and management of the data processing function of an organization.

If it is decided that an organization is to become computerized, the services of a data processing (DP) department are essential. The organization structure of a computer facility encompasses such decisions as the number of managerial levels, authority relationships, and the general pattern of functions performed by the members at all levels. The structure of a typical facility may have (1) the manager of the computer facility, (2) the supervisors for systems analysis and design, programming and computer operations, (3) support staff for performing the functions of systems analysis and design, programming and computer operations. It should be noted that this structure is a general model and it has many variations, depending on the size of the computer facility and the extent to which computer processing is centralized.

The personnel involved may be as many as hundreds or as few as half a dozen. The number obviously affects the structure of the department. For example, a computer facility utilizing a minicomputer may consist of a manager (who is also a systems analyst), one to three programmers, a console operator, and one to three key punch operators. In contrast, a large-sized computer facility may require hundreds of specialized personnel and support staff. Many a small business has insufficient work to justify the expense of installing its own computer facility but still requires access to a computer system. Computer service bureaux, which hire out time on a contract basis, have grown up to meet this situation. Whether data processing is handled in-house (within the organization) or externally (by a computer service bureau) there are three main areas in which computer personnel are involved: systems design, development and operation.

Activities in a Computer Centre

The various activities in a computer centre are:

1. Systems Study
2. Systems Development
3. Program coding and testing
4. Systems test run
5. Execution of jobs on Computer/Implementation
6. Inout/outnut control

PERSONNEL STRUCTURE

The most important resource for the EDP centre is the systems and programming personnel. The organization could train their own officers in systems and programming or recruit trained staff for these positions. There are merits as well demerits in both these approaches. The existing staff may or may not have the proper interest, aptitude and skills for this type of work. But they have an indepth knowledge of the organization's unique applications which is a primary requirement. If persons are recruited from outside, their knowledge about that organization will be inadequate to handle the applications and it will be difficult for the organization to offer them good promotional opportunities within the same department. But they are likely to have an indepth knowledge in computers and will be thorough professionals in that field. Organizations may have to adopt a balanced approach of getting some personnel from outside as well as training their own personnel in this field so that the organization can get the advantage of both.

Location of the Computer Function

We can list the following seven different ways of locating a data processing organization:

1. **Decentralized, reporting to each user**. This is the structure whereby data processing location is the decentralized location and each important user (e.g., accounting, engineering, etc.) has his own computer.

2. **Centralized, reporting to one user**. In this structure, the data processing organization reports to one user, mainly the largest.

3. **Centralized, reporting on a level with the user**. In this case, the data processing organization is centralized and reports to a Secretary for administration or directly to an executive officer of the organization. It is thus independent of any of its users.

4. **Centralized systems and programming, decentralised operations**. When an organization contains many geographically disparate elements, then it may be desirable to decentralise the operating function. The systems and programming function remain centralized but each decentralized unit is provided with assistance of its own capability.

5. **Centralized, above the user. In this type of structure, data processing dictates policy and applications**. A deep understanding of organizational problems by the data processing manager is needed to determine how the integration of data and applications will take place.

6. **Centralized operations, decentralized systems and programming**. It happens when each division or user has its own systems and programming capability and takes decisions independently on the type of applications and programs to be implemented. In this type of structure, operating functions are centralized and machine time on a service-bureau basis are sold to users.

7. **Centralized operations and programming decentralized systems**. We can have a structure in which programming and operations are centralized but where the user designs his own systems. For this, the systems function must be related closely to the user and programming must be related to the machine.

Advantages and disadvantages of each of the above alternatives

The decision of an organization regarding its own structure for data processing must depend on its own policy. However, to facilitate an organization make the best possible use of the computer to serve the organization, we list some of the advantages and disadvantages of each alternative type of organization structure.

Advantages of Centralization

Total centralization has the following advantages:

1. Centralization of equipment helps in significant economies of use. Fewer operators and less programming effort will be needed to deal with peak loads of work.

2. Shared use of centralized computers permits a higher utilization of the computer.

3. Centralized programming with centralized equipment can deal easily with peak loads, emergencies and swift maintenance and correction of errors.

4. Centralized installations will attract and offer challenging posts, higher pay, and simulation of working with high calibre computer professionals.

5. Centralization has better control and potential for total organizational planning.
6. In a centralized system, the systems people have access to information in many different areas of the country instead of being restricted to data arising from their own organizations.

Advantages of Decentralization

1. Systems technology is more closely related to user applications. The advantages of decentralized installations start with such items as responsiveness, flexibility and turn-around time. A decentralized unit that is controlled by the user, is responsive to the needs of that organization. Hence it maximizes satisfaction in the greatest number of people. Also, the user has to comply with the rules of centralized systems and hence has a difficulty in getting adjusted. Further, to get maximum use, a computer normally requires scheduling and the running of particular types of jobs concurrently. This combined with the necessity to use various communications media to get data into the computer and to transmit the results to the user, takes time, resulting in a longer turn-around time.
2. It is much simpler to budget for and to charge the costs of a decentralized, smaller computer than for a large computer running in a multi-programming mode.
3. The difficult problems of designing systems to serve multiple users disappear.

Examination of the advantages of centralization indicates that such advantages disappear if decentralization is selected. The main advantages of decentralized systems, viz., responsiveness, flexibility, and lower turn-around time can be had through centralized devices, such as time-sharing remote terminals and high-speed printers in the hands of users. It is responsive because the user has an access to the computer at his ease, it is flexible because time-sharing programs can be written that adjust to experience level of the user and finally, turn-around time tends to be rapid in time-sharing systems, unless the computer is loaded heavily with work. Centralization thus appears inevitable. However, in cases where the data processing manager is not sufficiently strong and efficient to provide strong control and incentive, the data processing organization will continue to report to a financial officer or to an engineering officer.

Except in cases where data processing is the main livelihood of the business, it does not seem appropriate that the data processing elements may be one level above the remaining user elements.

Also, in centralized operations and programming, with a decentralized system we have an obvious disadvantage that inter-divisional applications may not be easily implemented. The alternatives, which may be used, thus are the first, third, and fifth. Decentralization is possible in geographical distribution of systems because it is not practicable to obtain timely information centrally. However, geographically separate facilities can be centralized due to increases in data communication efficiency and reductions in data communication costs. On the other hand, the competence of the existing data processing management and circumstances determine whether the centralized data processing organization reports to a single user or directly to the management.

PATTERNS OF ORGANIZATION

The structure of the data processing organization depends upon the location of the organization, its type — centralized or decentralized, etc. We shall consider the following three organizational structures in a single centralized unit consisting of all elements of operation, programming and systems.

1. The Line Organization

It has three or more elements, normally a programming manager, systems manager, and an operations manager as three second-line managers reporting directly to the data processing manager. If the organization is small, even more units like a keypunch supervisor or production scheduler may report directly to the data processing manager. This structure is disad-vantageous in the sense that the data processing manager cannot spend sufficient time on liaison with users, in orientation of top management, and in planning and control - all being his duties, and not being discharged efficiently.

2. Line/Staff Organization

In this alternative, the data processing manager recognizes his inability to discharge many of his responsibilities for planning, control, training and other functions in an efficient way and hence establishes a staff function or functions each assuming direct responsibility for some of these functional elements. An operations control can be established responsible for production scheduling, input control administration of operating functions, etc., or a project control function being responsible for activities related to development projects, similar to those of operations control. It also assumes further responsibilities for personnel training, administration, and standards development and maintenance. Further, with the advent of fourth generation computers, maintenance functions are now assuming considerable importance because complexities in modem software requires it even within ihe user organization. This maintenance function normally serves both development and operating elements, both being users of software.

3. Functional Organization

The functional structure, a tripartite organization, comprises the elements of development, control and operations. In order to reduce the problems between systems and programming, these two arc combined under one development function. Taking the staff control elements, it is made a direct line function. The development function has responsibility for systems analysis, programming and the maintenance function. The control function and a direct line function takes responsibility for project control, production control, and research functions implied in software maintenance, standards and training. Finally, the operating function is responsible for the basic functions of operation although not for operations control.

SUCCESSFUL EDP FUNCTIONS

For an EDP function to be successful, it is imperative that top management gives its full support and commitment, the user management fully participates and uses the computer as a tool for effective decision making, and EDP personnel are fully qualified and experienced to handle the EDP effectively. To achieve this success, let us have a look at the role to be played by each type of management (top, user or operating, data processing level-management).

Role of top management

Top level management is responsible for running the organization as a whole and provides resources and people to meet the objective. Its failure would mean abject failure of the computer program. Further, they must carry out functions like planning, organization, staffing, direction, controlling, etc. Specific responsibilities of top management include:

1. To understand the computer process (implications, general resistance, major software activity, data security).
2. To establish controls (define requirements, realistic budgetary control, schedules control).
3. To obtain competent data processing managers (competency training).
4. To establish realistic personnel policy (shortage of personnel, policies to attract).
5. To provide management support (support managers, recognition of problems, complexities, time-frame).
6. To define objectives accurately (short and long range, current objectives of DP program, structure).
7. To perform post-installation management audit (identified objectives, targets, major responsibility).

8. To perform long-range planning (information systems).
9. To recognize organizational implications.
10. To establish data processing locations.
11. To plan for equipment.
12. To support user training.

Role of operating management

Operating managers are responsible for such functions as product development, marketing, manufacturing, branch operations. These responsibilities differ from top managers in that their primary responsibility is to use the resources assigned to them to perform a particular function that supports the organizations' overall objectives. Specific responsibilities of operating management include:

1. To identify applications (possible mechanization, imagination and understanding, benefits to entire organization, evaluation and priority).
2. To define requirements (precisely and realistically, participation in DP vital, overall benefit).
3. To recognise economics (properly justified applications).
4. To accept requirements freeze during implementation,
5. To establish controls (I/O controls, control procedures).
6. To acquire DP education (continuing education, planning and equipment changes).
7. To participate in implementation (specification, testing, audit, information systems for organization cooperation).

Role of data processing management

Data processing management is a demanding and challenging task. It is a fascinating job for those with aptitude and ambition. Routine responsibilities include the management of operations-, systems-, user support-group and continuous improvement of DP service.

1. Role of Operations Manager:

1. To manage the operations service staff.
2. To ensure that the efficient and effective performance is maintained for the entire system.
3. To ensure that the files and libraries are maintained in a secure and reliable manner.
4. To ensure that the operations service is run in a cost effective manner.
5. To ensure that proper control is kept of the resources available to the users.
6. To ensure that the consumable etc. required for the computer system are planned and procured in time.
7. To ensure that the maintenance service is efficient and effective.
8. To maintain the record of, and recover the charges for providing computing facility to the users.
9. To make recommendations for addition/change of software/hardware.

2. Role of Systems Software Manager:

1. To organise and manage the systems group.
2. To ensure that the necessary software for the computing service is developed, commissioned and maintained.

3. To ensure that documentation is maintained, and procedures developed for the operations of the software.
4. To provide specialist courses for in-house training of staff.

3. Role of User-Support Manager:

1. To organize and manage User-Support Group.
2. To develop and maintain documentation and standards for the computing facilities for users.
3. To assess and meet the software requirements and maintain software.
4. To ensure that technical advice is available and properly given on aspects of software used or supplied by the computer centre.
5. To ensure that the user community is kept informed fully of the developments and standards through lectures, seminars, discussions etc.

4. Non-routine responsibilities of data processing management:

1. To acquire education in management skills (plan, organize, control).
2. To develop standards (effective standards manual, smooth transition, implementation).
3. To select personnel (operating personnel, qualified and motivated).
4. To establish long-range resource (planning parallel to corporate, 5-8 year cycle lead times planning).
5. To establish profit and loss responsibility (economic justification for applications, budgetary charging).

COMPUTER CENTRE SITE PREPARATION

Designing and outfitting a computer facility requires creativity and the collaboration of a host of different parties. No matter what the size of the room or the budget, no computer room or relocation, renovation, expansion, or creation can succeed without meticulous planning and implementation. People are the key to success, even at a high-tech facility. Finding the people to manage a computer room overhaul or new construction is an immediate challenge. The first step is to designate a full-time project manager. Typically, he is drawn from inside the company, often from EDP/MIS ranks, and has an engineering background as well as from six to ten years of experience in managing/operating data centres. Managing the development of a new or upgraded computer centre is a basic, straightforward project-management function. A group of experts must then be assembled to work with the project manager, typically, an electrical engineer, a mechanical engineer, a securities specialist, an interior designer/architect, a lighting consultant, and an accoustical consultant. In addition, there is likely to be a need for someone who knows the local codes, a fire control consultant, and a telecommunication expert. Equipment suppliers will also give considerable help in designing the installation, and will probably provide a site preparation manual and site engineers to help with installing their equipment. Certain areas, such as the siting of collection and delivery points, may require liaison with user departments. It may be necessary to form a coordinating committee to ensure that all aspects are covered and synchronized.

A number of companies tap the expertise of existing staffers when they upgrade or construct new computer facilities. It has been seen that most aspects of building a computer centre, i.e., site selection, design, construction, can be handled internally. But there can be drawbacks to doing it all in-house. One consultant tells of being called in to analyze an air-conditioning at a small data processing centre — one of several that a major company had built without the advice of a consultant. It was discovered that the walls of the computer room went only as high as the dropped ceiling. The walls should be built slab to slab to isolate the room for environmental control, security, and fire protection. The problem was corrected, but it was costly and could have been avoided if the company had enlisted outside help earlier.

For companies that resolve to hire a professional, the best time to act is early in the game. The sophisticated client will normally take the help of professionals before he has made any commitments as to where he is going to put the computer room so that professionals can help him analyze the space and other needs. Candid communication between the consultant and the company is essential. It begins with a discussion of what is required in a computer centre at present and goes on to include a company's internal projections for growth in the future.

All information should go to the company's project manager before being passed on to the consultant and the consultant, in turn, should funnel all information through his own project manager. It is crucial that both the company's project manager and the consultant's project manager have decision-making authority. If they do not have decision-making authority, it may lead to delays and a communication gap. It is crucial to find out vendors' specifications as early as possible because their requirements are so precise, It is best if the computer vendor get involved with the architect from the beginning at where the disk drive and orinter are coins to be. how much oower is comine into the room, etc.

It has been seen that vendors can discourage clients from making a bad mistake, such as trying to run computers by tapping into power circuits that have other equipment on it. That may be cheaper but who can afford to have information that is flawed? Moreover, when it comes to air conditioning / temperature / humidity and electrical specifications, it is warranty suicide to take liberties. When new computers start pouring out electronic garbage, manufacturers are likely to point to every piece of support equipment and every engineer in the room before taking a look at their computers. They never say that they have got a rotten piece of equipment.

Obtaining vendors' specifications is considered necessary, however, one need not always have to rigidly follow all vendors[1] specifications. It is possible to negotiate with them on some points. Obtaining vendors' specifications is only one part of the assessment process. It is also important to discuss with nearly everyone who will be affected. People who work in the computer facility must be queried about their workload, work flow, and work habits. Management must determine how much downtime the company can afford. Someone has to figure out the cost in rupees and lost data if the system goes down for minutes, hours, or weeks or even a millisecond.

When preparing for computer centre site, one has to consider the following parameters in detail:

SPACE

It is always surprising to see how little space is taken up by the main-frame of even a very large and powerful computer. The room in which it stands seems enormous by comparison. Upon asking the purpose of the totally anonymous wardrobe-like boxes standing all around, you may well get vague-sounding answers such as: "We think they are channels, but we know we need them, the engineer was called to mend one only last week". The truth is that only the manufacturer really knows what is in each box. A cynical story circulates around the industry from time to time to the effect that most of the boxes are unnecessary (or empty), but that customers will not pay high prices for small packages. This is reinforced by stories of people ordering a more powerful machine and the engineer fiddling about in the bowels of the existing machine for five or ten minutes to achieve the desired effect. Some of these stories are untrue.

For a medium to large machine there is a large array of associated equipment of various sorts which take up the bulk of the machine room space. Such items as power supplies, channels, input/output control units, printers, tape units and disk units will all take more space than the central processor. Some of these associated boxes are, in fact, computers in their own right, taking decisions on their own initiative with only occasional reference to the main central processor.

Another powerful user of space is the 'service clearance'. You might well think that if you could get the cabinet door open that would be sufficient. Not so. It is on occasions necessary to have all the doors open and still have space for equipment such as oscilloscopes and independent controllers and drivers besides the patient. The manufacturer will do his level best to fit machinery into awkward or restricted spaces but there are limits along with air-conditioning, floor loading, etc., which are,

a. Cable length: Electricity travels at the speed of light still at a finite speed. The length of some cables, and the size of some boxes, is limited by design, to make the loss of time waiting for electrical signals to flow from place to place as small as possible. Other cable lengths are restricted to prevent voltage drop due to electrical resistance.

b. Physical restrictions, on size of box, or bends in cables, on height, etc.

c. Operator convenience, especially whether the operator can see what is happening on printers and tape units (there are ways round this such as intercom, CCTV, and repeater indicators, but these are expensive items which are best avoided if possible).

d. Services availability: Air intakes and power supplies can give problems. Some very large machines require chilled water supplies.

e. Supplies storage: Continuous computer stationery is a very bulky item but supplies of scratch tapes and storage of written tapes should also be in close proximity.

In any case you will want to leave room for expansion. It is best to orovide the manufacturer with a without support columns or dividing walls and let him plan the layout.

FLOORING

A computer room requires a false floor (also referred to as a cavity floor) to house cables. A false floor which easily allows rearrangement or augmentation of the computer equipment is preferable to cable trenches in the structural floor. Often, air ducts and services to room mounted conditioners must also run under the floor. The minimum clearance between the lowest part of the false floor and the top of the structural floor should be decided in consultation with the supplier of the computer, (100 mm is usual, but it may vary between 200 to 400 mm).

A raised floor is de rigueur in most computer rooms. It can range in height from 12 to 24 inches, depending on vendor specifications and the amount of equipment destined to be housed below. The point is to get power cables, telecommunica-tions lines, and fire protection equipment, among other things, out of the way and, at the same time, support heavy computer equipment. The space beneath is also used for air circulation. The floor must be raised high enough to let the air circulate freely past'pipes, wires, halon gas tanks, and whatever else has been placed there.

A raised floor does not affect the operation of a computer room unless the space underneath becomes so crowded that air is prevented from circulating. At one company, the pipes supplying chilled water for cooling units were laid five feet in from the room's walls, while the outlets for the underfloor air conditioner ducts were placed three feet in from the walls. The pipes were in the way, resulting in restriqted airflow and inadequate cooling. This type of error is likely to be common when a coordinated underfloor drawing is not part of the overall planning process. Best way is to plan ahead for all the things which are to be laid out in the tindertloor.

Suitable proprietary cavity floor systems (comprising of removable modular load bearing floor panels and M.S. (mild steel) channel framework supported on jacks) are available from specialists who supply and lay them. A floor of say 100 sq.m. area could be laid in about a week's time with" ready-to-install components. The work of a proprietary floor owner is preferable to assigning the task to a general contractor since the former has the necessary expertise to construct a cavity floor perfect in level, with uniform panels, avoiding gaps which could permit the entry of dust from the sub-floor. He can also ascertain the distributed load and point load requirements of the floor and deflection under load.

LOADING CONSIDERATIONS

The total weight of the floor should not exceed 40 kg. per sq.m. The floor should be capable of supporting a point load of at least 450 kg. in the centre of the panel, with a maximum deflection of 1.5 mm and a minimum distributed load of 800 kgs. per sq.m. One can cater for heavier loads by installing additional jacks (or using stronger panels). Floor panels are 610 mm squares, and are faced with PVC vinyl or asbestos vinyl tiles. High pressure decorative laminate is a new facing material which is fire resistant, has a high abrasion resistance value and an anti-static quality.

Obviously a number of floor panels must be cut to allow cables to pass into the computer equipment. The computer manufacturer will provide details of the holes to be cut. If the cuts are extensive, extra jack supports may be required. To prevent electricity hazards, no metal should be exposed to the walking surface. Also, in order to ensure a correct flow of electronic charges, lining for false floors should have an electrical resistivity between five to 10**5 and two to 100**10 ohms. Sweeping or applying wax on the floor panels must be avoided, mopping would be the best way of cleaning floors.

CEILING

A false ceiling is essential to reduce the volume of area to be airconditioned. The false ceiling may be provided with an anodized aluminum T-bar self-interlocking ceiling system with a modular grid. The tiles or panels used should be the lay-in type which could be easily removed and refixed. The most suitable panel would be a 19 mm thick particle board tile with rehatted edges, faced with PVC wall paper keeping the tile 6 mm below the T-bar surface. Or, alternatively, a dish type aluminum panel, plain or perforated, could be used.

Wherever the roof slab is exposed to the sun, the underside should have an under deck insulation of 50 mm thick fiber glass/mineral wool or 40 mm thick 100 per cent fire proof phenolic foam insulation slabs. For fixing insulation under the roof slab use Galvolok-type GI channels (50x20x24 mm with clamps at 610 mm centers in one direction only), thereby providing 100 per cent fireproof back framing and is more economical when compared to wooden framework.

ROOM LAYOUT

Ideally, a computer room should have no windows. So if your windows have been bricked up, skip this paragraph. However, existing ones should be closed by felt lining and tack welding; also, the windows ought to be double-glazed by fixing a glass panel on the inside over the sill with suitable aluminium framing. If the windows are exposed to the sun, a solar control film may be applied on the glass. Curtains must not be used in the computer room, though Venetian blinds can be fitted to prevent direct glare. The partitions and doors inside the room, and the front wall partition with the entrance door and air-lock, should be made of special aluminium partition and door sections, emphasis being laid on the thickness and weight. There must also be an emergncy door.

A rectangular room, free from columns, is most suitable for housing your computer since it is convenient and does not restrict the layout of equipment. The minimum height in the airconditioned area between the finished cavity floor (under which lie the cables) and the suspended ceiling (over which are the air ducts) is 2.6 meters. This would require a distance of at least 3.3 meters between the structQral beams and the structural floor.

AIR CONDITIONING

This is a major item of investment and is best avoided if possible. The smaller machines do not need air-conditioned space. In fact the amount of computing is not the main factor in small and medium machines, A more important consideration is likely to be the input and output devices; anything with an electric motor in it will increase the power consumption and cosequent waste heat output.

There is no way of avoiding the expense of air conditioning in the larger machine ranges. They still have a very high power consumption and are quite fussy about working temperature range. Another factor is the relative humidity. If this varies from the manufacturer's specification then all sorts of problems can occur. Tape errors are often the first sign.

If your requirement is in the medium to large machine range you should bear in mind that when the air conditioning fails, the machine stops soon after. Economies made in the specification of the equipment are likely to prove false if they cause lost time and revenue. Some computers will continue running at temperatures as high as 30 degree C but it is not advisable since this can cause problems of motor lubrication and read errors (for example), at a later date.

A small point often overlooked by manufacturers of air-conditioning equipment is the speed of air flow emerging from the ducting. If this is too high it can make the machine room unpleasantly draughty and noisy. It can be so bad as to make handling of continuous stationery into a spectacular exercise in gymnastics.

In order to decide the capacity of the air-conditioner, you may consult the vendors of air-conditioning equipment.

DUST-FREE

The computer room has to be absolutely free from excessive vibrations, air-pollution, dust, noise, electromagnetic radiations, mechanical shocks and risk of fire. When working on computer site preparation, consideration has to be given to the physical security of computers, the records and the plant itself. Only such materials and finishings ought to be used inside the room that enable it to remain dust-free, fireproof, and of course, maintenance-free. Dust caught between the magnetic taoe and the reading and writing heads on a tape may, in addition to permanently damage the tanpr, cause reading and writing errors. Dust between the surfaces of a disk or drum and the flying heads may cause the head to score the recording surface. The dust filters fitted on tape units prevent the entry of dust particles exceeding a certain size, but not the smaller particles. Moreover, when a tape unit is opened to mount or remove reels, dust may enter.

So how do we go about ensuring a dust-free environment? A huge placard, placed strategically on the front door, reading 'No Dust Please - We Are Computing', is certainly not going to help. Sources of dust in the computer room have to be minimized. Structural concrete or other dust producing surfaces under the cavity floor and above the suspended ceiling should be sealed by applying a rubber based paint, epoxy paint or sodium silicate. It is not advisable to paint the walls of the computer room as it may require a repainting job after a couple of years (not only will the equipment be exposed to dust, the entire operation may have to be shut down for painting). Covering walls and columns with decorative laminate panelling would provide i permanent maintenance-free surface. The floor panels must have an exposed hard PVC lipping or sealing strip so that when the panels are laid in position the under-floor is sealed off.

CLEANLINESS

Your expensive air-conditioning system will chill or warm the air, adjust the relative humidity and remove dust. There is not much point in taking the dust out of the air and then shipping in vast amounts in the continuous stationery boxes. Paper manufacturers do try to reduce the amount of dust associated with their products but you can achieve more by having a separate area for printers and paper.

The training of cleaning staff can be an unexpected problem. If you are unlucky enough to have a cleaner with a steel-woo! fetish, do try to get someone else to clean the machine room floor. In fact you may find that cleaners have their own subculture within your organisation. They will by-pass any security arrangements, smoking prohibitions and special requirements for air-conditioned space (like keeping doors shut), unless you make a positive effort at education. It is best not to allow smoking or food and drink in the machine room. The original reasons are not quite outdated because of hardware improvements but the resulting squalor which can result is both an additional cleaning load and a threat to safety.

One area which is sometimes overlooked is the space under the raised floor. This needs to be kept clear of dust build-up as it can become a serious fire risk.

SITING

As with the siting of most large permanent items, the ideal place is likely to be a compromise between conflicting requirements. And you have no space there anyway. The following requirements along with security, access, and safety need to be evaluated.

a. Floor loading: It is not uncommon to need additional floor reinforcement if you are converting normal multi-storey office space into computer machine space. It may be the air conditioning which gives the heaviest single loads and these items can go on a lower floor,,

b. Services availability: In addition to the normal services of lighting and power, the machines themselves should have their own circuit for power supply since most machinery of this nature is prone to malfunction with a fluctuating power supply. These fluctuations can be caused by other equipment in the same building unless the supply is independent. There may also be problems with the supply as delivered by the Electricity Board although this is usually not their fault. In any case, you should consider the desirability of an unintenruptable power supply (UPS). This can give independence of operation during short breaks of supply and also smooth out the variations in the supply voltage. This is a very expensive option needing a lot of space. Most people settle for an emergency generator or nothing at all.

ACCESS

More than people need to be considered under the heading of access. In fact you may well choose to restrict people access for security reasons. The following items will need to be moved in and out of the machine room:

a. **People**, both those who work in it all the time, those who come in and out to service and clean, and those who come looking for jobs which the machine room has lot. This latter class is far better restricted to a formal reception area where all jobs in and out of the machine room are logged. This same area can also serve as an access control area for visitors to sign in before entering the machine room.

b. **Machine boxes**: The installation of some of the larger machine boxes can be difficult in multi-storey buildings. A ground-floor machine room has many advantages regarding physical installation.

c. **Supplies of paper, tapes, cards**: Again a ground-floor situation helps here but try to keep paper-supplies out of the air-conditioned area if possible.

SECURITY

Physical security of the machine room is much easier if planned in advance. The classic 'shop-window' approach taken by people who want the world to know that their computer is bigger and better is not desirable. One or two people in that world may want to see your machine room as a smoking heap of rubble and it is on the whole best not to tempt fate. Site your machine behind concrete walls without windows of any sort, if you think you can get people to work in such an enclosed environment. Otherwise, go for rigid perimeter security and test it frequently to make sure that it still works. A reasonable compromise is possible with blank walls to the outside world but picture windows facing inwards to other work space.

All access to the machine room itself should be recorded or restricted in some way. Even if you opt for free access it is still worthwhile seeing who did go in and out. Badge locks seem to be the most common access control system but there are disadvantages. If the badge lock system is to be complex enough to stop abuse, such as passing the badge back to a following person, then it can be an expensive overhead. If you have good discipline and some people already in reception area it may be acceptable for the reception staff to sign visitors in and allow operations staff free passage. This is not recommended where more than 15-20 people are involved, excluding visitors.

Much research is in progress on physical recognition of human characteristics such as hand geometry, fingerprints and voice patterns. Some of these devices are now coming on to the market but more work is needed before a foolproof, easy system is found. The psychology of these security situations needs some research work as well. It may be that complex security devices are regarded as a challenge, especially by computer people. Certainly you will achieve nothing unless people are trusted, at least to a certain extent.

SAFETY

Computer equipment is very safe. Apart from the risk of electrocution, which is small if all the covers stay on, there is not much more risk than that of a normal office situation. Most of the threats to safety come from outside the machine room. The most serious of these is fire, both to the people in the area and to the machine itself. Having produced plans of where the machine will go, get your fire precaution officer to have a look. He will be able to point out little things like the paper store in the basement below the machine, the paint shop next door or the garage at the rear of your premises.

Surprising as it may seem, not every computer room has fire protection. Most building codes require some form of fire protection in computer rooms. Companies have a choice of either highly sophisticated electronic fire detection equipment or low-tech fire extinguishers. Sprinkler systems are recommended when a computer room contains an appreciable amount of combustible materials, or if the enclosure of the computer room is made of combustible materials.

There is a basic misconception about sprinklers. A lot of people feel that water and electronic equipment do not mix. They think that water will permanently harm equipment. But the point is that water won't be harmful to equipment that is de-energized first. If the power is on you will have problems; shorting, arcing, and ultimately damaged equipment. It is like throwing water on your toaster when it is on. But if a computer is de-energized and it gets wet, disassemble it, dry it out, put it back together again, and it will work just fine.

The one big disadvantage to water is that after a fire, time will be lost cleaning up and drying out - from one day to as much as several weeks, depending upon the equipment and the amount of water that is used. An alternative is halon gas, which requires no cleanup. Just exhaust the room and the halon is gone. The problem is that halon is far more-expensive than water. All these systems can be controlled by a microprocessor fire detection system, which can be designed and programmed to respond to a three-tier smoke detection system. Smoke detectors are placed below the raised floor, on the ceiling, and in the space between the hung ceiling and the ceiling itself. The system can be programmed to shut down computer equipment and air conditioners as soon as smoke is detected, as well as charge sprinkler systems or set off halon gas.

The only other safety hazard causing problems on a regular basis is that of flooding - not necessarily river overflow or rain-water but sprinkler malfunction and plumbing catastrophes as well. Good drainage is important. Water is a bigger risk to machines than human life and you should have carbon dioxide or halogen flooding equipment in preference to water sprinklers. Opinions vary as to whether inert gas systems should be left on as asphyxiation is real enough for many firms to switch to manual control (the alarms being left on), until the area is left empty and only then invoke the fully automatic protection. Some kind of water detection system is also advisable. Water can come from several sources, including air conditioning units, sprinkler systems, and building plumbing. The systems range from low-tech battery-operated alarms to high-tech point sensors, tape sensors, or moisture-sensitive cable, all of which are installed along the underflooring or above the hung ceiling. The most sophisticated systems not only detect a water leak, but also pinpoint its exact location; however, they are expensive.

The remaining threats to safety come into the category of Acts of God such as an aircraft landing on your machine room, lightning, earthquake, terrorism and civil commotion all of which can be described as Acts of the Devil. The insurance companies can compensate for damages under such circumstances if the equipments are already insured.

POWER AND LIGHTING

Discovering that there is not enough power for a computer room after signing a lease can be a disaster. Bringing in additional electricity can be costly; it may mean purchasing and installing new lines, transformers, and switch gears. It can also add as much as a year to construction schedule. The power requirements for a computer room are based on the quantity and type of equipment installed. A company must consider requirements for lighting, heat, air conditioning, convenience outlets, administrative office equipment, and future growth. Once power is determined to be adequate, there are other factors to address, such as figuring out how "dirty" the power is, the tolerance of the computers for the electricity, and what it will take to match the two.

If the vendor suggests purchase of a constant voltage transformer (CVT), motor generator, or UPS system along with the computers, it makes sense to check with a consultant. Outages and voltage problems can arise if systems are inappropriately matched to the power system required at the location. Regulating the temperature of the computer room is a top priority. If you do not put in an adequate cooling system, the computer will run hot and you will have increased downtime. Staying within safe limits depends upon the kind of computer that is being used and the building in which it is located. Backup for cooling and electricity is important, too. Some redundancy is relatively inexpensive, such as duplicate power lines into the computer room from different electrical panels. But other backup, notable an uninterruptible power supply, is to encounter after the computers are up and running. Low to moderate levels of RFI can cause read/write errors and highlevels can be hazardous to both operating personnel and equipment components. A solution can be very costly.

The best way to protect a computer centre from RFI is to carefully examine the room before beginning construction. Most major computer vendors have site survey teams that will check for RFI. If the room is already built, shielding is the best method of suppressing RFI. Ways of doing this include grounding anything in the room that is metal, providing a good earth-ground (isolated-ground) for the computer equipment, supplying copper screens for windows, and installing computer equipment as far away from any outside wall/window as possible.

Lighting the room requires careful planning. Operators and maintenance engineers should be provided with sufficient light in the right places without excessive contrast or glare. The computer console indicator fight must be visible without any difficulty. Also, the operator should not face a very bright area. For general illumination, large area lights which minimize glare and shadows, are preferable. An average illumination of at least 480 lux may be taken as a guide, this can usually be achieved by the usage of fluorescent lamps or tubes. Internal decoration on surfaces should be non-glossy and not very lightly coloured. The ceiling too, ought to be lit adequately.

USER CONTACTS

As already suggested, a compromise between total isolation and complete integration of computer people is desirable. Since the isolation, however slight, will cause problems, it is worth thinking out any remedial action which might be taken. Obviously it is only necessary to isolate the machine and the people directly working with it. Programmers, analysts, software programmers, management, should all be as accessible as possible. In any case, the same rules of access should apply to these people as to the rest of the company. The software programmer is likely to do more damage in less lime lhan anyone else if he is a 'disillusioned employee'. And sometimes when he is not. The idea of a formal reception area is good if it can be properly staffed. If this is not possible then it can cause frustration by giving the appearance of efficiency without the reality. It is important that a good two-way conversation is maintained between the users of your computing service and those providing it. Positive action may be necessary to break down the barrier imposed by security requirements. It helps if everybody knows everybody else's name rather than it being, 'that funny woman in payroll', or 'that long-haired operator who picks his nose'.

Certainly each of the major systems should have a contact list which is in effect an escalation chart. If the named person is not available then his manager or team-leader should be the next point of contact. In this-way problems can be resolved quickly without loss of valuable machine time. If it is necessary to run a night shift then it will occasionally be necessary to telephone people at home to ask advice. This can get out of control to the extent that some people may be called every night. If you pay them (say) one hour's overtime for each call you will then have an inbuilt financial control.

STAFF FACILITIES

In addition to all these considerations, there are employees to think about. People who are not satisfied with their surroundings may not work up to capacity or may quit. Sometimes management is often just not aware that workers are uncomfortable. They do not realize that their attention to human needs is paid back with increased productivity and job satisfaction. Noise has a lot to do with comfort. While standard soundproofing techniques can help to isolate the noise from surrounding computer room support areas and lounges, noise reduction is difficult within the computer room itself because of all the hard surfaces. Selecting a sound absorbent ceiling is important, as is choosing fabric covered chairs. Beyond that, colour, texture, and comfortable furnishings are all good for employees.

The computer room is often the only area in some companies to work a regular shift pattern. If it is necessary to work a full three-shift system then care should be taken to provide appropriate facilities. Meals at 3 a.m. can present problems but most people can cook steaks or eggs for themselves if you can organise this with your cafeteria manager. The ideal is to provide the same facilities to night-shift staff as enjoyed by those working in days. Similarly, microwave vending machines and other mechanical systems should only be used if this is the norm accepted by the majority of your employees. One particular danger is that the local pub will be more attractive to the evening shift unless adequate feeding arrangements are made.

Since you have already outlawed food and drink from the machine room, it will be necessary to provide a rest area for coffee and smoking. It is nicer for everyone if this is outside the immediate vicinity of the machine but sensible positioning is necessary to avoid the impression that 'the only time we see computer operators they are playing cards or having coffee'.

PLANNING

An integral part of the assessment process is projecting a company's growth. It is better to be prepared to expand the computer room later on than to follow a plan that would make expansion prohibitively expensive. Growth projections should be obtained from top management, and then the EDP/MIS people should determine how the computer facility has to change to accommodate that growth. Forecasts of data centre requirements begin with business plans, relationships between business indicators, and computer systems and known machine needs of existing systems. After figuring that out, new system needs can be determined. For example, if the business is growing from x customers to y customers, and the existing systems that support x customers consume p machine cycles, q megabytes of DASD, and r amounts of other resources, then a simple approach is to multiple existing usage by increase of y over x to project future needs.

There is one hard-and-fast rule about anticipating expansion; put the computer facility in a place where expansion is easy. This may seem obvious but consultants maintain that it is frequently overlooked. One company put a full-floor computer centre one floor below its cafeteria. Not only did that preclude the possibility of expanding the computer centre up to the floor immediately above, but there were also continuous leaks.

The assessment process serves several purposes; to get a broad understanding of what is important to the company, to determine the scope of the project, and to hammer out the technical details. This will be important as the next step - the hunt for space - begins. Site selection should involve the company project manager, the consultant and/or vendor, and any other appropriate specialist.

Sometimes sites are less than ideal. One company had to build its computer room underneath large water supply pipes because no other place in the building was available. As a precaution, it installed a second waterproof ceiling beween the actual ceiling and the dropped ceiling and pitched it to direct water away from the computer equipment in the event of a leak. In such cases, as in others where location is not a flexible issue, the challenge becomes retrofitting a building to accommodate

One common mistake in designing a computer room is to plan to put more people in the room than is necessary. People do not have to be co-located with equipment any more, they do not have to sit with the CPU and disk drives, since they do not have to read CPU consoles. Sometimes work flow is often not adequately understood. Some still think the best place to locate Ihe tape storage facility is next to the tape drive, for example.

And lastly, keep in mind that all these preparations are essential to assure longer and better working of your computer. Seek the advice of" professionals; integrated drawings showing the duct layout, position of grills, diffusers and return air, details of false ceiling grid, etc., must be prepared and co-discussed. Lack of understanding and coordination can just cause unnecessary delays.

Outfitting a computer room is expensive. But there are plenty of ways to cut the cost. Go without a consultant. Do not put in a UPS system. Kill the palm scanner, the ergonorm'c chairs, and the custom-designed lighting. Can the soundproofing. Substitute sprinklers for halon gas. Skip the water-detection system. But remember, planning and equipping the computer room is not a job for the fainthearted. It demands experience, organization, common sense, patience, a knack for getting along with other? flexibility, an instinct for cost control, and a commitment to perfection. After all, if a computer facility can not be perfect, it is got to be almost perfect, or it is not going to work.

Pre-Installation Site Requirements for the Computer System

1. Flooring. It is essential to keep the computer room free from dust as far as possible. The concrete or wooden floor should be covered with marblex (or equivalent materials) tiles.
2. Ceiling. False ceiling at the height of 8 to 9 feet with adequate lighting shall be provided in the computer room. Paint work should be firm and durable and rough surfaces should not exist on walls, ceiling plastic emulsion paints are to be used. Use of carpets, curtains is strictly avoided as these tend to collect dust and are sources of static electric charges generated due to friction.
3. Earthing. Good earthing for computer installation is required considering the nuisance that stray pick-ups can cause in data processing. Electrical ground for the equipment should be drawn from a separately constructed earthing pit. Method of constructing separate earthing is described below:
   i) Dig a pit having following dimensions: Length - 1.5 mtrs, Breadth - 1.5 mtrs, Depth - 1.5 mtrs minimum. If damp soil is not encountered even at this depth then it will have to be more.
   ii) At the bottom of the pit, form a layer of charcoal dust of 5 cms thickness, then form a 2.5 cms layer of common salt. On top of mis form one more 5 cms thick charcoal dust layer and then again 2.5 cms thick common salt layer. Finally form one more 5 cms thick charcoal dust layer.
   iii) Insert a 60cm x 60cm x 0.6cm Copper Plate into these layers vertically.
   iv) 30 AMP PVC Sheathed Copper wire should then be used for connecting this earthing plate to one of the terminals of isolation transformer secondary winding. This wire should be joined to the plate by means of a copper strip 25 mm wide x 3 mm thick brazed to the wire on one end and firmly rivetted as well as brazed to the plate on the other end. (see Figure 17.2.6).
4. Temperature. The room temperature should be maintained between 22 +/- 2 degree centigrade. To achieve this required number of window aircondiiioners of 1.5 tonne capacity each are to be used. A wet and dry wall thermometer should be provided to monitor the room temperature.
5. Relative Humidity. It should be 45 to 65 per cent RH Maximum non-condensing. Hygrometer (preferably of the digital type) should be installed to monitor the humidity.
6. Electrical Requirements. The three phases of power may be split as below:

   A. i) Dedicated Phase: It is strongly recommended to provide a dedicated single phase power supply line to connect the computer equipment. No other electrical equipment shall be connected on this phase.

   ii) The equipment must be put on stablized power supply using a 1 KVA Servo stabilizer and 1 KVA Isolation Transformer for (PC/XT or PC/AT). The specifications of which are given below.

iii) The airconditioner, lighting and other miscellaneous electrical load should be connected with the remaining two phases of AC Power.

B. The following general rules should be observed in power cabling:

i) 15 AMP PVC sheathed copper wires should be used to carry phase, neutral and earth lines to all the equipments.

ii) Wires should not be joined by twisting and taping. If length of wire falls short then it should be increased using on-line connectors.

iii) Wiring at every point in the distribution path is to be of the concealed type. Wherever wiring is on the surface, it should be in metallic conduits.

iv) Throughout the installation, following colour code of wiring should be followed:

v) At the destination, i.e., tables on which equipment will be placed, good quality preferably metallic sockets and plugs or 15 AMP/5 AMP/(Universa! Sockets) should be provided with independent switch, fuse/MCB with neon indicator.

7. Meters. A digital indication meter for mains voltage, frequency shall be installed on the wall inside the computer room.

8. Emergency Light. Two, of rechargeable type should be provided.

9. Fire Protection System. It should be installed inside the computer room and preferably be HALON or CO2 type.

10. Furniture. Necessary furniture in the form of wooden tables (5' x 3') and revolving chairs should be provided in the computer room.

11. General Instructions.

  1. Hydraulic door closer for the doors.
  2. Boards with "NO SMOKING", "NO SHOES INSIDE" and "ADMISSION RESTRICTED" instructions for the computer room.
  3. Door mats.
  4. Good quality Vacuum cleaner and air conditioners.

UNINTERRUPTIBLE POWER SUPPLY (UPS)

An Uninterruptible power supply (UPS), also known as a battery back-up, provides emergency power and, depending on the topology, line regulation as well to connected equipment by supplying power from a separate source when utility power is not available. It differs from an auxiliary or emergency power system or standby generator, which does not provide instant protection from a momentary power interruption. A UPS, however, can be used to provide uninterrupted power to equipment, typically for 5–15 minutes until an auxiliary power supply can be turned on, utility power restored, or equipment safely shut down.

While not limited to safeguarding any particular type of equipment, a UPS is typically used to protect computers, data centers, telecommunication equipment or other electrical equipment where an unexpected power disruption could cause injuries, fatalities, serious business disruption or data loss. UPS units come in sizes ranging from units which will back up a single computer without monitor (around 200 VA) to units which will power entire data centers, buildings, or even an entire city.

Common power problems

There are various common power problems that UPS units are used to correct:

Power failure

Voltage sag

Voltage spike

Under-voltage (brownout)

Over-voltage

Line noise

Frequency variation

Switching transient

Harmonic distortion

UPS units are divided into categories based on which of the above problems they address, and some manufacturers categorize their products in accordance with the number of power related problems they address.

Technologies

The general categories of modern UPS systems are on-line, line-interactive, and standby. An on-line UPS uses a "double conversion" method of accepting AC input, rectifying to DC for passing through the battery (or battery strings), then inverting back to 120v AC for powering the protected equipment. A line-interactive UPS maintains the inverter in line and redirects the battery's DC current path from the normal charging mode to supplying current when power is lost. In a standby ("off-line") system the load is powered directly by the input power and the backup power circuitry is only invoked when the utility power fails. Most UPS below 1 kVA are of the line-interactive or standby variety which are usually less expensive.

For large power units, Dynamic Uninterruptible Power Supply are sometimes used. A synchronous motor/ alternator is connected on the mains via a choke. Energy is stored in a flywheel. When the mains power fails, an Eddy-current regulation maintains the power on the load. DUPS are sometimes combined or integrated with a diesel-generator[clarification needed], forming a diesel rotary uninterruptible power supply, or DRUPS.

A Fuel cell UPS has been developed in recent years using hydrogen and a fuel cell as a power source, potentially providing long run times in a small space.

Offline / standby

The Offline / Standby UPS (SPS) offers only the most basic features, providing surge protection and battery backup. Usually the Standby UPS offers no battery capacity monitoring or self-test capability, making it the least reliable type of UPS since it could fail at any moment without warning. These are also the least expensive, selling for as little as US$40. The SPS may be worse than using nothing at all, because it gives the user a false sense of security of being assured protection that may not work when needed the most.

With this type of UPS, a user's equipment is normally connected directly to incoming utility power with the same voltage transient clamping devices used in a common surge protected plug strip connected across the power line. When the incoming utility voltage falls below a predetermined level the SPS turns on its internal DC-AC inverter circuitry, which is powered from an internal storage battery. The SPS then mechanically switches the connected equipment on to its DC-AC inverter output. The switchover time is stated by most manufacturers as being less than 4 milliseconds, but typically can be as long as 25 milliseconds depending on the amount of time it takes the Standby UPS to detect the lost utility voltage. Generally speaking, dependent on the size of UPS connected load and the sensitivity of the connected equipment to votage variation, the UPS will be designed and/or offered (specification wise) to cover certain ranges of equipment, i.e. Personal Computer, without any obvious dip or brownout to that device.

Line-interactive

The Line-Interactive UPS is similar in operation to a Standby UPS, but with the addition of a multi-tap variable-voltage autotransformer. This is a special type of electrical transformer that can add or subtract powered coils of wire, thereby increasing or decreasing the magnetic field and the output voltage of the transformer.

This type of UPS is able to tolerate continuous undervoltage brownouts and overvoltage surges without consuming the limited reserve battery power. It instead compensates by auto-selecting different power taps on the autotransformer. Changing the autotransformer tap can cause a very brief output power disruption, so the UPS may chirp for a moment, as it briefly switches to battery before changing the selected power tap.

Autotransformers can be engineered to cover a wide range of varying input voltages, but this also increases the number of taps and the size, weight, complexity, and expense of the UPS. It is common for the autotransformer to only cover a range from about 90v to 140v for 120v power, and then switch to battery if the voltage goes much higher or lower than that range.

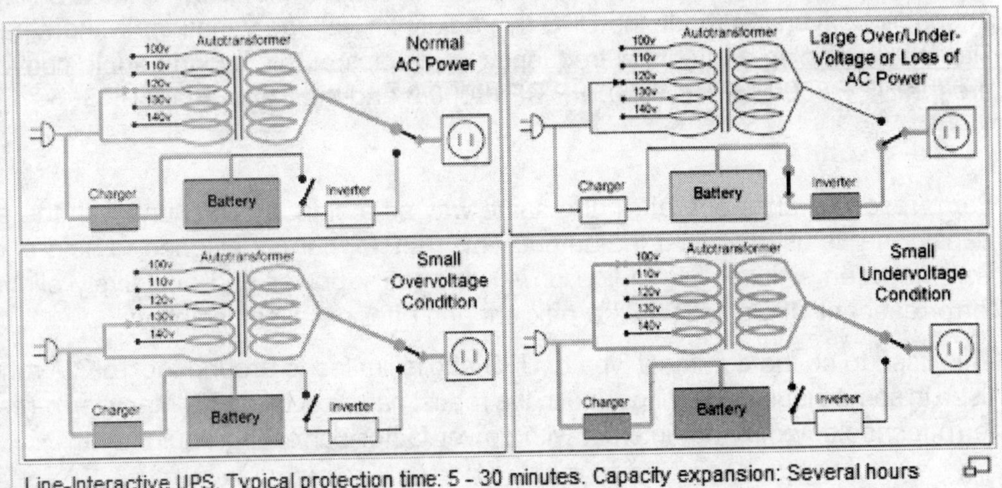

Line-Interactive UPS. Typical protection time: 5 - 30 minutes. Capacity expansion: Several hours

In low-voltage conditions the UPS will use more current than normal so it may need a higher current circuit than a normal device. For example to power a 1000 watt device at 120 volts, the UPS will draw 8.32 amps. If a brownout occurs and the voltage drops to 100 volts, the UPS will draw 10 amps to compensate. This also works in reverse, so that in an overvoltage condition, the UPS will need fewer amps of current.

Double-conversion / online

The Online UPS is ideal for environments where electrical isolation is necessary or for equipment that is very sensitive to power fluctuations. Although once previously reserved for very large installations of 10kW or more, advances in technology have permitted it to now be available as a common consumer device, supplying 500 watts or less. The Online UPS is generally more expensive but may be necessary when the power environment is "noisy" such as in industrial settings, for larger equipment loads like data centers, or when operation from an extended-run backup generator is necessary.

The basic technology of the online UPS is the same as in a Standby or Line-Interactive UPS. However it typically costs much more, due to it having a much greater current AC-to-DC battery-charger/rectifier, and with the rectifier and inverter designed to run continuously with improved cooling systems. It is called a Double-Conversion UPS due to the rectifier directly driving the inverter, even when powered from normal AC current.

In an Online UPS, the batteries are always connected to the inverter, so that no power transfer switches are necessary. When power loss occurs, the rectifier simply drops out of the circuit and the batteries keep the power steady and unchanged. When power is restored, the rectifier resumes carrying most of the load and begins charging the batteries, though the charging current may be limited to prevent the high-power rectifier from overheating the batteries and boiling off the electrolyte.

The main advantage to the on-line UPS is its ability to provide an electrical firewall between the incoming utility power and sensitive electronic equipment. While the Standby and Line-Interactive UPS merely filter the input utility power, the Double-Conversion UPS provides a layer of insulation from power quality problems. It allows control of output voltage and frequency regardless of input voltage and frequency.

Hybrid Topology / Double Conversion on Demand

Recently there have been hybrid topology UPSs hitting the marketplace. These hybrid designs do not have an official designation, although one name used by HP and Eaton is Double Conversion on Demand. This style of UPS is targeted towards high efficiency applications while still maintaining the features and protection level offered by double conversion.

A hybrid (double conversion on demand) UPS operates as an offline/standby UPS when power conditions are within a certain preset window. This allows the UPS to achieve very high efficiency ratings. When the power conditions fluctuate outside of the predefined windows, the UPS switches to online/double conversion operation. In double conversion mode the UPS can adjust for voltage variations without having to use battery power, can filter out line noise and control frequency. Examples of this hybrid/double conversion on demand UPS design are the HP R8000, HP R12000, HP RP12000/3 and the Eaton BladeUPS.

Ferro-resonant

Ferro-resonant units operate in the same way as a standby UPS unit with the exception that a ferro-resonant transformer is used to filter the output. This transformer is designed to hold energy long enough to cover the time between switching from line power to battery power and effectively eliminates the transfer time. Many ferro-resonant UPSs are 90-93% efficient and offer excellent isolation.

This used to be the dominant type of UPS and is limited to around the 15KVA range. These units are still mainly used in some industrial settings due to the robust nature of the UPS. Many ferro-resonant UPSs utilizing controlled ferro technology may not interact with power-factor-correcting equipment.

DC power

A UPS designed for powering DC equipment is very similar to an online UPS, except that it does not need an output inverter, and often the powered device does not need a power supply. Rather than converting AC to DC to charge batteries, then DC to AC to power the external device, and then back to DC inside the powered device, some equipment accepts DC power directly and allows one or more conversion steps to be eliminated. This equipment is more commonly known as a rectifier.

Many systems used in telecommunications use 48 volt DC power, because it is not considered a high-voltage by most electrical codes and is exempt from many safety regulations, such as being installed in conduit and junction boxes. DC has typically been the dominant power source for telecommunications, and AC has typically been the dominant source for computers and servers.

There has been much experimentation with 48v DC power for computer servers, in the hope of reducing the likelihood of failure and the cost of equipment. However, to supply the same amount of power, the current must be greater than an equivalent 120v or 240v circuit, and greater current requires larger conductors and/or more energy to be lost as heat.

High voltage DC (380 volts) is finding use in some data center applications, and allows for small power conductors, but is subject to the more complex electrical code rules for safe containment of high voltages.[4]

Rotary

A Rotary UPS uses the inertia of a high-mass spinning flywheel to provide short-term ride-through in the event of power loss. The flywheel also acts as a buffer against power spikes and sags, since such short-term power events are not able to appreciably affect the rotational speed of the high-mass flywheel. It is also one of the oldest designs, predating vacuum tubes and integrated circuits.

It can be considered to be online since it spins continuously under normal conditions. However, unlike a battery-based UPS, flywheel based UPS systems typically provide 10 to 20 seconds of protection before the flywheel has slowed and power output stops. It is traditionally used in conjunction with standby diesel generators, providing backup power only for the brief period of time the engine needs to start running and stabilize its output.

The Rotary UPS is generally reserved for applications needing more than 10,000 watts of protection, to justify the expense of an extremely large and heavy power system that can only be transported by forklift or crane. A larger flywheel or multiple flywheels operating in parallel will increase the reserve running time or capacity.

Because the flywheels are a mechanical power source, it is not necessary to use an electric motor or generator as an intermediary between it and a diesel engine designed to provide emergency power. By using a transmission gearbox, the rotational inertia of the flywheel can be used to directly start up a diesel engine, and once running, the diesel engine can be used to directly spin the flywheel. Multiple flywheels can likewise be connected in parallel through mechanical countershafts, without the need for separate motors and generators for each flywheel.

They are normally designed to provide very high current output compared to a purely electronic UPS, and are better able to provide inrush current for inductive loads such as motor startup or compressor loads, as well as medical MRI and cath lab equipment. It is also able to tolerate short-circuit conditions up 17 times larger than an electronic UPS, permitting one device to blow a fuse and fail while other devices still continue to be powered from the Rotary UPS.

Its life cycle is usually far greater than a purely electronic UPS, up to 30 years or more. But they do require periodic downtime for mechanical maintenance, such as ball bearing replacement. Battery-based designs do not require downtime if the batteries can be hot-swapped, which is usually the case for larger units. Newer Rotary units use technologies such as Magnetic bearings and air-evacuated enclosures to increase standby efficiency and reduce maintenance to very low levels.

Difficulties faced with generator use

The voltage and frequency of the power produced by a generator depends on the engine speed. The speed is controlled by a system called a governor. Some governors are mechanical, some are electronic. The job of the governor is to keep the voltage and frequency constant, while the load on the generator changes. This may pose a problem where, for example, the startup surge of an elevator can cause short "blips" in the frequency of the generator or the output voltage, thus effecting all other devices powered by the generator. Many transmission sites will have backup diesel generators - in the case of AM, the load presented by the transmitters changes in line with the signal level. This leads to the scenario where the generator is constantly trying to correct the output voltage and frequency as the load changes.

It is possible for a UPS unit to be incompatible with a generator or a poor mains supply; in the event that its designers had written the microprocessor code to require exactly a 50.0Hz (or 60.0Hz) supply frequency in order to operate; with this condition not met the UPS could remain on battery power, being unable to reconnect the unsuitable supply voltage.

This problem of input frequency requirements should not be an issue through the use of a Double Conversion / online UPS. A UPS of this topology should be able to adapt to any input frequency, using its own internal clock source to generate the required 50 or 60Hz supply frequency.

A problem in the combination of a "double conversion" UPS and a generator is the voltage distortion created by the UPS. The input of a double conversion UPS is essentially a big rectifier. The current drawn by the UPS is non-sinusoidal. This causes the voltage from the generator also to become non-sinusoidal. The voltage distortion then can cause problems in all electrical equipment connected to the generator, including the UPS itself! This level of "noise" is measured as a percentage of "Total Harmonic Distortion of the current" (THD(i)). Classic UPS rectifiers have a THD(i) level of around 25-30%. To prevent voltage distortion, this requires generators more than twice as big as the UPS.

There are several solutions to reduce the THD(i) in a double conversion UPS: Classic solutions such as passive filters reduce THD(i) to 5-10% at full load. They are reliable, but big and only work at full load, and present their own problems when used in tandem with generators. An alternative solution is an active filter. Through the use of such a device, THD(i) can drop to 5% over the full power range. The newest technology in double conversion UPS units is a rectifier that doesn't use classic rectifier components (Thyristors and Diodes) but high frequency components (IGBTs). A double conversion UPS with an IGBT rectifier can have a THD(i) as small as 2%. This completely eliminates the need to oversize the generator (and transformers), without additional filters, investment cost, losses, or space.

COMPUTER VIRUS AND ELIMINATION

Have you ever been bitten by a virus. Well the chances are that you have. So, would your computer say after some time. Computer virus though not very similar to the biological one, is probably more destructive. There are virus which can literally wash your hard disk clean. Let us try to understand how it gets generated and how it is treated.

Please ignore this section if you are not in a mood for lighter moments. Way back in 60s there was a film called Parakh, made by Mr. Bimal Roy. In this an old lady in her will had left some amount to be given to the best person of the village. So everybody of the village try to impress upon others to show his worthiness. The crux of story is that while trying to prove his worth, the Doctor of the village, introduces a certain type of medicine in the pond of the village. This results in people who are dependent on that water start falling ill and the doctor comes into the picture having the antidote of the same. No doubt his status in the eye of the villagers increases.

The main reason of my telling you this is that there is a saying that most of the Anti-virus software manufactures are the one who introduce the such viruses in the market and then sell their antidotes to make good money. How far is this true, well it is difficult to know but one thing is very clear, the computer virus is a man made thing. Man does make the virus and he makes the elimination possible too. But, in between the chances of losing data becomes very high. So keeping all this in mind one should be very careful about saving his computer from virus.

HISTORY OF VIRUS

The first computer virus for a personal computer was discovered (and created) around 1980. That means we've had about 29 years to get acquainted with them and used to their presence. Computer viruses are not a short-lived curiosity; they are today and will continue to be here for as long as anyone can foresee.

They are sufficiently widespread to be a real danger to most computers, requiring people using computers to have at least a basic knowledge of their workings if they want to avoid infections.

So the virus can be said to have the following properties.

1. A virus is a self-replicating program whose main purpose is to propagate itself to as many different places as possible.
2. A virus propagates itself by modifying another program to include itself.
3. A virus can only propagate itself by an (unknowing) act of a user of the system in which it exists.

How viruses actually work?

Virus are created using common programming tools, using knowledge that can be found in any computer book dealing with technical specifications on DOS/Windows.

Virus programming demands no special skills. Indeed, many viruses have shown such poor programming skills that it's a wonder they function at all. Yet virus programmers seem to have obtained the reputation of being master programmers.

How does a virus infect a computer?

The computes virus are of many types. There are some which would affect the boot sector of the computer, some would affect the executable files only, and so on. But, in most cases it is the data which is more likely to be affected since this is what you will have difficulty in creating. The software as such can be loaded again into the computer.

Then there are the partition and boot sector viruses. The partition sector/boot sector is the first part of any hard disk or floppy. It contains small programs, called the partition record/boot record, which is executed each time the computer is turned on. This program can, like normal files infected by the file infectors, be modified by a virus and thus infected. Viruses targeting the partition or boot sector are called partition-sector virus/boot-sector viruses.

Virus detection

For a virus to propagate, it needs to perform a number of specific actions, such as reading directory entries, opening files, writing to files, etc. Most of these actions are performed all the time by the system itself and other programs alike, although a few would not be performed under ordinary conditions.

Detection entails monitoring the system, to watch out for such dubious action. A dubious action could be opening (reading) a COM or EXE file in write mode, as one would not expect executable files to be modified.

All viruses cause some change to the system in which they infect. The change is almost always very easy to spot with normal DOS tools: **increase in file length** (use DOS command dir and a bit of arithmetic), **decrease in memory** (use chkdsk or mem), **change of time/date stamp** (use dir), etc.

For your to detect any change, it is of course required you have the initial state, file length, respectively mem-size before infection, to compare with which is not always possible. If you receive a disk from a friend or a commercial program, the size of the programs on the disk before any possible infection is not known. But even if you do not know if your system is virus free (has the initial state), it is possible to detect any further virus spread, when the virus changes the size of other, until now clean, files.

One of the most common virus protection schemes is called Stealth, Stealth is when a crafty virus uses interrupt hooking to run some of its own code that performs according to the virus's wishes. There are numerous ways to use and implement stealth and can, when performed right, be a very cunning way for the virus to hide itself. It is, however, not new thing.

One of the earliest viruses, Brain, used some stealth techniques. Brain redirected a request to read the boot sector (now infected) to the original boot sector and thus showed no infection. This would fool an antivirus program using a scan-string search and a checksum search.

Stealth is an active defence of the virus and requires that the virus have been run. As such it can easily be defeated using a know clean, uninfected, write protected disk to boot your computer.

Future of Viruses

As far as the computer goes there would always be viruses. So do not worry, take precautions. Have a good anti-virus program loaded into your computer all the time. There is something called Virus shield too, which would warn you when some virus infected is floppy is put in. But, remember nothing works better than precaution. Take care and enjoy.

Some popular viruses are listed below:

Scores Virus

These viruses are prevalent in Macintosh computers. Scores virus have a built-in time trigger that activates after two, four and seven days from the date when the disk becomes infected. The consequences are varied, ranging from printing problems and system crashes to malfunctioning of disk operations. This virus does not directly affect data files but detection of this virus requires detection of all files.

Brain Virus

This is one of the first viruses that come into existence. Also known as the Pakistani virus, it was, developed by Pakistani brothers to keep track of low cost software that were sold out of their outlet in Lahore. The virus pops up a screen saying, "Welcome to the Dungeon". This virus are known to destroy data and are highly contagious.

Lehigh Virus

This virus originated at the Lehigh University Computer Centre. The virus stays in the stack space of COMMAND.COM. When the PC is booted from an infected disk, the virus is spread through commands such as COPY, DIR, TYPE etc. On any other disk with COMMAND.COM the virus code gets copies to another disk and a counter is incremented on the parent. When the counter reaches a value of 4, all files of the disks gets erased. The boot sector gets ruined and the FAT is also corrupted.

Friday the 13th

The virus attacks only COMMAND.COM but also other executable files. When a Com or an EXE file is executed for the first time after booting the virus capture a specific interrupt and inserts its own code. After this whenever any EXE file is executed, the virus code is written to the end of the file, resulting in an enlargement in the size of the file by 1808 bytes. In COM files, the virus code is written to the beginning of the file.

The enlargement in the size of the EXE and COM files causes the program to become too large to be loaded into the memory. Also, after a certain interval of time, delays are inserted, resulting in considerable slowing down of the program. The worst disaster occurs when the infected EXE or COM file is executed and when the system date is Friday the 13th; on that day, all the first get deleted.

Sunnuvale Slug

This does a variety of things like displaying a message "Greeting from Sunnyvale. Can you find me?" and sometimes modifies the COPY command resulting in deletion of files instead of copying.

Raindrops

This virus infects COM files. It intercepts the load and executes the function of MS-DOS. It checks whether the file is an EXE file or not. If the file is not an EXE file, the first three bytes of the file are replaced by a jump instruction at the end of the file where it gets attached after encryption. This result is dropping or showering of characters on the screen like raindrops and is also accompanied by appropriate sound effects.

Happy Birthday 30th

This virus gets activated on January 5th, if any of the infected program gets executed and would ask the user to type Happy Birth 30th. It might destroy all the data stored on a disk. The symptom of this virus are that the computer memory is reported as 6KB lesser than actual; e.g. it would show a memory of 634 KB instead of 640 KB.

VIRUS PREVENTION AND ELIMINATION

Various measures of virus prevention are:

1. Legislation
2. Awareness of Users
3. Use of Anti-Virus Software
4. Use of Virtual Device Drivers
5. Use of Scanners
6. Checksummers

Let us look into each of them.

Legislation

You should use only legal software to prevent your system from viruses. The government must punish people who write virus programs. This will reduce the number of viruses written by various authors. However, it cannot slow down creation of new viruses.

Awareness of Users

Users do not regard computer problems as their own. They regard them as the domain of the MIS department. Users are too busy doing their jobs to pay any attention to looking out for viruses. Users can be given precise procedures to follow, to check all incoming software and about how to acquire software. Procedures tell users how to obey the rules. The procedure for checking disks should be written down in detail.

However, most of the users just ignore procedures. A user may see a virus once in many years. Thus, after say months of applying usch procedures, they learn that when you go through the procedures, you do not find any viruses. So the procedures fall into disuse. Procedures can be backed up some rules. A good set of rules might be as follows:

- Any incoming floppy disk must be virus-checked
- If your anit-virus software finds a virus, tell your PC Support department
- If the rules are broken, users can be 'puished'.

Use of Anti-Virus Software

Anti-virus software is the solution to many problems created by viruses. There are many kinds and brands of anti-virus software. You should use a scanner on any incoming software. In practice, it does not happen always as you do not always do as you are told, however, computers do. So, the best idea is to tell the computer to virus-check everything each time when it is loaded. This means that your programs will be checked more often than necessary, but that is irrelevant as compared to the damage caused by virus attacks.

Use of Virtual Device Drivers

On a Windows machine, you can install an anit-virus Virtual device driver (VxD). A VxD is a 32-bit device driver, which chekcs everything that arrives on the computer, whether it is a floppy disk, running programs or the accessed file.

You no longer have to rely on the user knowing what to do, that is built into the program. The user interface is simple—the user has to do nothing, just use their computer in the normal manner. If the VxD alerts, then it has found a virus and an alert is displayed on the user's screen and a network message can be sent to the supervisor. If a virus is found, there is also no option to allow the user to load it. On a Windows NT machine, you can install a File System Driver (FSD), which will provide similar cover.

So, anyone having a problem with the virus should install a VxD (or FSD) on all their computers and tell the network to update it regularly. This will strangle the virus to death. A VxD will check incoming files no matter where they come from, for example, via the Internet, via the parallel port, or via the floppy drive.

Use of Scanners

A scanner is a program that knows how to find a particular repetoire of viruses. Scanners are updated, quarterly or monthly. For many users, quarterly upgrades are sufficient, but every now and then, a new virus comes out and spreads very fast (for example, Tequila, or SMEG). In that case, you would be unable to detect this new virus for several weeks, depending on where you are in the update cycle. So you should subscribe to monthly upgrades to avoid this situation.

VirusGaurd (DOS) and WinGuard (Windows 3x, Windows 95 and Windows NT) are on-access scanners, and work continuously. As soon as any disk is accessed, it is checked for boot sector viruses; and as soon as any file is used, it is checked for file viruses. Both programs may be optionally configured to check files as they are written to the hard disk.

VirusGaurd occupies approximately 9KB of conventional (DOS) memory. VirusGaurd is a DOS TSR program. It does not have the full facilities of FindVirus. It is not able to find macro viruses (which do not work under DOS anyway) and a small percentage of extremely polymorphic virurses. VirusGuard will find polymorphic viruses in memory, if an infected program has been run.

WinGuard, which is a Windows-specific program, uses zero conventional memory. Any additional time-overhead involved in checking the disk or file is unlikely to be noticeable in most cases. WinGuard does not the constraints of a DOS TSR program and has the same detection capability as FindVirus.

Checksummers

A checksummer is a change detector. Executable files should not change, except for a good reason like updating of the software. A checksummmer aims to detect changes. The advantage of checksummers is that they do not detect a repetoire of viruses, so do not need updating. The downside of checksummers is that they are more of a hassle than scanners because files change on your computer more often than you might have thought, for good and valid reasons.

They also do not detect all viruses. For example, checksummers do not detect slow viruses, they do not detect all boot sector viruses (if the hard disk code is left unchanged) and they have problems with stealth viruses.

SUMMARY

1. With the information explosion taking place all over the world, computers are becoming a necessity rather than a luxury in most organizations.
2. The structure of a typical facility may have (1) the manager of the computer facility, (2) the supervisors for systems analysis and design, programming and computer operations, (3) support staff for performing the functions of systems analysis and design, programming and computer operations.
3. The most important resource for the EDP centre is the systems and programming personnel.
4. The decision of an organization regarding its own structure for data processing must depend on its own policy.
5. The advantages of decentralized installations start with such items as responsiveness, flexibility and turn-around time.
6. If the organization is small, even more units like a keypunch supervisor or production scheduler may report directly to the data processing manager.
7. This maintenance function normally serves both development and operating elements, both being users of software.
8. Taking the staff control elements, it is made a direct line function.

9. Top level management is responsible for running the organization as a whole and provides resources and people to meet the objective.
10. Operating managers are responsible for such functions as product development, marketing, manufacturing, branch operations.
11. Data processing management is a demanding and challenging task.
12. Finding the people to manage a computer room overhaul or new construction is the first challenge.
13. All information should go to the company's project manager before being passed on to the consultant and the consultant, in turn, should funnel all information through his own project manager.
14. For a medium to large machine there is a large array of associated equipment of various sorts which take up the bulk of the machine room space.
15. A computer room requires a false floor (also referred to as a cavity floor) to house cables.
16. A false ceiling is essential to reduce the volume of area to be airconditioned.
17. The computer room has to be absolutely free from excessive vibrations, air-pollution, dust, noise, electromagnetic radiations, mechanical shocks and risk of fire.
18. As with the siting of most large permanent items, the ideal place is likely to be a compromise between conflicting requirements.
19. All access to the machine room itself should be recorded or restricted in some way.
20. The only other safety hazard causing problems on a regular basis is that of flooding - not necessarily river overflow or rain-water but sprinkler malfunction and plumbing catastrophes as well.
21. The software programmer is likely to do more damage in less lime lhan anyone else if he is a 'disillusioned employee'.
22. Forecasts of data centre requirements begin with business plans, relationships between business indicators, and computer systems and known machine needs of existing systems.
23. An Uninterruptible power supply (UPS), also known as a battery back-up, provides emergency power and, depending on the topology, line regulation as well to connected equipment by supplying power from a separate source when utility power is not available.
24. The Offline / Standby UPS (SPS) offers only the most basic features, providing surge protection and battery backup.
25. The Line-Interactive UPS is similar in operation to a Standby UPS, but with the addition of a multi-tap variable-voltage autotransformer.
26. The Online UPS is ideal for environments where electrical isolation is necessary or for equipment that is very sensitive to power fluctuations.
27. A hybrid (double conversion on demand) UPS operates as an offline/standby UPS when power conditions are within a certain preset window.
28. A UPS designed for powering DC equipment is very similar to an online UPS, except that it does not need an output inverter, and often the powered device does not need a power supply.
29. The first computer virus for a personal computer was discovered (and created) around 1980.
30. All viruses cause some change to the system in which they infect.

REVIEW QUESTIONS

1. What is a business? What is a digital business?
2. What are the features of a digital business?
3. What are advantages of digital business?
4. What are four different types of Is for modern business?
5. What are functions of an information system in a business?
6. Explain the terms digital market, B2B, B2C, C2C and m-Commerce.
7. What is strategic information system? What are the common situations where it is frequently required?
8. How do strategic systems benefit society?
9. What are various information resources? Give a classified account of resources.
10. Give few examples of digital business, in the real life.

11. What are some of the benefits of information systems to an organization? Identify at least three intangible benefits of IS.
12. Describe agile manufacturing. What are the four key characteristics of agile manufacturing? Why is agile manufacturing sometimes called the "great equalizer"?
13. Why should manufacturing information systems be integrated with other systems in the organization? Describe MRP and MRP II.
14. What is the difference between manufacturing information systems and production system's? Can you give an example of a production system?
15. Briefly describe the five types of functional information systems. Is any one system more important than the other? Discuss.
16. What do we mean by a dedicated marketing information system? What are some of its subsystem? Do all organizations have dedicated marketing systems?
17. What are some subsystems of financial and accounting information systems? Describe any one subsystem of financial and accounting information systems.
18. What are the three competitive strategies of a firm? Why should a firm's competitive strategies be taken into account
19. Describe a GIS; identify some uses of GIS. What are some types of decision that rely on geographical data?
20. What is meant by vendor-managed inventory? Identify two advantages and two disadvantages of vendor- managed inventory.

CHAPTER 18

Managing Information Resources

LEARNING OBJECTIVES

After going through this chapter, you should appreciate the following:

- **Managing the Computer Function**
- **Managing Information Resources**
- **IRM**
- **Principles of Managing Information Resources**
- **Objectives of IRM**

  IRM Fucntions

  Technology Management

  Data Management

  Functional Management

  Strategic Management

  End-User Management

MANAGING INFORMATION RESOURCES

Earlier chapters of this book have emphasized the importance of information to the growth and success of an organization. Information must be managed and protected like any other corporate resource, such as manpower, machines, materials, and money. Many companies have succeeded through the innovative use of information systems and technologies. Thus, information, information systems, and information technologies should be treated as strategic resources and should be managed like other corporate resources, such as people, machines, materials, and money. The study of managing information and its associated components is referred to as information resource management (IRM).

Managing information resources requires a broad perspective on information, its uses, and its impact on the goals and the mission of the organization. Various entities that influence, and are influenced by, information, such as people, policies, procedures, products, and internal and external business entities, must collaborate for IRM to be effective. The story of the U.S. Treasury Department shows that the government invests large sums of money in information systems and technologies; in order to get good returns on these investments, it is essential to manage and monitor information-related resources. The Treasury Department is ensuring that it gets the best possible returns the establishing policies that require vendors to provide state-of-the-art technology at the best possible price, while protecting the agency from the risk of technological obsolescence.

Earlier chapters have emphasized the importance of promoting information stewardship rather than information ownership. Understanding the objectives, principles, processes, and philosophy of IRM is the first step toward being a good steward of information. The following forces that are shaping the way IRM is viewed by the organization.

- Information technology is growing and changing rapidly. Expectations as to what information systems can do for an organization have increased greatly in the last few years.
- Increasingly, top management is dissatisfied with the poor returns and inadequate performance of information systems. As corporate resources become tighter, there is increased pressure to put existing resources to better use.
- Information systems are no longer regarded as just an operational tool. More and more managers realize that if utilized creatively, IS can provide a strategic advantage that competitors find hard to overcome.

IRM

In broad terms, **information resource management (IRM)** refers to policies, principles, and processes that effectively manage all components of an organization that collect, store process, retrieve, and disseminate information. such as **IPS,** MIS, ISS, and OAS, management structures, strategic, information systems (SIS), IS personnel, and end-users. According to the office of Management and Budget (OMB), IRM can be defined as "the planning, budgeting, organizing, directing, training, and controlling of information systems and its associated elements. The term encompasses both information and its resources, such as personnel, equipment, funds, and technology". IRM is a multidisciplinary approach that is closely linked to the overall mission and objectives

The Paperwork Reduction Act of 1980 was the first major legislation that recognized information as a valuable resource. Under this act, agencies that managed information for the government were required to comply with the information policies, principles, standards, and guidelines prescribed by OMB. Today, all government agencies are required by law to report their IRM policies, plans, and procedures to Congress. This makes good sense, because information is the end product of many government agencies, so they should be evaluated according to how well they manage their information resources. The act also made many organizations take a good look at how they manage their information resource. Today, IRM is considered a vital part of good decision making.

PRINCIPLES OF MANAGING INFORMATION RESOURCES

Companies that are successful users of information, information systems, and information technologies follows well-established IRM policies and principles, and in particular, they share the four principles described below.

Principle 1: The IS department should be managed like any other unit or division of the business. Basic principles of management, such as planning organizing, staffing, directing, and controlling, that are applied to the various disciplines in an organization, (e.g., finance, production, marketing, and human resources) should also be applied to information systems and management. The argument that the IS department and its technical personnel cannot be managed using classic management principles is weak and disruptive and often leads to gross inefficiencies and mismanaged growth. This is not to say that the IS department does not have certain unique characteristics that separate it from other departments; only that these differences should not be used as excuses for managing the IS department poorly.

Principle 2: The sole purpose of information systems is to help the organization meet its goals and objectives. A common complaint of CEOs and other top managers is that the CIO and the IS personnel have a limited understanding of the business and the industry in which it operates, Top management often complains that IS personnel are more interested in acquiring the latest technology than in fully utilizing existing technologies. Technology for the sake of technology often results in a poor return on IT investments and leads to disillusionment about the power of technology in achieving the goals of the organization. Good IRM policies emphasize and promote aligning technology investments with business goals. In other words, IS personnel to organizations with good IRM practices often have a sound understanding of the business and its details and therefore strive continuously to find technologies that will enhance the strength of the company. When the IS department understands that its primary role is to support the rest of the organization in achieving its overall mission and goals, the CEO and the CIO become partners, rather than adversaries.

Principle 3: IRM is the responsibility of all managers, regardless, of their discipline or function. IRM is the responsibility of all functional managers who are involved, directly or indirectly, in the creation, collection, storage, use, manipulation, and dissemination of information. Treating IRM as a function of the IS department reflects a narrow and limited view, one that often results in gross inefficiencies and poor management of information and information-related resources. In chapter 3, Business Information Systems, we looked at the effects of information systems on the various functional areas in an organization; many examples showed the positive impact of information systems on profits, productivity, and people, emphasizing the active participation of all employees.

Most organizations that utilize the power and potential of information systems to achieve their goals firmly believe in and practice IRM policies and principles. In such organizations, IRM is an enterprise-wide effort. Therefore, it is not surprising that there is a tendency today to hold functional managers, regardless of their specialization, responsible not only for their own job functions but also for managing the information generated by their units. The efforts to build integrated, cross-functional, customer-oriented systems can be successful only if IRM becomes central to corporate life.

Principle 4: The commitment of top management is the key to realizing the full potential of information resources. Throughout this book, we have emphasized that the success of information systems and information technologies depends to a great extend on the commitment of top management to using technology in new ways to achieve the goals of the organization, A short-term commitment to some technologies will not do; neither will technology investments for the sole purpose of immediate gains help the organization. If top management is lukewarm in its commitment to IRM and in the implemehtation of IRM policies, employees will treat IRM as a "buzzword" that will eventually be forgotten. What is required'is a long-term commitment to technology; and this often demands vision, some risk taking, and the ability to apply technology in new ways. Often this requires that top management be well versed in the management of information systems and technology, though not necessarily in possession of detailed technical knowledge about information systems. Good IRM policies will shift technical responsibilities and decisions to the IS department, while providing top managers with good technology management skills.

OBJECTIVES OF IRM

Why does an organization need IRM and what are the objectives are IRM? Organizations need IRM so that they can be effective in managing their data, information, knowledge, information systems and information technology. The four main objectives of IRM are :

- To effectively utilize information resources in order to achieve the overall goals and mission of the organization.
- To inventory, document, and control all resources that create, process, store, and disseminate information.
- To create a model of the enterprise from an information point of view in order to improve communications, both within and outside the organizations.
- To emphasize the reusability of information, eliminate or reduce data redundancy, and ensure that all internal systems are developed within a common framework so that systems developed on different platform can communicate with each other.

The first objective of IRM is to use information in the most effective manner possible. This require that the right information, in (he right format, be made available to the right decision maker at the right time. Simply collecting data and generating reports is not enough; it is important to closely monitor the way those reports are used by decision makers and the additional information they need to increase the quality of their decisions. Second, as an organization grows and expands, it is easy to lose track of its information resources such as hardware, software, telecommunications, databases, and the like. When managers do not have a clear idea and a detailed accounting of existing resources, the result is often haphazard growth and incompatible systems. This can have a negative impact on Ihc overall productivity of the organization by creating major information-flow bottlenecks. Keeping an inventory of existing information resources is therefore more than just an accounting function. It can make all the difference in an organization's ability to build integrate systems rather than being burdened with incompatible systems.

One way to address this problem is through standardization, which requires the company to establish a set of plans and policies that guide the purchase of hardware, software, and other information-related items. For exampie,a company may establish a standardization policy for word processing packages that requires all employees to use only Microsoft Word or only WordPerfect; it may have a standardization policy for its PCs that requires them all to be IBM-compatible; and so on. There are other benefits of standardization. It provides an ethical framework for managers in the purchasing department of an organization and limits opportunities for favoritism or nepotism. Other benefits include lowering the costs of hardware and software, simplifying IS training needs, reducing maintenance costs, and increasing productivity. Unfortunately, despite the many benefits of standardization, only one in four Fortune 500 companies currently has standards for hardware and software.

Let us look at some companies that have benefits from standardization. Inland Steel Industries, a $4-billion company, founjd that although its computers were churning out about 84 million pages of data, employees were often complaining that theV did not gel the right information at the right time. When the company investigated the problem, it found (hat its systems fere highly compartmentalized and therefore decision makers could rarely get the information that would let them see the "big picture". Further, there was no strategic information plan detailing what the company should do to meet it current and future information needs, so individual departments within the organization were making their own technology decisions. In order to resolve this problem, the company formed an information technology council, made up of managers from all over the company, to coordinate investments in IT and ensure standardization of the company's information systems. The move increased productivity, reduced employee frustration, and led to increase utilization of information systems.

Another example of the benefits of standardization is provided by Grumman Data Systems, an aerospace and electronics defense contractor in Bethpage, New York. Some years ago, each business unit in the company made its own technology decisions without any concern for compatibility with existing systems in the organization. The company found that its 10 divisions had about 30 PC brand, making it increasingly difficult to monitor and approve new purchases, perform system maintenance, and provide technical training to employees. In 1987, in response to an urgent need to better manage its growing networks and to control costs, the company formed a standards committee, which standardized about 1,300 information-re-lated products and reduced the number of PC brands from 30 to 6. This standardization effort greatly reduced the cost of buying and managing information technologies and providing training. Productivity improved and the flow of information within the organization was greatly accelerated.

The third objective of IRM is to build a good understanding of the information inflow and outflow in an organization. Only when managers know the information inflow and outflow can they be successful at managing them. Managers should also be aware of who uses the information, when, how, and for that purpose. This is essential for employees to avoid becoming "paper pushers" and being overwhelmed by the number of reports generated in the organization. A good knowledge of data inflow and outflow is essential to an understanding of issues such as where to acquire information, how to use that information, who are the other decision makers in the organization who use that information, and so on. Finally, IRM aims to eliminate redundancy of information and increase the reusability of information that is already present within the organization. Today, reusability is an important consideration for IS managers as they search for ways to derive the maximum return from their investments in information systems and technologies. Reusability can be achieved only if the three objectives described above are achieved.

Why are IRM objectives so important to a company? Without IRM objectives and policies, decisions are of poor quality because decision makers do not get the right information at the right time or because information is undervalued in the company. Employees may have a very narrow view of information, seeing it as the responsibility of the IS department, and top managers may have little or no commitment to promoting the use of information systems and technologies to achieve the overall goals of the organization. Without clear objectives, organizations will be burdened with incompatible systems that create major information bottlenecks within the organization. Other problems inciude information mismanagement, acquiring technology for technology's sake, obsolescence, hostile relations between the IS department and end-users, and projects with cost overruns and missed deadlines.

For example, when HFSI, a subsidiary of Bull HN, in McLean, Virginia changed its business focus from selling hardware to providing system integration services, it first had to overhaul the company's 22 internal standalone business systems. The company realized that in order for it to be successful with its new line of services, it first had to establish sound IRM policies and principles. Based or interviews with 200 upper-level employees, IS planners prescribed specific tech-nologies that would effectively support and integrate different business functions. Today, HFSI has a set of well-integrated information systems that are well synchronized with the goals of the business,

IRM Fucntions

IRM can be broadly divided into six functions:

- Technology management
- Data management
- Distributed systems management
- Functional management
- Strategic management
- End-user management

Technology Management

Technology management is the process of managing the information technologies that an organization uses to meet its information needs, including hardware, software, telecommunications, and different types of information systems, such as TPS, MIS, ISS, OAS, and strategic information systems. As an organization grows in size and complexity, the task of technology management becomes more challenging. It managers must develop policies and procedures to ensure that existing technologies are put to the best possible use and closely monitor emerging technologies to make sure there is a good fit between new technologies and the information needs of the business. Technology inventory management and standardization are\also important aspects of technology management.

Data Management

Data management is the process of managing data and all resources that are used to create, process, store, disseminate, and maintain organizational data. Data may be in electronic or document form (up to 90% of information still takes the form of documents); data can be created manually or automatically. Regardless of the form or the medium used to create and maintain data, data are valuable organizational resources that must be actively managed, carefully protected, and efficiently utilized. Kaiser Permanente of Northern California is a chain of 30 hospitals and medical clinics, a $2.5million member health maintenance organization (HMD), and an insurance company. As the company diversified into different markets, hospital data was often stored in diverse, incompatible system, making the task of data management time-consuming and error-phone. The hospital integrated the data residing in different locations and provided users with a uniform and a single logical view of relevant data. It allows doctors to monitor the cost-effectiveness of different medical treatments and even to select the best combination of treatments for the patient.

In a centralized environment, all computer facilities, systems, and resources are installed in a central location and are then linked to other business units through telecommunications networks. A centralized environment provides users with access to large systems and resources that might otherwise be unaffordable. Further, since all resources are in one central location, it is often easier to manage and monitor them. Today, however, there are only a few organizations that still operate under a fully centralized environment, primarily because of significant advances in building small yet powerful machines, declining prices of computer hardware, the increasing sophistication of end-users, and continuous reengineering efforts. In a decentarlized environment, each individual site or business unit is free to acquire and develop systems that meet its local information needs; therefore, each business unit is responsible for the acquisition, development, and maintenance of its own systems. The greatest advantage of a decentralized approach to information systems is that end-users have greater control over their systems and the information they generate. Users can customize their systems to meet their own needs and often have easy and timely access to information.

The debate over centralization versus decentralization is an ongoing one; the pendulum swings from one environment to the other every few years. Both types of environments have Iheir advantages and disadvantages and are influenced by a number of factors such as organizational structure, management style, corporate culture, resource availability, and the information needs of decision makers. In order to possess the best of both worlds, some organizations centralize some IS functions and decentralize others. (For example, the payroll function may be centralized and marketing may be decentralized). Distributed systems are collections of systems developed by different vendors (such as IBM, Apple, DEC, Hewlett-Packard, and so on) on different types of computers (such as PCs, minicomputers, and mainframes) and linked together through telecommunications.

For example, Snapple, the manufacturer of a very popular juice drink uses the distributed systems to stay ahead in the highly competitive beverage market. Although the company's sales had doubled very year starting in 1988, in 1993, the company found itself facing stiff competition as giants such as Coca-Cola, Pepsi, Nestle SA, and Lipton entered the fruit juice market through strategic partnerships. Snapple recognized that one way to stay ahead of the competition was to say on the cutting edge of information systems and technologies, and made the decision to switch to a distrihuted environment. Now the company has electronic links with its suppliers and distributors; these links are essential if the company is to maintain its leadership. Companies frequently decentralize before they become distributed. Each user may get a PC as a first step toward decentralization, then after decentralization is achieved, companies may address the problems of linking these units. Clearly, this approach has its problems, since linking decentralized systems to build a distributed environment is not always as easy as starting from scratch.

Some advantages of distributed computing include lower operating costs, better customers service, and better information flow because of easier access to data. The disadvantages of distributed computing are that as employees gain access to information residing on multiple systems, problems such as data redundancy and security violations are likely to increase. Distributed management is the task of managing information resources in a distributed environment, which includes network administration, database administration, systems integration, system security, system maintenance, and end-user support.

Functional Management

This book has emphasized the importance of integrating the various-functional units in a business through cross-functional customer-oriented information systems. This is the only way to gain a total and uniform view of the customer. Although a number of systems, in the early days, were built as compartmentalized units, today the goal is to understand and manage the different functions and integrate them into a unified whole. This, as we have pointed out earlier, is not an easy task. Functional management is the task of integrating the information flows among the various functional units in a business.

Strategic Management

A system deliver information products and services that play a direct and prominent role in helping a firm achieve its strategic goals, is called Strategic Information System (SIS). An SIS also supplies an organization with business intelligence, or competitive information. Business intelligence consists of internal and external data used to assess and analyze oppor-tunities and threats in the business environment. If an information system helps a firm gain an edge over its competitors, or at the very least helps it to keep up with the competition, it can be viewed as a system of strategic importance.

It is important to recognize that an SIS is not a type of information system, like a TPS or an MIS. An information system is classified as a strategic system based on how it is used and on the benefits it provides to the organization. In other words, if an information system is used in creative ways to achieve the goals and fulfill the mission of the organization, it can be viewed as an SIS, whether it is a TPS, and MIS, or any other type of system. Strategic information systems can be external or internal systems. External strategic systems are used primarily by external entities in the business environment, such as customers, suppliers, and distributors, and have a value-added component that gives developers some time to reap the benefits of system innovation.

Internal strategic systems, on the other hand, are used by employees within the organization and do not have a value-added component. Instead, they focus on issues such as improving the quality of products and services and enhancing the decision-making capabilities of managers. Such systems are often used at all levels in the organization; they have long-term implications for the firm and for the business processes within the firm.

Strategic management is the task of managing strategic systems and all resources that the strategic for the success of the company. In particular, strategic information systems should be updated and maintained if they are to provide sustained benefits to the organization,

- Strategic systems need a sponsor at the highest level.
- Strategic systems have to be effectively marketed. Strategic systems should be built on an existing infrastructure.
- Strategic systems should be customer-oriented.

Sometimes strategic systems result from collaboration between allies; and in such cases, managing such systems becomes even more challenging. For example, the Electronic Joint Venture is a strategic systems that was initiated through the cooperative efforts of six Wall Street firms, which led to significant advantages that each firm operating individually could not have attained. However, the continued success of such systems requires careful management and monitoring by all parties involved.

End-User Management

In the 1960s and 1970s, the task of managing the information resources of an organization was strictly the job of the IS department. However, by the mid- 1980s, end-users had become active participants in developing and managing information systems, thus changing IRM from an IS function to a management function. Although there are many advantages to sophisticated end-users and end-user computing, end-user computing is a double-edged sword. If the end-users are not properly managed, the results can include ad hoc development of information systems, lack of system standardization, data redundancy, poor system maintenance, and security violations. IRM policies must ensure that end-users are equipped with the hardware and software necessary to effectively perform their job functions, keep them abreast of new technologies, and provide necessary job training and education on issues such as system maintenance, system security, and system integration.

SUMMARY

1. The study of managing information and its associated components is referred to as information resource management (IRM).
2. Today, IRM is considered a vital part of good decision making.
3. Basic principles of management, such as planning organizing, staffing, directing, and controlling, that are applied to the various disciplines in an organization, (e.g., finance, production, marketing, and human resources) should also be applied to information systems and management.
4. IRM is the responsibility of all managers, regardless, of their discipline or function.
5. The commitment of top management is the key to realizing the full potential of information resources.
6. The first objective of IRM is to use information in the most effective manner possible.
7. The third objective of IRM is to build a good understanding of the information inflow and outflow in an organization.
8. Technology management is the process of managing the information technologies that an organization uses to meet its information needs, including hardware, software, telecommunications, and different types of information systems, such as TPS, MIS, ISS, OAS, and strategic information systems.
9. A system deliver information products and services that play a direct and prominent role in helping a firm achieve its strategic goals, is called Strategic Information System (SIS).

REVIEW QUESTIONS

1. Define IRM and explain how it can help an organization to better manage its information resources. What are some of the components of IRM?
2. What is the Paperwork Reduction Act and how did the act promote IRM?
3. What are four objectives of IRM? What happens when a company does not have clearly stated IRM objectives?
4. What are some problems that manifest in companies that do not have well-established IRM policies and procedures?
5. Identify and describe the six functions of IRM. Why is end-user management an important IRM function?
6. Why is standardization of hardware and software an important part of technology management? What are some of the benefits of standardization?
7. What are distributed systems? What are some special issues that arise in managing these systems?
8. Define the terms centralized, decentralized, and distributed systems. Which approach, if any, is best?
9. What are the four principles of managing information resources? Discuss any one principle.
10. Who is the main advocate of IRM in an organization? Why?

CHAPTER 19

Computer Security, Crime and Ethics

LEARNING OBJECTIVES

After going through this chapter, you should appreciate the following:

- **Computer Security**
- **Why are Computer Systems Vulnerable**

  International Breaches by Employees
  Increased System Complexity
  Choices of System Components
  Network Vulnerabilities
  Sophisticated Hackers
  Complacent Management
- **Types of Computer Security Breaches**

  Accidental or Unintentional Errors
  Intentional Errors
  Cracking Passwords
  Natural Disasters
- **Security Controls**

  Application Controls
  Development Controls
  Physical Facilities Control
  Securing Computer Systems
- **Limits of Legislation to Control Computer Crime**
- **Hardware and Software Controls**
- **Ethics in Computing**
- **Managing the Work Environment**
- **Where is Computing Going?**

  Image Processing Technology
  Voice Processing Technologies
  Audio Response Devices
  Voice Recognition Devices
  Personal Information Managers
- **Cooperative Processing Systems**
- **The Challenge of Computer Systems**

INTRODUCTION

This chapter deals with the interaction of computers with society - the issues of computer crime, ethical issues in computer information systems, health and safety issues for people working with computers. We will also outline several important new computer technologies that are likely to change the way we use computers.

You have probably heard a friend or neighbour complain that computers are "taking over society" and that they "know too much about us." Whether you agree with this point of view or not, serious computer professionals recognize that current information processing trends, such as the emergence of massive credit databases containing the credit history of 150 million Americans, can potentially jeopardize our personal freedoms.

Although there is no reversing the trend toward large credit databases, their existence brings up two important social and organizational issues: privacy and security. Privacy is an individual concern; people need assurance that their personal information, such as employment and credit history, will be used properly. Security is an organizational concern; businesses need safeguards that protect computer systems and data from damage or unlawful use. As a result, security protects hardware, software, and data from natural disasters such as fire, flood, and earthquake; it also guards against sabotage and espionage, as well as various kinds of theft.

Computer crime, which results from the deliberate tampering with data, has become a costly trend for organizations ranging from small businesses to multinational corporations and the federal government. We will focus on methods that companies use to protect against computer crime; such methods will also help to protect data from natural disasters.

COMPUTER SECURITY

Computer security includes the policies, procedures, tools, and techniques designed to protect a company's computer assets from accidental, intentional, or natural disasters, including accidental input or output errors, theft, breakins, physical damage, and illegal access or manipulation.

Computer security is a complex and pervasive problem that often stumps many organizations, which struggle to balance proper security against the cost and inconvenience of providing it. It cannot be achieved through automation or sophisticated equipment alone; it also requires the active participation of employees with common sense, good judgement, and high moral values, because security is ultimately the responsibility of the individual using the computer. Therefore, it is not surprising that organizations that promote creativity, innovation, trust, and high ethical standards appear to be more successful in enforcing computer security than organizations with stifling cultures.

WHY ARE COMPUTER SYSTEMS VULNERABLE

here are a number of reasons why computer systems are vulnerable to security breaches.

International Breaches by Employees

Unfortunately, among the primary sources of security breaches are employees who are either callous or forgetful about security standards. In some cases, employees intentionally cause breaches, either for financial gain or for the fun of it. One of the best ways to reduce security breaches is to educate employees about security policies and to clearly communicate the penalties for violations.

Increased System Complexity

Today, wish the spread of end-user computing, the number of computer systems in the workplace has increased manyfold. Moreover, information systems have gone from being support systems to being the lifelines of many business, so the number of mission- critical systems has also increased significantly. Technological advances in computers have made many systems extremely complex and difficult to manage. A networked systems become the norm, the task of securing computer systems is becoming more and more challenging. Finally, users working on such systems have technical sophis-tication that can be misdirected.

Choices of System Components

In recent years, the number of hardware, software, and network options available to managers has increased manyfold. As IS managers attempt to integrate this wide variety of tools and techniques, providing system security is often a daunting task. Further, many systems run on different operating systems, and security considerations are often different for different systems. Network components and configurations have also increased, creating the opportunity to "mix and match" or "plug *n play". It is even more difficult to provide security for a diverse set of systems.

Network Vulnerabilities

Telecommunications, advances in networks and telecommunications have profoundly affected organizational productivity and decision making. The way companies do business has been completely revolutionized by telecommunications. Unfortunately, networks are also among the most vulnerable links in the security chain for computer systems—in fact, in a recent survey of CIOs, more than 90% of the respondents indicated that network security was a strategic concern for their organizations.

Networks are essentially sieves to anyone with minor technical skills and the desire to retrieve other people's information. The Internet is a vital link that connects people and organizations all over the world. However, in recent years it has been plagued with security problems as the number of Interest users has increased, the number of security breaches has also increased.

There are many reasons why networks are so prone to security violations. The arrival of cellular phones, radio modems, and sky pagers has created new points of vulnerability in the electronic exchange of information, since many unauthorized parties can tune into a company's voice or data transmissions. Second, in a distributed environment, there are innumerable opportunities for security breaches. "In contrast to the fortress-like architecture of the mainframe, security exposures in client-server computing almost defy identification". Third, networks transmit large amounts of data and information around the world and it is difficult to continuously keep track of who is doing what, where, when and how. Fourth, in many organizations network administrators are rewarded for providing easy access to the network, but not for tight security, and obviously the two do not go hand-in-hand. Fifth, many network users are ignorant of network security measures and, intentionally or unintentionally, can cause considerable damage. Users often view security policies and procedures are cumbersome and counterproductive, so they try to find short cuts or even to completely bypass security controls.

Sophisticated Hackers

They are given different —hackers, crackers, information warriors, cyberpunks, eyberterrorists, and phone freaks—but they are all people who violate computer security. A hacker is an individual who is knowledgeable enough to break into a computer system or facility, although he or she does not cause any harm to the system or the organization. A cracker, on the other hand, is a computer thief who breaks into a system with the intent of stealing passwords (sets of characters that allow users to log onto a system or to access a program), mail messages, files, programs, and so on, for fun or for profit. For example, in 1991, Pierre Marion, the former head of French intelligence, admitted that France had been spying on IBM, Corning, and Texas Instruments for almost a decade, causingTBM alone losses of billions of dollars. And why not? Marion asked. After all "in economics, we are competitors, not allies".

Crackers can cause financial damages and injure the competitiveness of a firm. For example, in 1991, when a security breach occurred at the research facility of a major U.S. automobile manufacturer, the company lost

$500 million worth of designs for future cars and suffered in the marketplace because its designs fell into the hands of competitors.

Complacent Management

In spite of the many highly publicized cases of security violations, top management in many organizations is oblivious to security violations and their ability to bring a corporation to its knees. They are often reluctant to invest in security because they do not believe it has a direct impact on profits. But unless management takes a vigilant and proactive approach to computer security, security breaches are like time bombs waiting to explode.

The challenges of securing computer systems in an organization are summarized as:

* Intentional breach by employees: A primary source of security breaches is the intentional or unintentional actions of employees.
* Increased system complexity: Open, integrated, mission-critical, and real-time systems are highly complex and difficult to monitor and manage.
* Too many choices in system components: The number of hardware, software, and network configurations has increased tremendously.
* Increased network vulnerabilities: Networks have become increasingly complex and difficult to manage.
* More skilled crackers: Crackers are better educated and more technically skilled, making it easier for them to break into computer systems.
* Complacent top management: Top managers often feel that security violations happen at other companies, not at theirs.

TYPES OF COMPUTER SECURITY BREACHES

The different types of computer breaches can be broadly classified into three categories: accidental or unintentional errors, intentional errors, and natural disasters.

Accidental or Unintentional Errors

Accidents in the workplace can cause security breaches; it is often said that the cost of intentional damage exceeds the cost of computer crime. Accidental security violations can be reduced by education and training, and by establishing and communicating security policies and procedures. Let us look at some types of accidental security violations.

Sometimes hardware components accidentally fail—the memory, keyboards, terminal emulators, LAN connection cards, network cabling, network servers, routers or bridges in networks, WANs, mainframe front-end processors, and a multitude of peripherals and accessories—causing a security breach. Cables, modems, fax machine, and cellular phones are particularly prone to failure. Countless cables installed underground or on building roofs link and support corporate networks; since they are not visible, they are often forgotten during development of security plans. However, cables can be accidentally cut or destroyed during building repairs and maintenance, so measures should be taken to protect them. Software errors—in input, processing, output, or storage—can also cause security violations.

Intentional Errors

Intentional damage to svstems is also common. It is widely believed that IS personnel are the greatest threat to system security, because they have intimate knowledge of the workings and the critical elements of a system. Intentional errors may take the form of illicit entry to a system, access to valuable proprietary corporate data, stealing passwords in order to snoop around, reading E-mail, or destroying important files. Regardless of the motives behind such acts, they are serious violations. They may go undetected for days, weeks, or even months, particularly if the violator is good at what he or she does. Let us look at some types of intentional security violations.

Cracking Passwords

Cracking, or decoding, passwords, which are the Achilles' heel of computer security, is one of the most common security violations, since hackers and crackers can easily guess passwords or capture them as they travel over the network. Once the super-user (the user, such as a system administrator, who has access to all passwords) password is cracked, the perpetrator has full control of the system and can set up accounts, use the system to uncover more passwords, and gain access to vital information, all without even being detected.

Breaking into Computer Hardware

Another type of intentional security breach is breaking into and damaging computer hardware. Modems, fax machine, and cellular phones are particularly vulnerable to this type of damage.

Millions of modems all over the country give employees and other level entities access to a company's computer system. Unfortunately, modems are also highly vulnerable to security breaches. For example, "demon dialers" are programs that first identify all the phone numbers connected to a modem and then break down passwords to gain illegal access to the system. Two hackers in Seattle used "demon dailers" to break into a federal court computer, decoded user passwords, and gained access to several files of national importance. Even worse, hackers often share phone numbers and passwords with other hackers for a price, further spreading the results of the crime.

Fax machines, the "long-distance copiers" of corporate America, are a weak link in computer security. Information sent through fax machines can be intercepted, copied, or rerouted to another machine. Although users rarely hesitate to give out their fax numbers, this practice can be a security threat. A risk management consultant tells the story of two U.S. companies that were negotiating merger terms through their law firms, located in Chicago and in New York. When clerks at the New York firm faxes sensitive contracts to Chicago, they misdialed the Chicago firm's fax number by one digit. The documents, instead of arriving at the Chicago law office, arrive at the office of The Wall Street Journal, which made the negotiations public. The merger fell through and one misdialed digit cost the company millions of dollars and irreparable damage to its competitive position.

Experts recommend that you never send anything confidential or proprietary by fax. "Assume that everything that you fax could go to the local newspaper", says one security expert. Also, documents received by fax should not be treated as original documents. Using a pair of scissors, a little bit of Scotch tape, and a falsified signature, a hacker persuaded a London bank to transfer $600 million into his account! Banks learned an important lesson in the process; today, the U.S. Uniform Commercial Code requires phone-call verification for any fax-based fund transfers.

Cellular phones are the weakest links in communication networks, because they are essentially software devices that can easily be accessed with a $100 scanner. Experts recommend that you should not discuss proprietary information over cellular phones and strongly urge strongly urge callers to use code words when discussing confidential matters.

Software Viruses

There are two primary sources of intentional software security breaches: computer viruses and "sniffer" programs.

The greatest threat to software is a computer virus, a program that causes a computer system to behave in unexpected and undesirable ways. Some signs of a virus include unexplainable loss of free memory, unusually long times for program loading or execution, changes in file or program size, print routines that stop working, computers "freezing up", strange beeps or messages, computer reboots in the middle of a process, and corrupted files. It is estimated that there are more/than 2,100 computer viruses and that about 50 new ones are created each month. When a virus is executed, it makes copies of itself and spreads from one system or application to another through networks and diskettes. It is precisely for this reasons that many companies strongly discourage the sharing of diskettes between systems.

Viruses are not easy to isolate and cure. A security manager at Nynex's New York headquarters recalls when a PC on his company's network became infected with the Jerusalem B virus. Every machine on the company's network, and all machines that shared potable disks, had to be examined. Four LAN administrators worked 2 full days plus overtime to isolate and clear the virus; a technician had to spend 9 hours clearing "trouble tickets;" a security specialist spent 5 hours on followups and reports; 200 users on the LAN each suffered at least 15 minutes of downtime.

Legal Implications of Spreading a Virus

Believe it or not, it is still legal in the United States to create a virus and inject it into any computer system, because the writing of software is protected by the First Amendment, although federal regulatory agencies are working hard to change this situation. There are other reasons why it is difficult to make viruses illegal. Researchers often use viruses for scholarly study, such as testing system security; this makes it difficult to ban them. Also, a law that makes it illegal to delete information, would make the popular delete function, DEL *.*, illegal! Further, with no uniform definition of a "malicious virus", it is difficult to prosecute those who create them. Every state except Vermont has its own definition of what constitutes a computer crime, so catching perpetrators is a legal battle that few are willing to wage.

To further aggravate the problem, when someone is convicted of injecting a system with a virus, the punishment is often light. For example, in 1988, Robert Morris actually brought down the Internet and other major networks around the country by injecting a virus into the network. Although this resulted in losses in the millions of dollars and loss of productivity for thousands of workers, he was given only 3 years' probation, a $10,000 fine, and 400 hours of community service. This is because the Computer Fraud and Absue; Act of 1986 uses the victims' dollar loss to determine the severity of the crime, rather than considering the larger consequences of the crime. However, a strong and concentrated effort is being made to make the writing of a virus illegal by focusing on the intent of the virus, not just the financial result.

The second type of intentional software security breach is using "sniffer" programs which explore the system to gather data about network users, their passwords, their access eodes, and the nature of their work. These programs, which are they useful for network administrators, can be dangerous in the hands of a hacker who stealthily monitors data transmissions.

Natural Disasters

The third type of security breach is caused by natural disasters, such as hurricanes, earthquakes, tornadoes, and floods. These can be so devastating that companies, and even entire cities, take a long time to recover from them. In 1992 alone, insurers in the U.S. handled a record $18 billion in natural-disaster claims.

Some less damaging natural disasters include those that affect power supplies, cooling systems, communication networks, alarm systems, lightning protectors, building structures, and other facilities that support computer systems.

Lightning is one form of natural disaster. Kcven L. Ervin Consulting Ecologists, a Fort Myres, Florida, firm, lost about $40,0000 worth of personal computer and network equipment when its installed lightning surge protectors failed. It took the firm 2 days to recover from the calamity and more than 6 months to recover from the problems of corrupted data.

Power outages are another common cause of computer downtime and lost productivity. They should not be taken lightly, because a power failure of just 50 milliseconds can result in at least 10 minutes of computer downtime, which can translate into losses of millions per minute for large financial institutions.[8] The average company loses 2% to 3% of its gross sales within 8 days of a sustained power failure; if the outage lasts longer than 10 days, the company may never fully recover from the loss. In fact, almost 50% of companies that suffer prolonged power outages are likely to go out of business within 5 years.

Telephone outages can cause major havoc and destroy the reputation of a company. For example, the Midwest Stock Exchange, with security transactions of close to $75 billion last year, knows that even a brief interruption in its telephone service can cause losses in the millions of dollars. The company therefore has a backup exchange. "We consider the telephone system the highest priority system in the exchange. Even when computers are down, we can continue to do trading manually, provided we have our telephone system operating".

Although the probability of a disaster is often at the core of cost-benefit analysis for disaster protection and recovery, this may not be the best approach. The first question should be "What is the probability of a disaster striking?". Instead, it should be "What is at risk if a disaster does in fact strike?" The following questions should drive home the dangers of a disaster much more poignantly and realistically than a cost-benefit model.

* What will be the loss in revenue if a given disaster strikes?
* How will the competitive position of the firm be affected?
* How will suppliers, creditors, and stockholders be affected?
* How will the firm's customers be affected?
* What will happen to the financial health of the firm?

Another conventional approach to calculating the expected value of a disaster is to multiply the probability of the disaster by the estimated magnitude of the loss:

Expected Value of Damage = Probability of Damage x Estimated Loss in Dollars.

In spite of the alarming statistics about disasters and their effects on a business, very few companies consider disaster avoidance and disaster recovery in their risk management plans. Top management often wrongly believes that the company is immune to disasters.

"An ounce of disaster prevention is worth a pound of disaster recovery cure. Physical disasters don't happen randomly. They are caused by preexisting, identifiable, disaster-prone conditions. Clearly, avoiding a corporate heart attack makes a lot more sense than the risk, pain, and expense of an attempt to recover after one strikes.

SECURITY CONTROLS

In this section, we look at some measures that organizations can take to reduce security breaches. Note that we use the word reduce, not eliminate, since it is impossible to eliminate all security violations; crackers always appear to be one step ahead of security experts!

Computer security controls are policies, procedures, tools, and techniques designed to reduce security breaches and system destruction, to prevent errors in data, software, and systems, to protect systems from accidental, intentional, and natural disasters, and to continually enhance system security. Controls may be manual or automated.

Application Controls

Application controls are policies and procedures that ensure the security and quality of system applications in the organization (such as payroll and inventory management). Application controls cover four primary areas of data processing: input, processing, output, and storage.

Input Controls

Input controls are designed to prevent users from entering incomplete, erroneous, unauthorized, or inappropriate data. There are four different kinds of input controls: access privileges, input authorization, data validation, and data format.

Access Privileges

Unique user IDs, aging passwords, smart cards, access control lists, and regular auditing and monitoring of potential security violations are some measures that organizations can take to ensure proper access privileges. Access privileges for vendors should also be closely monitored, since unscrupulous vendors can snoop around and gather intelligence on confidential data. Access privileges should be highly selective, closely guarded, and determined on a user-by-user basis or on a function-by-function basis, since most security breaches arc committed by insiders who know the weak points in a company's network.

Input Authorization

Data input must be authorized and monitored by appropriate authorities, failing which users with illicit motives may cause financial and legal problems for the company. For example, without proper input control, an unauthorized user can change payroll figures or other vital data.

In batch systems, where source documents are the primary source of data, input controls should monitor the movement of the source documents and the personnel who handle them. The source of each input should also be validated, particularly for critical systems or for those with major financial implications. For online systems, the primary source of input control is passwords.

Passwords, the most common type of authorization control, refers to a set of characters that acts like a key to unlock the system. Separate passwords can be used to access a system, an application, or even a file in a given application.

The success of this type of control depends on the ability of the user to create a password that is difficult to guess and to keep the password confidential. In order to ensure tight system security, many companies have policies that mandate the use of hard- to-guess passwords or randomly generated passwords, and require employees to change their passwords frequently. In recent years, with the increasing number of security breaches on the Internet, the idea of reusable passwords has come under close scrutiny and recommendations are being made that passwords be used only once, or that encrypted passwords be used, or both. Experts recommend that instead of a single word, a password should consist of a phrase, which more difficult to break. Some companies use "firewalls" which are security filters that apply a number of criteria before giving a user access to the network.

For example, Security Dynamics, in Cambridge, Massachusetts, has created a SecurID smart card, which displays a new, unpredictable six-digit password every minute. A corresponding feature on the network ensures that the password on the user's c&rd and the one on the host machine always agree. (A clock installed in the card is synchronized with access control hardware on the network). Security is further tightened by requiring the user to key in a secret personal identification number (PIN) so that in case the card is lost, the PIN will still prevent unauthorized users from gaining access to the system. The company claims that the odds of breaking into a system with SecurID are less than one in 14 billion.

But some experts caution that passwords often convey a false sense of security and recommend that companies use the principles of I & A: identification and authentication. I & A requires the use of three things.

1. Something you know. This would include things such as password, a PIN, or a phrase.
2. Something you own. This would include such things as a smart card or an ID card.
3. Something you are. This would include things like thumb prints, retinal scans, handwriting, and signatures.

These three measures, combined together, can significantly increase the security of a system. Obviously, not all systems require such rigid access controls, but for critical systems they may be a necessity.

Data Validation

Data should be validated before it is processed. This can be done manually by two employees who compare data, or automatically by a computer comparing the input data with existing master files. There are also programs that automatically compare data values against pre-established values: a long distance phone number should be 10 digits long, and so on. Usually, such checks are made by the DBMS so that the same checks can be applied uniformly to all applications.

Several data validation techniques are commonly used to detect input errors. Anticipation checks, which compare input values with expected or anticipated values, are particularly useful for checking for nonblank values, such as an employee name on a payroll check. Reasonableness checks are controls that check whether input values are within reasonable limits: for example, hours worked per week cannot be greater than, say, 80. Arithmetic proof checks ensure that arithmetic operations are properly executed: the sum of two positive numbers cannot be negative, and so on.

Data Format

Input controls should also check the format of the data, ensuring that there are no missing values and that data are in the right format (integer versus decimal values, for example), the right size, and the right type (for example, telephone numbers should not include alphabetic characters). Though the type and extent of controls vary from organization to organization, and even from application to application, IS managers must establish must establish and implement proper data controls. A distinction should also be made between policies that may be overridden under special circumstances and those that are strictly mandatory. Controls are also necessary to ensure that all errors are corrected. Cumulative errors lists that identify ali errors in a certain application are useful for corrective action. Clearly, only authorized people should be allowed to correct errors and notification of error correction should be documented and forwarded to the proper authority.

Process Controls

Process controls are policies and procedures that ensure that data are meaningful and reliable. These are designed to catch any errors that may have slipped through the input controls. For example, reasonableness checks can be incorporated into application processing so that any errors that may have gotten past the input controls are detected during processing. Other processing controls include ensuring that the right file or the most recently updated file is being processed and that the processing is accurate and timely.

Earlier in this chapter, we discussed some problems that an organization can face when its system is infected with a virus. What are some process controls that an organization can implement to protect itself from the dreaded virus? One of the most important steps toward eliminating viruses is to educate users about their effects and how to prevent them. In a recent survey of employees at a Fortune 100 company, 98% said that although they had heard about computer viruses, they were not sure as to what viruses do and many indicated that they had little or no knowledge of how to prevent or remove a virus. Education is vital to prevent infection by viruses. Second, a simple yet highly effective measure is to restrict the movement of diskettes from one system to another, this greatly reduces the chances of spreading viruses from one machine to another.

Also, there are many off-the-shelf virus detection programs that can be activated when the computer is first booted up as a way to prevent virus infection. Other steps that organizations can take to prevent virus attack are to mandate thai users change their passwords every 30 to 90 days, to establish strict guidelines for the user of "shareware", and to strictly prohibit access to "freeware" (software that is available at no charge).

Other process controls include frequent backups of important files. Making backups is creating duplicate copies of a file and storing them on a separate disk or medium, or even in a separate location. It is a way to protect files against accidental deletion, misplacement, and natural or man-made disasters. Take, for example, the case of the Rockland Community Action Council (ROCAC) administrative headquarters in Spring Valley, New York, where a fire started on a quiet Sunday morning. When it was put out later that day, seven PCs had gone up in flames and the CIO was convinced that the organization was ruined because its financial records, stored on those PCs' hard disks, were all gone. He suddenly remembered the fireproof filing cabinets, where some tapes had been stashed away ."My eyes nearly popped out when I realized the backup tapes were OK". The backup tapes contained all the vital records of the organization, which saved it from financial ruin.

It is also strongly recommended that the original file be checked for viruses before backups are made. Organizations that are data-intensive keep a long indicating when each backup was made, to avoid any confusion or overwriting. With the spread of end-user computing more and more organizations are shifting the responsibility of backups from the IS department to the end-user. When files are frequently backed up, the losses or damage from a virus are minimized, because only information generated since the last backup is lost or damaged.

Many organizations have written policies on the number and frequency of backups; some even state explicitly the penalty for failing to make backups. Although backups are vital, companies must perform cost-benefit analyses to determine which files are critical and to determine accordingly how frequently these files should be backed up (hourly, daily, weekly, monthly, semiannually, and so on).

Output Controls

The third type of application control is Output Controls, which ensure that system output is accurate and is disseminated to the right people at the right time and in the right format. The number and rigor of the output controls depend on the critically of the application; for critical or proprietary applications, output controls are likely to be more strict and rigid than for noncritical applications. If the output is confidential, such as nuclear facility designs or medical research findings,

In most case, output controls include at least a periodic review of system output by authorized individuals who check the timeliness, accuracy, and format of the output, identify any exceptions (such as overtime being five times the usual value), and make sure that no unauthorized programs were accessed during processing.

Storage Controls

The fourth type of application control is Storage controls, which ensure that the storage devices on which data and program are stored are safe, secure, and well protected from natural and man-made disasters. Storage controls mechanisms prevent unauthorized access to storage devices, as well as accidental or intentional deletion or manipulation of files. As you may recall, passwords and access privileges are two common and popular control measures that are effective storage controls. Backing up files is another control mechanism that helps organizations recover from damages to storage devices. Clearly, backup files should be stored on different devices from those that hold the original files, and in some cases should even be in a different location. File backups are discussed later in the chapter.

Development Controls

Control mechanisms for system security should not be an afterthought, but should be made an integral part of the development process, from product conception to product delivery. Development controls are controls built into each phase of the development cycle. The include measures such as establishing development standards (guidelines for developing systems), creating proper documentation, ensuring the security and reliability of data, establishing proper authorization for changes or additions to requirement specifications, and separation of duties.

Documentation

Proper system documentation is one way to control the quality of the development process and consists of detailed record keeping about the system, it logical and physical functions, its features, its interfaces, and any other elements that are essential to its smooth functioning and maintenance. Clear and well-written documentation should be developed for the entire system, for the various programs in the system, and for specific system operations. Documentations is an essential part of security control, because without it security experts may have to guess at the source, or even the indications, of a security breach. Moreover, when developers leave a project or leave the company, documentation is the only way to understand the intricacies and the possible weak links of the system so that proper security measures can be implemented. Though many developers view documentation as a boring task, it is so vital to the continued success of a system that some organizations hire a documentation specialist to ensure that all system are properly documented and that the documentation is frequently updated.

Data Security and Reliability

Data security and reliability are another development control mechanism that prevents unauthorized access to data. They are particularly critical in real- time distributed systems. Some measure to secure data are preventing viruses, establishing accessing privileges, securing physical facilities, and implementing user IDs and passwords.

Authorization Requirements

Authorization requirements are control mechanisms that allow only authorized users to access and use the system. These control all activities related to input, processing, output, dissemination, storage, and maintenance of data. Any installation of new programs and any system configuration should also require proper authorization.

Authorization controls are particularly essential for system changes, so that employees cannot accidentally or intention-ally change applications—for example, payroll or employee benefits.

Separation of Duties

Finally, separation of duties is another development related control mechanism, which reduces or eliminated conflicts of interest that can compromise the security and reliability of the system. For example, most organizations do not authorize system developers to give the final clearance on the quality and performance of the system. In other words, system testers should not be the same people as the system developers, because system developers have a personal stake in the perceived quality and reliability of the system.

In summary, there arc four main types of development controls: documentation, data security and reliability, authoriza-tion requirements, and separation of duties. Next, we look at the third type of control—control of physical facilities.

Physical Facilities Control

The primary goal of physical facilities control is to protect the physical facilities that house the computer and other related assets from theft, unauthorized access, natural disasters, and vandalism, through measures such as posting security personnel, installing fire alarms, security alarms, and hidden cameras, and requiring users to wear badges or use smart cards to gain access to the building. Most facilities also include environmental control device that monitor and control the air and the temperature in a building.

Although the reliability of physical support facilities is often overlooked, it is an important part of system security, particularly for real-time systems. Many support facilities were designed in the 1970s, when batch processing was the norm; when a system failed, the computer was simply shut down until the facility was restored. But today, many systems are 24-hour, real-time, mission-critical systems that simply cannot be interrupted.

In recent years, many computer failures have been attributable to failure of the support system, rather than of the computer system itself. For example, when an electrical fire broke out in the lower-Manhattan data center of Securities Industry Automation Corp. (SIAC) a few years ago, the New York and the American stock exchanges (NYSE and AMEX) came to a grinding halt and put transactions worth billions of dollars on hold for several hours. Although news reports attributed the disruption to the fire, the problem was traced to a faulty alarm system, which misinterpreted a blaze in the basement as a fire in the 14th-floor computer room and simply shut down the entire system.

Personnel Controls

Many security breaches are caused by employees within the company, either because they lack knowledge about system security or because they have illicit intentions. Some of the leading security concerns of CIOs in the U.S. are:

* Network security
* End-user security awareness
* Winning top management's commitment
* Using access-controlled software
* Distributed computing security
* Integrating security systems
* Monitoring user compliance with security policy

In fact educating end-users about computer security is one of the top three security concerns of CIOs in the U.S.

"There's a bigger security problem with insiders than with terrorists or industrial espionage. You can't worry about protecting against external forces if you have not protected yourself from within. We've seen cases where a disgruntled employee has gone in and wiped out all the information on a server", says a security expert at Coopers & Lybrand.

Controls are only as effective as the people who implement them. Training system users and communicating security policies are two types of personnel control.

Train System Users

Losses from network security breaches are estimated to be, in excess of $2 billion each year. This figure is expected to increase as companies move mission-critical data from mainframes to distributed environments and as the number of mobile users increases. Unfortunately, company employees are among the biggest threats to system data security., "The hackers you read about are by far the smallest threat. Many security breaches are caused by simple user errors". Hence, a key ingredient to achieving network security is regular and extensive user training on how to secure systems and data. Also, employees must be educated on the consequences of poor security and the penalties for failing to follow company policies.

Establish and Communicate Security Policies and Procedures

Security policies and procedures, combined with extensive user training, should precede any investment in security products. Establishing the security policy for a company is the first and most important step. The security policy should contain a mission statement, identify the security responsibilities of each employee, and address, in very specific terms,the ways to protect system hardware and software.

Securing Computer Systems

One study of 283 businesses and governmental institutions in U.S.A. found that half were victims of computer crime each year. Records show that while a bank robber armed with a gun steals an average of $1,600 from a bank, the white-collar criminal armed with a computer steals an average of $100,000! These statistics for white-collar crimes may in fact be low, because many organizations such as banks, fearing a loss of customer confidence, do not report all the crimes that occur.

Computer crime can be as small-scale as the unauthorized use of business computers for personal purposes, or as large as using computers to send corporate financial assets to a private Swiss bank account. Computer crime can include:

Theft of Computer Time. This common theft may be as simple as students doing term papers on computers at work or as great as someone stealing thousands of dollars of processing time for personal profit.

Manipulation of Computer Programs or Data. Remember the movie War Games, in which the protagonist changed his grades in the high school computer by using a modem at home? Unfortunately, such actions are all too common. Newspapers frequently print stories about computer enthusiasts, or "hackers", breaking into public and private databases -sometimes just for the technical challenge of it! Some hackers even plant "computer viruses" that tie up CPUs by commanding them to do such time-, consuming tasks as attempting to calculate the precise value of pi ~ thereby crippling enormous data networks.

Theft of Data and Assets. Legally called embezzlement computer theft often involves a trusted employee who cannot resist the temptation to steal. All too often, the theft is amazingly easy to carry out. For example, the chairman of the board and some of the executive officers of the Equity Funding Corporation - a publicly held mutual fund and insurance company in U.S.A. — used terminals to enter insurance policies for nonexistent people. By entering bogus data over a period of years, they greatly increased the company's apparent assets. Of the 97,000 insurance policies maintained by the computer, almost two-thirds were fictitious policies with a face value of $2.1 billion! Because the company appeared to be more profitable than it actually was, the stock of Equity Funding was greatly inflated; consequently, the officers, who were large shareholders, were able to sell their shares at considerable profits. The fraud went undetected because auditors consistently accepted the computer printouts that listed policyholders as beyond question. The crime was discovered by auditors and the police only when a former employee revealed the scheme.

Users Stealing Software. Are you stealing when you make a copy of word processing software for a friend to use? The law says you are. Yet many normally law-abiding people who would not dream of shoplifting see nothing wrong with making a copy of a $500 word processing package and giving it to a friend, despite the fact that it is in violation of the U.S. Copyright Code. Bootlegging software is clearly unethical, as well as illegal, yet it is so widespread that estimates suggest there may be as many as ten illegal copies for every legitimate, program sold.

To prevent bootlegging, software vendors sometimes copy protect software so that it cannot be copied to other disks -or can only be copied a limited number of times, generally twice. Copy-protected software is becoming rarer, however, as vendors respond to complaints from users that copy protection is a nuisance. Copy protection can make it difficult to do legitimate copying, such as creating backup disks or recovering from hard-disk failure. In fact, the lack of copy protection is often a selling feature for many programs.

LIMITS OF LEGISLATION TO CONTROL COMPUTER CRIME

Legislators in U.S. have been trying for years to enact laws to curb computer crime at the federal level, without success. The major stumbling block is the lack of a legal definition for "property" and "value" as they relate to computerized information. Prosecutors are also reluctant to take computer thieves to court because the computer security in an organization is typically so poor and computer crime laws so vague that they find it difficult to build good cases.

Because the U.S. federal government has not enacted effective laws in this area, many states are beginning to pass stronger legislation that protects companies from computer theft, deliberate destruction of data, and so on.

HARDWARE AND SOFTWARE CONTROLS

Precautions and controls can be employed for protecting hardware and software from illegitimate use. Access to a system and its data should be controlled, and secure backup copies maintained. Most electronic network packages include measures for controlling access to sensitive files. Other ways to reduce the risk of fraud are to rotate personnel in certain jobs and to separate important tasks so that no one person could complete a fraudulent transaction.

Controlled Access to Hardware and Software. If data or program security is important, systems analysts should ensure that unauthorized personnel cannot have physical access to the computer system. The system can be housed in a locked room to protect hardware from theft and to prevent unauthorized people from accessing data or programs. Specific physical and electronic access control techniques include keyboard locks, automatic logs, restricted access to systems, 'and limited after-hour use. Using passwords that change periodically can also help to keep a system secure.

Backup Copies of Data and Programs. Creating backups consists of making extra copies of programs or data. Backups safeguard against the loss of programs or data in computer memory, on hard disks, or on diskettes. Data should be backed up each time it is updated or changed in any way.

Security for Backup Copies. Because backups represent the safety net that will be used if original data or programs are destroyed, the backups must be protected with the same care as the originals. Protection techniques include keeping them under lock and key in a fireproof container and storing them in a location several miles from the originals. This protects files from natural disasters as well as computer crime.

Distributed Network Controls. Distributed processing and remote databases pose specific control problems for organizations because they are vulnerable to unauthorized access to data from remote locations. For example, a company trying to discover a competitor's confidential data might tap into the competitor's network and monitor transmissions for their own benefit. Two common controls are used for protecting networks: data encryption and callback systems.

— Data encryption involves encoding data so that it cannot be understood unless it is first decoded. To encrypt data, a program uses an algorithm to scramble, or encode, data before it is sent over the network. Another program at the receiving end then decodes the data. If an unauthorized person tapped into the database, the data would not be readable.

  Because data encryption is cumbersome and expensive, it is generally used only for sensitive data. Access to both the encryption and the decoding programs must be tightly controlled as well.

— A callback system ensures that a user calling in by phone is calling from an authorized telephone number. After validating user's password, the callback system breaks the phone connection and then immediately calls a previously stored telephone number linked to the password in the system's memory. If this is not the number where the person seeking access is located, entry to the system will not be permitted.

Separation and Rotation of Functions. Another way to ensure the security of computer systems is to segment the work done so that each task requires several different people. This separation of duties minimizes the risk of unauthorized and fraudulent use and/or modification of data as well as programs, because two or more perpetrators within the department would be required to commit a fraud. Separating tasks also reduces the risk of errors since one person can check the work of another.

In addition to separating duties, it is advisable to have duties rotated among individuals within each group from time to time. This arrangement is likely to thwart fraudlulent collusion among employees. If, for example, a particular data entry operator who enters only payroll data and a programmer who works exclusively on payroll programs intend to "work together to commit a computer crime, they may find it difficult to carry it out if their jobs are periodically rotated.

Safeguards such as these help honest people stay honest. Honest computer users often confront ethical challenges as well, and these issues are often not so clearly defined.

ETHICS IN COMPUTING

Ethical conduct goes beyond merely adhering to laws. All professions have a code of ethics that broadly sets standards for professionals; such ethical standards may not be covered by specific legislation. For example, what should you do if you are an analyst or programmer responsible for a program that invades privacy? Or how responsible are you if you create a software package that produces erroneous results? After all, is it reasonable to expect software packages to be totally free of errors?

There are, of course, no simple answers to questions such as these. Many people with high ethical standards have argued against holding computer professionals totally responsible for their work, because the way a system is used may not be under the programmer's or analyst's control. Some people argue that, just as Alfred Nobel cannot be held accountable for the immoral use of his invention of dynamite, computer professionals should not be held accountable for programs that are used illegally or unethically.

As the debate over these ethical issues goes on, many leaders in the computing field believe that a code of ethics is of primary importance and that it would be far better for professionals to police themselves before the government finds it necessary to pass laws.

MANAGING THE WORK ENVIRONMENT

The emergence of computers in the workplace has created a number of new organizational issues in such areas as space planning, health, and safety.

Consider what happened to a telephone company that installed an automated telephone system for its operators. Operator productivity suddenly decreased because:

— Light reflecting onto terminal screens from a large bank of windows bothered the operators. While the windows were a much desired change for the operators, the bright, natural light was sometimes so intense that it caused eye strain.

— The operators' workstations were designed for the average operator. There was little, if any, flexibility for changing the position of the screen, keyboard, or desk to satisfy individual tastes and desires.

— Each operator was given a U-shaped desk with side panels for privacy. Because the operators were accustomed to seeing their colleagues while they worked, they felt cut off from their peers.

What can be done to help users cope with the physical, menial and social problems caused by new office technologies? Ergonomics is the science of adapting machines and work environments to people. Ergonomic studies are designed to provide the best physical arrangement for people using computers and other technology for any length of time.

Reducing Office Glare. Perhaps the most obvious problem in the work environment - and the one easiest to deal with - is office lighting. Improper lighting conditions create glare on video display terminals. There are two common ways to reduce glare: provide indirect lighting, which may almost totally eliminate the problem, and/or provide anti-reflection filters that reduce glare on the screen but also reduce the intensity of the image.

The general trend is toward eliminating all direct overhead lighting, such as fluorescent lights, and substituting softer, indirect lighting in its place.

Reducing Sound Pollution. Well-planned offices eliminate distracting sounds yet make provisions for private conver-sations. Because office systems commonly result in noise created by keyboards, printers, and even the computer itself, an effective noise control program focusses on three areas: efficient sound-absorbing materials on furniture, walls, ceilings, and floors; sound-masking devices such as printer covers; and well-designed office layouts.

Designing Optimum Workstations. Workstations should be designed to allow users the greatest economy of move-ment. Factors such as sitting or standing heights, reach lengths, arm angles in keyboarding, and eye viewing angles all contribute to the comfort of performing necessary office tasks. Poor workstation design will ultimately result in user fatigue, a high rate of error, and slow task performance.

Reducing Hazards to Health. Many people are concerned that computer systems in businesses can be unhealthy for employees. Consider the experience of data entry operators whose input rate is closely monitored by automated equipment. The system keeps track of the average time it takes an operator to key in an order. If management has set strict standards for acceptable performance, such close monitoring can be devastating to the health of employees. It can induce stress, other health problems, feelings of powerlessness, and even complete apathy. As a result, organizational productivity can plummet.

Another hotly debated issue is whether video display terminals (VDTs) emit harmful radiation. Numerous studies conducted in the 1970s and early 1980s failed to detect radiation above acceptable levels, but these conclusions are now being re-evaluated. Questions center around the long-term biological effects of low-level radiation from VDTs on users, especially on whether prolonged exposure of pregant women to VDTs can cause birth defects. Until conclusive evidence is available to resolve these issues, a corporate policy requiring periodic testing for malfunctioning video display terminals that emit radiation above safety limits might be appropriate.

Employees' experience with computer systems affects their attitude toward new technology. In a poorly managed computer environment, employees may believe that their computer system displaces workers, affects their health, and limits their freedoms, or they may believe that computers provide new careers, enhance employee control over tasks, and improve their decision-making ability. The perception of the effects of computers in a given business depends on the leadership and vision of the company's managers as well as the computer professionals who plan and create these systems.

WHERE IS COMPUTING GOING?

The long-term goal of most advanced computer vendors is to create systems that are capable of handling compound documents that integrate data from different applications - text, data, spreadsheet, graphic, image and voice information -into a cohesive information system. Compound document systems conceivably allow an architect, for example, to:

1. Turn on the system and orally ask it to display sketches of a new amusement park, which are stored in the database.
2. Combine these sketches with photos of three proposed sites
3. Attach a written purchase order
4. Add a short oral note asking for comments
5. Send the whole package electronically across the country to the client's office.

While such futuristic document systems will not appear overnight, some compound technologies, such as word processing and spreadsheets, are well established. Other technologies such as image and voice processing may not mature for many years.

Following is an overview of areas in which we can expect to see advancements in the next decade.

Image Processing Technology

Beginning computer users are often surprised by how difficult it is to combine drawings, graphics, and photographs into documents. The technical problems arise from the huge amount of storage space required to store graphics; for example, while one page of text requires about two kilobytes of storage, an 8 x 10-inch photograph can require several megabytes -enough computer space to hold two or three thousand pages of text. Image processing systems that allow users to manipulate images in databases and combine them with text are slowly maturing, however, and will become more common throughout this decade.

Currenl image systems often employ workstations and laser printers; in addition, they may communicate with other devices via local and wide area networks. They often contain specialized devices such as scanners (devices that convert pictures and text into machine-readable information), optical disks (platters about the size of long- playing records that can contain about 40.000 pages of images and text), and jukeboxes that manipulate optical disks to process images. Scanners are now available tor microcomputer users for about $200.

A good image processing system also contains software that allows users to index, compress, edit, annotate, cut, paste, and route image information. In addition, image processing systems often contain word processors that allow users to combine text and graphics.

For image systems to work effectively in organizations, three technological hurdles must be overcome: data transfer rates must increase, users must be able to write to optical disks, and software tools capable of integrating images with other office information need to be developed.

Slow Data Transfer. The speed at which data moves between workstations through common LAN wiring such as twisled-pair and coaxial cable is sometimes too slow. These cables cannot accept information faster than 500,000 bits per second (hps), or about 3 1 ,000 bytes per second. This may sound fast, but it is too slow for image technologies that commonly use files of several million bytes. However, as LANs begin to use fiber optic cable, which is able to transfer data at much faster rates, image processing will become more practical,

Erasable Optical Disks. For image processing technology to be effective, users must be able to write and erase data on optical disks as easily as on magnetic media. Although it costs about one dollar to store one page of image-based information uu magnetic media and only about five cents to store the same information on an optical disk, optical disks are not yet fully practical because these disks can be written to only once but read any number of times (called WORM - write once, read many). Erasable disks that users can write to are becoming more common, however, and are likely to be important storage media for computers in the years ahead.

Manipulation Tools. Traditionally, users have not had the tools to edit, manipulate and integrate images easily with other information such as text, spreadsheets, and databases. However, public standards for using images in compound documents are being developed that allow users to pass graphic pictures, including photographs as well as drawings, back and forth between different systems.

Voice Processing Technologies

Like image processing systems, voice technologies - audio response and voice recognition - are still in the early stages of development. When these technologies mature, researchers expect them to become a major method for users to communicate with each other and with computer system components.

Voice processing technology turns analog, or sound, signals into digital information that machines can understand. This process is called voice input or voice recognition. The technology must then be able to interpret the digital information so that it can be output in a meaningful form. It may then process the output and provide a meaningful audio response - that is, turn the digital information into analog signals.

Audio Response Devices

Promising audio response (also called voice output) technologies are voice store-and-forward systems and voice synthesis systems.

Voice Store-and-Forward Systems. Voice store-and-forward systems turn analog voice signals into digital format so that voices can be stored, retrieved, and distributed like any other form of electronic information. A common store-and-for-ward system is a voice response system that turns words into digital information, compresses the digitized words, stores them in libraries of words and phrases, and later uses these words to build responses. The key part of a voice response system is the algorithm used to combine the words and phrases back into meaningful responses.

You have probably used one voice response system many times; most local telephone company directory assistance programs provide digitized directory information. The directory contains a database of telephone numbers and recordings of the first ten digits, zero through nine. To hear a telephone number, the operator identifies the requested number and the system then "speaks" each digit to you. More sophisticated algorithms can combine phrases from a database of 2,000 to 3,000 words into simple sentences.

Voice Synthesis Systems. Voice synthesis systems turn digital information into sound waves - an audible voice. Unlike voice response systems, which have a limited vocabulary, voice synthesis systems have a potentially unlimited vocabulary. Instead of storing words, a voice synthesis system stores the smallest units of sound used in speech (called phonemes) and uses a set of algorithms to put these basic sound units back together into words. Voice synthesis technology has two basic limitations: currently, the sound quality is poor, and it requires a heavy share of processing memory and secondary storage-space.

Voice Recognition Devices

While voice output technologies are complicated, they are relatively simple when compared to voice recognition systems.

Voice recognition turns human speech into computer-readable code. Because people talk in such hurried and varied ways, voice recognition technologies are extremely complex. Researchers may design voice recognition systems to be speaker-dependent (or independent), to recognize discrete (or continuous) speech, or both.

Speaker-Dependent Systems. Speaker-dependent systems require users to train the system to recognize their specific speech profiles. To train the system, a user speaks into a microphone, pronouncing each word he or she wants the system to recognize. Once trained, such a system recognizes only the intonations of the user it is trained to recognize - a security benefit in some cases, since it limits access to the system. For example, a system trained by an East Indian user who speaks English with a Hindu accent will probably not understand another user who speaks English with a British accent.

Speaker-independent systems allow anyone to use the system without training the system first.

Discrete Recognition Systems. Discrete recognition systems require the user to pause (possibly for only a fraction of a second) between words to help the system identify word breaks. Continuous recognition systems enable users to speak in a normal cadence with words running into one another.

Technical progress is slow in developing these systems because of the numerous complexities involved. Independent and continuous systems need to be able to process large and complex vocabularies, since a literate person's vocabulary may contain 100,000 words. In addition, people talk quickly - generally up to about 145 words a minute - and they often run words and sounds together.

Researchers estimate that a fully independent/continuous system will not be developed until the end of the century at the earliest.

Personal Information Managers

Many computer experts predict that personal information managers (PIMs) will be an exciting breakthrough in software for the 1990s. Currently, most PIMs are used basically as desktop organizers, but more powerful PIMs allow users to enter text information randomly into computers and quickly find it again. Unlike spreadsheets (which take the place of ledgers) or databases (which take the place of filing cabinets), personal information management software has no physical counterpart. It appeals to experienced users who spend most of their time at workstations and who store most of their information in digital form.

Personal information managers are designed to handle the small bits of text information that can get lost in traditional databases. For example, data that is ideal for PIMs include comments that a client made about his or her family during a golf date, or comments that serve as informal leads to potential new clients. The biggest conceptual challenge for those managing this kind of informal text is how to store it so that it can be easily retrieved. Although various personal information managers solve this problem in slightly different ways, they all combine three types of software; text and retrieval programs, freeform databases, and hypertext applications.,

Text and Retrieval Programs. Text and retrieval programs store the entire contents of a document in a database. These programs retrieve text either by searching from the beginning of a document to the end or by using special search algorithms. What distinguishes full text retrieval from traditional databases is that text can be completely unstructured and undefined -users do not have to remember a document number or name to retrieve information. You simply enter a keyword or phrase that you know is in the document, and the retrieval system tells you which documents in the database contain the specified word or phrase. For example, you can enter a client's name in a PIM record (Suresh Basandra, for example) and the fact that Suresh likes Manju and has a son going to the Indian Institute of Technology. Then, later, in another record, you can make a note to meet Suresh on Friday. When Friday comes, you can quickly locate all notes pertaining to Suresh.

Freeform Databases. Freeform database documents are structured similarly to the data fields and records of traditional databases: they allow you to sort, search, and manipulate documents as though they were database records. These programs create an actual text database of documents - not simply a collection of text files as in search and retrieval programs. Freeform databases allow users to specify certain words or numbers in a document as data fields, sort by those fields, and use Boolean operators (such as AND, OR, and GREATER THAN) just as you would with a traditional database.

Personal information managers that use freeform database concepts can manipulate text information extensively, but they are difficult to learn and are harder to use than search and retrieval programs. However, once mastered, they are also faster.

Hypertext. Hypertext is a form of DBMS that allows users to link screens of information (text, graphics, images, and even sound) together associatively. Hypertext products mimic our ability to store and retrieve information referentially for quick and intuitive access. Ted Nelson, who coined the term hypertext, defines it as a way of creating documents that can be read in relation to other documents. A common use for hypertext is for in-depth research. While displaying one document, a hypertext application refers readers to other documents, which in turn refer them to still other documents. Readers who want to check a reference might click a mouse button on the item to be referenced, and the referenced text will appear on the screen. In this way, all documents are linked to each other by association.

Many computer novices who use hypertext applications are impressed by its power. HyperCard is a popular hypertext application for the Macintosh. Many applications have been designed to take advantage of HyperCard's capabilities. These range from such business-related tools as medical dictionaries to games.

Personal information managers combine search and retrieval, freeform database, and hypertext techniques to allow systems users to organize the myriad tasks, ideas, and notes - even those created haphazardly - so that they can be retrieved quickly for current projects.

COOPERATIVE PROCESSING SYSTEMS

Many computer experts are currently combining the strengths of mainframes, minicomputers, and personal computers into cooperative processing systems. A good example of a cooperative system is Prodigy, the,subscriber service offered for microcomputer users by IBM and Sears. The Prodigy system consists of a central mainframe, several regional minicomputers, and software on the users' micros. Prodigy is designed so that each element of the system works in cooperation with each other element, and processing tasks are distributed to the most appropriate computer in the system.

For example, one of Prodigy's services is to allow users in any pan of the country to display a map of the country with local and national weather, and even ski conditions. Rather than store the maps, weather graphics, and current weather information at the central mainframe and then send it over the network to individual users, Prodigy stores the graphics map and menu displays at the users' computers; the mainframe sends users only the current weather information via the network, and the users' software overlays it on the resident maps. This substantially reduces processing and access times as well as the amount of storage space required on the mainframe.

Cooperative systems decrease the amount of data traffic and time needed to send data over networks. Each of the system's elements is used to perform the tasks for which it is most effective.

Analysts expect that powerful, multitasking operating system software such as OS/2 will make cooperative processing more common. Multitasking software takes advantage of increasingly powerful microcomputers and enables them to communicate and cooperate with mainframes as equals rather than simply as terminals or network nodes.

THE CHALLENGE OF COMPUTER SYSTEMS

As a result of the increasing power of image, voice, and expert systems, the day is coming when computer systems will provide many of the services now supplied by managerial support staff. Managers will rely on their computer systems to gather information, analyze it, and present it to workers and decision makers in immediately usable form.

A broad range of tools are converging on computer systems to create this level of support, which is likely to further revolutionize the work environment. These tools include compound documents, electronic messaging, interactive video teleconferencing, and intelligent networks that provide access to thousands of external public databases. They also include specialized workstation technologies such as legal, medical, and engineering expert systems that help professionals better use their creative capacities.

Such developments have significant influences on those who use computer systems, requiring them to ctiange from being merely participants in the system to becoming system designers themselves. Successful users will be those who are able to think and plan strategically, encourage innovation and develop computer solutions to their own business problems.

In many ways, computer systems are at the center of a technological and organizational revolution that is changing today's society. Those at the center of this revolution - those with the vision to see where computer technology is going and its power for constructive change - will be tomorrow's leaders.

SUMMARY

1. Although there is no reversing the trend toward large credit databases, their existence brings up two important social and organizational issues: privacy and security.
2. Computer security includes the policies, procedures, tools, and techniques designed to protect a company's computer assets from accidental, intentional, or natural disasters, including accidental input or output errors, theft, breakins, physical damage, and illegal access or manipulation.
3. Unfortunately, among the primary sources of security breaches are employees who are either callous or forgetful about security standards.
4. Technological advances in computers have made many systems extremely complex and difficult to manage.
5. Unfortunately, networks are also among the most vulnerable links in the security chain for computer systems.
6. They are given different —hackers, crackers, information warriors, cyberpunks, eyberterrorists, and phone freaks— but they are all people who violate computer security.
7. Accidents in the workplace can cause security breaches; it is often said that the cost of intentional damage exceeds the cost of computer crime.
8. Intentional damage to systems is also common. I
9. Cracking, or decoding, passwords, which are the Achilles' heel of computer security, is one of the most common security violations, since hackers and crackers can easily guess passwords or capture them as they travel over the network.

10. The greatest threat to software is a computer virus, a program that causes a computer system to behave in unexpected and undesirable ways.
11. Believe it or not, it is still legal in the United States to create a virus and inject it into any computer system, because the writing of software is protected by the First Amendment, although federal regulatory agencies are working hard to change this situation.
12. Power outages are another common cause of computer downtime and lost productivity.
13. Application controls are policies and procedures that ensure the security and quality of system applications in the organization.
14. Input controls are designed to prevent users from entering incomplete, erroneous, unauthorized, or inappropriate data.
15. Data should be validated before it is processed.
16. Input controls should also check the format of the data, ensuring that there are no missing values and that data are in the right format (integer versus decimal values, for example), the right size, and the right type (for example, telephone numbers should not include alphabetic characters).
17. Process controls are policies and procedures that ensure that data are meaningful and reliable.
18. Control mechanisms for system security should not be an afterthought, but should be made an integral part of the development process, from product conception to product delivery.
19. Data security and reliability are another development control mechanism that prevents unauthorized access to data.
20. Authorization requirements are control mechanisms that allow only authorized users to access and use the system.
21. Most facilities also include environmental control device that monitor and control the air and the temperature in a building.
22. Many security breaches are caused by employees within the company, either because they lack knowledge about system security or because they have illicit intentions.
23. Security policies and procedures, combined with extensive user training, should precede any investment in security products
24. To prevent bootlegging, software vendors sometimes copy protect software so that it cannot be copied to other disks -or can only be copied a limited number of times, generally twice.
25. Access to a system and its data should be controlled, and secure backup copies maintained.
26. Creating backups consists of making extra copies of programs or data.
27. Distributed processing and remote databases pose specific control problems for organizations because they are vulnerable to unauthorized access to data from remote locations.
28. All professions have a code of ethics that broadly sets standards for professionals; such ethical standards may not be covered by specific legislation.
29. The emergence of computers in the workplace has created a number of new organizational issues in such areas as space planning, health, and safety.
30. Well-planned offices eliminate distracting sounds yet make provisions for private conver-sations.
31. The long-term goal of most advanced computer vendors is to create systems that are capable of handling compound documents that integrate data from different applications - text, data, spreadsheet, graphic, image and voice information -into a cohesive information system.
32. Currenl image systems often employ workstations and laser printers; in addition, they may communicate with other devices via local and wide area networks.
33. The speed at which data moves between workstations through common LAN wiring such as twisled-pair and coaxial cable is sometimes too slow.
34. Traditionally, users have not had the tools to edit, manipulate and integrate images easily with other information such as text, spreadsheets, and databases.
35. Voice synthesis systems turn digital information into sound waves - an audible voice.
36. Speaker-dependent systems require users to train the system to recognize their specific speech profiles.
37. Text and retrieval programs store the entire contents of a document in a database.
38. Many computer experts are currently combining the strengths of mainframes, minicomputers, and personal computers into cooperative processing systems.

REVIEW QUESTIONS

1. What is the difference between hackers and crackers? Should an organization take measures to protect itself from both or just from one?
2. What is meant by application controls? Briefly describe the four primary areas of data processing that are covered by application controls.
3. What is meant by security controls? Briefly describe the five types of controls.
4. Define computer security. Explain why computer security cannot be achieved through automation alone. Identify any three reasons why computer systems are vulnerable to security breaches. Explain why networks are so prone to security breaches.
5. What are development controls? Identify and describe the four types of development controls.
6. What is meant by access controls? What are some measures that companies must take to ensure that passwords provide the necessary security?
7. What is a computer virus? What are some ways to prevent viruses?
8. What is a backup? Why are backups vital to computer system security?
9. What are some measures that managers can take to protect their networks from security breaches? Describe any two in detail.
10. What are the three types of security breaches? Give an example of each.
11. Why are fax machines and modems particularly vulnerable to security breaches? What measures can an organization take to secure these two types of hardware?
12. What are some data validation controls and how do they help to increase the security of input data?

CHAPTER 20

Robotics

Learning Objectives

After going through this chapter, you should appreciate the following:

- **Introduction**
  - Brief History
  - Historic Developments
  - Types of Robots
  - Polar Co-ordinate Configuration
  - Jointed Arm Configuration
  - Cylindrical Co-ordinate Configuration
  - Cartesian Co-ordinate Configuration
  - Technology of Robots
- **Basic Principles in Robotics**
  - Robot Programming
  - Manual Method
  - Leadthrough Method
  - Walkthrough Method
  - Off-line Programming
- **Applications of Robot**
  - Cutting Operations
  - Fettling and Cleaning
  - Inspection and Testing
  - Machine Loading and Unloading
  - Machining
  - Material transfer
  - Product Assembly
  - Surface coating
  - Welding

INTRODUCTION

There has been a rapidly growing and widespread interest in robots, mechanical manipulators and hands, mobile platforms, walking machines and many other so-called robotic devices and 'intelligent' systems. These robotic technologies combined with rapid advances in electronics, controls vision and other forms of sensing and computing have been widely recognized for their potential applications in almost all areas where machines enter our society.

In fact, it has been claimed that we are in the midst of a robotics revolution and this revolution will have more influence on human society than had the Industrial Revolution of the 17th and 18th centuries. Although the number of robots and their applications are proliferating the underlying science and to some extent the technology are moving at a much slower pace.

Brief History

The word robot came into English language in 1923 from the translation of a 1921 Czech play RUR. (Rossum's Universal Robot) by Karel Capek (Capek 1975). It is derived from the Czech word 'robota' meaning slave labour. The 'robots' in the play are designed to replace human workers and are depicted as very efficient and indistinguishable from humans except for their lack of emotions. In the play the robots rebel against their human masters and destroy the entire human race except one man so that he can continue making robots! Unfortunately, the formula gets lost in the destruction.

In contrast to the horrors of mechanization in Capek's play, in 1942, the science fiction writer Issac Asimov (Assimov 1970) in a story titled 'Runaround' coined the word 'robotics' to describe the study of robots and gave the three laws of robotics. In many of his stories dealing with robots, always designed on the basis of these three laws, Asimov portrays robots as harmless and totally under the control of human beings.

The modem industrial robot, as it first appeared, bore little resemblance to the science fiction-inspired vision of a robot. PUMA (Programmable Universal Machine for Assembly) and a **T3** (The Tomorrow Tool) robot are manufactured by Unimation Inc. and Cincinnati Milacron Inc., respectively and are seen extensively in textbooks, industry and academic and research institutions. Clearly, it is not even remotely similar to the human-like robots depicted in science fiction.

The modem industrial robot was patented by George C. Devol in 1954 and he called it a 'programmable articulated transfer device'. Engelberger and George C. Devol founded the world's first robot company, Unimation Inc., in 1956 and the first industrial robot, called Unimate, was purchased by General Motors and installed at an automobile plant in New Jelsey, USA, in 1961.

What is a robot in the modem sense of the word? There are several definitions.

Definition 1: ***The Webster dictionary defines a robot as 'an automatic device that performs functions normally ascribed to humans or a machine in the form of a human'.***

A more formal and restrictive definition comes from the Robot Institute of America (1969) defines robot as:

Definition 2: ***Robot is a reprogrammable, multifunctional manipulator designed to move materials, parts, tools or specialized devices through various programmed motions for the performance of a variety of tasks.***

The keyword in the definition is 'reprogrammable' and this word has closely linked the development of robots to the rapid development of the digital computer and developments in the art and science of computing. A computer or a microprocessor that allows running of different robot programs for the various applications is an essential component of a robotic system.

One of the first computers, ENIAC, was developed in the University of Pennsylvania in 1946 and in 1959 a programmable lathe was first demonstrated at MIT. It may be mentioned that the word 'reprogrammable' also distinguishes a robot from computer numerically controlled (CNC) machines since the level and sophistication of reprogrammability is significantly higher in an industrial robot.

In addition to the digital computer, the other key ingredient in the development of the modem industrial robot is the concept and implementation of feedback control. Feedback control allows the execution of the programmed or desired motion (chosen by a robot operator or another program called a task planner) with the required accuracy in spite of 'small' changes in the robot or the environment and thus improve the performance of robots. The first textbook on feedback control, Cybernetics or Control and Communication in the Animal, describing control in mechanical, electronic and biological systems, was written by Prof. Norbert Wiener of MIT in 1948. The use of feedback control is by no means limited to robots. Today, a whole range of CNC machines, automobiles, airplanes, missiles and spacecrafts and an ever increasing number of consumer products such as washing machines and microwave ovens use feedback control.

In the late 1980s and early 1990s, the growth in the use of industrial robots slowed down significantly, except in Japan. One of the main reasons was the inability of robots to perform tasks that human operators could perform quite easily, such as avoiding obstacles in a cluttered workspace, recognizing and manipulating objects such as screws, bolts and nuts and adapting and reacting quickly to changes in the environment. It was realized that most of the existing industrial robots were essentially blind, deaf and dumb and a great deal of effort was made to equip robots with sensors and computing resources so that the robots could sense, quickly process data from sensors and then interact intelligently with the environment.

Present-day industrial robots are often equipped with sensors to detect the presence or absence of the object to be manipulated, measure applied forces and moments and obtain the position and orientation of objects in its environment. Present-day industrial robots also come with a wide variety of end-effectors, hands and grippers (which are often equipped with sensing elements) to grasp and manipulate a wide variety of tools and objects. With the advancement in sensing and computing, the modem industrial robot is easier to program and use, more flexible and more intelligent. The late 1990s have seen a renewed interest in the use of robots.

Modern industrial robots are used in a variety of places and situations. These can be broadly classified into three categories. The first typical area is in an environment that is hazardous for humans to operate in, or an environment where the cost of protecting humans is very high. Examples are in handling of fuel and radioactive material in nuclear power plants and in space and underwater operations. For example, the satellites and experimental payloads in the space shuttle are often removed from the cargo bay by a mechanical manipulator operated by an astronaut from the safety of the cabin.

Note:➢ ***The pictures of the ocean liner Titanic and retrieval of portions of the Air India's Kanishka airplane, from great ocean depths, were taken by unmanned submersible robots.***

The exploration of Mars was done by mobile robots Sojourner in 1997 and Spirit and Opportunity in 2004, which not only beamed back spectacular pictures of the Martian landscape but also the data and the images sent by them allowed researchers to infer the presence of large amounts of water on the Martian surface in the past. Robots are also being used in environments not hazardous to human beings but where human beings are hazardous to the product-robots are being increasingly used in ultraclean rooms in the electronic industry as it is expensive to keep off dust and other foreign material carried and generated by human beings.

The second area where modem industrial robots have been employed in large numbers is in tasks that are repetitive, back-breaking and also boring for human beings. In these tasks, human beings cannot maintain the required accuracy or quality because of the monotonous and tedious nature of the task.

Typical applications can be seen in automotive industries where robots are often used for spray painting and welding of car bodies, in general manufacturing where robots are used for loading and unloading of material, parts and tools from other machines and more recently for assembly of components such as electric motors and computer peripherals.

The third area where robots are used is in manufacturing of consumer products where the number of items is not very large and the product or the model is frequently changing. Typical examples are television sets, cameras and other audio/video consumer products. Robots are ideally suited for these industries because of their ease of re-programmability. Reprogramming the robots to handle different parts of newer models can be done more easily than expensive retooling and changes in the assembly line and this allows a manufacturer to keep pace with the changing consumer tastes and stay competitive.

With the maturing of the technology, robots are finding their way into many other areas of human activity. To name a few, robots are arid have been used extensively for entertainment as evidenced by the Star War and Terminator series movies. The robot dog Aibo from Sony and the LEGO Mindstorms robot construction kit is very popular among children and adults. The humanoid robot P3 and Asimo from Hondahas appeared in advertising for a variety of products.

A robotic system called Da Vinci has been used for heart surgery, where it is programmed to follow the physician's hand movements very accurately and with no tremors (the tremors and unwanted movement can be removed with the help of a computer and the robot controller) and thus can be used to perform very delicate bypass and heart valve surgeries. Finally, robots are finding their way into human homes as robotic vacuum cleaners and lawn mowers which can clean the house or mow the lawns on their own when the occupant is away!

Japan, accounting for more than half the number of robots installed worldwide, is the largest user of robots, followed by the European Union and USA. To give an idea of the explosive growth in the use of robots in Japan, the number of robots in use in Japan went up from approximately 5,500 in 1980 to over 65,000 in 1985 and about 400,000 in 1995. Although the number of robots in use in Japan has not increased much during the last decade due to the retiring of older robots and the depressed economy, the number of robots in use have gone up in Europe and USA. It is forecast that there will be a dramatic increase, in tens of thousands, of robots for domestic and medical uses. In India (and other developing countries) too robots have found their way into a few industries such as for spray painting and spot welding of automobile bodies, handling of molten metals and other hazardous substances and in nuclear waste handling. The use, however, is insignificant compared to that in Japan, USA and Europe.

Historic Developments

Some of the important dates in the history of robotics are given below.

1770 Mechanism-driven life-like machines that can draw, play instruments and clocks made in Germany and Switzerland.

1830 Cam programmable lathe invented.

1923 Karel Capek's play RUR.

1942 Asimov coins the word 'robotics' and gives his three laws of robotics.

1946 ENIAC, the first electronic computer, developed at the University of Pennsylvania.

1947 The first servo electric-powered tele-operated robot at MIT.

1948 Book on feedback control, Cybernetics, written by Prof. Norbert Weiner of MIT.

1948 Transistor invented at Bell Laboratories.

1952 IBM's first commercial computer, IBM 701, marketed.

1954 First programmable robot patented and designed by Devol.

1955 Paper by J. Denavit and RS Hartenberg (Denavit and Hartenberg, 1955) provides a notation to describe links and joints in a manipulator.

1959 Unimation Inc. founded by Engelberger; CNC lathe demonstrated at MIT.

1961 General Motors buys and installs the first Unimate at a plant in New Jersey to tend a die casting machine.

1968 Shakey, the first mobile robot with vision capability, made at SRI.

1970 The Stanford Arm designed with electrical actuators and controlled by a computer.

1973 Cincinnati Milacron's (T3) electrically actuated, mini computer controlled industrial robot.

1976 Viking II lands on Mars and an arm scoops Martian soil for analysis.

1978 Unimation develops PUMA, which can still be seen in many research labs.

1981 Robot Manipulators by R. Paul, one of the first textbooks on robotics.

1982 First educational robots introduced by Microbot and Rhino.

1983 Adept Technology, maker of SCARA robot, started.

1995 Intuitive Surgical formed to design and market surgical robots.

1997 Sojourner robot sends back pictures of Mars; the Ronda P3 humanoid robot, started in 1986, unveiled.

2000 Honda demonstrates Asimo humanoid robot.

2001 Sony releases second generation Aibo robot dog.

2004 Spirit and Opportunity explore Mars surface and detect evidence of past water.

Types of Robots

Robots are generally classified according to their number of degrees of freedom or axes. The degrees of freedom of a robot roughly indicate the capability of a robot. A general task consisting of arbitrarily positioning and orienting an object or a tool can be achieved only by a six-DOF or a six-axes robot. Painting and simple welding can be done by a five-axes robot and often assembly robots have only four degrees of freedom. A five or a six-DOF welding robot is often mounted on a three-axes gantry, giving rise to an eight- or nine-axes robotic system for larger operating volume and flexibility.

Robots are available in variety of shapes and sizes. Although it varies widely in shape and size, they are generally grouped in one of four main robot configurations. It is noted that some robot may employ more than one configuration. Four basic robot arm geometries are used for industrial applications. These are:

Polar Co-ordinate Configuration

This configuration also known as the "Spherical Co-ordinate." The geometry of the polar configuration combines rotational movement in both horizontal and vertical planes with in and out movement of the arm. This type of robot has a rotary base and a pivot that can be used to raise and lower a telescoping arm. This is best suited to listing and shifting applications.

Jointed Arm Configuration

This configuration is also known as anthropomorphic. The jointed arm configurations comprises a number of rigid arms connecting rotary joints. The arm of the robot is mounted to a base which can be rotated to provide the robot with the capacity to work within a quasi- spherical space.

Cylindrical Co-ordinate Configuration

This type of configuration combines both horizontal and vertical linear movement, with rotary movement in the horizontal plane about the vertical axis. Cylindrical Co-ordinate robot is best suited for movement around a base.

Cartesian Co-ordinate Configuration

This is also known as Rectangular Co-ordinate configuration. This type of configuration provides for three linear axes of movement at right angles to each other. These type of robots can be used for tasks involving pick and place operations.

The term 'anthropomorphic' or 'articulate' is used for a robot because of its 'similarity' to a human arm and a SCARA (selective compliance adaptive robot arm) design is based on a folding door. In most manipulators, there are two or three additional joints after the first three joints, which form a wrist. The first three joints are typically used to position an object or a tool in the workspace of the manipulator, whereas the wrist joints are used to orient the tool or the object being manipulated.

All the above configurations are called serial manipulators since they have one fixed end, a free end which carries the end-effector or tool and no closed loops. Many present-day robots have one or more joints fixed to the ground and one or more closed loops. These are called parallel manipulators or robots.

According to the mode of operation in a playback robot, a robot is physically taken through each step of the desired motion by an operator and these recorded positions are simply played back by the robot on being signaled to do so. In a computer-controlled robot, the desired motion is obtained from 'a' computer after computations according to specified algorithms. An intelligent robot is equipped with sensors and processors and is capable of performing tasks such as avoiding obstacles, taking simple decisions based on sensor inputs and even 'learn' about the environment in which it operates.

In addition to the above classification, we also have other types of robots and robotic devices. To name a few, there exist multi-DOF walking machines, robots mounted on two- or three- DOF mobile platforms or Automated Guided Vehicles (AGVs) and multi-DOF mechanical hands with fingers attached to a robot

Technology of Robots

The technology and hardware of robots are changing continuously and we can, at best, describe briefly and qualitatively some of the main components of a robot. A typical robot consists of mechanical components, actuators, power transmission devices, sensors, an electronic controller and computers. The main mechanical components of a robot are links connected by joints. As mentioned earlier, in a serial manipulator, the links are arranged sequentially, starting from the base and ending in the end-effector with no loops. In a parallel manipulator, on the other hand, there can be one or more loops. Links are assumed to be rigid in most of this text and are generally made of metal such as steel or aluminum (cast or machined).

It is desirable that links be as lightweight as possible so that torque (force) requirements from an actuator are low and at the same time the links must have rigidity to achieve positioning accuracy. The joints allow relative rotation or translation between the connecting links and various types of bearings are used to ensure relatively free and smooth, motion. The end-effector carries the tool and is application specific. In painting or welding, the paint gun or the welding tool is fixed on the end-effector and the arrangement is made to continuously supply the paint or the welding wire. In material handling, often a two-fingered gripper is used to grasp objects.

Elements of robots are as follows:

- Power Supply
- Computer for the purpose of controlling—Manipulator
- End Effector etc.

The basic motions of the robots are six (Rotational traverse, Radial traverse, vertical traverse, wrist bend, Wrist yaw and wrist Swivel) which provide the capability to move the end effector through the required sequence of motions. Out of six three Co-ordinates can locate the centre of gravity of an object and another three can determine its orientation.

Six basic motions of the robot can be explained as following:

(1)	Rotational traverse	Rotation of arm about the vertical axis.
(2)	Radial traverse	Movement of the arm is in and out.
(3)	Vertical traverse	Motions of the arm is up and down.
(4)	Wrist bend	Bending movement in a plane vertical to the arm.
(5)	Wrist Yaw	Twisting movement in a plane horizontal to the arm.
(6)	Wrist Swivel	Swivel movement in a plane perpendicular to the end of the arm.

The links are moved by actuators, which are electric motors or pneumatic and hydraulic cylinders. Electric motors can be DC or AC servo-motors, or sometimes stepper motors. The motors required for robots should have ideally a low rpm (of less than 100), be lightweight and have high torque. Most lightweight DC servo-motors, however, run at a high speed of 3000 rpm or more and a suitable transmission has to be used to bring down the speed. Usual speed reduction approaches using standard spur gears, chains and sprockets or belts cannot be used since the accuracy is lost due to backlash or slippage. Special low-backlash gear sets, harmonic drives and ball screws are used for transmission of power and to reduce speed. Often brakes are present to stop the motion or to hold the robot when it is not in motion.

The speed and repeatability requirement vary with the nature of the task and the load-carrying capacity. The tip of a large welding Robot can move as fast as 2 m/sec although the welding process speed is much smaller at about 1-5 m/min) carrying a payload of 5-10 kg and can have a repeatability of less than 1 mm and a reach of 2-3 m. Typical speeds of material-handling robots are 1 m/sec carrying a payload of about 10 kg, with a repeatability of about 0.1 mm (thickness of a human hair) and a reach of 1-2 m. Finally, there are small electronic assembly robots which can have maximum speeds of more than 5 m/sec, a payload of less than 1 kg, a repeatability of 0.01 mm or less and a reach less than 1 m.

Most robots have sensors at joints, which measure rotation or translation at joints for feedback control. The angular rotation at a joint is measured by optical encoders and the angular velocity can be measured by tachometers. Translation and linear velocities can be measured by Linear Variable Differential Transformers (LVDTs) and video cameras. Force at the end-effector or at the links can be accurately measured by force-torque sensors, which use strain gauges.

Most controllers are implemented digitally using microprocessors and contain circuitry for analog to digital (AID) and digital to analog (D/A) conversions, memory and other electronics. Typically, the measured signals and the processing are digital (0/5 V and currents in milliamperes) whereas the input to the actuators are higher voltages (often 12 V or 24 V) and currents (in amperes) in analog form and hence carefully designed servo-amplifiers are used to drive actuators. The technology of controllers for robots is quite complex, difficult and expensive to develop and together with computers also makes up the bulk of the cost of a robotic system—the controller may cost as much as 60% of the entire robotic system.

In addition to the sensors required for control, most industrial robots have sensors required for the task and application for which the robot is being used. For example, an arc-welding robot will have sensors to maintain the arc length while the robot is moving along the required weld path. A few robots are equipped with simple vision systems. They are used to inspect or pick components not oriented in the desired way. Several research robots, at universities and research laboratories, have full-fledged vision systems or sonars which allow them to avoid obstacles and navigate in cluttered environments.

Two of the most important components in a robotic system are the computers and the software or the programs residing in them. Often there are two kinds of computers in a robotic system: one set performs the task of controlling the actuators in a robot and the other is a supervisory or a master computer where application programs can be developed and stored, fault detection, diagnosis and corrective actions can be taken, or where a high-level task planner or an expert system can reside.

At the actuator level, the programs are simple and the processing has to be very fast (typical sampling rates are about 50 – 100 Hz) and an assembly language programming is often used for achieving the fast processing requirements. At the supervisory level, the processing speed is much slower, but the programs are more complex. At this level, a user-friendly environment and a standard high-level language, such as C, or a robot programming language is available for developing application programs. There are two-way communication channels between the 'actuator' control computers and the supervisory computer.

Finally, an industrial robot is a complex and expensive machine. It is important to provide a user-friendly operator interface so that the robot operator can learn to use it easily and quickly. The commands to the robot to accomplish a given task must be simple and straight forward to the operator. The operator interface is normally through a teach pendant or through a computer. A large amount of careful programming, often including graphics, is required to build this user interface.

BASIC PRINCIPLES IN ROBOTICS

To understand how and why robots work, we have to understand the scientific principles that form the basis of robotics. Robotics is an interdisciplinary subject which drawing ideas and tools from mathematics, physics, engineering and computing. We take a brief look at some of the ingredients of robotics, namely, kinematics, dynamics, controls, sensing and intelligence.

Kinematics deals with the motion of rigid bodies (motion of the rigid links of a robot) in a three-dimensional (3D) space. A rigid body moving in a three-dimensional space has six degrees of freedom, or, in other words, a rigid body requires six independent parameters to be fully specified.

Three of the six parameters specify the position of a point of interest, which could be a point on the end-effector, or the tip of the paint or welding tool, or the centre of gravity of the part being moved. Three other parametres are required to specify the orientation of the same object.

In order to achieve these six degrees of freedom, a robot must have at least six independently actuated joints. In kinematics of robots we study the functional relationships between the motion at the joints and the motion of the end-effector or tool without reference to the cause (external forces and moments) of the motion. One can find and study, quantitatively, the motion at the end-effector for a given motion at the joints (the direct kinematics problem), the motion at the joints for a required motion of the end-effector (the inverse kinematics problem), the workspace or the volume in 3D space which a point of interest on the robot can reach and other issues related to the time derivatives of the position and orientation of the links of a robot, i.e., the velocity and acceleration.

Robot Programming

There are various methods by which robots can be programmed to perform a given task. These methods can be divided in mainly four categories:

Manual Method

Manual method is more like setting up a machine rather than programming. It is the procedure used for the simple type of robots. For example, for pick and place operations the manual method is more suitable.

Leadthrough Method

Because of its ease and convenience this method is more popular among all robot programming method. This method makes use of a teach pendent to power drive the robot through its motion sequence.

Walkthrough Method

This method is more suitable for arc welding and spray painting an walkthrough method, the programmer manually moves the arm and hand of robots through the motion sequence of the work cycle.

Off-line Programming

Similar to NC part programming off-line programming method involves the preparation of the robot program off-line.

APPLICATIONS OF ROBOT

Robots are used for a wide range of applications. The range of applications is very wide. It is employed in the agriculture, civil engineering, mechanical engineering, nuclear industry, household work and also security Supervision. The robot should be placed as a Substitute for the human worker, where there are potential dangers, workplace is uncomfortable or health hazards due to heat. A robot is also suitable for repetitive tasks, difficult handling for those human worker would need. Some form of mechanical assistance and multishift operation.

The wide ranges of industrial robot application are following:

Cutting Operations

The robot can cover a relatively large workspace and also has a higher flexibility. Applications of cutting operations are: Drilling, Laser beam cutting and Milling etc.

Fettling and Cleaning

Fettling is such type of process commonly associated with the cleaning up of casting. In this type of operation the control system needs to be capable of describing often complex continuous path movement.

Inspection and Testing

Industrial robots are also used for inspection and testing. This operations is also a new area of application of industrial robot. Dimensional checks also comes under application of this operation.

Machine Loading and Unloading

Machine loading and unloading has been a very popular application for robots. The machine loading and unloading tasks are carried by Stationary stand robot. For this type of operation robot need point-to-point control. These applications provide good economic returns by reducing the labour cost, high production rate and decreasing scrap. In this application the robot would grasp a raw workpart from a conveyor and load it into the machine. Robots are used for loading and unloading of the machines given below:

Forging machines

Metal cutting machines

Die Casing machines

Injection molding machines

Transfer molding machines

Glass processing machines

Inspection machines

Machining

Robots are used to transport cutting tools for performing machining operations. This operations are new area of application of robot. Routing, grinding, polishing, drilling is the common application of this operation.

Material transfer

In which the robot is used to move works parts from one location to another location. It includes transfer of parts from conveyor to conveyor.

Example of material transfer are:

Transfer of parts from conveyor to conveyor.

Pick - & - Place operations

Product Assembly

Assembly operations having large potential area for robot applications. Industrial robots are widely used in automobile assembly. For assembly functions large number of small servo controlled robots have been developed.

Surface coating

Coating is the second most application. This type of applications are found mostly in the automotive industry. Coating operations involve paint spraying, stain etc. Advantages of using robots for coating applications are more uniform surface coating, less energy used, greater productivity, saving of paint is more than 35%.

Welding

Welding are usually carried out by stand alone robots. This is an important application area for industrial robots. This process is generally divided in two categories first spot welding and second is arc welding.

Spot welding was the first application where robots were used. It is a process in which metal parts art fused together at localized points by passing a large electric current. Point-to- point control is mainly used for spot welding.

Arc welding is an area for extensive robotic applications. Most arc welding application are relatively simple. Arc welding processes includes gas Metal Arc Welding, Tungstan Inert Gas Welding, Gas Tungstan Arc Welding, Metal Inert Gas Welding. Arc welding requiring complex motions along a workpiece surface. Also arc welding is a fabricating process often used on low volume products. Continuous path control is mainly used for arc welding.

In practice most robots have an operation time approximately 12 per cent lower than that of skilled human welder. Also industrial robot gives higher quality welds, higher productivity and improved safety.

SUMMARY

1. Robots are programmable machines with some human like capabilities.
2. Robots can be programmed by several techniques.
3. Robots can be defined as "it is a programmable, multi-function manipulator designed to move material, parts, tools or special devices through variable programmed motions for the performance of a variety of tasks".
4. Robots can also be defined as "It is an automatic machine with a certain degree of autonomy, designed for active interaction into the environment".
5. Robots are used to get: Maximum payload, Accuracy , Reliability of operation, Flexibility, Repeatability, Availability for work, Predictable cycle times, Reductions in hidden costs and Running costs.
6. Among the various reasons for using Robots are: Robot brings improvements in quality of product, It relieves worker of hazardous or fatiguing tasks, Robot increases the output without increasing the worker, Robot offers opportunities for multi-machine manning for multishift operation, Where man cannot work, robot can work with high efficiency, Robot can lift very high weight easily, Robot saves money and time also and Robot with sensing power will find more applications.
7. Among the various characteristics of a Robot are: (i) Robot is multifunctional, it can be used in different ways, Robot can be programmed to perform a particular task, Robot is reprogrammable, It gives higher accuracy, Repeatability is the very important characteristic in determining the robot's ability, Robot can lift very high load, and Memory capacity is also one of the characteristics of robot, it determines the length and complexity of the operation that the manipulator is able to perform.
8. Robot programming can be done by 4 methods: Manual method, Leadthrough method, Walkthrough method and Off-line programming.
9. Basic elements of a Robot are: Power Supply, Computer for the purpose of controlling—Manipulator and End Effector.
10. Theres are six basic motions of the robot: Rotational traverse, Radial traverse, Vertical traverse, Wrist bend, Wrist Yaw and Wrist Swivel.
11. Robot is employed in the agriculture, civil engineering, mechanical engineering, nuclear industry, household work and also security supervision.

MULTIPLE CHOICE QUESTIONS

1. Robot can be programmed:
   (a) Yes (b) No
2. Robots's main parts are: Power Supply, Manipulator and ______________:
   (a) Data (b) End Effector (c) Communicator
3. Robot programming can be done by the following method too:
   (a) Online (b) Automatic (c) Manual
4. Robot can replace men in all fields:
   (a) Yes (b) No
5. Robot reduces cost of operations:
   (a) Yes (b) No

REVIEW QUESTIONS

1. What are Robots?
2. How can you program Robots?
3. What are the advantages of using Robots?

4. What are the characteristics of Robots?
5. What are the basic elements of Robots?
6. Which are the different motions of Robots?

ANSWERS

Multiple Choice Questions

1. a 2. b 3. c 4. b
5. a

CHAPTER 21

Index

D

E

F

G

H

I

N

O

P

Q

R

S

T

U

V

W

X

Y

Z